CANADIAN

PERSPECTIVES ON

INTERNATIONAL

LAW AND

ORGANIZATION

EDITED BY
R. ST J. MACDONALD
GERALD L. MORRIS
DOUGLAS M. JOHNSTON

Canadian Perspectives on International Law and Organization

UNIVERSITY OF TORONTO PRESS

© University of Toronto Press 1974
Toronto and Buffalo
Printed in Canada
ISBN 0-8020-1974-9 (trade edition)
ISBN 0-8020-1975-7 (student edition)
LC 72-98024

The support of the Canada Council in
the preparation of this volume is
gratefully acknowledged.

Contents

Contributors

GEORGE W. ALEXANDROWICZ is professor of law at Queen's University, where he has taught since 1967. His primary interests are in the areas of international law and environmental resources law. He has served as a consultant to the federal Department of the Environment and has been a member of Canadian delegations to international diplomatic conferences dealing with international environmental affairs and to the UN Seabed Committee.

CHARLES BEDARD is a graduate of Laval and Paris (LL D) and a member of the Quebec bar. Since joining Canada's Department of External Affairs in 1953 he has served in Los Angeles, Vietnam, Haiti, and Belgium. In Ottawa Dr Bédard has served in Legal Division, United Nations Division, and as Deputy Director of Cultural Affairs Division. He has lectured on international law at Ottawa university and his publications include a 1966 volume, *Le Statut juridique des Grands Lacs de l'Amérique du Nord et du Fleuve Saint-Laurent*. In 1973 he was appointed Canadian Representative on the Council of ICAO.

J. ALAN BEESLEY practised law in Victoria, British Columbia, for five years prior to joining Canada's Department of External Affairs in 1956. He served abroad in Tel Aviv (1957–60) and Geneva (1964–7). In Ottawa he served as Head of the UN and Law of the Sea Section in Legal Division (1960–4) and as Head of Legal Division (1967–71). In 1971 he was designated Legal Adviser and Director General of Legal Bureau. In 1973 he was appointed Canadian Ambassador to Austria and concurrently Permanent Representative to IAEA and UNIDO.

IVAN BERNIER est licencié en droit de l'Université Laval et détenteur d'un PH D de l'Université de Londres (London School of Economics). Il est professeur à la Faculté de droit de l'Université Laval depuis juin 1969. Spécialisé en droit international public, ses recherches actuelles portent plus particulièrement sur la pratique canadienne en matière de droit international économique.

EMILIO S. BINAVINCE is professor of law at the University of Ottawa and is a member of the Ontario bar. A graduate of Quezon (LL B), Tulane (MCL), and Harvard (LL M), he also holds the Certificate of Legal Studies from Bonn. He is faculty editor of the *Ottawa Law Review* and was a visiting professor of law at New York University in 1972.

C.B. BOURNE is a graduate in law of Toronto, Cambridge, and Harvard and is a member of the bars of Barbados and British Columbia. He taught at Saskatchewan

(1947–50) and has taught international law and Canadian constitutional law at British Columbia since 1950. While attached as adviser to the Legal Division at External Affairs in 1971–2, Dr Bourne was the Canadian draftsman and legal adviser to the Canadian team that negotiated the Great Lakes Water Quality Agreement with the United States.

JOHN E.C. BRIERLEY is a law graduate of the universities of McGill and Paris, and a member of the Quebec bar. For some years he has served as a member of Quebec's law reform body, the Office of Revision of the Civil Code. He collaborated with R. David in the work *Major Legal Systems* (1968). At present he is associate professor, McGill Law Faculty, Montreal, teaching Quebec civil law.

J.-G. CASTEL, SJD (Harvard), is professor of law at Osgoode Hall Law School, York University, and is a member of the Ontario bar. He is editor of the *Canadian Bar Review*.

MAXWELL COHEN, QC, LL D, is Macdonald Professor of Law and former Dean of the Faculty of Law and Director of the Institute of Air and Space Law, McGill University. He is a member of the bars of Quebec and Manitoba. An eminent and prolific scholar, he is the Past President of the Canadian Branch, International Law Association; former Chairman of the Section on Constitutional and International Law of the Canadian Bar Association; was a member of the Canadian Delegation to the 14th United Nations General Assembly; and was Director, Department of External Affairs project of the Royal Commission on Government Organization (1961). He is President, Quebec Advisory Council on the Administration of Justice; and Chairman, Advisory Committee on Marine and Environmental Conferences, Department of External Affairs.

MAURICE D. COPITHORNE was admitted to the bar of British Columbia in 1956 and joined the Department of External Affairs the same year. He served in Canadian diplomatic missions in Vientiane, Saigon, Tehran, and Kuala Lumpur. He was Head of the Treaty Section of the Legal Division in the Department (1962–4) and Deputy Head of Legal Division (1968–71) with particular responsibility for international claims. In February 1971 he was appointed the Director of the newly created Legal Advisory Division of the Department, a position he held until his assignment in June 1972 to the Canadian embassy in Peking as Counsellor.

CHARLES M. DALFEN, a professor of law at the University of Toronto, was previously the Legal Adviser to the federal Department of Communications and associate professor of political science at Carleton University. He has represented Canada in meetings of the UN Outer Space Committee, the UN Direct Satellite Broadcasting Working Group, UNESCO, INTELSAT, and the ITU. He is co-editor of the *Canadian Communications Law Review*, is a member of the Panel on International Telecommunications Policy, American Society of International Law, and was the designated Canadian representative to the Space Communications Section, Inter-American Bar Association.

ANDRE DUFOUR a obtenu sa licence en droit de l'Université de Montréal en 1961, avant d'aller poursuivre sa formation à Paris où il obtenait un premier Diplôme d'études supérieures en droit et un deuxiéme en science politique. De 1963 jusqu'a 1973 il était professeur titulaire enseignant le droit administratif et le droit international à l'Université Laval. Il est actuellement Directeur de la Recherche, Ministère de la Justice, Québec.

IVAN R. FELTHAM is Director of the Business Law Program of the Osgoode Hall Law School of York University, Toronto. He is a consultant on economic regulation and other aspects of business law and is counsel to the Select Committee of the Ontario Legislative Assembly on Economic and Cultural Nationalism

GERALD F. FITZGERALD is Principal Legal Officer of the International Civil Aviation Organization (ICAO) and a part-time lecturer at the Institute of Air and Space Law, McGill University. He is a member of the New Brunswick bar and Honorary Chairman of the Executive Committee of the Canadian Branch of the International Law Association (Canadian Society of International Law). Dr Fitz-Gerald is a frequent contributor to legal publications.

WOLFGANG G. FRIEDMANN (1907–1972) was trained in civil law in his native Germany but achieved his global reputation while teaching and studying in common law jurisdictions. He held appointments in England, Australia, and at Toronto before accepting the position of Director of International Legal Studies at Columbia University. Renowned for his wide-ranging scholarship, his lengthy list of published works includes *Legal Theory* and *The Changing Structure of International Law*. Revisions to his contribution to this volume had not been completed when death intervened. It may well be his last manuscript to be published.

ALLAN E. GOTLIEB was a Rhodes Scholar and fellow of Wadham College at Oxford, England, prior to joining the Canadian foreign service in 1957. In June 1967 he was appointed Assistant Under-Secretary of State for External Affairs and Legal Adviser. During the years 1967 and 1968, he was Canadian alternate delegate to the United Nations General Assembly. On 1 December 1968 he became Deputy Minister of the new Department of Communications. On 15 May 1973 he was appointed Deputy Minister of the Department of Manpower and Immigration.

L.C. GREEN has been a University Professor at the University of Alberta since 1969. After serving as a Deputy Military Prosecutor in India, he was successively lecturer in International Law, London (1946–60); professor of International Law, University of Singapore (1960–5); and professor, Department of Political Science, University of Alberta (1965–9). His published works include *International Law through the Cases* (3rd edition, 1970); and he has been rapporteur of the International Law Association's Committee on Asylum since 1961.

DAVID H.W. HENRY practised law for many years with the Department of Justice in Ottawa. From 1960 to 1973 he was Director of Investigation and Research under the Combines Investigation Act. For seven years during that period he was Chairman of the OECD Committee of Experts on Restrictive Business Practices. His research has focused on the Combines Investigation Act and restrictive business practices, both in the domestic and international fields. He was for some years a lecturer at the law schools of the University of Ottawa and McGill University. He is now a judge of the Supreme Court of Ontario.

JOHN P. HUMPHREY interrupted his teaching career at McGill University to spend twenty years (1946–66) as Director of the Division of Human Rights, United Nations Secretariat. He had joined the McGill law faculty in 1936 and was appointed Dean of the faculty shortly before joining the UN. Upon his return to McGill, Dr Humphrey was professor of law and political science (1966–71) and was visiting professor of law at Toronto in 1971–72. Since ending his full-time UN service, he has been a member of the UN Sub-Commission on the Prevention of Discrimination and the Protection of Minorities (1966–71) and its chairman in 1970; a member of the Royal Commission on the Status of Women in Canada; and President, Canadian Commission, International Year for Human Rights.

GEORGE IGNATIEFF, Provost of Trinity College, University of Toronto, since 1972, had a career of thirty-two years in the Canadian foreign service. During this period he occupied various posts relating to disarmament and defence problems. These included: principal diplomatic adviser to General A.G.L. McNaughton, Head of the Canadian Delegation to the UN Atomic Energy Commission 1946–8; Head of the Defence Liaison Division, Department of External Affairs 1954–7; Assistant Under-Secretary of State for External Affairs 1960–1; Canada's Permanent Representative to the North Atlantic Council 1961–5; Canadian Ambassador to the United Nations 1966–8; and Canada's Permanent Representative to the Geneva Disarmament Conference 1969–72.

DOUGLAS M. JOHNSTON is professor of law and political science at the University of Toronto and currently visiting professor of law at Dalhousie University. He has had faculty appointments at Harvard law school, New School for Social Research, Louisiana State University, and the University of Western Ontario. He served as Director of the China Programme of the Canadian Institute of International Affairs and has written extensively on the law of the sea, Chinese foreign policy, and international environmental problems.

FREDERICK J.E. JORDAN pursued studies in law at British Columbia and Michigan. He is a member of the Ontario bar. Since 1964 he has taught international, constitutional, and environmental law, first at Carleton University in Ottawa, and subsequently at Queen's University, Kingston. During this period he acted as a research consultant to the Canadian Section of the International Joint Commission. Professor Jordan is now on leave from Queen's University, working as a member of the Legal Research and Planning Section of the Department of Justice in Ottawa.

S. JOSHUA LANGER is a graduate of the University of Toronto, Osgoode Hall, and Columbia University Law School. His law teaching experience includes lecturing in international law at the universities of Manitoba and Windsor. His research has focused on legal issues related to natural resources, a subject which he has frequently discussed as a member of academic and professional panels and on television.

W.R. LEDERMAN, QC, was professor of law, University of Saskatchewan (1945–6 and 1948–9); Sir James Dunn Professor of Law, Dalhousie University (1949–58); and Dean of Law, Queen's University (1958–68). Since 1968 he has been professor of law at Queen's University. He is a member of the bars of Saskatchewan, Nova Scotia, and Ontario. His areas of special interest are federalism and the constitutional law of Canada, private international law, and jurisprudence.

EDWARD G. LEE is a graduate of British Columbia and Harvard and is a member of the British Columbia bar. He joined the Department of External Affairs in 1956 and has held positions abroad in Djakarta, Indonesia, and London, England. Since returning to Ottawa in 1969 he has been Director of the Legal Operations Division, Director of the Personnel Operations Division, and is now Legal Adviser to the Department of External Affairs and Director General of the Bureau of Legal Affairs.

LEONARD H.J. LEGAULT was admitted to the Alberta bar in 1961 and joined the Department of External Affairs the following year. He has held diplomatic assignments in Warsaw, New Delhi, and Geneva. He headed the Law of the Sea Section of the Legal Bureau of the Department of External Affairs for four years and has served on numerous Canadian delegations to various international conferences on maritime matters. He is now Director-General of the International Fisheries and Marine Directorate of the Department of the Environment, on secondment from the Department of External Affairs.

RONALD ST JOHN MACDONALD, QC, previously professor of law at Osgoode Hall, University of Western Ontario, and University of Toronto, is currently Weldon Professor and Dean of the Faculty of Law at Dalhousie University. Formerly Rapporteur and Vice-Chairman of the Third Committee of the General Assembly, he is at present a member of the Committee on the Elimination of Racial Discrimination, a member of the Council of Management of the British Institute of International Law, and the founding president of the Canadian Council on International Law.

BRUCE C. MCDONALD is a partner in the Toronto law firm of Lang, Michener, Cranston, Farquharson & Wright where he is engaged primarily in commercial litigation. He received his post-secondary training at the University of Manitoba, Queen's University (LL B), and, as a W.W. Cook Fellow, at the University of Michigan (LL M, SJD). From 1964 to 1970 he was a law professor at Queen's University. He has served as an adviser to the Department of External Affairs, the Department of Communications, and the Patent and Copyright Office.

GERALD L. MORRIS is a professor in the Faculty of Law, University of Toronto. He is also appointed in the University's Institute of Environmental Sciences. After qualifying in 1957 as a barrister and solicitor in Ontario, he spent the years 1958–66 with Canada's Department of External Affairs, serving in Ottawa, New Delhi, and New York. He has held his present appointment since 1966.

DONAT PHARAND is professor of Law at the Faculty of Law (Civil Law Section) of the University of Ottawa where he has been teaching since 1959, after postgraduate studies and four years of private practice. He wrote his doctoral dissertation in 1954–5 on the 'Sector Theory in the Arctic,' for which he was awarded a prize by the Law Faculty of the University of Paris, and has been writing extensively for a number of years on problems relating to the Arctic. He has recently completed a study on the 'Law of the Sea of the Arctic,' on which his contribution to this volume is partially based.

WILLIAM R. RAUENBUSCH graduated from Osgoode Hall Law School in 1971 and obtained his LLM from Harvard in 1972. He anticipates admission to the bar of Ontario in 1974.

LOUIS SABOURIN est directeur de l'Institut de Coopération internationale de l'Université d'Ottawa dont il a été le fondateur. Auteur de plusieurs volumes et d'articles en droit public et sur la politique canadienne et internationale, il a été auparavant directeur du département de Science politique avant de devenir doyen de la faculté des Sciences sociales de l'Université d'Ottawa. Membre du barreau du Québec, le professeur Sabourin a été président de la Société canadienne de Science politique ainsi que de la section d'Ottawa de la Société canadienne de droit international.

JOSEPH W. SAMUELS is associate professor of law, University of Western Ontario. He is the author of a *Draft Protocol on Weather Modification* (World Peace Through Law Center, Geneva, 1971) and Chairman of the Center's Committee on Weather Modification. He is also legal adviser to the Canadian Red Cross Society on international humanitarian law.

A.J. STONE, QC, is a graduate of St Francis Xavier, Dalhousie, and Harvard and is a member of the bars of Nova Scotia and Ontario. He teaches admiralty law at the University of Toronto and is former National Chairman, Maritime Law Section, Canadian Bar Association. He is a partner in the law firm of MacKinnon, McTaggart in Toronto.

MICHAEL J. VECHSLER graduated from the University of Toronto in arts and in law before joining the Department of External Affairs in 1969. He has served in the Department's Legal, Cultural Affairs, Aid and Development and Protocol Divisions and at the Canadian Embassy in South Africa.

ERIK B. WANG graduated from McGill University and was admitted to the Quebec bar before joining the Department of External Affairs as a foreign service officer in

1958. He served abroad in Copenhagen (1959), Oslo (1960–2), and New Delhi (1966–8). In Ottawa he was seconded to the Directorate-General of Plans, Canadian Forces Headquarters, Department of National Defence (1968–9), and served in Defence Relations Division, Department of External Affairs (1970–1). He is currently Counsellor at the Canadian Permanent Mission to the United Nations, New York.

D. COLWYN WILLIAMS (1916–1971) was Assistant Dean of Law, University of Saskatchewan, at the time of his sudden death in December 1971. He had held several prior academic appointments and was a barrister of the Middle Temple and a member of the Saskatchewan bar. He was President of the United Nations Association in Canada and Chairman of the International Law Section of the Association of Canadian Law Teachers. He had been Director and Vice-Chairman of Canadian University Service Overseas. He died shortly after completing the initial draft of his contribution to this volume.

J.P. WOLFE is a colonel in the Canadian Armed Forces serving as Deputy Judge Advocate General at Canadian Forces Headquarters in Ottawa. From January until July 1973, he was stationed in Vietnam as Legal Officer on the Canadian delegation and on the secretariat of the truce supervisory commission in that nation.

JOHN A. YOGIS is associate professor at Dalhousie Law School and a member of the Nova Scotia bar. He directs the Legal Research and Writing Program at Dalhousie and teaches Legal Process, Wills, Agency, and Public International Law. His published research has centred on Canadian fishery treaties and Canadian sovereignty in the Arctic.

Foreword

This volume is a co-operative venture. The thirty-eight papers, by as many authors, cover nearly all aspects of Canadian relations with international organizations and with other members of the family of nations.

One hesitates to suggest that a book is unique; but this one is certainly unusual. It is unusual in the vast scope of the subject matter of the papers. Any scholar who seeks to write a treatise that will serve the on-coming generation in the way that Oppenheim has served us will need to break away from traditional limitations and make a new framework taking in the constitution and functioning of international organizations, the relations of individuals and corporations with states other than those of which they are nationals, multinational corporations, control of the extraterritorial activities of individuals and corporations, pollution of the air, the fresh waters and the ocean, the seabed, the continental shelf, and the conservation of the fisheries. Such a scholar will find much of the material for such a framework in this book.

This book is also unusual in the matter of authorship. The contributors' list indicates that it is largely a co-operative venture between members of the academic community and officials of the Department of External Affairs. Nevertheless, it is noteworthy that there are contributions from officials of other departments, including the Judge Advocate General. The inclusion of the Judge Advocate General is especially important because the armed forces are so largely concerned with Canada's relations with other members of the family of nations, whether allies, neutrals, or enemies. Further, the laws governing such members have had an important impact on Canada in matters such as visiting forces, joint command, war trials, and the like. It is also important that this book contains contributions from jurists who bring a lifetime of experience in the field of international organization into the venture and, incidentally, that a new dimension, the air, is brought into the picture.

A number of the papers are by contributors whose background is the civil rather than the common law. International law was the brainchild of jurists with Roman law backgrounds. Its thought pattern was Roman rather than 'common.' In the early centuries, the thought pattern of diplomacy and the thinking of diplomats was almost entirely Roman and, even today, with the United States in the driver's seat and the United Nations in New York, the civil law way of thinking is still paramount.

The weakest point in our legal education, in provinces other than Quebec, is our neglect of the study of Roman law, legal history, and jurisprudence. This neglect is shared by most of the universities in the United States. It is for this reason that lawyers and judges and diplomats nurtured in the civilian tradition are apt to have some difficulty in understanding and fully appreciating legal propositions put forward by those of us who were indoctrinated from our childhood with the peculiar form of ancestor worship which is known as *stare decisis*. For such lawyers – and they may be a substantial part of our reading public – the contributions by our Canadian civilians may be doubly welcome, because of their intrinsic merit, and because the pattern of their argumentation will be familiar and readily comprehensible.

It would be invidious to make any comments on any of the papers or on any of the contributors. I am, however, impelled to say something about the venture. To me it is a milestone marking the progress made in dealing with Canadian relations with international organizations and with other members of the family of nations, whether on the academic or the public service level. Thirty years ago, it would not have been possible to assemble in Canada a comparable group of contributors. It might have been possible to gather together ten or twelve people with some knowledge of international law and organizations, but they would not have had the depth of experience both in active practice and in academic intercourse. They would have spent most of their efforts in establishing a position in which Canada was fully recognized as a member of the family of nations, and those who were in the academic world would have been living in a period when there were few opportunities to make contact with their opposite numbers in other countries in symposia or conferences. It is the members of this small group, however, who have been largely responsible for the sudden emergence of Canada into the international stream and for the important role played by this country during the last thirty-odd years. This enlarged role has led inevitably to awakened interest and experience in international matters and to the existence of a substantial group of persons who can speak with authority. It is for this reason that the editors have been able to assemble these chapters, all the product of the research of scholars and officials whose competence is beyond question.

JOHN E. READ

Introduction

This collection of essays brings together for the first time a comprehensive Canadian conspectus on current issues and developments in international law. We have been fortunate in obtaining contributions from more than thirty academic or government international lawyers and private practitioners. Ten years ago this figure would have represented almost the entire community of persons actively engaged in international law in Canada, but today it represents barely one-third. With so many at work in the field today we have had little difficulty in covering most areas of the subject by assigning a different chapter to each contributor.

As inevitably happens, illness, unexpected career developments, or other causes have prevented several authors from completing their chapters. Although replacements could not be arranged in time for inclusion in the volume, the gaps have been reduced in some measure by broadening the scope of related chapters. The low incidence of casualties among the planned chapters was remarkable, however, and the editors appreciate the great effort by contributing authors to meet editorial deadlines despite the heavy pressure of other obligations.

The production of so large a volume requires a number of months after receipt of the manuscripts by the editors. A few of the chapters relating to especially dynamic areas of international concern were revised during the last stages of editorial work, but other authors were unable to undertake a comprehensive review. Inevitably, some chapters may already have fallen behind the march of recent events. The essential significance of the volume, however, is hardly affected by incipient obsolescence with respect to chronological details. Our objective has been the achievement of a less ephemeral value: the sketching of a modern Canadian world view.

To the extent that the contributors emphasize issues of special interest in Canada or reveal Canadian assumptions and preferences, this book may be regarded as a fairly complete reflection of contemporary Canadian approaches to international law. We hope that the collection, seen in this light, will be useful to non-Canadian as well as Canadian readers who are interested in national and regional contributions to the development of the international legal order.

We hope also that these essays, taken together, will serve as a text for students of Canadian foreign policy as well as for Canadian students of international law and organization. Active involvement in international organizations, especially the organs and agencies of the United Nations, has been a conspicuous element in the political history of Canada since the end of World War II. To students of Canadian history interested in assessing the depth of Canadian commitment in the last three decades to the purposes of the organized world community, many of these chapters should be of value.

As they peruse this book, readers may wish to consider whether Canada has increasingly turned away from internationalism in the past few years in favour of unilateral pursuit of national goals. Have we, perhaps, long deluded ourselves concerning the extent of our objective altruism? Or are we assuming a growing role as a progressive voice in multilateral consultations on the numerous, complex problems facing the world? What attitude is appropriate for a middle power such as Canada?

The years immediately preceding the publication of this work have seen not only a rapid increase in the number of international lawyers in Canada but also their accelerated development as a nationally organized professional community. In the summer of 1972 the Canadian Council on International Law held its inaugural meeting and in October of the same year convened its first annual conference. Two years earlier the Canadian Bar Association had elevated its special committee on international and constitutional law to a continuing national section and began organizing provincial subsections. The Canadian Branch of the International Law Association continues its varied activities, including its extremely valuable support for the *Canadian Yearbook of International Law*. While financial limitations severely curtail the international law section of the Association of Canadian Law Teachers, its members have begun to explore means of developing year-round liaison on matters especially pertinent to teachers in the field.

It seems reasonable to hope that initiatives from these groups, and from interested official quarters, will carry Canadian research in international law and organization into a more vigorous and fruitful phase. This prospect is enhanced by the current willingness of officials of the Department of External Affairs and other federal agencies to keep their academic counterparts well informed on current issues through the supply of documents and by their own participation in conferences and seminars of joint interest to government and university specialists.

The scope of this collection is so vast that we have made no direct effort in the final chapter to draw themes or highlights together into a coherent whole. Instead we have chosen to review the history of international law teaching in Canadian universities and of federal government practice in the field so as to provide a background to a general examination of Canadian approaches to international law and organization and the presentation of some recommendations.

Although it would be impractical to attempt to acknowledge the assistance of all those who contributed in one way or another to the publication of this volume, a few names must be mentioned. Nancy Iacobucci undertook the very difficult task of substantially revising and polishing several manuscripts, when death or other imperative causes prevented their authors from completing the final draft. Claude Emanuelli accepted the challenge of preparing the bilingual subject index and the accompanying lists. And among those who toiled on our behalf at the University of Toronto Press, we wish especially to thank Jean Houston and Diane Nelles, who shouldered the main burden of shepherding the volume through the publication process.

Finally, we record our hope that this volume will stimulate further debate and research on issues relating to international law and organization. We solicit reactions and suggestions from readers.

R.St J.M., G.L.M., D.M.J.
June 1973

PERSPECTIVES

MAXWELL COHEN

1/Canada and the International Legal Order: An Inside Perspective

Over two centuries in search of an accommodation among English- and French-speaking Canadians; an almost equal length of time in search of a framework for coexistence with that part of the first British Empire in North America that turned to 'trans-aqueous separatism' in a thirteen colony solution to aspirations and resentment; a century of federal union that moved decisively from 'colony to nation' but has yet to achieve a sense of durable integrity in that nationhood; a universe comprising nation state-UN Charter systems facing nuclear weapons, white affluence and non-white poverty, escalating technology and environmental damage, the green revolution and population runaway; these are the gross historical profiles within which an emergent Canada now views itself and the world in the last third of the twentieth century.

But focusing primarily, as this volume does, on the relations of Canada to and its contribution towards international systems in general, and the international legal order in particular, the perspective must not only embrace the interplay between the domestic and the international but must pay special attention to the role of agencies in the public and private sectors which have helped form and inform the Canadian mind and national policies. Hence, the international legal order viewed from a Canadian standpoint is not merely a recitation of the evolution of the specific but varied forms of obligations undertaken by Canada. It is also, and perhaps of equal importance, a study of the professional interest and responses of the bench and bar; the development of scholarship in the law schools and related political science areas; and, finally, the extent to which the many intellectual and statecraft trends and experiences, evolving largely out of western developed societies, have been shared in by Canadians as they moved during the past century into the mainstream of international dealings. These, and the related flow of ideas from several disciplines, consciously or otherwise have shaped the image and the reality of the modern international legal order.

FROM COLONY TO COMMONWEALTH

In a sense Canadian experience with the international legal order is part of the very beginnings of Canada itself. Conquest, war-making, treaty law, and the rights of a new subject people related to a grand imperial-colonial design marked the beginnings of the experiment that was to become Canada. In a curious way the 'victories' of 1759 and 1760, the proclamations establishing the new imperial government, and the Treaty of Paris of 1763 all laid the foundations for what was then in fact a united, continental British North America, except for Spanish claims largely in the southern and southwestern territories and the Russian presence on the Alaska mainland for another century. But within less than two decades, in 1783, another Treaty of Paris climaxed the revolution of 1776, and British North America's ambitions now were split between a 'loyal' north and the rebellious south – the independent Thirteen, now the United States of America. Revolution, war, and new boundaries had reshaped the British North American remnant, infusing it with a deep and lasting imprint so that, in a sense, the creation of the components that one day were to become an independent Canada had first to be defined by an international legal settlement, itself the product of revolt, war, and dissolution of the first British Empire to be quickly replaced by the second.

Hence it may be said that Canada was sired in warfare, mothered in treaties, and nurtured in the delicate crèche of both imperial constitutional relations and international law as they were in the latter eighteenth century. To this day the most urgent and powerful concerns of Canadian policy, for its growth and identity, are an evolutionary reflection of these fractured imperial beginnings. Canada's boundaries were not made final until as late as the Alaska Panhandle dispute of 1903, and a continuing anxiety exists for the management of a society and an economy where the pull of continental integration was always to parallel the stress of searching for national self-definition and political autonomy. No one could have foreseen in 1776 or 1783 that the new, independent English-speaking United States would grow so rapidly as to overshadow quickly the imperial remnant to the north and create by these geopolitical facts the permanent crisis in Canadian life; namely, its development beside an immense neighbour who would outstrip Canada in everything, perhaps, but the determination to achieve an integrity of its own. It is no surprise, therefore, that the long-term Canadian international experience *par excellence,* and the concomitant political-legal preoccupation, should have been the form and substance for managing Canadian relations with the United States; and this remains true to the present day.

Yet side by side with these continental parameters, imposed by geography, politics, and law on an emerging Canada, there was an almost equally important school for that 'emergence' in the shift from Empire to Commonwealth. The dominant role played by the position of Canada in the evolution of the second British Empire, and its transformation in the latter half of the nineteenth century and the first quarter of the twentieth into the Commonwealth, proved to be a double training ground of paramount significance. For at one and the same time the movement from 'colony to nation' required a search for political and 'constitutional' solutions within the imperial system which slowly transformed dependence to independence for those British North American communities that remained outside the United States solution of 1783. That process trained Canadians to obtain in peace what their revolutionary cousins in the United States sought and only realized with war: responsible government, representative and essentially independent in the management of local life from a centralized, distant imperial control.

Hence, with responsible government in Nova Scotia in 1848 and the varied experiments with parallel developments in the Canadas, New Brunswick, and Prince Edward Island, there was laid the foundation for the united Canada of 1867, perhaps accelerated by annexation fears of and efforts from the United States and by the lessons of the civil strife there between north and south. Confederation thus reflected a triple process: increasing autonomy from imperial Britain; accommodation between French- and English-speaking peoples in Quebec as well as in New Brunswick and Ontario and later the Northwest; and finally, through unity as a barrier to the possible threat of absorption of people and territory by a rapidly expanding and expansionist neighbour.

Yet once Confederation resolved these various needs and absorbed the forces behind them into a new political entity, the altered relationships between the United Kingdom and the new dominion became the starting point not only for the development of a process leading to the transformation of 'Empire into Commonwealth,' but also a process of education in international dealings that the Commonwealth imposed on the United Kingdom and Canada and later on other member states. For the Empire-Commonwealth was not only a political system but a legal order, however specialized may have been some of the relationships between members *inter se* and, indeed, giving rise to the classical *inter se* doctrine. What was evolving from 1867 onward, from the international lawyer's point of view was a curious mixture of quasi-constitutional patterns among the members of the Empire-Commonwealth parallelled by international legal claims and positions, and principles of operation, as the independence features of the Commonwealth system began to outpace the imperial ones. Hence, members of the Empire-Commonwealth were becoming international legal persons in their own right while continuing their special status within the Commonwealth political-legal framework. In a sense, therefore, Canada has had a multiple perspective on her own international legal evolution. There has been the transition of individual, non-independent colonies to independence within a federal state, with all of the domestic and international problems and positions this has imposed upon leaders and governments. There has been the evolution of the Commonwealth itself with the particular intra-Commonwealth relationships that partook partly of a constitutional-like system of dealings as well as of an international system. And, finally, there has been the emergence of a sovereign Canada whose posture vis à vis the world and fellow Commonwealth members has been one of a classical independent nation state, qualified until recently by the curious anomalies of Commonwealth status. Until a generation ago this status permitted some legal theorists to pretend that the nation state, as a description of Canadian legal claims, was not precisely analogous to states without such a Commonwealth systemic origin.

All of these, cumulatively, have in fact given Canadian scholars, civil servants, politicians, and opinion-makers a fused, prismatic perception of the international legal order or orders to which they belong and the obligations that have conditioned their political and legal thought because of these linkages. Today the effect of this training process has been to make it possible for Canadians very quickly to assume multiple roles in the international legal order, to feel comfortable with old and new affiliations; for example, maintaining the Anglo-Commonwealth association while entering upon the Franco-Commonwealth experience with some 'feel' for what this may mean politically and juridically. At the same time, Canadians are able to participate intensively at two ends of the spectrum of international experience: intricate and vital bilateral relations with the United States in many sectors and equally intricate and significant multilateral relations regionally and universally with many states over all the world's subject matter and with varieties of social systems.

CANADA AND THE UNITED STATES: CONTINENTAL ACCOMMODATIONS

If the Commonwealth was the 'original' school for Canadian nationhood and for evolving international personality it was the United States that gave Canada its first taste of learning to live in the severe world of realpolitik where bilateral dealings with an immensely powerful neighbour were the basic geopolitical facts of life for Canada. It is no surprise, therefore, that some of the most important and creative international legal experiences for Canada have emerged from its almost two centuries of dealings with the sometime imperial brothers who went their own national way. Tariffs (and reciprocity agreements), boundaries, boundary waters, fisheries, immigration, and joint obligations to native peoples were all a product of the nineteenth-century process of Canada learning to live successfully with the United States. 'Continentalism,' no popular word today, was nevertheless destiny for both, and many legal arrangements were mirrors of that shared reality.

The twentieth century multiplied the interpenetration of the two societies, accentuated by two world wars and the military-economic-political co-operation to which these led. And so a complex regulatory network evidenced by instruments ranging from a simple exchange of notes to formal treaties marked the era of expanding involvement – in defence production, west coast fisheries, post-World War II military policy for the continent, resource development with the emphasis on mineral, petroleum, forest products, the energy demands from the United States (from the Columbia River Treaty to natural gas exports), and the St Lawrence Seaway. More recently contradictory trends have emerged such as the new limits on immigration and restrictive economic policies side by side with an immense common obligation to refresh the Great Lakes system from joint pollution over many years. Some interesting case law, through the arbitral process in one form or another, has come out of these relations, albeit infrequently. 'Hot pursuit' in the *I'm Alone,* poisonous fumes from the *Trail Smelter,* and the flooding of recreational shorelines by *Gut Dam* have resulted in doctrines and footnotes uniquely North American in their origin but perhaps universal in their significance. This is certainly true for the *Trail Smelter* case, the first transnational air pollution dispute to invite arbitration and become a precedent.

Most important of all have been the recent debates in Canada over foreign ownership and investment largely from the United States; over the impact on Canada's cultural integrity of United States media, from magazines to television; and over the powerful model the United States presents in almost all of its intellectual and personal lifestyles for emulation by Canada. At the moment of writing the economic vulnerability of Canada to US decision-making has become the primary point of focus. But long before this time Canadian imagination ought to have evolved some grand strategy for the evolution of an economy and a society. Although it might be dependent on the markets, the venture capital, the technology, and the managerial leadership of its neighbour, it should have somehow provided buffers more constructive than quotas or tariffs to assure the minimum of injury to Canada from unilateral United States decision-making, particularly on economic matters directly affecting Canadian exports or internal economic development. The failure to have evolved some counter-weight to the enormous impact of US economic behaviour on Canadian fortunes, not merely by seeking trade diversification multilaterally, which Canada has in fact done, but by evolving some common umbrella to share facts and to modify destructive unilateral action, has been perhaps the largest single failure of Canadian political imagination in its international dealings since maturity as a state was achieved.

Nevertheless, living with the United States has become Canada's principal teacher in the art of international 'self-protection' with all of the political and legal significance of that experience, and it is likely to be the most important single source of Canadian anxiety and Canadian training for the years to come.

SOVEREIGN CANADA: AT HOME AND ABROAD

It is difficult to estimate the precise effects of the interplay between the evolving quasi-constitutionalism of the Empire-Commonwealth framework of the nineteenth- and early twentieth-century period and the emergence of Canada as an international legal person in its own right and subject to the classical system. From most of the inside and outside perspectives, there were, to be sure, a number of anomalies conspicuous until the end of World War I, perhaps less so after the Statute of Westminster in 1931, and certainly reduced with the abolition of Appeals to the Judicial Committee in 1949. Untouched, as yet, however, is the gross anomaly of an amending power for the Canadian 'constitution' (the British North America Act *simpliciter*) remaining within the parliament of a 'foreign' sovereign state. There is a certain political and scholarly quaintness to this interplay between Canada as an international person with sovereign majesty evolving over the years and Canada as a Commonwealth member, subject to the very loose political rules of that unique multiracial club and also to some of the legal anachronisms carried over from an older day. Extradition, shipping, citizenship (until recently), and the amending power still bear the marks of the older imperial connection; indeed, it is probably true to say that it was a forceful intermingling of war-making, and more generally of political policy, which helped to bring about the last clear stages of an emerging sovereignty. Canadian tariff policy had been in the hands of local negotiators from the beginning of Confederation; even the Boundary Waters Treaty had as its principal negotiators Laurier and Pugsley, although the governor general from Ottawa and the British ambassador in Washington were the formal channels of communication and final treaty-making.

Hence, while it is true that responsible government and essential autonomy were *de facto* true by the third or fourth quarter of the nineteenth century, there were a number of imperial threads still tying the robust Canadian image to the 'Mother Country.' Good illustrations of this mixture of the imperial-Commonwealth procedures, and their effect on clear international personality as such, may be seen in the powers of the governor general, perhaps until 1947; the pre-World War I appointment of the commander in chief of the Canadian forces from among imperial officers, particularly the royal family; the disputes over the Canadian contribution to and management of its forces in the Boer War; the controversy over Canadian naval policy in the first years of the twentieth century; and the crucial role for the image and fact of sovereignty or independence played by military issues in World War I, since the independence of the Canadian Corps and the determination to have a separate identity for that corps had important psychological and political consequences. They probably influenced the legal-political decision for Canada to be a separate 'signatory' (through initials at least) to the Treaty of Versailles. And when to these events are added the Commonwealth conferences of 1926 and 1930 and the Balfour Resolution in 1926, climaxed by the Statute of Westminster in 1931, and the abolition of criminal appeals to the Judicial Committee in the same year – to which should be added the establishment of the Department of External Affairs as a working organism in 1928 (although the department itself was created in 1909), along with the Canadian treaty series – it is obvious how intermixed were the growth lines of a sovereign independent Canada with the evolutionary patterns of the Commonwealth itself.

World War II virtually destroyed any pretensions of 'automatic' political or military response to the policies of the United Kingdom or any juridical theories of 'subordination.' The insistence on a separate Canadian declaration of war on 9 September 1939, the determined position of the government with respect to status and command of Canadian troops, and the special case of the Royal Canadian Air Force, and even the insistent claims to independence for the Royal Canadian Navy were all part of the final erosion of umbilical links to London – as if the reality had not already been forecast by World War I, the Chanak incident over Turkey, and Canadian behaviour generally in the League of Nations and in the multilateral world of the interwar years. What became clear, however, was that the political, military, and legal fading of authority from United Kingdom, imperial-Commonwealth sources was being replaced by the voluntary alliances of the NATO-NORAD system and this, in effect, provided the primary focus of the new struggle for independence *de facto* if not *de jure,* together with economic questions to be turned now towards the American neighbour and away from the imperial 'mother.' But unlike the Commonwealth story, there were no historical-juridical anomalies to be resolved. United States-Canadian relations have been a case of bilateral dealings between sovereign equals on a plane of majestic inequality.

Enough has been said to indicate how significant has been this combined Empire-Commonwealth, and classical international law and legal personality experience, for the evolution of Canadian sovereignty and Canadian policy in the international arena. It was not difficult for Canada to make 'independent' claims to becoming a member of the League of Nations or to be a founding signatory for the Charter of the United Nations. The Commonwealth anomalies in the eyes of the international community were insufficient to offset the much stronger juridical image of independence. And although to the present day the role of the Queen, the Office of the Governor General, the problems of Letters of Credence and of 'full powers,' amendments to the British North America Act still vested in Westminster, the remnants of extradition, and *inter se* doctrines and procedures for Commonwealth members are all hangovers from an earlier time, they provide only cryptic reminders that whatever may be the dilemmas of internal Canadian unity, the external political image and reality, as an independent member of the international community, is long and firmly established.

THE INTERNATIONAL COMMITMENT

While other papers in this volume will deal with specific Canadian experiences with international organizations, 'peace-keeping' and perhaps the new framework of

Canada's second commonwealth – Francophonie – as well as with its 'second neighbourhood' – the Soviet Union and the Arctic – it is nevertheless worth reflecting for a moment on the complex web which Canada has deliberately woven, or inevitably become involved with, in these many multilateral and bilateral relations and systems.

The commitment to international organizations as such began, of course, with the League-ILO system in 1919-20, although Canada had been a member of the International Postal Union, now the Universal Postal Union, since the end of the nineteenth century. Moreover, the unique Canadian experience after 1909-10 with the Boundary Waters Treaty and the International Joint Commission had provided Canadians with a feel for a binational regulatory mechanism dealing with perhaps the most complex and lengthy water boundary system in the world, stretching from Cornwall to Lake of the Woods for thirteen hundred miles and with about a hundred and fifty lakes, rivers, and streams crossing the US-Canadian boundary from sea to sea.

It is perhaps too fanciful to suggest that this very special Canadian-US expertise in a limited field of boundary waters management – and other US (and Commonwealth) dealings – prepared Canada for its slow but steady involvement with the social and economic aspects of the League of Nations. Nevertheless, Canada assumed its obligations under the 'optional clause' of the International Court of Justice, and the Dandurand statement of 1929 dealing with Canadian reservations was limited to matters of domestic jurisdiction and intra-Commonwealth affairs, as well as matters where the parties agreed to some other method of peaceful settlement and to the special case where proceedings might be suspended in the case of disputes submitted to consideration by the Council of the League. But in 1939 when the optional clause of the League of Nations was renewed, Canada added that it would not regard this acceptance now as covering disputes arising out of events occurring in World War II.

Finally, it may be said with respect to the League of Nations-ILO system that the degree of political involvement and juridical obligation envisaged by Canada for itself was essentially limited. Canadian internationalism in the interwar years was skin deep and no better illustration of this comparatively cautious affiliation with this experiment in 'world order' may be recollected than Canadian treatment of sanctions against Italy in which the government of the day repudiated its League delegate in 1936 for daring to vote on the high ground of strengthened sanctions because of Italian transgression of the covenant through her invasion of Ethiopia.

But the colony-become-nation was learning and Canada's rapid engagement with World War II prepared her for the deeper commitment to the UN Charter system. Indeed, almost from the beginning, Canada's membership in the United Nations became a means of asserting a new sense of multilateral participation. It was not so much a simplistic faith in the para-constitutional world order of the charter, with its promise of a more effective regime of collective security and a more heightened awareness of economic, social, racial, and general human rights problems. For Canada it was a quite sound, instinctive judgment, characteristic of many small and middle powers, sensing the political asset that a universal system such as the charter provided for diplomatic entrée, for accelerated participation, indeed, for a role on the world stage that such countries could rarely, by themselves, have hoped to achieve. But the political system of the charter was a legal order as well, and the domestic political process of Canada as a federal state was peculiarly in tune with the evolving constitutional processes of the charter system which had to balance not merely organs within the system but the relations of the organization to member and non-member states as well – a problem not unreminiscent of the classical Canadian question in the relations of central to local governments. Of course, the scope and detail as well as the juridical traditions in this analogy are somewhat strained. But it remains nevertheless empirically visible that the multiple constitutional processes of a complex federal system, where the primary preoccupations are those involving the distribution of powers, are not unlike the now well-defined and still unresolved issues of the United Nations and the 'domestic jurisdiction' areas of controversy with member states.

Much will be said about Canada and the charter system in other contexts in this volume. It is sufficient to conclude here with the extraordinary and unexpected role which the mechanisms of the charter – particularly the work of the Sixth Committee, the International Law Commission, resolutions of the General Assembly, the Administrative Tribunal, the International Court of Justice, and, finally, law-making conferences sponsored by the United Nations based essentially upon resolutions of the General Assembly, (eg, law of the sea, diplomatic and consular immunities, and treaties) – had on the general development of international law whether stated in 'codification' or in 'progressive development' terms. Here the early Canadian interest in discovering the thrust of the Assembly as an 'authoritative' law-making or law-mirroring body, while not without enthusiasm was not particularly significant, except in the later years for vigorous contributions to the Law of the Sea conferences in 1958 and 1960 and in the preparations for the Stockholm (1972), Law of the Sea (1973-4), and IMCO (1973) conferences.

But Canadian reservations with respect to the compulsory jurisdiction of the International Court of Justice in the matters of the Arctic pollution zones legislation, as well as east and west coast fisheries control and pollution regulatory areas, doubtless have surprised some in the international community and possibly a substantial number of professional international lawyers in Canada itself. And yet so severe a step by a state with an otherwise credible image for the support of the international legal order may vaguely be defended in the face of the ambiguities with respect to present rules, or their absence, touching upon high seas environmental pollution hazards threatening coastal states and the non-existence of international machinery to regulate or abate such hazards even if the legal position were clear, which it is not.

Technology in this area is racing ahead, particularly in the matter of the seabed and subsoil exploration on the continental shelf, and therefore Canada with one of the largest shelf areas in the world, on three coasts and oceans, had very special reasons for its anxieties. In the Arctic it was the vulnerability and slow recovery capacities of the environment to petroleum and natural gas drilling and transportation hazards with the certainty of long-term effects from accidents on land or at sea. While on the east and west coasts the volume of traffic of a potentially hazardous nature, particularly petroleum transportation, threatened vital living resources and recreational facilities of coastal and over-the-shelf areas. In the absence of adequate international rules and controls, it is not surprising that Canada should have taken interim unilateral action. However there was no need for and little public debate about the hundred-mile Arctic pollution control zone that was adopted. A more flexible doctrine such as the 'priority of concern' concept in favour of a coastal state, without a specified limit as to mileage or distance, might have been more credible and realistic. It remains arguable, indeed, that the World Court may have been quite sympathetic to these special Arctic and east and west coast problems of environmental, habitat, pollution, and fisheries dangers, and that the expectations of Canada that the court would behave unpredictably were probably less than realistic in view of the fact that Canada was prepared to permit its new (and controversial) territorial seas limit of twelve miles to remain outside of its reservation and thus within the court's jurisdiction. Yet in view of the instability surrounding so much of the general debate over the Law of the Sea and international environmental questions generally, it is understandable that Canada should, after very serious consideration at the cabinet level, if not on the level of professional or public discourse, have decided to enter a 'reservation' on these actions to the court's jurisdiction, however unfortunate the result may have been for the parallel Canadian interest in strengthening the role of the court, as evidenced by its recent reply to the secretary general on the subject.

Finally, the charter system should be viewed in the light of the other systemic and bilateral experiences in Canada with the international legal order. Certainly at the multilateral level, while the Commonwealth retains a high priority in rhetoric, if not always in deed (trade preferences, conferences, scholarships, and general aid apart) for contemporary Canadian policy, it is the United Nations and its specialized agencies and other bodies and programs within the UN family that command the most elaborate and involved multinational institutional commitment of Canada. Yet, at the same time – again *pace* the Commonwealth – there is the very serious, and in the political-military sense perhaps the primary, Canadian international involvement through its NATO-NORAD obligations. Even if NORAD is regarded as primarily a bilateral Canada-US system, it is so keyed in with the whole of the North Atlantic Treaty mechanism that the combined effects in Canada are seen as a single overarching obligation. And, of course, the automatic effects of article V of the North Atlantic Treaty, creating an instant duty to come to the assistance of any member state under attack, – even though the degree of assistance seems to be left to the judgment of the signatory state concerned – has created a framework of commitment, through existent military forces in a common structure, that is more precise and more significant than any other Canadian security-political obligation.

While in a unique way the NATO structure, combined with the related NORAD political-administrative agreements with the United States, appears to be a self-contained framework, by the very language of the treaty itself, the intention has been to relate NATO, politically at least, to the charter system through the justifications and verbal linkages in the body of the treaty.

The other regional system to which Canada has something of a special relationship is, of course, the Organization of American States, where an 'observer status' does not signify that Canada has yet crossed the bridge of decision which would lead it towards full membership. Indeed, public opinion, facing both the political and economic effects of membership in the OAS, has held back accordingly even though there seem to be significant hemispheric reasons for keeping alive an alert and positive Canadian interest in membership. Curiously, an auxiliary reason for Canadian participation, at least indirectly, in some OAS activities is the long tradition of interest in international law characteristic of Latin America, inheriting nineteenth century legal classicism as part of the historic process of transforming a colonial continent into a hemispheric system of sovereign states. It has always seemed an intriguing accident of western, hemispheric, post-colonial, political development that North America should have emerged from empire into systems of continental federal states, while South America should have rejected empire in favour of sovereign states, although Bolivar and his contemporaries originally had hoped for something approaching a South American, continental federal structure.

Here are additional perspectives, therefore, which may be useful for the Canadian observer able to gain from these perhaps deeper insights into the Canadian position in the international legal order by being aware of the multiple approaches to that order through belonging directly or indirectly to differing 'systems.' For regional and ideological unities have created in fact 'diverse systems of public order.' It may not really be possible to perpetuate any simplistic view today of universal principles of international law as such. But it would be regrettable as value judgment, and incorrect as a fact judgment, to pretend that, despite this diversity, a considerable degree of universalism does not exist with respect to general principles of law to say nothing of those universal-multilateral treaties from the UN Charter to the Law of the Sea that provide 'universal' norms binding upon all states.

While it would be useful to explore the Canadian multilateral and bilateral experience in many functional and particularly economic areas from the General Agreement on Tariffs and Trade to the Automotive Products Agreement of 1965 with the United States, the truth is that no such detailed exposition is necessary here. What is significant, however, is not so much the descriptive detail as the awareness such data arouse with respect to the dimensions of the Canadian involvement with, and participation in, aspects of the international legal order generally and particularly. And in this process of involvement and commitment, Canada is caught up in making a choice of appropriate legal instruments that the subject matter, in a period of rapid political and technological change, inevitably imposes. That choice tends now to be reliance by Canada and, indeed by almost all states, on conventional international law, from simple declarations to exchanges of notes to formal treaties rather than on general principles of customary law as such – although these principles remain, in a variety of forms and sources, the substance and the spirit – the *fons et origo* – underlying the idea and the operations of the international legal system (or systems).

NEW FRIENDS AND RELATIONS

Some reference must be made to the juridical implications of two new Canadian experiments with international co-operation, the association with the French-speaking community – Francophonie – and the new agreements and protocols on trade, cultural and scientific exchanges, and political consultation with the Soviet Union. While in the case of Francophonie there are important political as well as cultural and developing-country aid problems, actual and potential, arising out of this new relationship, its most significant juridical consequence may be the effect it has had within Canada on the constitutional debate over the treaty-making power, and the indirect consequences of this debate on the general question of Quebec-federal relations both politically and constitutionally. Of course the formulas now evolved for Quebec, and joint Canada-Quebec representation and participation, have some significance for international law. But the place for this discussion will be more relevant in the following section on federalism and internationalism in the developing Canadian relationship to international political and legal systems. No serious juridical consequences flow from the association with Francophonie as a kind of second commonwealth, as it were, comparable to the variety of quasi-constitutional or inhibitory norms that characterized Canada's place in the Anglo-Commonwealth and Empire system for so long and, indeed, which continue in some forms to the present day.

In the case of the Soviet Union, fascinating prospects have been dangled before Canadian eyes as to the political, cultural, economic, and general possibilities this new relationship may offer. For the time being whatever may come of political consultation and the contributions to general detente it may provide, and, equally, whatever may arise from an intensive study of the possibilities of extending the scope of bilateral trade and cultural-scientific exchanges, it is clear that from the point of view of Canada's national and international interest, the most significant effect of this new relationship may be its development of the 'second neighbourhood' theory, through the Arctic Basin where both countries are the major sector powers. Put in the language of the international lawyer, these written agreements and perhaps their implications involve the potential of Canadian-USSR co-operation in the management of the Arctic Basin, its developmental, environmental, and pollution problems, with a common scientific input as well as a joint engineering effort towards the technology of sub-Arctic and Arctic development from urban growth to transportation and mineral exploitation. And although the Russians have refused so far to participate in an intergovernmental Arctic Basin conference and equally have refused to consider, for the time being, an Arctic Basin treaty, the Canadian initiative here is valuable. Friendly relations will keep open the avenues of discussion so that, at the very least, scientific management and co-operation between the two 'major' countries of the Arctic Basin increasingly will be possible. This will lead to a movement from purely bilateral dealings to including the Danes and the United States, the two other principal sector powers, because oceanic and habitat environmental questions can hardly be studied and resolved without the involvement in one way or another of all the basin states.

A new era thus has begun on various fronts for a variety of states, dramatized by the recognition of, and the presence of the government of the People's Republic of China in the United Nations; the Nixon visits to Peking and Moscow in 1972; the new US economics and its opportunities for (or threats to) the evolution of a more progressive and stable international monetary and trading system; the United Kingdom's entry into the Common Market with all of its implications for Europe, the Commonwealth, and Britain itself; the momentous rise of Japan largely unaffiliated in political or economic blocs, except for its special security and trade involvement with the United States, but soon to become the second industrial power in the world and already probably the first in Asia. Amidst all of these developments the Canadian initiatives towards the Soviet Union, and earlier towards China, have their significance for world politics and world order at least within the limited areas that a strategically located and affluent middle power ever can have on larger systems.

THE DEPARTMENT AND INTERNATIONAL LAW

In this study of the interaction of Canadian growth, affiliations, and policies, of its international legal and political posture and activities, it is important to examine, briefly, the role of the Department of External Affairs on one side, and the particular nature of Canadian federalism, as it affects Canada's international legal activities on the other.

The establishment of a foreign office presents no problems today for new states of whatever size coming to share in the multiple minuets of international relations. Yet it was not until 1909 that the Department of External Affairs was created by statute and not until 1928 that the department really began to function apart from the Prime Minister's Office to which until then it had been essentially subordinated (although the prime minister of Canada remained the secretary of state for external affairs until the separate appointment of Mr St Laurent after World War II). The files in the department, as a distinct entity, begin in that year, coinciding with the publication of the Canadian Treaty Series. The quality of the Canadian performance in international law matters was significantly affected by the paradox of early teams of devoted and competent departmental lawyers, of which Judge John Read was perhaps the best example of the period, and the relatively few numbers of full-time staff whose ability to function effectively required them to have some feeling for diplomacy, indeed a decent appreciation of their clients' business. But this process of training for the understanding and management of diplomacy as a regular foreign service officer raised questions about the ability of the department to satisfy the optimum needs of 'professionalism' as international lawyers side by side with the strong tradition of having such lawyers move about the service and bear their full share of functional and area experiences within the department as a whole and at its missions abroad.

It is not surprising that over the years there should have been a continuing and critical debate over the effect of the mixing of a generalist and professional pattern in the staffing and training of personnel for legal services and international law advisory duties at the highest level of continuing professional excellence. Nevertheless, no serious student of the department can avoid the impression that while the level of professionalism from time to time may have varied in quality, it has been a good deal higher than many of its critics were prepared to admit, judging by instruments drafted, advice given on crucial issues, and more recently on the intensity and quality of Canadian participation in international law-making forums, notably the United Nations and United Nations sponsored conferences.

A recent survey by the department of international law issues before the government of Canada, and the annual survey prepared by A.E. Gotlieb and later by J.A. Beesley of the department, for the *Canadian Year Book of International Law* covering varieties of legal matters arising out of state practice, reflect the very large range of problems demanding high competence and an understanding of the political, economic, and scientific substance of many issues ultimately taking juridical form

– again with the Law of the Sea a prime example. Then, too, the growing kinship between the department and the academic community, and occasionally the international legal community, is evidence of its recognition of the value of such co-operation and the desire to have a professional and intellectual ambience based upon the available Canadian professional resources. It would be improper, indeed impossible, to draw any conclusions from so short a review of the department's contribution to the international legal needs of Canada or to the development of international law generally, or to the rationale of Canadian state practice, or to the Canadian contribution generally to international legal discussions at the intergovernmental level since 1928. Nevertheless it is probably fair to say in the absence of a coherent and systematic study that, while the curve of excellence has varied, the general line of competence in the numbers of officers, full-time and part-time, involved in international law, shows a positive upward movement over the years. To this should be added a new problem, namely, the number of departments of the government of Canada that generally for their own substantive needs are also involved in international legal advisory services to the government of Canada – the Department of Justice, the Department of Environment, the Department of Energy, Mines and Resources, the Department of Indian Affairs and Northern Development, the Department of Transport, the Department of National Defence, and the Department of Finance and Industry, Trade and Commerce in their association with the International Monetary Fund, the Bank, GATT, and other agencies affecting Canada's international fiscal and monetary and commercial policies, and having a rule-making feedback affecting Canadian decision-making. The same 'rule-making' experience applies to the Department of Communications in relation to the International Telecommunications Union, the Department of Health and Welfare in relation with the World Health Organization, and the Ministry of Transport in relation to the International Civil Aviation Organization and IMCO.

The central and co-ordinating role of the Department of External Affairs for international policy-making, and the lead role it should have for international law-making, *simpliciter*, become a matter of some difficulty and delicacy in the face of the widening participation of other departments as described above. It has not been easy for External Affairs to preserve this departmental co-ordinating and lead role in the face also of the natural foreign policy interest and leadership of an activist prime minister and his Office. Yet it should be borne in mind that too great an insistence on co-ordination, and the lead-role position, could inhibit creative substantive initiatives by the departments directly concerned. At the same time while the cabinet and its committees provide, theoretically, the mechanism for assuring the synchronization of the departmental views leading to official Canadian positions, there is a great deal to be said for maintaining the primacy of a foreign office in the matter of both general diplomatic action and essentially legal advice for those issues clearly in the international forum, whether bilateral or multilateral.

FEDERALISM AND THE INTERNATIONAL LEGAL ORDER

There are some interesting perspectives to be observed in the evolution of the Canadian involvement with the international legal order as a reflection of the parallel evolution of a nation-state built upon a federal system. If it has taken over a century for Canadian federalism to evolve – without any guarantees at the moment as to the precise nature of its future – it is somewhat ironic that to others the image and activity of Canada as a nation state in the international forum most often appears secure, activist, and confident. Thus the questions to be asked about the interaction between the federal-political-legal development within Canada, and the emergence of Canada as an international legal and political person, are how far these two processes impinge, stimulate, inhibit, or otherwise affect each other.

At the outset it can be said that it may be easier to move backward in the analysis than forward because at this moment in time the legal entity or person known as Canada, in the international forum, has status, definition, and identity without question. But at this same moment in time the debate over the Canadian future as an internal experience has never been more acute. It takes both an urgent domestic form and a longer range continental form, but it is the domestic controversy, and its constitutional-political character, that may have more significance for this attempt to analyse the interactions of the international legal personality of Canada and the federal systemic reality.

The central point of this debate over the relationship of the federal reality to the international personality probably is to be found in the unfinished dialogue over a group of issues that includes the nature and scope of the treaty-making and treaty-implementing power; the legal position of the provinces in the international forum, if any; the special problem of Quebec in its relations to the world of Francophonie; the impact on theory of *de facto* administrative arrangements by provinces, for example, with bordering states of the United States for local functional needs; and, finally, the extent to which experience with the federal model tends to make Canada more sensitive to the operations of international organizations with respect to jurisdictional questions and, conversely, the extent to which international patterns controlling interstate, sovereign relations may indirectly influence Canadian constitutional thinking in the management of provincial-provincial relations and federal-provincial relations.

The treaty-making power has been the centrepiece of Canadian federal-constitutional debate with respect to the interplay between Canada, the state, and Canada, the federal system. Both state practice and, of course, the line of cases widely known as the continuing conventional wisdom on the issue – the *Radio, Aeronautics,* and *Labour Conventions* cases – all point to the standard position that probably holds 'true' today; namely, that while Canada may undertake any form of international obligation and, indeed, is exclusively empowered to do so in the international forum on behalf of the state and people of Canada, Canada (the federal executive and parliament) can approach the problem of 'implementation' only through the limitations of the internal constitutional structure. Assuming that 'ratification' is technically an executive act – however varying has been the federal practice here in referring certain treaties to parliament for 'ratification' – it cannot be doubted that the present distribution of powers does not permit the federal implementation of an international obligation, whether in a simple form such as in an exchange of notes or the most solemn of treaties, unless the subject matter is already within the jurisdiction of the parliament of Canada. And where it is not, then, although 'ratification' in the Canadian practice may be either an executive act, as an exercise of the prerogative or through the gesture of a parliamentary resolution, the legislatures of the provinces alone are competent to provide measures of implementation that have the force of law.

The Canadian treaty-making power is, therefore, caught within a continuing dilemma. Except for 'Empire' treaties under section 132, where parliament would have a general authority to implement whatever the subject matter – and this does not seem to apply, *pace* the *Aeronautics* case, to any instrument since the Boundary Waters Treaty of 1909 – the parliament of Canada cannot implement, in the case of the many subjects within provincial jurisdiction, what clearly the government of Canada in fact may be free in the international forum to negotiate for and obligate the state and people of Canada. This has been the classical Canadian position and debate for example with respect to ILO and human rights matters, except for that portion of Canada juridically or territorially that may come within federal jurisdiction and permit implementation within such federal limits otherwise not 'within' provincial competence. To that extent the Canadian constitution already has what may be described as a built-in 'Bricker Amendment,' which the United States barely avoided. For the efforts to amend the Constitution of the United States, led by Senator Bricker and stimulated almost a generation ago by the American Bar Association, did not succeed in weakening or destroying the present power of the United States executive to enter into 'treaties' by and with the consent of two-thirds of the Senate, the effects of which continue to provide for treaties becoming the 'supreme law of the land,' either 'self-executing' or by congressional action, and thereby overriding any otherwise valid state jurisdiction.

Hence, by contrast, two Canadian inhibitions remain. There is the implementation problem in a system of divided jurisdiction without any general theory of the supremacy or paramountcy of treaties (or even of federal law) *per se*. And, too, there is the fundamental Anglo-Canadian constitutional doctrine preventing treaties from being self-executing for obvious reasons of limiting the legal effects of the royal prerogative on the one hand and thus affirming the supremacy of parliament on the other, thereby preventing any executive act in dealings with foreign states to become a binding legislative norm without the due intervention of the legislative process.

This bifurcation of the treaty-implementation power – but not the treaty-making power itself – doubtless lies at the base of continuing provincial claims in Canada for some kind of international role. It has been dramatized by Quebec arguments, with particular reference to its dealings with the French-speaking world in particular – France, Belgium, and the French-speaking African communities. The difficulty has been to find a formula that would permit active intercultural relations between Quebec and any French-speaking community throughout the world whether it was a nation state or otherwise, without at the same time permitting such relations to be given that mark of formalism which, by delineating the legal capacity of Quebec so to deal with such entities, would in fact be suggesting that some degree of international legal personality or status attaches to a Canadian province, itself a member of a federal system. The present formulas that have evolved since 1964 range from the original federal *Loi Cadre* to permit cultural-educational arrangements between Quebec and France to the present membership in Francophonie associations by Quebec itself and to common or separate delegations from Canada and Quebec to 'international' meetings with voting procedures and representational techniques that seemed to vary with the importance, 'politically,' of the forum.

All of these devices are designed to preserve the strict position that there is only *one Canada* in the international forum able to create binding legal obligations for the Canadian people, but at the same time within the federal system, there are entities, eg, Quebec, that are legal persons within that federal system and hence may have certain limited and permitted dealings with other legal entities in the international forum or within other federal or imperial systems, eg, Louisiana in the us federal structure, or Martinique and Guadaloupe as Overseas Departments of the French Republic, or St Pierre and Miquelon as French overseas territories, or with sovereign members of the French Community (La Communauté), eg, Gabon or Niger. And this rather subtle-simple series of techniques evolving to meet immediate and longer run pretensions and realities on the issue has been buttressed, to some extent, by the *de facto* performance of other provinces, eg, Ontario, which have had 'direct' administrative dealings with states of the us federal system or with members of the Commonwealth, eg, the United Kingdom or member states of a federal system within the Commonwealth, eg, New South Wales in Australia. Such arrangements between some provinces and states of the us include traffic matters, joint recreational facilities, the sale of hydro electric power, etc (usually around their common boundary); and agreements between provinces and Commonwealth legal entities (from the United Kingdom to an Australian state) involving alimentary orders, etc. And of course there long has been the quite formal presence in London of governmental representation from Ontario, Quebec, Saskatchewan, and British Columbia, etc, and from Quebec in Paris.

The hope for a workable resolution of the issues raised by the complex questions embracing treaty-making, treaty-implementation, and international and provincial legal personality is not likely to be realized except by a quite systematic restatement in some future constitutional rewriting, or by the Supreme Court of Canada somehow shedding the weight of the *Labour Conventions* case and the general approach to Canadian treaty practice which it crystallized and has since influenced.

Perhaps a more revealing long-term perspective has to do with the extent to which Canadian federalism has prepared Canada for a more sensitive understanding of jurisdictional problems as international organizations broaden the scope of their claims and do, in fact, penetrate 'domestic jurisdiction' by debate or 'regulation.' In a sense the Canadian experience here is somewhat contradictory. *A priori* the Canadian management of its system of distribution of powers ought to have prepared it for the somewhat more delicate issue of 'supranational' or international versus 'domestic jurisdiction.' That preparation ought to have been reflected not so much in a simplistic yielding up of 'sovereignty' or independence in a world where the nation state is still the principal unit of sociopolitical organization; but rather it ought to have signified the capacity of Canada to understand more readily that participation in organs with decision-making, binding, or quasi-binding authority should in fact lead to a recognition that such processes are bound to involve degrees of intrusion on areas classically defined as 'domestic.' In fact, however, it was Canadian Secretary of State for External Affairs Mr St Laurent who in 1948 at the United Nations raised doubts about the suitability of the UN Charter being submitted to the International Court of Justice for interpretation particularly on questions involving the powers of its principal organs, especially those of the General Assembly and the Security Council. It was his position that essentially political organisms should in the early stages of their self-development decide jurisdictional questions for themselves as a matter of 'political' judgment rather than through third-party adjudication.

It might have been thought that with so much of a delicate Canadian federal structure in the hands of the courts, throughout almost eighty years at the time he spoke, he would have been ready for the experiment of some larger participation by the World Court in the interpretive function. At the same time it should be recalled that faith in the judicial process even within Canadian federalism has been often startlingly absent, as when the prime minister of Quebec in 1964-5 rejected the role of the Supreme Court of Canada as the proper forum to determine disputes between the federal and provincial governments over offshore mineral claims, asserting instead that these should be settled by political negotiations and not by the court – a view reiterated by others in recent years, particularly among the Atlantic provinces. In general, however, it is not possible to discount entirely the preparation of Canadian political thought and practice, through its federal experience predisposing it to an increasing understanding of some dynamic balance emerging in the ongoing relations between international organizations, with rule-making authority, and member states obliged increasingly to co-operate within the framework of such norms.

Finally there is the question whether Canadian international experience, both generally and juridically, may influence the course of Canadian federal thinking and practice itself. This is a quite difficult matter to explore since the empirical evidence, except on the treaty-making issue and the Quebec representation question, is not very extensive. Nevertheless, on one or two points the influence of such international activities already is evident. It is clear that Canadians are bound to ask themselves why their own constitutional processes do not provide for systematic adjudication in disputes between provinces or the provinces and the federal government when such a framework is available for disputes between nation states themselves through the mechanism of the International Court of Justice and more particularly, if narrowly, through new and extensive judicial mechanisms within the European Economic Community.

Equally it is likely that the entire human rights debate, internationally, and the force of international instruments, such as the two UN Covenants (unratified), the Rome Treaty (the European Convention on Human Rights), the standards provided by the Convention on Racial Discrimination, and the Draft Convention on Religious Discrimination, to say nothing of the 1948 Universal Declaration of Human Rights itself, are all bound to penetrate and are penetrating into the processes of Canadian law-making with new levels resulting in human rights standards. To that extent both the rhetoric and the rules touching on the Canadian constitutional and legislative future reflect this international experience and may have a curiously unifying result within Canadian federalism itself, simply because the human rights norms concerned are so generally applicable that whatever may be the distribution of powers which affect their implementation within Canada, the generality of the norms themselves, whether adopted at the provincial or federal level or both, must have an integrative impact on social attitudes as well as on legislation itself. It may be one of the unexplored ironies of Canadian international experience that her federal difficulties with the implementation of human rights obligations from the international forum, either accepted by Canada or open for acceptance, will feed back into the creation of a higher degree of common Canadian approaches, in spirit as well as in form, to human rights issues which, in the last analysis, deal with the place of the individual in society and his claims to decent and equal treatment and opportunity in a fortunate and largely affluent land.

BENCH AND BAR: OPPORTUNITY AND PARTICIPATION

It is now necessary to examine how far professional and intellectual structures in Canada have reflected this enlargement of international processes with which Canada is involved in an increasingly interacting world and with an ever-growing body of international legal norms influencing nation states in so many aspects of their existence. This really means exploring, briefly, the responses of the Canadian judiciary to international legal problems, the interest and activity of the bar measured both by the volume of actual international law problem-solving for clients, as well as the interest expressed through the voluntary work of professional organizations. Finally, there is the question of how far the law schools and universities themselves, through courses, research, and multidisciplinary programs and contact have come to reflect the demands of the international legal order on Canada, and on intellectual-social awareness, as trained intelligences in this sector, in particular. In short, what is the contribution that bar, bench, law schools, and universities in general are making towards the evolution and application of international legal ideas and the pressing forward of the horizons of thought and perception in these areas?

A review of the Canadian judgments of the last generation or two suggests that from the *Ottawa and Rockcliffe Reference* case to a series of sovereign immunity questions arising out of Cuban shipping confiscations on the one hand, and Expo 67 construction and architectural 'contracts' on the other, the Canadian courts have had an increasing opportunity to examine some classical doctrinal issues, such as the immunity of foreign sovereigns and their property from suit or seizures, and to explore the increasing dilemma of how, in essentially commercial transactions, to limit the scope of that immunity. On another level the courts have had opportunities to continue the examination of the rights of aliens and the status of foreign forces on Canadian territory. Exotic North American exercises in the legal validity of so-called treaties with native peoples have invoked both the analysis of the legal status of such peoples and their so-called agreements with the crown. These have been related to both Canadian domestic legislation and to us-Canadian treaties which were often the basis for such legislation, particularly in the matter of migratory birds as well as the much older and wider issue of the effect of the Jay Treaty (and others) on the rights of Indians to ignore the Canadian-us border for customs and travel purposes.

Interesting opportunities were afforded to Canadian courts to examine international law concepts in two important matters arising out of World War II; namely, the treatment and in due course the deportation of Japanese Canadians, and the Gouzenko spy trials which involved the status of so-called embassy archives and the general position of espionage in municipal law.

But overall, and subject to the usual peril of oversimplification, it is difficult to conclude that the Canadian courts have made any signal contributions to international law thinking even where so specific a question as the treaty-making and treaty-implementing power may have offered opportunities for some more experimental views about the interplay between international and federal systems within the framework of the constitutional structure of Canada. In general, the judicial process here – even in an independent and formally *Supreme* Court of Canada – continues to reflect, in a large measure, the well known Anglo-Canadian inhibitions towards frank policy discussion by courts, relieved only by an occasional cold wind of realism from a Northwest Territories judge examining Indian rights or an Ontario Supreme Court judge willing to absorb the Charter of the United Nations and the Universal Declaration of Human Rights into the concept of public policy in determining the validity of restrictive covenants. Even the Supreme Court's discussions of the important legal-historical basis for the offshore mineral rights reference, in the matter of British Columbia and federal claims, were disposed of by the court in very modest policy terms, however detailed the formal historical materials in the judgment may have been. But then there remains the weighty encumbrance of some of the Judicial Committee's tradition still to be borne by Canadian courts. It has only to be remembered how little attention the Privy Council paid to international law in the Japanese-Canadians case where virtually no understanding was disclosed with respect to the propriety of one state imposing its nationals, by deportation, onto the territory of the second state. At the same time the factums in the *B.C. Offshore Reference* case remain within the traditional Canadian mould and reveal a continuing reluctance by provincial and federal law officers of the crown – reflecting the prevailing attitudes, probably, of the bar itself – to incorporate policy discussion and references with frankness side by side with the usual technical forms of traditional drafting and argument. Whether a generation of younger judges will disclose a more determined willingness to explore both in method and substance the essential issues of international law that come before them remains to be seen, but such a candid exploration of issues is likely to develop much more promisingly than what has been accepted heretofore as the working professional parameters.

Turning to the role of the bar and professional bodies themselves there are two tests to be applied to their involvement with and contribution to Canadian thinking on international law and development. The first, of course, is the extent to which the bar increasingly has before it issues and problems which it recognizes as having a public international law content presented in the ordinary way by clients for disposition. Some years ago I attempted to estimate the number of matters having some international law components brought by clients to law offices (as distinct from private international law except for the overlapping questions of the 'recognition' of foreign judgments in relation to foreign 'acts of state'). At that time, 1954-5, I estimated that taking the number of reported cases in Canada as a base it would be possible to assume that for every reported case in each year there may have been at least ten matters requiring attention in each law firm, but that the firms never went to the point of filing an action or going to trial or judgment. If this quite arbitrary extrapolation had any validity it would be necessary to examine the total number of reported and unreported judgments since 1954 in Canada and to make certain further assumptions about the increase in the volume of matters affecting foreign sovereign immunity, transnational business, aliens, extradition, etc, and project from there on the basis of some new multiplier, the likely number of cases brought to law firms since that date on a per annum basis.

If to this list are added the public international law content of many maritime law cases then, of course, the figures could be considerably increased. But maritime law tends to have a large private law component in its 'collision' and 'carriage of goods by sea' issues which, together with questions arising out of 'chartering' etc, make up the majority of matters characteristic of maritime law practices. Nevertheless, even in maritime law, and to some extent in private international law, as well as in several areas of commercial law (and taxation) generally, there are now bilateral and multilateral treaties to which Canada is a party and where federal and provincial legislation may be reflecting the content of those treaties directly and indirectly. To that extent the bar often may be called upon, in what appear to be essentially private law matters, to deal with them from their treaty-law aspect and requiring, therefore, some understanding of the law of treaties, their interpretation and the approach that Anglo-Canadian courts have taken towards their absorption into municipal law. In the absence of any such survey since 1954, I will hazard no estimate, but it is probably fair to say that with the increasing volume of transnational business from metropolitan Canadian centers, and with the variety of sovereign immunity questions that have appeared, the bar in general may be becoming increasingly familiar with public international law issues, directly or indirectly arising from such varied transactions.

But from a review of the *International Law Reports* which annually collect cases from all jurisdictions, it would appear that Canada, comparatively, is still a relatively modest contributor to the total number of reported cases with a clear public international law content. Yet Canadian courts have been among the very few that have had an opportunity, for example, to test, in municipal law, the juridical status of the United Nations and the secretary general.

The bar has also had an opportunity in Canada, and particularly in Montreal, to have had direct experience with the operations of one specialized agency, the International Civil Aviation Organization, and equally the government of Canada, through its law officers, has had the opportunity to design rules within a federal system that would operate so as to give ICAO and its staff members the benefits of theory and practice touching on the privileges and immunities of a specialized agency and its staff. An indirect consequence of this status has been, of course, the bar's involvement with the immunity of the organization's staff from suits in the matter of ordinary commercial transactions, from varieties of taxation – federal, municipal, and provincial – the status of the premises of ICAO, etc. Exceptionally there has been the ability to observe what may be called the internal administrative law of an international organization, involving the powers of the secretary general to contract with and, particularly, to discipline staff members. When ICAO used *ad hoc* local procedures for appeals from the decisions of the secretary general on matters of his rulings affecting the rights and duties of the staff, those tribunals were comprised often of one or two members of the profession of Montreal, while counsel from the bar of Montreal appeared before the tribunal. To the extent that the Administrative Tribunal of the United Nations in New York became a more experienced and desirable forum, it seemed unnecessary to continue these *ad hoc* ICAO appeal tribunals, and these experiences ceased to be an available opportunity for the Montreal bar to participate in the administrative processes of an important international agency. Nevertheless, what experience there was should be added to the corpus of the bar's continuing education in the colourful diversity of international law activities increasingly available to it in Canada over the past generation.

These professional activities may be viewed also through the perspective of the organizational interests of the bar where two particular forums have been available – the Canadian Bar Association and the International Law Association. Perhaps to these should be added the quite extensive participation of the family of Canadian international academic lawyers in the newly created Canadian Council of International Law, in the work and proceedings of the American Society of International Law, and to a much lesser extent in l'Institut de Droit International and the activities of the Hague Academy.

It is not without significance perhaps that the Canadian Bar Association had an early 'activist' period at the end of World War II and afterwards, when it examined at least three subjects with some care; namely, the proposed Charter of the United Nations, the proposed Universal Declaration of Human Rights, and a proposed Statute for the creation of an International Criminal Court. Ironically, it was a strongly isolationist wing of the American Bar Association which attempted to influence Canadian professional thinking with respect to the Declaration of Human Rights and indeed subsequent UN deliberations on the covenants as well. But this attempt to affect Canadian thinking was without success and to its credit the Canadian Bar Association did not adopt an early anti-UN or anti-human rights stand that was characteristic of the American Bar Association until the influence of Charles Rhyne and Chief Justice Warren – plus the facts of life – led to a major conversion of the ABA by 1960 into a much more positive supporter of the international legal order, its methods, and its rules.

Nevertheless, in the 1950s, the role of international law in the Canadian Bar Association was sporadic, and not until the early 1960s was an effort made to enlist the support of the bar for a continuing professional concern with international law viewed particularly through the colourful if often distorted prism of the 'national interest.' And the result today is a reasonably effective forum for study by the bar of issues having both general international and specific Canadian significance.

Parallel to this activity has been the existence in Canada for a generation of the International Law Association, itself now a hundred years old, with branches in over forty countries, including the USSR, and comprising in its membership a very wide range of personnel from the bench, the practicing bar, the universities, and the public service, both national and international. The ILA has had a continuing influence upon developing Canadian thinking particularly on issues of direct concern to Canada, on a number of professional subgroups the ILA embraces, and finally on providing Canadians with valuable contacts with ILA branches of interested persons and working committees throughout the world. These include varieties of subject matter reflecting the most intensive transnational attention at any point in time, eg, antitrust questions, water resource problems, the multinational corporation, air and space law issues, oceanic and transboundary pollution matters, international monetary and trade law, etc. Indeed, when the work of the ILA's Committee on International Rivers – now the Water Resources Committee – was at its height in 1954-68 the local Canadian Committee, and individual Canadians on the International Committee, contributed substantially to the International Committee's thinking, largely because of the unique Canadian experience with its boundary waters and the International Joint Commission under the Boundary Waters Treaty. At present the Canadian contribution to evolving international water resources principles, now being considered by the ILA, is not unimportant. Similarly there have been useful Canadian contributions, at the ILA's international committee level, in the areas of UN Charter revision, air law, and outer space, enforcement of foreign judgments, peace-keeping within the UN, antitrust matters, human rights, etc. And while the membership and activity in the Canadian branch and city or provincial sections has varied, and the committee work on the national level has been somewhat uneven, nevertheless, the International Law Association is a permanent feature of the Canadian professional and scholarly landscape.

SCHOLARSHIP AND THE LAW SCHOOLS

An examination is necessary of the role of scholarship in the law schools and the universities and the contributions made over the years by Canadians to the continuing dialogue over the theory and practice of the law of nations. If the purely professional bar-oriented activity has shown a steady but modest rise in interest and involvement, what can be said of the academic community, linked to some extent with the neo-academics in the public service, is that here, at least, concern and contributions to international law thought and analysis show a coming of age.

It is difficult to measure such a statement, for the empirical indices tend to be those reflecting gross growth and by themselves may be of limited significance. Nevertheless, taking such factors as courses given, numbers of teachers, articles and books written, and the use of the products of Canadian-bred scholarship for purposes of bench, bar, and government – together with the total 'vector' consequences of these activities for what may be loosely described as the Canadian contribution to the international law family of thought and scholarship – there is much to be said for the argument that twenty-five years have made a difference. Every law school in Canada has either compulsory or optional international law courses and many of them offer postgraduate studies, at least at the master's level, and one or two at the doctoral. Some law faculties have reached a considerable level of sophistication in the range of courses offered and the graduate supervision provided by men of competence. But overall, any serious test would have to turn to the quality and variety of scholarship evidenced by projects, articles, monographs, and casebooks and perhaps also by the unpublished effects of advisory services to international institutions, foreign states, and to provincial and federal governments by trained Canadian international lawyers, essentially from the university family.

It is a far cry from pre-World War II days when H.A. Smith, Percy Corbett, and N.A.M. MacKenzie with John Read at External Affairs were perhaps the best known and almost the only significant figures, each making his respective impact in university and government. Today, with Bourne, Castel, Alexandrowicz, and others, the casebooks are beginning to proliferate, with MacKenzie and Laing now a valuable historical memento rather than an active classroom document. More important, perhaps, is the evidence of research in books, papers, and collections of essays (of which the present volume is likely to be the most elaborate presentation to date) as to where the Canadian level of performance now stands. To this should be added research projects such as Lawford's use of the computer at Queen's to explore and program the whole of the Empire-Commonwealth treaty structure in force today, in Canada, as ex-colony and successor sovereign state. The ability of McGill, for example, to sustain an Institute of Air and Space Law for over twenty years with an average annual class of postgraduate students ranging from twelve to twenty-five, and the presence of postgraduate candidates at the master's level in almost half of the sixteen Canadian law faculties are highly suggestive.

Before touching on the character and scope of the research being done by teachers and students, it may be worth observing that most of the younger contemporary international lawyers in faculties across Canada have increasingly had their postgraduate training at the front-rank US law schools rather than in the United Kingdom, although for some of the Quebec teachers in the French language civil law schools (including the University of Ottawa, Civil Law Section), France remains a prime source of graduate training. The effect of this shift to the United States, of course, is noticeable in the whole range of Canadian legal scholarship and not only in international legal studies. It has had important consequences for the Canadian approach to the use of casebooks with an increasingly heavy emphasis on Canadian materials and for a receptivity to and flexibility about other disciplines interested in international relations-international law as part of the complex of international studies; in general, it has pointed Canadian scholarship towards policy-oriented thinking which in the case of international law, as indeed elsewhere, is indispensable for any realistic rapport with materials or students.

While it is difficult without a detailed questionnaire or an examination of theses' titles, or a list of published monographs and articles, to state with precision the direction and quality of research studies, it is clear that there has been a constructive shift away from what was the singular Canadian preoccupation before World War II; namely, problems of the treaty-making power and evidences of Canadian sovereignty or limitations thereon. Now the concern is with a broad spectrum of issues, many having a specific Canadian content but nevertheless related in their implications or specifically to a more universal international law subject matter: human rights; international rivers; the multinational corporation; US-Canadian legal relations with particular reference to extraterritorial effects of US law in Canada; the multiple jurisdictional issues presented by the Arctic, east and west coast territorial sea, baselines, fisheries, and pollution questions; air law and related ICAO and IATA problems; inner and outer space issues; the new concern for continental shelf and bed of the sea exploitation; the World Court and reservation questions; friendly relations; the reopening of the debate on innocent passage in the Arctic straits, freedom of the seas, and the rights of coastal states in the age of pollution, conservation, and environmental needs; and finally disarmament, terrorism, and war crimes. All of these and more are to be found in increasing numbers and inproved quality in volumes and essays published since World War II.

But there are two deficiencies which should be recognized in any appraisal of that scholarly birth or rebirth. The first is the continuing reluctance of some faculties and teachers to participate in multidisciplinary activities where the richness in varieties of political science or more general behavioural science research might be absorbed into the teaching and scholarly works of Canadian international lawyers in the universities. Not enough of the diversity of schools of thought dealing with peace research, games theory, systems analysis, conflict resolution theory, etc, has made its apparent impact on either Canadian law courses, teachers and materials, or the working relations between faculties of law and the other departments experimenting with and developing these new behavioural science approaches to the international order.

Perhaps this may be too harsh a judgment, however, in the absence of a careful survey, if it is recognized that in a sense the younger international lawyers have often disclosed directly or indirectly a great deal of the Yale-McDougal-Lasswell influence. Their work represents perhaps one of the most progressive and experimental periods in both American legal education as a whole and the teaching and study of international law in particular. Probably more Canadian law teachers in the field are, in fact, policy and multidisciplinary oriented because of Yale than their formal relations with the behavioural scientists as such might indicate. Moreoever, the actual number of competent experimenters in the various behavioural sciences concerned with international studies may be limited in Canada, and opportunities for interplay with faculties of law or international lawyers may therefore be fewer than should be the case in this generation. However, the recent collection of papers on strategic studies, published in the *International Journal* by the Canadian Institute of International Affairs (Autumn 1971) and the continuing activities of the Canadian behavioural sciences – international studies – peace research family are highly suggestive of the available resources for interdisciplinary co-operation if there is the will to use them.

Perhaps these characteristics of Canadian scholarship, together with the general inhibitions which until recently overlay the Anglo-Canadian pattern, explain the absence of what would be the crown of such intellectual effort; the emergence of a body of respectable and respected theory from Canadian sources. It would not be unfair to say that while a good deal of theorizing has been done – and a review of the *Canadian Year Book of International Law* and other sources of the past eight or nine years would surely indicate this to be true – it cannot be seriously argued that a first-class Canadian theorist (Percy Corbett excepted) has emerged to demonstrate a capacity for model-building and broad analytical thinking that would make a contribution not only for international law but for the theory of law in general. Probably the next stage to be expected or, at least, to be hoped for is that the multiple interests of Canadian scholars deriving from federalism, the varied experiences on three oceans and with the Arctic Basin in particular, the unique bilateral problems in the US-Canadian continental context, and general Canadian multilateral involvement, classically and through the UN family, will in due course not only be reflected in the discrete topics analysed but in some comprehensive view of international law from a Canadian standpoint where the 'accidents' of national interest are converted into insights having some universal validity. It is possible, however, that this is a too cautious view of the Canadian achievement so far and that a more careful analysis of the literature might reveal a mind or two at work already climbing the heights and viewing the horizon beyond the territorial footnotes.

PROBLEMS IN THE WINGS

It may be desirable at this juncture to consider some of the main Canadian concerns with international law problems both uniquely its own as well as more universal. Bearing in mind contemporary Canadian international law issues – unilateral, bilateral, regional, and universal – it may not be too hazardous to attempt an outline of these questions and what they portend for the Canadian international lawyer of the future.

1 *The treaty-making power* Undoubtedly this will be troublesome for some time unless the Supreme Court of Canada or constitutional revision somehow simplify the present built-in limitations on the power of parliament to implement international law obligations undertaken by Canada.

2 *The international personality issue* The present formula with respect to the legal status of the provinces in their dealings with external entities, delineated particularly by the Quebec-Francophonie question, is a variant on the treaty-making theme but with its own special characteristics. The problem will be with us increasingly and again may require constitutional revision together with some Supreme Court judgments for clarification.

3 *Law of the Sea problems* These issues are likely to be central for some time as Canadian positions require mature study in connection with the Law of the Sea Conference (1973-5) and the IMCO Conference (1973). But the scientific, economic, political, and legal questions all have a powerful domestic political meaning in addition, or parallel, to their international status as issues and claims. For example, it is only to be remembered how unsettled are the problems of the exploitation of the continental margin (however defined); the prevention of pollution within reasonable distances of Canadian coasts; the spelling out and application of an acceptable baseline theory and practice; the proper scope for coastal control over fisheries, particularly in the waters superjacent to the continental margin; the regulation of navigation far out to sea where the construction of vessels or the content of their cargo present hazards to the coast and the role of the coastal state in the absence of adequate international rules or administrative-regulatory agencies; the development of a theory of preferences for coastal states in the proportion of their claims to the living resources of the sea for which they may take a primary responsibility in maintaining stocks, as well as responsibility for the related matter of ecological balance and 'integrity'; the exploitation of the continental margin, its seabed, and subsoil and the sharing of its revenues with less advantaged states without a shelf and without similar petroleum or mineral resources available to them for development; the technically abrasive issue of dividing lines between neighbours on the shelf which in Canada's case means Canada and the US on the east and west coasts, and Canada and France with respect to St Pierre and Miquelon, Canada and Denmark in the eastern Arctic, and Canada and the US in the western Arctic; the special problems of factory fleets on the high seas and specifically those of the USSR operating both on the east and west coasts in areas where Canadian conservation and coastal preferential theories would require a limitation of the Russian fisheries presence in otherwise high seas waters; the special jurisdictional problems of the Arctic affecting pollution control, navigation through the Northwest Passage, habitat protection, and exploitation regulation with the possibility of evolving an Arctic Basin treaty for Arctic Basin member states or, at the very least, a semi-voluntary Arctic Basin Council for the common developmental, protection, and information exchange purposes; and international rivers leading to the high seas, straits, the breadth of the territorial sea and the future of the doctrines of innocent

passage and contiguous zones, all are of the utmost significance to Canada's national interest. But the fulcrum on which they rest is the emergence of viable international conventional rules and possible varieties of international regulatory machinery.

4 *Canada-United States relations* Systematic thought will have to be given to the immense network of Canada-US relations which now are untouched by treaty or even simple exchanges of notes (which was enough for the St Lawrence River Seaway project) and which today are causing mounting irritation among greatly interdependent friends of long standing. Agreement on foreign and US investment; the future of possibly selected 'free trade' sectors comparable to the Agreement on Automotive Products of 1965; the extraterritorial operation of United States law both directly and through subsidiaries already well known in the case of antitrust laws, the sale of securities, trading with the enemy, and proscribed goods regulations; environmental disputes; foreign exchange and profit repatriation regulations (to which concessions were made in 1966-7 to Canada), the setting and removing of oil import quotas unilaterally, by the United States, energy policies, and the possibly severe impact on Canada of the Nixon economic measures to deal with US unemployment, inflation, and balance of payment questions – all of these require some systematic common approach between two neighbours that have more intertwined relations than may be the case even among the members of the European Economic Community.

Canadian international lawyers, in co-operation with the substantive experts, should be giving thought to the juridical framework for the optimum continental approach to these questions which would limit unilateral decision-making particularly by the United States where, if done without consultation with Canada and adequate notice, can be very harmful to Canadian life and the economy. Although 25 per cent of US exports are to Canada, over one-third of US foreign investment is in Canada, and the actual or potential resource deficit of the United States in many areas, notably petroleum, natural gas, minerals, forest products, hydroelectric power, and possibly water for irrigation, have Canada as their primary replacement source. The experience with the International Joint Commission, the Salmon and Halibut Commissions, the Permanent Joint Board on Defence, and other agencies suggests that the Canadian international lawyer has considerable expertise to contribute both in absolute North American terms and in comparative regional terms to the creation of appropriate machinery for this inevitable challenge to a more rational system of continental economic management. Here a joint economic and statistical commission is certainly a long overdue option to be considered.

5 *International economic institutions* Similarly the international lawyer in Canada will be giving considerable thought to their established scope and possible need for broadening the range of their jurisdiction as in the case of the World Bank, the Fund, the GATT, and all of the implications that may flow for the multinational corporation from the work now being done on UNCITRAL. Indeed, the comparativists here, for which Canadians are particularly well equipped as civilian and common law lawyers, should have a great deal to contribute to the development of a systematic body of international trade law and regulations first attempted by the abortive Havana Charter of 1948 which was revived in part by GATT and now is

desperately in need of a new juridical framework. For this conception must take account of the variety and volume of international trading transactions and the reality of the multinational corporation whose operations effectively bypass many sovereign states and their internal priorities in the absence of international regulatory mechanisms or rules binding upon states and such corporations together.

6 *The United Nations family of problems* Apart from the important and continuing work of the International Law Commission, on which Canada once had able representation, there are the challenges presented by the new interest in finding a more positive role for the International Court of Justice. Perhaps even more important is the recognition that the United Nations has become, through the resolutions of the General Assembly, an important source of direct or indirect international law-making. Not only may consensus be mirrored by General Assembly resolutions, thus crystallizing customary law, but the will of the assembly often leads to a new consensus and to conferences creating, through a supreme effort of clarification, a codified body of now conventional general principles. Already this has happened for the Law of the Sea, in part, for treaties, for consular and diplomatic immunities, for some environmental and pollution control (through Stockholm, and UN and IMCO sponsored conferences), and, undoubtedly, there will be others in the years to come. Here the preparatory work of the International Law Commission and the Sixth Committee (Legal) of the Assembly (the First Committee for Outer Space Matters and the Third Committee for Human Rights) will be of the utmost importance for Canadian participation. Whenever possible the marriage of the university to the foreign office in the exchange of ideas may be the measure of the Canadian contribution.

But also within the family of United Nations activity, the Canadian international lawyer may find ample scope for his imagination in the internal constitutional problems of the charter and the specialized agencies to avoid such damaging dilemmas as that posed currently for the United Nations by the peacekeeping and related financing questions. These have helped almost to bankrupt the organization, have interrupted its effectiveness in peacekeeping, and have caused large uncertainties as to its future role in this important sector. Equally inviting are the imaginative responses that may be foreseen to questions of human rights and disarmament, to say nothing of the subtleties that may or may not emerge in the area of general principles from doctrines rooted in the resolutions on 'friendly relations' and its successor concepts.

Indeed, the legal art of keeping the United Nations going at all in the face of its political and financial difficulties from ministates' applications to non-payment of assessments should stimulate thinking about international organization law, theory, and practice to the point where these become as significant to the international lawyer in Canada, to the law schools, and legal education as the central role of constitutional law long has become for the standard curriculum and for scholarship and for policy.

7 *Social change and social justice* Finally, the interpenetrating worlds of classical and UN Charter law and of customary and conventional law will be faced with social change and social demand on a politically and technologically escalating scale of urgent issues from population control to adjusting somehow international incomes through mechanisms that do not as at present allow 25 per cent of the

world's population to consume 75 per cent of its gross national product. The regional disparities which are of so much concern to Canada are nothing compared to disparities globally; and the nation-state system, while still the working jural-political fact of life in the international order, for as long as one can see, clearly is not an institution designed, from microstates to macrostates, to solve the enormities of social need and social changes confronting mankind. New institutions and advancing standards of international equity cutting into the autonomy of nation state decision-making where these have transnational effects, socially and economically, are in the offing if mankind is to be rescued from its own numbers and follies. And so whether it is the standard stuff of international law from state succession to diplomatic immunities to the breadth of the territorial sea or the more sophisticated advances toward interstate co-operation with varieties of supranational institutions, economic and political, universal or regional, the task of the international lawyer of the future and of the Canadian in particular – given his own regional and continental specialties – is without foreseeable limits as to the demands that it will make on scholarship and political imagination and its application to the short- and long-range problems of the national interest in the international forum, and of the international interest to be pressed upon the sometimes too chauvinist national forum itself.

CONCLUSIONS

In such a *tour d'horizon* there is little danger of escape from superficiality. But that is a price that has to be paid for an exercise that attempts to introduce a volume which explores elsewhere in more scholarly detail the achievements of this generation of Canadians who are concerned with the international legal order and inevitably its relation to the national interest. It would be satisfying to be able to conclude that the level of Canadian performance on the bench, at the bar, in the universities, and in government suggested a degree of maturity and skill that was not present a generation ago. That satisfaction cannot be entirely denied to any fair-minded surveyor of the Canadian record, a view which this volume hopefully will corroborate. But there is yet some distance to go before it can be said that the older blacklettered pragmatism of Canadian scholarship and the modest involvement of bench and bar have reached a plateau of interest and competence deserving comparison with even Holland or Scandinavia to say nothing of the larger European countries and, of course, the United States. Even Australia continues to have an image of scholarly output in several fields, not only in international law, that Canadians have not yet matched if the index here is to be large-scale and important enterprises such as those of Julius Stone and D.P. O'Connell. Nevertheless, the *Canadian Year Book of International Law,* the not-yet-failed *Yearbook of Air and Space Law,* some important collections of essays, the considerable variety of papers in all the almost two-score Canadian law journals, the cognate materials produced by political scientists, historians, and area specialists and others in the *International Journal,* the *Canadian Journal of Political Science,* the *Canadian Historical Review,* and elsewhere are a continuing witness to the volume and variety of studies in the international law-international relations intellectual complex. And to these should be added, of course, the number of university departments, institutes, and centres now devoted to a large spectrum of international political, legal, social, and area studies, and to methodology for investigation.

Indeed it is interesting to contemplate that the successes of Canadian scholarship and general professional interest in constitutional law in contrast to that of Latin American and west European states, mostly unitary in character, in international law, was a reflection of the geo-legal and geo-political realities of their respective continents. Canada and the United States are both large continental federal systems made up of numbers of member components – provinces and states, respectively – and the primary preoccupation of the majority of the public law specialists both in Canada and the United States tended, in the formative intellectual years of legal studies, and perhaps even unto the present day, to be those urgently confronting them in the constitutional law of their respective federal systems. By contrast, Latin America as the continent of a dissolved Hispano-Portuguese imperial system, turned to nation states for the solution of its organizational problems, and the necessary consequence of learning the art of dealing with each other dictated their professional and political concern with international law. If Latin America had been a continental federal state system the primary movement of its public law interests probably would have been the constitutional law of a continental federalism. Significantly, something of this process is to be witnessed now in the evolving quasi-federalism of the Common Market. For that group of classically sovereign nation states from which came almost the entire structure of modern international law is now moving from the international law of independence to the quasi-federal-constitutional law of a common market and potentially a 'federated' west Europe.

Some day soon a first-class Canadian theorist in law or international law or international relations *cum* law will emerge to give crown to this broadening intellectual interest. Meanwhile one central point of testing performance is likely to be found in the quality of general research and the positions taken by the government of Canada as it expresses high policy in the many forums in which it now must operate. But without basic research in the university, in the law schools, without the high sense of professional interest by bar and bench, government will not have the intellectual infrastructure upon which to rely, the streams from which to help nourish and make more fruitful the difficult doctrinal postures and strategies to which governments in the day-to-day affairs of state must resort.

For it remains the lasting paradox of international law that it at once should attract so much objective thought and subjective idealism when it may serve at moments as a base rationale for untenable national positions. A sacrificial goat for sometimes justifying unacceptable state action in the name of the 'national interest,' international law has long been exposed to suspicion, and, by its enemies, to ridicule. What is not admitted is that like Hamlet's mother, the world must assume the virtue of order even if it has it not – and there is really no evidence that it does not wish to have order. The long debate between the naturalist and positivist is not over. Both are wrong in their attempts to occupy the whole of history. Whether the behaviourists persuade us that we are programmed to respond to rewards and punishment or whether the bio-sociologists are more convincing in claiming that we are genetically programmed, through the eons of evolution behind us, it is likely that men will make the assumption that rationality is a human phenomenon and that deliberate choice is still a human attribute. In this act of faith about the nature of the human condition, it is possible to anticipate the evolution of some world order to manage the common affairs of mankind, and in this high task the international lawyer of the future, in Canada as elsewhere, should have a formidable share of the work and the glory.

WOLFGANG FRIEDMANN 2/Canada and
the International
Legal Order:
An Outside
Perspective

IS THERE A NEED FOR CANADA?

It might be as well to start this essay with straightforward and brutal questions. Is there a need for Canada? Would the world be shaken if Canada, as a political and international unit, disappeared from the world scene?

To ask such questions about a contemporary state is less absurd than in the last century, or even a generation ago, when the great majority of states – far less than half the present number – were well-established historical units or like Germany and Italy had emerged from protracted struggles to translate ethnic, linguistic, and historical links into political and legal reality. Today, the reality of individual statehood has been diluted by the sheer quantity, as well as by the suddenness of the transformation of obscure and often non-viable colonies or other dependencies into 'sovereign' states. It is one of the tragedies of the postwar movement of decolonization and self-determination that dozens of artificially and arbitrarily constituted colonies of the imperialist era, instead of merging into viable units, have become states with the same, often artificial, divisions and boundaries and fight for their borders with the same determination as their former colonial masters. Except as voters in the General Assembly of the United Nations, these states – for example, the majority of the thirteen West African ex-French colonies – are no more viable than they were as colonies and, in the absence of regional federations or associations, continue to survive by the support of their former masters. Nor would the disappearance of many of these states as political and legal units cause more than a ripple on the international scene.

Obviously, the disappearance of Canada, by its dissolution into two or three or even more separate states, would be in a totally different category. Whatever the internal stresses may be that could lead to such a development, virtually the entire outside world would regard the disappearance of Canada, as we now know it, as a major international tragedy. And it can be said with some confidence that such reaction would be shared by the western world, the communist world, and the 'Third World'; it can also be said that few states in the world would share this distinction. The disintegration of any of the old and established powers, such as the United States, the USSR, Britain, or France, would create a major international upheaval. But the *de facto* partition of Germany into two separate states which, as far as one can see, is likely to endure barring an international upheaval, is regarded with sorrow and apprehension by some and with satisfaction by others who continue to be afraid of the resurgence of an overpowerful state in the heart of Europe. It seems, therefore, worthwhile to analyse briefly the major reasons why the existence of Canada as an international political and legal unit is so important to the world.

In an elegant and witty essay on 'Defence by Other Means: Diplomacy for the Underdog,' Arthur Andrew, a Canadian foreign service officer, has given the following five criteria as 'providing a framework for discussing the sources of national strength in international affairs':

1 *Stability* – the internal stability which enables a state to act with confidence and flexibility in world affairs.
2 *Resources* – the cultural-intellectual and material resources a state can dispose of as compared with those at the disposal of other states.
3 *Environment* – geographical location, history, natural endowments in general; factors which affect a state's attitude to the world (and the world's attitude toward it) but which are not matters over which the state itself has much control.
4 *National goals* – the goals and the means of attaining them as adopted by the state's present government.
5 *Reputation* – the assessment of the preceding four factors as compared with other states, reached by the state itself and by other states, to produce assessments of reputation, prestige, or national honour.

Perhaps only the last of these five criteria, the most intangible, could be indisputably applied to Canada. It has, notably in the last quarter century since the end of World War II, acquired an international posture and reputation, which for reasons to be analysed later would make its disappearance an international tragedy. None of the other four criteria could be applied to Canada without serious questions. Canada's internal stability continues to be put into question by the division between its English-speaking provinces and Quebec, although other tensions have also appeared. And while this heterogeneity enriches 'cultural-intellectual' resources, Canada's great material resources are largely felt by Canadians to be overshadowed by, and dependent on, the vastly greater economic power of its great neighbour, the United States. Environment, in terms of 'geographical location, history, natural endowments,' is certainly a questionable foundation for the existence of Canada, whose identity unlike, for example, that of Britain is not cemented either by geographical separateness, history, or other 'natural factors.' Finally, the question of national goals is an elusive one, in a constantly changing world.

A general analysis of the reasons for the durability, continuity, and importance of a state has not, to my knowledge, been written; nor can it probably be attempted with any prospect of success, for the reasons why states do or do not survive seem to be highly individual, varying from case to case. Geographical separateness, ethnic or linguistic or religious homogeneity, climatic and economic conditions, as well as the sheer accidents of history, will play a part in differing mixtures. While the Scandinavian states may have a large degree of ethnic and religious homogeneity and enjoy at least in contemporary politics a relative remoteness from the main centres of power politics and international struggle, Switzerland has survived for more than seven centuries, despite its three major languages and ethnic groups and an almost even division between Catholics and Protestants. Germany and Ireland are each partitioned, despite many factors which push towards unification. Poland, a nation of respectable antiquity, religious homogeneity, and except for the recently incorporated territories of German tradition of fair ethnic homogeneity, was for centuries divided between its major neighbours.

It would therefore seem more profitable to survey briefly the specific reasons that account for Canada's importance and, indeed, necessity in the contemporary world. I would subsume the reasons why Canada as a political and legal unit fulfils an essential role in the contemporary world under two major categories. The first is what John W. Holmes in his essay *The Better Part of Valour*[1] has called 'Middle Powermanship.' The other is the probably unique and certainly precarious balance between contending pulls which enables Canada, to a considerable extent, to straddle the conflicting blocs and deep tensions that characterize the contemporary international scene.

CANADA AS A MIDDLE POWER

As a state with well over twenty million inhabitants, vast natural resources, a highly developed and still growing industrial, scientific, and intellectual potential, and as one of the world's major trading powers, Canada certainly ranks high in the league of 'middle powers': those that are not, on the one hand, powerful enough to be contenders for world or even regional domination or leadership of contending blocs; but, on the other hand, in terms of military, economic, and other resources are strong enough to enjoy more than nominal sovereignty. John Holmes has characterized 'middle powermanship' as dependent on two elements: first, 'the unformalized institution of maintaining peace by nuclear deterrents'; second, 'the formalized institution of the United Nations.' With regard to the former, he maintains that the need for the superpowers to exercise restraint by virtue of the very awesomeness of the destructiveness of nuclear power produces a stalemate 'that gives lesser powers enough of a feeling of security to raise their voices and pursue their interests.' With regard to the second, he asserts that the middle powers that profit from the nuclear stalemate could hardly exercise the functions they do exercise without the existence and framework of the United Nations.[2]

Both are increasingly precarious foundations for middle powermanship. The nuclear potential is now possessed by a growing number of powers – including, of course, Canada herself – and the availability of nuclear weapons is probably more dangerous today in the hands of smaller states less restrained by the world responsibilities of the superpowers than in the hands of the latter. And the United Nations, it has to be acknowledged with sadness, is becoming a less and less important factor in the vital decisions over peace and war, perhaps largely because of the proliferation of its membership and the disparity between actual power and nominal voting rights. Yet, this does not destroy the need for major middle powers such as Canada, a state which in terms of military power, economic resources, and the international respect it has acquired over the last quarter of a century can make its voice effectively heard without being suspected of 'imperialist' ambitions.

The Canadian military establishment is modest enough not to arouse suspicions of domination. Yet it has been tested in war and peace, and its equipment, while there is less of it, is technologically on the level of highly advanced military powers. This is the reason why Canada has been much in demand as a participant in the limited but important 'fire brigade' functions exercised by the United Nations which since 1956 have become a modest and inadequate substitute for the international security functions envisaged for the United Nations in its charter. It was a Canadian statesman, Lester Pearson, who played a leading role in the constitution of the first of these order forces, the now defunct UNEF constituted to defuse the Suez Canal conflict of 1956, a force that played a crucial part in maintaining peace in the Middle East until the troops were hastily withdrawn at the request of President Nasser immediately preceding the Six-day War with Israel in 1967. Canadian forces also participated in the ONUC, the UN Congo expeditionary force that intervened to prevent the secession of Katanga from the newly established Congo Republic. Canadians serve in the UN force in Cyprus that constitutes a vital barrier between the feuding Greek and Turkish communities on the island.

It now seems unlikely that the modest but important role of the United Nations in preventing the escalation of conflicts, using the military forces contributed by middle and small powers, will be extended or that this role can be much longer maintained at the present level. This may well be another victim of the decreasing influence of the United Nations as a peacekeeping authority and the tendency for vital conflicts to be settled, or fail to be settled, by direct confrontation and negotiation between the nations concerned. To that extent, Canada's role as a middle power will decline. Canadian military advisers may well continue to play a modest role in the training of forces of some developing countries, although their advisory function in Tanzania was recently terminated by a friendly and informal agreement between the two governments.

What probably accounts for the acceptability of Canadian military advisers or observers in contested zones, and in similar peacekeeping functions, as well as in developing countries is a reputation that Canada has generally gained as a power dedicated to the strengthening of international order and sympathetic to the aspirations of the newer and poorer states. This is an uncertain and shifting posture, but it extends far beyond the military and police functions that have just been mentioned. Guided by a small but exceptionally able and dedicated group of statesmen, diplomats, and civil servants, Canada has carefully and gradually moved to a position that, despite its close links with the western Atlantic group of nations and its important participation in NATO from its beginning in 1949, has enabled it to maintain a stance somewhat distinct from that of both Britain and, more important, the United States.

CANADA'S PRECARIOUS BALANCE

In my opinion, Canada's international posture is characterized by the combination and balance achieved in the face of conflicting pulls, affiliations, and orientations.

The first, and it is to be hoped the most enduring, of Canada's orientations is its active and responsible membership in the United Nations and its specialized agencies. As has been observed the role of Canada as a leading member of the 'fire brigade' will probably decline unless this function of the United Nations is revitalized, an uncertain prospect at this time. On the other hand, the role of the

specialized agencies – far and away the most important and constructive contribution to international organization and to law made by the United Nations – is likely
to be maintained and must indeed be greatly expanded if mankind is to survive. For
many years I have supported the functionalist, as distinct from the blueprint,
approach to world order[3] and am therefore in full agreement with John Holmes's
view that 'there is much to be said for the functionalist approach, strengthening and
multiplying international organizations for specific purposes.[4] Some further observations on this subject will be made later in this essay. Suffice it to say that Canada
has from the beginning been an active, though not a dominating member of the
World Bank and its more recent affiliates and of the International Monetary Fund,
and a Canadian, Brock Chisholm, served as director general of the World Health
Organization. In addition, the only League of Nations organization to survive
World War II and be reconstituted under UN auspices, the International Labour
Organization, had its headquarters in Montreal. At the present time Montreal is the
seat of one of the more important functional international organizations, the International Civil Aviation Organization (ICAO). A Canadian, Maurice Strong, was the
chief organizer and chairman of the International Conference on the Human Environment, held under UN auspices in Stockholm in 1972. In one of the most important
and most critical of contemporary international issues, the future of the ocean bed
and its resources, as well as of ocean fisheries, Canada is playing an important part
by virtue of its vital interests in the oceans; both its Atlantic and Pacific coastlines
are long and important politically, economically, and geographically. Canada's
fishing interests are extensive, as are its interests in the exploitation of ocean bed
resources and its capacity to utilize them. All these factors account for Canada's
active and major role in the UN Seabed Committee, and in other UN activities
designed to regulate the future of the oceans.

Canada's initiative in the founding of NATO and its active membership in that
organization would at first sight appear to be incompatible with the strengthening
of UN security functions. Although NATO is constituted somewhat artificially under
article 51 of the UN Charter, this collective defence organization was not part of
the originally contemplated role of the UN as a world security organization, but it
filled the void created by the collapse of the permanent military force envisaged in
article 42 of the charter. The failure of the UN force was an inevitable consequence
of the cold war, which split the major members of the Security Council. In the
absence of a UN security system, it can now be asserted with confidence in retrospect that the constitution of NATO, and its counterpart, the USSR-sponsored Warsaw
Pact, has served as a balancing factor. In Europe peace has been preserved because
of the existence of these organizations. And it is quite possible that from the basis
of these collective defence organizations, both of which are going through a state
of crisis, a relaxation of tensions and perhaps a mutual reduction of the forces in
that area can be secured. However, the peace of the world would be further imperilled if both, or even more if one of them, disappeared without its place being taken
by an alternative international arrangement. For this reason it must be hoped that,
although Canada has reduced its military commitment to NATO, it will maintain its
membership, while continuing to work for a relaxation of tensions.

The relationship of Canada to the United States has for a long time been a dominant political, economic, and physical problem for Canada. Since the turn of the

century, and increasingly since the end of World War II, the question of Canada's position vis a vis her neighbour has greatly overshadowed the gradually fading British and Commonwealth associations.

At this writing, the relation between Canada and the US is going through a particularly critical phase, the outcome of which cannot yet be clearly foreseen. But the US-Canadian relationship has long been the concern of Canadian historians and political scientists.[5] The factors that account for Canada's overwhelming preoccupation with the United States (hardly parallelled by a corresponding preoccupation of the United States with Canada) are evident enough: from the Atlantic to the Pacific the undefended and geographically unmarked frontier between Canada and the US extends for thousands of miles; the nuclear age has reinforced military and strategic interdependence, symbolized by the NORAD system (radar warning against impending hostile air attacks), located partly in Canada; Canada's major industries, and some of its utilities (oil, steel, automobile manufacturing, aircraft components, paper, and many others) are to a large extent financially and managerially controlled by US interests: trade with the US is a dominant aspect of Canada's international trade. In 1970 its exports to the US were valued at $11.1 billion, and far exceeded the nearest competitor, Japan; on the other hand, Canada is still the largest single recipient of US investment, and its largest trading partner.[6] Intellectually and culturally the influence of US news media and publications and, though to a decreasing extent, US universities has been a major factor in the shaping of Canadian habits and ways of life.

The impact of US economic control over major sectors of Canada's economic life was tellingly illustrated a few years ago when the Ford Motor Company sought to prohibit the export of Canadian-made Ford trucks to communist China. More recently, in September 1971, two of the United States' major companies, Chrysler and the McDonnell Douglas Company, sought to impose a three-month wage and price freeze decreed by President Nixon for the United States on their Canadian subsidiaries. This interdependence, however, is not entirely one sided. A few years ago, an agreement was reached between the US and Canada under which automobile parts manufactured in Canada by US-controlled companies would enter the United States free of duty, and this has not been affected by the 10 per cent surcharge on all imports which generally applies to Canada as it does to all other countries.[7]

The view that Canada's close but unequal association with the United States has heavily weakened Canada's national independence and identity was expressed vehemently in 1957 by D.G. Creighton, an eminent Canadian historian.

> The long association of Canadians with the government and people of the United States, their dependence upon American capital, their reliance upon American initiative and technology, their gradual acceptance of American standards and values, had given the Republic a large equity in the Canadian nation and a potent influence upon the Canadian national character. Continentalism had divorced Canadians from their history, crippled their creative capacity, and left them without the power to fashion a future for themselves. Even the will to defend their independence and protect their national identity had been weakened: they seemed scarcely to be aware of the danger in which they stood.

The problem of a separate Quebec had come to obsess and monopolize the minds of both English and French Canadians. It had distracted them from other and more vital tasks. It blinded them to the peril that threatened their existence as a separate nation in North America.[8]

What Canadians resent, not without reason, is that the ever-present consciousness of United States proximity and penetration is not reflected by an even remotely corresponding preoccupation of the United States with the Canadian position. It has been remarked, for example, that in the influential study of President Nixon's Adviser on Foreign Affairs, Henry Kissinger, Canada is not even mentioned.[9] There are, of course, exceptions to Canada's generally low place in the order of foreign policy priorities of the United States. Not surprisingly these involve direct economic or strategic interests. Examples are the growing water shortage in the western United States, which can be mitigated only by greatly increased supplies from Canada's abundant natural water resources, or the controversy about the status of the Arctic straits, with regard to which the US maintains a right of free passage (important because of recent oil discoveries in Alaska), while Canada claims them as part of its exclusive national jurisdiction. This dispute has led to important and critical developments in international law, to which we will come back later.

To anybody who has lived both in Canada and the United States, the strong impact of American ways of life, language, institutional patterns, and cultural influences, especially on the English-speaking parts of eastern and far western Canada, is evident enough. And this very fact has contributed to the increase of tensions between the English-speaking parts of Canada and Quebec, whose linguistic and cultural orientation is towards France, and not Britain or the United States.[10]

Is Canada's close relationship with, and dependence on, the United States likely to increase or decrease in our time? This is indeed a crucial question for Canada's survival, but the answer is far from obvious. As John W. Holmes wrote in an article first published in *Foreign Affairs* in 1967,[11] 'in the paradoxical continental partnership between the United States and Canada, there are always forces driving them together and apart.'[12] First, Canada's exceptionally close economic interdependence with the United States is not likely to be altered basically in the foreseeable future, although it is in the process of modification. As Lester Pearson observed a few years ago,[13] 'it is not a very comforting thought, but in the economic sphere, when you have 60% or so of your trade with one country, you are in a position of considerable economic dependence.' No doubt present and future Canadian government policy will, strongly supported by public opinion, seek to avoid any further intensification of Canadian dependence on the United States. In a few cases – such as the acquisition of a Canadian-owned oil producer, the threatened US acquisition of a Canadian-controlled publishing enterprise, or the foreign content of Canadian radio and television programs – the government has already intervened to prevent such alienation. It is quite likely that Canada will follow the example increasingly adopted by the vast majority of far less developed countries of requiring a 51 per cent Canadian interest in certain types of industries and basic utilities which are considered to be of vital national importance. There are obvious limits to such a process, as long as Canadian production and trade is so overwhelmingly oriented towards the United States.

Nevertheless, it is my strong conviction that growing independence rather than strengthened dependence on the United States will increasingly mark Canadian postures in foreign policy, international law, and economic transactions. The first reason for this is a general facet of international development in the postwar world, which is by no means confined to Canada but which strengthens the position of a major middle power such as Canada. This is the, at first sight, paradoxical fact that the enormous accumulation of destructive military potential in the hands of the two superpowers – both of which have the capacity not only to paralyze and largely destroy each other but also a large part of the rest of the world – has restricted rather than expanded their freedom of action. This, of course, is subject to the chastening reservation that a madman like Hitler may obtain absolute control in one of the present or future states equipped with overwhelming destructive power and set the world aflame. But for purposes of any rational analysis we have to ignore such a frightening prospect, and derive considerable comfort from the fact that in the years since the end of World War II conflicts and tensions that would have started major international wars at any other period have somehow stopped short of a general international conflagration. Granted the nuclear stalemate between the US and the USSR – and in a more complex fashion, the triangular balance of power that may dominate the next decade as China joins the other two superpowers in a precarious 'dance of the three,'[14] – other states unquestionably gain a greater measure of freedom of movement. This is a far cry from the hopes for an affective international authority that would control world affairs in vital matters of security and defence as was envisaged by the framers of the UN Charter, but it is the unquestioned reality of our day.

Evidence of such growing independence in the conduct of Canada's international relations was accumulated well before the attempt of the distinctly more national-minded Trudeau government. The two aspects of Canadian foreign policy most clearly at odds with US policy have been, first, the Canadian recognition of communist China years before the present reorientation of US policy; and, second, the absolute refusal of Canada, along with most but not all of the allies of the US, either to join the US in its Vietnam War, or even to support it ideologically. Indeed, Canada has, not only for reasons of geographical proximity, been the recipient of US draft resisters and other protesters against the war. The tensions undoubtedly caused by these major acts of independence in international relations may recede with the establishment of US diplomatic relations with China and as US involvement in the Vietnam War diminishes. But unquestionably these major independent actions have strengthened Canadian tendencies towards a more independent posture in international relations. Another recent manifestation of Canada's independence from and indeed opposition to US interests has been its assertion that the Arctic straits, through which ships must pass in order to reach Alaska, are Canadian and not international, and the declaration of a hundred-mile Canadian pollution control zone – which may very well expand into a full assertion of Canadian jurisdiction – and which has been strongly protested by the United States.

At the conclusion of this essay, some observations will be made on the tragic dilemma created by the discrepancy between the increasing interdependence of the nations for survival and the growing nationalism and indeed disintegration of vital aspects of international order in recent years. For the moment it may suffice to state that, for better or for worse, discrepancy of political and military power does not necessarily entail corresponding political domination, and that Canadian independence from the United States is likely to increase rather than decrease in the years to come.

Compared with the ever-present fact of the close links of Canada with the United States, its historical association with the British Empire, and subsequently the Commonwealth, is a factor of decreasing importance. Economically, this has long been evident, since the Canadian currency is based on the dollar, not on sterling, and since Canada's share in trade with the United Kingdom, while considerable, has always been far below its corresponding significance for the other white members of the Commonwealth, such as Australia and New Zealand. Canada does, of course, participate in the Ottawa Agreements of 1931, which created a general tariff preference for exports to the United Kingdom. But this is likely to decrease and eventually to vanish with Britain's entry into the European Common Market.

Politically and legally, the Commonwealth has become an increasingly loose and diverse association of states, with no central machinery of government or anything resembling a federal or even a confederate structure. Although the great majority of the newly independent former Asian and African colonies have chosen to remain within the Commonwealth, this amounts essentially to a periodic and formal machinery of consultation and the continuation of traditional links – mainly between the elites of the countries concerned – but with increasing divergence of policies and orientation. The Privy Council has virtually ceased to be an instance of judicial appeal, and even the remnants of a common nationality (British subjects or Commonwealth citizens) have decreasing significance, as the various members of the Commonwealth have created their own nationalities and, on the other hand, membership in the Commonwealth no longer gives automatic rights of entry to the UK (this in fact operates mainly against non-white members of the Commonwealth).

What remains are the uncertain and partly sentimental links between English-speaking Canada and Britain, and a certain familiarity that is likely to weaken in the next generation but will not easily be extinguished. However, the remaining symbolic links – notably the continuing titular position of the Queen as the common sovereign – cannot disguise the fact that the Commonwealth is a factor of steadily decreasing significance in Canada's policy. And this, of course, has been greatly increased by the growing assertion of Quebec autonomy and the Quebec orientation towards French rather than British associations.

Canada is not, of course, simply divided ethnically and culturally between English-speaking and French-speaking citizens, the latter concentrated though by no means exclusively in Quebec. More than a third of the Canadian population has diverse racial and ethnic origins – Dutch, German, Italian, Polish, Yugoslav, and many others – whose cultural and emotional links are neither with the anglophone nor the francophone sphere.[15] Nevertheless, the growing irredentism of Quebec remains by far the most important single factor in the reorientation of Canada's international position.

Quebec symbolizes the French history of that part of Canada. It is francophone,

Catholic, and oriented towards French cultural and intellectual influences. One of the most important distinctive features of Quebec is its legal system which, at least in the sphere of private law and to some extent in the organization of the legal profession (*notaive*), is an adaptation of the French legal system. The Quebec Civil Code of 1866 is a modified version of the French Code Civil. French textbooks and jurisprudential developments continue to have strong influence on the interpretation of the Quebec civil law, even though the latter is gradually developing a tradition of its own and has not remained uninfluenced by certain common law concepts and traditions.[16] The composition of the Supreme Court of Canada is carefully balanced to include both common law and civil law judges.

It is not, of course, the function of this survey to assess the manifold aspects of the Anglo-French dualism and tensions in Canada. At the very beginning of this survey, the conviction was stated that the disappearance as a political and legal unit – possibly as a result of the separation of Quebec and perhaps other parts from the rest of Canada – would be an international tragedy. The duality of French and English influences in Canada may prove a source of strength rather than weakness in its international posture.

The duality of the legal system which, of course, extends essentially to the civil sphere and not to the growing branches of public law, such as constitutional, administrative, and labour law, is in itself not a major factor in international law. Splits and divisions in international society, and the weaknesses of international law and organization in our time, do not follow the divisions of the world between the civil law and the common law spheres. The overwhelming international problems, such as the problems of disarmament and the restraint on the use of national force, the threat to the freedom of the seas, the need for closer international collaboration in matters of communications, health, pollution, finance and trade, and development aid, are not functions of the duality of the two basic legal systems of the world. Nor are the legal solutions sought on this basis for such outstanding problems of contemporary industrial society as the responsibility for motor car accidents or the liberalization of family law, or the legal responses to the threat to environment, basically different in such countries as Britain, France, Germany, the United States, or the Soviet Union. Differences are determined by political and social ideologies, and even these recede before the common disasters that threaten mankind.

Nevertheless, there is, between the countries of civil law and the common law systems a notable difference of style and language. The style of a French-type judgment is basically different from that of a common law judgment. The difficulty of translating the legal terminology of one system into that of the other has been the bane of many an international treaty and other documents. It is here that the duality of the civilian and the common law inheritance in Canada can become a major advantage in international diplomacy and the formulation of international treaties and other legal agreements. This, of course, presupposes that the French civilian tradition in Canada – which has so long been suppressed or neglected in Canada's international relations – acquires a full and equal place. Granted this now increasingly strong development, a Canadian delegation composed of its anglophone and francophone elements and their corresponding legal affiliations can play a very constructive role in the formulation and interpretation of international legal documents of general international concern.

In a broader international context it has been observed that cultural heterogeneity may have advantages rather than disadvantages in international relations.

> To achieve a reliable degree of stability, the heterogeneous state must have developed, for its internal purposes, techniques of negotiation and compromise of a high order and its citizens must have come to understand what they might think right or desirable. These attributes transfer readily to the international scene. The attendant risk is, of course, that heterogeneous nations are vulnerable to attacks on their basic internal stability by foreign opponents.[17]

And John Holmes has observed that 'Canada's existence as a bi-tribal state has not only tempered its international political awareness; it has also been a source of inspiration to new countries struggling against much greater odds to establish multi-tribal states. I have no doubt also that a stronger assertion of the French fact in Canada would strengthen Canada's diplomatic hand.'[18] We have here one of the many factors that, in the unique combination that prevails in Canada, is both a source of strength and weakness, depending on a delicate balance in the conduct of Canadian affairs as well as the many uncertainties of world politics.

In another sphere, considering Canada's continuingly close even though not entirely voluntary relationship with the United States, and its founding role in NATO, it is a remarkable achievement that Canada should have maintained, and recently strengthened, relatively friendly relations with the Soviet Union, although these have been marred by serious conflicts caused by the ubiquitous and often ruthless activities of Soviet fishing fleets off the Canadian coasts. More remarkable perhaps has been Canada's relationship with communist China, which has extended beyond mere formal diplomatic recognition. Over a number of years Canada has been a major supplier of wheat for China, and much of the scanty information that reached the West in the years when there was not only a total absence of diplomatic contacts between the United States and China, but when Britain's relations despite her formal recognition of communist China were near to hostility (partly because of communist activities in British-controlled Hong Kong), came from Canadian newspaper correspondents. Again it is probably the fact that Canada does not rank as a major power that made it easier for communist China to open its doors towards the West via Canada.

In realizing that the political, diplomatic, and legal isolation of the most populous country in the world from the rest of the world was a legal and political anachronism, and that a cautious opening of trade and industrial relations between China and the West could be possible, Canadian diplomacy provided encouragement and perhaps somewhat eased the belated steps taken by the United States in the summer of 1971. This does not, however, obscure the fact that ultimately Canada's major political, economic, strategic, and cultural alignments are with the western world, and that the extent to which Canada's relations with the communist powers will develop must essentially be dictated by the basic aspects of the relationship between the communist and western worlds. No doubt present Canadian policy will, far more than twenty or even ten years ago, tend to play down the remaining cold war aspects, which account for the confrontation of the NATO and Warsaw Pact forces in Europe, and support proposals for a reduction of the western military in

Europe, tending to take an optimistic view of Russian moves towards a détente. Nevertheless, it is highly improbable that Canada can in a deeper sense become an 'uncommitted' country.

Another dilemma for Canadian policy may arise from the growing antagonism between the Soviet Union and communist China. A positive aspect of this antagonism is the destruction of the lingering myth of a monolithic communism, which spawned the cold war containment policies that reached their climax under John Foster Dulles. The tragedy of the Vietnam War has been largely a product of this preoccupation with a non-existent monolithic communist front. Another consequence of the Soviet-China antagonism is that 'bipolarism' – which has long given way to a much more mobile play of forces in which the middle and smaller powers play a crucial role – is becoming obsolete and that the manoeuvering between the three major powers designed to avoid a firm alliance between the other two (in almost Orwellian fashion) can, if skilfully handled, provide a greater mobility in world politics. But it may well be that Canada, at some time, will have to decide on its preference between closer relationships with the USSR or Communist China. Here it would appear that the importance of Canadian contacts with the Soviet Union, their Arctic contiguity, and the potential conflict of their fishing and other ocean interests will make the relationship with the USSR the more vital one. As far as possible, however, Canadian diplomacy will almost certainly be directed towards maintenance of correct, if not friendly, relations with both the communist giants.

In view of this growing significance of the Arctic Basin Maxwell Cohen, in a recent essay on 'A Just Foreign Policy and the National Interest,' suggested a possible new vital role for Canada. As a consequence of the unlocking of the Arctic for purposes of navigation and the potentially enormous significance of Alaska as a source of oil and perhaps other natural resources, Canada is now a neighbour not only of the United States but also of the Soviet Union: 'The Arctic should be used as an entrée to the new polar neighborhood in cooperation with the other sector states, notably the USSR, and, of course, the U.S.A. We will be stronger in our dealings with the United States if we view the polar region in our own sector as a basin to be managed within some cooperative and internationally acceptable rules. And, above all, we will found on this basin policy a new neighborhood relationship with the Soviet Union with all of its implications – and its limitations as well.'[19] This is not an isolated opinion. In a recent interview with NBC's John Chancellor, John Holmes observed: 'The Arctic especially is our thing, and herein lies the basis of a curious affinity with the Soviet Union. In his recent visit to the USSR, Mr Trudeau constantly stressed that we were Arctic neighbors. Canadians really have a feeling about this.'[20]

This is no doubt to a large extent a vision for the future rather than a realistic view of the present. At this time Canada is essentially engaged in unilateral protective measures against both its powerful 'neighbours.' Its claim to priority interests in the waters of the Arctic island system, of which the one hundred mile Arctic waters pollution control zone proclaimed in 1970 is the prominent example, is essentially directed against US claims to free navigation through these Arctic waters and the dangers that might be caused by increasing navigation, especially of oil tankers, to the Arctic ecology. Canada's redefinition of its continental shelf, measured, as permitted by the Geneva Convention of 1958, from baselines, has been a protective step largely directed against the intrusions of Soviet fishing fleets. After years of fruitless negotiations, Canada has concluded bilateral agreements with the USSR defining their respective fishery rights. That an Arctic 'community,' in which Canada would both be a buffer between, and join both its powerful neighbours in a common endeavour for the scientific use and conservation of the biological, mineral, and ecological resources of the Arctic, would be an eminently desirable goal will scarcely be doubted; that it is an unlikely development in the near future is part of the trend in international legal relations to which we will revert at the end of this essay.

Turning now to Canada's relations with the Third World, reference has already been made to the fact that, by virtue of its middle power status, Canada has been in a favourable position vis à vis the large number of developing countries which now constitute a substantial majority of the membership of the United Nations. For this reason the armed forces of developing countries will agree to have Canadian advisers, and Canada is generally the most acceptable member among the western-oriented powers in international bodies, such as the largely impotent International Control Commission, established by the Geneva Accords of 1954 and consisting of Canada, India, and Poland. But this is not a static relationship. For this reason the gradually increasing role of Canada in international aid is a further important link with the developing world. This role – exercised through membership of the World Bank Group, through the essentially Commonwealth-based Colombo Plan, and through bilateral aid – has grown in relative significance as the United States has virtually abdicated its once predominant role in international development aid.[21] The flow of resources from the richer to the poorer countries consists of development aid – which is provided in grants or low-interest loans by governments or international organizations and is conceived of as public and relatively disinterested contributions of the richer countries to the economic development of the poorer ones – and investment, which is essentially a bilateral or multilateral transaction that private entrepreneurs pursue for business purposes, although the conditions under which they operate today generally make such investment part of national development plans in the developing countries. In this process, Canada's role does not, of course, compare with that of the United States or with Britain or France.

It has nevertheless not been inconsiderable. Among many examples of contemporary Canadian investment in developing countries, we may mention the Brazilian Power and Light Company (Brazilian Traction), a company formed in 1912 in Canada as a holding and management company for utility subsidiaries that had operated in Brazil since 1899. It developed into Canada's biggest single foreign investment operation, and its assets are estimated as well in excess of $1 billion. At one time Brazilian Light and Power completely controlled Brazil's utilities, but in 1962, after prolonged negotiations, it sold its telephone and telegraph interests to the Brazilian government. Part of the proceeds of the sale are being invested in smaller joint venture operations in Brazil. It is likely that gradually other utilities will be nationalized, as part of the now almost general policy of Latin American states to nationalize their public utilities and natural resources. However, this remains a very important economic link between Canada and Brazil. Canadian interests also played a pioneer part in the group that explored Liberian mining ore and eventually led to the formation of the giant multinational Lamco operation, whose assets are about $300 million, and whose operations have not only opened up a rich iron ore mountain in the interior of Liberia but also developed a whole infrastructure of railways, roads, harbours, schools, and other utilities. Canada also gives technical aid to the East African Common Services Organization as well as to its member states and is thus, for example, indirectly contributing to the building of the railway between Zambia and Dar-es-Salaam, Tanzania.

THE PROSPECTS FOR CANADA'S SURVIVAL

The previous sections have attempted to survey briefly what appeared to me the most important facets of Canada's unique international position. No other state manages to balance such different pulls, interests, and associations. The factors that account for this Canadian position are in part based on history, in part on geography, in part on racial and ethnic factors, in part on the remarkable stature of a succession of Canadian statesmen, and more recently, the distinction of a small but outstanding corps of diplomats. The factors just enumerated can as easily lead to weakness and disintegration as they can lead to an important international role of a people who, in the words of the Canadian historian A.R.M. Lower, 'have had to re-work the miracle of their political existence.'[22] From Macdonald and Laurier to St Laurent, Pearson, and Trudeau, Canada has had a succession of statesmen of vision. But the balancing act is so precarious that Canadians continue to discuss the problem of Canada's *survivance*.[23] Lower's assertion that 'Canada has been created because there existed within the hearts of its people a determination to build for themselves an enduring home; Canada is a supreme act of faith' is undoubtedly true. But whether this faith continues to exist, whether the centrifugal pulls will prevail over the centripetal ones, whether in particular the emergence of Quebec nationalism will tear this unity asunder are questions that Canadians as well as non-Canadians must constantly re-examine.

In former years the preoccupation of Canadian historians was, not unnaturally, the predominance of British power and culture as well as economic dominance. But this can no longer be a major concern of Canadians in the 1970s. Britain's power, in its own right and as the centre of an empire transformed into a commonwealth, has diminished. On the contrary, it would appear that at the present time at least English-speaking Canadians would welcome the preservation and possible strengthening of British intellectual, political, and even economic influences as a counterbalance to the overpowering influence of the United States.

The relationship of Quebec to France and the French-speaking world is a more serious challenge to Canadian unity. It is difficult for an outsider – as it is perhaps even for Canadians – to assess the depth and the durability of Quebec irredentism. Surely it is necessary to distinguish between two different aspects of Quebec nationalism: the desire for full status and equality, in political, economic, and cultural terms, with an English-speaking Canada that until recently has played by far the dominant role in economics and government; and the political orientation towards France as a possible counterpart to the once dominant association of

Canada with Britain. With respect to Quebec associations with the French-speaking world, it is again important to distinguish between any specific political association with France and a separate, though limited, association of Quebec in international organizations with the French-speaking states. The former is, in my opinion, not a serious prospect, though it was artificially inflated by the late General de Gaulle's sense of French grandeur and anti-Anglo-Americanism. 'Vive le Québec libre' appealed to French-Canadians but also made many of them realize that they were after all Canadians. And it would certainly take a great deal of self-deception to believe that the French people have, over the last century, had more than superficial links with Quebec or that they feel now as close to Quebec as they are, for example, to the French-speaking part of Belgium or even to the former French colonies in Africa, in their political, economic, or personal associations. De Gaulle's 'Vive le Québec libre' was a flash, an assertion of French grandeur rather than a serious move towards a new political alignment.

While it is certain that the transformation of Anglo-French relations in Canada will continue to cause severe stress, it seems now less likely than a few years ago that it will lead to the partition of Canada. There may be a further decentralization of powers, although this may not necessarily be a disadvantageous development; there will be further battles for greater equality, redistribution of financial resources, and perhaps – as has been suggested, for example, by Louis Sabourin – 'separate Quebec representation in certain international organizations and associations.' But Canada is likely to survive. The prospects of national survival are strengthened in my view because the submerging of Canada's political and economic identity in its more powerful American neighbour is at present a smaller threat than it was some years ago.

CANADA'S CONTRIBUTION TO THE DEVELOPMENT OF INTERNATIONAL LAW AND ORGANIZATION

Although the present volume is essentially devoted to the study of Canada's role in international law, no apology is made for the foregoing analysis of its political and international relations. International law does not exist in a vacuum. It is, far more than the more secure systems of municipal law, dependent on the state of society in which it operates. Present day international society is a still relatively loose association of 'sovereign' national states for which international law is at best a superstructure.

Arthur Andrew expressed the view that international law is used and twisted by governments ' ''more to buttress positions they have reached through policy decisions than to help them to reach international legal'' positions ... the legal experts of the ''foreign ministry may be consulted to put the best face possible on the pre-determined policy.'' '[24] Precisely because there is distressingly much evidence to support such a cynical view, it is necessary to expose its inadequacies. Examples in vindication of Mr Andrew's view are numerous enough: in recent years the US intervention in the Dominican Republic (1965) which, in President Johnson's plain admission was undertaken to thwart the installation of a left-wing government under Juan Bosch, was later justified by the legal adviser to the State Department as being an action contrary to 'any fundamentalist view of international law' but in the tradition of the common law; that is, as an attempt to bring 'a practical and satisfactory solution to a pressing problem.'[25] The Soviet military intervention in Czechoslovakia in August 1968, designed to oust a relatively liberal government that it was feared would stray from communist orthodoxy, was subsequently justified in the so-called Brezhnev Doctrine, which maintained that while 'the Socialist states respect the democratic norms of international law ... the picture changes fundamentally when the danger arises to socialism itself in a particular country ... Naturally, the communists of the fraternal countries could not allow the socialist states to be inactive in the name of an abstractly understood sovereignty, when they saw that the countries stood in peril of anti-socialism and degeneration.'[26] We might add the mutual disregard of international law by both the Arab States and Israel in their continuing conflict or, more recently, in the economic and financial sphere, the unilateral violations, by the US of her treaty obligations as a member of the ILO and the GATT. These are only some of the most flagrant examples of many attempts to twist or circumvent the norms of international law, for example, by invoking the *clausula rebus sic stantibus* or similar disguises for evading international obligations.

Nevertheless, there is abundant justification for the observation made by a realistic observer of the international legal scene: 'The mistaken impression of lawlessness may derive ... from a tendency to think of international law only in terms of major dramatic events ... It is fair to say that most nations observe most principles of international law and most of their international obligations most of the time.'[27] In matters of territorial jurisdiction, diplomatic relations, the great majority of international treaties, and other agreements observance is the overwhelming norm and violation the exception, occurring principally in matters affecting vital political issues. It is particularly important to stress this because Canada's international reputation rests largely on her generally highly creditable record in the observance of international law. Canada's recent tendency to resort to unilateral actions in matters of national jurisdiction, especially over the seas, endangers this reputation.

However, customary and treaty international law as it has been developed over the last few centuries is essentially a body of rules delimiting mutual sovereignties and jurisdictions; it almost entirely abstains from the regulation of matters affecting the lives of the peoples: trade, health, labour, and communications. It is in these spheres, in the elaboration of co-operative norms of behaviour in matters affecting the lives of the nations, whose interdependence for survival has been dramatically increased by modern technology and the revolution of communications, that the most vital problems of international law have arisen. Essentially the progress of international law depends on the progress of international organization. It is in this area that a middle power like Canada, which is directly involved in the problems of modern technology and industrialization but stands somewhere between the superpowers and the smaller and mostly underdeveloped nations, has played and can continue to play a vital role.

As early as 1909 the Boundary Waters Treaty between Canada and the United States established a model for the international organization of international river resources. The treaty established the International Joint Commission, composed in equal parts of Canadian and United States commissioners, which combines technical, administrative, and judicial functions. It has been described as 'a strong and flexible instrument for the settlement of international disputes.'[28] But the treaty remains an isolated instance of this type of international co-operation.

The functional organization of common international concerns – partly through the specialized agencies of the United Nations, and partly through regional and bilateral arrangements – has been one of the most significant international developments since the end of World War II. As has already been observed, the progress of such functional international arrangements is, in view of the collapse of any prospects for a more comprehensive political international structure, the only hope for civilized survival. Canada has been an active participant in all the specialized UN agencies. In the World Bank and its affiliates,[29] the International Atomic Energy Association (IAEA), where Canada is one of the 'five members most advanced in the technology of atomic energy, including the production of source materials' and therefore a permanent member of the Board of Governors, and the World Health Organization Canada has been conscious of the importance and urgency of functional international collaboration.

Today the concern with environment is, justifiably, looming ever larger as one of mankind's primary concerns. The recent series of papers entitled *Foreign Policy for Canadians* (1970) again and again stresses the environmental problem and the 'quality of life' as two of the principal concerns of Canadian foreign policy in the seventies. But the immensity of the task of developing solutions should not be underestimated. Environmental control means more than a more general international agreement on the elimination and control of oil spilling by tankers; it means more than a more effective enforcement of the woefully inadequate measures and institutions existing at this time to prevent overfishing and the extermination of entire species of fish by competing and highly industrialized trawler fleets; it means more than international agreement on the disposal of radioactive waste. All these are individual instances of a global and multidimensional problem: the finding of a better balance between production, consumption, and environment. And this balance, which no single state has as yet been able to achieve with the much stronger legal controls of a domestic legal system, must be found on a global scale. All the basic problems of environment of our time – overpopulation, urban conglomerations, pollution of the oceans and of the major international rivers, pollution of the atmosphere, the ecological alteration of such vital parts of our globe as the Arctic region, of the temperature of the oceans by thermal discharges, the balance and conservation of marine life – are interconnected aspects of the giant global problem of how we can control the drive for more and more production, increasing though very unevenly distributed consumer demands, the population explosion, and reckless waste – greatest in the most advanced societies – in order to preserve life on earth.

But although the urgency as well as the immensity of this problem is beginning to be recognized, the legal and political organization of mankind has hitherto prevented more than a few rudimentary beginnings of an international perspective and organization of these concerns. One of the most important aspects of a more comprehensive and more integrated approach to international organization will be the co-ordination of environmental concerns and development aid. There is growing recognition in the industrially developed countries that the preservation of environment and a better ecological balance may rapidly become a condition of survival and entail a drastic readjustment of priorities. But the developing countries not surprisingly take a different view. They are intent on rapid industrialization, which they regard as the quickest way to increase national productivity and wealth and to diversify essential rural and static economies. The need to bring together the viewpoints of the developed and the developing countries, and to adjust development assistance to the constantly growing danger of a destruction of the basic conditions of life, could be one of the major tasks of international environment law and organization. In this task, Canada, by virtue of its leading role in the UN sponsored Stockholm conference and because of its direct exposures to this problem, can become a leader.

CANADA: THE NEW NATIONALISM AND THE FUTURE OF INTERNATIONAL LAW

One of the great tragedies of our time, perhaps the ultimate tragedy, is the widening gap between mankind's need for greatly intensified worldwide and institutionalized co-operation on a widening range of matters and the actual policies pursued by the various nation states. These not only trail a long way behind the urgent need to organize such worldwide concerns as population and pollution control, international monetary stability, or the preservation of marine life, but increasingly threaten the achievements of international law attained over the last few centuries. The most important and threatening instance of this spread of nationalism, at the expense of existing as well as developing community interests of mankind, is the rapidly growing threat to the freedom of the seas. In view of Canada's exceptionally important position, as a state with long coastlines and fishery interests in both the Atlantic and Pacific areas and its vital economic and strategic interests in the Arctic Zone, Canada's posture in the years to come is of crucial importance.

This is not the place to analyse the gradual progress towards an at least partial partition of the oceans since the Truman Proclamation on the Continental Shelf of 1945.[30] Suffice it to say that an increasingly powerful and widespread trend has been a / for the technologically advanced powers to push outward and downward the exclusive rights over the exploitation of the seabed and subsoil resources, under the shelter of article I of the 1958 Geneva Convention on the Continental Shelf, which defined the continental shelf as referring 'to a depth of 200 meters, or beyond that limit, to where the depth of the superjacent waters admits of the exploitation of the natural resources of the said areas'; and b / for states which either have no extensive exploitable continental shelf areas or a dominant fishery interest or, as in many cases, a combination of both, to push outward the limits of exclusive national jurisdiction. The former has, under the pressure of petroleum and other industrial interests, and with the support of some legal scholars, led to the gradual substitution of the 'continental margin' for the 'continental shelf' concept; that is, to the advocacy of the national jurisdiction over seabed resources of coastal states up to the abyssal depths of the ocean.[31]

The latter approach, adopted first by the Latin American states, has induced an increasing number of states – essentially those with fishery interests and weak maritime power – to proclaim 100 mile, or even 200 mile, zones of exclusive national jurisdiction over the ocean areas adjacent to their coasts. Superficially the latter claims appear to be more extensive than the former. They extend radically from the surface to the bottom of the sea, whereas 'continental shelf' or 'continental margin' only extend to seabed and subsoil resources. However, not only may these reach in some cases well beyond the 200 mile limit; as the technological and industrial exploitation of seabed resources proceeds, industrial installations of all kinds will make the theoretically preserved freedoms of navigation and fishing increasingly theoretical. Recently, therefore, the concept of 'ocean space' has begun to replace the former, more limited, definitions.[32] The end result, as has indeed been proposed in the most recent proposals of Ambassador Pardo, may well be a general national jurisdiction extension of coastal states up to a limit of 200 miles from the coastal baseline. This would encompass the overwhelming majority of both biological and mineral resources and lead, in an economic if not in a geographical sense, to a new era of 'closed seas.'[33]

Where does Canada stand in this controversy, surely one of the most fateful for the future of international law and the political configuration of mankind? With regard to the expanding claims over seabed and subsoil resources, Canada took an intermediate position by proposing that all states should, by a certain deadline, state their maximum jurisdiction claims, and that from that date onward no further national extensions should be permitted.[34] Given the present climate, the acceptance of such a contention would almost certainly lead to a proliferation of claims to 200 mile limits from most coastal states, with the exception of the major maritime and technologically advanced powers, who are likely to compensate by extending their seabed resources claims to the edge of the continental margin.

More significant perhaps has been the much-discussed Canadian proclamation of an exclusive 100 mile Arctic pollution control zone. That Canada, at the same time, extended its territorial waters to a twelve mile limit and accepted the jurisdiction of the International Court of Justice for possible litigation arising out of that claim are of far less significance. The extension of territorial waters to a twelve mile limit is now all but universal, and those countries, like the United States, which do not yet adopt it openly have a contiguous nine mile zone adjoining the three mile territorial water zones, for which exclusive fishing rights and other exclusive powers are claimed. The submission of such a claim to the jurisdiction of the World Court would therefore be an empty gesture. Contrast with this situation the specific exclusion of such jurisdiction from the far more controversial 100 mile pollution control zone. The avoidance of a submission clearly indicates that Canada is not sure that such a claim would be compatible with existing international law but intends to adhere to it in any case. To that extent, Canada has undoubtedly joined the general race for an extension of national controls and a further reduction of the already lamentably weak sphere of international legal and administrative controls. Moreover, it would be surprising if, in line with the general developments sketched above, pollution control would not be gradually extended to other aspects, and the 100 mile zone would become one of exclusive jurisdiction over ocean space.

Nevertheless, there are extenuating circumstances. The danger through pollution from oil tankers which are likely to ply between the newly opened oil fields and the eastern coast of America is real. Interference with the ecology of the Arctic, which is as yet largely unexplored but certainly has a major effect on the climatic balance of the earth, presents grave dangers. And whereas even at the time of

Canada's action, jurisdictional claims exceeding twelve miles were still regarded as exceptional, they have now rapidly become the rule. In the absence of effective control measures and authorities, there is some justification for Canada's unilateral action.

Ultimately, of course, the question is whether this will be just one more move towards the partition of the seas by a state that has been, and in many respects still is, in the forefront of those fighting for a better and more comprehensive international organization. Or is it a prelude to some kind of regional organization, the 'Arctic Community?'

In the contemporary state of international society, there is somewhat more hope for regional community organization than for worldwide organizations. There is a greater community of interests between a limited number of states sharing certain common concerns, and the policing of any arrangements made with regard to fisheries, exploitation of minerals, or pollution control should be considerably easier than on a worldwide basis. Yet the example of the North Sea[35] shows that even in that area, bordered by states with many historic, economic, and other links, the best that could be attained was a peaceful and amicable delimitation of the respective national continental shelf zones, rather than a community approach. The latter – the principle of joint exploitation – was suggested, in Judge Jessup's opinion, as 'particularly appropriate in cases involving the unity of a deposit,' and as possibly having 'a wider application in agreements reached by the parties concerning the still undelimited but potentially overlapping areas of the continental shelf which have been in dispute.'

Of course, Canada cannot act alone in seeking community rather than national solutions. In the Arctic zone it depends on the collaboration of its neighbours, the US and the USSR. In any attempt to call a halt to the constant expansion of national exclusive fishery zones, Canada depends to a large extent on the attitudes of the world's most ubiquitous fishing fleets, notably those of the USSR and Japan. Nevertheless, Canada is strong enough not to be a mere passive spectator in the development of international relations.

CONCLUSION

The foregoing pages have sought to show that Canada's most characteristic contribution to the development of international law and a more peaceful world derives from the unique confluence of diverse ethnic, cultural, religious, linguistic, legal, and political factors. This has generally served to underline Canada's role as a balancer, a mediator, and a moderator. But it has not always meant bold leadership. In all too many cases, Canada has been a 'middle' power, not only in the physical and political sense. In the field of international human rights, as John Humphrey points out in this volume, Canada's record is less than inspiring. Although Canada has been one of the states that has accepted the so-called 'optional clause' – the compulsory jurisdiction of the International Court of Justice for disputes of a legal character – she expressly withdrew that acceptance in the case of her recent proclamation of a 100 mile exclusive Arctic pollution control zone.

But in both these as in many other spheres vital to the progress of international law Canada's record is certainly no worse than that of the major powers. None of them is prepared to translate the Universal Declaration of Human Rights into concrete and enforceable covenants of human rights which, though passed by the General Assembly in 1966, have no prospect whatsoever of ratification. And it should be remembered that the United States has not to this date found it possible to ratify even the Genocide Convention. Nor is the record more inspiring when it comes to the submission of vital disputes to adjudication by the International Court of Justice, which is severely underemployed. To this day both France and the Soviet Union have refused to comply with an advisory opinion of the International Court of Justice and a subsequent General Assembly resolution affirming the competence of the Assembly to assess members for their share of the cost of the United Nations Congo Expeditionary Force.

Canada, no less than other powers, will seek to pursue her vital national interests in preference to the ideals of a better international legal order. But at the same time the factors that have been briefly surveyed in this essay are likely to impel Canada more strongly than most other countries towards a leading role in the development of functional international co-operation on which the survival of mankind may well depend. Canada's initiative in the organization of the Stockholm Conference on the Human Environment is a good omen. It is out of the realization of *necessities* rather than *ideals* that a fuller international legal order of co-operation may emerge. And few other powers are better equipped than Canada to take a lead in this evolution.

NOTES

1 John W. Holmes, *The Better Part of Valour: Essays on Canadian Diplomacy* (1970).
2 Ibid, 20 ff.
3 See, most recently, 'The Reality of International Law' (1971), 10 *Col. J. Transnational L.* 46.
4 *Supra* note 1, at 63.
5 See, among many others, D.G. Creighton; *Canada's First Century* (1970); W.L. Morton, *The Canadian Identity* (1961); Ramsey Cook, *The Maple Leaf Forever* (1971); Holmes, *The Better Part of Valour, supra* note 1, at part J.
6 Canada's exports to the US account for about 70 per cent of its total exports. US exports to Canada constitute about 25 per cent of its total exports. *N.Y. Times,* 3 October 1971.
7 In a survey in the *N.Y. Times,* 13 September 1971, Brendan Jones estimated that the import levy does not apply to three-fourths of Canadian exports to the United States but that nevertheless some $2.5 billion of Canadian exports are subject to the surcharge and that these are mainly the products of industrial plants concentrated in Ontario and Quebec.
8 D.G. Creighton, in his presidential adress to the Canadian Historical Association, 1957, cited in Cook, *The Maple Leaf Forever,*

supra note 5, at 157.
9 *American Foreign Policy* (1969).
10 This does not, however, apply to the economic orientation of Quebec, whose desire for industrialization and foreign investment naturally directs her towards the United States more than any other country, including France, which obviously cannot meet the capital needs of an expanding Quebec economy.
11 Republished in Holmes, *The Better Part of Valour, supra* note 1, at 166 ff.
12 Ibid, at 167.
13 *Maclean's,* July 1967.
14 See *Economist,* 11 September 1971.
15 In a speech given to the Ukrainian-Canadian Congress at Winnipeg on 9 October 1971, Prime Minister Trudeau stressed the multiracial character of Canada: 'Canada's population distribution has now become so balanced as to deny to any one racial or linguistic component an absolute majority. Every single person in Canada is now a member of a minority group. Linguistically, our origins are one-third English, one-third French, and one-third neither.' He also announced that federal support would henceforth be available to all of Canada's cultures and seek to 'assist members of all cultural groups to

overcome cultural barriers to full participation in Canadian society, promote creative encounters and interchange among all Canadian cultural groups in the interest of national unity, and continue to assist immigrants to acquire at least one of Canada's official languages in order to become full participants in Canadian society.' This program was to be implemented by a number of separate programs all designed 'to recognize the importance to Canada of the many cultural and linguistic elements in our society, and to encourage their preservation and enhancement.'

16 The introduction of the common law concept of trust into the law of Quebec in 1879 (and added to the Code Civil itself in 1888) has remained something of an anomaly within the context of a civil law system. It is principally used for estate planning, in non-French milieux.

17 Andrew, 'Defence by Other Means,' at 9.

18 Holmes, *The Better Part of Valour, supra* note 1, at 26. As already observed, the characterization of Canada as a 'bi-tribal' state ignores the fact that more than one-third of Canadians are neither English nor French in background or orientation.

19 Maxwell Cohen, 'A Just Foreign Policy and the National Interest,' in Allen and Linden, eds, *Living in the Seventies* (1970).

20 (1971), *The Lamp* 3.

21 Canadian development aid – bilateral and multilateral – has grown from $338.7 million in 1969–70 to $424.4 million in 1971–2. OECD figures give the amount of official Canadian Development assistance in 1970 as $346 million US, as compared with $3,119 million for official US development assistance. More significant is the fact that in 1965 the corresponding figures were $96 million (Canada) and $3,465 million (US). While US assistance has declined absolutely and even more drastically as a percentage of GNP, Canadian assistance has almost quadrupled.

22 *Colony to Nation* (1946), at 561.

23 See Cook, *The Maple Leaf Forever, supra* note 5, at c 8 and 9.

24 Andrew 'Defence by Other Means,' *supra* note 18, at 88.

25 Meeker, 'The Dominican Situation and the Perspective of International Law' (1965), 53 *Dept State Bull.* 60.

26 *7 International Legal Materials* (1968) 1323.

27 Louis Henkin, 'International Law and the Behavior of Nations' (1965), 1 *Recueil des Cours* 179.

28 La Forest, 'Boundary Waters Problems in the East' in Deener, ed, *Canada-United States Treaty Relations* (1963) 36.

29 In the IBRD, the Canadian percentage of subscriptions, according to the 1969 *Annual Report,* was 3.44 per cent of the total, and Canada's voting power 3.17 per cent.

30 For some recent analyses, see Andrassy, *International Law and the Resources of the Sea* (1970), and Friedmann, *The Future of the Oceans* (1971), and idem 'Selden Redivivus' (1971), *Am. J. Int'l L.*

31 It should be noted, however, that the US State Department's Draft Convention of 1970 resists this trend, by restricting the continental shelf proper to a depth of 200 metres and establishing, between the limits of the continental shelf and those of the continental margin, an 'intermediate zone' in which the coastal state would exercise administrative 'trusteeship' powers subject to certain financial and other obligations to the international community. This approach was strongly attacked by the US Senate Subcommittee headed by Senator Metcalf (see Friedmann, 'Selden Redivivus,' *supra* note 30).

32 Eg, in the draft treaty proposed to the UN Seabed Committee in July 1971 by Ambassador Arvid Pardo.

33 The term is taken from John Selden's famous pamphlet, 'Mare Clausum,' published in 1639, in answer to Hugo Grotius' advocacy of 'Mare Liberum.'

34 See the statements of the Legal Adviser to the Department of External Affairs, J. Alan Beesley, in the UN Seabed Committee, March 1971.

35 See the *North Sea Continental Shelf* case, [1969] ICJ Rep. 3.

GERALD L. MORRIS

3/Canadian Federalism and International Law

THE CONSTITUTIONAL BACKGROUND

Canada's constitutional position on jurisdiction over treaty matters and other aspects of foreign affairs is probably the most complex of all the world's nations. The intricacies of the situation have a direct impact on Canadian approaches to the majority of important international issues facing the modern world.

The development of a federal state's international dealings normally raises delicate legal or practical questions because of the inevitable tensions flowing from the division of governmental powers between central and regional authorities. In Canada's case, however, the difficulty has been increased by the omission from our basic constitutional document, the British North America Act of 1867, of any provision clearly awarding jurisdiction over such matters to the federal government or to the provinces. Consequently, Canada has necessarily developed its practices relating to international affairs without the decisive assistance of plainly relevant textual provisions of the sort on which other federal states have been able to rely.

For Canada the central problem of foreign affairs revolved for many years around the treaty power. More particularly, the core issue concerned jurisdiction to implement treaties internally. In recent years other controversies (discussed later in this paper) have reached a level which challenges the primacy of the treaty question but are, in fact, closely linked to that problem. Certainly, the development and resolution of the treaty-implementation problem has decisively shaped modern discussion of the various aspects of the external competence of the provinces vis à vis the federal role.

When incurring treaty obligations, a state must not only concern itself with becoming a party to the agreement (commonly done through signature followed by ratification), it must also ensure that any required action is taken to carry the treaty commitments into domestic law. This internal implementation frequently, under the Anglo-Canadian system, requires the enactment of legislation. If there is any serious doubt as to the government's ability to bring about passage of the implementing legislation, the government will not wish to ratify the international engagements.[1] Controversy over the power to implement treaties internally arose as soon as Canada, following World War I, began the rapid process of asserting full capacity to conclude treaties in its own right.

EARLY DEVELOPMENT OF CONSTITUTIONAL PRACTICE

The one section of the BNA Act clearly relevant to Canada's external relations was section 132. It dealt with implementation, but only in a limited scope, giving

Ottawa the right to implement all commitments on behalf of Canada contained in treaties made by the Empire. It did not matter whether the subject matter of the treaty fell normally within the legislative jurisdiction of the provinces or of the dominion.

Given a more dynamic approach to constitutional interpretation, it might have been held that section 132, drafted when Britain retained responsibility for Canada's foreign relations, should be construed to give Canada equally broad powers of implementation when Britain ceased to conclude treaties for Canada. After some years of uncertainty, however, the courts held that construction to be invalid,[2] and it seems that section 132 must be considered obsolete except, perhaps, as an indication of the view which the founders of Confederation might have taken had they contemplated the possibility of a sovereign Canada in full charge of its international dealings.

Section 132 was by no means the only basis of the federal claim to plenary implementing power in pursuance of treaty obligations, and it was the other facets of the argument that proved most controversial. Canada's attainment of recognized sovereign status went hand in hand with achievement of sole control over treaty-making and foreign affairs in general. The constitutional justification for federal assumption of total competence has been discerned by some scholars in the general legislative power assigned by section 91 of the BNA Act (carrying with it similar executive competence under the *Bonanza Creek* doctrine[3]); by others in the gradual transfer from Britain to Canada of the royal prerogative in respect of foreign affairs (traceable through a number of major constitutional documents); and again by others in the mere fact of Canada's new sovereign independence, which automatically brought full power to deal effectively with the other nations of the world.

Whether one stresses one possible source over others, or relies on a combination of them, the fact remains that Canada succeeded during the 1920s and 1930s in satisfying virtually everyone in Canada and abroad that only Canada – and not the provinces – had the power to enter into bilateral or multilateral treaty relations with foreign governments.[4] This being so, the federal government was able, after considerable debate, to persuade itself that it must also have a parallel power to implement internally those external undertakings which it alone could accept. For this view support could certainly be found in the constitutional philosophy enunciated in the fundamental laws of the majority of other federal states.[5] Ottawa, however, was more strongly influenced by the apparent trend of judicial opinion following enactment of the Statute of Westminster in 1931.

Prior to the convening of the Imperial Conference of 1926, which expressly recognized the sovereign equality of Britain and the Commonwealth dominions, the prevailing judicial attitude seemed to favour a narrow view of federal competence. But by the time the Statute of Westminster gave legal form to the decisions taken in 1926, signs began to appear that indicated judicial cognizance and acceptance of Canada's enhanced status. In the *Aeronautics*[6] and *Radio*[7] cases, the Privy Council exhibited willingness to support wide federal powers of implementation. The following year, in *Croft* v *Dunphy*,[8] the Judicial Committee again evinced readiness to attribute broad sovereign powers to Ottawa in an analogous situation.

In these circumstances it is hardly surprising that the Bennett government felt confident in 1935 that it could adhere to and implement three conventions adopted by the International Labour Conference, even though they clearly dealt with matters falling within the normal scope of provincial legislative competence. The opinion rendered by Lord Atkin in the resulting *Labour Conventions* case created intellectual shock-waves in Canada. Without conceding any inconsistency with the language of the *Aeronautics* and *Radio* cases, he managed to distinguish them in terms which permitted a resurrection of the Judicial Committee's pre-1926 doctrine. In essence he held that: a / there was no separate category of 'treaty legislation' that could be claimed by the dominion as forming an invariably federal head of power; b / where the subject matter of the treaty came within internal provincial legislative competence, then only the province could enact implementing legislation and the federal authorities could not acquire a competence otherwise denied them by simply concluding an international agreement on the subject; c / only by federal-provincial co-operation could Canada carry out international commitments relating to provincial heads of power.

AFTERMATH OF THE LABOUR CONVENTIONS DECISION

No matter how reluctantly, federal officials bowed to the Privy Council's enunciation of restricted federal powers. Over the years they carefully avoided precipitating further courtroom tests on the issue. After canvassing the various procedural avenues open, they gradually settled on the formula of co-operative consultation with the provinces where valid provincial interests were involved. In addition, the use of mixed delegations of federal and provincial officials has been extended to a wide variety of negotiations involving matters wholly or partly within provincial jurisdiction.[9] Notwithstanding Ottawa's distress, therefore, Lord Atkin's opinion forms the basis of present Canadian practice in the field of treaty negotiation and implementation. Provincial officials welcomed the decision and most political leaders of French Canada, at both the provincial and federal levels, have made it clear that they regard the *Labour Conventions* doctrine to be a cornerstone of Canadian federalism. It can hardly be doubted that it is now part of the basic political fabric of the nation.

Unlike Canada, most federal states have secured to their federal authorities, either by judicial construction or by explicit constitutional text,[10] a clear legal power to override the normal jurisdiction of their constituent states, if necessary, to implement *bona fide* treaty commitments that are otherwise unobjectionable from a constitutional standpoint. Canada has been joined by West Germany and Nigeria in the tiny group of nations whose central governments do not appear to have the legal power needed for full control over all aspects of foreign relations. It is somewhat ironical that, in Canada's case, this result was triggered by a desire as laudable as the wish to adhere to three ILO conventions aimed at securing improvements in the basic rights of workers.

If Lord Atkin's opinion elicited little public criticism in government circles, the same was not true among constitutional scholars who felt free to speak out. Nor, so far as can be determined, has the attitude of the judiciary been free of doubt. Over the past thirty years a notably high proportion of Canada's most eminent students of the constitution have criticized the *Labour Conventions* decision.[11] Some have characterized it as a crippling blow to Canada's national integrity and international effectiveness, while others have pointed out that – whatever deficiencies in legal theory the decision may contain – the actual changes in Canadian practice because of the case are more limited than might at first be expected.[12]

Implied judicial criticism may perhaps be discerned in Lord Simon's return to the *Aeronautics* and *Radio* doctrine in his opinion in the *Canada Temperance Federation* case,[13] and in a comment by Chief Justice Kerwin in *Francis v The Queen*.[14] The possible significance of statements made by the Supreme Court of Canada in the *Offshore Minerals* case[15] is still being assessed.[16] Far more explicit criticism was provided by Mr Justice Rand[17] and by Lord Wright[18] (who sat with Lord Atkin on the board hearing the *Labour Conventions* appeal) in views expressed off the bench.

ANALYSIS OF THE LABOUR CONVENTIONS DOCTRINE

A careful reading of Lord Atkin's judgment suggests basic questions that his statements do not dispose of completely. Why was it necessary to hold that treaty legislation did not exist as a separate class? To put it another way, why must legislation designed to implement treaties be deemed to come within one of the 'heads of power' listed in sections 91 and 92 (or elsewhere) in the BNA Act, according to the subject matter of the treaty? Is such a rule justified sufficiently by the fact that implementing legislation relates to other legislative fields as well as to the treaty-making power (or the general foreign affairs power)?

A similar situation exists with respect to many legislative items without imposition of a rule that would declare *ultra vires* those legislative enactments validly based on a federal power but also affecting a provincial area of jurisdication. In fact, if section 132 has any continuing relevance, it may be as an indication that those who drafted the constitution were clearly of the opinion that there was a separate category of treaty legislation by which (to the extent foreseeable in 1867) the federal government must be able to impose necessary changes in internal law in order to carry out *bona fide* treaty commitments, even if such changes would otherwise come within normal provincial legislation.

A survey of other modern federal states shows that nearly all of them have, in their constitutional documents or their judicial interpretations, thought it necessary or appropriate to provide their central governments with this power.[19] They evidently saw nothing illogical in establishing a separate class of treaty legislation. Nor, apparently, did they see any serious threat to desired regional autonomy in giving an overriding power to the central authorities for this purpose. There may be some persuasive value for Canada in the fact of this heavy preponderance of opinion regarding a fundamental aspect of federalism.

When the BNA Act was passed, there was no reason to include provisions dealing with foreign affairs and treaty-making beyond section 132. Since London expected to retain control over Canada's international activities, no one could foresee a need to spell out a constitutional allocation of jurisdiction in foreign affairs save for an implementing power worded to accord with the treaty-making procedure of that day. Thus, while the omission of a broader implementing power and a general power over foreign relations was deliberate in one sense, it was at the same time analogous to the omission of specific powers to deal with aeronautics, radio communications, old age pensions and other matters, the future significance of which could not be foreseen.

The proper method of allocating jurisdiction over matters not specifically mentioned in the BNA Act is to determine whether the essential nature of the matter permits it to be placed within the scope of one (or possibly more than one) named head of power, or whether it must be treated as a head of power distinct from all the enumerated heads and therefore brought within the general power under section 91. Where the uncertainty is extreme or where policy reasons dictate that the result of ordinary interpretation be changed, recourse can be had to the amending procedure.

There would seem to be little reason to accept the suggestion that, because an unlimited power to implement treaties concluded by Canada was not spelled out in the BNA Act, no separate class of treaty legislation can possibly exist and reference must be had to the subject matter of the treaty to determine the relevant head of power. Undue concentration on the 'subject matter' of legislation – in the sense of the ultimate points of possible impact – at the expense of a straightforward appraisal of the immediate, essential nature and purpose of the enactment can lead a court badly astray. In most instances not involving treaties the courts have avoided this pitfall and have emphasized a sensible 'pith and substance' approach to the characterization of statutes.

Why should the Privy Council have established a contrary restrictive rule in regard to treaty legislation? Was the Judicial Committee hypnotized by the prospect – remote though it obviously must be – of the federal government's conspiring with other nations or international organizations to produce treaties for the principal purpose of intruding under false colours on provincial fields of jurisdiction? Or was the board hampered by an inadequate and antiquated view of the proper scope of international relations conducted *bona fide* in the modern world?[20] Perhaps it was a combination of the two, amounting to a failure to discern the true relationship of the concept of the sovereign national state to the fundamental elements of federalism.

If the Anglo-Canadian tradition of conservative statutory interpretation prevented a wide reading of section 132 which would have retained its effect in the unexpected new circumstances, then one might have anticipated a finding that capacity to implement resided in the general power. Indeed, even if the broad general power in section 91 were lacking and no clear guidance could be divined from other provisions, the basic theory of federalism would point to a finding that the implementing power rested solely with the federal authorities.

It could be suggested, perhaps, that there is an element of logical repugnancy in a federal constitution which declines to give full control over the processes of international relations to the central government but instead gives express implementing power to the constituent states. It would be asking far too much, however, to expect a Canadian court to fly in the face of express constitutional provisions. But where no explicit allocation of capacity to implement existed, there should have been little difficulty in resolving the issue in favour of the federal government.

THE PROSPECTS FOR A CHANGE IN DOCTRINE

It must be kept in mind that there is no visible reason to expect that Canada's federal and provincial political leaders might agree during constitutional discussions to alter the *Labour Conventions* doctrine in Ottawa's favour through a new constitutional provision. On the contrary, the pressure is currently in the other direction and it would seem politically to be a question of whether the federal government can retain the powers in respect of foreign relations which it now has.[21]

There would appear to be little realistic justification (despite the occasional judicial hints in past years) for discussing the possibility of meaningful change, were it not for the intriguing passage inserted more recently by the Supreme Court of Canada into the *Offshore Minerals* opinion.[22] It has been suggested that the remarks of the court represent a sharp departure from the *Labour Conventions* doctrine.[23]

In concluding that the federal government alone was entitled to exercise jurisdiction with respect to offshore mineral resources under the territorial sea and in the continental shelf beyond territorial limits, the Supreme Court appeared to rely on two essential premises: 1 / the historical record showed no indication that British Columbia had acquired sovereign or proprietary rights at any time over the offshore areas, while the available evidence supported a gradual accretion of sovereignty at the federal level; 2 / a general federal competence could be founded on the necessary implications of Ottawa's role as the authority responsible to the international community for the consequences of any national activity in offshore areas and able to engage in binding international agreements pertinent to those areas.

The opinion offered by the court drew a mixed reaction.[24] For one thing, in developing its first premise the court appeared to gloss over the proprietary aspect, while stressing legislative competence. The ambiguity attaching to key passages of the opinion relating to the second premise also gave rise to concern. Perhaps more important, the court's conclusions clearly supported the 'national concern' test,[25] which opens too wide a centralist door, in the eyes of many advocates of extended provincial competence. In addition, the importance attached by the court to the influence of international law and theory on the internal constitutional arrangements of a federal state was unacceptable to many.

Discussion of the latter aspect has focused on two passages in the Court's opinion:

1 Moreover, the rights in the territorial sea arise by international law and depend upon recognition by other sovereign States. Legislative jurisdiction in relation to the lands in question belongs to Canada, which is a sovereign State recognized by international law and thus able to enter into arrangements with other States respecting the rights in the territorial sea.

   Canada is a signatory to the Convention on the Territorial Sea and the Contiguous Zone and may become a party to other international treaties and conventions affecting rights in the territorial sea.[26]
2 ... it is Canada, not the Province of British Columbia, that will have to answer the claims of other members of the international community for breach of the obligations and responsibilities imposed by the [Continental Shelf] Convention.'[27]

Professor Head has termed these statements 'shocking in their impact' and 'inexplicable,' save on the basis that 'the Court was not cognizant of what it was saying.'

In his view, it is an apparent reversal of the *Labour Conventions* opinion, in that it may establish the 'revolutionary' position that 'the federal power, by virtue of a treaty obligation, assumes paramountcy over the provinces.'[28]

It would seem equally arguable, however, that the quoted passages at most imply continuing judicial disenchantment with the *Labour Conventions* philosophy and a readiness to limit its application to situations which cannot readily be distinguished. Here a distinction can be based on the geographical location on which the dispute centres, since the court has satisfied itself by other adequate evidence that the region is geographically outside that area which is subject to a constitutional division of powers between the two levels of government. In this analysis, the *Labour Conventions* issue does not arise and the views expressed by the court do not constitute a direct attack on the doctrine. In view of the court's rather cautious judicial tradition, this reading may be preferable to one which would justify such adjectives as 'shocking,' 'inexplicable,' and 'revolutionary.'

At the same time, it must be conceded that a reading of the opinion allows one to infer that the members of the court proceeded on the basis of a subjective assessment of the modern federal state which, while not explicitly articulated in the opinion, seems essentially hostile to Lord Atkin's pronouncement in 1937. Accordingly, the questions raised by Professor Head should perhaps be left open until the precise significance of the court's remarks becomes clearer.

It is almost amusing that a hesitant attempt by the Supreme Court to supplement more orthodox constitutional analysis by the development of a basic philosophy of modern federalism has resulted in controversy. This is probably the natural consequence of the traditional Anglo-Canadian judicial difficulty in perceiving the true nature of the federal state and the relationship between the federal entity and the world community.

Could it not be argued that the weaker ground of decision was in fact the historical review of statutory and judicial sources? That process renders more difficult the development of a consistent and adequate federal theory by the judiciary and permits the undesirable possibility of differing results in respect of the various provinces, even in the absence of explicit and unavoidable statutory provisions. It might have been preferable, if tradition could be ignored, to place less stress on the historical survey, while emphasizing in its place the view that the very act of federation brought a transfer of jurisdiction (whether actual or potential) over offshore areas from the component states to the federal authorities, subject to any consequent internal agreement concerning actual exploitation and control.

It is hardly surprising that Canadian judges seemed reluctant to spell out the subjective value judgments which they in fact appear to have made. Our judicial tradition discourages any admission that personal conceptions of the essential elements of federalism are being imprinted on the texture of Canadian jurisprudence by members of the court. But that, of course, is what happens and there are grounds for satisfaction that the Supreme Court in recent years shows signs, however ambiguous, of a tendency to contain, and possibly reduce, the logical aberration from rational federal theory represented by Lord Atkin's analysis. The political hostility which will certainly be engendered by such doctrinal rehabilitation should be overcome by appropriate co-operative political solutions along lines suggested later in this paper. In any event, there exists no compelling reason for construing occasional statements by the court so broadly as to constitute a decisive threat to the core of the 'watertight compartments' theory.

CONSEQUENCES OF DOCTRINAL CHANGE

It is widely conceded that a reversal of the *Labour Conventions* doctrine would hardly transform the practical situation in Canada.[29] Where serious public controversy might result, the same basic political realities would inhibit rash federal initiatives which might be portrayed as a trampling on provincial autonomy. There could be, nonetheless, limited but important situations in which a clear federal competence to act both internationally and domestically would offer practical advantages and might be utilized.

Occasions might arise in which prompt action could be seen to serve major Canadian objectives without undue risk of widespread political opposition. The ability of Canadian officials to respond quickly might be enhanced if they had no need to study the probability of persuading the courts to sustain federal action under such judicial criteria as demonstrable emergency or substantial national concern.

A more frequent, potentially beneficial situation might arise in respect of 'motherhood' issues which found federal and provincial authorities essentially *ad idem* concerning the acceptability of a proposed course of action. Where excessive delay in reaching formal federal-provincial agreement resulted mainly from bureaucratic inertia or political apathy in one or two provincial capitals, the leverage inherent in a judicially recognized federal competence might stimulate greater celerity in concluding our internal negotiations prior to action at the international level.

Similarly, where federal-provincial negotiations had settled matters of substance but were still enmeshed in matters of detail, it might be easier for Ottawa to proceed with signing and ratification. Where, for example, it was desirable internationally to act on a certain date, such as a United Nations or ILO anniversary, or to achieve the minimum number of ratifications needed to bring a convention into force, Canadian officials could proceed in the knowledge that allegations of bad faith or technical breaches of international commitments could be met with unilateral federal implementation on an interim basis, if necessary, should a negotiating impasse, a change in government, or some other unforeseen delay hold up necessary provincial action.

While these may be considered marginal situations, the Canadian experience reveals that the prospects for international action frequently turn on finely balanced factors. Any change which might reduce administrative complexity and official caution could have a significant effect in such an area of major current international activity as human rights. While Canada has achieved a certain prominence in the human rights field, this has probably been due more to the contribution of several individual Canadians to the work of the United Nations apparatus than to Canada's acceptance of binding international obligations.

Gotlieb, writing on human rights and federalism,[30] points out that Canada's record in the ratification of human rights treaties is reasonably good in comparison to other federal states. That, however, means that we can stand comparison only in a rather limited context, since the federal states generally have a rather mediocre record. Furthermore, the present constitutional situation may encourage Canada to ratify conventions without internal implementation of any sort, even where it may be needed. In that connection a question might be raised concerning our recent adherence, without specific implementation, to the Convention on the Elimination of All Forms of Racial Discrimination.[31]

Canada's performance with respect to ratification of human rights conventions may merit the rather negative assessment that it is no more subject to criticism than is the record of many other states. There is, however, an evident distinction between this faintly applauded position and the potential influence inherent in truly challenging leadership in the adoption and implementation of human rights treaties. The avoidance of comparative shame hardly gives cause for positive pride.

The human rights example illuminates the broader treaty problem faced by Canada. Under our present consitutional doctrine, it is just a little more difficult for any government of Canada, no matter how enlightened, to become an active world leader in the human rights field. The additional burden of a more cumbersome method of achieving the desired result may suffice, in fact, to render leadership impossible, so far as national compliance with evolving international standards is concerned. It must surely be conceded that this is a considerable price to pay for safeguarding regional autonomy, particularly if it should appear that, in view of the very real political factors protecting the provinces, there is little genuine need of those constitutional safeguards.

For a middle power urgently seeking an appropriate and significant role in the international arena, leadership in the effective realization of progressive international standards in such fields as human rights would seem to offer a worthy natural vehicle towards the achievement of its aspirations. So attractive does the role appear that, even within the constricting constitutional doctrine which seems our permanent lot, one may hope that the most strenuous efforts will be made to achieve the best possible approximation of that humanitarian leadership. The performance of most states with respect to human rights is so regrettably inadequate that even a modest improvement in Canada's record would place it near the progressive vanguard.

PROVINCIAL COMPETENCE TO CONCLUDE TREATIES

Reference has already been made to the increasing pressure in Canada, during recent years, directed towards a further dilution of the federal government's control of the conduct of international relations. A central element of this pressure has been the argument that the provinces were in fact constitutionally competent to negotiate, conclude, and implement binding international agreements with foreign sovereign states and international organizations, so long as the substance of the agreements fell within a provincial head of legislative power. From this conclusion flowed certain corollaries which led to the ultimate position that the provinces were entitled to a relatively free hand in international dealings relating to provincial fields of internal competence. Furthermore, the provinces must be entitled, in pursuance of this treaty-making right, to develop the diplomatic apparatus and relationships necessary for the purpose.

The challenge to Ottawa assumed serious proportions during the 1960s when several authoritative voices in Quebec spoke out persuasively and the Quebec government moved rapidly, and with every semblance of diplomatic formality, to develop its relationship with France and with various other francophone governments and institutions.[32] But although Quebec held the spotlight, it was not the only province to show an interest in expanding its international links. During the 1950s, to mention one example, the government of Nova Scotia signed an agreement with the Netherlands relating to immigration procedures. When Ottawa learned of this provincial initiative, federal disapproval was communicated to the Netherlands ambassador, who had signed the agreement, and to Nova Scotia in sufficiently vigorous terms that the agreement was thereafter treated as a dead letter by the parties. More recently, Ottawa has not always found the provinces so amenable to correction.

The arguments in favour of a provincial treaty-making competence and its consequences, as well as the arguments opposed, have been examined extensively.[33] This short paper on such a complex topic cannot review the elaborate expositions presented on both sides, but must remain limited to its assigned task of suggesting pertinent facets of the subject in outline form. It must suffice, then, to say that the argument for extended provincial competence has been constructed on four main bases:

a   An argument based on symmetry: A reading of the *Labour Conventions* case together with the *Bonanza Creek* decision is seen as supporting the view that the provinces have executive authority to conclude treaties co-extensive with their legislative power to implement them. The contrary argument is that the *Labour Conventions* decision is probably wrong in law and that there is no valid reason for extending the effect of the error. In any event, the Board hearing the case specifically declined to make any ruling on the treaty-making aspect. Nor can it be assumed that the general terms of the *Bonanza Creek* doctrine extend to treaty-making, since the foreign affairs power is considered by the majority of constitutional scholars (and is treated by most federal constitutions) as an exceptional power that is, indeed, somewhat *sui generis*.

b   A comparative argument, based on precedents allegedly found in other federal constitutional systems: It can be demonstrated rather persuasively that the precedents found in the Soviet, Swiss, and other systems are archaic, or misleading, or misconstrued, or so trivial in scope that they have no meaning when related to the sweeping claims made in the Canadian context. The federal German system, which looks more analogous, is far more restricted than the arrangement which provincial advocates in Canada call for, and treaty-making by German states in the postwar world has been insignificant. This is in line with the worldwide trend among federal states to closer central control of international relations.

c   An argument relying on article 5(2) of the International Law Commission's draft articles on treaty law: That provision indicated that federal component states could make treaties to the extent permitted by their federal constituion.[34] The argument became a central one in Quebec's aspirations, since it seemed to place no outer limit on the competence which a federal substate might attain. It was a major blow to Quebec's hopes when the Vienna Conference on Treaty Law deleted the provision entirely from the convention opened for signature.

While it can be argued that the deletion by the delegates resulted from uncertainty and lack of time rather than positive disapproval, there is little prospect that the provision will be reintroduced in a form which gives such open-ended discretion to the national constitution without a balancing reference to the limits imposed by the international legal system. It seems fair to suggest that the simplistic form of draft article 5(2) was possible only because the ILC rapporteurs were drawn from a unitary state and had limited experience in the realm of federalism. Even so, the rapporteurs were sharply divided on the question.

d   The argument of necessity: This boils down to a suggestion that federal systems are endlessly flexible. Consequently, there is no reason why the perceived needs of a people cannot be satisfied by the architects of a constitutional system. The argument ignores the fact that, whatever the internal flexibility of federal systems may be, the international community imposes fairly definite limits on the variety of external faces which federal states can develop. To be acceptable internationally, a state must (unless it is extremely powerful) abide by the somewhat rigid rules of the international club. The argument that 'we can do whatever we need to' is excessively introverted and ignores the realities of the modern world in favour of a nineteenth-century vision of a long-departed, intensely balkanized world.

PROBLEMS OTHER THAN TREATIES

Provincial offices abroad

Provincial agencies general have existed since the nineteenth century and a variety of provincial offices have been opened over the years. Ontario now has fourteen offices on three continents, with more planned.[35] Not all provincial offices in other countries create serious problems, particularly where they concern themselves with travel promotion, sales development, and similar matters.

Problems can become obvious where the provincial office consciously functions as an 'embassy' in competition with Ottawa's representatives. This is widely believed to have happened in recent years in Paris, where the office of the Quebec delegate general rivalled the Canadian embassy in staff, budget, and access to French officials. There are disturbing signs that more of the same could be in store, with Washington as the trouble spot. Premier Lougheed of Alberta and his minister of intergovernmental affairs have recently announced their intention to open a 'listening post' in Washington.[36] Its stated functions of obtaining information and making Alberta's interests and concerns better known sound rather like those of a diplomatic mission. Ontario has also indicated that it will have a listening post in Washington, although its planned functions sound more restricted than those of the Alberta office.[37] In May 1971 the premier of Nova Scotia announced that a 'permanent representative' of Nova Scotia would be located in Paris to encourage investment in the province.[38] The precise significance of these moves is unclear but Alberta and Ontario were motivated by impatience with the limited information available through federal channels concerning economic questions of importance to the provinces.[39]

The almost unique Canadian practice concerning provincial representation abroad might be contrasted with the German federal government's refusal to permit Bavaria to open an office in Brussels to deal with the secretariat of the European

Economic Community. It would seem that some agreed ground rules are needed in the Canadian context. Alternative solutions are also highly desirable, possibly including more provincial officers seconded to Canadian missions. Quebec already has an education counsellor at the Canadian embassy in Abidjan and can assign immigration officers to appropriate Canadian posts.[40]

Provincial participation in international conferences and organizations

For some years, signs have been discernible of provincial interest in a greater involvement in various international organizations. To some extent these pressures have been accommodated through the use of mixed federal-provincial delegations to the conferences of various agencies such as UNESCO.[41] Quebec has found this arrangement less than satisfactory and has voiced particular disapproval of federal involvement in educational and cultural organizations (eg the International Bureau of Education).[42]

Quebec has utilized *la francophonie* as a major vehicle for asserting its competence, and the publication in October 1971 of the agreement between Ottawa and Quebec concerning the 'modalities according to which Quebec is admitted as a participating government to the institutions, activities and programmes of the Agency for Cultural and Technical Co-operation' revealed a major effort by Ottawa to permit Quebec to function with as much autonomy as possible in the special circumstances of the Agency.[43] At the same time, Ottawa has retained its ultimate control over such activity and can therefore accept the measure of international responsibility with which it remains fixed for Quebec's international activities.

Aside from rare exceptions such as *la francophonie*, it remains doubtful that most members of the world community would accept direct participation by federal component states in international organizations.

THE LIMITS OF PROVINCIAL COMPETENCE: A REPRISE

Federal states cannot ignore the essential indivisibility of concern with foreign relations which is a basic reality of the modern world. Virtually every aspect of national life may impinge, at some point, on foreign policy considerations. Accordingly, Ottawa must be able to orchestrate 'total diplomacy,' with the total range of national sources of leverage being available to assist in achieving major national objectives.

Contrary to common belief, Canada has unusual need of all the 'diplomatic muscle' it can muster in support of important national interests. Canada is one of the few nations that does not belong to a natural bloc or alliance on which it can rely for almost automatic solidarity and support. Especially in economic and trade matters Canada must learn to stand alone in defence of its interests. We cannot look to Europe, to the Commonwealth, or to the US giant next door.

The provinces must learn to live with this reality. While some scope exists for quasi-diplomatic dealings with foreign states, there is sound reasoning behind the imposition of limits. Greater flexibility is possible in the area of informal arrangements of an administrative or reciprocal nature between provinces and foreign governments, as well as in respect of the wide range of mixed public and private activities often labelled 'transnational.'[44] Even here, however, an ultimate veto must reside in the federal power, if major Canadian interests on the international level are in jeopardy.

Something more is needed, in fact, than a simple *ex post facto* veto.[45] Once a province has committed itself to a course of action, it is on the record in a way which can render corrective action exceedingly difficult, for a sudden reversal of the adopted course can be embarrassing to the province. The federal government can also be embarrassed, since the change may reveal Canadian policy to foreign observers prematurely or turn a sophisticated diplomatic manoeuvre into a blatant, heavy footed exercise. Similarly, an obvious withdrawal from a known course of provincial conduct could spark an internal public debate as to the cause. This would hardly assist Canada's diplomatic operations.

The obvious need, of course, is for effective prior consultation and co-operation between the provinces and the federal government. Only in this way can the natural tensions of the federal system be harnessed and the international effectiveness of Canadian activity at all levels be maximized.

THE PARADOX BETWEEN THEORY AND PRACTICE

While the necessity of federal dominance in foreign affairs can be demonstrated to justify a strongly centralist legal theory, the story does not end there. Instead, there must be a substantial divergence between legal doctrine respecting the foreign affairs power and actual federal practice, in order to meet pragmatically the needs of a modern technological society locked into the artificial legal framework of an international order still based on the archaic, but cherished, concept of the sovereign national state.

As the recent complaints by Alberta and Ontario indicate, the provinces do have vital interests at stake in many international situations. Whether or not their views are deemed justifiable, and even if national interests ultimately require that the interests of one or more provinces must be subordinated, surely the province should have the right to voice its concerns and to make its assessment on the basis of reasonably accurate information.

Ottawa and Quebec, in particular, have displayed notable flexibility in devising forms and techniques for bringing the provinces into the international arena in a meaningful but suitably regulated way. Reference has been made to mixed delegations, the attaching of provincial officers to the staff of Canadian embassies, and to the modalities for Quebec participation in *la francophonie*. Another example is the umbrella agreement, or *accord cadre*.[46]

There has, however, been a difficulty with respect to the machinery of federal-provincial consultation and the flow of information to the provinces. The consultative machinery linked with the conferences of first ministers has been a start. Other arrangements, including the working group on international environmental questions, look good on paper, at least.[47]

Nevertheless, there seems to be a need for rapid improvement. The complaints by the provinces at the November 1971 federal-provincial conference make it clear that provincial leaders consider the situation unacceptable, particularly in the realm of economic issues. Also notable was the refusal of the federal minister of external affairs to let the provincial leaders know what was being discussed in the recent Canada-US trade negotiations.[48] National action in the human rights area may be another example of inadequate consultation.

CONCLUSION

The federal government must accept primary responsibility for making positive efforts to ensure that the federal system works. It should be prepared to allocate adequate resources to perfecting machinery for improved federal-provincial consultation on matters pertinent to foreign policy and to provide effective liaison once international action is undertaken at either level. The need to reassure the provinces about Ottawa's good faith and to instil in them a sense of meaningful involvement in the development of co-operative foreign policies far outweighs the risks or political drawbacks inherent in new consultative machinery.

What may be needed are provincial bureaux, located in Ottawa, to facilitate continuing face-to-face consultation. Possibly a federal department of federal-provincial affairs should be considered, although Germany has abandoned its experiment along those lines.[49] More joint committees with a real external relations function (even if it stops short of joint planning) should be set up; they should not be a sham device to 'keep the provinces quiet.' Consultation by correspondence or even by occasional telephone calls no longer can be thought of as adequate. A quiet revolution in co-operation is needed. The rewards should easily justify the expense.

NOTES

1 For more detailed discussion of the problems involved in treaty-making and treaty implementation, see A.E. Gotlieb, *Canadian Treaty-Making* (1968). Numerous references to the principal literature may also be found in Morris, 'The Treaty-Making Power: A Canadian Dilemma' (1967), 45 *Can. Bar Rev.* 478. For the broad context of the question, see the federal government's white papers *Federalism and International Relations* and *Federalism and International Conferences on Education* (both 1968).

2 Compare *In the matter of Legislative Jurisdiction over Hours of Labour*, [1925] S.C.R. 505 with *Attorney General for Canada v Attorney General for Ontario (Reference re The Weekly Rest in Industrial Undertakings Act, The Minimum Wages Act and The Limitation of Hours of Work Act)*, [1936] S.C.R. 461 and, in the Privy Council, [1937] A.C. 326. The latter reference is the well-known *Labour Conventions* case.

3 *Bonanza Creek Gold Mining Co. v The King*, [1916] 1 A.C. 566.

4 The contrary contention by provincial counsel in the *Labour Conventions* case (*supra* note 2) was largely ignored until nearly thirty years later.

5 See the survey in the annex to *Federalism and International Relations, supra* note 1.

6 *Re Regulation and Control of Aeronautics*, [1932] A.C. 54.

7 *Re Regulation and Control of Radio Communications in Canada*, [1932] A.C. 304.

8 [1933] A.C. 156.

9 For an outline of recent practice, along with indications of the proposed future trend, see the two federal white papers, *supra* note 1.

10 The United States is an example of the former category. See *Missouri v Holland* 252 U.S. 416 (1920). Austria's postwar constitution spells out in article 16 that the federal government can implement treaties if the constituent states have not discharged their obligation to do so within a reasonable time.

11 A number of references to the extensive literature are given by Laskin in *Canadian Constitutional Law* (3rd ed., 1966) 269–91.

12 See Gotlieb, *supra* note 1, at 76. Also, Gotlieb, 'The Changing Canadian Attitude to the

United Nations Role in Protecting and Developing Human Rights' in Gotlieb, ed, *Human Rights, Federalism and Minorities* (1970).

13 *Attorney General for Ontario v Canada Temperance Federation,* [1946] A.C. 193.

14 [1956] S.C.R. 618, at 621. Note also *Johannesson v Rural Municipality of West St. Paul,* [1952] S.C.R. 292, and *Pronto Uranium Mines Ltd.* v *Ontario Labour Relations Board,* [1956] O.R. 862.

15 *Reference re Ownership of Offshore Mineral Rights,* [1967] S.C.R. 792, at 817; (1968), 65 D.L.R. (2d) 353, at 376.

16 See I.L. Head, 'The Canadian Offshore Minerals Reference: The Application of International Law to a Federal Constitution' (1968), 18 *U. Toronto L.J.* 131. See also Morris, 'Foreign Relations and the Constitution' in the 1968 Canadian Bar Association papers (available from the CBA national office).

17 See I. Rand, 'Some Aspects of Canadian Constitutionalism' (1960), 38 *Can. Bar Rev.* 135.

18 See Lord Wright's tribute to the memory of Chief Justice Duff (1955), 33 *Can. Bar Rev.* 1123.

19 See *supra* notes 5 and 10; cf E. McWhinney, 'Federalism, Biculturalism and International Law' (1965), 3 *Can. Y.B. Int'l. L.* 100, and also McWhinney, *Comparative Federalism* (1962) 36–49. The logical difficulties of the *Labour Conventions* opinion clearly derive in part from a line of earlier Privy Council decisions which tended to emasculate the general or residuary power by placing undue stress (despite the plain wording of section 91) on the significance of the listed examples of the federal general power. See, for example, *Attorney General for Canada v Attorney General for Alberta,* [1916] 1 A.C. 588.

20 An argument that would support a federal 'total treaty power' (comprising both conclusion and implementation) is outlined in Morris, *supra* note 1, at 497, where the broad sweep of modern activity in international affairs is termed 'crucial, complex and all-pervasive.' On the federal government's need to have recourse to a wide range of measures (including inducements and deterrents in the cultural field) for the effective conduct of foreign relations, with the result that compartmentalization of jurisdiction into federal and provincial categories is both illogical and cumbersome, so far as it relates to foreign policy. See Morris, 'Les provinces et les affaires étrangères,' *Le Devoir* (Montreal), 19 April 1968, and 20 April 1968. But cf comment by J.-Y. Morin (1967), 45 *Can. Bar Rev.* 160. A report carried by press wire services on 3 September 1968 indicated that, as a result of its displeasure over Soviet actions in Czechoslovakia, the United States government was reviewing its cultural arrangements with the Soviet Union.

21 See pp. 13–15 of the Quebec government's 'Brief on the Constitution' submitted to the federal-provincial conference on constitutional review held at Ottawa, 5–7 February 1968. And see the views of P. Gérin-Lajoie, minister of education in the previous Quebec government, enunciated in an address to the Consular Corps of Montreal on 12 April 1965 (reported in *Le Devoir,* 14, 15 April 1965).

Subsequent to the drafting of this essay, the March 1972 *Report of the Special Parliamentary Committee on the Constitution of Canada* (the Molgat-MacGuigan report) was published. The very brief chapter on international relations contains recommendations which appear to endorse the basic *Labour Conventions* doctrine but stop short of the extended inferences concerning provincial treaty-making competence which some commentators in Quebec would seem to favour. The recommendations read as follows:

75 Section 132 of the British North America Act should be repealed.

76 The Constitution should make it clear that the Federal Government has exclusive jurisdiction over foreign policy, the making of treaties, and the exchange of diplomatic and consular representatives.

77 All formal treaties should be ratified by Parliament rather than by the Executive Branch of Government.

78 The Government of Canada should, before binding itself to perform under a treaty an obligation that deals with a matter falling within the legislative competence of the Provinces, consult with the Government of each Province that may be affected by the obligation.

79 The Government of a Province should remain free not to take any action with respect to an obligation undertaken by the Government of Canada under a treaty unless it has agreed to do so.

80 Subject to a veto power in the Government of Canada in the exercise of its

exclusive power with respect to foreign policy, the Provincial Governments should have the right to enter into contracts, and administrative, reciprocal and other arrangements with foreign states, or constituent parts of foreign states, to maintain offices abroad for the conduct of Provincial business, and generally to cooperate with the Government of Canada in its international activities.

Unfortunately, the text of the recommendations and the meagre explanatory comments in chapter 25 leave numerous unanswered questions which may limit the constructive value of the proposals. An intriguing example is recommendation 77, calling for formal treaties to be ratified by parliament rather than the executive. The precise meaning and consequences of such terms as 'ratified' and 'formal treaty' are not set out. Are we, in fact, to borrow part of the US practice by which the Senate gives advice and consent to (but does not ratify) treaties other than executive agreements? Would we find ourselves caught up in legal and political difficulties comparable to those engendered in the US by resort to the executive agreement procedure for major agreements akin to the Great Lakes Water Quality Agreement signed in Ottawa on 15 April 1972? The parliamentary report provides no answer.

22 *Supra* note 15.
23 Head, *supra* note 16, at 151–7.
24 Dr McWhinney, borrowing a phrase used by Charles Evans Hughes, has characterized the court's response to the request for an opinion as a 'self-inflicted wound.' E. McWhinney, 'Quebec and Non-Quebec elements in the Canadian Constitutional Revolution' (statement of 12 November 1970 to the Joint Senate and House of Commons Committee on the Constitution), 15.
25 Enunciated in a number of decisions, notably including *Munro* v *National Capital Commission* (1966), 57 D.L.R. (2d) 753 (S.C.C.).
26 (1968), 65 D.L.R. (2d) 353, at 376.
27 Ibid, at 380.
28 Head, *supra* note 16, especially at 147, 151, 155. But cf N. Caplan, 'Legal Issues of the Offshore Mineral Rights Dispute in Canada' (1968), 14 *McGill L.J.* 473, at 491 ff. Recommendation 72 of the Molgat-MacGuigan report (*supra* note 21) endorses federal

offshore legislative jurisdiction in terms consistent with the *Offshore* opinion.
29 See Morris, *supra* note 1, at 491. See also W. Friedmann, 'Canadian Approaches to International Law' (1963–4), 19 *International Journal* 77.
30 Gotlieb, 'The Changing Canadian Attitude,' *supra* note 12.
31 See R. St J. Macdonald, 'The Relationship Between International Law and Domestic Law in Canada' in this volume.
32 See the Quebec brief and Gérin-Lajoie, *supra* note 21, and, more generally, the sources listed *supra* note1. See also Morin, *supra* note 20, and Morin, 'La conclusion d'accords internationaux par les provinces canadiennes à la lumière du droit comparé' (1965), 3 *Can. Y.B. Int'l, L.* 126.
33 A few examples are listed *supra* note 32.
34 See the Quebec brief, *supra* note 21; Morin, *supra* note 20; and Morris, *supra* note 1.
35 Seven offices are in the United States, six are in western Europe, and one is in Japan.
36 See reports in the Toronto *Telegram*, 18, 19, 20 October 1971, and reports in the *Globe and Mail* (Toronto), 11 October, 8 November 1971, and 27 January 1972.
37 See the Toronto *Telegram* reports, *supra* note 36.
38 Reported in (1971), 2 *Int'l Canada* 128.
39 The Alberta government complained that it could not discharge its responsibilities when forced to rely on occasional Canadian Press dispatches from Washington for its factual information.
40 Agreement on the latter step was reported in (1971), 2 *Int'l Canada* 134.
41 See Department of External Affairs Press Release no 90 of 26 November 1971, which lists the Canadian delegation to the fourth session of the OECD's education committee. The delegation was led by Alberta's associate deputy minister of health and included Ontario and Quebec officials. Such examples are numerous.
42 See the Quebec brief, *supra* note 21.
43 See Department of External Affairs Press Release no 74, 8 October 1971, which sets out the modalities. More generally, see the immensely valuable work by L. Sabourin, 'Canadian Federalism and International Organizations: A Focus on Quebec' (1971 offset manuscript; under auspices of the Institute for International Co-operation at the University of Ottawa).
44 Note the endorsement of such activity, sub-

ject to federal veto, in recommendation 80 of the Molgat-MacGuigan report, *supra* note 21.

45 Cf R. Atkey, 'The Role of the Provinces in Foreign Affairs' (1970–1), 26 *International Journal* 249, at 270 ff.

46 See, generally, the elaboration of the *accord cadre* theory in the sources cited *supra* note 1.

47 The working group was described by a non-government member as 'nothing but a farce.' See Ottawa Citizen, 10 November 1971.

48 The federal explanation was that the position in the negotiations was unclear while they proceeded and, consequently, it was difficult to transmit meaningful information to the provinces. See *Globe and Mail*, 16 November 1971.

49 The Molgat-MacGuigan report, *supra* note 21, recommends appointment of a federal minister of state for inter-governmental affairs who would facilitate federal-provincial liaison and co-ordination.

AUTHOR'S ADDENDUM

This paper was prepared following a period of marked friction in federal-provincial relations pertaining to external affairs. Sources in the Quebec delegation at the constitutional conference in Victoria reported their shock and dismay at an allegedly rigid and regressive federal stance in the confidential discussions on competence in international relations. In subsequent months, occasional indications of co-operative progress seemed outweighed by a series of skirmishes involving Ontario, Alberta, Saskatchewan, Nova Scotia, and other provinces. There appeared to be some objective evidence of increasing federal impatience with provincial expectations when external issues of concern to one or more provinces arose.

In the months following submission of this manuscript, signs of a welcome improvement could be perceived. Although not all of the details were made known to the public, it was clear that official efforts to negotiate acceptable compromises tended to continue, even when political leaders were taking public positions in unqualified, challenging terms. Such modes of bargaining on two planes are common in intergovernmental relations, of course, but the process can sometimes become enmeshed in its own rhetoric. Federal and provincial negotiators, however, appear to have made significant progress towards accommodation, sometimes relying on bilateral, rather than multilateral, discussions.

Judging by published and other sources, it seems that some of the potential dangers in unrestricted use of provincial 'legations' have been obviated. Detailed federal proposals have increased the possibilities for seconding provincial officers to Canadian diplomatic and consular missions to perform various functions, including economic reporting. Isolated signs have been noted of a provincial interest in establishing offices that would provide a direct presence in the national capital. On the federal side, thought is being given to the stationing of experienced foreign service officers in provincial capitals to facilitate liaison and consultation. The flexible approach evinced by these developments deserves support and commendation.

ANDRÉ DUFOUR

4/Fédéralisme canadien et droit international

Alors que depuis des siècles certains l'ont considéré comme la solution aux problèmes internationaux et la forme de gouvernement la mieux adaptée aux relations internationales,[1] on pourrait croire, à entendre certaines critiques, que la structure fédérale d'un pays doit être maintenant reconnue comme une maladie ou une tare sur le plan des relations internationales.[2] Dans la mesure où le fédéralisme signifie partage de compétences entre deux ordres de gouvernement,[3] il semble en effet devenir un sérieux handicap dans les relations conventionnelles d'un Etat et devenir synonyme de frustrations continuelles.

Depuis près d'un demi-siècle déjà, le Canada fait l'objet de cette confrontation entre ses structures constitutionnelles et sa volonté de participation sur la scène internationale. C'est en effet depuis son appartenance à l'OIT, en 1919, que ces difficultés se sont faites jour et elles n'ont cessé de progresser.[4] D'abord divisé par le doute et l'équivoque quant à la lattitude des pouvoirs que lui accordait une indépendance progressive, le gouvernement fédéral se voit finalement débouté de ses prétentions par les plus hautes instances judiciaires vingt ans plus tard.[5] Puis, après l'intermède des années de guerre, le retour à l'exercice normal des pouvoirs fait renaître les compromis, les impossibilités et l'immobilisme d'un pouvoir tronqué, jusqu'à ce qu'éclate, au cours de la dernière décennie, un réel affrontement dont les conséquences et les possibilités de développement sont encore imprévisibles.[6]

POUVOIR DE CONCLUSION ET POUVOIR DE MISE EN ŒUVRE DES TRAITES

Au cours de ces dernières années, les problèmes ont surtout surgi à propos de la compétence de conclusion des traités. En effet, d'une part, le gouvernement central, tablant sur la dimension nationale de ses pouvoirs constitutionnels, sur l'expérience acquise en cette matière, sur l'unité d'une telle compétence et sur la pratique des autres Etats fédéraux, en revendique l'exclusivité[7]; d'autre part, le Québec, invoquant le silence de la constitution, le caractère administratif de ce pouvoir et la primauté de leur compétence législative, en tire la conclusion que ce 'treaty-making power' devrait lui appartenir, dans la limite des pouvoirs que lui accorde la constitution.[8] Ce débat a déjà fait l'objet de multiples discussions et études, et il s'est même concrétisé sur la scène internationale par des initiatives provinciales et de fracassantes prises de position du gouvernement fédéral.

Pourtant, l'opposition apparente des deux thèses ne fait que souligner davantage le caractère désuet, aujourd'hui, d'un partage de compétences exclusives en l'absence d'un mécanisme commun de coordination. D'où la nécessité, de part et d'autre, de chercher à satisfaire l'exercice de ses pouvoirs par l'adjonction des droits complémentaires. La différence fondamentale réside en ce que pour Ottawa l'essentiel demeure le pouvoir de conclusion des traités, l'accessoire étant le pouvoir de mise en œuvre, alors que pour les provinces, c'est la possession du pouvoir législatif qui doit, primer la conclusion de l'entente n'étant qu'un corollaire.

Toutefois, si l'on étudie attentivement les difficultés du fédéralisme canadien en matière de droit conventionnel international, ce n'est pas vraiment le *jus tractatuum* qui a jusqu'ici constitué la pierre d'achoppement de nos relations extérieures, mais ce fut beaucoup plus la compétence de mise en œuvre des ententes conclues. Certes, la dimension politique et le caractère spectaculaire des relations entre le Québec et la France ont-ils particulièrement mis en relief cette question, mais même si l'on arrivait à trouver une solution acceptable à ce problème, si même le gouvernement central se voyait reconnaître sans conteste le pouvoir de conclusion, il n'en reste pas moins que persisterait cette incapacité du gouvernement à mettre en œuvre les traités conclus dans des domaines qui relèvent des provinces sur le plan législatif. Or, ces domaines, qui échappent à Ottawa, sont de plus en plus importants au fur et à mesure que le droit international touche des domaines qui affectent directement les individus. De plus, l'importance législative des provinces se développe également dans la mesure où ces autorités interviennent de plus en plus dans la vie sociale, économique, et culturelle des individus, c'est-à-dire dans la mesure même où notre société accepte la venue d'une forme accrue de socialisme.

Contrairement aux tendances constitutionnelles contemporaines,[9] l'une des caractéristiques des relations conventionnelles du Canada, qui découle de son attachement politico-juridique aux institutions britanniques, est la nécessité où se trouve notre pays de transformer en droit interne les normes internationales auxquelles il adhère, pour en assurer l'exécution, si ces normes sont contraires au droit interne ou touchent les droits des individus.[10] Comme c'est de plus en plus le cas, le partage constitutionnel des compétences législatives prend donc une importance d'autant plus grande.

C'est même là une caractéristique fondamentale, si l'on cherche à comparer le fédéralisme canadien à celui des Etats-Unis. Des études de fédéralisme comparé[11] invoquent l'exemple de nos voisins du sud en omettant de préciser que, si le 'treaty-making power' américain est aussi efficace, cela découle bien sûr de sa centralisation entre les mains du président, mais également et peut-être surtout, du fait qu'en ce pays les traités ont valeur de lois, et que, mis à part certaines exceptions, ils ne nécessitent donc pas l'intervention du pouvoir législatif.[12] Si tel était le cas, on a démontré que les relations conventionnelles américaines seraient tout aussi compliquées et ardues qu'elles le sont pour nous, même si déjà elles le sont beaucoup plus que nous voulons bien le croire.[13]

Donc, puisqu'un engagement international ne peut avoir valeur, du point de vue juridique interne, que par un acte législatif de réception, il s'ensuit qu'un lien indissoluble unit le pouvoir de conclusion au pouvoir de mise en œuvre. Et puisque le jugement du Conseil Privé de 1937 a rendu inapplicable l'article 132 de notre constitution et qu'il a partagé le pouvoir de mise en œuvre selon la ligne de partage générale des compétences, en l'absence de toute autre disposition explicite en la matière, il en découle que le pouvoir central ne peut s'engager hors de ses compétences sans risquer d'être en faute.[14]

Jusqu'ici le gouvernement central s'est violemment opposé à tout partage du pouvoir de conclusion avec les provinces en appuyant sa position sur l'unité fondamentale du pouvoir en matière de relations extérieures[15] et sur la pratique des Etats fédéraux.[16] Sur le premier point, disons seulement que les 'relations extérieures' ne constituent pas un sujet de compétence prévu par la constitution canadienne contrairement à la constitution australienne et qu'il ne saurait donc servir de base à une argumentation juridique. Quant à la technique de droit comparé, elle servit de base à plusieurs études[17]: les unes pour en tirer la conclusion que ce qui se passait en d'autres lieux, où un partage existait entre les deux ordres du gouvernement, pouvait fort bien valoir chez nous,[18] les autres pour en déduire que la pratique réelle des Etats fédéraux conduisait en pratique au rejet de toute forme de partage.[19]

Il serait bien inutile de reprendre le débat, mais de récents exemples de réformes constitutionnelles en Tchécoslovaquie et en Yougoslavie nous invitent cependant à réfléchir sur la possibilité réelle de semblable répartition de compétences en matières extérieures et sur la vraisemblance d'une telle voie de solution. D'ailleurs, à ceux qui veulent ridiculiser cette solution en disant qu'il serait inacceptable de voir onze politiques extérieures différentes naître des onze gouvernements au Canada, il faut répondre que serait également invraisemblable onze politiques fiscales ou onze politiques sociales ou onze politiques culturelles et pourtant il s'agit là de domaines partagés! Au contraire, ce qui serait intolérable pour notre structure fédérale, ce serait l'unité des pouvoirs de conclusion et de mise en œuvre aux mains d'un seul gouvernement central.

C'est dans ce cadre qu'il faut aussi replacer le fameux débat qu'a soulevé le Canada, à la Conférence de Vienne, autour de l'article 5 du projet de convention sur le droit des traités. Après un premier échec,[20] la délégation canadienne parvenait, en 1969, à faire disparaître cette disposition qui reconnaissait aux Etats membres une capacité de conclusion 'si cette capacité est admise par la constitution fédérale et dans les limites indiquées par la dite constitution.'[21]

Il importe de se souvenir que, dans son rapport à l'Assemblée générale, la Commission prévoyait les objections qu'on allait lui opposer mais elle jugeait nécessaire de couvrir les cas qui se présentent dans la pratique de traités conclus avec des Etats étrangers par des Etats membres de certaines fédérations. Toutefois, elle y professait son respect du droit interne et de la constitution fédérale puisque c'est là que réside l'origine des pouvoirs en la matière. Et elle ajoutait:

> Le plus souvent, la capacité de conclure des traités appartient exclusivement au gouvernement fédéral, mais il n'y a pas de règle de droit international qui interdise aux Etats membres d'être dotés de la capacité de conclure des traités avec des Etats tiers. On peut se demander, dans certains cas, si l'Etat membre de l'Etat fédéral conclut le traité en tant qu'organe de l'Etat fédéral ou en son nom propre. Mais sur ce point également c'est dans les dispositions de la constitution fédérale qu'il faut chercher la solution.[22]

Lors de la deuxième session de la Conférence de Vienne, le représentant canadien, M Wershof, invoqua le danger d'intervention étrangère que pouvait soulever la rédaction proposée en permettant à un Etat tiers d'interpréter subjectivement la constitution fédérale selon ses propres intérêts. On aurait pu répondre à l'objection 'd'intervention' de M Wershof en plagiant l'article 46 (23) de la Convention qui présente le même problème, en disant que cette capacité de l'Etat membre devra être manifeste, c'est-à-dire qu'elle devra être: 'Evidente pour tout Etat se comportant en la matière conformément à la pratique habituelle et de bonne foi.' D'ailleurs, ce danger n'était pas si grand puisqu'en plus de son fondement constitutionnel, la capacité des Etats membres doit être reconnue par la communauté internationale, ce qui facilite l'identification de son caractère 'manifeste.'

On sait que finalement l'article 5 fut modifié pour exclure toute référence aux Etats membres d'une fédération. Or, si la disposition originale avait été adoptée, elle n'aurait pu, en elle-même, changer quoi que ce soit à la constitution canadienne ni accorder aux provinces le droit de conclusion. Conformément au droit international classique, elle s'en remettait au droit constitutionnel du pays, qui seul régit cette compétence et détermine à quel ou quels organes elle appartient.[24]

A l'inverse, il est donc faux de conclure que le rejet du paragraphe 2 de l'article 5 dans la version finale puisse manifester le retrait de tout pouvoir de conclusion aux autorités décentralisées d'une fédération,[25] tout comme on ne saurait tirer du rejet de la proposition autrichienne, visant à confirmer l'autorité du pouvoir central sur les activités conventionnelles des Etats membres, qu'il ne peut exister un tel contrôle chez certaines fédérations.[26]

L'impasse, le 'dilemme' persiste donc et pour respecter le principe 'pacta sunt servanda,' le gouvernement central s'est résolu jusqu'ici à adopter une politique qui limite ses engagements internationaux à la mesure de ses pouvoirs constitutionnels. Pour ce faire, il ne s'engage que dans des traités qui cadrent avec cette compétence ou bien il limite son adhésion par la réserve de la clause fédérale.[27]

Une telle politique est tout à fait conforme avec une conception statique et dépassée du fédéralisme qui conduit à concevoir le partage des pouvoirs comme une répartition de compartiments étanches. Elle conduit cependant au degré d'inefficacité et de frustration que nous connaissons maintenant. Et, elle est peut-être la cause des réclamations provinciales dans la mesure où ces autorités, se sentant exclues du domaine extérieur malgré les pouvoirs qu'elles possèdent, veulent promouvoir leurs compétences en devenant responsables de leur exploitation dans le domaine international.

Si au contraire, on avait mis dès le départ l'accent sur la complémentarité – sur la coopération, dirait le Conseil Privé – si le gouvernement central avait considéré les provinces comme des partenaires, on aurait sans doute réussi, malgré les difficultés d'entente et de fonctionnement, à développer en pratique des mécanismes de collaboration qui auraient permis au fédéralisme canadien de s'adapter à l'évolution du droit international conventionnel et qui auraient éviter que se développe un vacuum d'engagement à la dimension des pouvoirs législatifs provinciaux.[28]

Pour illustrer en pratique ces difficultés et ces occasions perdues, il n'est pas de plus bel exemple contemporain que le domaine des relations diplomatiques et particulièrement l'ensemble des normes internationales touchant les agents diplomatiques et consulaires étrangers qui sont en poste au Canada.

Jusqu'à ces toutes dernières années, ces normes internationales étaient composées de contumes qui jouissent dans notre système juridique d'une intégration directe en droit interne pourvu que ces règles soient reconnues par les tribunaux et qu'elles ne soient pas contraires à la législation existante.[29] Or, depuis que ces coutumes ont été rassemblées dans deux conventions, ces mêmes règles doivent alors faire l'objet d'une législation de mise en œuvre si le Canada les ratifie, et se pose donc le problème du partage des compétences.[30]

Si d'une part, ces agents diplomatiques et consulaires sont agréés par le gouvernement central et relèvent essentiellement de lui, d'autre part il est indéniable que les immunités dont ils ont besoin pour exercer leurs fonctions sont à maints égards soumis à l'autorité des provinces. Qu'il s'agisse de l'immunité fiscale, de l'inviolabilité des agents et de leurs locaux, de l'immunité de juridiction et même en certains cas de la liberté de communication, toutes ces mesures de protection sont susceptibles d'être plus ou moins respectées par les provinces si ces dernières sont exclues du cadre des engagements fédéraux à l'égard des pays étrangers. Grâce à leurs pouvoirs en matière d'administration de la justice, en matière de fiscalité, et en matière de droit civil, il leur est possible de réduire considérablement la valeur des Conventions de Vienne de 1961 et 1963 et de vider de leur contenu les immunités qu'elles prévoient.

FEDERALISME ET COORDINATION DES POUVOIRS CONSTITUTIONNELS

Les solutions pour pallier aux déficiences de notre forme de gouvernement ne se sont pas avérées jusqu'à maintenant valables à long terme. Si le gouvernement central jouit seul du pouvoir de représenter et d'engager le pays, il doit cependant se plier au partage des pouvoirs. Dès lors, il ne s'engage qu'à des ententes en son domaine, ou il restreint son engagement par le biais de la clause fédérale. Ou encore, il se voit forcé après coup d'assumer la paternité d'accords qui furent conclus dans son dos sur des domaines qui lui échappent.[31]

Comme nous l'avons vu, cela découle d'une conception statique du fédéralisme dont le caractère rétrograde est à la source des difficultés qu'il engendre puisqu'il prohibe toute capacité d'adaptation aux situations nouvelles. Au contraire, il faudrait faire prévaloir deux idées qui se marient facilement à la théorie du fédéralisme: souplesse et participation.

Si l'on continue de considérer le pouvoir de conclusion sous l'angle d'un pouvoir exclusif, cela va sûrement contribuer à déchirer la fédération si les provinces l'exercent, ou au mieux, cela conduira à l'impasse actuelle si Ottawa le conserve. Pour mettre fin à l'impasse, il faudrait donc octroyer au gouvernement fédéral le pouvoir de mise en œuvre ce qui aurait pour effet de détruire le fédéralisme aussi sûrement que par l'éclatement et l'indépendance des provinces.[32]

C'est ce que pourrait laisser entendre la dernière décision de la Cour Suprême dans l'affaire des droits miniers sous-marins[33] et l'on ne saurait trop souligner la confusion que cet arrêt démontre entre le gouvernement fédéral et l'Etat canadien.[34] Même si l'on peut en tirer des interprétations qui ne soient pas directement en conflit avec la jurisprudence antérieure, même si la décision ne révèle pas clairement un lien de cause à effet entre l'affirmation de souveraineté et l'attribution des droits au gouvernement canadien,[35] il n'en reste pas moins qu'il s'agit d'un facheux précédent dont la faiblesse du raisonnement juridique ne peut que laisser paraître la motivation politique.[36]

Admettons-le, il est tout aussi incongru de s'appuyer sur l'hypothétique et éventuelle responsabilité internationale du gouvernement central pour entirer la conclusion qu'il lui appartient d'exercer telle ou telle compétence, que de conclure, en droit civil, qu'une personne doit être considérée majeure parce qu'elle sera tenue responsable de ses actes! D'ailleurs si ce raisonnement avait la moindre valeur, il conduirait à conclure qu'étant donné l'éventuelle responsabilité du Canada sur la scène internationale, il lui appartient d'exercer la compétence en matière d'administration de la justice, en matière de santé ou d'éducation.

Si, au contraire, on considère le pouvoir de mise en œuvre comme partie intégrante du pouvoir de conclusion, il est alors possible de concevoir l'ébauche d'une coordination des compétences qui, à l'image même des organisations internationales actuelles, permettrait la participation des autorités provinciales en reconnaissant leurs compétences tout en assurant l'exercice de la pleine souveraineté du Canada par la voie d'un même organe.

La recherche de nouvelles solutions peut se faire tant à l'intérieur du cadre juridique actuel que dans la perspective de réformes constitutionnelles. Toutefois, les voies de solutions au sein du fédéralisme ne requièrent pas nécessairement, à mon avis, de modifications constitutionnelles, même si en certains cas il serait nécessaire d'institutionnaliser les relations fédérales-provinciales. On peut regrouper ces propositions en trois groupes principaux selon que la solution s'intègre à la situation actuelle et aux techniques déjà en usage, qu'elle cherche plutôt à accentuer la suprématie du gouvernement central ou enfin qu'elle vise à instaurer un nouveau type de coopération grâce à une révision des structures.

Le statu quo

Même si nombreuses furent les critiques du système actuel, il n'en demeure pas moins celui en usage et avant de le rejeter totalement, il serait bon de tenir compte des récentes suggestions visant à corriger certaines de ses lacunes, ou à explorer certaines de ces virtualités. Il s'agit surtout d'une révision de la clause fédérale de réserve et d'une exploitation nouvelle des possibilités législatives des provinces.

Rénovation de la clause fédérale
La plus récente étude en vue de pallier aux difficultés du partage des compétences dans la mise en œuvre des traités demeure celle de la Conférence des commissaires pour l'uniformisation du droit.

Depuis déjà longtemps[37] diverses autorités faisaient pression pour que le Canada tire profit des travaux de la Conférence de La Haye dans le domaine du droit privé et qu'il s'intègre aux courants mondiaux visant à uniformiser les règles de droit en cette matière ou tout au moins ayant pour but de réduire les points de conflit. C'est ainsi que notre pays décida d'adhérer à la Conférence de La Haye en 1968.

Comme il fallait s'y attendre le problème constitutionnel se posa dès le départ, puisque la très grande majorité des conventions qui y sont négociées et signées relèvent au moins partiellement de la compétence indiscutable des provinces.[38] Les trois premières conventions soumises portaient en effet réciproquement sur la reconnaissance des divorces et des séparations de corps, sur la loi applicable en matière d'accidents de circulation routière, et sur l'obtention des preuves à l'étranger en matière civile ou commerciale. C'est ainsi que suite au rapport de son délégué, la Conférence des Commissaires fut saisie du problème que posait au Canada l'adhésion et la mise en œuvre de ces conventions.[39] Et il est heureux que l'on se soit posé la question au niveau de ces problèmes, d'une part, parce que la compétence des provinces y est incontestable et, d'autre part, parce qu'on peut y saisir facilement les conséquences néfastes pour le fédéralisme canadien d'un abandon par les provinces de leur pouvoir de mise en œuvre. Un seul de ces traités permettrait au gouvernement central d'envahir de larges secteurs du droit civil et il faudrait peu de temps pour dénaturer totalement le partage constitutionnel.

Dans le rapport qui fut ensuite soumis, plusieurs possibilités furent successivement étudiées mais c'est surtout la réforme de la clause fédérale qui sembla retenir l'intérêt. En effet, dans la résolution qui fut par la suite adoptée, la Conférence 'recommande que les délégations canadiennes (aux prochaines négociations) fassent inscrire dans de telles conventions une disposition dite ''clause fédérale'' dont le texte aura été établi après de telles consultations et qui permettra la mise en application intégrale de ces conventions dans les provinces qui le désireront.'[40]

Pour bien comprendre la portée de cette recommandation, il ne faudrait pas croire cependant qu'il s'agisse de la clause fédérale conventionnelle, telle qu'elle apparaît à l'article 19 de la Constitution de l'OIT ou de celle qui fut incluse par le Canada dans sa ratification de la Convention sur les droits politiques de la femme.[41] On a déjà démontré l'inefficacité de cette réserve à faciliter la participation réelle des Etats fédéraux et l'agacement que soulève une telle stipulation dérogatoire à l'égard des autres parties au traité.[42]

Profitant des plus récentes expériences[43] en ce domaine, il s'agit de distinguer les deux ordres de gouvernement en permettant non seulement à l'autorité centrale de restreindre son engagement aux dimensions de sa seule compétence mais également de permettre aux Etats membres d'exprimer leur engagement librement et individuellement. La volonté des provinces peut alors s'exprimer soit par l'intermédiaire du gouvernement, soit directement comme partie à la convention.[44]

Ainsi, il ne serait plus nécessaire au gouvernement central de s'assurer d'une participation totale et complète des Etats membres et toute adhésion, même d'un seul gouvernement provincial, serait alors possible. De plus, la possibilité d'une participation directe serait aussi de nature à valoriser cette adhésion provinciale tout en réduisant les craintes d'intrusion du pouvoir central. En devenant l'intermédiaire entre les provinces et l'extérieur, le gouvernement central est continuellement informé des gestes posés et des actions envisagées par ces dernières. Par contre, une fois l'engagement fédéral donné à la convention, les provinces demeurent libre d'adhérer comme elles l'entendent au traité.

Toutefois, il reste encore que si cette technique permet à l'Etat fédéral de s'engager dans une convention malgré la carence de sa compétence législative, elle ne permet pas à l'Etat membre d'être partie à une convention sans adhésion fédérale, ou de forcer l'organe central à ratifier un accord auquel il désire ardemment participer.

Utilisation des compétences législatives provinciales
La situation des Etats-Unis face à ces conventions de La Haye en matière de droit privé est assez semblable à la nôtre malgré l'apparente clarté de la Constitution

américaine en matière d'engagements internationaux et le gouvernement de Washington, refusant de paraître empiéter sur la juridiction des états, s'est constamment abstenu de toute participation jusqu'en 1963.[45] C'est en ce sens que s'exprimait dès 1874 le Secrétaire d'Etat Fish à la suite d'une invitation des Pays-Bas à une conférence internationale sur la reconnaissance des jugements étrangers, alors qu'il attestait à la fois de la tradition et du caractère politique des réserves constitutionnelles qu'allègue son pays: 'The difficulties are so great in the way of carrying into effect the project, arising from the nature of the organic Constitution of the United States and the relations of the States to the Federal Government, that it is not thought best to attempt it.'[46]

Pour éviter ces difficultés, les représentants américains proposèrent d'abandonner la formule des conventions multilatérales pour utiliser la technique des 'lois modèles.'[47] Cette solution possède l'immense avantage politique de laisser les Etats maîtres de leurs compétences et de leur adhésion aux projets et, sur le plan juridique, cette méthode coincide chez nos voisins à une pratique interne presque centenaire: les 'model acts' rédigés depuis 1892 par la 'National Conference of Commissioners on Uniform State Law.'

Par contre, l'expérience canadienne en la matière[48] démontre qu'en pratique, et malgré l'avantage de son apparente souplesse, une telle solution contribuerait plutôt à réduire les possibilités d'unification au sein de la communauté internationale puisqu'elle entraînerait la multiplication des autorités législatives susceptibles d'adopter ces lois. La majorité des Etats fédéraux ont, en vertu des dispositions constitutionnelles, la compétence nécessaire pour lier leurs parties composantes. Ce mécanisme d'engagement unitaire ne pourrait plus être utilisé en l'occurrence, au détriment de l'efficacité acquise.

Enfin, cette technique multiplie les dangers de particularisme, en ce sens que les législatures et les parlements divers peuvent modifier à leur guise les dispositions de la 'loi modèle' et conduire ainsi à une diversité de régime qui soit contraire aux intérêts poursuivis et qui rende impossible toute réciprocité d'obligations entre les diverses parties. Il faut aussi ajouter que cette solution ralentie considérablement les rapports internationaux et que très souvent elle ne repose pas sur un engagement formel des parties excluant ainsi le sentiment d'obligation qui se dégage d'un accord conventionnel.

Quant à la technique de la 'loi uniforme'[49] qui contrairement à la précédente ne tolère aucune dérogation de la part des pays qui l'adoptent, elle serait carrément inapplicable au Canada, chaque fois qu'elle aurait pour objet un sujet relevant à la fois de la compétence du gouvernement fédéral et des provinces.

Il reste cependant que de sa seule compétence législative découle pour une province le pouvoir de s'engager par voie de législation réciproque avec une autorité étrangère et que cet engagement équivaut à une entente internationale si les deux parties le reconnaissent comme tel. Au lieu de se placer inutilement, comme l'a déjà fait la Cour Suprême, d'un point de vue formel[50] que ne reconnaît pas le droit international,[51] il vaut mieux constater qu'en pratique si une province s'entend pour accorder à un Etat étranger un avantage sous bénéfice de réciprocité, cet accord sera tout aussi efficace que s'il s'agissait d'un traité formel conclu par l'Etat fédéral. Tel serait le cas d'une reconnaissance mutuelle de diplômes, de jugements en matière de pension alimentaire, ou d'exemption contre la double taxation. On pourrait même ajouter que mieux vaut une réciprocité d'exécution reposant sur un accord verbal ou tacite qu'un accord formel sans possibilité d'exécution réelle.[52]

Suprématie du gouvernement central

Dans l'optique des propositions du gouvernement d'Ottawa, il est possible de concevoir que la solution réside dans la reconnaissance de la suprématie fédérale en matière de 'relations extérieures.' Il ne s'agirait pas, bien sûr, d'une compétence exclusive mais de la reconnaissance d'une responsabilité suprême qui coifferait les pouvoirs provinciaux.

Pouvoir exclusif de conclusion

Il s'agit là essentiellement de la thèse du pouvoir central qui désire ainsi conserver le contrôle formel des engagements provinciaux en encadrant les négociations et en s'assurant ainsi non seulement toute l'information requise mais également toutes les possibilités d'interventions. Puisqu'il demeure seul capable d'exprimer la volonté du pays, seul capable de lier l'un quelconque des gouvernements canadiens à un Etat étranger, le gouvernement central détiendrait ainsi le contrôle absolu des relations extérieures même dans les domaines qui ne relèvent pas de sa compétence.

Certes, c'est là une proposition concevable et qui correspond à la pratique internationale suivie par notre pays jusqu'à aujourd'hui et à la pratique suivie par la plupart des Etats fédéraux. Mais, elle témoigne d'une politique centralisatrice que certains désirent renverser et l'expérience passée a maintes fois démontré chez nous l'inefficacité de cette solution. L'exclusivité du pouvoir de conclusion peut certes être conçue dans un esprit de coopération qui vienne tempérer son exercice, mais n'oubions pas que c'est dans la mesure où l'initiative de s'engager par traité vient des provinces qu'il est difficile à soutenir. Si face aux demandes provinciales, le gouvernement central décide de bloquer une entente, il ne reste plus aux provinces comme pouvoir de marchandage qu'à refuser éventuellement le concours de son pouvoir législatif pour assurer l'exécution d'un traité d'inspiration fédérale. C'est vraiment très peu!

La théorie de l'accord cadre ou du 'parapluie' constitue une nette amélioration, en l'occurrence, puisqu'elle donne ouverture aux initiatives provinciales tout en protégeant l'exclusivité du pouvoir de conclusion. On peut donc croire que c'est là une formule d'avenir mais le seul exemple passé[53] est survenu dans des conditions telles qu'on peut se demander si le précédent se répétera[54], car la pluie avait commencé de tomber avant que ne s'ouvre le parapluie! Cela permet cependant d'ouvrir ainsi aux provinces des voies de négociations avec l'extérieur qui leur donnent une certaine marge de manœuvre à l'intérieur des programmes politiques fédéraux.

Cette formule n'est toutefois pas sans défaut et on peut se demander par exemple quelle valeur ont les engagements provinciaux sur le plan international et quels liens de responsabilité peuvent unir les provinces à Ottawa à l'intérieur de ces accords cadres? Enfin, qu'arrivera-t-il des accords provinciaux si l'accord cadre est annulé, vont-ils s'éteindre au même moment ou si leurs obligations peuvent se poursuivrent indépendamment?

Pour résumer, disons que cette solution semble offrir la garantie de l'unité des relations extérieures mais sans apporter de solution à nos problèmes internes. Le gouvernement central, ayant l'exclusivité de la conclusion, ne sera jamais obligé de conclure au nom d'une province et aucun mécanisme d'arbitrage ne viendra les départager, alors qu'à l'inverse il ne pourra rien conclure de sa propre initiative hors de son domaine sans l'appui provincial. En somme la conséquence est à l'image de la situation présente; chaque fois qu'un accord porte sur des compétences provinciales chacun peut empêcher qu'il se réalise alors qu'Ottawa demeure entièrement libre dans son champ de compétences. Il en découle nécessairement une recherche de liberté de la part des provinces, qui se sentent alors brimées, et que ne peut empêcher Ottawa, même avec son pouvoir exclusif de conclusion, car outre la procédure formelle d'engagement, il sera toujours possible comme nous l'avons vu à une province de s'entendre verbalement on tacitement avec l'extérieur et de conserver toute l'efficacité de son entente grâce à ses seuls pouvoirs législatifs et administratifs internes.

Rappelons-nous seulement l'incident des Trésors polonais où l'on assista à une dangereuse impasse entre Ottawa et Québec, le jour où contrairement au gouvernement central, le Premier Ministre provincial, M. Duplessis, refusa de reconnaître le gouvernement communiste de Pologne comme détenteur légitime du pouvoir au sein de l'Etat polonais, lui préférant le gouvernement en exil à Londres. Il s'agit là d'une opposition des plus caractéristiques qui priva jusqu'en 1959 Varsovie d'une certaine quantité de trésors artistiques nationaux, cachés au Québec durant la dernière guerre par le précédent gouvernement polonais.[55]

Il serait également vraisemblable que le Québec, ayant le monopole de la vente des alcools, veuille conclure une entente avec l'Algérie selon laquelle en échange d'un important achat de vin, le gouvernement algérien s'engagerait à acheter des contreplaqués produits par une société mixte québécoise comme la Société Générale de Financement (SGF).

Le pouvoir de désaveu

Il est également possible de faire revivre le pouvoir de désaveu en l'appliquant aux relations extérieures. Conforme à l'esprit de la constitution, il atteste de la suprématie du pouvoir central sans détruire le partage des compétences et dans l'espèce il permettrait de confirmer l'autorité d'Ottawa sans brimer l'initiative des provinces.

On sait que le principal argument en faveur de la centralisation du pouvoir en matières extérieures et de l'exclusivité du pouvoir repose sur le contrôle nécessaire qui doit permettre l'unité en ce domaine. Or, comme nous l'avons vu, ou bien les provinces sont brimées dans leurs initiatives, ou bien elles contournent le pouvoir central grâce à leurs compétences législatives. L'idéal serait donc de leur permettre l'autonomie extérieure tout en conservant une forme adéquate de contrôle. Et c'est justement ce que permettrait le pouvoir de désaveu puisqu'il touche précisément le pouvoir législatif des provinces.

Essentiellement passif, ce pouvoir ne permettrait pas au gouvernement fédéral d'envahir le domaine des provinces ou de légiférer à leur place mais prohiberait toute incartade sérieuse. Il rendrait impossible toute opposition majeure contre les objectifs poursuivis par le gouvernement central tout en plaçant sur les épaules de celui-ci le fardeau de démontrer l'incompatibilité. En ce sens, il s'agit d'une solution supérieure au pouvoir exclusif de conclusion puisqu'il ne permet pas de censurer l'action provinciale et qu'il permet l'arbitrage de l'opinion publique, dans l'appréciation de l'incompatibilité. Enfin, contrairement à la formule précédente, le désaveu touche directement le pouvoir législatif de mise en œuvre et dépasse le contrôle formel de la conclusion d'un accord. Jointe à la suprématie des pouvoirs fédéraux selon le préambule de l'article 91 de la constitution, cette solution constitue donc un contrôle complet et efficace.[56]

Il reste qu'à cause de la tradition qui entoure l'exercice de ce pouvoir, il faudra un motif sérieux pour désavouer l'action d'une province mais cette difficulté ne peut être qu'un gage de sécurité pour les gouvernements provinciaux sur qui pèsera la menace de l'annulation. Faute de mieux, c'est-à-dire faute d'une coopération plus positive, voilà sans doute la formule de contrepoids la plus cohérente avec notre régime fédéral.

La coopération intergouvernementale

Même si, dans les formules antérieures, il était possible de faire place à une coordination des politiques et même à une coopération entre les deux ordres de gouvernement grâce à la compréhension réciproque et à une mutuelle confiance, aucune de ces solutions n'intégrait vraiment les deux partie. Leur but était plutôt d'éviter les oppositions en limitant chacun dans son secteur ou de hiérarchiser les compétences, en confiant au fédéral le contrôle suprême.

Il est toutefois possible d'imaginer une coordination des compétences qui ne conduise pas nécessairement à une soumission des provinces et qui, tout en respectant l'autonomie des pouvoirs, conduise à une communauté d'action. Mais pour y parvenir, il faut espérer autre chose qu'une approche pragmatique[57] car, telle fût l'attitude de nos hommes d'Etat dans le passé et on en connaît le résultat.

Au contraire, il faudrait institutionnaliser cette coopération et formaliser les rapports de forces en procédant par analogie avec les organismes internationaux regionaux. Il faudrait essentiellement pallier au caractère exclusif du partage des pouvoirs par l'unité du mécanisme de prise de décision.

C'est donc dire que la consultation ne dépendrait pas uniquement de la bonne volonté du gouvernement central ou des provinces, comme c'est aujourd'hui le cas. En formalisant cette consultation, on lui donnerait un caractère institutionnel propre à de saines négociations, ce qui permettrait de publiciser les points d'accrochage et à l'occasion de se soumettre ainsi à l'arbitrage populaire. N'est-ce pas ce qui se produit présentement en matière fiscale ou dans le domaine du bien-être social?

Qu'il s'agisse d'un éventuel accord bilatéral ou multilatéral, son adhésion serait nécessairement précédé d'une consultation interne formelle et d'une entente fédérale-provinciale préalable à la signature et à la ratification. Ainsi, la ratification d'un traité par le Canada pourrait-elle prendre une nouvelle dimension dans la mesure où cette expression de volonté externe serait précédée d'une entente intérieure qui engagerait juridiquement les parties et qui lierait la responsabilité de ses auteurs. Si une province s'est formellement engagée à adopter telle législation à l'intérieur de tel délai, on pourra lui opposer son engagement devant les tribunaux. Par contre, il faudra que chacune des étapes de la conclusion de l'accord: pleins pouvoirs, signature et ratification, devienne le fruit d'une œuvre commune.

Si le Canada, par exemple, décide de jouer pleinement son rôle au sein de l'OIT, il ne se contentera plus d'informer *a posteriori* les provinces des nouvelles conventions adoptées en les priant de le tenir au courant des mesures qu'elles pourraient éventuellement prendre pour en assurer la mise en œuvre. Il cherchera au contraire à intégrer les provinces dans l'étude même des projets de convention, à intégrer les gouvernements provinciaux dans la délégation canadienne, pour finalement convoquer toutes les parties à une conférence plénière où serait décidée l'attitude à prendre et où chacun préciserait son engagement.

C'est en mai 1970 que pour la première fois une telle ébauche d'institutionnalisation fût tentée par une réunion des sous-ministres du travail à Ottawa. Auparavant, les consultations se réduisaient à un échange de correspondances. Or, si de telles rencontres peuvent se répéter et se donner un cadre permanent tout en élargissant la portée des sujets qui seront abordés, elles aboutiront nécessairement à l'objectif recherché: la création d'un organisme permanent de coordination fédérale-provinciale en matière de relations extérieures.

CONCLUSION

On nous place souvent devant l'alternative de confier tous les pouvoirs de conclusion et de mise en œuvre à Ottawa ou d'octroyer aux provinces l'autonomie extérieure de leurs compétences pour ensuite tirer la conclusion que cette dernière solution étant irréalisable, il ne reste plus que la première.[58] En fait, si l'autonomie extérieure des provinces 'conduisait à la dissolution du régime fédéral sur lequel le Canada est fondé,' comme on le dit, l'autre solution aurait le même résultat puisqu'elle abolirait tout partage interne de compétences.

Dans un cas comme dans l'autre la souveraineté canadienne ne peut être l'apanage d'un seul gouvernement aussi longtemps que nous voudrons vivre sous un régime fédéral car comme le dit Friedrich: 'No sovereign can exist in a federal system: autonomy and sovereignty exclude each other in such a political order.'[59]

Derrière la querelle sur la capacité de conclusion des traités se cache tout le problème des relations extérieures, et il paraît bien évident, à l'heure actuelle, qu'à moins d'une profonde modification constitutionnelle, les provinces conserveront un pouvoir d'initiative avec lequel Ottawa devra compter. Sans que formellement aucune entente ne soit conclue, il est possible pour le Québec de négocier un accord avec des agents commerciaux japonais aux termes duquel le Japon achètera les surplus québécois de production de poulets et qu'en retour les investisseurs japonais se verront octroyer certains privilèges fiscaux dans le domaine de l'automobile ou se verront faciliter l'obtention de permis d'exploitation en matière de richesses naturelles. Le gouvernement québécois ne vient-il pas de consentir à la France une augmentation de sa main-mise dans le commerce provincial du livre en échange d'une promotion du livre québécois en France?

Ces exemples démontrent qu'on ne saurait réduire le débat aux cadres formels du *jus tractatuum* et qu'au contraire les deux ordres de gouvernement possèdent à la fois tous les pouvoirs nécessaires pour se nuire ou pour collaborer. Partant de là, on doit en déduire que seule une coopération institutionnalisée sous la forme d'un conseil des relations extérieures et composée des plus hautes autorités des divers gouvernements peut constituer une solution véritable.

Il est possible de concevoir plusieurs techniques de coopération qui permettraient aux parties de préserver leurs compétences tout en constituant une seule entité sur la scène mondiale. Seule l'opportunité politique du choix de cette technique peut donc en retarder la mise en œuvre. Mais, il importe que ce choix soit l'œuvre d'une entente formelle et qu'il se fasse le plus tôt possible. Il ne saurait convenir que l'on compte encore sur l'interprétation juridiciaire en ce domaine, puisqu'il n'appartient pas aux tribunaux de créer les règles pertinentes en l'absence de toute disposition dans le cadre constitutionnel actuel.

Les tenants de la centralisation des pouvoirs ont raison lorsqu'ils prétendent qu'en matière de relations extérieurex tout est lié et qu'un accord culturel peut avoir autant d'incidences politiques qu'un accord de commerce. La conclusion qui s'en dégage à mon avis, si l'on croit encore au fédéralisme, repose dans un regroupement des organes compétents, non dans l'unité des compétences.

LES NOTES

1 Voir l'étude de André Bernard, 'Le fédéralisme dans les pays multinationaux: avantages et limites' ainsi que celle de Claude Corbo 'Socialisme et fédéralisme au xIxe siècle' dans *Fédéralisme et Nations* (1971). Voir également l'ouvrage collectif publié sous la direction de Gaston Berger, *Le fédéralisme* (1956).

2 Harold J. Laski, 'The Obsolescence of Federalism' (1931), 98 *New Republic* 367, ainsi que Carl J. Friedrich, *Trends of Federalism in Theory and Practice* (1968).

3 K.C. Wheare, *Federal Government* (1963), at 12: 'And the important point is whether the powers of government are divided between co-ordinate, independent authorities or not.' Et plus loin: 'What is necessary for the federal principle is not merely that the general government, like the regional governments, should operate directly upon the people, but, further, that each government should be limited to its own sphere and, within that sphere, should be independent of the other. Ibid, at 14.

4 J.P. Després, *Le Canada et l'Organisation Internationale du travail* (1947).

5 L'affaire des conventions internationales du travail: *A.G. for Canada* v *A.G. for Ontario,* [1937] A.C. 326.

6 Il est intéressant sur ce point de comparer l'opinion du professeur Corry en 1939 dans son étude 'Difficultés inhérentes au partage des pouvoirs,' présentée à la Commission Rowell-Sirois, avec celle de Laskin aujourd'hui dans *Canadian Constitutional Law* (3e éd, 1966), 288 à 291. Pour une étude récente des détails de l'évolution juridique du conflit et une bibliographie complète sur le sujet, voir: A.M. Jacomy-Millette, *L'introduction et l'application des traités internationaux au Canada* (1971).

7 Voir principalement le Livre blanc du gouvernement central, publié en 1968 par l'Honorable Paul Martin, 'Fédéralisme et relations internationales,' ainsi que son supplément, publié quelques mois plus tard par l'Honorable M. Sharp: *Fédéralisme et conférences internationales sur l'éducation* (1968).

8 Voir principalement le 'Document de travail sur les relations avec l'étranger,' présenté par le Québec, le 12 février 1969 à la conférence constitutionnelle d'Ottawa et publié dans *Le Devoir,* les 13 et 14 février 1969.

9 Comme, par exemple, l'article 55 de la Constitution française de 1958: 'Les traités et accords régulièrement ratifiés ou approuvés ont, dès leur publication, une autorité supérieure à celle des lois, sous réserve, pour chaque accord ou traité, de son application par l'autre partie.' Sur ces tendances, voir également Pierre Lardy, 'La force obligatoire du droit international en droit interne' (1966), *L.G.D.J.*

10 Voir ci-dessous l'article du doyen Macdonald sur les rapports entre notre droit interne et le droit international.

11 En particulier celle de J.N. Horak, *Les limitations constitutionnelles au pouvoir de traiter dans les régimes fédéraux* (1956).

12 Article 6 de la Constitution des E-U.

13 Voir plus loin les notes 45 et 46.

14 Comme c'est d'ailleurs toujours le cas auprès de l'OIT pour ces fameuses conventions ratifiées par le Canada en 1935 et non mises en œuvre. Voir E.A. Landy, *The Effectiveness of International Supervision: Thirty Years of I.L.O. Experience* (1966) 112.

15 Livre blanc sur le fédéralisme, *supra* note 7, à 15.

16 Ibid, 12.

17 Elizabeth Weiser, 'La conclusion d'accords internationaux par les Etats fédérés allemands, suisses et autrichiens' dans *Les pouvoirs extérieurs du Québec* (1967) 100, à 162.

18 J.-Y. Morin, 'La conclusion d'accords internationaux par les provinces canadiennes à la lumière du droit comparé' (1965), 3 *A.C.D.I.* 127.

19 G.L. Morris, 'The Treaty-Making Power: A Canadian Dilemma' (1967), 45 *Rev. Can. Bar.* 478.

20 Documents officiels, Conférence sur le droit des traités, première session, 1968, A/Conf. 39/11, 64 à 75. J.S. Stanford, 'United Nations Law of Treaties Conference: First Session' (1969), 19 *U. Toronto L. J.* 59; et C. Castilla, 'La Conférence de Vienne sur le droit des traités' (1969), 73 *Revue Gén. de D.I.P.* 790, à 794.

21 (1966), 2 *Annuaire de la Commission de droit international* 194.

22 Ibid, 209.

23 Qui était l'article 43 du projet.

24 On peut se demander où M. Wershof est allé chercher que 'ce doit être l'Etat fédéral qui confère cette compétence,' Documents officiels, deuxième session de la Conférence de Vienne, A/Conf. 39/11/ add. 1, 7.

25 'Supprimer le par. 2 de l'art. 5 ne porterait aucunement atteinte aux droits existants des membres d'un Etat fédéral quelconque.' Comme le disait le représentant canadien, à la septième séance plénière de la deuxième session, Documents officiels, at 7; et repris par J.S. Stanford, 'The Vienna Convention on the Law of Treaties' (1970), 20 *U. Toronto L. J.* 18, 29 à 31. Pourtant, voir la prétention contraire du secrétaire parlementaire M.

Goyer, devant la Chambre des Communes le 30 octobre 1969, et Ronald G. Atkey, 'The Role of the Provinces in International Affairs' (1970), 26 *International Journal* 249, à 262.

26 Documents officiels, *supra* note 20, à 75.

27 D'ailleurs l'article 27 de la Convention de Vienne stipule bien qu' 'une partie ne peut invoquer les dispositions de son droit interne comme justifiant la non-exécution d'un traité.'

28 A titre d'exemple, voir l'étude de L.M. Gouin et B. Claxton; 'Expédients constitutionnels adoptés par le Dominion et les provinces,' appendice 8, Etude préparée pour la Commission royale des relations entre le Dominion et les provinces (1939); et celle du doyen W.R. Lederman, 'Some Forms and Limitations of Co-operative Federalism' (1967), 45 *Rev. Can. Bar.* 409.

29 Voir en particulier 'In re Powers to Levy Rates on Foreign Legations and High Commissioners Residences' (1943), *R.C.S.* 208 et le commentaire de Christian Vincke; 'Certains aspects de l'évolution récente du problème de l'immunité de juridiction des Etats' (1969), 7 *A.C.D.I.* 224.

30 La Convention sur les relations diplomatiques, faite à Vienne le 18 avril 1961, fut signée par le Canade le 5 février 1962, ratifiée le 25 mai 1966, et est entrée en vigueur au Canada le 25 juin 1966. Par contre, la Convention sur les relations consulaires, faite à Vienne le 24 avril 1963, n'a pas encore été ratifiée par notre pays. Voir en pratique l'attitude du ministère des affaires extérieures au cours des dernières années dans *l'Annuaire canadien de droit international* et en particulier dans le vol 8 de 1970, aux 339 à 342. La seule loi de mise en œuvre qui existe présentement est celle du gouvernement fédéral: Loi sur les immunités diplomatiques (pays du Commonwealth), [1970] S.R.C. vol II, c D-4.

31 Comme ce fut le cas lors de l'entente France-Québec, de février 1965 et de son 'intégration' subséquente à l'échange de notes franco-canadien du 17 novembre 1965. Voir (1966), *Revue générale de droit international public* 532–3.

32 Le professeur Corry ayant dit: 'Quand le Dominion et les provinces se partagent la gestion d'une même fonction administrative, il semble en résulter inéluctablement la mésintelligence, le gaspillage et l'inefficacité.' La Commission Rowell-Sirois

recommandait qu'il soit 'loisible au Dominion de donner suite à toute convention ouvrière de l'Organisation Internationale du travail.' Tome II, 50.

33 In re Ownership and Jurisdiction over Offshore Mineral Rights, [1967] R.C.S. 792.

34 Voir Jacques Brossard, *Le Devoir*, 22 novembre 1967.

35 Ibid, 769.

36 I.L. Head, 'The Canadian Offshore Minerals Reference: The Application of International Law to a Federal Constitution' (1968), 18 *U. Toronto L.J.* 131. Jules Brière, 'La Cour Suprème et les droits sous-marins' (1967–8), 9 *Cahiers de Droit* 736: 'Ajoutant la caricature à l'erreur, elle [La Cour] fonde son attribution sur une expectative de droit: le Canada sera reconnu par le droit international donc l'Etat fédéral est exclusivement compétent. Le tout laconiquement, à la manière du législateur, sans souci d'étayer son raisonnement' (772).

37 Voir l'excellent article de J.-G. Castel, 'Canada and The Hague Conference on Private International Law, 1893–1967' (1967), 45 *Rev. Can. Bar.* 1.

38 Ibid, 18 à 23. Egalement François Knoepfler, *Les nouvelles conventions de La Haye de droit international privé* (1968).

39 Conference of Commissioners on Uniformity of Legislation in Canada, *Proceedings* (1969), 21 et 75.

40 *Proceedings* (1970) 42, version française.

41 [1957] *Recueil des Traités* no 3, 7: 'Vu que sous le régime constitutionnel canadien la compétence législative en ce qui concerne les droits politiques est partagée entre les provinces et le gouvernement fédéral, le Gouvernement canadien est tenu, en accédant à la Convention, d'apporter une réserve à l'égard des droits qui relèvent de la compétence législative des provinces.'

42 J.-Y. Morin, 'Le fédéralisme canadien: un dilemme en matière de traités' (1965), *Annuaire canadien de droit international* 130 à 139 et ss. Voir aussi R.B. Looper, 'Federal State Clauses in Multilateral Instruments' (1955–6), 32 *B.Y.I.L.* 162.

43 Article 38, Convention internationale relative au contrat de voyage, Bruxelles, 23 avril 1970. Il ne faudrait pas confondre avec la clause fédérale, cette disposition (art 39 de la convention précitée) qui permet à une partie de restreindre son engagement.

44 Cette variante fut soulevée par Gerald FitzGerald dans: 'Educational and Cultural Agreements and Ententes: France, Canada and Quebec – Birth of a New Treaty-Making Technique for Federal States' (1966), 60 *Am. J. Int'l L.* 529, à 535–6.

45 S. Mentschikoff et N. de B. Katzenbach, *International Unification of Private Law: Report of the American Bar Association Special Committee* (1961).

46 Ibid.

47 Voir le mémorandum de la délégation américaine relatif aux lois uniformes et aux lois modèles. Conférence de La Haye, *Actes de la Conférence* (1963) 273.

48 'Il faudrait peut-être ajouter ... que cette méthode propre à nos travaux dans le passé nécessiterait peut-être d'être révisée à la lumière des résultats obtenus.' *Proceedings, supra* note 40, à 172.

49 L. Kos-Rabcewicz-Zubkowski, 'The Possibilities for Treaties on Private International Law to Serve as Model Laws' (1969), 26 *Revue du Barreau* 229.

50 *Attorney-General of Ontario* v *Scott*, [1956] R.C.S. 137, et B. Laskin, 'The Provinces and International Agreements' dans Background papers and reports, Ontario Advisory Committee on Confederation, 1967, aux 110 et 111.

51 Voir *supra* note 22.

52 On pourrait citer dans ce cadre l'accord culturel conclu entre le Canada et la Belgique, le 8 mai 1967 sans la participation du Québec.

53 L'accord cadre franco-canadien du 17 novembre 1965.

54 Malgré l'optimisme de l'ancien sous-secrétaire d'état aux affaires extérieures qui disait, en parlant de l'accord culturel franco-québécois: 'Celui-ci a été négocié directement entre Québécois et Français mais, selon l'usage avant qu'il ne soit paraphé, le Gouvernement fédéral a signifié par note diplomatique au Gouvernement français qu'il donnait son accord. Pourquoi en aurait-il été autrement? Sur le fond, cet accord qui bénéficiait au Québec bénéficierait du fait même au Canada ... Ce simple paraphe avait valeur de symbole. Il était signe de coopération.' Marcel Cadieux, 'Le Québec dans le monde, mythe ou réalité' dans *Mythes et réalités: Individu-Etat, Communauté internationale*, études et conférences publiées par le Club des Relations Internationales (1972), à 135.

55 Débats de la Chambre des Communes du Canada 1948, vol II, 1915 à 1920 et *Keesing's Contemporary Archives* (8 janvier 1959) 16635.

56 Voir Atkey, 'The Role of the Provinces in International Affairs,' *supra* note 25, à 270.

57 E. McWhinney, 'Canadian Federalism, and the Foreign Affairs and Treaty Power: The Impact of Quebec's Quiet Revolution' (1969), 7 *A.C.D.I.* 3.

58 Livre blanc, *supra* note 7, à 32.

59 Friedrich, *Trends of Federalism in Theory and Practice, supra* note 2, à 8.

R. ST J. MACDONALD

5/The Relationship between International Law and Domestic Law in Canada

International law and domestic or municipal law interrelate along a wide and varied front, with the points of contact, though frequent, not forming any identifiable pattern. This lack of consistency makes the task of describing the relationship between these two branches of law necessarily complex. Further complication is added by the fact that international law springs from three different and important sources – custom, convention, and general principles – each having its own peculiar characteristics. In addition, there are at least three routes by which international law, whether customary, conventional, or general, can enter or interact with domestic law: the courts, the legislature, and the executive. Since it is obviously not possible to discuss all these aspects of the subject at the present time, this chapter will be confined to an examination of the impact of customary and conventional international law on the courts as they discharge their responsibility of settling disputes by applying and shaping the common law or interpreting and enforcing the statute law.

CUSTOMARY INTERNATIONAL LAW AND THE CANADIAN COURTS

Customary international law has been received and applied in English courts for at least two hundred years and in Canada for at least eighty. With this long history of dealing with international law, it may seem remarkable that the courts have not yet developed a clear and uncontroverted theory of the relationship between customary international law and municipal law. That they have not so done is evidenced by the on-going analyses of commentators, who continue to feel the need to explore this area and, more importantly, by the rather vague and ambiguous comments on the problem that have appeared in Canadian judgments over the past thirty years. But if this absence of theory is remarkable, it is also in keeping with what can only be described as the common law tradition of doing first and theorizing about it afterwards.

In any event, it might well be asked why we need such a theory. The courts seem to be applying international law in a more or less satisfactory manner, so what difference does it make how it gets into our municipal system? There are, it is submitted, at least three reasons why the relationship question should be examined and clarified.

First, and of foremost importance to the practicing lawyer, there is the need for as much certainty as possible in advising a client. If the client's problem turns, in any way, on the court's application or non-application of an international rule, then the way that the court will consider the rule becomes critical. Need it be proved as foreign law? Is it automatically part of our domestic law? Or must it have earlier been made part of our domestic law by some transforming act? If so, what if the rule has changed since the time of the act of transformation? Even if it is true, as sometimes suggested, that whatever way the court receives the rule, it will be applied, so long as it is a rule of customary international law, the practitioner will still find it essential to know something of its relationship to the municipal system in order to make sound predictions as to the way the rule will be interpreted.

Second, and of obvious relevance to the international community, there is a need to ensure that the municipal order in Canada conforms to the requirements of international law and organization and that Canadian processes and procedures for giving effect to international obligations, customary as well as conventional, are efficient, effective, and reasonably well-known. Like every other member state of the international community, Canada has a duty to carry out in good faith its obligations arising from treaties and other sources of international law. It is widely accepted practice and doctrine that a state cannot successfully offer its own internal arrangements as a reason for failing to perform this duty. If it purports to do so 'it will find that – apart from having broken its international undertakings in the specific case concerned – confidence in its word will have been shaken in the international community.'[1] It follows, therefore, that there is value in continuing to review and appraise the processes and structures that pertain to the internal application of international law in Canada, especially at a time of reconsideration and readjustment in the federal system itself. Conflicts between international law and Canadian law are less likely to occur when the relationship question is clearly articulated.

From a wider perspective, it is useful to remind ourselves that the relationship problem at the international level is not unlike the problem of the effective distribution of power within a federation at the domestic level. In McDougal's language, the problem is one of working out 'that balance between the inclusive competence of the general community of states and the exclusive competence of particular states which best promotes the total production, at least cost, of their shared values.'[2] The establishment and maintenance of such a balance, representing a moving line of compromise between complementary, contraposed policies, are of high interest to officials, scholars, and elected representatives alike.

Third, it is possible that an examination of the relationship doctrine in Canada will persuade us to seek its alteration by legislation or institutional change or to codify it as it now stands through either of these two methods. It has become rather common in western European countries, and in other countries as well, to provide formally in the national constitution for recognition and support for the principles of international law.[3] At a time when Canadians are attempting to reach agreement on new constitutional accommodations it would seem only reasonable to consider this significant, though frequently overlooked, area of our public law system. The tendency in Europe to provide, in the constitution, for the method whereby international law is made effective in the municipal system offers a large measure of certainty, though it can be argued that it also lacks flexibility.[4]

Even if it is concluded that the relationship doctrine requires neither change nor codification, it is nevertheless important that the public in Canada enjoy as full an understanding as possible of the ways in which the laws that govern us, including international laws, are formed and applied. This may sound like a plea for the open society, but it is more than that; for, as anyone who follows public events must be aware, there are growing demands around the world, especially in North America, for clear identification of the decision-making processes. As the interactions between nations increase, Canadians will want to know how and to what extent extranational sources shape their laws. To wait until the exact nature of this relationship becomes a national issue is to wait too long.

For these and other reasons, then, an inquiry into the nature of the relationship between customary international law and domestic law is important. Before examining the cases, it may be helpful, however, to consider a few preliminary points. The first of these is this question: What authority, if any, do the judges have to reach for international law? The judges as individuals and the courts as institutions are in a legal relationship with their own state, of which they are organs. They have, then, a formal obligation to perform their functions in the manner prescribed by law. If the powers and duties granted the courts are clearly set out, then the relationship question can be answered fairly quickly; but if the judges' obligations are uncertain, then they must construe their powers within the general limits of their authority; they must work out their own mandate as to what they are to do and as to what sources they are to consult.[5]

The place to begin, then, is with the statutes creating the courts and with any other rules that delimit their functions and define their sources. The BNA Act contains no provisions relating to the duties or responsibilities of the courts; section 101 merely states that there shall be a general court of appeal for Canada. The act establishing the general court of appeal is the Supreme Court Act; but the only reference in it to duties or powers is section 55(2), which states that 'where a reference is made to the Court under subsection (1) it is the duty of the Court to hear and consider it.'[6] A reference under subsection (1) is a reference by the governor general in council. Knowing that the court has a duty to consider does not help us appreciate what it is that it can or must consider.

Other statutes, such as the Judges Act,[7] the Exchequer Court Act,[8] the Federal Court Act,[9] and the County Judges Act[10] add nothing in the line of duties or responsibilities. Sections 17 and 18 of the Canada Evidence Act permit judicial notice to be taken of United Kingdom, Canada, and other Commonwealth statutes.[11] Section 7 of the Ontario Interpretation Act has similar provisions for acts and proclamations.[12] The Canada Evidence Act further permits evidence to be received of 'any proceeding or record whatever of, in, or before any court ... of record of ... any other foreign country.'[13] Interestingly, the Ontario Evidence Act has a similar provision listing the jurisdictions from which judgments under seal will be received, but not including, as did the federal act, foreign courts.[14] However, it is not important in regard to our quest here, since even the federal act does not include the decisions of international courts and tribunals, general principles of law, or text-writers, three of the most important sources of international law.

The Ontario Judicature Act contains in section 10 a similar oath requirement to the above-mentioned acts; and sections 13 and 14 provide that the courts shall continue to have all the power and jurisdiction they held on 31 December 1912 without specifying what that power or jurisdiction was. The rest of the act simply ensures that the courts will 'subject to the foregoing provisions for giving effect to equitable rights ... recognize and give effect to all legal claims and demands ... existing by the common law or created by any statute.'[15] It may well be that the rules of international law are brought in through this reference to common law.

The most promising statutory reference to legal sources is in the Law Reform Commission Act, which authorizes the federal Law Reform Commission to 'initiate and carry out ... such studies ... as it deems necessary ... including studies and research relating to the laws and legal systems and institutions of other jurisdictions in Canada or elsewhere.'[16] This is clear authorization to look to all sources including international sources; unfortunately for present purposes, the statute establishes a law reform commission, not a court. However, this specific reference in the Law Reform Commission Act emphasizes a pertinent silence on the point in statutes establishing the principal courts.

Those who take an oath according to the Oaths of Allegiance Act swear that they 'will be faithful and bear true allegiance to Her Majesty.'[17] Were judges obliged to take this oath, one might conceivably infer that, should an international rule conflict with a domestic rule, a judge's oath of loyalty to Her Majesty might preclude him from applying the international rule. However, judges do not take this oath. A judge of the Supreme Court of Canada promises and swears 'that I will duly and faithfully, and to the best of my skill and knowledge, execute the powers and trusts reposed in me as Chief Justice (or as one of the judges) of the Supreme Court of Canada. So help me God.'[18] The oaths required for the other courts are similar and thus we are no farther ahead since we do not know what these 'powers and trusts' are.[19]

In short, the statutes offer neither powers, limitations, duties, nor guidance to judges in their role as dispute-settlers and law-shapers. We must, it seems, go back to the generality that the courts interpret and apply the law of the land. This seems a neutral generality until it is combined with the classic and often quoted judgment of Lord Talbot in 1737 wherein he asserted that 'the law of nations, to its full extent, was part of the law of England.'[20] Or, as Blackstone put it, 'the law of nations ... is held to be a part of the law of the land.'[21] Assuming for a moment that this is a correct statement of the law, what does it mean? What are the implications of this doctrine?

Since (apparently) Canada has in no way limited the sources of which the judges may avail themselves, preferring merely to swear them to execute the powers and trusts of their office, can we say that Canada has impliedly assented to the rule in the *Barbuit* case as part of its general system of law? The rule existed for 140 years before Confederation. Surely Ontario, at least, adopted this rule when in 1791 it passed the Constitutional Act 'to introduce the English Law as the Rule of Decision in all Matters of Controversy, relative to Property and Civil Rights.'[22] If so, the courts, in consulting international law, are merely fleshing out their mandate. But, if they are so acting in fulfilment of a mandate, does this amount to much the same thing as an implied constitutional provision directing, or at least empowering, the courts to apply international law?

Further questions arise. If international law is part of the law of the land, who determines what international law is? The courts? The executive? The legislature? Or should it be a world court which would receive references from municipal tribunals asking what the customary rule is on a certain point? If it is to be the courts, then are the judges to take judicial notice of international law? This would seem to follow from saying that customary rules are part of the law of the land. This problem of judicial notice will be dealt with after we have examined the cases. If it is to be the executive that decides what is or is not international law, would it do so in advance or on request? Would it hear argument? If so, would the arguments be strictly legal – cases and, perhaps, text writers – or would the arguments tend to be based on national policy? Leaving the matter in the hands of the legislature would involve a full acceptance of the dualist theory since the legislature would never be at the beck and call of the courts and therefore would have to make advance decisions. Thus, any rule which had not been pronounced upon by the legislature would, in effect, not be part of the law of the land.

To refer these questions to a supranational body would involve a surrender of sovereignty, since the courts, in so doing, would be permitting a body over which neither they nor any group or individual in Canada has any control to determine what was Canada's domestic law. Full respect for international law would require this, but given the realities of today, it is most unlikely to come about. In fact, as we shall see, the courts determine these rules themselves and this brings us to the question of *stare decisis*. If international law is part of the law of the land, then, once it has been applied domestically, does it remain fixed in form until and unless another domestic court reinterprets it? Or does the rule in question remain subject to the ebb and flow of international legal opinion even while being part of the law of the land? Again, there is a question of surrender of sovereignty. This question of *stare decisis* will reappear at a later stage of our discussion.

One final question which arises is, perhaps, less difficult to handle. If international law is part of the law of the land, then, when domestic courts apply it, are they applying international or domestic law? Surely this is simply a terminological problem. If one defines municipal law as that law which is applied by municipal courts, the problem is obviated. If this solution is unsatisfactory, one can define municipal law as that law which springs from sources and customs within the jurisdiction of the municipal courts, or from sources outside the jurisdiction which are felt (by the judges?) to be appropriate bases of analogy. This would mean that the judges are still applying municipal law, but municipal law which has, as its source, a principle drawn from international law. A difficulty can arise only if one insists on this latter definition of municipal law, yet argues that international law, if it is part of the law of the land, must be accorded a status higher than that of analogy. But even here, if municipal law must come mainly from internal sources, surely that within the state which authorizes the court to treat international law as a part of municipal law is the proper internal source of the international rules. Thus, the courts are still applying municipal law.

It can be seen then that Lord Talbot's statement on the relationship between customary international law and domestic law is not without its difficulties even if it is fully accepted by Canadian courts. A theoretical discussion of these difficulties could continue indefinitely. It is, therefore, worthwhile at this point to examine briefly the background provided by the English case-law in order to discover the extent to which Lord Talbot's statement is followed in Canadian courts and, also, to see how these theoretical difficulties have been handled in practice.

Adoption and transformation

It is convenient, at least initially, to examine the cases within a framework provided by the distinction between adoption and transformation.[23] The doctrine of adoption apparently means that the rules of customary international law are applied as such;

they become the equivalent of municipal law, directly applicable to individuals, not by the creation of parallel municipal norms, but by direct application. The court would, in this case, not be applying municipal law, but international. The courts would apply these rules on their own; that is, not as the result of express constitutional or other legislation authorizing them to adopt international law, but as a result of common law doctrine and practice. Under the theory of adoption, the courts can bring about a sort of general reception of international law; they keep municipal law in step with changing international law and there is, therefore, considerable scope for a national judge who wants to develop international law.

Those who subscribe to a dualist point of view prefer the doctrine of transformation, which seems to imply that the rules of customary international law must be converted into rules of municipal law and that this can only be accomplished through an act of transformation performed under the laws of the state concerned. There must be parallel norms, created by municipal law, quite independent of international norms. It is often assumed that the act of transformation – the creation of the parallel norms – must be effected by the legislature, either through individual pieces of legislation, as in the case of a treaty, or as the result of an omnibus authorizing statute; however, there is some ambiguity here. As summarized by Seidl-Hohenveldern, the advantage of transformation is that it is certain: the citizen knows what rules will be binding on him; the municipal system is protected from inroads made by the application of international law that has not been duly approved by the legislature; the courts are kept in step with the government; the government knows exactly how to keep in step with the changing needs of the international order.

Of course it might also be argued that the executive is better informed as to changes in international law and that in the national interest (for example, ensuring that erroneous interpretations by the courts do not embarrass foreign relations) it would, therefore, be the better agency to transform. Or should the courts themselves be the agents of transformation, since the judges are more accustomed to establishing what the law is on any given point? This is where the ambiguity exists; for if the courts are permitted to transform, as they apparently are in England and in Canada,[24] then the strict dualist theory is evaded. It seems then that the framework must include not just adoption and transformation as strictly understood, but also a modified form of transformation by the courts. Nevertheless, it must be borne in mind that both adoption and transformation maintain the dependence of international law on municipal law. Adoption does not mean that international law is operative in the municipal sphere by virtue of independent and superior international rules. Like transformation, adoption requires the consent of the state; the difference being that, in adoption, the state consents to allow international rules to operate automatically, while, with transformation, the state might consent to the individual rules.[25]

The English background

The relationship between customary international law and the domestic law of England as expounded by the judges in England has been treated in depth by a number of commentators including Holdsworth, Westlake, Brierly, Lauterpacht, McNair,

McDougal, and Fawcett.[26] It is not intended, nor is it necessary, to repeat their findings here, but rather to emphasize the highlights of the English treatment and to discuss a few of the cases that have had a direct bearing on Canadian jurisprudence.

In 1765 Blackstone enunciated his view of the doctrine of adoption or, as he called it, incorporation of international law as part of the law of the land:

> the law of nations (wherever any question arises which is properly the object of its jurisdiction) is here adopted in its full extent by the common law, and is held to be a part of the law of the land. And those acts of parliament which have from time to time been made to enforce this universal law, or to facilitate the execution of its decisions are not to be considered as introductory of any new rule, but merely as declaratory of the old fundamental constitutions of the kingdom; without which it must cease to be a part of the civilized world.[27]

In making such a strong statement, Blackstone had at least two English decisions to support him. In *Buvot* v *Barbuit,* Lord Talbot had stated that 'the law of nations, to its full extent, was part of the law of England.' Lord Mansfield, who had acted as counsel in *Buvot,* supported this decision in *Triquet* v *Bath* in 1764. Lord Mansfield reinforced this view in at least two subsequent cases.[28] As Lauterpacht correctly points out, it is controversial whether Blackstone and Lord Mansfield were expressing an actual rule or were formulating a principle whose rationality appeared to them to be irrefutable. Lauterpacht continues: 'However that may be, the principle thus formulated proved an exposition of the law as it has been applied in the hundred and seventy years that followed.'[29] This statement is supported by a series of cases in the nineteenth century including *Emperor of Austria* v *Day and Kossuth* where the court, in enjoining the printing of money on behalf of Kossuth's revolutionary government, said that 'a public right, recognized by the law of nations, is a legal right; because the law of nations is part of the common law of England. These propositions are supported by unquestioned authority.'[30]

After more than one hundred years of consistently adopting international rules, the English Court for Crown Cases Reserved in 1876 handed down what at first sight seems to be an opposing judgment in *The Franconia, The Queen* v *Keyn.*[31] A foreigner, in command of a foreign ship which had collided with a British ship within three miles of England, in such a manner as to render the master liable for criminal manslaughter under British law, was duly charged and convicted by the Central Criminal Court. He appealed on the ground that that court had no jurisdiction since the offence was committed on board a foreign ship on the high seas; the crown responded that since the offence was committed within three miles of England, it was triable in England. By a seven to six majority the court held that the offence was not triable in England. The minority, consisting of Lord Coleridge CJ, Brett and Amphlett JJA, and Grove, Denman, and Lindley JJ, approached the problem in the same way: one hundred years after Blackstone, they felt no need to articulate the adoption method, but rather simply to employ it. The attitude of Brett JA is perhaps typical. He described his task in this way: 'It seems, therefore, necessary to determine, first, what is the authority of a common agreement or acquiescence of jurists; secondly, is there any such acquiescence or agreement with regard to three miles of open sea adjacent to countries; thirdly, if there is, what is the exact purport of such agreement.'[32] Having set out this task, Brett JA concluded that the agreement of writers, if enough of them agree, creates customary international law, that there was such agreement in regard to the littoral sea, and that the rule was that the adjacent state enjoyed sovereignty over the littoral sea and that this sovereignty imported jurisdiction. This rule was then automatically applied to the case at bar and the appeal was denied. Similar reasoning was employed by the other five judges in the minority.

For the majority, however, several speeches were delivered which have created difficulty, for at first glance they appear to be transformationist. Sir Robert Phillimore, with whom Kelly CB agreed, found it 'a most grave question whether, if this statement of international law were correct [three miles sovereignty], nevertheless an Act of Parliament would not be required to empower the Court to exercise jurisdiction.'[33] This question seems to imply that the rule of customary international law would not be part of the law of England unless transformed by an act of parliament. However, Sir Robert found that the rule itself did not exist in international law and thus never came to consider the question he had raised.

Cockburn CJ, with whom several members of the majority concurred, also appears to have opted for the transformation theory: 'This unanimity of opinion ... may go far to shew that, by the concurrence of other nations, such a state may deal with these waters as subject to its legislation. But it wholly fails to shew that, in the absence of such legislation, the ordinary law of the local state will extend over the waters in question.'[34] Again, the implication is that the existence of the international rule is insufficient in the absence of legislation.

Finally, Lush J delivered a seemingly strong speech in support of the transformation theory.

> I think that ... international law [has] appropriated these waters to the adjacent State to deal with them as the State may deem expedient for its own interests. They are, therefore, in the language of diplomacy and of international law ... the territorial waters of Great Britain, and the same or equivalent phrases are used in some of our statutes denoting that this belt of sea is under the exclusive domain of the state. But the dominion is the dominion of Parliament, not the dominion of the common law. That extends no further than the limits of the realm ... International law ... cannot enlarge the area of our municipal law, nor could treaties with all the nations of the world have that effect. That can only be done by Act of Parliament. As no such Act has been passed, it follows that what was out of the realm then is out of the realm now, and what was part of the high seas then is part of the high seas now.[35]

The fact of an international rule giving the adjacent state sovereignty does not enlarge the realm until and unless there is an act of parliament to that effect.

These judgments have been dealt with in detail since they have, it is suggested, been much misunderstood, particularly in Canadian jurisprudence. That they do not support the transformation theory becomes immediately clear when one considers the exact holding of the majority. First, not one judgment suggested that England had no sovereignty over a three mile territorial sea; if there was any confusion here it was whether the distance might be greater. Thus, there was implicit adoption of the customary rule that the adjacent state enjoyed such sovereignty. The diffi-

culty came with just what this sovereignty meant. Did it automatically confer jurisdiction on the court? Or was it permissive only, and therefore required legislation
to extend court jurisdiction? By a seven to six majority the court held that the customary international rule was a permissive one only. The question of the relationship of international to municipal law was never at issue. There was no doubt that,
whatever the rule was, it would be incorporated; the question was, did the rule itself
envisage further actions by the individual states?

The affirmative answer given to this latter question explains Sir Robert Phillimore's 'grave question,' which dealt not with the relationship of the rule to municipal law, but with the content of the rule. Again, Cockburn CJ, when he said that
'this unanimity of opinion that the littoral sea is ... subject to the dominion of the
local state, may go far to shew that, by the concurrence of other nations, such a
state may deal with these waters as subject to its legislation. But it wholly fails to
shew that, in the absence of such legislation, the ordinary law of the local state will
extend over the waters in question – which is the point which we have to determine'
was simply explaining his interpretation of the customary rule itself. He was saying
that the rule gives sovereignty but does not automatically extend jurisdiction.[36]
Lush J also admitted that the rule gives England sovereignty, but he made it clear
that this rule could not, nor would any customary rule (he is alone on this point),
enlarge the area of municipal law; that must await parliament. Again, this is
interpretation rather than relationship.

It can be seen then, that in fact the *Keyn* case does fall within the mainstream
of English incorporation theory. The basis of this theory was explained by Lord
Alverstone in 1905 in *West Rand Central Gold Mining Co.* v *The King*. In the course
of holding that there was no international rule which compelled an annexing state
to assume the liabilities of the annexed state, His Lordship added that 'whatever
has received the common consent of civilized nations must have received the assent
of our country, and that to which we have assented along with other nations in
general may properly be called international law, and as such will be acknowledged
and applied by our municipal tribunals when legitimate occasion arises for those
tribunals to decide questions to which doctrines of international law may be
relevant.'[37] Several points are worth noting in this remarkable passage: first, the
basis of adoption is the consent of the nation involved – a clear rejection of the older
naturalist theories – and the consent of that nation is a condition precedent to incorporation. Second, in order to qualify as customary law, a rule needs only the consent of 'other nations in general,' not the unanimous consent of the member states
of the international community. Third, 'will be acknowledged' presumably implies
that judicial notice will be taken of these rules. Fourth, 'and applied' is a clear
description of the adoption process. Finally, 'legitimate occasions' are not identified, but presumably refer to situations where the international rule is relevant and
is not contradicted by a statute of the *lex fori*. It may be suggested that precisely
such a situation arose in the *Keyn* case.

The adoption doctrine received further support in *Re Suarez* (1918) and *Engelke*
v *Musmann* (1928).[38] But, about this time, an interesting development began to take
place. The English courts continued to employ the adoption theory – indeed, they
never have done anything else – but they began to do so with greater and greater
reluctance, feeling obliged, while automatically applying customary rules, to warn

that they did not have to do so, that international law had no strength on its own, and that it was only by virtue of the consent of the United Kingdom that these rules had any validity in English law. Whether this was because customary international law had undergone such rapid change and expansion during the first half of the century, or because these changes were less influenced than previously by the United Kingdom, or for some other reason is difficult to say, but the reluctance is clear. Lauterpacht felt, in 1939, that adoption was becoming unpopular because of its early associations with the then-rejected natural law; and also because, with the increase in the quantum of treaty law, along with its requirement for implementing legislation, a dualist upswing was beginning.[39]

This trend began, perhaps, with *Mortensen* v *Peters* decided by the Scottish High Court of Justiciary in 1906. In support of its interpretation of a fisheries act in apparent contravention of international law, the court added the celebrated passage that 'it is a trite observation that there is no such thing as a standard of international law extraneous to the domestic law of the Kingdom, to which appeal may be made. International law, so far as this court is concerned, is the body of doctrine regarding international rights and duties of states which has been adopted and made part of the law of Scotland.'[40]

The first part of this quotation is ambiguous: If it means that there are no extraneous standards at all, it is clearly wrong; if it means that there are none to which appeal can be made directly, in the sense of there being immediate access to international courts and tribunals, then it is correct, for the appeal to international law must always be made through the municipal system, and, if we accept the terminology, through municipal law. However, the ambiguity is resolved by the second part of the quotation which is clearly a statement of adoptionist theory, made albeit in a somewhat grudging manner. If one reads 'judicially noticed' for 'adopted' and 'incorporated into' for 'made part of,' the last sentence becomes a classic exposition of the adoption theory.

In *Commercial and Estates Co. of Egypt* v *The Board of Trade,* the court had no trouble in adopting the international rule of angary to justify a seizure of the goods of a neutral brought into England against his will. Bankes LJ quoted with approval the passage cited above from *West Rand,* concluding that 'that right [angary] is so well established in international law that it forms part of the municipal law of this country.'[41] Atkin LJ shared the view that angary was a part of international law but felt obliged to warn that 'International law as such can confer no rights cognizable in the municipal Courts. It is only in so far as the rules of international law are recognized as included in the rules of municipal law that they are allowed in the municipal Courts to give rise to rights or obligations.'[42] Again, this first sentence is ambiguous; however, if one reads into it 'without the consent of the *lex fori*' it is perfectly correct; if it is meant as an absolute rule, it is clearly nonsense. The second sentence is reasonable and unobjectionable. An adoptionist interpretation of the first part of this passage was strengthened by Atkin LJ himself who, after first concluding that angary was part of international law then warning that international rules must be consented to by municipal courts, went on to conclude that 'the right of angary therefore is a right recognized by English law.'[43] As Lauterpacht says: 'Why "therefore"?'[44] Why indeed, unless he were applying the adoption theory?

In 1938 the House of Lords spoke unanimously in *The Cristina* of 'propositions of international law engrafted into our domestic law' and of 'a rule of international law' which 'is binding on the municipal Courts of this country in the sense and to the extent that it has been received [read judicially noticed] and enforced by these Courts.'[45] Yet, Lord MacMillan, before examining and applying directly the appropriate rule from international law (sovereign immunity of foreign commercial vessels) found it necessary to refer with approval to the first part of the above-quoted passage from *Mortensen* v *Peters*. That he understood this passage in the sense suggested above is borne out by considering how unlikely it would have been for His Lordship to have said in effect that 'there is no such thing as a standard of international law' and then to turn around and examine international authorities in order to establish and apply the correct international rule. Clearly he meant that the standards of international law must be applied by the courts.

The *Chung* case represents the most recent opinion of the English courts on the relationship problem, and, since the case has been much discussed in Canadian cases, although, interestingly, never again mentioned by the English courts, the ambiguous passages that it contains deserve close examination. The case concerned a Hong Kong criminal court's jurisdiction to try a murder committed aboard a foreign vessel within Hong Kong territorial waters. Lord Atkin delivered the judgment and seemed initially to be taking an adoptionist approach: 'The domestic Courts, in accordance with principles of international law, will accord to the ship and its crew and its contents certain immunities.'[46] But he continued with the warning that: 'It must be always remembered that, so far, at any rate, as the Courts of this country are concerned, international law has no validity save in so far as its principles are accepted and adopted by our own domestic law. There is no external power that imposes its rules upon our own code of substantive law or procedure.'[47] Again, this could be interpreted as transformationist but, as His Lordship explained on the next page, it is really a hesitant statement of the adoptionist view: 'The courts acknowledge the existence of a body of rules which nations accept amongst themselves. On any judicial issue they seek to ascertain what the relevant rule is, and having found it, they will treat it as incorporated into the domestic law, so far as it is not inconsistent with rules enacted by statutes or finally declared by their tribunals.'[48] From this last passage it is clear that once a rule of international law is ascertained, it is treated as automatically a part of domestic law so long as it is not inconsistent with a statute or a previously articulated common law principle.

After passing through this rather disturbing period, the English courts have not spoken on the point; in fact, not only has the relationship question not been in issue, but the (in Canada) controversial *Keyn* and *Chung* cases have not even been cited in England since 1927.[49] The law in England at the present time is probably accurately stated in *Chung*: having found a relevant rule of international law, the courts 'will treat it as incorporated into the domestic law, so far as it is not inconsistent with rules enacted by statutes or finally declared by their tribunals.' This is correct so long as 'finally declared by their tribunals' refers to long-standing common law traditions and not merely single contrary decisions.

That statute law, as suggested by this passage, is superior to international law is supported by the Scottish court in *Mortensen* v *Peters*, where the court said that 'for us an Act of Parliament duly passed by Lords and Commons and assented to by the King, is supreme, and we are bound to give effect to its terms.'[50] To like effect, Dr Lushington in *The Johanna Stoll* observed that 'the Parliament of Great Britain, it is true, has not, according to the principles of public law, any authority to legislate for foreign vessels on the high seas ... though if Parliament thought fit to do so, this Court in its instance jurisdiction at least, would be bound to obey.'[51] And, finally, in the very recent case of *Cheney* v *Conn (Inspector of Taxes)* the English court reaffirmed the old rule that international law is part of the common law but pointed out a clear restriction in regard to statute law when Ungoed-Thomas J said that 'International Law is the law of the land, but it yields to statute.'[52]

The problems that the latter relationship could generate have been obviated by a canon of construction which says that statutes will so far as possible be interpreted so as not to conflict with international law. This canon has been many times stated as, for example, by Cockburn CJ in *Keyn,* where he said that 'the true canon of construction is to assume that the legislature has not so enacted as to violate the rights of other nations.'[53] In the same case, Sir Robert Phillimore stated that 'it is an established principle as to the construction of a statute that it should be construed, if the words will permit, so as to be in accordance with the principles of international law.'[54] This canon is eminently reasonable for a jurisdiction which adopts international law automatically into its domestic law. Just as, in England, statutes are presumed not to be intended to violate long-standing common law traditions, so too they are presumed not to violate another branch of the common law, international law.

The Canadian cases

With such a solid English background of adoption on which to build, and with the tradition in Canada of following English case law, one might have expected the judges in Canada to have developed a clear record in favour of adoption. Such is not the case. In fact, the judgments on this point are so often contradictory, vague, and ambiguous that our adoption-transformation framework breaks down. For this reason, in the discussion that follows, no attempt will be made to categorize the cases, but I will simply state the views on the relationship point as they appear in the judgments. Having done this, I will then draw a few conclusions from what has been said.

The earliest Canadian case touching on the relationship of international to domestic law would appear to be *The Grace* decided in 1894. An American fishing vessel was brought in for adjudication under the Fisheries Act, R.S.C. c 94 (1886), for fishing in Canada's territorial waters. The defence was that, although the vessel was fishing on the Canadian side of the international boundary of Lake Erie, it was nevertheless outside the three mile limit of the Canadian coastline. MacDougal J rejected this argument and went to international law for the proposition that Canadian national territory extended to the boundary line. He continued: 'It is an axiom of international law that every state is entitled to declare that fishing on its coasts is an exclusive right of its own subjects.' There is no direct comment here on the relationship point, but clearly MacDougal J felt that the international rule was an integral part of Canadian law.[55]

The Fisheries Act was the subject of dispute ten years later, in *The North,* where the question arose whether a ship could be seized on the high seas for an offence committed within three miles of Canada's shore, the vessel having been pursued out to the high seas.[56] The seizure was justified by the customary international law rule on hot pursuit; the defence was that this doctrine was not automatically a part of Canadian law, but required a transforming act. In the lower court Martin J had pointed out that there was no case or statute law on this point and had gone to international law to determine and apply the rule: a clear case of implicit adoption.[57]

In the Supreme Court, the argument of the defence in favour of transformation was rejected by Davies J, with whom MacLennon J concurred, as he said that the 'Admiralty Court ... is bound to take notice of the law of nations ... The right of hot pursuit ... being part of the law of nations was properly judicially taken notice of and acted upon.'[58] It seems clear that in rejecting transformation, Davies J was opting for adoption. Idington J was more cautious, preferring to rest his judgment on statute interpretation and leaving the relationship point open: 'Without assenting to this [transformationist] proposition as being one of universal application I assume that for the purposes of this case the judgment must be rested upon the statute ... The general, though not universal, principle that municipal legislation is necessary to give effect to the doctrines of international law [probably] was assumed [by the lower court].'[59] Sedgewick J agreed with the court below, which means, in effect, that he accepted the adoption theory, and Girouard J, who dissented, apparently agreed with Davies J on the relationship point but felt bound to allow the appeal on a point of statute interpretation. This case is, therefore, a strong statement of the adoption theory, although it should be remembered that it was a decision in admiralty and admiralty law has closer ties with international law than has the ordinary common law.

In another Admiralty Court decision, *The King* v *The Schooner John J. Fallon*, Duff J concluded that the Island of St Paul's off Nova Scotia was part of Canada by resorting to international law, which he apparently assumed was binding in this case.[60] Again, though, it must be remembered that not only was this an Admiralty Court case, but that it also dealt with matters which were of an intrinsically international nature. In determining whether or not an island should be considered part of Canada, where else could one go but to international sources?

In *The Dunbar and Sullivan Dredging Company* v *The Ship Milwaukee* (1907) the court, in supporting the principle that no independent sovereign state is to be assumed to have contracted itself out of its sovereign rights, quoted with approval, first, *Hall's International Law*, to establish that this international rule existed, and, second, Lord Mansfield, in *Triquet* v *Bath*, that 'the law of nations to its full extent, is part of the law of England,' to establish that this rule was incorporated in the laws of Canada.[61]

In *The King* v *Boutilier*, the court canvassed various international authorities to establish that Canada had jurisdiction over St Margaret's Bay;[62] in implicitly adopting the customary rule, the court cited with approval the case of *Mason* v *Coffin*, where Harris CJ said: 'It is a rule of Customary International Law that within three miles of the sea-shore at low water mark a state may exercise any jurisdiction or do any act which it may lawfully do upon its own land territory.'[63] Harris CJ then proceeded simply to apply that customary rule in the *Coffin* case.

There are other cases of implicit adoption, such as *Rex* v *Furuzawa* and *Rex* v *The Kitty D.*,[64] but there seems to be no need to discuss them since it is clear that, at least until 1939, the English doctrine of adoption was well-established in Canada. It was only after the *Chung* decision in England that Canadian courts began to share the concern of the English courts about the significance of automatic incorporation.

In 1943 the Supreme Court of Canada considered the question of a foreign legation's liability for municipal taxation.[65] Although the properties in question would have been taxable ordinarily, the defence raised was that they were diplomatic missions and, as such, were exempt from taxation under the international doctrine of diplomatic immunity. Duff CJ found that such a rule was part of Canadian law and that therefore there could be no tax on the properties. But before reaching this conclusion he felt it necessary to quote the above-mentioned passages from *Chung* and *Mortensen* v *Peters,* complete with their caveats and, as I have argued, their subsequent support for the adoption theory. The chief justice then continued by stating that 'there are some general principles touching the position of the property of a foreign state and the minister of a foreign state that have been accepted and adopted by the law of England (which, except as modified by statute, is the law of Ontario) as part of the law of nations.' A little later he added that 'it is probable that the privileges attributed to foreign representatives by the law of England, as part of the law of nations are at least as liberal as those recognized by the law of any other country' and, in support of this statement, he quoted Lord Mansfield in *Heathfield* v *Chilton:* 'The law of nations will be carried as far in England, as anywhere.'[66]

Now, the *Mortensen* and *Chung* quotes are what I have described as grudgingly adoptionist, the last passage from Duff CJ's judgment and the *Heathfield* passage being adoptionist; but what needs explanation is the first Duff passage where he speaks of principles 'that have been accepted and adopted by the law of England.' If he is using 'adopted' as a term of art, why the word 'accepted'? Unless he means by 'accepted,' judicially recognized as a valid rule of customary international law. If this is so, then the entire judgment is adoptionist and is internally consistent. But, it could be argued that he was looking to English acceptance as a legal precedent to follow or even as an act of transformation to legitimize his use of these rules. In any case, there is ambivalence in, or at least reluctance to apply as he does, the adoption method. Rinfret J spoke similarly when he included the doctrine of immunity 'amongst the principles of international law which have acquired validity in the domestic law of England, and therefore, in the domestic law of Canada.'[67] Does 'acquired validity' refer to the court recognizing the rule as a valid one and automatically applying it? If so, it is adoption. Or, does it refer to some transformation process? Or merely the following of English precedent? Again, there is the absence of either a straightforward application or an explication of the adoption theory.

Taschereau J concurred with Duff CJ, speaking of 'settled and accepted rules of international law' (which are automatically part of our law?). Kerwin J simply accepted the international rule without comment – implicit adoption; and Hudson J found the Statute of Anne to be valid in Ontario and thus did not find it necessary to go to customary rules. This case, then, could be cited to support the adoption theory, but it is less than clear and less than overwhelming in its support of that doctrine, especially in view of the seventy years of quiet acceptance that preceded it.

Similar difficulties are to be found in the *Armed Forces* reference decided later in that same year.[68] The question there was whether or not Canada's criminal courts had jurisdiction to try American military personnel for offences committed in Canada. Duff CJ found that if the American military enjoyed an exemption from Canada's penal laws, the rule of exemption 'derives its validity solely from alleged principles of international law to which the nations, including the United Kingdom and Canada, are supposed to have agreed.'[69] That is, a principle cannot become a customary rule until and unless nations including the United Kingdom and Canada have consented to it; this is the basis of adopting the rule. But, the chief justice continued, it is a fundamental constitutional principle in England and, therefore, in Canada that the military not be exempt from the common law. In England, an act of parliament was required to overcome this principle, and no less would be required in Canada. In any case, there could be no such customary rule since 'the United Kingdom has never assented to any rule of international law by which British courts are restricted in their jurisdiction.'[70] The chief justice appears to have been willing to use adoption; although, as in the *Foreign Legations* case, he is less than direct and it could be argued that, in requiring an act, he was opting for the transformation theory.

Taschereau J saw his task as twofold: 'To seek if there exists and if the Court can acknowledge a body of rules accepted by the nations of the world, to the effect that the troops of a foreign sovereign visiting a country, with the consent of the latter's Government, are exempt from criminal proceedings prosecuted in that country. And secondly, having reached on that point an affirmative conclusion, the further question that must be solved is: Are these recognized principles of international law adopted by our domestic law?'[71] The fact that he asked such a question as the second shows at best an imprecise understanding of adoption (for, if a principle is recognized, it should be adopted automatically), and at worst a tendency to transformation, though not of the type which would require legislation.

Having consulted international authorities, Taschereau J decided that such a rule existed and turned to his second question. After first issuing the now common warning that 'I do not forget that international law has no application in Canada unless incorporated in our own domestic law,' and quoting the similar warning from the *Chung* case, he went on to quote Duff CJ in the *Foreign Legations* case to the effect that international law is recognized by the law of England and, consequently, by the law of Ontario. The reason for this being, as he said, that 'if not accepted in this country, international law would not be binding, but would merely be a code of unenforceable abstract rules of international morals.' Mr Justice Taschereau then quoted the second half of the *Chung* passage which is, as I have argued, the classic English position on adoption. His conclusion was that 'there exists such a body of rules adopted by the nations of the world.... I have to acknowledge their existence, and treat them as incorporated in our domestic law, following the direction given in the *Chung* case.'[72] Thus, although he showed some uncertainty in setting out his task and though he did warn that international law must be accepted by the nation concerned, Taschereau J did, in the end, come out clearly in favour of adoption. These warnings that both Duff CJ and Taschereau J felt obliged to offer must have been merely intended to assert Canada's sovereignty and demonstrate that we would accept these rules only with our own consent, a concept which is in no way inconsistent with adoption.

Rand J also felt the need to proceed with caution. In a judgment that is far from clear, he appeared to have thought that international rules were part of our law, but was quite concerned with the method of determining the rule in question. He referred to 'all immunities which by international law attached to them [the military]'; later in the same passage he stated: 'The conventions and usages of international law are of voluntary adoption by sovereign states as rules according to which international relations shall be governed.'[73] One of these, whose existence in Canadian law Rand J seemed to take for granted, is sovereign immunity. The only question remaining then was the extent of the immunity 'implied in the invitation' to a foreign army to come into Canada 'with its laws, courts and discipline.' Here, Rand J felt that he should apply 'the rule which reason and good sense ... would prescribe.' He then quoted the *Chung* passage complete with warning and adoption theory and commented:

> From that language, I do not understand that the ordinary methods of judicial determination are not to be resorted to. To insist upon precise precedent in usage would sterilize judicial action toward changing international relations: and in the reduction of terms of an implied arrangement the court must be free to draw upon all sources of international conventions, including 'reason and good sense.'[74]

These words do not refer to whether or not the customary rules are part of Canadian law; that is simply assumed. Rather, they refer to the determination of the scope of the rule. In determining the scope of sovereign immunity here, Rand J found, as did Duff CJ, that the rule conflicted with a fundamental constitutional principle that the civil law is supreme over the military arm. 'If that principle meets the rule of immunity to foreign forces arising in the circumstances stated, then the latter must give way.'[75]

This view is entirely consistent with English adoption theory as stated in the *Chung* case. The fact that Rand J would also, like Duff CJ, require an act of parliament to overcome this fundamental constitutional principle in no way alters the fact that both judges accepted the propriety of applying the adoption theory. Ordinarily, the rules are applied automatically with no need of a statute. Taschereau J did this; but if, as Duff CJ and Rand J found here, the customary rule conflicts with a fundamental principle ('as finally declared by our courts' in the *Chung* case) then a statute is required to help the customary rule to overcome this principle. Kerwin J simply adopted the sovereign immunity rule and applied it: 'These exemptions are grounded on reason and are recognized by civilized countries as being rules of international law which will be followed in the absence of any domestic law to the contrary.'[76] Hudson J concurred with the chief justice.

Thus, we have five judgments, three of them dealing with the relationship point in detail, all of which accept, albeit some with caveats, the adoption theory. The immunity was refused to the American military by a three to two vote not over the relationship issue, but because three of the judges felt the customary rule had to give way before a fundamental constitutional principle.

It is true that one could argue that by requiring an act to implement the immunity, these three judges were in favour of transformation, but this interpretation would require one to ignore their numerous statements and quotations of the adoption principle and the fact that they required legislation only because the immunity rule conflicted with a fundamental principle. This case has to stand with the *Foreign Legations* case and *The North* as an example of the express application of the adoption theory. These three cases become significant when one considers how rarely the courts explain what they are doing. In the bulk of the cases to follow, we must infer the theory by which the courts are operating.

One year after the *Armed Forces* case, the Supreme Court accorded sovereign immunity to the Polish government in a suit by a solicitor in Quebec for his fees. The immunity rule was accepted without comment save for Mr Justice Taschereau's statement that 'la jurisprudence l'a aussi adopté comme étant la loi domestique de tous les pays civilisés.'[77] It might be argued that he meant that Canada had adopted the rule because other civilized countries had done so; or that because other nations, including England, had adopted the rule it was transformed into Canadian law; or that he would simply follow precedent. But, given his adoptionist stance in the two reference cases, it is likely that Mr Justice Taschereau meant that, since most nations had adopted this rule, it was a customary rule and, therefore, part of Canadian law. This is, in fact, what he and the court did.

The famous Gouzenko spy exposé gave rise to two cases in which the papers Gouzenko removed from the Russian embassy were offered as evidence for the prosecution. In both cases the defence objected to the use of these documents on the grounds that, coming from the Russian embassy, they were privileged according to international law and therefore could not be admitted.

In the first of these, the *Rose* case, Barclay J would not even consider whether or not international law had been violated since 'the documents are legally before this Court and should be dealt with.'[78] This appears to be an implicit statement that international law is not part of domestic law; but this is not so, since this approach to illegally obtained evidence was a standard one for Canadian courts, whether the illegality stemmed from a violation of domestic or of international law.[79] Bissonnette J with whom Gagne J concurred, decided that the documents were not embassy documents and that therefore the immunity rule did not apply. He indicated that the rule was adopted into Canadian law by the manner in which he consulted international authorities, apparently assuming that these would be the law of Canada. For example, he said, 'it is recognized in the present state of international law,' and later, 'Canada has no particular legislation of public international law, so ... the general rules [of international law] must be applied here.'[80] In the second of these cases, *Rex* v *Lunan*, the court followed reasoning similar to *Rose,* but made its willingness to use adoption most explicit by citing *Halsbury* to the effect that 'the immunities ... which have come to be known as international law, are expressly recognized in the law of England.'[81]

In an Ontario High Court decision, *Yin-tso Hsiung* v *Toronto,* Smily J, in deciding whether the property occupied by a consul general was immune from municipal taxation on the basis of diplomatic immunity, found that 'the matter involves international law, and whether, if covered by international law, the principle in point has been accepted and adopted by our own domestic law.'[82] This is a disturbing passage since, on one reading, it could be interpreted as suggesting that there could be rules of international law which might not be accepted and adopted by Canada. On that interpretation, it would be a transformationist statement. However, a close reading of this passage reveals that Smily J thought the matter 'involved' international law and might be 'covered' by it. This does not imply that there necessarily is a customary rule covering it. Whether or not there is a rule depends on general acceptance, and in particular Canada's acceptance, of it. Once Canada is found to have accepted the rule, it is immediately adopted with no transforming act required. As an aid in determining which of these two interpretations of this passage is correct, we can look to what Smily J did. He cited the *Chung* passage and the *Foreign Legations* case with their adoptionist statements and then found that the immunity was well embedded in our law. Clearly, he was not applying transformation theory, since he never discussed a transforming act. Whether he was simply following precedent or was, as the *Chung* quotation would suggest, adopting international law is a moot point. In any case, the judgment does not, in fact, go against the adoption theory, but it may be ambivalent on it.

The question that was discussed in the *Keyn* case whether the customary international rule automatically extended the law of the littoral state to the three mile limit or whether legislation was required to effect this purpose arose in two cases on Canada's east coast. In the first case, *Gavin et al.* v *The Queen* (1956), seventeen lobster fishermen and three lobster canneries had been convicted of violating the Lobster Fisheries Regulations in regard to the length of the lobsters retained.[83] Campbell CJ of the Prince Edward Island Supreme Court followed the seven to six majority in *Keyn* and held that the customary rule was permissive and that legislation was required to extend the operation of the Fisheries Act (which authorized the regulations) beyond the coast of Canada. The chief justice found that the Fisheries Act, in fact, did authorize the governor general in council to issue regulations which would operate in the territorial sea; but he held further that the regulations that had been promulgated were vague and inadequate to so extend their operation, and he therefore quashed the fishermen's conviction.

Chief Justice Campbell had little to say on the relationship point; he apparently adopted, without question, the customary rule on the littoral sea and concerned himself, as had the judges in *Keyn*, with the content of the rule. His judgment, then, could be described as implicit adoptionist or the simple following of precedent, but not transformation, despite his requirement for an act to extend the operation of these regulations.

In 1963 the Nova Scotia Supreme Court, in the *Cape Breton* case, was asked to decide if certain underground mine workings which extended under the territorial waters were properly assessable under the Assessment Act of Nova Scotia.[84] Chief Justice Ilsley, with whom MacDonald J concurred on this point, followed the reasoning in the *Keyn* and *Gavin* cases in regard to the need for special legislation to extend the operation of Nova Scotian and Canadian law to the territorial sea. MacDonald J supported his argument for legislation by referring to the combined operation of section 7 of the BNA Act (1867) and section 3 of the BNA Act (1871) which, he held, required that specific legislation be passed to alter the boundaries of a province. Both judges apparently accepted the implicit adoption in the *Keyn* and *Gavin* judgments.

Patterson and Bissett JJ did not discuss this point, resting their agreements with

Ilsley CJ and MacDonald J (that the workings were not assessable) on other grounds. But Currie J dissented, not on the relationship point, but on the interpretation placed on the customary rule by the majority in *Keyn,* Campbell CJ in *Gavin,* and the two judges mentioned above. Pointing out that *Keyn* was a seven to six decision and that its result (though not its reasoning) had been reversed by the English parliament, Currie J went on to speak of 'my interpretation of the law of nations,' which was that the operation of legislation was automatically extended by international law to the territorial sea. There seemed no doubt in his mind that international law was part of the common law and that his role was simply to interpret the law. In this latter view he was joined by the two other judges who dealt with the point.

The Supreme Court of Canada had a further opportunity to deal with sovereign immunity in a municipal taxation setting in 1958 when the city of Saint John attempted to tax property leased to Fraser-Brace and other companies who were doing construction work for the American government in the province of New Brunswick.[85] The court unanimously followed the *Foreign Legations* reference and held that there could be no local taxation. The major (and very stimulating) judgment was delivered by Rand J who, as he had done before in the *Armed Forces* reference, was concerned not with whether customary international law is part of our domestic law (that he assumes) but with how to determine the scope and content of international law. Quoting Lord Mansfield in *Heathfield* v *Chilton,* that 'the law of nations will be carried as far in England, as anywhere,' Rand J continued that 'in this country, in the 20th century, in the presence of the United Nations and the multiplicity of impacts with which technical developments have entwined the entire globe, we cannot say anything less.'[86]

Having made it clear that international rules are incorporated into our domestic law, Rand J then stated that the *Foreign Legations* reference had clearly established that sovereign immunity was a customary rule, not on the basis of extraterritoriality – *Chung* had removed that – but on the basis of consent of the host nation as laid down by Marshall CJ in *The Schooner Exchange*.[87] The task then was to decide whether this rule applied to the facts at hand; to do this Rand J went back to his earlier formula in the *Armed Forces* reference: 'In the language of Sir Alexander Cockburn quoted by Lord Atkin in Chung Chi Cheung ... in the absence of precise precedent we must seek the rule which reason and good sense ... would prescribe.' This approach to evolving and reshaping customary rules which are incorporated into domestic law is characteristic of the adoptionist approach.

Locke J, with whom Cartwright J concurred, implicitly adopted the customary rule and canvassed international authorities to see if it applied here; he found that the immunity was based on consent and that therefore it applied to the *Fraser-Brace* facts. Abbott J concurred with Rand J, and Fauteux J agreed with the result without offering reasons. The case then is a very strong one for adoption especially when one reads Rand J's judgment which had Abbott J's concurrence.

The next case that touched on the relationship question was the *Off Shore Mineral Reference* of 1967.[88] Though this case said nothing specifically on the point under discussion, whatever inferences may be drawn from it suggest on first reading that the Supreme Court recognized and preferred the dualist theory as prevailing. The court noted that at common law the realm was restricted to the low-water mark. However, after the Statute of Westminster Canada was regarded in international law as sovereign over a territorial sea three nautical miles wide and, for this reason, Canada could legislate with respect to this area:

> Canada has now full constitutional *capacity* to acquire new areas of territory and new jurisdictional rights which may be available under international law ...

> ... the rights in the territorial sea arise by international law and depend upon recognition by other sovereign states. *Legislative* jurisdiction in relation to the lands in question belongs to Canada which is a sovereign state recognized by international law and thus able to enter into arrangements with other states respecting the rights in the territorial sea.[89]

Although international law regards the coastal state as the sole agent competent to deal with the territorial sea, the coastal state has merely a 'capacity' to 'legislate' with respect to the territorial sea in order that it might implement 'jurisdictional rights' which international law merely make 'available,' which rights international law does not implement of its own force. International law seems to be regarded as permissive only and of insufficient force to extend automatically the application of all general Canadian statutes. This is, of course, a reiteration of the holding, as argued above, in *Keyn*. In that case, it will be remembered, all of the judges felt that international law was incorporated into English law; but they differed on the meaning of the rule. The majority said that the rule was that a state had the capacity to legislate for the territorial sea; the minority said that the rule was that a state's laws automatically extended to the territorial sea. In Canada, on the authority of *Gavin, Cape Breton,* and now a dictum in the *Offshore Minerals* reference, it seems that we accept the majority statement of the rule in *Keyn*.

It was suggested earlier that one important difference between transformation and adoption was that if a rule were transformed it would be fixed until a new version was transformed, whereas, if the rule were adopted, as it changed internationally, it would also change in our domestic law. An interesting opportunity to observe a Canadian court's handling of this issue of a changed or changing customary rule presented itself in the case of *Venne* v *Democratic Republic of the Congo.*[90]

In *Venne* an architect was suing the republic of the Congo for his fees for the design of a pavilion at Expo 67. The defence was sovereign immunity. The architect argued that the property he had designed was not to be used for a public purpose, that the correct customary rule was that of limited, not absolute, immunity, and that, therefore, the latter defence was not available. Owen J observed that the Supreme Court of Canada had applied the doctrine of absolute immunity in the *Dessaulles* case, although it had hinted at a relaxation of the rule in *Flota Maritima.*[91] He then canvassed international authority and, observing a trend towards limited immunity, repudiated the absolute rule, saying that, 'in my opinion it is time our Courts repudiated the theory of absolute sovereign immunity as outdated and inapplicable to today's conditions.'[92]

Brossard J followed similar reasoning, saying that the court should look to 'reason and good sense' and to the 'general assent and reciprocity' criteria formulated by Rand J in *Fraser-Brace*. Taschereau J held in favour of a limited sovereignty rule but without offering extensive reasons. Thus, these three judges clearly felt that international law was such a part of the common law that, as it changed, so too would the common law. The appeal presented the Supreme Court with an excellent opportunity to discuss at least the problem of *stare decisis* as applied to customary international rules in domestic courts, if not the entire relationship point.

In May 1971 the Supreme Court handed down its judgments, which were disappointing to say the least. Mr Justice Ritchie, who delivered the reasons for the seven man majority, quoted the passage from Owen J's judgment cited above and then said that 'the problem so dramatically posed by Mr Justice Owen can only arise in this case if the Judges of the Court of Appeal were right in adopting, without discussion, the finding of the learned trial judge that ... the appellant (in employing respondent) ... was not performing a public act of a sovereign state.'[93] Later, he added that 'it therefore follows in my view that the appellant could not be impleaded in the Courts of this country even if the so-called doctrine of restrictive sovereign immunity had been adopted in our Courts, and it is therefore unnecessary for the determination of this appeal to answer the question posed by Mr Justice Owen and so fully considered by the Court of Appeal ... I think it would be undesirable to add further *obiter dicta* to those which have already been pronounced.'[94]

However, having said that, Ritchie J proceeded to criticize the lower court's use of American cases, pointing out that the so-called 'Tate letter' had created a different situation than that prevailing in Canada. He emphasized that he was not deciding the immunity point and that the *Flota Maritima* decision governed the facts at bar:

> I think the present circumstances are governed by the decision ... in *Flota Maritima Browning de Cuba S.A.* v *Republic of Cuba*, [1962] s.c.r. 598 where it was said of the ships whose seizure gave rise to the issue before the Court:
>> 'All that can be said is that they are available to be used by the Republic of Cuba for any purpose which its government may select and ... are to be regarded as public ships of a foreign state *at least until such time as some decision is made by the sovereign state in question as to the use to which they are to be put.*'
> Similarly in the present case ... [it] was a contract made by a foreign Sovereign in the performance of a public act of State and ... *whatever view be taken of the doctrine of sovereign immunity,* it was a matter in respect of which the Republic of the Congo cannot be impleaded in our courts.[95]

The *Flota Maritima* passage quoted by Ritchie J is the very passage used by the Quebec court to show that doubt had been cast on the absolute doctrine by that case. It is not the purpose of this chapter to explore the intricacies of the law of sovereign immunity and therefore it is best merely to point out that nothing in the judgment of the majority suggests that it would not be open to a Canadian court to revise a customary rule as the need arose. There was no mention of the need for *stare decisis*. The majority overruled the Quebec court on the basis that the trial judge's original finding of fact was incorrect and that, therefore, there was no need to decide the immunity question.

Thus, the reasoning of the lower court stands uncontradicted on the relationship point and has, in fact, been followed by the Quebec Court of Appeal in *Penthouse Studios Incorporated* v *Government of the Sovereign Republic of Venezuela et al.*,[96] a case also arising out of Expo 67. But, this reasoning was not only uncontradicted by the Supreme Court, it received positive support from Laskin J with whom Hall J concurred. Apparently assuming that the rule was part of our law, Laskin J continued: 'There is no doubt that there has been a shift in the positions of the domestic Courts of various countries.' Then he made clear that the courts were free to apply the latest developments in the rule: 'For Canada, at any rate, the [immunity] question is one for this court, subject to any binding Canadian treaty on the subject.' He then agreed with the majority that most American cases were not helpful, but found by consulting English and international authorities that a doctrine of restricted immunity should be applied.[97] We have then, two Quebec Court of Appeal judgments (*Venne* and *Penthouse*) and Laskin J's judgment in the Supreme Court saying that our law should be modified as customary rules change; the other Supreme Court judgments remain neutral, although they are implicitly adoptionist as well.

Conclusions from the Canadian cases

One must be very careful in drawing conclusions about the relationship point from twenty scattered cases, particularly when, apart from *The North* (an Admiralty case) the adoption-transformation distinction was never the central issue and the cases themselves were clustered about only three problems: admiralty law; extraterritoriality; and sovereign and diplomatic immunity. Nevertheless, there does seem to be a pattern in the courts' treatment of the relationship of customary international law to domestic law.

The four early Admiralty cases, *The Grace, The North, The John J. Fallon,* and *Milwaukee,* were all clearly in the English adoptionist tradition. *The North* specifically rejected a defence based on the transformation theory; the *Milwaukee* case supported its adoption with a quotation from *Triquet* v *Bath.* The judgments in *Boutilier, Coffin, Furuzawa,* and *The Kitty D.* were also implicitly adoption. It can be said, quite safely, then, that until the *Foreign Legations* reference, there was no question that in Canada customary rules were automatically adopted into domestic law.

It will be remembered that during the twenty or so years preceding the *Foreign Legations* case, the English courts had begun to issue caveats to the effect that international law was applied domestically only with the consent of the *lex fori*. Yet, after issuing these warnings, the English courts would invariably adopt the customary rule. This is apparently what began to happen in Canada with the *Foreign Legations* reference. All four judges who dealt with the problem on the basis of the customary rule of diplomatic immunity adopted the rule. But Duff CJ quoted the English caveats and used 'accepted and adopted' in a way that was at least ambivalent; yet later he quoted Lord Mansfield. Rinfret J also spoke ambiguously of principles which have 'acquired validity' in our domestic law. Taschereau J, although concurring with the chief justice, seemed to lean more to the adoption theory. Kerwin J simply adopted the rule. Thus, the worst that can be said about this case, from an adoptionist's point of view, is that some of the passages in the judgments were slightly ambivalent in their explication of the adoption theory. None of them articulated the transformation theory.

The *Armed Forces* reference cleared up much of this ambiguity. For here, Duff CJ with Hudson J concurring, spoke in clear adoptionist terms, and Rand and Kerwin JJ impliedly adopted the customary rule. Taschereau J explored the topic fully and, after initial confusion, emerged with a clear adoptionist approach taken directly from the *Chung* case. The holding was against the customary rule, but that was because it conflicted with a fundamental constitutional principle not because of any transformation doctrine.

In the *Dessaulles* case, Taschereau J's comment might be called ambivalent; but, given his clearly adoptionist comments in the previous case and the fact that he did adopt the customary rule, it seems reasonable to call his approach adoptionist. The *Rose* and *Lunan* cases were both cases of implicit adoption. But in *Yin-tso Hsiung,* Smily J of the Ontario High Court echoed Duff CJ's earlier comments about principles which have been 'accepted and adopted by our domestic law.' As was argued earlier, however, this passage could be interpreted as adoptionist and, in fact, the customary rule was adopted.

The *Gavin, Cape Breton,* and *Offshore Minerals* cases were all situations where it was held or suggested that specific legislation was required to extend the operation of domestic laws to the territorial sea. How one views these cases depends, to a large extent, on how one views the *Keyn* decision. In one view, by requiring legislation, the seven to six majority in *Keyn* was transformationist. This would make the three Canadian cases which explicitly or implicitly followed it also transformationist. But, as I have argued several times earlier, the relationship point was not at issue in *Keyn.* All the judments implicitly adopted the customary rule giving the littoral state sovereignty over the territorial sea. So did all the judgments in the three Canadian cases. The question was: Did this sovereignty extend the operation of domestic laws to the territorial seas? The majority in *Keyn* in effect said no, the customary rule does not say that; legislation is required to do that. *Gavin,* the majority in *Cape Breton,* and the dictum in *Offshore Minerals* agreed.[98] The question was, then, what the customary rule said, not whether it was part of our law. Therefore, all of these judgments are adoptionist.

In support of this argument, I would point out that the court in *The North,* in rejecting transformation, obviously did not feel that the *Keyn* case offered a transformationist stumbling block. The judgments in the *Foreign Legations* and *Armed Forces* references did not even mention *Keyn.* And when Currie J dissented in *Cape Breton* it was not on the ground that the *Keyn* case was transformationist, but because the majority in *Keyn* had interpreted the content of the customary rule incorrectly. He agreed with the minority's interpretation.

The three later decisions, *Fraser-Brace, Venne,* and *Penthouse,* were all clearly adoptionist and found no need even to discuss the *Gavin* and *Cape Breton* decisions, which they must have considered also to be adoptionist. However, even if this interpretation of the *Keyn* case is rejected, the most that can be said is that *Keyn* is an anomaly in English law and that a PEI and a split Nova Scotia court followed it and that a dictum in *Offshore Minerals* seems to support it. Against this we have a series of Supreme Court of Canada decisions from *The North* through the two references and the *Dessaulles* case to the *Fraser-Brace* decision all supporting the adoptionist theory.

The conclusion must be, it is submitted, that there is room for the view that the law on the relationship of customary international law to domestic law in Canada is the same as it is in England: customary rules of international law are adopted automatically into our law, amid a few caveats about sovereignty, and then directly applied unless they conflict with statute or some fundamental constitutional principle in which case legislation is required to enforce them. From the standpoint of international law, this is a favourable situation for it ensures maximum support for international rules. From the standpoint of Canadian law, it is probably preferable to transformation with its inherent rigidity and difficulties of application; and it is infinitely better than a situation where one is not certain which of the two theories will be applied. In short, despite some judicial hesitation, Canadian courts are not doing *too* badly in this area.

Judicial notice

Throughout our discussion of both the English and Canadian courts' handling of customary international rules, the concept of judicial notice has played a silent but fundamental role; for without it, the entry of these customary rules into our domestic law would be much more complicated. It would seem worthwhile, then, if we are interested in exploring the fundamental aspects of the interaction between domestic and international law, to examine this concept and its use in this area in some detail.

According to *Black's Law Dictionary,* judicial notice is

> the act by which a court, in conducting a trial, or framing its decision, will, of its own motion, and without the production of evidence, recognize the existence and truth of certain facts, having a bearing on the controversy at bar, which, from their nature, are not properly the subject of testimony, or which are universally regarded as established by common notoriety, *e.g.* the laws of the state, international law, historical events, the constitution and course of nature, main geographical features, etc.

This definition is in general accord with those offered by most commentators and can be used in this discussion after two clarifications.

First a court can be either the judge or the jury or both. Second, the 'certain facts' is a misleading phrase since it implies either that law is a fact (probably, judging by the examples, what was meant) or that law cannot be a subject of judicial notice. Both implications are incorrect. Law can be the subject of judicial notice; and it is not a fact, at least not in the sense that courts use the word fact; that is, as implying the need of strict proof. This may seem to be quibbling, but it highlights an important distinction between the judicial notice of facts and of law.

In regard to facts, the trier of fact, be he judge or jury, may take judicial notice; that is, he may assume notorious and indisputable facts or, as Morgan puts it, 'what everyone knows and uses in the ordinary process of reasoning about everyday affairs.'[99] This type of judicial notice does not concern us directly in our discussion of international and domestic law. What does concern us is judicial notice of law; the judge takes judicial notice of the domestic law and is bound to do so: 'In determining the content or applicability of a rule of domestic law, the judge is unrestricted in his investigation and conclusion.'[100] He may rely on the advice of counsel; or he may investigate on his own; or both. What is important is that it is the judge, as trier of law, who is in control of the law-determining process and it is he who determines how formal or informal the proof of domestic law is to be.

Foreign law, however, is considered in all common law courts to be a matter of fact which must be formally proved as must any fact. It is never indisputable and thus judicial notice cannot be taken of it as it can of certain types of facts. Nor can judicial notice be taken of it as a matter of law. In *Bondholders Securities Corp.* v *Manville et al.* (no 2), Martin JA said that

> In *Bremer* v *Freeman* (1857) 10 Moo. P.C. 306, 14 E.R. 508, the rule was laid down that foreign law is a matter of fact to be ascertained by the evidence of experts but that where the evidence of the experts is unsatisfactory and conflicting an appellate Court, not having had an opportunity of personally examining the witnesses to ascertain the weight due to each of their opinions, will examine for itself the decisions of the foreign Courts and the text writers in order to arrive at a satisfactory conclusion upon the question of foreign law.[101]

Another way of expressing this rule is to say that foreign law is presumed to be the same as domestic law; and if, therefore, one party-litigant wishes to rely on some difference he must plead and prove that difference.[102]

If customary international law were subject to the same requirement for formal proof that foreign law is, grave difficulties would arise. The 'experts' referred to in the *Bremer* case are easy to identify in the case of the law of another state; they are, generally speaking, those who have been licensed to practice law in that state. What would the equivalent be for international law? Those who have argued before the World Court? This would leave out many experts. In addition, international law is a system which relies very heavily on text writers, many of whom are dead or unavailable. Formal proof would require their attendance at court, or else their commentaries would be ignored. Also, much of customary international law derives from matters not susceptible to formal testimony, such as customs, changing world attitudes, and inferences and implications drawn from certain events. These are significant inputs into the process of formulating a customary rule, yet they could only be established in an informal (as with judicial notice of domestic law) rather than a formal (as with foreign law) manner.

Fortunately, it is true, as Lauterpacht pointed out, that 'international law need not be proved in the same way as foreign law or any other fact must be proved – apparently for the reason that it is not foreign law.' He continued: 'Judicial notice is taken of it as of Acts of Parliament or of any branch of the unwritten law, although having regard to the frequent absence of direct authority the range of judicial inquiry is wider and, on occasions, more laborious than in the case of ordinary rules of municipal law.' Lauterpacht could find no English judicial authority bearing directly on the matter, though he did cite two American cases to that effect, one of them holding that 'foreign municipal laws must indeed be proved as facts, but it is not so with the law of nations.'[103] It is a fact, however, that the practice of the English courts has always been as Lauterpacht suggested and the practice of judicially noticing international law is probably so well entrenched that no comment is necessary. This is borne out by the implicit equating of international and domestic law to be found in *Re Piracy Jure Gentium* where the Lord Chancellor said that 'in considering such a question, the Board is permitted [by what? its own rules of practice?] to consult and act upon a wider range of authority than that which it examines when the question for determination is one of municipal law only.'[104]

In Canada, also, the standard practice has been to notice judicially international law, although, as in England, the Canadian courts have not usually seen fit to comment on this point directly. There have, however, been several judicial comments which make clear that international law is judicially noticed in the same way that domestic law is. In *The North,* Davies J, in upholding the lower court finding, said that the hot pursuit doctrine 'being part of the law of nations was properly judicially taken notice of and acted upon.' This statement can only mean that customary rules which are part of international law are to be judicially noticed. In the *Armed Forces* reference, Taschereau J saw his task as, first, 'to seek if there exists' the customary rule in question. The implication in this statement is that it is the judge who must do the seeking, just as he does in domestic law; in fact, in domestic law, the task could be described using exactly the same words: to seek if there exists the domestic rule in question. The conclusion that international law is being treated as part of domestic law in this regard is inescapable.

But it was Rand J, in the *Armed Forces* reference and, later, in *Fraser-Brace,* who most clearly described the proper approach in judicially noticing international law, when, after quoting the *Chung* case, he said:

> From that language, I do not understand that the ordinary methods of judicial determination are not to be resorted to. To insist upon precise precedent in usage would sterilize judicial action toward changing international relations: and in the reduction of terms of an implied arrangement the court must be free to draw upon all sources of international conventions, including 'reason and good sense.'[105]

Just as in domestic law, the judges are free to go to whatever sources are available to them to determine what the appropriate customary rule is. He reiterated this formula in the *Fraser-Brace* case and it was picked up by Brossard J in the *Venne* case.[106] The *Venne* case itself is a classic example of the court accepting, without formal proof, a change in a previously accepted customary international law in the same way as, or even as part of, domestic law. Because it has access, in an informal manner, to the subtle developments and shifts in world opinion, the court is able to review and refresh the law in these areas and to keep it in accord with reason and good sense.

One might also note that the practice of judicially noticing international law is added proof that our courts adopt customary rules and treat them as part of the law of the land. For, if we required a transforming act, as was discussed earlier, the rule which was transformed would be rigid and changes in it could not be judicially noticed. In fact, it would be impossible to take judicial notice of anything other than the act of transformation itself. Customary rules would *per se* not be judicially noticed. However, since our courts clearly and consistently also take judicial notice of customary rules, one must conclude that they are adopting them.

CONVENTIONAL INTERNATIONAL LAW AND THE CANADIAN COURTS[107]

The attitude of English and Canadian courts to conventional international law is generally simpler and more clearly defined than it is with regard to customary international law. It is safe to say that, generally speaking, our courts have adhered to a dualist approach to conventional law and have required legislation to implement treaties which purport to change domestic law in any way. There are exceptions to this broad rule and, in addition, in Canada the matter is further complicated by the federal nature of our constitution. These problems will be best examined after a brief review of the English approach to conventional law.

The English background

The law in England is and has been for some time very clear that the power to make and ratify treaties lies with the crown exclusively.[108] This power to make treaties includes the power to conclude conventions, declarations, protocols, agreements, notes, and other similar arrangements which collectively comprise conventional international law. Many of these treaties have nothing to do with the law of the land and thus never come before a municipal court; such treaties would include guarantees and international neutralization agreements. However, many treaties do affect the law of the land, and if they purport to change it parliament must enact legislation so as to alter the law or empower the crown to enforce the treaty provisions.[109] If parliament refuses to enact enabling legislation for a treaty signed by the crown, then the crown should not ratify the treaty because it will not – cannot – be fulfilled and the crown should not leave it as a nullity. If the crown has ratified the treaty, then it is left with an international obligation and no means of fulfilling it.

The classic statement of this principle was delivered by Sir Robert Phillimore in *The Parlement Belge,* where the crown was opposing a motion for the arrest of a Belgian mailship on the basis of a postal convention agreed to by the king of Belgium with the British government.[110] This convention, which had not been accompanied by legislation, provided that these mailboats should be 'considered and treated [in British ports] as vessels of war and be there entitled to all the honour and privileges which the interests and importance of the service ... demand.' In a judgment which was reversed on other grounds by the Court of Appeal, Sir Robert allowed the warrant of arrest to issue saying:

> If the Crown had power without the authority of Parliament by this treaty to order that *The Parlement Belge* should be entitled to all the privileges of a ship of war, then the warrant which is prayed for against her as a wrong-doer on account of the collision cannot issue, and the right of the subject, but for this order unquestionable, to recover damages for the injuries done to him by her is extinguished. This is a use of the treaty-making prerogative of the Crown which I believe to be without precedent, and in principle contrary to the laws of the constitution. Let me consider to what consequences it leads. If the Crown without the authority of Parliament, may by process of diplomacy shelter a foreigner from the action of one of Her Majesty's subjects who has suffered injury at his hands, I do not see why it might not also give a like privilege of immunity to a number

of foreign merchant vessels or to a number of foreign individuals. The law of this country has indeed incorporated those portions of international law which give immunity and privileges to foreign ships of war and foreign ambassadors; but I do not think that it has therefore given the Crown authority to clothe with this immunity foreign vessels, which are really not vessels of war, or foreign persons, who are not really ambassadors.[111]

This rather long passage has been quoted in full since it not only states the law but also a few of the reasons behind it. The rule is one of constitutional law and is designed to prevent the crown from encroaching on the competence of parliament. In regard to customary international law, the rules are created not as directly by one of the three branches of government but by the consent of civilized states and thus there is less danger of encroaching on the preserve of parliament. The rule then, as outlined in *The Parlement Belge,* is that if the law is changed, legislation is required. Thus, in 1906, Anson stated that 'where a treaty involves a charge upon the people, or a change in the general law of the land, it may be made, but cannot be carried into effect without the consent of Parliament.'[112]

This rule, however, is not completely inflexible. In 1922, the English Court of Appeal in *Fenton Textile Association* v *Krassin* had to consider whether a Russian official agent, appointed under a 1920 Trade Agreement which had no legislative backing, was entitled to immunity from civil process.[113] The court held that he could receive no immunity either under the agreement or apart from it; but, in doing so, the court discussed the agreement as if it were actually binding on them. Atkin LJ could see 'no reason why sovereign states should not come to an agreement as to the rights and duties of their respective envoys, ordinary or extraordinary, and why such agreements should not enlarge or restrict the immunities which otherwise would be due under the well-established usage of nations.'[114]

In addition, in *Engelke* v *Musmann,* the House of Lords affirmed that it is the right of the crown to determine who is and who is not entitled to diplomatic immunity.[115] The appellant was a cipher clerk for the German embassy and was served with a writ. He made a conditional appearance and entered a plea of diplomatic immunity supported by the attorney general, who stated that it was the position of the crown that the appellant was so entitled. The respondent contended that his status could not be determined in this way, but must be established in the ordinary way according to the rules of evidence. Lord Buckmaster found that the principle was established by *Duff Development Co. Ltd.* v *Kelanton Government* that 'on any question of the status of any foreign Power the proper course is that the court should apply to His Majesty's government, and that in any such matter it is bound to act on the information given to them through the proper Department.'[116] He held that this principle authorized the crown to declare diplomatic immunity for the appellant.

While these two cases may appear to weaken the principle that legislation is required to change the law, in fact, they do not. In both cases, the rule of diplomatic immunity was already a part of domestic law and the only thing that the crown was attempting to do was to determine who qualified for the immunity. The crown was not attempting to create a whole new class of persons who enjoy immunity, as it was doing in *The Parlement Belge,* but rather was attempting to determine whether or not marginal persons (a Russian official agent in *Fenton*; a cipher clerk in

Engelke) came within an already established category. Both cases in fact come within the act of state doctrine. The crown's action in *Engelke* was clearly held to be permissible as an act of state; in *Fenton* this is not quite so clear although the case could certainly be read in that way. In any case, the comments in *Fenton* were *obiter* and they were never picked up in any subsequent case.

A real exception to the rule does exist, however, in the case of treaties affecting belligerent rights, since the waging of war is considered to be a royal prerogative. Thus, conventions regarding the rules of war, such as the Declaration of Paris of 1856 or the Hague Conventions, even though they affect domestic law, need no legislation.[117] For example, in *Porter* v *Freudenberg,* article 23(h) of chapter 1 of section 2 of the Hague Regulations respecting the Laws and Customs of War on Land was considered in relation to an old common law rule. The Hague Convention was held to have nothing to do with the old rule, but the point of interest is that, throughout the judgment, it was clearly assumed by the full Court of Appeal that the convention was, in fact, binding in English courts.[118]

In addition to treaties affecting the law of the land, that is to say, private rights, there are several other types of treaties which require legislation. Treaties which for their implementation require the accrual of new powers by the crown, as in the case of extradition treaties, require legislation.[119] Also, as was suggested by the passage quoted from *Anson,* any treaty which creates a direct or contingent financial obligation for England requires legislation. Both of these rules are directly explainable by British constitutional law and its requisite separation of powers. There is, finally, as McNair suggests, a practice, probably amounting to a binding constitutional convention, whereby treaties involving a cession of British territory are submitted for the approval of parliament by statute.[120] The crown, then, might well be left, as exceptions, with little more than the power to declare peace and war (though even the peace treaties of World War II were legislated) and to conclude alliances in addition to the rules of war.

The relationship between conventional international law and domestic law has come before the English courts in two recent cases. In the *Republic of Italy* v *Hambros Bank,* the Italian government was attempting to prevent Hambros Bank from dealing with certain moneys transferred to it by the Custodian of Enemy Property.[121] The basis of the action was a Financial Agreement of 1947 between England and Italy which had no implementing legislation. The Italian government argued that the Treaty of Peace (Italy), which had been implemented and thus was part of the law of the land, included this Financial Agreement implicitly. A clause in the treaty envisaged the possibility of such agreements existing, but the court found this to be permissive, not obligatory. Vaisey J went on: 'Secondly, if the Financial Agreement was intended to be referred to why was it not expressly mentioned? Thirdly, is there any authority or principle which enables me to hold that a contract such as the Financial Agreement made between high contracting parties and having all the appearance of a treaty can be imported into and incorporated in our domestic law by a mere vague allusion, when there would have been no difficulty at all in doing so expressly and when an obvious opportunity for doing so presented itself?'[122] Finding none, he held that the agreement was unenforceable for want of implementing legislation as required by the constitutional principles discussed earlier.

In *Cheney v Conn (Inspector of Taxes),* Cheney refused to pay his income taxes on the ground that the tax money was going to be used for an illegal purpose, namely, the manufacture of nuclear weapons in the United Kingdom.[123] He argued that such manufacture was illegal because it violated customary international law (not identified specifically) which was the law of the land, and conventional international law, namely, the Geneva Conventions, which were incorporated into English law by the Geneva Conventions Act of 1957. He rested his case primarily on an alleged conflict between the Geneva Conventions Act, 1957, and the Finance Act, 1967, under which he was being taxed.

Ungoed-Thomas J quickly disposed of the customary international law argument saying that 'International law is the law of the land, but it yields to statute.'[124] Thus, even if there were a conflict, the Finance Act would take precedence over any customary rule. Turning to the conventional law argument, Ungoed-Thomas J continued: 'Secondly, conventions which are ratified by an Act of Parliament are part of the law of the land. And, thirdly, conventions which are ratified but not by an act of Parliament, which thereby gives them statutory force, cannot prevail against a statute in unambiguous terms.'[125] He then quoted *Oppenheim's International Law* (8th ed, 1955), at 40, to the effect that 'such treaties as affect private rights and, generally, as require for their enforcement by English courts a modification of common law or of a statute must receive parliamentary assent through an enabling Act of Parliament.' Thus even if the manufacture of nuclear weapons were against the Geneva Conventions, the particular convention that was violated would have to be ratified by parliament. Ungoed-Thomas J held that the Geneva Conventions Act, 1957, did not ratify anything that would apply to nuclear weapons; therefore Cheney was liable for his taxes. It can be seen, then, that the law of England is, as was suggested earlier, clear and settled in relation to conventional international law.

Conventional international law and the Canadian courts

The law on treaties was definitively established for Canada and, indeed, for the rest of the British Commonwealth in *Attorney-General for Canada v Attorney-General for Ontario (Labour Conventions)* where Lord Atkin, in a classic passage said:

> It will be essential to keep in mind the distinction between (1) the formation, and (2) the performance, of the obligations constituted by a treaty, using that word as comprising any agreement between two or more sovereign States. Within the British Empire there is a well-established rule that the making of a treaty is an executive act, while the performance of its obligations, if they entail alteration of the existing domestic law, requires legislative action. Unlike some other countries, the stipulations of a treaty duly ratified do not within the Empire, by virtue of the treaty alone, have the force of law. If the national executive, the government of the day, decide to incur the obligations of a treaty which involve alteration of law they have to run the risk of obtaining the assent of Parliament to the necessary statute or statutes. To make themselves as secure as possible they will often in such cases before final ratification seek to obtain from Parliament an expression of approval. But it has never been suggested, and it is not the law, that such an expression of approval operates as law, or that in law it precludes the assenting Parlia-

ment, or any subsequent Parliament, from refusing to give its sanction to any legislative proposals that may subsequently be brought before it. Parliament, no doubt, as the Chief Justice points out, has constitutional control over the executive: but it cannot be disputed that the creation of the obligations undertaken in treaties and the assent to their form and quality are the function of the executive alone. Once they are created, while they bind the State as against the other contracting parties, Parliament may refuse to perform them and so leave the State in default. In a unitary State whose Legislature possesses unlimited powers the problem is simple. Parliament will either fulfil or not treaty obligations imposed upon the State by its executive. The nature of the obligations does not affect the complete authority of the Legislature to make them law if it so chooses.[126]

The question at issue in that case was whether the federal government could legislate on matters concerning labour relations, an area clearly within provincial competence, in pursuance of certain labour conventions it had signed. Having established the need of parliamentary implementation, Lord Atkin went on to hold that parliament did not have the competence to implement these conventions and that the legislation in question was invalid and the conventions internally ineffective. The rule thus stated is the law of Canada and has been consistently applied in a variety of stitutions.[127] Strictly speaking, of course, Lord Atkin's statement was *obiter,* since his actual holding was that the legislation was *ultra vires* because it was outside federal competence and the mere signing of a treaty could not increase that competence. However, if some dicta are stronger than others, then this one must rank among the strongest, for it is very close to being a fundamental step in Lord Atkin's reasoning. The Supreme Court of Canada five years earlier had held that 'in the absence of affirming legislation this provision of the treaty cannot be enforced by any of our courts whose authority is derived from municipal law,' and cited *Walker* v *Bird* as authority. This case – the *Arrow River* case – arose when the Ontario government authorized a company to charge tolls for lumber passing along certain rivers including the Pigeon River which was an international boundary river.[128] To charge such tolls would have been in violation of the Webster-Ashburton Treaty signed by Britain for Canada in 1842, under which such international waterways were to remain free and open to citizens of both countries. The federal government argued that the provincial legislation was *ultra vires* since it conflicted with the treaty; the provincial government answered that the treaty had not been implemented by legislation. In the Court of Appeal, Riddell J, speaking for a unanimous court, held that the county court judge should be restrained from authorizing tolls on the Pigeon River, as was required by the act, since the statute did not cover rivers not wholly in Ontario. To reach the conclusion that the Pigeon River was beyond the reach of the provincial statute, Riddell J employed a rule of statutory construction in relation to conventional international law which was not challenged by the Supreme Court, where the decision was reversed:

> The real argument is that the Treaty was made with Her Majesty, and is binding in honour upon Her Majesty's successor, his present Majesty, as it was upon his predecessor. Consequently, the Sovereign will not consider enacting anything that will conflict with his plain duty, unless the language employed in the statute is perfectly clear and explicit, admitting of no other interpretation ... the King cannot be thought of as violating his

agreement with the other contracting power; and if the [Ontario] legislation can fairly be read in such a way as to reject any imputation of breaking faith, it must be so read.[129]

Thus the Ontario statute was read in such a way as to avoid violating the treaty.

At the Supreme Court, Lamont J, with whom Cannon J concurred, found that the Ontario statute was clearly repugnant to the treaty but was within provincial competence under section 92 of the BNA Act. The act 'must therefore be held to be valid unless the existence of the treaty of itself imposes a limitation upon the provincial legislative power. In my opinion the treaty alone cannot be considered as having that effect ... the Crown cannot alter the existing law by entering into a contract with a foreign power.'[130] Thus the provincial act was valid and the toll could be assessed. Smith J, with whom Rinfret J concurred, also felt that the provincial act was intended to cover the Pigeon River, but he construed the treaty so as to avoid a conflict with the statute. Chief Justice Anglin agreed with both Lamont and Smith JJ but leaned towards the interpretation approach. In the result, the court unanimously allowed the tolls. From this case, it can be seen, first, that the English rule in regard to conventional international law applies in Canada; and, second, that the courts will strain very hard to resolve any conflict between a statute and a treaty.

The *Arrow River* case also touched on the interesting question of the ability of a province to legislate in violation of international law. Vanek has argued that neither the federal nor the provincial legislatures may so legislate; and La Forest has argued that the provinces are under that restriction.[131] It is submitted, with respect, that both these positions are incorrect, at least under present law. First, the dominion and provincial governments enjoy equal and plenary powers within their individual spheres of competence; thus if one may violate international law, so may the other.[132] Second, it is clear law that if the English parliament legislates in unambiguous terms contrary to customary international law that legislation is valid.[133] Third, there is no reason to believe that the English rule of the supremacy of parliament does not apply in Canada. Indeed the passage from *Chung* which sets out the English rule has been cited with approval several times by the Supreme Court of Canada.[134] In addition, this rule was articulated in *Rex* v *Meikleham*.[135] Fourth, the English parliament can override treaty obligations with clear legislation.[136] Fifth, the supremacy of Canadian federal statutes over treaties, that is, conventional international law, was recognized in the *Swait* case where Hyde J of the Quebec Court of Queen's Bench, in rejecting an argument that the Trustee Act violated Canada's international obligations, said that 'whatever may have been the case before the Statute of Westminster, 1931–32 (U.K.)., c 4, the laws of Canada are supreme within the framework of the B.N.A. Act and where Parliament has clearly legislated on some matter within its jurisdiction, the validity of that legislation cannot be affected by external treaties.'[137] Sixth, the only two judges on the Supreme Court who decided the point held that the province of Ontario could legislate in violation of the Webster-Ashburton Treaty in the *Arrow River* case itself.[138] Thus, it follows that both federal and provincial legislatures, in exercise of their supremacy, may legislate in violation of any form of international law.

The relationship of treaties to Canadian law came up again in *Bitter* v *Secretary of State of Canada,* where the Exchequer Court of Canada had to determine the effect of the Treaty of Peace (Germany) Order, 1920, in relation to the disposition of enemy (as defined by the order) property.[139] In discussing the treaty, Thorson J said that

> the Treaty of Peace itself contains provisions relating to the *situs* of certain kinds of property, which have a bearing on the question before the Court. What legal effect should be given to the terms of a Treaty of Peace is an interesting question. In *Secretary of State of Canada* v *Alien Property Custodian for United States,* [1931] 1 D.L.R. 890, at 902, S.C.R. 169, at 198, Duff J made the following striking statement: 'The treaty it is to be observed, being a Treaty of Peace, had the effect of law quite independently of legislation.' With the utmost respect, I venture the opinion that there is no authority for this statement and that it cannot be accepted without important qualifications. While a Treaty of Peace can be made only by the Crown, it still remains an Act of the Crown. While it is binding upon the subjects of the Crown without legislation in the sense that it terminates the war, it has never, so far as I have been able to ascertain, been decided or admitted that the Crown could by its own act in agreeing to the terms of a treaty alter the law of the land or affect the private rights of individuals.[140]

In *Bitter,* the Treaty of Peace (Germany) Order, 1920, was passed pursuant to the Treaties of Peace Act, 1919, and thus there was no question as to its validity. The question suggested by Duff J's comment was whether the provisions of the Treaty of Peace enjoyed a validity independent of the order. Thorson J, following the classical rule in regard to treaties which affect domestic law, said that they did not, save, as is always the case, to stop the hostilities. In the *Alien Custodian* case, Duff J was dealing with the same order which, as was stated, was a valid order under the Treaties of Peace Act. Since he decided the case by reliance on the legislatively supported Consolidated Orders, Duff J's comment, that 'the treaty it is to be observed, being a Treaty of Peace, had the effect of law quite independently of legislation,' was *obiter* and in no way fundamental to the result. It is accurate only to the extent that the crown is exercising its prerogative in regard to peace and war; if the treaty purports to affect private rights or to charge the people it must have legislation.

In criticizing the dictum of Duff J, Thorson J might have included the dictum of Angers J in *Ritcher* v *The King*, a case on the same point as the two previous cases and decided one year before *Bitter*.[141] There, Angers J said that 'in passing I will note that an Act was not necessary to bring into force the Treaty of Peace between the Allied and the Associated Powers and Germany in question in this case; a treaty of peace is law in itself, independently of any legislation on the subject: *Secretary of State of Canada* v *Alien Property Custodian for the United States,* [1931] 1 D.L.R. 890 at 913, S.C.R. 169 at 198.'[142] He then decided the case on the basis of the valid order in council.

To summarize: There have been three statements on the topic of peace treaties, all of them *obiter*. It is submitted that Thorson J in *Bitter* correctly stated the law; and that Duff J in *Custodian of Alien Property* (the other judges did not discuss the point) and Angers J in *Ritcher* were correct only in regard to the cessation of hostilities and not with regard to affecting private rights, because the latter are outside the prerogative of the crown.[143] Since these cases were decided all peace treaties have been legislated and thus the point may well be purely academic.[144]

In 1956 the Supreme Court of Canada considered the Jay Treaty, 1794, in connection with a claim by an Indian that he was exempted from customs taxes by that treaty. The court, in *Francis* v *The Queen,* rejected this contention on the ground that the treaty had no implementing legislation and had, in any case, outlived its usefulness.[145] In doing so, Chief Justice Kerwin, with whom Fauteux and Taschereau JJ agreed, stated that 'it is clear that in Canada such rights and privileges as are here advanced by subjects of a contracting party to a treaty are enforceable by the Courts only where the treaty has been implemented or sanctioned by legislation. This is an adaptation of the language of Lamont J speaking for himself and Cannon J in *Re Arrow River and Tributaries Slide & Boom Co.,* [1932] 2 D.L.R. 250, S.C.R. 495, 39 C.R.C. 161, and is justified by a continuous line of authority in England.'[146]

Rand J delivered a classical outline of the rule in regard to treaties and, incidentally, touched on the peace treaty controversy when he said that

> speaking generally, provisions that give recognition to incidents of sovereignty or deal with matters in exclusively sovereign aspects, do not require legislative confirmation: for example, the recognition of independence, the establishment of boundaries and, in a treaty of peace, the transfer of sovereignty over property, are deemed executed and the treaty becomes the muniment or evidence of the political or proprietary title ... Except as to diplomatic status and certain immunities and to belligerent rights, treaty provisions affecting matters within the scope of municipal law, that is, which purport to change existing law or restrict the future action of the Legislature, including, under our Constitution, the participation of the Crown, and in the absence of a constitutional provision declaring the treaty itself to be law of the state, as in the United States, must be supplemented by statutory action.[147]

This statement accords with the English rule and the rules stated in *Arrow River, Labour Conventions,* and *Bitter.* It also, I submit, supports the view taken in *Bitter* with regard to peace treaties; except to terminate hostilities or cede property (already a crown prerogative, though McNair suggests that legislation is becoming a tradition) peace treaties require legislation.

The rule in *Francis* was followed by the Manitoba Court of Queen's Bench in *R* v *Canada Labour Relations Board, Ex parte Federal Electric Corporation,* where it was held that an international agreement between Canada and the United States in regard to defence contract wages could have no effect without legislation.[148] Smith J stated that, 'in general, a Treaty is a contract between States ... a treaty binding the government does not, *ipso facto,* become part of our law and enforceable in the courts.'[149] In the *Offshore Minerals* reference, where the Supreme Court of Canada was faced with competing claims to the territorial seas between British Columbia and Canada, there was a unanimous ruling in favour of Canada for several reasons, including the fact that international law looked to Canada for responsibility for said seas. In support of this reasoning, the court stated that

> Canada has now full constitutional capacity to acquire new areas of territory and new jurisdictional rights which may be available under international law. The territorial sea now claimed by Canada was defined in the Territorial Sea and Fishing Zones Act of 1964

referred to in Question 1 of the Order-in-Council. The effect of that Act, coupled with the Geneva Convention of 1958, is that Canada is recognized in international law as having sovereignty over a territorial sea three nautical miles wide. It is part of the territory of Canada.[150]

It is clear from this reasoning that the SupremeCourt was assuming the need of legislation to implement the Geneva Convention.

The rule that conventional international law requires legislation to be implemented in our domestic law would appear, then, to be as well established in Canadian law as in English law. But, like any rule, it is not so absolute as to be without its exceptions or, at least, marginal cases. These have arisen out of a number of prisoner-of-war cases and restrictive covenant cases. In *Rex* v. *Krebs,* Galligan PM of the County Court of Renfrew was asked to decide whether a POW who escaped and broke into a dwelling-house for provisions to facilitate his escape was guilty of a crime.[151] Unable to find any precedent, save an English dictum favourable to his ultimate decision, Galligan PM reasoned that the POW owed no allegiance to Canada and thus had no need to obey our laws. This decision was not followed, however, in three subsequent decisions: *Rex* v *Brosig*; *Rex* v *Shindler*; and *Rex* v *Kaehler.*[152] In *Shindler,* an Alberta court, on similar facts, declined to follow *Krebs* on the ground that the police magistrate in *Krebs* had failed to consider the Geneva Convention of 1929 relative to the treatment of prisoners which, by its wording, clearly envisaged criminal prosecution of POWs in some situations. For example, article 53 read in part: 'Prisoners qualified for repatriation against whom any prosecution for a criminal offence has been brought may be excluded from repatriation until the termination of the proceedings.' There were other articles quoted of similar import. The police magistrate in *Shindler* made it clear that but for the Geneva Convention he would have followed *Krebs.* Yet at this time there was no legislation implementing the Geneva Convention of 1929. How, then, did it come to have the force of law? Identical reasoning was applied by a unanimous Court of Appeal of Ontario in *Brosig*; and in *Kaehler* the *Brosig* decision was cited and the chief justice of Alberta said: 'I think however, we are entitled to accept the decision as authoritative for the proposition that the Geneva Convention of 1929 is a part of the law of Canada, and that under it a prisoner of war has no immunity from the consequences of his committing an act which if committed by a member of one of our own armed forces would be punishable as a crime.'[153] The judgment here was also supported by reference to an order in council passed pursuant to the War Measures Act which provided in regulation 7 that POWs be treated as the members of Canada's forces would be. It was never suggested that this order in council implemented the Geneva Convention.

These three cases may be explained in three ways. First, it could be argued that the convention was used merely as a source of common law doctrine. Common law defences are available in criminal actions in Canada and the judges in being presented with a novel situation had to look where they could for principles to guide their formulation of the rule. Just as the judges look to conventions for aid in statute interpretation, so did they look to the Geneva Convention in these cases as an aid in the formation of a common law rule in regard to the immunity of POWs. This is plausible, but it does not account for the statement in *Kaehler* to the effect that the convention is 'part of the law of Canada,' something much more substantial than a source of common law. Of course, this statement might mean simply that, having been used as a source, this convention is now an intrinsic part of the common law; or the passage might simply be an incorrect statement of the law. However, the more likely conclusion is that this is not the best way to explain these three cases.

A second possibility is to call these cases an exception to the general rule and then to try to fit them into some new category. One might say that, although, generally, treaties require legislation to implement them, in the case of rights of prisoners of war there is an exception and treaties on these questions are regarded as part of our law upon being ratified. However, it is seldom a satisfactory solution to a problem to create new exceptions and this is especially so where, as here, there is no plausible rationale for the exception other than the fact that the cases went this way.

The third and, it is submitted, most satisfactory approach to these cases is to treat them as situations falling within the crown's prerogative in regard to peace and war. It is clear that in regard to the waging of war, the crown may tie its hands as to how it will conduct its operations.[154] The holding of prisoners of war, the exchanging of same, and the punishment of those prisoners of war who violate their rules of detention would also come under this war prerogative. In addition, the crown has a discretion in regard to prosecutions and thus it would exercise this discretion in favour of prosecuting or not prosecuting prisoners of war as it saw fit. Thus, when the crown ratified the Geneva Convention of 1929, it obligated itself to exercise its prerogative in this regard in accordance with the convention, and no implementing legislation was necessary. It would be in this sense that the convention was the law of Canada. Of course, the crown would be tying its hands internationally only; the domestic courts would not be able to comment on the exercise of the crown's prerogatives and the correspondence of this with the crown's international obligations.

Treaties and public policy

The restrictive covenant cases began with *Re Drummond Wren* where both vendor and potential purchaser of a parcel of real estate in Toronto attempted to have a restrictive covenant against selling the property to Jews struck down as contrary to public policy.[155] Mackay J found the matter to be one of 'first impression, because a search of the case law of Great Britain and Canada does not reveal any reported decision which would be of direct assistance in this proceeding.' Later, he continued, 'it is a well recognized rule that courts may look at various Dominion and Provincial Acts and public law as an aid in determining principles relative to public policy ... First and of profound significance is the recent San Francisco Charter, to which Canada was a signatory, and which the Dominion Parliament has now ratified.'[156] He then quoted certain sections of the Charter on Human Rights and Fundamental Freedoms. Next came 'the Atlantic Charter, to which Canada has subscribed,' with similar provisions. From these and certain statutes Mackay J concluded that to allow such a covenant to stand would be against Canada's public policy.

In *Re Noble and Wolf,* Schroeder J dealt with a similar fact situation except that, unlike the situation in *Drummond Wren,* counsel had argued the other side of the case.[157] After noting the judgment in *Drummond Wren,* he continued: 'The case cited [*Wren*] is a decision of a Court of co-ordinate jurisdiction and I am not necessarily bound by it ... I ... regret that I find myself in disagreement with it.' Reviewing Mackay J's list of authorities, Schroeder J continued: 'To these may be added art. 17 of the Bill of Human Rights.' But he doubted, on the basis of the *Labour Conventions* case, that the dominion parliament had the power to carry out these international obligations. He concluded that 'whether legislative jurisdiction to give effect to treaty obligations belongs to the Dominion Parliament or to the Provincial Legislatures, my attention has not been drawn to any of the obligations existing or which may be said to exist under the United Nations Charter. If the obligations arising under the Charter of the United Nations are in conflict with the internal law of a signatory power, it has evidently not yet been determined by agreement of the nations concerned that the internal laws should be overborne by the provisions of the Charter.'[158] He pointed out that a clause to this effect had been rejected at the San Francisco conference and he concluded that there was no public policy on the matter and that therefore the covenant could stand.

A few preliminary comments on these two cases are in order. First, Mackay J referred in *Drummond Wren* to parliament having 'ratified' the San Francisco charter. Had this, in fact, been done the charter would have had the force of law according to the rule discussed earlier. However, no legislation had been enacted at that time in regard to the San Francisco charter and thus it is difficult to know to what Mackay J was referring. In any case, he based his public policy on both the San Francisco and Atlantic charters, neither of which were implemented by legislation. Schroeder J rejected them on this basis in *Noble,* but then he implied that Canada might, by international agreement, arrange to have the terms of that agreement 'overbear' the internal law. This is contrary to the *Arrow River* rule and also contrary to Schroeder's own reasoning in the *Noble* case; he must surely have meant that Canada could do this by an agreement which was implemented by legislation.

The two cases are of co-ordinate jurisdiction and thus they stand side by side. In *Drummond Wren,* Mackay J seemed to be arguing that, since Canada had bound herself internationally to recognize certain rights, these rights were then part of Canada's public policy and were to be used as such as a source of common law doctrine. He, at no time, argued that the charters were actually part of domestic law in the way that the courts in the POW cases did. Thus, he was using conventional international law as an aid in the formulation of internal public policy.

Schroeder J, on the other hand, after concluding that these charters were not part of the domestic law of Canada, rejected their use even as a source of public policy. In fact he rejected the entire idea of basing common law doctrines of public policy on any such esoteric sources as public statutes and international obligations. It is submitted, with respect, that this is a far too narrow view of the legal process. It is true that public policy can be an 'unruly horse,' but this danger arises only when the judges are attempting to pluck public policy 'out of the air,' so to speak; that is, when they accept no guidance – or too little guidance – in their search for public policy other than their own intuition. This is certainly not the case in regard to public statutes: if parliament passes an act to prevent rats from running wild on the waterfront, a judge is not riding an unruly horse if he concludes that Canadian public policy favours the prevention of rats running wild on the waterfront; he would even be safe in surmising that public policy favoured preventing rats running wild on our streets or in our houses; he could probably conclude that our public policy was to reduce the incidence of rats running wild anywhere. Could he not draw the same conclusions if Canada signed an international convention on the control of rats? Leaving the constitutional question of the distribution of powers aside for the moment, is there any real difference between international conventions which have been signed and ratified, and statutes, as sources of public policy? And can public policy which may be ascertained so easily and accurately from these sources safely be ignored when a judge is formulating common law doctrine? It is submitted that the answer to the last question should be in the negative and that, therefore, the *Drummond Wren* decision was correct and *Noble and Wolf* wrong.

The *Wren* approach was adopted in *Brown* v *Beleggings-Societeit N.V.* where a confiscation of the shares of a German company by the Netherlands for war reparations was challenged on the grounds that the Dutch legislation was confiscatory and was, therefore, not enforceable by Canadian courts as against public policy.[159] McRuer CJHC found the legislation not to be against Canadian public policy on the grounds that Canada had similar legislation and also on the grounds that the Dutch legislation was in accordance with treaties and conventions – the Bretton Woods, Paris, and Brussels agreements – to which both Canada and the Netherlands were signatories.

It is true that the Bretton Woods Agreement was implemented by legislation,[160] but neither the Paris nor Brussels agreements were and, more importantly, it was on the basis of the ratified treaties themselves, not legislation, that McRuer CJHC based his findings of public policy. He made clear the approach he was using when he said that 'this agreement [Brussels] to which both Canada and the Netherlands were parties, was referred to in argument as evidence of a declared public policy.'[161] After quoting from the Brussels Agreement, he continued: 'These articles [of the agreements] all lead to the conclusion that it is the policy of Canada declared by solemn treaty to co-operate with the Netherlands not only in resolving conflicting claims between Canada and the Netherlands respecting German property for reparations no matter how it may be cloaked or disguised. In my view it would require very strong authority to hold that it is contrary to the public policy to give effect to a claim that is entirely consistent with the objects of this treaty.'[162]

If conventional international law can be used as a source of public policy on which to base common law doctrine, could it be used to create a new right of action?[163] In the *Wren* case there already was a rule that covenants against public policy could be struck down; the treaty merely aided in the determination of public policy on that point. Similarly, in *Brown* there was a rule already that foreign statutes would be enforced if they were not penal or revenue laws and were not against public policy; the treaty helped to determine whether the statute in question was against public policy. But new rights of action come from more than just public policy; they stem usually from an observation of certain legislative facts which lead the judge to conclude that a right of action (or a defence) which was not valid in the past has now become so because of changed and changing circumstances including public policy but also matters such as public social attitudes, changes in business operating methods, and technological developments.[164] Could a treaty ratified by Canada but not implemented by legislation lead a judge to such reasoning? The answer is far from clear, although the *Wren* case could be viewed as the creation of a new defence to a restrictive covenant violation.

Even if conventional international law can be used to found common law causes of action, its use would be restricted, since in many important areas, such as human rights and fundamental freedoms, the common law is ill-equipped to provide any remedy. What is required in these cases is a statutory right of action and a statutory remedy. Could a ratified treaty provide such a statutory right of action or remedy?[165]

This is a large step from common law doctrine and the answer seems clear that, if there is no implementing legislation, the court will not recognize a cause of action founded on an alleged treaty violation.[166] Yet, one may ask if this is the correct rule. It is true that, to allow the crown, by signing a treaty, to change the law of Canada would be unconstitutional. But is there not some meaning to Canada's having signed and ratified a treaty? Does not the crown have an obligation, after ratifying a treaty, at least to attempt to implement that treaty by legislation? To use an example, Canada, in October 1970, ratified the International Convention on the Elimination of All Forms of Racial Discrimination. No action has been taken to implement this convention with legislation, the unofficial explanation being that the standards against discrimination are, in each of the provinces, high enough to fulfil the convention. This may be true, but can this be what the other signatories anticipated when they spent months working out the exact wording of the articles of this convention? Surely the actual document has some significance!

What if the judgment on the state of the law in each province is inaccurate, with the result that it is possible for someone to be discriminated against in violation of the convention but not in violation of provincial law? The complainant could not cite the convention; he could not bring an action against the crown for not having protected him as it had promised other nations it would; and, finally, he could not even protect himself for the future by bringing mandamus against the crown to force it to attempt to implement the convention. The convention would indeed be meaningless.

The solution to this problem does not immediately present itself; however, it may be easier to deal with the problem if it is broken down into two parts. First, there is the separation of powers problem between the crown and parliament; this has been discussed as the basis of the rule requiring legislation. Second, there is the problem of the distribution of powers between the dominion and the provinces; this has been discussed in a previous chapter and will not be dealt with here, except to re-emphasize that it is Canada as a unit and not the provinces which is responsible to the international community. There is, in addition, the argument that if customary international law is permitted to override provincial jurisdictions, why should not conventional international law, so long as the dominion is restrained by the 'colourability' doctrine? This argument is partially answered by the proposition that customary law is created by forces outside Canada while conventional law is the creation of the dominion itself, but the argument is not as cogent as it was in the case of the crown versus the legislature. Besides, the dominion government can affect customary international law at least in a negative way by refusing to recognize a certain rule.

We must ask again, what domestic status should be accorded a signed and ratified treaty which has no legislative implementation? At present, according to the *Arrow River* rule, it has none if it affects a change in domestic law. The reasons for this were seen to be the problems pertaining to the separation and division of powers. It is submitted that, on the basis of the foregoing discussion, the division of powers difficulty should and could be done away with either by an overruling of the *Labour Conventions* case or by dominion-provincial negotiation. As to the separation of powers between the crown and parliament, it is submitted that this could be preserved while still enabling (and forcing) Canada to fulfil her international obligations by according ratified but unimplemented treaties a status superior to common law but inferior to statute. Thus, if a ratified treaty changed domestic law which was not covered by statute, the treaty would be effective even without legislation. If the treaty changed domestic law governed by statute, the statute and the treaty would be interpreted to avoid conflict, but if that were impossible then the statute would rule until and unless the treaty were implemented by legislation. Thus parliament would still have the final word, yet Canada's solemn international commitments would have some meaning. This change, as will be discussed later, would require or, at least, would be best accomplished by a constitutional amendment.

The United Nations Act, 1947

Before attempting to draw any conclusions from this examination of the relationship of conventional international law to domestic law in Canada, it is worthwhile to explore briefly the United Nations Act of 1947 which, although it does in one sense form a distinct area of impact between international and domestic law, is in a very real way a part of conventional international law.[167] Although all treaties represent a surrender of sovereignty in the sense that the state binds itself to do or not to do certain acts, the United Nations Act passed to implement article 41 of the United Nations Charter permits the governor general in council to pass orders and regulations to enforce or carry out measures determined not by Canada but by the Security Council of the United Nations. There is no actual surrender of sovereignty since the act is permissive rather than mandatory, but it does represent the implementation by parliament of a treaty the complete terms of which are not and could not be determined at the time of implementation since the Security Council can pass new resolutions at any time.

With regard to the two problems discussed above – separation and division of powers – the charter and the act present no difficulty in regard to the separation of powers. The crown signed and ratified the treaty, and parliament implemented its terms including the giving to the governor in council the power to make orders to apply future measures which the Security Council may decide are necessary. This is clearly within parliament's power. But, in regard to the division of powers, there may well be a question as to the competence of parliament not so much to pass the act itself, but to stand behind certain orders in council which clearly cover areas given exclusively to the provinces. This determination will require a closer look at the charter and the act.

Article 41 of the charter as printed in a schedule to the United Nations Act reads as follows:

The Security Council may decide what measures not involving the use of armed force are to be employed to give effect to its decisions and it may call upon the Members of the United Nations to apply such measures. These may include complete or partial interruption of economic relations and of rail, sea, air, postal, telegraphic, radio or other means of communication and the severance of diplomatic relations.

In 1947 parliament passed the United Nations Act, section 2 of which states that

When in pursuance of Article 41 of the Charter of the United Nations, set out in the schedule, the Security Council of the United Nations decides upon a measure to be employed to give effect to any of its decisions and calls upon Canada to apply such measure, the Governor-in-Council may make such orders and regulations as appear to him to be necessary or expedient for enabling such measure to be effectively applied.

The remainder of the statute provides for penalties ranging from fines up to $5000 to imprisonment of up to five years, or both, for violations of such an order (s 3) and for the tabling before parliament of any orders made pursuant to the act, parliament having forty days in which to annul the order.

This act was not used for the twenty years prior to February 1967; trade with communist countries had been restricted by orders issued under the Export and Import Permits Act.[168] When the situation in Rhodesia began to deteriorate, that country was added to the list of countries for which an export permit was required by the Export and Import Permits Act.[169] Later these permits were partially suspended.[170] On 16 December 1966 the Security Council decided that the situation in Rhodesia constituted a threat to international peace and security, that certain measures were to be taken to maintain international peace and security, and that all members of the United Nations were to apply such measures.[171] Two months later the governor in council enacted the United Nations Rhodesia Regulations pursuant not to the Export and Import Permits Act but the United Nations Act. These regulations prohibit the export and import and the shipment, transshipment, or diversion of any goods specified in the schedules attached, to or from Rhodesia respectively or the payment for same under penalty of fine, imprisonment or both. These regulations remain in effect.[172]

It is important to note at the beginning that there is no question as to the constitutionality of the United Nations Act itself; the act does not do or say anything save to empower the governor in council to issue regulations in certain circumstances and to provide for the enforcement of these regulations. But, until the regulations are made, the question of constitutionality cannot be decided and, even after they are made, it is not the act which would be examined, but the individual regulations made under it. Thus it is the Rhodesia regulations which must be considered.

The constitutional validity of these regulations might be attacked in two different situations. If an exporter or an importer were prosecuted for violating the regulations, he could raise as a defence that the regulations were *ultra vires* the dominion parliament. Alternatively, if a broker lost money on a contract cancelled by a Canadian exporter or importer who pleaded frustration due to the Rhodesia regulations, the broker could attack this defence on the basis that the regulations were *ultra vires* the dominion. The constitutional validity of the Rhodesia regulations depends on, first, whether or not these regulations can be distinguished from the legislation which was struck down in the *Labour Conventions* reference; and, second, if they cannot be so distinguished, whether the reasoning of that reference should be followed. As to the first point, the legislation struck down in the *Labour* case included an Act relating to Hours of Work in industrial undertakings, an Act relating to Weekly Rest in industrial undertakings, and an Act relating to Minimum Wages in industrial undertakings. It had been decided in *Re Legislative Jurisdiction over Hours of Labour* that 'the Legislatures of the Provinces were the competent authorities to deal with the subject matter "of these acts" save in respect of Dominion servants.'[173]

Despite this earlier ruling, the dominion insisted that it had competence to enact the legislation because it was doing so pursuant to three Draft Conventions that it had signed and ratified. The Privy Council's answer, that the signing of a treaty did not enlarge the sphere of competence of the dominion, has been discussed elsewhere. The matters covered by the dominion acts were assigned exclusively to the provinces by section 92 (13) of the BNA Act and the treaties could not change that. However, in the case of the Rhodesia regulations, it is submitted, the subject matter is not property and civil rights but import and export. Property and civil rights are affected only incidentally as they are in almost any legislation; the thrust of these regulations is the control of imports and exports to and from Rhodesia.

Imports and exports are clearly within federal competence by virtue of the trade and commerce power or the general power for peace, order, and good government.[174] The Export and Import Permits Act has stood unchallenged as a competent federal act. Thus the 'pith and substance' of the Rhodesia regulations is the control of imports and exports and this is within federal competence and, therefore, the regulations are *intra vires* the dominion. It might be argued that these regulations are ' colourable'; that is, that, under the guise of controlling imports and exports, they are in fact designed to promote Canada's foreign policy. Even if the 'colourable' argument were successful (a doubtful proposition after the *Reader's Digest* case[175]), the promotion of Canada's foreign policy is, itself, a dominion matter under the peace, order, and good government of Canada. The matter has never been decided by our courts but Professor Laskin (as he then was) has written that 'it should be clear that it is only the Dominion that may as a matter of domestic constitutional law, modify, abolish or extend the accepted common law rules of immunity ... How far the courts recognize, in domestic litigation, the principles of international law respecting immunity ... does not as such touch legislative power but it necessarily pre-supposes (unless this be another gap in law-making authority) that there is a competent legislature able to deal with those matters ... The constitutional value involved is surely a matter of the peace, order and good government of Canada.'[176] In addition, the passages quoted earlier from the *Offshore Minerals* reference support the view that the dominion has exclusive competence over foreign relations.[177] In either view, then, import and export or foreign relations, the regulations are *intra vires* the dominion, the interference with property and civil rights being incidentally necessary to the enforcement of this statute.

As to the second question, namely, the division of powers, it has already been submitted that the reasoning of the *Labour Conventions* reference is inadequate in this modern age and that the case should not and probably would not be followed today. But, in the case of the Rhodesia regulations, this would be unnecessary since the matters covered by the regulations are within federal competence.

CONCLUSIONS

We have, thus far, examined the relationship between customary international law and municipal law as applied by our domestic courts and the relationship between conventional international law and municipal law as applied by our domestic courts, including the related special case of the United Nations Act. In regard to customary international law, it was suggested that our courts, by adopting customary rules and incorporating them into our domestic law, were performing quite adequately. In regard to conventional international law, it was suggested that the combined force of the *Arrow River* rule, requiring implementing legislation before a court would enforce a treaty, and the *Labour Conventions* rule, preventing the dominion from legislating on provincial matters in pursuance of a treaty, placed the federal government at a decided disadvantage in its attempts to carry out its international responsibilities. It was further suggested that the *Labour Conventions* case is ready to be overruled, but that that might not be the most satisfactory method of dealing with it; and, finally, that the *Arrow River* rule could only be changed by constitutional amendment. In regard to the United Nations Act, it was argued that this statute is constitutionally sound both from a separation and division of powers point of view and that it does not represent a dangerous surrender of sovereignty in that the act confers upon the governor in council a discretion as to whether to enforce Security Council decisions and in that parliament has forty days in which to annul any regulations or orders made under the act. It is nevertheless a step in the direction of allowing international law a greater measure of authority in our domestic system.

At a time of continuing study of the Canadian constitution it is important for us to ask to what extent conclusions and suggestions contained in this review should be included in a new or modified constitution. It is submitted that whether or not one expects customary rules to recover their once-great influence in international law, an influence which is now eclipsed by that of convention, it would still be best to leave the handling of these rules to the courts. They have evolved, from Lord Mansfield's time, their own way of dealing with customary rules and it is wise to leave alone a system that has worked satisfactorily. It might be asked why we want a tighter control over the court's use of convention than of custom; surely it is the more fragile and less certain customary rules which should be controlled than fixed and carefully worded treaties? The answer to this question is that treaties are made by men at a specific point in time; these laws should be subject to some parliamentary scrutiny. Customary rules are generated by a process of consent at no particular point in time; these laws, being by definition more neutrally and deliberately arrived at, need less parliamentary scrutiny: they can be left in the hands of the courts.

It is submitted that a new constitution should contain a clear statement that the federal government has exclusive jurisdiction over external affairs affecting Canada as a whole and that it may enact any legislation it wishes in pursuance of its external affairs policy. No mention need be made of, but of course the courts would enforce, the control of the 'colourability' doctrine on this head of power as they do any other. In addition, another clause should be inserted which would make ratified treaties the law of the land subject only to valid, clear, and unambiguous provincial or dominion legislation. This would, as argued earlier, give a ratified treaty some meaning, but would leave parliament with its traditional check on the executive. If either provincial or dominion legislation conflicted with the treaty, that legislation would prevail until and unless the federal parliament enacted implementing legislation. If these recommendations were implemented then, it is submitted, Canada's treatment of international law would be both rational and balanced.[178]

NOTES

1 Ignaz Seidl-Hohenveldern, 'Transformation or Adoption of International Law into Municipal Law' (1963), 12 *I.C.L.Q.* 88–125, at 90 (a very useful paper).

2 Myers S. McDougal, 'The Impact of International Law Upon National Law: A Policy Oriented Perspective' in his *Studies in World Public Order* (1960) 157–236, at 159; see also 171.

3 D.R. Deener, 'International Law Provisions in Post World War II Constitutions' (1951), 36 *Cornell L.Q.* 505.

4 Seidl-Hohenveldern, 'Transformation or Adoption of International Law into Municipal Law,' *supra* note 1.

5 This is the approach of Professor Van Panhuys in (1964), 2 *Hague Recueil* 7.

6 The Supreme Court Act, R.S.C. c S-19, s 55 (2) (1970).

7 R.S.C. c J-1 (1970).

8 R.S.C. c E-11 (1970).

9 R.S.C. c 1 (1970).

10 R.S.O. c 95 (1970).

11 R.S.C. c E-10 (1970).

12 R.S.O. c 225 s 7 (1970).

13 S 23(1).

14 R.S.O. c 151, s 38 (1970).

15 R.S.O. c 228, s 18(7) (1970).

16 R.S.C. 1st Supp., c 23, s 12(1)(b) (1970).

17 R.S.C. c O-1, s 2 (1970).

18 The Supreme Court Act, R.S.C. c S-19, s 10 (1970).

19 The Federal Court Act, R.S.C. s 9(1) (1970); Exchequer Court Act, R.S.C. c E-11, s 11(1) (1970); County Judges Act, R.S.O. c 95, s 10 (1970).

20 *Buvot* v *Barbuit* (1737), 25 E.R. 777.

21 Blackstone, *Commentaries on the Laws of England*, book IV, c 5.

22 Constitutional Act, 1791.

23 The literature on the subject is extensive. See, for example: Seidl-Hohenveldern, 'Transformation or Adoption of International Law into Municipal Law,' *supra* note 1; H. Mosler, 'L'application du droit international public par les tribunaux nationaux' (1957), 1 *Hague Recueil* 680; E. Van Bogaert, 'Les antimonies entre le droit international et le droit interne' (1968), 72 *Rev. gen. de D.I.P.* 346–60; W. Wengler, 'Réflexions sur l'application du droit international public par les tribunaux nationaux' (1968), 2 *Ottawa Law Review* 265–319; and references in Erades and Gould, *The Relation Between International Law and Municipal Law in the Netherlands and in the United States* (1961).

24 In England, according to Felice Morgenstern, 'Judicial Practice and The Supremacy of International Law' (1950), 27 *B.Y.I.L.* 42, at 52, with the apparent exception of *R.* v *Keyn*, in no case has a court refused to give effect to a rule of customary international law because it had not been previously incorporated into national law; this despite many transformationist dicta.

25 In the *Schooner Exchange* v *McFadden*, (1812) 7 Cranch. 116, Chief Justice Marshall, after pointing out that 'all exceptions ... to the full and complete power of a nation, within its own territories, must be traced up to the consent of the nation itself,' went on to add that 'this consent may be either express or implied.' Surely an implied transformation is close to an adoption.

26 Lauterpacht, 'Is International Law a Part of the Law of England?' (1939), 25 *Transactions of the Grotius Society* 51; Westlake, 'Is International Law a Part of the Law of England?' (1906), 22 *Law Quarterly Review* 14; Brierly, 'International Law in England' (1935), 51 *L.Q.R.* 24; Holdsworth, 'The Relation of English Law to International Law' (1942), 26 *Minnesota L.R.* 141; McNair, 'The Method whereby International Law is Made to Prevail in Municipal

Courts on an Issue of International Law' (1944), 30 *Transactions of the Grotius Society* 11; Fawcett, 'The Judicial Committee of the Privy Council and International Law' (1969), 42 *B.Y.I.L.*, 229; Morgenstern, 'Judicial Practice and Supremacy of International Law' (1950), 27 *B.Y.I.L.* 42; Vanek, 'Is International Law Part of the Law of Canada?' (1949–50), 8 *U. Toronto L.J.* 251; Fawcett, 'Customary International Law in the Courts of the United Kingdom' (1968), 21 *Revista Espanola de Derecho International* 459; McDougal, 'The Impact of International Law Upon National Law: A Policy-Oriented Perspective,' *supra* note 2, at 157–236.

27 Blackstone, *Commentaries on the Laws of England, supra* note 21, at Bk IV, c 5, 67–8.
28 *Lockwood* v *Coysgarne* (1765), 3 Burr. 1676; *Heathfield* v *Chilton* (1767), 4 Burr. 2015.
29 Lauterpacht, 'Is International Law a Part of the Law of England?' *supra* note 26, at 53; for good discussion of the cases see C.E. Wilson, *Diplomatic Privileges and Immunities* (1967) 27 ff.
30 (1861), 2 Giff. 628, at 678, cited by Lauterpacht, ibid, at 56.
31 (1876), 2 Ex.D.63.
32 Ibid, at 127.
33 Ibid, at 68.
34 Ibid, at 193.
35 Ibid, at 239.
36 Ibid, at 193.
37 [1905] 2 K.B. 391, at 406–7.
38 [1918] 1 Ch. 176 (C.A.); [1928] A.C. 433.
39 Lauterpacht, 'Is International Law a Part of the Law of England?' *supra* note 26, at 77–84; see also Waldock, (1962), *Réceuil des Cours* 137.
40 (1906), 14 Scots L.T.R. 227.
41 [1925] 1 K.B.271, at 284.
42 Ibid, at 295.
43 Ibid.
44 Lauterpacht, 'Is International Law a Part of the Law of England?' *supra* note 26, at 83.
45 [1938] A.C. 485, at 502, per Lord Wright.
46 *Chung Chi-cheung* v *The King*, [1939] A.C. 160, at 167 (P.C.).
47 Ibid, at 167–8.
48 Ibid, at 168.
49 At least not according to the *All England Law Reports* Index and Noter-Up. A possible reason for the decrease in judicial activity is that many of the areas where an international rule might be applied to domestic law are now covered by statute; for example: Territorial Waters Jurisdiction Act, 1878 (U.K.) c 73,

which is consistent with the holding in *Keyn* but corrects the result; Geneva Conventions Act, 1957; Diplomatic Privileges Act, 1964. There are also a number of Canadian statutes which have the same effect of reducing the court's concern with the relationship distinction: Diplomatic Immunities (Commonwealth Countries) Act, R.S.C. c D-4 (1970); Geneva Conventions Act, R.S.C. 1970. In 1877 two courts composed of basically the same judges as sat in *Keyn* considered that case. In *Harris* v *Franconia* (1877), 46 L.J.Q.B. 363, the court felt that *Keyn* decided that the territory of England and the sovereignty of the Queen ended at the low water mark unless extended by an act of parliament. In *Blackpool Pier Co.* v *Fylde Union* (1877), 46 L.J.M.C. 189, the court on similar reasoning held that the Poor Law of 1867 did not apply to a pier which extended 500 feet beyond the low water mark.
50 (1906), 14 Scots L.T.R. 227.
51 Lush. 308.
52 [1968] 1 W.L.R. 242, at 245. See also *I.R.C.* v *Collco Dealings Ltd.*, [1962] A.C. 1, at 19 where the court quoted with approval from Maxwell, *Interpretation of Statutes* (10th ed, 1953), at 148: 'But if the statute is unambiguous, its provisions must be followed even if they are contrary to international law.'
53 (1876), 2 Ex.D.63, at 210.
54 Ibid, at 85.
55 (1894), 4 Ex.C.R. 283. Vanek, in 'Is International Law Part of the Law of Canada?' *supra* note 26, at 268 quotes the above passage and the next few lines, which read 'and therefore the Act respecting fishing by foreign vessels is strictly within the powers of the Parliament of Canada,' to argue that it was a federal rather than a provincial matter. If the judge meant what Mr. Vanek suggests, then he was according to Canada a lesser sovereignty than England, a proposition which might have been reasonable in 1894 but was certainly not the case in 1950, two decades after the Statute of Westminster. It is also suggested that such a crucial matter as this would hardly be decided finally in the Toronto District Admiralty Court. For contrary authority from an equally inferior court (Divisional Court of Ontario) see *Rex* v *Meikleham*, (1906) 11 O.L.R. 366, at 373 where Meredith CJCP in speaking of freedom of the high seas said that 'although that is, no doubt, a rule of international law, yet, where it is

plain, that the Legislature has intended to disregard or interfere with that rule, the Courts are bound to give effect to its enactments.'

56 (1906), 37 S.C.R. 385.

57 (1905), 11 Ex. C.R. 141 (B.C. Admiralty District).

58 (1906), 37 S.C.R. 385, at 394.

59 Ibid, at 397–8.

60 (1917), 55 S.C.R. 348.

61 (1907), 11 Ex. C.R. 179, at 188.

62 [1929] 2 D.L.R. 849 (N.S.S.C.).

63 [1928] 2 D.L.R. 263, at 264–5 (N.S.S.C.).

64 *Rex v Furuzawa*, (1930) 42 B.C.R. 548 (B.C.C.A.); *Rex v. The Kitty D.*, (1903) 2 O.W.R. 1065 (Tor. Ad. Ct.). See also *Brown v S.S. Indochine*, (1922), 21 Ex C.R. 406 (Que. Ad. Ct.), where sovereign immunity was accepted without question; and see too *Leonard v Premio-Real* (1885), 11 Quebec L.R. 128; *Maluquer v Rex* (1924), 38 Que. Reports (K.B.) 1; *Campbell v Cour des Sessions Générales de la Paix* (1930), 49 Quebec Reports (K.B.) 65; *Maass v Seelheim*, [1936] 4 D.L.R. 267 (Man. K.B.).

65 *Reference as to the Powers of the City of Ottawa and the Village of Rockliffe to Levy Rates on Foreign Legations and High Commissioners' Residences* [1943] S.C.R. 208.

66 Ibid, at 214.

67 Ibid, at 232.

68 *Reference as to whether the Members of the Military of the United States of America are exempt from Criminal Proceedings in Canadian Criminal Courts*, [1943] S.C.R. 484.

69 Ibid, at 490.

70 Ibid, at 496.

71 Ibid, at 511–12.

72 Ibid, at 517.

73 Ibid, at 520.

74 Ibid, at 524.

75 Ibid, at 525.

76 Ibid, at 502.

77 *Casimir Dessaules v The Republic of Poland*, [1944] S.C.R. 275, at 211. This case and reasoning was followed by *Mehr v The Republic of China*, [1956] O.W.N. 218 (Ont. H.C.).

78 *Rose v The King*, [1947] 3 D.L.R. 618, at 628 (Que. K.B.)

79 See, for example, *Lightheart v Lightheart*, [1927] 1 W.W.R. 393 (Sask. K.B.); stolen letters.

80 [1947] 3 D.L.R. 618, at 645.

81 *Rex v Lunan*, [1947] 3 D.L.R. 710, at 713 (Ont. C.A.).

82 [1950] 4 D.L.R. 209, at 210 (Ont. H.C.), following the *Foreign Legations* case.

83 (1956), 3 D.L.R. (2d) 547 (P.E.I. S.C.).

84 *Re Dominion Coal Co. Ltd. and County of Cape Breton; Re Nova Scotia Steel and Coal Co. Ltd. and County of Cape Breton* (1963), 40 D.L.R. (2d) 593 (N.S.S.C.).

85 *Municipality of Saint John v Fraser-Brace Overseas Co.*, [1958] S.C.R. 263.

86 [1958] S.C.R. 268, at 268–9.

87 *Supra*, note 25, at 267: 'What is substituted is the conception of an invitation by the host state to the visiting state ... When one state admits ... a foreign sovereign or his representative, the terms of that entry are to be gathered from the circumstances of the invitation and its acceptance.'

88 *In the Matter of a Reference by the Governor General in Council Concerning the Ownership of and Jurisdiction Over Off-Shore Mineral Rights*, [1967] S.C.R. 792.

89 Ibid, at 816–17 (emphasis added).

90 (1969), 5 D.L.R. (3d) 128 (Que. K.B.).

91 *Flota Maritima Browning de Cuba S.A. v Steamship Canadian Conqueror et al. and Republic of Cuba* (1962), 34 D.L.R. (2d) 628 (S.C.C.), per Ritchie J at 637–8.

92 (1969), 5 D.L.R. (3d) 128, at 138.

93 *Government of the Democratic Republic of the Congo v Venne* (1972), 22 D.L.R. (3d) 669, at 672 (S.C.C.).

94 Ibid, at 673.

95 Ibid, at 677–8 (emphasis added).

96 (1970), 8 D.L.R. (3d) 686 (Que. C.A.).

97 (1972), 22 D.L.R. (3d) 669, per Laskin J, dissenting, at 681.

98 The Supreme Court of Canada in the *Offshore* reference considered the *Keyn* case and the two later cases referring to it and concluded that the law was correctly stated by Coulson and Forbes in *Waters and Land Drainage* (6th ed, 1952), at 12: '(i) The realm of England where it abuts upon the high sea only extends to low water mark; all beyond is high sea. (ii) For the distance of three miles, and in some cases more, international law has conceded an extension of dominion over the seas washing the shores. (iii) This concession is evidenced by treaty or by long usage. (iv) In no case can the concession extend the realm of England so as to make the conceded portion liable to the common law, or to vest the soil of the bed in the Crown. This must be done by an Act of the Legislature.' [1967] S.C.R. 792, at 807. This is the exact interpretation of *Keyn* herein argued for.

99 Edmund M. Morgan, 'Judicial Notice' (1944), 57 *Harvard L. Rev.* 269–95, at 272.

100 Ibid, at 270.

101 [1935] 1 w.w.r. 452, at 457–8 (Sask. c.a.).

102 *Canadian National Steamships Company Ltd.* v *Watson*, [1939] s.c.r. 11.

103 Lauterpacht, 'Is International Law a Part of the Law of England?' *supra* note 26, at 59. The us cases were *The Scotia* (1875, 14 Wall. 170, at 187 and *The New York* (1899), 175 u.s. 187.

104 [1934] A.C. 586, at 588 (P.C.).

105 *Armed Forces Reference*, [1943] s.c.r. 483, at 524.

106 (1969), 5 d.l.r. (3d) 128, at 142, 146.

107 As to sources of international law other than custom and convention and the Canadian courts, there is very little to go on. Canadian courts already apply general principles of law and the principles of equity in their day to day decisions; there is nothing to suggest they would not continue to do this in a case with an international flavour: See *Armed Forces Reference*, [1943] s.c.r., at 524 per Rand j. The teachings of publicists and judicial decisions, whether of the International Court or a foreign court, are used as sources to determine the scope and content of customary rules. For a situation where a Permanent Court judgment was used as a source of Canadian labour arbitration doctrine, see *Re Oil, Chemical & Atomic Workers and Polymer Corp. Ltd.* (1959), 10 l.a.c. 51, at 59–60 per Laskin (chairman).

108 McNair, *The Law of Treaties* (1961), at 81; 1 *Bl. Com.* (14th ed) 256;

109 McNair, *The Law of Treaties, supra* note 108, at 81.

110 *The Parlement Belge* (1879), 4 p.d. 129, at 132.

111 Ibid, 154.

112 *Law and Custom of the Constitution* (3rd ed, 1908), vol 11 (The Crown); Part ii, at 109. Another frequently cited case in favour of this proposition is *Walker* v *Bird*, [1892] A.C. 491) where the crown was attempting to justify the seizure of a lobster factory on the basis of a *modus vivendi* worked out between England and France to avoid war. Counsel for the crown, under questioning by their lordships, was forced to admit that the crown could not sanction 'an invasion by its officers of the rights of private individuals whenever it was necessary to compel obedience to the provisions of a treaty' (497). His contention that this agreement was 'alien to a treaty of peace' was rejected by their lordships and the defence failed, although the status of a treaty of peace vis à vis legislation was left open.

113 (1922), 38 t.l.r. 259.

114 Ibid, at 262.

115 [1928] All E.R. 18.

116 Ibid, at 20.

117 McNair, *The Law of Treaties, supra* note 108, at 89, points out that these conventions can come before the courts, in addition to Prize Courts, as shown by the cases of *Hobbs* v *Henning* (1865), 34 l.j.c.p. 117 and *Seymour* v *London and Provincial Insurance Co.* (1872), 41 l.j.c.p. 193, both cases on policies of insurance. As for Prize Courts, which of course administer international law by their terms of reference, se *The Vryheid* (1778), Hay and Marriott 188, and *The Neptunes* (1807), 4 C. Rob. 403. In the *Zamora*, [1916] 2 h.l. 77, at 97, the Prize Court indicated that 'it will act on amount to a mitigation of the Crown rights in favour of the enemy or neutral as the case may be.' This is in keeping with the theory that war is a crown prerogative and if it wishes to tie its hands it may.

118 [1915] 1 k.b. 857.

119 *Reg.* v *Wilson* (1877), 3 q.b.d. 42; *In re Castioni*, [1891] 1 q.b. 149. In an article entitled 'Enforcement of Treaties by English Courts' (1958), 44 *Transactions of the Grotius Society* 29, at 31–2, Dr Mann argues that McNair's division of treaties requiring legislation into three categories (change in law; extra powers for crown; and charge on people) is unnecessary since the general principle that those treaties which require any change in the law of the land must be implemented by legislation covers all three and, in addition, turns the so-called exceptions into situations simply falling outside the rule. This is no doubt correct. I have retained McNair's distinctions, however, for the purpose of making clear all the implications of the rule.

120 McNair, *The Law of Treaties, supra* note 108, at 24.

121 [1950] 1 All E.R. 430.

122 Ibid, at 433.

123 [1968] 1 w.l.r. 242.

124 Ibid, at 245.

125 Ibid. This passage is interesting in that it suggests that treaties not ratified by parliament may have some value as law and would fail only before an unambiguous statute. This

is true in the sense that, if a treaty is in accord with domestic law, no parliamentary
implementation is necessary. It is also true
that an ambiguous statute will be interpreted
in accordance with international law (customary or conventional) rather than out of
accordance with it: *Maxwell's Interpretation
of Statutes* (11th ed, 1962), at 142 (customary); *Salmon v Commissioners of Customs
and Excise,* [1967] 2 Q.B. 116 (treaties).

126 [1937] A.C. 326, at 347–8.

127 *Missouri v Holland* is an opposite holding in
regard to the United States. The phrase 'if
they entail alteration of the existing domestic
law' is taken in the broad sense as used by Dr
Mann.

128 *Re Arrow River and Tributaries Slide and
Boom Co.,* [1932] 2 D.L.R. 250, at 260–1.

129 [1931] 2 D.L.R. 216, at 217

130 [1932] 2 D.L.R. 250, at 260.

131 Vanek, 'Is International Law a Part of the
Law of Canada?' *supra* note 26, at 251; La
Forest, 'May the Provinces legislate in Viola-
tion of International Law?' (1961), 39 *Can.
Bar. Rev.* 78.

132 If judicial support is needed for this proposition in addition to the BNA Act, 1867, itself,
see the *Labour Conventions* case, [1937] A.C.
326, and *Murphy v C.P.R.* (1958), 15 D.L.R.
(2d) 145, at 153.

133 *Chung Chi-cheung v The King*, [1939] A.C.
160, at 167–8 (P.C.). *Cheney v Conn*, [1968] 1
W.L.R. 242, at 245.

134 *Foreign Legations Reference,* [1943] S.C.R.
208, at 213–14; *Armed Forces Reference,*
[1943] S.C.R. 484, at 517.

135 (1905), 11 O.L.R. 366.

136 *The Vernon City,* [1943] P. 9.

137 *Swait v Board of Trustees of Maritime
Transportation Unions* (1967), 61 D.L.R. (2d)
317, at 322.

138 Vanek, 'Is International Law a Part of the
Law of Canada?' *supra* note 26, at 273, n 68
cites the cases of *R. v Wing Chong* (1885), 2
B.C.R. 150 and *Tai Sing v Maguire* (1878), 1
B.C.R. 101 as holding that provincial legislation imposing special taxes on the Chinese
was *ultra vires* the province on the ground
inter alia that it was in violation of a treaty
between Britain (for Canada) and China. In
the *Wing Chong* case, Crease J observed (at
161–2) that 'these obligations are binding
here and in other parts of the Dominion under
s. 132 of the British North America Act, and
no Province, or the Dominion itself, can lawfully pass laws interfering with that right

without a previous revision of the treaties by
the high contracting parties to them for that
purpose.' It is submitted that the holding of
ultra vires (eminently supportable on other
grounds also) was correct in these cases
since by section 132 of the BNA Act the
dominion parliament had '*all* powers necessary or proper for performing the obligations
of Canada, *or of any Province* thereof, as part
of the British Empire towards foreign
countries arising under treaties between the
Empire and such foreign countries'
(emphasis added). The suggestion that it was
beyond the power of the dominion so to act
is wrong except in the sense that royal assent
might have been refused had such legislation
been passed and that Britain did control
Canada's external affairs at that time. Thus
these decisions are correct on the basis of
section 132. But Vanek's suggestion that
they should have governed the *Arrow River*
case and made the provincial legislation
there also *ultra vires* misses the point that the
Webster-Ashburton Treaty was not made 'as
part of the British Empire' as was the case in
the Chinese treaties; it was made to apply to
Canada and the United States only and thus
section 132 would not have applied. And, of
course, since section 132 has lost meaning in
the modern age, these two cases cannot have
any relevance on this point.

139 [1944] 3 D.L.R. 482.

140 Ibid, at 497–8.

141 [1943] 3 D.L.R. 540.

142 Ibid, at 545.

143 This contention is supported by McNair,
The Law of Treaties, supra note 109, at 87,
n 3.

144 In *Francis v The Queen* (1956), 3 D.L.R. (2d)
641, Kerwin CJC, at 643 seemed to think there
was something special about peace treaties
though he did not specify what it was. Before
stating that the Jay Treaty of 1794 required
legislation to be implemented he stated that
'the Jay Treaty was not a treaty of peace.'
Had he said 'since' it was not a treaty of
peace it needed legislation, it would have
been a modern dictum against my contention. As it stands, it says nothing.

145 (1956), 3 D.L.R. (2d) 641.

146 Ibid, at 643.

147 Ibid, at 647.

148 (1964), 44 D.L.R. (2d) 440.

149 Ibid, at 453–4.

150 *Re Offshore Mineral Rights of British
Columbia,* [1967] S.C.R. 792, at 816.

151 [1943] 4 D.L.R. 553.
152 [1945] 2 D.L.R. 232; (1944) 82 C.C.C. 206; [1945] 3 D.L.R. 272.
153 [1945] 3 D.L.R. 272, at 277.
154 McNair, *The Law of Treaties, supra* note 108, at 89.
155 [1945] O.R. 778.
156 Ibid, at 781.
157 [1948] O.R. 579.
158 Ibid, at 592.
159 (1961), 29 D.L.R. (2d) 673.
160 S.C. 1945 c 11; now R.S.C. c B-9 (1970).
161 (1961), 29 D.L.R. (2d) 673, at 774.
162 Ibid, at 715.
163 Another use to which conventional as well as customary international law can be put is in the area of statute interpretation: see *Re Chateau Gai Wines and A-G Canada* (1970), 14 D.L.R.. (3d) 411; *Re Stegeman* (1966), 61 D.L.R. (2d) 340 (B.C.C.S.) upholding (1966), 58 D.L.R. (2d) 415; and see the *Report of the British Law Commission on the Interpretation of Statutes* (1969) 44–5.
164 For examples of this process see *Fleming* v *Atkinson* (1959), 18 D.L.R. (2d) 81, and *Applebaum* v *Gilchrist*, [1946] 4 D.L.R. 383.
165 This was what was attempted in *Cheney* v *Conn (Inspector of Taxes)*, [1968] 1 W.L.R. 242. There was no statute declaring nuclear weapons illegal, but Cheney relied on the Geneva Convention of 1957 as declaring them illegal. The court rejected this contention on the grounds that even if part of the convention outlawed nuclear weapons, that part had not been implemented by statute. This would most probably have been a Canadian court's answer also.
166 This was in fact the holding in *Re Arrow River and Tributaries Slide and Boom Co.*, [1932] 2 D.L.R. 260, and *Francis* v *The Queen* (1956), 3 D.L.R. (2d) 641.
167 R.S.C. c U-3 (1970).
168 P.C. 1954-792, 27 May 1954; SOR/54-204 *Canada Gazette*, part II, v 88. Passed pursuant to the Export and Import Permits Act. R.S.C. c E-17 (1970).
169 P.C. 1965-2252, 20 December 1965; SOR/66-4 *Canada Gazette*, part II, v 100.
170 SOR/66-89, 4 February 1966. *Canada Gazette*, part II, v 100.
171 P.C. 1967-323, 21 February 1967; SOR/67-93. *Canada Gazette*, part II, v 101.
172 It is interesting to note that in England where there is no act empowering the crown in advance to apply Security Council sanctions, the House of Lords almost refused to follow the Security Council resolutions. Had they done so, England would have been left in violation of her solemn promise to support and uphold the United Nations Charter, for it is clear that, in England, the charter has no strength of its own. Cf *Keesing's Contemporary Archives* (1968), at 2292–4.
173 [1937] A.C. 326 at 347, citing [1925] S.C.R. 505.
174 *Gold Seal Ltd.* v *Dominion Express Co. and A-G Alta.* (1921), 62 S.C.R. 424.
175 *A-G Can.* v *Reader's Digest Association (Canada) Ltd.* (1962), 30 D.L.R. 296 (S.C.C.). The magazine attacked part of the Excise Tax Act, R.S.C. c E-13 (1970) on the grounds that it was designed to help Canadian magazines compete with American ones. The court held this to be a valid exercise of the dominion's taxing power.
176 Laskin, *Canadian Constitutional Law* (1969), at 291.
177 This is not to comment on the vexed question of the provinces' ability to sign treaties on matters within their own competence. As to this question see Laskin, 'The Provinces and International Agreements' in *Ontario Advisory Committee on Confederation: Background Papers and Reports* (1967), at 101; Morin, 'Treaty-Making Power-Position of the Government of Quebec' (1967), 45 *Can. Bar Rev.* 160; Morris, 'The Treaty-Making Power: A Canadian Dilemma' (1967), 45 *Can. Bar Rev.* 478.
178 Among those who have had a hand at one time or another in the preparation of this manuscript, I wish to express my appreciation and acknowledge my indebtedness to Mr Peter Gilchrist, for his outstanding research assistance, and to Mr Peter Carter and Professor Gerald L. Morris, for their valuable suggestions.

W.R. LEDERMAN

6/The Private International Law System: Some Thoughts on Objectives, Methods, and Relations to Public International Law

INTRODUCTION

Somewhat recently in historical terms the world has witnessed the rise of the territorially based national state. Well over one hundred such states constitute the present membership of the United Nations, each with its own legal institutions. As Woodrow Wilson once put it, a state is a people organized for law within a definite territory. National legal systems differ considerably in detailed content and are in large measure mutually exclusive in the territorial sense. Probably this mutual exclusivity reached its zenith in the nineteenth century, but, in any event, it has never been complete. Overriding legal influences, transcending the particular distinctive legal systems of countries or regions or cities, have been present in some form from the days of the Roman Empire, and this has become increasingly true in the modern era of territorial national states. Especially is it true in this second half of the twentieth century when appropriate international legal responses are urgently necessary to meet the rapidly increasing extent to which many persons in all countries are in fact involved in border-crossing activities, occurrences, and relations. In general two forms of such interstate, transnational or international legal influences may be discerned. In the first place there have been some overriding substantive legal rules and principles recognized as the same for all countries. In the second place in certain limited but significant circumstances one country has recognized and given effect to the domestic laws of a second country, even though the laws of the second country differ from the first for the matter in hand. In this second case, there are no overriding substantive international principles for the subject in hand, so one is left with a choice between the two differing domestic laws, for persons and occurrences touching both countries. The overriding substantive international rules and principles first referred to are the primary area of Public International Law, whereas Private International Law comprises the indicative or selective rules and principles whereby, to an extent limited by specific subject categories and persons, the domestic laws of one country are in appropriate circumstances given effect in another country, by the courts of the latter country if need be.

Brief illustrations of these two forms of international legal influence would perhaps be helpful at this point. Public International Law, for example, lays down what immunities from local laws are enjoyed by diplomats stationed in every country. Also, as a result of treaties, Public International Law lays down what radio frequencies may be used by citizens of each country adhering to the treaty, when they propose to engage in the broadcasting of radio transmissions that may spill over national borders and affect broadcasting in other countries.[1]

An example of the operation of Private International Law may be found in the subject of marriage. When a man and a woman have married under the local marriage laws of one country (Whiteland), which at the time was their permanent home, and later they move to a second country (Redland) as their permanent home, will the second country legally recognize them as married persons, thus giving effect in the second country to the domestic marriage laws of the first country? This question arises because there is no overriding substantive Public International Law of marriage to govern the simple interstate situation postulated here. Thus, the choice for the Redland court, in this example, is either to recognize the result prescribed by the law of Whiteland for these former Whitelanders, or else to apply to them retroactively the Redland law as to marriage as if they had lived in Redland the whole time. The choice-of-law issue here is not critical if, in fact, the substantive domestic laws of Redland and Whiteland are the same, at least for the persons whose status is up for determination. But what if Whiteland's law permits cousins to marry one another, whereas Redland law forbids it; and the man and the woman (John and Mary) are indeed cousins? How does Redland resolve this conflict between its own domestic law and that of Whiteland? If Redland has the typical English Common Law rule of Private International Law to cover the situation, that rule says: where the issue is capacity to marry, the law of the permanent home (that is, domicile) of each party is to be applied to determine his or her capacity, even if that means applying a different marriage law than the domestic law of Redland respecting capacity to marry. So the cousins are legally married, even in Redland. This illustrates the nature of Private International Law rules as indicative or selective, and also shows us why this body of rules is known alternatively by the title of 'The Conflict of Laws,' meaning that they are rules for the resolution of interstate conflicts of domestic laws, as illustrated. Many other examples of such conflict-of-laws situations could be given; for instance, respecting the validity of title to movable goods taken across a border by persons moving from one country to another, or respecting business agreements (contracts) involving persons and performance in more that one country.

The basic question may be asked at this point whether the principles and rules of both Public and Private International Law are of overriding authoritative validity, so that they must be given effect within national states? For example, are the courts and the legislature of Redland *obliged* to give them effect, even if the results differ from those prescribed in Redland laws for corresponding situations that are entirely domestic to that country? Monistic theories concerning international law, though they have several variations, are to the effect generally that international laws, whether 'Public' or 'Private,' must be accepted at the national level as overriding. Thus, monistic theories hold that international law is of superior authoritative validity in relation to national law, and hence that international laws prevail, in the matters with which they deal, over national laws. Monistic theory contrasts with dualistic theory. The latter also has several variations, but the pervasive emphasis is that the legal autonomy or sovereignty of the national state is primary. Thus, dualistic theory holds that, while international laws (Public or Private) may be given effect by the courts or the legislature of Redland, it is the national law of Redland itself which allows or requires this result; there is not considered to be a superior quality in international law that compels such a result. Rather, in these latter circumstances, national law is supreme, and rules of Public or Private International law in effect in Redland take effect there because they are authoritatively sanctioned by the national legal customs, courts, or legislatures of the country.[2]

This main issue between monism and dualism is always with us, and we will have to return to it in general and in particular from time to time in this study. But I propose to attempt some analysis of the objectives and methods of the Private International Law system from a more pragmatic and particular point of view, setting aside for the moment the grand issue of high theory between monism and dualism.

My more pragmatic and particular hypothesis is this. As a matter of observable fact, the most fully developed and complete systems of law in the modern world are the domestic legal systems of territorially based national states. But, while these systems tend to be autonomous and mutually exclusive, they are by no means entirely so. When persons and facts are completely local to a single national state, then, true enough, only the domestic laws of that state govern those persons and facts. But of course interstate or transnational activities, movements, and transactions are common on a regular basis in great number and variety. Looked at from the point of view of a single national state, which we may call Redland, we find that the substantive domestic legal system of Redland undergoes some interpenetrations by laws from sources outside Redland, to take due account of these interstate or international factual elements. As explained earlier, these interpenetrations take two forms. In the first place some substantive rules of Public International Law, which are directly dispositive of rights, powers, and duties for persons, are effective in Redland; for example, concerning the tax immunity of foreign diplomats stationed in Redland, or limiting the frequencies available to national radio broadcasters there. Such laws come into Redland from the international realm and are recognized and given overriding effect there by the decisions of Redland courts or, at times, by an implementing statute from the parliament of Redland. But substantive Public International Law of this type is very partial and incomplete as to the range of matters with which it deals.

So we come to the second form of interpenetration, that effected by the indicative or selective rules of Private International Law which introduce into Redland, for particular persons on selected subjects, the domestic substantive laws of other countries, though they differ from the domestic laws of Redland. When there is no true substantive international law in effect, this seems the only alternative, where there are interstate elements deserving of attention at the national level in the name of justice. The example was given earlier of the marriage law of Whiteland taking effect in Redland for former Whitelanders now in Redland and, as indicated, many other examples could be given.

As a matter of analytical approach, my point is this. As one looks at the total operating Redland legal system, one sees that these interpenetrations from outside Redland in fact occur according to the terms of specific rules for priority or selection that operate in Redland to effect this result, as a matter of Public or Private International Law. Since the actual terms of these rules for priority or selection are known, their meaning and policy implications can be ascertained and analysis carried to quite an advanced point before the jurist engaged in such study will find it necessary to address himself to questions of the ultimate source of the legitimacy of Public or Private International Law. This later stage does come of course, as we shall see. Nevertheless, let us start with the modest approach, undertaking some analysis of the policy objectives and the methods of the typical private international law system as we see it operating in fact in national states, including relations to public international law at this level.

THE POLICY THRUST OF THE PRIVATE INTERNATIONAL LAW SYSTEM

At times policy is discussed as if it were something apart from and outside existing laws. That is not the approach here. I proceed on the footing that, for example, the substantive domestic laws of the countries Redland and Whiteland embody, crystallize, express, and imply the official policy objectives of Redland and Whiteland, item by item, as those respective domestic laws deal with many matters. The same can be said of the indicative rules making up the Private International Law systems of Redland or Whiteland, which we see operating in those two countries. Laws are for people, and realistic policy analysis is an attempt to assess the effectiveness of existing laws in advancing well being and justice for the people contemplated by their terms. Reformers may conclude that there are better ways of doing what existing laws seek to do, or that policies not yet legally sanctioned in any way should be given legal sanction and support. Of course some policy considerations do stand outside existing laws, but this is no excuse for neglecting the policy implications of the laws already on the books. To sum up, what I am trying to say here has been admirably expressed by Professor Hessel E. Yntema as follows: 'The conception that legal problems, including those arising in conflict situations, should be studied in terms of social policies, and not as mere exercises in deductive or intuitive manipulation of abstract principles of justice, represents a basic modern insight into the nature of law.'[3]

In this spirit then, let us turn to the policy considerations relevant to the typical Private International Law system. Let us look again at the simple example given earlier concerning the conflict of laws on capacity to marry between Redland and Whiteland. Whiteland was the permanent home of the cousins when they married, but later they made their permanent home in Redland, where the domestic law was to the effect that cousins were incapable of marrying one another. Nevertheless the Private International Law of Redland directs that this man and this woman are legally married in Redland. For these persons in these circumstances, Redland's Private International Law causes the domestic capacity-to-marry law of Redland to be displaced by the domestic capacity-to-marry law of Whiteland. In the result, the man and the woman concerned have married status in both countries, and a limping marriage, so called, is avoided. Notice that, in this interstate situation, Redland's Private International Law sacrifices Redland's local substantive capacity-to-marry policy to the conflicting local Whiteland capacity-to-marry policy, because uniformity of status for these persons in the two countries *on these terms* seems obviously to be just in the circumstances. So it may be said that interstate uniformity is the policy objective of Redland's Private International Law in such cases, whether the Redland Private International Law system is to be regarded as a branch of the national law of Redland, or as overriding international law, effective in Redland as well as in other countries. Setting aside this last issue then, let us look further at interstate uniformity of result as the policy objective of Redland's Private International Law system. 'Uniformity' here is not as simple a concept as it may seem at first sight.

As Professor Elliott I. Cheatham has shown,[4] uniformity as a policy objective in these circumstances is basically a derivative of the ideal of equality, or, in other words is a seeking after equal protection of the laws. The root idea seems to be that justice in the sense of consistency requires that, regardless of differences in time or place, persons in essentially similar circumstances should get the same treatment from the law. This objective has also been described, less adequately perhaps, as a search for stability or certainty or security in terms of the reasonable expectations of the parties. These are corollaries of the idea of equal protection of the laws. But the difficulty in an interstate conflict-of-laws situation is that full equality is not possible. Only if there were a single overriding substantive international law of capacity to marry, binding in both Whiteland and Redland, could you assure complete uniformity or equality before the law for all cousins in Redland and Whiteland respecting their capacity to marry one another. In the result, in this example, when it comes to achieving married status, cousins resident in Redland are not equal with John and Mary, the cousins in our example, whereas cousins resident in Whiteland are.

Nevertheless there are some other respects in which Redland's Private International Law system can and does achieve certain equalities. They may be explained as follows, again in terms of our standard matrimonial example.

1 For John and Mary, their marriage is recognized as continuing in Redland as well as Whiteland. This is equality as to *different places and times for the specific persons* now in Redland.
2 For other persons in essentially the same circumstances in Redland as John and Mary, Redland Private International Law promises the same result. So there is a measure of equality here for other couples with foreign connections who claim married status in Redland.
3 If Whiteland has the very same Private International Law rule concerning capacity to marry as does Redland, then equality in the form of reciprocity between the two countries enters the picture. Thus the equalities specified in paragraphs 1 and 2 as assured in Redland, in our standard example, would now be assured in Whiteland on a reciprocal basis. That is, on pricisely converse interstate facts, the same equalities would be assured in both countries, but this time in terms of Redland's domestic laws of capacity to marry. This follows if the Private International Law rules are in fact the same, regardless of why, in theory, they are the same.

These are important steps in the direction of equal protection of the laws, steps worth taking, even though perfection is out of reach, Indeed, the objectives given in paragraphs 1 and 2 are worth pursuing in Redland alone on the basis of Redland's Private International Law, as a branch of the national law of Redland, even though there is no international assurance of reciprocity as in paragraph 3 above.

But this is only one side of the coin so far as the policy content of Redland's Private International Law system is concerned. As we have seen, these partial equalities can only be obtained at the price of Redland tolerating conflicting differences between Redland's domestic laws and those of other countries, such countries being involved with Redland on interstate facts. As we shall see, there is a point beyond which this tolerance will not be carried as a matter of extraordinary public policy reservations in Redland. Nevertheless, within these broad limits we must regard tolerance of differences between domestic national laws as a principal policy thrust of Redland's Private International Law system, or of any Private International Law system. In other words, the typical Private International Law system is a system for mitigation of the harsher effects of these conflicts of national laws, for persons involved in interstate and international factual situations. Accordingly, the typical Private International Law system may be seen as a necessary complement to those parts of Public International Law that eliminate national legal differences by establishing overriding uniform international substantive laws on this or that subject. Since this part of Public International Law is very partial and incomplete in its coverage, the continuing need on into the future for the procedure and technique of Private International Law is obvious.

In summary, then, we see that the policy thrust of the typical Private International Law system is twofold. It seeks to provide equal protection of the laws as to different times and places for persons involved in interstate situations, and this it does by tolerating differences in substantive domestic national laws on a selective basis, and within the wide limits of the extraordinary public policy reservation mentioned earlier. These distinctions and reservations concerning 'policy' require further explanation, which I now give by quoting certain paragraphs I wrote in 1956 on this subject.

Very little has been said of policy considerations in the foregoing analysis of the legal techniques or procedures involved in private international law. Every rule of law expresses policy of some kind, but in connection with private international law, some careful distinctions should be made. Given a novel situation having factual connection with two or more countries, the legally significant connecting factor for the juridical question raised has to be chosen or compounded from these factual points of contact by the judge confronted with the need to formulate a new indicative rule. In effect, he should ask himself which of the countries concerned has the most important interest in the result – which country is most closely concerned with the result. Then, the factual connecting factor which will consistently point to this particular country in such matters should be selected as the legally significant one, and, thus, a judge-made rule to that effect would emerge as a new precedent. For instance, Dr Cheshire argues that the policy behind the choice of 'the intended matrimonial home' as the legally significant connecting factor for 'capacity to marry' is simply that that country is the one most closely concerned with the substantive marital standards to which the man and woman concerned should conform. Hence, it is sensible and just to frame the choice-of-law rule so that it will impose the laws of that country upon them. The 'proper law of the contract' doctrine of England and the Commonwealth countries is (on its objective side) an even more apt illustration. This, then, is the ordinary type of policy decision which lies behind the formulation of an indicative rule of private international law and which such rules embody and express once authoritatively formulated, whether by a judge or a legislature.

This ordinary indicative type of policy decision has to be distinguished from the substantive policy considerations which govern the formulation of national dispositive laws themselves by judges or legislatures. For England, for example, monogamy is deemed desirable and right in marital relations, and, hence, English domestic laws permit only monogamy. By contrast, in India, polygamy is regarded as proper, and certain domestic Indian laws are to that effect. However, in framing a choice-of-law rule for an international marital situation touching both England and India, ordinarily the policy issue is not whether monogamy is right and polygamy is wrong or vice versa; rather, it is simply the question which country has the more important interest in the marital standards of the people concerned, whatever may be the substantive matrimonial policy expressed in that country's domestic laws. Every time foreign laws differ from English ones on a given matter and, nevertheless, are given effect in England in a particular case, English substantive policy embodied in English domestic laws is to that extent displaced by the foreign substantive policy embodied in the foreign domestic laws. To effect this result in appropriate circumstances is the purpose of private international law. The only alternative is the intolerant and parochial one that 'whoso comes to Rome must do as Romans do.'

Even so, tolerance cannot be unlimited, and, thus, we find that as an extraordinary matter of ultimate reservations, substantive policy considerations do enter directly into some choice-of-law problems. 'Public policy,' as usually conceived in this regard, defines certain fundamentals implicit in our substantive laws and legal institutions and forbids the adoption by operation of our choice-of-law rules of any foreign laws which would work results repugnant to these basic concepts. The problem arises because our indicative rules, when they refer us to the laws of a foreign country, refer us to those laws, whatever they may be, at the material time. In this way, they rather call for a step in the dark. What ultimate public policy requires us to do is to look before we leap, and we are restrained from 'taking off' if the results would be too unpalatable. For example, where Russia was the intended matrimonial home, England would have no objection to giving effect to a Russian rule that persons under 20 years are incapable of marriage, though the English age of capacity is lower. But it might be very different with the recent Soviet decree that Russians are incapable of marrying any foreign nationals. This would likely be deemed a basically repugnant type of discrimination.

It is not the ultimate or extraordinary public policy here that is an 'unruly horse'; rather, the unruly horse is the uncertainty of substantive result implicit in our indicative rules, because they require us prima facie to adopt the laws of a foreign country at the material time, whatever their effect might be. The public policy reservation on the operation of these rules, then, is not the unruly horse, but the checkrein on the beast.[5]

The foregoing is what might be called orthodox theory concerning the various policy considerations of the typical Private International Law system. Yet this view has certainly not gone unchallenged. Some jurists would frankly assess the comparative justice of the conflicting and competing national domestic laws, and choose the better law. They would ask – is monogamy better than polygamy? They would ask – is the better law of marriage capacity that which allows cousins to marry?

They would then apply the *better law* in both Redland and Whiteland. Again we may quote Professor Yntema.

> Although equality is a prime ingredient of equity, it is not the only consideration to be taken into account in the administration of justice. As has been indicated, the attainment of security as a conflicts policy supposes that the conflicts rules administered in the different legal systems under considerations should be sufficiently ascertained. This is by no means universally true, since the cases are sporadic and new problems constantly arise. Moreover, the elaboration of law through judicial legislation is a slow process, which frequently hovers for some time between competing theories. Meanwhile, with changes in conditions of life or in the evolution of legal doctrine, the old solutions may become inappropriate or their over-technical application may produce harsh results. In such situations, comparative justice in the individual decision, by which is meant consideration of the desirable result as indicated by comparative study of the underlying policies of the domestic substantive laws, suggests itself as a criterion for the solution of conflicts cases.
>
> In effect, the principle of comparative justice serves in part to complement the principle of security and in part to correct improper effects thereof resulting from artificial applications of stare decisis and like doctrines. Thus, as the need to satisfy the reasonable expectations of the parties argues that there should be a corresponding degree of predictability in the adjudication of conflicts cases in the interests of security, comparison of the substantive law doctrines has significance in considering what may be reasonable in such expectations. In some situations, indeed, as Hancock and others have pointed out, careful analysis of the policies embodied in the competing laws may provide a just solution. On the other hand, where choice is to be made between the application of an obsolete or misconceived law and of more modern legislation, the comparative justice of the newer and better law may outweigh considerations of security, and courts will find ways by appropriate construction to decide as seems to them right.[6]

But really, one must have doubts about the 'comparative justice' approach. I do not believe that the study of comparative law, however sophisticated and distinguished, could or would produce philosophically obvious or politically acceptable criteria of comparative justice. Can an English court really deny the policy content of its own domestic laws in a conflict-of-laws case and say French domestic marriage law is better than English, so *for that reason* we apply French law in England? I doubt whether even an international court could go so far, if, for instance, the Private International Law system were true international law and were, moreover, entrusted to an international appellate judicial body for final interpretation and application. Even then, I suggest that the international judges would have to be supermen, if they were to be expected to choose the 'truly better' national laws and prefer them in conflicts cases. Many conflicting differences are going to remain indefinitely between national substantive laws, and no system for mitigating the undesirable effects of these differences that postulates the international judge or the comparative jurist as a philosopher king has any chance of juridical success or political acceptance.

Furthermore, if one examines the extensive writings of Professor Currie in the United States, one sees the warning flags flying about where the comparative justice approach would in fact lead us.[7] Professor Currie's elaborate (and tedious) reasoning about 'governmental interests' wears the colours of the comparative justice approach, but almost invariably it means in practice that one ends up applying the domestic law of the forum, the country of the court. Professor Currie admits and approves this as the result of his reasoning. So this road leads back to Rome: 'Whoso comes to Rome must do as Romans do.'

In other words, what I fear here is the intolerance that seems to lurk in Professor Currie's views. The comparative justice approach seems to postulate that there is just one 'better' or 'best' legal solution for this or that subject matter. It seems to deny that to an important extent there are high values in diversity – that foreign domestic laws different from those of the forum may be neither better nor worse, but just different. Hence to my mind assessing the comparative justice of the different domestic laws in conflict is something of a trap, if it is offered as the main policy basis of the typical Private International Law system. The more neutral approach of orthodox theory lets in comparative justice only occasionally, as a matter of the extraordinary public policy reservation explained earlier. It should be noted that obnoxious extremes of difference between a foreign domestic law and the law of the forum are reasonably perceptible by a judge. In any event, the occasional operation of this public policy exception is very different from attempting to assess comparative substantive justice every time and in every way as the heart of the process for choice of law. It is the latter to which I have been objecting. I reiterate then that, in my view, the only feasible policy basis for a choice-of-law system is toleration of differences between various domestic national laws, within the wide limits permitted by the extraordinary public policy reservation.

Nevertheless, I do not maintain that all is well with the orthodox approach, in spite of the fact that its main policy assumptions are sound. What then are the problems of the orthodox choice-of-law system and what are the prospects for improving it?

PROBLEMS OF METHOD IN PRIVATE INTERNATIONAL LAW

In countries that have inherited the English Common Law, Private International Law is mainly judge-made law and has the virtues and vices of this origin. Judicial decisions in various countries have afforded an important measure of international equality or uniformity in the senses explained in the preceeding section, and in so doing, the judges have exposed the problems of method that arise in the typical Private International Law system. These are very complex and can only be briefly sketched here. My general conclusion is that refinement and improvement of Private International Law now require international agreement and legislative law reform that is responsive to the terms of such agreements in the states, provinces, or countries affected. In spite of the accomplishments of the past, judicial law-making is too incremental and partial as the method for primary law reform in this field. This seems to be so because the refinement and development needed call for deliberate and systematic treatment in a comprehensive way, subject by subject. Let us consider first the technical improvement of choice-of-law rules, and then issues of assuring uniformity and reciprocity between states respecting such rules.[8]

Looking first at improving the technique of the typical Private International Law system, we note that the judge-made Common Law rules for choice-of-law are relatively few, depending on a small number of broad categories, each of which is linked to an apparently simple connecting factor. Contract issues are referred to the place of contracting, torts to the place where harm was suffered, title to land to the situs of the land, matrimonial status to domicile, and so on. It is true of course that the courts have carried the growth of Private International Law beyond these simple generalities in some respects. For example, in recent decades the courts in some Common Law countries have developed, for conflicts issues in contract and tort, the more sophisticated centre-of-gravity connecting factor. Briefly this means that, in a conflicts case, all the factual place elements in the situation, touching the country of the forum and other countries, are assessed for their dominant collective indication of *the one country* more or most closely connected with the persons and the matters involved. In contract issues, the intention of the parties, if made explicit, is relevant as one place element in the mix. Now this may be an improvement on attributing everything to place of contracting or place of harm, particularly if the weighing of place elements is neutral and objective. But there are also serious faults in this technique, relative to the policy objectives of Privace International Law. For one thing, comparative justice of the differing domestic national laws in conflict may re-enter here by the back door, to the detriment of proper toleration of such differences within the broad limits of the extraordinary public policy reservation. There would be a real tendency for a national court, in weighing a mix of place elements, to find that the centre of gravity favoured the country with the 'more progressive' or 'more just' domestic law. Moreover, as noted earlier, this would all too often turn out to be the law of the forum – the country of the court.

There is another more serious objection related to what has just been said. The theory of Private International Law is that, for example, in a tort situation connected with three countries by its various factual place elements, it should not matter to the result for the injured party in which country he seeks relief in the courts. This should follow, if each country has the same choice-of-law rule for tort. But if this uniform rule has the centre-of-gravity connecting factor, then judicial differences in weighing the relative influence of the various factual place elements in the mix could easily produce a different finding on centre of gravity, country by country.

What these considerations imply is that technical improvement in choice-of-law systems calls for movement in quite a different direction. Generally speaking, we should develop a greater number of choice-of-law rules, rules that are more specific and precise as to both categories of issues, and the significant connecting factors used for each category of issue. It is many years now since Professor W.W. Cook called for a multiplication of working categories in conflict-of-laws situations.[9] This points the way to a more detailed Private International Law system that could be made more responsive to the true variety of the social needs that arise. For example, it seems obvious that there should be several choice-of-law rules for torts, not just a single rule. Personal injuries, conversion of chattels, and defamation should all get different treatment for choice-of-law purposes. The same could be said of some different types of contracts. Law reform along these lines, as stated earlier, is for the most part beyond the capacity of national courts and requires international agreements and responsive legislation in the countries concerned.

Fortunately, in 1968, Canada joined the Hague Conference on Private International Law, and so is now collaborating in efforts along these lines. By way of example we find that in 1968 the delegates of some twenty-five countries at the session of the Hague Conference in that year agreed upon a draft convention concerning choice-of-law rules to deal with traffic accidents involving vehicles on public highways, the obligation being to submit the convention to their respective governments for consideration.[10] So we see this class of torts or delicts given separate treatment. Moreover, no centre-of-gravity connecting factor is used. Rather one finds that three quite precise connecting factors are specified: The state where the accident occurred, the state where a vehicle involved is registered, and the state where a vehicle involved is habitually stationed.

There is not much chance for courts to differ on the evidence concerning where these connecting factors point in a particular case. Moreover the above named place elements are specified to be used singly or in combination in quite definite ways, to choose the domestic law that is to determine liability in favour of or against a driver, an owner, a passenger, a pedestrian, or certain combinations of such persons. The scheme of this convention is rather complex at first sight, but the paradox is that this detail brings precision and certainty in choosing the applicable domestic law. Moreover this is to be done subject only to the extraordinary public policy reservation mentioned earlier. So it is apparent that this typical draft convention assumes and implements the orthodox policy thrust of Private International Law, that which pursues equality through tolerance of differences, as explained earlier. In 1972 the Hague Conference was scheduled to deal with a draft convention for determining products liability in interstate situations. No doubt the proposed draft on this subject will exhibit the characteristics just noticed in the convention on highway accidents.

There are some further reasons, resting on analytical jurisprudence, for believing that the approach of the Hague Conference to these problems of Private International Law is the correct and fruitful one. The Hague Conference emphasizes the importance of uniformity of Private International Law systems between countries, and strives to obtain this uniformity by conventions that will be ratified and implemented as treaties and thus acquire the full status of superior international law. On the other hand, if such rules for choice-of-law are national law only, then they may vary from country to country, and what are known as 'renvoi' situations may arise. For example, on particular facts, English Private International Law may refer a person's matrimonial status to the law of France as the law of the country of domicile, whereas French Private International Law would refer that same person's matrimonial status to the law of England as the law of the country of his nationality. If the English reference to French law includes the French Private International Law, then that law would refer the issue back to English law, and so a sterile oscillation of references would be set up for which there is no logical or sensible solution. Even if a Private International Law system is a national system only, its references to another country's laws should be taken as references to the domestic internal law of that other country only. Nothing else makes sense as a technique for serving the legitimate policy objectives of the typical Private International Law system, even if the authoritative status of that system is as a branch of the national law only. Of course, uniformity of Private International Law rules as between countries eliminates the possibility of 'renvoi' situations, and so avoids this trap of wrongful method or technique. Even so, no doubt out of abundant caution, we find that the Hague convention on highway accidents specifies that reference to the law of the place of the accident is a reference to the internal or domestic law of that country only. The same is true of the other place references in the convention.

Finally at the level of problems of technique, we should note that a common international appellate tribunal of interpretation is needed, even for internationally uniform rules of Private International Law, if such uniformity is to bring all the benefits it should in terms of equal protection of the laws. The same words or concepts may receive differing interpretations in different national courts, and only a common appellate tribunal can control this intractable element, to attain uniformity of interpretation. In this connection, it should be stressed that a uniform and restrictive interpretation of the extraordinary public policy exception is necessary to the full success of a uniform Private International Law system. An international appellate court could provide such uniform and restrictive interpretation.[11]

Some explanation should now be made concerning the scope of this essay. Consideration has so far been concentrated on the choice-of-law rules of the typical Private International Law system, but such a system also includes two other areas: i / rules for the assumption of jurisdiction by national courts to hear a case in the first place, and ii / rules for the recognition and enforcement of foreign judgments by the courts of a national state. I do not consider the former to be fundamental because, if the choice-of-law rules are the same for the courts of the different countries concerned, and if there is a common appellate tribunal, it does not matter in which country's courts the case is tried. Even if there is not uniformity of choice-of-law rules or a common appellate tribunal, provided the country of the court does have a well-articulated system of choice-of-law rules, that is the governing consideration in any event.

As for the recognition of foreign judgments by the courts of a given national state, there are certainly highly significant elements here, related to giving the root idea of *res judicata* some degree of international operation. But also, every foreign judgment involves the use by the foreign court that rendered the judgment of its own or another country's substantive domestic laws, to reach the result expressed in the judgment. So some choice-of-law system is usually vital in the background of the recognition cases in any event.

In short, as space is limited and as the choice-of-law rules are, in my view, the most fundamental part of the typical Private International Law system, this essay is confined to their significance. On this basis, the following final questions are relevant. What conclusions may we now draw about Private International Law, including its relations to Public International Law? What is the bearing of these conclusions on the future of Private International Law in Canada and the provinces?

GENERAL CONCLUSIONS:
PRIVATE INTERNATIONAL LAW IN CANADA AND THE PROVINCES

We may now return briefly to the question of the authoritative nature of the choice-of-law rules of Private International Law. Are they part of a true international law, or are they a branch of the national law of the state, and thus variable country by country? It must be conceded, in my view, that they have for the most part the latter character at present, though the total picture is a mixed one. As we have seen, a purely national choice-of-law system may take some special account of foreign facts, and thereby implement some important equalities for the persons involved in interstate situations. Thus national laws recognize that interstate situations may deserve different treatment from purely domestic situations. It is true that conditions of life in the modern world increasingly dictate that there should be such recognition, but these conditions, international though they be, are not in themselves superior international law. Such international influences, though very real, have not yet been precisely formulated in rules or principles widely accepted over a period of time. Without this, they cannot be characterized as international law. In other words, national law can respond to international facts and influences without itself becoming international law in the process.

Yet we have also seen that a Private International Law system best serves its purpose if there is uniformity of choice-of-law rules between different countries, backed up by uniform interpretation of evidence and concepts in a common international appellate tribunal. Only if this is so can there be reciprocity and uniformity of result, for the persons concerned, among different countries. Studies in comparative jurisprudence, however important and suggestive, will not themselves bring this reciprocity about. The uniform rules must be scientifically drafted and embodied in model codes or international conventions. As the model codes are widely adopted, or the international conventions ratified and implemented, true superior international law emerges. To a limited extent this has happened now, and more progress along these lines seems the hope of the future. So, in this sense, those who look for true international law here have the last word.

There are certainly some problems in all this for Canada. On many subjects, Private International Law is within provincial and not federal legislative jurisdiction under our federal constitution. For many if not most subjects, the provinces form separate law districts in Private International Law. Hence, giving legislative effect to the Hague conventions raises all the issues and problems of the power to implement treaties in Canada – the problems articulated in the *Labour Conventions* case of 1937.

We need not give up on attempting to secure ratification and implementation of appropriate Hague conventions, particularly since we are now helping to formulate them. Meanwhile, we can at least take the terms of the Hague conventions as model codes or statutes which may be enacted locally, apart from any international obligations to do so. An eminent Canadian authority, Dr Horace E. Read of Dalhousie University, sees much wisdom in the latter course. He has written as follows:

There are two ways in which Canada and its provinces can gain the advantages of membership in the Hague Conference. One is by Canada ratifying its conventions and implementing them by statutes enacted by the constitutionally competent legislatures. The other is by refraining from ratification and instead passing uniform acts that incorporate the provisions of the conventions. It is said that law reform is generally more easily attainable in Western Europe and the United Kingdom by adopting international conventions than by uniform legislation. The draw-back to ratifying conventions is that the adhering government loses its freedom of action and the law is frozen until the other adhering countries agree to amendment of the conventions. Among the provinces and territories of Canada uniform legislation has been used with considerable success. The Conference of Commissioners on Uniformity of Legislation in Canada was organized in 1918 and since then has contributed to law reform by preparing sixty-four model statutes, most of which have been enacted by a large majority of the provincial legislatures. This seems to indicate that in this country the advantages of membership in the Hague Conference could be better gained, not by formal adherence to the conventions but by active participation in its work and use of its conventions as models for uniform acts. In this way, perhaps with an occasional slight departure from uniformity, greater flexibility and adaptability to conditions peculiar to this country could be ensured.[12]

NOTES

1 *In re Regulation and Control of Radio Communication in Canada,* [1932] A.C. 304: 'Canada as a Dominion is one of the signatories to the convention. In a question with foreign powers the persons who might infringe some of the stipulations in the convention would not be the Dominion of Canada as a whole but would be individual persons residing in Canada. These persons must so to speak be kept in order by legislation and the only legislation that can deal with them all at once is Dominion legislation' (Viscount Dunedin, at 312).

2 D.P. O'Connell, *International Law* (2nd rev ed, 1970) vol 1, 38–43.

3 H.E.Yntema, 'The Objectives of Private International Law' (1957), 35 *Can. Bar Rev.* 721 at 731.

4 Elliot E. Cheatham, 'Problems and Methods in Conflict of Laws' in Academie de Droit International, *Recueil des Cours* (1960) tome 1, 233, especially chapter VI, 279.

5 W.R. Lederman, 'Conflict Avoidance by International Agreement' (1956), 21 *Law and Contemporary Problems* 581, at 595–6.

6 Yntema, *supra* note 3, at 737–8.

7 B. Currie, 'The Constitution and the Choice of Law: Governmental Interests and the Judicial Function' (1958), 26 *U. Chi. L. Rev.* 9. Also, see the criticism of Currie's views by M. Baer, 'Guest Statutes in Conflict of Laws' (1967), 16 *Buffalo L. Rev.* 537, at 573–8.

8 This subject was analysed more fully in my 1956 essay cited *supra* note 5.

9 W.W. Cook, *The Logical and Legal Bases of the Conflict of Laws* (1942).

10 *Proceedings of the Fifty-First Annual Meeting of the Conference of Commissioners on Uniformity of Legislation in Canada* (1969) 75. The text of the convention referred to begins at 86. See also J.-G. Castel, 'Canada and The Hague Conference on Private International Law' (1967), 45 *Can. Bar Rev.* 1 and *Proceedings of the Fifty-Second Annual Meeting of the Conference of Commissioners on Uniformity of Legislation in Canada* (1970) for 'Report of The Commissioners for Quebec on the Implementation of Conventions Adopted by The Hague Conference' 157, 177.

11 Lederman, *supra* note 5, at 603–4.

12 Quoted from the January 1969 issue of *The Ansul* (Dalhousie University Law School) by the Quebec commissioners in the *Proceedings* (1970), *supra* note 10, at 211–12.

PRACTICES

EMILIO S. BINAVINCE

7/Canadian Practice in Matters of Recognition*

It is desirable at the start to stake out the scope of this chapter. First, its discussion is confined to the recognition of states and governments. Other categories of recognition, such as the recognition of belligerency, insurgency, territorial change, and other relevant acts or events, cannot be treated, with the adequacy they deserve within the limits of this paper. Second, the object of this chapter is not to add to the already overwhelming periodical discussion of recognition, but rather to sketch the outlines of Canadian practice, with occasional doctrinal excursus to provide perspective.

Reliance has been placed in large measure on secondary materials for which at times no references can be given. The reason for this is that external affairs documents customarily bear the seal of secrecy for extended periods of time, after which they are published under the authority of the Department of External Affairs. The first set of volumes containing such documents was recently published, encompassing the period 1909 to 1925. For reasons which will become obvious, this period is – to put it bluntly – the time of doldrums in Canadian recognition practice. The end of World War II marks the beginning of intense Canadian interest in recognition. Unfortunately, documents relating to this period and to the present are not freely open to scrutiny.

RECOGNITION AND THE LEGAL ORDER

'Recognition' is a fundamental legal institution in both primitive and modern municipal legal systems. It operates as a formal machinery that marks the acquisition of legal personality, of the capacity to do certain acts with legal effects, or of the legitimization of certain acts or events. For instance, in primitive society, where a human being was not the same as a person, recognition marked the transition of a slave from chattel to person; in modern society, recognition confers legal competence in certain matters to a wife or an illegitimate child.

The early historical function of recognition in international law parallels its municipal law counterpart. The legal capacity to pursue a just war required, already in the middle ages, a recognized *auctoritas principis*; a ship that wanted to avoid the treatment of a pirate vessel must carry a recognized flag; and a ruler who wished to be treated as a sovereign must not recognize a superior authority.[1] In the nineteenth century, recognition acquired a new dimension of importance beyond

---

*In the course of the preparation of this article, Mr Lorne Clarke, Department of External Affairs, and Mr E. Haythorne have rendered invaluable assistance. Specifically, the references to government papers were supplied by Mr Clarke; Mr Haythorne undertook the collection of relevant materials. The section on 'Form of Recognition' is substantially based on Mr Haythorne's draft of the topic.

such traditional matters. The old Christian states of western Europe that formed the original Family of Nations in the nineteenth century resorted to recognition as a device to accord to a new state membership in the Family. At that time, the mere acquisition of statehood did not automatically confer membership in the Family of Nations; recognition by the original members of the Family of Nations was the crucial operative fact that effected the transition of a state from a legal non-entity into the status of a member of the international community. Within the limits of this historical context, Lauterpacht's somewhat sweeping statement must be conceded validity: 'A State is, and becomes, an International Person through recognition only and exclusively ... In fact it is difficult to see what the function of recognition could be if the mere claim of a community to be an independent State, in the meaning of International Law, gave it a right to membership of the Family of Nations. Through recognition only and exclusively a State becomes an International Person and a subject of International Law.'[2]

The resort to the machinery of recognition to confer membership in the Family of Nations rested on a fundamental consideration: the desire to limit the number of states that could claim rights and duties under what was then simply a 'European Law of Nations.' The fundamental statement that 'the States of the world form the community governed by international law,' contained in the Draft Declaration on Rights and Duties of States,[3] was not an axiom of international law. At that time, international rights and duties were propositions which flowed directly from international personality, and since international personality was conditioned by membership in the limited club of states that formed the original Family of Nations, an unrecognized state had neither international personality nor international rights and duties.[4]

It is today debatable whether recognition still exerts this limitative function; nonetheless recognition remains a significant institution of international law. Even on such matters as sources of international law, recognition possesses a fundamental role. Under article 38 of the Statute of the International Court of Justice, the court is directed to apply rules found in international conventions 'expressly recognized' by the contesting states and general principles of law 'recognized' by civilized nations. With respect to international customs, it is recognition of the general practice as a binding rule of law by the states that gives it its operative character.[5] The reason for the continuing and pervading importance of recognition in international law stems from the anarchic assumption of positivism upon which the authority of modern international law is theoretically founded. As J. Mervyn Jones explains:

> International law, except in so far as it has been modified by treaty provisions, leaves a state free to judge for itself whether a given state of facts fall within a given international legal category. The rule is that a state, subject to its treaty obligations, is not bound to accept a judgment other than its own upon a question of international law or international status. The importance of recognition in international relations and in national courts arises from this peculiar feature of the international legal order.[6]

CANADIAN SOVEREIGNTY, FOREIGN POLICY, AND RECOGNITION

The act of according recognition to a state, government, belligerents, and other relevant international law events is a significant incident of sovereignty. It is, like the power to declare war, a more unequivocal evidence of a sovereign government than the power to enter into international agreements.[7] It is thus somewhat surprising that the great mass of historical analysis on Canada's emergence to statehood, largely concentrated on the treaty-making power, has ignored the role of recognition.[8] Indeed, it is this overwhelming bias towards the treaty-making power that led the meetings of the heads of the Department of External Affairs in 1950 to go as far as to say that Canada did not acquire the power to accord recognition independently of the United Kingdom as late as the Imperial Conference of 1926. To clarify this point, it is necessary to deal briefly with Canada's first act of recognition.

In 1923 and the years preceding it, we find no evidence of Canada's attempt to claim the power to accord recognition. In matters of recognition Canada had not been as vociferous as she had been in her claim to enter into international agreements. For one thing, there had not been many occasions which confronted her that involved the exercise of the power to recognize. For another, the factors that shaped Canadian foreign policy had been largely identical with those of the United Kingdom. It was thus natural, and indeed more convenient, that British recognition practice was calmly accepted and considered as automatic Canadian recognition. For this reason, when Canada's first act of recognition was made in 1924, it occurred without dramatic repercussions; it was simply peripheral to the more urgent skirmishes on the treaty power.

On 16 March 1921 the United Kingdom and the Union of Soviet Socialist Republics entered into a trade agreement which, in accordance with the procedure then established, was subsequently endorsed and made applicable to Canada by Mackenzie King's government. As a result, a limited form of trade and consular relations had been established between Canada and Russia, with Russia appointing an official agent in Montreal. As early as 1921 the British government had accorded recognition to the Soviet government as *de facto* government in Russia and subsequently, on 1 February 1924, the Soviet government was recognized *de jure*. On 20 March 1924 Mr Yazikoff, the official agent of the Soviet Union in Canada, wrote to Prime Minister King as follows:

> Referring to the conference which I had with you yesterday, and wishing to have a more definite basis for trade negotiation and for the performance of my other functions, I would ask you to be good enough to inform me whether the *de jure* recognition of the Union of Soviet Socialist Republics by his Britannic Majesty's Government on first of February last, comprehends recognition by Canada.[9]

Mr Yazikoff was simply securing an endorsement of the British recognition by Canada.

Mr King's position, however, was that the British recognition was not automatically to be considered Canadian recognition and that it was not enough that Canada declared that the British action applied to Canada: it was necessary that Canada accorded separate recognition.[10] In his reply to Mr Yazikoff on 24 March, he said: 'Following up my conversation of a few days ago, and with special reference to your letter of the 20th instant, I have the honour, in the best interest of both countries, to represent that Canada is prepared to recognize the Union of Soviet Socialist Republics.'[11]

Mr King's letter is ambiguous, for it did not specifically state that, by his letter,

Canada was according formal recognition to the Soviet republic; it simply stated that 'Canada is prepared to recognize' it. One may assume that a formal recognition would subsequently be made, but no formal recognition followed this letter. This ambiguity was raised by the Consul General of Germany, Mr L. Kempff, who wrote to Mr King on 2 April 1924:

> The *Montreal Gazette* of March 27th, reprints your letter to Mr Alex Yazikoff, Agent in Canada of the Union of Soviet Socialist Republics, in which you represent that Canada is prepared to recognize the Union of Soviet Socialist Republics. On reading your letter it is not quite clear to me whether it expressed merely a preparedness on the part of Canada to recognize the Soviet Republic, so that formal recognition may be expected later, or whether it actually contains a definite recognition, as the *Gazette* seems to assume.
>
> As my government is naturally greatly interested to know whether the Union of Soviet Socialist Republics is formally recognized by the Canadian Government, I should be grateful if you would be so kind as to enlighten me on the subject.[12]

Joseph Pope, the undersecretary of state for External Affairs, argued in a letter dated 16 April that Mr King's letter of 24 March constituted formal recognition: 'In reply to your letter of the 2nd instant to the Prime Minister on the question of the recognition of the Union of Soviet Socialist Republics, I am desired by Mr. King to inform you that the Union of Soviet Socialist Republics is formally recognized by the Canadian Government.'[13]

Later, on 23 June 1924, the prime minister himself affirmed the formal recognition of the Soviet Union in a statement in the House of Commons in reply to Mr J.S. Woodsworth:

> Canada's formal recognition of the Union of Soviet Socialist Republics was conveyed to their official agent in Canada, Mr A. Yazikoff, in a letter from the Prime Minister dated the 24th of March 1924. Among the states included in the Union of Soviet Socialist Republics which Canada has recognized is a Ukrainian Socialist Soviet Republic. Canada has not, however, recognized the Ukrainian People's Republic.[14]

The selection of the Imperial Conference of 1926 as the decisive date of Canada's acquisition of her independent power to recognize is thus open to serious challenge, even if it is accepted as the date Canada acquired the power to enter into international agreements. The role of the United Kingdom as persuasive force on the conclusion of Canadian international agreements, then precariously supported by the slogan of avoiding embarrassment to the basic unity of imperial foreign policy, was already tenuous after World War I. The signing of the Halibut Convention with the United States in 1923 swept away, both in substance and form, this role of the United Kingdom. Although the Imperial Conference of 1923, which followed a few months later, piously declared a semblance of this role for the United Kingdom, it also approved the procedure adopted by Canada on the conclusion of the Halibut Convention.[15] Under the resolution of the 1923 Imperial Conference, the United Kingdom had no more significant influence on the negotiation of Canadian treaties than that possessed by the other dominions and India. Thus, it is fair to consider the subsequent developments brought about by the Imperial Conference of 1926 and the enactment of the Statute of Westminster in 1931 as simple and formal acknowledgments of the historic events that started with the signing of the Halibut Convention.

However, an independent foreign policy dimension in Canadian recognition practice emerged at a much later date than acquisition of the power to recognize. In the main the reasons were obvious enough and valid at the time. The imperialist attitude that Canada should follow the lead of the United Kingdom in the field of foreign policy in the belief that the long-range interest of Canada could best be served by this action was strong and remained a significant factor in Canadian foreign policy until after World War II. Necessarily, Canadian recognition relied heavily on British leadership. Although Mackenzie King asserted Canada's legal right to accord separate recognition to the Soviet republics, his government's recognition of the Soviet republics was based on the British foreign policy initiatives. When the British foreign policy towards the Soviet Union changed in 1927, it was to be expected that Canada's attitude to the Soviet Union would shift accordingly. In that year the British government decided to break off relations with Russia and required the withdrawal of the Russian mission because of alleged communist propaganda and espionage carried out under its auspices in London. Canada followed suit and secured a withdrawal of the trade delegation in Montreal. Although Mackenzie King protested that his government's action was not 'necessarily obsequious, a mere invitation, or, above all, that it is in any shape or form yielding to dictation,' and that the circulation of communist propaganda literature in Canada, among other actions, of the Russian trade mission in Montreal was a reason for the severance of Canadian relations with Russia, he conceded that after Great Britain had severed connections with it in the matter of trade, this country would have been left in the awkward position of being one part of the Empire which had maintained relations, a 'relationship which was likely to prove embarrassing to the rest of the British Empire.'[16] In 1931 Canada again calmly followed British leadership in the recognition of the new Spanish Republic; Great Britain, Canada, Australia, New Zealand, South Africa, and the Irish Free State accorded recognition in six separate documents.

On the surface one might notice a fragile assertion of autonomous Canadian recognition policy during the turbulence of World War II. The attitude of Canada from 1940 to 1942 towards the Vichy regime and General de Gaulle's government-in-exile in London appeared to veer away from British policy, and the opponents of the government of Prime Minister King found it a lever for criticism. On 24 February 1941 Mr Hanson, leader of the opposition, confronted Mackenzie King in the House about this situation: 'I do not think it is the clear duty of this government to take every action to strengthen the hand of Marshal Pétain and his government as at present constituted ... I would ask the Prime Minister to state to the House whether the present situation has the full consent and approval of the British government.'[17] The presence in Ottawa of a representative of the Vichy government and in Paris of a Canadian representative was asserted as an embarrassment. On 25 February the prime minister was pointedly asked: 'What exactly are our relationships with the two governments [Vichy, and the government of General de Gaulle]?'[18] Mackenzie King's reply to opposition questions asserted the consistency of this action with British policy:

> The leader of the opposition last night asked ... whether the action of the Canadian government in having Mr Dupuy as chargé d'affaires representing Canada at Vichy, as he has done, had the full approval of the government of the United Kingdom. I may say that not only has Canada's action been approved by the government of Great Britain but we have been thanked very warmly by the British Prime Minister for the services which we have been able to render at this time through the association which this country has maintained with France.[19]

As the war progressed, imperial policy as determined by London increasingly weakened as a factor in Canadian recognition practice. Two significant factors combined to bring about this situation. First, World War II had, with the weakness of Great Britain to hold its own against the Axis powers, transformed the imperial issues into international issues. Second, the United States had dominated all fronts encompassed by the war. Thus arose the two dimensions of Canadian foreign policy: the international and American relations, each alternating in significance from World War II to the present. The recognition of the number of governments-in-exile in London – Belgium, Czechoslovakia, France, Greece, the Netherlands, Norway, Poland, Yugoslavia – were accorded so as to facilitate the military and political cooperation that appeared necessary in waging the war. The recognition of Israel in 1948, Korea in 1949, West Germany in 1949, Japan in 1952, and the new African and Asian states in the 1950s and 1960s was a pattern of recognition practice where considerations of international relations and American attitudes emerged more significantly than the British imperial policy. In these cases Canadian practice had adequately deferred to American intentions before according recognition, although Canadian interpretation of international affairs loomed large in the background. In 1950 the British recognition of Red China finally crystallized the replacement of Great Britain by the United States in the foreign policy dimension of Canadian recognition practice. Canada, for a time, had seriously considered following the lead of the United Kingdom and extending recognition to the Peking government.[20] In the end, however, United States leadership, coupled with international considerations such as the intervention of the Korean War, the status of Formosa, and Peking's announced refusal to honour international obligations inconsistent with its own interest, prevailed.

Canadian dependence on United States initiative has, at times, been disturbingly excessive. With respect to Latin American countries, for instance, Canadian decision to recognize or not is, in essence, what the United States has decided. Even in other cases, Canada seems afraid to assume the responsibility of creative decision-making as a memorandum of the legal division of the Department of External Affairs frankly admits: 'In most instances of recognition the Canadian Government's decision *has ultimately hinged on a single criterion*, i.e. whether other countries, and particularly the U.S. had extended recognition or not.'[21] But since 1968, when the Trudeau government came to power, the delicate interplay of international and American considerations seems to have been resolved increasingly in favour of an autonomous Canadian definition of international relations. In October 1970 the crucial step to recognize Peking displayed indifference to United States attitude and was based solely on Canadian assessment. Although this step may well prove to be a Copernican turn, it is still premature to say that Canada has taken the decisive turn towards a creative role in world politics. Today, the United States occupies a position that Great Britain had earlier occupied in Canadian foreign policy:

> Since what Professor F.H. Underhill has called the revolution of 1940 the United States has come to occupy the position in the Canadian scheme of things formerly occupied by Great Britain. It is the position of an elder brother whose protection is expected and relied but whose tendency to dominate is feared ... In a sense Canada now wages against the United States the battle of status which it fought against the British prior to the Statute of Westminster, of 1931.[22]

THE INTERPLAY OF POLICY AND LEGALITY IN CANADIAN RECOGNITION PRACTICE

Lauterpacht's work, *Recognition in International Law*,[23] is a masterly endeavour to unravel the complex nature of recognition. The nature of recognition is the central issue in the debate of two contending theories: the declaratory theory and the constitutive theory. According to the widely accepted declaratory theory, the recognition of a state or government is simply an acknowledgment of the reality that a new state has emerged or that a new government had the actual capacity to act for the state it represents. The new state becomes a subject in international law if the organized community of people concerned satisfies all the conditions for statehood, regardless of recognition. In the same manner, a new government that came to power through unconstitutional means possesses the status of an organ of the state if it exercises over the populace and the territory an effective and reasonably stable control. In both instances, the presence of factual requirements creates personality or capacity to possess rights and duties even before recognition is received.[24] Theoretically, the declaratory theory is based on a natural law premise: insofar as personality and capacity are concerned, states or governments acquire them, like natural persons, automatically from mere factual existence. The will of other states (as expressed in recognition), though the fundamental basis of the authority of international law, is thus irrelevant.[25] Recognition is a unilateral act whose main function in international law is to remove any doubt that flows from the principle of effectivity; it is accorded so that the existence of the state or the status of a government can no longer be challenged.

The classical constitutive theory gave full force to the fundamental assumption of positivism that international law is founded on the consent of the states. Accordingly, recognition was conceived as a contract through which the recognized state or government is accorded personality or capacity to possess rights and duties in the community of nations. Although the bilateral nature of recognition has been somewhat modified to overcome logical objections, the main thesis of the constitutive theory remains unchanged: that recognition has a certain measure of creative character to the extent that, as in the original Family of Nations, it operates as the crucial machinery that effects transition in status.[26] The mere presence of all factual requirements of statehood or of a new government does not confer personality or capacity to possess rights and obligations in international law.[27]

The underlying reason for the wide acceptance of the declaratory theory in state practice and among scholars is the fact that the declaratory theory leaves to the recognizing state the freedom to treat recognition as a political act in which its interpretation of national interest can be brought to bear in international relations.[28] The constitutive theory, on the other hand, compels a decision to recognize on legal criteria, thus excluding the role of political considerations in recognition practice. To insulate the integrity of the legal criteria from politics, leading supporters of the constitutive theory argue for the existence in international law of a duty to recognize upon the presence of the legal criteria.[29] The legal nature of recognition, therefore, raises the problem of the nature of the act of recognition itself. As Rosseau accurately put it: 'Deux grandes théories sont ici en presence, celle de la reconnaisance acte politique et de la reconnaisance acte juridique.'[30]

Canadian practice on recognition reflects this interplay of politics and legality. It is impossible to find any evidence of the Canadian government according or refusing recognition expressly on the basis of political expediency. As a matter of procedure the political division of the Department of External Affairs, with the assistance of the Canadian mission abroad, assumes the function of ascertaining facts tending to establish the objective criteria. If the political division is satisfied that the criteria have been met, it advises the minister accordingly. At the same time, the political division brings to the attention of the minister any exceptional circumstances of a political nature, such as the intention of friendly states to recognize or not to recognize, which in its opinion should be taken into consideration by the minister before the Canadian government's decision to recognize is finally arrived at. In most instances, Canada had granted or refused recognition, with an adequate articulation of the observance of legality. In these cases, politics and legality often coincide, and Canada generally views non-recognition as disadvantageous to national interest. Reflecting this consideration, the minister of external affairs on the occasion of the NATO conference in February 1964, said:

> I think that it can safely be said that in general in assessing the important factors governing relations between governments there are certain disadvantages in non-recognition of a government. This non-recognition not only prevents first-hand observation of conditions within the state, but also discourages the contacts which may eventually help improve understanding, modify policy, and bring about better relations. Undoubtedly, the withholding of recognition may on occasion prove effective in the case of new regimes in small countries which have not established effective control over the territory by their own national means and which therefore depend to a considerable extent on support from the outside. For such cases there may be from time to time political advantages to the withholding of recognition from states or governments for a limited period of time in order to obtain concessions or modifications in policy. In general, however, unless there are exceptional circumstances, it is the Canadian view that the recognition of a government represents acknowledgment of facts, that is, of the establishment of effective control by that government. It certainly need not imply acceptance of all the territorial claims of the government being recognized.

In the few cases in which significant national interest and legality obviously clash, Canada has decided in favour of politics. To reach this result, Canada still manages to profess adherence to legality by adopting the technique usually practised by the United States: either by adopting an interpretation of one or more of the legal criteria in a way determined by political expediency, or by advancing an additional condition which, though not widely accepted as a rule in international law, offers an adequately plausible justification.

THE OBJECTIVE LEGAL CRITERIA OF RECOGNITION

It is a rule of international law that certain objective legal criteria of recognition of state or new government must be observed otherwise the recognition is invalid and can be considered as international delict of intervention. The fulfilment of these criteria makes the recognition both lawful and effective.[31] The states, however, enjoy a great degree of freedom in ascertaining the facts in each particular situation and in assessing whether these facts meet the legal criteria. This freedom opens the door for the role of political expediency.

The principle of effectivity

The principle of effectivity is the generally accepted minimum criterion for a valid and non-delictual recognition.[32] What, however, in particular are the requirements of the principle of effectivity is the subject of considerable debate. As a general proposition, it is stated that this principle, applied to new state, requires that it must possess all the necessary conditions for statehood; in the case of new governments, it must have effective and stable control of both territory and the people of the state.

Recognition of states

With respect to recognition of state, Canadian practice has given full scope to the principle of effectivity. In granting recognition to the new African and Asian states, the Canadian position was consistent with the practice of the majority of states in the world. The recognition of the state of Israel, however, did not come as readily as in the case of the African and Asian states. Canada took almost eight months to evaluate the situation and form a decision; when it did, it extended only *de facto* recognition. It was the territorial controversy that accompanied the establishment of the state of Israel that had given pause to the Canadian government. On 24 December 1948 the secretary of state for external affairs made the following announcement:

> The Canadian Government today informed the provisional government of Israel that the Canadian Government recognizes *de facto* the State of Israel in Palestine and that it also recognizes *de facto* the authority of the provisional government of Israel.
>
> The State of Israel was proclaimed on May 15, 1948. During the seven (7) months that have elapsed, the State of Israel has, in the opinion of the Canadian Government, given satisfactory proof that it complies with the essential conditions of statehood. These essential conditions are generally recognized to be external independence and effective

internal government within a reasonably well-defined territory.

The provisional government of Israel has been informed that the recognition given by Canada is accorded in the knowledge that the boundaries of the new State have not as yet been precisely defined, and in the hope that it may be possible to settle these and all other outstanding questions in the spirit of the resolution adopted by the General Assembly of the United Nations on December 11, 1948.

The following is the text of the message of December 24, 1948, from the Secretary of State for External Affairs to Mr Mohame Shertale, Foreign Secretary of the Provisional Government of Israel.

'I have the honour to inform you, on behalf of the Government of Canada, that Canada recognizes *de facto* the authority of the Provisional Government of Israel, of which you are a member. This recognition is accorded in the knowledge that the boundaries of the new State have not as yet been precisely defined, and in the hope that it may be possible to settle these and other outstanding questions in the spirit of the Resolution adopted by the General Assembly of the United Nations on December 11, 1948.'[33]

Mr Pearson also stressed that the recognition of the state of Israel was separate from that of Israel's admission to the United Nations. In the Security Council, Canada abstained from voting on Israel's admission to the United Nations because it believed that further time was required to examine the boundary issue. Because the boundaries established for the state of Israel were not acceptable either to Israel or the neighbouring Arab states, Canada was anxious not to be put into the position of appearing to accept them in voting for the Israel application.[34] It was not until 11 May 1949 that Canada extended *de jure* recognition which was implied in the Canadian vote in the General Assembly in favour of admitting Israel to membership as a state possessing the qualifications for membership.[35]

With regard to the recognition of East Germany as a state, the principle of effectivity was defined in terms of political expediency as determined by the wider western political and military strategy. The strategy proceeded from the assumption that Germany remains a single state and that its division is simply transitional: a reunited country under one democratic government was the ultimate objective of the western powers. At the London Conference of 28 September to 3 October 1954, the United States, France, and Great Britain declared: 'They consider the Government of the Federal Republic as the only German Government freely and legitimately constituted and, therefore, entitled to speak for Germany as the representative of the German people in international affairs.' The secretary of state for external affairs, on 24 October 1954, committed Canada to the above declaration: 'My own Government ... fully endorses and associates itself with the declaration which has been made; and we will do what we can, or should, to ensure that the objectives behind the declaration, to which we subscribe, are realized.'[36]

This strategy thus transforms the issue of recognition of East Germany as a state into the recognition of government, and by according recognition to the government sponsored by the western powers in West Germany, accompanied by a denial of any status to the Soviet supported government in East Germany, the assumption of the strategy is maintained. Accordingly, Canada granted recognition to the Federal Republic of Germany shortly after its proclamation on 21 September 1949, but withheld recognition of the German Democratic Republic which was established on 5 October 1949. In refusing recognition to the DDR, the position of Canada was stated as follows:

> The new 'Government' in spite of lavish claims to independence, was in fact permitted by Moscow only to assume the administrative functions formerly exercised by the Soviet Military Authority except in matters relating to the fulfillment of the Potsdam Resolutions and other four-power agreement in Germany. Early statements in the Communist press that this step would be followed by a peace treaty and a withdrawal of Soviet forces, have, so far, not been justified by Soviet statements or actions. It is clear that this body does not satisfy the Canadian government's views on the form of political organization for Germany as given in the government statement of January 30, 1947 (H.C. Debs. Jan. 30, 1947, p. 9, paras. 15–18). The government has therefore endeavoured to refrain from any act that could be taken as giving even limited recognition to this regime.[37]

This position has changed little; Canada remains indifferent, for instance, to the application of East Germany for United Nations membership.[38] Willy Brandt's recent venture into a new *Ostpolitik* has yet to influence Canadian attitude towards East Germany. In any event, it seems beyond challenge that if the principle of effectivity were objectively applied, Canadian non-recognition of the state of East Germany is difficult to justify: the DDR has as much effective government and control in East Germany and independence from the USSR as other eastern communist countries that Canada has recognized. It is likely that the House of Lord's judicial confirmation of the alleged Russian control of East Germany and of the fiction of the agency mandate of the DDR government in *Carl Zeiss Stiftung* v *Rayner*[39] will sustain for sometime the rejection of the principle of effectivity with respect to the state of East Germany.

In two recent secession attempts in Africa – that of Biafra and Southern Rhodesia – Canada adhered to legality in one case, defying significant popular sentiment in Canada, and allowed political expediency, consistent with world and Canadian opinion, to govern the other. In both cases, as in the case of East Germany, the issue of effective, organized, and independent government provided the legal leverage. In the case of Biafra, the government of Colonel Ojukwu was obviously lacking demonstrated effective control of both territory and people and was short of adequate administrative organization. The Canadian refusal to grant *de jure* or *de facto* recognition of his government, more so of the state of Biafra, was clearly legally well founded. In the case of Southern Rhodesia, however, politics was more apparent than legality. Considering the unquestionably demonstrated effective and organized government of Prime Minister Smith and his independent action in administering the country after its Unilateral Declaration of Independence, it seems difficult to contend that conditions of statehood do not exist. The Canadian policy towards Southern Rhodesia rules out – even given stronger evidence of the independence of Prime Minister Smith's government than now available – any Canadian recognition as long as independence is declared unilaterally and no form of majority rule is forthcoming. Indeed, even before the UDI of 11 November 1965 – on 30 April 1965 – the secretary of state for external affairs had unequivocally stated this position:

The Government has made clear on a number of occasions our view that a unilateral declaration of independence by the Rhodesian Government would be a deplorable act which would lead to very serious economic and international political difficulties in Rhodesia. Moreover, we think the repercussions throughout Africa, particularly in race relations, might be serious. We have conveyed our views to the Rhodesian Government. We earnestly hope that the Southern Rhodesian Government will take no such action. We have of course paid particular attention to the statement made yesterday in the British House of Commons.

In his statement in this House on July 17, 1964, following the Commonwealth Prime Ministers' meeting, the Prime Minister indicated that Canada would not recognize the validity of a unilateral declaration of independence by the Rhodesian Government. If such a declaration took place we would have to consider other measures, in consultation with other Commonwealth Governments.

I should, however, add that negotiations on independence between the British and Rhodesian Governments are still going on. I hope they will eventually result in agreement on a program which will lead to independence for Rhodesia within the Commonwealth, in the words of the communiqué issued by the Prime Ministers' Conference, 'at the earliest practical time on the basis of majority rule.'[40]

When UDI occurred, Canada took strong counter-measures to supplement its action of non-recognition: withdrew the Canadian trade commissioner in Salisbury, halted Canadian aid and export financing facilities, imposed an embargo on arms and military equipment, and lifted preferential tariff rates from Rhodesian goods.[41] Further, Canada supported the economic sanctions adopted by the United Nations.

The Rhodesian situation is an excellent illustration of the use in Canada of non-recognition as sanction and the confinement of legality on the basis of strong considerations of policy. Obviously, majority rule in Rhodesia is a principle that cannot be ignored. In effect, Canadian non-recognition of the independence of Rhodesia represented an insistence on an additional criterion, not yet recognized in international law, as a condition of recognition; hence it is not to be read as an outright rejection of legality.

With respect to the new state of Bangladesh, the Canadian attitude originally reflected a certain degree of ambivalence. Two factors militated against early recognition: 1 / the United States commitment to West Pakistan and its opposition to the Indian entry into the war; 2 / Pakistan's possible withdrawal from the Commonwealth if the major Commonwealth countries, such as Canada and Great Britain, recognized Bangladesh. On the other hand, worldwide sympathy for Bangladesh and the atrocities committed by West Pakistan in Bangladesh argued for early recognition. Unfortunately, the communist countries (except Red China, of course) had taken the first initiative in recognizing Bangladesh. Thus, for Canada to grant recognition, without other non-communist countries taking the same action, would have been awkward. During a television interview on Tuesday, 11 January 1972, Mr Sharp stated that early recognition of Bangladesh could not be expected because Bangladesh lacked the necessary condition of independence to be considered a new 'state.' In sixteen days, on 26 May 1972, with no substantial change of the condition in Bangladesh, Mr Sharp articulated a change of Canadian attitude: recognition of the Dacca government and the Bangladesh state would be made within 'a number of days.' The obvious reason for this change was that consultation with western and Asian countries, including the Commonwealth members, revealed the general desire to accord recognition. Canada subsequently recognized Bangladesh after these European and Asian non-communist countries had accorded recognition.

Recognition of governments

As a general proposition, it is often stated by responsible officials at the Department of External Affairs that four conditions must be satisfied before recognition of a government is accorded. In a statement to the House of Commons, the secretary of state for external affairs on 3 and 7 March 1950 summarized these conditions: 'The four conditions ... are as follows: One is the effectiveness of the authority of the government concerned. The second is the independence of the government concerned ... The third is the ability and the willingness of the government concerned to carry out its international obligations ... Finally, there is the question of the acceptability of the new government by the people over whom it exercises authority.'[42] Scholarly analysis has treated all or some of the last three conditions as simple aspects or manifestations of the principle of effectivity articulated as the first condition. In Canadian practice, however, the principle of effectivity does not seem to circumscribe this broad definition. The statement of Mr L.B. Pearson, then secretary of state for external affairs, made at St Francis Xavier University on 7 November 1954, articulates the ambit of this principle and outlines the method of its ascertainment.

> In the case of a revolution against a recognized government, it is very important to make sure that the revolutionary government possesses effective control and that the previous government offers no prospect of seriously resisting this new government; if the old government seems to have a chance of regaining control of power, recognition would be premature; this could be interpreted as interference into the affairs of a state by a foreign power, which is contrary to international law.
> A test which can be applied to determine whether the new government has effective control is to ascertain whether this government can organize and administer the legislative, judiciary and administrative branches of the government.[43]

If there were two competing authorities, Canada always insisted on the continuity of governments, thus continuing the recognition of the *de jure* government until strong evidence of the effectiveness and stability of the new government had emerged. The basis of this practice was outlined by Prime Minister Mackenzie King when, in spite of the action of other countries, Canada maintained for some time its diplomatic relations with the Vichy regime in France:

> The representation of one country in another is not to any particular government but to the country itself. One government may be in office at a particular moment and another government at some other time. Canada's representation to France is not to the government of France with which the government feels it is in a position to continue diplomatic relations. It is not in any sense representation to Vichy as against de Gaulle; it is representation to France itself. The fact that the government of unoccupied France at the present time is at Vichy and is headed by Marshal Pétain is, we have felt, the strongest reason

why we should seek to maintain as long as possible a relationship that will enable not only our government on our own behalf, but, I might say, in the interest of the whole British commonwealth to have immediate access to that government and to exchange information with it.[44]

This position is, of course, consistent with the well-established rule of international law that changes in the composition or in the form of a government do not affect the international personality of a state whether the changes taking place are in conformity with or in violation of the constitutional law of that state. As a matter of procedure, Canadian representatives where a revolution takes place are instructed that during the period of uncertainty they are to continue, without implying recognition to the new government, to have 'relations officieuses' with the new government on routine matters and on important matters which, by their nature, are impossible to postpone. The representatives are also instructed to refrain from discussing any matters of a political nature. In any case, all exchanges and acts are to be carried out as informally as possible.

Some states had, on a few occasions, refused recognition to new governments that, on the strict application of the effectivity principle, should have been granted recognition. To justify this position, they insisted on some normative qualifications of the scope of the principle of effectivity. These normative qualifications were either founded on internal factors within the state whose new government was to be recognized or on international factors that raised the international legality of the new regime. The first is the so-called 'legitimacy principle,' the latter the 'international legality principle.' It must be noted, however, that neither of these principles is considered separate from the principle of effectivity; they are utilized simply to qualify the criterion of 'effectivity' itself. These principles, in effect, define 'effectivity' not only in factual, but also in normative terms.

The classical legitimacy test was formulated to insulate the dynastic regimes of Europe from revolutionary changes; it found its most comprehensive expression in the Holy Alliance of 1815. Although the legitimacy test was discarded with the passing of the alliance, it left its legacy on matters of recognition. It is the source of today's distinction between *de jure* and *de facto* governments. Under the dynastic regimes, legitimacy of rule was reserved to the regime that assumed power by the recognized dynastic succession. For this reason, those who assumed power through revolutionary and illegitimate means were denied legitimacy of origin. This thought is maintained in today's distinction between *de jure* and *de facto* governments, except that today constitutional, rather than dynastic, origin of the government determines legitimacy.[45]

A complete and clearcut change of government according to the established constitutional process does not invite the granting of recognition. The issue of recognition arises generally only in cases of unconstitutional method of change in government. In effect, the insistence on the constitutional legitimacy of origin under the dynastic system meant the perpetual non-recognition of a *de facto* government that came to power through revolution. For this reason, the revolutionary movements in Europe towards the end of the eighteenth century and early part of the nineteenth rejected this thought. In the early part of this century, the doctrine of constitutional legitimacy became prominent in Central America, then plagued by revolutionary movements. To promote stability in Central America, Dr Tobar of Ecuador sought to revive the doctrine. Five Central America states entered into treaties in 1907 and in 1923 to arrest the increase of revolutionary regimes. The main thesis of the Tobar doctrine – the constitutional legitimacy of origin which perpetuates non-recognition of any revolutionary regime – was, however, not adopted; these treaties simply required a formal and subsequent constitutional legitimation.[46]

It is now well-established by most nations, including Canada, that constitutional legitimacy cannot be made a rule of the international law of recognition. International law cannot be subordinated to national constitutional determination; its acceptance would create instability in international relations because of its perpetuation of non-recognition of the new government. As the *Tinoco Arbitration* case held:

> To hold that a government which establishes itself and maintains peaceful administration with the acquiescence of the people for a substantial period of time does not become a *de facto* government unless it conforms to a previous constitution would be to hold that within the rules of international law a revolution contrary to the fundamental laws of the existing government cannot establish a new government. This cannot be, and is not true ... The issue is not whether the new government assumes power or conducts its administration under constitutional limitations established by the people during the incumbency of the government it has overthrown. The question is, has it really established itself in such a way that all within its influence recognize its control.[47]

The classical legitimacy test also inspired the emergence of a more fundamental qualification to the effectivity principle: democratic legitimacy. In this doctrine the freely declared approval of the new government by the people is the formula of legitimacy. It is conceded, of course, that there may be numerous means from which approval can be deduced and that degrees of approval or disapproval can occur, but it is also recognized that the 'test of popular consent' is susceptible to practical application in an objective manner.[48] Democratic legitimacy is thus advanced not to determine the legitimacy of the new government, but rather as a process through which a new government, admittedly illegitimate in origin, subsequently acquires legitimacy and thus is entitled to recognition.

Great Britain applied this test on a number of occasions by insisting that before recognition was granted there must be a satisfactory showing 'by some clear expression of national will that the ... Government enjoys the confidence of the country.'[49] The United States likewise, at least until after World War I, governed its actions in accordance with Jefferson's statement in 1792: 'It accords with our principles to acknowledge any government to be rightful which is formed by the will of the nation, substantially declared.'[50] Perhaps the best known support for the test of democratic legitimacy was embodied in the 1907 and 1923 treaties of five Central American states. Under these treaties, the contracting parties 'shall not recognize any other Government which may come into power in any of the five Republics as a consequence of a *coup d'état*, or of a revolution against the recognized Government, *so long* as the freely elected representatives of the people thereof have not constitutionally reorganized the country.'[51]

Canada does not seem to have expressly applied the notion of subsequent popular legitimation, in spite of the abundant British and American reliance on this notion before World War I. As the secretary of state for external affairs has stated, 'effective control does not mean necessarily acceptance of the new regime by the whole population. On this question Lauterpacht says: "Effectiveness in this connection, meaning of their effectiveness of power, pure and simple, regardless of any adequately expressed acquiescence of the population or, perhaps, more accurately, effectiveness based on popular consent which, as a whole, provides evidence of permanence." '[52] As a matter of practice, however, Canada tries to identify the support that the new government enjoys from the people, the prospects of an election and participation by political parties, and other related matters, without making its appraisal on any of these points determinative in the decision to recognize or not to recognize a government. In Canadian practice, therefore, this consideration is simply one of the many others that must be appraised in reaching a decision. In a statement to the House of Commons, the secretary of state for external Affairs, on 3 and 7 March 1950, stated:

> In deciding whether recognition should or should not be given to a new government, certain criteria – certain conditions, if you like – have been laid down by authorities on international law ... but these conditions, of course, have never been, and were never meant to be, applied rigidly and without exception ...
>
> In dealing with this ... question, acceptability ... Professor Lauterpacht ... has stated ... that acceptability does not necessarily mean now acceptability by – and I quote his words – 'freely expressed popular approval.' There must be other evidence. There must be the question of the people's resistance to the challenges of the government, or the reaction of the people to the new government – how they accept the new government's rule. But in dealing with this question the other night the leader of the opposition said that the United Nations resolution passed in 1946 establishes once again the principle that acceptability must be freely expressed popular approval ... He said ... that its purport was that a decision was made by the United Nations that there would not be recognition of the government of Franco Spain until it was a government with the consent of the governed. He then went on to argue that it altered the existing system of international law ... because this was a resolution of the United Nations ...
>
> On that point, I should only like to remark that resolutions of the United Nations do not make international law ...
>
> Furthermore this particular resolution had nothing whatever to do with recognition ... It did not concern in any way, shape or form the recognition of Franco.[53]

Canadian insistence on majority rule in the Rhodesian problem is perhaps its clearest commitment so far on the principle of democratic legitimacy. But even here, there are a number of stronger considerations aside from popular legitimacy which have influenced the Canadian position.

The Canadian stand accords with international law, since democratic legitimacy cannot be made as a maxim of recognition under international law: there is no rule in international law that ensures democratic government to all nations in the world.[54] International law is ideologically neutral, hence indifferent, to any form of government.[55] Lauterpacht seeks to skirt around this objection by saying that the test is to be 'regarded as insistence on proper evidence of effectiveness.'[56] This argument provides no justification for democratic legitimacy as a rule in the international law of recognition. There is no valid reason why democratic regimes have available to them this 'evidence' of effectiveness which is unavailable to other forms of government. This argument, therefore, establishes a bias for democratic governments. Besides, the governmental effectiveness has nothing to do at all with the presence or absence of popular support. Stalin's regime, in terms of effectiveness, was overwhelming yet had commanded minimal popular support; the nazi regime in Germany, communist governments in eastern Europe, and dictatorial regimes around the world today demonstrate the absence of correlation between popular support and effective government.

Recognition upon proof of the international legality of the event or act has also been practised by some states. These states are in effect insisting that the principle of effectiveness is inadequate; it is necessary to satisfy the international legality of the emergence of the new state or government. The famous example of this practice is the so-called Stimson doctrine announced by the United States in 1932 after the Japanese invasion of Manchuria. Foreign Secretary Stimson sent a note to the Japanese and Chinese governments on 7 January 1932, stating that the United States 'does not intend to recognize any situation, treaty, or agreement which may be brought about by means contrary to the covenants and obligations of the Pact of Paris of 27 August 1928, to which both China and Japan, as well as the United States are parties.' Shortly thereafter, the Assembly of the League of Nations also declared 'that it is incumbent upon the members of the League of Nations not to recognize any situation, treaty, or agreement which may be brought about by means contrary to the Covenant of the League of Nations or to the Pact of Paris.'[58] Article 17 of the Charter of the Organization of American States also subscribes to the requirement of international legality by providing that 'no territorial acquisitions or special advantages obtained by forced or by other means of coercion shall be recognized.'[59]

The nearest Canada came to adopting some form of argument on the condition of international legality was its declared reason for not recognizing Rhodesia. The seizure of power by a unilateral declaration of independence by Prime Minister Smith was seen, in a sense, as a violation of international law. White minority rule over the black majority attacks the fundamental principles that the United Nations Charter and other fundamental instruments in international law have guaranteed.[60] It can also be argued that a government, which under international law represents the state, must actually be representative of the people; since Smith's government can be considered as nothing more than a 'small tightly-organized minority ... it might well be argued that a treaty signed by such a government would be no more than a personal agreement of its officials, not binding upon the state they claim to represent.'[61]

The fulfilment of international obligations

In both recognition of state and recognition of government, some states have often insisted upon the fulfilment of international obligations as a condition of recognition. If the new state or government fails to provide guarantees that the obligations specifically contracted for by its predecessor or obligations imposed by general international law of special interest to the recognizing state would be fulfilled, recognition will be refused. In state practice, two techniques are used to refuse recognition in the absence of the guarantee. First, the state simply insists that the new state or government must have *capacity* or *ability* to meet these obligations and, as a general proposition, ignores the new state's or government's willingness or unwillingness to fulfil these obligations. The failure of the new state or government to demonstrate the requisite capacity would be taken as proof of its failure to satisfy the requirements of effectiveness. Although this might be true if the failure to fulfil the international obligation were attributable to the state's or government's lack of credible control over the territory and people, the inability of the state or government may stem from an altogether irrelevant factor. In this instance, states do not appear to insist vigorously on the application of this condition.

The other way in which fulfilment of international obligations is utilized in state practice proceeds from the assumption that this condition is not an aspect of the principle of effectivity but a separate and independent condition. For this reason, what is sought to be examined is not the capacity or ability of the new state or government, but simply its willingness to fulfil these obligations. The United Kingdom has followed this practice in the past, but it has refrained from insisting on this condition in recent practice. United States practice seems still to demand the satisfaction of this condition before recognition is granted.

Canadian recognition practice does not maintain any sharp distinction between ability and willingness to fulfil international obligations and has not followed any rigid rule as to their significance. As a matter of general practice, of course, ability and willingness to honour international obligations are usually expressed by the new state or government in a formal declaration which accompanies invitations to foreign governments to grant recognition. Accordingly, Canadian practice considers it somewhat imprudent to grant recognition before such a declaration is made. The Canadian government does not consider the declaration sufficient to ensure the real goodwill of the new state or government, but it looks upon the declaration as strong evidence of goodwill. This flexibility is evident in the statement of Mr Pearson, then secretary of state for external affairs, in the House of Commons, on 3 and 7 March 1950:

> The third [condition of recognition] is the ability and the willingness of the government concerned to carry out its international obligations. That condition, of course, cannot always be applied too rigorously and too exactly. If it were always applied in that way we might today be recognizing the government of Mr. Kerensky in Moscow.[62]

The role of the fulfilment of international obligations in Canadian recognition is evident in its practice of recognition of Latin American governments. For example, in the course of the exchange of views between the secretary of state for external affairs and the Canadian ambassador to Chile about the recognition of the Arias government in Panama, it was stated: 'It is evident that President Arias' regime is fairly well established, is in effective control of the administrative machinery of State, and has promised to live up to Panama's international obligations and agreements. Since, therefore, his government has fulfilled the requirements of international law ... '[63] The Canadian government generally acknowledges this willingness to fulfil international obligations in its message of recognition. The wording used in the recognition of Argentina in 1955 is typical of these cases: 'The Government of Canada is gratified to learn of the Government of Argentina's readiness to fulfil its international obligations including existing treaties and agreements between Canada and Argentina as well as multilateral agreements.'[64] In the recognition of the provisional government of Manuel Urrutia of Cuba in January 1959, the note handed by the Canadian ambassador in Havana to Urrutia contained acknowledgment in almost similar terms: 'I have been instructed by my Government to inform Your Excellency that they have noted with satisfaction the assurances given by the new Government of Cuba that all international obligations and treaties at present will be respected.'

In at least one instance, the case of Red China, Canada has used this principle not to decide on recognition with prudence, but to deny it for some time, against all realistic evidence. In this case, United States denial of recognition of Red China on the basis of lack of willingness to honour international obligations governed Canadian decision more than prudent consideration. The statement of the Liberal government's secretary of state for external affairs on 7 November 1954 echoed in substance the United States position on the recognition of Red China:

> We are all agreed, I think, that the Communist Government does control the actions of a majority of the Chinese people, whether we or they like it or not. But have the Chinese Communists shown up to now that they are prepared sincerely to assume the duties and responsibilities of membership in the international community?
>
> Furthermore, armed intervention by the Chinese Communist forces in Korea against the United Nations has, to say the least, raised grave doubts as to their peaceful intentions. For these reasons, the Canadian Government has taken the position that unless and until there is some evidence of a genuine disposition to follow the rules of acceptable international behaviour the Chinese Communist Government has no claim to our formal recognition. To specify in advance and in detail the conditions which would have to be met before such recognition could be given is difficult. Indeed, to try to do so would, as I see it, be neither entirely logical nor wise, in view of the traditional policy of this and most other free democratic countries of recognizing in our own interest certain Communist and other totalitarian regimes whose domestic and foreign policies are not more to our liking than those of Peking ...
>
> I would say therefore that if the Communist Chinese were sincerely to co-operate in the achievement of peaceful and honourable settlements to Far Eastern problems, and were to respect the agreements reached, then formal recognition, which however would not in any sense imply approval, of their Government by Canada could be looked at again. I do not think that we should go further than that in present circumstances. But equally, I do not think that we should tie ourselves down to any rigid commitments that never will we recognize any Communist Government in China.[65]

Even with the change of government, this policy did not change. Sidney Smith, secretary of state for external affairs in the Conservative government, said in the House on 26 February 1959:

> It seems to me, however, that in discussing this question we must make a clear distinction

between the legal factors which apply whenever Canada extends recognition to any new government, and the national and international considerations.

Let me deal with the legal aspects of the question first. It is true that recognition is usually extended to a government when that government exercises effective control over the territory of the country concerned, and when that government has a reasonable prospect of stability. Then, there is a second legal factor. The government of that country should indicate its willingness to assume international obligations inherited from its predecessor. So far as China is concerned, there is some doubt about the Peking government's willingness to assume the obligations and responsibilities of its predecessor. The Peking government made known, in September, 1949, that it would, in effect, regard as binding only those obligations which it considered to be in its own interest. There is little doubt, however, that the Peking government commands the obedience of the bulk of the population. It must be admitted, therefore, that most of the legal requirements for recognition have been fulfilled by the government of the people's republic. In any event, I say this: the Peking government has fulfilled its obligation to at least the same extent as some governments which we do recognize now, and about whose political systems we have the same kind of reservations.[66]

The weakness of the view that fulfilment of international obligations is a condition of recognition has been adequately exposed.[67] Perhaps its most glaring weakness is its wrong assumption that the new government has the power to repudiate the international obligations of its predecessor and that a declaration to this effect provides anything more fundamental than a mere psychological illusion that willingness to fulfil obligations can be guaranteed by a simple declaration.

Summary

The Canadian government, therefore, seems to be committed to the proposition that the so-called conditions of recognition are simply factors that should be examined in reaching, at a political level, the decision to recognize or not to recognize. Undoubtedly, the principle of effectivity is the most important factor and often closely examined, but even this principle is not vigorously applied if effective control over either the territory or the population exists and a relatively adequate control over the other, though indefinite or precarious, is apparent. If this is the situation, favourable evidence about other factors may influence a positive decision. This was well demonstrated in the recognition of the provisional revolutionary government of South Vietnam in 1963, at which time – indeed until today – it is unclear whether the South Vietnamese government exercised *effective* control over a substantial part of the population. At the granting of recognition, Mr Martin, then secretary of state for external affairs, said in the House of Commons:

The government has decided to accord recognition to the [provisional revolutionary] government of the republic of [South] Viet Nam. The considerations which the Canadian government examined were: The fact that the government is in actual control of the major part of the territory of the state; it has undertaken to observe international obligations entered into by its predecessors, and it has secured the acquiescence of the population. It has also promised to protect foreign lives and property and to guarantee fundamental freedoms 'within the framework of the anti-communist struggle and the security of the state.' Moreover, the Vietnamese government has undertaken to maintain co-operation with the international supervisory commission on which Canada serves.[68]

DE FACTO AND DE JURE RECOGNITION

In early practice the terms *de facto* and *de jure* have been used to characterize a certain government professing to act for a state and inviting, expressly or implicitly, recognition as that state's exclusive organ. As elsewhere discussed, these terms were used by the dynastic regimes in the earlier part of the nineteenth century in relation to their insistence on the classical legitimacy test: a *de facto* but illegitimate government was not entitled to recognition. In this usage the terms *de facto* and *de jure* had no special relevance to the recognition of states in international law. A state has no degree of existence and hence no international personality. With respect to government, however, the question of interest is its capacity, both in fact and in law, to act for the state. Capacity in fact and capacity in law were deliberately separated; capacity in fact was tested by the principle of effectivity, whereas capacity in law was determined by the dynastic rules of succession.

The practice of using terms *de facto* and *de jure* to characterize recognition itself is recent and has acquired wider currency only since World War I.[69] This usage of the terms *de facto* recognition and *de jure* recognition, instead of the terms *de facto* government and *de jure* government, has brought about confusion of thought in modern literature and practice in international law. One view maintains that '*de facto* and *de jure* recognition' is the same as '*de facto* and *de jure* government.' O'Connell's words typify this view: 'The expressions *de jure* recognition and *de facto* recognition are shorthand for recognition of a government as the government *de jure* and recognition of a government as the government *de facto*; there is nothing in the distinction descriptive of the form or character of the recognition but only of the entity recognized.'[70] The authors who support this view, however, differ on whether *de jure* and *de facto* recognition can apply only to governments as in the traditional usage; some limit the terms to recognition of governments, whereas others extend the usage to recognition of states. Another view maintains that the expressions '*de facto* recognition' and '*de jure* recognition' have totally separate meanings. 'Both these types [*de facto* and *de jure*] of recognition,' Kunz insists, have 'no exact relation to both [*de facto* and *de jure*] types of governments.'[71] The supporters of this view, however, differ as to the exact nature of these types of recognition. The majority of the authors hold the view that *de facto* recognition is provisional and can be withdrawn but *de jure* recognition is absolute, continuous, and cannot be withdrawn;[72] the minority view considers the distinction not one of substance but of politics, in that its relevance is only as an aid in the interpretation of the intentions of the parties involved in recognition.[73]

In British practice the distinction between *de jure* and *de facto* recognition has been observed, but it is not clear which of the contending views can claim support from it. In 1921 Great Britain accorded recognition *de facto* to the Soviet government of Russia, which it changed with recognition *de jure* in 1924.[74] United States practice rejects the distinction between *de facto* and *de jure* recognition; recognition extended is always a 'recognition *per se*, not *de facto* recognition.'[75] When it was suggested that the United States recognize the United Arab Republic but confine itself to *de facto* recognition, the Department of State stated that 'such a position, halfway between recognition and non-recognition, would not result in whatever benefits might reside in either of the latter attitudes, and that, instead, by indicating doubt as to the legal qualifications of the U.A.R. for recognition, irritation and resentment might be caused, making it difficult for states extending *de facto* recognition to transact business with the government thus recognized.'[76]

Canadian practice seems to have developed in two stages, roughly coinciding with the dominance of British or American influence in Canadian international practice in general. The instances in which *de jure* and *de facto* recognition have been extended by Canada have often involved territorial annexation. The Canadian reaction to the invasion and annexation by the Soviet Union of the Baltic states of Estonia, Latvia, and Lithuania in 1940 was conveniently accommodated by the distinction. The Baltic states were recognized by the United Kingdom in 1922, and Canada had maintained this recognition. In the *Estonian States Cargo and Passengers Line* v *S.S.Elise* case,[77] the solicitors requested the secretary of state for external affairs to answer some questions which were then material to the case. In replying, he resorted to the concept of *de facto* recognition with respect to Estonia's assimilation into the Soviet Union:

> Your letter of December 23 encloses four questions put jointly by you and Mr C.F. Inches, representing all parties in this action. You desire my answers to these questions for production to the court in this case.
>
> Question 1   Does the Government of Canada recognize the right of the Council of Peoples' Commissars of U.S.S.R. or any other authority of U.S.S.R., to make decrees purporting to be effectual in Estonia?
>
> Answer: The Government of Canada recognizes that Estonia has de facto entered the Union of Soviet Socialist Republics, but does not recognize this de jure. The question of the effect of a Soviet decree is for the Court to decide.
>
> Question 2   Does the Government of Canada recognize the existence of the Republic of Estonia as constituted prior to June 1940, and if not when did such recognition cease?
>
> Answer: The Government of Canada does not recognize de facto the Republic of Estonia as constituted prior to June 1940. The Republic of Estonia as constituted prior to June 1940, has ceased de facto to have any effective existence.
>
> Question 3   Does the Government of Canada recognize that the Republic of Estonia has entered the Union of Soviet Socialist Republics, and if so, as from what date, and is such entry recognized as being 'de facto' or 'de jure'?
>
> Answer: The Government of Canada recognizes that Estonia has de facto entered the Union of Soviet Socialist Republics but has not recognized this de jure. It is not possible for the Government of Canada to attach a date to this recognition.
>
> Question 4   Does the Government of Canada recognize the Government of the Estonian Soviet Socialist Republic, and if so, from what date?
>
> Answer: The Government of Canada recognizes the Government of the Estonian Soviet Socialist Republic to be the de facto government of Estonia but does not recognize it as the de jure government of Estonia. It is not possible for the Government of Canada to attach a date to this recognition.[78]

The Canadian government extended the status of Estonia to the other Baltic states.[79] The *de jure* recognition to the Baltic states has never been withdrawn by Canada. Later events, however, indicate that this *de jure* recognition has no real significance today. The inclusion of the honorary consuls of the Baltic countries in the official publication, *Representatives of Other Countries in Canada*, and their offices in Toronto, have now only a symbolic value. Canada has never permitted these consuls to perform any significant official functions. In matters that concern these countries Canada has always dealt with the government of the Soviet Union. In matters of visa and immigration, the Canadian embassy in Moscow negotiates with the foreign minister of the Soviet Union.[80] These facts show the anomalous position of Canada with respect to these countries. It is awkward to extend *de facto* recognition to one government and *de jure* recognition to another in the same territory; and it is more anomalous to extend *de jure* recognition as to the independent existence of a state and at the same time declare *de facto* recognition of its integration into another, especially if this state has no organized government.

The *de facto* recognition of the state of Israel in 1948, as earlier discussed, similarly involved a serious territorial question. This territorial question was unresolved in 1949 when Canada extended *de jure* recognition. Canada, it seems, was forced into granting *de jure* recognition because of the great number of states extending *de jure* recognition at that time. This practice further shows the questionable utility of *de facto* recognition: if Canada was quite uncertain of its position because the outstanding territorial question was considered significant, it should not have hastily extended recognition. Questions that appear significant at one time have – in international relations – often become insignificant as subsequent events unfold. The reverse is, of course, also true, and it seems to be the better part of prudence to wait for a relatively fixed and certain appreciation of the circumstances before a decision on recognition is actually made.

The preliminary skirmishes of the Axis powers before World War II – and to some extent their actual conduct of the war – occasioned other instances of Canada's applying the concept of *de facto – de jure* recognition. Between 1930 and 1945 Germany, Italy, and Japan embarked on forcible annexation of territories in Asia, Africa, and Europe. The Canadian reaction to these annexations was not marked with any consistent policy and, necessarily, its recognition practice was inconsistent. Japan's conquest of Manchuria in 1931 was never recognized by Canada. The annexation of Abyssinia by Italy, however, earned a different reaction. The United Kingdom recognized *de facto* the Italian annexation of Ethiopia and the Italian government as government of Ethiopia in 1936; in 1938, the recognition was made *de jure*. Following the British lead Canada, on 21 December 1938, also granted *de jure* recognition.[81] The German annexation of Austria, Poland, Czechoslovakia, Yugoslavia, and its occupation of France were similarly treated without discernible consistent policy. The *Anschluss* of Austria was recognized *de facto* by Canada on 27 March 1939.[82] The later annexation of Poland, Czechoslovakia, and Yugoslavia – then within the span of the war – were not considered within the context of recognition; these countries were characterized as 'territories occupied by the enemy' and their provisional governments in London were accordingly recognized *de jure*.[83] With respect to France, as earlier discussed, the Vichy regime was recognized *de jure* for some time. This recognition was withdrawn on 9 November 1942 and on 26 August 1943 the Comité français de liberation nationale under General de Gaulle was recognized.

After World War II, the practice of distinguishing *de facto* from *de jure* recognition seems to have diminished considerably. There was no *de facto* recognition of the People's Republic of China and *de jure* recognition of Chiang Kai-shek's government, and when Canada decided to recognize the Peking government, the recognition was nothing short of formal, *per se* recognition which compelled withdrawal of Canadian recognition from the Taipei government. The considerations that led to this procedure were largely legal in character. The recognition of the Peking government as the *de jure* government of China logically implied that formal relations with the Taipei government must be terminated. Under international law, the only possibility for Canada to sustain formal relations with Taipei was to recognize a new state of Taiwan. This obviously was unacceptable to both Peking and Taipei, since they persistently claimed the exclusive right to represent the state of China, of which Taiwan is but a part. Besides, the majority of the states of the world, largely in their desire to support the positions of either government, rejected the idea of a new state of Taiwan. The alternative of recognizing Peking simply as a *de facto* government of China and continuing *de jure* recognition of Taipei could not withstand objective legal analysis. To deny legitimacy to the Peking regime was to ignore reality and anchor recognition on the artificial qualifications to the principle of effectivity, such as the discredited test of constitutional legitimacy of origin or the unacceptable test of willingness to fulfil international obligations, while at the same time ignoring Taipei's lack of ability to fulfil its international obligations respecting China as a whole. If it was absurd enough to grant *de facto* recognition to Taipei because of its failure to meet the test of effectiveness, it follows that it was more absurd to grant to it the more superior status of *de jure* recognition. Logically, therefore, for Canada to support a two-China policy would have meant the assumption of a decision beyond its competence: the establishment of Taiwan as a new state against the will of Taiwan itself. As a consequence, Mr Sharp, on 29 May 1969, said: 'Canada has a one-China policy and, since the Nationalist Government purports also to be the Government of China, we cannot recognize Peking and Taiwan at the same time.'[84] The joint communiqué which recorded the Canadian and Chinese agreement reached in Stockholm provided as follows:

1   The Government of Canada and the Government of the People's Republic of China, in accordance with the principles of mutual respect for sovereignty and territorial integrity, non-interference in each other's internal affairs and equality and mutual benefit, have decided upon mutual recognition and the establishment of diplomatic relations, effective October 13, 1970.

2   The Chinese Government reaffirms that Taiwan is an inalienable part of the territory of the People's Republic of China. The Canadian Government takes note of this position of the Chinese Government.

3   The Canadian Government recognizes the Government of the People's Republic of China as the sole legal government of China.

4   The Canadian and Chinese Governments have agreed to exchange ambassadors within six months, and to provide all necessary assistance for the establishment and the perfor-

mance of the functions of diplomatic missions in their respective capitals, on the basis of equality and mutual benefit and in accordance with international practice.[85]

The Bangladesh government of Sheik Mujibur did not undergo any stage of *de facto* recognition; neither did those of Vietnam, Korea, and especially of East Germany, which remains unrecognized. One can attribute this new attitude to the United States practice of not distinguishing between *de facto* and *de jure* recognition.

THE FORM OF RECOGNITION

Recognition as a juridical act is a declaration of a will; its object is the determination of a relevant fact or event, such as the emergence of a state or government.[86] The branch or organ of government competent to extend recognition is usually the executive as a political organ of the state. In Canada, recognition usually emanates from the secretary of state for external affairs, the political official responsible for the conduct of Canada's foreign relations. In some instances, for instance upon a country's acquisition of independence, the prime minister of Canada sends a congratulatory message which expresses or implies recognition. No law requires that recognition should be submitted to the cabinet or parliament for prior or subsequent approval. If the recognition, however, can bring about a far-reaching impact in commerce, trade, finance, immigration, and other areas of government policy, or where a major change of foreign policy will occur, the recognition decision is usually reached only after consultation with the prime minister or with the cabinet. For example, the recognition of the People's Republic of China in October 1970 was obviously a major shift in Canada's foreign policy; recognition was extended only after study by the cabinet.

Like most declarations of will in law, recognition has to be communicated in a certain form which provides evidence of its contents. Usually the recognition is expressly granted in the form of communication to the appropriate official of the recognized state or government, public declaration of a competent official of the recognizing state or government, notice to a third state, or a recognition agreement among several states.[87]

In most cases, Canada sends a direct communication to the state or government. This communication usually takes the form of a message from the prime minister or secretary of state for external affairs to the head of government or the foreign minister of the state. In the cases of states acquiring independence, Canadian representatives are appointed to attend the independence ceremonies and then transmit the congratulatory message normally signed by the prime minister. If independence is acquired by the peaceful transfer of sovereignty, the prime minister also sends a message to the head of state of the mother state. The form and content of these congratulatory messages transmitted on the occasion of the independence of the Republic of the United States of Indonesia can be considered typical:[88]

TO THE PRIME MINISTER OF THE NETHERLANDS:
I take great pleasure in extending to you and to the Dutch people the most cordial greetings of the Government and the people of Canada on the occasion of the transfer of

sovereignty to the Republic of the United States of Indonesia.

I trust that the Netherlands-Indonesian Union thus established between the Netherlands and the Republic of the United States of Indonesia will contribute to peace and stability throughout the world.

I have just informed Prime Minister Hatta that the Canadian Government has extended full recognition to the Republic of the United States of Indonesia.

TO THE PRIME MINISTER OF THE REPUBLIC OF THE UNITED STATES OF INDONESIA:

Upon the proclamation of the independence of the Republic of the United States of Indonesia, I take great pleasure in extending to you and your people the cordial greetings and good wishes of the Government and people of Canada. The transfer of sovereignty which has just taken place constitutes a tribute to your statesmanship and that of your colleagues. We also welcome your voluntary association with the people of the Netherlands in the new Netherlands-Indonesian Union.

I hope that Indonesia will enter upon an era of peace and prosperity that will contribute to the well being and stability of all nations in the Pacific. I feel confident that by collaborating in the establishment of peace throughout the world, both your country and mine will be brought together in ever closer friendship for their mutual benefit.

This message may be regarded as giving full recognition by the Government of Canada to the Republic of the United States of Indonesia.

In cases of recognition of governments in states where Canada has diplomatic representatives, the Canadian ambassador or high commissioner, pursuant to an instruction from the secretary of state for external affairs, often transmits the recognition message. For instance, on 17 May 1957, the Canadian ambassador to Colombia called on the secretary general of foreign affairs of Colombia and handed him a note formally recognizing the new government of Columbia. The Canadian ambassador in Lima – also accredited to Bolivia – acted in similar function when, on 6 November 1964, the Canadian embassy in Lima received a note from the Bolivian minister of foreign affairs that on 4 November 1964 a military junta had assumed power. On instructions from the Department of External Affairs, the embassy acknowledged the receipt of the Bolivian note by a telegram to La Paz on 7 December 1964 which contained Canadian recognition of the new regime.

The cases of implied or tacit recognition have always raised difficult problems of interpretation of the evidence from which recognition is being deduced. As Lauterpacht says: 'The question of implied recognition resolves itself into an enquiry as to the kind and type of conduct which, in the absence of clear indications to the contrary, the law will interpret as amounting to recognition.'[89] Since this matter is an attempt to read an intention from a somewhat equivocal evidence, controversy has always surrounded it. It seems often unfair and unrealistic to impute evidence of recognition in many instances when convenient methods to express recognition are available to the parties who have chosen not to invoke it. The cases in which one can justly imply recognition should be limited and confined to the cases which Lauterpacht, after careful and incisive analysis, has identified: 'The only legitimate occasions for implying recognition are: 1 / the conclusion of a bilateral treaty which regulates comprehensively the relations between the two States (and which must be distinguished from temporary arrangements and agreements for limited purposes); 2 / the formal initiation of diplomatic relations and, probably, the issue of consular exequatur; and 3 / in case of belligerency, a proclamation of neutrality or some such unequivocal act.'[90]

The Canadian government has been very careful not to give a state or government the opportunity of inferring recognition from Canadian governmental action or from the conduct of Canadian representatives abroad. There have been, however, instances where Canada had taken action which clearly implied recognition. For instance, the Canadian government, after deciding to deal with the Romanian government in a way which implied recognition, took steps to revive the Extradition Treaty of 1893 and the pertinent Protocol of 1894. Pursuant to this decision, an exchange of notes with the Romanian minister was made in Washington in March 1948. The normalization of treaty relationships after the termination of the state of war amounted to implied recognition of the government of Romania. Similarly in 1945, Canada's action of reviving two prewar treaties with Hungary (an Extradition Treaty of 1873 and a Convention regarding legal proceedings in civil and commercial matters of 1935) constituted implied recognition of the then government of Hungary. As in the case of Romania, adequate evidence exists to show that Canada's purpose in taking this action was to normalize treaty relations with Hungary following the termination of the state of war with Hungary.

Diplomatic intercourse is the normal channel of inter-state relations; it presupposes, therefore, a recognition of the personality or capacity of the state or government to enter into normal international relations with other states. For this reason, the exchange of diplomatic representatives is regarded in Canadian practice as an evidence of an implied recognition. An instance of the exchange of diplomatic representatives as implied recognition in Canadian practice occurred in the autumn of 1955 when the Canadian ambassador, Mr Picard, presented his Letters of Credence to the new president of Argentina shortly after President Péron was overthrown. The Canadian action implied Canada's recognition of the new government as successor to the Péron regime. However, the mere retention of diplomatic representatives in the country where a revolutionary change of government has occurred is not considered implied recognition by Canada. In the main, the purpose of maintaining diplomatic representatives in the country in such cases is simply to open communications with one or both of the contending forces during the period of uncertainty. The Canadian representatives are, for this reason, instructed to act scrupulously so as to preclude the possibility of implied recognition. Furthermore, the absence of Canadian diplomatic representatives in a country does not imply non-recognition by Canada. Recognition does not create an obligation to establish diplomatic relations with the state or government recognized by Canada. Thus, Canada does not have diplomatic representatives in a number of states it has recognized, for example, Liberia and Saudi Arabia.

The issuance of a consular exequatur to a consular official of a foreign government is regarded in Canadian recognition practice as constituting implied recognition in the absence of an expression to the contrary. Recognition of the government of Nicaragua on 12 November 1948 and of the government of Venezuela on 28 June 1948 was implied when consular exequaturs were issued to their consular officials on those dates. In Canadian practice, an invitation to request the issuance of a consular exequatur can be construed as an implied recognition of the state or government to whom the invitation is directed. In December 1949, for example, a note was addressed to the minister for external affairs of Panama asking him whether the government of Panama intended to request the Canadian government for provisional recognition of the Panamanian honorary consul-general-designate. This note was considered within the Department of External Affairs to constitute implied recognition.

Canada's United Nations vote respecting the admission of a state to membership has been construed by Canada in two instances as recognition. Canada's vote in favour of admitting Israel to membership was implied *de jure* recognition of the state of Israel. Canada also voted at the United Nations in favour of resolutions affirming that the Republic of Korea was fully qualified for, and should be admitted to, United Nations membership; and that the government of the Republic of Korea was the only fully elected and lawful government in Korea. Thus, Canada had formally recognized the government of South Korea. On the other hand, its opposition to resolutions at the United Nations urging the admission of the Democratic Republic of Korea to membership in the United Nations clearly indicated non-recognition of both the state of North Korea and its Pyong-yang government.

Proceeding somewhat differently is Canada's approach to the government of the Mongolian People's Republic (Outer Mongolia). Canada has never taken any formal action to recognize this government; but most communist countries and a handful of non-bloc countries have recognized it. In 1955 Canada proposed and the United Nations General Assembly approved a resolution requesting the Security Council to consider a number of outstanding applications for membership, including that of Outer Mongolia. Outer Mongolian membership in the United Nations was approved by the General Assembly without a dissenting vote on 27 October 1961. The Department of External Affairs position is that while Canada has on occasion used the acceptance of a country's qualification for United Nations membership and its vote for such a country to indicate an implied recognition, it is generally accepted that, without the specific expression of an intention to extend recognition, a vote in favour of the admission of a new member to the United Nations cannot be construed as an act of recognition. This position accords with the general practice that admission of a state to the United Nations does not in itself entail recognition by the members of the United Nations. The Israeli and Korean recognitions can be interpreted, because of clear declarations to this effect, as express recognition, rather than as a return to Canada's position under the regime of the League of Nations that its vote in favour of the admission of a state to the League was a form of implied recognition.

Outside of the above situations, Canadian practice in international law has not accepted other ways by which recognition can be implied. Specifically, the following acts, among others, are not considered as constitutive of implied recognition:

1 The issuance of a visa to a person holding a passport issued by an unrecognized government.
2 Communication with unrecognized authorities such as the lodging of protests or representations on behalf of Canadians. The form and manner of communication are not significant.
3 Attendance of a Canadian government representative at a social function attended by or sponsored by representatives of an unrecognized authority.

4 The conclusion of commercial transactions between Canada and representatives of an unrecognized authority.
5 A vote by Canada in the General Assembly of the United Nations or in any of its specialized agencies in favour of the acceptance of credentials of representatives of a particular government.

CONCLUSION

Canadian practice in matters of recognition clearly indicates that recognition is considered a political act which should be decided after an assessment of a number of factors. For Canada, as an official of the Department of External Affairs stated, 'it would be much better to start from political realities and work back to Lauterpacht, than vice versa.'[91] Canada, however, attempts to establish an appearance of legality in reaching its decision, and it has always asserted that 'the granting of recognition by the Canadian Government to another Government is not viewed as signifying approval of the policies of that Government or, for that matter, of the political philosophy of that Government or of the manner in which it came into power.'[92] In interpreting the so-called legal conditions of recognition, Canada takes them not as rigid rules containing objective standards from which a duty to recognize can be founded, but as guidelines in which approval looms larger than anyone in the Department of External Affairs is willing to concede.

This conception of recognition by Canada and by most countries of the world precisely casts doubt on the usefulness of recognition – at least of states and governments – as an institution of international law: adherence to the standards is false, if not altogether hollow. The alternatives to the present status of the recognition of states and governments are just as difficult to support today, for one reason or another. First, we may admit frankly that recognition is truly a political act which carries no more legal significance than any other political acts of states today. This position has the merit of honesty; it would clearly concede the relative uselessness of the institution of recognition of states and governments and logically argue for the basic tenets and the procedure urged by the Estrada doctrine. Second, we may establish Lauterpacht's proposition that the regime of legality is paramount and the duty to recognize, based on agreed objective legal criteria, should exist. This would require, as a corollary, the institutionalization of the recognition of states and governments as a collective responsibility of the United Nations. This position will undoubtedly restore to recognition its pre-eminence in the ordering of international relations; it has my enthusiastic endorsement.

In its thrust, however, this view yearns for a return of the lost ideal of the old historical function of recognition in the original Family of Nations which appears now to be too remote in the past and too revolutionary for the present to inspire any vigorous and widespread acceptance. Perhaps there is, after all, an unstated merit in invoking a certain degree of self-delusion that governs the current practice and literature of recognition: this is the best that modern international law can produce to sustain an ordered regime in this area of international relations.

NOTES

1 For details, see the excellent study of E. Reibstein, (1963), 2 *Völkerrecht: Eine Geschichte seiner Ideen in Lehre und Praxis* 507–67.

2 L. Oppenheim, 1 *International Law* (8th ed, 1955) 125–6.

3 U.N. GA Res 375 (IV), December 1949.

4 On 15 April 1842 Secretary Webster, in a letter to the United States minister to Mexico, said: 'Every nation, on being received, at her own request, into the circle of civilized governments, attains rights of sovereignty and the dignity of national character, but that she limits herself also to the strict and faithful observance of all those principles, laws and usages which have obtained currency among civilized states, and which have for their object the mitigation of the miseries of war.' Moore, *Digest of International Law* (1906) 10. As to the standing of an unrecognized state in the international community, see Sharp, *Non-recognition as Legal Obligation, 1775–1934,* (1934) 199.

5 The English version of article 38(1)(*b*), uses the words 'general practice accepted as law,' and the French version states 'pratique générale acceptée comme étant le droit.' In German the word 'accepted' is generally translated 'anerkannt' (recognized). See G. Dahm, 2 *Völkerrecht* (1960) 32.

6 'The Retroactive Effect of the Recognition of States and Governments' (1935), 16 *Brit. Y.B. Int'l L.* 42–3.

7 The Permanent Court of International Justice said in the *Wimbledon* case that 'the right of entering into international agreements is an attribute of State sovereignty.' P.C.I.J. ser A, no 1, at 25. Canada's possession of the capacity to enter into international agreements, however, does not provide conclusive evidence of sovereign statehood for it is now widely accepted in international law that not only fully sovereign states can possess this capacity. See Lord McNair, *The Law of Treaties* (1961) appendix A, at 754–66.

8 The thrust of these studies, impressive as they are [for a bibliography, see J.-G. Castel, *International Law* (1965) 99–100], must be qualified by the fact that Canada had the power to enter into international agreements even at the time when, admittedly, Canada was still under the control of the United Kingdom.

9 Dept. of Ext. Aff., 3 *Documents on Canadian External Relations,* (1970), doc 829

[hereafter cited Ext. Rels. Doc.].

10 A.B. Keith, *The Dominion as Sovereign State* (1938) 45.

11 Ext. Rels. Doc. 831.

12 Ibid, 832.

13 Ibid, 833.

14 W. Riddell, ed, *Documents on Canadian Foreign Policy, 1917–1939* (1962), at 743–44.

15 M. Ollivier, *Problems of Canadian Sovereignty* (1945) 87–90.

16 Riddell, *supra* note 14, at 746.

17 1 H.C. *Debates* (1941), 948.

18 Ibid, 994.

19 Ibid, 995.

20 Dept. of Ext. Affairs, *Annual Report* (1950), at 21.

21 10 July 1964. File 20–14–1, vol 1.

22 D.C. Masters, 8 *Canada in World Affairs, 1953–1955* (1959), at 209.

23 Published in 1947 [hereafter cited Lauterpacht].

24 For a brief discussion of this theory, see ibid, at 41–51.

25 D. Anzilloti, *Corso di diritto internazionale* (4th ed, 1955) 155.

26 As Cavagliere says, recognition 'does not declare an existing quality; it creates and attributes it.' *Corso di diritto internazionale* (1934), at 204, quoted in Lauterpacht, at 40.

27 For a brief discussion of the constitutive theory, see Lauterpacht, at 38–41 and 52–8.

28 Zellweger, 'Die völkerrechtliche Anerkennung nach schweizerischer Staatenpraxis' (1954), 11 *Annuaire Suisse de droit international,* at 13–14.

29 J.C. Bluntschlli, *Das moderne Völkerrecht der zivilizierten Staaten als Rechtsbuch dargestellt* (3d ed, 1878) 75; P. Guggenheim, 1 *Lehrbuch des Völkerrechts* (1948), at 182, note 49; Lauterpacht, at 26–37, 158–65.

30 *Droit international public* (1953), at 293.

31 J. Spiropoulos, *Die de facto-Regierung im Völkerrecht* (1926) 20; Lauterpacht, at 7–12.

32 Lauterpacht, at 98–102; A. Jimenez de Arechaga, *Reconocimiento de gobiernos* (1947) 71.

33 (1949), 1 *External Affairs* 29.

34 Ibid, at 29–30.

35 1 H.C. *Debates* (1948), 219, 468.

36 8 Auge. 1960. File 10464–A–40, vol 6.

37 Department of External Affairs, *Report* (1949), at 21.

38 See Paul Martin's statement in the House of Commons on 2 March 1966. 2 H.C. *Debates* (1966), at 2055.

39 [1967] 1 A.C. 853, [1966] 2 All E.R. 536 (1966).
40 1 H.C. *Debates* (1965) 775–6.
41 Office of the Prime Minister, Press Release, 11 Nov. 1965 and Press Release, 26 Nov. 1965.
42 Dept. of Ext. Aff., Press Release no 50/7.
43 Dept. of Ext. Aff., Press Release no 50/49.
44 1 H.C. *Debates* (1941) 994–5.
45 J. Kunz, *Die Anerkennung von Staaten und Regierungen in Völkerrecht* (1928) 143–6.
46 Jiminez de Arechaga, therefore, correctly rejects the view that the Central American treaties of 1907 and 1923 embody or apply the Tobar doctrine: 'Se comete un grueso error cuando se afirma, como es frecuente, que los tratados centro-americanos de 1907 y de 1923 constituyeron la consagracion o la application practica de la doctrina Tobar.' *Reconicimiento de gobiernos* (1947) 156.
47 (1923), 1 *U.N. Int'l Arb. Awards Rep.* 369.
48 See Lauterpacht, at 115–40.
49 Instruction to the British minister in Durazzo, 28 July 1924, quoted in Lauterpacht, at 123.
50 Ibid, 126.
51 For the text of these treaties, see (1908), 2 *Am. J. Int'l L. Supp.,* at 229 and (1925), 19 *Am. J. Int'l L.,* at 164. For examples of the application of the Tobar doctrine, see Woolsey, 'The Non-recognition of the Chamorro Government in Nicaragua' (1926) 20 *Am. J. Int'l L.* 543.
52 Dept. of Ext. Aff., Press Release no 54/49.
53 Dept. of Ext. Aff., Press Release no 50/7.
54 H. von der Heydte, 1 *Völkerrecht* (1958) 202.
55 Contra: Chen, *The International Law of Recognition* (1951) 336.
56 Lauterpacht, at 115.
57 The note is reproduced in (1932), 26 *Am. J. Int'l L.* 342, followed by a comment by Quency Wright, 'The Stemson Note of January 7, 1932' ibid. See also, McNair, 'The Stimson Doctrine of Non-recognition' (1933), 14 *Brit. Y.B. Int'l L.* 65.
58 Quoted in Lauterpacht, at 417.
59 (1952), 46 *Am. J. Int'l L. Supp.* 43; for more instances, see Sharp, *supra* note 4, at 67.
60 See, eg, articles 1, 55, 73.
61 Fenwick, 'The Recognition of the Communist Government of China' (1953), 47 *Am. J. Int'l L.* 658, at 660.
62 Dept. of Ext. Aff., Press Release no 50/7.
63 Dec. 1949. File 5670–40C.
64 28 Sept. 1955. File 19464–A–401, vol 3.
65 Dept. of Ext. Aff., Press Release no 50/49.
66 2 H.C. *Debates* (1959) 1405–6.
67 See Lauterpacht, at 110–14.

68 5 H.C. *Debates* (1963) 4721.
69 von Bieberstein, *Zum Problem der völkerrechtlichen Anerkennung der beiden deutschen Regierungen* (1959) 54–8, with extensive literature at note 161.
70 1 *International Law* (2d ed, 1970) 160. See also Lauterpacht at 330. For other supporters, see the authorities in Chen, *supra* note 55, at 273.
71 Kunz, *Die Anerkennung von Staaten, supra* note 45, at 51.
72 Ibid at 52. Cf also Brierley, *The Law of Nations* (6th ed, 1963) 146–8.
73 See, eg 1 D. Anzilloti, *Corso di diritto internazionale* (4th ed, 1955) 160; cf also Brownlie, *Principles of International Law* (1966) 87–8.
74 For detailed discussion, see Wilson, 'British Recognition De Facto and De Jure of the U.S.S.R.' (1934), 28 *Am. J. Int'l L.* 99. *Luther v Sagor*, [1921] 3 K.B. 532, seems to support O'Connell's view. For a summary of British practice, see Lauterpacht, at 330–6.
75 Whiteman, 2 *Digest of International Law* (1963) 3.
76 Ibid, at 4.
77 [1949] S.C.R. 530, [1949] 2 D.L.R. 641.
78 Quoted in Kerwin J's judgment, [1949] 2 D.L.R. at 650–1.
79 5 H.C. *Debates* (1954) 4770; affirmed on 3 April 1957, 3 H.C. *Debates* (1957) 3004.
80 Legal Memorandum to Protocol Division (through European Division), 23 June 1958.
81 British *de jure* recognition was withdrawn in 1940, see *Azazh Kebbeda Tesema v Italian Government*, [1938–1940] *Ann. Dig.* case no 36, but Canada did not withdraw its recognition. See 8 Aug. 1949, File 10464–A–40, vol 1.
82 19 December 1958: File 10464–A–40, vol 1.
83 See 30 June 1958: File 9449–A–40, vol 2.
84 Quoted in (1970), 22 *External Affairs* 415.
85 Establishment of Diplomatic Relations With the Republic of China, Dept. of Ext. Aff., Press Release no 70/19.
86 For a discussion of recognition as determination of a relevant fact or event, see (1964), 1 *Wengler, Völkerrecht* 773–7.
87 See Chen, *International Law of Recognition* (1951); Whiteman, 2 *Digest of International Law* (1963) 51–9.
88 (1950), *External Affairs* 51.
89 Lauterpacht, at 369.
90 Ibid, at 405–6; see also Starke, *Introduction to International Law* (6th ed, 1967) 132.
91 28 March 1950. File 10464–A–40, vol 1.
92 21 March 1965. File 20–14–1, vol 1.

EDWARD G. LEE
AND MICHAEL J. VECHSLER*

8/Sovereign, Diplomatic, and Consular Immunities

This chapter examines Canadian developments with regard to sovereign, diplomatic and consular immunities. It is not meant as a general survey of all immunities accorded in Canada but instead it will analyse some specific problems concerning the granting of immunities. The related subjects of immunities of international organizations such as the United Nations and its family, including the International Civil Aviation Organization whose headquarters is located in Montreal, or the NATO Status of Forces Agreements, will not be examined in this chapter.

SOVEREIGN IMMUNITY

With the exception of questions governed by maritime law, there are no Canadian statutes or international conventions, to which Canada is a party, that purport to incorporate the international law rule of sovereign immunity into Canadian law or to codify that doctrine. On a number of occasions the Supreme Court of Canada has recognized the immunity of foreign states from the jurisdiction of Canadian courts,[1] but in so doing appears to have been applying the principle approved by Chief Justice Duff in the *Foreign Legations* case that 'the Courts acknowledge the existence of a body of rules which nations accept amongst themselves. On any judicial issue they seek to ascertain what the relevant rule is, and, having found it, they will treat it as incorporated into the domestic law.'[2] In short, the Supreme Court seems to have acknowledged the existence of an international law rule of sovereign immunity and has incorporated it into Canadian municipal law. However, as will be suggested below, the Supreme Court has so far not answered the important question whether the doctrine of sovereign immunity incorporated into Canadian law and in force in Canada today is the traditional rule of absolute immunity or the more modern concept of a restricted immunity.

Taschereau J enunciated the traditional rule of absolute sovereign immunity in the Supreme Court case of *Dessaules* v *The Republic of Poland* when he stated: 'It is well established that a sovereign state may not be sued in foreign courts. This principle is based on the independence and dignity of states, and international comity has always observed it.'[3] (Despite the apparent breadth of the rule of absolute sovereign immunity it seems to be generally recognized that it does not encompass litigation involving ownership or other interests in immovables in the territory or an interest in an estate locally administered.[4]) The absolute rule appears to have been justified at various times on a number of grounds including the principles of

*The views expressed in this article are solely the authors' and do not necessarily represent those of the Department of External Affairs.

the sovereignty, independence, and equality of states as well as reciprocity.[5] However, with the expansion of governmental activity beyond the traditional political realm, and particularly with its intrusion into the commercial field, it has been suggested that the doctrine of absolute sovereign immunity can no longer be justified and should now be restricted to public acts, with a state being liable before the courts of a foreign country for its private acts. In order to determine the current scope of the international law rule and the extent to which the absolute principle has given way to the restrictive concept it is necessary to examine 1 / international conventions, 2 / state practice, and 3 / the teachings of highly qualified publicists. Inevitably, in the space available, this examination cannot be exhaustive, but is merely intended to give an indication of trends.

International conventions

Conventional law appears to be confined to maritime matters. Articles I, II, and III of the 1926 International Convention for the Unification of Certain Rules Relating to the Immunity of State-Owned Vessels (Brussels Convention),[6] to which some twenty-three countries are now a party, restricts the applicability of the doctrine of sovereign immunity to state-owned or operated ships used, at the time the cause of action arose, exclusively for governmental and non-commercial purposes. Article 21 of the 1958 Geneva Convention on the Territorial Sea and the Contiguous Zone,[7] which entered into force in 1964 and has been ratified by thirty-nine states, permits coastal states to treat 'government ships operated for commercial purposes' as if they were non-government foreign ships with respect to executions or arrests constituting an element in civil proceedings. Finally, articles 8 and 9 of the Geneva Convention on the High Seas,[8] which entered into force in 1962 and has been ratified by forty-six states, by explicitly recognizing that warships and 'ships owned or operated by a State and used only on government non-commercial service' are completely immune from the jurisdiction of any state other than the flag-state, appear to acknowledge, *by implication* that state-owned or operated vessels engaged in non-government or commercial services are not entitled to like immunity. However, it should be noted that the USSR and a number of communist states which are parties to the Convention on the Territorial Sea and the Contiguous Zone and the Convention on the High Seas have all entered reservations regarding the above-mentioned articles indicating that they reject the restrictive concept of sovereign immunity which excludes state-owned or operated vessels used for non-governmental or commercial purposes. Canada is a signatory to the two Geneva conventions.

State practice

Turning to state practice, at least five countries (Italy,[9] Belgium,[10] Norway,[11] Sweden,[12] and Argentina[13]) have enacted legislation denying immunity to foreign state-owned or operated ships which are engaged in commercial operations. Section 43(7)(c) of the Canadian Federal Court Act (1970–1, Can., c 1) specifically states: 'No action *in rem* may be commenced in Canada against any ship owned or operated by a sovereign power other than Canada, or any cargo laden thereon, with respect to any claim where, at the time the claim arose or the action is commenced, such ship was being used exclusively for non-commercial governmental purposes.' By specifically excluding ships owned or operated by foreign states and 'used exclusively for non-commercial governmental purposes,' the new Federal Court Act may be interpreted as *implicitly* granting jurisdiction to the court over ships owned and operated by foreign states and used for commercial non-governmental purposes. It is perhaps also interesting to note in connection with shipping, that the representatives of Burma, Ceylon, and India to the first session of the Asian Legal Consultative Committee held in 1957 rejected the doctrine of absolute immunity of government ships. At that meeting, the representative of Indonesia, alone, expressed strict adherence to the doctrine of absolute immunity.[14]

The courts of at least eight countries (Argentina,[15] Austria,[16] Belgium,[17] France,[18] Greece,[19] Italy,[20] Netherlands,[21] and Switzerland[22]) appear to have accepted the restrictive doctrine. The lower courts of the Federal Republic of Germany also appear to be leaning towards the restrictive concept, and this tendency is now supported by a dictum of the Supreme Court.[23] The position of the English courts appears to be still unclear. There are some dicta in *Compania Naviera Vascongada* v *S.S. Cristina*[24] and in *Sultan of Johore* v *Abubakar Tunku Aris Bendahar*[25] (a Privy Council decision), suggesting that the House of Lords has not closed the door on the restrictive doctrine. These will be dealt with in greater detail below.

Following the decision of Chief Justice Stone in *Republic of Mexico* v *Hoffman*,[26] the position taken by us courts on the question of sovereign immunity became to a large degree academic. In that case, Chief Justice Stone stated:

> It is therefore not for the Courts to deny an immunity which our government has seen fit to allow, or to allow an immunity on grounds which the government has not seen fit to recognize.[27] … it is the duty of the Courts in a matter so intimately associated with our foreign policy and which may profoundly affect it not to enlarge an immunity to an extent which the government, although often asked, has not seen fit to recognize.[28]

In other words, Chief Justice Stone was saying that the courts would follow the advice of the executive branch of government (in practice, the Department of State) with regard to the granting of sovereign immunity.

However, there are some indications that the us courts may now be retreating slightly from the subordinate position assigned to them by Chief Justice Stone. In the case of *Victory Transport Inc.* v *Commissaria General de Abastecimientos y Transportes*,[29] decided by the United States Court of Appeal (second circuit) in 1964, Smith J gave the following interpretation of the dictum of Chief Justice Stone in *Republic of Mexico* v *Hoffman*:

> But we think it means at least that the Courts should deny immunity where the State Department has indicated, either directly or indirectly, that immunity need not be accorded. It makes no sense for the Courts to deny a litigant his day in Court and to permit the disregard of legal obligations to avoid embarrassing the State Department if that agency indicates it will not be embarrassed …

Where, as here, the Court has received no communication from the State Department concerning the immunity of the Commisaria General, the Court must decide for itself whether it is the established policy of the State Department to recognize claims of immunity of this type.[30]

In addition, to indicating that US courts may, in the absence of a suggestion from the State Department, make their own decisions in sovereign immunity cases, the *Victory Transport* case also follows the restrictive doctrine of sovereign immunity.

The policy of the State Department regarding sovereign immunity is set out in a letter dated 19 May 1952 from J.B. Tate, the Department's acting legal adviser, to the acting attorney general. The Tate letter, which adopts the restrictive doctrine, states that, in future the Department would only grant immunity to foreign states in respect of acts *jure imperii* (public acts) and not acts *jure gestionis* (private acts).[31] (In the US the absolute doctrine of sovereign immunity is applied with respect to executions.)[32]

It may be of interest to record at this point excerpts from a statement made by M.J. Belman, when he was deputy legal adviser at the State Department, regarding the approach at present adopted in the US to sovereign immunity cases:

> The Tate letter tried to draw a distinction between governmental and commercial activities. In today's world, this standard is extremely hard to apply ...
>
> The problem with the standard is that it creates too many anomalies. The purchase of rifles for a country's army is probably a governmental act ... but a purchase of rifles for a country's olympic team is probably not ...
>
> The Department of State has become ill-suited to decide sovereign immunity cases ... the Tate letter purported to eliminate the foreign relations criterion from the Department's consideration and rested the whole sovereign immunity decision on the governmental and commercial activities of foreign governments. In other words, the Department is now making legal judgements that fall within the province of the courts and can more satisfactorily be decided using judicial procedures.
>
> For some time, we in the State Department have been thinking about these issues and now have proposed remedial legislation.
>
> The proposal would modify the standards now applied in sovereign immunity cases ... and it would remove the State Department from any role in deciding sovereign immunity cases.
>
> ... the State Department proposal would require that foreign States answer in the courts of the United States in certain kinds of contract and tort cases. Sovereign immunity would not lie in any action founded upon express or implied contracts entered into, to be performed in, or arising out of transactions bearing a reasonable relation to the United States. Foreign States would also be unable to rely upon sovereign immunity as a defence to responsibility for the negligent torts of its officers, agents or employers ...
>
> As under present law, the property of foreign states would be immune from execution. This rule is consistent with our present law and practice and with that of many other countries. It is grounded on the belief that one state should not seize and sell the property of another state, since to do so would be severely detrimental both to good relations between the states and to the carrying on of appropriate functions by the state whose property is taken ... In practice we have found that the immunity from execution we now

accord foreign sovereigns has not resulted in their refusing to pay judgements against them, and we see no reason why the good faith of foreign states in this regard should not continue.[33]

Mr Belman has left the State Department and it is now only possible to conjecture whether the views expressed above are still held by the Department. The remedial legislation proposed has not been introduced.

Current US treaty practice appears to be in line with the present policy of the State Department except with respect to immunity from execution which, as was noted above, is normally granted in all cases involving foreign states. The US has established bilateral treaties of 'Friendship Commerce and Navigation' with Greece, Ireland, Israel, Italy and Japan. Article 18(2) of the treaty with Japan is typical:

> No enterprise of either party, including corporations, associations, and government agencies and instrumentalities, ... shall, if it engages in commercial, industrial, shipping or other business activities within the territories of the other party, claim or enjoy, either for itself or for its property, immunity therein from taxation, suit, execution of judgement or other liability.[34]

Even in the absence of recorded cases, it may still be possible to say that the communist states of eastern Europe, including the USSR, seem to adhere to the theory of absolute immunity.[35] As was noted above, these states entered reservations to those provisions of the Convention on the Territorial Sea and the Contiguous Zone as well as of the Convention on the High Seas which appeared to deny the applicability of the doctrine of sovereign immunity to cases involving state-owned or operated ships not engaged in governmental non-commercial activities. In practice it is only on the basis of reciprocity that foreign merchant ships enjoy immunity from arrest while in the waters of the USSR, and no distinction is made between merchant ships carrying commercial and non-commercial cargoes. However, the USSR has adopted the practice of owning its merchant ships through limited companies, and does not generally claim any immunity for them.[36] In addition, since before World War II the USSR has maintained a consistent policy of entering into agreements specifying that its trade delegations are not entitled to immunity from jurisdiction or execution with respect to commercial transactions.[37]

Views of scholars

An examination of the views of writers and of the resolutions of learned societies indicates that, with a few exceptions, scholarly opinion supports the restrictive concept of sovereign immunity. McNair,[38] Brierly,[39] Nielson,[40] Lalive,[41] Sorenson,[42] and Lauterpacht[43] all support the restrictive concept. However, Lauterpacht (like Mr Belman), while supporting the restrictive doctrine, questions whether the distinction between acts *jure imperii* and acts *jure gestionis* is practical since all private acts of a state are also in a real sense public acts.[44] Lauterpacht seems to believe that it would be better to start from the premise that a state enjoys no immunity subject to certain well defined exceptions: immunity must remain the rule with respect to a / legislative acts of a foreign state and measures taken in pursuance thereof; b / executive and administrative acts of a foreign state within its territory; c / contracts made with or by a foreign state except contracts concluded within the territory of the state whose court is assuming jurisdiction, or a contract to which the *lex fori* is applicable; d / diplomatic immunity, and e / warships or similar vessels and armed forces aircraft should be immune from actions *in rem*.[45] It is interesting to note that in the *Victory Transport* case Smith J approved the approach suggested by Lauterpacht.[46]

Articles 11 and 23 of the 1932 Harvard Research in International Law Relating to the Competence of Courts in Regard to Foreign States,[47] the Resolution on State Immunity adopted by the International Law Association at its 1952 Conference,[48] the Resolution on Immunity of Foreign States from Jurisdiction and Measures of Execution adopted by the Institut de Droit International at its 1954 Session,[49] and section 72 of the Official Draft Restatement of the Foreign Relations Law of the United States (whose publication was approved by the American Law Institute in May 1962)[50] all favour the adoption of the restrictive doctrine of sovereign immunity.

On the basis of the foregoing, it is probably at this time only safe to say that the whole international law doctrine of sovereign immunity is in a state of flux, and that therefore both the absolute and restrictive doctrine are compatible with international law in its present stage of development. However, there appears to be a clearly discernible trend away from the absolute theory and towards adoption of the restrictive doctrine. This trend seems highly justifiable in view of the ever-expanding realms of activity of modern states. It should also be noted that even where the restrictive approach has been adopted there does not appear to be any concensus regarding the correct test to use in determining whether in a particular case a state is entitled to immunity.

Canadian experience

During the past ten years the Supreme Court of Canada has on two occasions been asked to decide that a foreign state was not entitled to claim sovereign immunity since the act to which the litigation pertained was not a 'public act' of the defendant state. In other words, the Court was being asked to determine whether the restrictive doctrine of sovereign immunity has been incorporated into Canadian law or whether the absolute doctrine enunciated in such cases as *Dessaules v The Republic of Poland* still prevails. Regrettably, in both instances the majority in the Supreme Court studiously avoided answering this crucial question. They simply decided on the basis of the facts in each case that the questions at issue were 'public acts' so that even under the restrictive doctrine the foreign state would be entitled to immunity. However, the majority decisions in both cases do contain tantalizing *obiter dicta* relating to the status of the restrictive doctrine in Canada.

The first case, *Flota Maritima de Cuba S.A. v Steamship 'Canadian Conqueror' et al. and the Republic of Cuba*,[51] involved an action *in rem* against ships owned by the Republic of Cuba. As noted above, the majority decision, delivered by Ritchie J (Fauteux, Abbott, Martland, and Taschereau JJ concurring), was based on the ground that the subject matter of the case involved a 'public' act and, consequently, the Republic of Cuba would be immune even under the restrictive doctrine. However, in the course of delivering his judgment Ritchie J did state:

It has long been recognized that ships of war engaged in the service of a foreign state are to be treated as floating portions of the flag state and that as such in peacetime they are exempt from the jurisdiction of our Courts, and this principle has been extended to include the ships of a foreign state which are used for the public purposes of that state such as mail carrying packets (*The Parlement Belge* [1878], 5 P.D. 197) and ships carrying coal for public purposes (*The "Terraete"*, [1922] 259), but the proposition that trading vessels owned and operated by a foreign sovereign state are equally immune from the jurisdiction of our Courts rests in large measure upon the case of *The "Porto Alexandre"* ([1920] 30) decided in the English Court of Appeal and upon the minority opinion of Lord Atkin in *Compania Naviera Vascongado* v *S.S. "Cristina"* ([1928] A.C. 485).[52]

Ritchie J continued:

The majority of the judges in the House of Lords [in *"The Cristina"*] placed their judgements squarely on the ground that the ship was being employed for the public purposes of a sovereign state, and Lord Thankerton, Lord Macmillan and Lord Maugham expressly reserved their opinion on the question of whether such immunity from arrest would have attached to the ship if it had been engaged in trade."[53]

Ritchie J also quoted from the decision of Viscount Simon[54] who, when speaking on behalf of the Judicial Committee of the Privy Council in *Sultan of Johore* v *Abubakar Tunku Aris Bendahar*,[55] stated:

If, however, it had been definitely determined that in no case could a foreign sovereign be impleaded without his consent, there could be no justification for reserving the case of a sovereign's ship engaged in ordinary commerce – a reservation that was in fact made by the majority of the House of Lords in *The Cristina*. For a sovereign is impleaded by an action *in rem* against his ship, whether it is engaged in ordinary commerce or is employed for purposes that are more usually distinguished as public.[56]

Turning to the case of *Thomas White* v *The Ship Frank Dale*[57] in which Sir Joseph Chisholm held that *all* state-owned vessels are entitled to immunity, Ritchie J said:

When reference is made to the decision of Sir Joseph Chisholm, it is found that learned Judge must have been misled by the headnote in the *"Cristina"* ... because he says 'In the *Cristina* case the Court held that the immunity claimed extended and applied to ships engaged in trade and belonging to a foreign sovereign State.'[58]

Ritchie J noted that this interpretation of the *Cristina* was rejected by Sir Lyman Duff in the *Foreign Legations* case.[59] He next referred to the sixth edition of Cheshire's Private International Law (at 96–7) where Dr Cheshire expressed the view that it is unjust if not preposterous for foreign state-owned ships engaged in commercial undertakings to be granted immunity. Ritchie J concluded by stating:

With the greatest respect for those who hold a different view, I do not find it necessary in the present case to adopt that part of Lord Atkin's judgement in *The "Cristina"* in which he expressed the opinion that property of a foreign sovereign state 'only used for commercial purposes' is immune from seizure under the process of our Courts, and I would dispose of this appeal entirely on the basis that the defendant ships are to be treated as (to use the language of Sir Lyman P. Duff C.J.C.) 'the property of a foreign state devoted to public use in the traditional sense' and that the Exchequer Court was, therefore, without jurisdiction to entertain this action.[60]

In the second case, *Le Gouvernement de la Republique du Congo v Jean Venne*,[61] the plaintiff, an architect, brought an action to obtain payment for services performed for the Congolese Government in preparing sketches for the Congolese pavilion at Expo 67. The Quebec Court of Appeal decided in favour of the plaintiff on the basis of the restrictive doctrine,[62] but the Supreme Court upheld the immunity of the defendant. However, it again did so without denying the restrictive doctrine. In delivering the Court's decision, Ritchie J (Fauteux CJC, Abbott, Martland, Judson, Spence, and Pigeon JJ, concurring) stated: 'The appellant's employment of the respondent was in the performance of a sovereign act of state. It therefore follows in my view that the appellant could not be impleaded in the courts of this country even if the so-called doctrine of restrictive sovereign immunity had been adopted in our courts.'[63]

In the above two cases, the Supreme Court has definitely not closed the door on the restrictive concept but has left it open for the Court at a later date to decide that this doctrine has in fact been incorporated into Canadian municipal law. On the basis of a number of recent lower court decisions,[64] particularly in Quebec, it seems likely that the trend in Canada, as in international law generally, is towards the restrictive doctrine. However, in the meantime the law has been left in an unsatisfactory state of uncertainty. It is perhaps wrong to criticize the Court for leaving this uncertainty since its function is to reach a decision on the facts in a particular case. However, instead of having said, as the Supreme Court did, that the facts in these cases would permit the invocation of sovereign immunity even under the restrictive doctrine and in this way escaping the necessity of determining whether the restrictive doctrine has been incorporated into Canadian municipal law, the Court could have as easily first made a determination on the validity of the restrictive concept, and, if it decided that this doctrine had been incorporated, could then proceed to decide whether on the facts of the particular case the foreign state was entitled to immunity under the restrictive doctrine. This latter approach would seem to have the distinct advantage of resulting in the clarification of an important area of Canadian law.

While the above cases do not clarify the standing of the restrictive doctrine in Canada, they at least provide some indication of how the Supreme Court will interpret the restrictive doctrine should it be adopted. In *Flota Maritima Browning de Cuba S.A. v The Steamship "Canadian Conqueror" et al and the Republic of Cuba*, Ritchie J appears to have proceeded on the basis that there was no evidence before the Court regarding the purpose for which the ships would ultimately be used. In these circumstances he decided:

Although the ships might ultimately be used by Cuba as trading or passenger ships, there is no evidence before us as to the use for which they were destined, and ... I ... do not feel that we are in a position to say that these ships are going to be used for ordinary trading purposes. All that can be said is that they are available to be used by the Republic of Cuba for any purpose which its government may select, and it seems to me that ships which are at the disposal of a foreign state and are being supervised for the account of a department of government of that state are to be regarded as 'public ships of a sovereign state' at least until such time as some decision is made by the sovereign state in question as to the use to which they are to be put.[65]

The majority decision in *Le Gouvernement de la Republique Democratique du Congo* v *Jean Venne* stated:

The question of whether the contract in question was purely private and commercial or whether it was a public act done on behalf of a sovereign state for state purposes, is one which should be decided on the record as a whole without placing the burden of rebutting a presumption on either party.[66]

Previously, Ritchie J had mentioned

that the contract here in question was made in pursuance of the desire of a foreign sovereign state to construct a national pavilion at an international exhibition and to be thereby represented at that exhibition which was registered by the Council of the Bureau of International Exhibitions and which was to be held (in the words of s.3(1) of the *Canadian World Exhibition Corporation Act, supra*) 'in connection with the celebration of the centennial of Confederation in Canada in a manner in keeping with its national and historical significance.'[67]

He went on to say:

'I think that it is of particular significance that the request for the respondent's services was made not only by the duly accredited diplomatic representatives of the Congo who were Commissioners General of the Exhibition, but also by the representatives of the Department of Foreign Affairs of that country. This makes it plain to me that in preparing for the construction of its national pavilion, a department of the Government of a foreign state, together with its duly accredited diplomatic representatives, were engaged in the performance of a public sovereign act of state on behalf of their country and that the employment of the respondent was a step taken in the performance of that sovereign act.'[68]

Finally, Ritchie J noted: 'Here there is no evidence of a commercial venture.'[69]

In both cases the Supreme Court appears to have taken a broad view of 'public acts.' Despite what Ritchie J said in *Le Gouvernement de la Republique du Congo* v *Jean Venne* that there is no burden on either party to rebut a presumption, it seems clear that a burden was placed on the plaintiff in *Flota Maritima Browning de Cuba S.A.* v *The Steamship "Canadian Conqueror"* et al and the Republic of Cuba to rebut the presumption that the ships in question were to be regarded as 'public ships of a sovereign state.' In *Le Gouvernement de la Republique du Congo* v *Jean Venne* the Court appears to have decided, as Ritchie J suggested, 'on the record as a whole.' It did not look at the narrow purpose of the contract (ie construction of a building) but looked instead at the whole context of the contract (ie Expo 67), and such other factors as 1 / that it was entered into by a duly accredited diplomatic representative, 2 / the background of the Canadian World Exhibition Corporation Act, and 3 / that there was no evidence of a commercial venture.

Given the current state of flux in international law with regard to the absolute as opposed to the restrictive doctrine of sovereign immunity and also with respect to the test to be applied in determining whether a particular act falls within the restrictive doctrine, it seems probable that the Supreme Court of Canada's decisions in both *Flota Maritima Browning de Cuba S.A.* v *The Steamship "Canadian Conqueror" et al and the Republic of Cuba* and in *Le Gouvernement de la Republique du Congo* v *Jean Venne* must be regarded as consonant with international law. However, the Supreme Court does not seem to have tried in either case to determine the international law rule of sovereign immunity or the test to be applied in deciding whether a particular act falls within the restrictive concept. There was no visible attempt to examine the generally accepted sources of international law; namely, international conventions, state practice, or the writings of highly respected publicists. In both cases the majority opinions appear to refer only to British and Canadian precedents with the exception of single references to 1 / a US case, 2 / state practice in the US, and 3 / to a publicist. In fact, Ritchie J explicitly stated with regard to US decisions that

> in such cases the question to be determined ... is whether it is the established policy of the State Department to recognize the immunity claimed in any particular case. As no such question arises in this country, I take the view that cases concerning sovereign immunity decided in the courts of the United States in recent years are of little or no authority in Canada.[70]

One might almost think on the basis of the majority judgments that the Court believes it is deciding an ordinary Canadian municipal law case and not a case where it is first necessary to ascertain the international law rule so that that rule can then be incorporated into Canadian municipal law.

Conclusion

In conclusion, it is probably correct to say that at present there is not a great deal more uncertainty in Canadian municipal law regarding the doctrine of sovereign immunity than there is in international law generally. However, with the ever-expanding scope of state activities, particularly in the commercial realm, the inequity of the absolute doctrine becomes increasingly apparent. In addition, there is a need for persons dealing with foreign states to know the extent of their rights before entering into such contracts. This would seem to be especially true with respect to commercial transactions. Ritchie J may be correct in saying 'that immunity from the jurisdiction of our courts on the ground of sovereign immunity does not necessarily preclude the enforcement of a just demand through other channels.'[71] However, in practice such other channels (diplomatic) are often cumbersome and involve long delays without assurance of a successful outcome. (It is perhaps worth noting here that in Canada the law of sovereign immunity appears to be the same with respect to immunity from both execution and judgment. Presumably, therefore, if judgment were obtained execution could also be enforced. However, it will be recalled that Mr Belman is reported above as stating that in the us where immunity from execution is absolute little problem has been experienced in collecting judgments.)

In view of the need for certainty in this area of the law, and the apparent reluctance of the Supreme Court to provide such certainty, it seems that consideration should at some stage be given in Canada to enacting legislation clarifying the law of sovereign immunity. As noted above, such legislation has already been enacted in the maritime law field and it seems that the federal government would probably have the power to enact general legislation dealing with sovereign immunity under the heading of 'peace, order and good government.' If and when consideration is given to drafting legislation codifying the restrictive concept, it is to be hoped that considerable thought and care will be taken to devise a test, for the limits of the immunity, which will meet the requirements both of certainty and justice.

DIPLOMATIC IMMUNITIES

Immunities enjoyed by diplomatic agents in Canada were (at least until the ratification by Canada on 26 May 1966 of the Vienna Convention on Diplomatic Relations of 1961) based on generally recognized principles of internaional law which, in the light of the decision of the *Foreign Legations* case by the Supreme Court of Canada,[72] were considered incorporated into the domestic law of Canada insofar as such rules were 'not inconsistent with rules enacted by Statutes or finally declared by their tribunals.'

The written part of our law concerning diplomatic immunities consists of, *inter alia*, the United Kingdom Diplomatic Immunities Act of 1708 (7 Anne, c 12), which is regarded as applicable in all of Canada except the Province of Quebec. It is mainly declaratory in nature and restricted to immunity from civil process. Canada is not at present a party to any bilateral agreement governing the exchange of diplomatic privileges and immunities with a foreign country, although the Diplomatic Immunities (Commonwealth Countries) Act (Statutes of Canada 1953–54, c 54), was enacted in pursuance of intra-Commonwealth arrangements. That act provides for the special case of Commonwealth representatives, according to them the 'like immunities' as are granted to foreign envoys without, however, specifying the immunities.

The 1961 Vienna Convention on Diplomatic Relations codified the international law on diplomatic immunities. It did not set standards of immunity greater than those generally recognized already in Canadian practice and since the convention embodied practice and usage which had been long observed, the convention could be considered to be part of the common law in Canada in accordance with the *Foreign Legations* case, except where statutes or decisions of Canadian legislatures and courts establish rules to the contrary. For these reasons the Canadian government did not enact specific legislation to implement the provisions of the Vienna Convention on Diplomatic Relations, unlike the United Kingdom and Australia, whose parliaments enacted respectively the uk Diplomatic Privileges Act of 1964, and the Australian Diplomatic Privileges and Immunities Act of 1967. In any areas not dealt with by the provisions of the Vienna Convention the customary international law of course continue to govern.

While the Vienna Convention on Diplomatic Relations clearly accords to diplomatic agents immunities based on the functional approach (meaning that the immunities are granted to them in order to facilitate their work), and while the provisions of the convention are in most respects in line with Canadian practice, some problems have arisen from time to time. For example, some minor questions have arisen concerning the compulsory searching of diplomatic agents at Canadian airports as part of the procedures to deter the hijacking of aircraft. Problems have also arisen over the provincial governments' right to levy provincial sales taxes on diplomatic agents. There have also been occasional questions raised by diplomatic agents who have been required to pay the federal sales tax on wholesale purchases of furniture and paper products; the federal authorities deny the allegations of certain diplomatic agents who claim that the sales tax is a direct one because it appears as a separate item on the wholesale sales voucher and consequently that they should be exempted from that tax.

The question of the applicability of succession duties to foreign diplomatic agents and members of their families has also been the subject in the past of some discussion between the Department of External Affairs and diplomatic agents in Canada. The estate of a foreign diplomatic agent, although not that of members of his family, is exempted on a reciprocal basis from all federal taxes and duties on property acquired by him incidental to his residence in Canada as an officer of a foreign government. There are, however, no specific provisions in the provincial succession duty acts granting exemptions in favour of all persons falling within the scope of the Vienna Convention on Diplomatic Relations. In practice, however, whenever specific cases have arisen, provincial authorities have accorded sympathetic consideration to the amicable settlement of the relevant estate.

CONSULAR IMMUNITIES

In Canada no clearcut case has yet arisen which establishes that foreign consular officers are immune from the jurisdiction of the judicial or administrative authorities of Canada in respect of acts performed in the exercise of their consular functions. Nevertheless, we attempt to show here that article 43 of the 1963 Vienna Convention on Consular Relations represents a codification of generally accepted principles of international law which would be considered by a Canadian court as binding on Canada despite the fact the Canadian government has not yet signed or ratified that convention. Article 43 reads as follows:

1 Consular officers and consular employees shall not be amenable to the jurisdiction of the judicial or administrative authorities of the receiving state in respect of acts performed in the exercise of consular functions.
2 The provisions of paragraph 1 of this Article shall not, however, apply in respect of a civil action either:
   a / arising out of a contract concluded by a consular officer or a consular employee in which he did not contract expressly or impliedly as an agent of the sending state; or

b / by a third party for damage arising from an accident in the receiving state caused by a vehicle, vessel or aircraft.

Customary international law, like the common law, is a living organism which is constantly changing and evolving. Consequently, in order to determine the extent of the immunities which should be accorded to foreign consular officers in Canada, it is necessary to examine current state practice which can be found *inter alia* in the provisions of international conventions, municipal legislation, the decisions of municipal tribunals, and the statements of government spokesmen. In addition, the teachings of the most highly qualified contemporary publicists provide a subsidiary guide to the present state of customary international law on this matter.

International conventions

Turning to the question of consular immunity, and looking first at international conventions as indicators of state practice, W.E. Beckett[73] considers that nearly all modern consular conventions contain an express provision that 'Consuls shall not be subject to the jurisdiction of the State in which they reside officially as regards the carrying out of their official duties.' He cites the following examples and indicates that there are innumerable other instances: 'Article x of the Convention of March 25, 1925 between Germany and Estonia; Article 4 of the Convention of March 1924 between Italy and Czechoslovakia; Article 5 of the Convention of July 1924 between the u.s.s.r. and Poland; Article 4 of the Convention of December 1925 between France and Poland.'

Similarly, Luke T. Lee in his book *Consular Law and Practice* observes that

> Of the many consular treaties supporting the functional approach [ie that consuls should be exempt from the civil or criminal jurisdiction of the courts of the receiving State with respect to acts performed in pursuance of their official functions] two may be cited. The United Kingdom-Norwegian Consular Convention of 1951 (Article 13) provides:
> 1 A consular officer or employee shall not be liable, in proceedings in the course of the receiving state, in respect of acts performed within the functions of a consular officer under international law, unless the sending state requests or assents to the proceedings through its diplomatic representative.
> 2 It is understood that the provisions of paragraph (1) of this Article do not preclude a consular officer or employee from being held liable in a civil action arising out of a contract concluded by him in which he did not expressly contract as agent for his government and in which the other party looked to him personally for performance.
> The Polish-Soviet Consular Convention of 1958 (article 11) also provides that consular officers and employees who are nationals of the sending state are not subject to the jurisdiction of the receiving state in matters concerning their official activities.[74]

Finally, it should be noted that the us-ussr Consular Convention signed in Moscow on 1 June 1964 provides in article 19:

> 1 Consular officers shall not be subject to the jurisdiction of the receiving state in matters relating to their official activity. The same applies to employees of the consular establishment, if they are nationals of the sending state.

2 Consular officers and employees of the consular establishment who are nationals of the sending state shall enjoy immunity from the criminal jurisdiction of the receiving state.

3 This immunity from the criminal jurisdiction of the receiving state of consular officers and employees of the consular establishment of the sending state may be waived by the sending state. Waiver must always be express.

Two important multilateral conventions also contain parallel provisions. The Pan-American Convention on Consular Agents adopted in Havana on 20 February 1928 and ratified by Brazil, Colombia, Cuba, Dominican Republic, Equador, El Salvador, Haiti, Mexico, Nicaragua, Panama, Peru, and the United States provides in article 16 that 'consuls are not subject to local jurisdiction for acts done in their official character and within the scope of their authority. In case a private individual deems himself injured by the consul's action, he must submit his complaint to the Government, which, if it considers the claim to be relevant, shall make it valid through diplomatic channels.' The Consular Relations Convention, which was adopted by the United Nations Conference on Consular Relations held in Vienna in 1963, entered into force on 19 March 1967 and has now been signed by fifty-one states and ratified or acceded to by forty-one states. The United States is a party to the convention, and the United Kingdom a signatory. In 1968 the United Kingdom enacted the Consular Relations Act which states in the preamble that it is 'An Act to give effect to the Vienna Convention on Consular Relations.' Section 1 (1) of this act accords article 43 of the convention the force of law in the United Kingdom.

Governmental statements and regulations

With respect to official statements by governments and municipal laws and regulations as evidence of international custom, Beckett[75] points out that there are many official statements and regulations issued by governments which state generally that consuls cannot claim diplomatic immunity and are subject to the jurisdiction of the local courts and make no special reference to process relating to acts performed in their official capacity. However, there would appear to be no statements or regulations which deny immunity specifically with regard to acts done in the performance of consular functions, and immunity from process in respect of official acts is specifically recognized in the following official statements and regulations.

United Kingdom   The Consular Relations Act 1968, referred to above, provides that consular officers and consular employees shall not be amenable to the jurisdiction of the judicial or administrative authorities of the receiving state in respect of acts performed in the exercise of consular functions.

Denmark   Resolution of 25 April 1821: 'Foreign consuls (whether of Danish or other nationality) do not come under the jurisdiction of the country so far as their consular affairs are concerned.'

Italy   Memorandum of October 1930 from the Italian government to the United States ambassador: 'As regards the prerogatives of consuls, it is to be noted that they are more restricted than those of diplomats ... Immunity from the local jurisdiction is limited to acts performed by the consuls in the exercise of their functions, aside from special conventions.'

Sweden   Memorandum of April 1930 from the Swedish government to the

American legation: 'Through the application of international usage, as well as by virtue of various treaties, according to consuls under the conditions of reciprocity the benefit of the most-favoured-nation treatment, the Swedish authorities would probably recognize for them exemption from jurisdiction for all acts attaching to their quality of public agents.'

Switzerland A letter from the Swiss Federal Political Department to the judge of a court of the Canton of Berne who had asked a question about consular immunity gives the following ruling: 'In principle consuls are subject to the jurisdiction of the receiving State except with regard to acts done in the exercise of their official duties and within the sphere of their authority.'

USSR Regulations of 14 January 1927: 'Article 11   The consular representatives of foreign States enjoy on a basis of reciprocity the rights and privileges attached to their functions in conformity with the rules of international law. In particular the consular representatives ... are not subject to the jurisdiction of the judicial institutions of the U.S.S.R. and of the Federated Republic because of offences committed in the discharge of their office.''

In addition, the laws and regulations of the following countries direct their consuls to claim in foreign countries as essential for the discharge of their functions the freedom of those acts appropriate to their consular character': Bolivia (Regulation 1887, article 21); Chile (Regulations 1915, article 113); Costa Rica (Regulations 1888, article 27); Dominica (Law 1887, article 18); Ecuador (Regulations 1870, article 17); Uruguay (Regulations 1917, article 57).

Legal decisions

The decisions of national tribunals also provide evidence of international practice.

United Kingdom   While it is clear that the United Kingdom courts have decided that consuls are not entitled to *diplomatic type immunity* (ie immunity from judicial and administrative process whether the relevant acts were performed in the course of official functions or not), we have not been able to discover any cases where the courts have denied that consuls are immune from jurisdiction with respect to acts performed in the course of official duties.[76] Indeed, the statement of Lord Ellenborough in *Viveash* v *Becker* that consuls enjoy special protection under the law of nations including the right to the liberty and safety necessary for the discharge of their functions appears to recognize the existence of *consular immunity* (ie that consuls are immune with respect to acts performed in the course of their official duties). If consuls were not immune from the jurisdiction of the courts of the receiving state with respect to acts performed in the course of their official duties, they would not have that liberty and safety necessary for the discharge of their functions to which Lord Ellenborough refers.

The House of Lords in the case of *Engelke* v *Musmann,* [1928] All E.R. 18, dealt with the question of diplomatic immunity but did not deny the existence of consular immunity. The distinction between these two types of immunity is very crucial. Diplomatic immunity confers on the beneficiary immunity from judicial and administrative process whether he was acting in the course of his official duty or not (see 1961 Vienna Convention on Diplomatic Relations, article 31). Consular immunity, on the other hand, is different in kind and merely confers immunity on the beneficiary with respect to acts performed in the course of his official duties. It is not, moreover, applicable to civil actions arising out of a contract concluded by a consular officer or a consular employee in which he did not contract expressly or impliedly as an agent of the sending state or to civil actions brought by a third party for damages arising from an accident in the receiving state caused by a vehicle, vessel, or aircraft (see Vienna Convention on Consular Relations, article 43).

In the case of *Engelke* v *Musmann,* a consular secretary on the staff of the German ambassador was claiming immunity from suit resulting from an action arising out of a lease into which he had entered. There is no indication in the report that he entered into the lease contract either expressly or impliedly as an agent of the German government, or that he was even acting in the course of his duty. It, therefore, seems clear that consular immunity would not have been applicable in this case and, consequently, does not appear to have been pleaded.

The inapplicability of consular immunity explains the implication found in the report that if Engelke were not entitled to diplomatic immunity he would not be immune from suit. It is true that Lord Dunedin states at page 22 that 'The respondent tried to convince us that, if this case was decided in favour of the appellant, it was opening the door to the granting of diplomatic privilege to the consular service.' Similarly, Lord Phillimore comments at page 23: 'The description which the defendant gave of himself and which has been given of him by the Foreign Office is, that he is a Consular Secretary on the staff of the German Ambassador and the argument for the plaintiff rested on the expression "consular" with a suggestion that an attempt was being made to get diplomatic privilege for a person who was not truly diplomatic, but only in the consular service.'

In our view, these two statements at most indicate that consuls are not entitled to dipolmatic privileges and immunities. Since diplomatic immunity and consular immunity are two entirely distinct and separate principles, one cannot interpret the above statements as in any way denying that consular officials are entitled to consular immunity.

Mauritius   In the case of *Dangin* v *Paturau* decided in the Supreme Court of Mauritius in 1949, Brouard J stated at page 302:

> It appears that consuls, although not entitled to the privileges of personal immunity enjoyed by the diplomatic service, are, nevertheless, according to international courtesy and usages, granted a certain protection when acting in their official capacity. That protection, according to the learned authors, seems to be based on reciprocity. I find from the cases of *Murphy* v *Lee Fortin* and *Princess Zizianoff* v *Bigelow* that the British Consuls in France have already been granted that '*immunité de jurisdiction*' when acting in the performance of their official duties. Were I to apply that principle of reciprocity, it is evident that a French Consul in a British Colony should be allowed *l'immunité de jurisdiction.* Further, it seems logical that if 'muniments and papers of a consulate are inviolable', consuls should not be requested to explain before a foreign court acts done by them under instructions in the performance of their official duties.[77]

Canada   In *Maas* v *Beelheim* [1936], 4 D.L.R. 267, the German consul did not plead consular immunity, but did plead qualified privilege in respect of a defamatory statement made in the course of his official duties. The consul was successful on the plea of qualified privilege. In three other cases involving consuls – *Campbell v Cour des Sessions générales de la Paix,* 49 Quebec Law Reports, Kings Bench 65:*Maluquer v R,* [1924], Quebec Reports, Kings Bench 1; *Leonard v Premio Real,* [1885] 11 Quebec Law Reports 128 – consuls were held to be subject to the jurisdiction of municipal courts. However, in none of these cases did the consul involved plead that the act at issue had been undertaken in the course of his official duties; indeed, on the facts of the cases such a plea would seem impossible. It is true that in *Maluquer v R* the court stated that consuls possess no 'personal immunity' from suit. However, in our view this statement does not conflict with the principle of consular immunity. Brouard J, in the above excerpt from the Mauritius case of *Dangin v Paturau,* characterized diplomatic immunity as 'personal immunity' and acknowledged that consuls were not entitled to this type of immunity. Nevertheless, he considered that they were entitled, on the basis of reciprocity, to immunity in respect of acts performed in the course of official functions. In other words, when the court in *Maluquer v R* commented that consuls do not possess 'personal immunity' it was merely stating that consular officials are not entitled to diplomatic immunity. It was not deciding that consular officials are not entitled to consular immunity which does not confer 'personal immunity' but only immunity in respect of acts performed in the course of official duties. There do not seem to be any Canadian cases which hold that consuls are not immune from the jurisdiction of municipal courts in respect of acts performed in the course of their official functions.

United States In *Landley v Republic of Panama,* Annual Digest, 1938–40, Case No. 175, decided by the District Court of the Southern District of New York, an action was brought against the Republic of Panama, its consul general at New York, and other defendants registered with the Department of State as accredited agents of the Republic of Panama. The plaintiff undertook to set up two causes of action: 1 / to recover $10,750 on a *quantum meruit* for services in investigating alleged maladministration of the so-called 'Panama Fund'; and 2 / to recover the same amount in an action against G.L. Fabrega, individually and as consul general. In granting motions of the named defendants challenging the jurisdiction, the court said:

> There is no allegation in the complaint that the Republic of Panama has consented to be tried, and it cannot be otherwise, and the motion is granted as to it. While Fabrega is sued individually as well as in his official capacity, it seems clear from an analysis of the complaint that the action is directed against him based upon the duties performed by him as the Consul-General of his country, and the motion is granted as to him.

It is possible that this decision was based on the Pan-American Convention on Consular Agents, noted above, although the court does not appear to have referred specifically to that convention. However, in another case to which no convention applied, namely *Waltier v Thompson and the Dominion of Canada,* 31 *International Law Reports,* at 397, the United States, District Court, Southern District, New York, stated unequivocally that 'A consular official is immune from suit when the acts complained of were performed in the course of his official duties.'

In *France,* the rule that under international law and apart from convention a French court has no jurisdiction to entertain proceedings against a foreign consul in respect of official acts seems to be firmly established and regularly applied, as may be seen from the following cases: *Murphy* v *Lee Jortin. Clunet* (1900), *Journal de droit international* at 130, 958, and *Wemberg* v *Hellevig*, decided by the Civil Tribunal of Marseilles on 28 December 1912 (Beckett, 'Consular Immunities' (1944), 21 *British Y.B. Int'l L.* 34, at 45).

The position seems to be the same in the courts of Italy – *Mazzucchi* v *American Consulate* [1933–34] Annual Digest (No 68).

Scholastic writings

Turning lastly to the teachings of the most highly qualified publicists, Lauterpacht indicates that:

> Apart from the special protection due to consuls according to International Law, there is neither a custom nor universal agreement between the Powers to grant them ordinary diplomatic privileges. Such privileges of a diplomatic character as consuls actually enjoy are granted to them either by courtesy or in compliance with special stipulations in a commercial or consular treaty between the sending and admitting State. However, consuls do in fact enjoy the jurisdictional immunities granted to diplomatic representatives inasmuch as, according to the generally accepted practice, they are not liable in civil nor, perhaps, in criminal proceedings in respect of acts which they perform in their official capacity on behalf of their States and which fall within the scope of consular functions as recognized by International Law.[78]

In a similar vein B. Sen comments that:

> Consular officials, unlike diplomatic agents, are not immune from the jurisdiction of local courts, civil or criminal. Whatever privileges and immunities they do enjoy with regard to exemption from local jurisdiction rest upon provisions of treaties, reciprocity, courtesy, national laws and regulations, and the policy of the receiving state. Nevertheless, it seems to be recognized in the practice of states as well as in the writings of jurists that if an act is performed by a consul in the course of his official functions, he should be exempt from local jurisdiction in respect thereof, the reason being that a consul in discharging his official duties is acting on behalf of his home state which cannot be sued without its consent.[79]

In his latest edition Brierly states that:

> Consular immunities have been much less well defined than those of diplomats and, according to a former Foreign Office Legal Adviser (Sir E. Beckett, *B.Y.I.L.*, 1944, p. 35), nowhere were they at a lower ebb than in the United Kingdom. Even so, two rules had, he thought, become established in customary law – the first was the inviolability of consular archives and correspondence, and the second the immunity of consular officers from either criminal or civil proceedings in respect of acts performed in their official capacity. Furthermore, during the past fifty years there has come into existence a large network of bilateral consular conventions setting out in considerable detail the privileges and immunities which the contracting parties were prepared to concede to each other's

consuls; and these conventions show that there was more common ground in regard to consular status than had formerly been supposed. The International Law Commission, in preparing a Convention on Consular Intercourse and Immunities, has drawn largely upon the principles contained in these conventions without attempting to determine to what extent each one has already been accepted in customary law ... The Commission's draft convention admittedly contains a number of elements of 'progressive development' of the law which go beyond existing practice in regard to immunities of consuls (it should be noted that the International Law Commission, as was stated above, expressly viewed article 43 as a codification of existing customary international law, and, consequently at least that provision of the draft convention was not a 'progressive development'), and it remains to be seen how far it will commend itself to governments.[80]

Customary international law

In the light of the foregoing analysis it would appear that international custom and state practice recognize the immunity of consuls with respect to acts performed in the course of their official duties. Moreover, this principle finds support in the teachings of the most highly qualified publicists. Consequently, we submit that there is a principle of customary international law, binding on Canada, which provides that consular officers and consular employees are immune from the jurisdiction of the judicial or administrative authorities of the receiving state in respect of acts performed in the exercise of consular functions.

While under article 43 of the Consular Relations Convention consuls are only immune in respect of acts performed in the course of consular functions, we do not consider that this immunity is confined to civil actions but rather that it could encompass criminal activities if those acts were performed in the course of consular functions. Paragraph 1 of article 43 provides: 'Consular officers and consular employees shall not be amenable to the jurisdiction of the judicial or administrative authorities of the receiving state.' The words 'jurisdiction of the judicial or administrative authorities' are not qualified and therefore should be read as encompassing both civil and criminal proceedings. This interpretation would appear to find support in the wording of paragraph 2 of article 43 which states: 'The provisions of paragraph 1 of this Article shall not, however, apply in respect of a *civil* [our emphasis] action.' If paragraph 1 of article 43 were only applicable to civil actions there would be no reason for including the word 'civil' when limiting the scope of paragraph 1 in paragraph 2. The omission of any qualifying word in Paragraph 1 coupled with the use of the qualifying word 'civil' in paragraph 2, when attempting to restrict the scope of paragraph 1, suggests that paragraph 1 applies to both criminal and civil actions. It is true that articles 41 and 42 contain provisions concerning the arrest of consular officers. These articles clearly indicate that consular officers may in certain circumstances be arrested, which implies that they are subject to the criminal jurisdiction of the receiving state. However, there is no suggestion in these articles that a consul can be arrested for a criminal act performed in the course of his duty, and article 43 clearly provides that a consul is not subject to the criminal jurisdiction of the receiving state with respect to such acts. Moreover, it is possible for a consular officer to commit an illegal act in the course of performing his consular duties, and in such a case international law requires that he be held immune from the jurisdiction of the judicial authorities of the receiving state. However, article 55 of the convention places a duty on persons enjoying privileges and immunities to respect the laws of the receiving state. If members of a consular post engage in illegal activities in Canada, diplomatic representations would probably be made to the sending state and the consular officer may well be sent home to receive his due punishment from his own authorities.

Conclusion

We conclude from the foregoing that article 43 of the Consular Relations Convention is merely a restatement of an existing rule of international law. International law is incorporated into the law of Canada except in those cases where it is specifically excluded either by statute or by judicial decision.[81] As was noted above, there would not appear to be any Canadian or British judicial decisions which deny the immunity of consuls with respect to acts performed in the exercise of their official duties. Consequently, unless relevant provincial statutes explicitly provide that they are applicable to consular officials, it would seem that they would have to be interpreted as preserving a consular officer's or employee's right to immunity from jurisdiction with respect to acts performed in the course of his official duty. However, this is not only a question of the correct legal interpretation of provincial statutes. The granting of immunity clearly benefits Canadian local governments and communities by enabling foreign consular officers and employees to carry out their functions of facilitating *inter alia* international commerce and tourism. In addition, under the doctrine of reciprocity, Canadian consular officials abroad are provided with equivalent immunities and are thus able to protect the interests of Canadians in other countries.

Finally, mention should be made of an important procedural problem. In accordance with the House of Lords decision in *Engelke* v *Musmann* cited above, it is up to the courts and not the secretary of state for external affairs to determine whether a particular individual is entitled to immunity. The sole function of the secretary of state in these cases is to inform the courts about the status of a particular individual. However, it would appear that neither the UK nor the Canadian courts have decided how they would determine whether a consular official was acting in the course of his duty. In the United Kingdom, this problem has now been resolved by section 11 of the Consular Relations Act which provides:

> If in any proceedings any question arises whether or not any person is entitled to any privilege or immunity under this Act, a certificate issued by or under the authority of the Secretary of State stating any fact relating to that question shall be conclusive evidence of that fact.

United States courts, in the absence of statute, appear to have decided that they will accept a consular officer's statement as to whether or not he was acting in the course of his official functions and will not inquire further into the matter.

If a consul were required to prove, factually, that he had been acting in the course of his official duty in order to obtain immunity, it might necessitate, in certain circumstances, the disclosure of classified information. Rather than make such a disclosure, the consul might prefer not to challenge the court's jurisdiction. Clearly, such indirect pressure would contravene the spirit of the international law rule which provides for consular immunity. This procedural aspect of consular immunity still remains to be clarified in Canada.

NOTES

1 *Saint John et al.* v *Fraser-Bruce Overseas Corporation et al.*, [1958] s.c.r. 263.
2 *Foreign Legations* case, [1943] s.c.r. 203, at 213–14.
3 *Dessaules* v *The Republic of Poland*, [1944] s.c.r. 172, at 277.
4 J.M. Sweeney, *The International Law of Sovereign Immunity* (1963) 20.
5 *Dessaules* v *The Republic of Poland.*
6 176 L.N.T.S.
7 [1965] GR. BRIT. T.S. 3.
8 [1953] GR. BRIT. T.S. 5.
9 T.K. Thommen, *Legal Status of Government Merchant Ships in International Law* (1962) 30.
10 Ibid, 30.
11 Ibid, 34.
12 Ibid, 35.
13 Ibid, 37.
14 Ibid, 37–8.
15 Sweeney, *supra* note 4, at 32–3. (*Picardo y Cia* v *Administrazione Autonoma dei Monopoli di Strato,* 1941 decision of the Supreme Court.)
16 Ibid, 30 (*Dralle* v *Republic of Czechoslovakia,* a 1950 decision of the Supreme Court [1950] *International Law Reports* 155).
17 Ibid, 27–8 (*Societe Anonyme de Chemins de Fer Liégeois Lumemborgeuis* v *The State of the Netherlands,* a 1903 decision of the Supreme Court [1943] *Pasierisie Belge* I).
18 Ibid, 31–2 (*USSR* v *Association France-Export,* a 1929 decision of the Supreme Court).
19 Ibid, 30 (*x* v *USSR,* a 1928 decision of the Supreme Court [1927–28] *Ann. Dig.* 172).
20 Ibid, 26–7 (*State of Rumania* v *Trutta,* a 1926 decision of the Supreme Court (1932) 26 *Am. J. Int'l L. Supp.* 629).
21 Ibid, 33–4 (*Krol* v *Bank of Indonesia,* 1958 decision of the Court of Appeals of Amsterdam).
22 Ibid, 31 (*Yugoslav State* v *S.A. Sogerfin,* a 1938 decision).
23 Ibid, 33 and 36–8 (*Confiscation of Trade Mark,* a 1955 decision of the Supreme Court [1955] *International Law Report* 17).
24 *Compania Naviera Vascongado* v *S.S. Cristina*, [1938] A.C. 485.
25 *Sultan of Johore* v *Abusbakar Tunku Aris Bendahar*, [1952] A.C. 318.
26 *Republic of Mexico* v *Hoffman*, (1944) 324 U.S. 30.
27 Ibid, at 35.
28 Ibid, at 38.
29 *Victory Transport Inc.* v *Commissaria General de Abastecimientos y Transportes*, (1964) 336 Fed. Rep. [2d], 354.
30 Ibid, at 358.
31 M.M. Whiteman, (1968), 6 *Digest of International Law,* 569.
32 M.J. Belman, 'New Departures in the Law of Sovereign Immunity' (1969), *Proc. Am. Soc. Int'l L.* 182, at 186.
33 Ibid, 183–7.
34 Thommen, *supra* note 9, at 41.
35 Ibid, 43–5.
36 Ibid, 44.
37 Sweeney, *supra* note 4, at 42.
38 W.L. McNair, (1948), 34 *Grotius Society* 43.
39 Brierley, *The Law of Nations* (5th ed, 1955) 193.
40 Nielsen, (1919), 13 *Am. J. Int'l Law* 20.
41 Lalive, (1953), 84 *Receuil de Cours* 205.
42 Sorensen, (1960), 101 *Receuil de Cours* 1.
43 Lauterpacht, (1951), 28 *Brit. Y.B. Int'l L.* 220.
44 Ibid, 224.
45 Ibid, 237–9.
46 *Victory Transport Inc.* v *Commissaria General de Abastecimientos y Transportes*, (1964), 336 Fed. Rep. [2d], 354, at 360.
47 (1932), 26 *Am. J. Int'l Supp.* 451, at 457.
48 (1953), *International Law Association Report* vii, viii.
49 Sweeney, *supra* note 4, at 43–4.
50 Ibid, 35.
51 *Flota Maritima de Cuba S.A.* v *Steamship "Canadian Conqueror" et al. and the Republic of Cuba* (1962), 34 D.L.R. (2d) 628, and *Le Gouvernement de la Republique du Congo* v *Jean Venne* (1972), 22 D.L.R. (3d) 669.
52 Ibid, 634.
53 Ibid, 635.

54 Ibid, 636.

55 *Sultan of Johore* v *Abubakar Tunku Aris Bendahar,* [1952] A.C. 318.

56 Ibid, 344.

57 *Thomas White* v *The Ship Frank Dale,* [1946] Ex. C.R. 555.

58 *Flota Maritima de Cuba S.A.* v *Steamship "Canadian Conqueror"* et al. *and the Republic of Cuba,* at 636.

59 *Foreign Legations* case, [1943] S.C.R. 203, at 491–2.

60 *Flota Maritima de Cuba S.A.* v *Steamship "Canadian Conqueror"* et al. *and the Republic of Cuba,* at 638.

61 *Le Gouvernement de la Republique Democratique du Congo* v *Jean Venne* (1972), 22 D.L.R. (3d) 669.

62 *Venne* v *Le Gouvernement de la Republique du Congo* (1969), 5 D.L.R. [3d] 128.

63 *Le Gouvernement de la Republique du Congo* v *Jean Venne,* at 673.

64 *Venne* v *Le Gouvernement de la Republique du Congo* and *Allan Construction Ltd.* and *Le Gouvernement du Venezuela,* [1968] Que. S.C. 523.

65 *Flota Maritima de Cuba S.A.* v *Steamship "Canadian Conqueror"* et al. *and the Republic of Cuba,* at 634.

66 *Le Gouvernement de la Republique Democratique du Congo* v *Jean Venne,* at 674.

67 Ibid, 672.

68 Ibid, 673.

69 Ibid, 674.

70 Ibid, 675.

71 Ibid, 677.

72 *In the Matter of a Reference as to the Powers of The Corporation of the City of Ottawa and the Corporation of the Village of Rockcliffe Park to Levy Rates on Foreign Legations and High Commissions,* [1943] S.C.R. 208, the opinion of Duff CJ, which espoused the theory of incorporation or reception of international law into the domestic law, contains a thorough discussion of diplomatic immunities in Canadian law and is regarded as the landmark of Canadian judgments in this field.

73 W.E. Beckett, 'Consular Immunities' (1944), *21 Brit. Y.B. Int'l L.,* 41.

74 See Luke T. Lee, *Consular Law and Practice* (1961), at 248. Lee also mentions the following conventions which support this contention: Italy-Latvia, 1932, arts 12, 13; Poland-Bulgaria, 1934, arts 11, 12; Czechoslovakia-Soviet Union, 1935, arts 4, 5; Poland-Hungary, 1935, arts 10, 11; UK-Norway, 1951, art 13 (1)(2); US-UK, 1951, art. 11 (1)(2); UK-France, 1951, art 14 (1)(2); UK-Sweden, 1952, art 13 (1)(2); UK-Greece, 1953, art 13 (1)(2); UK-Mexico, 1954, art 13 (1)(2); UK-Italy, 1954, art 13 (1)(2); US-Iran, 1955, art 18; France-Italy, 1955, art 13; France-Sweden, 1955, art 15; UK-Federal Republic of Germany, 1956, art 11 (1)(2); Hungary-German Democratic Republic, 1957, art 6; Poland-German Democratic Republic, 1957, art 11 (1); People's Republic of China-Soviet Union, 1959, art 6.

75 W.E. Beckett thoroughly examines official statements and national laws and regulations on this subject. Beckett, *supra* note 73, at 39–41.

76 The basic view taken by UK courts with respect to consular immunity is succinctly described by Beckett in his article 'Consular Immunities' at 35 as follows:

> At the end of the eighteenth and the beginning of the nineteenth centuries the question was debated amongst the publicists and in the courts whether consuls were 'public ministers' and as such entitled to all the privileges and immunities of diplomatic representatives, which include complete immunity from process in respect of official or private acts. After some divergence of opinion the view prevailed everywhere that, as consuls had no 'representative character' (i.e. were not intermediaries through whom matters of State were discussed between Government and Government), they were not 'public ministers' and therefore could not claim the general immunity and 'Exterritoriality' which attaches to diplomatic representatives ...
>
> For a short time after this it seems to have been concluded that since they could not claim privileges as 'Public ministers', they could not claim any privileges at all. The old English cases of *Heathfield* v *Chilton,* 4 Burr. 2015, and *Buvot* v *Barbuit,* Cases t. Talbot 281, belong to this stage of development. Subsequently, the view prevailed that, though consuls were not 'public ministers' they had a status of their own under international law. They were appointed by commissions from their own Sovereigns, and received 'exequaturs'

from the Sovereigns of the foreign country of their residence to perform important duties as State agents ... It was consequently recognized that consuls enjoyed under international law such protection and immunity as is required for the performance of those duties ... the beginning of the view that consuls have some privileges is seen in the judgement of Lord Ellenborough in *Viveash* v *Becker,* (1814) 3 M. & S. 285, where a resident merchant of London who was a consul of a foreign prince was held not to be entitled to immunity from arrest on mesne process in respect of a private trading debt. In this case Lord Ellenborough laid down that the consul enjoys a special protection under the law of nations, *including the right to the liberty and safety necessary for the discharge of his functions* and to safe conduct to enter and leave the country. In *Clark* v *Cretico,* 1 Taun, 196, where the issue was the right of a consul to claim immunity from arrest, the court was at pains to decide on the ground that the man was no longer a consul rather than to deny any right for a consul to claim any privilege from arrest.'

77 (1949), *Annual Digest,* case no 105.
78 Lauterpacht, 1 *Oppenheim's International Law* (8th ed, 1955), 840–1.
79 B. Sen, *A Diplomat's Handbook of International Law and Practice* (1965) 249–50.
80 Brierley, *The Law of Nations* (6th ed, 1963) 264–5.

The International Law Commission's Commentary on Draft Article 43 of their Draft Articles on Consular Relations which formed the basis of, and is virtually identical to, Article 43 (1) of the Vieenna Convention on Consular Relations states:

'(1) Unlike members of the diplomatic staff, all the members of the consulate are in principle subject to the jurisdiction of the receiving State, unless exempted by one of the present rules or by a provision of some other applicable international agreement. In particular, they are, like any private person, subject to the jurisdiction of the receiving state in respect of all their private acts, more especially as regards any private gainful activity carried on by them.

(2) The rule that, in respect of acts performed by them in the exercise of their functions (official acts) members of the consulate are not amenable to the jurisdiction of the judicial and administrative authorities of the receiving State, is part of customary international law. This exemption represents an immunity which the sending State is recognized as possessing in respect of acts which are those of a sovereign State. By their very nature such acts are outside the jurisdiction of the receiving State, whether civil, criminal or administrative. Such official acts are outside the jurisdiction of the receiving State, no criminal proceedings may be instituted in respect of them. Consequently, consular officers enjoy complete inviolability in respect of their official acts.'

81 *Foreign Legations* case, [1943] S.C.R. 213–14.

M.D. COPITHORNE*

9/State Responsibility and International Claims

THE LAW OF STATE RESPONSIBILITY

The branch of international law described variously as the law of international claims, the diplomatic protection of citizens abroad, or the responsibility of states for injuries to aliens traces its origin back to Vattel's famous remark that 'quiconque maltraite un Citoyen offense indirectement l'Etat, qui doit protéger ce Citoyen.'[1] In due course the Permanent Court of International Justice proclaimed: 'It is an elementary principle of international justice that a state is entitled to protect its subjects, when injured by acts contrary to international law committed by another state from whom they have been unable to obtain satisfaction through the ordinary channels.'[2]

One of the most significant events in the historical development of the subject and one of particular interest to Canada, was the Jay Treaty of 1794 which, in establishing three international claims commissions, marked the introduction of a means of adjustment of disputes arising out of the protection of citizens abroad and more generally of the modern use of arbitration for settling international disputes. The commissions were concerned with the claims of United States and British subjects arising out of the capture of ships in earlier hostilities, with debts owing to British subjects, and finally with the definition of the border between what are now New Brunswick and Maine along the St Croix River.[3]

In the succeeding years, national and international commissions created a body of precedents with the gradual result that demands for redress became assertions of legal rights rather than appeals to international comity and the maintenance of friendly relations.[4] However, while there developed much useful analysis of the rights of aliens and the equitable application of general principles to specific cases, state responsibility remained a neglected area until Borchard's classic treatise appeared in 1915.[5]

The first codification efforts were as recent as 1930, but the appearances that state responsibility was ready for this process were deceiving. In 1930 a Codification Conference in the Hague failed to produce a convention, a failure generally attrituted to the absence of consensus on the vital question of whether aliens were or should be entitled to an international standard of justice or alternatively to the national standard of the host state. Canada was one of the majority group that pressed for recognition of an obligation to maintain a standard 'in conformity with the rules of law accepted by the community of nations.'[6] The opposing point of view adhered to in particular by the Latin American states was that aliens should receive no better than national treatment.

*The views expressed in this chapter are not necessarily those of the Department of External Affairs.

Following the postwar nationalizations in eastern Europe and the trend to similar acts in other parts of the world, renewed efforts were made to formulate the rules of state responsibility, particularly a state's liability for the taking of foreign property. The first of these was the attempt made by the International Law Commission in response to a request by the United Nations General Assembly in 1953 to undertake the codification of the principles of international law governing state responsibility. By 1962 the commission had received six reports on the subject from its special rapporteur Garcia-Amador[7] but, while some of them produced detailed debate, it was clear that the fundamental problem which defied the Hague Conference was no closer to resolution. In view of the breadth of state responsibility as a subject, the special rapporteur had decided to deal first with the responsibility of state for damage caused to the person or property of aliens. The inconclusive nature of the commission's discussion led him to narrow his subject further to the international responsibility of states for injuries to aliens. The rapporteur tried to bridge the gap between national and international standards by the use of human rights to assure the protection of legitimate human interests regardless of nationality.[8]

This approach met with opposition from several quarters, particularly the communist states which were resisting the development of international human rights and which now rejected the concept of state responsibility for damage to aliens as an attempt by capitalist states to use international law for the protection of their own interests.[9] There was also opposition from the newer states which questioned whether they should be bound by traditional rules to which they had not consented.[10] These states showed a preference for negotiation rather than arbitration and for resolving disputes through political rather than legal means. This reluctance was viewed sympathetically by the Canadian secretary of state for external affairs who suggested that it may result from a conclusion that the definition of issues in legal terms obscures rather than clarifies the realities involved, or that the applicable rules are unjust or inadequate.[11]

Under these influences there had developed by 1963 a consensus in the commission that the topic it should be studying was the definition of the general rules governing interstate obligations.[12] This shift in focus away from the traditional body of rules relating to damage to aliens has been interpreted as a reflection, in part at least, 'of a diminution of interest in human beings and an enhanced preoccupation with the rights and duties of states,'[13] Since then, the commission has put aside its studies of state responsibility in favour of other more pressing assignments, but when it does return its new orientation seems likely to involve it in areas already otherwise occupied such as the principles of friendly relations and the definition of aggression.[14]

A second major codification work in the field of state responsibility has been the Harvard Draft Convention on the International Responsibility of States for Injuries to Aliens for which Professors Sohn and Baxter served as reporters.[15] The declared purpose of the draft was to 'codify with some particularity the standards established by international law for the protection of aliens and thereby to obviate as far as possible, the necessity of looking to customary international law.'[16] The draft incorporated the principle of an international minimum standard in terms of 'the principles of justice recognized by the principal legal systems of the world.'[17] While introducing some interesting new thoughts, the draft's essentially traditional approach has had its share of critics.[18]

A third attempt to reformulate the rules in the field is the American Law Institute Restatement of the Foreign Relations Law of the United States.[19] The reporters, who declared their intention to identify and restate rather than codify,[20] relied heavily on the Harvard Draft Convention in that part of the restatement concerning state responsibility for injuries to aliens. The restatement incorporates an international standard of justice which it defines as that body of norms established by: a / the applicable principles of international law as established by international custom, judicial and arbitral decisions, and other recognized sources or, in the absence of such applicable principles, b / analogous principles of justice generally recognized by states that have reasonably developed legal systems.[21] The restatement applies this international standard to three areas: discrimination against aliens, denial of procedural justice, and injuries to the economic interests of aliens. With regard to the latter, it describes its rules as representing the weight of authority but objections have been made that such authority 'does not reflect a consensus adequate to support, or to bring into existence, an international legal norm.'[22]

The view of the capital exporting states was clearly reflected in the 1967 OECD Resolution and Draft Convention on the Protection of Foreign Property. Article 1 of the convention, which has not been opened for signature, provides for 'fair and equitable treatment' to the property of nationals of other parties. The convention's 'Notes and Comments' on this article add that this phrase 'indicates the standard set by international law for the treatment due by each State with regard to the property of foreign nationals ... The standard required conforms in effect to the "minimum standard" which forms part of customary international law.'[23] The Draft Convention does not purport to codify or restate customary international law but is rather a proposed set of contractual obligations between parties who would expressly consent to be bound by them.

Many of the states which have indicated a reluctance to be bound by customary international law have come to regard private foreign investment as a major source of developmental capital. The problem has been how to reconcile the seemingly conflicting interests of the states concerned with those of the investors. One group requires the recognition of their sovereignty and in particular the right to take private property; the other requires acknowledgement of the right to a reasonable level of security and profit. In the United Nations, the debate led up to the Declaration on Permanent Sovereignty over Natural Resources.[24] This declaration sets out the basic principles for the exercise of sovereignty over natural resources subject to the requirement that they be in conformity with duties of states as defined by existing international law. More particularly, compensation is to be paid in accordance with the rules in effect in the taking state and with international law. Where the question of compensation gives rise to controversy, local remedies are to be exhausted and, with the agreement of the parties, these are to be followed by recourse to arbitration.[25] This was a compromise solution to the debate that had gone on for some years as to whether a state's sovereignty over its resources was to be qualified by its duties under international law. The focus was on the existence of a duty to pay compensation and, while the result reflects the reluctance of many states to be bound by compulsory arbitration as a general proposition, it leaves the door open for binding investment agreements between states and private parties which could include arbitration provisions such as recourse to the International Center for the Settlement of Investment Disputes set up under the IBRD Convention on the Settlement of Investment Disputes.[26]

Thus, the problem remains of defining what responsibilities customary international law spells out for injury to the interests of aliens. Perhaps all that can be concluded as to the present state of international law is that traditional concepts are in doubt and they may well now lack a consensus sufficient to preserve their standing as norms of general application in the settlement of international disputes.[27]

CANADIAN CLAIMS PRACTICE: LUMP SUM SETTLEMENTS

Canadian practice in the field of international claims has in large part evolved in the period since World War II. Canadians have not traditionally had sizeable investments abroad and, while this is changing, Canada today remains a net importer of capital. Over the same period Canada has received large numbers of immigrants who have left property behind in their countries of origin.[28] In general Canadian practice has developed along lines consistent with the traditional concepts of state responsibility. While as indicated earlier these older rules have resisted codification, many of them traditionally enjoyed sufficient respect to constitute widely recognized precepts of customary international law. The secretary of state for external affairs has stated that Canada 'sees considerable value in the older rules as providing a fair and just basis for adjusting the interests of the state concerned.'[29] In the following paragraphs some of the more important elements of Canadian practice will be outlined.

Assuming that they are meritorious, international claims brought to the attention of the Department of External Affairs are normally dealt with in one of four ways. If the claim appears to arise out of an isolated act of the state concerned, which has likely affected one or at most a few Canadian citizens and that the claimant has exhausted his local remedies,[30] the individual claim or claims may be espoused by the government; that is, submitted to the foreign government with a demand for redress. If on the other hand the claim appears to arise out of one or more state acts of general application, such as nationalization decrees, so that the interests of many Canadian citizens may be affected and no effective local remedies are available, then the claim is likely to become part of a package to be espoused by the Canadian government and settled on a lump sum basis. A third variant is that of agreement between the governments concerned to submit the claims to international adjudication, but this is little used today, chiefly because of the scarcity of disputes between states which are prepared to see them resolved by international adjudication. A recent example of this process was the agreement of 25 March 1965 between Canada and the United States to establish the Lake Ontario Claims Tribunal to arbitrate the Gut Dam claims.[31] In that case, however, at the tribunal's suggestion, the parties negotiated a lump sum settlement of the claims.[32] A fourth possibility is the exercise of good offices, an informal measure which is traditionally distinguished from 'the more juridical concept of formal diplomatic espousal.'[33] Such assistance may take a variety of forms including 'an enquiry by the Canadian consulate in the locality as to the present status of a dispute, a request for a review of an administrative decision, or a request for information as to the regulations or procedures which a Canadian should follow in order to press his own claim under local laws.'[34]

The use of international arbitration has been in decline for some fifty years, and the particular device of international claims commissions has fallen on especially hard times since 1945.[35] In part at least, its place has been taken by the lump sum or global claims settlement and the national claims commission.[36] The reasons for this development are many and include the inherent defects in the mixed commission process that had been pointed up in the settlement of World War I claims, the need to cope with the vast numbers of claims arising under postwar nationalization measures at first in eastern Europe and later in parts of the developing world, and finally the reluctance and in many cases the outright refusal of such states to have the claims settled by recourse to international adjudication. The essential advantage of the lump sum settlement procedure is the general acceptability that it has earned in the postwar years among both claimant and respondent states. The reasons for this include the comparative simplicity of fixing the quantum as an approximate amount of the sum claimed, the relative speed with which this can be accomplished, the capability of the agreement to be interpreted as including or excluding compensation for doubtful claims according to the needs of the parties, the usefulness in terms of bilateral relations of settling all outstanding claims at once, and the simplified arrangements that can be made to meet the foreign exchange requirements.[37]

However, there is as yet little agreement on the jurisprudential worth of such settlements and the decisions of national claims commissions. The International Court has described such agreements as *lex specialis*,[38] and a number of writers have noted that the operation of various national commissions could lead to increasing divergence in the construction of international legal rules and that the decisions would be more relevant if the commissions were mixed.[39] On the other hand, one expert in the field describes them as 'a growing edge of international law.'[40]

In addition to these conceptual difficulties with the process of lump sum settlements as a source of law, it has been argued that they undermine the well known view, which will be considered later, that international law requires the payment of 'prompt, adequate and effective' compensation.[41] On the other hand there is no doubt that it was the widespread resistance encountered in the implementation of the rule that led to the search for other solutions. As their critics suggest, lump sum settlements are undoubtedly compromises in terms of the quantum of compensation, but they do testify to the general acceptance of the principle of paying compensation, though not necessarily to a liability to do so. Thus, the real issue is sometimes posed as disagreement over valuation methods.[42] It has been pointed out by a British official that 'there is no internationally acceptable measure of appropriate compensation and that it is difficult to achieve a ''restitutio in integrum'' for the claimant where the whole basis of market values has been fundamentally altered by a complete change in the economic structure of the country where the property was confiscated or expropriated. This problem of finding an agreed basis of value between two negotiating states has only been overcome by compromise solutions.'[43]

As noted earlier the communist states have resisted the codification of the customary international law rules concerning state responsibility for damage to aliens. In their view, 'a state has the exclusive right to regulate questions regarding property rights and in particular to establish the content and nature of the rights of ownership, to regulate acquisition, transfer and loss of ownership and hence to nationalize properties and to determine the terms of nationalization etc.'[44] Thus the payment of partial compensation to aliens does not flow from a recognition of an international obligation but from political considerations, specifically the need to normalize and improve relations between the states concerned.

The existence of extraneous economic and political factors has raised serious doubts as to the correlation between the merit of the claims and the amount of the lump sum.[45] In some cases, claimant states have received substantial while in others very modest returns. In general there seems to have been a significant relationship between the inducements the claimant state has been able to offer and the percentage compensation it has obtained. Thus, each settlement stands in the context of its own time and circumstances.[46] To some critics, claimants have often been sacrificed for foreign policy objectives.[47] On the other hand, the claiming state may have found it necessary to buy a settlement, however unsatisfactory it may seem, with trade or other concessions which could for example have entailed expenditures from government revenues. The United States-Poland claims settlement provided for the payment of a lump sum of $40 million; awards against the fund totalled slightly over $100 million, resulting in a percentage return of approximately 40 per cent. However, in reaching agreement, the United States government used economic lures of various kinds including the provision of very substantial credits and it is perhaps fair to speculate that without such inducements the settlement would have been if not impossible very much reduced in size.[48]

Such criticism has not hindered the usefulness of the lump sum approach in the eyes of the states concerned. Since the war there have been at least 130 such agreements.[49] For its part, the Canadian government, after successful experience in settling war claims against Italy and Japan[50] by the lump sum procedure, adopted the same approach in its negotiation of nationalization claims. It has so far concluded four lump sum settlements with eastern European states: Bulgaria (30 June 1966),[51] Hungary (1 June 1970),[52] Romania (13 July 1971),[53] and Poland (15 October 1971).[54] Negotiations to the same end are in hand with Czechoslovakia, Yugoslavia,[55] and Cuba. Some 3,700 individual claims have been brought to the attention of the Department of External Affairs under these lump sum settlement programs.

In most cases Canada has been among the last to reach settlements not because of any indifference to the matter but because of a lack of inducements to compel recognition of the claims.[56] The assets of the nationals of these states under Canadian control have been of relatively small value, and trade is of little importance. However, in the last decade the international perspective of the eastern European states has changed and with it has come a desire, in some cases an eagerness, to establish first diplomatic and commercial relations with Canada and then to build a substantial export market in Canada. Faced with the need to improve relations with Canada generally and to settle claims in particular if the desired access to and development of the Canadian market was to be achieved, these states have been prepared to settle the outstanding claims.[57]

LUMP SUM SETTLEMENTS: REGISTRATION AND ADJUDICATION

As a first step in launching lump sum claims negotiations, Canadian authorities have found it useful in most cases to obtain an agreement in principle to negotiate a general settlement. Such preliminary agreements are then publicized with a notice to file claims. Inquirers are sent questionnaires with detailed instructions.[58] The claims are individually reviewed by the Claims Section of the Legal Advisory Division of the Department of External Affairs and in most cases the claimants are provided with assessments of their claims, usually accompanied by requests for clarification or supporting documentation. This process is deemed a purely administrative one with the adjudication proper taking place after the settlement has been reached.[59] The Canadian practice of registration and preliminary examination is designed to elicit a clear understanding of the number and size of the claims that are likely to be admitted on adjudication and secondly to obtain as much information as possible for the use of negotiators. The purpose of separating the adjudication process is to ensure that the claims are accorded consistent and equitable treatment, that is as far as possible in accordance with generally accepted jurisprudential norms and free from the extraneous influences that, as indicated above, are usually associated with the conclusion of the settlements. It should be noted however that adjudication may be carried out before a settlement is achieved. The United States has used the preadjudication process for a number of its lump sum claims programs.[60] Britain has adjudicated after settlement but in most cases has also utilized a presettlement registration system.[61]

In Canada adjudication is carried out by an independent quasijudicial body.[62] In the case of the Bulgarian settlement, an 'adviser on claims' was appointed to examine the claims and make recommendations to the minister of finance and the secretary of state for external affairs, concerning the validity of the claims under the agreement, the amount to which the claimant was entitled under the agreement, and the division as between claimants of the monies to be paid out by the minister.[63] The adviser, Chief Justice Thane A. Campbell of Prince Edward Island, who had earlier been chief war claims commissioner,[64] recommended that of the twenty-eight claims received, eight were acceptable, and by September 1968 the distribution of the $40,000 lump sum to these eight claimants had been completed.[65]

These arrangements, while clearly appropriate to the small size of the Bulgarian settlement, were considered to be insufficient to cope with the task of adjudicating the more than fifteen hundred claims against the $1.1 million Hungarian settlement. Further, in anticipation of other equally substantial claims settlements that were expected to follow, the government decided to establish the Foreign Claims Commission. This was effected by the appointment of two commissioners under part I of the Inquiries Act with the powers of hiring staff etc.[66] The commissioners were Chief Justice Campbell who had by then retired from the bench and T.D. MacDonald, QC, a former deputy solicitor general and assistant deputy minister of justice. The commissioners were charged with inquiring into and reporting upon 1 / claims made by Canadian citizens and the government of Canada against Hungarian citizens and the government of the Hungarian People's Republic, and 2 / any other claims that might be referred to the commission by the governor in council for which compensation might be paid out of the Foreign Claims Fund. The commissioners were required to report to the secretary of state for external affairs and the minister of finance stating whether in their opinion each claimant was eligible to receive a payment out of the fund, the reasons for their opinion, and their recommendation as to the amount that should be paid in respect of each such claim. At the same time, there were promulgated the 'Foreign Claims (Hungary) Settlement Regulations' which deal with such matters as notice of claims, eligibility of claimants, nature of the chief commissioner's report, and payments out of the Foreign Claims Fund.[67]

After the Romanian and Polish settlements were completed, the government of Canada referred to the commission claims against Romania and Poland by orders in council dated 28 March 1972 and 21 September, respectively. The three sets of claims were being reported on concurrently.

CANADIAN CLAIMS JURISPRUDENCE

The Department of External Affairs examines four elements of claims submitted to it: nationality, ownership, loss, and valuation. The criteria applied are substantially the same whether the claim is submitted under a lump sum program or *ad hoc*.

Nationality

The well established customary international law on nationality, which eastern European states have found it to their interests to recognize in form if not in principle, is that a state may only espouse the interests of persons who were its nationals at the time of taking, espousal, and settlement.[68] In the case of lump sum settlements, Canadian practice has accorded with this rule[69] for the very pragmatic reason that to insist for example on the inclusion of persons who had become Canadian citizens at a point in time between the dates concerned would undoubtedly have put off the achievement of the settlements indefinitely into the future. As a state with a proportionately large number of recent immigrants, Canada has found that this onerous rule works a hardship on many of its prospective claimants. The government has made clear where its sympathies lie:

> To say that the Government of Canada has recognized the generally accepted rules as to nationality is not also to say that it is satisfied with them. Great injustice may be done someone who through inadvertence or accident of time does not fit within the rule. At the root of the Government's dissatisfaction is a fundamental dissent from the Marxist doctrine that it is fair or just to deprive any person of his property without fair and reasonable compensation. But while the Government of Canada remains most sympathetic to the plight of Canadian citizens deprived of property in their lands of origin, the generally accepted rules of international law have become too well established in this area to avoid. Canada has had to make a realistic appraisal that the best interests of a majority of claimants would be served by accepting the more limited class of claimant as defined by international law.[70]

Several modifications of the traditional nationality rule have been suggested, but sufficient consensus has not yet been reached to permit their introduction in practice.

One area of particular hardship has been the traditional requirements rule that 'a person having dual nationality cannot make one of the countries to which he owes allegience a defendent before an international tribunal.'[71] In the Canadian lump sum claims programs, many of the claimants could fall afoul of this rule for a very high percentage of them were emigrants from the states against which they were claiming and those states imposed severe limitations on the right of expatriation. Fortunately, however, the doctrine of dominant or effective nationality has provided relief for those persons who have clearly cut their ties with their former state.[72] The doctrine has received judicial recognition in the Nottebohm decision[73] and comparable treatment in the Mergé decision of the United States-Italian Conciliation Commission.[74] In Canada the doctrine has received tacit approval by the Department of External Affairs.[75]

In the case of the Hungarian and Romanian claims programs, nationality requirements were somewhat complicated by the possibility of bringing claims under the respective treaties of peace. Many claimants under these programs as well as some under the earlier Italian war claims program could not meet the customary law requirement of Canadian citizenship at the time of loss but submitted their claims under the treaties which appeared to create certain exceptions to the nationality requirement. In particular, article 26 of the Hungarian treaty provided for the restoration in Hungary of the legal rights of persons who were nationals of member states of the United Nations, and article 27 provided for restoration or, if impossible, compensation for the loss of property, legal rights, or interests in Hungary of persons under Hungarian jurisdiction which had been the subject of measures of sequestration, confiscation, or control on account of the racial origin or religion of such persons.[76] The comparable articles of the Romanian peace treaty are 24 and 25.[77] Those persons who had acquired the nationality of one of the member states of the United Nations by the date of the peace treaties – 10 February 1947 – and had subsequently become Canadian citizens appeared to be *prima facie* eligible under articles 26 and 24 respectively. In practice, there were so few such claims that there was no difficulty in including them in the settlements.[78]

Claims under articles 27 and 25 posed greater difficulties. To begin with, there were a large number, at least under the Hungarian treaty. Second, the Hungarian authorities insisted that their government had discharged all its obligations under this article. Third, no other state appeared to have succeeded in obtaining compensation for claims under this article. The Canadian government thus concluded that 'it was not in a position to insist that the Hungarian authorities change their attitude to these claims and that, on the basis of the arguments available to Canada, there was no realistic expectation of bringing about such a change.'[79] Thus, faced with the hard decision of postponing a settlement of all claims indefinitely and prejudicing otherwise valid claims, the government decided that claims under article 27 would have to be excluded. After prolonged negotiation this was accomplished by omitting any reference to article 27 claims in the agreement and covering them instead in an attached exchange of letters in which the Hungarian signator stated that the Hungarian government had fulfilled its obligations and the Canadian signator stated that he had noted this statement. The result is that, while not included, such claims have not been extinguished as have been the claims admitted to the settlement and there remains the possibility that a remedy might become available through other channels. In the case of Romania there was a different solution mainly because there appeared to be few if any claims that could be brought within article 25. The Romanian agreement settles all peace treaty claims.

Shareholder and Corporate Claims

Claims arising out of a corporate shareholding are an important and controversial class.[80] The recent Barcelona Traction decision of the International Court turned largely on whether Belgium as the state of nationality of 88 per cent of the shareholders of a Canadian company doing business in Spain had *jus standi* to bring an action against Spain for allegedly wrongful acts towards the company. The court's reply in the negative has provoked wide and generally unfavourable comment.[81]

It is of course far beyond the scope of this chapter to discuss this complex decision with its many unanswered questions. Suffice it to note two particular points: the reaffirmation of the traditional rule that apart from certain exceptions only the state of incorporation may espouse an international claim arising out of wrongdoing to a corporation;[82] the confirmation of a state's right to establish its own criteria for espousing the claims of its corporate nationals. Recent Canadian practice has not been consistent with the first conclusion; the Department of External Affairs has expressed itself willing in principle to espouse the interests of Canadian shareholders in non Canadian companies.

> Where a Canadian national has an interest, as a shareholder or otherwise, in a foreign company and where the state under the laws of which that company was incorporated and of which it is therefore a national, injures the company, the Canadian Government may intervene to protect the interests of the Canadian national. The Canadian Government may also intervene on behalf of a Canadian shareholder in a foreign state if that company is injured by the acts of a third state. In such case, the intervention may be made in concert with the government of the state in which the company was incorporated.[83]

The trend of recent US practice has been in the same direction.[84] However, both British and French practice would seem to have been contrary.[85]

The second proposition concerns the right of the state to establish conditions for the espousal of the claims of its own corporations.[86] States have adopted various criteria. The United States, Great Britain, and since World War II, Switzerland have required that their nationals hold a substantial beneficial interest in the company.[87] Some other European states continue to look to their domestic law norm of examining the company's *siège social*.[88] Canada has exercised this discretion in requiring a substantial Canadian beneficial interest in the company.[89]

> According to Canadian practice, claims of corporations are espoused by the Canadian Government only where there is a 'substantial' Canadian interest in the company. Whether such 'substantial' Canadian interest exists so as to justify Canadian diplomatic intervention depends on such questions as the place of incorporation of the company, and whether or not it carries on business and active trading interests in Canada, and the extent to which the company is beneficially owned in Canada. Insofar as the place of incorporation is concerned, the Canadian Government can only espouse claims in respect of property nationalized abroad (including companies incorporated abroad) where the

claims belong to a company incorporated under the laws of Canada or of any province of Canada and which was so incorporated on the date on which the claim arose.[90]

Ownership

The second element of the claim to be established is that of ownership. Most claimants under the eastern European claims programs have encountered problems arising out of the difficulty of obtaining proof of former title. This is the result in part of the wartime destruction of records, in part the lapse in time between the taking of the property and the submission of the claims, and in part the apparent reluctance of some respondent states to provide aliens with documentary information concerning property rights. In these circumstances it has had to be recognized that the claimants were often at some disadvantage in trying to document their claims through no fault or lack of effort on their part. For these and other reasons very few claims under these programs met the rules of evidence that would normally be required by a national or international tribunal. Otherwise sound claims for which the claimants have attempted and failed to obtain proof of ownership are usually put forward for discussion and if the other side chooses to challenge every imperfection, no progress would be possible. Often the respondent state produces records which show that the claimant was indeed at one time the owner of the property, but in some cases there is also evidence that the claimant transferred title or gave a power of attorney to do so to another person, often a relation. A particularly difficult class of cases involves inheritance. In the wartime and postwar dislocation of population that occurred in many states of eastern Europe, particularly Poland, there have been many cases in which only a few family members survived. Wills were not widely used in some of these states nor was it possible in most cases to establish with any certainty the death of the original owner or of other potential heirs. In such cases, every effort is made to test the basic credibility of the claim, by for example requiring affidavits from neighbours, members of the family, or other knowledgeable persons.

Loss

The third element to be examined is that of loss. In most cases, this consists of establishing that the property was taken over by the respondent state. With regard to the effective date of the taking, there are three possibilities: the date on which the claimant lost control, the date on which title was registered in the name of the state, and the effective date of the legislation or administrative decree. The latter date usually proves to be the simplest to apply. In some cases the legislation or decrees appear to require a subsequent implementing act applying the general law to the specific property. Difficult cases arise when the claimant has acquired citizenship between these two dates; to ensure that provision is made in the quantum for such claims, it is sometimes necessary for the claiming state to invoke the concept of unjust enrichment.

In other cases, the property may have been placed under state administration or transferred to the name of a collective farm. In such circumstances, the property may have been subject to a constructive taking. On the other hand, the property may have been taken by the state under abandoned property rather than nationalization legislation. Given the obvious need for such legislation in a postwar situation, and a failure by a claimant to give notice of his interest in the property within the specified period which in the case of Poland was ten years, it is difficult to find that the property has been nationalized in the usual sense of the word. Similar problems arise in the case of claimants whose property was taken over first by the occupying state and then confiscated by the respondent state as having been registered in the name of a national of the occupying state. Such persons often failed to take advantage of the restitution legislation designed to enable the original owners to regain their property. Examples of all these types of cases are before the Foreign Claims Commission for decision.

Some of the claims submitted to the Department of External Affairs arose out of the taking of property in the Baltic states and those portions of Poland, Czechoslovakia, and Romania which had been ceded to the Soviet Union, as well as portions of Hungary ceded to Czechoslovakia. In these cases the question was whether liability for the taking lay with the former or the current sovereign. Sometimes the factual situation was complicated by the wartime reoccupation of the territory by the ceding state. For example, a number of claims concerned the taking of real property in Northern Bukovina, an area ceded to the USSR in June 1940. Romania reoccupied the territory from mid-1941 until early in 1944 but its retroactive transfer to the USSR was confirmed by article 1 of the Romanian treaty of peace.[91] The department concluded that the occupation by Romanian forces did not affect the 1940 transfer of sovereignty and that, although the claimants may have been deprived of their property while the territory was under occupation, the claims should be directed against the USSR as the state which had sovereignty over the territory at the time the taking occurred and which continued to benefit from the taking.[92]

While the physical loss of immovable property usually poses few problems of proof, the loss of movables is more complex. The difficulty is proving the existence of the movables and their subsequent loss through nationalization. In the case of claims arising in a wartime context there existed the real possibility that the movables were either looted or destroyed and that the claim was thus more properly one for war damage rather than for nationalization. The Canadian practice has been to insist that claimants produce some evidence that the movable property in question survived the war and secondly that it was taken by some government agency.[93]

Valuation

Canadian claimants are asked to indicate a valuation of their losses both in local currency and in Canadian dollars. Canadian practice has been to follow established principles of international laws, under which values are normally based upon the reasonable or fair market value of the property concerned at the time of the loss, nationalization, or confiscation. However, where market values of the properties concerned at the time of loss are unknown or are considered to be unrealistic in the absence of normal market conditions, or where currency inflation throws doubt on the accuracy of monetary valuation in a particular period, other information and evidence are sought as to the reasonable market value of the properties during the last period of relative economic stability, normally before the outbreak of war.

Values of properties from earlier prewar purchase price as set out in a deed, an insurance appraisal, or a tax assessment together with supporting documentation (photocopies of prewar deeds, etc) are used.[94]

CLAIMS PRACTICE: OTHER ASPECTS

It is well established that a state owes no duty at international law nor it would seem under any domestic law that has yet been tested to accord diplomatic protection to the interests of its citizens.[95] Moreover, if a state does accord protection, it may waive, settle, or compromise the claim and extinguish it. The explanation of this authority seems to be that 'the power of a state in international law to make arrangements concerning the affairs of its nationals in relation to other states is unlimited.'[96] In general, governments are capable of binding their states and even if the government lacks authority, the states' international obligations are nevertheless engaged.[97] It is of course a matter of domestic law whether a government acts within its competence when it assumes international obligations and, for example, extinguishes the claims of its citizens. In the recent *Aris Gloves* case, the United States Court of Claims dismissed an action for damages arising out of the United States government's waiver under the Potsdam Agreement of certain claims by United States citizens.[98] And a British Foreign Office legal adviser wrote, 'the Government, in practice, is able to deal with the claim of an individual without his consent, although normally an individual claim would only be taken up, presented to a foreign government and settled at the wish of the individual concerned.'[99]

Lump sum claims settlements are just that: settlements of all claims within specified categories arising before the date of the coming into force of the agreement, whether presented or not. In a large program, only a sample of the cases can be discussed at the negotiating table. The agreements also provide expressly that all the claims covered by the agreements are extinguished.[100] There is no agreed record of the claims that are considered compensable and the distribution of the proceeds of the settlement is left to the exclusive responsibility of the claiming state.[101] While Canadian claims agreements are lump sum settlements and while they reflect in a general way the number and value of claims submitted by the Canadian government, they are not regarded as the sum total of the individually accepted claims.[102] Thus the advancement of the claim during the negotiations and its acceptance or rejection by the respondent state are not conclusive. Moreover, a recommendation of the Foreign Claims Commission does not in itself create a right to an award.[103]

However, it should be noted that some claims may not be covered by such settlements. Defaulted bonds and commercial debts are examples of types of claims often omitted from lump sum agreements, usually because it is more convenient to deal with them otherwise. On the other hand, omission may arise from a failure of the parties to agree on the admissibility of a particular category and the parties, in effect, agree to leave the category aside for the time being.[104] Whatever the motives for omission may be, such claims are clearly not extinguished by operation of the agreement.

The exact status of the proceeds of lump sum settlements has been the subject of dispute. There have been repeated efforts to revive earlier recognition that the receiving governments were trustees for the claimants but these have been defeated in both United States and British courts. The United States Supreme Court has declared that the fund in question was 'a national fund to be distributed by Congress as it saw fit ... no individual claimant had, as a matter of strict legal or equitable right, any lien upon the fund awarded nor was Congress under any legal or equitable obligation to pay any claim out of the proceeds of the fund.'[105] In a British case that went to the House of Lords, Lord Atkin stated that on the facts it was impossible 'to impute to the Crown the position either of trustee or of an agent.'[106] The making of the settlement has been described as an exercise of the crown prerogative and 'even where the Crown or the executive has negotiated and concluded with a foreign government a settlement of claims on behalf of its subjects, it still retains full discretion as to how and to whom the funds obtained thereby should be distributed. Similarly under Canadian law, the prerogative of the Crown is the source of authority for the exercise of the treaty making power, and the Canadian citizen cannot compel the Canadian Government to take up his claim at the diplomatic level. Nor under the same principle can he insist on the Government allowing him to share in any overall settlement of claims that it might negotiate (although, of course, he may have a moral right to participate in the proceeds negotiated on his behalf).'[107]

Reference has been made earlier in this chapter to the view that international law requires that compensation for nationalization be 'prompt adequate and effective.'[108] The existence of such a rule has most recently been reiterated by President Nixon in the following terms: 'Under international law the United States has a right to expect that the taking of American property will be non-discriminatory; that it will be for a public purpose; and that its citizens will receive prompt, adequate and effective compensation from the expropriating country.'[109] However, a commissioner of the United States Foreign Claims Settlement Commission has observed that 'despite strenuous efforts by the Department of State, prompt, adequate and effective payment has been the exception rather than the rule.'[110] Moreover, the accuracy of this view of the law has been challenged[111] and state practice suggests it should be defined with considerable flexibility:

a   the quantum of compensation deemed adequate in the case of nationalization is not 'full market value' of the property ... It is rather a substantial proportion of the value of the property, such value being probably determined by the fair market value of the property ...[112]
b   As for the form of compensation, the principle is not that the alien must necessarily receive the compensation in the currency of his national state, but that he must be able to use the compensation to his benefit. Generally this would require payment in a convertible currency, though there may be exceptions to this rule.
c   Promptitude in payment is apparently not required. Exigencies of the international situation permit payment over a period of time and it has been submitted that this must be a 'reasonable period', such period being one which never exceeds 10–12 years and 'reasonableness' depending on all the circumstances of the case ... Interest must be paid from the date of nationalization as it falls due and adequate guarantee must be given that future payments will in fact be made.[113]

CONCLUSION

It has been suggested earlier in this chapter that there is no immediate prospect for the codification of the law of state responsibility. The broad approach to the subject recently favoured by the International Law Commission is likely to involve directly or indirectly all the rules of international law and to raise a number of politically sensitive issues. Nothing in the history of United Nations efforts to come to grips with politically charged topics such as the definition of aggression holds out a promise of quick or easy results in an area in which many of the rules are in a state of evolution. It is perhaps equally unlikely that a codification confined to responsibility for injury to aliens can succeed in the near future in view of the widespread indifference and from some quarters opposition to the customary concepts. Moreover, there exist substantial areas of difference even among the adherents of the rule of customary international law as to what those rules are.

The prospect for the time being is that the international community will have to rely on norms of international conduct that are uneven in vigour and uncertain in application. There will continue to be some claims that will lend themselves to resolution by international adjudication and others to lump sum settlement. There is likely to be expanded use of investment disputes settlement procedures. In addition, confidence in domestic law systems is likely to be increased as the rights of aliens become more clearly recognized. In short, while the advance of the rule of law in the area of state responsibility is not likely to be forthright, the search will continue for effective dispute resolution procedures.

NOTES

1 Vattel, *Le droit des Gens ou principes de la Loi Naturelle*. 71, 1758 text, *Classics of International Law*.
2 the *Mavrommatis Concessions* case, [1924] P.C.I.J., ser A, no 2, at 12.
3 An account of the proceedings of the latter commission is to be found in Corbett, *The Settlement of Canadian–American Disputes* (1937), which provides a comprehensive view of its subject from the Jay Treaty down through the Pecuniary Claims Agreement of 1910 to the well known *I'm Alone* and *Trail Smelter* cases.
4 For a brief account of the history of state responsibility, see Lillich, 'Toward the Formulation of an Acceptable Body of Law concerning State Responsibility' (1965), 16 *Syracuse Law Review* 720–37.
5 Edwin M. Borchard, *The Diplomatic Protection of Citizens Abroad* (1915).
6 Parliamentary Report of the Canadian Delegates quoted in Corbett, *supra* note 3, at 84.
7 See (1956), 1 *International Law Commission*

Yearbook 228–49; (1957), 2 ibid 104; (1958), 2 ibid 47; (1959), 2 ibid 1; (1960), 2 ibid 41; (1961), 2 ibid 1.
8 Garcia-Amador's approach to codification was a liberal one: he defined the task as 'bringing the principles governing state responsibility into line with international law at its present stage of development.' (1956), 2 *International Law Commission Yearbook* 176. For a further elaboration of Garcia-Amador's views on the profound transformation of certain concepts and principles of international law as they throw into doubt certain traditional concepts of state responsibility, see his '*The Role of State Responsibility in the Private Financing of Economic and Social Development*' (1965), 16 *Syracuse Law Review*.
9 G.I. Tunkin (1960), *Soviet Yearbook of International Law* 101–4.
10 'As the international community was confined, during by far the longest period of its growth, to the Western Christian Powers, the bulk of international law, if not the whole of

it, represents their common customs and traditions which need not be, and in most cases are not, the common customs and traditions of the other Powers, and, in any event, the Powers that secured their admittance to the Family of Nations after World War II were not parties to the agreements and understandings on which, after all, international law is, in its last analysis, based.' Guha Roy, 'Is the Law of Responsibility of States for Injuries to Aliens part of Universal International Law?' (1961), 55 *Am. J. Int'l L.* 867.

11 Hon. Paul Martin, 'International Law in a Changing World: Value of the Old and the New' (1964), 16 *External Affairs Bulletin* 586–96, at 587.

12 The commission's decision in 1963 was '1 / That, in an attempt to codify the topic of State responsibility, priority should be given to the definitions of the general rules governing the international responsibility of the state, and 2 / That in defining these general rules the experience and material gathered in certain special reports, especially that of responsibility for injuries to aliens, should not be overlooked and that careful consideration should be paid to the possible repercussions which developments in international law may have had on responsibility.' *International Law Commission Report* (1963), UN Gen. Ass. Off. Rec. 15th Sess, supp no 9, at 36 (A/5509).

13 R.R. Baxter, 'Reflections on Codification in Light of the International Law of State Responsibility for Injuries to Aliens' (1965), 16 *Syracuse Law Review* 745–61, at 746. Baxter considers in some detail suitable criteria for determining the appropriate dimensions for an international law subject to be codified and concludes that the law of states responsibility as now understood by the commission does not meet them. He argues forcefully that the law of state responsibility for injuries to aliens 'possesses a separate identity which sets it apart from the rest of the law of state responsibility' (751).

14 The Declaration on Principles of International Law concerning Friendly Relations and Cooperation among states in accordance with the Charter was adopted by the General Assembly on 4 November 1970 (res 2625 (xxv)). Canada played an active role in the Special Committee on Friendly Relations which had been considering the subject since 1964. The declaration incorporates seven principles including in particular the non-use of force, the peaceful settlement of disputes, and non-intervention.

The Special Committee on the Question of Defining Aggression, established in 1967, has made substantial progress towards clarifying the elements to be included in a legally adequate definition of aggression and towards developing and expanding the political basis for agreement on a definition but the objective is probably still some years off.

15 Reproduced in Sohn and Baxter, 'Responsibility of States for Injuries to the Economic Interests of Aliens' (1961), 55 *Am. J. Int'l L.* 545.

16 Ibid, at 547.

17 See, eg, Convention, article 10(5)c.

18 Lillich, *supra* note 4, at 729, estimates that the draft followed traditional rules 90 per cent of the time (729).

19 *Restatement of the Law, second: Foreign Relations Law of the United States as Adopted and Promulgated by the American Law Institute* (1965).

20 Lillich, *supra* note 4, at 731.

21 *Restatement, supra* note 19, at s 165(2).

22 C.F. Murphy, 'State Responsibility for Injuries to Aliens' (1966), 41 *N.Y.U.L. Rev.* 125–47, at 136.

23 For text and commentary, see (1968), 2 *International Lawyer* 326.

24 Document 1803 (XVII) adopted 14 Dec. 1962. A summary of United Nations consideration of permanent sovereignty is set out in 8 Whitman, (1967), *Digest of International Law* 1024–32.

25 Paragraph 4 of the declaration is as follows: 'Nationalization, expropriation or requisitioning shall be based on grounds or reasons of public utility, security or the national interest, which are recognized as overriding purely individual or private interests, both domestic and foreign. In such cases, the owner shall be paid appropriate compensation, in accordance with the rules in force in the State taking such measures in the exercise of its sovereignty and in accordance with international law. In any case where the question of compensation gives rise to a controversy, the national jurisdiction of the State taking such measures shall be exhausted. However, upon agreement by sovereign States and other parties concerned, settlement of the dispute should be made through arbitration on international adjudication.'

26 A discussion of the more particular international attempts to encourage the use of arbitration and conciliation procedures, and through them the flow of private investment capital, is beyond the scope of this article. See however the article elsewhere in this volume by John E.C. Brierley.

27 'Rules of law, opinions of authoritative writers and decisions of international judicial or quasijudicial bodies no longer have a persuasive ring, when dealing with the status of private property, particularly of private capital investment, in international law.' N.R. Doman, 'New Developments in the field of nationalization' (1970), 3 *N.Y.U.J. Int'l L. & Pol.* 307.

28 E.B. Wang, 'Nationality of Claims and Diplomatic Intervention in Canadian Practice' (1965), 43 *Can. Bar Rev.* 136.

29 Martin, *supra* note 11, at 591.

30 The local remedies rule has been the subject of much literature; see in particular C.F. Amerasinghe, *State Responsibility for Injuries to Aliens* (1967) C V, VI, and VII; I.L. Head, 'A Fresh Look at the Local Remedies Rule' (1967), *Can. Y.B. Int'l L.* 142; for a comparative study of the procedures available for the protection of the private rights of aliens, see F.G. Dawson and I.L. Head, *International Law, National Tribunals and the Rights of Aliens* (19??); in the case of lump sum settlements, the usual absence of adequate remedies in the respondent state brings into effect the futility exception to the rule which states in effect that 'the alien need not seek to exhaust justice where there is no justice to exhaust' (Head, 154).

31 [1966] CAN. T.S. no 22; text also appears in (1965), *Can. Y.B. Int'l L.* 283–4; see Lillich, 'The Gut Dam Claims Agreement with Canada' (1965), 59 *Am. J. Int'l L.* 892.

32 (1968), *Can. Y.B. Int'l L.* 317–18; for a description of the arbitration and the settlement, see Kerley and Goodman, 'The Gut Dam Claims: A Lump Sum Settlement Disposes of an Arbitrated Dispute' (1970), 10 *Virginia J. Int'l L.* 300; for a Canadian view of the dispute written before the parties reached a settlement, see D.S. MacDonald, 'Canada's Recent Experience in International Claims' (1966), 21 *International Journal* 324.

33 Lillich and Christenson, *International Claims: Their Preparation and Presentation* (1962) 99.

34 (1966), 18 *External Affairs Bulletin* 11.

35 See for example comments of Baxter, *supra* note 13, at 757.

36 Lillich, in his 'International Claims: Their Settlement by Lump Sum Agreements' in *International Arbitration, Liber Amicorum for Martin Domke* (1967), at 145 refutes the suggestion that lump sum settlements are a postwar phenomenon and traces their use back to the Jay Treaty. See also the same author's *International Claims: Their Adjudication by National Commissions* (1962) 5–15. Lillich establishes that the earliest United States commission was that created in 1803 to distribute the proceeds of an agreement with France settling claims arising out of the French revolution. The first British commission appears to have been established in the same year. See Lillich, *International Claims: Postwar British Practice* 3–4.

37 I. Foighel, *Nationalization (1957)* 98.

38 Barcelona Traction Light and Power Company, Limited (New Application: 1962) (*Belgium* v *Spain*) Second Phase, Judgement, 5 February 1970, at 40.

39 Baxter, *supra* note 13, at 757: 'On the international plane the decisions of Commissions can never command the same weight as those of international tribunals.' Murphy, 145 considers that negotiated lump sum settlements combined with preadjudication procedures 'have overtones which are not conducive to the development of international order.'

40 B.H. Weston, *International Claims: Post War French Practice* (1971) 7.

41 For a fuller discussion of these various views, see Lillich, *International Claims: Their Settlement by Lump Sum Agreements,* who suggests that inquiry might more usefully be directed to the construction of a standard of just compensation to regulate future takings of property.

42 See in particular Sweeney, 'Restatement of the Foreign Relations Law of the United States and the Responsibility of States for Injury to Aliens' (1965), 16 *Syracuse Law Review.*

43 Brooks, 'Registration of International Claims under the Foreign Compensation Act, 1950' (1959), 44 *Transact. Grot. Soc'y* 187–8.

44 G.E. Vilkov, 'Nationalization and International Law' (1960), *Soviet Yearbook of International Law* 76.

45 For example A. Martin in the 'Distribution of Funds under the Foreign Compensation Act' (1950), 44 *Transact. Grot. Soc'y* 243,

observes that 'the size of a compensation fund obtainable from an expropriating Government is determined neither exclusively nor predominantly by the particulars which can be presented of the claims put forward.'

46 See Foighel, *supra* note 37, at 79–85 for an analysis of the apparent motives behind a number of settlements.

47 Lillich, 'International Claims Practice' in *This Fire Proof House* (1967) 118–19, comments that 'persons holding international claims should not be required, through an inadequate settlement of their just grievances, to pay the entire price of better relations themselves.'

48 For a table of percentage returns on United States claims settlements, see Freidberg, 'A New Technique in the Adjudication of International Claims' (1970), 10 *Virginia J. Int'l L.* 299; for a discussion of the inducements in United States claims agreements, see Lillich, *International Claims: Their Adjudication by National Commissions*, at 106–8; for a description of inducements used by the British, see Lillich, *International Claims: Postwar British Practice*, at 137–9.

49 See Weston (1971), 65 *Proceedings, A.S.I.L.* 343.

50 For a description of these settlements, see C.V. Cole, 'A Generation of Canadian Experience with International Claims' (1965–6), *British Y.B. Int'l L.* 380 and 383–5.

51 Agreement between the Government of Canada and the Government of the People's Republic of Bulgaria relating to the Settlement of Financial Matters, [1966] CAN. T.S. no 14.

52 Agreement between the Government of Canada and the Government of the People's Republic of Hungary relating to the Settlement of Financial Matters, [1970] CAN. T.S. no 14.

53 Agreement between the Government of Canada and the Government of the Socialist Republic of Romania concerning the Settlement of Outstanding Financial Problems, [1971] CAN. T.S. no 30.

54 Agreement between the Government of Canada and the Government of the Polish People's Republic Relating to the Settlement of Financial Matters, [1971] CAN. T.S. no 47.

55 Canadian citizens participated in the Anglo-Yugoslav claims settlement of 23 December 1948, [1948] CAN. T.S. no 29. This single postwar example of including Canadian claims in

a British settlement has been described by Wang as a legacy of the earlier period of dependency on British diplomacy (*supra* note 28, at 145). The current negotiations are confined to claims that have arisen since 1948.

56 See Macdonald, *supra* note 32. There was however, one exception, that of the Protocol of 19 Sept. 1944 between Canada, the United Kingdom, and the Soviet Union providing for the payment of compensation by the Soviet government to the Canadian government for Canadian owned interests in nickel mines in the territory of Petsamo which was ceded by Finland to the Soviet Union in 1944, [1944] CAN. T.S. no 29.

57 In the case of Bulgaria, the secretary of state for external affairs tabled in the House of Commons on 4 July 1966 agreements between Canada and Bulgaria on the establishment of diplomatic relations, on the settlement of claims, and understandings concerning consular protection, reunification of families, and the status of dual nationals (H.C. *Debates* (Can) 1966, at 7113). In the case of Hungary, the secretary of state for external affairs announced in the House of Commons on 11 June 1964 that representatives of the government had been discussing 'problems of common interest in the fields of trade, financial claims, consular matters and diplomatic relations' and that agreements had been reached in all these areas (H.C. *Debates* (Can) 1964, at 4177). In the case of Romania, the secretary of state for external affairs announced in the House of Commons on 9 May, 1967 that following the exchange of letters tabled in the House on 4 April concerning the establishment of diplomatic relations between Canada and Romania, he was tabling a consular understanding and an exchange of letters setting out an agreement to negotiate a lump sum settlement of claims (H.C. *Debates* (Can) 1967, at 1). The Romanian claims agreement was signed on 13 July 1971 and a trade agreement three days later. Instruments of ratification for both agreements were exchanged on 14 Dec. 1971.

58 The text of the Polish notice is reprinted in (1965), *Can. Y.B. Int'l L.* 330; the texts of other notices are similar, varying only in details of application to the particular state. For comparable United States procedure, see Lillich and Christenson, *supra* note 33, at c VI and appendices. For British procedure, see F. Vallat, *International Law and the*

Practitioner (1966) appendices XI to XIV.

59 The Department of External Affairs has stated: 'It should be emphasized that we do not seek to adjudicate or pass judgement on the merits of individual claims nor are we empowered to do so. Our only concern, at present, is to assist claimants with advice about the kind of information and documentation which may be relevant and which may ultimately be required in support of their claims.' (1968), *Can. Y.B. Int'l L.* 263.

60 Claims against Yugoslavia and Panama were adjudicated after settlements were achieved. Polish claims were registered before the settlement but adjudicated afterwards. Claims against Bulgaria, Hungary, Romania, and Czechoslovakia were preadjudicated and to date settlements have been achieved only with Bulgaria and Romania. Claims against Cuba and China are in the process of preadjudication. For an evaluation of the preadjudication process, see Lillich, *The Protection of Foreign Investment: Six Procedural Studies* (1965) 167, at 181–8; Re, *The Presettlement Adjudication of International Claims in International Arbitration Liber Amicorum for Martin Domke*, 214, 217–20; S. Freidberg, *A New Technique* (1967) 282–98.

61 Claims against Yugoslavia and Czechoslovakia were adjudicated after settlements were achieved. Presettlement registration was utilized in the cases of Bulgaria, Hungary, Romania, and additional claims against Czechoslovakia and the Soviet Union. See Lillich, *The Protection of Foreign Investments: Six Procedural Studies* 177–9; and Martin, 'The Distribution of Funds under the Foreign Compensation Act, 1950' (1959), 44 *Transact. Grot. Soc'y* 243.

62 In the United states the Foreign Claims Settlement Commission carries out the adjudication function. The work of the commission and its predecessors the War Claims Commission and the International Claims Commission, together with the relevant agreements, legislation, regulations, and leading decisions are set out in *Foreign Claims Settlement Commission of the United States: Decisions and Annotations* (1969); see also Lillich, *International Claims: Their Adjudication by National Commissions*. In Great Britain, the Foreign Compensation Commission carries out the adjudication function, see Lillich, *International Claims: Post War British Practice* 1–23.

63 See Cole, *supra* note 50, at 393–4 for a description of the Bulgarian distribution arrangements and the full text of the Foreign Claims (Bulgaria) Regulations established by order in council P.C. 1966–2062 of 3 November 1966, S.O.R. 66–506.

64 Cole, *supra* note 50, at 379–85, describes the process under which war claims were settled.

65 See Department of External Affairs, *Annual Report* (1969) 83.

66 P.C. 1970–2077 of 8 December 1970.

67 Order in council P.C. 1970–2078 of 8 December 1970, S.O.R. 70–527.

68 See Wang, *supra* note 28, and (1967), *Can. Y.B. Int'l L.* 265–7. More generally, see C. Joseph, *Nationality and Diplomatic Protection* (1969) 1–32.

69 See Agreements with Bulgaria, article III; Hungary, article III; Romania, article II; Poland, article II.

70 Macdonald, *supra* note 32, at 324. For critical views of the rule, see M.D. Copithorne, 'International Claims and the Rule of Nationality' (1969), 63 *Proceedings, A.S.I.L.* 30–5 and S. Freidberg, 'Unjust and Outmoded: The Doctrine of Continuous Nationality in International Claims' (1970), 4 *International Lawyer* 835.

71 Borchard, *supra* note 5, at 588. See also article 4 of the Convention on Certain Questions Relating to the Conflict of Nationality Laws, signed in the Hague, 12 April 1930, [1937] CAN. T.S. no 7.

72 Z.R. Rode, 'Dual Nationals and the Doctrine of Dominant Nationality' (1959), 53 *Am. J. Int'l L.* 139–44.

73 *Liechtenstein v Guatemala* (1959), *International Law Reports* 349.

74 *Claim of the United States ex rel Florence Strunsky Mergé v Italy* (1953), case no 3, decision no 55, Third Collection of Decisions of the Italian-United States Conciliation Commission 1, 12–14. For a discussion of the Nottebohm and Mergé cases as well as the Flegenheimer case, see Joseph *supra* note 68, at 11–22.

75 The United States State Department has also approved the doctrine (see 8 Whitman (1967), *Digest of International Law* 1252); the Foreign Claims Settlement Commission has made awards to dual nationals. (See Lillich, *International Claims: Their Adjudication by National Commissions* 83–5). British practice appears to accord with the traditional rule. (See N.H. Moller, 'Compensation for

British Owned Foreign Interests' (1959), 44 *Trans. Grot. Soc'y* and Vallat, *supra* note 61, at 24.) Danish practice is believed to be similar and to have been upheld in the courts.

76 [1947] CAN. T.S. no 5.

77 [1947] CAN. T.S. no 6.

78 Article I (4) of the Hungarian Agreement and article I (c) of the Romanian Agreement.

79 (1971), *Can. Y.B. Int'l L.*

80 See L. Calfisch, *La Protection des sociétés commerciales et des entérêts indirects en droit international public* (1969).

81 *Barcelona Traction Light and Power Co.* case (*Belgium v Spain*) Second Phase (1970) I.C.J. 4. For comment, see A.M. Susman, 'Notes' (1971), *Har. Int'l L. J.* 91; C.W. Brownfield, 'Recent Decisions' (1971), 5 *J. Int'l L. & Econ.* 239; H.B. Reimann, 'Notes' (1970), *Journal of World Trade Law* 719; J-V. Louis, 'Jurisprudence International Interessant la Belgique' (1971), 7 *Belgium Review of Int'l L.* 347; R. Higgins, 'Aspects of the Case Concerning the Barcelona Traction, Light and Power Company, Ltd' (1971), 11 *Virginia J. Int'l L.* 327; H.W. Briggs, 'Barcelona Traction: The Jus Standi of Belgium' (1971), 65 *Am. J. Int'l L.* 327; 'Round Table' (1971), 65 *Proceedings, A.S.I.L.* 333; 'Notes' (1971), 3 *Law and Policy in International Business* 542; 'Notes' (1970), 3 *N.Y.U.J. Int'l L. & Pol.* 390.

82 See for example, J.M. Jones, 'Claims on Behalf of Nationals Who are Shareholders in Foreign Companies' (1949), 26 *British Y.B. Int'l L.* 225. The rationale advanced for the rule has usually been the multiplicity of claims that could otherwise arise.

83 (1968), *Can. Y.B. Int'l L.* 265.

84 The State Department has adopted a 'substantial and bona fide interest' test. Congress has had a variable approach to the standards it has instructed the FCSC to enforce but 'the trend is toward the allowance of direct stockholder claims regardless of the American interest in the corporation concerned.' Lillich, *International Claims, their Adjudication by National Commissions* 86–94, at 94. However, two years after Lillich's comment, Congress established a requirement in the Cuban claims program that United States citizens own 25 per cent of the Beneficial interest in non-United States corporations. See Friedberg, *supra* note 58, at 285, n 14.

85 For a discussion of British practice see, Lillich, *International Claims: Postwar British Practice* 40–52; Weston, *supra* note 40,

167–71 states that French commissions have consistently refused to accept such claims.

86 See Calfisch, *supra* note 80, at 130–43 for a discussion of the theories favouring the existence of an international law norm for the establishment of the nationality of companies. He concludes: 'la "nationalité" des sociétés de capitaux et de personnes est déterminée par référence à la législation de l'Etat dont la "nationalité" est en cause. Cette "nationalité" est opposable à des Etats tiers-et doit être reconnue par eux – si elle est basée sur l'un (ou plusiers) des éléments suivant: incorporation ou constitution, siège administratif réal, centre d'exploitation, contrôle, ou sur tout autre critère qui revêt un certaine effectivité minimum. Ce principe appelle une seule réserve: la "nationalité" conférée à une enteté par un Etat sur la base du critère de l'incorporation ou de la constitution est inopposable à l'Etat dont les ressortissants exercent un contrôle direct ou indirect sur la société' (ibid, 145–6).

87 Ibid, at 116–29.

88 'The siège social of a company as that term is understood in continental systems of law is the place where the company exercises legal, financial and administrative control over its operations.' G. White, *Nationalization of Foreign Property* (1961) 63.

89 Note however, that such a condition was not imposed in the *I'm Alone* claim. For a discussion of the result of that case in the context of the espousal of corporate claims, see Calfisch, *supra* note 80, at 104–11.

90 (1968), *Can. Y.B. Int'l L.* 265.

91 [1947] CAN. T.S. no 6.

92 (1970), *Can. Y.B. Int'l L.* 357–8.

93 Ibid, 360.

94 See (1966), *Can. Y.B. Int'l L.* 267. For United States valuation methods, see Lillich and Christensen, *International Claims: Their Preparation and Presentation* 74–81, and Friedberg, *supra* note 58.

95 See authorities quoted by Wang, *supra* note 28, at 148; also views expressed at 'Round Table' (1971), 65 *Proceedings, A.S.I.L.* 332; Vallat, *supra* note 61, at 21 states:

Since the claim when presented as an international claim is that of the State and not of the individual, it follows that its presentation is a matter within the discretion of the Government. It is necessary for the practitioner to be quite clear on this point, because sometimes the refusal of the Government to sponsor a claim is regarded as an injustice if not actually unlawful. It should be remembered that there are various factors which may govern the presentation of a claim. Thus, although the claim may appear to be a valid one from the point of view of private law, the necessary conditions for an international claim may not have been fulfilled. For example, although the claim may at the time of presentation be vested in a British national, it may not have been British in origin. Again, there may be overriding political factors which make it undesirable to present the claim: for example, because to do so might tend to imply recognition of a regime or an acquisition of territory which the Government is not prepared to recognize. Again, the time may not be propitious. Patience is essential. Much damage can be done by pressing claims when the political climate is wrong. These are all matters which are and must be within the judgement of the Government. Some of them are of a legal character and some of them are of a political character.

96 Foighel, *supra* note 37, at 101.
97 *Eastern Greeland* case (1933), P.C.I.J. ser A/B no 53.
98 *Aris Gloves Inc.* v *United States* 420 F.2d 1386; for case note, see (1970), 64 *Am. J. Int'l L.* 948.
99 Vallat, *supra* note 61, at 39.
100 Bulgaria, article IV; Hungary, article IV(1); Romania, article IV; Poland, article IV(1).
101 Bulgaria, article V(1); Hungary, article V; Romania article V; Poland, article V.
102 (1970), *Can. Y.B. Int'l L.* 362-3.
103 Sec 8(2) of the *Foreign Claims (Hungary) Settlement Regulations*.
104 For example, article 27 peace treaty claims were not included in the Canadian claims settlement with Hungary. See discussion of this exclusion in the section on Canadian claims juris prudence.
105 *Williams* v *Heard* 140 U.S. 529 (1891) quoted in Lillich, *International Claims: Their Adjudication by National Commissions* 27.
106 *Civilian War Claimants Assoc., Ltd.* v *The King* (1932), A.C. 14; see also *Rustomjee* v *The Queen* (1876), 1 Q.B. 487; both cases are discussed in Moller, at 236–40; the same conclusion has been reached in the Dutch courts, see *Trustee in the Liquidation of Mendelssohn & Co. Amsterdam* v *the State*

of the Netherlands (1966), N.J. no 230, summarized in (1968), 15 *Netherlands Int'l L. Rev.* 434.
107 Wang, *supra* note 28, at 149.
108 The usual authority for this expression is the note sent by Cordell Hull in connection with the Mexican expropriations: 'The right of a sovereign state to expropriate property is coupled with and conditioned on the obligation to make adequate, effective and prompt compensation.' Hackworth, (1942), 3 *Digest* 288, at 662.
109 Official text, President Nixon's policy statement, 19 January 1972, on Economic Assistance and Investment Security in Developing Nations.
110 Freidberg, *supra* note 58, at 282.
111 See Dawson and Weston, 'Prompt, Adequate and Effective: A Universal Standard of Compensation?' (1962), 30 *Fordham Law Review* 727; B.A. Wortley, *Expropriation in Public International Law* (1959) 33–5, for a list of writers supporting and opposing the rule; G. White, *Nationalization of Foreign Property* (1961) 11–18, at 15 submits that the 'classic formula should be recognized as the expression of the desired aim rather than a technical rule for the measurement of compensation.'
112 However, the Hickenlooper amendment to the Foreign Assistance Act specified 'speedy compensation for such property in convertible foreign exchange, equivalent to the full value thereof, as required by international law.' See Lillich, *The Protection of Foreign Investment: Six Procedural Studies* 117, for a generally critical study of the amendment; the American Law Institute *Restatement, supra* note 19, at ss 186, 187, 188, endorses the full value standard; Bin Cheng, 'The Rationale of Compensation for Expropriation' (1959), 44 *Proc., Grot. Soc'y* 293–5, concludes that while compensations must be 'just,' 'fair,' or 'equitable' they need not be 'full'; White agrees that compensation need not amount to the full value, and concludes from an examination of state practice that states have paid or accepted amounts of compensation 'in accordance with economic, political and other non legal motives' (14). The OECD Draft Convention provides for the payment of 'just' compensation which 'shall represent the genuine value of the property affected' (article 3(iii)). The convention's 'Notes and Comments' add that

'as a rule, this will correspond to the fair market value of the property without reduction in that value due to the method by which the payment is calculated; to the manner in which it is made; or to any special tax or charges levied on it ... The determination of the "genuine value" must initially be referred to the national body to which is entrusted the task of assessing compensation' unless another process is stipulated in an 'undertaking' (paras 9(a) and (b)).

113 Amerasinghe, *supra* note 30, at 167.

A.E. GOTLIEB

10/Canadian Treaty-Making: Informal Agreements and Interdepartmental Arrangements

The dominant feature of Canadian treaty-making is 'the informal and pragmatic approach that has characterized, over the years, the actions taken by Canada in developing effective and simplified methods for making treaties.'[1] This conclusion, which I emphasized in *Canadian Treaty-Making* in 1968, is evident in a wide range of characteristics of Canadian treaty-making. The Canadian government was able, through various techniques and arrangements worked out over many years, to pass from the use of formal and sometimes cumbersome methods of concluding international agreements, such as treaties in head of state form, to treaty-making in the form of a variety of entirely intergovernmental agreements which in turn simplified the often complex procedural requirements for full powers, signature, and ratification of treaties. In thus avoiding the delays of satisfying formal constitutional requirements involving the taking of steps in London as well as in Ottawa, Canada, as an independent member of the international community, was able to move effectively and relatively swiftly to equip itself to meet the needs of contemporary international dealings.

There has been no diminution whatever of the trends, evident for over a century, to extend the areas of international co-operation into virtually all aspects of the affairs of the state. Each year that passes reveals new focal points of international regulation which result from problems that surpass the boundaries of a single state, even large and important ones. Most recently, we see an increasing need for greater international regulation in a number of areas that are subject to rapid technological change such as telecommunications and the utilization of the seas and of space, as well as in fields of growing social concern such as the preservation of man's environment against the damage caused by industrial development and of various forms of pollution. Inevitably, the very rhythm of international co-operation affects the timing of national plans and programs and may require the preparation of government positions and arrangements with the least possible delay. These international exigencies are often continuing to be met by informal methods in the preparation and adoption of international agreements and arrangements.

The review of Canadian practice which follows demonstrates, I believe, that the Canadian approach to treaty-making is and has been a very flexible one. Forms are adapted to meet international requirements, whatever they may be. The accent is both on informality and flexibility.

At the same time as these trends towards informality and flexibility exist, Canada has taken steps to ensure that its treaty-making procedures as a whole conform to the international law of treaties. Since publication of *Canadian Treaty-Making,* Canada has taken the significant step of acceding, on 14 October 1970, to the Vienna Convention on the Law of Treaties. The convention is not yet in force but is already

1 Canadian exchanges of notes 1966–70[3]

Year	Bilateral agreements	Exchange of notes
1966	31	13
1967	29	16
1968	19	9
1969	27	15
1970	22	10
Total	128	63

having an influence on international treaty practice and is likely in the years to come to have a profound influence on Canadian practice.

EXCHANGES OF NOTES: RECENT TRENDS

Just as procedures developed to reduce dependency on formal engagements by transferring normal authority to enter into treaties from the head of state to the government, procedures also evolved during the past half-century to move treaty-making from the level of full-fledged intergovernmental agreements (whether in the form of 'treaties,' in the formal sense of the term, or conventions, protocols, or 'agreements') to the exchange of notes form of arrangements. Elsewhere, I have shown that an extremely high proportion of all Canadian treaties in the two-decade period of 1946 to 1965 were in the form of exchange of notes. Of a total of 494 bilateral agreements that I have identified as being concluded by Canada in this twenty-year period, 351, or approximately 71 per cent, were in the form of exchange of notes or, rarely, of letters.[2] But it is not possible to generalize about trends without running the risk of inaccuracies.

It is rather surprising that in the period 1966 to 1970 the proportion of the total number of exchange of notes entered by Canada, in relation to the total number of its bilateral agreements, has declined. As will be seen from Table 1, Canada in this period entered into 128 bilateral agreements, of which only 63 were in exchange of notes form. Thus, exchanges of notes constitute approximately only 49 per cent of the total number of bilateral agreements made by Canada in this period, in comparison with a percentage of approximately 67 per cent of the total number of bilateral agreements in the period 1956–65 and of approximately 74 per cent in the years 1947–55. It is difficult to find an explanation of this decline in favour of the use of exchange of notes in the last few years. The decline is all the more mysterious considering that the exchange of notes form remains particularly predominant in the case of Canada-US bilateral agreements.

Table 2 shows the annual number of Canada-US treaties in the period 1947–65, as well as the annual number in exchange of notes form.[4] Thus, in the period 1947 to 1965, almost 83 per cent of all agreements made with the US were in exchange of notes form – over 12 per cent above the average percentage of exchange of notes agreements (71 per cent) in relation to all bilateral agreements made by Canada in this period.

In the years 1966–70 the same pattern emerges for Canada-US agreements (Table

2 Canada-US treaties 1947–65

	Canada-US treaties	Exchange of notes
1947	9	7
1948	7	7
1949	10	9
1950	5	3
1951	8	6
1952	13	10
1953	8	7
1954	4	4
1955	12	8
1956	6	5
1957	7	5
1958	6	5
1959	12	11
1960	9	8
1961	8	8
1962	6	3
1963	8	8
1964	15	13
1965	11	9
	164	136 (83%)

3 Canada-US agreements 1966–70

	Agreements	Exchange of notes
1966	7	5
1967	9	7
1968	3	3
1969	7	7
1970	7	5
Total	33	27 (82%)

3). Thus the proportion of Canada-US agreements in exchange of note form in relation to all of Canada's bilateral agreements with the US is approximately 82 per cent, only one per cent below the average of 1947–65.

If we compare the proportion of bilateral agreements in exchange of notes form with the total number of Canada's bilateral agreements with all other countries we detect the proportions as shown in the accompanying Table 4. Thus in the period 1947 to 1965, agreements in exchange of notes form constituted only approximately 65 per cent of the total number of informal bilateral agreements with these same countries – a significantly lower proportion than the 83 per cent figure for US treaties in the same period.

In the years 1966–70, statistics emerge for all Canadian bilateral treaties with countries other than the US as in Table 5.

Thus it appears that in the period 1966–70, only about 38 per cent of all bilateral agreements between Canada and countries other than the US were in exchange of notes form. This compares with the proportion of 82 per cent for Canada-US agreements in exchange of notes form in the same period.

4 Bilateral agreements between Canada and all countries other than the US 1947–65[5]

	Total number of agreements between Canada and countries other than the US	Exchange of notes
1947	19	9
1948	11	6
1949	18	14
1950	16	13
1951	22	14
1952	13	12
1953	16	14
1954	6	5
1955	17	12
1956	21	13
1957	23	15
1958	24	15
1959	12	7
1960	14	8
1961	9	5
1962	12	8
1963	16	5
1964	15	12
1965	11	3
Totals	295	190 (65%)

5 Bilateral agreements between Canada and countries other than the US 1966–70

Year	Total number of bilateral agreements between Canada and countries other than US	Exchange of notes
1966	24	8
1967	20	9
1968	16	6
1969	20	8
1970	15	5
Total	95	36 (38%)

These figures reflect the emergence of a substantial variation between Canada-US treaty practice and Canadian treaty practice vis à vis countries other than the US in the 1966–70 period. The low proportion – 38 per cent – of exchanges of notes between Canada and all countries other than the US in this period should also be compared with the far higher figure of 65 per cent for exchanges of notes between Canada and all states other than the US in the period 1947–65. If we examine the period of the early sixties we can perceive the beginnings of this definite swing away from agreements in exchange of notes form between Canada and countries other than the US, the trend becoming more prominent in the last six years. In contrast, the exchange of notes form in Canada-US treaty practice continues to predominate to an almost overwhelming degree. Whether this trend is likely to continue is difficult to predict.

AGREEMENTS

If we look at the form of the agreements that are not exchanges of notes, we find an increasing tendency to use the term 'agreement.' A bilateral agreement is usually a single document consisting of a number of articles, most commonly is not subject to ratification, and is signed by authorized representatives of the two parties. 'Agreements' normally contain final clauses about when they come into effect and terminate and whether and how they can be renewed or renounced.

In 1970 Canada entered into nine bilateral 'agreements'; in 1969, 11; in 1968, 9; in 1967, 9; in 1966, 16. Thus, out of a total of 128 bilateral agreements with all countries in the years 1966–70, 54, or somewhat over 42 per cent were called, and were drawn up in the form of, 'agreements.' If, however, we compare another active five-year period of treaty-making – 1956–60, when 134 bilateral agreements were made with all countries – we find the following annual number of treaties called agreements: 1956, 8; 1957, 6; 1958, 9; 1959, 5; 1960, 5. Thus, only a total of 33 treaties called agreements were entered into by Canada during these years, or somewhat under 25 per cent of the total number of bilateral agreements between Canada and other countries.

The head of the Economic and Treaty Section of the Department of External Affairs has commented on the use of the term 'agreement.'

> There is an increasing tendency to use the term 'agreement' as descriptive of the bilateral treaty which is not an exchange of notes. It is here where I believe simplicity, and flexibility, in Canadian practice and in the practice of a large number of Canada's treaty partners, are having the greatest effect. The usefulness of the agreement, as an international instrument establishing obligations between governments, containing the requisite language versions, lending itself to a variety of procedural requirements, including external ratification, if required, is clearly recognized. The ease of attaching annexes or appendices to such agreements, and the possibility of separate amendment procedures for annexes and appendices also lends itself to use of this form of treaty-making. In addition, the agreement, at signature, may more readily lend itself to the political visibility often favoured by governments. On the basis of present evidence I would anticipate that the use of the agreement will increase, even to the point, perhaps, of displacing the exchange of notes form of treaty-making, for the agreement can be as simple or complex as required in the individual case.

AGREEMENTS SUBJECT TO RATIFICATION: NEW TRENDS

Another curious feature of Canadian treaty-making since the end of World War II is the fact that the percentage of bilateral and multilateral treaties subject to ratification, ie treaties of a more formal character, has, contrary to what might have been expected, not been declining. Of course, there is always a partner or partners to such agreements and their constitutional requirements for ratification must also be taken into account. Thus it is difficult to generalize about the possible significance of these tendencies in the area of formal bilateral and multilateral treaty-making by Canada.

6 Bilateral treaties subject to ratification

Year	Number of bilateral agreements	Number subject to ratification
1966	31	2
1967	29	6
1968	19	2
1969	27	4
1970	22	2
Totals	128	16 (12^1/$_2$%)

7 Informal multilateral agreements 1966–70

Year	Total number of multilateral agreements	Number of formal multilateral agreements
1966	16	7
1967	16	4
1968	18	12
1969	15	6
1970	21	3
Totals	86	32 (37%)

In respect of bilateral treaties, in the period 1926–35 only about 11 per cent of Canadian treaties were subject to the ratification process or to accession, acceptance, or approval. This ratio increased to 12^1/$_2$ per cent in the decade 1936–45, went down to 7 per cent in the period 1946–55, and, surprisingly, increased to 13 per cent in the decade 1956–65.[6] Statistics for the period 1966–70 are as in Table 6. Thus, in this five-year period, approximately 12^1/$_2$ per cent of Canada's bilateral treaties were subject to ratification – the proportion of formal agreements thus remaining almost the same, although very slightly lower, than during the years 1956–65.

When multilateral agreements are examined it appears that in the decade 1926–35 approximately 69 per cent of total number of such treaties were formal, or subject to the ratification process; the percentage declined to about 43.5 per cent in 1936–45, rose to slightly over 44 per cent in the years 1946 and 1955, and increased further to approximately 51 per cent from 1956 to 1965. Thus in the multilateral area, as in the bilateral, Canadian practice showed signs of a trend towards greater formality during the late fifties and early sixties.[7] When we examine the years 1966–70 (Table 7), we can detect a substantial decline in formality in Canadian practice, a swingback to trends in the forties and fifties towards informality in multilateral treaty-making. The proportion of 37 per cent formal to the total multilateral treaties was lower, it should be noted, than in any ten-year period during the past fifty years.

It is not surprising to see the possible re-emergence of a trend towards informality in multilateral treaty-making, although it is too early to pronounce on the likelihood of such a trend continuing. Over a period of half a century informality has, in a general way, been the dominant international tendency in the multilateral field, which seems natural and logical in view of the exigencies of worldwide co-

8 Subject matter of formal bilateral treaties 1946–65[8]

Taxation and fiscal matters	17
Trade	11
Fisheries, waters, etc	6
Atomic energy	6
Air service	6
Extradition	1
Radio	1
Industrial property	1
Settlement of disputes	1

In the period 1966–70, the pattern is very similar (Table 9).

9 Subject matter of formal bilateral treaties 1966–70

Trade	5
Taxation	4
Extradition	3
Radio	2
Fisheries, waters	1
Economic cooperation	1
Culture	1
Diplomatic immunities	1

operation, increasing technicality, and the growing ambit of transnational regulation.

But it is difficult to account for what might be a reverse tendency – although again generalizations here are very hazardous – towards somewhat greater formality in bilateral treaty-making in the period 1965–70. Formality may possibly be observed in the declining use of exchange of notes in the bilateral field and in the emergence of a higher percentage of bilateral treaties subject to ratification than in late pre-World War II years. Perhaps it may be surmised that the increasing emphasis in Canadian foreign policy on the political and economic significance of strengthening and developing of Canada's bilateral relations with a wide number of countries outside of North America is reflected in this manner in the processes of its treaty-making. However, emphasis on strengthening bilateral ties is not reflected in any significant increase in this period in the total annual number of bilateral agreements. On the other hand, it is interesting to note that 1970 saw the highest number of multilateral treaties (21) ever entered into by Canada in a single year. The second highest number also appears in this period (18 in 1968), which seems to suggest an increasing level of multilateral treaty-making on the part of Canada.

SOME OTHER FEATURES OF BILATERAL TREATIES

So far as concerns both the subject matter of Canadian bilateral treaties and the identity of Canada's treaty partners, no significant new trends seem to have appeared in this same five-year period. With regard to Canada's formal bilateral treaties, the topics have remained virtually the same. In the period 1946 to 1965 Canada entered into fifty bilateral treaties subject to ratification, acceptance, approval, or confirmation in some other form. These break down as in Table 8.

These tables show the continuation of the same major trends with respect to formality of treaty-making, the main areas that Canadian treaty practice singles out
for the ratification process being trade and tax matters.

No new significant features have emerged in the period 1966–70 with respect to
the profile of Canada's treaty practices. In 1968 I listed 70 postwar treaty partners
of Canada with which Canada had between 1946–67 entered into 555 bilateral
agreements.[9] If prewar treaty partners are added, the total is 77. To that number,
should be added the Asian Development Bank, Barbados, Brazil, Singapore,
Panama, Thailand, Cameroon, and Uganda, making a total of 85 treaty partners of
Canada at end of 1970.

NEW TECHNIQUES FOR AUTHORIZING SUBSIDIARY AGREEMENTS

In *Canadian Treaty-Making*, I described the general practice, in the field of interna-
tional co-operation and aid, to adopt understandings with countries which were not
intended to be binding or which were of a contractural or private law character.
Such understandings have not appeared in the Department of External Affair's
Treaty Register or the Canada Treaty Series. Until the end of 1967 the Canadian
International Development Agency (CIDA) and its predecessor, the External Aid
Office, had entered into 68 loan agreements, 35 technical assistance agreements,
and approximately 190 memoranda of understanding on capital projects. There
were however only 4 formal treaties in this area – with India, Pakistan, Ceylon, and
the former Federation of the West Indies.[10]

An interesting development in recent practice reflects a special method for
achieving both a state of formal obligation and informal co-operation in economic
and technical matters with developing countries. This technique might possibly
have had its origins in earlier economic development agreements but appears most
similar to that used in the France-Canada cultural agreement of 17 November 1965
to which was appended an exchange of notes authorizing the provinces to enter into
ententes falling within the framework of the cultural agreement.[11] In the field of
economic co-operation the government of Canada entered into an agreement in
1970 with the government of the Federal Republic of the Cameroon for economic
and technical co-operation which provides a binding legal framework governing
several modalities of co-operation and which at the same time makes provision for
subsidiary but non-binding agreements. Article 4 of the agreement provides that 'in
pursuance of the objectives of the present Agreement, the Government of Canada
and the Government of the Federal Republic of the Cameroon, acting directly or
through their competent agencies, may in due course conclude secondary agreements, evidenced by letters, notes or memoranda in writing relating to [various
aspects of conditions of service, personal loans, subsidies, etc].' Article 6 of the
agreement then provides that 'unless the text thereof expressly states the contrary,
subsidiary agreements concluded in accordance with Article 4 of this Agreement
shall be considered to be administrative arrangements only and not formal agreements binding the Parties in international or domestic law.'[12] The Canada-
Cameroon agreement is, it may be noted, more explicit than the Canada-France cultural agreement in defining what is the legal status of subsidiary arrangements made
within the framework of the agreement. In the case of the Canada-Cameroon agree-

ment the competence is, of course, conferred not on the provinces but on federal agencies.

It remains to be seen to what extent this agreement will serve as a model for further types of umbrella arrangements between Canada and other countries for economic and technical co-operation. It seems a sensible way of underlining the importance which each country attaches to the agreement, of setting out the basic overall framework of co-operation and, at the same time, facilitating the making of detailed administrative arrangements of a less significant character between agencies of the two parties.

Canada has also sought methods for arranging administrative co-operation between the provinces and bodies or agencies of a foreign country. It is well known that Canada has pioneered the development of the technique of the *accord-cadre* and of agreements in the form of an exchange of notes to serve as an umbrella for the authorization of provincial administrative arrangements.[13] Of course, many jurisdictions in federal states enter into informal administrative arrrangements of a reciprocal character where there is no document specifying the nature of the agreement between the jurisdictions. Such types of co-operation are found, for example, in the areas of reciprocal enforcement of maintenance orders, licensing regulations, driving privileges, etc. A recent exchange of notes between Canada and the United States for forest fire protection, which has no specific precedent in Canadian practice, again shows the flexibility of Canadian treaty-making methods. On 29 January 1970 Canada and US representatives exchanged notes governing the participation by New Brunswick and Quebec in the northeastern forest fire protection compact. This agreement authorized both Quebec and New Brunswick to sign the North Eastern Interstate Forest Fire Protection Compact of 1949. Quebec adhered to the compact on 23 September 1969, four months before the federal exchange of notes; New Brunswick has not yet done so. The interstate agreement of 1949 had been authorized by an act of the United States Congress.[14]

The Canada-US exchange of notes brought out an interesting point of jurisprudence concerning Canadian practice: that the signature of the Canadian provinces presumably does not take legal effect until the date of the authorizing agreement, unless otherwise specified by the exchange of notes. In the case of the North Eastern Interstate Forest Fire Protection Compact, the US note expressly provided that 'I am also pleased to confirm that the United States Government accepts the view of the Canadian Government that, in accordance with Canadian law, the signing by these two Provinces takes effect on the date of this exchange of Notes or on the date of their signature of the Compact, whichever is the later.'

This is the first occasion on which the technique of an exchange of notes on the federal government level has been used to authorize adherence of a province to a multilateral arrangement.

TREATIES AND CONTRACTS

Another area which provides some flexibility with regard to the making of international obligations is that of international arrangements in private law. It is usually said that states are competent to enter into 'contracts' governed by an appropriate domestic law and not just international agreements governed by public international law.[15] Nevertheless, examples of this latter type of arrangement are rarely given and seem equally hard to find in Canada as well as in international practice.

A Canadian illustration is a document stated to be a 'contract' between Her Majesty the Queen in right of Canada and the State of Alaska containing a variety or stipulations about the maintenance (in the form of snow removal) of a portion of the Haines Road. Article 10 of the document provides that 'this contract shall be interpreted and the rights and obligations of the parties construed in accordance with the law of Canada and for the purpose of adjudicating any dispute arising out of this contract, Alaska will submit to the jurisdiction of a Canadian Court.' The document is signed by the deputy minister and secretary of public works of Canada and the governor of Alaska and commissioner of highways of Alaska. The Canadian agreement to this arrangement is contained in a note of 29 September 1964, dealing with snow removal on other parts of the Haines Road, which is not registered in the Department of External Affairs Register but is referred to in [1964] Canada Treaty Series No 27.

It is apparent that the distinction between a contract and a treaty may be of significance from the standpoint of federal states, as most federal constitutions do not recognize the right of the constituent parts to conclude agreements and when they are so allowed may do so only on rather stringent conditions. When legal adviser of the Department of External Affairs, I found few other examples of what were clearly contractural arrangements formally subject to private law entered into by Canadian jurisdictions.

INTERDEPARTMENTAL ARRANGEMENTS: MINISTERIAL RESPONSIBILITIES

It is also difficult to obtain evidence about the practice of government departments and agencies in the making of international arrangements. It is probable that the files of many government departments contain a substantial number of interdepartmental agreements and arrangements of a wide variety. As these are not normally regarded as creating binding international obligations they are never listed in the Treaty Register of the Department of External Affairs; nor are they ever published in the Canada Treaty Series or registered with the United Nations. When legal adviser of the Department of External Affairs, I again turned up few examples.

Accordingly *Canadian Treaty-Making* does not provide much insight into the nature, variety, or extent of this practice. The only indication I was able to obtain of the extent of interdepartmental arrangements was the list of 293 memoranda of understanding technical assistance and loan agreements entered into by the Canadian International Development Agency (CIDA) with other countries and their agencies up to the end of 1967. *Canadian Treaty-Making* also notes the great rarity in Canadian practice of the use of the exchange of notes form of agreement by departments other than External Affairs or their foreign counterparts. In fact, only three examples have been found: one involving social security, which, in fact, was an exchange of letters registered by the United Kingdom in the United Nations Treaty Series; the second involved compensation for war damage; and the third, which occurred in 1970, concerned a flight test project involving Canada and the United States.[16]

Occasionally, parliament has expressly granted authority to specific ministers to make international agreements or international regulations but this has not happened too often. An example of a specific authority to make international agreements is found in the Canada Pension Plan in which parliament authorized the minister of national health and welfare to enter in agreements with foreign governments for the making of certain reciprocal arrangements relating to the administration or operation of the Canada Pension Plan or similar laws of foreign states.[17] Authority to make international postal agreements is specifically granted by parliament to the postmaster general,[18] and power to make agreements with foreign governments for exchange of information concerning taxation of estates has been granted by parliament to the minister of national revenue.[19] The power to secure 'by international regulation or otherwise; the rights of Her Majesty in respect of Her Government of Canada in international air traffic' has been assigned to the minister of transport under the Aeronautics Act.[20] Similar powers are given to the minister of communications under the Radio Act which provides that 'the Minister shall take such action as may be necessary to secure, by international regulation or otherwise, the rights of Her Majesty in right of Canada in telecommunications matters and shall consult the Canadian Radio-Television Commission with respect to all such matters that, in her opinion, affect or concern broadcasting.'[21] A similar provision is also contained in the Department of Communications Act, which speaks more broadly of communications matters.[22] In such areas of ministerial responsibility, it is not necessarily the case that all international agreements are signed by the minister identified in the act of parliament. In respect of telecommunications matters, the minister of transport and, subsequently, the minister of communications have made international agreements; for example, the agreement between Canada and the United States for the provision of safety on the Great Lakes by means of radio, signed by the minister of transport in 1952,[23] and the International Telecommunications Union Convention of 1965, signed by the director of the Telecommunications Branch of the Department of Transport.[24] But the secretary of state for external affairs also makes such agreements; for example, the agreement between Canada and United States concerning Pre-Sunrise Operation of Certain Radio Stations.[25] A study of Canada's telecommunications agreements over the years indicates that the majority of these agreements are made by the secretary of state for external affairs or Canadian diplomatic representatives abroad.

The governor in council might also, of course, authorize any particular minister to sign an international agreement on any particular subject. This would normally be done on the advice of the secretary of state for external affairs. An example of this practice may be noted in a variety of fields. On 29 October 1968 the minister of industry, trade and commerce signed at Caracas, a Reciprocal Amateur Radio Operating Agreement between the government of Canada and the government of Caracas.[26] An agreement of 24 April 1970 between the government of Canada and the government of the United States on Reciprocal Fishing Privileges in certain areas off their coasts was signed for Canada by the deputy minister of fisheries.[27]

In cases where an order in council is issued on the advice of the secretary of state for external affairs authorizing another minister or departmental representative to sign an agreement, whether or not such minister or department has statutory responsibilities, there is full co-operation between the Department of External Affairs and the other department involved to ensure that the forms of the agreement and all related documents conform to proper international practice and that, so far as the substance of the agreement is concerned, all requisite steps have been taken to ensure its conformity with Canadian foreign policies. Canadian practice here, as in other fields, reflects both the flexibility and adaptability of Canadian treaty methods.

When agreements are made by ministers or representatives of departments which have the express authority of parliament to enter into such agreements, the instruments are normally binding in international law. The authority to sign by a minister is usually by order in council signed or co-signed by the secretary of state for external affairs and the agreement is usually listed in the Department of External Affairs Treaty Register, although it may not be published in the Canada Treaty Series. Canada's postal agreements, for example, which are made by or under the authority of the postmaster general, are rarely listed in Canada's Treaty Series, although information about them can be obtained from the department's Treaty Register.

Given the international competence or responsibility of a specific minister of the crown, it is to be expected that the departments or agencies for which they are responsible would from time to time have occasion to enter into less formal international arrangements. But it is very likely that such arrangements are also entered into by departments and agencies which do not have specific grants of authority by parliament to conclude international agreements. Very few government departments or agencies have responsibilities which do not involve some area of international co-operation and there is no doubt that many, if not most, agencies make arrangements with representatives of entities of foreign jurisdictions both at the senior and working level. These are commonly of a routine administrative type. In saying that such agreements are of an administrative character it should not, however, be thought that they are necessarily lacking either in political or policy significance. The use by government departments of exchanges of letters between officials signifies less the absence of political importance than the desire to avoid binding arrangements and the need for flexibility and speed of response. But major new directions in departmental policies in specific areas would not normally be reflected in working level exchanges of letters.

CANADIAN PRACTICE IN THE FIELD OF TELECOMMUNICATIONS:
INTERDEPARTMENTAL ARRANGEMENTS[28]

Analysis of the practices of the Department of Transport when it was responsible for telecommunications matters and more recently of the Department of Communications reveals the variety of circumstances in which interdepartmental agreements and arrangements may be made. It also reveals the different techniques involved, with their varying degree of informality.

The government of Canada might, of course, enter into agreements of a fully binding character in the field of telecommunications. As previously noted such agreements may be signed by the secretary of state for external affairs or members of his department or the minister of communications or his representatives. Of course, such agreements may or may not be subject to ratification.

Another binding method of treaty-making which is, however, of a less formal character is the signature of a memorandum of understanding between departments or agencies covered by an exchange of notes. The memorandum of understanding governs the detailed modalities of co-operation and is then made an annex to the exchange of notes. Thus the interagency agreement is enshrined in a more formal and hence, in a sense, more political context and, at the same time, is given international legal effect. The technique of an exchange of notes between diplomatic representatives of Canada and the United States was used on 6 May 1964 to cover the Memorandum of Understanding between the Canadian Defence Research Board and the United States National Aeronautics and Space Association, dated 23 December 1963, concerning the Alouette–ISIS ionospheric monitoring program.[29] This technique was also used in notes of 21 April and 27 April 1971 to embrace the Memorandum of Understanding between the Canadian Department of Communications and the United States National Aeronautics and Space Association, dated 20 April 1971, concerning co-operation in an experimental communications technology satellite for launching into geostationary orbit.[30]

Having regard to the subject matter of the arrangement and to the need to meet specific time requirements, a department might enter into an interdepartmental or interagency arrangement which is not binding under international law and is not published in the Canada Treaty Series or maintained in the Treaty Register of the Department of External Affairs. Nevertheless for reasons of simplicity of presentation, the arrangement might be drawn up in the form of articles and contained in a single document. This is the case in connection with the Memorandum of Understanding between the Office de Radiodiffusion-Télévision Française and the Canada Department of Communications which was signed in Paris in a French and English version on 5 November 1971. This document, which relates to the allotment and utilization of television channels of St Pierre and Miquelon and neighbouring parts of Canada, is a highly complex instrument of twenty-one pages containing a considerable amount of statistical data.

A further example of the use of the memorandum of understanding is the arrangement dated 22 August 1962 between the deputy minister of transport and the commandant of the United States Coast Guard concerning the co-ordination of the Marine Radio Beacons of Canada and the United States. This memorandum is somewhat less structured than the memorandum between the Office de Radiodiffusion–Télévision Française and the Department of Communications although in some ways it follows similar lines.

Some points of practice should be pointed out. The memorandum of understanding concerning Marine Radio Beacons came into effect 22 August 1962, but it was signed at dates several months apart by representatives of the two agencies. The memorandum was signed by the Coast Guard on 18 April 1962 and for the Department of Transport on 22 August 1962. It should also be noted that this document replaced another document entitled the 'General Principles Recommended for the Coordination of the Marine Radio Beacons of the United States and Canada' agreed upon by representatives of the Canada Department of Marine and the Lighthouse Service, Department of Commerce, United States, in 1935 and revised in 1939. This indicates that the practice of interdepartmental arrangements, so far as Canada is concerned, is indeed of long standing. An additional feature of interest is that the memorandum of understanding concerning the co-ordination of radio beacons contains no final clauses while the later memorandum between the Department of Communications and the Office de Radiodiffusion-Télévision Française concerning frequency co-ordination in the areas of St Pierre and Miquelon contains a final clause specifying the duration in force of the agreement, the fact that it can be renewed by tacit agreement or denounced.

There are also several examples of interagency arrangements in the form of exchange of letters – the most informal method available to departments and agencies. One such example is an exchange of letters dated 20 June 1960 and 2 September 1960 between the director of the Telecommunications Electronics Branch of the Canadian Department of Transport and the acting secretary of the Federal Communications Commission in Washington concerning frequency plans for the railroad radio service in the United States and Canada. Another example of a non-binding international arrangement is an exchange of letters between the assistant deputy minister, Canadian Department of Communications, dated 10 December 1969 and a letter from the chairman of the federal Communications Commission in Washington, which appears to be undated but was received on 20 January 1970, concerning principles for the co-ordination of the proposed maritime mobile use of UHF channels excluded from arrangement (A) in the US-Canada co-ordination agreement for frequencies above 30 mc/s. In this case an annex is attached to the Canadian letter which is described as 'principles of Federal Communications Commission-Department of Communications Understanding etc.'

A further example is an exchange of letters between the director general Telecommunications Regulation Branch, Department of Communications, dated 9 August and the chief engineer of the Federal Communications Commission dated 20 August 1971, concerning principles relating to provision of transborder radio paging services by Canadian and US licensees. In this instance, the Canadian letter specifies that, together with an earlier Federal Communications Commission letter on 25 June, it might constitute an 'informal agreement.'

It may be seen from this outline of the ways in which federal government departments enter into international arrangements that there is a wide variety of methods which can be used ranging from formal agreements binding in international law to very informal methods with no legal standing. It would be desirable for such arrangements to be collected in a central source in the federal government and, at least where no national security arrangements are involved, made available to members of the public. Until that time no definitive assessment of the extent of Canadian practice in the making of interdepartmental and interagency agreements can be made.

CONCLUSION

A review of Canadian practice in various areas of Canadian involvement in the making of international agreements confirms the difficulty of perceiving any broad or uniform trends during the past few years in respect of the forms of concluding international agreements and arrangements. There is a continuation of the major thrust of Canadian practice over the past fifty years of developing new informal and flexible methods for enabling bilateral and multilateral international agreements to be made quickly and effectively, but there also appears to be a tendency, evident in very recent practice, to attach new value or importance to certain formalities in the bilateral treaty-making process.

There is substantial evidence that a number of departments and agencies of the federal government make many international agreements with counterpart bodies in other countries. Where such agreements are binding in international law, the authority is usually derived from an act of parliament and there is full consultation with the secretary of state for external affairs and his department whose legal authority is also involved as part of the process of authorization. Many departments also make interdepartmental arrangements which are not binding in international law. There is a wide variety of methods for making such arrangements, with their own varying degrees of formality. Not enough is known about such arrangements to determine the full extent of the practice or whether it is growing. These practices again reflect the flexibility of Canadian methods of entering into international agreements.

NOTES

1 A.E. Gotlieb, *Canadian Treaty-Making* (1968) 84.
2 Ibid, 57.
3 Throughout this chapter the information concerning Canada's treaties in the period 1966–70 is taken from the annual reports of the Department of External Affairs for the years 1966, 1967, 1968, 1960, 1970.
4 All statistics are taken from Gotlieb, *supra* note 1.
5 See note 4.
6 Gotlieb, *supra* note 1, at 51–4.
7 Ibid, at 51.
8 Ibid, at 58–9.
9 Ibid, at 60–1.
10 Ibid, at 63.
11 Signed at Ottawa, 17 November 1965; in force 6 December 1965; [1965] CAN. T. S. no 21.
12 Agreement on Economic and Technical Co-operation between the Government of Canada and the Government of the Federal Republic of Cameroon, signed at Toronto, 15 September 1970. Provisionally in force as of 15 September 1970.
13 Gotlieb, *supra* note 1, at 22–32.
14 See 63 US Statutes 271 and 66 US Statutes 71. The Canada-US agreement is set out in an exchange of notes between Canada and the US concerning Participation by New Brunswick and Quebec in the North Eastern Interstate Forest Fire Protection Compact, done in Washington, 29 January 1970, in force 29 January 1970. [1970] CAN. T. S. no 3.
15 See International Law Commission commentary to article 2 (paragraph 6 of commentary) General Assembly Official Records 21st Session, supp 9 (a) – 6309 rev 1; also, D.P. O'Connell, 1 *International Law,* (1965) 224;

and Gotlieb, *supra* note 1, at 24.
16 Gotlieb, *supra* note 1, at 33, footnote 14.
17 Sec 109(1) of the Canada Pension Plan, 1964–5, Can., c 51.
18 Under the Post office Act, R.S.C. s 5(1)(j) (1970), the postmaster general may 'make and give effect to any postal agreement or arrangement with the government or postal authorities of any country or independent postal administration.'
19 1958, Can., c 29, s 56(2).
20 Aeronautics Act, R.S.C. s 3(h) (1970).
21 Radio Act, R.S.C. s 8(i) (1970).
22 R.S.C. s 5(f) (1970).
23 Signed at Ottawa 2 February 1952; instruments of ratification exchanged and in force 13 November 1954 [1952] CAN. T. S. no 25. For a further list of treaties in the area of telecommunications, together with information about signatures, see Telecommission Study 3(a), 'International Implications of Telecommunications: The Role of Canada in Intelsat and other Relevant International Organizations' (1971).
24 Signed at Montreux, 12 November 1965; entered into force January 1967.
25 Exchange of notes of 31 March and 12 June 1967 [1967] CAN. T. S. no 11.
26 Signed at Caracas, 29 October 1968. Entered into force, 13 November 1968 [1968] CAN. T. S. no 13.
27 [1970] CAN. T. S. no 9.
28 For a record of Canada's treaties in the field of telecommunications, see the Department of Communications Study 3(a), *supra* note 23.
29 [1964] CAN. T. S. no 6.
30 Agreement signed 21 and 27 April 1971.

L.C. GREEN

11/Immigration, Extradition, and Asylum in Canadian Law and Practice

From the point of view of the individual and of the state the problems of immigration, extradition, and asylum are almost inextricably interwoven. The individual coming from abroad seeks to be admitted as an immigrant to the country of his choice, hoping that the country in question will not extradite or deport him to a country to which he does not wish or is afraid to go, and will instead grant him asylum allowing him to stay as long as he wishes. In this statement, terms which enjoy a particular meaning in law have in fact been used in a general and completely untechnical fashion.

IMMIGRATION, EXTRADITION, AND ASYLUM IN INTERNATIONAL LAW

General principles

Nationality and immigration
According to international law, states are exclusively competent over matters concerning their internal affairs and falling within their domestic jurisdiction, subject to limitations in accordance with customary or conventional international law. In the absence of such limitations, international law concedes that states have authority to decide whom they admit into their territory and the requirements that such persons must fulfil before being admitted, so long as such requirements are applied on a non-discriminatory basis as between the nationals of different states. However, some discriminatory situations do exist. Since international law allows states to regulate their own nationality legislation,[1] provided certain minimum requirements are satisfied,[2] it may well happen that so far as a particular state is concerned some people are counted as nationals and entitled to immigration rights, even though they are also considered to be nationals of other countries with which they might even have closer ties. This situation is perhaps most clearly illustrated in the case of the British Commonwealth, for by the 1948 British Nationality Act[3] the citizens of all Commonwealth countries are *ipso facto* British subjects;[4] hence, until the enactment of restrictive legislation[5] directed at reducing the number of Commonwealth citizens from overseas entering Britain and claiming a right of permanent residence, all such persons were automatically entitled to immigrate into Britain and were entitled to exercise all the rights of British subjects. Moreover, for historical reasons, certain persons now classified as aliens may enjoy a right of immigration not possessed by the majority of aliens. This is the case with citizens of Eire seeking to enter the United Kingdom, for, bearing in mind the links that existed between Britain and Southern Ireland before the establishment of the

republic and the extent to which the Irish economy and labour force were interwoven with those of England, it was decided that while the Irish were not British they would not be treated as aliens.[6]

It is not only in accordance with a particular municipal law that an apparently discriminatory position is created in favour of particular aliens granting them the right of immigration. By virtue of the multilateral treaties which set up the European Community,[7] mobility of labour has been decreed among the labour forces of the member countries,[8] thus giving their nationals entry rights which are not extended to others. In fact, among the objections that have been raised to British entry into the Common Market by some British critics is the contention that by virtue of such membership aliens from Europe will now be in a better position with regard to immigration and labour permits than are Commonwealth citizens.

Since the right of immigration is discretionary and states may grant it on such terms as they please, it is not granted to those who are considered 'undesirable.' Undesirability may depend on matters relating to the individual as such; thus immigration regulations may forbid the entry of persons suffering from certain diseases or whose general health is such that the local state considers it deleterious to public welfare to allow them in. Also, the moral record of the applicant may be of a kind not considered conducive to the public good; at the present moment, many countries are exercising their right to exclude on this ground 'hippies,' drug addicts, and the like. Among aliens most regularly denied the right of immigration are those who possess criminal records, although states differ as to the crimes which are considered as constituting disqualifications for this purpose; few states, for example, will regard motoring offences as being sufficient. Particulary in times of economic stress, countries of immigration have tended to exclude those who are indigent or so unskilled that they are unlikely to secure gainful employment and are therefore potential burdens on the economy.

Undesirability may also be dependent upon local conditions within the state to which immigration is sought and the impact of large-scale immigration upon that state, even though there is no reason of a personal character to deny immigration to certain immigrants. This may be the result of xenophobia on the part of local inhabitants, or sometimes it results from an unwillingness on the part of the immigrant state to take any step which might aggravate its relations with the emigrant state. More usually, such steps are taken because the number of immigrant applicants, or their desire to settle as a group within a defined locality, is such as to give ground for fear that the economy of the state or the district concerned may be jeopardized. This type of problem becomes important when entry is sought by large numbers emigrating from one state, usually on account of political or religious persecution, or bad economic conditions therein; or because, as with Asian inhabitants of certain African countries, the local government is no longer prepared to afford them residence or work permits, even though they may have been born in the territory before it achieved its independence.

Thus, while Pufendorf, one of the great 'fathers' of international law writing at the end of the seventeenth century, was of opinion that 'humanity engages us to receive a small number of Men, expelled from their Home, not for their own Demerit and Crime, especially if they are eminent for Wealth or Industry, and not likely to disturb our Religion or our Constitution,' he nevertheless pointed out that

> no one will be fond of asserting, that we ought in the same manner to receive and incor-
> porate a great Multitude ... since it is scarce possible, but that their Admission should
> highly endanger the Natives. Therefore every State may be more free or more cautious
> in granting these Indulgences, as it shall judge proper for its Interest and Safety. In order
> to which Judgment, it will be prudent to consider, whether a great increase in the Number
> of Inhabitants will turn to Advantage; whether the Country be fertile enough to feed so
> many Mouths; whether upon Admission of this new Body, we shall be strained for room;
> whether the Men are industrious, or idle, whether they may be so conveniently placed
> and disposed, as to render them incapable of giving any Jealousy to the Government. If
> on the whole, it appears that the Persons deserve our Favour and Pity, and that no Re-
> straint lies on us from good Reasons of State, it will be an Act of Humanity to confer
> such a Benefit on them, as we shall not feel very Burthensome at present, nor are likely
> to repent of hereafter. If the Case be otherwise, we ought to temper our Pity with Pru-
> dence, as not to put ourselves in the ready way of becoming Objects of Pity unto others.[9]

It is not surprising that most states refuse to grant immigration rights to applicants with a criminal record. Many countries when questioning potential immigrants inquire about their past records and indicate that entry will be denied to those who have been found guilty of certain crimes, while others refuse to admit persons who may be considered morally rather than legally corrupt. Further, the discretion enjoyed by a state enables it to expel an alien who it finds, subsequent to his entry, has in fact been guilty of some action which, had this been known in advance, would have warranted a denial of entry. It is but a short step from this to acceding in the request from another country for the expulsion or return of one whom the applicant state would like to have in its custody.

Extradition

Since all states profess to be interested in the need for the suppression of crime,[10] at least the more serious types, and since all nowadays pay lip service to their belief in the supremacy of the rule of law, it is perhaps not surprising that customary techniques have developed whereby a state, whose criminal law has been offended, is enabled to recover the alleged offender even though he has departed from its juris-diction. In the absence of any treaty requiring such surrender, the decision will be made purely in accordance with the discretion of the host state, subject to any municipal legal requirements which may have been enacted; while it may be an unfriendly act to deny such a request, there is in customary international law no obligation upon the receiving state to comply with it.

It may happen that a country will not surrender its own nationals, a practice that is believed to have stemmed from the relations of France and the Low Countries.[11] In Roman days Romans were surrendered if their offence was directed against foreign ambassadors, even though the offence was committed in Rome;[12] and if any ally of Rome complained of the conduct of a Roman citizen, the *Feciales* would investigate the complaint and, if true, had power to hand the offender to the com-plainant.[13] Likewise, a country may deny extradition – 'the act by which one nation delivers up an individual, accused or convicted of an offence outside of its own territory, to another nation which demands him, and which is competent to try and punish him,'[14] normally because the offence has actually been committed within its territory[15] – because the alleged offender is amenable to its own jurisdiction and it proposes trying him itself, as would be the case, for example, with pirates *jure gentium*.[16] It may also happen that the country to which the request for surrender has been made does not consider the offence sufficiently grave to warrant such extreme action,[17] or does not consider that any offence at all has been committed,[18] or regards the proposed penalty as contrary to its own public policy.[19] Surrender may also be denied because it is felt that the fugitive would be denied a fair trial,[20] because there is fear that he may in fact be wanted for some other offence for which his extradition would have been denied,[21] because of a fear that the risk involved in not punishing the fugitive was less than the risk of his being subjected to inhumane treatment if extradition were granted,[22] or because it was suspected that his return was required in order to subject him to political rather than legal justice.[23] In such cases, however, the state of refuge may rid itself of undesirables by using the process of expulsion[24] or by denying entry when it is requested.[25]

Asylum

When there appears to be some ground for believing that a fugitive is likely to be persecuted for political or religious reasons if he is returned to his own state, even if the country of refuge declines to keep him, there is a growing tendency not to return him to that state but, in accordance with the doctrine of *non-refoulement*,[26] to allow him to name the country to which he would like to go. This is in conformity with the general principle that persons accused of political offences should be afforded asylum, as also should non-criminal fugitives claiming the same privilege. In fact, the Universal Declaration of Human Rights,[27] having proclaimed in article 2 that 'everyone is entitled to all the rights and freedoms set forth in this Declaration, without distinction of any kind, such as race, colour, sex, language, religion, political or other opinion, national or social origin, property, birth or other status,' goes on to provide in article 14 that 'everyone has the right to seek and to enjoy in other countries asylum from persecution.' Recognizing, however, that in customary law the grant of immigration rights is purely discretionary, the declaration makes no attempt to impose an *obligation* on any state to grant asylum. Even the General Assembly resolution known as the Declaration on Asylum[28] provides in its first article that 'it shall rest with the state granting asylum to evaluate the grounds for the grant of asylum ... [which is] granted by a state in the exercise of its sovereignty,' while the International Covenant on Civil and Political Rights,[29] drawn up and adopted by the United Nations in 1967 and the only document which purports to impose legal obligations, makes no reference whatever to any right of asylum.

While there is no obligation in international law for any state to grant asylum, there is nothing to stop it from making such a grant if it so wills.[30] Some states, in fact, have gone so far as to embody a right to asylum in their constitutions, and such provisions may be found in the constitutions of countries of varying political ideology; clauses of this kind are to be found in, for example, the constitutions of the Soviet Union (1936), the German Federal Republic (1949), the Chinese People's Republic (1954), Venezuela (1961), and the United Arab Republic (1964).[31] The

Soviet and Chinese provisions reflect the political character of the state, for the former 'affords the right of asylum to foreign citizens persecuted for defending the interests of the working people, or for scientific activities, or for struggling for national liberation,' and the latter 'grants the right of asylum to any foreign national persecuted for supporting a just cause, taking part in the peace movement or engaging in scientific activity'; similar clauses are to be found in the constitutions of the other people's republics. The constitutions of non-communist states are phrased far less specifically and are apparently open to all who may be seeking asylum. However, since the determination of who is a political fugitive is to be made in the case of an offender by the courts and in the case of a refugee by the administration, it frequently happens that only persons whose political allegiances are sympathetic to or approved by the state of refuge are the ones to receive asylum – unless, although politically opposed to that state, the fugitive is seeking asylum from a country which is the refuge state's ideological antagonist, and it is believed that the defection of the fugitive is likely to have some propaganda or other advantage. The years since the end of World War II have witnessed many such examples in the practice of countries both east and west of the iron curtain, perhaps the leading example being the asylum granted to a Soviet agent whose disclosures led to the expulsion of more than one hundred Soviet representatives from the United Kindom.[32]

Political considerations

General
Normally speaking, states do not envisage being faced with requests for asylum against countries or governments with which they are allied or politically sympathetic.[33] It is perhaps not surprising, therefore, that there is no reference to asylum in the European Convention on Human Rights of 1950.[34] It is interesting to note that in 1971 the European Commission on Human Rights was faced with allegations that the British refusal to allow entry to Kenyan Asians who were at the same time British nationals was a breach of the convention. Since the Fourth Protocol of 1963,[35] which provides in article 3(2) that 'no one shall be deprived of the right to enter the territory of the State of which he is a national,' has never come into force, the allegations were based on specific articles of the parent convention. It was alleged[36] that denial of a permanent right of residence constituted breaches of articles 3 (degrading treatment), 14 (discrimination), 5 (security of the person), and 8 (respect for private and family life, since some of those denied entry already had families resident in the United Kingdom) – hardly the basis for asserting a legal right to immigration.

There is no reason why states should not recognize that fugitives might be political offenders or refugees from a friendly government. Revolution is a common phenomenon in Latin America and is becoming increasingly so in Africa, and attempts have been made to institutionalize the concept of asylum in a regional fashion. Thus, the Latin American countries have entered into a number of conventions whereby they have extended the concept of asylum from the territorial to the diplomatic level;[37] that is, for those who have accepted the obligation the territorial government agrees to recognize asylum extended by a Latin American diplomat in his embassy, with the concomitant undertaking to provide safe conduct to enable the refugees to depart. Normally speaking, such asylum tends to be extended only to leading local political figures.[38] Despite the long practice of the states concerned in this matter, in the *Asylum* case[39] between Colombia and Peru the International Court of Justice adopted an approach which tended to deny any legal obligation either to grant or to recognize such asylum:

> The Court cannot admit that the States signatory to the Havana Convention intended to substitute for the practice of the Latin-American Republics, in which *considerations of courtesy, good-neighbourliness and political expediency* have always played a prominent place, a legal system which would guarantee to their own nationals accused of political offences the privilege of evading national jurisdiction. Such a conception, moreover, would come into conflict with one of the most firmly established traditions of Latin-America, namely non-intervention. [Emphasis added.]

It is interesting to note that the judges from Brazil, Chile, and Colombia dissented from this judgment.

The dispute in this case was not so much about the grant of asylum itself, as about the right of the ambassador unilaterally to qualify as 'political' the offence with which the fugitive was charged. This problem was settled, for those states (not including Peru) ratifying it, by the Caracas Convention, which stipulated that 'it shall rest with the State granting asylum to determine the nature of the offence or the motive for the prosecution'; however, the value of the convention is somewhat vitiated by article 2 which states that 'every state has the right to grant asylum, [but] it is not obliged to do so or to state its reasons for refusing it.' The American Convention on Human Rights,[40] which was signed by twelve Central and South American states[41] in 1969, does not carry the matter any further; once again the right to receive asylum is conceded, but no obligation to grant it is created, although the principle of *non-refoulement* is accepted. Article 22 is concerned with freedom of movement and residence, and while it does not grant a right of entry it does attempt to forbid arbitrary expulsion of aliens lawfully present; expulsion is allowed only 'pursuant to a decision reached in accordance with law,' which may presumably be by administrative decree. It goes on to provide that

> 7 Every person has the right to seek and be granted asylum in a foreign territory, *in accordance with the legislation of the state* and international conventions, in the event he is being pursued for political offenses or related common crimes.
> 8 *In no case may an alien be deported or returned to a country,* regardless of whether or not it is his country of origin, *if* in that country *his right to life or personal freedom is in danger of being violated because of his race, nationality, religion, social status, or political opinions.* [Emphasis added.]

The question of who determines the nature of the offence is also dealt with in the 1971 Canadian-United States Extradition Treaty: 'If any question arises as to whether a case comes within the provisions of [the] subparagraph ... [concerning political offences], the authorities of the Government [*quaere* courts] on which the requisition is made shall decide.'

Political sympathy is perhaps most clearly evident when examining the fashion in which African states exercise their discretion with regard to asylum. Despite their common membership in the Organization of African Unity, Guinea did not hesitate to grant hospitality to Nkrumah after his overthrow in Ghana, while Tanzania gives asylum to Obote and apparently still regards him as president of Uganda. On the other hand, Lybia did not hesitate to interfere with the international flight of a scheduled British aircraft in order to take off and surrender to the Sudanese government the named president of what appeared to be a successful coup d'état.

This latter action is similar to the practice of some communist states which have been willing to promote the 'international solidarity of the working class.'[42] Thus, in November 1962 Wynne, a British businessman, was arrested in the streets of Budapest and handed over to the Soviet Union where he was tried and sentenced for espionage; he was stated to have been handed over in accordance with a Soviet-Hungarian extradition agreement[43] with regard to persons accused of committing crimes which were offences in both countries, although there is no evidence to suggest that there was ever any judicial process in Hungary before the extradition was effected.[44] It should be borne in mind that, as the *Eisler* case has shown,[45] the fugitive need only be passing through the state from which extradition is requested. In that case there was no extradition agreement between either the United Kingdom or the United States and eastern Germany, any more that there was an extradition treaty between the United Kingdom and the Soviet Union.

The political relationship that exists between some states has led to the suggestion that both sides in a worldwide confrontation might well be justified in pursuing a policy of not affording asylum.[46]

> At the present time an act of espionage or some other political offence on behalf of the Soviet Union or any of the Communist States against a non-Communist State is a threat to the security of such a State on behalf of that State's potential enemy. Further, in view of the commitments under such agreements as NATO, CENTO and SEATO, as well as the 'inherent right of self-defence' on an individual or collective basis, recognised in the Charter of the United Nations, such a threat is also a threat to all other democratic States. This is especially so when the State in which the fugitive is claiming refuge is an ally of the country from which he is in flight. Further, from the point of view of the State of refuge, the State on behalf of which the offence has been committed is its potential enemy too. In view of this, it is carrying concepts of liberalism too far to expect such a State to give asylum to the fugitive. The time may be ripe for democratic countries to amend their criminal law so as to grant jurisdiction to their courts to try offences directed against the security of their allies. If this be considered too revolutionary, then extradition treaties may have to be amended so as to limit the exception in respect of political offences to afford no protection to one who, in view of his political affiliations, had he been in the State of refuge might have committed the offence there; or in respect of an offence committed on behalf of a foreign power and aimed either immediately or indirectly against the safety of the State of refuge. Until such amendments have been made, States may have no option but to pursue a policy of exclusion, involving the return of the undesirable alien to the country from which he has come, usually that which is seeking to prosecute him.

Such a policy was followed by the United Kingdom with Soblen and by Canada with Paterson.[47]

War criminals

Shortly after World War II some allied countries, in connection with the extradition of alleged war criminals, adopted an attitude which had much in common with that just suggested. Thus, in the *Extradition of Greek Nationals (Germany)* case,[48] the German Federal Supreme Court granted the extradition of a Greek national who claimed that the offences which he was alleged to have committed in Greece in 1944 were political, and that he was thus protected by the asylum clause in the federal constitution. The court did not consider that this clause in any way conflicted with article 3 of the German Extradition Law, 1925,[49] which permitted extradition in respect of an offence, which would *prima facie* be a political offence, if it 'constitutes a deliberate offence [*Verbrechen*] against life, unless committed in open combat.' Similarly, in *Re Spiessens*[50] the French Cour d'Appel at Nancy had to consider a Belgian request for extradition of a national charged with collaborating with the enemy in both Belgium and France. The court stated:

> Collaboration with the enemy is not considered by French legislation or judicial decisions to be a political offence. Moreover, in time of war, in a country occupied by the enemy, collaboration with the latter excludes the idea of a criminal action against the political organisation of the State which characterises the offence. These considerations lead us to include collaboration with the enemy amongst common crimes, particularly when, as in the present case, the offence was committed in time of war *both against an ally and against France, whose interests were linked.* [Emphasis added.]

A similar judgment had been delivered two years earlier by the Cour d'Appel, Paris, in *Re Colman*,[51] but without any suggestion that the offender had committed any offences in or against France. There is a similar dictum to be found in the decision of a United States Circuit Court of Appeals in *Chandler v United States:*[52] 'An asylum State might, for reasons of policy, surrender a fugitive political offender – for example, *a State might choose to turn over to a wartime ally a traitor who had given aid and comfort to their common enemy*' [emphasis added]. This attitude is also seen in the commentary of the draftsmen of the Harvard Draft Convention on Extradition[53] explaining why their article on political offences was expressed in a permissive and not a compulsive form: 'There is no reason why a State should be precluded from surrendering, if it so chooses, a person sought for a political offence. It may well be that some States because of close association or because of the close similarity of their political institutions, would find the extradition of political offenders desirable.'

It should also be mentioned that war criminals have long been the subject of specific international agreements. As long ago as 1661 and 1662, Charles II made treaties with Denmark and the States-General whereby the latter undertook to surrender the regicides.[54] More recently the members of the United Nations entered into a number of mutual undertakings, both during World War II and after, whereby they agreed to surrender war criminals to each other and to refuse to give them asylum.[55]

Hijackers

Under the impact of the spate of aerial hijackings experienced in the late sixties, the majority of the countries of the world, regardless of their ideologies, undertook in the 1970 Convention for the Suppression of Unlawful Seizure of Aircraft[56] to amend their laws so as to deny asylum to any hijacker, to prosecute him themselves[57] if he is not extradited, to amend all their extradition treaties so as to include hijacking as an extraditable offence, and to include it similarly in all future treaties. Moreover, the convention provides that countries which make extradition dependent upon a pre-existing treaty may, at their option, treat the convention as the basis for acting on a request from a contracting party with which no other extradition treaty exists. At the same time, however, the convention reserves all the local legal requirements in regard to extradition, and so presumably leaves open the possibility for a hijacker to contend that his act was indeed political and that he is therefore protected from extradition by local legal requirements.

Even before the convention came into force Canada was seeking to bring its principles into operation by means of bilateral arrangements, as in the case of her discussions with Cuba.[58] In her 1971 Extradition Treaty with the United States,[59] Canada extended her territorial scope to include her airspace and aircraft registered in Canada even when in flight, defined as the time between 'the moment when power is applied for the purpose of the take-off until the moment when the landing run ends,' thus including flight over the high seas. The treaty also includes offences directed against the passengers or crew of one of her aircraft, or offences on board an aircraft if the aircraft landed within her territory with the alleged offender still on board. Further, the schedule of extraditable offences attached to the treaty expressly includes 'any unlawful seizure or exercise of control of an aircraft by force or violence or threat of force or violence, or by any other form of intimidation, on board such aircraft.' This treaty requires ratification, however, and an amendment of the Criminal Code was needed to make the clause in the convention effective.

Summary

It would appear that customary international law imposes no obligation upon any state to grant entry to any person seeking it, although it has generally been understood that states will not refuse to admit their own nationals, except in the case of the British Commonwealth Immigrants Acts, which deviate from this practice. As a concomitant to their discretion in the field of immigration, states are also entitled to expel whomever they like but, in the absence of a treaty, are under no obligation to return any person to another state requesting his surrender, regardless of the reasons for the request. Since states are under no obligation to surrender those within their territorial limits, they are equally free to determine whether they will extend asylum to fugitives, whether from justice or persecution, and to determine the conditions upon which such asylum will be granted. Nowadays, the majority of states have entered into treaty relations regulating the basis on which requests for extradition will be satisfied. Normally speaking, such grants will be made only if the alleged offence is contrary to the law of both states and provided that there is *prima facie* evidence for the fugitive to stand trial, that he is to be tried only for the offence for which he is surrendered, that the offence with which he is charged is listed as an extraditable offence in the treaty, and, for those countries whose law so requires, that the offence is also listed in the legislation regulating the application of extradition processes. In most treaties there is a reservation on behalf of those alleged to have committed political offences, but there is nothing compulsive to this effect and the definition of whether the offence is political or not rests with the courts before which the extradition proceedings have been launched. In view of this, there is no rule of law which forbids a country from stating that particular offences, or offences committed against particular countries, will not be regarded as political and will not therefore be so protected. In some cases, as with war criminals and aerial hijackers, such a provision may be embodied in a multilateral treaty. If asylum is claimed by a refugee on racial or political grounds it is for the state to which the claim has been addressed to decide whether such asylum will be extended. For countries which recognize the legality of diplomatic asylum, there is some doubt whether the diplomat granting such asylum is alone competent to decide that the refugee is in fact a political fugitive.

Since the whole basis on which extradition and asylum rest is discretionary or, at most, contractual, it is not possible to lay down any specific statement and describe that as constituting the law on the subject. As a result, there is nothing contrary to international law for a state, in the absence of an extradition treaty or, if such a treaty exists, if it is felt that the normal processes would not serve a political purpose and the country of refuge wishes to satisfy the country of request, to declare an applicant an undesirable and to refuse him entry. All one can say of the practice of any particular country is that it does or does not coincide with what is generally regarded as international practice in these matters, bearing in mind that, in the absence of treaty, 'the giving up of criminals, fugitives from justice, is agreed and understood to be a matter in which every nation regulates its conduct according to its own discretion. It is no breach of comity to refuse such surrender.'[60] On the other hand, there may well be substance in the suggestion of Lord Brougham that a general obligation *should* exist for the mutual surrender of fugitive offenders as between neighbouring countries:

> He thought the interests of justice required, and the rights of good neighbourhood required, that in two countries bordering upon one another, as the United States and Canada ... there ought to be laws on both sides giving power, under due regulations and safeguards, to each government to secure persons who have committed offences in the territory of one and taken refuge in the territory of the other.[61]

IMMIGRATION, EXTRADITION, AND ASYLUM IN CANADIAN MUNICIPAL LAW

Immigration and deportation

General principles
From what has been said it is evident that *prima facie* the regulation of immigration, extradition, and asylum depends on the municipal law of the country to which the applicant is seeking entry. This principle may be limited or conditioned by treaty, but to the extent that there is no treaty provision dealing with a matter, it is munici-

pal and not international law which governs. An early statement of this principle in the field of immigration is found in the comments of Secretary of State Frelinghuysen in February 1883 when refusing a request for the surrender of an escaped convict put forward by the Portuguese minister:

> The immigration act[s] of March 3, 1875, and of August 3, 1882, authorize the return of foreign convicts to the country to which they belong and from which they come. Construed as a whole, the intent of the act clearly is that persons of the described classes shall not be permitted to land in the United States, but shall be returned at the expense of the vessel which brought them. As the act does not take the place of a convention of extradition, the responsibility of the Secretary ... is necessarily limited to preventing the landing of the persons who come within the prohibition. His obligation is not an international one, but domestic.[62]

More recently the Israeli minister for the interior has made a somewhat similar remark, pointing out that he interpreted the Law of the Return to mean that Israel was open to any Jew wishing to live a Jewish life, religious or cultural: 'Israel was established for any Jew who was hounded as a Jew. If anyone is hounded as a criminal and not because he shares my religion, nationality, history and destiny, it's a different matter.' He said that each case would be decided on its own merits, indicating that it would be for the minister to decide whether the individual would be allowed to remain either as a tourist or an immigrant.[63] Indeed, speaking generally, in any case in which the minister concerned exercises his discretion to deny an applicant's wish to stay, the question of the finality of that decision or the possibility of an appeal against it will depend solely upon the local law.

Any country's policy with regard to immigration is a reflection of its attitude towards population and the intensity thereof, its views as to the economic and other development of its country, and the extent to which it may regard 'racial purity' as essential or desirable. The Canadian law regarding immigration is found in the Immigration Act[64] and the regulations[65] made in relation thereto, of which it has been said that 'the Parliament of Canada, acting well within its right, has prescribed the condition upon which an alien may enter or be permitted to remain in Canada.'[66] This is in line with classical doctrine, for Vattel wrote in 1758 that 'one of the rights possessed by the supreme power in every State is the right to refuse to permit an alien to enter that State, to annex what conditions it pleases to the permission to enter it, and to expel or deport from that State, at pleasure, even a friendly alien, especially if it considers his presence in the State opposed to its peace, order and good government, or to its social or material interests.'[67] At the same time it must be borne in mind that immigration laws often have to be examined in the light of policy statements, especially when there is provision for any exercise of discretion by those called upon to carry them out. From this point of view, the statement of Prime Minister Mackenzie King in May 1947,[68] which reflected many of the points made by Pufendorf at the end of the seventeenth century,[69] is still important. The prime minister said:

> The policy of the Government is to foster the growth of the population of Canada by the encouragement of immigration. The government will seek by legislation, regulation, and

vigorous administration, to ensure the careful selection and permanent settlement of such numbers of immigrants as can be absorbed in our national economy.

Like other major problems of today, the problem of immigration must be viewed in the light of the world situation as a whole. A wise and productive policy for Canada cannot be devised by studying only the situation within our own country ... Among other considerations, it should take account of the urgent problem of resettlement of persons who are displaced and homeless, as an aftermath of the world conflict ...

Canada is not obliged, as a result of membership in the United Nations or under the constitution of the international refugee organization, to accept any specific number of refugees or displaced persons. We have nevertheless, a moral obligation to assist in meeting the problem, and this obligation we are prepared to recognise ...

The government's long term programme ... is based on the conviction that Canada needs population. The government is strongly of the view that our immigration policy should be devised in a positive sense, with the definite objective of enlarging the population of the country ...

The fear has been expressed that immigration would lead to a reduction in the standard of living. This need not be the case. If immigration is properly planned, the result will be the reverse. A larger population will help to develop our resources. By providing a larger number of consumers, in other words a larger domestic market, it will reduce the present dependence of Canada on the export of primary products. The essential thing is that immigrants be selected with care, and that their numbers be adjusted to the absorptive capacity of the country ...

With regard to the selection of immigrants, much has been said about discrimination ... Canada is perfectly within her rights in selecting the persons whom we regard as desirable future citizens. It is not a 'fundamental human right' of any alien to enter Canada. It is a privilege. It is a matter of domestic policy. Immigration is subject to the control of the parliament of Canada. This does not mean, however, that we should not seek to remove from our legislation what may appear to be objectionable discrimination.

One of the features of our legislation to which strong objection has been taken on the ground of discrimination is the Chinese Immigration Act.[70] This act seems to place persons from one particular country in an inferior category. The government has already initiated the repeal of that statue [so as allow Chinese residents to become naturalized and bring into Canada their wives and unmarried children under 18].

The East Indians legally resident in Canada are British subjects who have resided here for many years. They are therefore Canadian citizens. As such, their wives and unmarried children under 18 are admissible.

With regard to the Japanese, I stated, on August 4, 1944, at which time we were at war with Japan, that the government felt that in the years after the war the immigration of Japanese should not be permitted. This is the present view and policy of the government. It will be for future parliaments to consider what change, if any, be made in this policy.

There will, I am sure, be general agreement with the view that the people of Canada do not wish, as a result of mass immigration, to make a fundamental alteration in the character of our population. Large-scale immigration from the orient would change the fundamental composition of the Canadian population. Any considerable oriental immigration would, moreover, be certain to give rise to social and economic problems of a character that might lead to serious difficulties in the field of international relations. The government, therefore, has no thought of making any change in immigration regulations which would have consequences of this kind.

... Canada recognizes the right of all other countries to control the entry or non-entry of persons seeking to become permanent residents. We claim precisely the same right for our country.

... the Canadian government is prepared, at any time, to enter into negotiations with other countries for special agreements for the control of admission of immigrants on a basis of complete equality and reciprocity.

The prime minister's reference to the exclusion of Orientals has now become primarily of historical interest. By section 61(g) of the 1952 Immigration Act, the governor in council may make regulations 'prohibiting or limiting [the] admission of persons by reason of (i) nationality, citizenship, ethnic group ... or geographical area of origin'; and in *Narine Singh* v *Att'y Gen. of Canada*,[71] the Supreme Court applied the Oxford dictionary definition of 'ethnic' as being 'pertaining to race,' so as to hold that Indians of Trinidad were in fact Asians and covered by the limitation found in section 20 of the Immigration Regulations. This qualification has been abolished and the regulations, despite section 61, no longer make any reference to racial origin; all aliens seeking admission to Canada are now treated on an equal basis with regard to their ethnic origin. Nevertheless, it could happen that security considerations become of such a character as to involve the reintroduction of discriminatory measures,[72] even to the extent of making Canadian citizens liable to the provisions of the Immigration Act.

Discretion of immigration officials: Judicial review
Prime Minister Mackenzie King's statement received judicial recognition when it was referred to by Sullivan J in the Supreme Court of British Columbia in *Re Hanna*.[73] The learned judge applied the new legislation to a stateless person and held that

no Canadian court has power to assist Hanna in his plea that he be given right of residence in Canada. That is a decision for immigration officials, and for them alone, to make. Similarly all right of exercise of discretionary power to exempt from strict compliance with the Immigration Act or regulations made thereunder is vested in and is the prerogative of only the minister, deputy minister, director or such other persons as may be authorised to act for the director. The jurisdiction of the court in all matters relating to immigration is controlled and restricted and for the most part ousted by ... [section 39[74]] of the Act ... That is the law of Canada as the people have enacted it through their Parliament, and the sole duty of this court is to enforce the law of Canada as so enacted ... it would be highly improper ... for any judge to suggest to an immigration officer of whatever rank, that he would personally like to see executive discretion exercised in a certain manner in any given case.

Nevertheless, the learned judge pointed out that under the deportation order in question it appeared as if Hanna was condemned to perpetual sailing in the ship which had brought him to Canada, and 'so far as Hanna is concerned, this deportation order amounted to a sentence of imprisonment aboard the *Gudveig* for an indefinite time, and ... no immigration officer has the legal right to exercise such drastic power.'[75] He therefore discharged the order, pointing out that his decision gave no right of entry, for this remained with the immigration officers. In the meantime, since the order was illegal, Hanna was to be released from arrest, but the immigration officers were free to take him into custody again pending deportation, provided the order was in due form.

The wide discretion of the immigration officials was not reserved merely for aliens but extended to all persons not Canadian citizens or domiciled in Canada. Duff J, as he then was, commented on this situation in *Samejima* v *R*.:[76] 'I am horrified at the thought that the personal liberty of a British subject [not a Canadian citizen] should be exposed to the hugger-mugger which, under the name of legal proceedings, is exemplified by some of the records that have incidentally been brought to our attention.'

This statement was made in 1932, but the situation does not seem to have improved under the new legislation. In 1955 *R.* v *Spalding*[77] concerned the appeal of an Australian woman against whom a deportation order had been made. O'Halloran JA of the British Columbia Court of Appeal commented that the hearing before the special inquiry immigration officer had been 'conducted in violation of the essentials of justice ... In true effect it was not a valid hearing at all ... [Therefore,] there was no jurisdiction to make the deportation order ... and hence there was nothing to appeal from [to the Minister].' He then dealt with the nature of the 'appeal' to the minister provided for in section 31, pointing out that

there is nothing to indicate that the appeal to which it refers, is anything more than a documentary review of the proceedings by the Minister, in his own private office, in his own time, as part of his multifarious administrative and executive duties. There is nothing to prevent him then ... from listening to unsworn representations about the case, written or verbal, by people unknown to the person ordered to be deported and of whose representations to the Minister such person may never learn. In fact even if the Minister should disapprove of the grounds for deportation in the order he may nevertheless uphold it for reasons based upon information adverse to the deportee, of which the latter may never learn in specific terms. In short, the review by the Minister is not an 'appeal' in the legal sense, but is only the exercise of an executive or a political act (in its high sense) by the official who occupies the Cabinet post to which departmental matters must be referred finally for review or decision. Moreover there is no suggestion in this case that the conduct of the Special Inquiry Officer could be so patently outrageous to the Minister that the decision would be rectified ... by the Minister. There is nothing in the record to indicate that the officer's conduct in the proceedings was not in accord with customary departmental instructions to its officers. One would assume that an officer deputed to conduct such a hearing and with power to order immediate deportation must be an experienced officer well acquainted with the regular departmental procedure. If that is so, the likelihood of the Minister interfering with his decision would be less and less; such a specialised officer would very likely have much more experience and knowledge in such matters than the Minister himself whose duties are multifarious and on much higher level. It is not to be overlooked, in *Samejima* v *R.*,[78] where the Minister upheld the deportation order, Sir Lyman Duff described the proceedings as 'hugger-mugger'. This is said, not as reflection in this case upon the Immigration department, but as an illustration of the obvious necessity of recognition of *certiorari ex debitio justitiae* in this type of case.

In 1962 Ilsley cj hinted in the Supreme Court of Nova Scotia that the situation might have changed with the enactment of the Canadian Bill of Rights,[79] section 2(e) of which provides that 'no law of Canada shall be construed or applied so as to ... deprive a person of the right to a fair hearing in accordance with the principles of fundamental justice for the determination of his rights and obligations.' While the learned chief justice held in *Re Fraser*[80] that he was 'unable to find anything in the Canadian Bill of Rights which would invalidate a deportation validly made before the Canadian Bill of Rights was passed or to require a hearing before such order is carried into effect,' he refused to commit himself on what the position would be with regard to an order made after the bill had come into effect.

It might have been thought that the enactment of the Immigration Appeal Board Act[81] – repealing the appeal to the minister and setting up an Appeal Board as a court of record, holding public hearings, and with an ultimate appeal to the Supreme Court – would have remedied the situation. This does not, however, seem to have been the case. In *Ex parte Hosin*[82] in 1970, Wright J of the Ontario High Court had some very strong comments to make on this matter:

> Once it has been established ... that the Immigration Appeal Board as now constituted is an additional Court for the better administration of the laws of Canada ... it is in no sense an inferior Court over which this Court has jurisdiction to apply extraordinary remedies to its normal work ... I ask who is there to require the Immigration Appeal Board to do its duty and to do its duty properly or to protect the public against abuses? There is, of course, the process of appeal under s.23 of the Immigration Appeal Act [by leave, to the Supreme Court] ... But what power is there otherwise to exercise any control over the work of the Immigration Appeal Board and like bodies, in any matter which does not involve a decision of the Board on an appeal [for by s.22 of the Act the Board 'has sole and exclusive jurisdiction to hear and determine all questions of fact or law, including questions of jurisdiction'] or of other bodies in their proper work? ... Although the Immigration Appeal Board is a Court of record ... the members are not in the same position as Judges, and do not share our powers and independence ... as long as we have available in our country, methods of judicial review, and as long as we maintain the authority of our Courts, tyranny can be defeated. But when we set up groups of men with full powers over the future of their fellow men but subject to no judicial power except by way of statutory appeal from their decisions, we open the door to illegality if it is minded to come in ... I consider that every public officer should be subject to the jurisdiction of some impartial Court in connection with matters directly involving the fundamental freedom of his fellow citizens. In this case, it appears to me that the Immigration Appeal Board, if it chose, could fail to deal entirely or conscientiously with appeals brought before it and there would be no power that I can see in any Court to force it to do its duty. The only remedy would be the removal of the members by the Governor in Council for cause. This is not the same guarantee of our freedoms that the traditions of our Courts and justice provide.

This statement was basically only a reiteration of a statement made three years earlier by Munroe J of the Supreme Court of British Columbia in *Re Edery*:[83]

> This court is without jurisdiction to grant the relief claimed herein ... This court's jurisdiction in certiorari is ousted in immigration matters by virtue ... of the Immigration Appeal Board Act. Likewise ... the court is without jurisdiction in prohibition to hear and determine any question of jurisdiction arising under the Immigration Appeal Board Act. Such jurisdiction is now vested solely in the immigration appeal board, a court of record newly created by parliament in 1967.

The non-judicial character of immigration proceedings before a special inquiry officer, as distinct from the Immigration Appeal Board, and the non-applicability thereto of the Bill of Rights were also explained in 1971 by Dryer J of the Supreme Court of British Columbia in *Ex parte Paterson*,[84] a case arising out of the refusal to allow immigration rights to the hijacker of a United States aircraft. In this case, counsel for the applicant had been delayed by weather conditions and it was alleged that the hearing which had proceeded in his absence was in breach of section 2(c)(ii) which provides that 'no law of Canada shall be construed or applied so as to ... deprive a person who has been arrested or detained ... of the right to retain and instruct counsel without delay,' and of section 2(f) that 'no law of Canada shall be construed or applied so as to ... deprive a person charged with a criminal offence of the right to be presumed innocent until proved guilty according to law in a fair and public hearing by an independent and impartial tribunal.' Mr Justice Dryer commented:

> The right to retain and instruct counsel is one thing. The right to prevent a hearing from proceeding in the absence of counsel could very well be another. S. 2(f) applies only to 'a person charged with a criminal offence' and does not apply here ... [The Special Inquiry Officer] was not ... conducting an inquiry or holding a hearing. He was not required to do so. In the case of a person entering Canada from the United States of America, since he can be readily returned to the 'place whence he came,'[85] the Special Inquiry Officer is not required to hold an inquiry. S. 24(1) says that, in the case of persons from the United States of America, after receiving the report of the immigration officer, the Special Inquiry Officer 'shall, after such further examination as he may deem necessary ... admit such person ... or make a deportation order against such person.' 'Examination' I interpret as meaning an examination of the facts and not (certainly not necessarily) something in the nature of a trial or hearing although it may, of course, include hearing the applicant and other persons. Whether the Special Inquiry Officer hears counsel for the appellant or any other person depends upon whether he deems it necessary. He is not obliged to do so ... On habeas corpus, without certiorari in aid, the court cannot go behind the order of deportation.

And as already noted in *Re Edery* and *Ex parte Hosin,* the Immigration Appeal Board Act had ousted the court's jurisdiction *in certiorari*. At this point, despite the Bill of Rights, immigration officers enjoy perhaps an even wider freedom than they did under the unamended Immigration Act, subject only to the statutory supervision of the Board and the Supreme Court. It has also been held, in *Re Prata and Minister of Manpower and Immigration,*[85a] that s 21 of the Immigration Act, concerning limitations on the Immigration Appeal Board's power to stay or quash deportation orders concerning persons thought by the minister to be among those 'it would be contrary to the national interest for the Board to take such action,' was not contrary to the Bill of Rights, for there is 'no absolute, basic, universal right in an alien to enter Canada. It is for Parliament to decide whether or not permission to enter will be granted, and if permitted, the terms and conditions of such entry.'

Nevertheless, the discretion may not be completely unfettered, but must be exercised within the terms of the act. An attempt to ensure this compliance with the act was made by the Ontario Court of Appeal in *Chan* v *McFarlane*.[86] The appellant had been born in China in 1931 and had gone from there to Hong Kong. He went to the United States in 1949 and entered Canada in 1959, only to be subjected to a deportation order naming Hong Kong as his destination, since the United States declined to readmit him. The court was concerned with the validity of this order. Speaking for the majority, Kelly JA said:

> Canada, as a Sovereign power, has a right to exclude from her borders those who have not by nationality or citizenship a claim to admission [and the] power to remove those whose entry has not been authorized ... Although deportation may commonly be thought of as the removal of an unacceptable person from Canada, an act which would be complete when the person concerned was placed beyond the boundaries of Canada, under the Act[87] deportation is so defined that an order for deportation is an order for the removal under the Act from any place in Canada to the place whence he came to Canada, the country of his nationality or citizenship, or to the country of his birth, or to such other country as may be approved by the Minister under the Act. Deportation thus defined embraces removal from Canada to a destination which must be one falling within the categories set out in [the act] ...
>
> Deportation as contemplated by the Act includes the initiating of the removal in Canada and also the termination of such removal in a destination, either statutory or approved. The naming of the destination is essential to the process and no order for deportation would be enforceable until some destination is specified; similarly every step in the enforcement of an order for deportation must be one in a continuing process originating in Canada and concluding in some one of the designated destinations.
>
> Where the place named as the destination of a deportee is one of the statutory destinations, the order for deportation does not require to be supplemented by any approval of the Minister as to the destination and its validity cannot be questioned on account of the destination.
>
> What must be decided in this case is whether, Hong Kong not being a statutory destination, power rests in the Minister to approve Hong Kong as a country to which the respondent may be deported, that power having been conferred on the Minister by the Act, or vested in him as a power inherent in his office as Minister.
>
> The Minister's action in approving Hong Kong cannot be supported as flowing from any inherent power. Parliament, having seen fit to provide by the Act for the exclusion or removal of non-acceptable persons seeking to enter or remain in Canada and having vested in the Minister and his officers mentioned in the Act certain powers spelled out in the Act with some particularity, it must be assumed that the powers conferred by the Act on the Minister and his servants are all that Parliament intended should be exercised by them for the purpose of carrying out the Act.
>
> ... If one were to accept the contention that s.36(1) conferred an unrestricted power

on the Minister to approve in the course of removing an unacceptable applicant for admission, any country whatsoever as a destination to which he was to be conveyed from Canada, this power would necessarily extend to authorize the Minister to approve at will any country regardless of whether such country had an obligation or was willing to accept the deportee. Since the deportation must include the removal from Canada to some one of the destinations, the unfettered discretion of the Minister to approve of any country would be exercisable to authorize the removal of a person from Canada to some place which could not be compelled or was unwilling to accept the deportee. Such an order might well be incapable of performance. I cannot convince myself that a Parliament that was so solicitous as to provide that deportation would include not only the removal from Canada but the removal to some other place would have intended to put in motion a process which could not have carried out Parliament's expressed intention that the deportee be removed from Canada to some specified destination.

The opinion then referred to section 40 of the Immigration Act which deals with cases in which the United States refuses to allow back into that country persons against whom deportation orders have been made, such persons having come to Canada through the United States.

S.40(1) is clearly inapplicable since the respondent was not a person who came to Canada through the United States of America; 'through' to me implies continuous transit through that country in the course of a journey from without the borders of that country to Canada, and not a movement which has been interrupted by a ten-year stay. In the light of his ten years' sojourn in that country he must be considered to have come to Canada from and not through the United States of America.

Under s.40(2) the approval of the Minister cannot be given spontaneously whenever the Minister in his discretion deems it useful or convenient that it should be given; as a condition precedent to the Minister's approval there must be a request by the transportation company which brought the person to Canada that the deportation may be made to a country other than one which is a statutory destination, which alternative country is acceptable to the person concerned and which country is in its turn willing to receive him.

Even if Hong Kong be willing to accept the respondent, two of the three relevant conditions remain unfulfilled; there had been no request from any transportation company and Hong Kong is not a country acceptable to him. Therefore, the purported approval evidenced by the direction of [the minister] ... was not an approval by the Minister under the Act and there [thus] existed no authority to deport the respondent to Hong Kong ...

In the result the respondent's contention must prevail. That does not mean, however, that the respondent has established any legal right to enter or remain in Canada. It is for Immigration officials and for them alone to grant or withhold that privilege. The order for deportation itself has not been questioned ... and the right of the appropriate officers to take whatever action is authorized by the Act in the carrying out of that order should not be interfered with.

Shortly after the decision in *Chan v McFarlane* had been rendered, the Supreme Court in *Rebrin v Bird and the Minister of Citizenship and Immigration*,[88] a judgment which made no reference to the *Chan* case, pointed out that section 61 of the act authorized the governor in council to make regulations, and regulation 13 permitted the minister to prescribe the form of words to be used in a deportation order; and the court accepted as valid an order made without naming any place to which the deportation was to be directed. This verdict was followed by the Supreme Court in *Moore* v *Minister of Manpower and Immigration,*[89] which concerned an order made against a man who had come from Panama, to which he wished to return, but who was wanted in the United States to stand trial for offences committed there. He had originally been deported from Canada and had returned using a Canadian passport which he obtained wrongly. The minister's order did not specify the place to which he was to be deported, but the minister had indicated to his counsel that it was intended to send him to the United States. Cartwright cj declared that 'the Minister has not as yet made an order naming the country to which the appellant is to be deported, but the question as to whether the Minister or the appellant has the right to choose the destination is one of law depending on the construction of the Act and the regulations. ... The conclusion to be drawn from the wording of the Act is that the choice rests with the Minister.' The learned chief justice, accepting the reasoning in *Ex parte Soblen,*[90] held that the appellant had not satisfied the burden of proof incumbent upon him concerning his allegation that the minister had not acted *bona fide,* and continued: 'Once it has been held that a valid deportation order has been made which does not name the destination to which the deportee is to be sent, and that in such circumstances Parliament has committed to the Minister the choice as to what that destination shall be ... the Minister's mode of exercising that choice does not raise a question of law which is reviewable by this Court upon an appeal [under section 23 of the Immigration Appeal Board Act].' The chief justice accepted as his own the comments made by Judson j to the effect that section 36(2) ('unless otherwise directed by the Minister or an immigration officer in charge, a person against whom a deportation order has been made may be requested or allowed to leave Canada voluntarily') and the last part of section 40(2) ('to a country that is acceptable to such person, and that is willing to receive him')

> are permissive only and do not compel the Minister to act under them. The definition of 'deportation' [in section 2(d)] and s.36(1) state four possible destinations: (a) the place whence he came; (b) the country of which he is a national or citizen; (c) the country of birth; (d) such country as may be approved by the Minister under the Act. The sections do not state that the Minister may make a choice, if the facts of a given case permit a choice. Neither do they impose any limitation upon the power of a Minister. We have here a valid deportation order. There are four stated destinations. My conclusion on this legislation is that the choice rests with the Minister and not with the person to be deported. He has the power and its mode of exercise does not raise a question of law which is reviewable by this Court ... the discretion given to the Director [of the Immigration Branch of the Department of Manpower and Immigration] under s.26 ... is purely administrative and is not subject to judicial review.

Section 26 provides that the director 'shall upon receiving a report ... and *where he considers that an inquiry is warranted*, cause an inquiry to be held' (emphasis added).

As a result of the *Rebrin* and *Moore* decisions, it would appear that the Supreme

Court has, without even referring to that judgment, completely rejected the attempt made in *Chan* to limit the exercise of discretion by the minister, at least when it cannot be proved that he is acting *mala fide*. Presumably, however, the *Chan* interpretation of section 40(1), in the case of a deportee coming 'through' or 'from' the United States and whom the United States will not readmit, is still valid. At least so far as the special inquiry procedure is concerned, it would also seem that a deportee would still be protected by the principles of natural justice. Thus in *Re Brooks*[91] it was held that 'the principles of natural justice as applied to administrative tribunals or inquiry boards provide that the subject of the inquiry is entitled to be present, to have a chance to be heard in person or by counsel,[92] to be made aware of the charges that are alleged against him, and to hear the evidence and be given an opportunity to meet and counter such evidence.' The standing of the Immigration Appeal Board as a court of record, and the appellate powers of the Supreme Court over it, would tend to ensure that these requirements are in fact met.

Canadian citizens

The Immigration Act of 1952[93] was intended to give effect to the policy outlined by Mackenzie King in 1947 and covers both immigration to and deportation from Canada and provides for the administration of these processes, as well as for examination and appeals. The act clearly asserts (section 3) that 'a Canadian citizen has the right to come into Canada.' Since this right is established by statute, it can be taken away only by parliamentary action or in accordance with parliamentary authorization.

Nevertheless, one of the conditions attached in 1970 to the immunity from prosecution granted to the kidnappers of James Cross, a British diplomat in Quebec, was that they would never attempt to return to Canada. This raises interesting issues. Clearly, a government may enter into such arrangements as it pleases with its own citizens; and if the citizens concerned were to disregard such arrangements, the government would resume all rights which it had agreed to waive. Therefore, should the individuals in question return to Canada, they would presumably find that their immunity from prosecution no longer existed. However, as regards any other country such an agreement is *res inter alios acta*. No state is entitled to make an arrangement with its citizens which adversely affects the rights of another sovereign state. So long as Cuba, which agreed with Canada to accept the persons involved, is prepared to allow them to remain, no problem will arise. But it has never been made clear whether Cuba entered into a binding obligation to this effect with Canada or merely acted out of comity to assist Canada in solving a difficult problem, while retaining its right to resume freedom of action towards these 'visitors.' According to international law, the only country which is obliged to accept the entry of an individual who is denied admission to or expelled from another country is the country of which the individual is a national; this in fact is the problem with Asians expelled from Africa and denied entry into Britain in accordance with the latter's immigration legislation, despite the fact that these Asians possess no nationality other than British. In the case of the Cross kidnappers, Canada might well find herself in difficulties if she were to persist in refusing to receive back such individuals if they should leave or be expelled from Cuba and find themselves unable to secure entry into some other country. In view of the fact that, in such a case, they would not be returning of their own volition, it might well be questioned whether it would not be a breach of faith on the part of Canada if she sought to try them for the kidnapping. It is difficult to see, however, what principle of law, municipal or international, would be broken by such an exercise of jurisdiction.

It is perhaps of interest to note that article 4 of the 1971 Extradition Treaty between Canada and the United States[94] provides that '(a) kidnapping, murder or other assault against the life or physical integrity of a person to whom a Contracting Party has the duty according to international law to give special protection, or any attempt to commit such an offence with respect to any such person,' shall not be considered as political in character, entitling the offender to immunity from extradition. This means that if, after the treaty has been ratified and come into force, a kidnapper were to escape from Canada to the United States, or *vice versa,* the country of refuge would be obliged to surrender him by way of extradition. If, however, the victim were, let us say, a United States diplomat in Canada and the kidnapper remained in Canada, the treaty would not prevent Canada from making an arrangement whereby he would be given safe conduct providing he never returned to Canada, even though under United States law attacks on her diplomats abroad were crimes, and she were willing to try the kidnapper herself.

In spite of what has been said above, it would appear that even Canadian citizens may be subjected to deportation from Canada, as happened with Japanese Canadians after World War II. In *Co-operative Committee on Japanese Canadians* v *Attorney General of Canada*[95] Lord Wright, speaking for the Privy Council, recognized that

it may be true that in construing legislation some weight ought, in an appropriate case, be given to a consideration of the accepted principles of international law, but the nature of the legislation in any particular case has to be construed in determining to what extent, if at all, it is right on a question of construction to advert to those principles ... Those principles find no place in the construction of the War Measures Act.[96] The Act is directed to the exercise by the Governor in Council of powers vested in the Parliament of the Dominion at a time when war, invasion, or insurrection or their apprehension exists. The existing rules of international law applicable in times of peace can hardly have been in contemplation, and the inference cannot be drawn that the Parliament of the Dominion impliedly imposed the limitation suggested [that only aliens and no citizens can be deported] ... Commonly it is only aliens who are made liable to deportation, and, in consequence, where reference is made to deportation, there is often imported the suggestion that aliens are under immediate consideration ... As a matter of language, their Lordships take the view that 'deportation' is not a word which is misused when applied to persons not aliens. Whether or not the word 'deportation' is in its application to be confined to aliens or not remains therefore open as a matter of construction of the particular statute in which it is found. In the present case, the Act is directed to dealing with emergencies; throughout it is in sweeping terms ... The general nature of the Act and the collocation in which the word is found, establish ... that in this statute the word 'deportation' is used in a general sense and as an action applicable to all persons irrespective of nationality. Nationality *per se* is not a relevant consideration.

While it is true that the federal parliament may enact measures which would subject citizens to deportation, or which might be in breach of international law, and that the courts would have to ensure that such statutes were obeyed, the Privy Council did not attempt to deal with the possible international consequences for Canada of such legislation.

Perhaps here it should be pointed out that when the War Measures Act was invoked at the time of the Cross and Laporte kidnappings, the regulations made thereunder[97] made no provision for the deportation of any person from Canada, whether alien or citizen.

Canadian domiciliaries

In addition to giving a right of entry to citizens, section 3 of the Immigration Act affirms that persons possessing Canadian domicile although not citizenship also enjoy such a right. However, any such person who has assisted Canada's enemies or 'performed for or rendered to a country other than Canada any military service or other aid or assistance that is prejudicial to any action taken by Canada under the United Nations Charter, the North Atlantic Treaty or other similar instrument for collective defence that may be entered into by Canada,' or who leaves the country with such an object in view, will be allowed to return only if specifically so authorized by the minister. This, of course, raises difficulties for any domiciled alien who may be a citizen or a sympathizer of a country against which the United Nations may decide to take action in which Canada is participating. Thus, any Rhodesian domiciled in Canada who disagrees with the United Nations decision – accepted by Canada – to apply sanctions against Rhodesia and who endeavours to evade such sanctions might find himself denied the right to return to Canada; and problems might easily have arisen for many Canadian residents had the Soviet Union not vetoed the resolutions of the Security Council directed against India during the 1971 war with Pakistan.

For the purposes of the act, domicile is acquired 'by a person having his place of domicile for at least five years in Canada after having been landed in Canada'; but any period during which he was not a free agent, such as by reason of detention in an asylum or gaol, will not be included in this computation, nor will any period between the making and execution of a deportation order, nor will he attain domicile if his residence in Canada is under permit, for example, as a tourist. Such domicile is lost by the person concerned being out of Canada voluntarily and with the intention of making his domicile elsewhere. It may also be lost if the individual takes part in any activities or belongs to any organization threatening the security of Canada or involving disaffection to the queen, or if he has been found guilty of an offence under narcotics legislation.

Several cases have arisen involving domicile problems. For example, in *R.* v *Jawala Singh*[98] it was held that a British Indian who had entered Canada in 1908, entered the United States by stealth in 1926, and then returned to Canada also by stealth in 1935 had lost his Canadian domicile by long residence in the United States, and that, having returned by stealth he could not be considered to have 'landed' so that there was no possibility of his reacquiring domicile. However, a deportation order must be carried out with alacrity, or else the deportee may acquire Canadian domicile and become exempt from deportation. This occurred in *Re Nikola Ferenc,*[99] which concerned an application by an appellant who had been subjected to a deportation order in 1932 and again in 1938. Robson JA said:

> The Act shows a parliamentary intention that deportation proceedings shall be carried out with reasonable promptness; it cannot be the intention that deportation orders shall lie dormant for [five] years ready to be revived at any time the department sees fit ... Common justice requires that the alien shall not remain in a state of uncertainty for perhaps years and the obligation of the steamship company must surely end some time. ... [In fact] I do not think it was necessary for Ferenc [who had been domiciled in Canada more than five years] to bring any proceedings to have the earlier order set aside as lapsed or abandoned.

Other aliens in Canada

Vaaro v *The King*[100] concerned the deportation of a group of aliens alleged to be members of a group favouring the overthrow of the government, and it demonstrates how far in such cases the courts are prepared to accept the discretion of the authorities and their unwillingness to examine the facts for themselves. Lamont J declared that

> broadly speaking every alien, who has been admitted into and is actually in Canada and is taken into custody on a charge for which he may be deported, is entitled to the benefit of the writ of habeas corpus to test in court if his detention is according to law. If it is not, the applicant may be released. If, however, his detention is authorised by law, his application must be refused. All that is necessary in the complaint ... is that the allegation shall make known with reasonable certainty to the person against whom the investigation is directed, the conduct on his part, in violation of the Act, to which objection is taken. There is no analogy between a complaint under the Immigration Act and an indictment on a criminal charge ... The object of making provision for a Board of Inquiry is to have at hand a tribunal which can without delay inquire into the truth of the allegations made in the complaint ... [As to the contention] that the evidence does not warrant the finding of the Board ... as a general rule in habeas corpus matters we are not entitled to look at the evidence to see if it is sufficient to justify the decision arrived at ... The sufficiency of the evidence is a matter with which the Minister [and now the Immigration Appeal Board] can deal with in the appeal, but unless he reverses the finding of the Board [of Inquiry] its decision is final.

Interesting cases have arisen concerning deportation orders made against aliens who have come into Canada in possession of documents, or who applied for immigration when already in the country. In *Masella* v *Langlais*[101] the court did not sustain the appellant's contention that 'because he was allowed to land in Canada on the strength of a visa and a certificate of medical examination assumed to have been legally issued no complaint to the Minister can be validly laid under ... the Act.' Abbott J said:

> The legality of his entrance to Canada was subject to question at any time until he had acquired Canadian domicile within the meaning of the Act. Immigration to Canada by persons other than Canadian citizens or those having a Canadian domicile is a privilege

determined by statute, regulation or otherwise, and is not a matter of right.[101a] In the Immigration Act, Parliament has set up the machinery for the control of immigration to this country and for the selection of prospective immigrants. To accomplish this purpose, very wide discretionary powers are given under the Act, to the Governor in Council and to the Minister ... In order to provide for the effective administration of an Act such as this, it would seem not unreasonable that the Immigration authorities should be in a position to insist upon strict compliance abroad with the requirements of the Act or regulations ... in order to determine the suitability of a proposed immigrant ... In this case it was established to the satisfaction of the board of inquiry that these regulations had not been met. In my opinion the proceedings before the board of inquiry were regularly taken and a proper investigation made of the subject-matter of the complaint in accordance with the provisions of the Act ... Where a board of inquiry has taken evidence in good faith and has otherwise complied with the provisions of the statute, a court has no jurisdiction to substitute its judgment for that of the board.

Taschereau J was to the same effect:

Si le comité d'enquête a suivi les prescriptions qu'ordonne le statut, il est clair que les tribunaux ne peuvent pas intervenir ... Il me sera suffisant de dire que l'ordonnance du commité, confirmée par le Ministre, me paraît avoir été émise en conformité des dispositions de la loi de l'Immigration, et qu'il n'appartient pas aux tribunaux d'intervenir et de decider si en fait un immigrant est desirable ou ne l'est pas.

Masella v *Langlais* was applied in *Re Mannira*[102] in the case of an alien who was already in Canada as a non-immigrant and who, it was held, would have to satisfy all the immigration conditions concerning immigrant visa, health certificate, and the like if he wished to stay; and he would have to be in possession of these at the time of his arrival. This decision was confirmed by the Supreme Court in *Espaillat-Rodriguez* v *R.*[103] Although the situation was temporarily changed, a visiting alien cannot acquire immigrant status without departing from Canada.[104]

Another problem situation is the case of the convicted alien who has been subjected to a deportation order but whose sentence is remitted as an act of clemency. *Re Veregin*[105] concerned an applicant who on 6 May 1932 had been sentenced to eighteen months for perjury and was therefore subjected to a deportation order. On 20 January 1933 the solicitor general approved the remission of the sentence, as Veregin's Russian passport was due to expire in March and there was some reason to believe that it was not likely to be renewed. In the Supreme Court of Nova Scotia, Mellish J held that 'the prisoner cannot be deported or held imprisoned for deportation [since] his "sentence or term of imprisonment" expired within the meaning of [the Act] ... On this ground alone ... the prisoner is entitled to be discharged ... it need hardly be said that the policy of the Government as expressed in relation to the prisoner is immaterial except in so far as such policy can be legally implemented.' He held, therefore, that the extension to the prisoner of mercy or a pardon terminated the entire sentence, including the recommendation for deportation. As a result of this decision, the Supreme Court of Canada was asked for its opinion; and in *Re Royal Prerogative of Mercy upon Deportation Proceedings*,[106] Duff CJC pointed out that the prerogative of mercy is in fact a royal prerogative, so that 'the act of clemency in releasing a convict from prison prior to the completion of the term of his sentence may be valid and effective in law without the consent of the convict.' Further, 'the phrase "sentence or term of imprisonment", in s. 43 [of the 1927 act, now s. 35(2)], is intended to embrace both the case where the convict has undergone the full term of imprisonment imposed by the sentence and the case where the term of imprisonment has been reduced by the operation of some general statutory provision or by a valid act of clemency.' The result was that the minister could still authorize the deportation; moreover, since the deportation was administrative and not attaching to the punishment *de jure,* it was not affected by the pardon.

Deportation of related persons
During his judgment on behalf of the Supreme Court in *Vaaro* v *The King,* [107] Lamont J reiterated that 'it is generally considered that by the law of nations, the supreme power in every state has the right to make laws for the exclusion and expulsion of aliens and to provide the machinery by which these laws can be lawfully enforced ... By the British North America Act, 1867, the exclusive legislative jurisdiction over "Naturalization and Aliens" was given to the Dominion, s.91(25). In the exercise of the power thus given Parliament passed the Immigration Act.' Whatever may be one's feelings of moral criticism of exercising punitive action against innocent third parties, whether by way of judicial decision or administrative decree, there is in the Immigration Act (section 37) power to include within a deportation decree all the dependent members of the deportee's family, if the deportee is head of that family. Similarly, if a deportation order has been made against a dependent member of a family on the ground that he has become a public charge, the special inquiry officer has power to include within the order any members of the family whom he regards as having wilfully neglected to support such person although they were morally bound to support him. Thus if the person held to be wilfully neglectful is the head of the family, it is possible to expel from Canada the entire family of a person deported as a public charge. Also, if the dependents of a deported head of family had not been included in the original deportation order, they might subsequently find themselves liable to deportation for having become public charges.

Other provisions
For the main part, the remaining sections of the Immigration Act lay down the rules that govern hearings and the execution of immigration orders, and these sections must be read in conjunction with the Immigration Regulations. Thus, the latter give details of the persons who may be 'sponsored' by Canadian citizens or persons lawfully resident in Canada, and specify the norms of assessment to be taken into consideration by immigration officers when examining the claim of nominated relatives or independent applicants. The act also recognizes that, in accordance with the normal practices of international law, a transportation company is liable for removing any deportee for whose arrival their facilities have been used. However, this liability is not absolute or indefinite, and the act provides that if the deportation is ordered more than five years after the deportee was admitted or for reasons that arose after such admission, then the company would not be liable.

The Immigration Act was summed up in the judgment of the Supreme Court in *Gana* v *Minister of Manpower and Immigration,*[108] when Abbott J stated:

> The scheme of the Immigration Act is relatively simple. The only persons entitled to enter Canada as of right are Canadian citizens and persons having a Canadian domicile. All others must obtain permission to enter from the Minister of Manpower and Immigration acting, of course, through his departmental officials. Those coming for a temporary stay are given permission to do so for a limited period as a visitor, a student, a tourist or for some other purpose. Would-be immigrants, however, are subject to examination as to their suitability on medical grounds, educational qualifications and the like and, if found satisfactory by the examining officer at the point of entry, are granted permission to enter and to remain in Canada as landed immigrants. The decision to grant or refuse such status in accordance with the Act and the Regulations, is made in the discretion of the immigration officer at the port of entry, and is an administrative decision. It is not subject to review, judicial or otherwise, by anyone other than the Minister. In many cases, would-be immigrants are examined abroad as to their suitability and, if found to be acceptable, are granted a visa authorizing them to enter Canada as landed immigrants. If permission is refused that is the end of the matter. Once a person is in Canada, having been granted the status of a landed immigrant, he can only be deprived of that status and ordered to be deported after a hearing before an officer of the department described in the as a Special Inquiry Officer. If deportation is ordered, that order is subject to an appeal to the Immigration Appeal Board. Prior to 1967, would-be immigrants who applied outside Canada or at border points, and those already in Canada on a temporary basis, were treated on the same basis. But, as a result of amendments to the Immigration Regulations ... made in 1967 ... a person who has been allowed to enter Canada as a visitor or on some temporary basis may now apply to an immigration officer in Canada before the authorized period of his stay has expired, for admission to Canada as a landed immigrant.

This relaxation of the regulations was removed by the amendments that came into force at the beginning of 1973, and it is no longer possible for the temporary visitor to apply, while already in Canada, to remain as a landed immigrant.

Summary
It would appear that there is nothing in any of the legislation relating to immigration into and deportation or exclusion from Canada that is in any way inconsistent with international law. Canada is not a party to any international convention requiring her to grant entry to any alien, although the Refugees Convention of 1951[109] does appear to limit her complete freedom of action is this field: it provides that if refugee seamen are sailing on a vessel flying a Canadian flag, Canada is required to 'give sympathetic consideration to their establishment on its territory ... or their temporary admission to its territory particularly with a view to their facilitating their establishment in another country.' In the same way, the absolute discretion of the minister as to the place of destination for a deportee is limited in the case of convention refugees, since 'no Contracting State shall expel or return (*refouler*) a refugee in any manner whatsoever to the frontiers of territories where his life or freedom would be threatened on account of his race, religion, nationality, membership of a particular social group or political opinion.'[110] However, 'the benefit of the pres-

ent provision may not be claimed by a refugee whom there are reasonable grounds for regarding as a danger to the security of the country in which he is, or who, having been convicted by a final judgment of a particularly serious crime, constitutes a danger to the community of that country.' There is no attempt made to define what is meant by 'a particularly serious crime.' Moreover, it may well be questioned whether, in view of the decision of the International Court of Justice in the *Southwest Africa* cases,[111] the provision in the convention that any disputes concerning its application may be referred to the World Court by any party is of more than ideological significance.

Asylum and extradition

General principles of asylum
The ban on *refoulement* is intended to impose an international obligation to grant refuge to one who is in danger in the country to which he might normally be sent and is intimately tied in with the concept of asylum. Requests for asylum may arise when an application has been made from abroad for the extradition of an alleged fugitive from criminal justice; or an individual may request asylum from the authorities of the country in which he is present on the ground that he is likely to suffer discrimination if he returns to his own state, or that, for some political reason appealing to the local state, he wishes to stay within its territory; or a person may seek refuge in an embassy in the country in which he is present on the grounds that his life or liberty is endangered on political, national, or some other ideological ground, either by the territorial state or by the state of which he is a national and to which he does not wish to return.

Obviously, if a request for asylum locally made is denied the applicant is likely to be deported. This fact is recognized in the Canadian Immigration Appeal Board Act,[112] which grants the right of appeal to the board to any person denied asylum in Canada. The board's decision in such a case is binding, and the appeal may, in accordance with section 15(1)(b)(i), be allowed 'in the case of a person who was not a permanent resident at the time of the making of the order of deportation, having regard to the existence of reasonable grounds for believing that if execution of the order is carried out the person concerned will be punished for activities of a political character or will suffer unusual hardship.' Presumably the concept of 'unusual hardship' is wide enough to enable the board to grant asylum for such reasons as racial or religious persecution.

The decision to grant asylum to any applicant is not appealable and is made by the government purely on discretionary grounds, but the board should not disregard 'credible' evidence, and 'must be accorded the trust in its careful and fair dealing with the cases that come before it for ... relief as its status as an independent Court of record demands.'[112] A good example of government discretion was the decision made by Great Britain in 1971 to afford asylum to Oleg Lyalin, a Soviet defector, dropping driving charges against him; those who were alleged to have imparted official secrets to him were prosecuted, but no accusation of espionage was brought against Lyalin himself.[113]

While, as has been seen, there tends to be a practice in Latin American countries to grant diplomatic asylum in embassies, even there it has not hardened into a rule of law. And in the rest of the world there is general refusal to recognize that diplomatic premises may be used in this way, unless the applicant for asylum is in imminent danger of his life. Even then, once the danger has receded the asylum should be brought to an end.

Statements have occasionally been made on an official level indicating the Canadian view concerning diplomatic asylum. Thus, in 1961 the undersecretary for external affairs stated:[114]

> our files have no record of a Canadian national having sought asylum in a foreign embassy in Canada. However ... on February 15, 1961, following the death of Patrice Lumumba, the Belgian Embassy in Cairo was set on fire and one or more staff members sought and was granted refuge for a number of hours in the neighbouring Canadian Embassy. The position that Canada takes is that our consulates and diplomatic missions abroad may not grant asylum on the premises of a post except in extraordinary circumstances. The sort of circumstances we have in mind is where temporary asylum would be granted on humanitarian grounds to a person whether a Canadian citizen or not, if he is in imminent personal danger to his life during political disturbances or riots, with care being taken to ensure that the humanitarian character of the mission's intervention should not be misinterpreted. The Cairo incident ... is ... a good case in point. The Government of Canada has not signed or ratified any international convention establishing a right of asylum, Canada's position concerning asylum being based upon general principles of international law which recognise that the right of asylum may be exercised under very exceptional circumstances.

A somewhat similar statement was made some five years later[115] to the effect that

> no general right of asylum on diplomatic premises is recognised in contemporary international law. However ... in exceptional cases, temporary asylum may be granted for humanitarian reasons where not only the life, liberty or person of an individual seeking such asylum is threatened by violence, but when the life of such a person is actually in imminent danger. Such incidents, in which Canada's representatives abroad have granted asylum, are ... extremely rare. As far as concerns the right of a foreign mission to grant asylum in Canada, we are not aware of any instances in which this has occurred. It is, however, not likely that Canada would recognise such a right, in view of the principle cited, if such occasion were to arise.

The nearest instance of such an occasion arising is perhaps that of the Quebec kidnappers. At the time that their hiding place was discovered, they had in their custody a British diplomat whom they had kidnapped. In return for his release unharmed, the government agreed not to bring proceedings against the kidnappers and to allow them to leave Canada on condition that they never returned. It was further agreed that certain of the members of their families would be permitted to join them and leave with them. The surrender of the kidnapped diplomat was to be made to the Cuban consul in Montreal, who would then take the kidnappers and others involved into his protection and arrange for their safe removal from Canada. The governments of Canada and Cuba agreed that the transfer would take place at the former Cuban pavilion at the site of the Montreal Exhibition 'Man and His

World,' this pavilion being given diplomatic immunity for the purpose. This was not a simple case of a local resident, Canadian or otherwise, seeking asylum in diplomatic premises. In order to deal with an extremely difficult and sensitive problem, the governments of Canada and Cuba agreed to deal with the issue on an emergency *ad hoc* basis.

It is clear that any decision with regard to asylum is made on basically political grounds and is completely discretionary. However, attempts have been made to bring some element of judicial control into the matter. Frequently fugitive offenders whose extradition has been requested by some foreign state put forward the contention that they are not really common criminals but political offenders. They sometimes contend that the offence with which they are charged is really an inherent part of a political act, or is nothing more than a trumped-up excuse to secure their recovery in order to try or otherwise proceed against them for political reasons. This factor has become so important in connection with extradition that most municipal statutes regulating the surrender of fugitive criminals, as well as the treaties embodying a legal obligation upon the parties to effect such surrenders, make provision for the immunity of those charged with political offences. This means that when a request for surrender comes before a court, accompanied by sufficient evidence to ground a *prima facie* case against the accused or to warrant his going to trial, the judge may decide that the offence is in fact political and that the fugitive is not to be extradited. If the judge decides the other way, however, there is nothing to stop the government from deciding, nevertheless, to afford asylum to the fugitive and deny his extradition. Moreover, it is even possible for a court so to interpret the provisions governing extradition that asylum is granted even in cases where it would initially appear that surrender would be justified.

Development of extradition in Canada
According to the Jay Treaty, 1794,[116] the first governing the mutual surrender of fugitives between Great Britain as sovereign of Canada and the United States, fugitives charged with murder or forgery were to be surrendered. This expired in 1807. Then by article x of the Webster-Ashburton Treaty, 1842,[117] it was agreed

> to deliver up to justice all persons who, being charged with the crime of murder, or assault with intent to commit murder, or piracy, or arson, or robbery, or forgery, or the utterance of forged paper, committed within the jurisdiction of either, shall seek asylum, or shall be found within the territories of the other; provided that this shall only be done upon such evidence of criminality as, according to the laws of the place where the fugitive or persons so charged shall be found, would justify his apprehension and commitment for trial, if the crime or offence had there been committed.

In 1833 a statute was passed[118] whereby Canada undertook

> to deliver up to justice any person who may have fled to this province or who shall seek refuge therein, being charged with murder, forgery, larceny or other crime, committed without the jurisdiction of this province which crime if committed within this province would by the laws thereof be punishable by death, corporal punishment, by pillory or

whipping, or by confinement at hard labour, to the end that such person may be transported out of this province to the place where such crime shall have been charged to have
been committed.

It also provided that arrest could take place before any application was received
from abroad, and that surrender could be denied if the governor and council deemed
that expedient. Although this statute was superseded by the Webster-Ashburton
Treaty insofar as the United States was concerned, it governed the situation
between Canada and the rest of the world until its repeal in 1860.[119]

It appears to have been the general view at the time that co-operation between
the United States and Canada concerning fugitive criminals should be encouraged,
even when no treaty existed. In 1818, when Canada requested the surrender by
Massachusetts of an American citizen who was charged with forgery in Lower
Canada, John Quincy Adams refused the request,[120] but a year later, in *Re
Washburn*,[121] Chancellor Kent approved the extradition of a fugitive from Canada
on a charge of theft, for 'it is the law and usage of nations, resting on the plainest
principles of justice and public utility, to deliver up offenders charged with felony
and other high crimes, and fleeing from the country in which the crime was committed, into a foreign and friendly jurisdiction.' This dictum was expressly approved
by Reid CJ in *Re Fisher*,[122] when he granted the extradition of a Prussian who had
fled from the United States to Upper Canada. The chief justice held that

> the right of surrender is founded on the principle, that he who has caused an injury is
> bound to repair it, and he who has infringed the laws of any country is liable to the punish-
> ment inflicted by those laws; if we screen him from that punishment, we become parties
> to his crime,   we excite retaliation, – we encourage criminals to take refuge among us.
> We do that as a *nation*, which as individuals it would be dishonourable, nay, criminal
> to do. If, on the contrary, we deliver up the accused to the offended nation, we only fulfil
> our part of the social compact, which directs that the rights of nations as well as individu-
> als should be respected, and a good understanding maintained between them; and this
> is the more requisite among neighbouring states, on account of the daily communication
> which must necessarily subsist between them.

When it was suggested that Fisher's offence was not serious enough to warrant his
extradition, Reid CJ replied that once the right was established the matter was
ended. And when it was pointed out that no demand had come from the United
States, he replied that this did not concern him, since the prisoner was held under
a warrant from Dalhousie as governor in chief, Canada. Again, in 1826, after the
murder of the master and mate of the American cruiser *Fairy* off Newfoundland,
and the flight of the crew to Cape Breton where they were imprisoned, Secretary
Clay offered to transport the wanted men if they were surrendered, and the lieutenant governor of Nova Scotia handed them over.[123]

However, while Canada might have been willing in the absence of a treaty to surrender an alien to the United States, she adopted a somewhat different attitude
when the fugitive was British. In 1833 Lord Aylmer, governor of Lower Canada,
refused to surrender Figsby and others who were wanted for murder on the ground

that such surrender, in the absence of a treaty, would contravene the rights of British subjects to seek a writ of habeas corpus.[124]

Although Canada and the United States appeared willing to help each other to recover common criminals, difficulties arose in connection with fleeing slaves. As early as 1829 a request had been made for British good offices in recovering one Vallard, who had stolen a female slave and fled to Canada. Vaughan, the British minister, replied by quoting part of a report of the Executive Council of Lower Canada:

> In former cases the committee have acted upon the principle, which now seems to be generally understood, that, whenever a crime has been committed, and the perpetrator is punishable according to the *lex loci* of the country in which it was committed, the country in which he is found may rightfully aid the police of the country against which the crime was committed in bringing the criminal to justice; and, upon this ground, have recommended that fugitives from the United States should be delivered up.

But he pointed out that the offence must be *malum in se,* usually admitted to be a crime in every nation; and since Canada did not admit that property could be had in a human being, there was no ground to justify a surrender in this instance.[125]

Another slave case arose after the 1842 treaty had come into force. Anderson, a fleeing slave, killed the man who, in accordance with the law of Missouri, sought to deprive him of his liberty and return him to his owner. Anderson fled to Upper Canada and his extradition was sought. The governor general was instructed to take such measures as were authorized by the law of Canada 'to deliver up the fugitive,' who sought his release by way of habeas corpus. The Court of Queen's Bench remanded him for extradition,[126] and Anderson gave notice of appeal. The secretary of state for the colonies instructed the governor that

> if the result of the appeal be adverse to the prisoner, you will bear in mind that, under the Treaty of Extradition, he cannot be delivered over to the United States authorities by the mere action of the law. That can only be done by a warrant under the hand and seal of the Governor. The case of Anderson is one of the greatest possible importance, and Her Majesty's Government are not satisfied that the decision of the court [of Queen's Bench] at Toronto is in conformity with the view of the Treaty which has hitherto guided the authorities in this country. I am, therefore, to instruct you to abstain in any case from completing the extradition until Her Majesty's Government shall have had further opportunity of considering the question, and, if possible, of conferring with the government of the United States on this subject.[127]

In the meantime, however, Anderson had obtained from the Court of Common Pleas his release on habeas corpus because of irregularity in the proceedings,[128] and no further action was taken.

It is perhaps of interest to note the comments of Dr La Forest on this case:[129]

> In Canada, the institution of slavery did not exist and there was, of course, no law requiring citizens to apprehend escaping slaves. Had the incident occurred in Canada, there-

fore, Anderson might well have been justified in killing the victim in order to retain his liberty. It was nevertheless held by a majority of the Court of Queen's Bench of Upper Canada that it had to deal with the case on the assumption that the victim had been acting with legal authority. That being so, the fugitive should be extradited; a person who in Canada killed a person who was attempting to apprehend him under legal authority would be guilty of murder ... The approach taken in *Re Anderson* seems to be the only logical one; the institutions and laws of the foreign country must necessarily form the background against which to examine events occurring in that country.

It is submitted that while this may be superficially attractive, Dr La Forest has tended to reduce the significance of the wording of the 1842 treaty, which expressly provides that extradition 'shall only be done upon such evidence of criminality as, according to the laws of the place where the fugitive or person so charged shall be found, would justify his apprehension and commitment for trial, if the crime or offence had there been committed.' It is difficult to see how one can gather from these terms that a free man, threatened in his freedom by one who in 'the place where the fugitive ... shall be found' would have no right or power of arrest, can be charged with murder if, in the course of resisting such unlawful arrest, he killed the person seeking to detain him.

Dr La Forest would apparently contend that in every case, including those in which Canadian law would say that a particular action was completely justifiable, a Canadian court would be obliged to import into Canadian jurisprudence some completely alien concept because the action in question was defined as an offence in the law of the country where it occurred. He states that 'no one would argue that a person making a false oath before a qualified official in the United States could not be extradited for perjury on the ground that had the oath been taken before the official in Canada it would not have been valid.' It is interesting in this context to compare the Eisler case in England,[130] in which it was held that the particular oath, though amounting to perjury in the United States, was not perjury in England, and that therefore Eisler could not be extradited. The 1971 treaty with the United States, however, covers 'perjury in any proceeding whatsoever [and] making a false affidavit or statutory declaration for any extrajudicial purpose.'

A statement by Duff J in *Re Collins* (No. 3)[131] was cited by Dr La Forest in support of his views:

one may look at it in two ways. One may take it that one is to apply one's mind to the conditions existing in the demanding State, or that one is to conceive the accused, and the acts of the accused, transported to this country. In the first case, one is to take the definition of the imputed crime in accordance with the law of Canada, and apply that to the acts of the accused in the circumstances in which these acts took place. If in those acts you find that the definition of the crime is satisfied, then you have the statutory and Treaty requisites complied with. In the second case, if you are to conceive the accused pursuing the conduct in question in this country, then along with him you are to transplant his environment; that environment must, I apprehend, include, so far as relevant, the local institutions of the demanding country, the laws affecting the legal powers and rights, and fixing the legal character of the acts of the persons concerned, always excepting, of course, the law supplying the definition of the crime which is charged.

However, nowhere does the learned justice suggest that this transposition extends to principles or institutions of law which would be contrary to the public policy of Canada. And slavery is such an institution.

War crimes
In the *Vallard* case it was pointed out that to be extraditable, an offence must be *malum in se*. It might well be thought that war crimes of the type committed during World War II might fall within this definition, especially in view of the various undertakings given by the United Nations with regard to the surrender and punishment of these individuals.[132] The Canadian attitude in this matter may be seen from a letter of the Department of External Affairs in 1966,[133] to the effect that 'war crimes, as such, are not listed in the schedules of extradition treaties or in our Extradition Act. However, specific acts, such as murder, of which a war criminal could be accused, are listed.' If war crimes were listed *per se,* it would not be possible for the defence of 'political offence' to be raised in connection with them;[134] to deal with them merely as specific crimes, with no mention of their being war crimes, leaves this loophole available.

Extradition in the absence of a treaty
While there was a time when Canada was prepared to surrender fugitive criminals, at least to the United States, without a treaty, the view gradually developed that surrender could take place only if a treaty existed and in accordance with its terms. Nevertheless, some Canadian judges were acutely aware of the difficulties in preserving the rule of law presented by the proximity of Canada to the United States and by their long land frontier. At the same time there has been full recognition of the fact that extradition is directed against the liberty of the individual and that, therefore, it is essential that every attention be paid to the *minutiae* of formality and procedure. This recognition is well brought out in the comments of Osler J in *Re Parker*[135] when he said:

> I regret it, if there really be any foundation for the charge, but if parties who are concerned in prosecuting it will not take common pains to make it, and are content to rest upon depositions only,[136] which turn out to be insufficient, they must take the consequences. For myself, I shall be glad to see the day when 'free trade' in criminals shall exist, but so long as there is an extradition law under which a criminal whose extradition is sought has rights to be observed here, he is entitled to have those rights administered by our courts.

As recently as 1960 the Department of External Affairs expressed its sympathy for something similar to Mr Justice Osler's 'free trade,' pointing out that there is more need today for international co-operation in the field of extradition.

> In an age when it is possible to travel in a few hours by commercial jet air liners to the far corners of the earth, it is important that formal arrangements exist for the extradition of fugitives who might otherwise go unpunished. The existence of these arrangements

also no doubt serves as a deterrent to persons who might think that in committing a crime they could not be brought back to face punishment once they had sought refuge in another country ... This is not to say that the person committing a crime has only in order to escape justice to choose a country as a refuge with which his own country has no extradition treaty ... a country may grant extradition under its municipal laws in the absence of treaty. Moreover, it is possible that the authorities of the country of refuge may institute deportation proceedings against the offender with a view to his return to his own country. The existence of extradition treaties, however, offers a substantial guarantee that fugitive criminals will not escape justice.[137]

In view of the acknowledgement in this statement of the possibility that states may, by virtue of their municipal law, extradite without treaty, it is of interest to bear in mind that part II of the current Extradition Act[138] is headed 'Extradition Irrespective of Treaty.' Section 35(1) of the act provides, however, that 'this Part shall not come into force, with respect to fugitive offenders from any foreign state, until it has been declared by proclamation of the Governor General to be in force and effect as regards such foreign state, from and after a date to be named in the proclamation,' and its scope is limited only to offences which are listed in the Third Schedule of the act, which is narrower than the list in the First Schedule and may well be narrower than the list appearing in normal extradition treaties to which Canada is a party and for which 'treaty offenders' are liable to extradition. By section 2(c) of the act ' " extradition crime" may mean any crime that, if committed in Canada, or within Canadian jurisdiction, would be one of the crimes described in the First Schedule; and, in the application of this Act to the case of any extradition arrangement, "extradition crime" means any crime described in such arrangement, whether or not it is comprised in the said Schedule.' However, part II of the act has never come into force, although it could become more important when Canada becomes a party to the international agreements concerning the treatment of aerial hijackers or any other offenders against international criminal law.

Procedure for extradition
Perhaps it may be as well to give some indication of the procedure which is followed in securing the extradition of offenders to and from Canada. These measures are taken in accordance with the stipulations in the legislation, and are somewhat formal in character.

If a foreign state desires the extradition from our country of one of its criminals, it will instruct its diplomatic mission in Ottawa to make a formal request to the Department of External Affairs for the return of the person sought. The Department of External Affairs transmits the request with accompanying evidence relating to the crime to the Department of Justice which in turn, notifies the attorney general's department of the province where the offender resides. Instructions are then issued for his arrest by the police and he is brought before the extradition judge,[139] who – in the common law provinces – is usually a county court judge but may be a Supreme Court judge, depending upon who is available. [In the Province of Quebec, judges of the Superior Court act in extradition cases.] The country requesting extradition appoints counsel to present the evidence upon which the request for extradition is based. The extradition judge, after the hearing, either commits the accused or orders his release. If committal is ordered, the accused cannot be extradited until 15 days have elapsed in order to provide time for the making of a writ of habeas corpus. After the 15 days have elapsed, the Minister of Justice may issue a Warrant of Surrender, which is sent in duplicate to the Secretary of State for recordation and transmission to the counsel retained by the foreign country. One copy of the Warrant of Surrender is given to the gaoler and the other to the escort taking into custody for delivery to the foreign country.[140]

The normal procedure for securing the extradition from a country of a fugitive wanted in Canada is as follows:

i The Canadian police (provincial or federal, depending on the nature of the offence) communicate directly with the police authorities where the fugitive is or is suspected of being, providing details of the crime for which he is sought. (It is open to the Canadian authorities to make the initial communication through diplomatic channels, although this is not the normal practice.)

ii The foreign police either arrest the fugitive on their own, on a 'holding charge', or, more frequently, on a provisional extradition warrant issued by the local authorities. (In the majority of cases the Attorney-General of the province in question requests the foreign police by telegraphic communication to obtain the provisional arrest of the fugitive.)

iii A hearing is held by the foreign court to determine whether the case falls within the Extradition Treaty in question.

iv If the foreign court decides that the fugitive be held pending a formal extradition hearing, the documentation which forms the basis for the issue of a warrant of arrest in Canada (information and complaint, deposition, related testimony and documents, etc.) is forwarded to the provincial Attorney-General.

v The documents in question are then certified by the Lieutenant-Governor of the province seeking the extradition, (the certification providing that justice has been done insofar as concerns the procedures carried out).

vi The duly certified material is then sent by the provincial Attorney-General to the Federal Department of Justice.

vii The Department of Justice transmits the documents to the Secretary of State for certification by the Governor-General of the signature of the Lieutenant-Governor.

viii The duly certified documents are then forwarded by the Department of Justice to the Department of External Affairs together with a covering letter asking that the formal requisition for the surrender of the fugitive be made to the appropriate authorities of the country in question. Alternatively, the formal request is passed on to External Affairs by Justice without the necessary documents being attached, in the understanding that such documents will be transmitted by the appropriate provincial authorities directly to the provincial legal agents in the country concerned.[141]

The latest statement with regard to the procedure is to be found in the 1971 Treaty of Extradition signed with the United States.[142]

9 1 The request for extradition shall be made through the diplomatic channel.

2 The request shall be accompanied by a description of the person sought, a statement of the facts of the case, the text of the laws of the requesting State describing the offence and prescribing the punishment for the offence and a statement of the law relating to

the limitation of the legal proceedings.

3 When the request relates to a person who has not yet been convicted, it must also be accompanied by a warrant of arrest issued by a judge or other judicial officer of the requesting State and by such evidence as, according to the laws of the requested State, would justify his arrest and committal for trial if the offence had been committed there, including evidence proving the person requested is the person to whom the warrant of arrest refers.

4 When the request relates to a person already convicted, it must be accompanied by the judgment of conviction and sentence passed against him in the territory of the requesting State by a statement showing how much of the sentence has not been served, and by evidence proving that the person requested is the person to whom the sentence refers.

10 1 Extradition shall be granted only if the evidence be found sufficient according to the place where the person sought shall be found, either to justify his committal for trial if the offence of which he is accused had been committed in its territory or to prove that he is the identical person convicted by the courts of the requesting State.

2 The documentary evidence in support of a request for extradition or copies of these documents shall be admitted in evidence in the examination of the request for extradition when, in the case of a request emanating from Canada, they are authenticated by an officer of the Department of Justice of Canada and are certified by the principal diplomatic or consular officer of the United States in Canada, or when, in the case of a request emanating from the United States, they are authenticated by an officer of the Department of State of the United States and are certified by the principal diplomatic or consular officer of Canada in the United States.

11 1 In case of urgency a Contracting Party may apply for the provisional arrest of the person sought pending the presentation of the request for extradition through the diplomatic channel. Such application shall contain a description of the person sought, an indication of intention to request the extradition of the person sought, and a statement of the existence of a warrant of arrest or a judgment of conviction against that person, and such further information if any, as would be necessary to justify the issue of a warrant of arrest had the offence been committed, or the person sought been convicted in the territory of the requested state.

2 On receipt of such an application the requested State shall take the necessary steps to secure the arrest of the person claimed.

3 A person arrested shall be set at liberty upon the expiration of forty-five days from the date of his arrest pursuant to such application, if a request for his extradition accompanied by the documents specified in Article 9 shall not have been received. The stipulation shall not prevent the institution of proceedings with a view to extraditing the person sought if the request is subsequently received.

After all these steps have been taken, the municipal law of the country to which the request has been made comes into operation, and the local courts will usually be the decisive agency for authorizing extradition on the ground that the offence charged and the request are in accordance with the treaty.

Defences to extradition
The most usual defences put forward to a claim for extradition are that there is no

treaty, that the treaty does not apply, that the extradition legislation has not been complied with in some respect, that the offence is not an extradition offence, or that, while the offence *prima facie* appears to be extraditable, this is not the case since it is political in character.

The last defence is in accordance with section 27 of the act which provides that 'no fugitive is liable to surrender ... if it appears (a) that the offence in respect of which the proceedings are taken under this Act is one of a political character, or (b) that such proceedings are being taken with a view to punish him for an offence of a political character.' This section is based on section 3 of the British Extradition Act of 1870,[143] which was dealt with by Denman J in *Re Castioni*.[144] The learned judge held that

> it must be shown that the act is done in furtherance of, done with the intention of assistance, as a sort of overt act in the course of acting in a political manner, a political rising, or a dispute between two parties in the State as to which is to have the government in its hands ... The question really is, whether, upon the facts, it is clear that the man was acting as one of a number of persons engaged in acts of violence of a political character with a political object, and as part of the political movement and rising in which he was taking part.

As a result of this emphasis on the need for organization, it has been held that an offence committed by an anarchist in furtherance of the 'political aims' of that 'movement' could not enjoy the rights of protection extended to a political offender, for 'to constitute an offence of a political character, there must be two or more parties in the State, each seeking to impose the Government of their own choice on the other ... if the offence is committed by one side or the other in pursuance of that object, it is a political offence, otherwise not.'[145]

There have been very few cases in which the plea of political offence has been raised in a Canadian court. *Re Federenko*[146] concerned a request, in accordance with the Anglo-Russian Treaty of 1886,[147] for a fugitive charged with murder. The accused was a member of the Social Democratic party which, undoubtedly, sought to alter the form of government and had in fact carried out a number of revolutionary outrages. The fugitive, while in an area under martial law, killed a local constable who, unaware of his political affiliations, had asked him to identify himself. Having cited Mr Justice Denman's definition in *Castioni,* Mathers CJ of the Manitoba King's Bench inquired:

> was the crime of the accused committed in the furtherance of a political object? He belonged to the social democratic party, whose object was, not only to alter the form of government, but also to do away with private property. A propaganda was carried on by them throughout the country and numerous revolutionary outrages were perpetrated by them ... [In view of the circumstances of the death,] can it be said that the killing was in furtherance of a political object? I think not. Nor do I think the fact that the crime of the accused would, in the demanding State, be called a political crime and be tried by a special tribunal make it a crime of a political character within the meaning of the ... [Treaty].[148] The crime of killing a policeman by a person in no way identified with any political movement would in Russia be so described, and would be tried by the same tribunal.

This decision raises nice issues in connection with any possible future claim for asylum as a political offender by a member of the Black Panthers or the Weathermen fleeing from the United States and charged with the murder of a police officer.

At one time it might have been thought that if a similar case had arisen again in Canada, and particularly if it had gone to appeal, a more liberal approach might have been adopted. The Lord Chief Justice in *Ex parte Kolczynski*[149] recognized that nowadays the political situation in some countries, as for example in eastern Europe, precluded the possibility of an organized attempt by an organized party to overthrow the government and take the reins of power to itself, and held, by looking at the character of the accused themselves, that they were in fact political offenders. Commenting on the impact of this case upon *Federenko*, La Forest states that 'it would seem better in such cases to err on the side of mercy, and it is submitted that *Ex parte Kolczynski* should be followed even where as in the *Federenko* case the cause of the fugitive is unpopular in the country, to which the demand for extradition is made.'[150] Unfortunately, however, *Castioni* seems to have established itself as the authority among most jurisdictions: a United States Circuit Court of Appeals has expressly rejected *Kolczynski* and continued to apply the *Castioni* principle;[151] and the House of Lords in *Schtraks* v *Government of Israel*[152] reaffirmed the authority of *Castioni*, although Viscount Radcliffe recognized that

> if ... the idea of 'political offence' is not altogether remote from that of 'political asylum,'[153] it is easy to regard as a political offence, an offence committed by someone in furtherance of his design to escape from a political regime which he found intolerable. I have no criticism to make of the decision in ... *Kolczynski,* but the grounds on which it was decided are expressed too generally to offer much guidance for other cases in the future ... The idea that lies behind the phrase 'offence of a political character' is that the fugitive is at odds with the State that applies for his extradition on some issue connected with the political control or government of the country.

It would appear that the Canadian courts accept this latter idea rather than the narrower concept of *Castioni* when met with the defence of political offence from, for example, a 'radical' fugitive charged with killing a police officer. Thus, in *Re Commonwealth of Puerto Rico and Hernandez*[152a] it was held, on the basis of *Schtraks*, that the killing of a police officer during riots by members of a Puerto Rican independence movement directed against the activities of the ROTC on a university campus, was not 'political.'

> The question in issue should be determined by looking primarily at the events of the day and the actual circumstances of the murder. The actual political climate of Puerto Rico at that time is of secondary interest. It is important only if it is a predominant factor in the circumstances of the murder. It is not relevant that the act subsequently became a major political issue if it was not of a predominantly political character at the time of the act ... What took place ... was not to overthrow the government but rather to force the university authorities to divorce the R.O.T.C. from the campus ... One cannot deny that political considerations were involved in the antagonism towards the cadets, but I cannot feel persuaded that this could be considered a political uprising against the government or that the murder ... could be considered an act in furtherance of a political uprising.

Moreover, in *Re State of Wisconsin and Armstrong*,[152b] concerning charges of murder and arson during campus rioting, it was held that the burden of proof was upon the fugitive, and, in the light of *Castioni, Federenko,* and *Schtraks,* this was found not to be discharged: 'The offences ... are not of a political character and the proceedings are not taken with a view to prosecute or punish the respondent for an offence of a political character.'

Perhaps the most frequent ground put forward against extradition is that the crime alleged is not within the terms of the relevant treaty. This may be on the ground that the nomenclature is wrong, or that the crime alleged is not an offence under Canadian law. This latter contention has already been illustrated by the discussion concerning *Re Anderson.*[154] In *Re Brooks,*[155] Garrow J of the Supreme Court of Ontario, applying the principles laid down by Duff J in *Re Collins,*[156] held that for extradition from Canada to take place, the demanding country must establish: '(1) that the imputed crime is a crime within the Extradition Treaty; and (2) within the Extradition Act; and (3) within the law of ... [the demanding state]; and (4) that there was such evidence of criminality before the learned Judge as, if the crime had been committed in Canada, would, according to Canadian law, have justified the committal of the accused for trial.' It would appear that the learned judge has gone too far in the postulation of his second principle, unless he means it in the most formal sense, for, as has been seen, by section 2(c) extradition will lie even in respect of crimes not specified in the act if they are included in the relevant treaty. The evidence required by his fourth postulate is 'such as to justify a magistrate in a similar case under our law committing him for the purpose of standing his trial,'[157] or, as it was put by Wells J of the Ontario High Court: 'My duty is to determine whether on the findings of fact of the learned Commissioner [of extradition], there is any evidence which could go to a jury and upon which a jury, properly directed, could convict;'[158] it does not have to be evidence showing guilt, merely sufficient to leave to the jury.

There have been a number of interesting cases in which it has been alleged that the offence was not properly named. In *Re Arton*[159] an English court held that exact identity of nomenclature was unnecessary. This principle has also been followed in Canada, and in *Re Insull*[160] it was held that 'an offence shown to be according to the laws of the State of Illinois embezzlement, larceny or larceny by a bailee is theft in that State and in Canada, and, therefore, an extraditable crime.' And Associate Chief Justice Scott of the Quebec Supreme Court has expressly stated[161] that 'it is not necessary that the crime alleged be described in identical language in both countries, provided that in substance it is the same.' This type of problem has also arisen in connection with persons who have been extradited to stand trial in Canada. The Extradition Treaty with the United States refers to fraud by a banker,[162] and the accused in *R. v Nesbitt*[163] was charged with the statutory offence of 'wilfully' making a false return under the Bank Act.[164] But the indictment was quashed, the court declaring that 'the Crown has substituted for the word "wilfully" the word "fraudulently"; and so for the purpose of bringing the matter within the Extradition Treaty, charges the accused with something different from the statutory offence of which he may or may not be guilty.'

Along similar lines, *Buck v R.*[165] was even more emphatic. Buck had been extradited to Canada from the United States on a charge of fraud arising from a statement published in the *News-Telegram*. He was convicted, however, of 'concurring in publishing a false statement' in the *Albertan,* which had not been mentioned in the extradition proceedings. In the Supreme Court, Fitzpatrick CJ held:

> The person surrendered shall not be triable for any offence other than the offence for which he was surrendered, until he shall have an opportunity of returning to the country by which he was surrendered ... The publication of a statement on one day in a newspaper cannot be said to constitute the same offence as the publication in another newspaper on another day of a statement which may or may not be to the same effect or identical with the first. On the extradition proceedings, the only statement proved was the one published by T in the *News-Telegram*. At the trial the statement relied upon, which was said to be the subject of the charge, was that published by C in the *Albertan,* which was not before the extradition commissioner, and it cannot, therefore, be said that he was extradited for concurring in the publication of that statement.

Anglin J expressed it in more general terms:

> 'The offence for which (the accused) was surrendered'[166] means the specific offence with ... which he was charged before the extradition commissioner (in the surrendering state) and in respect of which that official held that a prima facie case had been established and ordered his extradition, and not another offence or crime, though of identical character and committed about the same time and under similar circumstances.

Dubuc DCJ of the Alberta District Court considered *Re Neilsen*[167] to be the converse of *Buck*. Denmark had applied for Neilsen's extradition for fraud and larceny under the Anglo-Danish Treaty of 1873,[168] which includes larceny and fraud by a bailee. It was held that there was insufficient evidence to sustain the fraud charge, and the judge said:

> The accused is charged with larceny, and the evidence suggests, that if he committed an offence, that offence was fraud by a bailee ... This is the converse case [of *Buck* v *R.*], and I do not think I would have authority to extradite a prisoner for an entirely different offence than that with which he is charged. Conversion by a bailee was not larceny at common law, and whilst it now constitutes theft by reason of The Criminal Code ... there is no evidence before me that the Danish law includes conversion by a bailce under the term of larceny ... where facts only constitute a crime in this country because of statutory provision, it should be proven that the foreign country has also included such facts within the purview of its statutory law ... If it had been proven that fraud by a bailee was included under 'larceny' in Denmark, the fact that it is included under 'theft' in Canada, would not help the prosecution. But in the absence of evidence that the facts suggested in the foreign depositions constituted the offence of larceny, which is the offence charged, ... the prisoner should be discharged.

The learned judge went on to say, in words reminiscent of Osler J in *Re Parker,*[169] that

> when a foreign state demands the extradition of a person who, encouraged by our immigration policy, has gone so far as to establish himself as an industrious and law-abiding

citizen here [since Neilsen had been in Canada only one year, the Judge must have meant 'resident'], the demanding state must be prepared to prove all the formalities preliminary to an order for extradition, and while the evidence upon the merits of a charge only needs to prove a case sufficient for committal for trial in Canada, the prisoner should be given the benefit of the doubt as to whether the foreign law covers his case, or as to any other formalities which must be strictly proven or complied with, before extradition will be ordered. He is entitled to protection from prosecutions here or abroad which are not fully substantiated by the preliminary requisites of law.[170]

The foreign law must be proved by proper expert evidence. In *Re Low*[171] the statement of a United States customs officer as to the law under the Tariff Act of that country was not accepted:

In the absence of evidence of his qualifications it cannot be assumed as a fact that he possessed that legal knowledge necessary in order to qualify him to give evidence as to the laws of the United States respecting the charge of bribery in question here. In order to be entitled to extradition of the accused, it was necessary for the United States to prove that at the time of the committal by the accused of the alleged acts of bribery the same were criminal according to the United States. There was no evidence that at that time there existed any law in the United States making them criminal. Moreover, even if ... [the customs officer's] evidence was construed as an expression of his opinion that such a law then existed, he was not qualified to prove that law.

In her treaty practice as it is now developing, Canada demands a copy of the legislation under which the charge is laid to accompany the request for extradition.[172]

It sometimes happens during a criminal trial that, while the evidence is insufficient to prove the offence charged, it is clearly enough to prove some lesser offence. This may also happen during the trial of one who has been returned to Canada to face charges. In *R. v Flannery*[173] the accused had waived his rights during extradition proceedings in the United States but before an order for surrender had been made. Thus there would be no breach of faith, as far as the United States was concerned, if Canada tried him for any offence under the Criminal Code. The conviction of the accused for attempted murder was set aside, as there was no evidence of an intent to kill; and the Court of Appeal favoured a new trial for grievous bodily harm, which did not figure in the Extradition Treaty.

Where the accused has been extradited under the treaty there cannot be a conviction for a lesser offence included in the offence for which the accused was extradited unless the lesser offence is itself extraditable. In this case it is not. The trouble [is] ... whether the accused was ever 'surrendered by a foreign state in pursuance of an extradition agreement.'[174] ... At some stage the accused consented to come back with the Canadian officer ... Certainly American authority in some form had been exercised to arrest and detain the accused ... If the accused had insisted on formal extradition proceedings and the Judge there had taken the same view as we had done of the evidence, he would ... have held that there was nothing upon which he could reasonably be convicted of the crime charged and would have refused extradition ... The question of good faith towards the accused is one which, as a matter of law, under the treaty the Court cannot properly consider ... It is only good faith with the other contracting country which must be preserved at all costs; and ... it does not appear that the extradition authorities of the United States were ever approached at all. So that I do not think we ought to hesitate to grant a new trial on any legal ground referable to the interpretation of the treaty or of our statute passed in consequence of it.

In fact, the court decided on other grounds to exercise its discretion under section 1018 of the Criminal Code and refused a new trial.

Extradition in narcotics cases
In recent years both the United States and Canada have become concerned about the traffic in narcotics, and this concern has been reflected in Canadian extradition practice. The history of extraditable offences, particularly with regard to narcotics offences, was outlined by McRuer CJHC, Ontario, in *Re Brisbois*.[175] He explained that

the first Treaty between Her Britannic Majesty and the United States of America was entered into in 1842.[176] It related to seven offences: murder, assault with intent to commit murder, piracy, arson, robbery, forgery and utterance of forged paper, and was confined to persons charged with these crimes. In 1889 a Supplementary Convention[177] was entered into which added several other crimes and extended the Treaty to persons convicted of the crimes respectively named. Among the crimes added in 1889 were included 'crimes and offences against the laws of both countries for the suppression of slavery and slave-trading.' It will be noted that this clause is general in its terms and does not purport to detail the precise crimes that come within it. A further Supplementary Convention was entered into in 1900[178] adding other enumerated crimes. In 1905 the crime of bribery was added as an extraditable crime together with 'offences if made criminal by the laws of both countries against bankruptcy law.'[179] In 1922 a Supplementary Convention[180] added wilful desertion or wilful non-support of minor and dependent children and by a Convention of 1925[181] 'crimes and offences against the laws for the suppression of the traffic in narcotics' were made extraditable and added as clause 17 of the Convention of 1889 ... In this Convention the high contracting parties adopted the language that had been used in the Supplementary Convention of 1889 with respect to crimes and offences against the laws for the suppression of slavery and slave trading and did not attempt to spell out or define either the crimes, offences or laws 'for the suppression of the traffic in narcotics.' In my view this was done designedly so that the Treaty would broadly comprehend all crimes and offences for which persons may be convicted in the course of the direct suppression of the traffic in narcotics.

In this case it was suggested that the United States indictment was not sufficiently specific, but

such an argument would place much too narrow an interpretation on the broad language of clause 17 of the Convention. Crimes against the laws for the suppression of the traffic in narcotics are the crimes and offences that are made extraditable. These words encompass any laws that Parliament has made directly available to the law enforcement agencies for the suppression of the traffic in narcotics ... When the Convention of 1925 was entered into, many forms of dealing and trafficking in narcotics were indictable offences under the Opium and Narcotic Drugs Act.[182] Likewise it was an indictable offence to conspire with anyone to commit any of ... [those] indictable offences ... There is no essential difference between the law of the United States of America and the law of Canada in this regard ... [In the British Extradition Act, 1870, section 26[183]] the term 'extradition crime' means a crime which if committed in England or within English jurisdiction would be one of the crimes described in the first schedule to the Act. Thus ... it is the Act that governs and not the Treaty. This is not so in Canada. Under s.2(c) of the Extradition Act an extradition crime is defined in this manner '... whether or not it is comprised in the said Schedule.' The last portion of this definition does not appear in the British Act and in fact one does not find anything in the First Schedule to the Canadian Act that refers to the suppression of traffic in narcotics nor to many other crimes that are now made extraditable by treaty, Convention or arrangement ... The prisoner has been convicted of an offence that comes within the terms of the Treaty existing between Canada and the United States of America.

The learned chief justice specifically accepted the unreported decision of Spence J in *Re Agucci* to the effect that 'conspiring to traffic in narcotics is within the class "crimes and offences against the suppression of the traffic in narcotics" (Art. 1, Supp. Conv., 1925), despite the fact that the crime of conspiracy does not appear by name in any schedule to the main Convention.'

While the 1967 treaties with Austria and Israel refer, *simpliciter,* to 'offences in connection with the traffic in dangerous drugs,' that of 1971 with the United States is more detailed: 'offences against the laws relating to the traffic in, production, manufacture, or importation of narcotic drugs, Cannabis sativa L., hallucinogenic drugs, amphetamines, barbiturates, cocaine and its derivatives.'

Interprovincial rendition and Commonwealth fugitives
What has been said so far relates only to the extradition of fugitives between Canada and foreign countries. Interprovincial rendition has applied since 1796,[184] including after the British North America Act made the criminal law federal. The Imperial Fugitive Offenders Act of 1881[185] provided for rendition among the territories that then comprised the British Empire. This was immediately followed by the Canadian Fugitive Offenders Act, 1882,[186] which was intended to assert Canadian competence in this area. By virtue of the Colonial Laws Validity Act, 1865,[187] however, the Canadian statute could apply only to the extent that it was not repugnant to the British act, which otherwise prevailed.[188] In the 1970 Revised Statutes of Canada the Canadian act is re-enacted,[189] and it has been suggested that 'the British statute only applies [now] to a limited extent within Canada, for the Statute of Westminster, 1931,[190] provides that the Colonial Laws Validity Act no longer applies to Canadian statutes.'[191]

By section 2(c) of the Canadian act, ' "fugitive" means a person accused of having committed an offence to which this Act applies in any part of Her Majesty's dominions, except Canada, and who has left that part'; and by section 3 the act

applies to treason and to piracy, and to every offence whether called felony, misdemeanour, crime or by any other name, that is, for the time being, punishable in the part of Her Majesty's dominions in which it was committed, either on indictment or information, by imprisonment with hard labour for twelve months or more, or by any greater punishment; and ... rigorous imprisonment, and any confinement in a prison combined with labour, by whatever name it is called, shall be deemed to be imprisonment with hard labour.

Section 4 broadens the act even further, providing that it 'applies to every such offence, notwithstanding that, by the law of Canada, it is not an offence or not an offence punishable in manner aforesaid.' The scope of the Fugitive Offenders Act is therefore far wider than is that of the Extradition Act.

There is no provision in the Imperial or the Canadian Fugitive Offenders Act recognizing immunity for political offences, on the somewhat out-of-date assumption that an act directed against the government or political regime in any of Her Majesty's dominions is an offence against Her Majesty and is not in any way altered by taking up residence in some other of Her Majesty's territories. Apart from the political unreality of such an approach, it is clear that there can be no validity to this theory in those dominions which have become republics and can no longer really be described as 'Her Majesty's dominions' in the sense of the statute.

Starting with India, various Commonwealth countries have introduced legislation whereby fellow members of the Commonwealth are, from the point of view of extradition, treated in exactly the same way as other foreign countries, necessitating ordinary extradition treaties instead of the Fugitive Offenders system. This matter was referred to the Commonwealth Law Ministers' Conference of 1966, which

> considered that Commonwealth extradition arrangements should be based on reciprocity and substantially uniform legislation incorporating certain features commonly found in extradition treaties, e.g., a list of returnable offences, the establishment of a prima facie case before return, and restrictions on the return of political offenders. The meeting accordingly formulated a scheme[192] setting out principles which could form the basis of legislation within the Commonwealth and recommended that effect should be given to the scheme in each Commonwealth country.[193]

As yet, Canada has not enacted any legislation of the kind here envisaged, nor has she entered into any extradition arrangement with any Commonwealth country. The old Fugitive Offenders Act still governs and will do so even for Commonwealth countries which have replaced it, with the result that there is no possibility of reciprocal treatment.

An interesting case illustrating the interplay of interprovincial rendition and the operation of the Imperial Fugitive Offenders Act was the British Columbia decision in *Re McDougall's Habeas Corpus Application*.[194] The applicant was wanted in Alberta for theft and while on bail went to Scotland. While still in Scotland he was charged in British Columbia with armed robbery and possession of stolen property, and that province secured his return in accordance with the imperial act. The applicant contended that he had been returned to stand trial for certain offences in British

Columbia and opposed his surrender by that province to Alberta, only to be met by the judge's comment:

> I am of the opinion that it is impossible to read a provision similar to s.33 of the Extradition Act[195] into the Fugitive Offenders Act, 1881, by necessary implication of law or otherwise, and thus limit the obvious intention of parliament to make a surrendered fugitive amenable to the law of the requisitioning country for any offence that he may have committed; the statute has made no restrictive provision in his favour.

In 1966 the Canadian government made a statement in reply to a query as to the present scope of the Canadian Fugitive Offenders Act to the effect that it was not clear to which Commonwealth countries the act still applied, as this 'depends on the judicial interpretation of the meaning of 'Her Majesty's dominions' and ... the status of certain Commonwealth countries which have become republics is no longer clear in that respect. Any particular case might have to be decided on its merits by a Canadian court.'[196] If the Canadian court in question seeks guidance on this matter, it may find it in the decision of the English courts in *Re Armah and Government of Ghana,*[197] in which it was held that the imperial act still applied as between Britain and Ghana even though the latter had become a republic.

Summary

As is its position with the law concerning immigration and deportation, Canada's law and practice with regard to asylum and extradition are in no way out of line with what is generally regarded as being consistent with international law. This does not mean that they are identical with the law and practice of the rest of the world, nor is there any reason why they should be. Most countries regard asylum as a matter of political discretion. Each will, therefore, afford asylum to fugitives purely for its own reasons, and its practice will, of necessity, reflect its own prejudices and ideologies. Insofar as political offenders are concerned, as distinct from asylum-seekers not charged with any offences, Canada appears to follow the general practice which regards as essential some organized effort on behalf of an organized movement aimed at the overthrow of the established government. If Canada is in the future faced with the 'political offence' defence to an extradition request, it may well be desirable for her courts to adopt a more liberal approach recognizing the realities of modern politics, acknowledging that there are some countries in which an opposition movement cannot exist, and perhaps even accepting that at the present time those who describe themselves as anarchists may also be politically motivated. Indeed, there are even some Commonwealth countries which do not tolerate any opposition, and it is perhaps time that Canada, between herself and other Commonwealth countries, abandoned the old imperial practices which are no longer of practical validity, and brought her practice in the area of inter-Commonwealth rendition into line with her normal extradition processes.

In view of the nature of modern international travel it may be that Canada should take to heart the opinion of Osler J in the nineteenth century and take the first steps towards introducing a 'free trade' with regard to fugitive criminals. So long as the Extradition Act, which already recognizes the possibility of extradition without treaty, is observed and its provisions strictly interpreted, there are probably sufficient safeguards to protect those who should not be extradited, while it could be ensured that no person who should be sent back to stand trial receives hospitality on the sole ground that Canada has no treaty with the country seeking his return. If necessary, a reciprocity section could be written into the legislation so that Canada would surrender her fugitive criminals without a treaty to any country which under its laws would extradite in the absence of a treaty. It would be relatively simple in any given case to obtain from the local embassy a certificate that the requisitioning state has similar legislation.

IMMIGRATION, EXTRADITION, AND ASYLUM IN CANADIAN TREATIES

The treaty that is perhaps regarded as possessing the greatest significance at the present time is the Charter of the United Nations, which, however, makes no provision for immigration, deportation, extradition, or asylum. Nevertheless, the members of the United Nations have undertaken to recognize the immunity of international civil servants. In view of this 'the Canadian Government, notwithstanding treaty arrangements between Canada and the United States providing for extradition, will not seek to extradite persons who are in the United States on invitation of the United Nations organization during a period of time reasonably related to such invitation.'[198]

While the charter is silent on the matters with which this discussion has been concerned, there are some multilateral treaties to which Canada is a party that do have provisions relating to the issues under consideration. They are few, however, and reflect a comparatively new development. Traditionally, the discretion of countries on these matters is limited only by bilateral arrangements, and such arrangements have tended to be restricted to extradition. The practice of Latin America[199] and the Extradition Treaty drawn up under the auspices of the Council of Europe[200] are unique, the exceptions that prove the rule.

Bilateral treaties

General
Until comparatively recently, Canada had not become a party in her own name to any bilateral extradition treaties. Two such treaties were signed in 1967, one with Israel in March[201] and the other with Austria in May.[202] This latter, although it does not expressly say so, replaced the 1873 treaty between the United Kingdom and Austria-Hungary,[203] which was suspended by the outbreak of World War II and not revived for Austria, although it was revived in the case of Hungary by article x of the Peace Treaty.[204] The latest bilateral extradition treaty to be signed by Canada is that of December 1971 with the United States.[205] Apart from these treaties, as the Department of External Affairs has stated,[206] 'Canada is bound by extradition treaties with approximately 40 other countries but all of these are in whole or in part older British treaties,[207] which were extended to apply to Canada in the 19th century or in the earlier part of the 20th century.' The continued validity of these treaties becomes clear from a statement by the undersecretary of state for external affairs, who wrote on 13 October 1967[208] in reply to an inquiry about extradition from Canada to Mexico:

An extradition treaty was concluded in 1889 between Britain and Mexico.[209] This treaty applies to a number of offences including fraud, false pretenses and crimes against bankruptcy laws. ... Once ... [the alleged fugitive wanted by the Toronto police] has been located and arrested the Government will, of course, take the appropriate steps under the extradition treaty with Mexico to arrange for his return to Canada.

British treaties

Before the signature of the 1971 treaty with the United States, and in fact earlier than the treaties with Israel and Austria, Canada had herself been the signatory to two Supplementary Conventions with the United States, amending the original treaty of 1842: as was pointed out in the outline history of Canadian-United States extradition relations provided by Chief Justice McRuer in *Re Brisbois*,[210] drug-trafficking was made extraditable in 1925; and in 1951[211] a further Supplementary Convention was signed extending the 1900 Supplementary Convention to

obtaining property, money or valuable securities by false pretences or by defrauding the public or any person by deceit or falsehood or other fraudulent means, whether such deceit or falsehood or any fraudulent means would or would not amount to a false pretence ... [and] [m]aking use of the mails in connection with schemes devised or intended to deceive or defraud the public or for the purpose of obtaining money under false pretences.

It is clear that the governments of both the United States and Canada were of the opinion that the 1842 Webster-Ashburton Treaty continued in full force.

In 1953, however, an attempt was made to deny the validity of this opinion – an attempt which, if successful, would have invalidated every extradition treaty by which Canada then regarded herself as bound. In *Ex parte O'Dell and Griffen*[212] it was contended on behalf of the applicants who were wanted for murder in New York

that there was no subsisting extradition treaty or convention between Canada and the United States ... [since] the only treaty or convention in existence within the meaning of the Extradition Act of Canada, is the Ashburton Treaty of 1842, which was entered into between Her Britannic Majesty and the United States of America ... It is urged ... that since the enactment ... of the Statute of Westminster the Ashburton treaty ceased to have any validity in Canada; that Canada had only colonial status when that treaty was made, but since the enactment of the Statute of Westminster Canada has been an independent and self-governing nation. It is argued that ... the present relationship between the Crown and this country is completely different from the relationship which existed in 1842 when Canada was only a possession of Her Britannic Majesty in America and that consequently the Ashburton Treaty, not being a treaty made by Her Britannic Majesty on behalf of Canada as a self-governing and independent nation, no longer has any force and effect.

After this outline of the applicant's case, the court continued:

It is undoubtedly true that since 1931 Canada has been independently represented in the United States and in other foreign nations by her own diplomatic representatives and has entered into treaties with foreign countries through her own ministers of state without reference to the Government of the United Kingdom, but I am quite unable to apprehend how ... the Statute of Westminster can possibly have the effect ascribed to it ... It is declared and enacted that the Parliament of a Dominion has full power to make laws having extraterritorial operation ... [and] that no Act of Parliament of the United Kingdom thereafter passed shall extend or be deemed to extend to a Dominion unless it is expressly declared in that Act that the Dominion has requested and consented to the enactment thereof. Had it been intended that the Ashburton treaty or any other convention which had been entered into ... by the Imperial Government ... prior to this time, affecting Canada or any of its Provinces, should cease to have validity, one would expect to find express provision for it in the Statute of Westminster or in some other statute. There is nothing to prevent Canada from entering into a new treaty with the United States or substituting some other extradition arrangement for the one which is now [covered by] the Ashburton treaty, but until that is done that treaty remains in full force and effect and is binding upon the signatories thereto, including Canada. Indeed it would be a startling and extraordinary thing if Canada and the United States had been without an extradition arrangement for a period of approximately twenty-two years. Many extradition proceedings have taken place during that period and it is rather astonishing, if this point has any merit in it, that it was not at least raised before this date.

This judgment, which is beyond question a correct exposition of the law, might have been further strengthened had Schroeder J pointed out that the extradition arrangement of 1951 was signed by L.B. Pearson and Stuart S. Carson for Canada, that the instruments of ratification were to be exchanged in Ottawa, and that its official title is 'Supplementary Convention to the Supplementary Convention between Her Majesty and the United States of America for the Mutual Extradition of Fugitive Criminals signed at Washington, December 13, 1900.' Obviously the two governments were convinced that the earlier agreement was unaffected by any statutory of constitutional changes that might have taken place since 1900 and was therefore still valid. The same must be true of the Supplementary Convention of 1889 since that of 1900 is declared to be intended to add to the list of crimes in the earlier agreement, which in turn expressly extends the scope of the Ashburton treaty. The fact that the 1971 treaty with the United States, when ratified, will replace the Webster-Ashburton Treaty with all its supplementary conventions does not in any way affect the validity of the reasoning in this judgment with regard to the other extradition treaties signed by Britain and extended to Canada. Perhaps it should be pointed out that the application for extradition in *Re State of Wisconsin and Armstrong*[212a] was lodged under the Webster-Ashburton Treaty.

Treaties with Israel and Austria
Although the treaties with Israel and Austria were entered into almost simultaneously, their terms are not identical. In the first place, the crimes listed in the Israeli treaty do not include bigamy, or 'unlawful and wilful seizure of an aircraft [or] unlawful and wilful acts that are intended or likely to damage an aircraft or endanger its occupants.' In view of the hijackings that have been directed against Israel, it might have been thought that this offence would certainly be included; and if it were argued that these hijackings were political offences and so not extraditable, article 4(d) of the Israel treaty would apply. Article 4 is the non-extraditability provision

of each of the conventions, but they differ in their ambit. The Austrian treaty does not permit the extradition of any person whose offence is 'solely against military law,' nor 'if the act for which his extradition is sought was not punishable, at the time it was committed, by the law of the requesting and requested State.'

It would appear, therefore, that the principle of double criminality applies in the case of Austria, but not in the case of Israel; however, the same effect may well be achieved by virtue of the fact that by article 8(a) of the treaty with Israel, a judicial officer in Canada may issue a warrant 'on production of a warrant of arrest issued in Israel, or upon an information or complaint ... upon such evidence as, in the opinion of such authority, would justify the issue of a warrant if the offence of which the person is accused or is alleged to have been convicted had been committed in Canada.' Article 5 of the Austria treaty provides that 'neither State shall be obliged to extradite its own nationals,' but this provision is missing from the Israel treaty. Both treaties allow extradition to be refused if the offence for which the fugitive is requested carries the death penalty in the requesting country, but not in the country requested.

As far as political offences are concerned, both treaties recognize this exemption; and they also grant protection to an individual if the extradition request has been made 'for the purpose of prosecuting or punishing him on account of his race, religion, nationality or political opinion or his position may be prejudiced for any of these reasons.' Both treaties preclude a trial for any offence other than that for which the fugitive was surrendered; they also prohibit his surrender by the requesting state to a third state, unless he has failed to leave the requesting state within the time specified – in the case of the Israel treaty sixty days, but only thirty in the case of the treaty with Austria. The Israel treaty permits trial on a different charge if the fugitive leaves the territory of the requesting state after extradition and then voluntarily returns thereto. And in both treaties, the requested state may give permission to the requesting state for prosecution on a different charge or for extradition to another state.

Despite these differences the treaties are very close to each other and broadly reproduce the articles which formerly appeared in the imperial treaties to which Canada succeeded.

1971 treaty with the United States
The 1971 treaty with the United Utates which replaces the earlier series of arrangements contains certain peculiarities of its own. These may well act as precedents for Canada's future treaties, and may even serve as models for the treaties to be entered into by other states and which are intended to deal with some of the realities of modern international life.

In the first place, the treaty's territorial scope extends to the airspace and to the territorial waters of the parties, to vessels and aircraft bearing their nationality, and to aircraft leased without crew to lessees having their permanent place of business or permanent residence in their territory, if the aircraft is in flight or the vessel is on the high seas when the offence is committed (the definition of flight being that found in the 1970 Hague Convention for the Suppression of Unlawful Seizure of Aircraft[213]). While such offences are considered to have been committed within the territory if the aircraft lands therein with the offender still on board, if the offence has been committed outside the territory of the requesting state, 'the executive or other appropriate authority of the requested State shall have power to grant the extradition if the laws of the requested State provide for jurisdiction over such an offence committed in similar circumstances.' Further, the treaty provides for surrender in respect of 'any of the offences listed in the Schedule ... provided these offences are punishable by the laws of both Contracting Parties by a term of imprisonment exceeding one year'; and among the offences listed in the schedule is 'any unlawful seizure or exercise of control of an aircraft by force or violence or threat of force or violence, or by any other form of intimidation, on board such aircraft.' It should be noted that insofar as these hijacking provisions are concerned, the Canadian Criminal Code required amendment for them to become effective.

The treaty also covers attempts and conspiracy to commit any of the scheduled offences, and extends to 'any offence against a federal law of the United States in which ... [any of these] offences ... is a substantial element, even if transporting, transportation, the use of the mails or interstate facilities are also elements of the specific offence.'

As with the treaties with Austria and Israel and the earlier treaties affecting Canada, this one also exempts political offenders; but there is no reference to protection for one who might be in danger on account of his race, religion, nationality, or political opinion, an exclusion which might prove of importance in connection with some recent entrants into Canada from the United States. On the other hand, reflecting the Cross kidnapping and similar phenomena, especially in Latin America, the treaty expressly provides that 'a kidnapping, murder or other assault against the life or physical integrity of a person to whom a Contracting Party has the duty according to international law to give special protection, or any attempt to commit such an offence with respect to any such person,' shall not be regarded as of 'a political character.' By restricting this exception to those to whom there is a 'duty according to international law to give special protection,' the treaty acknowledges that the kidnapping or murder of a local politician, as happened with Pierre Laporte, might well be political in character entitling the offender to protection from extradition. This provision is in line with the proposal submitted to the Hague Conference of the International Law Association in 1970 by its committee on the legal aspects of the problem of asylum, although the draft convention prepared by that committee recognized that the kidnapping of a diplomat possessing the nationality of the kidnapper might in fact be regarded as a political offence.[214] Strangely, the treaty also specifically excludes from the concept of political offences those relating to the traffic in narcotics if committed on board an aircraft engaged in commercial services carrying passengers.

Like the treaty with Israel, and unlike that with Austria, the treaty with the United States does not exclude the surrender of nationals. In fact, in view of the nature of the relations between Canada and its neighbour, the length of their common frontier and the facility with which nationals cross from one country to another, such a limitation would largely render the treaty useless. There is, however, an exception which does not appear in the earlier treaties. If the person whose extradition is requested is under the age of eighteen, or was under that age at the time of the commission of the offence, 'and is considered by the requested State to be one of its residents, the requested State, upon a determination that extradition would disrupt the social readjustment and rehabilitation of that person, may recommend to the requesting State that the request for extradition be withdrawn.'

For the main part, the remaining provisions of the 1971 treaty are similar to those in the earlier treaties, save that the list of extradition offences in the schedule is somewhat different, reflecting perhaps some of the special conditions existing between the two countries. There is no reference to abortion, nor is bigamy mentioned; and the offence of unlawful sexual acts with minors is not confined to girls under sixteen, makes no reference to the sex of the victim, and postulates 'the age specified by the laws of both the requesting and requested States.' It also makes the wilful non-support of a minor extraditable when it is likely to result in injury or danger to his life. Further offences listed include acts done with intent to endanger the safety of any person travelling by any means of transportation; use of the mails in connection with schemes intended to deceive or defraud the public or obtain by false pretences; making or possessing explosive substances with intent to endanger life or cause severe damage to property; and obstructing the course of justice by seeking to dissuade a witness by corrupt means, or attempting to influence a juror, or for corrupt consideration abstaining from giving evidence or doing anything as a juror. In addition, as has been seen,[215] the provisions concerning narcotic drugs are more specific than in earlier treaties.

Multilateral arrangements

It has been in the humanitarian field that Canada has been prepared to undertake extradition or asylum commitments as a result of multilateral engagements. It has already been pointed out that the Universal Declaration of Human Rights[216] asserted that everyone had the right to seek and enjoy asylum from persecution. Canada voted in favour of this resolution of the General Assembly; but since it imposes no concomitant legal obligation upon states to grant the asylum which is sought, she is in breach of no commitment in continuing her policy of granting asylum according to her discretion. The Genocide Convention[217] which was adopted by the General Assembly the day before the Universal Declaration, is a treaty and has been ratified by Canada. While it imposes no obligation upon the parties to extradite those alleged to have committed genocide, it does provide that genocide shall not be considered a political crime for extradition purposes – a somewhat more positive approach than that indicated in the 1966 statement of the Department of External Affairs as being Canadian policy regarding the extradition of war criminals.[218]

In some treaties to which she is a party, Canada has undertaken an obligation to make specific acts extraditable offences. This is the case in regard to white slaving,[219] as to which she agreed that 'the offences mentioned ... shall ... be deemed ipso facto to be included among the offences giving cause for extradition according to the already existing Conventions between the Contracting Parties.' Since the other parties to the extradition conventions in question would also be parties to the white slavery agreement and, therefore, bound by the same obligation, this is an example of a multilateral treaty being used as an amending process to bilateral treaties of a more general character which already exist among some of the parties to the later multilateral agreement. The 1936 Convention concerning Illicit Traffic in Dangerous Drugs[220] is even wider in its effect, since article 9(1) provides that 'the offences set out in Article 2 shall be deemed to be included as extradition crimes in any extradition treaty which has been or may hereafter be concluded between any of the High Contracting Parties.' This convention, therefore, not merely amends existing treaties, but obliges the parties to include drug offences in their future extradition treaties, although should they fail to do so the convention will operate to fill this *lacuna*. It would appear as if the 1961 Single Convention on Narcotic Drugs[221] retreats somewhat from this commitment, for article 36(2)(b) merely makes it 'desirable' that narcotics offences be included as extradition crimes in any 'treaty which has been or may hereafter be concluded.' Canada is a party to the Narcotics Convention; but as was illustrated by *Re Brisbois* and *Re Agucci,*[222] Canada had passed her own narcotics legislation in 1923 and made narcotics offences extraditable as far as the United States was concerned by the Supplementary Convention of 1925, this commitment being widened in the 1971 treaty. It may be safe to assume, therefore, that the treaties with Austria and Israel would have included drug offences in the list of extradition crimes even if Canada had not become a party to any international agreement in this field.

The most recent attempt on a multilateral level to impose an obligation to extradite has been in connection with aerial hijacking. The first international agreement to be concerned with this problem was the 1963 Tokyo Convention on Offences and Certain Other Acts Committed on Board Aircraft,[223] which was ratified by Canada in February 1971. Although 'nothing in this Convention shall be deemed to create an obligation to grant extradition,' it gives the commander of an aircraft the right to call upon a contracting party in whose territory he has landed to take custody of the alleged offender in accordance with the local law 'for such time as is reasonably necessary to enable any criminal or extradition proceedings to be instituted.' Moreover, in order to facilitate extradition proceedings, offences committed on aircraft belonging to contracting parties are to be treated as if they had been committed both in the place where they occur as well as in the state of registration.

The matter was carried further by the Hague Convention for the Suppression of Unlawful Seizure of Aircraft,[224] which by 10 August 1971, had been signed by seventy-eight states and by 14 October 1971 was in effect for eleven. Canada is not included in this latter group, although 'the Canadian Delegation to The Hague Conference played an active role in promoting a generally acceptable treaty and was particularly instrumental in securing adoption of the strong prosecution provision … The Canadian Government will now make a close study of the convention with a view to ascertaining what national legislation will be required. When the required legislation has been enacted and other steps necessary to permit ratification have been taken, it is expected that Canada will become a party.'[225] Legislation was necessary to give effect to that provision of the convention which obliges parties to make it an offence punishable by severe penalty if one 'unlawfully, by force or threat thereof, or by any other form of intimidation' seizes or takes over control of an aircraft in flight, or attempts so to do, or acts as an accomplice of anyone so doing. Legislation still appears necessary to establish criminal jurisdiction over a hijacker who is present in Canada, if that hijacker is not extradited, unless the flight in question terminated in Canada. However, no legislation would be necessary to give effect to that part of the convention which, like the White Slave and Narcotics Conventions, seeks to amend all existing extradition treaties in force between contracting states so that an offence of this character shall be extraditable; and the parties have undertaken to include this offence in all future extradition treaties to which they become parties – and Canada has already taken steps to that effect.

The convention, however, goes somewhat further than its precursors, in that it provides that those countries which make extradition conditional upon the existence of a treaty may, at their option, treat the convention as the basis for acting upon a request from a country, party to the Convention, with which no other extradition treaty exists. This treaty, therefore, serves not only to amend existing bilateral treaties between its parties, and to impose an obligation to embody its stipulations in future such treaties, but it creates a treaty obligation to extradite for all those parties who have no other extradition commitment. There is no reason to doubt that the Hague Convention will serve as an arrangement referred to in section 2(c) of the Extradition Act as creating extradition offences irrespective of the first schedule of the act. Moreover, it must be borne in mind that the treaty with Austria already lists 'unlawful and wilful seizure of an aircraft' as extraditable, and presumably both the governments concerned anticipate that Canadian courts will be made competent to give effect to this requirement, as will be the case when the Criminal Code is amended. Further, Canada has sought to give effect to the provision of the convention by initiating bilateral discussions to this end,[226] and the treaty with the United States is the first result of such discussions. It should also be noted that the convention does not attempt to interfere with local extradition procedures and requirements. Presumably, therefore, a hijacker whose extradition is sought from Canada might be able to contend that his offence was political in character.[227]

The only multilateral treaties to which Canada is a party that go any way towards recognizing a right of immigration or residence are the 1951 Refugees Convention,[228] the Protocol of 1967,[229] and the 1957 Convention on Refugee Seamen.[230] As a result Canada is committed to affording 'stateless persons regularly serving as crew members on board a ship flying the [Canadian] flag ... sympathetic consideration to their establishment on its territory and the issue of travel documents to them in their temporary admission to its territory particularly with a view to facilitating their establishment in another country.' She has further agreed 'not [to] expel a stateless person lawfully in ... [her] territory save on grounds of national security or public order ... [She will] also allow such a stateless person a reasonable period within which to seek legal admission into another country.' She has also agreed that, if she finds it necessary to deport a refugee, she will not 'expel or return (*refouler*) ... [him] in any manner whatsoever to the frontiers of territories where his life or freedom would be threatened on account of his race, religion, nationality, membership of a particular social group or political opinion.' However, she need have no compunctions of this kind in the case of 'a refugee whom there are reasonable grounds for regarding as a danger to the security of ... [Canada], or who, having been convicted by a final judgment of a particularly serious crime, constitutes a danger to the comminity of ... [Canada].'

SUMMARY AND CONCLUSION

There seems little question that the Canadian law and practice with regard to immigration, deportation, asylum, and extradition are fully in accord with any requirements that may exist in international law. Moreover, whereas international law gives a state complete discretion as to whom it allows to remain within its territory, Canada has by legislation introduced a number of safeguards for the individual concerned, limiting her own freedom of action.

In relation to extradition, she has gone further than many countries. By not insisting that extradition crimes be listed in both the local legislation and the extradition arrangement, she has opened the door to a vital and developing extradition policy, which will permit extradition for offences that may not have been sufficiently serious to be listed in her legislation, so long as an extradition convention or supplementary convention is directed towards dealing with them. In this way, Canada has been able to accept the obligations in a limited number of multilateral treaties dealing with such matters as white slavery and narcotics, as well as being able to sign a treaty making aerial hijacking extraditable, and, even before the entry into force of that treaty, she did not hesitate to include this offence in her extradition treaty, which came into force before her ratification at the Hague Convention. Finally, part II of the Extradition Act, although it has never been brought into operation, suggests that, given reciprocity and co-operation from others, Canada would be perfectly willing to see the institution of a system of mutual surrender of fugitive offenders, even though no treaties existed to bring an extradition system into operation.

NOTES

1 See, eg, Israel Law of the Return, 1950, United Nations, *Laws Concerning Nationality* (1954) 263.
2 See, eg, *Nottebohm* case *(Liechtenstein v Guatemala),* [1955] I.C.J. Rep. 4.
3 *Laws Concerning Nationality, supra* note 1, at 468.
4 See, eg, *Sayce* v *Ameer of Bahawalpur,* [1952] 1 All E.R. 326 (K.B.), [1952] 2 All E.R. 64 (C.A.).
5 Commonwealth Immigrants Act, 1962, c 21; 1968, c 9; Immigration Act, 1971, c 77.
6 British Nationality Act, s 32(1): ' "Alien" means a person who is not a British subject, a British protected person *or a citizen of Eire.'* (Emphasis added.)
7 Schuman Plan Treaty (European Coal and Steel Community), 261 U.N.T.S. 140; Rome Treaties, 298 U.N.T.S. 11 (European Economic Community); 298 U.N.T.S. 176 (EURATOM); 298 U.N.T.S. 267 (Common Institutions).
8 See, eg, EEC Treaty, article 48.
9 S. Pufendorf, *De Jure Naturae et Gentium* Lib III, s 10 (1688), Kennedy/Carew translation 246 (1728), Oceana Reprint 366–7 (1964).
10 See Opinion of Att'y Gen. Cushing, 4 Oct. 1855: 'The object to be accomplished in all these [extradition] cases is alike interesting to each government – namely, the punish-

ment of malefactors, the common enemies of every society.' J.B. Moore, *A Treatise on Extradition and Interstate Rendition* (1895) 5 [hereinafter cited as *Moore*].
11 A. Billet, *Traité de l'extradition* (1874) 39.
12 Dig 50, 5.17. See G.C. Lewis, *Foreign Jurisdiction and Extradition of Criminals* (1859) 51 n.
13 *Moore,* at 9–10; C. Phillipson, 1 *The International Law and Custom of Ancient Greece and Rome* (1911) 364–5.
14 *Moore,* at 3.
15 See eg, *Att'y Gen., Hong Kong* v *Kwok-a-Sing* (1873), L.R. 5 P.C. 179.
16 See eg, *In re Tivnan* (1864), 5 B. & S. 645. See also *Att'y Gen.* v *Kwok-a-Sing, supra* note 15.
17 In practice, states carefully list which offences are considered extraditable in the legislation regulating the process. See, eg, Canadian Extradition Act, R.S.C. E-21, 1st Schedule (1970). However, this statute provides that extradition may also be granted for offences listed in a treaty, even though not in the act, s 2(c). *Re Brisbois,* (1962) 133 C.C.C. 188.
18 Legislation usually provides that the alleged offence shall also be an offence according to the local law. See, eg, Canadian Extradition Act ss 2(c), 10(1). However, this does not

mean that there must be exact identity of nomenclature. *See Re Arton* (No 2), [1896] 1 Q.B. 509; *Re Insull*, [1934] 2 D.L.R. 696.

19 Nowadays, countries which have abolished the death penalty tend to refuse surrender to countries which still exact it. See Canadian treaty with Israel, 1967, *infra* note 201; Canadian treaty with Austria, 1967, *infra* note 202. Sometimes, however, the latter undertake that this penalty will not be enforced. See Anglo-Israel Extradition Treaty, [1960] Gr. Brit. T. S. no 77 (1960), Cmnd. no 1223; Canada-United States Extradition Treaty, 1971, article 6, Can. Dep't of External Affairs, *Canada Communiqué No. 92*, 3 Dec. 1971.

20 See *Re Government of India and Mubarak Ali Ahmad*, [1952] 1 All E.R. 1060, 1063 (refusal of Goddard LCJ to accept such allegations re judges in India); and *Re Commonwealth of Puerto Rico and Hernandez*, (1972) 30 D.L.R. (3d) 260, at 269.

21 See *In re Grandi* (1934), 7 *Ann. Dig.* 340 (Switzerland); *Jimenez* v *Aristeguieta* (1962), 311 F.2d 547, 49 *Dep't of State Bull.* (1963) 364; *R* v *Governor, Brixton Prison, ex parte Enahoro*, [1963] 2 Q.B. 455, 675 *Hansard* (Commons) col 581–682 (21 March); col 1271–87 (26 March); col 1287–1369 (Prime Minister's reference to assurances); col 1290 (10 April). See also *Armah* v *Government of Ghana*, [1966] 3 All E.R. 177, *sub. non. R.* v *Governor, Brixton Prison, exparte Armah and Government of Ghana*, [1968] A.C. 192: In this case the government of Ghana stated that Armah would be prosecuted under the Criminal Procedure Code and not the Corrupt Practices Prevention Act, 1964; and if he was tried and acquitted, the government undertook that he would not be taken into protective custody and would be allowed to leave. The majority of the House of Lords considered 'it very undesirable that a foreign government should be encouraged to offer not to apply the ordinary law of its country to one of its own subjects if he is to return to that country. There may not be the same objection to the foreign government stating that it does not intend to take certain executive action with regard to the accused person.' [1966] 3 All E.R., at 188, [1968] A.C., at 235–6 (*per* Lord Reid). See also [1966] 3 All E.R. at 201, [1968] A.C., at 256 (Lord Pearce); [1966] 3 All E.R., at 205, [1968] A.C., at 262–63 (Lord Upjohn); [1966] 3 All E.R., at 196, [1968] A.C., at 247 (Lord Morris of

Borthy-Gorst dissenting). See also discussion between United States and Canada re Winslow and Lawrence, 1875–6, *Moore*, at 145–215; *Commonwealth* v *Hawes*, (1877) 3 Bush. 697 (accused extradited from Canada to United States); *United States* v *Rauscher*, (1886) 119 U.S. 407; *Re Woodall*, (1888) 59 L.T. 549 (effect of *Rauscher* case in England).

22 Thus, in May 1949 the British government announced that no further war criminals would be handed over to a demanding state for trial in the absence of a satisfactory explanation for the delay, 162 *Hansard* (Lords) col 388. See also *Daily Telegraph* (London), 13 March 1961 (British rejection of Soviet demand for surrender of Ain Erwin Merl). Similar refusals have been made by Australia and the United States, *The Times* (London), 10 Jan. 1962, 13 Oct. and 21 Dec. 1961. See also *Zacharia* v *Republic of Cyprus*, [1963] A.C. 364; 658 *Hansard* (Commons) col 811 (1 May 1962)(British refusal to surrender two Cypriots despite judicial decision in favour of extradition).

23 In fact, since states refuse to extradite political offenders, applicant states frequently base their request on an offence which is described as a common offence. See Green, 'Hijacking and the Right of Asylum' in E.W. McWhinney, *Aerial Piracy and International Law* (1971) 124. See also *Re Giovanni Gatti* (1947), 14 *Ann. Dig.* 145 (Italy).

24 See Decree of General Légitime, Port-au-Prince, Haiti, *Le Moniteur* (Port-au-Prince), 2 May 1899. See also *Holmes* v *Jennison*, (1840) 14 Pet. 540, 568 (*per* Taney J).

25 Eg, *R.* v *Governor, Brixton Prison, ex parte Soblen*, [1963] 2 Q.B. 243. See also Canadian action re Paterson, a United States citizen who hijacked an American aircraft and sought admission as a landed immigrant in Canada: *Globe and Mail* (Toronto), 2, 3, 9 March 1971; *Ex parte Paterson*, (1971) 3 C.C.C.(2d) 181.

26 See, eg, statement by British home secretary, 26 March 1958, 583 *Hansard* (Commons)(Written Answers) col 153: 'If it is reasonable to suppose that the result of refusing admission to a foreigner would be his return to a country in which, on grounds of political opinion, race or religion, he would face danger to life or liberty, or persecution of such a kind and extent as to render life insupportable, he would normally be admitted.' See also Draft Convention on Ter-

ritorial Asylum, *The Declaration of Buenos Aires* art. 9, Int'l L. Assoc., *Report of the 53rd Conference, Buenos Aires, 1968*, at 277: 'Should the asylum-granting State decide to terminate the asylum, it may not return the asylee to the State from which he fled or any other State in which he might be subject to persecution.' Article 33 of the Refugees Convention, 1951, expressly forbids the *refoulement* of refugees. 189 U.N.T.S. 150. See also S.P. Sinha, *Asylum and International Law* (1971) 159–61 [hereinafter cited as *Sinha*]. See Immigration Appeal Board Act, R.S.C. I-3, s 15 (1)(b)(i) (1970), and *Re Daniolos* (1971), 2 *I.A.C.* 434.

27 G. A. Res 217(III)(1948).

28 G. A. Res 2312(XXII)(1967).

29 G. A. Res 2200(XXI)(1966).

30 See Green, 'The Right of Asylum in International Law' (1961), 3 *Univ. of Malaya L. Rev.* 223; Int'l L. Assoc., Committee on Legal Aspects of Asylum, *Report of the 51st Conference, Tokyo, 1964*, at 246; *Sinha*, at 18, 155.

31 For details of some typical constitutional provisions of this kind, see Green, 'The Nature of Political Offences' (1964), 3 *The Solicitor Quarterly* 213, 217–20. For a fairly comprehensive list, see *Sinha*, at 54 n 5.

32 See, eg, *The Times* (London), 2 Oct, 1971. See also *Rose* v *The King*, [1947] 3 D.L.R. 618 (Canadian case arising from the defection of Gouzenko).

33 For an interesting instance of avoidance of this, see the Eisler incident between the United Kingdom and the United States: *The Times* (London), 28 May 1949; Finch, 'The Eisler Extradition Case' (1949), 43 *Am. J. Int'l L.* 487; Green, 'Recent Trends in the Law of Extradition' (1953), 6 *Current Legal Problems* 274, at 284–7.

34 (1950), *Y.B.H.R.* 420.

35 (1964), 58 *Am. J. Int'l L.* 334.

36 See *The Times* (London), 2 Oct. 1971.

37 Havana Convention, 1928, M.O. Hudson, 4 *International Legislation* 2412; Montevideo, 1933, 6 ibid, at 608; Montevideo, 1939, 8 ibid, at 405; Caracas, 1954, United Nations (1955), *Yearbook on Human Rights* 330.

38 During the hostilities in East Pakistan (Bangladesh) in 1971, similar asylum seems to have been extended to local political figures by the International Red Cross.

39 [1950] I.C.J. Rep. 266, 285.

40 (1970), 9 *Int'l Legal Materials* 99.

41 Chile, Colombia, Costa Rica, Ecuador, El Salvador, Guatemala, Honduras, Nicaragua, Panama, Paraguay, Uruguay, and Venezuela.

42 Constitution of R.S.F.S.R., 1924, article 58, T.A. Taracouzio, *Soviet Union and International Law* (1935) 147.

43 It is perhaps of interest to note that extradition does not figure in J.F. Triska and R.M. Slesser, *The Theory, Law and Practice of Soviet Treaties* (1963), while no extradition treaty to which the Soviet Union is a party is cited by Taracouzio, *supra* note 42, and only one – that with Czechoslavakia, 1957 – is specifically mentioned in Academy of Sciences of the USSR, Institute of State and Law, *International Law* (1961) 169, although it is hinted that the Soviet Union has signed such treaties with the other People's Democracies (ibid). The treaty with Hungary, for example, was signed in 1958.

44 See *The Times* (London), 24, 27 Nov. 1962.

45 *Supra* note 33.

46 Green, *supra* note 31, at 237–8. The quotation which follows is taken from that article.

47 See *supra*, note 25.

48 (1955), 22 *Int'l L. Rep.* 520, 524.

49 (1935), 29 *Am. J. Int'l L. Supp.* 385.

50 (1949), 16 *Ann. Dig.* 275, 276.

51 (1947), 14 *Ann. Dig.* 139.

52 (1948), 171 F.2d 921, 935.

53 (1935), 29 *Am. J. Int'l L. Supp.* 110.

54 *Moore*, at 10 note 4.

55 For discussion of these, see Green, 'Political Offences, War Crimes and Extradition,' (1962) 11 *I.C.L.Q.* 329, at 345 *et seq.*; *Sinha*, at 200 notes 131–3.

56 (1971), 10 *Int'l Legal Materials* 133; McWhinney, *supra* note 23, appendix 6, at 171.

57 The Canadian delegation played a particularly active role with respect to the prosecution provisions of this convention. See *infra*, note 225.

58 Can. Dep't of External Affairs, *Canada Communiqué No. 12* (22 Feb. 1971). In 1973 it was announced that agreement had been reached.

59 Can. Dep't of External Affairs, *Canada Communiqué No. 92* (3 Dec. 1971).

60 Letter from Daniel Webster to Lord Ashburton, 1 Aug. 1842, 6 *Webster's Works* 311. See also letter from Daniel Webster to M. d'Arguiz, 21 June 1842, ibid, at 399, 405; *United States* v *Rauscher, supra* note 21, at 411–12 (Miller J).

61 14 Feb. 1842, 60 *Hansard* (3d ser)(Lords) col

319–20. A somewhat similar view had been expressed by Secretary of State Jay as early as 1786 when advising that, in the absence of a treaty, the United States should not ask for the surrender of John Phelan, believed to have absconded to Canada:

> If nations were by general consent to refuse an asylum to each other's fugitive offenders, and on requisition deliver them up to justice, it would doubtless much discourage the commission of crimes. If such a practice would be beneficial to society in general, it could not be improper for any particular nation to set the example and begin it, and as the United States border an extensive dominion of the King of Great Britain, a proper agreement on this subject might be convenient and useful to both.

2 *Reports of the Secretaries of State* no 81, at 175 (6 Sept. 1786); *Moore,* at 26 note 2.
62 Ibid, at 38–9.
63 *The Times* (London), 9 Oct. 1971. See also *Ex parte Soblen, supra* note 25.
64 R.S.C. c 325 (1952), as amended; Stats. Can. cc 25, 90 (1966–7); Stats. Can. cc 1, 37 (1967–8), now R.S.C. I-2 (1970).
65 1962–7, Cat. No YX74–325/1967–8 (Can. Gov't Pub. 1968), amended 1972, SOR 73–20, 20 December 1972.
66 *R.* v *Alamazoff* (1919), 47 D.L.R. 533, 534–5 (*per* Mathers CJKB). See also *Re Prata and M.M.I.,* (1972) D.L.R. (3d) 465, at 478 (Sweet DJ).
67 E. de Vattel, *Le Droit des Nations* Liv I, s 231, Liv II, s 125 (1758), as paraphrased by the Privy council in *Att'y Gen., Canada* v *Cain,* [1906] A.C. 542, 546.
68 Can., H.C. *Debates,* 1 May 1947, 3d Sess, 20th Parl, vol III, at 2644–6.
69 *Supra* at note 9.
70 R.S.C. c 95 (1927), repealed, Stats. Can. (1947) c 19, s 4.
71 [1955] S.C.R. 395, 397.
72 See *The Cooperative Committee on Japanese Canadians* v *Att'y Gen., Canada,* [1947] A.C. 87.
73 (1957) 8 D.L.R. (2d) 566, 568–9.
74 This gave certain appellate functions to the minister, but has now been replaced by the Immigration Appeal Board Act, R.S.C. I-3 (1970).
75 8 D.L.R. (2d), at 574.
76 [1932] S.C.R. 640, 642.
77 [1955] 5 D.L.R. 374, 375, 376, 377–8.

78 *Supra* note 76.
79 Stats. Can. c 44 (1960); R.S.C. app III (1970).
80 (1962) 40 D.L.R. (2d) 380, 383.
81 R.S.C. I–3 (1970).
82 (1970) 12 D.L.R. (3d) 704, 706, 707–8.
83 (1967) W.W.R. 553, 555.
84 *Supra* note 25, at 185, 186.
85 Immigration Act, s 24.
85a (1972) 31 D.L.R. (3d) 465, at 474 (Jackett CJ), at 478 (Sweet DJ).
86 (1962) 34 D.L.R. (2d) 179, 185, 186–8, 189.
87 Ss 2(d), 36(1).
88 [1961] S.C.R. 376, 381.
89 [1968] S.C.R. 839, 842, 844 (Cartwright CJ), 847 (Judson J).
90 *Supra* note 25, at 281.
91 (1965) 55 W.W.R. 174. See also *Gooliah* v *Minister of Citizenship and Immigration* (1967), 63 D.L.R. (2d) 224.
92 See *Re Kokorinis* (1965), 53 W.W.R. 427 (held that the applicant should be told that 'counsel' is one who is legally qualified, and not that 'he need not be a lawyer,' at 430–1).
93 R.S.C. c 325, (1952), as amended, now R.S.C. I–2 (1970).
94 Can. Dep't of External Affairs, *Canada Communiqué No. 92,* 3 Dec. 1971.
95 *Supra* note 72, at 104–5.
96 R.S.C. c 206 (1927), now R.S.C. W–2 (1970).
97 Public Order Regulations, SOR/70–444 (1970), *Canada Gazette,* part II, vol 104, no 20, 28 Oct. 1970.
98 [1938] 4 D.L.R. 381.
99 [1938] 4 D.L.R. 697, 700–1 (Man. CA).
100 [1933] S.C.R. 36, 39, 42–3.
101 [1955] S.C.R. 263, 280–1, 266, 268.
101a See *Re Prata and Minister of Manpower and Immigration,* (1972) 31 D.L.R. (3d) 465, at 478 (Sweet DJ).
102 (1959) 17 D.L.R.(2d) 482.
103 [1964] S.C.R. 3.
104 P.C. 1967–1616, SOR/67–434. See *Gana* v *Minister of Manpower and Immigration* (1970), 13 D.L.R. (3d) 698, 700 (*per* Abbott J). See, now, SOR 73–20, 20 December 1972.
105 [1933] 1 D.L.R. 362, 364–5.
106 [1933] 2 D.L.R. 348, 350, 355, 358, 362.
107 *Supra* note 100, at 40.
108 *Supra* note 104, at 700.
109 360 U.N.T.S. 117, amended by Protocol 1967, 606 U.N.T.S. 267.
110 A similar provision against *refoulement* is to be found in the Convention on Refugee Seamen (1957), 7 *I.C.L.Q.* 344, to which Canada became a party in 1969.

111 [1966] I.C.J. Rep. 6.
112 R.S.C. I–3 (1970). See *Re Daniolos, supra* note 26.
112a *Boulis* v *Minister of Manpower and Immigration*, (1972) 26 D.L.R. (3d) 220, at 223 (*per* Laskin J).
113 Parliamentary Answer by Att'y Gen., U.K., in House of Commons, 8 Nov. 1971, *The Times* (London), 8 Nov. 1971.
114 J.-G. Castel, *International Law Chiefly as Applied and Interpreted in Canada* (1965) 541.
115 1 April 1966, (1967), 5 *Can. Y. B. Int'l L.* 274.
116 1 BFSP 784.
117 [1952] CAN.T.S. no 12; 30 BFSP 360.
118 Statutes of Upper Canada, 2d Sess., 11 & 12 Parl., 2–3 Wm. IV, 1831–1837, repealed, Statutes of Province of Canada, 23 Vict., 1860, at 91.
119 See eg, *R.* v *Tubbee*, (1852) 1 P.R. 98.
120 *Moore*, at 30–1.
121 (1819) 4 *Johns Ch.* 105, 112.
122 (1827) STU. K.B. 245 (italics in original).
123 *Moore*, at 46.
124 E. Clarke, *Treatise upon the Law of Extradition* (1888) 89.
125 *Moore*, at 671–2.
126 *Re Anderson*, (1860) 20 U.C.Q.B. 124.
127 [1861] *Annual Register* 520.
128 *Re Anderson*, (1860) 11 U.C.C.P. 9.
129 La Forest, *Extradition To and From Canada* (1961) 38–9.
130 *Supra* note 33.
131 (1905) 10 C.C.C. 80, 103.
132 See Green, *supra* note 55, at 345 *et seq.; Sinha*, at 200 notes 131–3.
133 16 Sept. 1966, (1967), 5 *Can, Y. B. Int'l L.* 270.
134 See Green, *supra* note 55; *Sinha*.
135 (1882) 9 P.R. 332, 335.
136 *Compare Miller* v *R.* (1963), 42 W.W.R.(N.S.) 141 (attempt to depend solely on interrogatories).
137 (1960), 12 *External Affairs* 784, 788.
138 R.S.C. E–21 (1970).
139 Section 9 provides:
    (1) All judges of the superior courts and of the county courts of a province, and all commissioners who are, from time to time, appointed for the purpose, in a province by the Governor in Council, under the Great Seal of Canada, by virtue of this Part, are authorized to act judicially in extradition matters under this Part, within the province; and every such per-
son has, for matters under this Part, all the powers and jurisdiction of any judge or magistrate of the province.
    (2) Nothing in this section shall be construed to confer on any judge any jurisdiction in habeas corpus matters.
140 (1960), 13 *External Affairs* 784.
141 Statement by Legal Division, Can, Dep't of External Affairs, 31 Aug. 1967 (1968), 6 *Can. Y. B. Int'l L.* 268.
142 *Supra* note 59. Similar provisions are to be found in the 1967 treaties with Israel, *infra* note 201, and Austria, *infra* note 202.
143 33 & 34 Vict., c 52 (Imp'l).
144 [1891] 1 Q.B. 149, 156, 159.
145 [1894] 2 Q.B. 415, 419 (*per* Cave J).
146 (1910) 17 C.C.C. 268, 270–1.
147 Acts of Canada, 1887, at xcix, 17 *Hertslet's Treaties* 920. This treaty is now tacitly regarded as inoperative by Great Britain: 478 *Hansard* (Commons) col 462 (1950).
148 This comment is of interest when compared with the discussion concerning the *Anderson* case. *Supra* at notes 126–31.
149 [1951] 1 Q.B. 540.
150 La Forest, *supra* note 129, at 46.
151 *Karadzole* v *Artukovic* (1957), 247 F.2d 198, 203. See also *United States* v *Karadzole* (1959), 170 F.Supp. 388, 392.
152 [1964] A.C. 556, 591.
152a (1972) 30 D.L.R. (3d) 260, at 268 (*per* Honeywell Co Ct J, Ont.) (unaffected as to substance, 30 D.L.R. (3d) 613).
152b (1972) 28 D.L.R. (3d) 513, at 520 (*per* Waisberg Co Ct J, Ont.) (unaffected as to substance, 30 D.L.R. (3d) 527).
153 For a wider discussion of the concepts of 'political asylum' and 'political offence,' see Green, *supra* note 23; Green, *supra* note 30; Green, 'Piracy of Aircraft and the Law, (1972), 10 *Alta. L. Rev.* 72. See also *Sinha*, esp. chap. 8.
154 *Supra*, at notes 126–31.
155 (1934) 54 C.C.C. 334, 338.
156. *Supra* note 131, at 85.
157 *Re Latimer*, (1906) 10 C.C.C. 244, 247. See also *Re Clair*, [1969] 1 N.B.R.(2d) 26.
158 *Ex parte Pendergast*, [1964] 2 C.C.C. 264, 267.
159 *Supra* note 18.
160 *Supra* note 18, at 700 (*per* Matlock CJC).
161 *United States* v *Novick* (1960), 128 C.C.C. 319, 322.
162 Section 16 of the schedule to the 1971 treaty.
163 (1913) 11 D.L.R. 708, 709 (*per* Middleton J).

164 R.S.C. c 23 (1906) now R.S.C. B-1 (1970).
165 (1917) 55 S.C.R. 133, 134, 135 (*per* Fitzpatrick CJ), 145 (*per* Anglin J).
166 See Extradition Act s 33:

> Where any person accused or convicted of an extradition crime is surrendered by a foreign state, in pursuance of any extradition arrangement, he is not, until after he has been restored or has had an opportunity of returning to the foreign state within the meaning of the arrangement, subject, in contravention of any of the terms of the arrangement, to a prosecution or punishment in Canada, for any other offence committed prior to his surrender, for which he should not, under the arrangement, be prosecuted.

167 [1922] 1 W.W.R. 515, 516–17.
168 *Canada Gazette* VI, at 229; 14 *Hertslet's Treaties* 258.
169 *Supra* note 135.
170 [1922] 1 W.W.R. at 518.
171 [1933] 2 D.L.R. 608, 614 (*per* Matlock CJO, Ont. CA).
172 The treaties with Israel, Austria, and the United States require a copy of the legislation concerned.
173 [1923] 3 D.L.R. 689, 693–4 (*per* Stuart JA, Alta. Sup. Ct., App. Div.). See also *R.* v *Corrigan,* [1931] 1 K.B. 527.
174 R.S.C. c 155, s 32 (now s 33) (1906).
175 *Supra* note 17, at 191–2, 195–6.
176 [1952] CAN.T.S. no 12; 30 BFSP 360. The learned judge ignored the Jay Treaty.
177 [1952] CAN.T.S. no 12; 81 BFSP 41.
178 [1952] CAN.T.S. no 12; 92 BFSP 72.
179 [1952] CAN.T.S. no 12; 98 BFSP 385. See *United States* v *Stegeman,* (1966) 57 W.W.R. 267, 58 W.W.R. 62.
180 [1952] CAN.T.S. no 12; 116 BFSP 508.
181 [1952] CAN.T.S. no 12; 116 BFSP 508.
182 1923, c 22; R.S.C. c 201 (1952) 1960–1961, c 35, now R.S.C. 1970, N-1, Narcotic Control Act.
183 33 & 34 Vict., c 52 (Imp'l).
184 36 Geo. III, c 12 (N.B.).
185 44 & 45 Vict., c 69 (Imp'l).
186 45 Vict., c 21.
187 28 & 29 Vict., c 63 (Imp'l).
188 See, eg, *Re Whitla* (1916), 28 D.L.R. 402.
189 R.S.C. F-32 (1970).
190 22 Geo. V, c 2, s 2 (Imp'l).
191 La Forest, *supra* note 129, at 13.
192 See Cmnd. no 3008 (U.K.).
193 Can. H.C. *Debates,* 11 May 1966, vol V, at 4993.
194 (1965) 53 W.W.R. 618, 625 (*per* Branca J).
195 *Supra* note 166.
196 15 March 1966, (1967), 5 *Can. Y. B. Int'l L.* 273.
197 *Supra* note 21.
198 Letter from secretary of state for external affairs to US ambassador, 1964, (1965), 3 *Can. Y. B. Int'l. L.* 336.
199 See Pan-American Union, *Inter-American Treaties and Conventions on Asylum and Extradition* (1967).
200 1957, 359 U.N.T.S. 273.
201 To be published as [1969] CAN.T.S. no 25; Gov't of Israel, Reshumot Kitvei Haamana, no 721, vol 21.
202 To be published as [1969] CAN.T.S. no 24; 79 Austrian Gazette, 3 Sept. 1969, no 324 (ratified in 1969). It is perhaps of interest to note that the Canadian Department of External Affairs has wrongly described the treaty with Israel as the 'more recent' (1968), *Can. Y. B. Int'l L.* 269
203 Acts of Canada, 1875, at xvii, 63 BFSP 213, amended by U.K.T.S. no 13, Cd no 1078 (1902).
204 41 U.N.T.S. 273.
205 Can. Dep't of External Affairs, *Canada Communiqué No. 92.* 3 Dec. 1971.
206 (1968), 6 *Can. Y. B. Int'l L.* 269.
207 A list of these treaties appears in La Forest, *supra* note 129, at appendix II, part A, 156–65.
208 (1968), 6 *Can. Y. B. Int'l. L.* 269.
209 *Canada Gazette* XXII, at 2242; 8 *Hertslet's Treaties* 849.
210 *Supra* note 17. See *supra,* note 175.
211 [1952] CAN.T.S. no 12.
212 (1933) 3 D.L.R.(2d) 207, 208, 210–11 (per Schroeder J, H.C. Ont.). See also *Re Brassey's Settlement,* [1955] 1 W.L.R. 192; *Armah* v *Government of Ghana, supra* note 21.
212a *Supra* note 152b.
213 (1971) 10 *Int'l Legal Materials* 133; McWhinney, *supra* note 23, appendix 6, at 171.
214 Int'l Law Assoc., *Report and Draft Conventions on Diplomatic and Territorial Asylum* (1970) art. 2(d).
215 See *supra* notes 175–84.
216 General Assembly res 217(III)(1948). See *supra* note 27.
217 1948, 78 U.N.T.S. 277.
218 *Supra* note 133.

219 Convention for Suppression of the White Slave Traffic, 1910, 103 BFSP 244, as amended by the Protocol of 1949, 99 U.N.T.S. 103, article 5.

220 108 U.N.T.S. 300.

221 166 BFSP 188.

222 See *supra,* text to notes 175–84.

223 (1964), 3 *Int'l Legal Materials* 1042; McWhinney, *supra* note 23, Appendix 1, at 147.

224 1970, (1971), 10 *Int'l Legal Materials* 133; McWhinney, *supra* note 23, appendix 6, at 171.

225 Can. Dep't of External Affairs, *Canada Communiqué No. 86* (16 Dec. 1970). Canada ratified 10 June 1972.

226 Eg, Can. Dep't of External Affairs, *Canada Communiqué No. 12* (22 Feb. 1971) (Cuba).

227 See *supra,* text to notes 143 *et seq.* But see also *supra* note 23; *supra* note 153.

228 360 U.N.T.S. 117.

229 606 U.N.T.S. 267.

230 (1958), 7 *I.C.L.Q.* 344.

AIR, COMMUNICATIONS,

AND WEATHER LAW

GERALD F. FITZGERALD*

12/International
Air Law in
the 1970s

The rapid development of aviation technology poses great challenges for the air lawyer. He is faced with the task of applying incomplete and sometimes conflicting norms that have grown up *ad hoc* and, at the same time, developing more complete and mutually compatible norms. Some of the problems that will have to be solved in carrying out these tasks are examined in this chapter.

PUBLIC LAW

Introduction

At the present time, the basic institutional framework for intergovernmental co-operation in civil aviation is provided by the International Civil Aviation Organization which has its headquarters in Montreal. ICAO was established by the Convention on International Civil Aviation[1] and, at the end of 1971, had 122 member states.[2] In the private sector, there are many international organizations catering to the needs of various interest groups, such as the International Air Transport Association,[3] representing the scheduled international air carriers, the International Federation of Airline Pilots' Associations,[4] and a host of other bodies. Scheduled international air transport is regulated by a complex network of bilateral agreements,[5] while, at least in the ICAO family, non-scheduled international air transport is governed by article 5 of the Chicago Convention. As the most important legal norms governing international civil aviation are developed under the auspices of ICAO, the bulk of this chapter will be devoted to ICAO's role in this field.

ICAO and the Convention on International Civil Aviation

ICAO

ICAO functions through an Assembly, which is open to all 122 contracting states; it normally meets once every three years, and it lays down broad policies to be followed by the organization.[6] There is a Council of twenty-seven contracting states;[7] this number will increase to thirty once a recent amendment has been ratified by eighty states.[8] The Council is elected every three years, holds at least three sessions a year at ICAO headquarters, and is presided over by an elected official who holds office for a three-year term.[9] The chief executive officer of the organization and the head of the Secretariat is the secretary general, who is elected for a term which may vary from three to five years.[10] The development of standards, practices, and

---

*This article was written in a private capacity.

procedures governing international air navigation is in the hands of the Council, a twelve-member Air Navigation Commission[11] (which will have fifteen members as soon as a recent amendment to the convention has been ratified by eighty states),[12] and a variety of technical bodies, some open to a limited number of members. Working through the Council, the Air Transport Committee, and related bodies, the organization also establishes norms in the facilitation field whereby it cuts out red-tape in immigration, health, and related procedures.[13] Through its Legal Committee and diplomatic conferences held under its auspices, ICAO is the prime instrument for the development of conventions on international air law.[14] Canada has been active in this work from the inception of ICAO.

Examples of constitutional questions arising in ICAO
During the 1970s Canadian government lawyers concerned with ICAO as an intergovernmental organization may from time to time have to advise on such constitutional problems as 1 / the methods whereby states become parties to the Chicago Convention and state succession thereto;[15] 2 / denunciation of the convention;[16] 3 / circumstances under which a state may appropriately hold that the convention does not apply between it and another member state;[17] 4 / the structure of ICAO; new bodies are frequently created and the membership of other bodies is increased to meet new types of needs; representation is being broadened as the developing countries seek their place in the sun;[18] 5 / the status of ICAO, its representatives, observers, and secretariat; the question of status is of particular interest because ICAO headquarters is located in Montreal;[19] 6 / finances, for example, the question of the maximum contribution of a state;[20] 7 / relations with other international organizations; for example, the alleged conflict between ICAO and the United Nations in respect of an abortive attempt to develop in ICAO a convention for the taking of concerted action against states which hold aircraft, passengers, crew, and cargo for international blackmail purposes, or harbour hijackers;[21] 8 / the amendment of the Chicago Convention.[22]

We may now turn to a more detailed examination of selected public air law topics in respect of which Canadian lawyers may be called upon to make a contribution within the framework of an international organization as exemplified by ICAO.

Impact of the Vienna Convention on the Law of Treaties
on the interpretation and application of the Chicago Convention
The Vienna Convention on the Law of Treaties,[23] which contains a concise statement of the rules governing the preparation, adoption, and ratification of international conventions, as well as such related matters as their interpretation, application, and amendment, provides a new context in which the constitutions of organizations like ICAO must be viewed. The Vienna Convention has become one of the most frequently cited documents in ICAO debates on legal matters. For example, in the debates in the ICAO Subcommittee on the Council Resolutions of 1 October 1970, when the question arose as to concerted action against states which used hijacking for blackmail purposes or were hijacker havens, reference was made to various articles of the Vienna Convention as supporting the view that the United Nations charter had primacy over the Chicago Convention.[24] Accordingly, participants in ICAO legal debates in this decade will profit from a close study of the Vienna Convention.

Work of the International Law Commission on the development
of a statement of rules governing the legal status and privileges
of international organizations and their personnel
Canada being the host state to ICAO has concluded with the organization a headquarters agreement specifying the privileges, immunities, and facilities extended
to ICAO, national representatives, and ICAO personnel. Canada is also a party to the
Convention on the Privileges of the Specialized Agencies, which applies to ICAO.[25]
Therefore, it is of direct concern to Canadian lawyers that the International Law
Commission has, for some time, been working on the topic 'Relations between
states and international organizations.'[26] In order to bring its studies to a successful
conclusion the commission will have to ensure that its proposals do not impinge
on existing treaty regimes, such as those found in the Headquarters Agreement and
in the convention.

ICAO's norm-creation functions in the technical field
These are concerned with development and implementation of i / International
Standards and Recommended Practices (SARPS), Procedures for Air Navigation
Services (PANS), and Regional Supplementary Procedures (SUPPS) to meet the
changing needs of international air navigation; and ii / Regional Air Navigation
Plans for air navigation facilities and services.

Annexes, PANS, SUPPS, extent of obligation   The SARPS are adopted by the
ICAO council in accordance with articles 54(1), 37, and 90 of the Convention on
International Civil Aviation and are designated, for convenience, as annexes to the
convention. So far there have been sixteen of these annexes, fifteen dealing with
technical air navigation matters and one with the facilitation of international air
transport (reduction of red-tape in immigration and related matters). The uniform
application by contracting states of the specifications comprised in the International
Standards is recognized as necessary for the safety or regularity of international
air navigation; on the other hand, uniform application of the specifications in the
recommended practices is regarded as desirable in the interest of the safety, regularity, or efficiency of international air navigation.[27]

The provisions in annexes are not binding on states unless voluntarily
implemented. With one exception, standards are adopted on a 'contracting-out'
basis and thus states may notify the Council of differences between their national
provisions and the standards in the annexes.[28] The exception relates to the standards on the rules of the air which, when adopted by the ICAO council, are applicable
over the high seas without deviation.[29] Although the recommended practices and
the provisions included in the PANS and SUPPS are of a lower category, and states
are not obliged to notify differences that may exist between their national provisions and the lower category material, states have in the past been encouraged to
notify the differences that did exist in order that the whole international aviation
community might have full knowledge of local deviations. But this practice has
been abandoned since it was found impossible for ICAO to publish the differences
on an up-to-date basis.

Regional plans   The details of the facilities, services, and procedures required
for the nine regions into which ICAO has divided the world of air navigation are
included in regional plans. Each plan contains recommendations which govern-

ments can follow in programming their air navigation facilities and services so that such facilities and services will form, with those of other states, an integrated system adequate for the foreseeable future. These plans are approved by the Council.[30]

Sanctions for non-compliance The remarkable thing about many of the ICAO-adopted norms is that they have little binding force between the organization and its member states, the result being that the penalty for non-compliance is not strictly legal but, rather, the natural sanction inherent in the state's inability to participate effectively in aviation if it does not meet the prescribed norms. In other words, non-compliance with basic technological norms invites the sanction of non-participation in the benefits of international civil aviation.[31] While ICAO has functioned well for over a quarter of a century without need of a more solidly based system of sanctions, the lawyers of the 1970s may well have to consider the need for more 'teeth' in the system in order to ensure more effective compliance. In the final analysis, it may be that the penalties which will have the greatest effect will be those provided for under national laws, in which the ICAO norms are included.[32] However, it would not be inappropriate for lawyers to examine the possibility of developing appropriate international sanctions by international organizations themselves.

Problems of implementation A distinction must be drawn between non-compliance in the legal sense and the inability of a state to implement ICAO norms.[33] The technological gap between developed and developing states is nowhere more dramatically illustrated than in the aviation field, since manufacturing states in this field are few in number.[34] For this reason, an extensive program of international aid is directed towards improving the capacity of developing states to implement SARPS, PANS, and SUPPS.[35] Similarly, states are faced with the heavy burden of providing facilities and services under Regional Air Navigation Plans; so much so that, at the eighteenth session of the ICAO Assembly, in 1971, it was pointed out that 'states were being faced with ever-increasing demands for new facilities and services and resulting increased expenditures, and it was essential to ensure an acceptable balance between operational requirements and the States' capacity to meet them.'[36] It is obvious that international norms will not be effective unless implemented. Therefore, lawyers could increasingly be called upon to join aviation administrators and those in charge of aid programs with a view to assisting developing nations to overcome the gap caused by the lack of trained men, matériel, and money, the so-called 3-M gap.

Amendments That the ICAO annexes and other regulations, which form the backbone of so many national aviation laws, have not been frozen is obvious from the frequent amendments to the documents containing them. There is a constant race to keep up with the requirements of an ever-changing technology. On the other hand, the question arises as to the capacity of even technologically advanced states to absorb frequent amendments. Thus, the latest guideline, adopted by the Assembly at its eighteenth session in 1971, reiterates an earlier guideline in stipulating that, 'unless exceptional circumstances dictate otherwise, the applicability dates of amendments to SARPS and PANS shall be so established as not to require the Contracting States to amend their national regulations more often than once per year.'[37] Whether and to what extent it is practicable to lock amendments of this kind into a rigid time frame is a matter for lawyers and technical personnel to work out. It is apparent that governments prefer to have an annual date for implementation of

ICAO material rather than being obliged to issue piecemeal amendments to their own laws. This problem is not peculiar to aviation; it is a reflection of the ever-burgeoning explosion of knowledge.

Adaptability of ICAO in developing Annex material That ICAO has been adaptable in the reorientation of its annex material has been demonstrated over the years. For example, annex 8 – Airworthiness – underwent a change in the 1950s when there was a shift away from the concept of developing airworthiness requirements for ICAO-type aircraft to streamlined standards and broadly stated Acceptable Means of Compliance (AMCs) in substitution for detailed technical standards.[38] The annex is now being rethought and the new approach is a matter of more than passing interest. The ICAO Airworthiness Committee, in 1970 reached the majority conclusion that the present concept of AMCs should be abandoned, since the broad and objective standards in annex 8, together with the requirement that each state establish its own code of airworthiness (or select a code established by another contracting state) meet the objectives of articles 33 and 37 of the Chicago Convention. However, with a view to facilitating the development and uniformity of national codes by contracting states, the committee recommended that provision be made for the publication by ICAO of an airworthiness manual to include guidance material of a non-regulatory nature.[39] Canadian air lawyers will note for future reference that any shift away from the inclusion of detailed standards in annex 8 itself will have an impact on the obligations of states under the convention. This is seen from the undertaking in article 33, which provides for the international recognition of airworthiness certificates as follows:

> Certificates of airworthiness and certificates of competency and licences issued or rendered valid by the contracting State in which the aircraft is registered, shall be recognized as valid by the other contracting States, provided that the requirements under which such certificates or licences were issued or rendered valid are equal to or above the minimum standards which may be established from time to time pursuant to this Convention.

A further example of new activity in the development of annexes is found in the now fashionable topic of the environment. ICAO adopted a new annex on Aircraft Noise in 1971.[40] This annex includes noise certification standards for future subsonic turbojet aeroplanes, recommends practices relating both to noise measurement and an international noise exposure reference unit, and contains material on aircraft noise abatement operating procedures. The annex became applicable on 6 January 1972. During the coming decade it will attract increasing attention as new types of aircraft are planned and brought into service.

The future The lawyer who deals with the technical side of air navigation will be wise not to restrict his attention to national air regulations and associated material as though they existed in a vacuum;[41] instead, he will wish to examine the impact on these documents of the ever-growing ICAO material which, in large measure, shapes the content of those regulations. He will make a real contribution in the 1970s if he can bring his lawyership to bear on many of the problems mentioned above.

Amendment of the Chicago Convention
General comments In spite of its age one does not look for a major overhaul

of the Chicago Convention during the next few years. The ICAO system tends to work quite well in view of the liberal application of the convention. The tendency has been to amend the convention only when necessary and then, for the most part, only in connection with matters of a housekeeping nature, such as frequency of Assembly sessions, increase in membership of the Council and Air Navigation Commission, and cognate matters.[42] One exception was the (highly political) article 93 bis adopted in 1947 in order to exclude from ICAO states disapproved of by the United Nations.[43] Such political amendments have not had too successful a history since then. In 1965 a thirty-one nation move to amend the convention with a view to expelling South Africa failed to secure the required two-thirds vote of the Assembly,[44] although a resolution condemning South Africa's policies of apartheid and racial discrimination was adopted. By 1971 the countries opposed to apartheid and the like had abandoned the attempt to amend the convention, but in that year they secured the adoption of a resolution which had the effect of cutting off invitations to South Africa to attend certain ICAO meetings, other than those which South Africa had a right to attend because specifically mentioned in the convention, and of preventing the circulation of certain ICAO documentation to that country.[45] A similar resolution in respect of Portugal narrowly failed of adoption.[46]

Reluctance of states to make substantive amendments States are reluctant to make substantive amendments to the convention. For example, in 1968 and 1971, Sweden proposed to amend article 7 so as to enable a state to grant cabotage privileges to foreign operators on an exclusive basis instead of being obliged to give such privileges to all operators if it gave them to one. This proposal failed, on both occasions, to receive the necessary two-thirds vote of the Assembly.[47]

Settlement of differences Recent experience with chapter XVIII (articles 84–9) of the Chicago Convention, which provides for the settlement of disputes over the interpretation or application of the convention and its annexes, has uncovered differences of opinion on the manner in which the ICAO Council should carry out its judicial functions under this chapter.[48] In 1971 Pakistan filed an application concerning, *inter alia,* a dispute with India over the interpretation or application of certain provisions of the convention and of the International Air Services Transit Agreement. India raised preliminary objections to the Council's jurisdiction. The Council having ruled that these objections could not be accepted, India then appealed to the International Court of Justice. This case may produce new insights into the provisions of chapter XVIII and the Council's role thereunder.[49] Canadian lawyers will no doubt be moved to take a careful look at the procedure for settling disputes under the convention in the light of the ICJ's judgment.

Unlawful seizure of aircraft and unlawful interference with international civil aviation During the extraordinary session (seventeenth) of the Assembly, convened in June 1970 to discuss measures for the prevention of unlawful seizure of aircraft and unlawful interference with international civil aviation, Switzerland presented some amendments to the Chicago Convention aimed at countering the wave of violence against international civil aviation.[50] It is always possible that, in the next few years, amendments of this nature may come up for consideration. Meanwhile, some of the annexes to the convention have been amended so as to permit more effective measures to be taken against hijacking and other forms of unlawful interference with international civil aviation and its facilities.[51]

Ratification of amendments The requirement that two-thirds of the contracting states must ratify an amendment before it can come into force can frustrate quick action.[52] For example, the amendment increasing the number of Council members from twenty-seven to thirty was adopted by an extraordinary session of the assembly on 12 March 1971 and eighty ratifications were specified for its coming into force. By the time of the next Council election, three months later, only forty ratifications had been deposited, leaving the council with twenty-seven members in spite of the fact that the well-attended Assembly which had adopted the amendment had unanimously expressed its will that the Council should have thirty members. A similar amendment, adopted by the Assembly in July 1971, increasing the size of the Air Navigation Commission from twelve to fifteen, also requires eighty ratifications before it will come into force. Could the experience gained in respect of these two amendments lead to an altered procedure whereby, for certain types of amendments, where there is a high degree of consensus in the assembly, fewer ratifications may be required?

The future
The foregoing discussion of ICAO and the Chicago Convention indicates that Canadian air lawyers familar with the public law aspects of international civil aviation will face many problems in the coming years. In order to keep up with aviation technology, ICAO will continue to engage in mind-stretching activities. The lawyer will have his role to play both in the creation of new norms governing aviation and in determining the organizational machinery to be used for their creation.

International civil aviation and the environment

Like other forms of modern technology, civil aviation is concerned with the relationship between technological advancement and the human environment. However, the effects of present generation aircraft on the environment are minor, if not negligable, in comparison with the impact that the requirements of aircraft approach, landing, ground handling and take-off have on the communities in the vicinity of airports. It is particularly at the airport that the air transportation system and community meet, and it is there that the interests of both interact most intensively, in some respects in competition, and in other more fundamental respects, to their mutual benefit. In regard to the airport, questions for consideration include aircraft noise, land use, ecology, air pollution, transportation capacity, rate of adjustment of the community, and airport planning.[53]

In particular, the work of ICAO with regard to aircraft noise concentrates on the protection of the people in the vicinity of the airport. As a result of a resolution of the ICAO Assembly in 1968,[54] a worldwide conference was convened in 1969 to deal with various aspects of aircraft noise in the vicinity of airdromes.[55] International agreement has now been reached on the manner in which aircraft noise is described, measured, and monitored. Important human aspects have been studied from the medical point of view. Recommendations have been formulated for the reduction of ground run-up noise and for operational procedures to be complied with to reduce noise levels around airports. Definite noise limits requiring international compliance have been established for future subsonic jet transport.[56] ICAO is also considering aircraft noise certification matters and retrofitting of existing subsonic jet aircraft.

At the Eighteenth Session of the Assembly in 1971, ICAO adopted resolution A18–11, in which it decided to inform the 1972 United Nations Conference on the Human Environment, that: the Convention on International Civil Aviation places on ICAO the responsibility to guide the development of international civil aviation in such a manner as to benefit the peoples of the world; in fulfilling this role ICAO is conscious of the adverse environmental impacts that may be related to aircraft activity and of its responsibility and that of its member states to achieve maximum compatibility between the safe and orderly development of civil aviation and the quality of the human environment; in discharging its responsibility, ICAO is already assisting and will continue to assist states by all available means, in order that they may increasingly reap the benefit of the potential which civil aviation offers for improving living conditions. The Council later approved a statement for inclusion in the documentation of the Stockholm conference.

In resolution A18-12, the Assembly requested the Council, with the assistance and co-operation of other bodies of ICAO and of other international organizations, to continue with vigour the work related to the development of standards, recommended practices, and procedures and guidance material dealing with the quality of the human environment and urged contracting states to adopt, where appropriate, the ICAO measures and procedures so developed. By the end of 1971 the council had approved a plan of action on both the technical and non-technical aspects of the continuing work.

As to aircraft en route, the view has been expressed that thus far they interact with their environment in a minor way, although this may not be true for future generations of aircraft.[57] During its 1968 meeting, ICAO stated that it attaches great importance 'to ensuring that no unacceptable situation for the public is created by sonic boom when supersonic aircraft are introduced into commercial service.'[58] The Sonic Boom Panel, established in 1969, has already carried out the first part of a program aimed at ensuring that international standards would take due account of the problems which the operation of supersonic aircraft may create for the public, the taking of action to achieve international agreement on the measurement of sonic boom, the definition of the expression 'unacceptable situation for the public,' and the establishment of corresponding limits. The panel has prepared a detailed report on the effects of sonic boom and the ranges of sonic boom values likely to emanate from known supersonic transport designs.[59] In the next phase of the study, operational, economic, social, and legal experts have been added. The panel has been replaced by the interdisciplinary Sonic Boom Committee which is now at work on the above-mentioned problems.[60]

Problems arising out of leases, charters, and interchange of aircraft in international operations

It has long been known that problems are likely to arise when an aircraft registered in one state is operated by an operator belonging to another state. Leasing and exchanging of aircraft is increasing and this may produce complex problems in the legal and technical fields.

As early as 1950 ICAO added a note to annex 6 to the Chicago Convention in which it was suggested that, when an aircraft was chartered, the state of registry might consider delegating some of its responsibilities to the state of the operator.[61] The International Conference on Private Air Law (Guadalajara, Mexico, 1961) covered certain private law aspects of the question when it adopted the Convention, Supplementary to the Warsaw Convention, for the Unification of Certain Rules Relating to International Carriage by Air Performed by a Person Other than the Contracting Carrier.[62] This conference also adopted resolution B, which urged ICAO to study 'the legal problems affecting the regulation and enforcement of air safety which have been experienced by certain states when an aircraft registered in one state is operated by an operator belonging to another state.'[63]

An ICAO Legal Subcommittee later drew up two reports on the subject, one for presentation to the Tokyo Conference of 1963, in which it suggested a text for inclusion in the Tokyo Convention, that text not being adopted; and the other dealing with a number of legal problems affecting the regulation and enforcement of air safety in cases of lease of aircraft; for example: amendment of the Chicago Convention; delegation of functions of the state of registry to the state of the operator; inclusion of a standard in annex 13 providing for representation of the state of the operator at accident inquiries.[64] The Legal Committee at its fifteenth session in 1964 took the following action: it agreed that the European Civil Aviation Conference could also study the problem (and this body has continued to do so); it decided that the best way of solving the problems in question would be the delegation of functions of the state of registry to the state of the operator of the aircraft concerned; it decided that the subcommittee should prepare model bilateral agreements to provide for such delegation (a task which the subcommittee did not carry out because the item was given low priority on the Legal Committee's work program); and it decided that a questionnaire seeking information should be sent to states (this was not done because of the low priority given to the subject).[65]

The subject languished in ICAO until the seventeenth session of the Assembly, convened in 1970 to discuss ways and means of curbing violence against international civil aviation. In resolution A17-5, the Assembly recommended that contracting states adopt certain measures to alleviate the consequences of an unlawful seizure of aircraft and called upon the state of registry to take certain actions. This resolution also contemplated that, where an aircraft is leased to and operated by a carrier of a state other than the state of registry, the state of the carrier should have the same rights and responsibilities as those recommended in the resolution for the state of registry. Further, the Convention for the Suppression of Unlawful Seizure of Aircraft (The Hague, 1970) lists as one of the states required to establish jurisdiction in the event of the unlawful seizure of aircraft, the state of the operator in cases 'when the offence is committed on board aircraft leased without crew to a lessee who has his principal place of business or, if the lessee has no such place of business, his permanent residence in that State.'[66]

At the eighteenth session of the Assembly, in 1971, emphasis was placed on the examination of technical problems arising out of leases, charters, and interchange of aircraft in international operations. In the Technical Commission of the Assembly it was recognized that the root of the problem was in the Chicago Convention, which places the responsibility for discharging certain functions on the state of registry of the aircraft and does not generally provide for the situation of an aircraft being leased, chartered, or interchanged by an operator of a state other than the state of registry.[67] Problems are particularly evident when the aircraft is leased without a crew, the so-called dry-lease.

By way of short-term solution, the Assembly, in resolution A18-16, urged that, where arrangements for the lease, charter and interchange of aircraft (particularly aircraft without crew) would be facilitated, the state of registry of such an aircraft, to the extent considered necessary, delegate to the state of the operator its functions under annex 6 of the Chicago Convention. It also urged that in such cases the state of the operator change, if necessary, its national regulations to the extent required to empower it to accept such delegation of functions and to oblige the operator to fulfil the obligations imposed by annex 6. Having in mind a long-term solution, the Assembly, in the same resolution, directed the ICAO Council: to examine the annexes to the Chicago Convention with a view to making recommendations for their amendment as soon as practicable; to examine that convention as well as any other relevant convention and to submit a report on the subject at the next session of the Assembly at which a Technical Commission is established which will probably be in 1974; and to obtain and distribute to contracting states information concerning national laws and regulations pertaining to lease, charter, and interchange of aircraft, taking into account the financial implications of this directive. It is not improbable that there will be an opportunity for Canadian aviation experts (technical, legal, and economic) to make their contribution to the solution of the problems posed by resolution A18-16.

Unlawful interference with international civil aviation

During the last two decades, international civil aviation has faced serious problems arising out of incidents of unlawful seizure of aircraft (commonly known as hijacking) and other forms of unlawful interference. ICAO has been active in seeking solutions for these problems.

Convention on Offences and Certain Other Acts Committed on Board Aircraft (Tokyo 1963)

The Convention on Offences and Certain Other Acts Committed on Board Aircraft (Tokyo 1963),[68] drawn up under the auspices of ICAO, contains specific provisions on the unlawful seizure of aircraft. In particular, article 11 provides that when a person on board an aircraft has unlawfully committed by force or threat thereof an act of interference, seizure, or other wrongful exercise of control of an aircraft in flight or when such an act is about to be committed, contracting states shall take all appropriate measures to restore control of the aircraft to its lawful commander or to preserve his control of the aircraft. In such cases, the contracting state in which the aircraft lands shall permit its passengers and crew to continue their journey as soon as practicable and shall return the aircraft and its cargo to the persons lawfully entitled to possession. The convention also provides for the taking of the suspected hijacker into custody and for disposal of him thereafter.[69] Unfortunately, states were slow to ratify the Tokyo Convention. Hence, when the wave of unlawful seizures hit the aviation world in the latter half of the 1960s, the useful legal tool represented by the convention could not be put to work because it entered into force only on 4 December 1969 and then only for the twelve states that had ratified it. Fortunately, the convention has become more widely accepted. As at 31 December 1971 it was in force for 48 states. Canada became a party with effect from 5 February 1971.

Convention for the Suppression of Unlawful Seizure of Aircraft (The Hague 1970)
With incidents of hijacking reaching epidemic proportions in the late 1960s, the ICAO Assembly, meeting in Buenos Aires in 1968, called for the preparation of a special convention on unlawful seizure. On 16 December 1970, ICAO's work on the subject culminated in the signature of The Hague Convention for the Suppression of Unlawful Seizure of Aircraft.[70] The 77 states attending the conference reached near unanimity, 50 of them signing the convention at the close of the conference. As of 31 December 1971 a total of 81 states had signed the document and this augurs well for its wide acceptance. The convention came into force for 11 states on 14 October 1971 and many states are taking the necessary legislative steps prior to ratification.

Briefly, the convention describes, along the lines found in article 11 of the Tokyo Convention, the acts which constitute unlawful seizure.[71] The convention applies if the place of take-off or the place of actual landing of the aircraft on board which the offence is committed is situated outside the territory of the state of registration; and it is immaterial whether the aircraft is engaged in an international or domestic flight.[72] Also, the articles on the taking of the offender into custody, the requirement to extradite him or prosecute him, and the furnishing of assistance between states in connection with criminal proceedings all apply whatever the place of take-off or the place of actual landing of the aircraft, if the offender or the alleged offender is found in the territory of a state other than the state of registration of the aircraft.[73]

The convention obliges each contracting state to take such measures as may be necessary to establish its jurisdiction over the offence of unlawful seizure and other acts of violence against passengers or crew committed by the alleged offender in connection with the offence in specified cases.[74] Upon being satisfied that the circumstances so warrant, any contracting state, in the territory of which the offender or the alleged offender is present, shall take him into custody or take other measures to ensure his presence.[75] This far-reaching provision is intended to eliminate 'hijacker havens.'

The convention contains carefully drafted compromise provisions on prosecution and extradition, Thus, the contracting state in the territory of which the alleged offender is found shall, if it does not extradite him, be obliged, without exception whatsoever and whether or not the offence was committed in its territory, to submit the case to its competent authorities for the purpose of prosecution. Those authorities must take their decision in the same manner as in the case of any ordinary offence of a serious nature under the local law.[76] The convention contains a provision similar to article 11 of the Tokyo Convention on continuance of the journey of the aircraft, crew and passengers.[77] As an indication of the gravity with which the states at The Hague Conference viewed acts of unlawful seizure of aircraft, the convention is open to 'all states' for signature in Moscow, London, and Washington.[78] This formula was adopted in spite of the declared interest of many states in preserving the Vienna formula, found in the Convention on the Law of Treaties, 1969.[79]

The foregoing summary of some of the main provisions of the convention indicates that its effective implementation by Canada and other nations will require some rethinking of relations between states in the criminal law area in relation to acts of unlawful seizure of aircraft.

Convention for the Suppression of Unlawful Acts against the Safety of Civil Aviation

The seventeenth session (extraordinary) of the ICAO Assembly met in June 1970 after the international community had been shocked by the mid-air bombing on 21 February 1970 of two civil aircraft in western Europe, one of the aircraft crashing with the loss of all crew and passengers.[80] The Assembly, faced with what came to be called 'acts of unlawful interference against civil aviation and its facilities,' called for a convention on this subject.[81]

Working on the basis of a draft convention prepared by the ICAO Legal Committee at London in September-October 1970,[82] a diplomatic conference developed and adopted, at Montreal, in September 1971, the Convention for the Suppression of Unlawful Acts against the Safety of Civil Aviation.[83] Opened for signature at Montreal, on 23 September 1971, this convention is intended to ensure that persons committing acts endangering the safety of civil aviation, other than acts contemplated by The Hague Convention, will be unable to find a haven where they will escape punishment.

The convention is concerned with unlawful and intentional acts committed against persons on board aircraft, if such acts are likely to endanger the safety of the aircraft; destruction and damaging of aircraft in service; the placing of devices or substances on board aircraft which are likely to destroy or damage them; destruction or damaging of air navigation facilities or interference with their operation; and communication of false information. Attempts and complicity are considered to be offences for the purposes of the convention.[84] As in the case of The Hague Convention, each state party to the Montreal Convention undertakes to make the offences mentioned therein punishable by severe penalties.[85]

The convention contains detailed provisions about its application. For example, it will apply to most offences covered by it, irrespective of whether the aircraft concerned is engaged in an international or domestic flight only if the place of take-off or landing, actual or intended, is situated outside the territory of the state of registration of the aircraft, or the offence is committed in the territory of a state other than the state of registration of the aircraft. In the case of offences against air navigation facilities, the convention applies only if the facilities are used in international air navigation.[86]

In regard to jurisdiction,[87] apprehension of the alleged offender,[88] prosecution,[89] extradition,[90] continuation of the journey of the aircraft, passengers, and crew,[91] the Montreal Convention contains provisions similar to those found in The Hague Convention. Like the latter, the Montreal Convention also contains the ''all-states'' clause which, through use of a triple depositary, enables it to be open for signature in Moscow, London, and Washington.[92]

Concerted action
Tragic and destructive events occurred in September 1970, when four aircraft were hijacked to the Middle East and blown up while passengers and crew members were held as hostages against the release of seven Palestine guerrillas detained in western Europe.[93] On 1 October 1970 the ICAO Council called for concerted action against states which, where aircraft and persons on board are held for international black-mail purposes, give refuge to the malefactors.[94] The Legal Committee, meeting in London, was immediately given a United States draft convention, which took a multilateral approach to the question of concerted action,[95] and a Canadian pro-posal, which aimed at the same result through the inclusion of a standard clause in bilateral air transport agreements between states.[96] The Legal Committee reached no conclusion except to establish a subcommittee to study the matter. The report of the subcommittee, prepared in April 1971, raised many difficult ques-tions.[97] The main question was whether ICAO, rather than the United Nations, was the competent body to work on the preparation of a convention which would in effect be concerned with sanctions. After a lengthy debate at the eighteenth session of the Assembly in 1971, the subject of concerted action was placed in the non-current part of the Legal Committee's work program,[98] the Canadian delegation being strongly opposed to that decision.

The future
From what has been stated above, it is seen that, during the 1970s, Canadian lawyers will have to work out the techniques for implementing the conventions already adopted for the purpose of curbing attacks against the safety of civil aviation; they could also be called upon to work on the subject of concerted action, although the forum in which such work would take place is, at the present time, uncertain.

Canada and agreements for the exchange of commercial rights in international civil aviation

For the sake of completeness, mention may be made of agreements for the exchange of commercial rights in international civil aviation. Non-scheduled flights internationally are permitted under article 5 of the Chicago Convention subject to certain qualifications. Article 6 of the convention stipulates that no scheduled inter-national air service may be operated over or into the territory of an ICAO contracting state, except with the special permission or other authorization of that state and in accordance with the terms of such permission of authorization.[99] The Interna-tional Air Services Transit Agreement, to which Canada and seventy-nine other states are parties, grants the right of overflight and technical non-commercial stops to the scheduled international air services of the parties. In the case of Canada in mid-1971, a network of bilateral air transport agreements covered these two so-called freedoms, as well as the commercial rights involving the picking up and set-ting down of passengers. Two of these agreements (with New Zealand and the Netherlands) have been abrogated, although air services between Canada and the Netherlands have continued, and two (with Austria and Greece) have not been signed. One (with Turkey) has not been ratified. Over and above the twenty-eight bilateral agreements, there are special permits whereby Canadian Pacific Airlines operates to Spain, Chile, and Argentina.

There has been pressure by foreign airlines to have Canada throw open the Toronto market to them. A recent government policy statement (1969) is that Canada is not prepared to open bilateral negotiations on this matter and that the Canadian government would expect any foreign government to submit, as a basis for negotiation, a concrete proposal indicating reciprocal concessions equivalent in value to landing rights at Toronto.

These are matters of greater interest to aviation economists and government policy-makers than they are to Main Street lawyers, although government lawyers will be called upon to play an important role both in negotiating bilateral agreements and putting them into words.

PRIVATE LAW

International recognition of rights in aircraft

The Convention on the International Recognition of Rights in Aircraft (Geneva 1948),[100] drawn up under the auspices of ICAO, provides for recognition and enforcement of property and other rights in aircraft created in conformity with the national law of the state in which the aircraft is registered, so that even if the aircraft crosses a national frontier the interests of holders of such rights will be protected. This convention was prepared in the hope that acceptance of its principles would encourage investors to make financial assistance available to operators for the purchase of new aircraft to be used internationally. The basis of the convention was that the interest of investors would be protected no matter where the aircraft went, provided it was within the territory of a party to the convention. Apart from the convention, charges or encumbrances attaching to an aircraft under the law of one state would not necessarily be recognized in another state. Canada is not a party to the convention, which thirty-five states have now accepted. Hence if a Canadian-registered aircraft, put up as security for a loan in Canada, flies abroad, it would be subject to seizure in execution proceedings in another state and the Canadian lender could be left out in the cold. The foreign purchaser of the aircraft would be under no legal obligation to honour the unsatisfied claim of the Canadian lender.

From time to time the Canadian Bar Association has pressed the Canadian government to establish a central register where property rights in aircraft could be recorded, it being realized that until such a register is established Canada cannot effectively become a party to the Geneva Convention.[101] However, constitutional objections have been raised to the establishment of a central register of the kind envisaged, even though property rights in ships are recorded in a central register kept in Ottawa. This is a matter which Canadian air lawyers should keep under study during the coming years; the establishment of a machinery for the international recognition of property rights in aircraft could be of some help to export sales of the Canadian aircraft industry.

Liability of the air carrier in respect of the international carriage by air of passengers and baggage

In spite of the recent activity aimed at revising the liability rules governing the international carriage by air of passengers and baggage, the air lawyer will find that the dream of unification is far from being realized. The discussion that follows will show why this is so.

Warsaw Convention, 1929
The hope of air lawyers in the pioneer days of international air transport was to have a system of unified liability rules governing the relationships between international air carriers and their users. The Convention for the Unification of Certain Rules relating to International Carriage by Air (Warsaw 1929),[102] if taken alone, would appear to have made this dream come true, since as at 31 December 1971 there were no less than ninety-six parties to it, including Canada. However, on closer examination it is seen that today the Warsaw Convention is but part of a very complex network of conventions and arrangements which make a lottery out of the legal regime that will apply to the international carriage by air of passengers and baggage. The contents of this network may now be briefly examined.

The Warsaw Convention contains a presumption of liability for the air carrier when, during international carriage by air, a passenger is killed or injured, or baggage or cargo are lost or destroyed. The carrier is also liable for damage occasioned by delay in the carriage by air of passengers, baggage, or cargo. The liability is subject to the following limits: for each passenger, 125,000 gold francs ($8,300 US); for each kilogram of checked baggage and cargo, 250 gold francs ($16.58 US); for possessions which the passenger carries with him, 5,000 gold francs ($331.67 US). The carrier loses the benefit of these limits if the documents of carriage are not issued or are defective in certain respects. He also loses the benefit of the limits in the case of his so-called wilful misconduct or equivalent conduct, the whole being defined in article 25 of the convention. The carrier's basic defence under the Warsaw Convention is that he or his agents took all necessary measures to avoid the damage or that it was impossible for him or them to have taken such measures. A further defence is that the damage was caused or contributed to by the negligence of the person suffering the damage.

The Hague Protocol, 1955
The Hague Protocol of 1955[103] amends the Warsaw Convention by doubling the limit per passenger to 250,000 gold francs ($16,600 US); by providing that the carrier loses the benefit of the passenger limit if the passenger ticket is not delivered and a specified notice concerning the limitation of liability is not given; and by specifying in an amended article 25 that the carrier will lose the benefit of limited liability if (and this is a substitution for the wilful misconduct formula) it is proved that the damage resulted from an act or omission by him, his servants, or agents, with intent to cause damage or recklessly and with knowledge that damage would probably result. As at 31 December 1971 seventy-two states, including Canada, were parties to the Hague Protocol.

Montreal Agreement, 1966

The story did not end there and a further complication arose. Under the threat of denunciation of the Warsaw Convention by the United States, the so-called Montreal Agreement,[104] developed by airlines in May 1966, was approved by the United States Civil Aeronautics Board barely in time to head off the denunciation. Under this agreement, which constitutes a *de facto* amendment of the Warsaw-Hague regime, airlines whose flights touch the territory of the United States are subject to absolute liability with limited defences. They have a limit of liability for each passenger for death, wounding or other bodily injury in the amount of $75,000 US, inclusive of legal fees and costs or, where appropriate, $58,000 US, exclusive of legal fees and costs. The agreement also requires that a more prominent and understandable notice concerning the limitation of liability be furnished with the ticket. This accounts for the notice included within air tickets in recent years in large type and headed 'Advice to International Passengers on Limitation of Liability.' As at 1 November 1971 some 434 airlines had notified the United States authorities that they had accepted the Montreal Agreement.

Guatemala City Protocol, 1971

The Montreal Agreement was but a stop-gap; and, during the late 1960s, there was pressure to amend the Hague-Warsaw system of liability in respect of passengers. Beginning in February 1966 negotiations were carried on in a series of ICAO meetings between the United States, on the one hand, and other parties to the Warsaw-Hague system, on the other. As negotiations progressed, the difficulty of having a universal system of liability on a worldwide basis was highlighted, particularly since the developing countries indicated that high limits of liability could be a severe hindrance to the development of their civil aviation. The negotiations culminated with the adoption of the Guatemala City Protocol to Amend the Convention for the Unification of Certain Rules Relating to International Carriage by Air Signed at Warsaw on 12 October 1929, as Amended by the Protocol Done at The Hague on 28 September 1955.[105] The Guatemala City Protocol was opened for signature on 8 March 1971 and was signed by twenty-one states, including Canada. Some of the highlights of this protocol are described below.

Absolute liability   The Guatemala City Protocol radically revises the Warsaw-Hague system. It provides for the absolute liability of the air carrier in the international carriage of passengers and baggage.[106] It does not deal with the carriage of cargo. It preserves the defence of contributory negligence, but omits in respect of the carriage of passengers and baggage – except in the case of delay – the defence that the carrier, his servants, or agents took all necessary measures to avoid the damage or that it was impossible for him or them to have taken such measures.[107]

Limits of liability for passengers   The protocol provides an unbreakable limit of 1,500,000 gold francs ($100,000 US) for the aggregate of claims, however founded, in respect of damage suffered as a result of death or personal injury of each passenger.[108]

National supplementary system   A novel provision in the protocol contemplates a national supplementary system of compensation.[109] This is the main provision that made the protocol acceptable to the United States at the Guatemala City Conference. According to this provision, nothing in the convention prevents a state from establishing and operating within its territory a system to supplement the compensation payable to claimants under the convention in respect of death or personal injury of passengers, provided the system fulfils stipulated conditions.

Conference for review of passenger limit   There is a provision[110] for convening conferences of parties to the protocol during the fifth and tenth years from the date of entry into force of the protocol for purposes of considering devaluation and increases in the cost of living, and for reviewing the passenger limit, although at each of these conferences the limit in force at the respective dates of the conferences will not be increased by an amount exceeding 187,500 gold francs ($12,500 US). There will be an automatic increase by $12,500 US on 31 December of the fifth and tenth years respectively, unless the review conferences decide otherwise by a two-thirds majority.

Settlement inducement clause   Associated with the passenger limit is a settlement inducement clause that enables courts to award costs in addition to damages unless the carrier has, at a stipulated time, made an offer of settlement.[111]

Additional forum   In the case of passengers and baggage, the Guatemala City Protocol adds to the fora contemplated in article 28 of the Warsaw Convention as amended by The Hague Protocol, the following forum: the court within the jurisdiction of which the carrier has an establishment, if the passenger has his domicile or permanent residence in the territory of the same High Contracting Party.[112]

Delay   The Guatemala City Protocol retains in the case of delay of passengers and baggage the old Warsaw-Hague regime of presumed liability of the carrier and establishes a new limit of 62,500 gold francs ($4,150 US) in the case of delay in the carriage of persons.[113]

Baggage   In the carriage of baggage, the liability of the carrier is limited to 15,000 gold francs ($1,000 US) in the case of destruction, loss, damage, or delay.[114]

Unbreakability of limits applicable to passengers and baggage   The most noteworthy of these provisions limits the application of the escape clause in article 25 of The Hague Protocol to the carriage of cargo,[115] with the result that even an act or omission described in that article will not lead to a loss of the carrier's limitation of liability with respect to passengers and baggage. It is also provided that, in the carriage of passengers and baggage, any action for damages, however founded, whether under the convention or in contract or in tort or otherwise, can only be brought subject to the conditions and limits of liability set out in the convention, without prejudice to the question as to who are the persons who have the right to bring suits and what are their respective rights. It is further stipulated that the limits of liability constitute maximum limits and may not be exceeded whatever the circumstances which gave rise to the liability.[116] The provisions on the liability of the servant or agent of the carrier have been adjusted in the light of the foregoing.[117]

Application clause   The protocol also has its application clause which provides that the Warsaw Convention, as amended at The Hague in 1955 and by the Guatemala City Protocol, shall apply to international carriage as defined in article 1 of the convention, provided that the places of departure and destination referred to in that article are situated in the territories of two parties to the new protocol or within the territory of a single party to the protocol with an agreed stopping place in the territory of another state.[118]

Entry into force   The protocol will enter into force on the ninetieth day after the deposit of the thirtieth instrument of ratification 'on the condition, however, that the total international scheduled air traffic, expressed in passenger-kilometres, according to the statistics for the year 1970 published by the International Civil Aviation Organization, of the airlines of five states which have ratified this Protocol, represents at least 40% of the total international scheduled air traffic of the airlines of the member states of the International Civil Aviation Organization.'[119]

Guadalajara Convention The Warsaw-Hague-Guatemala City system is further complicated by the existence of the Convention, Supplementary to the Warsaw Convention, for the Unification of Certain Rules Relating to International Carriage by Air Performed by a Person Other than the Contracting Carrier (Guadalajara 1961).[120] However, Canada is not yet a party to this convention,[121] although thirty-nine states are.

Problems arising out of the Warsaw-Hague-Guatemala City system The legal rules applicable to the international carriage by air of passengers and baggage are now so complicated that the average passenger will find it most difficult, if he does not have access to an up-to-date list of parties to the various instruments concerned, to know exactly what regime will apply to any given carriage. By way of example: a passenger purchasing an air ticket in Montreal for a one-way trip to a state that has accepted only the Warsaw Convention, may find that he is subject to the Warsaw regime with its $8,300 limit of liability; if he is flying to a state which has accepted The Hague Protocol, he may have a $16,600 limit; but if he is going to that state by way of New York, the Montreal Agreement will intervene with its $58,000 to $75,000 limits; and at some future date, when the Guatemala City Protocol will have come into force, he would have the benefit of the $100,000 limit, which may be even higher if the national supplementary compensation system has been applied. Then, too, there are states which are not parties to any of the instruments pertaining to the Warsaw regime; in this case, the passenger may be subject to widely differing national liability regimes. Whether the Guatemala City Protocol will become so widely accepted as to absorb all of the widely differing regimes applicable to the international carriage of passengers and baggage by air remains to be seen.[122] Meanwhile, Canadian air lawyers will be called upon to advise whether Canada should ratify the Guatemala City Protocol and the Guadalajara Convention, while, at the same time, they will have to steer their clients, whether carriers, users, or insurers, through a thicket of disparate legal regimes and limits of liability.

Liability of the air carrier in respect of the international carriage of cargo by air

The question of the revision of the Warsaw Convention in regard to the international carriage of cargo by air is on the work program of the ICAO Legal Committee, and computerization of cargo operations will, it is expected, have its effect on the traditional form of the air waybill.[123] Means of preserving a legally acceptable record of information concerning cargo shipments, other than by detailed entries on pieces of paper, will have to be found if speedier methods of cargo handling are to be effectively implemented. A related question, now under active study by the transportation community, is that of the preparation of a convention on the international combined transport of goods, particularly in the case of container traffic. Canada was an active participant in the Joint IMCO/ECE Meeting which prepared a draft of the above-mentioned convention.[124] The ICAO Legal Committee has under consideration the implications of such a convention for international civil aviation. At the time of writing, the schedule of the United Nations called for the adoption of the convention on combined transport by a conference on international container traffic convened for November 1972.

Damage Caused by Foreign Aircraft to Third Parties on the Surface

The Convention on Damage Caused by Foreign Aircraft to Third Parties on the Surface,[125] opened for signature at Rome, on 8 October 1952, has to date been ratified or adhered to by twenty-five states, including Canada. As this convention may be amended in the present decade, reference will be made to some of the reasons for amendment after first describing the convention in brief.

The Rome Convention of 1952 is a revision of the corresponding Convention of 1933 and of the Brussels Protocol of 1938 regulating certain insurance aspects of the earlier convention. The Rome Convention provides for absolute liability of the aircraft operator for damage caused to third parties on the surface.[126] In return for acceptance by the operator of this rule of liability, along with a restricted number of defences,[127] the convention provides that the operator's liability shall not exceed certain monetary limits calculated in relation to the weight of the aircraft causing the damage. The limits run from 500,000 gold francs ($33,168 US) for aircraft weighing 1,000 kilograms or less, to 10,500,000 gold francs ($696,528 US) for aircraft weighing 50,000 kilograms, with a further increase of 100 gold francs ($6.63 US) per kilogram for aircraft in excess of 50,000 kilograms. The liability in respect of life or personal injury is not to exceed 500,000 gold francs ($33,168.00 US) per person killed or injured.[128] The convention applies unlimited liability to the operator in certain cases as well as to the unlawful user of an aircraft causing damage to third parties on the surface.[129] It also provides that any state party may require that the operator of an aircraft registered in another state party shall, in respect of damage on the surface that might be caused by such aircraft, be secured by means of insurance, or, in lieu thereof, a cash deposit, a bank guarantee, or a state guarantee.[130] A novel provision in this convention is the undertaking by states as to recognition and execution of foreign judgments on claims arising under the convention.[131] When it was adopted two decades ago, this provision represented the greatest advance made up to that particular time by any multilateral convention in respect of the recognition and execution of foreign judgments. A judgment under the convention rendered in the court of one state will be capable of execution in any other state party to the convention, subject to certain specified conditions.

In 1964 the ICAO Legal Committee,[132] acting at the request of the ICAO Council, placed the question of the revision of the Rome Convention on the work program of the committee, partly because of the lack of wide acceptance of the convention; a subcommittee was established to study the convention. The subcommittee held sessions in 1965 and 1966.[133] Canada, which is a party to the convention, was represented on the subcommittee. In 1967 the Legal Committee examined the work of the subcommittee particularly in regard to the questions of sonic boom, nuclear damage, and limitation of liability.[134] As to sonic boom, the committee noted, in relation to article 1(1) of the convention, that there was a problem concerning damage resulting from sonic boom. The committee was divided on whether claims on account of such damage should be left to be determined by national laws or should be regulated by the convention. The subcommittee was asked to continue its work on this question in the light of developments such as further comments from states and experience of supersonic flights.

In considering the question of nuclear damage, the committee noted that the Vienna Convention on Civil Liability for Nuclear Damage, 1963,[135] and the Paris Convention on Third Party Liability in the Field of Nuclear Energy, 1960,[136] as well as the Brussels Protocol of 1963,[137] channelled liability to the operator of the nuclear installation and excluded the liability of all other persons, an exclusion which would apply to the operator of an aircraft. Article II.5 of the Vienna Convention provides that the exclusion is not to affect the application of any international convention in the field of transport in force or open for signature on 21 May 1963. There is a corresponding provision in the Paris Convention. The ICAO Secretariat was requested to ascertain the extent to which these instruments had been ratified and to transmit the information received to the subcommittee. The committee thought that the question of the limits under the convention should be further examined, but it did not think that it was advisable for the subcommittee to attempt to determine, at that time, specific figures for the limits. The committee also noted that one of the topics that could be studied by the subcommittee was that of a standard form of a certificate of insurance or other security. In the event, it transpired that during the late 1960s and early 1970s, the energy of the ICAO legal community was channelled towards the revision of the Warsaw Convention and solving the crisis arising out of unlawful seizure of aircraft and unlawful interference with international civil aviation.

At its eighteenth session in 1971, the ICAO Assembly placed the study of the Rome Convention as the third subject in the active part of the work program of the Legal Committee, although it did not rule out the possibility of a consolidated regime embodying the Rome Convention, the draft convention on aerial collisions, and the subject of liability of air traffic control agencies. Since 1952, when the rate of increase in the limits of liability of the operator was flattened out at $6.63 per kilogram for aircraft in excess of 50,000 kilograms, the aviation world has progressed from the DC6B which weighed 48,125 kilograms (106,000 pounds) to the giant aircraft like the Boeing 747 weighing 351,540 kilograms (775,000 pounds).[138] Any revision of the Rome Convention which still related the limits of liability of the aircraft operator to the weight of aircraft would have to take these new circumstances into account. Whether and to what extent damage attributable to noise and sonic boom should be covered by a revised Rome Convention is a question that will require careful attention by those called upon to revise the Rome Convention as well as by those engaged in interdisciplinary studies on the impact of civil aviation on the environment.[139] Moreover, the sublimit of $33,168 per person stipulated by the Rome Convention at a time when the Warsaw limit was only $8,300 is no longer realistic in view of the Guatemala City limit of $100,000.

A further and fundamental point may require consideration. While the limits of liability established for the aircraft passenger by the Guatemala City Protocol are unbreakable, this is a *quid pro quo* for the relatively high limit of $100,000 and the absolute liability rule that the carrier would accept by contract. In view of this new posture of the contractual rules, careful thought will have be given to the circumstances in which any new limits of the Rome Convention could be broken. At the same time, it must not be forgotten that overall damages may reach astronomical sums in today's society. In this regard, one need only advert to a discussion in Kennelly's *Litigation and Trial of Air Crash Cases* where the author contemplates damages in the order of a quarter of a billion dollars for a single accident.[140] It is no exaggeration, therefore, to state that, once current work on legal controls over aviation violence and the Warsaw Convention is concluded, Canadian air lawyers of the 1970s will have a challenging task ahead of them in the revision of the Rome Convention.

Other liability questions

Other liability questions on the work program of the ICAO Legal Committee relate to aerial collisions and air traffic control agencies. Much work on the first item was carried out in ICAO during the period 1947–64;[141] the second item was studied extensively at the subcommittee level in the 1960s.[142] These items may well come up for study during the current decade; a fresh look at them may have to be taken in view of the radical changes to the Warsaw liability system wrought by the Guatemala City Protocol.

CONCLUSION

The foregoing description of the state of air law makes it abundantly clear that this branch of the law is in a state of flux. The public law problems are difficult and varied and it is expected that Canadian air lawyers will continue, as in the past, to make their contributions (chiefly through ICAO) to the solution of these problems. But the lawyer will not be alone in his task, since it must not be forgotten that, in the technical field, norm creation is more often than not in the domain of the technician, although it is often the product of teamwork between technicians and lawyers, as in the case of hijackings where the technical experts are in control of developing preventive measures and the lawyers are responsible for the task of preparing legal deterrents.

The private law problems pose great challenges for the future. In particular, it is to be hoped that more unification will be achieved in the rules governing the liability of the air carrier in the carriage of passengers and baggage internationally and that the radical reforms found in the Guatemala City Protocol will pave the way for this unification. That any revision of the cargo provisions in the Warsaw Convention should not be such as hinder the development of the air cargo business goes without saying. These are problems that in the immediately ensuing years will require close attention in Canada.

The use of a multidepartmental approach to Canadian representation at ICAO legal meetings indicates that the Canadian approach to unification in the field of air law will continue to be a balanced one. As in the past, it may be expected that Canadian delegations will, when the need arises, be composed of representatives from the Departments of External Affairs, Justice, and Transport as well as from the Canadian Transport Commission and major airlines.

In sum, while it cannot be said that the Canadian air lawyer will have any greater virtue than air lawyers of other nationalities in shaping the air law of the future, it can be said that, living as he does in a country which is one of the major civil aviation powers and the home of two great legal systems, he is in a unique position to play an important role in this process.

NOTES

1 Unless otherwise indicated all documents are ICAO documents. Doc 7300/4; 15 U.N.T.S. 295; [1944] CAN. T.S. no 36.

2 The USSR joined ICAO in 1970. On 25 October 1971 the United Nations General Assembly, by resolution 2758 (XXVI) recognized the representatives of the People's Republic of China as the only legitimate representatives of China in the United Nations. On 19 November the ICAO Council decided, for matters within its competence, to recognize the representatives of the government of the People's Republic of China as the only legitimate representatives of China to ICAO and requested the secretary general to communicate this decision immediately to all contracting States.

3 The IATA, which has its head office in Montreal, had, as at 23 December 1971, 106 scheduled international airlines as members. It was incorporated by federal statute: An Act to Incorporate International Air Transport Association, 9–10 Geo. VI, c 51. Assented to on 18 December 1946.

4 The IFALPA, which has its headquarters in London, England, represents 47,000 pilots grouped in sixty member associations. For a short description of the work of the IFALPA, see 'Pilots' Federation Represents 47,000 Globally' (1971), *ICAO Bulletin* 16–18.

5 Provision for registration of these agreements with ICAO is made in articles 81 to 83 of the Chicago Convention. See Doc 6685 c/767 6/4/49 Rules for Registration with ICAO of Aeronautical Agreements and Arrangements.

6 Chicago Convention, article 49.

7 Ibid, article 50(a).

8 Doc 8970. This amendment was adopted on 12 March 1971. By 31 December 1971 it had been ratified by 56 states.

9 Chicago Convention, articles 50–1.

10 Ibid, article 54(h). The procedure for the election of the secretary general is found in Doc 8665-c/970, Action of the Council, 59th Session (1966) 2–4.

11 Chicago Convention, article 56.

12 Doc 8971. This amendment was adopted on 5 July 1971 and the related protocol signed on 7 July 1971. By 31 December 1971 it had been ratified by 21 states. Because of the small number of ratifications, when the election of a new Air Navigation Commission took place on 24 November 1971, only a twelve-member body could be elected.

13 Chicago Convention, articles 22–24 and annex 9-Facilitation.

14 The Legal Committee was established in 1947 as the successor to the *Comité international technique d'experts juridiques aériens* (CITEJA), an intergovernmental body which developed many conventions during the period 1926–47. The ICAO Legal Committee is open to all ICAO contracting states, although in practice it has yet to be attended by as many as half of them. Nevertheless, the big aviation powers and a good cross-section of the world's legal systems are present at its meetings. For the Constitution of the Legal Committee, the procedure for approval of draft conventions and the Committee's Rules of Procedure, see Doc 7669-LC/139. When the Legal Committee prepares the final draft of a convention or protocol of amendment to a convention, the draft is sent to the ICAO Council which decides whether or not to convene a diplomatic conference to consider and adopt the convention or protocol in authentic form.

15 Chicago Convention, articles 91–3. During the 1970s there would be relatively few states left to join ICAO since it already numbers 122 members. Article 92 provides for admission of a so-called ex-enemy state of World War II subject, *inter alia*, to approval by the United Nations, a four-fifths vote of the ICAO Assembly and the consent of any state invaded or attacked by the ex-enemy state. In recent years, article 92 has not been strictly applied. Although this provision was applied rigorously just after the World War II, when certain ex-enemy states were admitted to ICAO, it was not applied at all to the admission of Romania in 1965

(A15-WP/177 P/32) and Bulgaria in 1967 (A16-WP/26 AD/12). As to questions of state succession, involving in particular the succession of India and Pakistan to the old India in 1947 and the establishment and dissolution of the United Arab Republic in 1958 and 1961 respectively, see R.H. Mankiewicz, 'Air Law Conventions and the New States' (1964), 29 *J. Air L. & Com.* 52–64, at 54–7. During the 1970s there may well be further regroupings of states and the problem of state succession in regard to membership will have to be faced by ICAO.

16 Denunciation of the convention may not necessarily be recognized. Thus, when the Republic of China (Taiwan) denounced the convention on 31 May 1950 with effect from 31 May 1951, this denunciation was not recognized by a number of states (eg the United Kingdom) which, at the time, recognized the Peking government.

17 This question arose in 1971 on the occasion of a dispute between Pakistan and India concerning the interpretation or application of the Chicago Convention in connection with the suspension of the overflight of Indian territory by Pakistani aircraft. Pakistan brought the matter before the ICAO council and India pleaded, *inter alia,* that, because of the relations between the two countries, the convention had been terminated or suspended between them. Accordingly, argued India, the council had no jurisdiction over the dispute. The council, having ruled that it had jurisdiction, India took the matter to the International Court of Justice. (ICJ Communiqué no 71/11, 1 September 1971.)

18 In this aspect of its work, ICAO shows how a functional international organization working in a changing field has to be adaptable to changes in aviation technology. Aside from bodies working on a broad range of basic problems, there are such bodies as the panel on automated data interchange system, the panel on the application of space techniques relating to aviation, the air traffic control automation panel, the technical panel on supersonic transport operations, the committee on aircraft noise, and the panel on sonic boom.

19 See Doc 7147 21/4/51 Agreement between the International Civil Aviation Organization and the Government of Canada regarding the Headquarters of the International Civil Aviation Organization, 96 U.N.T.S. 155. It entered into force on 1 May 1951. See also Privileges

and Immunities (United Nations)Act, R.S.C. c 219 (1952); Order-in-Council P.C. 1954–71, 18 November 1954; Statutory Orders and Regulations, volume III, 2589; Privileges and Immunities (International Organizations) Act, 13–14 Eliz. II, c 47; and Privileges and Immunities (International Organizations) Act, R.S.C. c P-22 (1970). As for Quebec, see Order-in-Council 1174, dated 20 July 1966, and 527, dated 13 March 1968. See Poeliu Dai, 'The Headquarters Agreement between Canada and the International Civil Aviation Organization' (1964), 2 *Can. Y.B. Int'l L.* 205–14.

20 In recent years, the United States has been endeavouring to reduce its percentage of the total contributions to the regular ICAO budget. In resolutions A11–14, A14–48, A15–36 and A16-54, the Assembly decided that, in principle, the contribution to be paid by any one contracting state should not, in any one year, exceed 30 per cent of the total contributions assessed. In spite of this, the United States assessment remained above 30 per cent for many years: 1965–7 at 31.28 per cent; 1968–70 at 30.87 per cent. At the eighteenth session of the Assembly, in 1971, the United States sought unsuccessfully to have its assessment lowered to 26.85 per cent and, after a bitter battle, the amount fixed for the period 1972–4 was 28.75 per cent (see resolution A18-26).

21 On 1 October 1970 the ICAO council adopted two resolutions concerning this type of international blackmail, one being concerned with a United States proposal for a multilateral convention on the matter, the other being concerned with a Canadian proposal to have a standard clause on the matter inserted in bilateral air transport agreements. During discussions on this matter in the ICAO Legal Committee, an ICAO legal subcommittee, and the ICAO Assembly (see note 24 below), it was argued that the taking of concerted action was a form of sanction and that this subject matter was more properly within the domain of the United Nations, the charter giving the Security Council primacy in regard to sanctions.

22 Article 94 of the convention provides that the number of states required to ratify an amendment shall not be less than two-thirds of the total number of contracting states. Two amendments made to the Chicago Convention during 1971 illustrate the difficulties inherent in requiring a relatively high number

of ratifications in order that the amendments may enter into force. On 12 March an extraordinary session of the Assembly adopted an amendment whereby the number of Council seats would be increased from 27 to 30. By the time the eighteenth session of the Assembly, convened three months later, was ready to proceed to the triennial election of the Council, only half of the instruments of ratification (ICAO then had 120 members) required to bring the amendment into force had been deposited and the Assembly was able to elect only 27 members to the Council in spite of the fact that the extraordinary session had unanimously adopted the amendment. Similarly, the Assembly, on 5 July adopted an amendment increasing the number of members of the Air Navigation Commission from 12 to 15, specifying 80 as the number of ratifications (ICAO then had 120 members) required to bring the amendment into force. When the Council proceeded to the triennial election of the commission, on 24 November, only 15 instruments of ratification had been deposited and it was able to elect only 12 members to the commission.

The Chicago Convention was opened for signature on 7 December 1944 in the English language only. An authentic trilingual text in English, French, and Spanish was adopted only in 1968 at Buenos Aires. By 31 December 1971 the text had been accepted by 63 states. For the text of the Buenos Aires Protocol and the Authentic Trilingual text, see Doc 7300/4. For a description of the protocol and some of the problems encountered in its preparation, see Gerald F. FitzGerald, 'The Development of the Authentic Trilingual Text of the Convention on International Civil Aviation' (1970), 64 *Am. J. Int'l. L.* 364–71.

23 (1969), 8 *I.L.M.* 679; Cmnd. 4140.
24 Doc 8910 LC/163 Summary of the Work of the Legal Committee during Its Eighteenth Session 34. For later discussions, see LC/SC CR – Report 27/4/71 Report of the Subcommittee on the Council Resolutions of 1 October 1970 (Montreal, 14–27 April 1971) 11; Doc 8954 A18-LE Assembly, 18th Session, 1971, Report and Minutes of the Legal Commission, 13–36; Doc 8963 A18-Min P/1-16, Assembly, 18th Session (1971), Plenary Minutes, 12th Meeting, paras. 38–67.
25 For reference to Headquarters Agreement, see *supra* note 19. The Convention on the Privileges and Immunities of the Specialized Agencies is found in 33 U.N.T.S. 261. Canada became a party with effect from 29 March 1966. As at 31 December 1971, 65 states had accepted the convention is respect of ICAO.
26 For a convenient summary of the work on this topic and related matters up to early 1971, see U.N. Doc A/CN.4/245 23 April 1971 International Law Commission, Twenty-third Session, 26 April 1971 – 30 July 1971, Survey of International Law, Working Paper prepared by the Secretary-General in the light of the decision of the Commission to review its programme of work, pages 176–185 (paras. 340–56).
27 Definitions of these expressions are found in ICAO Assembly resolution A18-13, appendix D as well as in the forewords to the various annexes to the convention. For the procedure followed in the adoption of annexes, PANS, and SUPPS and the extent to which this material binds states, see M. Sheffy, 'The Air Navigation Commission of the International Civil Aviation Organization' (1958), 25 *J. Air L. & Com.* 281–327 and 428–43; Jochen Erler, 'Regulatory Procedures of ICAO as a Model for IMCO' (1964), 10 *McGill L.J.* 262–8; Thomas Buergenthal, *Law-Making in the International Civil Aviation Organization* (1969) 57–122, Edward Yemin, *Legislative Powers in the United Nations and Specialized Agencies* (1969) 114–60, and Gerald F. FitzGerald, 'The International Civil Aviation Organization: A Case Study in the Implementation of Decisions of a Functional International Organization,' in Stephen M. Schwebel, *The Effectiveness of International Decisions* (1971) 156–205, at 168–80.
28 Chicago Convention, article 38.
29 Article 12 of the Chicago Convention provides that 'over the high seas, the rules of the air in force shall be those established under this Convention.' The Rules of the Air in annex 2 adopted by the Council are the 'rules' to which reference is made in article 12. Therefore, when the 27-member ICAO Council adopts rules of the air in the form of standards, they are applicable without deviation over the high seas, ie seven-tenths of the surface of the globe, surely a remarkable legislative jurisdiction for such a small body. See J. Carroz, 'International Legislation on Air Navigation over the High Seas' (1959), 26 *J. Air L. & Com.* 158–72.
30 For information on the adoption and implementation of Regional Plans, see Fitz-

Gerald, *supra* note 27, at 170, 181–6.

31 For a discussion of the question of sanctions, see FitzGerald, *supra* note 27, at 160–3.

32 National civil aviation laws and regulations implementing ICAO annex material include sanctions for violations.

33 This inability has been recognized in the report of the ICAO Special Implementation Panel (1956–9) Doc 7966 A12–EX/1. A summary of the main points made in this report is found in FitzGerald, *supra* note 27, at 181–4.

34 Considering the jet component of the commercial air transport fleet of ICAO states, 'it may be noted ... that by the end of 1970 an accumulated total of 4,503 of these aircraft had been ordered by commercial operators of ICAO contracting states, excluding the USSR, and 3,897 had been delivered. Of the total aircraft ordered, 2,183 (49 per cent) were Boeing, 1,325 (29 per cent) McDonnell Douglas, and 278 (6 per cent) other types of aircraft manufactured in the United States. The remaining 16 per cent were from the United Kingdom (405), France (274), and the Kingdom of the Netherlands (38).' Doc 8918 A18–P/3 March 1971 Annual Report of the Council to the Assembly for 1970, 38.

35 The main elements of this aid are given multilaterally through the United Nations Development Programme which includes the ICAO Technical Assistance Programme component and the ICAO Special Fund component.

36 Doc 8961 A18–TE, Assembly, 18th Session (1971), Report of the Technical Commission, paragraph 17.9.2.

37 Assembly resolution A18–13, appendix D, Associated Practice (8).

38 For an explanation of the use of Acceptable Means of Compliance, see the foreword to annex 8–Airworthiness of Aircraft, 5th edition (incorporating Amendments 1–86). April 1962.

39 Doc 8918 A18–P/3 March 1971, Annual Report of the Council to the Assembly for 1970, 64–5.

40 Meanwhile, the Committee on Aircraft Noise is examining the application of noise certification standards to existing turbojet airplanes, including the Boeing 747, and is also considering the future production and developed versions of all such airplanes. For the early work of this committee, see Gerald F. FitzGerald, 'Aircraft Noise in the Vicinity of Aerodromes and Sonic Boom' (1971), 21

U. Toronto L.J. 54–68. The committee met in September-October 1970 and November 1971. See also the reports of the Sonic Boom Panel in SBP–WP/15 17/10/69 and Doc 8894, SBP/II (1970). On 6 December 1971 the ICAO council decided that the Sonic Boom Committee which has replaced the old panel, should meet in May 1972. See, generally, L.S. Fink, 'Canadian Law and Aircraft Noise Disturbance' (1965), 11 *McGill L.J.* 55 and Michel Pourcelet, 'La responsabilité pour les dommages résultant des vols supersoniques' (1970), *Revue juridique Thémis* 413–39.

41 Because of the increased amount of so-called guidance material being published by ICAO in technical manuals as a supplement to the more mature material in the standards and recommended practices in certain of the annexes, the lawyer will not want to neglect this paralegal material which, because of the necessity for flexibility in the face of rapid technological changes, must be in such form as to permit of quick amendment. See Assembly resolution A18–13, appendix s and resolution A18–14 which relate to ICAO technical manuals.

42 In Assembly resolution A4–3 (1950) it is stipulated that 'an amendment to the Convention may be appropriate when either or both of the following tests is satisfied: (1) when it is proved necessary by experience; (2) when it is demonstrably desirable or useful.' The following is the list of amendments adopted up to the end of 1971 showing the year of adoption and the number of ratifications deposited to date and indicating whether or not the amendments are in force: article 93bis–1947, 65 ratifications; article 45–1954, 91 ratifications; articles 48(a), 49(e), 61–1954, 95 ratifications; article 50(a)–1961, 98 ratifications (these are all in force). Article 48(a)–1962, 60; article 50(a)–1971, 56; article 56–1971, 21 (these are not yet in force).

43 Adoption of this amendment was a condition precedent for conclusion of the relationship agreement between ICAO and the United Nations. See Doc 7970 Agreement between the United Nations and the International Civil Aviation Organization; 8 U.N.T.S. 315. The protocol in pages 1–5 of Doc 7970 recites the sequence of events leading up to the adoption and entry into force of the agreement. There is also a supplementary agreement: 21 U.N.T.S. 347.

44 Doc 8522 A15–EX/43 Assembly, 15th Session

(1965), Report of the Executive Committee, paras. 60–7; Doc 8516 A15–Min.P/5, Assembly, 15th Session (1965), Plenary Minutes, 10th Meeting (paras. 45–61), 11th Meeting (paras. 37–42) and 12th Meeting (paras. 2–28); resolution A15–7.

45 Doc 8960 A18–EX Assembly, 18th Session (1971), Report of the Executive Committee, paras. 39–46; Doc 8963 A18–Min.P/1–16, Assembly, 18th Session (1971), Plenary Minutes, 14th Meeting, paras. 12–37.

46 The resolution seeking to impose restrictions on Portugal was rejected in a plenary meeting of the Assembly by a vote of 41 to 40, with 6 abstentions. See Doc 8963 A18–Min.P/1–16, Assembly, 18th Session (1971), Plenary Meetings, 13th Meeting (paras. 4–33) and 14th Meeting (paras. 1–11).

47 Doc 8711 A16–EX, Assembly, 16th Session (1968), Report of the Executive Committee, paras. 39.1–39.6; Doc 8775 A16–Min.P/1–9, Assembly, 16th Session (1968), Plenary Minutes, 7th Meeting, paras. 19–25; Doc 8960 A18–EX, Assembly, 18th Session (1971), Report of the Executive Committee, paras. 37.1–37.7; Doc 8963 A18–Min.P/1–16, Assembly, 18th Session (1971), Plenary Minutes, 12th Meeting, paras. 1–11.

48 As there have been very few cases brought before the council, the literature on the council's judicial functions is scanty. See Thomas Buergenthal, *Law-Making in the International Civil Aviation Organization* (1969) 123–97; Bin Cheng, *The Law of International Air Transport* (1962) 100–4; R.C. Hingorani, 'Dispute Settlement in International Civil Aviation' (1959), 14 *Arb. J.* 14; L. Kos-Rabcewicz-Zubkowski, 'Le règlement des différends internationaux relatifs à la navigation aérienne civile' (1948), 2 *Revue française de droit aérien* 340.

49 One problem which arose involved the voting majority of the Council in disputes arising under the Chicago Convention and the International Air Services Transit Agreement (1944) and complaints arising under the Transit Agreement. Article 52 of the convention requires that decisions of the Council be taken by a 'majority of its members.' This means that, in a Council of twenty-seven members, fourteen votes would be required for a decision. But according to articles 53 and 84 of the convention a member of the Council is disqualified from voting if it is a party to a dispute, while, under article 62, a member of the council cannot vote if its vot-

ing power has been suspended by the assembly because of failure to discharge its financial obligations to ICAO. Similarly, article 66(b) of the convention states that members of the Council that have not accepted the Transit Agreement shall not have the right to vote on any questions referred to the council under the provisions of the agreement. It is therefore for consideration whether the foregoing provisions would not so operate as to reduce the possibility of obtaining the majority vote of fourteen members of the Council in a case where a substantial number of the twenty-seven council members were disqualified from voting. On 17 November 1971 the council debated the problem but reached no conclusion (C–Min. LXXIV/15).

A further problem which has arisen is whether a decision of the Council on the question of its jurisdiction in the case of a dispute or complaint should, if appealed to the International Court of Justice, be suspended until the appeal is decided. This problem involves consideration of the second sentence of article 86 of the convention which reads: 'On any other matter, decisions of the Council shall, if appealed from, be suspended until the appeal is decided.' The Council has not reached a decision on this matter.

50 A17–WP/27.

51 For example, in December 1970, the ICAO Council adopted an amendment to annex 9 (Facilitation) in the form of a recommended practice containing certain specifications and practices relating to the carriage of weapons on board aircraft and the segregation, guarding, and advance notification of aircraft which might be liable to attack. In December 1971 the Council included in annex 6 (Operation of Aircraft-International Air Transport Services) a recommended practice to the effect that in all passenger-carrying airplanes the flight crew compartment door should be capable of being locked from within the compartment. Also, in December 1971, the Council included in annex 14 (Airdromes) provisions relating to security within the perimeter of international airports to prevent incidents of unlawful interference with civil aviation and its facilities.

52 Chicago Convention, article 94(a).

53 For more details on the question of ICAO and the environment, see the following papers presented to the Eighteenth Session of the

Assembly in 1971: A18–WP/40 (ICAO Council), A18–WP/32 (Switzerland), A18–WP/65 (United States of America), and A18–WP/80 (United Kingdom).

54 Resolution A16–3: Aircraft Noise in the Vicinity of Airports.

55 Doc 8857, NOISE (1969), Report of the Special Meeting on Aircraft Noise in the Vicinity of Aerodromes.

56 A18–WP/40 EX/11, appendix I, at I–1 to I–3 (paras. 5–9).

57 A18–WP/40 EX/11, appendix I, at I–6 (par. 21).

58 Assembly Resolution A16–4: Commercial Introduction of Supersonic Aircraft: The Problem of Sonic Boom.

59 See SBP–WP/15 17/10/69 and Doc 8894, SBP/II (1970).

60 The interdisciplinary Sonic Boom Committee, appointed to take into account technical, economic, legal, and social considerations, met in May 1972. Canada is represented on this committee.

61 This note was inserted primarily to take care of the case of the aircraft operated by the Scandinavian Airlines System (SAS) consortium whose aircraft are registered by approximately 3/7 of each type of aircraft in Sweden, by approximately 2/7 in Denmark, and by approximately 2/7 in Norway.

62 Doc 8181; 500 U.N.T.S. 31. As at 31 December 1971 Canada was not yet a party to this convention, although 39 states were.

63 Doc 8182 Final Act of the International Conference on Private Air Law Held under the Auspices of the International Civil Aviation Organization at Guadalajara, 1961.

64 The reports are found in Doc 8582–LC/153–2 Legal Committee, 15th Session (1964), volume II–Documents, 123–43.

65 Doc 8582–LC/153–1, Legal Committee, 15th Session (1964), volume I–Minutes, (xi).

66 Doc 8920; (1971), 10 *I.L.M.* 133–6. Article 4(1)(c). The Convention for the Suppression of Unlawful Acts Against the Safety of Civil Aviation (Montreal, 1971) also contains a similar provision in article 5(1)(d): Doc 8966; (1971), 10 *I.L.M.* 1151–6.

67 Doc 8961 A18–TE, Assembly-Eighteenth Session (1971), Report of the Technical Commission, at 37 (para. 21:3).

68 Doc 8364; (1964), 58 *Am. J. Int'l L.* 566; (1963), 2 *I.L.M.* 1042.

69 Articles 12–15.

70 Doc 8920; (1971), 10 *I.L.M.* 133–6.

71 Ibid, article 1.

72 Ibid, article 3(3).

73 Ibid, article 3(5).

74 Ibid, article 4(1).

75 Ibid, article 6(1).

76 Ibid, article 7.

77 Ibid, article 9.

78 Ibid, article 13(1).

79 According to the Vienna formula, the convention would have been open for signature by all states members of the United Nations or of the specialized agencies or of the International Atomic Energy Agency or parties to the Statute of the International Court of Justice, and by any other state invited by the General Assembly of the United Nations to become a party to the convention. See article 81 of the Vienna Convention.

80 For a description of these incidents, see *Keesing's Contemporary Archives* 7–14 March 1970, at 23,867–8.

81 Resolution 17–20.

82 For the text of the draft convention and a commentary thereon, see Doc 8910 LC/163, Summary of the Work of the Legal Committee during Its Eighteenth Session (1970), 19–31, and (1970), 9 *I.L.M.* 1183–93. For a discussion of the draft convention see Gerald F. FitzGerald, 'The London Draft Convention on Acts of Unlawful Interference against International Civil Aviation' in Edward McWhinney, *Aerial Piracy and International Law* (1971) 36–54.

83 Doc 8966; (1971), 10 *I.L.M.* 1151–6.

84 Ibid, article 1.

85 Ibid, article 3.

86 Ibid, article 4(2) and (5).

87 Ibid, article 5.

88 Ibid, article 6.

89 Ibid, article 7.

90 Ibid, article 8.

91 Ibid, article 10.

92 Ibid, article 15(1).

93 For details of these events, see *Keesing's Contemporary Archives* (26 September–3 October 1970) 24,203–9, and *Time* (Canada) (21 September 1970), at 14–15, 20–7.

94 For the text of the two resolutions adopted by the Council, see Doc 8849–c/990/2 2nd Edition, Action by the Council and Other Decisions Taken and Work Done by ICAO on the Subject of Unlawful Interference with International Civil Aviation and Its Facilities 17–18; (1970), 9 *I.L.M.* 1286–7.

95 Doc 8910 LC/163, *supra* note 82, at 41–7 and (1970), 9 *I.L.M.* 1201–6.

96 Doc 8910 LC/163, *supra* note 82, at 53–4 and (1970), 9 *I.L.M.* 1210–11.

97 LC/SC CR–Report 27/4/71 Report of the Sub-committee on the Council Resolutions of 1 October 1970.

98 Doc 8954 A18–LE Assembly, 18th Session (1971), Report and Minutes of the Legal Commission, at 13–36; Doc 8963 A18–Min. P/1–16, Assembly, 18th Session (1971), Plenary Minutes, 12th Meeting, paras. 38–67. For a more extended history of the subject of concerted action in ICAO in 1970–1, see Gerald F. FitzGerald, 'Toward Legal Suppression of Acts Against Civil Aviation' in 'Air Hijacking: An International Perspective' (1971) *International Conciliation* 42–78.

99 The exchange of commercial rights is usually effected through bilateral air transport agreements. For a discussion of the methods used to obtain permission to operate scheduled international air services, see A.B. Rosevear, 'Scheduled International Air Transport: A Canadian Analysis,' in Edward McWhinney and Martin A. Bradley, eds, *The Freedom of the Air* (1968) 123–39. See also R. Azzie, 'Specific Problems Solved by the Negotiation of Bilateral Air Agreements' (1967), 13 *McGill L.J.* 303–8.

100 Doc 7620; 310 U.N.T.S. 151. For a description of the convention, see R.O. Wilberforce, 'The International Recognition of Rights in Aircraft' (1948), 2 *Int'l L.Q.* 421–58 and B. Hofstetter, *L'hypothèque aérienne* (1950).

101 See David I. Johnston, 'Legal Aspects of Aircraft Finance' (1963), 26 *J. Air L. & Com.* 161–81, 299–327, especially at 319–26 (IV. Legislation for Canada-Establishment of Canadian Registry for Rights in Aircraft) and Roman B. Karpishka, (1967), *Can. B. Papers* 9.

102 For the text of the Warsaw Convention, see Schedule One to The Carriage by Air Act, R.S.C. c C–14 (1970); 137 L.N.T.S. 11. See L.M. Bloomfield, 'La Convention de Varsovie dans une optique canadienne' (1961), 37 *Thémis* 7; Gerald F. FitzGerald, 'Liability Rules in the International Carriage of Passengers, Luggage or Goods by Aircraft – Warsaw Convention: The Carriage by Air Act, 1939' (1948), 26 *Can. Bar. Rev.* 861; N. Mateesco Matte, *Traité de droit aérien-aéronautique* (1964) 375–441; Alistair Paterson, 'An Outline of the Law on Carriage by Air' (1954), 32 *Can. Bar. Rev.* 982; M. Pourcelet, *Transport aérien international et responsabilité* (1964). For an additional list of writings on the Warsaw Convention found in Canadian sources up to 1964, see J.-G. Castel, *International Law (Chiefly as interpreted and applied in Canada)* (1965) 265.

103 For the text of the Hague Protocol, see Schedule to An Act to Amend the Carriage by Air Act, 12 Eliz. II, c 33 (Canada 1963); 478 U.N.T.S. 371. For a description of the protocol, see Gerald F. FitzGerald, 'Aviation-Liability Rules in the International Carriage of Passengers, Baggage or Goods by Aircraft: The Hague Protocol of 1955 to Amend the Warsaw Convention of 1929' (1956), 43 *Can. Bar Rev.* 326–34. See also, M. Pourcelet, 'La responsabilité illimitée du transporteur aérien dans la Convention de Varsovie de 1929 et le Protocole de La Haye de 1955' (1963), 23 *La Revue du Barreau* 149.

104 See Agreement CAB no 18900 approved by the United States Civil Aeronautics Board on 13 May 1966. The CAB order is found in 2 Avi. 14,285–6. For the story of events leading up to the conclusion of this agreement, see Gerald F. FitzGerald, 'Liability Rules in the International Carriage of Passengers by Air and the Notice of Denunciation of the Warsaw Convention by the United States of America' (1966), 4 *Can. Y.B. Int'l L.* 194–215. A description of the agreement is found in Gerald F. FitzGerald, 'Current Developments in the Revision of Rules Governing the Liability of the Air Carrier in respect of the International Carriage of Passengers by Air' (1968), 6 *Can. Y.B. Int'l L.* 188–211 at 189–92.

105 Doc 8932; (1971) 10, *I.L.M.* 613–16. The work in ICAO up to the eve of the Guatemala City Conference is described in Gerald F. FitzGerald, 'The Revision of the Warsaw Convention' (1970), 8 *Can. Y.B. Int'l L.* 284–306. A description of the Guatemala City Protocol and an examination of its legislative history is found in Gerald F. FitzGerald, 'The Guatemala City Protocol to Amend the Warsaw Convention' (1971), 9 *Can. Y.B. Int'l L.*

106 Guatemala City Protocol, Article IV (article 17).

107 Ibid, article VI (article 20).

108 Ibid, article VIII (article 22(1)(a)).

109 Ibid, article XIV (article 35A).

110 Ibid, article XV (article 42).

111 Ibid, article VIII (article 22(3)).

112 Ibid, article XII (article 28(2)).

113 Ibid, article VIII (article 22(1)(b)).

114 Ibid, article VIII (article 22(1)(c)).
115 Ibid, article x(article 25).
116 Ibid, article IX (article 24(2)).
117 Ibid, article XI (article 25A).
118 Ibid, article XVI.
119 Ibid, article XX(1).
120 Doc 8181; 500 U.N.T.S. 31.
121 J.G. Gazdik, 'The Conflicts and State obligations under the Warsaw Convention, the Hague Protocol and the Guadalajara Convention,' (1961), 28 *J. Air L. & Com.* 373; M. Pourcelet, 'Transporteur contractuel et transporteur de fait dans la Convention de Guadalajara (18 septembre 1961)' (1963), 9 *McGill L.J.* 317.
122 In the Legal Commission of the eighteenth session of the Assembly in June-July 1971, the Bulgarian delegation presented a draft resolution which reflected uneasiness with the Guatemala City Protocol and was aimed at obtaining information from governments as to whether they intended to become parties to the protocol (A18–WP/84 LE/9). After a hot debate, the Bulgarian proposal was rejected in the Legal Commission by a vote of 19 in favour (including many developing countries) and 23 against, with 5 abstentions.
123 Studies have been carried out in the London and Paris areas with a view to finding a solution to the processing problems arising out of the administration of commercial documents connected with the movement of air cargo on the international level. One such document is the air waybill. The role of the air waybill in an automatic data processing system has been examined in connection with the International Air Freight Computer System Project (SOFIA) for possible application to airports in the Paris area and with the London Airport Cargo Electronic Data-Processing System (LACES).
124 This question has been under study in the International Institute for the Unification of Private Law (UNIDROIT) since 1957. It was later studied by the International Maritime Committee. The UNIDROIT draft convention on the international combined transport of goods was studied and revised by a Joint IMCO/ECE Committee which held four sessions from November 1970 to November 1971. See United Nations Document E/CONF.59/3 and addenda 1–4 thereto.
125 Doc 7364; 310 U.N.T.S. 181. See also Schedule to the Foreign Aircraft Third Party Damage Act, 3–4 Eliz. II (Can. 1955),

c15. For a short description of the convention, see Gerald F. FitzGerald, 'Aviation-Liability Rules Governing Damage Caused by Foreign Aircraft to Third Parties on the Surface – Rome Convention of 1952' (1953), 31 *Can. Bar Rev.* 90–8. For a very detailed study of the convention, see de Michel Juglart, *La Convention de Rome du 7 octobre 1952 relative aux dommages causés par les aéronefs aux tiers à la surface* (1956).
126 Rome Convention, article 1(1).
127 Ibid, articles 5 and 6.
128 Ibid, article 11.
129 Ibid, article 12.
130 Ibid, articles 15–18.
131 Ibid, article 20.
132 Doc 8582–LC/153–1–2 Legal Committee, 15th Session (1964), volume I–Minutes, xii, and volume II–Documents, 161–213.
133 Doc 8787–LC/156–2 Legal Committee, 16th Session (1967), volume II–Documents, 256–95.
134 Doc 8787–LC/156–1 Legal Committee, 16th Session (1967), volume I–Minutes, xxv–xxvi.
135 IAEA Legal Series no 4, International Conventions on Civil Liability for Nuclear Damage, 3–17.
136 Ibid, 21–34.
137 Ibid, 45–57.
138 The figures given represent maximim take-off weight. For the DC6B figure, see *Jane's All the World's Aircraft 1958–1959,* 300 and for the Boeing 747, see *Jane's All the World's Aircraft 1969–1970* 281.
139 In resolution A18–12, the Assembly requested the Council to develop standards, recommended practices, procedures, and guidance material dealing with the quality of the human environment. The Sonic Boom Committee is, by definition, working on a problem that will have to be considered in dealing with possible amendments to the Rome Convention.
140 Chapter II, 47.
141 Gerald F. FitzGerald, 'The Development of International Liability Rules concerning Aerial Collisions' (1954), 21 *J. Air L. & Com.* 203–10; Gerald F. FitzGerald, 'The Development of Liability Rules Governing Aerial Collisions' (1961), 2 *Current Law and Social Problems* 154–76; T.J. Kelliher, 'The Draft Convention on Aerial Collisions: Some Textual Conclusions' (1966), 32 *J. Air L. & Com.* 564–70; M. Miyagi, 'Applicable

Limits of Liability under Article 8 of the 1964 Draft Convention on Aerial Collisions' (1966), 32 *J. Air L. & Com.* 195–221.

142 For reports of subcommittee and Legal Committee action thereon, see Doc 8582–LC/143–1–1 Legal Committee, 15th Session (1964), volume I–Minutes, x, and volume II–Documents, 10–121; Doc 8787–LC/156–1–2 Legal Committee, 16th Session (1967), volume I–Minutes, xxvii–xxviii, and volume II–Documents, 296–360.

13/Telecommunications

International law in relation to communications has, like its domestic complement, developed in a continuing and cumulative response to the needs and the problems generated by advances over the past century or more in the multifaceted technology of communications.[1] Like the technology itself, the curve of legal development was at first a gradual one as initial telegraph networks were established in the mid-nineteenth century. The curve sweeps upwards with the invention of radio and the establishment of numerous activities based on radiocommunication, most notably broadcasting; it skyrockets as artificial earth satellites were launched into operation. When to the actual and potential legal issues raised by these central communications modes are added those relating to computers performing international tele-processing activites, to multiple-capacity undersea and coaxial cables carrying transborder voice, record, video, and data messages, and to laser beams and their new potential, it becomes increasingly possible to consider the growing field of international communications law as a substantial subdiscipline of general international law.

This is not to suggest that juridical concepts have in fact played a very important role in international communications or that there is a single or stable body of international communications law. It is to suggest rather that there is now a greatly increasing consciousness of the important role that law can play in the orderly development of international communications, and that this in turn is giving rise both to a reappraisal of existing international norms and to the development of appropriate new ones. These norms are emerging in the context of existing universal international conventions relating directly to communications, such as the International Telecommunication Convention and its annexed Telegraph, Telephone and Radio Regulations, in related general international conventions such as the Outer Space Treaty,[2] and in particular multilateral agreements such as those governing the International Telecommunications Satellite Organization (INTELSAT) and the European Broadcasting Union (EBU).

In this norm-creating process the Outer Space Committee of the United Nations and its various subcommittees and working groups have played a central role.[3] A significant number of communications-related recommendations and draft conventions prepared in the Outer Space Committee have found their way into General Assembly resolutions and in turn into full-fledged international conventions, and this work continues.[4]

In the mainstream of legal and regulatory development is the 140-member International Telecommunication Union (ITU), the major international communications organization and a specialized agency of the United Nations. The purposes of the union are: a / to maintain and extend international co-operation for the improvement and rational use of telecommunications of all kinds; b / to promote the development of technical facilities and their most efficient operation with a view to improving the efficiency of telecommunication services, increasing their usefulness, and making them, so far as possible, generally available to the public; and, c / to harmonize the actions of nations in the attainment of those common ends.[5] Since its founding over a century ago, the ITU, in carrying out these purposes and the particular functions with which it is charged, has continuously developed and updated regulations, principles, procedures, and standards for the effective international utilization of various communications modes, and has in essence served as the prime author of international communications law, particularly as regards its administrative and regulatory aspects. In addition, international organizations such as UNESCO and the International Civil Aviation Organization dealing with certain aspects of communication in terms both of its 'hardware' and 'software'[6] and with objects ranging from research to regulation have, in their own particular areas, also contributed to the evolving body of communications norms. Finally, communications has become the subject of a growing legal literature.

This essay recognizes the many legal 'grey' areas that exist and that result as norms evolve through legal literature and in international meetings and conferences. It recognizes also that international law relating to communications is not necessarily any more effective or more firmly underpinned by compulsory processes or sanctions than in other areas. Perhaps the only difference is that, as in other technological areas, the dictates of effective communications are fairly clearcut, and a test of the suitability of legal provisions is the extent to which they respond positively to those dictates. In relation to communications, the tendency has not generally been for the law to over-react or to repress technological innovation. It has been rather to respond perhaps too slowly and without a clear conception of the appropriate legal framework within which international communications can most effectively operate and develop.

This chapter attempts an examination of the central themes that have emerged in international communications law in relation to both hardware and software aspects. In both areas two major international legal principles can be discerned as coexisting and as having coexisted, at times uneasily, since the conclusion of the first International Telegraph Convention in 1865. The first can be characterized as an international right of individuals to communicate; the second as an international right of states to control communications. Both principles are examined below as is their interrelationship, which has tended to oscillate between polarity and complementarity, depending on the subject. In a significant way the dynamic tension between the two principles has generated the energy for the development of international communications law.

Finally, the essay will also present, where appropriate, Canada's contribution to the process of developing the different facets of international communications law. In the past few years two significant developments have induced Canada to play an active and quite significant role in this process. The first was the establishment in 1969 of the Department of Communications under a minister of communications required by law to: 'Take such action as may be necessary to secure, by international regulation or otherwise, the rights of Canada in communication matters.'[7] The second was the advent of communication satellites, in the development and application of which Canada is playing a very active role. Two of the most important Canadian projects have been the establishment in 1969 of the Telesat Canada Corporation, to own and operate a trans-Canadian domestic communications satellite system, and the current development – in large part in the laboratories of the Department of Communications – of a multiexperiment Communications Technology Satellite in co-operation overall with the United States and in respect of particular experiments with the European Space Research Organization (ESRO). Outer space is fundamentally an international realm beyond state jurisdiction and its effective exploitation and regulation require international co-operation and norms.

Communications cannot be said to be the top foreign policy priority of the Canadian government. However, with the emergence of satellite technology and Canada's operational and experimental projects, Canada is playing an important role in developing appropriate rules and principles to govern international communications, through the major forums involved in this process.

COMMUNICATIONS: GENERAL PRINCIPLES

The International Telecommunication Convention, constituting the ITU, is an instrument which has been reconcluded at plenipotentiary conferences at irregular intervals since the first International Telegraph Convention in 1865. The present version, concluded at Montreux in 1965, is the ninth convention[8] and is itself scheduled to be reviewed in 1973. At the 1965 Plenipotentiary Conference, it was agreed to study the question of whether the ITU should have a permanent constitution.[9] The 1973 convention could probably be concluded to comprise such a constitution.

With the invention and spread of telegraphy in the middle years of the nineteenth century, telegraph lines and networks within countries developed rapidly. These links terminated at national frontiers, however, and an international telegraph message had to be transmitted to the borders of a country, written out, carried across the demarcation line, retransmitted in the neighbouring country by wire, and so on till it reached its destination. The conclusion of the International Telegraph Convention in 1865 was the first important step towards removing artificial barriers to communications and paving the way for the long-distance exchange of messages without regard to political boundaries.[10] In so providing, however, this first convention embodied both the principles of state control on the one hand and the right of individuals to communicate internationally on the other that have been passed on virtually unchanged into succeeding conventions including the present one.

The signatories to the convention of 1865 regarded telecommunications as a matter solely for governments and not for private enterprise. So strongly was this view held, that England and the United States, whose telegraph services were in the hands of private companies, were not even invited to attend. During the next few decades this line softened, the two errant capitalist countries acceded to the convention, and its advantages were accorded to private companies. With the advent of radio, however, the state was again required to play an important role in communications – in a regulatory as well as an operational capacity. The compromise finally settled upon is reflected in the preamble to the present convention wherein the signatories 'fully recognize the sovereign right of each country to regulate its telecommunication,'[11] without being concerned about whether national communications services are operated by state-run or private enterprises.[12] At the same time as the convention recognizes this government role, it also tries to direct this role towards the purpose of facilitating communications between people in different countries. Focusing on the international telecommunication message, it establishes principles and procedures which can be said to amount to an internationally recognized individual right to communicate.

What is significant about this is first that an international treaty among sovereign states, sensitive to the need for a strong state role in telecommunications, should confer such a right on individuals. What is also significant is that these principles and procedures have remained constantly and clearly articulated in subsequent conventions for more than a hundred years.

This right to communicate can be broken down into a number of elements. The first in article 31 of the present convention is the stated principle of the right of the public to correspond internationally. The second pertains to rates, as article 4(2)c envisages collaboration among ITU members 'with a view to the establishment of rates at levels as low as possible.' Third is a criterion of non-discrimination as familiar in utility regulation as the objective of low rates and expressed in article 31 as follows: 'The services, the charges and the safeguards shall be the same for all users in each category of correspondence without any priority or preference.' The fourth element deals with the means of communication; article 36 provides that administrations shall take necessary measures to ensure the establishment, operation, and protection under the best conditions 'of the channels and installations necessary to carry on the rapid and uninterrupted exchange of international telecommunications.' The fifth element is a type of 'provision of service' requirement embodied in article 4(1)b and providing for services to be made 'generally available to the public.' Sixth is an 'extension of service' provision in article 4(2)d by which the union is required to 'foster the creation, development and improvement of telecommunication equipment and networks in new or developing countries by every means at its disposal, especially its participation in the appropriate programmes of the United Nations.' And a seventh element is the secrecy of communications, at article 35 of the present convention, which is reiterated at article 17 of the Radio Regulations.

The right to communicate, however, is restrained and mitigated in a number of ways under the convention. The first category of restraints is that flowing from the contending principle of state control over communications embodied in the convention. Thus, under article 32(1), members of the ITU 'reserve the right to stop the transmission of any private telegram which may appear dangerous to the security of the State or contrary to their laws, to public order or to decency.' Article 33 reserves their right to suspend international telecommunications services indefinitely and without having to provide any justification. And article 34 exempts them from responsibility towards users of international telecommunication services, particularly as regards claims for damages.

Second, the provisions are often expressed more in hortatory than obligatory language. Thus article 35(1) providing for secrecy does not state clearly that all international communications shall be secret. What it does say is that 'Members and Associate Members (of the ITU) agree to take all *possible* measures, *compatible* with the system of telecommunication used, *with a view to* ensuring the secrecy of international correspondence' (emphasis added). Third, although article 31 mentions 'no priority or preference' among users in each category of correspondence, articles 39 and 40 provide that safety of life shall have 'absolute priority' and government communications 'shall enjoy priority over other telegrams when priority is requested for them by the sender.'

The convention itself is completed by appropriate Telegraph Regulations spelling out technical standards and operating criteria for effective international telegraphy. While these rules were initially based on telegraphy, the invention of the telephone required very little conceptual change in order to formulate appropriate telephone regulations. The case was similar with respect to undersea cables, which from the point of view of international regulation required merely the application of the existing Telegraph and Telephone Regulations.

RADIOCOMMUNICATION

Unlike the cases of telegraphy, telephony, and cable, where messages are guided by wire or other means between two points, radiocommunication messages can be transmitted into the atmosphere and be received by anyone with an appropriate receiver within the coverage area. Radio thus knows no national frontiers.

Each radiocommunication takes place on a particular radio frequency. While the number of frequencies that can be generated is virtually unlimited, the number of radio channels of varying widths available for efficient communications within a given geographical area at any one time is limited. The totality of these channels (a totality which increases as technology permits radiocommunication on increasingly higher frequencies) comprises the radio frequency spectrum. Given the limited number of frequencies available and the wide range of demands for frequencies, it becomes important to regulate usage in such a way that users throughout the world can carry on a wide diversity of radiocommunication services free from mutual interference.

An international regulatory regime for radiocommunications has thus been established on the basis of the ITU Convention and the Radio Regulations which complete it. The regulations are updated at frequent intervals by Administrative Radio Conferences in response to technological developments and new requirements of communications in various parts of the world. Many aspects of this regulatory regime have important legal implications. Due, however, to the practice of setting forth 'guides' to action rather than absolute rules, to the frequent use of such phrases as 'so far as practicable' or 'so far as possible,' and to the virtual absence of lawyers at ITU conferences, law has played a relatively minor role in the ITU and there is considerably less legal precision than there might be.[13]

Fundamental to the regulatory regime is the conception of the spectrum as an international resource, responsibility for the management of which rests with all states.[14] It requires that the spectrum be allocated in a rational and binding manner among potential and actual users and that as new services emerge as a result of new technology, frequencies be allocated to these as well. It requires further that all countries commit themselves to the goal of preventing and eliminating harmful interference among users of the spectrum and to appropriate rules and measures to achieve it.[15] It has accordingly become the major function of the union to effect the allocation – both globally and regionally – of different portions of the radio spectrum and this is embodied in the convention at article 4(2)a. The basis for the allocation is by class of radiocommunication service (eg maritime mobile, broadcasting, etc) rather than by country, and the Radio Regulations contain a Table of Frequency Allocations to services throughout the world. Within each country, national administrations are responsible for assigning frequencies to particular users, subject to a number of requirements of the ITU convention.

Article 48 of the convention provides that all stations, whatever their purpose, must be established and operated in such a manner as not to cause harmful interference to the radio services or communications of others. This is completed by article 3 of the Radio Regulations which requires at no 113 that assignments capable of causing harmful interference to stations in other countries conform to the ITU's Table of Frequency Allocations. No 115 provides that in any case where there is an assignment in derogation from the table, this can only be 'on the express condition that harmful interference shall not be caused to services carried on by stations operating in accordance with' the convention. Article 46 then provides for limiting the number of frequencies and the spectrum space used by these to the minimum essential – in the light of the latest technical advances – to provide the necessary services in a satisfactory manner.

Once the national administration has made an assignment, if the assignment is for international radiocommunication, or if it is capable of causing harmful interference to any service of another administration, or if the administration desires international recognition for the assignment, it notifies the ITU's International Frequency Registration Board (IFRB). Depending on the assignment, the IFRB carries out a technical examination, formulates a 'finding' on the conformity of the assignment with the convention and regulations and the probability of harmful interference to previously recorded assignments, and circulates this among the members. If there are no problems of harmful interference envisaged, it then records the assignment in the Master International Frequency Register with the date of its coming into operation. If there are objections from any other administration, these are raised by the IFRB with the notifying administration and an attempt is usually made to eliminate problems through mutual accommodation. Nevertheless the IFRB cannot refuse to register a frequency if the first administration insists even if the other administration continues to object to it.[16]

With respect to the legal status of assignments, this is not adequately outlined in the convention or the regulations. Nowhere in the convention, for example, is there any obligation on members to recognize the assignments made by other members. Also, while the recording of assignments is meant to confer upon them 'formal international recognition' or the right to 'protection,' the precise meanings of these terms are not adequately spelled out.[17] Nevertheless it can be stated as a general rule, which has emerged in the course of settling many interference disputes over the years, that any assignment in conformity with the convention and regulations, and recorded in the Master Register has, vis à vis any assignment recorded and put into use later, the right of precedence, irrespective of whether the later assignment is in conformity with the convention and regulations.[18] This means that where the later assignment causes harmful interference to the former, it must, as a general rule, cease its emissions.

The ITU dispute settlement provisions are based on article 28 of the convention which prescribes diplomatic channels, procedures established in bilateral or multilateral treaties, or any other method. In practice, in cases for example where harmful interference is alleged, dispute settlement consists essentially of non-binding procedures of IFRB study and recommendation. If, however, the latter are unacceptable to the parties to the dispute, the study is closed.[19] Article 28(2) provides for arbitration as outlined in annex 3 to the convention or in its Optional Additional Protocol, but there are a number of loopholes in the arbitration procedure, such as the possibility of a party's refusal to appoint an arbitrator. Finally, neither article 28 of the convention nor annex 3 rule out the possibility of submitting disputes to the ICJ, and the ITU could itself turn to the ICJ for an advisory opinion. These alternatives have never been utilized.

The ITU is also charged under article 4(2) with the co-ordination of efforts to eliminate harmful interference between radio stations of different countries and to improve the use made of the spectrum. It attempts this through its International Radio Consultative Committee (CCIR), which sets standards governing frequency usage to prevent harmful interference. Through the IFRB, the ITU co-ordinates efforts to eliminate harmful interference, and the Radio Regulations contain detailed rules, procedures, standards, and criteria for providing communications free of harmful interference and for co-ordinating radiocommunication among administrations.

In addition to the provisions governing spectrum allocation and management and the prevention of harmful interference to registered frequency assignments, there are a number of other principles embodied in chapter v of the convention containing special provisions for radio. Here again, the two contending principles reappear as article 47 enunciates the principle of intercommunication among mobile services to facilitate international correspondence while article 48(2) provides that states require the operating agencies they recognize to observe the requirements of interference-free radiocommunication. Article 51 then spells out the principle generally accepted as fundamental in international communications law and enunciated in article 22, that the provisions of the convention do not apply to military radio stations. Thus article 51(1): 'Members and Associate Members retain their entire freedom with regard to military radio installations of their army, naval and air forces.'[20] The article goes on to mitigate this principle to some degree, however, in subparagraphs 2 and 3:

2 Nevertheless, these installations must, so far as possible, observe statutory provisions relative to giving assistance in case of distress and to the measures to be taken to prevent harmful interference, and the provisions of the Regulations concerning the types of emission and the frequencies to be used, according to the nature of the service performed by such installations.
3 Moreover, when these installations take part in the service of public correspondence or other services governed by the Regulations annexed to this Convention, they must, in general, comply with the regulatory provisions for the conduct of such services.

Finally, article 50 provides for the only case of content regulation in the convention, as it requires members to take the steps required to prevent the transmission or circulation of false or deceptive emergency signals and to collaborate in locating and identifying stations transmitting such signals from their own country.

As may be evident from the above, the principles of the right to communicate and of state control have in respect of radiocommunications come to complement rather than combat each other as the achievement of the former depends on the latter. It is only through state regulation and co-operation among administrations that radio frequencies can be allocated internationally and assigned domestically and that the prevention of harmful interference can be achieved. And it is only once both these functions have been adequately performed that the right to communicate effectively by radio can be guaranteed.

SATELLITES

The advent of space communications has led to a new consciousness of the importance of communications law, both for the effective operation of communications and other satellites and for all types of space activity and exploration which depend upon reliable radiocommunications as their lifeline.

Space radiocommunications were recognized as a valid matter for the ITU after the launching of Sputnik I, and its response has been positive and ongoing.[21] Three World Administrative Radio Conferences have now dealt with space radiocommunications – the Ordinary Radio Conference of 1959, the Extraordinary Radio Conference (EARC) of 1963, and the World Administrative Radio Conference on Space Telecommunications of 1971. While the problems of frequency allocation and harmful-interference-avoidance familiar in terrestrial radiocommunications have emerged here as well, the space dimension has lent them unprecedented magnitude and importance.

For one thing, space communication has given rise to a greatly increased demand for radio frequencies. This has arisen not only for messages to and from astronauts in spacecraft and for communicating voice, video, and data messages via space satellites, but also for purposes of tracking, command, and communications on a worldwide basis. With regard to certain types of specialized satellites, eg meteorological, navigation, and earth resources, channels are also required for the transmission of intelligence data. Moreover, since because of variations in propagation characteristics only waves of certain lengths can pass through the atmosphere and the ionosphere, only selected frequencies within the radio spectrum can be used for communication between space vehicles and points on earth. Second, the co-ordination of terrestrial radio stations to ensure that they do not cause each other harmful interference is a matter usually confined to a relatively small area and hence to a very few states. However the co-ordination of space systems – in view of their vast coverage – is now a global business requiring co-ordination with a large number of administrations. Third, the location of terrestrial radio stations so as to transmit efficiently without causing interference is very seldom a problem since these stations can be placed in various alternative locations and can in the final analysis be moved. In space communications, however, one series of locations for space stations – along the geostationary equatorial orbit – is far more desirable, for a multiplicity of satellite communication purposes, than any other. The problem is that positions along this orbit are relatively scarce and available to only very few systems. Thus whereas in terrestrial communications there is really one potentially scarce commodity – namely the radio frequency spectrum – in space communications a second potential scarcity has now arisen requiring equitable distribution criteria and measures of general resource conservation. This has been especially important in view of the fears of many of the smaller states that by the time they are ready to employ communication satellites, the most desirable orbit locations will have been pre-empted by the space powers. Finally, the clearly international nature of satellites has given rise to the need not only for international regulation but for truly international operating entities such as INTELSAT which have also had a distinct impact on international law.

The Radio Regulations adopted at the three ITU conferences which have dealt with space have attempted to cope with these problems in a comprehensive manner. The regulations drawn up at the 1959 conference contained for the first time in any multilateral agreement explicit provisions applicable to outer space activities. Thirteen bands of radio frequencies were allocated under shared channel arrangements (either worldwide or regional) to two new services – space to space and earth to space – 'for research purposes' but for no other existing or anticipated services.[22]

The 1963 Extraordinary Administrative Radio Conference (EARC) carried further the allocation of frequencies for operational space communication services which were immediately required (such as communication satellites, meteorological satellites, etc) as well as for space research. All of these allocations (but for a very few exceptional exclusive ones) were made on the basis of equal rights for the space stations with those in the fixed and mobile services. The conference accordingly amended the Radio Regulations to provide procedures for co-ordination among satellite earth stations and terrestrial stations in the same bands such that they could be established without causing harmful interference to each other.[23] This meant that where administrations had earth stations or terrestrial stations within a technically defined co-ordination distance of each other, they would co-ordinate these stations. The procedure did not, however, extend to space stations. The EARC also adopted a number of other revisions to the Radio Regulations concerned, *inter alia,* with the assignment and use of frequencies. The 1971 World Administrative Radio Conference on Space Telecommunications (Space WARC), with eight more years experience and far more space activity undertaken, dealt with matters in much greater detail. The conference provided an entire list of new terms and definitions for space, aligned the nomenclature of space services with their terrestrial counterparts, provided detailed sharing criteria for space services, and allocated a large number of bands to space communications.

In the regulatory area, one innovation was the introduction of an advance publication procedure to take place prior to the commencement of co-ordination. Canada was one of the countries which proposed this procedure, the purpose of which it saw as enabling an administration planning to establish a satellite system to inform other administrations of its plans, provide them with certain details of its proposed system (as prescribed in appendix lb to the Radio Regulations), and invite their comments. This could save it the trouble and cost of proceeding into great detail with plans which might later be hindered by unforeseen objections of other administrations. The advance knowledge of such systems would also be of benefit to other administrations in their own plans. This procedure would not, however, entail any legal commitment on the part of either the notifying or the responding administration. The aim was to keep the procedure as preliminary, flexible, and general as possible, leaving detailed co-ordination for the next phase.

With respect to the co-ordination procedure introduced at the EARC, this was extended to include co-ordination among space systems. Moreover, an administration would seek co-ordination not only with those administrations with assignments already in the Master Register but also those who had themselves begun co-ordination. This would take account of all administrations seriously on their way towards establishing geostationary satellite systems and would avoid late-stage confrontations. Provision was also made at no 639AM for an administration which felt that it had been wrongly left out of the co-ordination procedure to request that it be brought in.

One important legal question which the conference dealt with in two of its aspects concerned the status of assignments registered in the Master Register. The same question of the legal status of these assignments as had arisen regarding terrestrial stations and as was noted earlier arose here as well. In view of the cost and the technical complexity of satellite systems, however, and the requirements for this detailed co-ordination with other satellite and terrestrial systems, the Canadian delegation attempted to have explicitly stated in the regulations that earlier recorded satellite systems assignments in conformity with the convention and regulations would enjoy prior rights to protection against later recorded assignments. While this is – as noted earlier – a recognized principle of telecommunication law, and while no delegation disagreed with the *de facto* validity of the principle, there was hardly any support to render it explicit.[24]

The second aspect of the status of assignments which the conference dealt with concerned the question of the deletion from the Master Register of assignments to satellite systems no longer in use, whether because of the expiry of their life, the loss of control over them, or for any other reason. It was the view of the Canadian delegation that to retain these assignments in the register along with their *de facto* prior rights was highly undesirable in that these 'deadwood' assignments could obstruct new systems from getting registration clearance and in that they rendered planning for other systems more complex and costly than necessary. In short, they were unjustifiable occupants of possibly valuable frequency assignments and geostationary orbit locations. The original Canadian proposals sought the radical solution of simply deleting all deadwood assignments no longer in use for a year. However, the compromise finally agreed to in nos 639DK, 639DL, and 639DM of the regulations provided for the drastic reduction in the status (though not the formal deletion) of assignments not in use for two years where the administrations responsible for them have been approached after eighteen months to indicate whether the assignments will be brought back into use.

With respect to the geostationary orbit, the conference had before it a US proposal on the possible relocation of satellites along the orbit. The sensitivity of many states, especially smaller states, to the possibility of the pre-emption of this orbit had frequently been expressed. At the 1963 EARC, while nothing concrete had been decided upon, there had been some consideration given informally to the notion that 'slots' be allocated along the orbit to each state in advance so that all would be assured of a place on it.

The United States, mindful of this type of sentiment, but convinced that this 'parking slot' approach was both a wasteful and inefficient way of allocating this scarce resource attempted a different approach at the WARC. The gist of the US proposal was that where an administration with a satellite in the geostationary orbit could operate just as effectively elsewhere on the orbit, it would be obliged to move its satellite to another location in order to accommodate a new system which required the very location used by the first system and which could not use any other. Originally intended for detailed embodiment in the regulations and in a resolution as a mandatory procedure, the concept was introduced by the US as a voluntary matter. In the course of the conference the proposed resolution was withdrawn, but relocation was introduced into the Radio Regulations at no 639AF. It is there provided that at this stage, prior to co-ordination, a newcomer must exhaust all possibilities for accommodating itself without adjustments to other systems. Once having done so, it may approach other administrations, and under no 639AF(b) explore with them all possible means of meeting its requirements, 'for example,' by the other administration 'relocating one or more of its own geostationary space stations.' No 639AF(c) then provides that 'the administrations concerned shall together make every possible effort to resolve these difficulties by means of mutually acceptable adjustments.'

Intelsat

In the area of operations as distinct from regulation, and with respect particularly to communication satellites, resolution 1721(D) of 20 December 1961 was passed by the UN General Assembly, 'believing that communications by means of satellites should be available to the nations of the world as soon as practicable on a global and non-discriminatory basis.' And resolution 1802(XVII) of 14 December 1962 emphasized 'the importance of international cooperation to achieve effective satellite communications which will be available on a world-wide basis.'

While these resolutions did not embody any concrete legal obligation on states, an International Telecommunications Satellite Consortium (INTELSAT) was set up on an interim basis in August 1964, 'recalling the principle set forth in Resolution No. 1721(XVI) of the General Assembly.' The main purpose of INTELSAT was to establish 'a single global commercial communications satellite system' to provide expanded telecommunications services to all areas of the world and to contribute to world peace and understanding. In line with both a basic principle of space law and with international communication law, it sought 'to provide, through the most advanced technology available, for the benefit of all nations of the world, the most efficient and economical service possible consistent with the best and most equitable use of the radio spectrum.' INTELSAT is now operating its fourth generation of satellites.

On 20 August 1971 definitive agreements converting the consortium into a permanent International Telecommunications Satellite Organization were opened for signature by all states who are members of the ITU. For their investment they obtain 'consequent participation in the design, development, construction, including the provision of equipment, establishment, operation, maintenance and ownership of the system.' The definitive agreements entered into force on 12 February 1973.

The INTELSAT arrangements create legal obligations only on the parties to the agreements. Moreover, other organizational arrangements for international satellite communications may be (and in certain cases have been) set up.[25] However, the fact remains that INTELSAT is the only entity successfully operating a worldwide system in conformity with the principles of space and communications law. And in so doing, it is establishing novel and significant patterns of co-operation and of effective operation and management – through joint ownership of the space segment, through a multilateral body for controlling the system, through governments and national telecommunications organizations co-operating on a number of levels, through the attempt to blend the principles of commercial viability and sovereign equality, and in numerous other ways. INTELSAT will therefore undoubtedly make important contributions to the evolution of a general regime of international law relating to satellite communications.

Two points at which INTELSAT is likely to interface with the ITU are in respect of attempting to acquire status in the latter organization and in attempting to play a regulatory role in respect of the satellite communications of its members. As regards the first, it is still the case that only individual state administrations have status under the ITU regulations in respect of notifying assignments to the IFRB for registration and of submitting proposals to radio conferences. It might be expected that proposals will be made to permit international organizations with juridical personality like INTELSAT to participate more directly in these ITU functions.[26] With respect to a proposed regulatory role for INTELSAT, it was proposed by the US early on in the negotiations that INTELSAT should be responsible for the technical co-ordination of other satellite systems in which its members participated.[27] This was modified, however, on the grounds that this was properly an ITU function. The definitive INTELSAT agreements do, however, contain the following provision at article 14D:

> To the extent that any Party or Signatory or person within the jurisdiction of a Party intends individually or jointly to establish, acquire or utilize space segment facilities separate from the INTELSAT space segment facilities to meet its international public telecommunications services requirements, such Party or Signatory, prior to the establishment, acquisition or utilization of such facilities, shall furnish all relevant information to and shall consult with the Assembly of Parties, through the Board of Governors, to ensure technical compatibility of such facilities and their operation with the use of the radio frequency spectrum and orbital space by the existing or planned INTELSAT space segment and to avoid significant economic harm to the global system of INTELSAT. Upon such consultation, the Assembly of Parties, taking into account the advice of the Board of Governors, shall express, in the form of recommendations, its findings regarding the considerations set out in this paragraph, and further regarding the assurance that the provision or utilization of such facilities shall not prejudice the establishment of direct telecommunication links through the INTELSAT space segment among all the participants.

While the assembly will issue recommendations only, this can have important legal significance for members establishing or participating in other satellite systems, in terms of fulfilling their treaty obligations as INTELSAT members.

BROADCASTING

With the advent of radiocommunication, radio, and later television, broadcasting soon developed as messages could now be transmitted to the general public.[28] The ITU limited its concern with broadcasting to the allocation of appropriate frequencies to the broadcasting service.

Nevertheless to many countries, broadcasting gave rise to certain important legal and political problems arising from the fact that programs broadcast in one country could be received in another either deliberately by design or simply by virtue of the spillover of the signal into the neighbouring country. As with respect to the hardware, the process of developing international norms relating to broadcasting has reflected an ongoing attempt to balance the avowed desire on the part of states to communicate with each other against the practice of certain governments of controlling or of censoring broadcasts from outside their territories. There are certain types of broadcasts that are regarded as offensive, varying in time, place, and context, and ranging from the incitingly aggressive (such as war propaganda) to the merely foreign (such as US programs in Canada) and from the morally objectionable (such as bullfighting in India) to the economically unacceptable (such as the advertizing carried by pirate radio stations to Britain). But there is in addition the general desire based on state sovereignty alone not to have to justify opposition to receiving foreign broadcasts.

As in the entire field of communications generally, different technologies have carried with them both new possibilities for transmitting more messages to a wider public and new fears of cultural invasion via the airwaves. High frequency radio, television, powerful offshore transmitters, cable television, and satellites have each introduced and created a temporary disequilibrium (real or perceived) to which international norms have had to respond in such a way as to retain the balance between the ideal of the free flow of communications and that of sovereign inviolability from foreign broadcasts.

The Universal Declaration of Human Rights[29] provides at article 19 that 'everyone has the right to freedom of opinion and expression; this right includes freedom to hold opinions without interference and to seek, receive, and import information and ideas through any media regardless of frontiers.' This has been interpreted, despite the absence of legal sanctions as providing for freedom of international broadcasting 'through any media' regardless of questions of national sovereignty.[30] As against this, there is Oppenheim's 'principle of exclusive sovereignty in the air space for the subjacent state which enables that state to prohibit the disturbance of the air space over its territory by means of Hertzian waves caused for the purpose of wireless communication and emanating from a foreign source.'[31] The principle means of 'prohibiting the disturbance of the air space over its territory' would be by jamming.[32]

The process of moving in from the extremes to norms in some equilibrium between the two principles has involved various attempts at mutual modification among them. Thus the unbridled right to prevent foreign broadcasts has been limited in the view of some writers by the need to show 'injurious effects' on the welfare of the state receiving them.[33] This amounts to a kind of 'abuse of rights' doctrine even though these injurious effects have nowhere been definitively specified and are obviously susceptible to subjective interpretation on the part of states.

The free flow principle for its part has been modified in the Covenant on Civil and Political Rights of the UN General Assembly.[34] Thus article 20 provides that '1 / any propaganda for war shall be prohibited by law; 2 / any advocacy of national, social or religious hatred that constitutes incitement to discrimination, hostility or violence shall be prohibited by law.' In 1936 there had been a Convention on the Use of Broadcasting in the Cause of Peace which *inter alia* prevented broadcasting from inciting war. This was never signed by Canada and is currently in force among only twelve states. In addition resolution 110 (II) of the UN General Assembly was passed in 1947 condemning propaganda designed or likely to provoke or encourage any threat to the peace, breach of the peace, or act of aggression. It has since been incorporated into the preamble to the Outer Space Treaty and made applicable to outer space. The possibility has also been raised that there is an obligation on states not to permit the establishment and operation in its territory of radiocommunications designed to produce injurious effects in other states.[35]

Two areas that have emerged as potential problem areas as a result of technological advances in terrestrial broadcasting are pirate radio transmitting operations and community antenna television (CATV). CATV does not involve transmitting unwanted broadcasts to another country, but rather of a party in one country erecting large antennas to receive transmissions from stations in another and then to disseminate these programs by coaxial cable to a large number of homes. Except for the question of copyright, which is dealt with to some extent through the rediffusion provision under the 1967 Stockholm revision of the Berne Convention[36] (to which, however, Canada has not acceded), international law is as yet quite silent on the matter.[37] Pirate broadcasting has involved setting up powerful transmitters beyond the boundary waters of certain European countries, particularly England, Holland, and Denmark, and transmitting programs into the state on unused broadcasting or maritime mobile frequencies.[38] The mechanisms of the ITU are not really adequate for dealing with this type of problem and European states accordingly in 1965 concluded a European Agreement for the Prevention of Broadcasts Transmitted from Stations Outside National Territories. This agreement is directed not against the content of the broadcasts but the fact of the broadcasts itself.

In all, however, a body of comprehensive international norms relating to broadcasting has yet to emerge, and there does not appear to be any single point of equilibrium between the principles of the free flow of communications and of the protection of sovereignty. It is generally accepted that states should not deliberately beam hostile programs to other countries and that in principle their citizens should be able to receive broadcasts from other countries where these are not injurious or offensive. In general, transmitting states should behave with consideration for the rights of their neighbours and receiving states with restraint.

Co-operation in broadcasting has been facilitated through various international broadcasting organizations, themselves often varying greatly in status, financing, and policy. These have resulted in rules and procedures regarding, *inter alia,* technical, administrative, financial, programming, and legal co-ordination. While the co-operative patterns have been most marked in Europe, under the European Broadcasting Union (EBU), they have also emerged through the Organisation Internationale de Radiodiffusion et Télévision (OIRT), the Asian Broadcasting Union (ABU), and the Union de Radiodiffusion et Télévision Nationales Africaines (URTNA). It has been this active and positive co-operation that has been the basis on which international broadcasting has developed rather than any strict adherence or resort to a very partially developed international law.

BROADCAST SATELLITES

Satellites capable of broadcasting have linked together the hardware and software strands in both technological and legal terms and have become the focal point of great attention by the international community. As 'hardware' they have been recognized as the most significant type of radiocommunications apparatus that the ITU has had to deal with, to the extent that even the Space WARC – dealing only with space systems – attached a qualitatively different degree of importance to them than to any other type of satellite system. As 'software' their legal, political, social, and cultural importance has been recognized in the establishment of a special United Nations Working Group on Direct Satellite Broadcasts.

Broadcast satellites are potentially more powerful than communication satellites in that they will be capable of broadcasting signals to smaller and smaller antennas first for community reception and ultimately directly to home receivers.[39] And one satellite in geostationary orbit will theoretically be able to blanket a third of the earth with its signals. In view of this tremendous potential, the Space WARC of the ITU regarded broadcast satellites as a matter deserving of special treatment in the Radio Regulations.

Some delegations had submitted documents to the effect that there should be no satellite broadcasting until after world plans were adopted which would allocate frequencies and orbit positions throughout the world to satellite broadcasting.[40] The compromise finally agreed to came down on the side of the right to communicate, permitting such systems, though suggesting that world and regional planning conferences be called to establish appropriate planned allocations, rules, and procedures for broadcast satellite systems.[41] Although the questions of co-ordination were very similar to those relating to communication satellites, broadcasting satellites were excepted from the purview of article 9A. The precise procedures were, however, reintroduced into resolution Spa G along with additional procedures for co-ordination between broadcasting satellites and terrestrial services which were not provided for in the Radio Regulations.

With respect to software questions relating especially to television broadcasting from satellites, these have for a number of years now been considered matters of importance in the United Nations. As early as November 1963 the Brazilian delegate to the Outer Space Committee suggested that the draft Declaration of Legal Principles Governing the Activities of States in the Exploration and Use of Outer Space should incorporate a ban on the utilization of a communication system based on satellites for purposes of encouraging national, racial, or class rivalries. The declaration, adopted a month later, contained no such provision, but merely referred in its preamble to resolution 110(II) of 3 November 1947 on war propaganda, declaring it applicable to outer space.

That the UN should consider the question of satellite broadcasting was reiterated in various ways at meetings of the Outer Space Committee and its Legal Subcommittee over the next few years.[42] In response to this demand, the Outer Space Committee, on a joint proposal of Canada and Sweden to its 11th session in 1968, established a Working Group on direct satellite broadcasting 'to study and to report to the Committee on the technical feasibility of communications by direct broadcasting from satellites and the current and foreseeable developments in this field as well as the implications of such developments, including comparative user costs and other economic considerations, as well as social, cultural, legal and other questions.'[43] The Working Group has now met in three sessions and out of these a general legal trend can be discerned. In the tension of the two polar principles of free flow and of sovereign rights to prevent unwanted programs, it was generally recognized that the technology should be permitted to develop and should not be artificially curbed or restrained; that there were real benefits of cross-cultural communication to be achieved through direct satellite broadcasting; and that extreme countermeasures (such as jamming) against unwanted transmissions should be avoided. At the second session of the Working Group a catalogue of programs of possibly unacceptable content was reported and was divided into three types: political, social-cultural, and legal.

Under undesirable political content were included programs interfering in the internal affairs of states, inciting racial or religious intolerance, violating fundamental human freedoms, using subliminal techniques, or purveying war propaganda.[44] Solutions envisaged at the session for coping with these problems included French and Australian suggestions of a code of conduct or program standards,[45] and a UK proposal for bans on specific activities.[46] Scepticism was expressed, however, notably in the Canadian-Swedish paper, as to whether generally acceptable and sufficiently exhaustive standards could be prepared and implemented, given differing national views and laws regarding free speech, censorship, and media control and given changing situations which any code of standards would have to cover.[47] Moreover, the interpretation of any standards would be immensely difficult as would the imposition of any sanctions for their violation. On propaganda, the reference to GA/Res 110(II) in the preamble to the Outer Space Treaty was noted,[48] but the Working Group report suggested further consideration of the entire question by the Outer Space Committee.

Under the cultural and social heading, the group noted that direct broadcasting could disturb cultural, religious, and social mores, particularly if programs ridiculed the beliefs of others or contained items involving obscenity, violence, or horror. Problems might also be caused by exposure to material emphasizing inequalities of standards of living.[49] And a final problem area could arise with respect to differing laws regarding libel, slander, right to privacy, and right of reply and rectification, where programs lawful in the country of origin would be unlawful in receiving countries. Few paths towards solution were proposed, although various studies such as those being carried on by UNESCO were recommended in the report with a view to concluding international agreements.

The commercial problems that the content of broadcasts might give rise to were seen as having to do primarily with advertising and its financial and trade effects. Solutions suggested ranged from a basic international code of advertising standards,[50] through the harmonization of international advertising codes, standards, and legislation,[51] to the banning of any advertising not consented to by the receiving state,[52] and finally to a complete ban on commercial advertising.[53] The report recommended further study,[54] and there was a general feeling that it was premature to lay down hard and fast guidelines regarding content on the grounds that they would be only hypothetical and possibly inapplicable to future real situations. These solutions were based on the assumption that satellite broadcasting was a legitimate activity which could and should be carried on. They recognized that with technological advances, broadcasting entities would have the capacity to perform certain technical operations, such as adjusting the direction, diameter, and power flux of broadcast beams to try and confine coverage to designated geographical areas. But they also realized that notwithstanding even the most rigorous attempts at technical control, it would not be possible – in view of the nature of broadcast beams under present technology and given numerous irregular borders – to avoid some 'spillover' of such broadcasts into neighbouring countries.[55] The content of such broadcasts might give offence to states affected by it and the solutions proposed would try to minimize if not eliminate the potential offence.

More radical than these solutions, however, were those which sought to get right to the source of the broadcasts. Certain delegations accordingly suggested at both the second and third sessions of the Working Group that, on the basis of the international legal principles of sovereignty and non-intervention, there should be a prohibition on broadcasts beamed from satellites by one state to others without the explicit prior consent of the governments concerned. Others suggested that rather than placing the onus on the broadcasting state to obtain consent from recipients, the onus should be on the recipient state which would have a right to refuse particular broadcasts.[56] The problem with both suggestions is that they would provide every state with a veto on broadcasts which other states covered by the beam would want to receive. This would be both unfair and would virtually eliminate international programming. The solution that the Working Group envisaged was one based on positive co-operation among countries and among broadcasting organizations, perhaps at a regional level, to establish systems among themselves and to agree on the programs that would be broadcast. As the third report stated:

> The Working Group considers that, while further exploration of various approaches to international co-operation in respect of broadcasting satellite systems continues to be desirable, co-operation and participation on the regional level, at least as a first step, appears to be the most practical and advantageous means of achieving desired results. Such participation in the establishment and operation of regional satellite broadcasting services and/or in programme planning and production, in most cases, would tend to meet the programme requirements and objectives of countries. Accordingly, the Working Group recommends that Member States and regional and international organizations should promote and encourage regional co-operative arrangements both on the governmental and non-governmental level, in order, *inter alia,* to increase the existing co-operation on a regional and international level among broadcasters and their associations for the future use of broadcasting satellite systems.[57]

This was seen not only as a solution to the problem of receiving undesirable content, but also to the problem of access.

This latter problem was given voice to both at the Working Group and at various other conferences on the part of those states not yet at the point where they could hope to have systems of their own. They did not wish to be mere 'consumers' of programs produced in the more advanced countries.[58] The solution to have them participate in regional or other groups to establish satellite systems in their region would mean that they would not only get access to these systems as receivers of programs but would also share in program production, engineering, finance, and the management of the system as well as decide on the programs to be shown. Solutions to the related problems of content and access would in this way be meaningfully limited. This approach very closely reflected the recommendations of the third Canada-Sweden working paper.[59]

A final legal problem relates to the protection of the transmissions of broadcast setellites from their being received and carried far beyond the territory from which they were intended. This is a magnified version of the problem relating to the importation of signals via CATV undertakings. At conferences in Paris and Lausanne an examination was made of the relevant copyright and related conventions, and it is now expected that a new international convention on the protection of all satellite transmissions will be concluded.[60] The solution recommended by the Working Group was not based on law so much as on positive co-operation, and it represented not a global but a regional approach. It sought not to develop actual legal norms but rather an institutional framework based on interstate co-operation within which norms might develop. What has been emphasized is a desire on the part of the international community to facilitate the technology and the advent of satellite broadcasting without erecting barriers to communications, bearing in mind that there are legitimate sovereign interests to be protected.

CONCLUSION

International communications law is developing through a number of organizations and in various forms. It is in a state of flux and evolution as normative principles emerge and are tested against competing principles, against technological realities and against national interests. Its essential dynamic is based on a tension between the principles of the right to communicate and the free flow of information on the one hand and of national sovereignty and state control on the other. Its development has so far been characterized by pragmatism rather than ideological concern, by an accent on working co-operative arrangements rather than on strict legal norms, and by a willingness in most cases to facilitate rather than restrain the technology.

Looking towards the future, it appears quite clear that with outer space activities having dramatically underlined the essential importance of communications, increasing attention will be paid to international legal developments affecting it. Communications has become a lifeline, both physically in that space activity is fundamentally reliant upon it and culturally in that understanding between peoples is dependent upon clear and effective communications links among them. Can we not then look forward to a greater community-oriented approach to the regulation of international communications? Can we not envisage a legal environment conducive to a freer flow of information across borders? Can we not, on the hardware side, foresee a more legally binding regulatory regime than under the present ITU to protect international communications facilities, to punish administrations that cause harmful interference, and to permit a compulsory framework for the settlement of disputes? Can we not envisage an international communications law based on the promise that the technology and the regulatory framework should be directed to the sole end that people are able to communicate freely, cheaply, and efficiently with each other through a multiplicity of media? In short, will we reach the point when the principle of state control is not regarded as the antagonist of the right to communicate but as its servant?

The aggregate answer is probably that we are not likely to see this kind of community orientation in the very near future. There is still far too much mistrust and fear on the part of many states that, however positive one's own intentions are, others might take advantage of a lowering of communications barriers for propaganda, cultural offence, or 'economic assault.' Thus the Working Group on Direct Broadcast Satellites, having raised a variety of potential fears about allowing foreign programs and rejected a number of negative and limiting solutions, did not progress to the point of framing a community oriented legal approach or positive principles of the freer flow of broadcasts across frontiers. The ITU will be holding a Plenipotentiary Conference in September 1973 and will probably adopt a permanent constitutional charter for the union. From the preliminary soundings, it is unlikely that the ITU will deviate very greatly from the kind of consensus-based technically oriented organization that it is at present, although there may be some changes reflecting a greater awareness of international community.

In the final analysis, whatever progress is made in the evolution of legal rules will not result from an *a priori* statement of principles, but will probably emerge from co-operative working arrangements to optimize communications technology. It is in this connection that INTELSAT can be regarded as a barometer, in that it both records – in international treaty form – a positive level of co-operative achievement at the same time as it underlines the limitations on that achievement in terms *inter alia* of membership and of the powers conferred on the INTELSAT organization. Nevertheless such co-operative arrangements hold forth the possibilities of reducing mistrust, of evolving proper and adequate rules for the particular activity undertaken, and of facilitating the access to the activities by additional states. It appears to be the case in international communications law that active co-operation is more likely to yield satisfactory legal norms than the *a priori* framing of norms, however satisfactory they may appear, is likely to lead to active co-operation.

Canada has consistently been a firm advocate of this approach emphasizing actual and ongoing co-operation as the solution to potential legal and related problems. The Canadian delegate to the UN Working Group on Direct Satellite Broadcasts summarized the point as follows:

Together, Canada and Sweden share a fundamental belief in the positive and immensely beneficial potentialities which direct satellite broadcasting offers to mankind. We believe that the development of satellite systems should thus inspire enthusiasm, even though it may also pose specific problems ... In seeking possible guidelines (for maximizing advantages and benefits and for minimizing whatever problems might arise) Canada and Sweden believe that the keynote should be international cooperation and that it would be both practical and advantageous to build upon the foundations of cooperative achievement already laid.[61]

This approach, which Canada has taken in relation to international communications generally, suggests that the solution to possible legal problems relating to rapidly developing technology does not lie in rigid rules or codes, which may themselves become quickly outdated in the face of technological change. Rather, it lies in co-operative arrangements which can maintain flexibility, a sense of experimentation, and a workable operational framework. By means of these cooperative arrangements, potential problems can either be avoided entirely, or at least settled amicably in the spirit of the joint enterprise and with a view to its success.

NOTES

1 In this chapter, communications is treated as synonymous with telecommunications. A telecommunication is defined as follows in article I, no 2 of the Radio Regulations of the International Telecommunication Convention: 'Any transmission, emission or reception of signs, signals, writing, images and sounds or intelligence of any nature by wire, radio, visual or other electromagnetic systems.' This is virtually the same definition as is found in Canadian federal statutes. See The Radio Act, R.S.C. c R-1, s 2(1) (1970).

2 Treaty of Principles Governing the Activities of States in the Exploration and Use of Outer Space, Including the Moon and Other Celestial Bodies. The treaty was opened for signature in January 1967 and came into force in October 1967. Canada ratified the treaty on 10 October 1967.

3 The UN Committee on the Peaceful Uses of Outer Space was constituted as a permanent committee under General Assembly resolution 1472(XIV) of 12 December 1959. It has established a Legal Subcommittee and a Scientific and Technical Subcommittee as well as a number of working groups.

4 The Outer Space Treaty is a good example of this process.

5 The International Telecommunication Convention, Montreux, 1965, article 4(1). Hereafter 'ITU Convention.'

6 'Hardware' refers to the technology, the instruments, and the physical facilities of communications. 'Software' refers to the content of transmissions. In McLuhanese, the distinction is one between the medium

and the message.

7 Department of Communications Act, R.S.C. c C-24, s 5(1)(f) (1970). The minister shares responsibility for developing appropriate international rules with the secretary of state for external affairs.

8 The predecessors to the present convention have included the International Telegraph Conventions of 1865 (Paris), 1868 (Vienna), 1872 (Rome), 1875 (St Petersburg). In 1927 a separate Radio Telegraph Convention was concluded at Washington. This and the 1875 Telegraph Convention were fused in 1932 into the International Telecommunication Convention (Madrid) which has since been reconstituted in 1947 (Atlantic City), 1952 (Buenos Aires), 1959 (Geneva), and 1965 (Montreux).

9 See resolution 35 of the Montreux Conference entitled 'Preparation of a Draft Constitutional Charter.'

10 See Henry J. Glazer, 'The Law-making Treaties of the International Telecommunication Union Through Time and in Space' (1962), 60 Michigan Law Review, at 271–2.

11 ITU Convention, Preamble.

12 Today, telecommunications services are run by the state in nearly all countries except for the US and Canada. In Canada there is a mixed situation with certain federally incorporated crown corporations such as the Canadian National Railway Company and certain provincial crown corporations such as Alberta Government Telephones providing telecommunications services alongside private companies like Bell Canada

(federally incorporated) and Québec-Téléphone (provincially incorporated).

13 See D.M. Leive, *International Telecommunications and Intentional Law: The Regulation of the Radio Spectrum* (1970), at 44. At the World Administrative Radio Conference for Space Telecommunications, lawyers for the first time participated on a number of delegations including those of Canada, the US, and France.

14 See C.H. Alexandrowicz, *The Law of Global Communications (1971), at 30*–1 for the view that world radiocommunication is co-ordinated on the basis of 'the concept of *res communis* or quasi-*res communis*.'

15 Harmful interference is defined at article 1, no 93 of the Radio Regulations as: 'Any emission, radiation or induction which endangers the functioning of a radionavigation service or of other safety services or seriously degrades, obtructs or repeatedly interrupts a radiocommunication service operating in accordance with these Regulations.'

16 See Radio Regulations, article 9 for details on the above procedures.

17 One exception is in respect of assignments recorded in column 2A of the Master Register. See Leive, *supra* note 13, at 155 *et seq* for details.

18 This is so despite no 705 of the Radio Regulations which provides that 'in the settlement of (harmful interference) problems, due consideration shall be given to all factors involved, including the relevant technical and operational factors such as: adjustment of frequencies ...'

19 See Radio Regulations, article 9, no 634.

20 For certain doubts as to the distinction between military and non-military radiocommunications, especially where space vehicles are concerned, see Glazer, *supra* note 10, at 295.

21 Any doubt as to whether the Radio Regulations applied to outer space was removed by the decisions taken at the 1959 Ordinary Radio Conference. Prior to that time, the two major space powers, the US and USSR, had selected their own frequencies for space research without any international regulations and the matter had not been considered very pressing in any other country. *Cf* the acceptance as a matter of principle that the UN Charter and the ICJ Statute were not limited in their operations to the confines of the earth (U.N. GAOR 14th Session, annexes, agenda item 25).

22 Certain bands, however, were 'reserved' for the radio astronomy service.

23 The procedure does not impose on an administration any obligation to agree to another's proposed operations, but only an obligation to make a good faith effort to do so. Nor is the successful completion of co-ordination a prerequisite either to the recording of an assignment in the Master Register or to subsequent protection of it. See Radio Regulations, article 9A *passim*.

24 All that was finally accepted (in no 639DD) was the attenuated principle that where a system which was established in conformity with the regulations, etc, suffered interference from one which had been recorded by insistence (having failed in one or more of the tests of conformity with the regulations) *and* had been recorded at a later date, the later system should cease the harmful interference.

25 On the global level, there is 'Intersputnik,' the USSR-sponsored global communications system, which was announced in the summer of 1968. The Intersputnik agreement was opened for signature in Moscow as of 15 November 1971. The main distinguishing features of the proposed scheme are that it provides for the membership of all states (v INTELSAT, which is open to ITU members only) and that there is to be no weighted voting in its organs of decision (v INTELSAT, where use is related to investment and investment to voting). On a regional level, the European space organizations are discussing a television distribution satellite system. On a bilateral level, the Franco-German 'symphonie' project might be noted. And on a domestic level the Telesat Canada Corporation has been established to own and operate Canada's domestic satellite system.

26 Cf Canadian recommendation proposed to the 1963 EARC which went part way in this direction but which was later withdrawn. It stated in part:

> ... recognizing that, in the establishment of space telecommunication systems involving more than one Member ... it appears necessary to state which of the participating Administrations will notify the frequency assignments to the space stations concerned; recommends that Administrations establishing a joint space telecommunication system should designate one of their number to be responsible

for submission of all notices of frequency assignments to space stations of the system, and to advise the Board accordingly.

1963 Space Conference, Committee 6, Draft Recommendation Relating to the Notification of Frequency Assignments for Joint Space Telecommunication Systems, Doc no 149, 31 October 1963. It is the case now that organizations like ICAO and IMCO have observer status in the ITU, including the CCIR, and are often rather active observers. It is not unreasonable to expect that INTELSAT will also be accorded observer status at least.

27 See in this connection INTELSAT Preparatory Committee Document P.C.(II)/49, at 63, para 207, b(ii); issued as an annex to Doc P.C.(III)/62 of 11 December 1969.
28 A broadcasting service is defined at article 1, no 28 of the Radio Regulations as 'a radiocommunication service in which the transmissions are intended for direct reception by the general public. This service may include sound transmissions, television transmissions or other types of transmissions.' Cf the Broadcasting Act, R.S.C. c B-11, s 2 (1970), where broadcasting is defined as 'any radiocommunication in which the transmissions are intended for direct reception by the general public.'
29 Accepted unanimously by the UN General Assembly on 10 December 1948. U.N. GAOR, 3rd session (I) resolutions.
30 See Delbert D. Smith, *International Telecommunication Control* (1969), at 11 and note 22.
31 Oppenheim, *International Law* (8th ed, Lauterpacht, 1955) vol I, at 529.
32 See Jessup and Taubenfeld, *Controls for Outer Space, as quoted in Smith, supra* note 30, at 5: 'The delivery of protests and the use of jamming techniques represent the limits of current protection of borders against the unwelcome onslaught by radio.'
33 See J. Evensen 'Aspects of International Law Relating to Modern Radio Communications,' Académie de Droit International (La Haye) Recueil des Cours II 1965, 477 at 525-7 and 559-60.
34 Annex to U.N. GA Resolution 2200(XXI) adopted 16 December 1966.
35 Briggs, *The Law of Nations* (2nd ed, 1952) 325.
36 Berne Convention for the Protection of Literary and Artistic Works of September 9,

1886 ... revised at Stockholm on 14 July 1967, article 11 bis.
37 Canada has numerous CATV systems receiving signals from US stations. The Canadian policy of limiting foreign signals which can be imported on the grounds of audience fragmentation, American advertizing spillover, and possible prejudice to the development of alternative Canadian service raises some interesting questions. See *Policy Statement on Cable Television*, CRTC announcement, 16 July 1971. Of relevance here is article 19 of the Civil and Political Rights Covenant referred to earlier which provides that:

2 Everyone shall have the right to freedom of expression; this right shall include freedom to seek, receive, and import information and ideas of all kinds, *regardless of frontiers*, either orally, in writing or in print, in the form of art or through the media of his choice.
3 The exercise of the rights provided for in paragraph 2 of this article carries with it special duties and responsibilities. It may therefore be subject to certain restrictions, but these shall only be such as are provided by law and are necessary:
a for respect of the rights or reputations of others:
b for the protection of national security or of public order (ordre public) or of public health or morals.

Canada has not adhered to these covenants.
38 See on this subject the note on European Agreement (1969) 117B *EBU Review* 56.
39 The First Report of the UN Working Group on Direct Broadcast Satellites reported that direct broadcast of television into augmented home receivers could become feasible technologically as soon as 1975, though with respect to unaugmented home receivers not before 1985. UN Doc A/AC 105/51, para 9. (References in footnotes 26–39 below are all to UN documents.)
40 Cf 1971 Space WARC documents 26 (Argentina), 72 (Brazil), and 90 (France).
41 Space WARC, resolution no Spa F.
42 See Gotlieb and Dalfen, 'Direct Satellite Broadcasting: A Case Study in the Development of the Law of Space Communications' (1969), *Can. Y.B. Int'l L.* 40 *et seq.*
43 UN Doc A/7285, at 5–6.
44 A/AC 105/66, para 32.
45 A/AC 105/62, section V. (2) and A/AC 105/63,

para 6 respectively. Cf USSR at 3rd session A/AC 105/W.G.3/C.R.P.1, re general standards governing program content.

46 A/AC 105/65, para 18.
47 A/AC 105/59, at 21, para 14.
48 A/AC 105/66, 24.
49 Ibid, para 34.
50 A/AC 105/63, para 6.
51 A/AC 105/65, para 23.
52 A/AC 105/62, sec v (3).
53 A/AC 105/65, para 23.
54 A/AC 105/66, para 63.
55 Cf A/AC 105/59, at 20, para 11.
56 A/AC 105/66, para 23. Cf Brazilian, French and Argentinian proposals to the 1971 Space WARC (Docs 72, 43, and 23 respectively) which would have required prior agreement between a transmitting administration and the administrations of those countries covered by a broadcast satellite beam. This was rejected by the WARC largely on the grounds that this was a matter beyond the competence of the ITU, since it did not relate to a broadcasting satellite system causing harmful interference to the services of other administrations, but rather to questions of program content.

57 A/AC 105/83, at 16, para 5.
58 See, for example, the Final Report of the UNESCO Meeting of Governmental Experts on International Arrangements in the Space Communication Field, Paris, 2–9 December 1969. UNESCO Doc COM/MD/15, 6 February 1970, at 16.
59 A/AC 105/WG 3/L 1, at 24–7, 30–3, and 36.
60 See Report, Committee of Governmental Experts on Problems in the Field of Copyright and of the Protection of Performers, Producers of Phonograms and Broadcasting Organization Raised by Transmission Via Space Satellites, (Lausanne, 21–30 April 1971), Doc UNESCO/WIPO/SAT/22, 30 April 1971 (issued as annex to UNESCO Doc 88 EX/13, 16 August 1971), at para 14.
61 Quoted in Gotlieb and Dalfen, supra note 42, at 37–8.

JOSEPH W. SAMUELS

14/International Control of Weather Modification Activities

At the Bangkok Conference on World Peace Through Law, 7 to 12 September 1969, the United Nations Committee of the World Peace Through Law Center recommended 'the establishment at the earliest possible date of a Convention on Weather Control pursuant to which international machinery would be set up requiring the strict registration and advanced licensing of all weather control activities having possible international consequences, guaranteeing the use of weather control for peaceful purposes only, and for the betterment of mankind as a whole.'[1]

In the Appeal of Bangkok adopted at the conclusion of the conference, the participants resolved that

> *Whereas,* weather control can be either a threat to international peace, or a means of bettering mankind's condition,
>
> *Resolved,* that the Bangkok Conference instruct the President of the Center to appoint a committee of experts to draft a treaty on transnational weather control providing for the establishment of international machinery for the regulation of all weather control activities having possible international consequences in order to insure their use for peaceful purposes only, and for the betterment of mankind as a whole; and
>
> *Further Resolved,* That the United Nations is urged to take appropriate action to implement the foregoing objectives.[2]

I was asked to prepare a draft convention for the World Peace Through Law Center and this chapter is, in a sense, a working paper on principles and problems that we meet when trying to draft such a convention. The agreement itself has been published by the center and is entitled 'Draft Protocol on Weather Modification'[3] (hereinafter referred to as the 'draft'). The present paper does not merely reflect the position taken in the draft but takes into account comments upon the draft made to me personally or in discussion at the World Peace Through Law Center's Conference at Belgrade in July 1971.

The technology of weather modification is in its infancy, but it poses several fundamental problems for man. To what extent can we permit tampering with our environment in the interest of a so-called better world for mankind? In what way can we regulate the use of this technology so that there is indeed a mutual co-operation and international benefit rather than increased tension as a result of the use of this science? We have here an almost unique opportunity, for the problem is not yet upon us. While in almost all other areas – pollution, arms, uses of the seabed, and so on – the international lawyer and politician are scrambling to cope with the problems already posed by advancing technology, in the field of weather modification, the lawyer and politician have the opportunity to create a legal order in advance of the real problems before interests have become fixed and immovable. At this point in time, it seems that we are on the threshold of a scientific advance that will see major weather experiments whose effects will spill over national frontiers to become primary sources of international discord.[4] Yet there has been no real attempt to provide for the political and legal framework necessary to cope with this development.[5]

The position of the Canadian government reflects current thinking. At the end of 1971 parliament passed the Weather Modification Information Act.[6] This piece of legislation is aimed at giving the government the information it needs to plan future policy in this field. Persons who wish to engage in weather modification activities in Canada must inform the administrator (as designated from time to time by the governor in council) of the proposed operation setting out:

a the date and time when and the place where the activity is to be carried out;
b the names and addresses of the persons by and for whom the activity is to be carried out;
c the purpose of the proposed activity;
d the equipment, materials and method to be used; and
e the geographic area that may be affected.[7]

Daily records of the activity must be kept, showing

a the location and operation of any equipment used,
b any meteorological observations made in the geographic area affected by the activity, and
c the chemical nature, physical properties and quantities of any substances emitted into the atmosphere for the purposes of weather modification.[8]

Finally, a report must be submitted to the administrator within the first two weeks of the month following the month in which the operation took place.[9]

While no special provision has been made to plan for or deal with the problem of international co-operation in this field, already a spirit of co-operation has been established between the Canadian Atmospheric Environment Service and the like bodies in the United States. When the United States Great Lakes Snow Redistribution Project was undertaken, full information was provided to the Canadian government, and the government was asked for its permission in advance for any activities which might have affected Canada.[10]

SCIENTIFIC PROBLEMS

While much has been done in the field of experimentation in weather modification,[11] the present situation involves several uncertainties. In the first place, there is great difficulty in predicting the effects of weather modification efforts before the operations are undertaken, and in analysing the effects after the operations are completed.[12] Second, we are not sure where our scientific quest will lead us in the future. Present experiments, successes and failures, will condition the avenues to be pursued in the years ahead.[13] Third, we are unsure of the ramifications of inadvertent weather modification through urbanization, air and water pollution, and so on.[14]

These scientific problems create difficulties for the politician and lawyer attempting to design a framework for organized control of weather modification activities. Given the uncertainty of predicting the effects before operations, or analysing the effects after them, what kind of decision-making process can be established to pass upon applications to undertake weather operations? The greater the uncertainty and chance involved, the more difficult a decision to permit operations becomes. The difficulties which have already been experienced in determining legal liability for damage purportedly resulting from weather modification activities will present themselves in any system of compensation for losses established under an international regime for the control of these activities. Preparation of the draft and the provisions in it are, in a sense, an 'act of faith' that while present technology is not capable of handling an accurate control system for weather modification, the competence will be achieved in the future. It is strongly urged that the opportunity to have a control framework ready before the really urgent problems are upon us demands that such an 'act of faith' be made. The position taken should be 'what kind of system should we have, given the necessary technical competence?' This point of view is not one shared by several experts within the World Meteorological Organization who, in responding to the draft which gives this organization the principal role in the proposed system, commented:

> It seems decidedly inadvisable to base international law on such flimsy a base as our present knowledge – or ... ignorance – in this field ... It would seem ... much better ... if the proposal for a protocol on weather modification were not raised until such time as clear-cut and positive effects could be produced by weather modification experiments on a scale which demonstrates that effects of activities in one country may extend to another ... It seems ... desirable that care should be taken that a legal framework is not built up which assumes a technical ability which we do not possess.[15]

The uncertainty as to the future of weather modification gives rise to the question: Will a system of control established today be capable of coping with unexpected scientific developments in the future? Or, at the least, will the framework of control be sufficiently flexible to adapt to these unexpected developments? To date, operators have tried to: 1 / modify precipitation by manipulating clouds, principally by artificial nucleation; 2 / supress hail; 3 / suppress lightning; 4 / dissipate fog; 5 / suppress or divert storm systems.[16] The future may bring attempts to modify whole weather systems so that the climate of whole regions will be drastically altered.

LEGAL AND POLITICAL PROBLEMS

Our first legal difficulty is what should be the definition of the activities intended to be controlled. The weather is a very complicated result of atmospheric conditions. Modification in the weather can result from deliberate attempts to change it or as a by-product of other life processes, such as urbanization, agricultural activity, and air transportation. The former is known as advertent and the latter as inadvertent weather modification. Do we submit both kinds of activity to the same control framework?

Then there is the difficulty resulting from the varied interests in the weather. Should a weather modification control system be part of a general package dealing with the environment because weather is part of the environment and many activities which directly affect the environment in one way (eg, air and water pollution) may also indirectly affect the weather? Or should the control system be part of an air and outer space regime because most of the weather modification activities take place in the air today and may take place in outer space tomorrow? Or should we be concerned only with advertent weather modification activities and link a control system with the present international weather framework of the World Meteorological Organization? Or should the weather modification control system be part of a water resources control regime because one of the principal measures of weather modification is to change the amount of precipitation in an area and thereby change the nature and quantity of the water resources?

The major difficulty is to develop a delicate balance between the benefit for some which will result from scientific achievement and the detriment to others. If clouds which pass over state A then state B are made to drop their water over state A, state B will lose some of its potential rainfall. If a hurricane is diverted from state A onto the territory of state B, again there is benefit for one and harm to the other. Countless illustrations of this balance could be drawn. How do we measure the relative gains and losses? Or should we establish a regime which merely preserves the *status quo* because of the near impossibility of establishing a proper balance?[17] Indeed, to preserve the *status quo* itself is to involve us in a measuring of gains and losses because a state which is in need of weather modification at present is deprived when the means of improvement are available yet must lie idle.

What principle of state responsibility should be used in a regime to govern weather modification activities? A leading statement of the present position is found in the *Trail Smelter* decision: 'No state has the right to use or permit the use of its territory in such a manner as to cause injury ... to the territory of another or the properties or persons therein, when the case is of serious consequence.'[18] Is this principle too restrictive in light of the potential benefits for all mankind of weather modification? Is there a point here where the rights of an individual state must be overcome for the greater benefit of the international community as a whole?

Our approach to this problem can and must be an innovative and imaginative one.[19] We are not restricted to the application of existing principles of state responsibility and neighbourhood law. The great advantage of having a treaty governing the control of weather modification operations is that we can fashion a suitable regime unfettered by existing principles. This does not mean that existing principles offer nothing to us here. They stand as guides to future principles. Most of the law we now have on weather modification has been developed in the United States.[20] The few cases that have come to the courts involving weather modification have been decided upon the general tort concepts of trespass and negligence. However other possible analogies have been suggested.[21] For example, one might create a property interest in clouds (or other elements of the atmosphere) which is subject to a body of law similar to that governing riparian rights.[22] Or one could create an interest in clouds as part of a state's interest in air and outer space.

Satterfield suggests four theories advocated for the ownership of airspace.[23] 1 / The zone theory whereunder 'the airspace above the land is divided into two layers, with the owner of the land owning absolutely that in the lower layer, but not that in the upper layer. The line drawn between the two layers is that of the owner's "effective possession", or the extent to which it is necessary for him to own the airspace in order to use the land below.'[24] 2 / The regime adopted by the Uniform State Law for Aeronautics whereunder 'the surface owner has an unlimited ownership of the upper airspace subject only to a privilege of flight by the public.'[25] 3 / 'The limitation of the surface owner to that portion of the upper atmosphere which he actually uses.'[26] 4 / The nuisance theory whereunder the ownership of the upper atmosphere is recognized and a remedy for nuisance is granted when the owner suffers actual interference with his rights.[27]

What means should be used to provide compensation for individuals and states which suffer harm from weather modification activities? Do we establish a new tribunal to handle such claims? We have already alluded to the present difficulty of proving the relationship between the damage and the weather modification operations. What standard of proof will we require in the international system? And who should pay the compensation? The operator? Where the activities benefited many states perhaps there should be some form of collective responsibility for the losses incurred?

SUGGESTED SOLUTIONS AND PRINCIPLES

Definition

It is suggested that a weather modification control system concern itself solely with advertent weather modification activities. The sources of inadvertent changes – urbanization, and so on – are so vast and complex that they do not admit of control in the same sense as do the deliberate weather-changing operations. No one body, no simple mechanism, can control the processes of urbanization and agricultural activity. It may well be advisable for the body entrusted with the regulation of advertent weather modification to gather information and conduct scientific research on the effects of these inadvertent weather modification activities. However, regulation of these activities must be found elsewhere, if at all.

Institutional framework

It is suggested that the administration of the international control system be brought within the existing World Meteorological Organization. This point of view is taken for two reasons: first, if it is possible, the proliferation of institutions, with inherent overlapping of jurisdictions and internecine struggles, should be avoided; second, use should be made of existing expertise. The WMO was established 'with a view to co-ordinating, standardizing, and improving world meteorological activities.'[28] One of its purposes is 'to further the application of meteorology to aviation, shipping, agriculture, and other human activities.'[29] Thus, here we have an existing intergovernmental organization, a specialized agency of the United Nations,[30] established to cope with such matters as the international control of weather modification. However, thus far the WMO has not provided itself, or has not been provided with, the machinery to exercise this control. None of the present organs of the institution is really equipped to deal with this problem.

The Congress consists of delegates of all the members.[31] It has the broadest of powers,[32] including the ability to amend the convention itself.[33] This organ is too large and unwieldy to exercise the day-to-day control that might be necessary under a regime governing weather modification. Indeed, ordinarily the Congress meets only every four years.[34] However, it is to the Congress that we must look for an amendment to the convention bringing in a system of control of weather modification.

The Executive Committee consists of the president and vice-presidents of the organization, the presidents of the Regional Associations created under the convention, and twelve directors of meteorological services of members of the organization elected by the Congress.[35] The Executive Committee conducts the business of the organization between the meetings of Congress. The Executive Committee does not have an appropriate constitution for the regulation of weather modification. Judgments as to the desirability of modification operations must be made not only by meteorological experts but also by politicians and other social scientists who are not at present represented on the Executive Committee. The scientist's role is to inform of the possible physical effects of the activities. However, he is not necessarily in the best position to judge the social and economic consequences. Apart from its constitutional inadequacies, the Executive Committee meets normally only once a year.[36]

The Regional Associations are composed of members of the organization whose territories lie within the areas defined for each region.[37] These associations are essentially regional discussion groups whose function it is to promote the execution of the resolutions of Congress and the Executive Committee in their regions, and to explore and make recommendations concerning matters within their own regions.[38] The associations have no real administrative powers and consequently are unsuited to carry the burden of implementing a system for control of weather modification.

The Technical Commissions consist of technical experts brought together to study and make recommendations to the Congress and the Executive Committee on any subject within the purposes of the organization.[39] Members of the organization have the right to be represented on the Technical Commissions.[40] Because of this right of broad representation, these commissions are too unwieldy for the purposes of weather modification control. Also, as mentioned above, our administrative agency must be more than a collection of technical experts. These commissions meet only once every four years.[41] Finally, none of the present commissions encompasses the whole problem of weather modification. There are now Technical Commissions for synoptic meteorology, climatology, instruments and methods of observation, atmospheric sciences, aeronautical meteorology, agricultural meteorology, hydrometeorology, and maritime meteorology.[42]

The Secretariat consists of the secretary general and such technical and clerical staff as may be required for the work of the organization.[43] It was not established, nor is it constituted, for the kind of administrative decision-making necessary in a system for international control of weather modification.

A new administrative body for our purposes would need to fulfil the following functions: 1 / setting out international standards for the licensing of weather modifiers; 2 / passing upon applications for permission to perform weather modification operations involving possible international effects; 3 / collecting and disseminating information concerning weather modification activities and scientific knowledge of weather modification; 4 / perhaps handling claims for compensation arising out of weather modification operations. Such a body could be established within the WMO by an amendment to the convention according to article 27. Perhaps the amendment could take the form of a Protocol on Weather Modification. The expenses of the new body could be borne by the members of the organization who agree to the amendment. The new body could be called the Committee on Weather Modification.

The composition of such a body should take into account three considerations. In the first place, while the control system is placed within the framework of the World Meteorological Organization, there must be representation from those other international institutions which have a particular interest in the weather. For instance, the Food and Agriculture Organization is interested in the weather as one resource input for the production of food. Decisions concerning weather modification activities should take into account this use of the weather and the opinion of the FAO on these activities. Secondly, because of the complexity of the effects of weather modification operations, decisions should be taken by a group with the varied expertise needed to cope with this complexity. Thirdly, there should be no domination by any particular group in the decision-making process.

The states represented on this committee would be chosen by the Congress from the states which are parties to the amendment. It is suggested that there be equal representation of states undertaking substantial weather-making operations at the time of the selection and those likely to be affected by such operations. A state which falls within both categories should be represented only in the former capacity. The delegation from any one state on the committee should consist of varied expertise, such as a meteorologist, an economist, a lawyer, and perhaps others. Each state would have one vote but decisions of the committee would need a majority of each group, the states undertaking weather modification operations and those likely to be affected by them.

The total size of the committee should be kept within manageable bounds, perhaps twelve states. Any state not on the committee but likely to be affected by a proposed modification scheme could appear for the deliberations but in a non-voting capacity.

In this way, it might be possible to have an administrative body with the necessary overall expertise to make the difficult decisions involving scientific and social problems. The decisions would not be imposed by a group dominated by advanced, weather-modifying states, or by less advanced states worried about the effects of weather modification.

The committee could draw up its own regulations for procedure as long as these regulations did not conflict with the laws and principles established by the amendment to the convention. The committee should be available either as a whole or as a working group to attend to day-to-day business. Perhaps the small working group could decide upon some applications for permission to conduct weather modification operations within firm guidelines set out by the committee as a whole in accordance with the principles of the amendment. The committee would report to the Executive Committee once a year, and to the Congress once every four years. It could draw upon the existing Technical Commissions and Regional Associations for advice, if necessary.

Because the weather modification regime would be part of the World Meteorological Organization framework, it would be subject to the provisions in the WMO Convention dealing with amendments[44] and interpretation and disputes.[45]

On the municipal level, the international administrative body could work through national governmental agencies. These agencies would administer a national licensing system for weather modifiers according to the standards established at the international level. Requests for approval of proposed weather modification operations involving international consequences and claims for compensation arising out of such operations would be presented to the committee by the national agencies. The state agencies would also be responsible for full reports at regular intervals of the weather modification activities undertaken and planned within their territory or by nationals over territory not under the sovereignty of any state.

Fundamental principles

Today there is growing concern with the damage man is doing to his environment. In an effort to change nature to suit himself, man is instead destroying the ecological balance he needs for survival. It is almost as if man and nature are incompatible.[46] Now we stand on the threshold of major scientific advances in the field of weather modification. We are about to tamper directly and deliberately with the environment. It is necessary to stand back and ask: Should we do so? Must we do so? Is it time to say 'Enough'? Is it time we learned to live with nature rather than in spite of nature? These questions are vital when we contemplate a legal regime for the international control of weather modification activities.[47]

It is true that we have been careless in our use of the earth's resources. We have taken measures whose possible consequences we were not aware of, nor did we care about them, and they have turned out to be disastrous. For instance, we used DDT to check insects which spread malaria and now we find that DDT may wipe out our birdlife and deform man himself. But must this always be the case? Is it not possible that our scientific advances will open opportunities to achieve the benefits we want without the harmful by-products? It will take us longer to explore all the consequences of future measures, but it will be worth it in the long run.

Must we tolerate the hurricane's ravages if we can avoid it without greater damage in some other way? Must we let deserts lie unproductive if we can bring increased precipitation and life to them? The great problem with out scientific thrust thus far has been our total inability to use the knowledge wisely. We unlocked the atom with its unbelievable store of energy so that we could build nuclear arsenals to preserve the peace through a balance of terror. But this need not be so. Perhaps it is possible for us to exercise wisdom in the use of our scientific advances.

The possibilities of weather modification are upon us. Where there is felt to be a great need to use these possibilities, they will be used. We can hope to control this use. It is pointless to forbid weather modification activities involving international consequences because such a prohibition will not be observed and there are situations which merit modification.

The international regime for the control of weather modification should take into account the following principles. First, the international community should interest itself, at this stage, only in those activities which have effects beyond the borders of the state in which they are undertaken. Second, weather modification should be restricted to peaceful uses; that is, it should not be used as a weapon against any state. This would still permit such military uses as fog-clearing around an airbase to facilitate the landing of aircraft. Third, it must be agreed upon that where the impact of the activity is transnational, then the decision concerning that activity must be international as well. This would involve a duty to inform the international community where it is likely that a weather modification operation will have international consequences.

In the light of these considerations it is suggested that we permit measures undertaken in good faith which offer general benefit to mankind or which may be harmful to some but for which adquate compensation is provided. This was the position taken, on a municipal level, in *Slutsky* v *City of New York*.[48] The plaintiffs, owners of a country club, sought an injunction to prevent the city from undertaking experiments to induce rain during a serious water emergency. The court held that it

> must balance the conflicting interests between a remote possibility of inconvenience to plaintiffs' resort and its guests with the problem of maintaining and supplying the inhabitants of the City of New York and surrounding areas, with a population of about 10 million inhabitants, with an adequate supply of pure and wholesome water. The relief which plaintiffs ask is opposed to the general welfare and public good; and the dangers which plaintiffs apprehend are purely speculative. This court will not protect a possible private injury at the expense of a positive public advantage.[49]

A similar approach of balancing conflicting interests should be taken at the international level.

If weather modification activities are to be permitted where the general welfare is served, there must be a system of compensation for those individuals and states who suffer from the changes made. It is suggested that when the public good is served, it is the whole community that should provide the compensation. One possibility is to compensate on an *ad hoc* basis for each operation undertaken. This would be unwieldy. A better method would be for the parties to an agreement governing weather modification to establish a compensation fund with contributions according to the size of a state's gross national product, its activity in the weather modification field, its potential gains from weather modification, and perhaps other factors. Out of this fund would be paid compensation for damage resulting from weather modification operations undertaken by another state with the approval of the international administrative body. Where this approval was not received, or where the operations were carried out in a manner not in accordance with the approved plan, the liability of the state undertaking the weather modification operation should be governed by the present international law of state responsibility.

Where the operations fall within the newly established international regime, the community as a whole should bear the responsibility for loss.

It is suggested that the Committee on Weather Modification of the World Meteorological Organization proposed above should administer the compensation fund. One may question the propriety of having the same body pass upon the request to undertake modification activities (and if it gives its approval thereby engage a responsibility on behalf of the world community) and then decide upon compensation claimed because of the approval which it granted in the first place. It is a bit like being judge and jury in one's own cause. However, it is suggested that the committee would have the integrity to assess properly claims for compensation. This is especially so when one bears in mind that a claim for compensation is not a slur upon the judgment of the committee. The whole purpose of an international control system for weather modification activities is to balance conflicting interests. It is expected from the outset that there will be gains and losses. It would be the committee's role to approve proposals which appeared to offer general benefit and to award compensation to the losers in the balance.

There are, of course, two problems here. First, there is the difficulty of proving the causative connection between the damage suffered and the weather modification operation. Second, there is the possibility of staggering losses which would swamp any compensation fund. These two problems will be dissipated by the advance of meteorological knowledge. The more we know about the phenomena of our weather, the better we will be able to predict the possible consequences of weather modification activities and the more able we will be to establish the causative links between purported damages and weather modification operations.[50] Until this knowledge is ours, the committee will have to refuse permission for weather modification operations which may involve massive unexpected consequences. Where the possible harm is small, we will have to live with the present difficulty of proving that the damage resulted from the artificial changes. Compensation should involve not only pure money payments but technical assistance to aid in rehabilitation as well.

What if the harm occurs to a state which is not a party to the weather modification agreement? It is suggested that the same principle of collective responsibility should be applied. Where the community approval is received, and where the common benefit is served, it is not right that the weather-modifying state bear the losses simply because the harm resulted to a non-party to the agreement. The same considerations prevail no matter what state suffers the damage. The community good has been served; the community should bear the responsibility for compensation.

Of course, if a non-party undertakes weather modification activities with international consequences, it must bear the responsibility for compensation according to the present rules of international law.

Two rules should be established in recognition of the doctrine of sovereignty. First, no modification operations may be undertaken over the territory of a state without its permission. This is to be distinguished from the *effects* of the operations which may occur in a state without its permission. Second, as has been mentioned, it is obvious that a state engages no international responsibility for weather modification activities undertaken within its own territory and affecting only the people and property within its own territory. The result of these two rules is to permit weather modification operations, according to the international regime, over territory not subject to the sovereignty of any state, such as the high seas. But where the *effects* of the operations are felt anywhere else but within the territory of the modifying state, the state must receive the approval of the international administrative body.

Finally, insofar as the fundamental principles of weather modification control are concerned, the responsibility of a state for activities must be engaged as long as they are undertaken on its territory whether or not the state itself is conducting the operations and whether or not the operations are lawful according to the law of that state. This would mean that responsibility is basically territorial rather than personal. The nationality of the operator would be irrelevant when the operations are conducted on the territory of a state. However, if the operations are undertaken over territory not subject to the sovereignty of any state, then a state's responsibility should be engaged if the acts are done by a national of that state.

CONCLUSION

Scientific advances in the field of weather modification will bring us shortly to the point where these activities will involve international consequences and will be a possible source of discord. The political scientist and lawyer must develop a framework within which this scientific progress can be channelled to peaceful purposes for the benefit of all mankind. To this end, it is suggested that the following course of action be adopted: 1 / An international agreement on the control of weather modification activities should be added by way of protocol to the existing WMO convention. 2 / The agreement should bring under international control all those weather modification operations which have effects beyond the frontiers of the state within which the operations are undertaken, and these operations should be limited to peaceful purposes. 3 / The agreement should establish a Committee on Weather Modification to operate within the framework of the WMO. The functions of the committee would be to set out international standards for the licensing of weather-modifiers, to approve proposals for weather modification operations involving possible international consequences, to collect and disseminate information concerning activities and knowledge in the weather modification field, and to administer a compensation system. 4 / This committee should operate on the municipal level through national agencies. 5 / Weather modification operations should be permitted where the common good of mankind is served though some individuals or states may suffer damages. Compensation should be provided out of a community-established fund for those who suffer harm arising out of weather modification operations approved by the committee. 6 / States must be responsible for all weather modification operations undertaken on their territory by anyone, or undertaken by their nationals on territory not subject to the sovereignty of any state. 7 / No weather modification operations should be undertaken on or over the territory of a state without its consent. 8 / Non-parties to the agreement should receive compensation for damage out of the community fund where the operations are undertaken with the approval of the committee.

At the Belgrade Conference on World Peace Through World Law, in July 1971, the delegates adopted the following resolution:

WHEREAS the Center recognizes the potential international problems that may arise from weather modification activities,

WHEREAS the Center takes note of the Bangkok Resolution #14 concerning the international control of these activities,

WHEREAS the Center desires to begin the processes of international control of weather modification activities and to examine the possibility of placing this control within the system of the World Meteorological Organization;

RESOLVED, that the Draft Protocol on Weather Modification be circulated to interested parties as a basis for the development of a method of international control, while realizing the very great difficulty of applying the provisions of the present Draft Protocol in the light of the state of weather technology. The Center also directs the Committee to continue its studies and revise the Protocol, as necessary.[51]

In addition, in the Pledge of Belgrade, it was said: 'We urge acceptance of world or multi-national authority ... to fix international standards and guidelines for the control of science and technology as it affects the control over or modification of the weather in any part of the world.'[52]

NOTES

1 From a mimeographed sheet produced for the conference (6/PP-E-3).

2 Resolution 14 of *The Appeal of Bangkok and Resolutions Adopted* published by the World Peace Through Law Center, Geneva.

3 World Peace Through Law Center, pamphlet series, no 15.

4 This warning is sounded in R.F. and H.J. Taubenfeld, 'The International Implications of Weather Modification Activities,' a study prepared for the Office of External Research, US Department of State, June 1968. The study largely reiterates the discussion in H.J. Taubenfeld, 'Weather Modification and Control: Some International Legal Implications' (1967), 55 *Calif. L. Rev.* 493.

The point is also made in the Final Report of the Panel on Weather and Climate Modification to the Committee on Atmospheric Sciences, National Academy of Sciences, US National Research Council, *Weather and Climate Modifications: Problems and Prospects* (NAS-NRC pub no 1350, 1966) v 1 (Summary and Recommendations), at 27–8. See also Peters, 'Change the Weather, Change the World' (1967), 234 *Harper's* 98.

5 Some guiding principles, with which I disagree, were put forth in the David Davies Memorial Institute of International Studies, *Draft Rules Concerning Changes in the Environment of the Earth* (undated). The subject is also mentioned briefly in a later study by the same Institute, *Principles Governing Certain Changes in the Environment of Man* (undated), at 31–2.

6 S.C. 1970–71, c 59. Royal assent was given on 15 December 1971. This act follows upon the Weather Modification Background Reports prepared in November 1967 by the Meteorological Service of Canada.

7 Ibid, s 3.

8 Ibid, s 4(1)(a).

9 Ibid, s 4(1)(b).

10 This was mentioned in a letter to me from the Honourable Jack Davis, minister of the environment, Canada, 23 November 1971.

11 For an outline of present developments see M. Neiburger, *Artificial Modification of Clouds and Precipitation* (1969) World Meteorological Organization, technical note no 105, WMO – no 249. TP 137; W.O. Roberts, 'The State of the Act in Weather Modification' in H.J. Taubenfeld, ed, *Weather Modification and the Law* (1968), at 1–21; National Science Foundation, *Weather Modification* (10th Annual Report, 1968, NSF

69–18); and the following chapters in R.G. Fleagle, ed, *Weather Modification: Science and Public Policy* (1969): R.G. Fleagle, 'Background and Present Status of Weather Modification,' at 3–17; P.V. Hobbs, 'The Physics of Natural Precipitation Processes,' at 18–29; and idem, 'The Scientific Basis, Techniques, and Results of Cloud Modification,' at 30–42.

12 Neiburger, *supra* note 11, at 28 says, 'In the case of precipitation – augmentation and hail – suppression, it is not known under which circumstances and by what techniques operations will lead to success, and when opposite effects will result.' See also the discussion of the difficulties involved in proving the effects of weather modification in E.A. Morris, 'Preparation and Trial of Weather Modification Litigation' in Taubenfeld, *supra* note 11, at 163–84. Insofar as large-scale changes are concerned, the following appears in *Weather and Climate Modification, Problems and Prospects, supra* note 4, at 8:

It can be stated categorically that there is, at present, no known way deliberately to induce predictable changes in the very large-scale features of climate or atmospheric general circulation. While man may attain the technological capability to induce perturbations sufficient to trigger massive atmospheric reactions, we cannot now predict with certainty all the important consequences of such acts. As long as our understanding is thus limited, *to embark on any vast experiment in the atmosphere would amount to gross irresponsibility* [italics in the original].

In a statement adopted by the Executive Committee of the World Meteorological Organization at its twenty-second session (1970) and slightly amplified and confirmed by its Sixth Congress (1971) entitled 'Present State of Knowledge and Possible Practical Benefits in Some Fields of Weather Modification' (unpublished), the organization emphasized and re-emphasized the need for further research to assess the impact and validity of weather modification activities. In the general part of the statement appears the warning: 'It is important to emphasize that weather modification is still largely in the research stage. For this reason, operational

efforts should be undertaken only after the most careful study of the particular situation by experts and with the understanding that the desired end results may not always be achieved.'

14 Two looks into the future are: T.F. Malone, 'Weather' in Foreign Policy Association, ed, *Toward the Year 2018* (1968), at 61–74; and R.C. Sutcliffe, 'Artificial Modification of Weather and Climate' (1965), 12 *International Relations* 787.

15 See *Weather and Climate Modification, Problems and Prospects, supra* note 4, at 10–12; David Davies Memorial Institute of International Studies, *Principles Governing Certain Changes in the Environment of Man* (undated), at 31–2.

15 These comments appear in unpublished letters and papers.

16 See note 6.

17 The David Davies Memorial Institute, *Draft Rules Concerning Changes in the Environment of the Earth* (undated), at 4, suggests: 'No State or international body shall engage in, or within the limits of its authority permit, operations which can cause changes in the environment of the Earth ... 2. if the changes may be reasonably expected ... b. to modify the climate or weather of any region of the earth.'

18 (1941) 3 R.I.A.A. 1905, 1965. Note should also be made of the following two principles in the Declaration on the Human Environment coming out of the UN Conference on the Human Environment, Stockholm, June 1972:

'States have, in accordance with the Charter of the United Nations and the principles of international law, the sovereign right to exploit their own resources pursuant to their own environmental policies, and the responsibility to ensure that activities within their jurisdiction or control do not cause damage to the environment of other States or areas beyond the limits of national jurisdiction.'
'States shall co-operate to develop further the international law regarding liability and compensation for the victims of pollution and other environmental damage caused by activities within the jurisdiction or control of such States to areas beyond their jurisdiction.'

19 E.A. Morris, 'Institutional Adjustment to an Emerging Technology: Legal Aspects of

Weather Modification' in W.R.D. Sewell, ed, *Human Dimensions of Weather Modification* (1966) 279–88 at 287: 'Legal theories which are original and even a complete departure from prior decisions should be explored. Then the economists, the social and political scientists can study the economic, social and political ramifications which might follow from each suggested possible legal approach.'

20 See H.J. Taubenfeld, *Weather Modification: Law, Controls, Operations* (Report to the Special Commission on Weather Modification, National Science Foundation, NSF 66–7, 1966); R.W. Johnson, 'Legal Implications of Weather Modification' in H.J. Taubenfeld, ed, *Weather Modification and the Law* (1968), at 76–102; R.J. Davis, 'Special Problems of Liability and Water Resources Law,' ibid, at 103–140; R.S. Hunt, 'Weather Modification and the Law' in *supra* note 11, at 118–37; D. Frenzen, 'Weather Modification: Law and Policy' (1971), 12 *Boston College Industrial and Commercial L. Rev.* 503; and H.J. Taubenfeld, ed, *Controlling the Weather: A Study of Law and Regulatory Procedures* (1970).

21 A discussion of the earlier cases and the principles which have underlain them is to be found in L.O. Satterfield, Jr. 'Legal Problems of Weather Control' (1960), 12 *Baylor L. Rev.* 113. See also the sources mentioned *supra* note 15, and V.C. Ball, 'Shaping the Law of Weather Control' (1949), 58 *Yale L.J.* 213, 227–37.

22 See Satterfield, *supra* note 21, at 114–17. See also the comment on *Southwest Weather Research, Inc.* v *Rounsaville* (1959) 320 s.w. (2d) 211, 'Are there individual property rights in clouds?' (1960), 15 *Wyo, L.J.* 92. Other comments on this case are at (1959), 4 *Vill. L. Rev.* 603; (1960), 36 *Nor. Dakota L. Rev.* 72. See also *Southwest Weather Research, Inc.* v *Duncan* (1959), 319 s.w. (2d) 910, and comments on it at (1959), 37 *Tex. L. Rev.* 799; (1959), 4 *S. Texas L. J.* 400. These two cases were affirmed in the Texas Supreme Court *sub nom. Southwest Weather Research, Inc* v *Jones* (1959), 327 s.w. (2d) 417. See also 'Who owns the clouds?' (1948), 1 *Stan. L. Rev.* 43.

23 Satterfield, *supra* note 21, at 117–22.

24 Ibid, at 118.

25 Ibid.

26 Ibid.

27 Ibid, at 119.

28 Preamble, *Convention of the World Meteorological Organization*, 77 U.N.T.S. 143 published in *Basic Documents* (Ed. 1963, WMO – no 15. BD1), at 4.

29 Ibid, article 2, paragraph (d).

30 See the *Agreement between the United Nations and the World Meteorological Organization*, 123 U.N.T.S. 245, published in *Basic Documents, supra* note 28, at 117.

31 WMO Convention, article 6.

32 Ibid, articles 7, 22–3.

33 Ibid, article 27.

34 Ibid, article 9.

35 Ibid, articles 12 and 7(i).

36 Ibid, article 14.

37 Ibid, article 17, paragraph (a).

38 Ibid, paragraph (d).

39 Ibid, article 18, paragraph (a).

40 Ibid, paragraph (b).

41 Regulation 154 of the *W.M.O. General Regulations* found in *Basic Documents, supra* note 28, at 25–89.

42 For their terms of reference see ibid annex II.

43 WMO *Convention*, article 19.

44 Ibid, article 27.

45 Ibid, article 28.

46 This is the theme of an excellent, haunting work by R. Edberg, now in an English translation. *On the Shred of a Cloud* (1969).

47 See W.R.D. Sewell, 'Weather Modification: When Should We Do It and How Far Should We Go?' in Fleagle, *supra* note 11, at 94–104.

48 (1950), 97 N.Y. Supp. (2d) 238 (Supreme Court).

49 Ibid, at 240.

50 See the World Meteorological Organization's *Second Report on the Advancement of Atmospheric Sciences and their Application in the Light of Developments in Outer Space* (1963). See also two chapters in Fleagle, *supra* note 11; J.E. McDonald, 'Evaluation of Weather Modification Field Tests,' at 43–55; and D.G. Chapman, 'Statistical Aspects of Weather and Climate Modification,' at 56–68.

51 Resolution no 13, found in a mimeographed sheet labelled Misc/E-17.

52 Misc/E-18.

TERRITORIAL CONSIDERATIONS

L.H.J. LEGAULT*

15/Maritime Claims

This chapter attempts a brief review of Canada's maritime claims and their evolution from the colonial period to the present. The intention is not to give a history of those claims or an analysis of their legal merits; rather it is proposed to examine Canada's claims to either maritime sovereignty or jurisdiction (or both) in the light of the factors which have determined both the claims themselves and the policies adopted in seeking to advance them.

Fisheries have occupied an important place in Canada's economic history and foreign relations from the colonial period to the present. Fishing, and not the fur trade, is Canada's oldest primary industry. The first treaty negotiated by Canada in its own right was the International Pacific Halibut Convention with the United States in 1923 (which, however, required ratification by the British government, coming as it did three years before the Imperial Conference of 1926 had accepted the equal status of the dominions and the mother country).[1] Canada is a member of nine international fisheries commissions established under various international conventions,[2] and in the two years from April 1970 to March 1972 Canada entered into nine new bilateral agreements related to fisheries.[3]

Self-evident though it may be, it is important to emphasize that Canada's maritime claims from the outset have been related to the use and protection of the living resources of the sea off its coasts. Despite the relative decline in the importance of commercial fishing to Canada's economy, and despite the fact that the annual cost of government services for the fisheries ranges from 25 to 35 per cent of the gross value of commercial fishery production on the Atlantic coast, fishing is still of vital importance to Canada's coastal provinces in both social and economic terms.[4] The resource orientation of Canada's maritime policy remains strong, and has been broadened with technological development to include offshore mineral as well as living resources. In addition, environmental concerns, which are intimately related to the protection of living resources, have recently assumed equal or greater importance.

BRITISH INFLUENCE

The basic Canadian concern for the protection of coastal resource interests has been a decisive factor in the evolution of Canadian maritime claims. Indeed the history of those claims may be described as being in large part the result of the interplay between Canada's preoccupation with coastal resource interests and the different and wider range of maritime interests of Great Britain and the United States.

*The opinions expressed here are solely mine.

It is one of the anomalies of history that Canada's maritime claims in some cases rest on earlier British claims but that, on the other hand, the advancement of Canadian claims was for a long period circumscribed and restricted (but also protected) by British policy. This is true not only for the period when Britain itself was largely responsible for Canada's maritime policy but also to some extent for part of the period following the achievement of Canadian autonomy in external affairs. For the legal heritage Canada acquired from Britain included the British view of the law of the sea, and its influence, as well as the influence of the other links with Britain, remained great in the determination of Canadian policy. Nevertheless, divergences between the views of the two countries in maritime matters appeared even before 1926 and were to widen thereafter.[5]

Notable examples of extensive early British claims to maritime areas adjacent to the Canadian coast include Hudson Bay and Strait, Conception Bay (and other bays of Newfoundland), the Bay of Fundy, and the Gulf of St Lawrence. English claims to sovereignty of the sea on the other side of the Atlantic go back to the tenth century,[6] and similar ambitions in North American waters were evident in the early colonial period. And from the early 1700s to the early 1800s when, as a result of naval interests, Britain was attempting to establish the freedom of the seas and restrict to three miles the marginal belt, the British were at the same time claiming increasingly wide customs jurisdiction to protect their fiscal interests that were being prejudiced by smuggling activities.[7]

As Professor Morin points out, the factors that influenced Britain to restrict its claims off its own (metropolitan) coasts do not appear to have been as decisive to its claims in the colonies, at least in the earlier period.[8] Full sovereignty over Hudson Bay and Strait was claimed by both Britain and France, and the 'restoration' of British sovereignty over these waters was recognized by France in the Treaty of Utrecht of 1713.[9] The British claim to Conception Bay (and other bays of Newfoundland) dates back to at least 1819 and was upheld by the Privy Council in the 1877 case of *Direct US Cable Company* v *The Anglo-American Telegraphic Company*.[10] Similarly Britain asserted sovereignty over the waters of the Bay of Fundy in the eighteenth and nineteenth centuries.[11] Britain (and earlier France) in the eighteenth century also claimed the Gulf of St Lawrence; the Treaty of Paris of 1763 would seem to indicate that both countries then acknowledged that these waters were 'national' and that access to the fisheries therein was a privilege to be granted by the territorial sovereign.[12]

After Trafalgar, however, British policy emphasized the freedom of the high seas and resisted claims to 'domination' beyond the three-mile marginal sea. This process culminated in the Customs Consolidation Act of 1876 after which, according to Colombos, 'the invariable practice of Great Britain has been to uphold the three-mile distance.'[13]

The effects of the new British policy for Canada were soon felt. Nevertheless, British influence remained important for a considerable period. In 1930 the answers of both Canada and Britain to the questionnaire circulated prior to the Hague Codification Conference reflected the same approach to the law of the sea (with the exception, however, that Canada listed 'geographic' as well as historic bays as being exempt from the ten-mile baseline rule).[14] It was not until the years following World War II that the divergences between the respective maritime policies of the two countries were to lead them to quite opposite stands on issues of coastal jurisdiction.

UNITED STATES INFLUENCE

As Canada's neighbour, and ultimately as the world's leading maritime power, the interests and policies of the United States have provided the other important element in the interplay of factors which have influenced Canada's maritime claims. Shortly after attaining independence the United States espoused the doctrine of the three-mile limit for 'exclusive pretensions to the sea,' although the United States has not considered it inconsistent with that position to claim certain rights of jurisdiction and control beyond that limit.[15] However, while being in essential agreement on this approach, the United States and Britain (on behalf of Canada) nevertheless became involved in a century-long conflict over the Atlantic fisheries of British North America. After the War of Independence, the new American republic was anxious to preserve for its nationals the same right to fish in British North American waters which they had enjoyed as British subjects. This led to a series of disputes and treaties culminating in the 1910 North Atlantic Coast Fisheries Arbitration heard before the Permanent Court at the Hague and revolving about the interpretation and application of article I of the Convention of 20 October 1818 between Britain and the United States.

In its decision the court upheld the right of the United States to common enjoyment of the inshore fisheries along certain areas of the Canadian Atlantic coast pursuant to the 1818 Convention, as well as the right of the British to regulate those fisheries in a reasonable and equitable manner. For those areas of the Canadian coast in which the United States under the 1818 Convention had renounced its 'liberty' to fish, the court decided that the line of exclusion should be i / three miles from a straight line drawn across the entrances to bays at the place where they ceased to have the configuration and characteristics of a bay, and ii / in all other cases, three miles from the sinuosities of the coast. The findings of the court were substantially incorporated in the Treaty of Washington of 1912, together with the court's recommendation that, in every bay not specifically provided for, the closing line should be drawn in the part nearest the entrance at the first point where the width did not exceed ten miles. (The 1912 treaty did not deal with Hudson Bay or delimit the bays of Newfoundland.)[16]

The decision in the North Atlantic Coast Fisheries Arbitration is of fundamental importance in the history of Canada's maritime claims. It may be seen both as having substantially recognized the principal Canadian claims at issue in the case and as having confirmed the limitations upon them vis à vis the United States. And it marked the end of a bitter controversy with the United States over the North Atlantic fisheries (a result which in the long run may have been assisted by the fact that United States fishermen gradually began to lose interest in those fisheries). It did not, however, completely lay to rest the underlying differences of views on maritime policy which continued sporadically to trouble the otherwise harmonious fisheries relations of the two countries on the west coast and appeared at the 1958 Law of the Sea Conference.

One of the early problems to appear in fisheries relations on the west coast was the Bering Sea fur seal controversy. In this case it was a United States claim rather than a Canadian one which precipitated the dispute. Some time after the acquisition of Alaska the United States sought to put an end to pelagic sealing in the Alaskan portion of the Bering Sea, on the grounds of urgent conservation needs, while allowing American nationals to take seals on the Bering Sea islands. These attempts to stop pelagic sealing were resisted by Canada in the name of freedom of the high seas, and Canadian vessels were regularly arrested for violating United States sealing regulations. An arbitral tribunal was established to resolve the dispute in 1892. In the light of later developments the arguments put forward in support of the United States and Canadian positions are particularly fascinating. The United States claimed a property right in the fur seals based on a vital territorial link with their place of origin and probable return. The United States also argued the right of self-protection or self-defence against activities threatening the extinction of an industry vital to the economic life of the nation. The British, on behalf of Canada, denied these claims and asserted the right of all states to fish on the high seas. The tribunal upheld the British-Canadian case in deciding that the United States had no right of protection or property in the fur seals outside the three-mile limit and could not regulate the fishery against foreign nationals.[17]

Some years after the Bering Sea arbitration, in 1911, a Convention respecting Measures for the Preservation and Protection of the Fur Seals in the North Pacific Ocean was signed by Britain, the United States, Russia, and Japan. This treaty (ultimately replaced by the 1957 Interim Convention on the Conservation of the North Pacific Fur Seals) was the first of a series of remarkable bilateral and multilateral conventions for the fisheries of the north Pacific. What is significant about these conventions is that despite difficulties and problems, some of which persist to this day, Canada and the United States were able to work out unusually co-operative and innovative arrangements for the conduct of important west coast fisheries. This is due perhaps in part to the parallel interests of the two countries in some important aspects of the development and exploitation of the fisheries concerned – for example, the principle of abstention.

Perhaps the most troublesome factor in the Pacific fisheries relations of Canada and the United States has been the question of Canadian claims to sovereignty over the waters of Dixon Entrance and Hecate Strait. Canada has regarded the line fixed by the 1903 Alaska Boundary Award (the A–B line) as constituting the international maritime boundary in these waters, running from Cape Muzon, Alaska (point A), almost due east to what the tribunal decided was the mouth of the Portland Canal (point B). The Canadian position has been that the waters, and not only the lands, lying south of the A–B line (comprising all the waters of Dixon Entrance and Hecate Strait) are Canadian waters. In this way the Unites States' Dall Island and Prince of Wales Island would be deprived of part of the territorial sea which would normally appertain to them in the absence of an agreement or other disposition to the contrary. This view, however, was not supported by the British, and in 1910 the law officers of the crown in London dismissed the Canadian claim as being unjustified under international law or by treaty rights.

The United States position has been that the 'A–B line' divides only the land territories of the two countries and not their territorial waters, although in the Canadian view this position was advanced by the United States only some years after the 1903 award. United States fishermen throughout the century have fished in the waters of both Dixon Entrance and Hecate Strait up to three miles from the Canadian shore. In addition, the extent of 'Canadian waters' in Dixon Entrance and Hecate Strait was temporarily restricted for customs purposes without 'foregoing any Canadian rights in respect of the waters thus restricted.'[18] Nevertheless, although Canada has not enforced its fisheries regulations against United States nationals (nor its customs regulations against foreign nationals generally) beyond three miles from shore in Hecate Strait and Dixon Entrance, the Canadian government since the 1890s has maintained that these are Canadian waters. Incidents have occurred from time to time to keep the issue alive.[19]

In summary, it can be seen that Canadian fisheries claims, and the underlying claims to sovereignty over wide areas of the sea, came into conflict with United States fishing interests shortly after the United States won its independence. That conflict has been a thread that has intermittently woven its way in and out of the otherwise generally harmonious pattern of fisheries relations between the two countries up to the present.

In addition, as the United States attained to prominence as a world power, and especially as a naval power, fisheries relations became complicated by strategic considerations. United States security interests have been seen as demanding the maximim freedom and range for American warships and aircraft and, as a corollary, the minimum assertion by states of coastal jurisdiction beyond three miles. In the wake of unilateral claims made by other states (especially of Latin America) following the equally unilateral 1945 Truman Proclamations on the continental shelf and on fisheries conservation, the United States has been concerned with the phenomenon of so-called 'creeping jurisdiction' and its possible effects on the mobility of its nuclear submarines.[20] As an ally of the United States in NATO and NORAD, Canada has shared the concern of the United States for North American security, but that common concern has not meant identical views on maritime policy and has not prevented the two countries from taking quite opposite positions on issues of coastal jurisdiction.[21]

POSTWAR DEVELOPMENTS

In the years following the end of the World War II Canada, like many other smaller and younger powers, became increasingly preoccupied with the question of extending its jurisdiction over coastal fisheries. Foreign fishing activities off both the Atlantic and Pacific coasts were expanding rapidly and gave rise to serious concern. Numerous precedents were set of unilateral claims to maritime sovereignty or jurisdiction out to twelve miles and well beyond following the Truman Proclamations on the continental shelf and on fishing. As a condition of the entry of Newfoundland into Confederation the Canadian government agreed to apply the headland-to-headland rule for the measurement of the territorial waters along the coasts of the new province. With the fundamental change in circumstances brought about in the Gulf of St Lawrence with Newfoundland's entry into Confederation, Canada (following the much earlier British lead) announced its intention to claim and seek acquiescence in the claim that the gulf should become an 'inland sea.' The 1951 *Anglo-Norwegian Fisheries* case, which upheld Norway's application of the straight baseline system for the measurement of the territorial sea along its coast, was seen by the government as having important implications for the Canadian coastline and as being applicable to 'many parts of the Canadian shores.'[22]

This, then, was the immediate background to the 1958 and 1960 Conferences on the Law of the Sea. Canada, in common with many other states, wanted greater protection for its coastal fisheries. Unlike some other states, however, it was not prepared to claim that protection unilaterally, and the government made clear that its intention was to seek multilateral agreement on 'territorial waters.' Out of concern for the security interests so heavily emphasized by Britain and the United States, and taking into account that the basic Canadian interest lay in resources rather than extensions of sovereignty, Canada proposed at the UN General Assembly in 1956 a formula whereby a fishing zone could be established beyond the traditional three-mile limit of the territorial sea. This separation of specialized jurisdiction from sovereignty had its roots, of course, in both British and United States practice. Neither Britain nor the United States, however, was prepared to go all the way with Canada at the 1958 conference. The United States introduced its own proposal for a six-mile territorial sea (thus abandoning the three-mile limit before Canada) and a six-mile contiguous fishing zone in which 'traditional rights' would be recognized in perpetuity. Britain for its part proposed a six-mile territorial sea which was in effect a three-mile territorial sea with an additional three-mile fishing zone. Accordingly Canada converted its own proposal to the six-plus-six formula but, in the face of opposition from the United States, Britain, France, the USSR, and others, was unable to obtain the necessary two-thirds majority. At the 1960 conference the United States and Britain ultimately supported a slightly modified compromise version of the Canadian six-plus-six formula, which failed by one vote to obtain two-thirds approval.[23]

The failure of the 1958 and 1960 Conferences on the Law of the Sea to resolve the question of the territorial sea and fishing limits marked an important turning point in the evolution of Canada's maritime policy and maritime claims. Until that point Canada had generally followed the path of negotiation, arbitration, and bilateral and multilateral agreement in respect of its claims. That path was not abandoned in the years following the 1958 and 1960 conferences, but a further element was added or at least reinforced: unilateralism. In effect Canada then dipped into one of the 'two parallel streams' of the history of the law of the sea as described by Lauterpacht; namely, the unilateral assumption of protective jurisdiction for special purposes within zones contiguous to the territorial sea.[24] This phenomenon – whose origins and attempted suppression owe so much to British and United States practice – was to become an essential element in Canadian law of the sea policy, without, however, entirely displacing the traditional basic emphasis on bilateral and multilateral agreements.

1964 LEGISLATION

After 1960 the Canadian government made one more attempt to find a multilateral solution to the coastal fisheries problem which the 1958 and 1960 conferences had failed to provide. Despite the failure at Geneva, Canada joined with Britain in canvassing countries around the world to ask them to join in a multilateral treaty based on the six-plus-six formula. This effort was supported by more than forty countries but not by the United States, and so came to nothing. Accordingly, by 1963 the Canadian government had decided that the protection of Canada's resources necessitated the establishment of a fishing zone without awaiting international agreement.[25] A bill to this effect was introduced in mid-1964.

The 1964 Territorial Sea and Fishing Zones Act provided the first general purpose definition of the breadth of the Canadian territorial sea, retaining the traditional three-mile limit.[26] It made the straight baseline system applicable to the Canadian coasts (with implementation of this provision left to the governor in council). And it established a nine-mile fishing zone contiguous to the three-mile territorial sea. By order in council the fishing vessels of the United States were allowed to continue to fish in the contiguous fishing zones on both the east and west coasts, and the fishing vessels of France, Britain, Portugal, Spain, Italy, Norway, and Denmark on the east coast, pending the conclusion of negotiations under way with each of these countries.[27] It was made clear that France and the US, the only two countries having treaty rights to fish in Canadian waters, would be allowed to continue their activities in the areas concerned, subject to agreed arrangements and conservation regulations, but that the traditional fishing practices of the other countries named in the order in council would be subject to phasing-out arrangements.[28]

Some three years later, in October 1967, the first list of geographical co-ordinates of points for the establishment of straight baselines was issued by the governor in council.[29] That list established straight baselines for the measurement of the territorial sea along the coast of Labrador and the eastern and southern coasts of Newfoundland. A second list was issued in 1969 establishing straight baselines along the eastern and southern coasts of Nova Scotia and the western coasts of Vancouver Island and the Queen Charlotte Islands.[30]

These various measures left unresolved questions associated with some of Canada's major claims to maritime sovereignty or jurisdiction, namely the claims relating to the Bay of Fundy, the Gulf of St Lawrence, and Dixon Entrance and Hecate Strait, all areas for which no baselines were promulgated in 1967 and 1969 (together with Hudson Bay and Strait and the waters of the Canadian Arctic archipelago). The Canadian claim to Dixon Entrance and Hecate Strait has already been discussed. It has also been noted that in 1949 the Canadian government had announced its intention to claim the Gulf of St Lawrence as an 'inland sea.' As for the Bay of Fundy, it came into prominence in November 1962 when the Canadian prime minister made clear in the House of Commons that this bay constituted Canadian internal waters and that Soviet trawlers which had been sighted there would be requested to leave.[31]

At about this same time, however, yet another claim began to emerge, that to Queen Charlotte Sound on the Pacific coast. This claim, which had no apparent antecedent in British or Canadian practice, was suggested in a brief submitted to the Canadian government by the Fisheries Council of Canada in January 1963.[32] The Fisheries Council recommended that straight baselines be drawn, *inter alia,* across the entrances to Queen Charlotte Sound, Dixon Entrance-Hecate Strait, the Bay of Fundy, and the Gulf of St Lawrence. Although the government had indicated that it would accept the council's recommendations as the basis of its negotiations with other countries,[33] these areas, as already noted, were not included among those covered in the 1967 and 1969 orders in council. However, in announcing the promulgation of the 1969 baselines to the House of Commons on 4 June 1969, the secretary of state for external affairs declared that the government would deal with these 'gaps' by an amendment to the Territorial Sea and Fishing Zones Act that would permit them to be enclosed within 'fisheries closing lines' without affecting the limits of Canada's internal waters and territorial sea.[34]

1970 LEGISLATION

It was against this background that the Canadian government introduced two bills before parliament in April 1970: the Bill to amend the Territorial Sea and Fishing Zones Act, and the Arctic Waters Pollution Prevention Bill. These received royal assent on 26 June 1970, with the latter providing one of the rare examples of an item of legislation being unanimously approved by parliament.[35] It is with the introduction of these statutes that new, environmental concerns come to assume equal if not greater prominence than resource interests as the essential foundation of Canadian maritime policy.

The amended Territorial Sea and Fishing Zones Act extended Canada's territorial sea from three to twelve miles, thus bringing Canadian practice into line with that of the now prevalent international practice and, incidentally, eliminating Canada's former nine-mile contiguous fishing zone. The act also authorized the establishment of new fishing zones in 'areas of the sea adjacent to the coast of Canada.' New fishing zones have since been created within 'fisheries closing lines' established across the entrances to the bodies of water not enclosed within territorial sea baselines by the 1967 and 1969 orders in council, that is, the Bay of Fundy, the Gulf of St Lawrence, Dixon Entrance-Hecate Strait, and Queen Charlotte Sound.[36] Subsequently, amendments to the Canada Shipping Act extended Canada's jurisdiction over both Canadian and foreign vessels in these newly created fishing zones for the further purposes of prevention and control of marine pollution.[37]

The Arctic Waters Pollution Prevention Act added two new dimensions to the international law doctrine of innocent passage. First, it posited that a passage threatening the environmental integrity of the coastal state could not be regarded as innocent. Second, it implied the applicability of the doctrine of innocent passage (which traditionally applies only to the territorial sea in contradistinction to the doctrine of freedom of navigation which applies to the high seas) independent of any claim of sovereignty. Thus, the legislation was another manifestation of the functional approach whereby a particular form of jurisdiction, rather than full sovereignty, is claimed and exercised for special purposes. Under the terms of the legislation, the waters of the Arctic archipelago, and the Northwest Passage in particular, are open to shipping subject to the necessary conditions for the protection of the ecological balance of Canada's Arctic islands and the adjacent marine environment. Commercially owned shipping entering waters designated by the Canadian government as shipping safety control zones is required to meet Canadian design, construction, equipment, manning, and navigation safety standards. These zones extend up to a hundred miles offshore. Ship and cargo owners are obliged to provide proof of financial responsibility and are liable for pollution damage caused by them; this liability will be limited by order in council but does not depend upon proof of fault or negligence. The legislation also extends to land-based activities which could affect the Arctic waters, and to exploration and exploitation of the mineral resources of Canada's Arctic continental shelf.[38]

While stressing the functional approach underlying the Arctic waters legislation and the fisheries provisions of the amended territorial sea legislation, the Canadian government was careful to point out that the establishment of pollution control zones in the Arctic waters and exclusive fishing zones in other bodies of water, could not be construed as being inconsistent with or as an abandonment of claims to sovereignty over the Arctic waters or such other special bodies of water as the Gulf of St Lawrence. The 1910 North Atlantic Coast Fisheries Arbitration was cited as authority for the view that a state may, while claiming sovereignty over the whole of a sea area, exercise only so much of its sovereign powers over all or part of that area as it deems desirable without thereby prejudicing its claim to full sovereignty.[39]

With the introduction of these two items of legislation, the Canadian government also submitted a new declaration of acceptance of the compulsory jurisdiction of the International Court of Justice. The new declaration contained a reservation excluding from the jurisdiction of the court 'disputes arising out of or concerning jurisdiction or rights claimed or exercised by Canada in respect of the conservation, management or exploitation of the living resources of the sea, or in respect of the prevention or control of pollution or contamination of the marine environment in marine areas adjacent to the coast of Canada.'[40] The government indicated that while remaining attached to the rule of law and maintaining its respect for the International Court of Justice, it was not prepared to litigate on vital issues where the law was 'inadequate, non-existent or irrelevant' or did not provide a firm basis for decision.[41] Ministers also pointed out that the new reservation did not apply to claims to maritime *sovereignty* such as, for instance, the extension of the territorial sea to twelve miles.[42]

The amended Territorial Sea and Fishing Zones Act and the Arctic Waters Pollution Prevention Act met with a prompt response from the United States and led to what may be one of the more acerbic exchanges in the history of diplomatic communications between the two countries. (The 1964 territorial sea legislation had also aroused public objections by the United States, and Canadian government spokesmen did not miss the opportunity to point out, in introducing the 1970 legislation, that the United States had adopted a nine-mile contiguous fishing zone in 1966 after having expressed disagreement with the same action by Canada in 1964.)[43] In a press release giving the substance of its official note to the Canadian government, the United States declared that international law provided no basis for these 'unilateral extensions of jurisdictions on the high seas' and that the United States could 'neither accept nor acquiesce in the assertion of such jurisdiction.' Concern was expressed that this action by Canada would be taken as a precedent in other parts of the world for 'other unilateral infringements of the freedom of the seas' and for claims to exercise jurisdiction for other purposes, 'some reasonable and some not, but all equally invalid according to international law,' with the result that 'merchant shipping would be severely restricted, and naval mobility would be seriously jeopardized.'[44] In its reply the Canadian government made clear that it could not accept the United States government's views concerning the Arctic waters legislation and the amendments to the Territorial Sea and Fishing Zones Act, and it cited United States precedents with respect to the exercise of jurisdiction beyond a three-mile territorial sea as indicating that the United States itself did not adhere to these views in practice. The Canadian reply characterized the Arctic waters legislation as a lawful extension of a limited form of jurisdiction to meet particular dangers and thus as being of a different order from 'unilateral interferences with the freedom of the high seas such as, for example, the atomic tests carried out by the US and other states.' The Canadian note went on to stress the inadequacies of international law with respect to the protection of the marine environment and the conservation of fisheries resources, and declared that the Canadian government was not prepared to abdicate its own responsibilities in these matters while awaiting the gradual development of international law. The note also emphasized the importance of state practice in the development of customary international law and justified the Arctic waters legislation as being based on the 'overriding right of self-defence of coastal states to protect themselves against growing threats to their environment.' Finally, the note argued that traditional concepts of the law of the sea were particularly irrelevant to the unique characteristics of the Arctic marine environment and reaffirmed the Canadian position that the waters of the Arctic archipelago, and the Northwest Passage in particular, are not high seas but Canadian waters.[45] (Following this exchange a further press release was issued by the Department of State on 18 December 1970 expressing the United States' objections to the Canadian government announcement of the establishment of 'fisheries closing lines' in the Gulf of St Lawrence, Bay of Fundy, Dixon Entrance-Hecate Strait, and Queen Charlotte Sound.)[46]

The negotiations begun in 1964 with respect to the traditional fishing practices of Britain, Norway, Denmark, France, Portugal, Spain, and Italy, and with respect to the treaty fishing rights of France, had not been concluded when the amended Territorial Sea and Fishing Zones Act was introduced in 1970. The Canadian government indicated, however, that the new legislation would help to bring these negotiations to an end, while reaffirming its intention to respect the treaty rights of the United States and France.[47] Indeed, an agreement had already been concluded with the United States allowing the fishermen of both countries to continue, on a reciprocal basis, the commercial fisheries which they had carried out up to three miles off the coasts of the other country prior to the first establishment of exclusive fishing zones by either Canada or the United States.[48] Subsequently, agreements were also concluded with Britain, Denmark, Norway, and Portugal concerning their traditional fishing practices in the Gulf of St Lawrence and the outer nine miles of the territorial sea off Canada's east coast; an agreement was also signed with France concerning its treaty fishing rights.[49]

The agreements with Britain, Denmark, Norway, and Portugal provided for the gradual phasing out of the traditional fisheries of these countries in the east coast areas concerned, with the latest terminal date being before the end of the present decade. The agreement with France provided for the termination of fishing activities by metropolitan French trawlers in these same areas but allowed continued fishing by a limited number of St Pierre and Miquelon vessels, subject to reciprocal treatment for Canadian vessels in the waters off the coast of the French islands; this same agreement also fixed the territorial sea dividing line between

Newfoundland and St Pierre and Miquelon (but not the continental shelf boundary south of the French islands). The fisheries phasing-out agreement with Norway was accompanied by a separate agreement on Norwegian sealing operations which provided for conservation measures to ensure the protection of seal stocks in the northwest Atlantic and allowed Norwegian sealing operations in the Canadian territorial sea on the east coast on an occasional and strictly regulated basis and subject to termination by 1978 if so desired. With regard to Spanish fishing practices, the negotiation of an agreement took somewhat longer; that agreement is generally similar to those dealing with traditional fishing practices of other countries but contains a number of special provisions. No announcement has been made about possible negotiations with Italy; that country appears, in any event, to have discontinued its traditional fishing practices off Canada's east coast.

PRESENT STATUS OF CLAIMS

Newfoundland Bays

All of the bays on the south and east coasts of Newfoundland have now been enclosed within the straight baseline system and so constitute internal waters of Canada. A new order in council was issued on 9 May 1972 revoking orders in council [1967] P.C. 2025 and [1969] P.C. 1109 and reissuing essentially the same geographic co-ordinates as had been included in the latter orders with certain minor revisions respecting the use of low-tide elevations as baselines for measuring the breadth of the territorial sea.[50] In addition, the new order incorporates the territorial sea dividing line between Newfoundland and St Pierre and Miquelon recently negotiated with France and establishes straight baselines for Fortune and Connaigre Bays on the south coast of Newfoundland (which had not been covered by the earlier orders in council).[51]

Bay of Fundy

This area has now been established as an exclusive fishing zone by a 'fisheries closing line' drawn from Whipple Point, Nova Scotia, to Garnet Rock, then to Yellow Ledge, Machias Seal Island and North Rock, and thence along Grand Manan Island to the Canada/United States boundary in Grand Manan Channel. Within this area, Canada also exercises comprehensive anti-pollution authority over all vessels pursuant to the 1971 amendments to the Canada Shipping Act. That the assertion of these special jurisdictions is not inconsistent with Canada's historic claim to the Bay of Fundy was emphasized in statements by government ministers referring to the principle established by the 1910 North Atlantic Coast Fisheries Arbitration. In any event, even if the territorial sea in the Bay of Fundy were to be measured from the sinuosities of the coast, the entire bay (with the exception of a small area that could be regarded as a 'high seas enclave' assimilated to the territorial sea entirely surrounding it) would fall under Canadian sovereignty with the adoption of the twelve-mile limit. It is perhaps important to note that the territorial sea, and hence Canadian fisheries jurisdiction, extends beyond the 'fisheries closing line' drawn across the entrance to the bay.

Gulf of St Lawrence

This area has been established as an exclusive Canadian fishing zone by a 'fisheries closing line' across Cabot Strait and the Strait of Belle Isle. As in the case of the other new fishing zones, Canada now also exercises anti-pollution authority in respect of all vessels within the gulf. Again, it appears that the assertion of special jurisdictions within the Gulf does not constitute an abandonment of the underlying claim to full sovereignty.

Dixon Entrance-Hecate Strait

This area has been established as an exclusive Canadian fishing zone by a 'fisheries closing line' from Langara Island (Queen Charlotte Islands) to point A (Cape Muzon, Alaska) of the A–B line' established by the 1903 Alaska Boundary Award. The amendments to the Canada Shipping Act already referred to also provide for the exercise of Canadian anti-pollution authority over all vessels in these waters. Recent incidents involving interference with Canadian vessels by the US Coastguard south of the 'A–B line' have led to reaffirmations of Canadian sovereignty over the area. According to government spokesmen, Canada has indicated its willingness in principle to hold talks with the United States with a view to avoiding further incidents and achieving a 'satisfactory resolution of the Dixon Entrance problem.'[52]

Queen Charlotte Sound

This area has been established as an exclusive fishing zone by a 'fisheries closing line' extending from Winifred Island (Vancouver Island) to Beresford Islands, Sartine Islands, and Triangle Islands and thence to the Kerouard Islands and Kunglit Island (Queen Charlotte Islands). Again, Canada now exercises anti-pollution authority in these waters under the Canada Shipping Act. As already noted, this claim was first proposed by the Fisheries Council of Canada in 1963 and appears to have no previous historic antecedent.

Arctic waters

Under the Arctic Waters Pollution Prevention Act, Canada will exercise jurisdiction over all vessels within one hundred miles from shore in the waters and ice adjacent to the Canadian Arctic islands for purposes of navigation safety and the prevention of pollution. While emphasizing that this legislation did not represent an assertion of sovereignty, government ministers have also affirmed that Canada has always regarded the waters between the waters of the archipelago as being Canadian waters. Particular emphasis has been laid on the implications of the twelve-mile territorial sea with respect to the Northwest Passage, where the new limit brings part of Barrow Strait as well as the whole of Prince of Wales Strait within full Canadian sovereignty under 'any sensible view of the law,' whether or not it might be alleged 'that other waters are not Canadian.' It has also been suggested that the status of the waters of the Arctic archipelago might fall 'somewhere between the regime of internal waters and the regime of the territorial sea.'[53] (For a further discussion of questions relating to the Arctic waters see the separate chapter by Professor Pharand.)

Hudson Bay and Strait

No straight baseline (or 'fisheries closing line') has been drawn across the entrance of Hudson Strait under the 1964 or 1970 legislation. However, a 1906 amendment to the Fisheries Act made clear that 'Hudson Bay is wholly territorial water of Canada,'[54] and an order in council of 18 December 1937 established a territorial waters baseline across the eastern entrance to Hudson Strait, from Button Island to Resolution Island.[55] There would appear to be no doubt that this claim is firmly established in both law and practice.

CONTINENTAL SHELF CLAIMS

In addition to the traditional fisheries claims already discussed, Canada's attention since World War II has been increasingly drawn towards the potential mineral wealth of the seabed adjacent to its shores. In his report to the House of Commons on Canada's participation in the 1958 Law of the Sea Conference, the Minister of Northern Affairs and National Resources, Mr Hamilton, stressed the 'particular significance to Canada' of the Convention on the Continental Shelf and indicated that it could have 'consequences of far-reaching importance to Canada in the development of underwater oil and mineral resources.'[56] Since that time, the pace of exploration activities in Canada's offshore areas has increased rapidly. In a statement to the House of Commons on 9 March 1970 the Minister of Energy, Mines and Resources, Mr Greene, noted that oil and gas permits had been issued, some at depths as great as twelve thousand feet, for 'more than half the total area of Canada's continental margin,' which he described as comprising a total area of 1.5 million square miles.[57]

Canadian policy with respect to the development of an international regime for the resources of the seabed and ocean floor beyond the limits of national jurisdiction is discussed in a separate chapter. What is of interest from the point of view of Canadian maritime claims is the Canadian position on the limits of national jurisdiction, bearing in mind the elastic definition of these limits in the 1958 Convention on the Continental Shelf (ie, the two hundred metre isobath or, beyond, to the limits of exploitability). While it is established doctrine that Canada like every other coastal state enjoys exclusive sovereign rights in respect of the exploration and exploitation of its continental shelf, differences of views exist as to how far out these rights extend under existing law and how far out they should extend under the new legal regime under discussion in the United Nations. On this question the Canadian position has been described as being founded on both the provisions of the Continental Shelf Convention and the decision of the International Court of Justice in the *North Sea Continental Shelf* cases. Canada's claim to the 'submerged continental margin' has been reiterated on a number of occasions and the margin has been defined as consisting of the 'continental shelf and slope and at least part of the rise.'[58] It is understood that the part of the rise in question is that part overlying the slope. On this basis Canada's continental shelf would extend only a few miles off the Queen Charlotte Islands and, if Flemish Cap is included, more that four hundred miles offshore due east of Newfoundland.

Of equal interest is the Canadian view of the nature as well as the geographic extent of the coastal state's jurisdiction. The interpretative declaration appended to Canada's ratification of the Seabed Arms Control Treaty is of particular significance in this regard.[59] The declaration enunciates Canada's view that: a / the Seabed Arms Control Treaty cannot be interpreted as allowing states to place non-prohibited (ie, conventional) weapons on the seabed and ocean floor beyond the limits of national jurisdiction (ie, beyond the juridical limits of the continental shelf), or to use this area for anything but peaceful purposes; b / the treaty cannot be interpreted as allowing any state other than the coastal state to place non-prohibited weapons on its continental shelf; and c / the treaty cannot be interpreted as in any way restricting the right of the coastal state to carry out inspection and removal of any weapons or installations on its continental shelf.[60]

While it is beyond the scope of this chapter to deal with questions relating to the delimitation of Canada's continental shelf boundaries with neighbouring states, it should be noted that the need for such delimitation arises in respect of the following areas: with the United States, in the Beaufort Sea, in the regions of Dixon Entrance and Juan de Fuca Strait, and in the Gulf of Maine; with France, in the area southwards of St Pierre and Miquelon (the territorial sea boundary between St Pierre and Miquelon and Newfoundland already having been delimited as noted above); and finally, with Denmark, in the area between Greenland and northern Canada.

CONCLUSION

Canada's maritime claims may well be among the largest in the world, embracing as they do such vast expanses as Hudson Bay and the Gulf of St Lawrence. They have their origins in resource interests, geography, and in history, many of them dating back to the British colonial period. They have occasioned differences with some of Canada's closest friends and allies and especially the United States, particularly in recent years when Canada has felt obliged to advance and protect its interests by unilateral action. It is important, however, to look behind the controversial term 'unilateralism' for a proper understanding of Canada's actions.

To begin with, Canada did not take unilateral action without having made exhaustive multilateral efforts over a period of many years to secure what it considered to be its legitimate interests. The background to Canada's unilateral ventures was well described by Senator Robichaud in the Senate on 10 June 1970 in the following terms:

These [multilateral] efforts, I believe, have failed largely because the major maritime states have been rigid and inflexible in their views. They have too often confused national interests with international imperatives. As a result there has developed what has been called the 'tyranny' of the traditional concept of the freedom of the seas. Although some concessions have been made to the interests of the newer states and the new needs arising from developing technology, these concessions have been too modest, they have come too late, and they have had too many strings attached.[61]

Another important consideration to be taken into account in assessing Canada's actions is the role of state practice in the development of international law. On this question the Canadian view was succinctly expressed in a statement to the United Nations General Assembly on 4 December 1970:

> The contemporary international law of the sea comprises both conventional and customary law. Conventional or multilateral treaty law must, of course, be developed primarily by multilateral action, drawing as necessary upon principles of customary international law. Thus multilateral conventions often consist of both a codification of existing principles of international law and progressive development of new principles. Customary international law is, of course, derived primarily from state practice, that is to say, unilateral action by various states, although it frequently draws in turn upon the principles embodied in bilateral and limited multilateral treaties. Law-making treaties often become accepted as such not by virtue of their status as treaties, but through a gradual acceptance by states of the principles they lay down ... Unilateralism carried to an extreme and based upon differing or conflicting principles could produce complete chaos. Unilateral action when taken along parallel lines and based upon similar principles can lead to a new regional and perhaps even universal rule of law. Similarly, agreement by the international community reached through a multilateral approach can produce effective rules of law, while doctrinaire insistence upon the multilateral approach as the only legitimate means of developing the law can lead to the situation which has prevailed since the failure of the two Geneva Law of the Sea Conferences to reach agreement upon the breadth of the territorial sea and fishing zones.[62]

Finally, it is important to note that Canada has sought to accommodate as much as possible the interests of other countries affected by Canada's unilateral initiatives, often at the cost of severe domestic political criticism. This accommodation of the interests of other countries has led, first of all, to restrictions on the qualitative scope of the Canadian claims. Thus they have been limited generally to extensions of functional jurisdiction for special purposes and cannot be said to have had any significant impact on freedom of navigation responsibly exercised. By way of further accommodation, Canada has not sought to terminate unilaterally either treaty fishing rights or traditional fishing practices; the former have become the subject of new arrangements and the latter are being phased out gradually and by agreement.

It is, of course, to the 1951 *Anglo-Norwegian Fisheries* case that Canada owes the recognition of the straight baseline system which Canada has used to its advantage. Canada, however, has not simply ignored the other principle established by that same case, namely that the delimitation of sea areas 'cannot be dependent merely upon the will of the coastal state as expressed in its municipal law.' Much the same point was made by Prime Minister Trudeau in the House of Commons in October 1969:

> Membership in a community ... imposes – and properly – certain limitations on the activities of all members. For this reason, while not lowering our guard or abandoning our proper interests, Canada must not appear to live by double standards. We cannot at the same time that we are urging other countries to adhere to regimes designed for the

orderly conduct of international activities, pursue policies inconsistent with that order simply because to do so in a given instance appears to be to our brief advantage. Law, be it municipal or international, is composed of restraints. If wisely construed they contribute to the freedom and the well-being of individuals and of states. Neither states nor individuals should feel free to pick and choose, to accept or reject, the laws that may for the moment be attractive to them.[63]

This recognition of the restraints imposed upon states by law remains an important element in the Canadian approach to the law of the sea and, in particular, to the Third Conference on the Law of the Sea scheduled for 1974. Canada was instrumental in bringing about agreement on the UN resolution calling for this conference and Canada has played a leading role in the preparations for the conference within the United Nations Seabed Committee.[64]

In these preparations Canada has sought to devise a new way of approaching the problems of the law of the sea and to establish new ground for an accommodation in the increasingly sharp conflict between coastal interests, on the one hand, and flag or distant-water interests on the other. To this end Canada has advanced the concepts of 'custodianship' and 'delegation of powers' as vehicles for the development of the future law of the sea. The essence of the policy summarized in the terms 'custodianship' and 'delegation of powers' is simple but nevertheless of fundamental importance: first, the primary or priority interests of the coastal state in all activities in areas of the sea adjacent to its shores must be reflected in international law; second, much of the administration of the law of the future must be 'delegated' to the coastal state and must be based on resource management and environmental management concepts; third, the basis for an accommodation between conflicting interests in the uses of the sea must lie in a better balance between the rights and consequent responsibilities of states, and hence the coastal state must exercise both its existing sovereign powers and its future 'delegated' powers not only in its own interests but as 'custodian' of vital community interests in the uses of the sea, on the basis of internationally agreed principles to this end.

This Canadian policy, and the twin concepts in which it has been encapsulated, applies to the whole range of issues of the law of the sea. Where acquired well-established rights are concerned, as in the case of the coastal state's sovereignty over the territorial sea or its exclusive sovereign rights over the continental shelf, the notion of custodianship implies that the coastal state must exercise those rights with due regard to the shared interest of all states in, for instance, innocent passage through the territorial sea and freedom of navigation in the superjacent waters of the continental shelf. From this point of view the notion of custodianship has a self-denying effect; it highlights the limitations already inherent in various recognized forms of maritime sovereignty and jurisdiction under traditional law, and presents them as positive duties owed by the coastal state to the international community. Where new or extended rights are sought to be acquired, such as anti-pollution authority in areas adjacent to the territorial sea, custodianship rides piggyback on the concept of delegation of powers (which, of course, does not apply to sovereign powers already acquired). Thus, on the one hand the concept of delegation of powers is acquisitive in effect and serves as a legal fiction (in the best sense of that term) under which legitimate aspirations of the coastal state can be satisfied; on the other hand it also carries with it the self-denying aspects of custodianship and hence does not open the door to unbridled arbitrary action by the coastal state. The idea, of course, is that states should not claim benefits without accepting corresponding obligations. (The concepts of custodianship and delegation of powers can, of course, be applied even to the right of flag states to navigate the high seas, which should also entail certain duties and responsibilities.) That some states may claim the obligations in order to gain access to the benefits in no way detracts from the essential objective of balancing rights and responsibilities.[65]

It is worth noting that the concept of custodianship is fundamental to perhaps the most important initiative which Canada has ever taken in its domestic maritime legislation, the Arctic Waters Pollution Prevention Act. In discussing the alternative approaches available with respect to the pollution of Arctic waters, Prime Minister Trudeau described Canadian policy in terms which aptly describe what is meant by custodianship:

> To close off those [Arctic] waters and to deny passage to all foreign vessels in the name of Canadian sovereignty, as some commentators have suggested, would be as senseless as placing barriers across the entrance to Halifax and Vancouver harbours ... On the other hand, if we were to act in some misguided spirit of international philanthropy by declaring that all comers were welcome without let or hindrance, we would be acting in default of Canada's obligations not just to Canadians but to all of the world ... For these reasons ... Canada regards herself as responsible to all mankind for the peculiar ecological balance that now exists so precariously in the water, ice and land areas of the Arctic archipelago.[66]

These concepts of custodianship and delegation of powers underlie Canada's policy in response to new demands for further extensions of Canada's fisheries jurisdiction. For, the old Canadian claims having been effectively secured, new claims are being pressed upon the government by the Fisheries Council of Canada which is now seeking to have established Canada's ownership of the non-sedentary species inhabiting the waters above the Canadian continental shelf.[67] However, rather than asserting such a claim to ownership, Canada is pressing for international agreement on the concept that the coastal state has a special interest in and special responsibility for the conservation and management of the living resources of the sea adjacent to its coasts beyond its territorial sea and exclusive fishing zones. The Canadian approach distinguishes between coastal, anadromous, and oceanic species and the management systems to be devised for each of these. With regard to coastal species – that is, the free-swimming or non-sedentary species that inhabit the relatively shallow waters adjacent to the coast – Canada has proposed a resource management system under which the coastal state would assume the responsibility, and be 'delegated' the required powers, for their conservation and management as 'custodian' for the international community. Under this system the coastal state would not have the exclusive right to exploit the non-sedentary species of its continental shelf. It would, however, obtain preferential rights and a preferential share – which could be as much as 100 per cent in some cases – in the harvest of those stocks of particular importance to the coastal population. The coastal state would, moreover, have the clear authority to regulate and control the exploitation of coastal species on the basis of internationally agreed principles, subject to review of the exercise of that authority by an international tribunal in the event of disputes with other states. This approach, in essence, would more clearly define the special interest of the coastal state already recognized in the 1958 Geneva Convention on Fishing and the Conservation of the Living Resources of the High Seas, and would give it effect in a practical, workable way while retaining the necessary safeguards against unreasonable action.[68]

Canada – and indeed the international community as a whole – is entering a new phase in the history of maritime claim and counter-claim. Canada is bringing to this new phase an approach which remains founded on national interests in the protection of coastal resources and the coastal environment. At the same time, however, Canada brings to the preparations for Third Law of the Sea Conference an imaginative, constructive approach which recognizes that there are limits to what can or should be done by unilateral action; that beyond the necessary accommodation between various national interests there are overriding international interests that must be secured; and that to the old concept of freedom of the seas there must be allied concepts of rational, responsible management not only of marine resources but of the marine environment as a whole. It is now more than ever essential that a new order be developed for the seas and oceans of the world before chaos, anarchy, and conflict take over Britannia's old job of ruling the waves. In the end, it is only in international agreement that an abiding solution can be found for the problems underlying the maritime claims of Canada and other countries.

NOTES

1 J.-Y. Morin, 'Les eaux territoriales du Canada au regard du Droit international' (1963), *Can. Y.B. Int'l. L.* 86.
2 *Canada Yearbook* (1970–1) 651.
3   i Agreement between the Government of Canada and the Government of Denmark concerning Fisheries Relations between the Two Countries (Ottawa, 27 March 1972).
  ii Agreement between Canada and France on their Mutual Fishing Relations (Ottawa, 27 March 1972).
  iii Exchange of Notes between the Government of Canada and the Government of Norway constituting an Agreement with respect to Norwegian Fishing Practices off the Atlantic Coast of Canada (Ottawa, 15 July 1971).
  iv Agreement between the Government of Canada and the Government of Norway on Sealing and the Conservation of Seal Stocks in the Northeast Atlantic (Ottawa, 15 July 1971).
  v Exchange of Notes between the Government of Canada and the Government of Portugal concerning Fisheries Relations between the Two Countries (Ottawa, 27 March 1972).
  vi Exchange of Notes between the Government of Canada and the Government of the United Kingdom concerning Fisheries Relations between the Two Countries, (Ottawa, 27 March 1972).
  vii Agreement between the Government of Canada and the Government of the United States of America on Reciprocal Fishing Privileges in certain areas off their Coasts (Ottawa, 24 April 1970).
  viii Agreement between the Government of Canada and the Government of the U.S.S.R. on Co-operation in Fisheries in the Northeastern Pacific Ocean off the Coast of Canada (Moscow, 22 January 1971).
  ix Agreement between the Government of Canada and the Government of the U.S.S.R. on Provisional rules of Navigation and Fisheries Safety in the Northeastern Pacific Ocean off the Coast of Canada (Moscow, 22 January 1971).
4 See W.C. Mackenzie, *Fishery Problems in*

the Atlantic Provinces, prepared for the Conference concerning Canada-U.S. Law of the Sea Problems, University of Toronto, 15–17 June 1971.

5 Morin, *supra* note 1, at 86, 145–6.

6 C.J. Colombos, *International Law of the Sea* (6th rev ed, 1967) 48.

7 See W.E. Masterson, *Jurisdiction in Marginal Seas* (1929).

8 Morin, *supra* note 1, at 91.

9 G. Chalmers, ed, *A Collection of Treaties between Great Britain and Other Powers* (1790) VOL I, 379–81.

10 N. MacKenzie and L.H. Laing, eds, *Canada and the Law of Nations* (1938) 88–91.

11 Morin, *supra* note 1, at 104–5; J.-G. Castel, *International Law, Chiefly as Interpreted and Applied in Canada* (1965) 346–8.

12 L. Hertslet, *A Collection of Treaties and Conventions and Reciprocal Regulations between Great Britain and Foreign Powers* (1840) vol I, 239–40.

13 Colombos, *supra* note 6, at 94.

14 For text of Canadian Reply to the Questionnaire see L.N. Doc C 74(a), M 39(a)(1929) V. This difference between the Canadian and British replies is brought out in an unpublished report prepared by Dean G.F. Curtis for the government of Canada in 1954.

15 See P.C. Jessup, *The Law of Territorial Waters and Maritime Jurisdiction* (1927) 49–60.

16 *Ibid,* 363–82; D.M. Johnston, *The International Law of Fisheries* (1965) 190–205; Castel, *supra* note 11, at 294–304, 443–9.

17 See L. Oppenheim, *International Law,* vol I, 499; Johnston, *supra* note 16, 205–10; *British and Foreign State Papers* (1892–93) vol LXXXV, 1158–67. It is another of the anomalies of history that the right of self-defence should have been one of the major arguments invoked by Canada against the United States, and rejected by the United States, in the exchange of communications between the two countries in respect of Canada's 1970 Arctic Waters Pollution Prevention Act. The analogies between the United States position in the fur seal dispute and the Canadian position in the current controversy with Denmark over high seas fishing for Atlantic salmon are obvious. One difference of fundamental importance, however, is that Canada has recently put severe restrictions on its own Atlantic salmon fishing effort, even in its territorial waters, whereas the United States did not forbid other than

pelagic sealing by its own nationals at the time of the fur seal dispute.

18 *Canada Gazette* vol 71, 1929. A proclamation, dated 29 January 1938, to Canadian Order in Council, [1937] P.C. no 3139.

19 For a recent official statement of the Canadian position see the statement by Albert Béchard, parliamentary secretary to the minister of justice, Canada, H.C. *Debates,* 20 September 1971, 8013.

20 See E.D. Brown, *Arms Control in Hydrospace: Legal Aspects* (1971) 90–6; also J.A. Knauss, *Factors Influencing a U.S. Position in A Future Law of the Sea Conference,* Law of the Sea Institute, Occasional Paper no 10 (1971); L.S. Ratiner, 'United States Ocean Policy: An Analysis' (1971); 2 *Journal of Maritime Law and Commerce*; a somewhat unorthodox military view, at least for the time, is given by G.E. Carlisle, US Navy, in 'Three-Mile Limit: Obsolete Concept' (1967), *U.S. Naval Institute Proceedings* 25–33.

21 See statement by the Honourable Mitchell Sharp, secretary of state for external affairs, on introduction of the Arctic Waters Pollution Prevention Bill, in Canada, H.C *Debates,* 16 April 1970, 5952: 'Security factors are vital to us as well as to others. It is because we share the concern to head off developments undesirable for common interests that we ask other states to adopt a flexible attitude which is responsive to new needs and special circumstances, and that we seek the cooperation of other states and offer them ours.'

22 See A.E. Gotlieb, 'The Canadian Contribution to the Concept of a Fishing Zone in International Law' (1964), *Can. Y.B. Int'l L.* 58–62.

23 Ibid, 64–71; see also *The Law of the Sea: A Canadian Proposal* (1962), and Canada, H.C. *Debates,* 25 July 1958, 2678–85.

24 See H. Lauterpacht, 'Sovereignty Over Submarine Areas' (1950), 27 *Brit. Y.B. Int'l L.* 404–7.

25 Canada, H.C. *Debates,* 30 January 1963, 3261; Canada, H.C. *Debates,* 20 May 1964, 3409–10; see also Gotlieb, *supra* note 22, at 74–5.

26 1964, Can., c 22.

27 Canadian Order in Council, [1964] P.C. no 1112.

28 Canada, H.C. *Debates,* 20 May 1964, 3408–12.

29 Canadian Order in Council, [1967] P.C. no 2025.

30 Ibid, [1969] P.C. no 1109.
31 Canada, H.C. *Debates,* 15 November 1962, 1650, and 16 November 1962, 1699–1700.
32 See appendix A, *Proceedings of the Senate Standing Committee on Banking and Commerce,* 7 May 1964, 38–44.
33 Proceedings of the Senate Standing Committee on Banking and Commerce, 7 May 1964, 20.
34 Canada, H.C. *Debates,* 4 June 1969, 9717–18.
35 An Act to amend the Territorial Sea and Fishing Zones Act, 1964, Can., c 63; An Act to Prevent Pollution of Areas of the Arctic Waters adjacent to the Mainland and Islands of the Canadian Arctic, 1970, Can., c 47.
36 Canadian Order in Council, [1971] P.C. no 366. The term 'fisheries closing lines' does not appear in the act or the order in council but is in common usage.
37 1971, Can., c 27.
38 See 'Background Notes on the Arctic Waters Pollution Prevention Bill and the Territorial Sea and Fishing Zones Bill' issued by the Department of External affairs, 8 April 1970; also Canada, H.C. *Debates,* 16 April 1970, 5948–53.
39 Canada, H.C. *Debates,* 16 and 17 April 1970, 5948–53 and 6014–15 respectively; also Senate Debates, 10 June 1970, 1198.
40 (1970–1), 25 *International Court of Justice Yearbook* 49.
41 Canada, H.C. *Debates,* 16 April 1970, 5952.
42 See address by Prime Minister, the Right Honourable Pierre Elliott Trudeau, to the Annual Meeting of the Canadian Press in Toronto on 15 April 1970. Department of External Affairs, *Statements and Speeches,* no 70/3.
43 Canada, H.C. *Debates,* 17 April 1970, 6013.
44 See appendix A: U.S. Press Release on Canada's Claim to Jurisdiction over Arctic Pollution and Territorial Sea Limits. Canada, H.C. *Debates,* 15 April 1970, 5923–4.
45 See appendix: Summary of Canadian Note handed to the U.S. Government. Canada, H.C. *Debates,* 16 April 1970, 6027–30.
46 See Department of State Press Release, no 357, 18 December 1970.
47 Senate *Debates,* 10 June 1970, 1199–1200.
48 Agreement between the Government of Canada and the Government of the United States of America on Reciprocal Fishing Privileges in certain areas off their Coasts (Ottawa, 24 April 1970); extended for one year as of 24 April 1972.
49 *Supra* note 3, i-vi.
50 Canadian Order in Council, [1972] P.C. no 966.
51 *Supra* note 3, ii.
52 Canada, H.C. *Debates,* 20 September 1971, 8013.
53 Ibid, 16 and 17 April 1970, 5948–53 and 6012–17 respectively.
54 1906, Can., c 13.
55 Canadian Order in Council, [1937] P.C. no 3139.
56 Canada, H.C. *Debates,* 25 July 1958, 2680.
57 Ibid, 9 March 1970, 4568–70.
58 See notes for an address, 'Law and Arms Control on the Seabed,' by the Honourable Mitchell Sharp, secretary of state for external affairs, to the International Law Association, Toronto, 5 Nov 1969.
59 Seabed Arms Control Treaty, signed at London, Washington, and Moscow, 11 February 1971. Canadian ratification deposited at London, Washington, and Moscow, 17 May 1972. In force on 18 May 1972.
60 See text of Canadian Declaration attached to Canadian ratification of Seabed Arms Control Treaty.
61 Canada, Senate *Debates,* 10 June 1970, 1196.
62 See statement by Mr J.A. Beesley, Canadian representative in the First Committee, on item 25. Law of the Sea, Press Release no 50, 4 December 1970.
63 Canada, H.C. *Debates,* 24 October 1969, 39.
64 See G.A. Res. 2750, 25 U.N. GAOR (1971). The Canadian role in bringing about agreement on this resolution was stressed in the US State Department's Press Release no 357 of 18 December 1970, which noted that 'Canada, perhaps more than any other country, played a very important lead role in achieving a commitment by the international community to resolve these issues multilaterally.'
65 See statement by Mr J.A. Beesley, legal adviser to the Department of External Affairs and Representative of Canada to the United Nations Committee on the Peaceful Uses of the Seabed and Ocean Floor beyond the Limits of National Jurisdiction, Plenary Session, Geneva, 5 August 1971.
66 Canada, H.C. *Debates,* 24 October 1969, 39; see also J.L. Hargrove, ed, *Law, Institutions, and the Global Environment* (1972) 101, in which the concept of custodianship with respect to the environment is discussed in the following terms in a report on the Conference on Legal and Institutional Responses to Problems of the Global Environment, jointly sponsored by the Carnegie Endow-

ment for International Peace and the American Society of International Law, and held in September 1971: 'The delegation by the international community of authority to the coastal state to act as environmental ''custodian'' over a portion of the ocean adjacent to its own coasts, currently suggested by some, could be predicated on the theory of an international community interest, although in practical fact its proponents are understandably more likely to be motivated by an interest in self-protection than in protecting the community at large.'

67 See Resolution, adopted at the 1972 Annual Meeting, in *Fisheries Council of Canada Bulletin* (1972) 11.

68 See statements by Dr A.W.H. Needler, deputy representative of Canada to the United Nations Committee on the Peaceful Uses of the Seabed and Ocean Floor beyond the Limits of National Jurisdiction, Sub-Committee II, Geneva, 6 August 1971 and by Mr J.A. Beesley, legal Adviser to the Department of External Affairs and Representative of Canada to the United Nations Committee on the Peaceful Uses of the Seabed and Ocean Floor beyond the Limits of National Jurisdiction, Sub-Committee II, New York, 15 March 1972.

J.A. YOGIS

16/Canadian
Fisheries and
International Law

Canadian fisheries and international law have acquired new interest since 1964 when the Territorial Sea and Fishing Zones Act established a twelve-mile exclusive fishing zone and made the straight baseline method applicable to the Canadian coastline.[1] The act was amended in 1970 to extend Canada's territorial sea to twelve miles and to permit the creation of fishing zones in areas of the sea adjacent to the coast of Canada.[2] This legislation is a reflection of the current Canadian practice of recognizing the coastal state's right to exercise fisheries jurisdiction in areas of the sea beyond the traditional three-mile limit.

Two historic principles of international law have had a bearing upon ocean fisheries: first, the principle that within an area of the sea adjacent to its coast a state possesses exclusive rights, and second, the principle that outside such areas the seas are free to all. However, a problem arises from the fact that ocean fisheries are exhaustible.[3] Unless effective means are adopted to prevent them from being overfished, they will be brought to the point of destruction.[4] Canada has been aware of this problem. Participation by foreign fishermen in the fisheries off the east and west coasts has increased significantly since the end of World War II,[5] and to have permitted foreign vessels to continue to take larger and larger catches would have meant an eventual depletion of major stocks. Accordingly, this chapter will discuss Canada's approach to the development of the international law of fisheries.

THE HIGH SEAS FISHERIES TREATIES

It is well accepted that every state has the exclusive right to manage the fisheries within its own territorial waters, subject only to outstanding treaty arrangements. The problem is to determine the extent of territorial waters. How far do they extend and from what line are they to be measured? The United States, Great Britain, Canada, and many other states traditionally favoured a narrow territorial belt; this seemed to be in accord with self-interest and contemporary international practice. At the 1958 and 1960 Geneva Conferences on the Law of the Sea, the proposals that received the widest degree of acceptance called for a territorial sea of from three to twelve miles.[6] While there still does not appear to be any general principle of international law on a precise limit of territorial waters, article 24 of the Convention on the Territorial Sea and the Contiguous Zone may indicate that twelve miles is the presently acceptable maximum limit of the territorial sea.[7] Beyond a state's contiguous waters are the high seas whose resources are traditionally regarded as open to exploitation by all nations. The most recent expression of the principle of freedom of the seas is found in the 1958 Geneva Convention on the High Seas which purports to be declaratory of established principles of international law.[8]

In recent years as technological advances in ocean harvesting have increased fishing intensity, the problem of conserving marine resources has become acute. This situation poses a problem for the international lawyer who must try to determine whether a high seas fishery can be subjected to regulation without violating such established principles as the freedom of the high seas. One way in which high seas fisheries can be regulated is by treaty. If the states whose nationals are prosecuting a particular fishery agree to regulations uniformly applicable to all, allegations of a violation of international law can be avoided. Most of the fishery treaties to which Canada has been a party in the twentieth century have dealt with the management of fisheries on the high seas.

Bilateral treaties

The Pacific halibut fishery
The 1923 treaty between Canada and the United States for the preservation of the halibut fishery of the North Pacific Ocean represents the first attempt in international law to regulate a high seas fishery.[9] The halibut fishery of the north Pacific had been prosecuted by the nationals of Canada and the United States since 1888. Declines in the annual catch were observed before World War I, with a steady fall in yield particularly evident in the period following 1915. Conservation of the fishery was first discussed in 1918, and finally in 1923 a treaty was agreed to by the two governments.[10] The treaty provided for the appointment of an International Fisheries Commission, now the International Pacific Halibut Commission, whose functions were to make investigations and recommendations on the regulation of the halibut fishery of the north Pacific Ocean, including the Bering Sea, which seemed to be desirable for its preservation and development.[11] Subsequent agreements changed the character of the commission from a body that merely investigated and made recommendations to one that was empowered to put regulatory measures into effect. The commission may now carry out such functions as dividing convention waters into areas; limiting the catch to be taken from such areas; and fixing the size and character of halibut fishing appliances.[12] The treaty also authorized the seizure of the nationals or vessels of either party illegally engaged in halibut fishing in extraterritorial waters.[13] Prosecutions, however, could only be carried out by the authorities of the state to which such persons or vessels belonged.

As a result of various bilateral treaties, international regulation of the Pacific halibut fishery has been remarkably successful. When the commission began managing the fishery in 1923 the total annual catch by fishermen of both countries was about 44 million pounds. As a result of conservation measures, the halibut stocks were rebuilt, so that the fishery now yields a total annual catch in the vicinity of 65 million pounds.[14]

The Fraser River sockeye salmon fishery
A second successful example of international management of a fishery, part of which is found on the high seas, involves the sockeye salmon of the Fraser River system. As with the Pacific halibut, the question of protecting the fishery from overexploitation posed an international problem. The fishery is prosecuted by the fishermen of both Canada and the United States, and any regulatory scheme would be

futile unless it were made applicable to the fishermen of both nations.

The Sockeye-Salmon Fisheries Convention, ratified in 1937, established the International Pacific Salmon Commission with authority to limit or prohibit the taking of sockeye salmon in any of the waters described in the convention.[15] The commission may make regulations regarding salmon fishing gear and appliances used on the high seas. As in the Pacific Halibut Convention, duly authorized officers of either party were given the authority to seize any person or vessel engaged in salmon fishing on the high seas in contravention of the convention. Because of the commission's conservation program, a substantial increase in the population of the Pacific salmon has been realized. The number of sockeye salmon returning to the Fraser River is climbing steadily, and there is every indication that the fishery will regain its peak pre-World War I condition. There is also evidence of an increase in the stocks of pink salmon as a result of measures taken since 1956.[16]

The Pacific halibut and salmon conservation treaties are significant for international law purposes because they illustrate programs for managing high seas fisheries that can be carried out in accordance with generally accepted principles. They show, for example, that the problem of conservation can be met while at the same time maintaining the principles of freedom of the seas. The method devised for dealing with offenders is an effective and acceptable international procedure. While authorized officials of either Canada or the United States may seize such offenders on the high seas, they must be turned over to the authorities of their own country who alone have jurisdiction to conduct prosecutions. In this way there is as little interference as possible with the principle that only the state to which a person or vessel belongs has authority to regulate its activities on the high seas.

Multilateral conventions

Management of a high seas fishery in which several nations participate is more difficult; there is a need for more elaborate administrative mechanisms and there is the problem of finding and effecting regulations acceptable to all parties concerned.

The Northwest Atlantic Fisheries Convention
The International Convention for the Northwest Atlantic Fisheries represents the most ambitious attempt to date to manage fisheries in international waters.[17] It was apparent before the signing of the convention that measures would have to be taken to conserve existing stocks (cod, haddock, and red-fish) or to rebuild an almost depleted stock (the halibut).[18] These fisheries are found mainly in the high seas off the west coast of Greenland, Labrador, Newfoundland, Nova Scotia, and New England. Both Canada and the United States participate in these fisheries. However, several other nations are involved: Denmark, France, Iceland, Italy, Norway, Portugal, Spain, and the United Kingdom. As a result of a conference attended by these parties, a Northwest Atlantic Fisheries Convention was concluded at Washington on 8 February 1949. The convention entered into force on 3 July 1950.[19] In addition to the parties mentioned, the governments of the Federal Republic of Germany, the USSR, Poland, and Japan have also ratified the treaty.

The convention established the International Commission for the Northwest

Atlantic Fisheries (ICNAF).[20] The commission is responsible for promoting and co-ordinating scientific studies on stocks which support international fisheries in the northwest Atlantic.[21] It may recommend the application of specified measures in order to keep these stocks at a level permitting the maximum sustained catch.

The commission has six panels, five of which review the status and make proposals for the wise management of the fisheries in a geographic subarea of the convention area, while the sixth reviews the status and submits recommendations respecting harp and hood seals in the convention area.[22] Each panel, upon the basis of scientific investigations, may recommend to the commission, which may in turn recommend to the contracting governments, joint action designed to achieve the optimum utilization of the stocks of those species of fish which support international fisheries in the convention area.[23]

The commission has no direct regulatory powers. Each of its proposals becomes effective for all contracting governments six months after the date of notification from the depository government, the United States.[24] Provision is made for any contracting government affected by a proposal to present an objection to the depository government within the six-month period. A proposal becomes effective for all contracting governments, except those governments which have presented objections within the time period for objecting. A proposal does not become effective if objections have been presented by a majority of governments concerned.

To ensure adherence to its conservation measures, the commission approved unanimously the adoption of an international scheme for inspection at sea.[25] Each contracting government may, under arrangements approved by the commission, appoint inspectors with authority to board a foreign vessel employed in fishing in the convention area. The inspector may make such examination of catch, nets, or other gear, and such relevant documents as he deems necessary, in order to verify the observance of the commission's recommendations in relation to the flag state of the vessel concerned. He must report his findings to the authorities of the flag state of the vessel as soon as possible. Contracting governments must consider and act on reports of foreign inspectors on the same basis as if these reports were reports of national inspectors. Contracting governments must collaborate in order to facilitate judicial or other proceedings arising from a report of an inspector.

Since 1951 ICNAF has in the main carried out studies on the stocks of fish in the convention area, collecting, analysing, and publishing scientific data. As a result of recommendations made to the member countries, regulations regarding the size of the mesh used in taking the more important species have generally been put into effect in the various subareas. While mesh size regulation has been found to be an important conservation measure, it has not been enough to reduce the results of intensive fishing efforts.[26] The commission has introduced additional measures, such as closed areas and closed seasons for particular species of fish. It continues to study the effects of fishing and it reviews the possibility of additional measures. For example, the commission is now attempting to develop principles and concepts that would allow it to set national quotas, taking into account such factors as those countries having special needs in a particular fishery.[27]

Because of geographic proximity and economic necessity, Canada has been active in attempting to have the objectives of the convention realized. Canada's particular concern has been with the serious depletion of the cod and haddock stocks and, more recently, the Atlantic salmon fishery. Recognizing that these and other stocks are of importance to the peoples of the Atlantic provinces, Canada has worked actively in the commission for the application of the commission's research to a rational program of exploitation of these resources. She has found that the application of international conservation measures is often slower than might be desired. Unfortunately measures are sometimes not taken until particular stocks have been seriously overfished.[28]

Canada's position has been that of a nation urging the adoption of regulatory measures designed to rebuild seriously depleted stocks. Canada, as the first state to advocate an international enforcement regime in order to ensure compliance with the commission's recommendations and proposals, was somewhat encouraged when the commission's International Joint Inspection Scheme came into effect on 1 July 1971.[29] However, she has been frustrated by the policies of some states whose failure to adopt restrictive measures may jeopardize the survival of the entire fishery. In December 1971 a joint Canadian-United States statement said that international efforts to achieve a ban on high seas fishing of Atlantic salmon (the fishery is concentrated along the west coast of Greenland) threw into question the survival of the fishery. Denmark and Norway, two of the states chiefly involved in salmon fishing, have objected to an ICNAF ban. Since ICNAF rules apply only to countries which accept them, the prohibition is not binding on two of the states most directly concerned. Such lack of co-operation demonstrates one of the principal difficulties of attempting to provide maximum fishery protection by international convention.

The north Pacific fisheries convention

Perhaps the greatest present problem pertaining to the control and conservation of high seas resources concerns the right of a state or states to restrain the fishing activities of other states when these activities are regarded as a threat to the protection of the stock in question. Early in the 1930s large floating canneries from Japan appeared off the North American coast in the vicinity of Alaska. It was evident that unless restrictions were imposed on Japanese activities, the halibut and salmon fisheries, which were being rebuilt through Canadian-American conservation programs, were liable to be destroyed.[30]

A Tripartite Conference held in Tokyo after World War II produced the International Convention for the High Seas Fisheries of the North Pacific Ocean.[31] This convention is particularly significant because it introduced the principle of abstention into international fisheries agreements. In effect, the convention provides a formula by which any of the contracting parties may be requested to abstain from participating in a fully utilized fishery, if such fishery has been subjected to an extensive conservation program by one or both of the other parties. Japan agreed to abstain from fishing, and Canada and the United States agreed to continue to carry out necessary conservation measures with regard to the halibut, herring, and salmon stocks in specified parts of the convention area off the coasts of Canada and the United States.[32] Canada and Japan agreed to abstain from fishing for salmon in the convention area of Bristol Sea off Alaska, and the United States agreed to continue to carry out there the necessary conservation measures.[33] The convention contained an enforcement procedure similar to that contained in the halibut and salmon conventions between Canada and the United States.[34]

Delegations representing the three parties met at Washington in June 1963 (at Japan's request) to discuss revisions to the convention. All delegations agreed on the continuing need for a treaty, and the Canadians and Americans asserted that conservation was best achieved by retention of the abstention principle.[35] The Japanese argued in favour of discarding the formula on abstention, which Japan regarded as monopolistic and contrary to the generally accepted principle of freedom of fishing on the high seas. No agreement was reached on modifications to the convention.

Following later meetings, near agreement was reached on a formula by which Japan would continue to recognize the conservation operations being carried out by the commission on behalf of Canada and the United States. No further meetings have been held and the existing convention remains in effect.[36] Although Japan has been critical of the abstention principle, it is incorrect to suggest that therefore the convention is a failure. Japan has not chosen to exercise her right to terminate the convention; on the contrary, Japan recognizes the continuing need for a treaty. The fact that in the future the conservation of these resources will probably be sought by means of a convention is one indication that the present treaty has enjoyed a measure of success. It is encouraging to note that any new agreement will probably continue to recognize the long-established conservation programs of Canada and the United States.

It is likely that, for the near future at least, the simplest method of reducing high seas fishery problems will be through bilateral and multilateral conventions. In this regard, Canadian experience provides a number of interesting precedents. In situations not covered by treaty, I believe less opposition is likely to be encountered by states that adopt non-exclusionary procedures, such as those contemplated by the Geneva Convention on Fishing and Conservation of the Living Resources of the High Seas.[37]

CANADIAN PARTICIPATION IN THE GENEVA CONFERENCE ON THE LAW OF THE SEA

Not all of the subjects discussed at Geneva in 1958 and 1960 were of equal importance to Canada. Matters concerning the territorial sea, the contiguous zone, and high seas fishing were, however, of particular interest; and, as is well known, Canada played an important part in the discussions on these subjects.

The fishing zone concept

Canada believed that a twelve-mile limit was necessary to protect her fishing interests. She recognized, however, that an extension of the territorial sea to twelve miles might jeopardize the interests of nations, such as the US, that wished to maintain a narrow territorial belt in the interests of freedom of the seas and freedom for air navigation over the seas. In an attempt to reconcile the interests of those supporting a narrow territorial sea with the needs of those advancing the interests of coastal states, the Canadian government proposed that there should be a contiguous zone of twelve miles within which the coastal state would enjoy exclusive fishing rights.[38] Although this proposal failed to receive the required two-thirds majority, it is undeniable that it introduced a concept that affected the whole course of the discussions on the territorial sea. It became a feature of all plans put forth to solve the problem of the breadth of the territorial sea.

The second conference, convened in 1960, considered the two main items left unsolved by the first conference: the breadth of the territorial sea, and the establishment of fishing zones by coastal states in the high seas contiguous to, but beyond, the outer limit of the territorial sea. After extended negotiations, the Canadians and Americans submitted a joint proposal calling for a six-mile territorial sea and a six-mile exclusive fishing zone, with a provision for recognition of historic rights. This proposal failed by one vote.[39]

The failure of the fishing zone proposal was a disappointment for Canada. However, it cannot be said that because the proposal was not incorporated as a convention article the proposal itself must be regarded as a failure. That fifty-four states were in favour of the proposal (only one vote short of the required majority) represents a wide measure of agreement. In addition, soon after the 1958 conference a number of states either claimed a territorial sea of twelve miles or established twelve-mile fishing zones, unilaterally or in bilateral and multilateral agreements.[40]

The conclusion to be drawn fron these trends is that a maximum limit of three miles can no longer be validly asserted (if it ever could) as a rule of international law.[41] It may also be concluded that a fishing zone concept distinct from the concept of the territorial sea is in conformity with contemporary international thought. In this respect, Canada's effort may be regarded as an important contribution to the development of the international law of the sea.

High seas fishing

The Convention on Fishing and Conservation of the Living Resources of the High Seas stemmed from the work of the 1958 conference.[42] It attempts to specify what country or countries may lawfully enact and apply conservation rules, either by statute or agreement, and to indicate the conditions in which such rules may be applied to foreign vessels.

Canada's main contribution to the debates lay in its efforts to get the conference to adopt the 'principle of abstention.' The Canadian representative, Mr Ozere, explained this principle as follows: 'Where a stock of fish was under such scientific investigation, management and regulation as was required to obtain the maximum sustainable yield, and where an increase of fishing would not be expected to result in any substantial increase in the sustainable yield, the states whose nationals had not in recent years participated in the fishery should abstain from fishing the stock.'[43] Mr Ozere stated that the adoption of such a principle was essential if certain fisheries, such as the salmon and halibut fisheries in the north Pacific, were to be preserved. However, a draft resolution on the principle of abstention failed to obtain the required two-thirds majority.[44] The Canadian government was not greatly disappointed with the result,[45] because the doctrine of abstention is relatively new to international law, originating in treaties between Canada, the United States, and Japan regulating the salmon, herring, and halibut fisheries in the north Pacific. The attention given to it at the conference and the support that it received was regarded as having enhanced its status.

The straight baseline system

The Canadian government has expressed satisfaction with the adoption by the conference of the principle of drawing straight baselines from headland to headland in the case of deeply indented coastlines for purposes of establishing the boundary of the territorial sea.[46] As we know, article 4 of the Convention on the Territorial Sea and the Contiguous Zone attempted to reflect the ruling in the *Anglo-Norwegian Fisheries* case.[47] This provision was important to Canada because certain of her coastlines seemed to qualify for application of a straight baseline system.

FISHERIES: UNILATERAL ACTION BY CANADA

Canadian participation at both conferences represented a further effort to seek solutions through multilateral agreement. Although Canada was, in general, pleased with the outcome of the first conference, no agreement was reached on two questions with which Canada was particularly concerned: the breadth of the territorial sea, and fishing limits. Since 1960 Canada's preoccupation in this area has been to obtain wider jurisdiction over fisheries in adjacent seas. Aware that an international convention on the extent of jurisdiction over adjacent waters for territorial and fishing purposes was unlikely for some time,[48] Canada decided in 1964 to declare unilaterally that her territorial sea extended three miles and that she possessed exclusive control over fishing in a nine-mile zone adjacent to her territorial sea. The straight baseline method was declared to be applicable to the Canadian coast.[50]

The Territorial Sea and Fishing Zones Act was amended in 1970 to provide for the extension of the territorial sea to twelve miles and the creation of fishing zones in areas of the sea adjacent to the coast of Canada.[51] The secretary of state for external affairs indicated that the 1970 legislation would allow the government to complete the delimitation of Canada's exclusive fishing zones in coastal areas where straight baselines had not been drawn, such as the Gulf of St Lawrence, the Bay of Fundy, Dixon Entrance-Hecate Strait, and Queen Charlotte Sound. However, the legislation is worded broadly enough to permit expansive assertions of maritime jurisdiction.

To some, unilateral action 'is uncomfortably reminiscent of early Latin-American justification for 200 mile jurisdictional claims.'[52] I concede that certain aspects of Canada's recent fisheries legislation are regrettable from an international lawyer's point of view, particularly the entering of a reservation to the acceptance of the compulsory jurisdiction of the International Court of Justice. However, this is not to deny that there are some arguments supporting the Canadian position in terms of a traditional international law approach. For example, with regard to exclusive fishing zones, it may be pointed out that the Canadian position is in conformity with the general tendency, since the Truman Proclamation of 1945, to permit the partitioning of areas of the ocean for purposes of conserving and protecting fisheries. The claims of the coastal state were further strengthened by the Geneva Convention on Fishing and Conservation of the Living Resources of the High Seas. While the Canadian assertion differs from previous formulations, it may be argued that the juridical basis has now been established for a claim by the coastal state to a special interest in the fisheries of the high seas adjacent to its coasts. The extensive claims of several countries in Latin America indicate that state practice is not uniform on the method by which a coastal state may effect an extension of its maritime jurisdiction. Finally, the Canadian government may take the position that the concept of a contiguous fisheries zone, in addition to a state's territorial sea, has become well established in international law, being recognized even in American domestic law since 1966. The Canadian legislation might be said to be merely a new application of the contiguous zone principle which in essence is a means of separating fisheries jurisdiction 'from the bundle of jurisdictions which constitute sovereignty.'[53]

The preceding paragraph refers merely to a few of the reasons that might justify Canada's recent fisheries legislation. It is my opinion, however, that justification for unilateral action of this nature cannot realistically be found in traditional law of the sea principles. Canada's expansionist claims represent a departure from the traditional dichotomy between the territorial sea and the high seas. The Canadian approach is perhaps best viewed as an example of national action being regarded as the only available solution to problems of fisheries conservation, management, and exploitation.

As a coastal fishing state, Canada has been acutely conscious of the depletion of the resources of the sea by the fishing activities of foreign states. This was an important factor in the decision to resort to unilateral action. Perhaps the most that can be said is that international law considerations played a part in the shaping of Canadian policy. The utilization of the fishing zone concept, for example, illustrates a conscious effort to effect changes by a method familiar to international lawyers. It is significant that those responsible for the legislation have attempted to make clear that regulation is to apply only to certain bodies of water in which Canada believes she has a special interest. (With regard to the Bay of Fundy, Canada could probably assert a territorial claim rather than the lesser claim of fisheries jurisdiction.) In other words, there is evidence to suggest that unilateral action was taken to accomplish a change with a minimum of interference with traditional principles.

It should also be noted that most writers concerned with resource conservation stress that new legal concepts are urgently needed to ensure the survival of existing fisheries stocks.[54] It may no longer be wise even to ask whether a program for managing fisheries is in conformity with established international law. Perhaps it is better to ask first whether state action, either unilaterally or multilaterally, contributes to the development of a rational conservation program. Though motivated primarily by nationalistic considerations and accomplished unilaterally, it is not thought that the present Canadian approach to fisheries jurisdiction creates a dangerous precedent. Even if support cannot be found in customary or conventional international law, the Canadian action demonstrates one way in which present day fisheries problems can be handled without involving an excessive assertion of jurisdiction or a complete disregard of international law. In an area where new principles and approaches are urgently needed the Canadian action may best be viewed as a reasonable and functional approach to an increasingly complex international and domestic problem.[55]

CONCLUSION

The early experience of Canada and the United States with regard to the halibut and salmon of the Pacific coast demonstrates that in certain circumstances conservation can be successfully achieved within the framework of traditional international law principles. Bilateral treaties provided the means by which the two nations were able to restore and protect the fisheries in question. These treaties suggest a formula that other states may wish to study in order to protect the fisheries in which they themselves have a stake. Where several nations are interested in exploiting a fishery on the high seas, management is made more difficult by such problems as the need for a more complex organizational structure, additional national pressures, and the complexity of putting into effect regulations which will cover all fishermen concerned.

It is impossible at the moment to state categorically that the Northwest Atlantic Fisheries Convention has solved the problem of fishery conservation in the area concerned. However, the seemingly high degree of co-operation and good will among the member countries suggest the possibility of a successful program being carried out even where several parties are involved and the area is extensive. One weakness in procedure is the inability of the commission to implement conservation measures without the approval of a majority of the member countries concerned. The reluctance of the state to delegate its authority to an international commission, thereby empowering it, for example, to regulate the activities of its fishermen on the high seas, is regrettable from a conservationist's point of view. For the immediate future it is likely that the commission's main work will be the carrying out of scientific investigations and the making of recommendations.

The International North Pacific Fisheries Convention, designed to cope with a threat to a conservation program already underway, introduced into international law a new concept for the regulation of fisheries. Known as the doctrine of abstention, it was aimed at restraining from participation in certain high seas fisheries those states which had not contributed to the development of the fishery, but which other states had subjected to conservation regulation. The doctrine stands as an example of a possible way in which international law could develop in the area of high seas management. As with the halibut and salmon treaties, these conventions attempt to achieve beneficial conservation results in accord with generally accepted principles of international law.

In the years following the Geneva conferences, Canada found it necessary to seek solutions to fisheries problems by methods which, while not overly radical, might be contested by other states. The fishing zone concept was an acknowledgement of the need to approach fisheries problems from a functional rather than a purely legalistic point of view. By recognizing that jurisdiction for fisheries purposes need not correspond to the territorial sea, a departure was made from the traditional approach. In its present application, the fishing zone concept might be regarded as an even more controversial method of exercising jurisdiction.

Canadian policy is influenced by the needs of Canada's fishing communities and by the dangers inherent in uncontrolled exploitation. Where multilateral agreement appears to be an impossibility (or at least too slow to meet urgent requirements) Canada is no longer reluctant to proceed unilaterally. Such measures as have been taken are generally in accordance with a policy that does the least disservice to international law. By asserting claims that are neither excessive nor unreasonable, Canada's policy may be justified as in accord with a present trend in international thought; this trend recognizes that conservation of the oceans' resources cannot be solved by an application of historical rules and principles.

NOTES

1 R.S.C. c T-7 (1970).
2 1969–70, Can., c 68.
3 Jozo Tomasevich, *International Agreements on Conservation of Marine Resources* (1943) 50.
4 Scientific evidence has shown that 'for any particular population of fish there is an optimum point of fishing intensity which, if sustained, will yield the maximum crop of fish year after year. Less fishing is wasteful for the surplus fish dies from natural causes without benefit to mankind; more fishing is wasteful because it depletes the population and so results actually in a smaller crop.' Walter M. Chapman, 'United States Policy on High Seas Fisheries' (1949), 15 *Dept. of State Bull.* 67, at 68.
5 A.E. Gotlieb, 'The Canadian Contribution to the Concept of a Fishing Zone in International Law' (1964), 2 *Can. Y.B. Int'l L.* 55, at 60.
6 Ibid, 69, 70.
7 Article 24 of the Convention on the Territorial Sea and the Contiguous Zone provides that a state may exercise control in relation to customs, fiscal, immigration, or sanitary matters in a zone of the high seas which does not exceed twelve miles from the baseline from which the breadth of the territorial sea is measured. It is difficult to conceive of a state with a territorial sea extending *beyond* twelve miles if it cannot there exercise control over the matters specified in article 24.
8 Article 2.
9 Treaty Between Canada and The United States of America For Securing the Preservation of the Halibut Fishery of the North Pacific Ocean, signed 2 March 1923. Ratified 21 October 1924, IV *Trenwith* 3982. *Treaties and Agreements Affecting Canada in force between His Majesty and the United States of America ... 1914–1925* (1927) 505.
10 *Supra,* note 3, 125; Douglas M. Johnston,

The International Law of Fisheries (1965), at 373–4.
11 Article 3.
12 Convention between Canada and the United States of America for the Preservation of the Halibut Fishery of the Northern Pacific Ocean and Bering Sea, signed 2 March 1953, ratified and in force 28 October 1953. [1953] CAN. T.S. no 14.
13 *Supra* note 9, article 2.
14 Johnston, *supra* note 10, at 379.
15 Convention between His Majesty and the United States of America for the Protection, Preservation and Extension of the Sockeye Fisheries in the Fraser River System, signed 26 May 1930, ratified 28 July 1937. [1937] CAN. T.S. no 13.
16 Johnston, *supra* note 10, at 390.
17 Signed 8 February 1949, in force 3 July 1950. 157 U.N.T.S. 157; [1950] CAN. T.S. no 10; (1951), 45 *Am. J. Int'l L. Supp.* 40.
18 Erik M. Paulsen, 'Conservation Problems in the Northeastern Atlantic,' paper presented at the International Technical Conference on the Conservation of the Living Resources of the Sea, January 1956 U.N. Doc A/Conf. 10/7, 183, at 188–92.
19 The Canadian Instrument of ratification of 9 June 1950 contains the following observation: 'That ratification by Canada of the Convention extends to Newfoundland and that any claim Canada may have in regard to the limits of territorial waters or to the jurisdiction over fisheries particularly as a result of the entry of Newfoundland into Confederation, will not be prejudiced.' [1950] CAN. T.S. no 10 (addendum).
20 Article II(1).
21 Article VI(1).
22 Article I(3) (the subareas were defined in section I of the annex to the convention); amended by Protocol of 9 June 1961, respecting harp and hood seals, which entered into

force 29 April 1966. ICNAF Handbook, 1969 revision, 29–31.

23 Article VIII(1).

24 Protocol of 6 June 1964 relating to entry into force of proposals adopted by the commission, which entered into force, 19 December 1969. ICNAF Handbook, 1969 revision, 35–7.

25 Protocol of 7 June 1963 relating to international enforcement which entered into force 19 December 1969 and became operative 1 July 1971 ICNAF, (1970), *Annual Proceedings* 20–2.

26 Memorandum relating to ICNAF activities from the Office of the Commission, 27 August 1968.

27 ICNAF, (1970), *Annual Proceedings* 25–6.

28 Ibid, at 15.

29 Ibid.

30 Gordon Ireland, 'The North Pacific Fisheries' (1942), 36 *Am. J. Int'l L.* 400, at 410.

31 Signed 9 May 1952, in force 12 June 1953. 205 U.N.T.S. 65; [1953] CAN. T.S. no 3; U.S. TIAS 2786, 4 U.S.T. 380, no 3; (1954), 48 *Am. J. Int'l L. Supp.* 71–81.

32 Annex 1.

33 Annex 2.

34 *Supra*, 399 et seq.

35 Hugh J. Lawford, 'Canadian Practice in International Law During 1963' (1964), 2 *Can. Y.B. Int'l L.* 271, at 291–5.

36 North Pacific Fisheries Convention, (1964), 16 *External Affairs* 550.

37 *Infra*, 404.

38 U.N. Doc A/Conf. 13/39, 51–3.

39 U.N. Doc A/Conf. 19/8, 30.

40 Gotlieb, *supra* note 5, at 72, 73.

41 Philip C. Jessup, 'The United Nations Conference On the Law of the Sea' (1959), 59 *Colum. L. Rev.* 234, at 264.

42 U.N. Doc A/Conf. 13/L. 54 (see A/Conf. 13/38, 139).

43 U.N. Doc A/Conf. 13/42, 22.

44 U.N. Doc A/Conf. 13/38, 47.

45 'International Conference on the Law of the Sea' (1958), 10 *External Affairs* 21, at 89.

46 Ibid.

47 [1951] I.C.J. Rep. 116.

48 Following the second conference, Canada tried to get support for a multilateral treaty between the states which had voted in favour of the Canada-US proposal, but her efforts were unsuccessful.

49 1964–5, Can., c 22 ss 3, 4.

50 Ibid, s 5.

51 *Supra* note 2, s 4.

52 Commander William R. Palmer, 'Territorial Sea Agreement: Key to Progress in the Law of the Sea' (1970–1), 25 *JAG J.* 69, at 73.

53 'Some Examples of Current Issues of International Law of Particular Importance to Canada,' Dept. of External Affairs Legal Division, 10 June 1970, part 1: Law of the Sea (pages unnumbered).

54 See eg, L.F.E. Goldie, 'The Ocean's Resources' (1969), 8 *Colum. J. Trans. L.* 1; 'The Law of The Sea: The Future of the Seas's Resources,' proceedings of the Second Annual Conference of the Law of the Sea Institute, 26–9 June 1967, University of Rhode Island.

55 For attempted justification of Canada's maritime zone of limited jurisdiction for environmental protection, see the statement by Professors R. St J. Macdonald, Gerald L. Morris, and Douglas M. Johnston in (1971), 21 *U. Toronto L. J.* 75.

17/Canadian Approaches to the Seabed Regime

The exploitation of the Canadian continental shelf goes back some one hundred years to the underwater extensions of coal mines in the Cape Breton Island region. However, it was not until the late 1950s and the early 1960s that Canada became fully aware of the potential of the resources of its continental shelf. It also became aware that a policy had to be developed at the federal level to deal with issues that had arisen both domestically and internationally. Domestically the federal government had to contend with a policy by British Columbia of issuing 'offshore crown petroleum and natural gas permits,' and internationally it had to consider the implications of the newly adopted Geneva Convention on the Continental Shelf. As the 1960s progressed, the involvement and interest of the federal government in the administration of the offshore areas became more and more extensive.[1] Technological advances rendered more acute the necessity for the solution of the domestic problem and the adoption of a policy with regard to the international issues. In 1967 a sharper focus was provided for both issues. In the fall of that year the Supreme Court of Canada delivered its opinion in the constitutional reference case respecting ownership of mineral rights off the west coast,[2] and the United Nations on the initiative of Ambassador Pardo of Malta established a committee to study 'the question of the reservation exclusively for peaceful uses of the seabed and the ocean floor, and the subsoil thereof, underlying the high seas beyond the limits of present national jurisdiction and the use of their resources in the interests of mankind.'[3]

In view of these developments the federal government had to undertake the very difficult task of elaborating a policy which would be flexible but would safeguard what it considered to be vital interests. This policy was translated into legal norms by the Canadian delegation to the United Nations over a period of some four years. The process will not be completed until the Third Law of the Sea Conference when, it is hoped, a legal regime for the seabed will be adopted. It is this process of integrating domestic and foreign policy and the expression of it in a legal framework that is the subject of this study, completed in May 1972.

POLICY CONSIDERATIONS UNDERLYING CANADIAN APPROACHES
TO A SEABED REGIME

The primary factor which influences the Canadian position towards an international regime and the determination of limits of national jurisdiction is the geography of Canada's offshore areas. These geographic features are well known. Canada has a continental shelf which is the second largest in the world, covering an area equivalent to 40 per cent of Canada's total land area.[4] Off the west coast the continental shelf is rather narrow, but off the east coast it reaches as far as four hundred miles from shore. A brief glance at a bathygraphic chart will also reveal the existence of a number of other features which will influence the Canadian policy-makers.[5]

The physical structure of the geological continental shelf must of necessity influence Canadian policy since there are a number of underlying emotional issues connected with the delimitation of these offshore areas into spheres of national and international jurisdiction. The Canadian government must face the possibility that it would be subjected to criticism for 'giving away a piece of Canada' if it were to adopt a policy which might in some way draw the lines of national jurisdiction short of the geological continental shelf. This type of attitude was perhaps best exemplified by the commentator on a recent CBC documentary entitled 'Who owns the sea'[6] when he described the continental shelf as 'the forty per cent of Canada which no one sees.' The International Court of Justice has added a legal foundation to this attitude by stating in the *North Sea Continental Shelf* cases, that 'the right of the Coastal State to its continental shelf areas is based on its sovereignty over the land domain, of which the shelf area is the natural prolongation into and under the sea.'[7] Ultimately it is the economic importance of the Canadian offshore areas and the concentration of resources on the geological continental shelves[8] and slopes which affect the policy of Canada with respect to the determination of the zone of national jurisdiction and the nature of the regime beyond this zone. Although these economic factors have tended to focus the attention of policy-makers on the determination of the limits of national jurisdiction in geographic terms, it could be suggested that it is the accrual of economic benefits to Canada rather than of territory or even of resources that should be uppermost in their minds. Their energies would then be concentrated on the elaboration of a regime which would ensure that Canada obtained an equitable share of the revenues produced from areas adjacent to its coasts.

However, the Canadian government has an interest in preserving as many of these resources under its direct jurisdiction as possible. When these resources become commercially exploitable the government can count upon large amounts of revenue from leases and royalty payments, as well as tax revenues from income of enterprises extracting these offshore resources. More important are the indirect effects on the Canadian economy that could result from a large-scale oil strike in the offshore area. These indirect benefits are already being felt in connection with the exploratory program which has been undertaken off the east coast, and the onshore preparations which are also being made for the expected flow of oil to nearby provinces.[9] There is also expectation that heavy capital investment and continuing revenues will be generated from secondary industries locating in these areas. These factors are extremely important in view of the depressed economic state of the maritime provinces. The possibility of developing export markets in the oil-hungry eastern seaboard of the United States is also a factor in the development of Canadian government policies, as an aggressive export program which provides needed foreign exchange has been one of the major objectives of Canadian governments. The reduction of imports to preserve foreign exchange would also be achieved through supplying of oil to eastern Canadian markets from domestic sources. This has been even more important in the recent past when oil importing nations have been forced to acquiesce in price increases dictated by oil exporting countries.[10] The importance of having a secure source of supply for eastern markets is a further consideration in Canadian thinking, although admittedly this is not as much a concern as it is in the United States, as Canada could divert western oil production (but at a substantial cost) to its eastern markets. Finally, transportation costs from offshore oilfields would be substantially less than those for Venezuelan oil; however, some of the savings would be offset by the generally higher development costs of offshore oil installations.

Not only is the government concerned with the economic benefits of the type described above, but it is also concerned with exercising direct control and jurisdiction over activities in areas of the ocean adjacent to its shores. This control is essentially of two kinds: economic and environmental. The economic controls are primarily concerned with Canadian ownership of resource exploitation companies and with resource development policies. The importance that the government places on Canadian participation in and control of the extractive industries is evident not only from its legislation but also from such ventures as the Canadian Development Corporation and the joint private industry-government consortium known as Panarctic Oils Limited.[11] Through these devices the government hopes to exercise a more effective and a more flexible control on corporations engaged in offshore operations than would otherwise be possible through the traditional, but more heavy handed, manipulation of conditions attaching to exploration and exploitation permits. The Canadian government is also aware of the possible effect of offshore production on world and domestic prices of minerals produced onshore and the repercussions that this might have on the economy of areas that are heavily dependent upon mineral extraction. The ability to control and regulate the offshore production would, of course, be highly desirable from the point of view of a government that is committed to the implementation of a rational mining and energy policy.

The policy of the Canadian government of extending environmental control to areas of the ocean adjacent to Canada is amply demonstrated by the Arctic Waters Pollution Prevention Act[12] and the recent amendments to the Canada Shipping Act.[13] The regulations dealing with drilling in offshore areas[14] are heavily influenced by environmental considerations and are not only among the most stringent and well-designed in the world but are amply policed. The Canadian ministry responsible for the safety and environmental supervision of offshore installations would be extremely unhappy to have the controls developed by them become less stringent or more laxly enforced. Similarly the Canadian government would not wish to lose control over transportation facilities associated with offshore installations such as shipping or pipeline terminals which might present potential pollution hazards. These considerations are extremely significant where the offshore installations are in important fishing areas, such as the Grand Banks, or in areas that are particularly susceptible to environmental damage, as in the Arctic.

There also exist a number of other considerations which affect the attitude of the Canadian government towards issues connected with the determination of a regime. Chief among these are defence policy and fisheries policy. Thus, although Canadian policy has staunchly supported various aspects of disarmament proposals, and Canada was extremely active in the negotiation of the seabed arms control treaty,[15] the government is very concerned that it retain sufficient control of adjacent continental shelf areas to enable it to use these areas for the establishment of detection and defensive devices. Because of the importance of living resources that can be found on and above the Canadian continental shelves, and the substantial role that these play in the economy of some regions of Canada, the government would take a negative view towards any proposal which would limit the control that it could exercise over these resources.[16]

In addition to these factors, the Canadian policy-makers must also take into consideration a number of political and diplomatic realities on the international scene. Canada is seen by many nations of the world as a 'have' country, blessed with a small population and an extremely large land area particularly rich in mineral and other resources. Thus, any attempt by Canada to arrogate to itself any large part of the seabed, especially if it is rich in mineral resources, would be regarded with suspicion, if not hostility, by a large segment of the international community. Canada also has to bear in mind that this suspicion has been further heightened by its extension of jurisdiction over fisheries and environmental matters in recent times. Canadian initiatives with respect to environmental issues, which would grant additional rights to coastal states, have confirmed in the minds of certain countries that the ultimate aim of Canada is to exclude all other countries from participation in the exploitation of a sizeable portion of the world's continental shelves.[17] Canada is becoming more and more concerned with this image of avarice which is appearing to displace the traditional self-image of generosity which has been a source of pride to Canadian administrations.

As far as the type and role of international organization which would be created to administer the seabed area are concerned, several considerations seem to be uppermost in Canadian thinking. The underlying premise appears to be that an international organization with broad powers and an independent source of income, with limited dependence on member states, is not politically acceptable, either to Canada or to the greater part of the world community. Apart from this consideration, the Canadian policy towards the type and role of the projected international institution is fairly flexible. But it must be remembered that this flexibility is limited by the awareness of policy-makers of certain basic Canadian approaches to international affairs in general and to ocean management in particular. The role of the organization to be established is of particular concern, as the attitude towards such an international organization will be coloured not only by 'seabed considerations' but also by other political, economic, and environmental factors. Thus, Canadian attitudes will significantly differ if the organization is given total ocean management jurisdiction in areas adjacent to Canada or if it will be restricted to a simple registry of national claims. Another concern that needs to be taken into account in the development of policy towards the international seabed regime is the possibility that the international organization, by an evolutionary process, might extend its jurisdiction beyond spheres and areas which Canada was prepared to assign to it at the time of its creation. Thus, the composition and the powers of the decision- and rule-making bodies of the organization are also extremely important. Canadian policy should also attempt to ensure that the organization is technically equipped to apply sound resource administration policies to the areas submitted to its jurisdiction and is substantially divorced from political pressures which would paralyse its operation. On the other hand, the technical experts to whom the day to day administration of the international organization would be entrusted must be provided with effective supervision and overall political guidance by member states. Thus, if, as is hoped, the international organization is to have universal participation, provision must be made for executive control by a relatively small number of nations. Canadian policy naturally strives to ensure permanent representation or the possibility of fairly frequent representation on this executive body. Canada is also interested in preventing a possible monopoly of control over the operations of the organization by such technological giants as the United States and the Soviet Union.

These basic policy questions faced the Canadians as they participated in the work of the various United Nations committees charged with the task of elaborating a regime for the seabed. As will become apparent from the analysis of the Canadian participation, the development of these policies and the selection of priorities among them as far as the government of Canada was concerned was slow and very cautious. This was basically the result of lack of information with respect to such crucial questions as the location and extent of offshore resources and the existence of conflicts among the various departments with respect to policy priorities. However, as the work of these committees progressed, the Canadian delegation was able to provide them with a comprehensive statement of Canadian objectives as these were being developed by the government.

CANADIAN PARTICIPATION IN THE SEABED COMMITTEE[18]

Determination of the limits of national jurisdiction

As is apparent from the discussion of the policy considerations respecting the approach that the Canadian delegation could be expected to take in relation to the seabed question, the crucial issue would be the determination of the limits which would separate the area under national jurisdiction from that which would be assigned to the international community. Thus the position taken by the Canadian delegation from the earliest UN meetings was very cautious and conservative and tended to underline that, although Canada was interested in pursuing the idea underlying Ambassador Pardo's proposal, it was not willing to negotiate with respect to areas it regarded as its own under international law.[19] This was made very clear right from 1967 when the matter was first brought up in the First Committee and where Mr Gotlieb, the Canadian delegate, insisted that the mandate of the Seabed Committee which was to be established should be limited to discussion of questions concerning 'abyssal depths' and the 'deep ocean floor.'[20] At first Canada did not make clear what it regarded to be the division line between the area in which coastal states had 'rights' and where the 'abyssal depths' began. However, it was clear from Canadian actions that Canada regarded the whole of the physical continental shelf area, as a minimum, to be subject to Canadian sovereignty and that Canada was encouraging early exploitation of it for the benefit of its citizens.

As the Seabed Committee began its meetings in the spring of 1968, Mr Ignatieff, the Canadian representative, sought to sketch out in broad terms Canadian thinking on the question of limits: 'In the view of the Canadian authorities there is no doubt that the areas over which coastal states possess sovereign rights under international law in respect of the resources therein include the continental shelf and slopes.'[21] From that statement, it became apparent that Canada would be advocating a criterion based on geological factors rather than one based on depth, distance from shore, or gradient to serve as the means in the drawing of limits between the national and international areas. It should also be noticed that at that early stage of the committee's work, Canada was not in a position to state firmly the outer limits which it felt coastal states were entitled to assert but was merely stating the minimum. This became even clearer in later statements by Canadian officials.[22]

As the work of the Seabed Committee progressed, the issue of defining the area subject to national jurisdiction became more acute and ever greater pressure was being exerted by delegations from developing countries to limit claims which restrict the 'common heritage of mankind.' In response to this pressure Canada attempted to allay fears that it would make claims substantially beyond the geological continental shelf and slope, but reserved the possibility of doing so. Mr Beesley, who had taken over as the chief Canadian delegate to the Seabed Committee, explained his government's position as follows:

> Canada has nevertheless taken the position that irrespective of what may be permissible under existing customary international law – and, as I said before, it has been argued that, under existing international law, a coastal state can legally extend its jurisdiction as far as it can exploit subject only to the median line – the limits of national jurisdiction need to be clarified and related to more precise and firmer legal criteria. Canada is not about to claim the large chunk of ocean floor beyond the geographical shelf. However, although we have done some preliminary studies of the Canadian shelf, we are not yet in a position to lay down any rule as we do not yet know, at least in any precise way, what the over-all picture may be and what type of criteria would meet the widely different geographical circumstances of the rest of the world.[23]

As other delegations began putting forward proposals for the resolution of this issue, Canada adopted a low profile and did not speak out at length on the question of limits during the later deliberations of the committee. It is apparent that this is the key question in the view of the Canadian government, and that there is not likely to be any change or softening of the Canadian position as might be the case with respect to other issues under discussion in the committee. Canada would find it extremely difficult to accept a formula based on gradient, as this would entail a major expenditure of time and effort to chart the vast area of ocean bottom adjacent to its shores with adequate precision to comply for example with the gradient requirement of the Nixon proposal.[24] Similarly the adoption of a depth criterion would require extensive mapping and would most probably result in the loss of some portion of the continental margin. As far as a distance from shore criterion is concerned, Canada would find that the distance which currently appears to have a certain amount of support, ie 200 miles,[25] was not acceptable because it would mean the loss of certain potentially oil-bearing portions of eastern continental shelf especially in the Flemish Cap and Tail areas of the Bank. The use of the geological criterion, although lacking the precision and simplicity of being able to draw a line a certain distance from shore, does have the advantage of reserving to Canada areas which it considers to be of vital importance for its economic development, and of providing an objective measuring device which is also suitable for use in the determination of the limits of other coastal states.

Although Canada might be criticized for selecting a criterion which favours it, a close examination of other criteria proposed by various governments in the committee discloses that they also reflect the interests of their proponents. Canada's inflexibility on this question, as will be seen, does not necessarily extend to the question of the destination of the revenues from the area assigned to the coastal states, and it is probable that with respect to the question of the determination of the limits of national jurisdiction, Canada might find it acceptable to agree to grant to an international organization a certain proportion of revenue arising from the area over which it would retain jurisdiction.

The 'Common Heritage of Mankind'

Coupled with the issue of the determination of the limits of national jurisdiction, there exists the issue of the determination of the nature of the regime which will govern the area beyond. From the beginning of the work of the Seabed Committee the Canadian delegation took the position that the development of the abyssal depths should be carried out 'in accordance with the United Nations Charter and for the benefit of all mankind.'[26] Although the Canadian delegation in the early proceedings of the committee was not in a position to describe the type of regime it envisaged, it did adopt a rather cautious and negative approach to the concept of 'common heritage of mankind' which the Seabed Committee sought to develop. This scepticism was generated by the fact that the Canadian delegation felt that the concept had no legal content or precedent in international law. It took the position that it would oppose the inclusion of the concept in any statement of principle until a precise legal definition was achieved, because to do so would have 'far-reaching juridical implications whose precise nature was as yet unknown.'[27] However, this preliminary position was softened in the light of developments, and soon thereafter some concession was made that such a concept might indeed exist.[28]

This grudging concession was followed by a warmer and warmer espousal of the concept[29] until the Canadian delegation in 1971 was able to incorporate it into a theoretical framework which they had devised and referred to not only as 'the most fundamental principle to be embodied in the future treaty' but also that it 'may come to be or indeed may already be regarded as [a] principle of customary international law.'[30]

The acceptance of this principle, however, was not without qualification. First and foremost, the Canadian delegation was concerned that this principle not be used in order to encroach on coastal state jurisdiction over undersea resources by permitting the delimitation of national offshore boundaries without the assent of such state and that it not predetermine the nature of the regime which would be adopted for the area described as the 'common heritage of mankind.' In particular the Canadians did not wish the concept to be used as a cloak under which the principle of freedom of the sea would be expanded to become the legal regime which would govern the exploration and exploitation of the ocean floor.[31] Similarly, they did not wish it to be used as a device by which sovereignty in the international area would be vested in the United Nations, as some delegates to the committee had suggested. They also were very careful to point out that the principle must refer only to the resources of the international area and not to the area itself, as this might lead to the establishment of a comprehensive superagency controlling every aspect of ocean use rather than the limited resource management machinery which the Canadians favoured. They feared that such a link between territory and the common heritage of mankind would also preclude the acceptance of such of their initiatives as the elaboration of juridical norms which would permit the establishment of pollution control zones, under the jurisdiction of coastal states, which might extend further seaward than the limits of national jurisdiction for purposes of resource exploitation.

The Canadian approach to this question shows that Canada was much less rigid and more willing to modify its policy in response to developments in the international arena than in respect to the determination of limits of national jurisdiction. The Canadian delegation understood the depth of feeling with which some delegations viewed this concept and sought to guide its development in a direction that would accommodate these views and yet retain its own basic policy objectives. Although the committee has not yet fully defined the scope of the concept, it was apparent from Canadian endorsement of many of its components that Canada had shifted from an aloof cautious posture to a more co-operative and influential position in the further development of this new area of international law as it is being developed in the Seabed Committee.

The moratorium on activities of exploitation of the resource of the area of the seabed beyond national jurisdiction

The work of the Seabed Committee proceeded very slowly as many delegations proceeded as cautiously as the Canadian delegation and many countries found it impossible to enunciate coherent national policies with respect to issues that were being considered in the Seabed Committee. Because of this a number of delegations were concerned that exploration and exploitation activities, which were proceeding very actively in many areas of the oceans, would be presented as a *fait accompli* and that the committee would not be able to push back the limits of national jurisdiction shoreward of then existing exploitation facilities.

In order to preclude this a number of nations in the fall of 1969 introduced a resolution into the First Committee whose purpose was to limit further national claims to the seabed in areas which were considered to be beyond national jurisdiction. The operative section of the resolution read as follows:

> The General Assembly ... *Declares* that pending the establishment of the ... international regime:
> a States and persons, physical or juridical are bound to refrain from all activities of exploitation of the resources of the area of the sea-bed and ocean floor, and the subsoil thereof, beyond the limits of national jurisdiction;
> b No claim to any part of that area or its resources shall be recognized.[32]

The Canadian delegation rejected emphatically the formulation of the moratorium concept enunciated in the draft resolution. It was primarily concerned about the adverse effects that the resolution might have on the exploration and exploitation of its own continental shelf which was progressing very vigorously.[33] In particular, the Canadians were very apprehensive that exploration would be severely curtailed by exploration companies who would fear that exploitation permits which they would ultimately obtain, although properly issued by Canada, might not be recognized by the international regime when it came into being and thus would frustrate the domestic Canadian policy of fostering agressive exploration programs. These considerations were not enunciated by the Canadian delegation which did, however, warn that a moratorium resolution in the form proposed would ultimately either prejudice future decisions establishing the limits of the international area or would, because of the imprecision of what was prohibited, encourage states to encroach on ever greater portions of the seabed. In either event the Canadians felt the result would not be consistent with policies they were seeking to develop in the committee. In the event that the resolutions were interpreted, according to one possible view proposed by some delegations, this would result in the loss to Canada of areas then 'beyond limits of national jurisdiction.' As no definitive conclusion had been reached by Canada at that time as to the limits of its own national jurisdiction, Canada would be precluded from making such a determination of its limits at a future date in the light of new policy considerations. On the other hand, Canada recognized that an area existed beyond national jurisdiction which was not the subject of appropriation by coastal states, and it was opposed to the creation of a situation which would encourage the making of extensive claims to national jurisdiction and which would impede approach to the definition of these limits.[34]

As an alternative, Canada put forward a moratorium proposal which, even it conceded, was 'radical.' Mr Kaplan of the Canadian delegation outlined the plan, which he qualified as having the advantages of certainty, simplicity, and equity:

> All we need to do is accept the principle that every ocean and every sea of the world shall have the same percentage of its underwater acreage reserved for the benefit of mankind ... we would be abandoning notions of territoriality, jurisdiction, and sovereignty which find their way into every distance, depth or other continental shelf formula. Why, in principle should it make any difference whether a shelf is shallow or deep? Consensus as to distance from shore would become unnecessary. Let us begin out in the centre of every sea in the world, be it Atlantic, the Pacific, the Arctic, the Mediterranean, the North Sea, the Persian Gulf, the Red Sea, the Baltic, the Caribbean, the China Sea – I could go on – and reserve out of each the same percentage – say 50, 60 or even 80 percent – of the underwater acreage.[35]

Despite able advocacy by the delegation, the Canadian suggestion did not obtain meaningful support and the moratorium resolution as originally drafted was adopted both by the First Committee and the General Assembly over the objections of Canada and of a substantial number of other countries.[36]

At the Seabed Committee sessions of March 1970, the Canadians once again revived the suggestion that a certain proportion of the total seabed and ocean floor in various maritime basins be reserved for the international community, but the delegation did not further elaborate on the precise method by which the area which would be available to coastal state for the purposes of exercising their national jurisdiction would be determined. The Canadians did, however, admit that some areas which were then under national jurisdiction of coastal states would be included in the international area. Mr Legault, the Canadian representative, in describing the benefits of the Canadian proposal, stated that the Canadian approach 'would be infinitely more effective than any now being considered since it would encompass areas in smaller and shallower seas which were already being exploited but which under other approaches would not fall within the region beyond national jurisdiction and would continue to be exploited for the exclusive benefit of the coastal nations.'[37] The vagueness of the proposal as well as the fact that nations whose continental shelf lay in ocean basins of larger oceans such as the Pacific and the Atlantic, as for example Canada, would not be affected as drastically as the nations to which Mr Legault referred, led to the same lack of enthusiasm and response that had met the original proposal.

Canadian proposal to resolve the impasse reached in the Seabed Committee

The major Canadian initiative in proposing its version of the 'moratorium' arose not only from the dissatisfaction it felt with the moratorium resolution as adopted, but also from a sense of frustration with the impasse which seemed to have been reached in the Seabed Committee because of the inability of the committee to resolve the twin problems of the determination of the limits of national jurisdiction and the definition of the nature of the regime in the international area. The Canadians in the spring 1971 meeting of the Seabed Committee pointed out that the slow progress of the committee was caused by the dilemma which plagued all the members of the committee including Canada. Until the question of limits was settled, states were uncertain as to the sort of broad guidelines they wished to lay down for the area beyond national jurisdiction; at the same time, until the question of the regime was settled, states were uncertain as to the precise limits they wished to fix for the area within national jurisdiction. The frustration felt by the Canadians was graphically illustrated by Mr Beesley, the head of the Canadian delegation:

> If we fail to break away from the pattern we have followed so far, we may continue to be working in a vacuum, in an atmosphere of unreality, not only attempting to build a house without knowing the size of the lot on which it will be situated but, worse yet, without knowing if we have any lot at all on which to place it, let alone who will carry out the task, and with what resources, and who will pay the cost.[38]

To solve this problem and to enable the committee to carry on with its work pending the final solution of the problem in the Law of the Sea Conference, then scheduled for 1973, the Canadians proposed a refinement of the moratorium proposal that they had first made in 1969.

Not giving up the concept of reserving a certain proportion of the world's ocean basins for the international regime, they proposed an immediate step which would deal with the basic difficulty of the original proposal, that of defining precisely the limits of national jurisdiction. This step would be a resolution calling on states to define their continental shelf claims by a certain date or, alternatively, stating that national claims on a date already past were deemed to have been frozen. The central idea would be modified by specifying that such claims were not immutable but were subject to alteration by the negotiations that would take place at the Law of the Sea Conference. For states that were not yet in position to make such a determination, because their policy had not yet become firm, the Canadians offered the option of permitting them to state a limit beyond which they undertook not to make claims. The Canadians pointed out that it would be difficult for states to make exorbitant claims in compliance with the call for the determination of these national limits because of international pressure not to exceed the largest claims made at the time of the proposal, ie 200 miles for some countries and the outer edge of the continental shelf for some other countries. Even if such larger claims were made, the Canadians did not necessarily see this as being altogether undesirable, as at least a frank statement of national interests would have been achieved. Furthermore, the international area would have been precisely delimited for the purpose of the work of the committee, and nations would be for all practical purposes stopped from in the future making claims which would encroach on the large proportion of the ocean basins which had been reserved for the international community by the adoption of this scheme. In any event, the claims as was pointed out above would be subject to reduction when the final agreement on the limits of national jurisdiction was negotiated.

This proposal was coupled with the suggestion that, simultaneously with its implementation, a first-stage machinery would come into operation for the international area as then defined and that it would be empowered to collect from coastal states a certain fixed percentage of all the revenues that they derived from the whole of seabed areas claimed by them beyond the outer limits of their internal waters.[39] The proposal would require such payments from countries which were actually receiving revenues from the exploitation of ocean resources and would satisfy the principle of equity by not making distinctions between narrow or wide shelf countries or making payment dependent upon the distance from shore that the development was taking place. The payment of what the Canadians termed a 'voluntary international development tax' would continue until the machinery and regime came into full operation, at which time the fees paid over to the organization would replace the voluntary payment.

This idea put forward by the Canadian delegation had the merit of not only satisfying the need for providing an immediate share of revenues from ocean resources, but also permitting the regime and machinery in their formative states to be financed from a new source of revenue, without the necessity of having recourse to already strained budgets of international organizations. This independent source of revenue also permitted flexibility in the selection of the type of organization that would administer the seabed, as there would not be any compulsion to link it in some fashion to the parent organization which had been providing funds in the interim period. As far as Canada was concerned, the imposition of the tax would not cause even temporary dislocation as there was no commercial exploitation of resources off the Canadian coast. The tax would take effect gradually as the exploration phase was completed and the production stage began. It was designed to show good faith on Canada's part as it would demonstrate that Canada was willing to consider the sharing of revenues with the international community from an area which it was claiming to be under its sole jurisdiction. The Canadian proposals, put forward at a very late stage of the committee's spring meeting, did not receive very much comment, though it was obvious that they would not be greeted with unanimous support. The third proposal, particularly, would meet with some resistance as it would have an immediate effect on nations with extensive offshore development programs and would require payment from some developing countries.

In the next session of the committee held in July and August 1971, the Canadian delegation again pointed out the urgency for the establishment of the interim machinery. It acknowledged the lack of support by the committee for their proposal and the serious objections that had been levelled by some of the coastal states especially with respect to the 'voluntary international development tax.' In order to attract a more positive response the Canadians further refined the proposal by defining the nature and role of the transitional machinery with more precision and sought to make their 'voluntary international development tax' suggestion more palatable. They conceded that they would be prepared to see the payments made in respect of exploitation seaward of a belt of twelve miles from shore rather than in respect of the whole continental shelf as they had earlier suggested, although they wondered why countries whose offshore development was concentrated in this twelve-mile belt should be exempted from payment of the tax.

This concession to those who argued that the whole concept of an 'international tax' was a violation of state sovereignty when applied to areas over which state sovereignty applied such as the territorial sea dealt a blow to the basic premise on which the whole Canadian concept was based – that of equity and simplicity.[40] The delegation took great pains to point out the irrelevance of this argument, put forward by opponents of the plan, which appealed to the highly emotional issue of state sovereignty. It drew the analogy of payments to the interim seabed organization to the contributions made by states to the United Nations, the source of which were revenues generated wholly within areas under national jurisdiction. In addition the delegation pointed out that no question of violation of sovereignty could arise, as the whole scheme was based upon voluntary contributions. The Canadians, however, refused to make a further concession, that of exempting developing countries from the voluntary contribution scheme. This, they argued would be a very serious blow to the principle of equity which required a contribution in proportion to the benefit derived from ocean resources and that the special position of developing countries should be taken into consideration at the stage of distribution of funds by the organization rather than at the stage of contributions. This would ensure that consideration could be given to determination of relative need of the various developing countries and would more equitably redistribute the available funds to those countries needing it most.

The modified version of the interim machinery proposal received study by members of the committee, but failed to attract any widespread support[41] and was consequently not implemented in any form, although Canada is continuing its major diplomatic initiative to have the proposal accepted in some form. Canada, in putting forward this program showed imagination and vitality in its attempts to advance the work of the committee and if it persists in its efforts may be able to provide a means to obviate the impasse which presently exists. To do this, it may have to streamline its proposal even further and to abandon completely the proportional reservation of the ocean basin proposal in order to concentrate on the moratorium and voluntary international development tax proposals.

International institutions for the management of the seabed

In the earliest proceedings of the Seabed Committee the Canadian delegation began its consideration of the institutions necessary for the management of the seabed by speculating whether such machinery was necessary at all. In view of the fact that most nations accepted the necessity of machinery of some sort, the Canadian delegation began to explore the nature of such machinery. The prime Canadian concern was that the proposed machinery not be paralysed by an excessively cumbersome bureaucracy or one which was too subject to political pressures. On the other hand, they wished to give to machinery an adequate structure in order to permit it to operate an effective resources management system. According to their conception this mechanism should be one which struck a 'balance somewhere between' simple registry of national claims and a full-blown international administrative mechanism.[42] The Canadians also adopted the position that the handing over of the tasks of the machinery to existing organizations would be unsatisfactory in view of the fact that 'the nature of the tasks required of the proposed machinery was so radically different from that at present undertaken in the UN family.'[43] They also advanced a more telling reason for the establishment of a new mechanism, the freedom which it would enjoy from the 'traditions and established practices'[44] of existing UN bodies. In the Canadian view this freedom would ensure impartiality, equity, efficiency, and practicality as well as objective operation without political pressures – in other words, a business-like approach.

The Canadians also proposed that the machinery should at its inception be rather rudimentary, merely providing facilities for the registration of national claims and the control of exploration. However, as the offshore operators moved into a second exploration phase, prior to the actual exploitation of seabed resources, the mechanism would be permitted to develop more mature and sophisticated forms. This idea was explained more fully in conjunction with the Canadian moratorium proposal. The first stage machinery which would serve as a skeleton and an experimental prototype of the permanent machinery would be composed of an executive council and a resource management commission and would rely on the existing machinery of the International Court of Justice for dispute settlement. The '*ad hoc* executive council' would be composed of members appointed by the United Nations General Assembly, but there was no indication of the possible size of the council. Most probably it would resemble in its composition the Seabed Committee before its last expansion.[45] The 'transitional resource management commission' would be appointed by the executive council and would be essentially a technical body composed of technical experts and scientists who would discharge a number of obligations[46] using the Seabed Principles[47] as a framework.

This transitional machinery would serve as a nucleus for the permanent machinery, which would adopt the orderly system of administration and the experienced technical staff from the interim body when it began its expanded operation. The permanent Seabed Organization, as envisaged by the Canadian delegation, would be constituted in such a way as to ensure its ability to function effectively as a resource administration agency and, although necessarily of political nature, it would be 'more like an enterprise, than an ordinary UN agency.'[48] It would have a juridical personality and have capacity to contract, hold property, sue, and be sued. It would be free of privileges and immunities that would not be in keeping with what would be essentially an international commercial enterprise generating revenues for the international community.

Two problems had to be faced by the Canadians when characterizing the organization as an 'enterprise.' The first of these was the reconciliation of roles as both a 'commercial' exploiter of the area's resources and an independent regulatory and administrative body. This conflict would be most obvious in situations where the commercial interest conflicted directly with environmental interests. Additional problems would also arise if the organization were to be given the power to engage in exploration and exploitation activities in direct competition with entrepreneurs sponsored by member states or the member states themselves.

For reasons which were stated earlier, the Canadians did not wish the organization to be associated closely with existing structures. Therefore, they proposed a completely independent structure which would have as its legislative body an assembly composed of all states parties to the treaty and which would take decisions on the basis of a two-thirds majority. The executive body or council would be the central decision-making body. It would make the major policy decisions with respect to the operation of the regime and would according to the Canadian suggestion even make decisions as to the manner of distribution of benefits. The Canadians had a vital interest in being represented continually on this body, but they were also concerned that the body not be paralysed because of excessive representation of member states. The formula proposed by Canada was that the council should have no more than thirty members composed of two classes: those 'designated' by the assembly, and those elected by the assembly. The number of designated states or of elected states was not specified, though of course Canada would prefer to be among the designated states and hold what would be essentially a permanent seat on the council. It rejected the criterion of 'highest gross national product' chosen by the Americans[49] for selection to the council and substituted criteria which in its eyes would be much more relevant and also are more favourable to Canada. These would be 'level of state expertise in offshore technology and resource management, length of coastline, area of continental shelf, land-locked or shelf-locked status and level of economic development.'[50] The Canadians were also wary of the possible domination of the council by the technological giants such as the US and the USSR, rejecting categorically any suggestion that systems of weighted voting be adopted.[51] Decisions would be taken by a two-thirds majority, thus ensuring that policy decisions could be made even in the face of objections by the superpowers.

The other organs of the proposed international machinery also reflect the Canadian concern for efficiency in the operation of the whole system. The day to day management of the system would be entrusted to a technical body composed of experts who would report directly to the council. This body, known as the resource management commission, would be kept small and would perform a number of specific administrative functions.[52] This commission could easily be supplemented by other bodies which would be brought into being when necessary to undertake tasks not specifically assigned to the resource management commission and by regional organizations if these should prove to be useful and necessary. The international machinery would also be provided with an administrative tribunal to deal in a summary fashion with disputes that had arisen with respect to the workings of the machinery or other aspects of the regime. This administrative tribunal would not supplement entirely the traditional modes of dispute settlement but would make the cumbersome procedures much less attractive. The machinery would also be provided with a secretariat of modest proportions to carry out tasks assigned to it by the various organs. Earlier the Canadians had also suggested the establishment of a separate inspection and enforcement authority which they dubbed 'seaguard,' but they abandoned this proposal when it did not receive any favourable response.[53]

Functions of the international seabed authority

The Canadians regarded the proposed seabed authority as a resource management organization charged only with the supervision of the exploration and exploitation of the mineral resources of the seabed. They were not inclined to accept the granting to the authority of jurisdiction over living resources of the seabed, much less the creation of a general ocean superagency which they described as possibly having powers 'surpassing those combining the Security Council, I.M.C.O., I.C.A.O., W.H.O., the I.T.U., G.A.T.T. and the I.A.E.A.'[54] This opposition was generated not only by the fear of a powerful independent supranational organization, with an inefficient bureaucracy, but also by the possibility that such an approach would lead to the vesting of jurisdiction over marine areas in the superauthority, to the prejudice of interests of coastal states. As far as Canadian policy and strategy are concerned, apprehension about the creation of a superregime is reasonable and expected, but consideration should be given to whether a review of this position ought not to be undertaken at some time in future in order to place the seabed problem within a totally integrated approach towards the marine environment and submit the whole administration of the area to a single organization.

The dangers in the Canadian approach are that agreement at an early date may be achieved with respect to seabed problems at the expense of freezing progress on other aspects of the Law of the Sea and that the concentration of attention on the petroleum and mineral extractive aspects of ocean use may lead to the development of juridical norms which give preference to these uses in fact, if not in law, over other uses of the sea such as fisheries.[55] The Canadian delegation would deny this danger pointing out that Canadian policy is equally concerned with these other uses of the sea and that equal pressure is being exerted within the international community for the simultaneous development of regimes for other uses of sea.[56] As a matter of fact, the Canadian delegation sees the danger lying in the other direction, namely that the attempt to include other issues in a comprehensive regime would indefinitely postpone any possibility of progress on the establishment of a regime to govern resource exploitation.

With respect to the issue of whether the seabed authority should be authorized to conduct exploration and exploitation activities on its own behalf, the Canadians took a very cautious approach, warning against the escalation of administrative staff and costs as a result of the grant of such powers.[57] However, in response to the pressure of some members of the committee the Canadians modified their stand sufficiently to be able to say to the February 1972 Seabed Committee meeting: 'We share in the view that it is imperative to ensure full and genuine participation by the developing countries in the exploration and exploitation of seabed resources and that some system of joint ventures with the international machinery could be one method of attaining this objective.'[58]

The Canadian delegation was very insistent that seabed authority administer a resource management system which would provide the greatest net benefit not only to entrepreneurs, who would be encouraged to divert their energies to offshore areas, and to coastal states, but ultimately to the whole international community and developing countries in particular. The specific system which the Canadians put forward was based on one which is operating domestically in Canada and is acknowledged to be among the most sophisticated in the world.[59] This is a system which distinguishes among the various phases of the exploration and exploitation process and which does not impose undue burdens on operators during the exploration phase but which provides for adequate revenues once a discovery is made. In addition, the system ensures a tight control through licensing and supervision of every aspect of the process through to the production stage. The Canadians also pointed out that, like the domestic system, they would prefer to see the primary concern of the organization, at least in early stages, to be the encouragement of exploration and exploitation of resources.

The Canadians also acknowledged that the authority would have to deal with such complicated economic issues as the effect that offshore production might have on world markets and the setting of required contributions, as well as the distribution of funds acquired by the authority. Although the Canadians expressed some concern about the disruption to existing market patterns which would be caused by large-scale exploitation of ocean resources, the level of concern did not approach that of some single resource countries.[60] As far as the other two economic issues were concerned, these were coupled with the often expressed desire for the recognition of a special status for developing countries in the operation of the regime.

For the resolution of this conflict the Canadians reverted essentially to the resource management system which they had outlined. They argued for realistic scales of contribution which would take into account the high development costs of offshore production and yet would provide the greatest amount of revenue to the machinery for its purposes. The Canadians also took the position that distribution of revenues to member states should only occur when the proper costs chargeable to the operation of the machinery were satisfied. These would include not only current operating costs, but also costs of financing protective measures with respect to possible dangers to the marine environment caused by the exploration and exploitation of the seabed, as these are legitimate costs which should be borne by the regime as well as by the entrepreneurs. Revenues should also be used for ancillary purposes such as scientific research in the area and to provide technical assistance to member states. The net revenue after allocation of reinvestment capital would then be distributed for the benefit of mankind as a whole irrespective of the geographical location of states, whether landlocked or coastal, and taking 'into particular consideration the interests and needs of the developing countries.'[61] It should be noted that the Canadians regard that it is only at this stage that these special considerations should apply and not at the time of allocation of licenses or determination of conditions, although they do state that steps should be taken to encourage developing countries to participate in the exploration and exploitation process. The Canadians also made brief mention of the possibility of incorporating the voluntary international development tax scheme into the permanent regime by suggesting that provision be made for coastal states to make a certain proportional payment into the regime machinery of revenues generated from the exploitation of areas under their national jurisdiction. The Canadians seemed also to imply that the net revenues of the regime would in large part be reserved for developing countries either directly or through international development programs.[62] These last two suggestions in some measure could make more palatable to the developing countries the extensive claims to national jurisdiction asserted by Canada.

The nature of coastal state rights under the regime

From the early stages of the work of the committee, the Canadian delegation used it as a forum to elaborate a doctrine under which the coastal states would be given a special status in the area beyond national jurisdiction. This concept was first raised in the summer session of the committee in 1969, when the possibility was suggested by the Canadian delegation that for purposes of pollution control 'there should be some mechanism to allow individual coastal states a degree of special rights within an adjacent zone beyond the limits of national jurisdiction at least as regards the control of exploration and exploitation operations.'[63] This idea was later broadened to include other aspects of the Law of the Sea. Thus Mr Legault of the Canadian delegation later spoke of the necessity for the transformation of the doctrine of the high seas in a manner that 'its essential features [would] be preserved but in a form which would provide greater flexibility for the protection not only of coastal states but of the international community as well.'[64]

Spurred by the controversy generated by enactment of the Arctic Waters Pollution Prevention Act[65] and the amendments to the Canada Shipping Act,[66] the Canadian delegation in the summer session of the Seabed Committee in 1971 tried to rationalize the various initiatives into a 'conceptual' statement. The main thrust of this theoretical analysis was that the development of law ought to establish a new balance between coastal interests and maritime or flag interests. In this connection, the Canadians put forward their understanding of the manner in which this balance would operate with respect to resources of the seabed. The basic means by which there could be a rationalization of the divergent interests would be the delegation of certain rights to the coastal states by the international community, in return for which the coastal states would be expected to undertake certain responsibilities and duties. The coastal state would be required to manage the resources entrusted to its jurisdiction not only for its own benefit, but for that of the whole of the international community under a system that the Canadians termed 'custodianship.' Thus, with respect to the continental shelf there would not be any question of surrendering any existing rights to the international community, merely the acceptance by the coastal state of a restriction of the uncontrolled enjoyment of benefits for the purpose of the international community, as for example by the payment of a portion of the revenues such as the voluntary international development tax. Mr Beesley in a later statement made very clear what he considered to be the limits of the terms 'custodianship' and 'delegation of powers':

> We should like to point out, however, that we do not interpret these concepts as some other delegations may do, as implying that coastal states would have or now have no rights except those which may be specifically delegated to them by the international community. On the contrary we would refer delegations to the present regime of the territorial sea as a kind of precedent to bear in mind in considering the concepts we have outlined. A coastal state now has sovereignty over its territorial sea, subject, however, to a particular limitation of that sovereignty, namely, the right of innocent passage. The coastal state, as we see it, acts as a custodian of the community rights of innocent passage. On a similar basis, we would envisage the recognition of sovereign rights of coastal states in specific areas and for specific functions, subject to certain limitations on these sovereign rights, which would be spelled out. Thus the rights themselves would not be subject to examination, renunciation or review by an international tribunal but the exercise of such rights, including in particular, the duties of custodianship would be subject to examination and review. The distinction may appear to be a nice one but it is a vital one.[67]

This approach, which the Canadians applied not only to the continental shelf but to other interests of coastal states in the sea, was consistent with the basic position of reserving to the coastal state a great amount of responsibility, subject to a certain amount of overall review by the international community. It served Canada's interests very well, but it left Canada open to the criticism that it was merely constructing an elaborate self-serving theory to justify what some nations considered to be unwarranted extensions of coastal jurisdiction in areas which had hitherto been, or could possibly be regarded, as part of the international community. As far as the seabed beyond national jurisdiction was concerned, the Canadians stated that the concepts of custodianship and delegation had to be applied in conjunction with the principle of the common heritage of mankind.[68] These principles would provide the theoretical framework under which the international machinery could devolve some of its authority upon member states in some areas of the ocean in return for the assumption of certain duties and responsibilities by those states. In this, the Canadian proposal resembled the various proposals of 'trusteeship' that had been submitted to the committee; however, the Canadians did make a point of distinguishing their proposal by the deliberate avoidance of the term 'trusteeship' and the connotation it had acquired.[69]

Environmental concerns

As far as the environmental aspects of the management system were concerned, the Canadians urged strong controls and, of course, insisted on the rights of coastal states to establish pollution control zones, but other suggestions were vague and disappointing. In the major statement dealing with the seabed regime only the following part of the comprehensive statement is devoted to environmental concerns:

> ... the treaty should establish safety standards and provide for their effective enforce-
> ment, with respect to blow-out prevention and mud circulation systems; casing practices;
> testing and plugging programmes; seaworthiness of platforms and other facilities; recog-
> nition of seabed geological hazards in the positioning of production and storage equip-
> ment, anchoring of drilling vessels, laying of pipelines; and so on[70]

One suggestion that could have been made to render more meaningful the provisions to mitigate pollution damage that might be done to coastal state and other
maritime interests would have been to set up a compensation fund, administered
by the international machinery, whose purpose would be to provide truly comprehensive coverage to states and individuals affected by pollution resulting from
exploration and exploitation of seabed resources. Such a fund financed partly
through revenues and partly through subrogation to rights against states and
individuals[71] would provide immediate and adequate payment covering not only
direct clean-up costs but also indirect economic damage such as loss of livelihood
to persons adversely affected. The fund would also be available to compensate
individuals or states which had been injured by chronic small scale pollution resulting from offshore exploitation and exploration but which was not attributable to any
particular entrepreneur or state. The organization could also be required to devote
some of its revenues to the establishment of standby emergency crews which could
be rushed to the site of a marine disaster, whether in the international area or in
areas under national jurisdiction. Further, the international machinery itself should
have the authority to prescribe and enforce the standards and conditions for the
exploration and exploitation of the resources concurrently with the member states.
Stringent penalty clauses providing for fines for non-compliance with these standards should be directly imposed by the international machinery on either the
entrepreneur or the state responsible for them, and provision should also be made
for the suspension of rights of member states and for the revocation of entrepreneur's licenses in cases of gross or persistent violations in this regard. It is also
very important that the treaty establishing the seabed regime deal with these
environmental matters, rather than leaving them for elaboration and implementation by the international machinery whose primary bias would be towards the
efficient extraction of resources from the seabed area.[72]

Scientific research, living resources, and military uses of the seabed

At the July 1971 meeting of the committee, the Canadian delegation dealt briefly
with other uses of the seabed which would be affected by the acceptance of the
regime and the machinery. These were, in particular, scientific research exploitation of living resources and military activity. As far as scientific research was concerned, the Canadians were in substantial agreement with the provisions of seabed
principle 10,[73] which dealt with this question but which avoided the many
difficulties which plagued the discussion of this issue in other fora. The only Canadian concern was that the stringent controls that they hoped would be applicable
to exploration and exploitation activities for the purpose of preventing pollution
should also be applied to scientific research, especially where this entailed drilling

into the ocean floor. The Canadians recognized that the acceptance of the regime would have a bearing on the legal norms that affect sedentary species. However, they pointed out that this was one of the remaining few areas where they had not developed any firm policies and that they probably would not do so until they had some indication as to where the limits of national jurisdiction were likely to be drawn.[74]

From the earliest stages of the discussions in the Seabed Committee the Canadian delegation had taken the attitude that questions of the regulation of the military uses of the marine environment should be dealt with by the Eighteenth Disarmament Commission. In that commission the Canadian delegation took a leading role in the negotiation of the treaty which prohibited the emplacement of nuclear weapons and other weapons of mass destruction on the seabed. The main Canadian concern, that appropriate verification procedures be incorporated into that treaty, was echoed in Canada's discussion of the seabed principle, which dealt with the reservation of the international area for peaceful uses. The Canadians stated that they were inclined to the view that the seabed machinery 'should be granted at least the same powers of verification of suspect activities as are granted to states parties under the seabed arms control treaty,'[75] but did not go to explain how this attitude was consistent with their statement that the role of the machinery ought primarily to be that of an 'enterprise.' They also took the opportunity to reaffirm that any expansion of seabed arms limitation agreements should not prohibit 'permissible defensive activities on the continental shelf [of] the coastal state concerned.'[76]

CONCLUSION

From the examination of the part played by the Canadian delegation in the Seabed Committee, there can be seen a transition from a passive cautious role into a role of leadership fostered by imaginative proposals. Though these proposals may not have been wholeheartedly accepted, they played a useful role in focusing the attention of the committee on crucial issues in its work. As far as Canada's position with respect to the question of coastal rights and the limits of national jurisdiction is concerned, it is reasonable to assume that there will not be a softening of position because of Canada's perception of its own needs and its feeling that international jurisdictional institutions in the foreseeable future will be inadequate to ensure that special coastal state interests will be protected. But this is not to say that Canada will not be more willing to be more generous in the sharing of offshore revenues. This is made quite clear by the Canadian delegation in a recent intervention when it stated: 'We believe that since the coastal state enjoys special rights and privileges with regard to the resources of the continental shelf, it could recognize some duty towards the international community as a whole, and particularly the developing countries, and contribute to them at least some benefits from these rights and privileges enjoyed by coastal states.'[77]

NOTES

1 The earliest attempt to stimulate federal interest in offshore development that was being planned off the coast of British Columbia was the introduction in the Senate of an act which would claim offshore lands for the federal government, an Act to Amend the Territorial Lands Act, introduced on 27 October 1957 and known as Bill L. The first

federal regulations to deal with offshore development were the Canada Oil and Gas Land Regulations, issued on 13 April 1960, s.o.r./1960/182. These were later superseded by amended Canada Oil and Gas Land Regulations issued on 28 June 1961, s.o.r./1961/253. Active involvement with offshore areas occurred early in 1960 when the federal Minister of Northern Affairs and National Resources, F.A.G. Hamilton, wrote to the Richfield Oil Corporation which held twelve permits issued by the British Columbia government covering some 700,000 acres on the west coast continental shelf and requiring them to obtain oil and gas permits. For a reference to this correspondence, see *Reference Re Ownership of Offshore Mineral Rights* case, 432. By 1964 some 70 million acres were being held under exploratory permits issued by the federal government and this figure had reached some 240 million acres by 1967. In 1966 the first two exploratory wells were drilled under federal supervision on the Grand Banks off the east coast, followed by the drilling of two exploratory wells off the west coast in 1967.

2 *Reference Re Ownership of Offshore Mineral Rights*, [1967] s.c.r. 192.

3 g.a. Res 2340, 22 u.n. gaor Supp 16, at 14, u.n. Doc a/6716.

4 Excluding Hudson Bay and Strait, the area of the Canadian physical continental shelf is some 847,000 square nautical miles or 1,117,000 square statute miles or 29 per cent of the land area. When the continental shelf underlying Hudson Bay and Strait is included, the total area of the Canadian physical continental shelf exceeds 1.5 million square statute miles. The size of Canadian physical continental shelf is second only to that of the ussr which exceeds 2.2 million square statute miles. The area of physical continental shelf and margin off Canada excluding Hudson Bay and Strait is 1,240,000 square statute miles or 1,577,000 square nautical miles. Including Hudson Bay and Strait, the area of the physical continental shelf and margin is in the neighbourhood of 2 million square statute miles. Canada's offshore extensions represents an area equivalent to the combined land areas of the provinces of Ontario, Quebec, Manitoba, Saskatchewan, and Alberta.

5 A sizeable proportion of the Canadian continental shelf lies beyond the two hundred meter isobath. In the Arctic and off the east coast over one-third and off the west coast over one-fifth of the continental shelf lies deeper than two hundred meters. The eastern continental shelf extends from up to 170 miles from the shore of Nova Scotia to approximately 400 miles off Newfoundland in the Flemish Cap area. In the Arctic the shelf extends to a distance from 50 to 300 miles beyond the islands of the Arctic archipelago. The Canadians have only recently undertaken large-scale mapping and surveying of their continental shelves and have made available large-scale bathymetric charts of limited areas of the Canadian offshore areas. See for example the Bathymetric Chart of the East Coast, Bay of Fundy to Gulf of St Lawrence, and of the Newfoundland Shelf issued by the Canadian Hydrographic Service, Marine Sciences Branch, Department of Energy, Mines and Resources, Ottawa, in 1969 and 1970, as no 801 and no 802 respectively.

6 Broadcast on the cbc television network on 29 February 1972.

7 *North Sea Continental Shelf* case, [1969] i.c.j. 3, at 39.

8 For an assessment of the oil and gas potential of the Canadian offshore areas see, Canadian Petroleum Association, 'Potential Reserves of Oil, Natural Gas and Associated Sulphur in Canada' prepared by the cpa Geological Reserves Committee, D.W. Axford chairman, submitted to the Canadian cabinet in Calgary in 1969. This assessment was reviewed in the light of information available from east coast drillings programs, but the cpa in oral submissions to various government officials indicated that its earlier estimates were substantially correct. See also D.W. Smith, 'The Potential of Canada's Offshore Mineral Resources' and D.G. Crosby, 'A Brief Look at Canada's Offshore.' Institute of Mining and Metallurgy Symposium, Ottawa, 13 February 1969.

9 For example, Gulf Canada has built a refinery at Point Tupper, ns. Another refinery in under construction at Come-By-Chance, Newfoundland. A third refinery is being planned by Continental Oil Company at Saint John, New Brunswick. Although, these ostensibly were built to handle imported oil, planning has taken into consideration the possible oil flow from Canadian offshore production. Similarly the Halifax shipyards are in the process of building their third and

fourth offshore platforms used in exploration and exploitation. It is interesting to note that one of these is being constructed for exploration and exploitation work in areas other than those off Canada.

10 The most recent agreement was that with the Persian Gulf States on 14 February 1971. This was followed by agreements with other countries such as Libya, Nigeria and Iraq later in 1971. A later agreement on 20 January 1972 was reached in which the importing nations agreed to compensate the exporting nations for losses resulting from the devaluation of the American dollar.

11 The acquisition of an oil or gas lease is restricted by s 55(2) of the Canada Oil and Gas Land Regulations (*supra* note 1) to Canadian citizens and to corporations incorporated in Canada. The corporation incorporated in Canada in order to obtain an oil or gas lease must satisfy the minister that at least 50 per cent of its shares are beneficially owned by Canadian citizens or that its shares are listed on a recognized Canadian stock exchange and that Canadians will have an opportunity to participate in the financing and ownership of the corporation. The Canada Development Corporation was established by the Canada Development Corporation Act, Bill c-219 passed by the House of Commons on 9 June 1971. Panarctic Oils Limited was established as a government-private industry consortium in order to facilitate exploration and exploitation of the Canadian Arctic. One of the chief reasons for its establishment was to ensure that this potentially important aspect of Canadian development remains in Canadian hand.

12 R.S.C. c 2 (1st Supp.) (1970).

13 Bill C-2, An Act to Amend the Canada Shipping Act, passed by the House of Commons, on 1 March 1971.

14 Canada Oil and Gas Drilling and Production Regulations, issued on 28 June 1961, S.O.R. 1961/253.

15 Treaty on the prohibition of the Emplacement of Nuclear Weapons and other Weapons of Mass Destruction on the Seabed and the Ocean Floor and the Subsoil Thereof. The text of the treaty is annexed to G.A. Res 2660, 25 U.N. GAOR Supp 28 at 11, U.N. Doc A/8028.

16 Although fisheries contribute to less than one per cent of the Canadian GNP, several provinces are heavily dependent on them for economic survival. For example, fisheries contribute in the neighbourhood of 10 to 16 per cent of the value added in commodity producing industries in the provinces of Nova Scotia, Prince Edward Island, and Newfoundland. Some communities in these provinces are totally dependent on fisheries. These figures become much more important when it is considered that because of the geographic isolation of the industry and the socioeconomic characteristic of the population presently engaged in fishing, a large portion of this labour force is not mobile and cannot be retrained to engage in other forms of employment.

17 The total area of the world's physical continental shelf and margin is in the neighbourhood of 18 million square nautical miles. Excluding Hudson Bay and Strait, Canada has 7–8 per cent of this area off its shores.

18 Pursuant to G.A. Res 2340, *supra* note 3, the General Assembly established an *Ad Hoc* Committee to study seabed question. This committee and its successor committee are referred to throughout as the Seabed Committee.

19 Statement made in the First Committee by Mr Allan Gotlieb, on 15 November 1967. Canadian Mission to the United Nations Press Release no 77, 5. Reported in 22 U.N. GAOR, U.N. Doc A/C. 1/P.V. 1529, 16, par 179.

20 Ibid, 4; 16, par 178.

21 Statement made in the *Ad Hoc* Committee on the Seabed and Ocean Floor, by Mr George Ignatieff, on 21 March 1968. Canadian Mission to the United Nations Press Release, no 8, 8. Reported in U.N. Doc A/AC, 135/SR. 4, 24.

22 See, for example the statement of Mr Sharp, the secretary of state for external affairs, in a speech to the International Law Association, Toronto, on 5 November 1969, in which he said:

We are taking the position that the redefinition of the continental shelf must recognize coastal-state rights over the 'submerged continental margin', which consists of the continental shelf and slope and at least part of the rise. Any arbitrary distance-plus-depth formula which disregarded existing international law and geographical geological factors would be unacceptable to Canada, and doubtless to a significant group of other coastal states.

Department of External Affairs, Information

Division, *Statements and Speeches,* no 69/19, 2.

23 Statement made by Mr J.A. Beesley on 13 February 1969, to the Symposium of the Canadian Institute of Mining and Metallurgy in Ottawa, entitled 'Contemporary International Law on the Seabed and Ocean Floor,' at 15. See also, A. Gotlieb, 'Recent Development Concerning the Exploration and Exploitation of the Ocean Floor, (1969), 15 *McGill L.J.* 260, at 274, on which the Beesley statement was based.

24 See the draft treaty presented by the US delegation, 24 U.N. GAOR, U.N. Doc A/AC. 138/25.

25 See for example the Draft Ocean Treaty presented by Dr Arvid Pardo, and submitted by the delegation of Malta, 25 GAOR, U.N. Doc A/AC.138/53.

26 *Supra* note 21, at 5.

27 23 U.N. GAOR, U.N. Doc A/AC.138/SC. 1/SR.13, 18.

28 See 24 U.N. GAOR, UN Doc A/C.1/P.V. 1682, 28.

29 24 U.N. GAOR, U.N. Doc A/AC.138/SR.24, 80.

30 Statement made in the Preparatory Committee for the Third Law of the Sea Conference, Sub-Committee I, by Mr J.A. Beesley on 30 July 1971, 3. Reported also in 25 U.N. GAOR, U.N. Doc A/AC.138/SC.1/SR. 10. The working paper can be found in 25 U.N. GAOR, U.N. Doc A/AC.138/59, dated 24 August 1971, 1. It is interesting to note that the Canadian delegation began to refer to the Seabed Committee as the Preparatory Committee for the Third Law of the Sea Conference, although the official name of the committee remained: the Committee on the Peaceful Uses of the Seabed and the Ocean Floor Beyond the Limits of National Jurisdiction.

31 *Supra* note 29, at 81.

32 24 U.N. GAOR, U.N. Doc A/AC.1/L.480/Rev.1. This draft resolution was sponsored by Brazil, Ceylon, Chile, Ecuador, Guatemala, Guyana, Kuwait, Mauritania, Mexico, Peru, and Trinidad and Tobago.

33 During 1968 eight exploratory wells were drilled off the west coast, and one on Sable Island. During 1969 four exploratory wells were drilled off the west coast, one off the east coast, and two in the Hudson Bay and Strait area. Plans were then being made for drilling some dozen or more exploratory wells in 1970 off the east coast.

34 See 24 U.N. GAOR, U.N. Doc A/C.1/P.V.1709, 28.

35 24 U.N. GAOR, U.N. Doc A/C.1/P.V. 1682, 28.

36 Draft resolution A/C.1/L.480 was adopted by 52 votes to 27 with 35 abstentions. Canada voted against this resolution. see *Supra* note 39, at 67–70. Canada also voted against the draft resolution which incorporated this First Committee resolution. See 24 U.N. GAOR, U.N. Doc A/P.V. 1833, 17. The resolution, which became G.A. Res. 2574D, 24 U.N. GAOR, Supp 30 at 11, U.N. Doc A/7630, was adopted by 62 votes to 28, with 28 abstentions. See 24 U.N. GAOR, U.N. Doc A/P.V. 1833, 18.

37 *Supra* note 29.

38 Statement made in the enlarged United Nations Committee on the Peaceful Uses of the Seabed and the Ocean Floor Beyond the Limits of National Jurisdiction by Mr J.A. Beesley on 24 March 1971, 20.

39 Ibid, at 25. Reported in 25 U.N. GAOR, U.N. Doc A/AC.138/SR.58, 201. It is interesting to note that the summary records the words 'beyond the outer limit of their territorial waters' in place of the words 'beyond the outer limits of their internal waters' which appear in the text of Mr Beesley's speech.

40 *Supra* note 30, at 32 *et seq*; 17 (prov); 20.

41 See the statement made in the Preparatory Committee for the Third Law of the Sea Conference, Plenary Session by Mr J.A. Beesley on 18 August 1971, 2, reported in 25 U.N. GAOR, U.N. Doc A/AC.138/SR.65, 15 (prov.), where he states

'we are somewhat disappointed by the lack of comment on our proposal that every coastal state make a voluntary contribution to the international community of a fixed percentage of its revenue from offshore mineral exploitation. We are particularly grateful to the delegations of Argentina and Algeria for the support they have given to the first part of our proposal, namely, the moratorium. We have, however, heard comments from a very few delegations expressing reservations about the first and second elements of our proposal ... But such delegations have not commented on the third element in our proposal.

42 Statement made in the Committee on the Peaceful Uses of the Sea-bed and Ocean Floor Beyond the Limits of National Jurisdiction, Economic and Technical Sub-Committee by Dr D.G. Crosby on 20 August 1969. Canadian Mission to the United Nations Release, 2. Reported in 23 U.N. GAOR, U.N. Doc A/AC.138/SC.2/, SR.21, 88.

43 24 U.N. GAOR, U.N. Doc A/AC.138SR.36, 98.

44 Ibid.

45 That is, forty-two states. See G.A. Res 2467, 23 U.N. GAOR Supp 18, at 15, U.N. Doc A/7218.

46 For a list of these, see *supra* note 30, at 24; 16 (prov); 20.

47 G.A. Res 2749, 25 U.N. GAOR, Supp 28, at 24, U.N. Doc A/8028.

48 *Supra* note 30, at 2; 11 (prov.); 14.

49 See article 36 and appendix E of the US draft convention. *Supra* note 24.

50 *Supra* note 30, at 23; 13 (prov); 16.

51 In a statement made in the United Nations Seabed Committee (Preparatory Committee for the Third Law of the Sea Conference) Sub-Committee I, by Dr D.G. Crosby on 23 March 1972, 1, reported in 26 U.N. GAOR, U.N. Doc A/AC.138.SC.1/SR.43, 2 (prov), the Canadian delegation stated that 'proposals for weighed voting would appear to be incompatible with the fundamental principle of the sovereign quality of States and the concept of the common heritage of mankind.' This position seems to have been reached after a certain amount of vacillation in the Canadian delegation, which previously had seemed to favour such a system, as it would ensure that the dominant influence in the organization was technical and economic rather than political.

52 These would be the issuance of licenses, inspection of operations, enforcement of standards, collection of fees, and recommendation of amendments to operation and safety standards established by the treaty. See *supra* note 30, 24; 14 (prov); 17.

53 *Supra* note 43, at 99.

54 Statement made in the Preparatory Committee for the Third Law of the Sea Conference, Plenary Session, by Mr J.A. Beesley on 5 August 1972, 6, reported in 25 U.N. GAOR, U.N. Doc A/AC.138/SR.63, 9.

55 Such approach appears to be adopted by the US draft convention. See *supra* note 24.

56 *Supra* note 51.

57 *Supra* note 30, at 21; 12 (prov); 15.

58 *Supra* note 51, at 1; 2 (prov).

59 A description of this system can be found in 24 U.N. GAOR, U.N. Doc A/AC.138/SR.38, 43 *et seq.*

60 See for example, the statement made in the First Committee by Mr Kaplan of the Canadian delegation where he stated that 'while the Canadian delegation agrees that it is desirable to guard against the disruption of world markets, we do not consider this objective should be permitted to override the paramount need to develop resources for the benefit of mankind and the developing countries in particular.' 24 U.N. GAOR, U.N. Doc A/C.1/P.V.1779, 7. It was only in the spring of 1972 that a much more sympathetic approach to this question was taken by the Canadian delegation. Dr Crosby said: 'Surely when we say that these resources are to be developed and exploited for the benefit of mankind, we must preclude the possibility that such exploitation would be to the detriment of states already producing such materials. We must not allow the situation to arise where some states bear the brunt of such socio-economic damage and dislocation for the benefit of others.' *Supra* note 51, at 4; 4 (prov).

61 Seabed principle 7. *Supra* note 47.

62 *Supra* note 30, at 10; 6 (prov); 6.

63 *Supra* note 42.

64 *Supra* note 29, at 81.

65 *Supra* note 12.

66 *Supra* note 13.

67 *Supra* note 41, at 1; 14.

68 *Supra* note 54, at 10; 12 (prov).

69 The term was most frequently linked to the 'Nixon proposal' and the draft treaty presented by the US delegation (*supra* note 24). Similarly the Canadians distinguished the 'custodianship' concept from the concept of an 'intermediate zone' proposed by some delegation in that, for them, custodianship did not imply the creation of zones of mixed coastal and international jurisdiction. Because of their belief that no consensus had been reached on the intermediate zone approach, they opposed an attempt to create a working group to explore this approach. *Supra* note 51, at 8; 6 (prov).

70 *Supra* note 30, at 16; 9 (prov).

71 The Canadian delegation underlined what it felt was the scope of international responsibility of states under its comments to principle 14. Ibid, at 19; 11 (prov); 13.

72 Such approach appears to be adopted by the US draft convention. See *supra* note 24.

73 *Supra* note 47.

74 *Supra* note 15. Canada ratified the Seabed Arms Treaty on 17 May 1972. The ratification was accompanied by an interpretive statement which reiterated the position that Canada had expressed both in the Seabed Committee and the Disarmament Commission. See (July-August 1972), *International Perspectives.*

75 *Supra* note 30, at 11; 6 (prov); 7.

76 Ibid, at 11; 6 (prov); p 7.

77 *Supra* note 51, at 7; 5 (prov).

DONAT PHARAND*

18/The Arctic Waters in Relation to Canada

The Arctic waters were not discussed at the Law of the Sea Conferences of 1958 and 1960. Having regard to the Arctic developments which have taken place in recent years, the legal status of some of those waters and the jurisdiction of states in relation to them might well be raised, at least indirectly, at the upcoming Third Law of the Sea Conference. The Arctic developments envisaged here refer mainly to three events: the 1968 discovery of vast oil reserves at Prudhoe Bay on the north slope of Alaska; the 1969 and 1970 voyages of the s.s. *Manhattan* in the Northwest Passage; and the adoption of two laws by Canada in 1970, one extending its territorial sea from three to twelve miles and the other establishing an antipollution zone of one hundred miles off its Arctic coasts. These developments have in turn raised three main issues of international law: the legal status of the Northwest Passage, the legal status of the Arctic Ocean, and the jurisdiction of coastal states such as Canada in the matter of oil pollution control in waters adjacent to their coast. I have recently published an article on this last question; thus only the first two issues will be examined here.

LEGAL STATUS OF THE NORTHWEST PASSAGE

Brief description of the Northwest Passage

There are four potential routes through the Northwest Passage, which spans the Canadian Arctic Archipelago from Baffin Bay to the Beaufort Sea.[2] However, the only feasible route for the moment goes through Prince of Wales Strait, east of Banks Island. Consequently, the Northwest Passage being studied here commences in the east with Lancaster Sound, continues directly west through Barrow Strait and Viscount Melville Sound, and then in a southwesterly direction through Prince of Wales Strait; finally, it crosses Amundsen Gulf and continues along the coast of the Yukon Territory and Alaska in the Beaufort Sea as far as the Bering Strait. Lancaster Sound is a wide strait, averaging about thirty-five miles in width, which joins Barrow Strait where the passage is narrowed to about fifteen miles between Young and Lowther Islands. The route continues into the immense Viscount Melville Sound and turns southwest into Prince of Wales Strait. This strait averages only about ten miles in width and the passage narrows to approximately five miles at the half-way point in the strait because of the two small Princess Royal

*The writer is greatly indebted to Lt Cmdr A.D. Taylor, naval international law specialist, Legal Operations Division, Department of External Affairs, for having read the manuscript and made numerous helpful suggestions.

Islands. M'Clure strait north of Banks Island would be the natural western end of the Northwest Passage instead of Prince of Wales Strait, if it were not for the fact that it usually remains choked with polar ice coming from the Beaufort Sea. It is therefore most difficult for surface navigation, as was shown by the attempt made by the *Manhattan* in 1969.

The ice conditions in the Northwest Passage[3] vary somewhat from east to west, becoming less favourable in Viscount Melville Sound. The ice in Lancaster Sound does not normally consolidate in winter so that the sound is usually open water from mid-July to the end of October. In Barrow Strait, the ice consolidates usually in December and remains in that condition until mid-July. The ice conditions in Viscount Melville Sound vary from year to year, but the ice usually is cemented together from the latter part of October until the middle of August, most of the ice being more than one year old. The ice conditions in Prince of Wales Strait are comparatively good since the ice is generally locally formed, except for some older ice floes entering at the northern end from M'Clure Strait. The break-up occurs in late July and the strait remains reasonably clear until late September. Amundsen Gulf is usually closed to navigation from late October to late June. September is normally the best month for navigation as the gulf is then usually ice free.

It is obvious from the above brief description that navigation in the Northwest Passage must normally be limited to the summer months and that only a very capable icebreaker or ice-strengthened ship could possibly negotiate the passage in winter conditions. The Humble Oil Company decided to modify the *Manhattan* for service as a giant icebreaker and made a voyage in September 1969, in order to determine the feasibility of year-round surface navigation in the Northwest Passage. In spite of the assistance of the Canadian icebreaker *John A. Macdonald,* the *Manhattan* was not able to negotiate the M'Clure Strait, but it did not have much trouble through the Prince of Wales Strait and the rest of the route. According to Captain Thomas Pullen, the Canadian government representative aboard the *Manhattan,* the main cause of the *Manhattan*'s failure to make the M'Clure was the lack of adequate shaft horsepower, which must be considerably more than for the conventional type of icebreakers.[4]

Nevertheless, the 1969 voyage of the *Manhattan* through the Northwest Passage, as well as her second voyage the next year in the eastern part of the passage, provided data which should eventually permit the building of a ship able to operate on a year-round basis. This is the conclusion of Captain R. Maybourn who states as follows:

> In the 2 years that have since elapsed the two voyages of the *Manhattan* to the Arctic, and the studies and reconnaissances associated with those voyages, have extended knowledge to the point where it may be stated with some confidence that, given a ship of the right design with the proper operational support, navigation throughout most of the Arctic on a year round basis is now possible.[5]

It would therefore appear that the Northwest Passage is navigable through the Prince of Wales Strait and that it is only a matter of time for surface navigation to take place through the M'Clure Strait.[6] The officers of the *Manhattan* would have been delighted to conquer the M'Clure Strait not only to demonstrate the ice capability of the ship, but also to be able to say that they remained on the high seas throughout the passage. This, of course, they could not claim after being diverted to the Prince of Wales Strait where the ship had to go through Canadian territorial waters. Territorial waters could not be avoided because of the presence of the Princess Royal Islands, although Canada still claimed only a three-mile territorial sea at that time.

Effect of a twelve-mile territorial sea on the Northwest Passage

On 17 April 1970 the Secretary of State for External Affairs, the Honourable Mitchell Sharp, moved the second reading in the House of Commons of Bill c–203 to amend the Territorial Sea and Fishing Zones Act, so as to extend the territorial waters of Canada from three to twelve nautical miles. The minister explained the effect of the new twelve-mile territorial sea limit with respect to the Northwest Passage in the following terms: 'Since the 12-mile territorial sea is well established in international law, the effect of this bill on the Northwest Passage is that under any sensible view of the law, Barrow Strait, as well as the Prince of Wales Strait are subject to complete Canadian sovereignty.'[7]

What the minister was saying in effect was that the distance between Young and Lowther Islands in Barrow Strait being only fifteen miles, there would now be an overlapping of territorial waters at that juncture of the strait, thus forming a sort of 'gateway' in the eastern section of the Northwest Passage, in addition to the existing 'gateway' in Prince of Wales Strait. The term 'gateway' was used by Mr J.A. Beesley, legal adviser of the External Affairs Department, when he described the legal implications for the benefit of the Standing Committee on External Affairs and National Defence: 'This has implications for Barrow Strait, for example, where the 12-mile territorial sea has the effect of giving Canada sovereignty from shore to shore. To put it simply, we have undisputed control – undisputed in the legal sense – over two of the *gateways* to the Northwest Passage.'[8]

With the coming into force of the new legislation, the validity of which is virtually impossible to challenge in international law, considering the great number of states already subscribing to a territorial sea limit of twelve miles or more, it is no longer possible to speak of a strip of high seas throughout the Northwest Passage, when avoiding the Prince of Wales Strait and passing by M'Clure.[9] Consequently, even if a tanker such as the *Manhattan* were to manage to negotiate the M'Clure Strait – which such a tanker is bound to do eventually – it would have to go through the territorial waters of Canada. In these circumstances, the coastal state may adopt measures to ensure that the passage of a foreign ship is an innocent one and is not prejudicial to its security. Indeed, if it is essential for the protection of its security, the coastal state may go so far as to suspend temporarily the innocent passage of foreign ships.[10] Such suspension, however, could not be imposed by Canada if it should be found that the Northwest Passage is a strait that has been used for international navigation.[11] In other words, there could be no suspension of the right of innocent passage in the Northwest Passage, if the latter constitutes an international strait. This is the effect of the relevant provisions of the 1958 Territorial Sea Convention which, though not ratified by Canada, are considered as having become part of general international law.

Is the Northwest Passage an international strait?

The answer to the question whether or not the Northwest Passage may be regarded as an international strait depends on two subquestions. First, is it used for international navigation, and second, does it connect one part of the high seas to another part of the high seas or the territorial sea of a foreign state?[12] The second subquestion will be examined later when the legal status of the Arctic Ocean is studied.

In its note handed to the United States government on 16 April 1970, Canada explained its position on this question:

> The Canadian Government is aware of USA interest in ensuring freedom of transit through international straits, but *rejects any suggestion that the Northwest Passage is such an international strait* ... The Northwest Passage has not attained the status of an international strait by customary usage nor has it been defined as such by conventional international law.[13]

The same opinion was reiterated by Mr J.A. Beesley, testifying before the Standing Committee on External Affairs and National Defence the following week.[14]

One has to agree that the simple fact is that no convention or agreement of any kind has ever defined the Northwest Passage as an international strait. The only other way for the Northwest Passage to be classified as an international strait is to show that it is in fact used for international navigation. The use does not have to be extensive for the non-suspension provision to apply, but there has to be some use. The International Law Commission had suggested in its draft of the Territorial Sea Convention that the non-suspension provision be limited to straits which are 'normally used for international navigation.'[15] However, the 1958 conference decided to remove the qualifying adverb 'normally.' Consequently, the test of usage to be applied is that formulated by the International Court of Justice in the *Corfu Channel* case:

> It may be asked whether the test is to be found in the volume of traffic passing through the Strait or in its greater or lesser importance for international navigation. But in the opinion of the Court the decisive criterion is rather its geographical situation as connecting two parts of the high seas and the fact of its being used for international navigation. Nor can it be decisive that this Strait is not a necessary route between two parts of the high seas, but only an alternative passage between the Aegean and the Adriatic Seas. It has nevertheless been a useful route for international maritime traffic.[16]

It follows from this test that, although the use need not have been extensive, it must have actually served as a route for 'international maritime traffic.' An examination of the known completed crossings which have taken place since Amundsen's first sailing of the passage (Lancaster Sound, Barrow Strait, Peel Sound, Franklin, James Ross, and Rae straits) in 1906 reveals that only seven of them have been made.

1 RCMP Schooner *St Roch* (1940–2): Amundsen's route east, except that it went through Bellot Strait and Prince Regent Inlet instead of Peel Sound.

2 RCMP Schooner *St Roch* (1944): Lancaster Sound, Barrow Strait, Viscount Melville Sound, and Prince of Wales Strait.
3 H.M.C.S. *Labrador* (1954): same route as the St Roch in 1944.
4 U.S.C.G.S. *Spar, Bramble,* and *Storis* (1957): same route as the St Roch in 1940–2.
5 U.S.S. *Seadragon* (1960): following the Parry Channel (Lancaster Sound, Barrow Strait, Viscount Melville Sound, and M'Clure Strait) and remaining underwater throughout, except for one surfacing at Resolute Bay.
6 S.S. *Manhattan* (1969): same route as that of the St Roch in 1944, for the return voyage as well.
7 C.S.S. *Hudson* (1970): Amundsen's route, except that it crossed Victoria Strait instead of going around King William Island through James Ross and Rae Straits.

Of those seven crossings, only numbers 4, 5, and 6 involved foreign ships and all of them were American. Number 4, the crossing of the three US Coast Guard icebreakers, was accomplished with the assistance of the Canadian naval ice-breaker *Labrador*[17] so that the US ships could manage to cross Bellot Strait, a narrow and key link in the route being followed. Number 5 was a crossing by the U.S.S. *Seadragon,* a 2360-ton nuclear submarine, whose official orders were to 'investigate the feasibility of a submarine passage through the Parry Channel.'[18] It is my understanding that the passage was made with the consent and assistance of the Canadian government. Number 6, the voyage of the *Manhattan,* was made, as already mentioned, with the assistance of the Canadian icebreaker *Macdonald.* As for the nature of these three crossings, 4 was reportedly a joint effort by the United States and Canada to establish an alternative route to service the Distant Early Warning line radar outposts.[19] Number 5 was to test the feasibility of submarine navigation throughout Parry Channel, in particular the shallow waters of Barrow Strait, and 7 was to determine the feasibility of year-round surface navigation.

Thus the various crossings of the Northwest Passage have all been exploratory in nature, and the only three made by foreign ships since Amundsen's discovery of the passage have taken place with the acquiescence and assistance of Canada. Of those three, only the voyage of the *Manhattan* was by a commercial ship and it was strictly an experimental one. In these circumstances, it is clear beyond doubt that the Northwest Passage has never been 'a useful route for international maritime traffic' as the Corfu Channel had been and is not a strait 'used for international navigation' envisaged by the 1958 Territorial Sea Convention. By the same token, it could not have acquired the status of an international strait by custom. This presupposes, by definition, a practice which has acquired force of law by long usage and acquiescence. This conclusion,[20] of course, does not mean that a foreign ship does not have the right of innocent passage in the Northwest Passage or that Canada does not recognize such right.

Is innocent passage applicable to the Northwest Passage?

The least that can be said about the right of innocent passage in a strait made up of territorial waters is that it is as applicable there as in ordinary territorial waters.

To apply this principle to the Northwest Passage presumes, of course, that the waters of the Canadian Arctic Archipelago in general, and those of the Northwest Passage in particular, cannot be considered to have a more restrictive status than that of territorial waters. If Canada could establish proof of historic title to those waters by the exercise of exclusive authority and control over a long period of time, accompanied by the acquiescence of foreign states, particularly those affected by the claim, the waters in question would then have the status of internal waters[21] and the right of innocent passage would not apply. Another method of giving those waters the status of internal waters would be to draw straight baselines around the whole of the Canadian Arctic Archipelago in order to delimit Canada's territorial waters. However, in this latter case, by virtue of article 5 of the 1958 Territorial Sea Convention, the establishment of such straight baselines – even presuming their validity in international law – would not bar the right of innocent passage, if the waters in question were previously considered as part of the territorial seas or the high seas.[22]

The Canadian government's position, repeated on a number of occasions by the secretary of state for external affairs, has been that 'Canada has always regarded the waters between the islands of the Arctic Archipelago as being Canadian waters.'[23] However, this convenient expression 'Canadian waters' has never been defined in relation to the Arctic, and one does not know if it means territorial waters, internal waters, or both. Guidance could perhaps be obtained by looking at the Customs Act which defines 'Canadian waters' as meaning 'all waters in the territorial sea of Canada and all internal waters of Canada.'[24] The fact remains, however, that this definition is for the purpose of customs' enforcement only and, even if it were of general application, the definition would not assist in determining whether Canada considers the waters of the Canadian Arctic Archipelago as internal or territorial. However, one thing is clear: Canada does recognize the right of innocent passage through the Northwest Passage. The note of 16 April 1970 to the United States stated: 'The Canadian Government reiterates its determination to open up the Northwest Passage to safe navigation for the shipping of all nations subject, however, to necessary conditions required to protect the delicate ecological balance of the Canadian Arctic.'[25]

But Canada insists that the recognition of such right cannot preclude the coastal state from exercising pollution control in the waters being traversed. The secretary of state for external affairs made Canada's position on this question very clear in the House of Commons: 'Certainly Canada cannot accept any right of innocent passage if that right is defined as precluding the right of the coastal state to control pollution in such waters. The law may be undeveloped on this question, but if that is the case, we propose to develop it.'[26] And Canada's legal adviser in the Department of External Affairs expressed the same view in front of the Standing Committee on External Affairs and National Defence: 'Canada has taken the position publicly that it does not consider that a passage through any body of water by a ship giving rise to a danger of pollution is an innocent passage. Such a ship is an inherently dangerous object. It represents a threat to the security of the state.'[27]

In other words, it is Canada's position that the present provision that 'passage is innocent so long as it is not prejudicial to the peace, good order or security of the coastal state'[28] should be given a restrictive interpretation, by restricting the meaning of 'innocent' and enlarging the notion of 'prejudicial.' It considers that a ship carrying inherently dangerous cargoes or substances such as oil and not conforming with certain anti-pollution standards prescribed by the coastal state creates a sufficiently serious threat to constitute a prejudice to the security of the coastal state. Certainly, such a ship attempting to negotiate the Northwest Passage, with the prevailing ice conditions, would constitute a threat to the marine environment of Canada and would be prejudicial to its environmental integrity, thereby resulting in a non-innocent or 'offensive' passage.[29] This Canadian position is, of course, diametrically opposed to that of the United States which considers the Northwest Passage an international strait.

The United States made it clear in the UN Seabed Committee that it would like to establish a right of 'free transit' in international straits and introduced the following provision as a part of draft articles on the question: 'In straits used for international navigation between one part of the high seas and another part of the high seas or the territorial sea of a foreign state, all ships and aircraft in transit shall enjoy *the same freedom of navigation and overflight,* for the purpose of transit through and over such straits, *as they have on the high seas.'*[30] In the draft articles the concept of international strait contained in the Territorial Sea Convention is preserved, but the right of innocent passage is replaced by a right of 'free transit.' This would give foreign ships and aircraft 'the same freedom of navigation and overflight ... as they have on the high seas.' The claim is, therefore for some kind of 'high seas corridors.' However, the draft articles would allow coastal states to 'designate corridors suitable for transit by all ships and aircraft through and over such straits' and, in straits where there are channels that are customarily used by ships in transit, the corridors should include such channels. As explained by the American legal adviser, the coastal state, while retaining its right to enforce 'reasonable safety traffic regulations,' could not use them 'as a way of impairing the right of free transit.'[31] This is really tantamount to saying that the foreign ship in such straits would enjoy virtually the same freedom of passage as on the high seas. This point was made quite clearly by Mr Stevenson in his address to the American Society of International Law, in April 1971, when he explained that 'the right of innocent passage which does not include the right of overflight is too circumscribed in its scope and has been subjected to too many different interpretations to constitute an adequate substitute for the effective exercise of the freedom of navigation of the high seas.'[32]

It seems, therefore, that 'free transit' through territorial sea straits used for international navigation means complete freedom of passage for all ships and aircraft as if they were actually on the high seas. No notice to the coastal state would be required and, since it would apply to 'all ships and aircraft,' it would include passage of military ships and overflight of military aircraft. Two observations should be made in this regard: first, the right of innocent passage does not presently extend to any aircraft and, second, the right of innocent passage for warships does not have a very clear status. It is true that such a right was recognized by the International Court of Justice in the *Corfu Channel* case in 1949,[33] but the 1958 Territorial Sea Convention is not really clear as to the scope of the right accorded to warships. Some maintain that prior permission must be obtained,[34] and a number of countries such as the USSR have attached a reservation as to warships to their instrument of ratification. Although the convention provides that 'the coastal State may require the warship to leave the territorial sea' if the latter does not comply with its regulations 'concerning passage,'[35] it is unclear as to how stringent those regulations may be. Surely they should permit the coastal state to ensure its national security and territorial integrity. This fundamental right of states must be respected in any discussion relating to the right of innocent passage of ships in general and of military ships in particular.

LEGAL STATUS OF THE ARCTIC OCEAN[36]

As was indicated earlier when examining the question of whether or not the Northwest Passage was an international strait, in strict logic one should first determine whether in fact the passage does constitute a link between two parts of the high seas. Is it really a strait in the legal sense? No one questions that the eastern end of the passage leads into the Atlantic Ocean through Baffin Bay and Davis Strait. However, some doubts have been expressed as to whether the western end of the passage leads into what could be considered as part of the high seas. Perhaps the Arctic Ocean in general and the Beaufort Sea in particular would not qualify as high seas because of the presence of ice. Consequently, it becomes important to examine the main characteristics of the Arctic Ocean and determine if in fact navigation is possible, since this is the underlying reason for the very existence of the principle of the freedom of the high seas.

Brief description of the Arctic Ocean

Unlike the Antarctic, which is a continent surrounded by a vast maritime belt, the Arctic is an ocean surrounded by a vast and nearly continuous continental mass. Whereas the South Pole rests on over 3000 metres of land covered by a solid ice cap, the North Pole rests on over 4000 metres of water covered by moving pack ice. This pack ice consists of ice floes whose average thickness is approximately 3 metres, and it covers nearly 90 per cent of the Arctic Ocean. It must be emphasized, however, that the ice cover is neither compact, uniform, permanent, nor immobile, these and similar adjectives having been used by several legal writers.

This ice cover of the Arctic Ocean is not compact, and it is inaccurate to speak of an 'ice pack' and even less of an 'ice cap.' The ice floes are not firmly packed together, but are separated by a number of water openings resembling lakes and rivers. Soviet scientists as far back as 1957 described the ice cover of the Arctic Ocean in the following terms: 'The ice-cover of the Central Arctic is not a continuous massif of old ice. On the contrary, the ice is inhomogeneous. It consists of icefields and fragments of different thickness and age, with open leads between all the mobile floes, no matter what their thickness, degree of hummocking, geographical position, or season of the year.'[37] The accuracy of this description has been confirmed many times since by scientists from a number of countries, in particular the United States and the USSR.

The ice of the Arctic Ocean is neither uniform nor permanent. The average thickness of an ice floe is about 3 metres, but it varies considerably, particularly where hummocking is found; such hummocking is due to fracturing of the ice and pressure ridging because of the action of strong current and wind. The ice itself is not permanent since there is a process of ablation by melting of the upper surface in summer and an accretion of the lower surface by freezing in winter. The process is repeated every year so that the ice floe normally attains an equilibrium thickness during the course of a year.[38] The mean lifetime of Arctic sea ice is estimated to be less than ten years, so that in reality it is not the ice itself which is permanent but rather its presence.[39]

Furthermore, the Arctic pack ice is not immobile. The ice floes are in constant motion all over the surface of the Arctic Ocean. There are two main ice circulation patterns: one called the *Transpolar drift,* carrying ice from the general area of the East Siberian Sea, passing across the North Pole, and continuing into the Greenland Sea; the other major drift follows a clockwise movement north of Alaska and the Canadian Arctic Archipelago and is known as the *Pacific Gyral.* As a consequence of these two dominant movements, most of the ice export goes into the Greenland Sea, but some polar ice does come through the numerous channels of the Queen Elizabeth Islands, as well as into the wide M'Clure Strait.[40]

Insofar as the *water masses* under the ice cover are concerned, they are basically no different than in any other ocean. There is an undersea mountain extending from the New Siberian Islands to Ellesmere Island, and the sea floor reveals a physiographic complex of basins and ridges, but there is nonetheless a displacement of water masses as in other oceans, although probably to a lesser degree. The relatively low communication of the water masses of the Arctic Ocean with the Pacific and the Atlantic explains in good part the low salinity of the surface layer of the Arctic Ocean and its being subject to ice formation. Nevertheless, in all other respects, it is water pure and simple.[41]

Is navigation possible in the Arctic Ocean?

With this combination of water and ice, the question arises whether or not navigation is possible.

Three types of navigation have been taking place in the Arctic Ocean: drift surface navigation, subsurface navigation, and conventional surface navigation. Drift surface navigation is accomplished by drifting in an icebound vessel or on an ice floe[42] in order to carry on various scientific investigations such as those relating to the ice, the water, and the ocean floor. Soviet and American scientists[43] have been carrying on such scientific investigations for a considerable number of years, but we are not concerned here with this special type of navigation and therefore only the ordinary types of navigation will be studied.

The experiments on subsurface navigation which have been carried out by the United States since 1957 have proved beyond any doubt that nuclear-powered submarines can be operated in any season of the year in the Arctic Ocean, as well as in the Northwest Passage, even in the shallow areas of Barrow Strait. In 1958 the U.S.S. *Nautilus* cruised without difficulty from the Bering Sea to the Greenland Sea, passing under the North Pole, thus, in the words of her captain, blazing 'a new submerged Northwest Passage.'[44] This first crossing was followed by a second one in the same year, that of the U.S.S. *Skate*; the latter repeated the feat in March 1960. The captain of the *Skate* reported that water openings were numerous enough to surface even in the middle of winter and, in fact, he did surface in the Arctic Ocean some fifteen times during the voyage.[45] In 1960 the u.s.s. *Sargo* carried out a thirty-one day cruise under the ice of the Arctic Ocean during January and February. On her trip to the North Pole and back she surfaced some twenty times, twice through ice three feet thick.[46] Also in the fall of the same year, the u.s.s. *Seadragon* recorded a first by crossing the Northwest Passage from east to west, following the Parry Channel throughout, and then made a quick trip to the North Pole.[47] As recently as March 1971 the British submarine *Dreadnought* also made a trip to the North Pole.

At the moment, a number of feasibility and cost studies are being carried out with a view to using giant submarine tankers to transport oil not only through the Northwest Passage to the American east coast, but also through the Arctic Ocean to western Europe.[48] With the improvement of submarine hull design, the development of better under-ice sonar, and the ever-increasing knowledge of the Arctic basin, it is not impossible to envisage the use of the giant submarine tanker as the principal means of transporting petroleum products from the Arctic.

In recent years the development of icebreakers and ice-strengthened ships has made conventional surface navigation a real possibility in Arctic waters. Very significant northings have already been attained by a number of icebreakers, particularly in the Chukchi and Beaufort seas.[49] In 1961 the nuclear-powered icebreaker *Lenin* made a high-latitude expedition of over 8000 miles, most of which was through ice. In the Laptev sea, the u.s.c.g.s. *Northwind* reached a latitude of 81°37.7′N in 1965 while going around the tip of Severnaya Zemlya. In 1964 the Canadian icebreaker *Labrador* set a Canadian record by reaching 81°47′N in Robeson Channel between Ellesmere Island and Greenland; but, more recently another Canadian icebreaker established a new record for Canada by attaining 82°56′N in the same channel.

With the development of ice-strengthened ships, such as the *Manhattan* which was able to traverse the greater part of the western end of the Northwest Passage where a good deal of polar ice was met, it is certainly possible that an improved design of such a ship could also negotiate the Arctic Ocean itself. As pointed out by Captain Maybourn in relation to the Northwest Passage, 'at its most severe this ice is comparable to the ice of the polar pack and, indeed, the westernmost 500 miles or so are through a section of polar pack.' Captain Maybourn concluded his article on the problems of operating large ships in the Arctic by saying: 'Once navigation is established along the North-West Passage route it can only be a matter of time before the logic of opening routes across the pole to Europe, or from Baffin Island's rich iron ore mines to Japan through the Bering Strait, is accepted.'[50]

Is the Arctic Ocean 'high seas?'

Having completed this brief review of the possibility of navigation in the Arctic Ocean, the question remains whether or not it can be considered as high seas.

The term 'high seas' is defined in the Convention on the High Seas as meaning 'all parts of the sea that are not included in the territorial sea or in the internal waters of a state' (art 1). The convention is general and makes no reference to specific oceans. It is argued by some, however, that the traditional freedom of navigation, which is one of the main freedoms of the high seas, is not applicable to the Arctic Ocean.[51]

The Canadian government does not seem to have adopted a clearly defined position on the legal status of the Arctic Ocean, including the Beaufort Sea with which we are particularly concerned here because it affects the status of the Northwest Passage. However, a number of statements have been made by government officials which would indicate that the Arctic Ocean, including the Beaufort Sea, would not be considered as high seas. On 15 April 1970 Prime Minister Trudeau, speaking to the Annual Meeting of the Canadian Press on Canada's fight against pollution, stated that 'only by an examination conceptually removed from reality can Beaufort Sea be described as "high sea." '[52] The next day Canada sent a note to the United States which contained the following statement relating to the freedom of the high seas in the Arctic:

> It is idle ... to talk of freedom of the high seas with respect to an area, large parts of which are covered with ice throughout the year, other parts of which are covered with ice most of each year, and where the local inhabitants use the frozen sea as an extension of the land to travel over it by dogsled and snowmobile far more than they can use it as water. While the Canadian Government is determined to open up the Northwest Passage to safe navigation, it cannot accept the suggestion that the Northwest Passage constitutes high seas.[53]

If the 'area' in question is the one defined by the Arctic Waters Pollution Prevention Act as 'Arctic waters,' then it includes part of the Beaufort Sea. However, it is possible that the passage just quoted relates only to the waters of the Northwest Passage itself between the Canadian Arctic islands, or perhaps the statement is meant to refer to both bodies of water.

In any event, the Canadian legal adviser, a short time later, speaking to the Standing Committee on External Affairs and National Defence, referred specifically to both the Arctic Ocean and the Beaufort Sea. In discussing the question of whether or not the Northwest Passage could be considered as an international strait, he stated: 'The conventional law does not settle the question one way or the other because it talks about joining two bodies of the high seas, as I think one would have to stretch the definition rather widely to refer to the Beaufort Sea or the Arctic Ocean as a high sea because much of them are covered with ice during most of the year.'[54] He amplified Canada's view of the Arctic waters in April 1971 in his statement at the Ditchley Conference. Having stated that 'the Arctic waters and ice do not constitute high seas to which the traditional freedoms apply,' he specified that 'so far as Canada is concerned, the special characteristics of the Arctic waters and ice combine to give them a special status – however defined – which implies special rights and responsibilities for the Arctic coastal states.'[55] It would seem that the 'Arctic waters' envisaged here did include the Arctic Ocean as well as the Beaufort Sea, since specific reference had been made to them before the passage just quoted. In particular, Mr Beesley quoted from a statement from Professor Douglas Johnston: 'The Arctic Ocean is largely hypothetical, a peculiar combination of hypothetical waters and hypothetical islands, the distinction mostly covered over by large masses of ice.'[56]

Although it is true that the Beaufort Sea is in good part filled with heavy ice floes for most of the year, navigation is usually possible along the coast from the end of July to early September.[57] The following report found in *Pilot of Arctic Canada* is significant:

> Easterly or northeasterly winds carry the main pack away from the land and in some years have been known to drive the Beaufort Sea ice so far offshore that a direct passage could easily be made from Point Barrow to Cape Bathurst. Eastward of Herschel Island, Larsen reports that on several occasions he made the passage through to Amundsen Gulf and onwards, without seeing a piece of ice from late July to the first week of September.[58]

In these circumstances and in light of the evidence, it is difficult for me to accept the proposition that the Arctic Ocean and the Beaufort Sea should not be considered as high seas and that the Northwest Passage does not connect two parts of the high seas.[59] The Northwest Passage connects two parts of the high seas whether one goes through M'Clure Strait or Prince of Wales Strait, the only difference being that in the latter case one must cross Amundsen Gulf before reaching Beaufort Sea. The entrance of that gulf is ninety-three miles wide and it has not yet been closed off. But, regardless of the precise status of the waters of this gulf, it is the only link with the Beaufort Sea when using Prince of Wales Strait.

To continue regarding the ice floes of the Arctic Ocean as constituting some quasi land mass seems rather unrealistic when one considers the present and future possibilities of navigation both surface and subsurface. It becomes all the more unrealistic in the light of the studies now being made in order to raise the temperature of the waters of the Arctic basin and increase their salinity, with a view to reducing or perhaps removing altogether the ice cover from the Arctic Ocean.[60] Not only would it be possible to reduce the ice cover in the Arctic Ocean by pumping warm waters from the Pacific into the Arctic basin, but it could also be done by injecting heat and carbon dioxide into the atmosphere. The following passage taken from a recent study on man's impact on climate is very revealing:

> There is a distinct possibility – according to some a probability – that a temperature rise associated with the anticipated injections of heat and CO_2 into the atmosphere in the next century would result in the summer melting of arctic ice. The mean lifetime of arctic sea ice is less than 10 years, and it is possible that the transition from ice-covered to an ice-free ocean would occur quite suddenly – within a few years.[61]

Parallel research is being carried out also to determine the climatological changes which would occur as a result of a complete or partial melting of the Arctic sea ice. No consensus has yet been reached in the scientific community on the possible consequences of such melting but studies are continuing. In the meantime, technology is developing so as to ensure that the presence of ice in the Northwest Passage and the Arctic Ocean is not an unsurmountable obstacle to the marine transportation of petroleum products found in the Arctic.[62]

CONCLUSION

Certain basic propositions emerge from this study, and an attempt is made here to formulate them by way of conclusion.

1 The Arctic Ocean, including Beaufort Sea, constitutes high seas.
2 The Northwest Passage connects two parts of the high seas.
3 The Northwest Passage is not an international strait.
4 Two 'gateways' of territorial waters now exist in the Northwest Passage: the new one in Barrow Strait and the old one in Prince of Wales Strait.
5 The right of innocent passage applies to the Northwest Passage and is properly recognized by Canada.
6 The Northwest Passage being bordered throughout by Canadian territory, Canada is entitled to take reasonable measures of self-protection against non-innocent passage.
7 The passage of a ship in the Northwest Passage which threatens the environmental integrity of Canada should be considered as being prejudicial to its security and, therefore, non-innocent.
8 The Northwest Passage not being an international strait, Canada may temporarily suspend the innocent passage of foreign ships if such suspension is essential for the protection of its security.

NOTES

1 See D. Pharand, 'Oil Pollution Control in the Canadian Arctic' (1971), 7 *Texas Int'l L.J.* 45. For an excellent discussion of the Canadian legislation against the general background of the Law of the Sea, see also R. Bilder, 'The Canadian Arctic Waters Pollution Prevention Act: New Stresses on the Law of the Sea' (1970), 69 *Mich. L. Rev.* 1. Another article on the same subject is that of Gary Sutton, 'Pollution Prevention in the Arctic: National and Multinational Approaches Compared' (1971), 5 *Ottawa L. Rev.* 32.

2 For a description of those four potential routes, see *Pilot of Arctic Canada* (2nd ed, 1970) Vol I, 131.

3 See ibid, at 144–8 and 149–50.

4 See 'Arctic study airs many subjects' in *Oilweek,* 15 December 1969, where Capt Pullen is reported as stating, in reference to the *Manhattan,* that 'her major deficiency was having stern power only one third of power ahead.' See also text of an address by Capt Pullen, 'Northern Waters,' on 20 February 1971, to the University of Toronto, University College Alumnae Association, at 3–4 (unpublished).

5 R. Maybourn (Capt), 'Problems of Operating Large Ships in the Arctic' (1971), 24 *Institute of Navigation Journal* 135, at 136.

6 It should not be forgotten either that subsurface navigation is also possible through the Northwest Passage, as was shown in 1960 by the U.S.S. *Seadragon,* a 2360-ton nuclear submarine. It is also interesting to note that

General Dynamics Corporation announced in the latter part of 1969 that it had made proposals to five oil companies to build 170,000-ton nuclear-powered submarine tankers. These would measure 900 feet long, with a beam of 140 feet and hull depth of 85 feet. See 'Transportation' (1970), *Canadian Petroleum,* at 14–15; the same report appears in 'Arctic Transport' *Oilweek,* 22 December 1969, at 12–13.

7 See H.C. *Debates,* 17 April 1970, 6015.

8 See Standing Committee on External Affairs and National Defence, *Minutes of Proceedings and Evidence,* no 25, 29 April 1970.

9 See my 'Innocent Passage in the Arctic' (1968), 6 *Can. Y.B. Int'l L.* 3, at 58.

10 See article 16(3) of the Convention in the Territorial Sea and the Contiguous Zone (1958).

11 Ibid, article 16(4).

12 Those are the two conditions contained in article 16(4), ibid.

13 See 'Summary of Canadian Note Handed to the United States Government on April 16, 1970,' H.C. *Debates,* 17 April 1970, appendix, at 6028 (emphasis added).

14 *Supra* note 8, at 19.

15 Article 17, [1956] 2 I.L.C.Y.B. 258

16 [1949] I.C.J. 28.

17 See 'Cutters Conquer Arctic Passage, (December 1957), *Polar Times,* at 9.

18 This is a quotation cited by its captain. See G.P. Steele, *Seadragon under the Ice,* (1962), at 164.

19 See *supra* note 17.

20 J.-Y. Morin, in his extensive study 'Le progrès technique, la pollution et l'évolution récente du droit de la mer au Canada, particulièrement à l'égard de l'Arctique,' also arrives at the conclusion that the Northwest Passage is not an international strait. See (1970), 8 *Can. Y.B. Int'l L.* 158, at 219.

21 For a study of this question see my 'Historic Waters in International Law with Special Reference to the Arctic'(1971), 21 *U. Toronto L.J.* 1. It is interesting to note that the Canadian legal adviser, J.A. Beesley, is reported as mentioning the possibility of considering those waters not only as 'internal' but also as 'historic territorial waters' (see *supra* note 8). Professor Morin similarly suggests that foreign states, if excluded from the passage, might contend that the waters have been treated by Canada as territorial rather than internal waters, even while admitting their historic character. Ibid, at 240–1.

22 Professor Morin has envisaged the possibility of drawing such baselines, but concludes that it would be wiser for Canada to wait for a consolidation of its historic rights over those waters. Ibid, at 242.

23 One occasion was on 16 April 1970. H.C. *Debates* 5948.

24 See 2(1), Customs Act, R.S.C. c 58 (1970).

25 *Supra* note 13, at 6029.

26 *Supra* note 7.

27 *Supra* note 8, at 19.

28 *Supra* note 10, at article 14(4).

29 This interpretation is also supported by Professor Goldie who maintains that a non-innocent passage 'would include any activities which the coastal state may regard as polluting its territorial or maritime environment.' See L.F.E. Goldie, 'International Law of the Sea: A Review of State's Offshore Claims and Competences' (1972), 24 *Naval War College Review* no 6, 43, at 45.

30 See article II of 'Draft Articles on Territorial Sea, Straits and Fisheries,' U.N. doc. A/AC. 138/SC. II/L.4, reproduced in (1971), 65 *Dep't State Bulletin* 266 (emphasis added).

31 See Statement by John R. Stevenson, in the UN Seabed Committee, reproduced in (1971), 65 *Dep't State Bulletin* 263.

32 (1971), 65 *Proc. Amer. Soc. Int'l Law* 113.

33 [1949] 1 I.C.J. 27.

34 See G. Tunkin, 'The Geneva Conference on the Law of the Sea' (1958), 7 *Int'l Affairs* 47, at 49.

35 *Supra* note 10, at article 23.

36 I have dealt with aspects of this subject in a

previous publication and have taken the liberty to draw upon it without always referring to the article in question. See 'Freedom of the Seas in the Arctic Ocean' (1969), 19 *U. Toronto L.J.* 210.

37 V.F. Burkhanov, 'Soviet Arctic Research' translated from (1967), *Priroda* 5, at 21–30 by E.R. Hope, Defence Research Board of Canada T265R (Nov. 1957) unpublished.

38 For a description of this melting and freezing process, see Dr N. Untersteiner in *Proceedings of the Arctic Basin Symposium* (1963), at 220.

39 See *Inadvertent Climate Modification: Report of the Study of Man's Impact on Climate (SMIC)* (1971), at 160.

40 For a description of the ice circulation pattern, see Dunbar and Wittmann 'Some Features of Ice Movement in the Arctic Basin' in *Proceedings of the Arctic Basin Symposium* (1963), at 90.

41 There are three water masses or layers of water in the Arctic Ocean and they have been described in a number of publications. For a recent and succinct description, see *The Arctic Basin* (1969) co-ordinated by J.E. Sater.

42 This could be an ice island such as T-3 used by American scientists and presumably detached from the ice shelf off Ellesmere Island. See my 'The Legal Status of Ice Shelves and Ice Islands in the Arctic' (1969), 10 *Les Cahiers de Droit* 461, at 467.

43 For an account of scientific activities on drifting ice stations by Soviet scientists, see N.A. Ostenso, ed, *Problems of the Arctic and Antarctic* (1966). See also Treshnikov *et al*, 'Geographic names of the main features of the floor of the Arctic Basin' in *Problems of the Arctic and Antarctic* (1967). As for activities of American scientists, see *Arctic Drifting Stations* (1968) co-ordinated by J.E. Sater.

44 Wm. R. Anderson (Capt) *Nautilus 90° North* (1959), at 224.

45 J. Calvert (Cmdr), *Surface at the Pole* (1960), at 204.

46 See (1960), 66 *The Polar Record*, at 279.

47 J.T. Strong, 'The Openings of the Arctic Ocean' (1961), 87 *U.S. Naval Institute Proceedings*, at 63.

48 See for instance 'Polar Route for Supertankers' in *Oilweek*, 25 November 1968, 14–16.

49 See table showing the latitute reached by twenty-three ships of various types from 1849 to 1961, in W.I. Wittmann *et al*,

'Proposed Arctic Drift Ship Station Study' in unpublished report no 19–61 (June 1965).

50 R. Maybourn (Capt). *Supra* note 5, at 142.

51 For my review of the doctrinal opinion on this question, see 'Freedom of the Seas in the Arctic Ocean' (1969), 19 *U. Toronto L.J.* 210, at 211–14.

52 P.E. Trudeau, 'Canada Leads the Fight Against Pollution' in *Statements and Speeches* (1970) no 70/3, at 4.

53 See *supra* note 7, at 6028.

54 Beesley, *supra* note 8, at 19–20.

55 See J.A. Beesley, 'Rights and Responsibilities of Arctic Coastal States: The Canadian View,' (1971), 3 *Journal of Maritime Law and Commerce* 1, at 5.

56 Ibid, at 3. The reference given by Mr Beesley for this statement of Professor Douglas M. Johnston is an article entitled 'Canada's Arctic Marine Environment: Problems of Legal Protection' in Canadian Institute of International Affairs, (1970), 29 *Behind the Headlines*. No page reference is given but at page 4, I was able to find the following brief statement: 'The Arctic Ocean is largely hypothetical.'

57 See *Pilot of Arctic Canada* (2nd ed, 1968) vol 3, 1–2.

58 Ibid, at 2.

59 It should be mentioned that Professor J.-Y. Morin, who has been writing on the Canadian aspects of the Law of the Sea for a number of years, also comes to the conclusion that 'le caractère de haute mer de l'océan Glacial ne peut manquer de s'imposer.' See 'Le progrès technique, la pollution et l'évolution récente du droit de la mer au Canada, particulièrement à l'égard de l'Arctique' (1970), *Can. Y.B. Int'l L.* 158, at 238.

60 For literature on this subject, see the following: L.G. Toporkov, 'Is it possible to remove the ice cover of the Northern Arctic Ocean' (1961), *Priroda*, at 93–7, translated by us Air Force, Cambridge Research Lab. (1964); L.K. Coachman *et al,* 'On the water exchange through Bering Strait' (1966), 2 *Limnology and Oceanography,* at 44–59; and M.J. Dunbar, *Second Report on the Bering Strait Dam* (1962).

61 See *supra* note 39, at 159–60.

62 Of course, this mode of transportation is of legitimate concern to Canada, whose Northwest Passage is envisaged as a route from Prudhoe Bay to the east coast of the United States. The possibility of a major oil spill from a huge tanker poses a real danger to the Arctic ecology, and Canada had little choice but to adopt anti-pollution legislation. This legislation compels foreign ships wanting to traverse waters adjacent to Canada's Arctic coasts to conform with certain prescribed standards. It was adopted as a matter of self-protection and, considering the urgency of the situation and the reasonableness of the legislative provisions, it finds considerable support in international law. For a discussion of the legal basis of Canada's oil pollution control legislation in the Arctic, see my article, *supra* note 1, at 67–72.

A.J. STONE

19/International Maritime Law

International maritime law in its various aspects is far too broad a subject to be dealt with adequately in one short chapter, and no attempt will be made to do so here. Instead, this chapter will endeavour to discuss a few aspects of that law which are of importance to the practicing bar in Canada, to those involved in the administration of that law, and to those concerned with the development of policy regarding sea commerce within Canada and between Canada and other nations. For convenience this chapter will be divided into three main parts: the first concerns the rules relating to the carriage of goods by water and the enforcement of the rights of the parties under Canadian law; the second concerns the general subject of other claims against ships, with particular reference to collisions, jurisdictional considerations, and the right of shipowners in some circumstances to limit liability; and finally, a brief reference is made to the doctrine of innocent passage as it is affected by recent anti-pollution legislation.

Although these comments are directed to the applicable Canadian law, the reader should bear in mind that many of the rules which relate to the subjects discussed in this chapter are a product of international agreement falling generally within the category of public international law. Indeed, maritime law is by nature international, so that international co-operation and uniformity of approach are not only desirable but mandatory. Ships of many European countries as well as those of Africa, Asia, Australia, and other countries of the western hemisphere are frequent visitors to Canadian ocean and inland ports, carrying the produce of foreign lands to Canadian markets and carrying away with them the products of this country; hence there is clearly a need for internationally accepted rules respecting the rights, duties, and immunities of ships and their owners and operators respecting the cargoes carried by them and the damage done by them to each other and to other property.

CARRIAGE OF GOODS BY WATER

Development of uniform rules

The pressure for adoption of uniform rules relating to the international carriage of goods by ships must be viewed against the background of earlier developments. The common law had come to regard a sea carrier of goods as an 'insurer' (except for acts of God or of the king's enemies) and, as such, liable for any loss or damage to the goods occurring after the time they were received by him until the time they left his custody.[1] In response to this development, the carrier introduced in the contract of carriage evidenced by the bill of lading increasingly sweeping exceptions which were designed generally to absolve carriers from every kind of liability for cargo loss or damage that might fall upon the carrier.[2] This development, in turn, threatened to undermine overseas sea commerce, which had come to depend largely on a system of credit in which the bill of lading played an important part as a negotiable instrument and document of title; these bills of lading became the medium through which mercantile contracts were established. The extent to which the carriers had excluded their liability was succinctly summarized by the chairman of the Bill of Lading Committee of the International Chamber of Commerce, who wrote at the time:

1 That carriers have unfairly exempted themselves from practically all liability for the faults of their servants in the stowage, custody and delivery of cargo by negligence clauses, or, where such clauses are prohibited by law, have limited their liability to a wholly inadequate figure – $100 or less per package;
2 That carriers have unfairly evaded the payment of just claims by bill of lading stipulations requiring claims to be presented within an impossibly short period;
3 That carriers have evaded the payment of claims for pilferage and similar losses, and have even encouraged such losses by casting an impossible burden of proof upon cargo owners;
4 That carriers have improperly stipulated in their bills of lading for the benefit of insurance effected by the shippers.[3]

The uncertainty brought about by exculpatory clauses and by inconsistent language tended to hamper international trade, and it soon became apparent that some agreement as to the general terms and conditions of carriage must be reached by the parties concerned. These parties consisted mainly of two groups: first, the parties to the contract of carriage itself, namely the shipper and the shipowner; and second, the third parties to the contract – the consignee of the goods, bankers, and others. In fact, it is mainly the parties in this second group, along with the carrier and the insurers (of goods and of the carrier), who were concerned. In most cases the shipper would have no further interest in the goods after shipment and hence little or no interest in the terms and conditions of the bill of lading; but consignees, bankers, and others, once the goods were shipped, became immediately concerned with the nature of the security provided by the bill of lading as a negotiable instrument and document of title. It thus became clear that legislative action was required to remove the discontent and lack of uniformity.

No doubt differing national interests have had an important influence on the move towards greater uniformity. In the early part of this century Britain held unchallenged superiority as a seapower, while other countries, including the United States, were developing their external trade. This contest between promoting shipowning interests, on the one hand, and international trade and commerce on the other became the subject of a comment by Lord Justice Scrutton in *Gosse Millard* v *Canadian Government Merchant Marine*:

For reasons it is unnecessary to indicate, the United States of America have not been, except in some exceptional periods, a shipowning country, and they have approached shipping matters from the point of view of the cargo-owners. I cannot think that their decisions, while treated with great respect, should necessarily control the shipping decisions of the Courts of the greatest shipowning country in the world.[4]

The attitude reflected in these words of one of Britain's foremost maritime law scholars is to be compared with more recent judicial utterances on both sides of the Atlantic which reflect the generally prevailing attitude at this time regarding the desirability of uniform interpretation. An illustration of this new attitude is found in the judgment of Viscount Simonds in the case of *Scruttons Ltd.* v *Midland Silicones Ltd.*:

> In consideration of this case I have not yet mentioned a matter of real importance. It is not surprising that the questions in issue in this case should have arisen in other jurisdictions where the common law is administered, and where the Hague Rules have been embodied in the municipal law. It is (to put it no higher) very desirable that the same conclusions should be reached in whatever jurisdiction the question arises. It would be deplorable if the nations should, after protracted negotiations, reach agreement, as in the matter of the Hague Rules and that their several courts should then disagree as to the meaning of what they appeared to agree upon: see Riverstone Meat Co. Pty. Ltd. v. Lancashire Shipping Co. Ltd. (1961) A.C. 807; (1961) 2 W.L.R. 278; (1961) 1 All E.R. 495, H.L. and cases there cited. It is therefore gratifying to find that the Supreme Court of the United States in the recent case of Robert C. Herd & Co. Inc. v. Krawill Machinery Corporation, (1959) 359 U.S. 297; (1959) 1 Lloyd's Rep. 305, not only unanimously adopted the meaning of the word 'carrier' in the relevant Act, which I invite your Lordships to adopt, but also expressed the view that the Elder, Dempster decision (1924) A.C. 522 did not decide what is claimed for it by the appellants.[5]

In 1893 the United States had already taken action designed to deal with problems of bills of lading by passing the Harter Act,[6] which unified the terms and conditions of the contract of carriage and maritime commerce from and between ports of the United States and ports of foreign countries. This act was judicially extended to cases of carriage of goods into the United States, with the result that regardless of the nationality of the ship or its owners, the Harter Act automatically became part of the contract of carriage whenever sea commerce with the United States was involved. This lead taken by the United States was followed by Australia, Fiji, Canada, and New Zealand. In 1920 the government of the United Kingdom appointed an Imperial Shipping Committee to review the position; in 1921 that committee recommended that there should be uniform legislation throughout the British Empire and suggested that it be based on the Canadian Water Carriage of Goods Act of 1910.[7] Shortly afterward, the aid of the International Law Association and the Maritime Law Committee of that association were called upon, and in due course the association passed a number of resolutions adopting 'the Hague Rules 1921,' which would have only voluntary application. It became apparent, however, that a binding effect was needed, and pressure began to build for international agreement. This eventually led to the conference on maritime law held at Brussels in 1922, and ultimately to the adoption on 25 August 1924 at Brussels of the International Convention for the Unification of Certain Rules Relating to Bills of Lading (the Hague Rules).[8] Although many of the signatory nations have ratified the convention, Canada has not done so but rather in 1936 enacted the Water Carriage of Goods Act,[9] which gave effect to the Hague Rules included in the schedule.

Canadian legislation

It will be useful at this juncture to note a number of outstanding features of the Canadian legislation. In the first place, the Carriage of Goods by Water Act and the rules incorporated in it do not apply to goods carried under bills of lading from ports outside Canada to ports or places in Canada. However, most of the leading maritime nations have adopted the Hague Rules, which therefore apply to bills of lading covering shipments originating in those foreign jurisdictions.

Second, the rules in the schedule to the act by article I(c) do not apply to live animals or to 'cargo which by the contract of carriage is stated as being carried on deck and is so carried.' This is one of the most important exclusions so far as carriage of goods is concerned. But if goods carried on deck are to be excluded, care must be taken to comply with the provisions of the Rules: all bills of lading issued in respect of deck cargo should therefore have stamped on their face the words 'carried on deck.'[10] Once they are excluded by making it clear that the goods under the bill of lading are carried on deck, a number of protective provisions with regard to such cargo can be included in the bill of lading.

Although on deck carriage of goods has generally been important in water transport, its importance today has taken on new significance with the use of the container, which has prompted a revolution in international sea carriage affecting all concerned, including the shipper, the carrier, the cargo handlers, the port operators, and, of course, the insurers and bankers. These containers, which are stuffed at the point of shipment, are carried through a system which often includes railways, trucks, barges, and ships. It is now common to carry these containers on deck with resulting problems, some of which have already been dealt with by maritime courts.[11] This on deck problem and other problems to which container and other intermodal concepts of carriage have given rise are now the subject of much international debate.

In certain circumstances the rules in the schedule do not apply to goods carried under a non-negotiable document. The authority for such a document arises in article VI of the rules, as amplified by section 5 of the act, and the position of goods carried under such documents is somewhat complicated. Under article VI the rules do not apply if there is no bill of lading, and a non-negotiable receipt is issued on particular goods not considered an ordinary commercial shipment. Section 5 broadens the scope of article VI with respect to goods carried from one place in Canada to another (or in what is known as Canadian coasting trade) by excluding the requirements that there should be particular goods and that there should be other than normal commercial shipments involved. These provisions have special applicability to carriage of goods by water to or within remote areas of Canada such as the Northwest Territories.

By article VII the rules in the schedule are not required to apply to liabilities arising 'prior to the loading on and subsequent to the discharge [of the cargo] from the ship.' This is one of the most important and significant exclusions from the rules, for it enables a carrier to exclude the application of the rules except for the period from the time of loading to the time of the discharge of the cargo from the ship. This is interpreted to mean that the rules apply only when the ship's tackle is hooked on and ceases at discharge when it is unhooked or, in other methods of loading, when the cargo is actually received on board the ship and when it leaves it. In most cases of maritime transport the carrier does not control the goods prior to loading or after unloading; and it is usually at pains in the clauses of bills of lading specifically to exclude the application of the rules and to include protective clauses regarding such parts of the carriage. The Canada Shipping Act makes carriers responsible 'not only for goods received on board their vessels, but also for goods delivered to them for conveyance by any such vessel, and they are bound to use due care and diligence in the safekeeping and punctual conveyance of such goods,' but this responsibility is expressly made subject to the Carriage of Goods by Water Act.[12]

The rules themselves do not exhaust the terms and conditions that may be included in the contract of carriage, and, although all contracts of carriage are subject to the rules, other obligations may be accepted by the carrier, for, as was stated by Mr Justice Devlin, 'the Act is not intended as a code. It is not meant altogether to supplant the contract of carriage, but only to control on certain topics the freedom of contract which the parties would otherwise have.'[13] Hence in some cases the carrier will by the bill of lading accept obligations beyond those imposed by the rules; for example, carriers have sometimes accepted responsibility for lightrage service in some ports or places. But instances of extension of the carrier's responsibility beyond that imposed by the rules are very few.

Article III imposes a number of liabilities on the shipper and the carrier. One of the major liabilities of the shipper is described in rule 5, which provides that:

> The shipper shall be deemed to have guaranteed to the carrier the accuracy at the time of shipment of the marks, number, quantity, and weight, as furnished by him, and the shipper shall indemnify the carrier against all loss, damages, and expenses arising or resulting from inaccuracies in such particulars. The right of the carrier to such indemnity, shall in no way limit his responsibility and liability under the contract of carriage to any person other than the shipper.

Rules 1, 2, 3, and 4 provide for liabilities of the carrier:

1 The carrier shall be bound, before and at the beginning of the voyage, to exercise due diligence to,
   (*a*) make the ship seaworthy;
   (*b*) properly man, equip, and supply the ship;
   (*c*) make the holds, refrigerating and cool chambers, and all other parts of the ship in which goods are carried, fit and safe for their reception, carriage and preservation.
2 Subject to the provisions of Article IV, the carrier shall properly and carefully load, handle, stow, carry, keep, care for and discharge the goods carried.
3 After receiving the goods into his charge, the carrier, or the master or agent of the carrier, shall, on demand of the shipper, issue to the shipper a bill of lading showing among other things,
   (*a*) the leading marks necessary for identification of the goods as the same are furnished in writing by the shipper before the loading of such goods starts, provided such

marks are stamped or otherwise shown clearly upon the goods if uncovered, or on the cases or coverings in which such goods are contained, in such a manner as should ordinarily remain legible until the end of the voyage;

(*b*) either the number of packages or pieces, or the quantity, or weight, as the case may be, as furnished in writing by the shipper;

(*c*) the apparent order and condition of the goods:

Provided that no carrier, master or agent of the carrier, shall be bound to state or show in the bill of lading any marks, number, quantity, or weight which he has reasonable ground for suspecting not accurately to represent the goods actually received or which he has had no reasonable means of checking.

4 Such a bill of lading shall be *prima facie* evidence of the receipt by the carrier of the goods as therein described in accordance with paragraph 3(*a*), (*b*), and (*c*).

Article IV extends certain rights and immunities to the carrier (rules 1, 2, 3, and 5):

1 Neither the carrier nor the ship shall be liable for loss or damage arising or resulting from unseaworthiness unless caused by want of due diligence on the part of the carrier to make the ship seaworthy, and to secure that the ship is properly manned, equipped and supplied, and to make the holds, refrigerating and cool chambers and all other parts of the ship in which goods are carried fit and safe for their reception, carriage and preservation in accordance with the provisions of paragraph 1 of Article III.

Whenever loss or damage has resulted from unseaworthiness, the burden of proving the exercise of due diligence shall be on the carrier or other person claiming exemption under this section.

2 Neither the carrier nor the ship shall be responsible for loss or damage arising or resulting from,

(*a*) act, neglect, or default of the master, mariner, pilot or the servants of the carrier in the navigation or in the management of the ship;

(*b*) fire, unless caused by the actual fault or privity of the carrier;

(*c*) perils, danger, and accidents of the sea or other navigable waters;

(*d*) act of God;

(*e*) act of war;

(*f*) act of public enemies;

(*g*) arrest or restraint of princes, rulers or people, or seizure under legal process;

(*h*) quarantine restrictions;

(*i*) act or omission of the shipper or owner of the goods, his agent or representative;

(*j*) strikes or lock-outs or stoppage or restraint of labour from whatever cause, whether partial or general;

(*k*) riots and civil commotions;

(*l*) saving or attempting to save life or property at sea;

(*m*) wastage in bulk or weight or any other loss or damage arising from inherent defect, quality or vice of the goods;

(*n*) insufficiency of packing;

(*o*) insufficiency or inadequacy of marks;

(*p*) latent defects not discoverable by due diligence;

(*q*) any other cause arising without the actual fault and privity of the carrier, or without the fault or neglect of the agents or servants of the carrier, but the burden of proof shall be on the person claiming the benefit of this exception to show that neither the actual fault or privity of the carrier nor the fault or neglect of the agents or servants of the carrier contributed to the loss or damage.

3 The shipper shall not be responsible for loss or damage sustained by the carrier or the ship arising or resulting from any cause without the act, fault or neglect of the shipper, his agents or his servants ...

5 Neither the carrier nor the ship shall in any event be or become liable for any loss or damage to or in connection with goods in an amount exceeding five hundred dollars per package or unit, or the equivalent of that sum in other currency, unless the nature and value of such goods have been declared by the shipper before shipment and inserted in the bill of lading.

This declaration if embodied in the bill of lading shall be *prima facie* evidence, but shall not be binding or conclusive on the carrier.

By agreement between the carrier, master or agent of the carrier and the shipper another maximum amount than that mentioned in this paragraph may be fixed, provided that such maximum shall not be less than the figure above named.

Neither the carrier nor the ship shall be responsible in any event for loss or damage to or in connection with goods if the nature or value thereof has been knowingly misstated by the shipper in the bill of lading.

These are not all but are among the more prominent features of the rules. Two of the most important protections accorded the carrier are rule 5 in article IV, which in most circumstances limits the carrier's liability for cargo claims to five hundred dollars per unit, and rule 6 of article III, which for the most part discharges the carrier and the ship from all liability in respect of loss or damage 'unless suit is brought within one year after delivery of the goods or the date when the goods should have been delivered.' In practice the carrier or his Canadian or other agents will, if requested, generally agree to extend the time for suit without prejudice to any other defence that may be available under the Rules or the bill of lading. However, if the extension is not granted and an action is not brought within the prescribed period, the carrier and the ship are absolutely discharged from liability and the claim is thereby extinguished. Moreover, the right of the shipowner to limit liability under the Canada Shipping Act[14] is preserved.[15]

Marine cargo claims

The practical application of these rules and of the Hague Rules to marine cargo claims has formed the basis of several works both abroad[16] and at home,[17] so that nowadays a useful collection of pertinent literature is available to the practitioner. If the claims cannot be settled out of court, they may be pursued in the ordinary courts or in the Admiralty Court (the Federal Court of Canada). Many contracts of carriage contain a so-called 'jurisdiction' clause purporting to give exclusive jurisdiction to foreign courts, usually but not always to the courts of the country of ship ownership. These generally are regarded with some suspicion by the Canadian courts whose jurisdiction they purport to deny so that the tendency of our courts nowadays is to disregard them.[18] Thus in most cases claims are justiciable in the courts of this country, provided, of course, that the actions are brought within the one-year limitation prescribed by rule 6 of article III unless extension is granted.

Under Canadian law as developed under our federal system both the ordinary courts and the Federal Court may hear and determine marine cargo claims. However, the territorial limits on the exercise of the jurisdiction of the provincial courts, including the provincial superior courts, often leads to these kinds of actions being brought in the Federal Court; and the same applied to its predecessor, the Exchequer Court of Canada, which was abolished on 1 June 1971 when the new Federal Court came into being. This new court exercises broad maritime jurisdiction which is conferred by the Federal Court Act[19] within the limits imposed by the British North America Act. Under section 22(1) a general grant of jurisdiction over shipping and navigation matters is made to the Trial Division; and section 22(2) confers particular jurisdiction on the Trial Division with respect 'to any claim or question' arising out of one or more of the matters enumerated in that provision.

One of the advantages of taking suit in the Federal Court is that, unlike the provincial courts, its writ runs throughout the country. Thus, for example, damaged cargo destined inland, discharged at an ocean port, may become the subject of an action taken in the court at the place of destination. Another advantage of proceeding in the Federal Court is that by virtue of its being the Admiralty Court it may exercise its maritime jurisdiction not only *in personam* but also *in rem*. Thus claimants may in some circumstances enforce their so-called 'statutory liens' for cargo damage against the ship itself, provided the ship has not changed ownership since the damage occurred. Moreover, when instituting an action *in rem* the plaintiff need not be concerned with vexing questions of ownership, charter, mortgage, and lien. In some cases the availability of the *in rem* proceeding is a decided advantage in that security for the claim and for costs is given at the time the action is commenced.

An action *in rem* can be brought only if the ship which is the subject of the action is within the territorial jurisdiction of the court at the time the action is commenced. Under the court's rules of practice and procedure the action is commenced with the issuance of a declaration or statement of claim, after which a warrant for arrest of the ship is applied for at the local or principal registry of the court. The warrant can then be served on the ship, which is thereby placed under arrest of the court and cannot thereafter be moved without the court's prior consent. But in practice, in many cases the warrant of arrest is not taken out or is not served. Instead, the ship's insurers, usually the Protection and Indemnity Clubs, will authorize Canadian solicitors to undertake to enter an appearance, submit to the jurisdiction of the court, accept service, and put in bail for the value of the claim if and when called upon by the claimant to do so. These arrangements are important, for they avoid the necessity of tying up the ship and the inconvenience and expense that flow from arrest, but at the same time they assure the claimant of having the security that arrest itself provides.

OTHER CLAIMS AGAINST SHIPS

Collisions; 'Rules of the Road'

Again in this area, as has been seen with carriage of goods by water, Canada's domestic laws have been greatly influenced by international agreement. The problems arising out of collisions of ships require approaches and solutions that were not generally available under purely domestic legal regimes important particulars of which often differed from country to country. These include problems of jurisdiction, of damage, of lien and mortgage, of ownership, of charter, and of limitation of liability.

Of fundamental importance to the safety of navigation have been the formulation and adoption of 'rules of the road.' The first of these were made by Great Britain in 1863 and were adopted by the United States in 1864 and subsequently by other maritime nations. However, there was concern that nations engaged in sea commerce should do more to promote adoption of a common agreement, with uniform principles and rules directed towards promotion of safety of life at sea. To this end many international conferences were held. The most important of these conferences was held in London in 1948 and resulted in the adoption of the International Convention for the Safety of Life at Sea,[20] which came into effect in Canada on 19 November 1952. The 1948 conference also adopted a new set of collision regulations, which were entitled 'The International Regulations for Preventing Collisions at Sea, 1948.' These took effect in Canada on 1 January 1954 by virtue of an order in council dated 13 August 1953, made under the authority of the Canada Shipping Act of 1934.[21] The International Collision Regulations apply and have force in all navigable waters within Canada or within the jurisdiction of parliament, with two major exceptions: the waters of the Great Lakes, including Georgian Bay and the connecting and tributary waters, and the St Lawrence River as far east as the lower exit of the Lachine Canal and the Victoria Bridge at Montreal. These two areas are governed by purely Canadian sets of collision regulations, known respectively as 'Rules of the Road for the Great Lakes'[22] and the 'St Lawrence River Regulations.'[23] Additionally, the government of Canada has issued certain small boat regulations which are designed to promote the safety of those using the waters for recreational purposes.[24]

International conventions

On 23 September 1910 the International Convention for the Unification of Certain Rules of Law with Respect to Collisions Between Vessels was signed at Brussels.[25] Although Canada was not a signatory and has not ratified the convention, it acceded to it on 25 September 1914. The 1910 convention dealt with certain substantive rules such as that the vessel at fault should be liable for the damage (article 3); that fault should be apportioned if two or more vessels are at fault (article 4); that liability of shipowners for death or personal injury should be joint and several (article 4); and that actions for recovery of damages arising out of collision are time-barred after an interval of two years from the date of the casualty (article 7). These provisions are now part of Canadian domestic legislation in part XIV of the Canada Shipping Act.

On 10 May 1952, three additional international conventions relevant to collisions and other claims against ships were signed at Brussels. These were the International Convention Relating to the Arrest of Seagoing Ships (Arrest Convention);[26] the International Convention On Certain Rules Concerning Civil Jurisdiction in Matters of Collision (Collision Convention);[27] and the International Convention for the Unification of Certain Rules Relating to Penal Jurisdiction in Matters of Collision or Other Incidents of Navigation (Penal Jurisdiction Convention).[28]

The first of these three conventions represented an attempt at the international level to deal with vexing and practical problems of arrest, for ships, like persons, have from earliest times and for very practical reasons been subject to arrest. Ships engaged in international sea commerce come and go, and they are capable of vast destruction in circumstances where they are negligently operated. Thus the common law, in order to protect the interests of nationals, saw fit to develop the concept of 'lien' and concomitantly that of arrest to enforce the lien. In this way problems of security for claims and some difficult questions of charter, ownership, mortgage, and lien were overcome. The main object of the 1952 Arrest Convention was to catalogue those claims which in any of the contracting states would be considered a basis for the arrest of a foreign ship by the courts of the contracting state. These are listed in article 1(1) of the Arrest Convention, which defines 'maritime claim' as

(a) damage caused by any ship either in collision or otherwise;
(b) loss of life or personal injury caused by any ship or occurring in connection with the operation of any ship;
(c) salvage;
(d) agreement relating to the use or hire of any ship whether by charterparty or otherwise;
(e) agreement relating to the carriage of goods in any ship whether by charterparty or otherwise;
(f) loss of or damage to goods including baggage carried in any ship;
(g) general damage;
(h) bottomry;
(i) towage;
(j) pilotage;
(k) goods or material wherever supplied to a ship for her operation or maintenance;
(l) construction, repair or equipment of any ship or dock charges and dues;
(m) wages of Masters, Officers, or crew;
(n) Master's disbursements, including disbursements made by shippers, charterers or agents on behalf of a ship or her owner;
(o) disputes as to the title to or ownership of any ship;
(p) disputes between co-owners of any ship as to the ownership, possession, employment or earnings of that ship;
(q) the mortgage or hypothecation of any ship.

Canada was not a signatory to this convention, nor has she ratified or acceded to it. However, the list of claims set forth in the convention for which arrests may be made are those that have been generally recognized under Canadian maritime law as giving rise to a right of arrest whether or not such claims give rise to what are known as maritime liens, statutory liens, or possessory liens. The Arrest Convention does not attempt to add to the list of claims that give rise to the maritime lien, which is regarded as the highest form of lien recognized under maritime law in that it runs with the ship; these have been limited to crew's wages, master's wages, master's disbursements, damages, salvage, bottomry, and respondentia.

Although Canada has neither ratified nor acceded to the Arrest Convention, it is noteworthy that in the recent overhaul of maritime jurisdiction now contained in the Federal Court Act many of the claims for which arrest is provided in the convention may be the subject of arrest in an action in the Federal Court. Although each of the nineteen particular heads of jurisdiction contained in section 22(2) of the Federal Court Act deals with claims which may be the subject of an action *in rem* and therefore of arrest, in ten of these instances the right of arrest is denied unless at the time the action is commenced 'the ship, aircraft or other property that is the subject of the action is beneficially owned by the person who was the beneficial owner at the time the cause of action arose.'[29] These ten instances are claims for damage sustained by or for loss of a ship, claims arising out of an agreement relating to carriage of goods on or in a ship under a through bill of lading, claims for loss of life or personal injury occurring in connection with the operation of a ship, claims for loss of or damage to goods carried in or on a ship, claims arising out of an agreement relating to the carriage of goods in or on a ship or to the use or hire of a ship, claims for towage, claims for necessaries, claims for constructing, equipping or repairing a ship, claims by a master, charterer, or agent of a ship for disbursements or by a shipper in respect of advances, and finally claims arising out of or in connection with a contract of marine insurance.[30] One of the incidental effects of these provisions is to abolish in Canada the maritime lien status which has for centuries applied to a master's disbursements. It is also interesting to note that although the convention permits the arrest of another ship which is in the same ownership, this so-called 'sister ship rule' has yet to be adopted in Canada; but it is anticipated that Canada will adopt such a rule when the Canada Shipping Act which is now under review is next revised and brought up-to-date.

The 1952 Collision Convention has likewise been neither ratified nor acceded to by Canada. As its full name indicates it is concerned with jurisdiction as distinguished from matters of substance dealt with by the 1910 Collision Convention. In general it embodies principles which have been applied in Canada, such as, for example, that the courts of this country have jurisdiction in collision matters if the ship is arrested or the collision occurs in Canada's internal waters (article 1). In addition, the convention prevents 'forum shopping' by prohibiting a plaintiff who has brought an action in one jurisdiction from bringing an action against the same defendant on the same set of facts in another jurisdiction without first discontinuing the action already instituted; a similar prohibition is now contained in the Federal Court Act.[31] The convention expressly applies to an action for damage caused by one ship to another or to the property or persons on board such ship 'through the carrying out of or on the omission to carry out a manoeuvre or to a non-compliance with regulations even when there has been no actual collision;' this substantially is now included in the Federal Court Act,[32] with the word 'law' substituted for the word 'regulations' appearing in the convention. These provisions of Canadian domestic legislation are apt illustrations of Canada's general approach to international conventions; that is, to take from such conventions that which is considered appropriate to Canada's own particular domestic needs and circumstances and to legislate in this limited way.

The final 1952 Brussels convention, the Penal Jurisdiction Convention, provides that penal or disciplinary proceedings in the event of collision or other navigation incident are to be instituted only by the flag state. However, this convention has also neither been ratified nor acceded to by Canada, and Canada does assume jurisdiction in penal or disciplinary matters arising out of collision cases involving foreign ships.

Limitation of liability

Ship operations are considered to give rise to onerous risks, not the least of which are those that fall upon the carrier. For more than a century the public policy of the United Kingdom has been to recognize these risks by providing the carrier with a measure of protection against potentially ruinous loss. The general basis of this policy is that exposure of carriers to such loss would likely discourage ship owning and operation to the detriment of the national interest. Thus developed, the concept of limitation of liability is well-known and widely applied today.

At the international level this general concept was approved and adopted in the International Convention for the Unification of Certain Rules Relating to the Limitation of Liability of Owners of Seagoing Vessels,[33] signed at Brussels on 25 August 1924, and in the more recent convention, the International Convention Relating to the Limitation of the Liability of Owners of Sea-Going Ships[34] adopted at Brussels on 10 October 1957, and to which Canada is a signatory. This latter convention provided for limitation of shipowners' liability against claims for loss of life or personal injury, damage to property, and expenses for removal of wreck (article 1). However, there can be limitation of liability under the convention only if the occurrence giving rise to the claim did not result from 'the actual fault or privity of the owner.' If limitation applies, the owner can limit his liability in accordance with article 3(1) of the convention:

> The amounts to which the owner of a ship may limit his liability under Article 1 shall be:
> (*a*) where the occurrence has only given rise to property claims an aggregate amount of 1,000 francs for each ton of the ship's tonnage;
> (*b*) where the occurrence has only given rise to personal claims an aggregate amount of 3,100 francs for each ton of the ship's tonnage;
> (*c*) where the occurrence has given rise both to personal claims and property claims an aggregate amount of 3,100 francs for each ton of the ship's tonnage, of which a first portion amounting to 2,100 francs for each ton of the ship's tonnage shall be exclusively appropriated to the payment of personal claims and of which a second portion amounting to 1,000 francs for each ton of the ship's tonnage shall be appropriated to the payment of property claims. Provided however that in cases where the first portion is insufficient to pay the personal claims in full, the unpaid balance of such claims shall rank rateably with the property claims for payment against the second portion of the fund.

For the purpose of ascertaining the limit of an owner's liability the tonnage of a ship of less than 300 tons is deemed to be 300 tons. In terms of Canadian currency the limitation for property damage claims is $87.18 per ton and for personal injury or death claims $270.26 per ton, while the 300 ton absolute floor amounts to $26,154 and $81,078 respectively.[35]

Although Canada has not ratified or acceded to the 1957 convention, parliament by appropriate amendments to the Canada Shipping Act has given effect to these provisions.[36] The basic limitation provision is section 647(2), which provides:

2 The owner of a ship, whether registered in Canada or not, is not, where any of the following events occur without his actual fault or privity, namely,

(a) where any loss of life or personal injury is caused to any person on board that ship;

(b) where any damage or loss is caused to any goods, merchandise or other things whatever on board that ship;

(c) where any loss of life or personal injury is caused to any person not on board that ship through

(i) the act or omission of any person, whether on board that ship or not, in the navigation or management of the ship, in the loading, carriage or discharge of its cargo or in the embarkation, carriage or disembarkation of its passengers, or

(ii) any other act or omission of any person on board that ship; or

(d) where any loss or damage is caused to any property, other than the property described in paragraph (b), or any rights are infringed through

(i) the act or omission of any person, whether on board that ship or not, in the navigation or management of the ship, in the loading, carriage or discharge of its cargo or in the embarkation, carriage or disembarkation of its passengers, or

(ii) any other act or omission of any person on board that ship;

liable for damages beyond the following amounts, namely,

(e) in respect of any loss of life or personal injury, either alone or together with any loss or damage to property or any infringement of any rights mentioned in paragraph (d), an aggregate amount equivalent to 3,100 gold francs for each ton of that ship's tonnage; and

(f) in respect of any loss or damage to property or any infringement of any rights mentioned in paragraph (d), an aggregate amount equivalent to 1,000 gold francs for each ton of that ship's tonnage.

The procedure applicable in limiting liability is a matter of some technicality. However, in a recent case in the Exchequer Court of Canada Mr Justice Noel had occasion to review the relevant legislation (then sections 657 *et seq* of the Canada Shipping Act) and the decided cases, and arrived at the following conclusions, as His Lordship put it, 'on a tentative basis':

(a) section 657 limits the liability of the owner of a ship in the circumstances and to the amount set out therein;

(b) where the owner anticipates a claim from only one person, and is not concerned about protecting himself against other possible claims, he can avail himself of the limitation of liability by merely pleading it as a defence to an action;

(c) where the owner anticipates claims from more than one source, some procedure is required to distribute the fund among the various claimants, and such procedure is supplied by section 658;

(d) notwithstanding the express reference to the judges of the court, the 'application' contemplated by section 658 may be made to the Exchequer Court of Canada but, in the absence of direction under sub-section (2), the court can only act upon such an application when the President or one of the puisne judges of the court is sitting;

(e) if the owner wishes to be protected as against claims by persons who have not been made a party to the proceedings the Exchequer Court can only properly provide such protection by making an order under which the owner will have to advertise for possible claimants and give them a stipulated time in which to put in their claims (compare Order 75 Rule 35 of the English Rules);

(f) in a case where the owner is satisfied that all possible claimants are parties to the proceedings he may be satisfied to proceed without obtaining an order for advertising, in which case he will not have protection as against any claimant who might subsequently appear and put forward a claim;

(g) where there is more than one possible claimant, but they have all joined as plaintiffs in an action commenced in the central registry of this court against the owner, it would seem to be appropriate procedure for the owner to counter-claim for an order under section 658 limiting his liability and distributing the amount of the fund among the plaintiffs;

(h) where an action has been begun against the owner, either

  (i) in this court where all the claimants are not plaintiffs, or

  (ii) in some other court (including an action in a district registry in Admiralty), the appropriate procedure would seem to be for the owner to make an application to this court by proceedings launched in the central registry for an order under section 658 of the Act – such an application can be made by way of an originating motion or an action commenced by writ or by statement of claim;

(i) upon such an application, the court should be asked for directions and an order should be made setting out the course the matter is to take, which should be adjusted to the circumstances of the particular case; this might follow the English rules (0.75 r. 35) or might be worked out to suit the circumstances of the particular case having regard to the above conclusions. (None of the cases examined contain any helpful discussion of the procedure to be followed under either the English or the Canadian provisions and the matter can therefore be dealt with as though there were no authority).[37]

POLLUTION AND INNOCENT PASSAGE

The right of foreign ships to innocent passage through Canadian waters, with attendant risks of fisheries depletion and pollution, has been the subject of much comment in the Canadian press and of legislation by parliament. The issue usefully illustrates one of the ways in which international maritime law evolves through the assertion of rights by one state and, after perhaps an initial period of uncertainty, acceptance or rejection of those asserted rights by the international community.

Canadian pollution prevention legislation

On 26 June 1970 the Arctic Waters Pollution Prevention Act[38] received royal assent. On 19 October 1970 Bill C-2, 'An Act to Amend the Canada Shipping Act,' was introduced in the House of Commons. This legislation, which took effect on 1 July 1971,[39] also deals with pollution prevention, but whereas the earlier act applies only to Arctic waters, the Canada Shipping Act amendments apply to other Canadian waters and depend on exceptions that may be contained in regulations made under the amendments. The application of the amendments is set forth in new section 736(2):

2 Except where otherwise provided in this Part or in any regulation made thereunder, this Part and any regulations made thereunder apply
    (*a*) to all Canadian waters south of the sixtieth parallel of north latitude;
    (*b*) to all Canadian waters north of the sixtieth parallel of north latitude that are not within a shipping safety control zone prescribed pursuant to the *Arctic Waters Pollution Prevention Act*;
    (*c*) to any fishing zones of Canada prescribed pursuant to the *Territorial Sea and Fishing Zones Act*; and
    (*d*) to all ships in waters described in paragraphs (*a*) to (*c*).

The amendments apply to what are generally referred to as territorial waters, internal waters, and other waters,[40] and also to 'any fishing zones of Canada' prescribed pursuant to the Territorial Sea and Fishing Zones Act.[41] This last inclusion is of great interest and importance. On 25 February 1971 the government of Canada issued an order in council pursuant to section 5A of the Territorial Sea and Fishing Zones Act 'prescribing certain areas of the sea adjacent to the coast of Canada' as fishing zones, effective 10 March 1971.[42] By this order in council certain fishing zones were delineated to include what have traditionally been regarded as areas of open sea in the Gulf of St Lawrence, the Bay of Fundy, and the Queen Charlotte Sound, Hecate Strait-Dixon Entrance, the effect of which is generally to convert the Gulf of St Lawrence, the Bay of Fundy, and the Queen Charlotte Sound into fishing zones for the purpose of the fishing zones legislation and hence also for the purposes of the new part of the Canada Shipping Act. The combined effect of this legislation is that Canada now asserts jurisdiction in pollution prevention matters over large areas of the open sea.

The significance of this development is pointed up by the wide powers over shipping which may be conferred upon the pollution prevention officer, who will be responsible under the legislation for bringing about compliance with the legislation and with the regulations made thereunder. These powers are contained in new sections 741 and 769 of the Canada Shipping Act.

741 (1) A pollution prevention officer may
    (*a*) require any ship that is within waters to which this Part applies or that is about to enter any such waters to provide him with information concerning the condition of the ship, its machinery and equipment, the nature and quantity of its cargo and fuel and the manner in which and the locations in which the cargo and fuel of the ship are stowed and any other information that he considers appropriate for the administration of this Part;
    (*b*) go on board any ship that is within waters to which this Part applies and that he suspects on reasonable grounds is bound for a place in Canada and conduct such inspections of the ship as will enable him to determine whether the ship complies with any regulations made under this Part that are applicable to the ship;
    (*c*) order any ship to proceed out of waters to which this Part applies by such route and in such manner as he may direct, to remain outside such waters or to proceed

to and moor, anchor or remain for a reasonable time specified by him and in a place selected by him that is within waters to which this Part applies,

(i) if he suspects, on reasonable grounds, that the ship fails to comply with any regulation made under this Part that is or may be applicable to it; or

(ii) if, by reason of weather, visibility, ice or sea conditions, the condition of the ship or any of its equipment, or any deficiency in its complement or the nature and condition of its cargo, he is satisfied that such an order is justified to prevent the discharge of a pollutant;

(*d*) order any ship that he suspects on reasonable grounds is carrying a pollutant to proceed through any waters to which this Part applies by a route prescribed by him and at a rate of speed not in excess of a rate prescribed by him; and

(*e*) where he is informed that a substantial quantity of a pollutant has been discharged in waters to which this Part applies or has entered waters to which this Part applies, or where on reasonable grounds he is satisfied that a grave and imminent danger of a substantial discharge of a pollutant in waters to which this Part applies exists,

(i) order all ships within a specified area in waters to which this Part applies to report their positions to him, and

(ii) order any ship to take part in the clean up of such pollutant or in any action to control or contain the pollutant.

(2) Compensation shall be paid by the Crown for the services of any ship which has complied with an order issued under subparagraph (ii) of paragraph (*e*) of subsection (1) ...

769(1) Whenever a pollution prevention officer suspects on reasonable grounds that

(*a*) any provision of this Part or of any regulation made thereunder has been contravened by a ship, or

(*b*) the owner of a ship or the owner or owners of all or part of the pollutant that is carried thereon has or have committed an offence under paragraph (*b*) of subsection (1) of section 762,

he may, with the consent of the Minister, seize the ship, and any pollutant that is carried thereon, anywhere in waters to which this Part applies or to which the *Arctic Waters Pollution Prevention Act* applies.

(2) Subject to subsection (3) and section 770, a ship and any pollutant seized under subsection (1) shall be retained in the custody of the pollution prevention officer making the seizure or shall be delivered into the custody of such person as the Minister directs.

(3) Where all or any pollutant seized under subsection (1) is perishable, the pollution prevention officer or other person having custody thereof may sell the pollutant or the portion thereof that is perishable, as the case may be, and the proceeds of the sale shall be paid to the Receiver General or shall be deposited in a chartered bank to the credit of the Receiver General.

The purpose of this chapter is not to comment on whether the provisions are justifiable as domestic legislation to meet the threat of pollution. It does appear, however, that these provisions mark a new departure in what this nation will regard as innocent passage in the circumstances to which new part XIX applies, namely, the prevention of pollution of coastal waters and coastal property.

Effect on innocent passage

The history and extent of the traditional concept of innocent passage has been the subject of much discussion in recent times, and no attempt will be made here to examine its proper limits in any detail.[43] However, it is noteworthy that among the provisions of the 1958 Convention on the Territorial Sea and Contiguous Zone,[44] the following are among those which concern the right of innocent passage:

14 1. Subject to the provisions of these articles, ships of all States, whether coastal or not, shall enjoy the right of innocent passage through the territorial sea.
2. Passage means navigation through the territorial sea, for the purpose either of traversing that sea without entering internal waters, or of proceeding to internal waters, or of making for the high seas from internal waters.
3. Passage includes stopping and anchoring, but only in so far as the same are incidental to ordinary navigation or are rendered necessary by *force majeure* or by distress.
4. Passage is innocent so long as it is not prejudicial to the peace, good order or security of the coastal State. Such passage shall take place in conformity with these articles and with other rules of international law.

'Foreign ships exercising the right of innocent passage' are by article 17 required to 'comply with the laws and regulations enacted by the coastal State in conformity with these articles and other rules of international law and, in particular, with such laws and regulations relating to transport and navigation.' The coastal state is empowered by article 16 to 'take the necessary steps in the territorial sea to prevent passage which is not innocent.' Further, as to the contiguous zone (the area extending seaward not more than twelve miles beyond the baseline from which the territorial sea is measured), article 24 provides:

1. In a zone of the high seas contiguous to its territorial sea, the coastal State may exercise the control necessary to:
    (*a*) Prevent infringement of its customs, fiscal, immigration or sanitary regulations within its territory or territorial sea;
    (*b*) Punish infringement of the above regulations committed within its territory or territorial sea.

The width of the territorial sea, for many years a three-mile limit, has been changing so that now a twelve-mile limit is widely recognized and accepted.

The 1970 amendments to the Canada Shipping Act appear to make substantial inroads into what the 1958 convention seems to contemplate in the matter of innocent passage, unless the passage of oil-laden tankers is *ipso facto* not to be regarded as innocent but 'prejudicial to the peace, good order or security' of Canada. The Canadian government has in fact expressed great concern about the traditional right of innocent passage and the consequential threat to coastal states and coastal property by maritime pollution.

The traditional law of the sea in general is oriented towards the concept of unfettered freedom of navigation on the high seas and thus favours flag-state jurisdiction while seeking to limit the jurisdiction of coastal states. As a result this essentially laissez-faire system is inadequate in its provisions for the prevention and control of marine pollution. Those provisions, as they are found in various conventions, do not properly recognize the paramount need for environmental preservation and do not strike a proper balance between the interests of the flag states in unfettered rights of navigation and the fundamental interest of the coastal states in the integrity of their shores. Flag-state jurisdiction does not carry with it, for instance, the logical consequence of flag-state responsibility for damage to the environment.[45]

These new amendments requiring compliance by ships operating into Canadian ports will affect the cost of ship operations and hence may, to that extent, prejudice seaborne trade into and out of Canadian waters. On the other hand, technological innovations required for the enforcement of these amendments, such as shore-based radar installations, may well enhance both the safety of the ship and the safety of the cargo to the benefit of all concerned in matters of this kind.

NOTES

1 See, eg, *Paterson Steamships, Limited* v *Canadian Co-Operative Wheat Producers, Limited*, [1934] A.C. 538, at 544–5 (*per* Lord Wright).
2 Ibid, at 545. See also *Trainor* v *The Black Diamond Steamship Company of Montreal* (1888), 16 S.C.R. 156.
3 Quoted in Astle, *Shipowners' Cargo Liabilities and Immunities* (1954), at 2–3.
4 [1928] 1 K.B. 717, at 732.
5 [1962] A.C. 446, at 471.
6 46 U.S.C. ss 190–6.
7 R.S.C. c 207 (1927).
8 N. Singh, 'International Conventions of Merchant Shipping' (1963), 8 *British Shipping Laws* 1080–7 [hereinafter cited as 8 *British Shipping Laws*].
9 1936, Can., c 49; now Carriage of Goods by Water Act, R.S.C. c C-15 (1970).
10 A general clause included in the other terms and conditions of carriage is not a statement that the goods are in fact being carried on deck. *Svenska Traktor & Maritime Agencies*, [1953] 2 Lloyd's List L.R. 124, at 130 (*per* Pilcher J). See the recent discussion of this general problem in *A. Couturier & Fils Ltée* v *St. Simeon Navigation Inc.*, [1970] Ex. C.R. 1012, and in *Grace Plastics Limited* v *The 'Bernd Wesch'* (1971), F.C. 273, at 280–3.
11 See, eg, *Mormaclynx*, [1970] 3 A.M.C. 1310, and other cases referred to therein. See also the *Mormacvega* case (1972), A.M.C. 2369, the *Royal Typewriter* case (1972), A.M.C. 1995, and the unreported decisions of the

Federal Court of Canada in *J.A. Johnston Company Limited* v *The Ship 'Tindesjell' et al.* (3 July 1973).
12 R.S.C. c S-9, s 657 (1970).
13 *Chandris* v *Isbrandtsen Moller Co. Inc.*, [1951] 1 K.B. 240, at 247.
14 Canada Shipping Act, R.S.C. c S-9, ss 647–55 (1970).
15 Carriage of Goods by Water Act, *supra* note 9, at article VIII. See also *Falconbridge Nickel Mines Ltd.* v *Chimo Shipping Limited et al*, [1969] Ex. C.R. 261. Appeal to the Supreme Court of Canada was dismissed (unreported).
16 Eg, R.P. Colinvaux, 'Carriage By Sea' (1963), 2 & 3 *British Shipping Laws*; Astle, *Shipowners' Cargo Liabilities and Immunities* (3d ed, 1967); Ivamy, ed, *Payne's Carriage of Goods by Sea* (8th ed, 1968); Knauth, *Ocean Bills of Lading* (14th ed, 1953).
17 Eg, Tetley, *Marine Cargo Claims* (1965).
18 See, eg, *A.S. May & Co. Ltd*, v *Robert Reford Co. Ltd. et al*, [1969] O.R. 611.
19 1970, Can., c 1.
20 8 *British Shipping Laws* 114–274. The most recent international conference on the subject was held in London in 1960 when the Brussels Regulations of 1910, which were revised in 1948, were further revised.
21 The present statutory basis of these and other federal collision regulations applying in Canada is section 635 of the Canada Shipping Act. See text of International Collision Regulations in S.O.R./55 Cons. (1955), 248–62.

22 Ibid, at 501–15.

23 Ibid, at 468–70.

24 Small Vessel Regulations, S.O.R./69–97 (1969), 103 *Canada Gazette,* part II, at 383 (4 March 1969).

25 8 *British Shipping Laws* 1047–51.

26 Ibid, at 1126–30.

27 Ibid, at 1131–4.

28 Ibid, at 1134–6.

29 S 43(3).

30 *Supra* note 20, at ss 22(2) (*e*), (*f*), (*g*), (*h*), (*i*), (*k*), (*m*), (*n*), (*p*), (*r*).

31 S 43(6).

32 S 43(8).

33 8 *British Shipping Laws* 1051–58.

34 Ibid, at 1058–64.

35 Under section 651 of the Canada Shipping Act, the governor in council is empowered to specify the amounts deemed to be the equivalents of 1000 and 3100 gold francs. The figures given are approximate and are subject to daily fluctuations.

36 Ss 647–55.

37 *Saint John Tug Boat Company Limited* v *Flipper Draggers Limited,* [1969] 1 Ex. C.R. 392, at 397–99. See also *Margrande Compania Naviera S.A., et al.* v *The Leecliffe Hall's Owners,* [1970] Ex C.R. 870; the *Nord-Deutsche* case (1971), F.C. 528.

38 1969–70, Can., c 47.

39 1970–71, Can. c 27. However, section 745, dealing with evidence of financial responsibility, is to come into effect on a date or dates fixed by separate proclamation.

40 See, eg, Federal Court Act, *supra* note 19, at s 43(4)(*b*).

41 R.S.C. c T–7 (1970).

42 S.O.R./71 171–81 (P.C. 1971, 366), 105 *Canada Gazette,* part II, no 5.

43 See, eg, Jessup, 'Sovereignty Over Territorial Waters' in *The Law of Territorial Waters and Maritime Jurisdiction* (1927), at 115, 211; Fitzmaurice, 'Some Aspects of the Geneva Conference on the Law of the Sea' (1959), 8 *Int'l & Comp. L.Q.* 73, at 90; Pharand, 'Innocent Passage in the Arctic,' (1968), 6 *Can. Y.B. Int'l L.* 3.

44 8 *British Shipping Laws* 1139–45.

45 Beesley, 'Rights and Responsibilities of Arctic Coastal States: The Canadian View' (1971), 3 *J. of Maritime Law and Commerce* 1.

C.B. BOURNE

20/Canada and the Law of International Drainage Basins

I

It is in the nature of things that water will always be an important issue in Canada-United States relations. This is so because those who fixed the boundary betwe⸍ .ı the two countries took no account of the geographical unity of drainage basins. Of the 5525 miles of boundary lines,[1] no less than 2198 miles pass through rivers and lakes, which thus are known as 'boundary waters';[2] elsewhere, the boundary cuts across many rivers so that they flow from one country into the other.

For a hundred years after the United States became an independent state, the main problem concerning the use of water in the relations of the two countries was navigation. It was a subject of concern from the very beginning of their international relations, being dealt with in the Treaty of Peace of 1783 in which Great Britain recognized the independence of the United States. Article VIII of this treaty, based on the erroneous assumption that the Mississippi River had origins in Canada, declared that navigation of it 'from its source to the ocean, shall forever remain free and open to the subjects of Great Britain, and the citizens of the United States.'[3] Since then navigation has been dealt with in many treaties between the two countries.

The principle of free navigation, first applied to the Mississippi River, was extended to all boundary waters by article III of the Jay Treaty of 1794;[4] it remains the rule today.[5] The British government, however, was reluctant to grant American citizens the right to navigate non-boundary waters, in particular the section of the St Lawrence River situated solely in Canada. It did grant them a limited right to navigate the St Lawrence by article III of the Jay Treaty, confining the privilege to 'small vessels trading *bona fide* between Montreal and Quebec,' but this was regarded by the British as having been abrogated by the war of 1812 and the issue was contentious for many years.

The United States government pressed its claim on the ground that 'the right of navigating the river is a right of nature, pre-existent on point of time, not necessary to have been surrendered up for any purpose of the common good, and unsusceptible of annihilation'; that upper riparians have by 'the law of nature and nations' this right to use the river in the territory of other riparians to reach the sea.[6] The British government, however, rejected this argument out of hand.[7] It did not change this position until the Reciprocity Treaty of 1854, by which it granted American ships the right of navigation on the St Lawrence River in Canada on an equal footing with Canadian ships in exchange for a similar right for British ships on Lake Michigan,[8] but the privilege of suspending these rights was expressly reserved. As things turned out, this right ended in 1866 when the Reciprocity Treaty was terminated.

By this time, however, the British government had given up its hostility to the American claim of free navigation and, in article xxvi of the Treaty of Washington of 1871,[9] it was provided that 'navigation of the River St. Lawrence, ascending and descending ... from, to, and into the sea, shall forever remain free and open for the purposes of commerce to the citizens of the United States, subject to any laws and regulations ... of Canada, not inconsistent with such privileges of free navigation.' By the same article British subjects were granted a similar right on the Yukon, Porcupine, and Stikine rivers and, in addition, their right of navigation of Lake Michigan was restored for the term of the treaty by article xxviii. This latter right is now provided for in article i of the Boundary Waters Treaty of 1909.[10]

Thus the contentious issue of free navigation was substantially disposed of by 1871. From time to time since then, navigation has been the subject of discussion and even of treaties between Canada and the United States; most of these treaties were designed to improve navigation on the Great Lakes and the St Lawrence River which have now become a deep-water highway from the sea to the heart of the continent, used not only by Canadian and American ships but those of all states.[11]

As the twentieth century approached, problems concerning non-navigational uses of water came to the fore in North America. Advances in technology, together with rapidly growing populations, increased enormously the utilization of water resources. More and more water was needed for domestic uses, for sanitation, for industry, for recreation, for irrigation and for the generation of hydroelectric power. At the same time rivers and lakes, traditionally the convenient dumping grounds for the sewage and other wastes of society, were becoming increasingly polluted. In these circumstances, competing uses usually lead sooner or later to conflicts of interest and to disputes about water utilization. In fact, this is what happened in the case of the waters in the international drainage basins shared by Canada and the United States.

Some illustrations of the issues that arose in the late nineteenth century are given here. The harbinger of diversion disputes came in 1841 when the waters of the Allegash River in Maine were diverted from their natural channel by a canal built between Lake Telos on the Allegash River and Webster Pond on the Penobscot River; these waters used to flow into the Saint John River and thus into Canada, but by this canal they were made to flow into the Penobscot River and thus through Maine into the sea.[12] Great Britain instructed its ambassador at Washington to protest this diversion, but there is no record that he did so. The impact of the diversion was insignificant and presumably the matter was not pressed. Before many years had passed, diversions and proposed diversions for irrigation purposes of the waters of the St Mary and Milk rivers in the state of Montana and the provinces of Alberta and Saskatchewan became a subject of conflict between the citizens and governments of the two countries.[13] And in the 1890s diversions of Great Lakes waters which would affect the generation of hydroelectric power at Niagara Falls and the division of the waters of Niagara River to be used for that purpose were matters of concern to persons on both sides of the boundary.[14] At this time too the growing city of Chicago was implementing plans to divert increasingly large quantities of water from Lake Michigan to carry away its sewage through a drainage canal connecting that lake, by way of the Chicago and Illinois rivers, with the Mississippi River. Water had in fact been taken out of the Great Lakes system since a canal had been completed in 1848; the volume diverted had been increased slowly over the years, but a large drainage canal was begun in 1892 and put into operation in 1900.[15]

Of course, diversions of boundary waters and the placing of obstructions in them, affected the levels of these waters and were the subject of complaints. For example, since 1888 Americans on the Minnesota side of the Lake of the Woods had been complaining that their lands were being flooded as a result of a dam built at the outlet of the lake in Canada.[16] There had been similar complaints by Americans about a dam built by Canadian authorities at the head of the Beauharnois Canal in Canada.[17]

By 1900, then, there was a growing number of disputes between Canada and the United States about the utilization of waters. In the words used by Sir Wilfrid Laurier in speaking of these disputes a few years later, 'the conditions existing were intolerable.'[18] In both Canada and the United States the need was felt for some mechanism and for some principles for solving these water problems without the direct involvement of the two governments. The impetus for the development of new institutions and new laws was strong.

The first step in this development was taken in 1894 at an irrigation congress at Denver, Colorado, convened by the United States and attended also by representatives of Canada and Mexico. The desirability of creating an international organization to regulate international rivers in North America was first discussed there with approval. The United States and Mexico had already started to experiment with an international agency as a means of solving their international river problems; in 1889 they had established the International Boundary Commission to deal primarily with diversions of water from the Rio Grande. This commission, however, had not removed all difficulties and the Mexicans were still complaining bitterly in the mid-1890s about the injury they suffered as a result of diversions of water in the United States.

The first concrete step in establishing a Canada-United States agency was taken at the International Irrigation Congress held in 1895 at Albuquerque, New Mexico, which was attended by representatives of the Canadian and Mexican governments. This congress was persuaded to adopt unanimously a motion asking for the 'appointment of an international commission to act in conjunction with the authorities of Mexico and Canada in adjudicating the conflicting rights which have arisen, or may hereafter arise, on streams of an international character.' The Canadian government approved the idea of an international commission at once and asked the British ambassador at Washington to take the matter up with the United States government. The latter government, however, was unwilling to proceed at that time and so the matter rested for some years. In 1902 the Congress of the United States requested the president to invite the British government to 'join in the formation of an international commission' which would have the duty 'to investigate and report upon the conditions and uses of the waters adjacent to the boundary lines between the United States and Canada.' This request was acted on eventually and thus the International Waterways Commission came into existence in 1905.[19]

This commission, composed of three Americans and three Canadians, was soon to be displaced by the International Joint Commission. During its short life, however, it did valuable work, presenting to the two governments a number of reports dealing with such subjects as the diversion and division of waters at Niagara, and the diversions of waters at Sault Ste Marie and at Chicago.[20] Almost immediately after it started work, the commission became aware of the lack of principles governing international water resources and the inadequacy of its own powers in the face of the problems to be dealt with. It therefore soon recommended that a joint commission be established to supervise the enforcement of its recommendations, or that it be given this power itself, and that a treaty be entered into to 'settle the rules and principles upon which all such questions may be peacefully and satisfactorily determined as they arise.'[21]

The two governments recognized the soundness of these recommendations and entered into negotiations for a treaty during 1907 and 1908. The negotiations were difficult.[22] The Canadians wanted a permanent commission that would have jurisdiction over all boundary water problems and would settle them in accordance with established principles; the Americans preferred *ad hoc* commissions to deal with particular problems. The Canadians supported the principle prohibiting diversions of waters that would injure public or private interests in the other state; the Americans insisted upon the principle that a state can do as it pleases with the water in its territory. In the end, the Americans agreed to a permanent commission and the Canadians reluctantly accepted the American view on diversions. And so the Boundary Waters Treaty was signed on 11 January 1909, was duly ratified, and came into force on 9 May 1910.

This treaty was a watershed in Canada-United States relations. Thereafter, disputes between the two countries about the use of the waters of their international rivers and lakes could be dealt with at a level below that of the two governments. Even if a problem could not be taken directly to the International Joint Commission, which was created by the treaty and held its first meeting on 10 January 1912, it could be sent there by either government on a reference under article ix of the treaty.[23] Thus issues that might rouse passions on either side of the international boundary could be studied by the commission, talked about in its quasijudicial atmosphere, and eventually returned to the governments with recommendations that most often had already been found acceptable to both the Canadian and American members of the commission. On rare occasions when the commission could not agree, as in the case of the Columbia River, its studies provided reliable information which, by elucidating the issues, made it easier for the two governments to find common ground and reach agreement.[24]

Canada and the United States, then, found in the 1909 treaty a satisfactory means of dealing with their common water problems. This does not mean that all these problems were thereby solved. Acute problems clearly still exist. Pollution of boundary waters in particular has gone from bad to worse and it is now realized that only drastic measures can stop the degradation and restore the quality of these waters. It does mean, however, that Canada has had a rich experience in the management of international water resources, especially since about 1900. A study of this experience will contribute to a better understanding of the nature of international water problems and thus to their solution.

II

The International Joint Commission has been involved in most of the international drainage basin problems between Canada and the United States and between their citizens since its inception in 1912.[25] It would therefore be possible to gain an appreciation of the Canadian experience in this field by examining the record of the commission. It is not intended, however, to deal with the subject in this manner; the work of the commission and its role having been fully discussed elsewhere[26] will be touched on here only incidentally. Rather, it is proposed to examine a number of particular aspects of the law of international drainage basins with a view to ascertaining Canada's view of this law and its contribution to it.

Theoretical basis of the law

It is hardly an exaggeration to say that there was no law governing international drainage basins as late as the end of the nineteenth century. At that time, a few authors had asserted that states could not utilize the waters of rivers flowing in their territory if their doing so would injure co-basin states,[27] and some states had protested utilizations by co-basin states on the ground that they violated international law. But others had maintained that states could utilize the waters of rivers in their territories without incurring liability to co-basin states for any harmful effects of their doing so.[28]

The situation may be illustrated by an example taken from United States-Mexico relations. The Mexicans, who had been protesting American diversions of the waters of the Rio Grande since 1880, argued in 1895 that 'international law would form a sufficient basis for the rights of the Mexican inhabitants ... Their claim to the use of the water of that river is incontestable, being prior to that of the inhabitants [of the United States] by hundreds of years.'[29] This claim by Mexico was referred by the United States secretary of state to Attorney General Judson Harmon, for an opinion on it. The attorney general responded with the classic statement, known as the Harmon doctrine, that 'the rules, principles, and precedents of international law impose no liability or obligation upon the United States,' and that the recognition of the Mexican claim would be 'entirely inconsistent with the sovereignty of the United States over its national domain.'[30] In short, the United States could do as it pleased with the waters in its territory.

Whether or not the Harmon doctrine was an accurate statement of the law, it was at that time and for many years thereafter the view adhered to by the United States, at least when its utilizations were questioned by other states.[31] It thus affected Canada directly. This was seen in the cases of the diversion of waters at Chicago, of the proposed diversion of waters from the St Mary River to the Milk River which Congress had authorized by act in 1902,[32] and of the diversion of waters from Birch Lake, a tributary of the Lake of the Woods which is a boundary water, proposed in 1904 by the Minnesota Canal and Power Company.[33] Concerning the latter diversion, Chandler Anderson, the New York lawyer who advised the United States government on Canada-United States water problems, wrote an opinion for Secretary of State Elihu Root in which he asserted that 'the jurisdiction of the nation within its own territory is necessarily exclusive and absolute ... no restriction upon the use of these tributary waters within the borders of the United States can be admitted. The United States is fully committed to this proposition, not only as a matter of principle, but in actual practice and as a matter of policy.'[34] It was, of course, Mr Anderson who later drafted article II of the Boundary Waters Treaty of 1909 which embodies the Harmon doctrine and makes it a fundamental principle of the treaty law governing diversions of waters which flow across the Canada-United States boundary or into boundary waters.

The Harmon doctrine, so firmly held by the United States, influenced the thinking of those concerned with Canada-United States water problems. In its 1906 opinion on the proposed diversion of waters in Minnesota from Birch Lake by the Minnesota Canal and Power Company, the International Waterways Commission advised against it because it would interfere with navigation contrary to article II of the Webster-Ashburton Treaty of 1842, but in doing so it expressed the view that the Harmon doctrine was settled international law and that, consequently, apart from treaty, states had a sovereign right to divert waters even though the diversion injured co-basin states.[35] The commission was alarmed at the dangers that this permissive law posed for boundary waters and lakes. It therefore recommended that 'a treaty be entered into which will settle the rules and principles upon which all such questions may be peacefully and satisfactorily determined, as they arise,' and that some enforcement powers be given to it or to another joint commission established to replace it.[36] This recommendation bore fruit and subsequently led to the creation of the International Joint Commission and the establishment of a number of principles by the Boundary Waters Treaty of 1909.

The territorial sovereignty theory expressed by Attorney General Harmon was accepted by a number of Canadians, perhaps less from conviction than from resignation in the face of stubborn American adherence to it. Sir George Gibbons, a member of the International Waterways Commission and a key negotiator of the 1909 treaty, accepted it. In notes on the treaty prepared by him for the prime minister, he wrote: 'There is no limitation on the sovereign right of each nation over waters within its own territory any more than over its lands,'[37] a view he repeated on other occasions.[38] Mr Aylesworth, the minister of justice,[39] and Mr Pugsley, the minister of public works,[40] took the same view. So too did the governor general.[41]

It would be wrong, however, to conclude from these statements, two of them made by members of the cabinet, that Canada officially took the view that the Harmon doctrine was a correct statement of international law. In the first place, the statements must be read in the context of Canada-United States relations in water resources matters. When that is done, it is seen that they were made largely to justify Canada's acceptance of article II of the 1909 treaty. This article recognized the unfettered right of the parties to divert waters flowing across the boundary or into boundary waters, although it did impose a qualification on that right by giving a measure of protection to private interests that may be thereby injured in the other country. The argument justifying it was in substance this: article II is not what we wished, but we accepted it because it gives Canadians greater protection than they would have under customary international law – at least under the American view of that law, which, in the light of the primitive state of international institutions is the view that one has no choice but accept. This was not put bluntly by Mr Pugsley and Mr Aylesworth in their speeches in the House of Commons, but as Mr Borden, the leader of the opposition, said, that was what their argument came to in the last analysis.[42] Moreover, Sir George Gibbons always made it clear that he regarded the Harmon doctrine with distaste, even though at times he paid it lip service. In a memorandum to Mr Root in 1908, he stated that the adoption in the treaty of the rule that no diversion could be undertaken by one state to the injury of public or private interests in the other without the consent of the other would be a correct declaration of international law.[43]

Sir Wilfrid Laurier, the prime minister, did not accept the Harmon doctrine. In the debate in the House of Commons, he expressly stated that he agreed with the view of the law taken by Mr Borden, that is to say, a state can use the water in its territory as it pleases so long as it does not do so to the detriment of another state.[44] Mr Borden had challenged Mr Aylesworth's and Mr Pugsley's assertions of the Harmon doctrine, quoting the opposite principle from Oppenheim's textbook.[45] There is little doubt that Laurier's view stated here represented the official stand of Canada on this issue. In the negotiations of the 1909 treaty, Canada had strongly urged the adoption of the substance of an article which would have prohibited diversions of waters that materially interfered with the natural flow 'to the injury of the other country, or of its citizens' without the consent of such other country.

Canada has consistently maintained this view of the law throughout the years in its protests that the Chicago diversions are contrary to international law. For example, in 1913 Ambassador Bryce presented the Canadian protest against the diversions to the State Department on the ground that, apart from the treaties, it was contrary to recognized principles of international law; in 1926 the British ambassador stated in protest that Canada believed 'it to be a recognized principle of international practice that unless by joint consent, no permanent diversion should be permitted to another watershed from any watershed naturally tributary to the waters forming the boundary' between Canada and the United States.[46]

Canada, then, has never supported the theory of absolute territorial sovereignty and yielded only reluctantly to the modified version of it that appears in article II of the Boundary Waters Treaty of 1909. Her early preference was for a principle of 'absolute territorial integrity' or a 'riparian rights' rule similar to that of the common law. Under that rule, a state cannot lawfully utilize the waters of an international drainage basin in its territory if its doing so will cause injury in the territory of a co-basin state unless that co-basin state consents to the utilization.

Taken to its logical conclusion, the theory that a state cannot undertake a utilization of the waters of a drainage basin that will affect prejudicially its co-basin states without the consent of these states, in effect gives them a veto over proposed utilizations. This doctrine of consent is the opposite of the Harmon doctrine. Under the latter doctrine, a state can do as it pleases with the waters in its territory no matter what injury is done elsewhere; under the former, it can do nothing that would expose co-basin states to injury without their consent no matter how reasonable it may be.

The truth of the matter is that the international law of rivers and lakes was only in its very early stages of evolution in the early 1900s when these contentious water issues between Canada and the United States arose. Without firmly established legal principles and without sufficient forethought about the implications of various legal solutions, both countries seized upon fragments of law developed in other contexts and used them to further their national water policy. With the passage of time, however, neither of the two doctrines was acceptable to the international community. The Harmon doctrine, which was tantamount to a denial of the existence of any law applicable to international drainage basins, was rejected as being 'radically unsound' and 'intolerable';[47] the consent doctrine was rejected because it would lead to delay and frustration in exploiting the riches of international drainage basins and give an unfair advantage to downstream states.[48]

The doctrine that has attracted overwhelming support and may now be said to be an established principle of customary international law is that of 'equitable utilization' or, as it is sometimes called, of limited territorial sovereignty. Its beginnings can be seen dimly in *Aargau* v *Zurich,* the decision of a Swiss court in 1878.[49] But it was the Supreme Court of the United States that first clearly stated the doctrine in 1907 in *Kansas* v *Colorado,*[50] and since then it has elaborated and refined it, notably in *Wyoming* v *Colorado,*[51] and *Nebraska* v *Wyoming.*[52] The doctrine attained a firm place in international law when, after lengthy study, it was incorporated into the 1961 Salzburg Resolution of the Institute of International Law[53] and into the Helsinki Rules adopted by the International Law Association in 1966.[54]

The essence of the doctrine of equitable utilization, found in article IV of the Helsinki Rules, is that 'each basin State is entitled, within its territory, to a reasonable and equitable share in the beneficial uses of the waters of an international drainage basin.' Article V provides that 'what is a reasonable and equitable share within the meaning of Article IV is to be determined in the light of all the relevant factors in each particular case'; it then lists some of the factors that are deemed to be relevant, concluding with a paragraph stating that 'the weight to be given to each factor is to be determined by its importance in comparison with that of other relevant factors.' The remaining thirty-two articles of the Helsinki Rules are mere glosses on articles IV and V and add little to their substance.

The doctrine is therefore rather vague. It merely introduces into this branch of international law 'the reasonable man test' for determining what is lawful or unlawful conduct. It demands that states sharing a drainage basin act reasonably in their utilization of its waters, and it instructs courts to determine the reasonableness of any utilization by weighing all relevant factors and by comparing the benefit that would flow from the utilization with the injury it might do to the interests of other co-basin states.[55]

There is some evidence that even the United States has abandoned its adherence to the Harmon doctrine and now accepts the doctrine of equitable utilization. Some of the statements made to the Senate Committee on Foreign Relations when it was considering the United States-Mexico Treaty of 1944 suggest this.[56] These statements, however, are equivocal,[57] and there is still room for doubt about the United States position. In proceedings before the International Joint Commission[58] as late as 1950 and 1951, counsel for the United States was still invoking the Harmon doctrine in substance by relying on article II of the Boundary Waters Treaty of 1909; and unilateral diversions are still being made at Chicago. The most recent official statement on the subject is the 1958 memorandum prepared by Mr William Griffin of the State Department. In opposing Canada's claims about Columbia River development, he argued in favour of the equitable utilization rule, interpreting it so as to give a high degree of protection to existing uses downstream; surprisingly, he also argued in favour of an interpretation of article II of the 1909 treaty that would render a party to the treaty liable for damage caused to the other party by a unilateral diversion, which is a far cry from the Harmon doctrine on which article II was based.[59] It is a fact, of course, that the United States did enter into treaties with Mexico and with Canada which were inspired by a sense of equity, but this is not a clear indication of its position on the prescriptions of customary international law. It should perhaps also be said that the Harmon doctrine was never applied to the 'boundary waters' between Canada and the United States, as distinct from waters flowing across the boundary and waters tributary to boundary waters; the provisions of the Boundary Waters Treaty of 1909 accord with this position.

There is little concrete evidence that Canada has accepted the doctrine of equitable utilization. Its relations with the United States concerning water resources are now so largely based upon treaties that discussions and differences of opinion about proposed projects usually involve, from the legal aspect, only points of treaty interpretation. For example, as late as the 1920s Canada invoked, in its notes protesting the Chicago diversions, a rule of customary international law to the effect that a state could not make a permanent diversion of waters without the consent of a co-basin state.[60] But by the 1950s its protests were based squarely on the treaty obligations of the United States; the diversions were contrary to the 'agreed regime' applicable to the Great Lakes watershed, it was asserted.[61] In its dealings with other problems, Canada has also relied on existing treaty rights and obligations. For example, she has claimed the right unilaterally to divert waters by virtue of article II of the 1909 treaty, as the Americans have done. She did so in the Souris River reference.[62] The government of the province of Saskatchewan had asserted its right to all of the waters of this river rising in the province and in 1957 the Canadian government informed the Canadian Section of the International Joint Commission that it agreed with Saskatchewan. No attempt, however, was in fact made to take these waters unilaterally. In the case of the Columbia River, Canada did study the feasibility of diverting waters from it for exclusive use in Canada, but the matter never got beyond that point. She held the opinion that article II of the 1909 treaty would justify this diversion; it was argued that the diversion could also be justified under the doctrine of equitable utilization.[63]

An indication of the modern attitude of the Canadian and United States governments may be deduced from the pronouncements of the International Joint Commission, bearing in mind its composition and the deference it pays to the views of the two governments. When the commission was asked in 1959 to prepare a statement of principles for determining and apportioning benefits from co-operative use of the waters of the Columbia River, it prefaced its list of principles with the statement that it 'was guided by the basic concept that the principles recommended herein should result in an equitable sharing of the benefits attributable to their co-operative undertakings.'[64] This is a good statement of the doctrine of equitable utilization.

While it is not possible to ascribe to Canada any clear espousal of the doctrine of equitable utilization, it is indisputable that she has always asserted that a state's exploitation of the waters of an international drainage basin is subject to international law, in particular, that a state is under a legal obligation to take account of the interests of co-basin states and not heedlessly and unreasonably inflict serious injury on them.

The unity of the 'drainage basin' concept

Once it is granted that there are rules of international law governing the utilization of the waters of international drainage basins, the question arises whether that law treats the basin in question as a single unit that must be viewed from all aspects. Or does it treat it in a piecemeal fashion, concentrating on a particular part or, perhaps, on a particular type of utilization?

In former times, when the capacity to interfere with the natural state of drainage basins was limited, disputes about the waters of rivers, especially large rivers, usually concerned problems affecting particular localities. Thus the solutions to these problems were also local in scope, and there was no need to worry about the entire basin. In the past century, however, owing to technological advances, man acquired the capacity to interfere greatly with nature. Vast dams, huge diversion schemes, and other works became commonplace. Today, it is true that the various parts of a drainage basin are interdependent. A utilization of water in one part often affects the water in another part, especially downstream from the utilization. Recognizing this interdependence, jurists have argued with force since the Congress of Vienna in 1815 that a drainage basin must be treated 'as a unity' or, as it is sometimes put, as a whole.[65]

This concept has never achieved the status of a rule of law. This is just as well, for it is not fully in accord with reality. It is apparent today that the development of an international drainage basin may affect not only persons and things within the basin but persons and things without the basin. It may have important regional or even national implications. When a utilization of waters is being planned, therefore, a wise state will study the project in the light of its effect on the basin as a whole and of the possibility of utilizing its waters otherwise, and also will consider it in the larger context of a regional or national water resources development plan.[66]

In the Boundary Waters Treaty of 1909, Canada and the United States deliberately rejected the concept of the unity of a drainage basin. In it they separated boundary waters from tributary waters flowing into boundary waters and from waters flowing out of boundary waters.[67] In one respect, however, they did recognize the interdependence of all waters in the basin; in article II, they qualified the right of one state to divert non-boundary waters by providing that it could not exercise this right so as to cause 'material injury' to the navigational interests of the other state anywhere in the basin.

This artificial division of a drainage basin is unreal and impractical. Few activities in a tributary will fail to affect to some degree the waters in the main channel of a river or lake. This interdependence cannot in fact be ignored. This is illustrated by a proceeding before the International Joint Commission. The Greater Winnipeg Water District applied to the commission in 1913 for permission to divert water from Shoal Lake. Since that lake, which is entirely in Canada, only connects with the Lake of the Woods and therefore seems to fall into the excluded class of tributary waters, a preliminary question was raised whether or not the commission had jurisdiction. The difficulty was overcome by the Water District's application being amended so that the diversion was said to be from Shoal Lake and from the Lake of the Woods. On this basis the commission proceeded to deal with the application, evidently taking the view that the two lakes were so closely connected that a diversion from one could be treated as a diversion from the other.[68] It would seem a fair deduction from this case that the commission regards itself as having jurisdiction over anything done in waters connected with boundary waters and affecting them.[69] This sensible stand, however, can be supported only by a most liberal interpretation of the treaty.

Although the 1909 treaty for the most part disregarded the unity of drainage basins, this is no proof that Canada rejected the principle. The record shows that Canadians were fully aware of the relationship between all parts of a drainage basin, in particular of the direct relationship between the diversions of the waters of Lake Michigan at Chicago and the volume of water available for power production and for navigation in the boundary waters of the Great Lakes and the St Lawrence River downstream. For example, Canadian members of the International Waterways Commission had insisted on including in one of the commission's reports the following principles:

1 In all navigable waters the use for navigation purposes is of primary and paramount right. The Great Lakes *system* ... should be maintained *in its integrity*.
2 Permanent or complete diversions of navigable waters or *their tributary streams* should only be permitted for domestic purposes and for the use of locks in navigation canals.[70]

Sir George Gibbons certainly appreciated the interdependence of a river system and fought to bring all parts of it under the rule of law. In a memorandum on a draft of the proposed Boundary Waters Treaty of 1909 which he submitted to Secretary of State Root, he wrote: 'As Lake Michigan and Georgian Bay are a part of [the Great Lakes] system, the component parts of which are *interdependent*, your Commission suggested ... that the privileges which the citizens of each country had with regard to the rest of the system should be extended to these waters. *Nature has made them inseparable*.'[71] The United States, however, did not agree and refused to give up the idea that a state is free to do as it pleases with the non-boundary waters in its territory. In these circumstances, as Sir Wilfrid Laurier in effect told the House of Commons in the debate on the treaty, Canada reluctantly agreed to the treaty on the ground that it was better than having no treaty at all.[72]

Canada has been consistent in its view of the interdependence of a drainage basin. This is seen in its statements and attitudes on a number of occasions. For example, in the negotiation of the convention on the regulation of the levels of the Lake of the Woods, Canada accepted the proposal of the United States that the international waters in question 'should be considered and treated as one general problem,' and proceeded to enter into a treaty governing the entire 'Lake of the Woods Watershed,' placing both its boundary and tributary waters under the jurisdiction of the International Joint Commission and thus departing significantly from the Boundary Waters Treaty of 1909.[73] Again, in the prolonged discussions and study of the development of the Columbia River, Canada and the United States both recognized the unity of that river's basin when they asked the International Joint Commission to study and make recommendations about its most advantageous development for both countries.[74] During the 1950s, the subject became a matter of controversy. Canada insisted that she would not allow developments of the river in Canada unless the United States shared with her some of the benefits that would result from these developments. She argued that not only the injuries caused by works in one state to co-basin states but the benefits thereby conferred on them had to be taken into account. This view was, in essence, a logical deduction from the concept of the unity of a drainage basin. More recently, the recommendations of the International Joint Commission have emphasized that the problems of pollution of the Great Lakes must be tackled on a basinwide basis,[75] and both Canada and the United States seem to be willing to take that approach to them.[76]

It was argued above that it was desirable, in considering a project to utilize the waters of a drainage basin, to look beyond the limits of the basin and to take regional and even national plans into account. But does the law permit a state to do so? On this question, Canada has been inconsistent. On the one hand, one of her reasons for condemning the Chicago diversions was the 'principle of international practice that no permanent diversion should be permitted to another watershed from any watershed naturally tributary to the waters forming the boundary between two countries.'[77] On the other hand, she contended that the International Joint Commission should include in its studies of the best way of using the Columbia River waters the advantages and disadvantages of transferring them from the Columbia River to the Fraser River basin. In other words, Canada was taking a regional view of the proper utilization of her Columbia River water resources and wished the commission to do likewise; her right to divert these waters out of their basin could be based on article II of the Boundary Waters Treaty of 1909, and perhaps also on the doctrine of equitable utilization.[78] The United States, of course, has been equally inconsistent, asserting the right to make out-of-basin transfers in the case of the Chicago diversions, but denying the legality of such transfers in the case of the Columbia River. It refused to allow the commission to include the Columbia-Fraser rivers diversion proposal in its study.

This view that out-of-basin water transfers are contrary to international law is not supported by state practice. These transfers are now common,[79] and some are explicitly sanctioned by treaty. For example, by article VI of the Boundary Waters Treaty of 1909, Canada and the United States agreed to treat the St Mary and the Milk rivers and their tributaries 'as one stream for the purposes of irrigation and power' and allowed the waters of the two rivers to be connected. Others are not thus sanctioned, for example, the Chicago diversions, and their validity must depend upon customary international law. That out-of-basin water transfers may be legal under customary international law is supported by statements of the tribunal in the *Lake Lanoux* arbitration between France and Spain referring to them with approval.[80] There are several examples of these water transfers in the United States.[81] In Canada 5000 cubic feet per second of water have been diverted from the Albany River, which flows into Hudson Bay, and transported by the Long Lac-Ogoki works into Lake Superior with the agreement of the United States,[82] and a much larger scheme to transfer surplus waters, perhaps more than 75,000 cubic feet per second, from rivers now flowing into James Bay to the Great Lakes basin has been studied.[83] Mention might also be made of the grandiose scheme that would initially take 110 million acre feet of water from Alaska, the Yukon, and British Columbia and distribute them among seven Canadian provinces and thirty-three states in the United States as far east as the Great Lakes, and among three northern states in Mexico.[84] It reflects the 'continental' approach to the development of drainage basins as distinct from the more limited drainage basin, regional, and national approaches.

There is little in this story about diversions of water, then, to suggest that Canada attributes any overriding significance to the concept of the unity of a drainage basin.

Priorities

Cheap and easy transportation of people and goods is a prime factor in the social and economic development of a nation. Historically, it has been provided best by ships. Consequently, navigable rivers have from earliest times served as highways and their use for that purpose became tremendously important. In the case of some rivers, such as the Rhine or the Danube, navigation is even today their prime use.

This early importance of navigation led many persons to conclude that the use of a river for navigation has priority over all other uses.[85] However, when technology added new dimensions to the utilization of the waters of rivers and lakes in the late nineteenth and early twentieth centuries, other uses became increasingly important and the primacy of navigation was soon challenged successfully. Most persons now deny that priority to navigation is a rule of international law,[86] although many treaties still give it that status. There is, in fact, overwhelming support for the proposition that international law denies priority to any use of the waters of international drainage basins. This is reflected in the writings of jurists[87] and in the declarations and statements of principles adopted by leading learned associations and institutes.[88] Article VI of the Helsinki Rules, for example, categorically states that 'a use or category of uses is not entitled to any inherent preference over any other use or category of uses.'

This rejection of a rule of priorities is understandable. Water is used for many purposes and the importance of a particular use varies from place to place and from time to time. A rigid rule of universal application is therefore unworkable. Under the principle of equitable utilization, the priority of a utilization is a flexible matter, depending upon what is reasonable in the light of all relevant circumstances. Broadly speaking, a statement of the United States Bureau of Reclamation puts the matter in proper perspective when it states that 'in planning the control and utilization of the waters ... the widest range of multiple benefits should be sought ... To the extent, however, that several functions of water control and utilization are conflicting, preference should be given to the functions which contribute most significantly to the welfare and livelihood of the largest number of people.'[89]

In early Canada-United States relations, it seems to have been assumed that navigation had the highest priority. As we have seen, the main emphasis in the treaties relating to water matters in the eighteenth and nineteenth centuries was on ensuring freedom of navigation. When other uses began to compete with navigation and each other, those concerned with Canada's water resources soon called for the establishment of legal principles to guide them. But the primacy of navigation was not to be shaken easily. Even the members of the International Waterways Commission, who led the movement for legal principles which culminated in the Boundary Waters Treaty of 1909, placed navigation first in a list of suggested principles, saying that 'in all navigable waters the use for navigation purposes is of primary and paramount right,' and that nothing is to be done that would injuriously affect navigation.[90]

This philosophy was projected into the 1909 treaty. In that treaty Canada and the United States dealt with the problem of priorities in the following manner. In the first place, they provided by article I that navigation of all boundary waters 'shall forever continue free and open' and that Lake Michigan shall be similarly open during the life of the treaty. Furthermore, by article II, they qualified their unfettered right to divert waters that flow across the boundary into boundary waters by prohibiting, in effect, diversions that would cause material injury to navigation interests. Then, by article VIII, they provided as follows:

> The following order of precedence shall be observed among the various uses enumerated hereinafter for these waters, and no use shall be permitted which tends materially to conflict with or restrain any other use which is given preference over it in this order of precedence:
> (1) Uses for domestic and sanitary purposes;
> (2) Uses for navigation, including the service of canals for the purposes of navigation;
> (3) Uses for power and for irrigation purposes.
> The foregoing provisions shall not apply to or disturb any existing uses of boundary waters on either side of the boundary.

It is still difficult to interpret these articles. It would be easier to determine their effect if navigation were dealt with separately. But as a result of the saving clause in the last sentence of the passage from article VIII just quoted, non-navigation uses are divided into two categories: those existing at the date of entry into force of the Boundary Waters Treaty of 1909, and those that have come into existence since that date. The former are given a special status: the priority rules set forth in article VIII do not apply to them and must not disturb them. To illustrate this let us suppose that a city proposes to divert water from boundary waters for its waterworks system and this diversion will 'materially' conflict with an existing hydroelectric power plant. If the power plant existed in 1910 when the 1909 treaty came into force, the International Joint Commission could not use the priority provisions of article VIII against it, for it would be protected from injury by the saving clause. On the other hand, if it came into existence after that date, the commission would have to apply the order of priority of that article. Since domestic and sanitary uses are to be ranked first and uses for power purposes third, the commission would have to allow the city's waterworks scheme to proceed, perhaps subject to the payment of compensation to the injured power plant.

The matter is more complicated in the case of navigation. At first glance, articles I and II appear to give navigation priority over all other uses. And yet article VIII specifically refers to navigation and ranks it second in the order of precedence. These articles therefore are in apparent conflict. The saving clause partly reconciles them, for it protects all uses existing on the date the treaty came into force in 1910 and this would include a navigation use existing at that time, at least such a use at the level at which it then existed. Suppose, however, that a post-1910 navigational use would be injured by a proposed utilization for domestic and sanitary purposes.

Would article VIII nevertheless require the International Joint Commission to give priority to the work for domestic and sanitary purposes, subject perhaps to the payment of compensation to the injured navigation interests? To answer this question with an unqualified 'yes' would be to say that, if in the last analysis there is an irreconcilable conflict between a navigation use of certain waters and a use of those waters for domestic and sanitary purposes, then the navigation use must cease. This answer is not satisfactory; at best it reduces article I merely to an assertion that, *if there is navigation,* the citizens of both countries are to be treated equally. This is hardly a proper interpretation of that article, which unquestionably does guarantee some navigation. One must therefore seek another answer to the question. Since article VIII expressly ranks navigation after domestic and sanitary uses, the parties clearly did not intend to give navigation an absolute priority. It would be wrong, therefore, to say that navigation interests must never be interfered with or damaged in any way. A better way of putting it would be to say that they must not be unreasonably interfered with. This statement, however, cannot be taken to its logical conclusion. Article I must be taken to guarantee some irreducible minimum level of navigation; it thus prevents the commission from destroying navigation altogether, even if it would be reasonable in the circumstances to do so in favour of a utilization for municipal or sanitary purposes. In the end, then, there seems to be an unavoidable contradiction between articles I and II on the one hand and article VIII on the other.

Another difficulty is inherent in article VIII itself. Immediately preceding the order of priorities, one finds these words: 'The High Contracting Parties shall have, each on its own side of the boundary, equal and similar rights in the use of waters herein before defined as boundary waters.' The relationship between this provision and the order of priorities that follows it is not clear. Let us suppose that one country has fully utilized its share of the rights in the use of the waters and that it then wishes to undertake a further utilization that has a higher priority under the order of precedence in article VIII than does a conflicting prior or contemporary utilization of the other country. In these circumstances would the International Joint Commission have to refuse permission to undertake the work with the higher priority because it would contravene the principle of 'equal and similar rights' for both parties to the treaty, or would it have to grant its permission because not to do so would contravene the order of precedence? One has no guide but the language of the article in answering this question. On balance, it is thought the equality of rights of the parties is the fundamental principle and the order of precedence should not therefore be used to subvert it.

The order of precedence in article VIII has had little practical effect. The International Joint Commission seems to have been guided by it in making its recommendations under the reference of 15 January 1940 concerning the apportionment of the waters of the Souris River and its tributaries which flow through Saskatchewan, North Dakota, and Manitoba to Hudson Bay.[91] North Dakota used much of these waters to support wildlife sanctuaries there. Saskatchewan, the upstream state, claiming the right to utilize the waters of the river to meet increasing demands for water for municipal and industrial purposes, argued that its uses for these human needs had priority over North Dakota's uses for wildlife, and in this was supported by the government of Canada. In its last report on the subject to the Canadian and

United States governments, made on 19 March 1958, the commission recommended an apportionment of the waters which took into account the list of priorities in article VIII and therefore gave a higher priority to human needs than to the needs of ducks.[92] The commission also paid its respects to the order of precedence in article VIII when it made its 1952 order approving the hydroelectric power works associated with the building and operation of the St Lawrence River Seaway; it made its approval conditional upon these works being constructed and operated without injury to those uses accorded a higher priority by that article.[93]

On the whole then, the provisions in the Boundary Waters Treaty of 1909 establishing an order of precedence for the utilization of waters of drainage basins have not played any significant part in the solution of Canada-United States water problems. They may, of course, be of crucial importance in the future when the demand for water for multiple uses exceeds its supply; whether or not they will be beneficial is a matter of doubt. The fact that many other water treaties contain provisions on priorities[94] indicates that many states still believe that an order of priorities fixed by law is beneficial. As has been said, however, the principle of equitable utilization rejects any rule fixing the priority of uses of water.

Diversion

The diversion of the waters of international drainage basins, particulary those shared by Canada and the United States, has been covered to a considerable extent in the discussion above. That discussion has shown that, under the general principles of international law, these diversions are not *ipso facto* illegal, as some would have it, nor always legal, as others would have it; their legality or illegality is determined by the application of the principles of equitable utilization. It has also shown that the Canada-United States rule on the subject of water diversions, which is found in article II of the Boundary Waters Treaty of 1909, was largely influenced by the adversary situations in which the United Sates, as the upstream state, found itself at the turn of the century vis à vis Mexico and Canada. A fuller discussion of the present Canada-United States law is needed to complete the picture.

This law is found in the treaties between the two countries, particularly in the Boundary Waters Treaty of 1909. This treaty divides the waters of Canada-United States drainage basins into two classes: boundary waters and non-boundary waters (preliminary article). It prohibits diversions of boundary waters that will affect their natural level or flow, except with the approval of the International Joint Commission (article III). On the other hand, it allows diversions of non-boundary waters subject to two provisoes: first, that such a diversion must not cause material injury to the navigation rights of the other country; and, second, that a person who is injured in the other country by such a diversion shall have the same legal remedies as if his injury had taken place in the country where the diversion occurs (article II). It is thus seen that the basic rule is that, apart from prior rights of navigation, non-boundary waters may be diverted at will; the only area of uncertainty is the extent of the liability for injuries to private persons injured by a diversion, a matter that was keenly debated during the controversy about Columbia River development.[95]

These prescriptions of the 1909 treaty have been amended slightly by subsequent treaties dealing with particular bodies of water. In the Lake of the Woods Convention, diversion of any water from that basin was prohibited except with the approval of the International Joint Commission;[96] thus, the non-boundary waters of this basin were placed on an equal footing with boundary waters. And, by the Columbia River Treaty of 1961, Canada's right of diversion under article II of the 1909 treaty or under customary international law has been restricted. In accord with the treaty, since Libby Dam is being built, there can be no diversion of the waters of the Kootenay River within twenty years from the ratification date of the treaty; thereafter an increasing amount of water may be diverted from the Kootenay to the Columbia River, so that after eighty years, if Canada wishes, not more than 1000 cubic feet per second may be left to flow across the boundary into the United States.[97]

These restrictions, however, do not apply to diversions for consumptive uses.[98] The diversions that are authorized by the Columbia River Treaty, not being subject to article II of the 1909 treaty, do not give rise to any liability to private persons in the United States who may be injured by it.[99] It may be argued, however, that article II of the 1909 treaty automatically revives on the termination of the 1961 treaty by virtue of its article XVII and will then apply to these diversions.[100] The success of such an argument is doubtful.

These treaty provisions deal only with diversions of waters *out* of international drainage basins. Is there any law governing diversion of waters from elsewhere *into* these basins? A diversion of this sort has been undertaken by Canada. By an agreement with the United States in 1940, some 5000 cubic feet per second of the waters of the Albany River, which flows into Hudson Bay, are transferred by means of the Long Lac-Ogoki works into Lake Superior.[101] This practice of transferring water from one drainage basin to another increases as governments take a more comprehensive and rational view of the development of the water resources under their jurisdiction; it is the inevitable result of technological competence and planning on a larger scale. It is not surprising today to hear proposals for taking vast quantities of water from the northern regions of the North American continent to places as far south as Mexico.[102]

The legal problems involved in adding to rather than subtracting from the waters of an international drainage basin have hardly been touched. In most cases the addition would have the consent of co-basin states, as the Canadian addition to the Great Lakes by the Long Lac-Ogoki works has done. If the transaction is in essence a sale of water by one state to another, the agreement of sale will determine the rights and obligations of the parties. In the absence of an agreement, however, legal solutions will have to be found in the general principles of international law.

The first relevant principle is that a state will be liable for damage caused by its flooding the territory of a neighbouring state. This is explicitly stated in article IV of the Boundary Waters Treaty of 1909 which prohibits one party from unilaterally flooding the lands of the other by backing up water across the boundary; article III also prohibits raising the level of boundary waters unilaterally. This principle is firmly established in Canada-United States international water law. It led to Canada's having to pay compensation to United States citizens whose properties on the American shores of Lake Ontario were injured by the increased level of the waters of the lake caused by Gut Dam, a Canadian-built obstruction in the St Lawrence River downstream.[103] Even Attorney General Harmon admitted in his famous opinion of 1895 that flooding the land of a neighbouring state was illegal,[104] a proposition that is universally recognized as sound doctrine.

A second relevant principle is that waters introduced artificially into an international drainage basin belong to the state introducing them. These waters are analogous to timber that is severed from land situated in a state and placed into an international river for transportation to another place in that state. Co-basin states can no more appropriate or claim rights in waters added to the basin than they can do so in this timber.

The application of these two principles leads to the conclusion that a state is entitled to add waters to an international drainage basin to transfer it to another part of its territory or elsewhere, perhaps to use it there for power production, for irrigation, or for some other purpose, provided that its doing so does not injure co-basin states. As a corollary of this, co-basin states are not entitled to take any of this additional water for their own use. They might, of course, be the passive beneficiaries of the increased flow of water; the question would then arise whether they would be liable to pay for these 'downstream benefits,' a subject to be examined below.[105]

These conclusions are supported by the practice of states as seen in their international agreements. They are in accord with the 1940 Canada-United States agreement concerning the Long Lac-Ogoki diversion works referred to above and with the Niagara River Water Diversion Treaty of 1950,[106] article III of which provided that the waters added to the Great Lakes by the Long Lac-Ogoki works were not to be included in the water to be allocated. In other words, the added waters were treated not as part of the waters of the drainage basin to be shared by Canada and the United States, but as exclusively Canadian waters. Furthermore, article VIII (b) of the 1941 agreement relating to the Great Lakes-St Lawrence waterway project, which was not ratified by the United States and lapsed when other arrangements were made in the 1950s for the building of the St Lawrence Seaway, provided that

> (b) in the event of diversions being made into the Great Lakes System from other watersheds lying wholly within the borders of either country, the exclusive rights to the use of waters which are determined by the Governments to be equivalent in quantity to any waters so diverted shall ... be vested in the country diverting such waters, and the quantity of water so diverted shall be at all times available to that country for use for power below the point of entry, so long as it constitutes a part of boundary waters.[107]

A similar provision is found in article 9 (h) of the 1944 United States-Mexico Treaty, which provides that waters diverted into the Rio Grande River or its tributaries belong to the country making the diversion.[108]

To the extent that this Canada-United States treaty law makes diversion subject to the approval of the International Joint Commission, it is in accord with the best opinion of modern international law scholarship. It is otherwise, however, with its fundamental principle of the right of unilateral diversion of non-boundary waters embodied in article II of the Boundary Waters Treaty of 1909.

Pollution

The pollution of the waters of international drainage basins is governed by the law applicable to utilizations in general.[109] Modern problems of pollution are so numerous and pose such hazards to the health and well being of man and his environment, however, that the vague principles of equitable utilization need to be elaborated quickly and bolstered by effective machinery of enforcement. This is evident in the growing number of treaties dealing with the subject.[110]

Canada and the United States may be said to have tackled the problem head-on in the Boundary Waters Treaty of 1909, for they provided in article IV that 'the waters herein defined as boundary waters and waters flowing across the boundary shall not be polluted on either side to the injury of health or property on the other.' As a statement of intention, this was admirable; as a legal proposition, however, it was totally ineffective. Pollution is far too complex to be dealt with by the simple edict, 'thou shall not pollute.'

There was concern about the quality of some of the waters of the Great Lakes at the time of the 1909 treaty, but it was not a prime concern of those who negotiated this treaty. The prohibition against pollution in article IV seems to have been an afterthought; it was inserted at the end of article IV which deals with a matter entirely unrelated to pollution, namely the raising of the level of waters across the boundary by dams or obstructions. Pollution was not referred to elsewhere in the treaty and the International Joint Commission was given no jurisdiction over it.

Although the subject was dealt with so casually in the treaty, the two governments have, by means of references under article IX, involved the commission since its earliest days in questions of pollution. On 2 August 1912, seven months after the commission started its work, they asked it to investigate and report on the extent, causes, and locality of pollution of boundary waters between Canada and the United States that creates injury to public health, and to recommend ways and means of remedying or preventing this pollution. Since then, they have given the commission an increasing responsibility for this subject which now seems destined to become even more important.

The commission issued its final report on this first reference in 1918.[111] It was followed by other references on the same subject. On 1 April 1946 the commission was asked to study and report on pollution of the boundary waters connecting Lakes Huron and Erie; this reference was extended on 2 October to the St Mary's River between Lakes Superior and Huron and again on 2 April 1948 to the Niagara River between Lakes Erie and Ontario.[112] The commission's report on this reference was submitted to the governments on 11 October 1950.[113]

Pollution of the St Croix River was referred to the commission on 10 June 1955, of Rainy River and Lake of the Woods on 30 May 1959,[114] and of the Red River on 1 October 1964. The commission submitted reports on these three references on 7 October 1959, 24 February 1965,[115] and 11 April 1968, respectively. The most recent reference was made on 7 October 1964, concerning pollution of Lake Erie, Lake Ontario, and the international section of the St Lawrence River. The commission, having already produced three interim reports under this reference, submitted a final comprehensive report at the end of 1970.[116]

The question of air pollution has also been referred to the commission under article IX of the Boundary Waters Treaty. The first reference concerned a particular case: the fumes from the Trail smelter in British Columbia. The commission was asked on 7 August 1928 to examine and report on, *inter alia*, the extent to which property in the United States was damaged by the fumes from the smelter and the amount of compensation that should be paid for past damage. The commission reported on 28 February 1931, recommending the payment of $350,000 for damages suffered up to the end of 1931.[117] A reference made on 12 January 1949, concerning air in the vicinity of the cities of Windsor, Ontario, and Detroit, Michigan, referred especially to smoke from vessels using the Detroit River;[118] the commission reported with recommendations on 31 May 1960. A more comprehensive reference concerning air in the vicinity of Port Huron-Sarnia and Detroit-Windsor was made on 23 September 1966. At the same time the commission was requested to take note of air pollution problems in other boundary areas that may come to its attention from any source and, if considered appropriate, draw such problems to the attention of the governments.

Initially, this work of the commission had little success. After the Canadian and United States governments had received the commission's report on the first reference in 1918, they requested it to draft either reciprocal legislation to be enacted by the appropriate legislatures of each country or a treaty to implement its recommendations for remedying and preventing the pollution in question. A draft treaty was prepared and submitted to the two governments, but it was never implemented by them.

The subsequent references on water pollution, however, ended more happily. In its 1950 report, the commission recommended for the connecting channels of the Great Lakes the adoption of certain 'Objectives for Boundary Waters Quality Control,' setting forth the criteria to be met in order to maintain these boundary waters in satisfactory condition, as contemplated in article IV of the Boundary Waters Treaty, and requested that it be authorized to establish and maintain continuing supervision over boundary waters pollution through boards of control appointed by it.[119] These recommendations were accepted and the commission now supervizes the implementation of the water quality control objectives through an International Board of Control.[120]

Later, in its 1965 report, the commission recommended adoption of its suggested water quality control objectives for the Rainy River as the minimal criteria to be used by the enforcement agencies in both countries and that it be given the task of continuing supervision to ensure maximum practicable progress towards meeting these objectives.[121] These recommendations have also been accepted and acted on by the two governments. The 1959 and 1968 reports similarly resulted in the adoption of water quality objectives for the St Croix River and the Red River at the boundary, with the commission specifically authorized to maintain continuing supervision over pollution of these waters to ensure progress towards accomplishment of the objectives. And in its 1970 report the commission recommended the adoption of water quality control objectives for Lake Erie, Lake Ontario, and the international section of the St Lawrence River and the connecting channels of the Great Lakes, the commission to be made responsible and given the means for co-ordination, surveillance, monitoring, implementation, reporting, and making recommendations to government.[122] On the whole, then, this record of the commission's accomplishments on the control of pollution, always a most difficult matter, is praiseworthy.

The commission's success, however, must not be exaggerated. In spite of its achievements, the level of pollution of some of the boundary waters between Canada and the United States is still intolerably high. Neither international law nor the work of the commission, the best of its kind anywhere, has been able to stem the increasing deterioration of the quality of these waters. It is therefore evident that the two governments must now take drastic measures if further degradation of waters is to be stopped and their quality enhanced. The favourable reception they gave to the commission's 1970 report raises hope that its recommendations will be implemented. Indeed, negotiations between the two governments for this purpose were carried on during 1971. The commission's report therefore foreshadows an agreement between Canada and the United States giving the commission the powers it has indicated it should have and providing for the adoption of water quality objectives and of programs and other measures needed to achieve these objectives.

The scheme recommended by the commission and likely to be adopted by the two governments contemplates no international legislative or enforcement machinery. The commission's role would be one of study, surveillance, and making recommendations; water quality objectives would be reached by agreement of the parties; and the programs and other measures to achieve the objectives would remain the responsibility of each government. No new principle of international law on the liability of a state to co-basin states for injury caused by pollution of waters, then, is likely to be promulgated, and article IV of the 1909 treaty will remain the applicable rule.

Such a scheme, however, would not be without legal effect; it would breathe life into article IV. The weakness of that article has been that it simply prohibits pollution and says no more. But what is pollution in the eye of the law? The term must be defined with some precision before it can become a practical guide for a state's conduct. If the recommendations of the commission concerning defined water quality objectives were adopted, these objectives would be in themselves a definition of pollution and thus give meaning to that term in article IV. In a sense, therefore, although these objectives would not have international legislative effect by virtue of the agreement between Canada and the United States under which they would have been adopted, they would have some indirect legislative effect by virtue of article IV of the 1909 treaty. After their adoption, it would be easier for one of the parties to that treaty to invoke article IV successfully.

Some would question whether pollution of an international drainage basin can be dealt with effectively by parallel action by co-basin states. One author, for example, has argued that the best way of getting abatement and control of water pollution within the United States is by federal river basin authorities that would fix standards and own and operate treatment plants and so on, to be financed by charges for services.[123] Another has suggested that the International Joint Commission be given that sort of power.[124] This solution to the problem at the international level is not likely to find favour with states. The money needed to clean up a body of water as large as the Great Lakes runs to billions of dollars; furthermore, measures of pollution control have enormous implications for the economy of states. It is difficult to imagine states being willing to surrender the necessary taxing power and power of economic regulation to an international agency like the International Joint Commission. Under the circumstances, therefore, the commission's modest recommendations are more realistic and, if faithfully carried out, seem to have a good chance of success.

Downstream benefits

Perhaps the greatest contribution that Canada and the United States have made to doctrine in the field of international water resources law is the principle of downstream benefits.[125] The essence of this principle is that, when a basin state does or refrains from doing an act and thus confers a benefit on a co-basin state, the latter state is obliged to share this benefit with the former.

In tracing the evolution of the principle in Canada-United States water law, one should start with article VIII of the Boundary Waters Treaty of 1909. This article provides that, when one country raises the level of waters in the other by dams or other works, the International Joint Commission 'shall require, as a condition of its approval thereof, that suitable and adequate provision, approved by it, be made for the protection and indemnity of all interests on the other side of the line which may be injured thereby.' This provision in substance requires the state benefitting from storage provided by the other state to compensate that state for any injury or inconvenience caused by the elevation of the water. Article VIII, then, may be said to be an expression of the principle of downstream benefits; but it is so only in a limited way, for it is linked with the notion of compensation for injury suffered, whereas the principle embraces the wider notion of a state's right to a reasonable and equitable share of the beneficial uses of the water of a drainage basin whether or not it has suffered an injury.

The link between article VIII and the evolution of the principle of downstream benefits is clear; the substance of the principle was first argued before the International Joint Commission when it was considering the indemnity that it should require under article VIII. In 1925 the New Brunswick Electric Power Commission applied to the International Joint Commission for approval, under article IV of the 1909 treaty, for a power development at Grand Falls on the Saint John River which would back up the waters of the river and raise its level at and along the international boundary. At the hearings, counsel for the United States, Mr Hackworth, claimed that the United States was entitled to a certain percenage of the power generated at Grand Falls. In substance, the claim was to all of the power whose generation was made possible by the storage of water on American soil, which he called 'an encroachment on sovereignty.' As it was a boundary water, the United States was entitled to only half of the waters and, therefore, only claimed half of the power made possible by backing up the waters of the river. Canada and New Brunswick argued against the claim. The commission, however, did not have to decide the issue because the applicant entered into an agreement with American interests to make certain power available for use in Maine; and the order of the commission merely noted this agreement.[126] Although there was no decision on this question in the Grand Falls Power Dam application, it is an instance of acquiescence in a claim for compensation for downstream benefits and of compensation being made in the form of power rather than cash.

While it was the United States that first made the argument claiming downstream benefits, it was Canada that put it forward strongly as a principle of law and popularized it. She relied heavily on the *Grand Falls Power Dam* case as a precedent supporting her claims to recompense for downstream benefits that would accrue to the United States from the development of the Columbia River in Canada. When she referred to it in argument in the Libby Dam application, the United States denied its applicability, contending that there is a distinction between the claims that may be made when waters are backed up into boundary waters and when they are backed up across the boundary. The basis of this argument is that article VIII of the 1909 treaty expressly provided that there must be 'an equal division' of boundary waters between the United States and Canada and that both have 'equal and similar rights in the use' of these waters; hence, power generated in boundary waters must be shared. But since the treaty did not provide for sharing the waters of transboundary rivers, power produced in one country does not have to be shared with the other country.[127]

This argument was correct as far as it went, but it did not go far enough to dispose of Canada's claim to share downstream benefits. The United States is undoubtedly entitled to all of the hydroelectric power that can be generated in the United States without assistance from Canada and with the water that she is legally entitled to. But if the United States seeks to generate power beyond the amount that can be thus generated, either by invoking Canada's aid in regulating the flow of a river by the storage of water in Canada (for example, behind Libby Dam or Mica Creek Dam), or by seeking to use waters that Canada is exclusively entitled to and wishes to use (for example, by diversion from the Columbia River to the Fraser River), should she not expect to pay a price for it? There is no warrant in the treaty or elsewhere for saying that the United States is entitled to that aid or those Canadian waters; or that she is under no obligation to give something in return for the benefits that she would derive from such aid or such waters. It must be remembered that article II tolerates unilateral diversions of transboundary rivers and so it is not inappropriate to speak of Canadian waters. Was there, then, any real difference between the argument of the United States in the Grand Falls Power Dam application and that of Canada in the Libby Dam application and in other discussions about developments on the Canadian portion of the Columbia River? In both instances, the governments were claiming the right to a share of the hydroelectric power made possible by the use of their resources.

As time passed the United States softened its position and eventually accepted the idea that simple equity required some compensation to be paid for the benefits received from upstream developments; after all, within the United States itself, upstream states had been successfully claiming a share of benefits conferred on downstream states by works in the upstream states. The issue became not the right to compensation but the amount and method of compensation. So it happened that in 1959 the two governments asked the International Joint Commission to recommend the principles to be applied in determining the benefits that would result from the co-operative use of storage of waters and electrical interconnection with the Columbia River system, and the apportionment between the two countries of such benefits.[128] Later that year the commission submitted its report setting forth a number of principles that should be followed. In doing so, it said, it was guided 'by the basic concept that the principles recommended herein should result in an equitable sharing of the benefits attributable to their co-operative undertakings.'[129]

With these principles to guide them the two governments were soon able to reach agreement and entered into the Columbia River Treaty in 1961.[130] By this treaty, Canada was declared to be entitled to one-half of the downstream power benefits and to a sum of about $64 million for flood control benefits accruing to the United States from the construction and operation of dams on the Columbia River in Canada (articles v and vi). By a further agreement in 1964, Canada sold its power benefits under this treaty to the United States for $254 million.[131]

The Columbia River Treaty marks the acceptance of the principle of downstream benefits by Canada and the United States. If one may judge from the many treaties by which states have agreed to share the benefits of a project utilizing the waters of an international drainage basin,[132] the basic idea underlying the principle finds favour with the international community of basin states. The wide acceptance of the 1966 Helsinki Rules also indicates this, for these rules are founded on the principle that the beneficial uses of the waters of a drainage basin must be shared reasonably and equitably by co-basin states.

As for the actual division of downstream benefits, it is impossible to prescribe a formula of general application. As we have seen, the International Joint Commission suggested some guidelines to deal with power and flood control benefits, but they are imprecise. The fact is that an equitable sharing of benefits can only be determined in the light of all the relevant facts of a particular case. It is a question of what is reasonable in the circumstances. In practice, it will usually be a matter decided by negotiation between interested co-basin states. The only rule that comes close to having the status of a legal formula is the one adopted in the Columbia River Treaty for power and flood control benefits; namely, that they should be shared equally.

In this discussion, it is of course assumed that there are 'downstream benefits' to be shared. It should not be overlooked that determining the amount of these benefits is a difficult and complicated matter on which experts often disagree. Arguments still persist on whether or not Canada made a good or bad bargain concerning Columbia River development; they arise from a difference of opinion about the actual value of the benefits conferred on the United States by the development of the Columbia River basin in Canada.[133]

As for the form the benefits should take, practice reveals no clear pattern. Again, then, the rule of reason is all that one can appeal to. There is perhaps a trend in support of Canada's view that, in the case of power benefits, they should be paid for by a share of the power rather than by cash.[134] In the Columbia River Treaty negotiations, Canada carried the point, but in 1964, on the insistence of British Columbia, she sold her share of the power for cash.

One aspect of the principle of downstream benefits needs further consideration. The principle clearly applies when the act or abstention from action is done at the request of a co-basin state. A benefit is thus gained by the requesting state and it is reasonable that it should pay a fair price for it. The same is true when the act or abstention from action is part of a co-operative scheme of development, as in the case of the Columbia River. Does the principle apply, however, when a state on its own initiative acts and incidentally makes it possible for a co-basin state to derive a benefit? Suppose, for example, that Canada had decided to meet its power needs by building dams and hydroelectric works on the Columbia River without any request or encouragement from the United States to do so. The resulting power benefits to United States interests would have been substantial, as they are from the development of that river under the 1961 treaty. Would Canada in these circumstances have been entitled to a share of the downstream benefits? There is no authority on this question. The most one can say is that in some circumstances Canada ought to be so entitled, for example, when waters are added to a basin and the United States takes advantage of the increased volume and flow.[135] The extent to which this rule would apply is uncertain.

Joint planning, administration, and adjudication

As we have seen, Canada and the United States chose the path of co-operation in dealing with problems relating to their common water resources. This became manifest at the end of the last century when they created the International Waterways Commission in 1905 and its successor, the International Joint Commission, seven years later. To the first of these bodies they gave only the power to make investigations and to report its conclusions and recommendations to them. To the second they gave not only investigative powers but also some judicial and administrative powers.

Under articles III, IV, and VIII of the Boundary Waters Treaty of 1909, the International Joint Commission exercises a judicial function in relation to diversions from boundary waters and to obstructions and new uses affecting the level or flow of boundary waters or of waters flowing across the boundary. Its jurisdiction over these matters is compulsory. In addition, under article X, it may adjudicate any matter voluntarily referred to it by agreement of the two governments, a role that it has never been called on to play.

The investigative role of the commission springs from article IX. Under this article, any question or matter of difference between the parties involving their rights, obligations, or interests along their common frontier 'shall be referred ... to the ... Commission for examination and report, whenever either ... Government shall request that ... [it] be so referred.' In practice, this provision is interpreted as requiring the consent of both governments to a reference; it would seem, however, that it would be a violation of an obligation under the article if one government were to refuse the request of the other to refer a matter to the commission.[136]

Canada and the United States have referred many of their international water problems to the commission under article IX and are doing so more frequently as the years pass. Of the fifty cases dealt with by the commission before 1944, only eleven were references; of the thirty-two cases dealt with between 1944 and 1946, twenty were references. This increasing use of the reference procedure is commendable; it allows the commission to perform the functions for which a joint commission of its kind is best suited; namely, that of fact-finder and conciliator.[137] A commission contributes immensely to the satisfactory solution of water problems by bringing its expertise and experience in these problems to bear on the particular problem submitted to it, by studying it and furnishing the parties with facts and recommendations about it, and by providing a forum in which contentious issues can be debated and selfish interests subjected to the light of rational argument without directly involving those at the highest level of government.[138] This may be illustrated by the part played by the International Joint Commission in the ultimate settlement concerning the development of the Columbia River basin, and also by the impact its recent report on the pollution of the lower Great Lakes is having in shaping the policy of the two governments on this vexed question.

In addition to its judicial and investigative functions, the commission has administrative functions in relation to the St Mary and Milk rivers under article VI of the 1909 treaty. Under this article, the waters of the two rivers are to be 'apportioned equally between the two countries,' the measurement and apportionment to be made by the appropriate officials of the two countries 'under the direction of the International Joint Commission.' The commission began this task within a few months of its coming into existence in 1912 and, after careful investigation, consultation with appropriate officials, public hearings, and listening to arguments from both governments, it made its order for measurement and apportionment on 4 October 1921.[139] Since its duty under article VI is a continuing one, it provided that any future disagreement about the matter should be brought to its attention.

Under the provisions of the 1909 treaty and of some other treaties subsequently entered into by Canada and the United States, the commission supervises a number of continuing control boards.[140] This aspect of its work is becoming more important as the two governments attempt to abate and control pollution of water and air along their boundary, for, as the commission itself has said recently, 'continuous surveillance ... must be provided to detect any changes in quality, to assess the effectiveness of remedial measures undertaken and to determine the need for further control measures to attain the agreed objectives.'[141] At the commission's own request, it has been given the task of supervising, through an International Board of Control,[142] the implementation of the water quality objectives for the channels connecting the Great Lakes. Recently, it has requested that it be given a similar task concerning the lower Great Lakes.[143] If this recommendation is accepted, the scale of the commission's work and importance will be magnified.

In sum, the commission has had a remarkable record of success in discharging the responsibilities placed upon it by the two governments. In over eighty cases dealt with, it was divided on national lines or failed to reach agreement in only three. More importantly, the manner of its disposition of the questions submitted to it has earned it the confidence of the governments and citizens of both countries.

III

Canada and the United States have faced as many problems in the utilization of the waters of international drainage basins as have any other basin states. Although some of these problems have been of tremendous consequence to them, they have dealt with them successfully and without disturbing the good relations between the two countries. The story of their experience in this field has been told above. It only remains to sum up the lessons in it for those who seek the orderly development and management of international water resources.

It is apparent that legal doctrine has not been the dominant factor in the settlement of Canada-United States water problems. No doubt the importance of equity in the utilization of the waters of international drainage basins had a place in the minds of those who had the responsibility of disposing of these problems. In that sense, the principles of equitable utilization have been influential. And, of course, the law of the Boundary Waters Treaty of 1909 has guided the parties and the International Joint Commission. The crucial factor, however, has been the willingness of the two countries to establish a joint commission, to use it fully, and to heed most of its recommendations. The wisdom of the decision to do this is borne out by the results.

Canada and the United States thus have demonstrated that co-operation among co-basin states makes for the harmonious and satisfactory utilization of the waters of an international drainage basin, and that co-operation can be achieved best by a joint institution having, at the least, ample powers of investigation and, preferably, some judicial and administrative power too. Fortunately, the significance of this demonstration has not escaped notice. Many states have already seen fit to follow the example set by Canada and the United States; they have established no less than eighty-nine joint agencies concerned with non-navigational uses.[144] The mere existence of an institution, of course, does not guarantee its success; that depends in the last analysis upon the spirit of those who use it. Nonetheless, their existence is a good sign. It gives hope that the immense problems relating to water utilization in an age of rapid population growth and industrialization will be overcome.

NOTES

1 For sources of information about the fixing of the boundary between Canada and the United States, see 3 Whiteman, *Digest of International Law* (1964) 722–7. Of the 5525 miles of boundary, about 3986 are between the Atlantic and the Pacific and about 1539 between the Pacific and the Arctic. These distances given here were obtained from the office of the Canadian Section of the International Joint Commission.

2 The meaning of 'boundary waters' in Canada-United States water law is now found in the Treaty relating to boundary waters and questions arising along the boundary between the United States and Canada, 11 January 1909, Preliminary Article. 36 Stat. 2448; T.S. no 548; III Redmond 2607; *Treaties and Agreements Affecting Canada In Force between His Majesty and the United States of America, 1814–1925* (1927), at 312 (hereinafter cited as *Treaties and Agreements*). This article provides as follows:

> For the purposes of this treaty boundary waters are defined as the waters from main shore to main shore of the lakes and rivers and connecting waterways, or the portions thereof, along which the international boundary between the United States and the Dominion of Canada passes, including all bays, arms, and inlets thereof, but not including tributary waters which in their natural channels would flow into such lakes, rivers, and waterways, or waters flowing from such lakes, rivers, and waterways, or the waters of rivers flowing across the boundary.

For a comment on the meaning of this article, see Bloomfield and FitzGerald, *Boundary Waters Problems of Canada and the United States* (1958) 22–3.

3 1 Malloy, *Treaties, Conventions, International Acts, Protocols and Agreements between the United States of America and Other Powers* (1910) 586, 589 (hereinafter cited as Malloy).

4 Malloy 592.

5 See the Boundary Waters Treaty of 1909, article I, *supra* note 2.

6 For these arguments see (1831–2), 19 *Brit. and For. State Papers* 1067–75. See also *American State Papers, 1789–1859, Foreign Relations*, vol 1, at 253–4, 439, and vol 6, at 757. For a brief account of the St Lawrence navigation controversy, see I Moore, *International Law Digest* (1906) 631–5.

7 See (1831–2), 19 *Brit. and For. State Papers* 1075–88.

8 Reciprocity Treaty as to Fisheries, Duties and Navigation British North America, concluded 5 June 1854, article IV, Malloy 668, 671.

9 *Treaties and Agreements* 37, 45; Malloy 700, 711; (1870–1), 61 *Brit. and For. State Papers* 40.

10 *Supra* note 2.

11 For a discussion of the right of American ships to use the St Lawrence today, see H.J. Lawford, 'Treaties and Rights of Transit on the St. Lawrence' (1961), 39 *Can. Bar Rev.* 577, 578–89; for a discussion of the right of other foreign ships to do so, see ibid, 589–602.

12 Bloomfield and FitzGerald, *supra* note 2, at 43.

13 For some account of this, see *Hearings of the International Joint Commission, St. Mary and Milk Rivers* (1915) 62–3. See also *Foreign Relations of the United States, 1929*, vol 2, at 97–111.

14 See I Moore, *supra* note 6, at 657–8.

15 For the early history of the Chicago diversions, see *Wisconsin v Illinois*, 278 U.S. 367 (1929). See also Paul L. Adams, 'Diversion of Lake Michigan Waters' (1959), 37 *U. Det. L.J.* 149.

16 See P.E. Corbett, *The Settlement of Canadian-American Disputes* (1937) 53–4.

17 See I Moore, *supra* note 6, at 658.

18 *Documents on Canadian External Relations*, vol 1, *1909–1918* (1963), at 363.

19 For an account of the creation of the Canada-United States International Waterways Commission, see Chacko, *The International Joint Commission between the United States of America and the Dominion of Canada* (1932) 71–7; Corbett, *supra* note 16, at 50–1; and Bloomfield and FitzGerald, *supra* note 2, at 8–10.

20 For a conspectus of the commission's work, see *Compiled Reports of the International Waterways Commission, 1905–1913*.

21 Ibid, for 1906, at 368.

22 For an account of the negotiations, see Bloomfield and FitzGerald, *supra* note 2, at 11–13.

23 *Supra* note 2.

24 For a discussion of the helpful part played by the commission in the settlement of the Columbia River dispute, see Bourne, 'Mediation, Conciliation and Adjudication in the Settlement of International Drainage Basin Disputes' (1971), 9 *Can. Y. B. Int'l L.* 119–22.

25 The International Joint Commission has not dealt only with water problems; it has had referred to it by the Canadian and American governments, pursuant to article IX of the Boundary Waters Treaty, a number of air pollution problems.

26 See F.J.E. Jordan, 'Canada-United States Boundary Relations' *infra* chapter 22; Bloomfield and FitzGerald, *supra* note 2; Chacko, *supra* note 19.

27 For some of these authors and their statements, see Berber, *Rivers in International Law* (1959) 19–40.

28 Ibid, at 14–19.

29 Letter from the Mexican Minister at Washington, Romero, to Richard Olney, secretary of state, 21 October 1895, S Doc no 154, 57 Cong., 2d Sess., XIII (4428), at 7, 8.

30 *Treaty of Guadalupe Hidalgo – International Law*, 21 Ops. Att'y Gen. 274, 282–3 (1895).

31 When Canada threatened to divert waters of the Milk River flowing from Canada into the United States, the United States protested, Secretary of State Hay writing that the waters of the river were already put 'to beneficial use by the inhabitants of the Milk River Valley long prior to any diversion of the river in Canada. Under the laws and customs which have grown up in the arid region and which are in force in Canada, priority of appropriation and use has been recognized.' See *Hearings of the International Joint Commission, St. Mary and Milk Rivers, supra* note 13. While thus denying Canada's right to divert the waters of the Milk River, the United States was asserting the right to divert the waters of the St Mary River to the Milk River in the United States, which would have interfered with prior users in Canada.

32 Ibid.

33 See *supra* note 20, at 354–68 (1906).

34 Chandler P. Anderson, Opinion dated September 1907: In the Matter of the Application of the Minnesota Canal and Power Co. (State Department File no 1718/27, National Archives). The sentences quoted may be found in Scott, '*Kansas* v. *Colorado* Revisited' (1958), 52 *Am. J. Int'l L.* 432.

35 *Supra* note 20, at 363–6 (1906).

36 See Chacko, *supra* note 19, at 76–7.

37 *Supra* note 18, at 368.

38 Ibid, 376 and 419. See also *Papers Relating to the Work of the International Joint Commission* (1929) 10.

39 *Supra* note 18, at 389–90, 393. See also his statements in debates in the House of Commons on the Boundary Waters Treaty: Can. H.C. *Debates* 1910–11, vol I, at 908–10.

40 Can. H.C. *Debates* 1910–11, vol I, at 870–3, 906–7.

41 *Supra* note 18, at 379.

42 See Can. H.C. *Debates* 1910–11, vol I, at 906–12.

43 See Griffin, *Legal Aspects of the Use of Systems of International Waters. Memorandum of the State Department*, S Doc no 118, 85th Cong., 2d Sess., 32, 42 (1958).

44 Can. H.C. *Debates* 1910–11, vol I, at 911–12.

45 Ibid, 895–6, 900.

46 Canada, *Sessional Papers* (1928) no 227, at 19 and 60. See also Simsarian, 'The Diversion of Waters Affecting The United States and Canada' (1938), 32 *Am. J. Int'l L.* 488, 508, and 511. A similar protest was made in 1927: see *Foreign Relations of the United States, 1927*, vol 6, at 484–7.

47 These were the words Professor H.A. Smith used to describe it. Smith, *The Economic Uses of International Rivers* (1931) 8, 145–7.

48 For a discussion of these two doctrines and their rejection, see Bourne, 'The Right to Utilize the Waters of International Rivers' (1965), 3 *Can. Y. B. Int'l L.* 187, 204–8, 222–7.

49 See Schindler, 'The Administration of Justice in the Swiss Federal Court in International Disputes' (1921), 15 *Am. J. Int'l L.* 149, 169–72.

50 206 U.S. 46 (1907).

51 259 U.S. 419 (1922).

52 325 U.S. 589 (1945).

53 Resolution on the Utilization of Non-maritime International Waters (except for Navigation), adopted by the Institute of International Law at its Session at Salzburg (4–13 September 1961)(1961), 49 *Annuaire de l'Institut de Droit International*, tome II, 381.

54 *Report of the Fifty-Second Conference of the International Law Association Held at Helsinki, August 14–20* (1967), at 484.

55 For a definition of equitable utilization, see Bourne, 'International Law and Pollution of International Rivers and Lakes' (1971), 6 *Univ. Brit. Col. L. Rev.* 115, 121–2. For a fuller discussion, see Bourne, *supra* note 48, esp. at 228–37, 245–64.

56 See *Hearings Before the Senate Committee on Foreign Relations on the Treaty with Mexico Relating to the Utilization of the Waters of Certain Rivers*, 79th Cong., 1st Sess., pt. 1, at 19–21, and 1738–82, esp. 1745, 1753, and 1761 (1945).

57 See Austin, 'Canada-United States Practice and Theory Respecting the International Law of International Rivers: A Study of the History and Influence of the Harmon Doctrine' (1959), 37 *Can. Bar Rev.* 393, 430–1, on this point, and ibid, 393–443 on the history of the Harmon doctrine generally.

58 See the Waterton-Belly Rivers Reference, Docket no 57 of the International Joint Commission (1948), and the Waneta Dam and Reservoir Application, Docket no 66 of the International Joint Commission (1951), in Bloomfield and FitzGerald, *supra* note 2, at 177 and 196 respectively.

59 See *supra* note 43, at 57–62, 63, 89–91.

60 See *supra* note 46.

61 See the 1959 Canadian notes protesting the Chicago diversion, (1959), 11 *External Affairs* 129–30, 324–26.

62 Docket no 41 of the International Joint Commission (1940), in Bloomfield and Fitz-Gerald, *supra* note 2, at 154–7.

63 See Bourne, 'The Columbia River Controversy' (1959), 37 *Can. Bar Rev.* 444, 449.

64 *The Columbia River Treaty, Protocol and Related Documents* 40 (issued by the Departments of External Affairs and Northern Affairs and National Resources, February 1964).

65 See Bourne, 'The Development of International Water Resources: The "Drainage Basin Approach" ' (1969), 47 *Can. Bar Rev.* 62, for a full discussion of this concept.

66 Ibid, esp. 83–7.

67 See the Preliminary Article of the treaty, *supra* note 2.

68 See Bloomfield and FitzGerald, *supra* note 2, at 22 and 85 n 1.

69 Ibid, 22–3.

70 *Supra* note 43, at 7–8 (emphasis added).

71 Ibid, 31 (emphasis added).

72 *Supra* note 44.

73 See Order in Council, P.C. 648, dated 13 April 1923, *supra* note 18, vol 3, *1919–1925*, at 889, 891, and the Convention between Canada and the United States of America to regulate the level of the Lake of the Woods, 24 February 1925. 44 Stat. 2108; T.S. no 721, 43 L.N.T.S. 251.

74 For the reference, see *supra* note 64, at 17. The controversy about the matter in the

1950s resulted from Canada's insistence that not only the injury downstream caused by upstream works but their benefits had to be taken into account. In essence, this viewpoint took the concept of the unity of a drainage basin to its logical conclusion.

75 See recommendations 20 to 22 of the commission's report in *International Joint Commission: Canada and the United States. Pollution of Lake Erie, Lake Ontario and the International Section of the St. Lawrence River, 1970*, (1971), at 92.

76 For an indication of the Canadian government's acceptance of the 'drainage basin approach' to the development of water resources, see the Canada Water Act, R.S.C. c 5 (1st Supp.) (1970).

77 *Supra* note 18, vol 3, *1919–1925*, at 851, 852.

78 For a discussion of this Canadian proposal, see *supra* note 63, at 448–50, and 457–61. See also *supra* note 65, at 74–5, and 3 Whiteman, *Digest of International Law* (1964) 981–84.

79 *Supra* note 65, at 72–8.

80 24 I.L.R. 101, 124–5 (1957).

81 See *supra* note 48, at 196–8, and *supra* note 65, at 83–5. See also Teclaff, *The River Basin in History and Law* (1967) 184–92.

82 See *supra* note 65, at 73 n 38, and 3 Whiteman, *Digest of International Law* (1964) 809–12.

83 Ibid. See also Bourne, 'Energy and a Continental Concept' (1965), 8 *Can. Bar J*. 158, 159–60.

84 This scheme, known as NAWAPA, has been spoken of favourably by some in the United States, but it has aroused little enthusiasm and considerable hostility in Canada. See *supra* note 65, at 73 n 37, and 83–4, esp. n 74.

85 For a discussion of this, see Smith, *supra* note 47, at 136–43. The Institute of International Law took the same view in article II, paragraph 4, of its 1911 Madrid Declaration. See International Regulations regarding the Use of International Watercourses for purposes other than Navigation, adopted by the Institute of International Law at Madrid, 20 April 1911 (1911), 24 *Annuaire de l'Institut de Droit International* 365–7.

86 Ibid. See also Sevette, *Legal Aspects of Hydro-Electric Development of Rivers and Lakes of Common Interest,* U.N. Doc no E/ECE/136, at 26–37 (1952); Sauser-Hall, 'L'utilisation industrielle des fleuves internationaux' (1953 II), 83 *Recueil des Cours* 471, 527. The Convention and Statute on the Regime of Navigable Waterways of International Concern, Barcelona, 20 April 1921,

article 10(6) of the statute, 7 L.N.T.S. 36, 57–9, also recognized that the right of navigation was not absolute.

87 For example, see Smith, *supra* note 47, at 143, and Sevette, *supra* note 86, at 30.

88 For that of the International Law Association, see article VI of the Helsinki Rules of 1966, *supra* note 54. For that of the Institute of International Law, see (1959), 48 *Annuaire de l'Institut de Droit International*, tome I, 186 and 194–5.

89 H.R. Doc no 475, 78th Cong., 2d Sess., 7. The bureau went on to say in this statement that, in its opinion, the waters of the Upper Missouri Basin were 'more useful to more people if utilized for domestic, agricultural, and industrial purposes than for navigation-improvement purposes. To the extent that these uses are competitive, domestic, agricultural and industrial uses should have preference.' This was a value judgment appropriate to the particular circumstances of the period in which it was made; it may not be appropriate in the changed circumstances of the future. This view of the bureau has been adopted in several acts of Congress, such as the Flood Control Act, 58 Stat. 887 (1944).

90 *Supra* note 43, at 8.

91 Bloomfield and FitzGerald, *supra* note 2, at 154–7.

92 See *Report of the International Joint Commission on the Souris River, March 19, 1958*, at 7, 10.

93 See (1952), 27 *Dept. State Bull*. 1019–22.

94 See, for example, Treaty between the United States of America and Mexico relating to the utilization of the waters of the Colorado and Tijuana rivers, and of the Rio Grande, 14 November 1944, 59 Stat. 1219; T.S. no 994; 3 U.N.T.S. 313.

95 See *supra* note 63, at 450–7. Cf Griffin, *supra* note 43, at 59–62.

96 Article XI of the convention, *supra* note 73.

97 Treaty relating to co-operative development of the water resources of the Columbia River Basin, 17 January 1961, with related agreements effected by exchange of notes at Washington 22 January 1964, and at Ottawa 16 September 1964, article XIII, [1964] CAN. T.S. no 2; 542 U.N.T.S. 244; 15 U.S.T. 1555.

98 Ibid, article XIII (1) and Protocol, article 6(1). According to article I, a consumptive use means 'use of water for domestic, municipal, stock-water, irrigation, mining or industrial purposes but does not include use for the generation of hydroelectric power.'

99 See the statement of Mr Fulton, who was minister of justice and chairman of the Canadian delegation that negotiated the treaty, on this point: *Minutes and Proceedings of the Standing Committee on External Affairs, House of Commons, May 11 and 12, 1964*, 2nd Sess., 26th Parl., 1155–6.

100 See *supra* note 97, article XVII, which is as follows:

(1) Nothing in this Treaty and no action taken or foregone pursuant to its provisions shall be deemed, after its termination or expiration, to have abrogated or modified any of the rights or obligations of Canada or the United States of America under then existing international law, with respect to the uses of the water resources of the Columbia River basin.

(2) Upon termination of this Treaty, the Boundary Waters Treaty, 1909, shall, if it has not been terminated, apply to the Columbia River basin, except insofar as the provisions of that Treaty may be inconsistent with any provision of this Treaty which continues in effect.

(3) Upon termination of this Treaty, if the Boundary Waters Treaty, 1909, has been terminated in accordance with Article XIV of that Treaty, the provisions of Article II of that Treaty shall continue to apply to the waters of the Columbia River basin.

101 See *supra* note 82.

102 See *supra* notes 83 and 84.

103 For a discussion of this, see 3 Whiteman, (1964), *Digest of International Law* 768–71, 862; and 'Report of the Agent of the United States before the Lake Ontario Claims Tribunal' (1969), 8 *Int'l Leg. Mat.* 118–43.

104 See *supra* note 30.

105 For a discussion of these problems, see Bourne, *supra* note 83, at 166–8. See also Piper, *The International Law of the Great Lakes* (1967) 103.

106 [1950] CAN. T.S. no 3; 132 U.N.T.S. 223; 1 U.S.T. 694.

107 3 Whiteman, (1964), *Digest of International Law* 809.

108 *Supra* note 94.

109 See Bourne, 'International Law and Pollution of International Rivers and Lakes' (1971), 6 *Univ. Brit. Col. L. Rev.* 115; 3 Whiteman, (1964), *Digest of International Law* 1040–50.

110 See Bourne, *supra* note 109, at 131–2.

111 For a synopsis of this reference, see Bloomfield and FitzGerald, *supra* note 2, at 76–9.

112 Ibid, 172–3.

113 *Report of the International Joint Commission on the Pollution of Boundary Waters* (1951).

114 See *Report of the International Joint Commission on the Pollution of Rainy River and Lake of the Woods* (1965) 7.

115 For this report, see ibid.

116 *Supra* note 75.

117 Bloomfield and FitzGerald, *supra* note 2, at 137–8.

118 Ibid, 183–5.

119 *Supra* note 113, at 18–19, 21–2.

120 For an indication of the extent to which the water quality control objectives are being met, see *supra* note 116, at 4.

121 *Supra* note 114, at 16.

122 *Supra* note 116, at 149, 156.

123 M.J. Roberts, 'River Basin Authorities: A National Solution to Water Pollution' (1970), 83 *Harv. L. Rev.* 1527.

124 *Montreal Star*, 10 April 1971, Letter to the Editor from Gerald F. FitzGerald.

125 Much of the material to be used here is taken from my article, *supra* note 63, at 462–5.

126 See Bloomfield and FitzGerald, *supra* note 2, at 113–15.

127 Ibid, 190–5.

128 *Supra* note 64, at 39.

129 Ibid, 40.

130 *Supra* note 97.

131 Ibid.

132 These treaties are too numerous to catalogue here. Two may be mentioned as examples. Article 358 of the Treaty of Versailles, 1919, gave France the exclusive right to use the waters of the Rhine for power production, subject to paying Germany one-half the value of the energy produced: 11 Martens, *N.R.G.*, 3rd Ser., 323. The Barcelona Convention, 1921, article X, also contains the idea of sharing downstream benefits; it provides that where a state is obliged under the convention to take steps to improve the river or is put to expense to maintain it for navigation, it is entitled to demand a reasonable contribution to the costs involved.

133 For the view that the Columbia River Treaty was a bad bargain for the United States, since it could have achieved the same results more cheaply by other means, see Krutilla, 'The International Columbia

River Treaty: An Economic Evaluation' in
A.V. Kneese and S.C. Smith, eds, *Water
Research* (1969) 69, at 95–6. For a strongly
held opinion that Canada made a very bad
bargain, see Donald Waterfield, *Continental Waterboy: The Columbia River Controversy* (1970). There was a difference of
opinion among Canadian officials about the
percentage of downstream benefits which
Canada derived under the treaty. General
McNaughton stated various figures: 40 per
cent, only two-fifths, and finally 32 per cent
of the total benefit. See *supra* note 99, at 92,
1323, 1397, 1437–8. Cf ibid, 1360–2, 1365,
1368–72.

134 See Sevette, *supra* note 86, at 179.
135 Piper, *supra* note 105, at 103.
136 See Chacko, *supra* note 19, at 241–5.
137 For a discussion of the commission as conciliator, see *supra* note 24, at 119–22.
138 Ibid, 122.
139 Bloomfield and FitzGerald, *supra* note 2, at
87–93.
140 Ibid, 40–2, 51–2.
141 *Supra* note 75, at 77.
142 *Report of the International Joint Commission on the Pollution of Boundary Waters*
(1951) 18–19, 21–2.
143 *Supra* note 75, at 78–9, 92.
144 See *supra* note 24, at 118–19.

CHARLES BÉDARD

21/Le Régime juridique des Grands Lacs

Etant donné, d'une part, leur situation particulière, enfermés qu'ils sont dans le territoire de deux états et reliés à la mer par un fleuve, en partie international, canalisé sur tout son parcours et, d'autre part, leurs dimensions considérables et leur immense potentiel industriel, les Grands Lacs et leur déversoir (le St-Laurent) offrent au juriste international un visage complexe, inusité, et plein d'intérêt.

A la question primordiale que soulève l'exercice de la souveraineté des états riverains sur cette immense nappe d'eau et son lit, se greffent tout naturellement celles de leur juridiction et de leur droit d'usage, ce dernier se dédoublant lui-même en droit de navigation et en droit d'exploitation et d'utilisation industrielle. Nous serons ainsi amenés à examiner successivement la question de la frontière et de la juridiction, celle de la navigation commerciale, et du sauvetage des épaves, de la marine de guerre, de la pêche, et enfin de l'utilisation des eaux et du lit.

La matière à examiner est aussi diverse qu'abondante. Elle comprend toute une série d'instruments bilatéraux: des traités, des conventions, des protocoles et échanges de notes entre la Grande Bretagne et les Etats-Unis, et, à une époque plus récente, entre le Canada souverain et les Etats-Unis. Là où l'instrument fait défaut, nous devrons, pour déterminer la règle de droit, faire appel aux mesures législatives réciproques édictées dans les deux pays ainsi qu'à la jurisprudence de leurs tribunaux. Tout ce matériau s'échelonne sur une longue période allant de 1783 – année de la signature du Traité de Paris dans lequel, pour la première fois, il est fait mention du statut des Grands Lacs et du Saint-Laurent – jusqu'à aujourd'hui.

FRONTIÈRE ET JURIDICTION

Frontière

La question du tracé de la frontière sur les Grands Lacs et la section internationale du St-Laurent s'est posée pour la première fois lors de la rédaction du Traité de Paris de 1783 qui mettait fin à la guerre de l'indépendance américaine. Cet instrument établissait dans la région des Grands Lacs (Lac Michigan exclus) et la section internationale du St-Laurent une frontière d'eau courante 'au milieu' du fleuve, des lacs, et des rivières qui les relient.

Cette délimitation assez sommaire de la frontière devait bientôt s'avérer insuffisante. On rapporte, en effet, que la Grande Bretagne continua jusqu'en 1796 à occuper tous ses postes sur les Grands Lacs et que les commerçants britanniques allèrent même jusqu'à proposer de repousser la frontière américaine jusqu'à la rive sud de ces Lacs. Les droits des Etats-Unis ne purent être complètement assurés que grâce à l'action conjuguée de la flotte et de la diplomatie américaine pendant la guerre de 1812.[1] Un nouveau traité, dit 'de paix et d'amitié' entre la Grande

Bretagne et les Etats-Unis, qui fut signé à Gand en 1814 et qui mettait fin à la deuxième guerre anglo-américaine, allait se charger de compléter et de préciser la définition de la frontière donnée par le traité précédent.

On formait à cette fin une commission de type paritaire à qui on confiait la charge de faire disparaître les doutes qui existaient des deux côtés quant à la détermination précise 'du milieu' des lacs, rivières, et voies d'eau. Cet organisme, dit 'Commission Mixte,' formé de deux représentants, dont l'un canadien et l'autre américain, devait fixer le tracé définitif de la frontière et déterminer, selon l'esprit du Traité de Paris de 1783, la possession de nombreuses îles que l'on se disputait le long de celle-ci.

Ses pouvoirs, voisins de ceux d''amiables compositeurs,' étaient très étendus et ses décisions, irrévocables, si adoptées à l'unanimité. Un excellent mécanisme subsidiaire d'arbitrage par un tiers était en outre prévu pour le cas où les commissaires ne parviendraient pas à s'entendre. Les deux riverains manifestaient ainsi de façon tangible leur volonté de régler définitivement le délicat problème de démarcation de la frontière sur les Grands Lacs.

La région à démarquer avait été divisée en deux tronçons. Le premier comprenait la section internationale du St-Laurent (ie, à partir du village de St Régis, situé à quelques milles de Prescott sur la rive opposée), jusqu'à la rivière Ste Marie et, plus précisément, jusqu'au Neebish Channel (dans la rivière Ste Marie). Le second couvrait le reste, soit la rivière Ste Marie, à partir du Neebish Channel et le lac Erié, la rivière Détroit, le lac et la rivière Ste Claire, le lac Huron, et une partie de la rivière Ste Marie. Mais que fallait-il entendre par l'expression 'milieu de la rivière?' Pour le commissaire britannique, c'était une ligne équidistante des deux rives; cependant que pour le commissaire américain, c'était le milieu du chenal, quelle qu'en fût la proximité de l'une des rives.[2]

L'échange de vues qui précéda le règlement définitif démontre qu'à défaut d'entente sur le principe, l'accord entre les deux commissaires se fit de façon empirique, sans autre règle que celle-ci, à savoir, que la frontière devait toujours être une frontière d'eau, sans jamais couper les îles. Et c'est ainsi que, les géomètres ayant déterminé la position respective des îles, du chenal, et de la ligne médiane, les commissaires démarquèrent à leur tour la frontière 'par le milieu,' sans toutefois entendre ces mots du Traité de Paris dans toute leur rigueur mathématique, mais uniquement en tâchant de répartir équitablement entre les deux riverains les îles en litige.

La première tâche ainsi terminée, les commissaires se réunirent de nouveau afin de poursuivre leurs travaux dans le second tronçon. Toutefois, incapables d'en arriver à un accord, ils se séparèrent en 1827. C'est ainsi que la question ne sera reprise et réglée définitivement que quinze années plus tard, lors de la signature par la Grande Bretagne et les Etats-Unis du traité ou convention dite 'Ashburton-Webster,' le 9 août 1842.

Le nouvel instrument adoptait cette fois comme principe de démarcation de la frontière, non plus celui du milieu de la rivière, comme pour le premier tronçon, mais plutôt celui du milieu du chenal, de manière à partager également la ligne de navigation entre les deux riverains. On note ici la succession de deux principes témoins de différentes époques. En effet, pour le premier tronçon de frontière soumis aux dispositions du Traité de Gand de 1814 et au sujet duquel les commissaires étaient parvenus à s'entendre, la nouvelle convention consacrait le critère du milieu de la rivière, tandis que pour le second, au sujet duquel il y avait eu disses-sion, elle apportait une solution différente, celle du milieu du chenal.

D'un point à l'autre, le principe variait: jusqu'au Neebish Channel en 1822, la démarcation s'était faite suivant le principe des vieux traités et des auteurs anciens (Grotius et Vattel), ie le milieu du fleuve, tandis qu'à partir de ce chenal, en 1842, le principe devenait celui des nouveaux traités (notamment celui de Lunéville en 1801, d'Arrau en 1808, et de San Stephano en 1878) et des auteurs plus récents, ie le milieu du chenal ou l'axe du thalweg.[3]

Nous verrons plus loin, en traitant de la navigation, que cette même convention de 1842 faisant perdre à l'ancien critère du milieu de la rivière la quasi totalité de sa portée pratique en établissant le principe de la liberté de navigation dans la sec-tion du St-Laurent et des Grands Lacs (premier tronçon) où le tracé de la frontière ne suivait pas le chenal.

La nécessité de stabiliser la frontière ainsi démarquée donna lieu par la suite à la signature d'un certain nombre d'accords entre la Grande Bretagne et les Etats-Unis. Une commission conjointe, dite 'internationale des voies navigables,' fut instituée en 1905. C'est à cet organisme que le traité de démarcation de la frontière internationale (article 4) signé à Washington en 1908 confiait la tâche de vérifier et rétablir le tracé de la frontière sur le St-Laurent et les Grands Lacs. Après avoir effectué diverses rectifications d'ordre secondaire et procédé à certaines démarca-tions requises, la commission soumit son rapport aux deux gouvernements, puis fut dissoute en 1915.

Toutefois, le traité de 1908 ne contenait pas de disposition concernant l'entretien de la ligne frontière, une fois terminés les relevés et les délimitations prévus. Or, pendant les années qui suivirent la cessation des fonctions de la commission, on constata le long de cette partie de la frontière qu'un grand nombre de bornes avaient besoin d'être déplacées ou réparées. De plus, on construisait sur les cours d'eau de jonction des ponts où rien n'indiquait la ligne frontière, cependant que la végéta-tion masquait déjà une grande partie du tracé.

La nécessité de garder à la frontière son caractère concret donna lieu, en février 1925, à Washington, à la signature d'un autre traité 'de démarcation de la frontière.' La tâche qui, aux termes mêmes du nouvel instrument, consistait à 'maintenir en tout temps et partout une ligne concrète entre les Etats-Unis et le Canada, et entre le Canada et l'Alaska,' fut cette fois confiée à la 'Commission de la frontière inter-nationale' qui déjà, depuis 1908, exerçait ses fonctions sur toute la longueur de la frontière canado-américaine, à l'exception bien sûr de la région des Grands Lacs et du St-Laurent, laquelle était désormais placée sous sa juridiction. Cet organisme est toujours en fonction aujourd'hui.

Juridiction

Comme conséquence des divers traités qui ont fixé la frontière internationale au milieu du St-Laurent, des Grands Lacs, et des cours d'eau de jonction, la Grande Bretagne (puisque le Canada n'existait pas encore à l'époque comme état souverain) et les Etats-Unis ont été amenés à considérer comme intégrée à leur ter-ritoire respectif la portion des eaux et du lit des Grands Lacs, sise de leur propre côté de la frontière[4] et à y exercer une juridiction territoriale aussi exclusive[5] que si cette surface d'eau était de la terre ferme. On est même aller jusqu'à utiliser pour qualifier les Grands Lacs, l'expression de 'propriété privée[6] des deux états riverains.

Toutefois, une ère nouvelle, en ce qui a trait à la question de la juridiction sur ces eaux (en particulier la juridiction criminelle), devait s'ouvrir avec la convention de 1842. On remarque, en effet, à partir de cette date, une préoccupation croissante chez les tribunaux des deux pays à se référer, sans doute par analogie, à la doctrine en droit public de la mer – et plus particulièrement à celle touchant le régime juridique de la mer territoriale – lorsqu'ils sont appelés à statuer sur leur compétence juridictionelle à propos d'offenses criminelles commises sur les Grands Lacs ou sur les cours d'eau de jonction. Certains cas typiques, comme *People* vs *Tylor* (1859)[7] et *U.S.* vs *Rodgers* (1893)[8] du côté des Etats-Unis, ainsi que *Rex* vs *The Ship North* (1905)[9] et *Rex* vs *Meikleham* (1905)[10] du côté canadien, illustrent fort bien cette tendance parfois assez confuse des tribunaux à transposer dans le domaine lacustre des concepts et théories propres au domaine maritime. Quoi qu'il en soit des principes et théories divergents mis en cause d'un côté et de l'autre de la frontière, il n'y eut jamais, comme conséquence de ces décisions – c'est du moins ce qui ressort d'une étude d'ensemble de la matière[11] – de conflits sérieux de juridiction entre les deux états riverains.

NAVIGATION COMMERCIALE ET SAUVETAGE DES EPAVES

Navigation

C'était très tôt dans l'histoire des relations amicales entre la Grande Bretagne et les Etats-Unis que fut reconnue la liberté pour les citoyens des deux pays riverains, de naviguer sur les Grands Lacs ainsi que sur les voies d'eau qui les relient. Une disposition précise du traité dit 'Jay' de novembre 1794 accordait, en termes très généraux, aux deux riverains un droit égal de navigation commerciale sur toute l'étendue des eaux traversées par la frontière. C'était ainsi que, à partir de cette date et, du moins, jusqu'à la guerre de 1812,[12] les Grands Lacs et leurs communications ont été considérés en quelque sorte comme des eaux internationales ouvertes à perpétuité à la navigation pacifique de tous les riverains.[13]

Comme nous l'avons mentionné précédemment, c'est à la suite de certaines difficultés relatives au tracé de la frontière que la Convention Ashburton-Webster de 1842 avait confirmé aux navires, vaisseaux, et bâteaux des deux riverains la liberté de navigation sur toute l'étendue des Grands Lacs (sauf, bien sûr, le lac Michigan, sis entièrement du côté américain de la frontière), dans les chenaux des cours d'eau de jonction, ainsi que dans ceux de la section internationale du St-Laurent. Mais, pour que le droit ainsi conféré pût s'exercer d'une façon efficace, il fallait en outre garantir l'accès par la mer – soit par le St-Laurent depuis son embouchure – de même que l'usage des canaux existants et ceux qu'on construirait à l'avenir sur toute l'étendue du réseau. Ces étapes allaient être franchies graduellement au moyen de concessions réciproques entre les deux riverains.

Par un premier traité, signé à Washington en mai 1871, les Etats-Unis accordaient à la Grande Bretagne le privilège de navigation sur le St Clair Flat Canal (construit entièrement du côté américain de la frontière) et sur le lac Michigan, privilège assujeti toutefois aux restrictions et règlementations locales, révocable après dix ans avec préavis, et concédé sous condition expresse de réciprocité de la part de la Grand Bretagne sur le canal Welland et le fleuve St-Laurent. Il était même question, du côté britannique, d'étendre ces concessions à tous les canaux du Dominion et, du côté américain, à tous les canaux d'Etats-Unis.

Signalons en passant que cette disposition du traité de 1871 qui accordait aux navires américains le privilège de libre navigation commerciale sur toute l'étendue du St-Laurent ('from, to and into the sea'), sans préjudice des lois et règlements du pays riverain compatibles avec tel privilège, mettait fin à une longue dispute entre le gouvernement de sa majesté et celui des Etats-Unis, lequel réclamait, depuis 1823, l'usage du fleuve sur toute son étendue, comme une sorte de servitude (de passage) naturelle découlant de son droit de libre navigation sur les Grands Lacs.[14]

Ce dernier instrument poussait encore plus loin la volonté de bonne entente entre les deux riverains en matière de navigation: l'une de ses dispositions allait même jusqu'à garantir aux citoyens de chaque pays une certaine participation dans le commerce côtier de l'autre. Toutefois, ce privilège quelque peu exorbitant devait être retiré douze années plus tard, à la suite d'une résolution du Congrès américain. Comme, depuis lors, aucune nouvelle entente n'est venue le rétablir, on peut dire qu'aujourd'hui le droit de libre navigation commerciale sur toute l'étendue des Grands Lacs et du St-Laurent ne comprend pas le cabotage qui demeure réservé aux navires nationaux de chaque côté de la frontière.[15]

La liberté de navigation sur tout le réseau des Grands Lacs et la partie internationale du St-Laurent fut de nouveau reconnue et rendue plus explicite dans l'important traité des eaux limitrophes (ie, celles à travers lesquelles passe la frontière internationale) signé à Washington en 1909. Cet instrument confirmait 'à perpétuité' sur l'ensemble des eaux limitrophes, la liberté de navigation commerciale déjà acquise en vertu des traités antérieurs, en y ajoutant un élément nouveau: cette liberté s'exercerait 'sans discrimination aucune,' mais conformément aux lois et règlements en vigueur dans chaque pays, lesquels s'appliqueraient sans distinction aux sujets, citoyens, ou navires des deux riverains.

Comme les eaux limitrophes excluaient de leur définition le lac Michigan et les canaux déjà existants, une disposition spéciale fut insérée au traité selon laquelle la liberté de navigation conférée sur toute l'étendue des eaux limitrophes était étendue au lac Michigan ainsi qu'à tous les canaux (reliant des eaux limitrophes) existant à l'époque de même qu'à ceux qui pourraient être construits à l'avenir de chaque côté de la frontière. De plus, les riverains conservaient le droit de règlementer l'usage des canaux sur leur propre territoire et le soumettre au besoin au péage, à condition toutefois qu'aucune discrimination n'en résulte, puisque les citoyens et navires des deux riverains étaient désormais placés sur un pied d'égalité absolue quant à l'usage des canaux.

Ces dispositions du traité des eaux limitrophes furent reprises et renforcées dans le 'Traité relatif à la canalisation du St-Laurent' de juillet 1932 ainsi que dans 'l'Accord relatif à la canalisation du bassin des Grands Lacs et du fleuve St-Laurent' de mars 1941, lesquels, faute d'approbation par le Sénat américain, n'entrèrent jamais en vigueur.

La situation en ce qui a trait à la navigation commerciale est donc aujourd'hui sans équivoque: 1 / la liberté pour les deux riverains de naviguer librement sur toute l'étendue du réseau des Grands Lacs et leur déversoir, le St-Laurent, est le fruit de concessions réciproques; 2 / aucun autre état n'ayant été partie aux divers traités et conventions qui l'ont établie, cette liberté demeure en principe, exclusive aux deux riverains; 3 / enfin, l'extension d'une telle liberté à un état tiers ne pourrait avoir lieu sans consultation et entente préalable entre les deux riverains.

Toutefois, si en principe, la situation se présente ainsi, on sait qu'en pratique, bon nombre d'états ont été, au cours des années, amenés à participer à cette liberté de navigation des riverains. D'abord, avant l'avènement du Canada comme état souverain, la Grande Bretagne avait signé avec un certain nombre d'autres puissances des traités dits 'd'Empire' qui concédaient à celles-ci le droit d'accès, pour leur commerce, aux ports et rivières accessibles par mer du Dominion du Canada. En outre, le Canada et les Etats-Unis ont signé, chacun de leur côté, une série de traités[16] octroyant à des pays comme la France, l'Espagne, la Pologne, la Norvège, l'Irlande, et le Japon le traitement de la nation la plus favorisée, sinon le traitement national. Ajoutons à ceci l'Accord sur la marine marchande britannique qui lie le Canada depuis 1931 et permet le libre accès aux ports canadiens de tous les navires et bâteaux enregistrés dans les autres parties de la Commonwealth, sur un pied d'égalité avec ceux enregistrés au Canada.

A ces traités bilatéraux qui lient, chacun de leur côté, les deux riverains à des pays tiers, s'ajoutent encore les obligations générales qui découlent de l'Accord général sur les tarifs douaniers et le commerce de 1947 ainsi que la convention de 1948 relative à la création d'une organisation maritime internationale. Ces instruments multilatéraux ont pour effet d'ouvrir à la navigation commerciale de tous les états signataires, sur un pied d'égalité, toutes les eaux intérieures et ports du globe, accessibles par mer. Ainsi se trouvent pour ainsi dire, nivelées en pratique les conditions dans lesquelles s'exerce la navigation de tous les pavillons dans les voies d'eau d'intérêt international, y compris le bassin des Grands Lacs et du St-Laurent.

Sauvetage

La question de l'aide à apporter aux navires naufragés sur les Grands Lacs, très tôt soulevée au Congrès américain et longuement débattue entre les riverains, ne fut réglée de façon définitive qu'au début du siècle. Tout comme les autres questions que nous venons d'examiner, elle met en lumière chez les parties, deux attitudes bien définies et parfois contradictoires, à savoir: un fort attachement au vieux principe de la souveraineté territoriale, et une volonté ferme de bonne entente.

La correspondance diplomatique[17] de l'année 1878 révèle que les Etats-Unis avaient fait une première tentative pour en venir à une entente avec la Grande Bretagne sur la question. Celle-ci toutefois, jugeant sans doute la tentative prématurée, ne répondit pas aux avances américaines et les choses en restèrent là. Entretemps, l'expérience ayant démontré que cette lacune avait été préjudiciable aux intérêts du commerce américain sur les Grands Lacs, en particulier par les nombreuses pertes qu'elle lui avait fait subir, le gouvernement américain prit l'initiative d'une nouvelle démarche. C'est ainsi que, par un acte en date du 24 mai 1890, il accordait, sous réserve de réciprocité, aux navires canadiens, le privilège de procéder à des opérations de sauvetage dans les eaux américaines. De son côté, trois ans plus tard, le gouvernement canadien se rendait à la requête américaine et accordait, par arrêté en conseil, la réciprocité demandée.

La question ne devait toutefois être réglée de façon définitive et formelle que le 18 mai 1908, lors de la rédaction d'un traité 'concernant les droits réciproques de sauvetage des navires et de destruction des épaves dans les eaux contiguës à la frontière entre le Dominion du Canada et les Etats-Unis.' C'est ainsi que les navires ainsi que le matériel de sauvetage de chaque pays sur les Grands Lacs peuvent tirer ou détruire toute épave, de même que porter secours et assistance à tout navire 'naufragé, désemparé ou en détresse' dans les eaux ou sur le rivage de l'autre pays.

Ce privilège réciproque comprend également toutes les opérations de remorquage s'y rapportant, mais il est soumis à une restriction spécifique: les navires de l'un et de l'autre pays doivent, aussitôt que possible après la fin des opérations, faire un rapport complet à la station de douane la plus rapprochée dans le pays sur les eaux duquel le sauvetage a été effectué.

Enfin, en mai 1951, les deux pays tinrent une 'conférence sur la sécurité de la vie humaine et de la propriété sur les Grands Lacs,' faisant ainsi, en quelque sorte, la mise au point du traité de 1908. Il fut alors convenu de rendre obligatoire, sur les navires jaugeant 500 tonneaux brut ou plus et sur tous les bâteaux de passagers de plus de 65′ de longueur, l'installation d'appareils radio-téléphoniques. En outre, tous les navires circulant sur les Grands Lacs, ainsi que tous les ports, étaient désormais requis d'être aux écoutes pour les appels de détresse.

MARINES DE GUERRE

Lors des négociations qui ont précédé le Traité de Paris de 1783, les Etats-Unis avaient suggéré que l'on procédât à un désarmement pur et simple sur les Grands Lacs.[18] Cette suggestion ne fut toutefois considérée de façon pratique qu'après la guerre de 1812, lors de l'échange de notes des 28 et 29 avril 1817, connu sous le nom de 'Convention Rush-Bagot.' Conçu tout spécialement dans le but de prévenir tout conflit susceptible de surgir sur les Grands Lacs, ce document établissait, à proprement parler, un régime de limitation des armements, régime sensiblement différent de celui, plus communément connu, de 'démilitarisation' qui supprime toute force armée. Ses dispositions principales étaient les suivantes: A / chaque pays consentait à réduire ses forces navales sur les Grands Lacs de la façon suivante: a / sur le lac Ontario: à un bâtiment de guerre d'au plus 10 tonneaux, armé d'une seule pièce de 18 livres; b / sur les lacs dits 'd'en haut' (Upper Lakes; l'expression ayant été interprétée par la suite comme comprenant tous les autres lacs, le lac Michigan inclus) à deux bâtiments de même déplacement et armés de façon identique; B / tous les autres bâtiments de guerre sur les Grands Lacs devaient être désarmés; et C / interdiction était faite d'y construire et d'y armer à l'avenir d'autres bâtiments.

Il est à noter que, bien qu'elle ne contenait aucune stipulation expresse en ce qui concerne les pataches de douane, la convention limitait les bâtiments armés à la taille nécessaire pour des opérations de police et de protection contre la contrebande. Les deux parties auraient du reste, par la suite, toujours considéré que les bâteaux affectés au service des douanes ne faisaient pas partie de la marine de guerre et qu'ils étaient de ce fait exclus du nouveau régime.[19] En outre, aucune mention spéciale ne fut faite des fortifications qui existaient à l'époque sur les Grands Lacs. De l'avis des deux parties, la fin de la guerre de 1812 avait apporté une période de détente qui rendait inutile, pour l'avenir, le maintien des bases navales existantes.[20]

Cet instrument constitue, à notre avis, un phénomène unique dans l'histoire des relations internationales. On connait de nombreux précédents à la neutralisation d'une zone le long d'une frontière terrestre et quelques cas de neutralisation garantie de petits états ou territoires (tels que la Belgique et la Suisse), mais il n'y a aucun précédent connu au document de 1817. Ce procédé qui avait pour effet d'abolir pratiquement deux marines rivales sur une grande voie de communication par eau, même s'il brisait avec plusieurs des vieilles maximes de la diplomatie, était en parfaite harmonie avec l'esprit des temps nouveaux.

Maintes fois et à plusieurs époques, on dérogea de chaque côté de la frontière aux stipulations de la convention (comme pendant la crise de 1835 à 1842 et la guerre civile américaine de 1861) sans qu'aucune partie n'élevât d'opposition sérieuse ou ne menaçât l'autre de dénoncer l'instrument. Toutefois, on rapporte que, peu de temps après la crise canado-américaine de septembre 1864, les Etats-Unis auraient songé à l'abroger, mais que, par prudence sans doute, on en aurait rien fait.[21]

Comme, à la fin du siècle dernier, il apparaissait aux riverains que l'interdiction faite en 1817 de construire des navires de guerre sur les Grands Lacs ne correspondait plus à une situation qui avait beaucoup évolué (ceux-ci offrant des avantages marqués pour la construction d'une certaine classe de bâtiments), l'idée fut pour la première fois émise de réviser la convention.[22] Toutefois, pour des motifs d'ordre divers, dont la plupart se ramènent à la crainte que les deux pays avaient de bousculer de si sages dispositions, le vieil instrument demeura sans modification jusqu'à la deuxième guerre mondiale. C'est alors que, par un long échange de notes, les deux pays, tout en se gardant de l'abroger, procédèrent à la révision et aux remaniements qui s'imposaient[23] et qui portaient notamment sur cinq questions principales: 1 / le nombre et la dimension des navires de guerre, 2 / leur disposition, 3 / leurs fonctions, 4 / leur armement, et 5 / leur construction dans les chantiers maritimes des Grands Lacs.

Relativement à la première question, la Convention de 1817 spécifiait, d'abord, quant au nombre, un bâtiment sur le lac Ontario et deux sur les lacs 'd'en haut.' Or, la marine américaine possédait déjà en 1939 cinq navires non classés sur les Grands Lacs, ce qui constituait une dérogation de fait aux dispositions de la convention. Ces derniers servaient à l'instruction des réservistes et leur nombre s'avérait déjà insuffisant pour cette tâche. Ainsi donc, puisque depuis de nombreuses années déjà, ces navires étaient demeurés en service sans opposition de la part du Canada, les parties convinrent d'entériner cette pratique, tout en interdisant qu'on en augmente le nombre à l'avenir.

Quant aux dimensions, la note américaine précisait que les cinq navires en question jaugeaient plus du maximum permis (de 100 tonneaux). On estimait toutefois que cette disposition de la convention de 1817 était tombée en désuétude depuis le début du siècle du fait de la substitution de l'acier au bois dans la construction des navires. De plus, ces bâtiments que depuis longtemps la marine américaine utilisait sur les Grands Lacs n'avaient pas plus de 14′ de tirant d'eau, ce qui les rendait impropres à la guerre moderne; tout au plus pouvaient-ils encore servir à l'instruction élémentaire des réservistes de la marine. Et c'est ainsi que, sous condition de réciprocité, les deux riverains consacrèrent la pratique existante en ce qui a trait au nombre et à la dimension des navires, bien que, à leur connaissance, cette pratique outrepassât les dispositions de la convention, parce qu'elle était 'en parfaite harmonie avec l'opinion publique de l'heure.'

A propos de la deuxième question, la convention stipulait: 'un bâtiment sur le lac Ontario et deux sur les lacs d'en haut.' La raison géographique de cette clause était qu'à l'époque de la négociation de la convention, les Grands Lacs étaient d'immenses nappes d'eau sans communication avec l'océan et, pour la plupart, sans communication entre elles. Cette situation avant été modifiée depuis, notamment par le creusage des chenaux et la construction de nombreux canaux; la note américaine informait le gouvernement canadien que les Etats-Unis ne considéreraient pas comme déraisonnable et contraire à l'esprit de la convention 'le fait pour les vaisseaux des deux parties de circuler librement sur les Grands Lacs ou de stationner dans un port quelconque de ceux-ci,' ce à quoi le gouvernement canadien acquiesça.

Quant à la troisième question relative aux fonctions, il s'agissait surtout de savoir si la convention permettait les exercices de tir. Vu le silence de l'ancien instrument sur ce point particulier; il semblait aux deux parties que 'selon son esprit et sa lettre,' elles pouvaient, dans leurs eaux respectives, 'utiliser les navires de guerre pour l'instruction de leurs réservistes de même que pour toute autre initiative normale, y compris les exercices de tir.' Ici encore le jeu de l'interprétation assouplissait la lettre.

Relativement à la quatrième question, la convention stipulait que les trois vaisseaux de guerre, dont le maintien en service était autorisé pour chaque pays, pouvaient être armés chacun d'un canon à boulet de 18 livres.

Or, l'obus d'un canon de 3″ pesait 14 livres, tandis que celui d'un canon de 4″ en pesait environ 30. Donc, selon la convention, seuls seraient utilisables les canons de 3″. Toutefois, les officiers de la marine des deux pays estimaient que seulement le canon de 4″ pouvait d'être considéré à l'époque comme 'équipement règlementaire,' propre à assurer l'instruction des réservistes. Il fut donc décidé de commun accord que 'l'esprit de l'ancien instrument s'accommoderait d'une entente en vertu de laquelle trois des navires de guerre de chaque pays sur les Grands Lacs seraient munis de deux canons de 4″, tous autres armements étant formellement exclus' et sous les conditions suivantes, à savoir: a / les exercices de tir ne pourraient avoir lieu que dans les eaux territoriales de chaque pays; b / les canons de 4″ seraient démontés, sauf pendant la période d'instruction des réservistes.

Concernant la cinquième question enfin, la convention portait interdiction totale de construire des bâtiments sur les Grands Lacs. Or, en 1939, la question revêtait une importance sans précédent pour les deux gouvernements, puisque les chantiers maritimes des Grands Lacs étaient en mesure de produire une certaine classe de bâtiments dont on avait urgent besoin pour la guerre. C'est pourquoi, on convint qu'il faudrait, dans l'interprétation de cette disposition, tenir compte du fait que les conditions qui existaient à l'époque de la signature de la convention (où les Grands Lacs étaient pratiquement sans voie d'accès par mer) étaient fort différentes en 1939, alors que des navires de 14′ de tirant d'eau pouvaient remonter le St-Laurent sur tout son parcours.

Une solution, jugée conforme aux intentions des négociateurs et à l'esprit de la convention de 1817, fut donc ('pour répondre aux nécessités de l'heure') adoptée de commun accord, solution selon laquelle serait permise la construction, dans les chantiers maritimes des Grands Lacs, de navires 'incontestablement destinés à ne servir que dans les eaux maritimes,' mais sous trois conditions: a / que chaque gouvernement communique à l'autre, avant la mise en chantier, des renseignements complets sur tous les navires de guerre dont on projette la construction dans les ports des Grands Lacs; b / que les armements soient installés de façon à ne pouvoir servir immédiatement pendant la période où les navires doivent demeurer sur les Grands Lacs; c / enfin, que les navires ainsi construits et armés quittent les Grands Lacs le plus tôt possible après leur parachèvement.

Les riverains firent une dernière mise au point après la guerre, par un échange de notes en date des 18 novembre et 5 décembre 1946 qui réglait, conformément à l'esprit du vieil instrument (bien qu'en dérogation de ses dispositions), le sort des vaisseaux placés en station sur les Grands Lacs pour l'instruction du personnel de leur réserve navale. Une telle mise en station était désormais permise, 'pourvu que tous renseignements utiles concernant le nombre, l'affectation, les fonctions et l'armement desdits vaisseaux soient communiqués par chaque gouvernement à l'autre au préalable.'

Et c'est ainsi que, par un système souple d'interprétation qui gardait intact le fond, les deux riverains ont procédé graduellement à l'ajustement d'un accord international dont la plupart des dispositions étaient déjà tombées en désuétude.

PECHE

A défaut de traité ou convention explicite entre les deux riverains réglementant le droit de pêche sur les Grands Lacs, la pratique admet la juridiction exclusive de chacun sur les eaux sises de son propre côté de la frontière internationale. Ainsi, chacun est-il maître de règlementer comme bon lui semble et de réserver à ses seuls nationaux le droit de pêche sur les Grands Lacs, jusqu'à la frontière internationale, tout comme si cette nappe d'eau faisait partie intégrante de son territoire.

Le caractère fluide et difficilement identifiable de la frontière (la médiane) sur les Grands Lacs, ne pouvait manquer de conduire à des tensions et affrontements entre riverains, particulièrement en matière de droit de pêche. On rapporte qu'au cours de la deuxième partie du siècle dernier, il y eut, comme résultat de lois discordantes dans les deux pays, des frictions. En effet, tandis que le gouvernement canadien avait, au moyen d'une règlementation, tenté d'enrayer le dépeuplement des Grands Lacs, la pêche était demeurée libre du côté américain où se trouvaient les terrains de frai. Cette liberté avait entraîné certains abus et on se plaignait du côté canadien 'des pillages' auxquels se livraient les pêcheurs américains outre frontière. Survint une migration massive du poisson dans les eaux canadiennes, laquelle fut aussitôt suivie par des pêcheurs clandestins d'outre frontière. Et c'est ainsi que plusieurs équipages furent appréhendés par les autorités britanniques, des bâteaux et équipements confisqués et des pêcheurs détenus pendant un certain temps.[24]

Un des cas les plus retentissants qui a été soumis en 1894 à la Cour d'Amirauté de Toronto[25] illustre bien l'état du droit sur la question. Il s'agit du bâteau de pêche américain, *Grâce,* dont l'équipage avait été incarcéré en Ontario pour avoir pêché sans autorisation dans la partie canadienne du lac Erié. L'affaire fit grand bruit et donna lieu à un long débat au cours duquel s'affrontèrent juristes et théoriciens du droit international.

La couronne invoquait pour soutenir sa thèse, l'autorité de deux juristes de renom, Bar et Hall,[26] cependant que la défense cherchait, à la lumière de la jurisprudence de *U.S.* vs *Rodgers,*[27] à faire dévier le débat sur le plan du droit public de la mer. Comme le *Grace* avait été capturé à neuf miles du littoral canadien, cette dernière évoquait l'argument des trois miles marin pour le soustraire à la juridiction canadienne. Dans sa décision, rendue la même année et jamais contestée outre frontière, le tribunal canadien maintenait l'application de la loi interne et sanctionnait la capture. C'était consacrer de nouveau le principe que la réglementation du droit de pêche sur les Grands Lacs relève de la souveraineté territoriale exclusive des riverains et que, en conséquence, aucune des règles du droit public de la mer ne peut s'appliquer sans leur consentement exprès.

Toutefois, la situation des pêcheries des Grands Lacs continuait à préoccuper les riverains. Il y eut au début du siècle une première tentative de réglementation conjointe du droit de pêche, avec la signature en 1908, puis la ratification par les deux, d'une convention 'relative à la protection du poisson comestible dans les eaux contigües à la frontière.' Toutefois, cet instrument n'entra jamais en vigueur et devint caduc suite à l'impossibilité des deux gouvernements de s'entendre sur les modalités d'application (règlements).

On reprit de nouveau l'expérience une quarantaine d'années plus tard, soit le 2 avril 1946, et les deux pays signaient à Washington une convention relative aux pêcheries des Grands Lacs qui s'apparente beaucoup à une édition révisée de la convention de 1908 et qui, toujours non ratifiée, pourrait bien connaître le même sort que la précédente.

Toutefois, si les riverains ne sont pas encore parvenus à s'entendre sur le plan d'une réglementation générale de la pêche sur les Grands Lacs, ils se sont attaqués avec succès à un problème particulier, celui de la protection des pêcheries des Grands Lacs menacée par la lamproie de mer parasite. Ils ont à cet effet signé, le 10 septembre 1954, une convention sur le sujet et formé en 1955 une commission conjointe dite 'commission des pêcheries des Grands Lacs.' Cet organisme composé d'abord de trois membres, puis de quatre à partir de 1967, est doté de vastes pouvoirs pour mener les enquêtes nécessaires et faire les recommandations qui s'imposent dans le but de remédier à cette situation alarmante. C'est là un important acquit qui pourrait bien un jour ouvrir la voie à un accord plus général sur la pêche elle-même dans les Grands Lacs.

UTILISATION DES EAUX ET DU LIT

La matière touchant cette question est particulièrement abondante: elle comprend des traités, des conventions, des échanges de notes, et autres instruments mineurs qui tous gravitent plus ou moins autour d'un instrument-clef, le traité des Eaux Limitrophes de 1909. L'importance de ce document tient à la fois du but d'ordre très général[28] qu'il se propose et de l'instrument remarquable – La Commission Mixte Internationale – qu'il crée pour sa réalisation.

Les problèmes, que pose l'utilisation de l'eau et du lit des Grands Lacs sont multiples et variés: construction de canaux, de barrages, de ports, de jetées, de brise-lames, dérivations pour usage hygiénique, pour la production d'électricité, pour l'irrigation, etc. Le traité de 1909 contient les éléments essentiels pour la solution de tous ces problèmes. *Grosso modo,* il stipule que les deux riverains se réservent le droit d'utiliser et de détourner à leur seul profit les eaux situées de leur propre côté de la frontière,[29] pourvu que ces utilisations ou détournements n'aient pas pour effet d'exhausser le niveau ou de nuire au débit ou à la pureté des eaux de l'autre côté de la frontière.

Cinq dispositions de base du traité nous intéressent ici de façon plus particulière. Une première (par. 1, art. 2) en vertu de laquelle chaque riverain conserve, de son propre côté de la frontière, la juridiction et l'autorité exclusive sur toute utilisation ou dérivation 'temporaire ou permanente' des eaux. Toutefois, dans le cas où ces travaux auraient des résultats préjudiciables de l'autre côté de la frontière, les parties lésées jouiraient des mêmes droits et pourraient se prévaloir des mêmes recours que si le préjudice leur était causé dans le pays même où se situent les travaux. Cette disposition a donc ceci de particulier qu'elle confère, dans les cas mentionnés, aux riverains canadiens le droit de demander aux tribunaux américains de redresser des torts, de réparer des dommages subis au Canada et vice versa pour les riverains américains. De plus, une réserve spécifique protège le droit de chaque riverain de s'opposer à 'toute ingérence ou toute dérivation' de l'autre côté de la frontière, susceptible de porter un préjudice réel aux intérêts de la navigation de son propre côté.

Une deuxième disposition (par. 2, art. 2) se rapporte aux travaux de réparation et d'entretien destinés à améliorer la navigation et les services portuaires que chaque riverain peut entreprendre sur son propre territoire. Ceux-ci sont permis, pourvu qu'ils ne modifient pas 'de façon perceptible' le niveau ou le débit des eaux de l'autre côté de la frontière ni ne gènent l'usage domestique ou sanitaire de ces eaux. Sont également permises (par. 1, art. 3), mais assujetties à une réserve encore plus rigoureuse, celle de ne pas modifier, affecter, ou 'influencer' le débit ou le 'niveau naturel' des eaux de l'autre côté de la frontière, les utilisations, obstructions ou dérivations nouvelles des eaux limitrophes.

L'établissement ou le maintien d'ouvrages de protection ou de réfection, de barrages ou autres obstacles dans les déversoirs ou 'eaux qui sortent' des Grands Lacs (ou dans le cours inférieur des rivières successives) est en outre permis (par. 1, art. 4), mais à la condition que ces ouvrages n'aient pas pour effet 'de hausser le niveau naturel des eaux de l'autre côté de la frontière.'

Une cinquième disposition (par. 2, art. 4) enfin, interdit expressément aux riverains de contaminer les eaux limitrophes et celles qui coupent la frontière au détriment de l'hygiène publique ou des biens situés de l'autre côté de la frontière.

Le traité ne se borne par à énoncer des principes généraux touchant l'utilisation des eaux. Il aborde également, en cherchant à les résoudre, quelques questions concrètes, notamment celle de la dérivation pratiquée dans l'un des cours d'eau de jonction, le Niagara (en amont des chutes), pour la production d'énergie électrique (art. 5). Sous réserve des détournements qu'il pourrait être nécessaire d'effectuer, soit pour fins domestiques ou sanitaires, soit pour le service des canaux ou pour la navigation en général, le volume d'eau détournable du Niagara était alors fixé à 20,000 pieds cubes à la seconde pour les Etats-Unis et 36,000 p.c.s. pour le Canada.

Cet arrangement considéré comme transitoire devait, peu de temps après, être remis en question et faire l'objet de nombreux pourparlers et négociations entre les deux riverains. Suffise de mentionner que les six échanges de notes et de memoranda ainsi que la convention et l'accord qui suivirent eurent pour effet d'augmenter successivement sur une période de quarante ans le volume d'eau détournable par chaque pays, jusqu'à la signature en 1950 du Traité de dérivation des eaux du Niagara, lequel faisait en quelque sorte, en les abrogeant, la synthèse des instruments en vigueur sur le sujet,

Ce nouvel instrument établissait, sous réserve de la quantité d'eau utilisée ou nécessaire pour les besoins domestiques et sanitaires, que le volume d'eau disponible pour la production de l'énergie électrique en amont des chutes serait désormais constitué par le débit total du lac Erié, ce volume d'eau étant lui-même partagé également entre le Canada et les Etats-Unis. Aucun aspect du problème n'avait été négligé: le nouveau document contenait certaines mesures transitoires en ce qui a trait à l'utilisation du volume d'eau disponible, une clause d'exonération de responsabilité pour dommages causés aux tiers, ainsi qu'un mécanisme d'abrogation après cinquante années. Enfin, certaines dispositions visaient même à protéger la beauté panoramique des chutes en fixant un minimum au-dessous duquel on ne pourrait réduire leur débit. Ainsi prenait fin un débat qui avait duré près d'un demi siècle.

Plusieurs importantes dispositions du traité de 1909 ont trait aux pouvoirs et au fonctionnement de l'organisme intergouvernemental auquel il confie plus directement la réalisation des objectifs qu'il s'assigne, la Commission Mixte Internationale, dont le rôle dans l'harmonie des relations inter-riveraines a été et demeure toujours primordial. Son étude mériterait qu'on s'y arrête longuement, mais nous n'y consacrerons que quelques paragraphes essentiels à notre sujet, afin de ne pas empiéter sur l'étude plus spécifique de la question qui a été confiée au professeur Jordan.

Cet organisme de type paritaire est formé de six commissaires, dont trois sont canadiens et trois américains, qui agissent conjointement et doivent s'efforcer, dans l'exercice de leurs fonctions, de garder une attitude américaine au sens continental de l'expression, en considérant que les populations des deux côtés de la frontière ont un droit égal à l'équité de leurs jugements. Ils représentent en quelque sort une vaste circonscription internationale et il est très significatif que, dans les cas examinés jusqu'ici, leurs décisions aient été à peu près unanimes.

Le traité donne une longue énumération de matières qui sont de la compétence de la Commission Mixte. Disons, pour résumer, que son autorisation est requise de façon expresse dans deux cas principaux:

1 / Celui où l'un ou l'autre riverain se proposerait d'utiliser, d'obstruer, ou de dériver d'une façon quelconque ('temporaire ou permanente') les eaux des Grands Lacs, si ces travaux sont de nature à affecter ou influencer le débit ou le niveau naturel des eaux de l'autre côté de la frontière (art. 3, par. 1). Cette disposition semble, à première vue, faire double emploi avec celle que nous mentionnions plus haut (art. 2, par. 1). Toutefois, à l'inverse de celle-là, son but est uniquement préventif et elle ne s'adresse plus aux tiers lésés.

2 / Celui où l'un ou l'autre riverain se proposerait d'entreprendre, de son propre côté de la frontière, dans les Grands Lacs ou dans les eaux en provenance de ceux-ci, des travaux destinés à améliorer la navigation ou les services portuaires, si ces

travaux ont pour résultat de modifier sensiblement le niveau des eaux de l'autre côté de la frontière ou de nuire à leur usage domestique et sanitaire (art. 3, par. 2).

Notons ici la différence entre les deux cas. Dans le premier on lit 'travaux de nature à influencer le niveau' et dans le second, travaux ayant pour résultat de 'modifier sensiblement le niveau.' La règle apparaît beaucoup plus rigide dans le premier et semble indiquer que le législateur donne une préférence aux travaux destinés à améliorer la navigation. Soulignons de plus que l'autorité de la commission peut être en tout temps écartée, lorsqu'il existe ou intervient entre les deux riverains un arrangement spécial sur un point relevant normalement de leur compétence respective. Sa compétence est enfin écartée en ce qui a trait aux cours d'eau tributaires des Grands Lacs.

Ses pouvoirs dans la formulation d'un règlement, dans l'établissement d'une règle de conduite et dans la fixation d'une indemnité ou compensation sont très vastes; ils sont sur de nombreux points, voisins de ceux des 'aimables compositeurs.' Comme unique règle de droit susceptible de guider la commission dans l'examen des questions qui lui sont soumises, les rédacteurs du traité ont statué que les deux riverains auraient, chacun de son propre côté de la frontière, des droits égaux (identiques et similaires, pour employer l'expression même du traité) en ce qui concerne l'utilisation des eaux limitrophes.

Le traité établit aussi un ordre de priorité dans les utilisations diverses que la commission peut avoir à autoriser. Cet ordre, qui doit être considéré comme absolu par les deux parties, est le suivant: 1 / usage de l'eau à des fins domestiques et sanitaires; 2 / usage de l'eau pour la navigation, y compris l'alimentation des canaux pour la navigation; 3 / usage de l'eau pour la production d'énergie électrique et pour l'irrigation.

Ainsi donc, après le droit prioritaire d'usage pour fins domestiques, c'est la navigation qui a le pas. Quant aux eaux excédentaires qui peuvent servir à la production d'énergie électrique ou à l'irrigation, c'est le principe du partage égal qui s'applique. Toutefois, pour importants qu'ils soient, ces préceptes sont, en pratique du moins, loin de restreindre complètement l'initiative de la commission, laquelle demeure entière dans le cadre des mesures concrètes à édicter dans chaque cas particulier.

Nous croyons utile, avant de clore cette dernière partie de notre étude, de faire un bref exposé de deux questions impliquant certaines des dispositions du traité de 1909 que nous venons d'examiner et qui ont revêtu une importance toute particulière pour les riverains depuis le début du siècle. Il s'agit de la dérivation de Long Lac-Ogoki et de celle de Chicago. Deux autres questions, enfin, celles du niveau et de la pollution des eaux des Grands Lacs, dans la solution desquelles la Commission Mixte est largement impliquée, mériteraient également, par leur ampleur et leur actualité, d'être traitées ici sommairement; nous ne ferons toutefois que les effleurer, afin d'éviter un double emploi possible avec certains passages de l'étude du Professeur Jordan sur les problèmes relatifs au bassin de drainage des Grands Lacs.

Dérivation de Long Lac-Ogoki

La première question de la dérivation de Long Lac-Ogoki est étroitement liée à celle des détournements du Niagara pour la production d'électricité que nous venons d'examiner. Il s'agissait pour le Canada de détourner vers le bassin des Grands Lacs, via Long Lac, les eaux de la rivière Ogoki, un tributaire de la rivière Albany qui se jette elle-même dans la baie James, ce qui devait avoir pour effet d'augmenter le 4000 p.c.s. le débit du bassin des Grands Lacs et de leur déversoir, le St-Laurent. Le gouvernement canadien désirait faire de même avec un autre tributaire de la rivière Albany, la rivière Kenogami, et utiliser, comme dans le premier cas, le volume d'eau disponible (de 1200 p.c.s.) pour la production d'énergie électrique du côté canadien.

Comme aucune des dispositions du traité de 1909, pas plus d'ailleurs que des traités précédents, ne s'appliquait aux affluents supérieurs des Grands Lacs et ne couvrait cette nouvelle situation, les riverains, après de longues négociations, estimèrent nécessaire do conclure une entente particulière sur le sujet. C'est ce qu'ils firent par un échange de notes, les 14 et 31 octobre 1940, en vertu duquel les Etats-Unis consentaient, tenant compte du nouveau volume d'eau ainsi rendu disponible, à ce que le Canada procède à une dérivation additionnelle de 5000 p.c.s. en amont des chutes, pour la production d'énergie électrique. Dix ans plus tard, une disposition (art. 3) insérée dans le traité de dérivation du Niagara de 1950 excluait spécifiquement du partage des eaux des Grands Lacs, pour la production d'électricité, 'les eaux qui sont détournées dans le bassin naturel des Grands Lacs, par les aménagements existant de Long Lake-Ogoki,' l'utilisation de ces eaux continuant à être régie par l'échange de notes ci-haut mentionné.

Dérivation de Chicago

La deuxième question, celle de la dérivation de Chicago[30] qui s'est posée au début du siècle, a fait l'objet, en particulier entre 1912 et 1927 et plus récemment au début des 1960s, d'une volumineuse correspondance diplomatique entre les deux riverains et n'a jamais pu être réglée dans le cadre du droit conventionnel en vigueur entre eux. Retraçons brièvement l'historique de cette intéressante question.

En 1889, la législature de l'état d'Illinois créa une corporation du nom de 'Sanitary District of Chicago' qui entreprit la construction d'un canal de drainage, allant du lac Michigan à la rivière Desplaines et destiné à servir d'égout industriel principal à la ville de Chicago. Ces travaux eurent pour résultat de détourner une partie des eaux du lac Michigan vers le bassin du Mississippi. En 1907, on développa même ce système de canaux pour la production d'énergie électrique. Mais l'affaire ne s'arrêtera pas là et, en mars 1925, le secrétaire de la guerre des Etats-Unis autorisait une dérivation totale de 8500 p.c.s. par jour. Deux ans plus tard, cédant à une active campagne de presse, le Congrès américain autorisait la construction d'une voie d'eau navigable de 9' de profondeur, en spécifiant toutefois que 'rien dans cette loi ne pourrait être interprété comme autorisant une dérivation d'eau du lac Michigan.' C'était, reconnaître de façon tacite, mais un peu tardive, après l'acte unilatéral posé par le secrétaire à la guerre en 1925, que le problème débordait des cadres de la souveraineté nationale et que, par conséquent, on ne pouvait autoriser une nouvelle dérivation des eaux du lac Michigan sans consultation préalable avec le gouvernement canadien.

Du côté du Canada, les réactions devant le geste de 1925 avaient été assez vives, dûes au fait d'un affaissement de niveau de plus de 4″ dans le port de Montréal, ce qui portait préjudice à la navigation. Le contrecoup se faisant même sentir sur la production d'énergie hydro-électrique et les aménagements existant dans la section canadienne du St-Laurent accusaient une perte de puissance de près de 100,000 chevaux-vapeur. L'on se trouvait, semble-t-il, en présence d'une sorte de quasi-délit engageant la responsabilité des Etats-Unis.

Or, aucun des traités ou conventions en vigueur à l'époque entre les deux riverains ne semblait pouvoir s'appliquer à pareille situation et encore moins donner ouverture à un recours en droit contre les Etats-Unis.

En effet, le seul instrument susceptible de servir de base à une réclamation en justice canadienne, le traité des eaux limitrophes de 1909, excluait de sa définition le lac Michigan. Il semblait donc que cette étendue d'eau, géographiquement partie intégrante du bassin des Grands Lacs, mais sise entièrement en territoire américain, échappait de fait aux dispositions du traité régissant l'utilisation des eaux limi-trophes, dont elle ne pouvait même pas être considérée comme tributaire ou affluent, voire au sens large. On fut alors tenté de recourir aux dispositions plus générales du droit des gens, mais force fut de constater que la doctrine, tout comme la juris-prudence, dans ce domaine étaient (comme ils le sont encore aujourd'hui d'ailleurs) pleins d'incertitudes.

On admettait généralement que la souveraineté territoriale d'un état était limitée par la grande maxime tirée du droit romain *sic utere tuo ut alienum non laedas*; en outre, quelques cas de jurisprudence étaient venus fixer quelque peu la doctrine. Toutefois, les anciennes décisions des tribunaux allemands et américains qui recon-naissaient le principe de la répartition équitable des eaux entre les divers riverains d'un fleuve international ne pouvaient s'appliquer comme telles au litige en ques-tion.[31]

Il semblait donc, dans les circonstances, aux deux parties que la meilleure solu-tion serait, comme pour la question précédente de la dérivation de Long Lake-Ogoki, de conclure un accord particulier sur le sujet. Et c'est ainsi qu'une disposi-tion fut insérée dans le traité 'relatif à la canalisation du St-Laurent' de 1932, laquelle, concordant avec un arrêt rendu par la Cour Suprême des Etats-Unis deux années auparavant dans un litige sur la question entre états riverains,[32] réduisait considérablement (soit de 8500 p.c.s. qu'il était à 1500 p.c.s. par jour) le volume d'eau détourné du réseau des Grands Lacs par le canal de drainage de Chicago. Des mesures compensatoires étaient en outre prévues à l'égard du Canada pour le cas où l'on se verrait forcé à l'avenir d'augmenter le débit du canal et un dédommage-ment était accordé pour le préjudice déjà causé. L'entente allait même jusqu'à réglementer pour l'avenir les détournements des eaux du Lac Michigan qui, comme on le sait, n'entraient pas dans la définition du traité de 1909. Toutefois, faute d'ap-probation par le Sénat des Etats-Unis, ces équitables dispositions ne furent jamais mises en application, pas plus d'ailleurs que celles identiques contenues dans l'Ac-cord sur la canalisation du Bassin des Grands Lacs et du St-Laurent de 1941 qui, lui non plus, n'a jamais pu obtenir la majorité des voix requises au Sénat américain. Le problème demeurait donc entier.

Comme par la suite, la situation demeurait stationnaire entre les deux riverains, le débat reprenait sur le plan interne aux Etats-Unis entre l'Illinois et les six autres états riverains de la fédération. Ces derniers demandaient qu'on limite, dans l'intérêt même de la navigation sur les Grands Lacs et de la production d'énergie électrique dans la section internationale du St-Laurent, le volume d'eau détourné du lac Michigan à Chicago. L'audition de ces divers dossiers, commencée à Chicago en 1959 s'est poursuivie pendant plusieurs années, au cours desquelles le gouvernement canadien, par le truchement du State Department de Washington, eut l'occasion de faire connaître ouvertement son 'opposition irréductible' à tout détournement, unilatéralement décidé, du bassin des Grands Lacs à Chicago, dont l'effet réduirait 'forcément le volume des eaux qui demeurent dans ce bassin, à quelque point de vue que l'on se place.' Les notes canadiennes (de 1961 et 1964) de ton très ferme, faisaient notamment appel à cinq instruments bilatéraux[33] signés depuis le début du siècle, lesquels reconnaîtraient, implicitement du moins, l'existence d'une relation de cause à effet entre, d'une part, des dérivations du bassin des Grands Lacs et, d'autre part, les effets nuisibles subis par la navigation canado-américaine et les aménagements hydro-électriques des deux pays.

La Cour suprême désignait par la suite un conseiller spécial chargé de recueillir la preuve des deux côtés et de formuler ses conclusions. Alors que le tribunal examinait le rapport de son conseiller, l'Illinois et les six autres états riverains concluaient entre eux une entente sur la base même des recommandations contenues dans le document. Cette entente était notamment à l'effet que le volume d'eau détourné journellement à Chicago n'excèderait pas, en tout et pour tout, 3200 p.c.s., ce qui n'altérait pas de façon substantielle les arrangements déjà en vigueur depuis de nombreuses années sur le sujet. Par décret, en date du 12 juin 1967, la Cour suprême entérinait cet accord qui entrait en vigueur le 1er mars 1970, scellant ainsi l'issue de ce grand procès.

Niveau des eaux

La troisième question, celle du niveau des eaux des Grands Lacs ou, plus précisément, de leur étiage a été à l'étude de façon intermittente depuis le début du siècle et fait, en particulier depuis 1952, l'objet de recherches et travaux suivis et approfondis de la part de la Commission Mixte Internationale.

En effet, l'utilisation de cet immense bassin hydrographique que constituent les Grands Lacs se trouve gravement contrariée, voire menacée, par des accélérations et des diminutions du cycle hydrographique qui affectent de façon sensible et pour une période de temps parfois considérable son approvisionnement en eau. Ce problème d'étiage des lacs et de leurs affluents préoccupe – tout comme celui que créait pour leur niveau même les dérivations de Long Lake et de Chicago – à juste titre les riverains qui, en vertu des dispositions (arts. 3, 8, et 9) du Traité des eaux limitrophes de 1909, en ont confié l'étude à la Commission Mixte Internationale. Cet organisme a déjà fait un certain nombre de recommandations en ce qui a trait au niveau du lac Ontario et au débit du fleuve St-Laurent et établi plusieurs commissions d'experts ainsi qu'un organisme de contrôle. Mais la tâche qui reste encore à accomplir est colossale; le problème est très complexe et il ne semble pas y avoir de solution en vue, à court terme du moins. On parle encore, en guise de palliatif, de la possibilité (avec le consentement bien sûr des provinces canadiennes concernées) de détourner vers le bassin des Grands Lacs les eaux de certaines rivières qui se déversent dans la baie James ou la baie d'Hudson. Toutefois, on doute que de tels détournements puissent rien régler: un nouvel apport d'eau provoquerait indubitablement des crues qui obligeraient à aménager dans les Grands Lacs et les cours d'eau de jonction toute une série d'ouvrages destinés à les contrôler. Est-ce là opération rentable ou même possible? Les recherches qu'on poursuit en ce sens ne sont pas encore assez avancées pour permettre d'en juger de façon certaine. On demeure toutefois confiant de pouvoir en arriver, à la longue, à une solution satisfaisante de ce problème.

Pollution des eaux

La quatrième et dernière question, celle de la pollution des Grands Lacs est à l'étude, plus spécialement depuis 1946. Elle s'inscrit du reste dans le cadre des nombreux travaux sur l'environnement humain qui se poursuivent un peu partout de nos jours. Notons ici que, bien que le traité de 1909 (art. 4, par. 2) interdise de façon expresse la contamination des eaux limitrophes et de celles qui 'coupent la frontière,' la Commission Mixte n'avait pas pour autant juridiction sur la matière. Ce n'est d'ailleurs que par le truchement d'une disposition plus générale du traité, celle de l'article 9,[34] que les deux gouvernements parvinrent à saisir celle-ci de cette importante question. Dans son rapport déposé en 1950, cet organisme recommandait bon nombre de mesures, entérinées par la suite par les deux gouvernements, destinées à réduire la pollution de ces eaux, dont la création d'une commission de régie (ou conseil consultatif) qui soumet un rapport sur la question à la commission deux fois par année.

En 1964, devant l'urgence du problème, les deux gouvernements revenaient à la charge et confiaient à la commission un nouveau mandat, celui de faire des recherches sur le degré de pollution des lacs Erié et Ontario ainsi que la section internationale du St-Laurent et de formuler, en tenant compte de tous les aspects du problème, des recommandations sur les mesures susceptibles de remédier à cette situation. Cette étude minutieuse dont la commission a chargé deux conseils consultatifs interriverains – l'un pour le lac Erié et l'autre pour le lac Ontario et le St-Laurent – devait s'échelonner de 1964 à 1970. Le rapport final qui a été déposé en janvier 1971 conclut que les eaux des lacs Erié et Ontario sont gravement polluées, en particulier par les déchets industriels et ceux déversés par les municipalités riveraines. Il recommande notamment; a / que les deux gouvernements concluent des accords pour l'exécution, dans des délais déterminés, des programmes de répression de la pollution qu'elle préconise; b / que la commission soit dotée des moyens nécessaires pour surveiller et contrôler la qualité de l'eau et réaliser de façon efficace les programmes en question; c / enfin que le mandat de 1964 soit reconduit, afin que la commission puisse poursuivre son enquête sur la pollution dans le reste des eaux du bassin des Grands Lacs, y compris leurs tributaires.

Enfin, à l'occasion de la visite du Président Nixon au Canada, du 13 au 15 avril 1972, un important accord sur la régénération des Grands Lacs a été signé, lequel faisait suite aux recommandations de la commission mixte internationale. Cet instrument établit un ensemble d'objectifs communs portant sur la qualité des eaux des Grands Lacs et engage les deux pays à mettre sur pied, d'ici 1975, des programmes[35] en vue de la réalisation de ces objectifs.

Dans ce cadre, le Canada a, d'une part, accepté de mener à bon terme dès 1975 un programme accéléré de l'ordre de $250 millions pour la construction d'installations de traitement des eaux d'égout municipales dans la région des Grands Lacs d'aval. On s'attend à ce que de leur côté, les Etats-Unis consacrent aux mêmes fins, d'ici le milieu de 1974, deux milliards de dollars. L'accord stipule de plus que les deux pays devront prendre des mesures pour préserver la qualité de l'eau là où elle n'est pas polluée. Cette disposition vise plus particulièrement les Lacs Supérieur et Huron où, en général, la qualité de l'eau est supérieure aux normes prescrites dans les objectifs. Une autre stipulation de l'accord est que chaque pays, indépendamment de la densité de sa population, continuera à jouir des mêmes droits et à respecter les mêmes obligations que ceux établis en vertu du traité des eaux limitrophes de 1909 ainsi que du droit international en vigueur.

De son côté, la commission mixte se voit attribuer les pouvoirs nécessaires pour analyser l'application des programmes de chaque pays et contrôler les résultats dans les lacs. En somme, il s'agit ici d'un instrument dynamique spécialement conçu de façon à incorporer au fur et à mesure le fruit des nouvelles découvertes scientifiques et technologiques dans le secteur de la pollution des eaux.[35]

CONCLUSION

Il est certain que, depuis le Traité de Paris de 1783, tout le droit international relatif aux Grands Lacs a sensiblement évolué: ses formules dans plusieurs domaines se sont graduellement élargies et précisées dans un sens à la fois progressif et libéral. Toutefois, nous sommes encore loin de la cohérence et de l'homogénéité qu'on pourrait souhaiter et toute cette matière demeure encore, dans une large mesure, informe et difficile à classifier.

On a noté plus haut, en traitant de la frontière, le manque d'uniformité dans les critères de démarcation. Cette anomalie, n'eut été le palliatif fourni par le Traité de 1842, aurait pu affecter sérieusement la liberté de navigation des riverains sur l'ensemble des lacs. De son côté, l'épineuse question de juridiction, enchevêtrée qu'elle était au début du siècle dans des considérations relevant du droit maritime international, s'est graduellement résorbée, tant et si bien que la compétence de chaque riverain est aujourd'hui aussi exclusive et absolue de son propre côté de la frontière sur les Grands Lacs que sur le reste de son territoire.

La situation, en ce qui a trait à la liberté de navigation commerciale des riverains, a, comme on l'a vu, évolué progressivement depuis deux siècles jusqu'à englober de plus en plus de pays tiers et présenter aujourd'hui à peu près tous les avantages d'un régime d'internationalisation, sans les inconvénients inhérents à ce régime sur le plan de la souveraineté territoriale. Celle concernant la navigation de guerre correspond à un régime mitigé de démilitarisation, ou plus précisément à une limitation des armements. Elle s'est considérablement assouplie au cours des années, en particulier à l'occasion des deux dernières grandes guerres et semblerait correspondre maintenant assez bien aux besoins de l'époque.

Quant au droit de pêche, on n'est malheureusement pas encore parvenu à s'entendre pour le réglementer en commun. La seule entente – de portée fort limitée – à laquelle ont pu en arriver les riverains se situe dans le domaine de la conservation de la faune et a trait au contrôle de la lamproie parasite. Nous sommes encore très éloignés de l'idée de communauté de pêche bien connue en Europe et préconisée, dans le domaine de l'énergie motrice, par le traité des eaux limitrophes de 1909.

Au domaine, enfin, de l'utilisation des eaux et du lit, les formules mises à l'avant sont nettement progressives et en général satisfaisantes, encore que certaines lacunes importantes[36] subsistent et qu'on ait peut-être trop tendance à éviter la vraie difficulté – celle de la déficience des structures juridiques – en s'en référant pour un nombre de plus en plus considérable de solutions à la commission conjointe formée aux termes du traité de 1909. Cet excellent organisme, soucieux avant tout d'efficacité, a joué – et c'est indéniable – depuis sa création, un rôle primordial dans le fonctionnement harmonieux des relations inter-riveraines. On peut toutefois regretter que ses décisions n'aient pas davantage fait la part du juridique et contribué à clarifier de façon plus systématique et à ordonner le contenu de l'instrument large et souple dont il est issu.

L'ensemble de cette matière, marquée au sceau de la transaction et du compromis, où filtre sans cesse, à la façon d'un postulat et d'un impératif, l'idée d'amitié indissoluble entre les riverains, mériterait à notre avis, d'être abordée de façon moins empirique et plus systématique. Loin de nous l'idée, à brève échéance du moins, d'une refonte globale de tout le droit conventionnel des Grands Lacs, d'une sorte de Charte des Grands Lacs. Ne pourrait-on pas toutefois s'écarter un peu des sentiers traditionnels et songer à réviser le traité de 1909? Ce serait, par exemple, l'occasion de faire la mise au point du mécanisme déficient de règlement des conflits et de régler l'épineux problème des affluents supérieurs des eaux limitrophes, lequel demeure sans solution depuis les deux tentatives infructueuses de 1932 et 1941. On pourrait, par la suite, élargir graduellement le cadre de l'instrument révisé pour y réglementer la police des infractions, la navigation, la pêche, le sauvetage et même les armements, faisant ainsi disparaître petit à petit l'indétermination gênante qui s'attache toujours à de trop nombreux chapitres de cette importante matière.

LES NOTES

1 J.M. Callahan, *The Neutrality of American Lakes and Anglo-American Relations* (1898) 10–27.

2 Lapradelle et Politis, *Receuil des arbitrages internationaux* (1905) t I, 311, et Moore, *International Arbitrations* (1906), t I, c v–vi, et t VI, carte.

3 IE, 'le chemin variable que prennent les bâteaux quand ils descendent un fleuve ou plutôt le milieu de ce chemin.' Kluber, *Droit des Gens*, 133. Voir également à ce sujet, Lapradelle, *La Frontière: Etude de droit international* (1928) 203; Westlake, *International Law* (1904–7), t I, 141 et note 1.

4 *Lake Front* case, 146 U.S. 387.

5 Limitée seulement par les principes du droit des gens et, en matière criminelle, par les conventions particulières entre les deux pays concernant l'extradition.

6 *Lake Front* case, *supra* note 4.

7 7 Mich. 160.

8 150 U.S. 249 (14 S. Ct. 109, 37 L. Ed. 1071). Voir à ce sujet, Mackenzie and Laing, *Canada and the Law of Nations,* a selection of cases in international law affecting Canada and Canadians, decided by Canadian Courts, by certain of the higher courts in the United States and Great Britain and by international tribunals (1938) 73 ss.

9 *Rex* v *The Ship North* (1905), 2 Ex. C.R. 141. Voir également à ce sujet, R. St J. Macdonald, 'Public International Law Problems arising in Canadian Courts' (1956), 11 *U. Toronto L.J.*

10 *Rex* v *The Ship North* (1905), 2 O.L.R. 366. Dans l'affaire *Rex* v *The Kitty D,* jugée par la Cour d'Amirauté de Toronto, (1905) 2 O.W.R. 1065, le juge amiral Hodgins précise

que 'on landlocked lakes surrounded by several States, the same principles as regulate the application of territorial law on dry land must rule, in so far as there are distinct boundary lines recognized.'

11 C. Bédard, *Le Régime juridique des Grands Lacs de l'Amérique du Nord et du Saint-Laurent* (1966) 19–22; D.C. Piper, *The International Law of the Great Lakes: A Study of Canadian-United States Co-operation* (1967) 21 ss; H.E. Hunt, 'How the Great Lakes became High Seas and their Status Viewed from the Standpoint of International Law' (1910), *Am. J. Int'l L.* 308.

12 Hackworth, *Digest* (1944), t I, 380–3.

13 Moore, *Digest* (1906), t I, 675 note 138; Hershey, *Essentials of International Public Law and Organization* (1927) 306 ss.

14 Pitt Cobbett, *Leading Cases in International Law* (1922), t I, 119–27.

15 Hershey, *supra* note 13; Moore, *supra* note 13; Fauchille, *Le Droit International Public,* t I, 420.

16 Bédard, *supra* note 11, 34–5.

17 Lettre en date du 18 juillet 1878 adressée par F.W. Seward, agissant comme secrétaire d'état des Etats-Unis, à Sir Edward Thornton, représentant diplomatique britannique à Washington.

18 Edgar McInnis, *Canada: A Political and Social History* (1947) 197 ss.

19 Callahan, *supra* note 1, à 10–27.

20 McInnis, *supra* note 18.

21 Callahan, *supra* note 1; Moore, *supra* note 13, à t I, 696.

22 Moore, *supra* note 13, à 698.

23 Echange de notes (9 juin 1939; 30 octobre 1940; 2 novembre 1940) concernant l'application et l'interprétation d'une convention (1817) au sujet des forces navales qui seront maintenues sur les Grands Lacs.

24 Callahan, *supra* note 1, à 10–27.

25 *Rex* v *The Ship Grace* (1894), 4 Ex. C.R. 283.

26 Bar, *International Law* (1910) 1067; Hall, *International Law* (1924) 104: 'The territorial property of a State consists in the territory occupied by the state community and subject to its sovereignty; and it comprises the whole area, whether of land or water, included within the definite boundaries as ascertained by occupation, prescription, or treaty.'

27 *Supra* note 8.

28 Soit, aux termes mêmes du préambule: 'Prévenir tous différends relativement à l'usage des eaux limitrophes et pour régler toutes les questions qui sont actuellement pendantes

entre les Etats-Unis et le Dominion du Canada impliquant les droits, obligations, ou intérêts de l'un ou l'autre pays relativement à son voisin et à ceux des habitants des deux pays le long de la frontière commune et dans le but de pouvoir à l'ajustment et au règlement de toutes questions qui pourraient survenir dans l'avenir.'

29 Article 2: 'et qui, en suivant leurs cours naturel, couleraient au-delà de la frontière ou se déverseraient dans les eaux limitrophes.'

30 Voir H.A. Smith, 'The Chicago Diversion' (1929), *B.Y.B.* 144–57; Sauser-Hall, 'L'utilisation industrielle des fleuves internationaux' (1953), 83 *Rec. des cours de l'Académie de droit international de La Haye* 512–17; Simsarian, 'The Diversion of Waters Affecting the United States and Canada' (1938), 32 *Am J. Int'l L.* 488.

31 *Stollmayer* v *Trinidad Petroleum Co.,* 1918 A.C. 485; *Kansas* v *Colorado,* 185 U.S. 125.

32 *Wisconsin* v *Illinois and Sanitary District of Chicago,* 281 U.S. 696; C.P. Wright, *The Saint Lawrence Deep Waterway: A Canadian Appraisal* (1935) 418–25.

33 1 Traité entre le Canada et les Etats-Unis d'Amérique relatif à l'utilisation des eaux du Niagara. Signé à Washington le 27 février 1950, [1950] R.T.C. 3.

2 Traité entre la Grande-Bretagne et les Etats-Unis d'Amérique relatif aux eaux limitrophes et aux questions se posant le long de la frontière entre le Canada et les Etats-Unis. Signé à Washington le 11 janvier 1909, [1927] C.U.S. 312.

3 Echange de notes entre le Canada et les Etats-Unis d'Amérique concernant la construction de la voie maritime du Saint-Laurent. Signé à Washington le 30 juin 1952 et le 11 janvier 1952, [1952] R.T.C. 30.

4 Echange de notes entre le Canada et les Etats-Unis d'Amérique portant modification de l'echange de notes du 30 juin 1952 concernant la construction de la voie maritime du Saint-Laurent. Signé à Ottawa le 17 août 1954, [1954] R.T.C. 14.

5 Echange de notes entre le Canada et les Etats-Unis d'Amérique relatif au bassin des Grands Lacs et du Saint-Laurent (Niagara, travaux de Long Lac Ogoki-Bassin de la rivière d'Albany). Signé à Washington les 14 et 31 octobre et le 7 novembre 1940, [1940] R.T.C. 11.

34 En vertu duquel la commission est dotée de vastes pouvoirs d'enquête (et peut faire des recommandations) concernant toute ques-

tion ou tout différend 'impliquant des droits ou obligations' le long de la frontière commune.

35 Pour de plus amples renseignements concernant ces programmes, voir (1972), 27 *Bulletin hebdomadaire canadien,* ainsi que le texte lui-même de l'accord.

36 On songe, par exemple, ici aux problèmes de la dérivation de Chicago qui s'est avérée impossible à résoudre dans le cadre du droit conventionnel en vigueur, à celui de la dérivation de Long Lac Ogoki et, en général, à tous ceux que peut soulever l'utilisation des affluents des Grands Lacs. On songe enfin au côté trop précaire du mécanisme de règlement des conflits mis en place par le traité de 1909 (art. 9) et qui, en définitive, repose sur la seule bonne volonté des parties.

F.J.E. JORDAN*

22/The International Joint Commission and Canada-United States Boundary Relations

NATURE OF CANADA-UNITED STATES RELATIONS

The extent and complex nature of relations between Canada and the United States are well-known; indeed, the unique relationship is the substance of nearly every communiqué issued by the leaders of the two nations following meetings between them. The extent and character of this mutual involvement of the countries was examined at length by two senior diplomats from Ottawa and Washington in 1964–5, and it was their conclusion that the two governments should foster the well-developed practice of establishing and utilizing special joint machinery to deal with particular areas of interaction between Canada and the United States, in addition to relying upon the usual diplomatic channels of intercourse.[1] Only in this way could the vast range of mutual interests and problems be most effectively considered and resolved.

As the facets of interaction between the two countries have multiplied in number and complexity, Washington and Ottawa have increasingly turned to the establishment of permanent joint agencies that can deal directly and expertly with particular areas of mutual concern on a continuing basis, building a degree of familiarity with the subject matter in question that would be difficult, if not impossible, to achieve at the general diplomatic level. This is not to suggest that such specialized agencies supplant the regular channels of diplomacy; rather they are supplemental and in many cases provide preparatory services for traditional negotiations and consultations.

The purpose of this chapter is twofold. First, to describe briefly a number of the more siginificant joint agencies that Canada and the United States have created in order to provide an appreciation of the kinds of interaction with which they deal. Second, to examine in depth the functioning of the oldest of these bodies, the International Joint Commission, to understand how such an agency may facilitate resolution of common problems along the international boundary according to rules established in advance by the two countries or evolved *ad hoc* by the commission itself.

JOINT CANADA-UNITED STATES AGENCIES

The most informal of Canada-United States joint bodies, the Interparliamentary Group, was formed in 1958 by concurrent resolutions of Congress and parliament

*This chapter was prepared for publication before I joined the Department of Justice, and the views expressed herein are solely mine.

to facilitate an interchange of ideas and views on a broad range of interests at the legislative level between the two countries. The group is composed of twenty-four legislators from each country and it meets once a year in plenary and committee sessions. The discussions are conducted in closed session and negotiations, agreements, formal actions, or resolutions do not occur. However, each section of the group does issue a report to its respective legislative bodies. Matters discussed by the group are wide-ranging, covering most issues of common concern that are of current interest to the legislative bodies, ranging from balance of payments to resources development and in each discussion the object is 'to exchange information and to promote better understanding of our common interests and accomplishments, as well as our differences and difficulties.'[2]

There are two agencies that operate on a continuing basis at the ministerial level, one dealing with economic matters and one with defence problems. The Joint Committee on Trade and Economic Matters was formally established in 1953 by an exchange of notes to consider matters affecting harmonious economic relations, to exchange information and views on matters that might adversely affect trade between the countries, and to report to the governments on the discussions with a view to improving economic and trade relations.[3] This joint committee, which meets at least once a year, is composed of the cabinet officers of each country who are responsible for matters of finance, trade and commerce, agriculture, fisheries, and such other cabinet officers as may be designated from time to time. Each delegation is headed by the foreign affairs minister and the committee meets alternately in Washington and Ottawa. The committee meets not to negotiate and conclude agreements but 'to help avoid future disagreements, and to smooth the way for more formal negotiations,' and the range of matters discussed is broad. For example, in 1970, the ministers discussed the economic and financial positions of the two countries, enlargement of the European Community, the GATT negotiations, foreign aid policies, East-West trade, Great Lakes pollution, continental energy issues, and the automotive trade agreement.[4]

In 1958 the two governments by an exchange of notes formally constituted the Committee on Joint Defence to consult periodically on any matters affecting joint defence of the two countries, to exchange information and views on problems with a view to strengthening close and intimate co-operation on joint defence matters, and to report to the governments on measures that may be appropriate or necessary to improve defence co-operation.[5] The notes pointed out that with the agreement to undertake a plan for integrated, continental air defence, it was essential to supplement existing channels of consultation and ensure periodic review at the ministerial level of the military, political, and economic aspects of joint defence problems. The committee, composed of cabinet officers responsible for foreign affairs, national defence, and finance from each country, is required to meet once a year or more often, alternately in Washington and Ottawa.[6]

Besides the cabinet-level Committee on Joint Defence, Canada and the United States have two lower-level joint agencies that concern themselves with North American defence matters. The first, the Permanent Joint Board on Defence, was initially created by President Roosevelt and Prime Minister Mackenzie King under the Ogdensburg Agreement of 1940 as a wartime body, directed to study and advise on military problems relating to the defence of North America. It is composed of four or five members from each country, mainly from the military services.[7] Each national section is composed of a civilian chairman, representatives from the branches of the armed forces, a representative from the foreign affairs office and sometimes representatives from other related departments. The board makes joint recommendations to the governments after reaching unanimous agreement on defence policy planning issues. In recent years the board's role has been 'helping to mesh military requirements with political, economic and other considerations in order to facilitate the implementation of continental defences programmes.'[8]

In 1957 Canada and the United States announced a plan to integrate their North American air defence systems, and the next year an agreement was concluded to establish the North American Air Defence Command (NORAD), a body composed of senior officers of the Canadian and American air forces, headquartered in Colorado Springs.[9] The purpose of the joint military agency is to replace co-ordinated air defence plans with a single integrated operation whereby common plans for North American air defence determined by the governments can be executed by the NORAD commanders acting in unison. The agreement establishing this second military joint agency was extended in 1968 for a period of five years.[10]

There are three bilateral joint agencies that concern themselves with fishing matters common to the two countries. Two administer fisheries on the Pacific coast, the other deals with fishery problems in the Great Lakes.

The Pacific Halibut Fisheries Commission, established in 1953, is charged with the task of preserving halibut fisheries in the northern Pacific Ocean and the Bering Sea.[11] It consists of six members, three appointed by each government, and its decisions require a majority of four, two affirmative votes from each section. The agency has two primary tasks. The first is to conduct studies designed to illuminate the life cycle of halibut in the convention waters and to publish information thereon. Second, to ensure a maximum sustained yield from the fishery, the commission is empowered, with the concurrence of the governments, to limit the catches that may be taken from the fishery.

The structure of the International Pacific Salmon Fisheries Commission, established in 1937, is similar to the Halibut Commission and takes its decisions by the same majority. Its task is to preserve the sockeye and pink salmon fisheries on the Pacific coast and in the Fraser River.[12] Under article III of its convention, the commission is charged with investigating the life cycle of the salmon and reporting thereon. It is empowered to improve spawning grounds, to develop and operate hatcheries, to stock convention waters, and to recommend to the governments the means to improve migration routes of the fish. Under articles IV and V, the agency can make regulations limiting or prohibiting the taking of salmon in any convention waters and may prescribe the size of fishing nets. However, under the 1957 Protocol, all regulations adopted by the commission must be approved by the governments, save those dealing with the establishment of the fishing season dates.

The Great Lakes Fishery Commission was set up in 1955 by the two governments in recognition of the need for joint and co-ordinated efforts of the two countries to preserve the declining fisheries of the Great Lakes.[13] This commission is composed of two national sections, each section having a maximum of four members appointed by its government. Each section has one vote and the commission's decisions and recommendations must have the approval of both. The agency must meet once a year at least. Under article IV of the convention establishing this commission, it is empowered to formulate and to carry out or co-ordinate research programs designed to determine the measures necessary to ensure a maximum sustained production of fish stocks of common concern to both countries. It is further authorized to recommend to the governments measures designed to preserve the fisheries and to carry out a comprehensive program of sea lamprey eradication in the Lakes. To carry out its functions the commission is authorized to hold public hearings and to co-operate with interested public and private organizations. Its jurisdiction covers all of the Great Lakes and the international section of the St Lawrence River. Since its inception the commission has been concerned with the lamprey eradication program, fisheries restocking programs, and pollution abatement.

Two joint agencies deal specifically with problems along the international boundary between Canada and the United States: the International Boundary Commission, and the International Joint Commission. In 1908 the two countries agreed that each would appoint an expert geographer or surveyor for purposes of completing the task of establishing. marking, and mapping the international boundary between the two countries.[14] By article IX of the treaty, the commissioners were authorized to proceed with their duties and, where they failed to agree, they were to make separate reports to their respective governments. Under a subsequent treaty in 1925 the commissioners appointed under the 1908 treaty were constituted as a permanent body to maintain an effective boundary between the two countries, inspecting the boundary, repairing markers, keeping the boundary vistas open, and determining any particular points along the boundary from time to time.[15]

INTERNATIONAL JOINT COMMISSION

Of all the joint agencies that have been established to deal with particular classes of problems arising in relations between Canada and the United States, none has a broader mandate, greater independence, or a longer and more impressive record of accomplishment than the International Joint Commission. Its tasks of seeking an accommodation of common interests or a resolution of common problems along the international boundary have involved the IJC in a variety of cases ranging from the relatively simple to the exceedingly complex. While it has encountered failure or deadlock in a few instances, in the vast majority of cases the IJC has resolved the issues satisfactorily or has provided the governments with the necessary guidance by which to reach a mutually beneficial agreement.

The International Joint Commission was created in 1909 by Canada and the United States as a permanent joint body to perform a number of functions under the Boundary Waters Treaty, an agreement that was concluded 'to prevent disputes regarding the use of boundary waters and to settle all questions which are now pending between the United States and the Dominion of Canada involving the rights, obligations or interests of either in relation to the other or to the inhabitants of the other, along their common frontier, and to make provision for the adjustment and settlement of all such questions as may hereafter arise.'[16] Composed of six members, three appointed by the president of the United States and three appointed by the Canadian governor in council, the commission is vested first with a *specific* jurisdiction to rule upon all proposals for the use, obstruction, or diversion of boundary and transboundary waters where the use on one side of the boundary would affect the level of the waters on the other side in the case of boundary waters (article III), and where the level of the waters would be raised in the upstream country by construction downstream in the case of rivers crossing the boundary (article IV). In each of these cases, in the absence of a special agreement between Canada and the United States, an application for approval of the project must be made to the IJC before any work may be undertaken.[17]

In considering applications for approval of projects falling under articles III and IV of the treaty (such applications may come either from individuals or from governments, but must in every case be transmitted to the IJC by the appropriate national government), the commission is required to observe and apply a number of legal principles set out in article VIII. In cases involving the use of boundary waters, the IJC must ensure that to each country is preserved, on its own side of the boundary, equal and similar rights in the use of the waters.[18] The commission is further directed in cases dealing with boundary waters to observe a precedence of uses that gives domestic and sanitary needs first priority, navigation uses second priority, and power and irrigation uses lowest priority.[19] In cases of material conflict between uses, the order of precedence must be enforced. Existing uses in boundary waters, however, are not to be disturbed.[20] Finally, the IJC is empowered in all cases to make its approval of an application conditional on suitable and adequate provisions being made to protect and to indemnify all interests in either side of the boundary adversely affected by the project.[21] In cases where the natural elevation of the water is to be raised by the project, the commission must impose such conditions.[22] When the IJC renders a decision on an application under articles III or IV, it acts by a simple majority vote. Where the commissioners are evenly divided on a case, each section of the commission is directed to make a report on the matter to its respective government.[23]

Beyond the specific jurisdiction conferred on the IJC to decide applications for projects on boundary and transboundary waters, the commission is vested with a general jurisdiction, on the initiative of either national government in each instance, to examine and to report with recommendations to the two governments on 'any other questions or matters of difference arising ... along the common frontier' that may be so referred to it.[24] On reference cases arising under article IX of the treaty, the commission reports to the governments by simple majority agreement, and in the event of an equal division of opinion, the commissioners on each side file separate reports with their respective governments. Reports by the IJC under an article IX reference are not considered to be decisions on questions of fact or law and the governments are not bound to accept or to act upon the recommendations made therein by the IJC.

In conducting studies under references sent to it by the governments, the commission is not governed by any specific legal rules except as these may be formulated in the particular terms of reference. There are, however, two rules in the treaty that do guide the commission in studies involving the uses of boundary and transboundary waters. Article I of the treaty provides that all navigable boundary waters are to continue free and open for navigation by both countries equally for all time. Article II preserves to each country the right, subject to possible legal claims by the injured parties in the other country, to use and to divert all waters on its own side of the boundary which in their natural course would flow across the boundary or into boundary waters.

Although the IJC is divided into Canadian and United States sections for administrative purposes and the sections are geographically separated, in carrying out the treaty functions the commission operates only as a single agency with joint chairmen elected by each section. The commissioners are drawn from a variety of backgrounds, but many have tended to be lawyers, a number are engineers, and frequently the commissioners are men experienced in political life. To carry out its functions relating to applications under articles III and IV and to conduct studies for the governments under article IX, the IJC is empowered to employ support personnel, to conduct open hearings where all interested parties may appear, to take evidence under oath, and to adopt procedures consistent with 'justice and equity.'[25]

When the IJC entertains an application it normally holds one or more hearings at which the applicant and all other interested parties present briefs supporting or opposing the project. The commission then takes the matter under advisement in executive session and, if it grants approval of the application, the commission frequently constitutes a subordinate international technical board (called a Board of Control) to exercise, on the IJC's behalf, continuing supervision over the implementation and operation of the project, according to the terms and conditions stipulated by the commission in its order of approval.[26]

The procedure of the IJC is rather different when it is dealing with a reference from the governments where it is usually requested to evaluate a potential project and to formulate a set of project plans for consideration by the governments. The initial engineering, scientific, and economic studies required are conducted by one or more joint boards of experts composed of personnel seconded from the public services of both countries to the commission. Once the studies are completed they are released to the public after which the IJC proceeds to hold an extensive series of public hearings in or near the vicinity of the area under study. The commission next proceeds to evaluate all of the data, information, and opinions thus assembled and to submit a report of its conclusions and recommendations to the two governments. If the governments agree to adopt some of all of the commission's proposals, they frequently request the IJC to exercise, through the aegis of an international joint board created by the commission, continuing surveillance over the implementation of the program approved by the governments.[27]

Since beginning its functions in 1912, the International Joint Commission has handled some one hundred cases, all of which, with the exception of four (three dealing with air pollution along the boundary, and one concerned with the problems of Point Roberts' residents), have been concerned with one or more present or proposed uses of waters along the international boundary by governments or by individuals. Sixty per cent of the cases have been applications under articles III and IV of the treaty and 40 per cent of the cases have been by way of reference under article IX. In the earlier years the bulk of the cases were applications for approval of projects. For example, of the first fifty cases (1912–42), thirty-nine were applications. More recently, however, the emphasis has been on reference cases from the two governments, with less than one-third of the last thirty cases (1952–72) being applications. The cases before the IJC tend to divide, with some exceptions, into two broad categories: those involving a proposal for a single-use development on a body of water, such as a power dam or flood control structures, and those that involve a consideration of multiple-use planning and development of a water basin.

The application cases have generally been of the first category, for example, a request for permission to construct a dam, to place log booms in a river, to dredge a navigation channel, or to reclaim submerged lands. In such cases, the commission's concern is not with determining the 'best' use to which the particular water should be put or with considering the overall development of the water resources. Rather, its attention is directed only to the proposed use and how it might adversely affect other uses of the water in that vicinity, according to the rules laid down in article VIII of the treaty. On the other hand, many, though not all, of the reference cases from the two governments have involved, either implicitly or explicitly by the terms of reference, a consideration of the multiple uses to which a water basin along the boundary may be put, thus involving the IJC in an attempt to devise a plan of development or control which provides for the optimum beneficial uses of the water resources of the basin from the international point of view. The reference cases consequently have been much more complex and extensive than the application cases and have obliged the commission to evolve principles for co-operative development of water resources without any guiding rules in the treaty.

Selected cases

To demonstrate the scope of the International Joint Commission's functions in handling the different types of cases that come before it, a selected number of cases are considered below. The first group includes cases where the commission has been concerned with a single-use development of water resources. The second group involves the multiple-use water resources planning cases. Finally, the cases concerning boundary air pollution and the peculiar case of Point Roberts are mentioned briefly.

Single-purpose projects
Hydroelectric power Despite the low priority assigned to hydroelectric power development by article VIII of the Boundary Waters Treaty, nearly forty of the cases to come before the IJC have been concerned primarily with this water use. The cases have arisen at all points along the boundary, save the prairies, and have ranged in magnitude from a dam for a small grist mill to the massive development of the international St Lawrence River. In dealing with water power cases, the commission has been concerned primarily with ensuring that the proposed power development does not interfere unduly with higher priority uses and with protecting affected riparian rights. In some cases, however, the IJC has been involved in a broader-based planning role.

Columbia-Kootenay power development The transboundary Columbia-Kootenay River system was ultimately considered for multiple-use development in 1959, but prior to this time the IJC entertained a number of applications for approval of individual projects for power development on both rivers. In these cases the major concern of the commission was to protect affected riparian interests.

The first application in 1929 was a request by West Kootenay Power and Light Company of Trail, BC, for approval of a power dam on the Kootenay River in BC, the effect of which would be to raise the river level upstream in BC and Idaho. Initially, Idaho opposed the application on grounds that reclaimed farm lands in the state would be flooded by the project, and in 1934 the application was withdrawn.[28] Later, when it became apparent that the upstream interests might receive some benefits from stabilized water levels, Idaho farmers withdrew the outright opposition, and in 1938 the power company renewed its application. After hearings, the commission issued an order of approval, subject to several conditions imposed under article VIII of the treaty. The applicant was ordered to enlarge the outlet capacity of Kootenay Lake and to pay to the state of Idaho compensation of up to $3000 per year for any remedial measures required upstream to protect farmlands. The applicant was also required to carry out its power and storage works in a manner which minimized the risk of upstream flooding, under the direction of the International Kootenay Lake Board of Control established by the IJC.[29] Since 1941 the power company has made several supplementary applications for approval to store additional waters above the dam. In each case the commission has granted interim approval, conditional on the applicant compensating adversely affected upstream landowners in Idaho and BC.[30] Claims for compensation were to be heard and determined by the Board of Control.

In 1940 the United States government requested approval of the IJC to operate the Grand Coulee Dam on the Columbia River in Washington state in a manner that might at certain times increase the levels of the river upstream in BC. The commission was unable to ascertain in advance what the upstream effects might be so it granted the approval in 1941 and appointed the International Columbia River Board of Control to determine the adverse effects, if any, when the dam was producing power and to advise the commission so that it might prescribe the appropriate protective measures. The commission's order of approval also provided that the future power development interests on the tributaries of the Columbia River in BC must be protected, and the commission retained jurisdiction to make future indemnification orders in this respect.[31]

Such a future power development materialized in 1951 when Cominco Ltd (then Consolidated Mining and Smelting Company) of Trail, BC, applied to the IJC for approval of a power dam on the Pend d'Oreille River, a Columbia tributary flowing from Washington into BC. The dam would flood several acres of land in Washington. After hearings, the commission issued an order of approval which expressly reserved to the United States all rights under article II of the Boundary Waters Treaty to use and divert any of the waters before they flowed into Canada. The commission's order incorporated the provisions for compensation which had been made by Cominco and provided that any upstream interests further affected by the project when it was in operation could apply to the commission for relief.[32]

St Lawrence power development   The IJC's involvement with water power development on the international section of the St Lawrence River related to concern both for affected riparian interests and for navigation uses of the waterway. In 1920 the two governments requested the IJC to undertake a major study and to advise them on the best plan of development of the St Lawrence River for navigation and power uses. The commission carried out major engineering and economic studies and held extensive hearings in both countries. In 1922 the commission reported that full development of the waterway was desirable and recommended plans for joint and integrated navigation and power projects.[33]

Opposition in the United States Congress to development of the proposed St Lawrence Seaway delayed the project until 1952, when Canada announced plans to proceed independently with construction of the seaway. Canada and the United States then concluded arrangements for joint development of power resources of the St Lawrence.[34] Under this 1952 agreement, the governments of Canada and the United States filed joint applications with the IJC, detailing their proposals for constructing adjoining dams across the international rapids of the St Lawrence and for operating power generation facilities at the site. After studying the plans submitted and holding public hearings, the commission in October 1952 approved the applications, subject to stringent conditions. The agencies designated by the governments to construct and operate the facilities must provide adequate indemnification and protection in all cases of injury arising from construction and operation of the works. The works must be located and operated so as not to conflict with or restrain uses of the waters given a preference under article VIII of the treaty. The agencies must operate the works in such a manner as to safeguard the rights and lawful interests of present and future developers of water power downstream and so far as possible the rights of riparian interests upstream that could be affected by changes in water levels. Finally, the works must be constructed and operated under the supervision of the International St Lawrence River Board of Control, a body created by the IJC and charged with ensuring compliance with the provisions of the order of approval relating to water levels and flow regulation.[35]

Passamaquoddy power development A unique proposal for boundary waters power development came before the IJC in 1956 when the governments of Canada and the United States requested the commission to evaluate the economic feasibility of co-operative development of the tidal power potential at Passamaquoddy Bay in the Bay of Fundy. The governments wished to ascertain the cost of such a project, the impact of the project on the local and national economies, and the effect that the project would have on fisheries in the region.[36]

The IJC established an Engineering Board and a Fisheries Board and after their studies were completed it held public hearings. The commission reported in 1961 that development of the power potential was not economically feasible when compared with the cost of obtaining power from alternate sources. The commission also concluded that the project would have no long-run benefits for the economies of the region. On the basis of these findings, the IJC recommended that the project not be undertaken until such time as other less costly sources of power had been utilized.[37] This recommendation was accepted by the two national governments.

Navigation
The IJC has handled nine cases wherein navigation has been the primary concern and all of the cases have arisen in the Rainy River and Great Lakes-St Lawrence regions of the boundary. In substance, the cases range from those where the commission sought to protect navigation interests from undue encroachment by other uses to those involving the planning of the optimum development of boundary

waterways for navigation purposes.

Rainy River booms   Two early applications before the IJC in 1912 and 1916 sought approval to locate, in the boundary Rainy River, log booms in which to store and sort logs for milling operations. In both cases the issue of protecting existing and future navigation on the river was raised and in each order of approval the commission stipulated modifications of the plans proposed to ensure that the booms would pose no obstruction to navigation on the waterway.[38] In the 1916 case, the commission retained jurisdiction to order subsequently the shifting of the booms to accommodate navigation activities on the Canadian side of the river.[39]

Champlain Waterway   The IJC has conducted two major feasibility studies of developing a deep navigation waterway from the St Lawrence River to New York City via the Richelieu River, Lake Champlain, and the Hudson River, in addition to having considered the question in the context of the 1920–2 study of the St Lawrence waterway. In 1936, under the first reference from the governments, the commission concluded that, while development of the waterway was practicable from an engineering viewpoint, its economic viability could not be evaluated meaningfully until the St Lawrence Seaway was constructed and operating. Thus the commission recommended that further consideration of the project be deferred for evaluation at a later date.[40] After the St Lawrence Seaway was operating, the two governments in 1962 requested the commission to re-examine the Champlain waterway proposal, considering the economic value of the development to both countries, bearing in mind the potential benefits of such development to conservation, recreation, and other uses. The commission established the International Champlain Waterway Board to conduct engineering and economic studies and itself conducted numerous public hearings to gather views on the proposed project.

On the basis of the information obtained, the commission concluded in 1967 that there was no strong evidence that an improved commercial waterway would contribute measurably to the economy of either country. It was further of the opinion that additional commercial development would adversely affect the ecology of the waterway. In consequence, the IJC recommended that the governments take no steps to improve the waterway for commercial navigation purposes and that they adopt common policies designed to preserve and enhance the natural environment for recreation uses. The commission further proposed that it be requested by the governments to carry out a joint study of the waterway for the purpose of advising the governments on joint measures to achieve the objective.[41] The governments have not acted on this latter recommendation.

Fisheries

The one application that has come before the IJC concerning the protection of fisheries is interesting if only because no mention of this use of boundary waters is made in the list of priority uses found in article VIII of the treaty. In 1923 the state of Maine sought permission from the IJC to require two power dam operators on the St Croix River, a boundary water, to reconstruct and maintain fish ladders on their dams to enable the passage upstream of migratory fish. The power dam operators objected to the application on the ground that the expenditures involved outweighed the value of the fish seeking passage upstream. The commission, satisfied that the proposed structures would not materially affect the levels of the boundary waters, rejected the contentions of the objectors and issued an order of approval in 1924.[42]

Irrigation

Not surprisingly, all irrigation cases before the IJC have come from the prairies and have involved disputes between farmers on opposite sides of the boundary over the division of the scarce water supplies for irrigation purposes. The task of the IJC in these cases is to devise an equitable allocation of the waters. The Sage Creek reference is illustrative of the problems.

In 1946 the governments asked the IJC to investigate complaints by farmers in Montana that they were being deprived by Alberta users upstream of their share of Sage Creek waters, a stream flowing intermittently from Canada to the United States. The commission was requested to use its good offices to bring about a 'mutually satisfactory agreement' on sharing the waters. After several years of measurement and studies by the International Sage Creek Engineering Board, the IJC concluded that the unregulated flow of the stream was not sufficient to carry out a satisfactory apportionment and proposed that the Canadian government construct a storage dam upstream to capture waters during spring runoff to permit apportionment during the irrigation season. The proposal was unacceptable to Canada because the cost of building the dam was greater than the irrigation benefits to be derived. In view of these circumstances, the IJC in its final report of 1967 concluded that there existed no 'mutually satisfactory' solution to the problem and recommended that the governments of Montana and Alberta continue to co-operate in their efforts to ensure that all water users in the basin were fairly treated.[43]

Domestic supply

The commission has had only two cases dealing specifically with the use of boundary waters for domestic purposes. The first was an application in 1914 by the city of Winnipeg to divert waters from Shoal Lake (a boundary water in the Lake of the Woods region) a distance of one hundred miles to Winnipeg for domestic use. Opposition was voiced by a number of riparian and navigation interests at the Lake of the Woods on grounds that the diversion would lower the boundary waters levels. The commission, conscious that the use for domestic purposes of boundary waters was given first priority under article VIII, found that the proposed withdrawal, if limited to 100 million gallons per day, would not affect appreciably the boundary waters levels for other users and approved the application.[44]

In 1968 the IJC received from the city of Winnipeg a new application for approval to increase the daily withdrawal from Shoal Lake to 300 million gallons per day.[45] At the subsequent request of the applicant, the scheduled hearing by the commission was postponed until the city notified the IJC that it was prepared to proceed with the application.

Conservation

The commission has dealt with over twenty cases concerning conservation measures for boundary and transboundary waters. The cases range through reclamation of wetlands, flood control, recreation, scenic protection, and water pollution control, and the problems have arisen at many points along the boundary. Of the cases, only two are selected to illustrate the functions of the IJC in this area. One involves the attempts to preserve the scenic splendor of Niagara Falls; the other considers the efforts to control water pollution in the Great Lakes.

Preservation of Niagara Falls   The main concern of Canada and the United States with Niagara Falls has been to achieve a balance between exploitation of the power potential and preservation of the scenic spectacle created by the waterfalls. This balance was sought by article V of the Boundary Waters Treaty in 1909 and was adjusted to accommodate increased diversions for power in 1950.[46]

It was evident by 1950 that the rock formations at the crest of Horseshoe Falls were being badly eroded to the detriment of the scenic beauty and in that year the governments asked the IJC to report on the remedial works necessary to preserve and enhance the beauty of the falls while keeping in mind the power generation interests. The task of the commission was twofold: to create a more even distribution of the remaining waters over the Horseshoe crest of the falls and to arrest the erosion at the centre of the Horseshoe. The commission set up a joint engineering board to carry out tests, and on the basis of its findings the IJC recommended in 1953 that the two governments construct a control structure above the falls and undertake remedial works on the flanks of the falls, the effect of which would be to distribute the water flow more evenly and to reduce erosion.[47]

In 1961, following water shortages experienced by the power companies during the winter months, the IJC was again asked to consider additional measures which might be undertaken beyond those recommended in 1953 to preserve the scenic beauty of the falls while yet allowing fuller use of the waters allocated in 1950 for power generation. An interim report by the IJC in 1961 recommended that the present control structures could be extended and several measures could be taken upstream to achieve the dual objectives of power and scenic beauty. It further proposed that all works be placed under the supervision of its International Niagara Board of Control.[48]

More recently, the governments turned their attention to the American falls and requested the IJC in 1967 to study and report on measures necessary to preserve and enhance the beauty of these falls, bearing in mind the importance of protecting both the conservation and the power interests in the vicinity of Niagara Falls and River. In this reference, the commission construed its mandate broadly and, through its American Falls International Board, has been looking at both the engineering aspects of the problem (removal of talus, retarding future erosion, and raising the levels of the Maid of the Mist pool) and the broader environmental setting of the scenic spectacle. In particular the commission has been considering the possible impairment of the natural beauty of the falls caused by industrial and commercial development in the vicinity.[49] The commission has not yet reported to the governments under this reference.

Great Lakes water pollution   Over the years the IJC has, under several references from the two governments, investigated water pollution problems in boundary and transboundary waters extending from the Red River on the prairies to the Saint John River in the east. The commission's largest and most significant pollution study has been in relation to the Great Lakes–St Lawrence River basin.

The commission first examined the problem of sanitary pollution in the Great

Lakes system in 1912 when the governments requested the agency to ascertain the extent to which water pollution along the boundary was causing injury to public health and to recommend means by which such pollution might be prevented. The commission employed scientists to carry out the massive sampling and analytical studies and reported in 1918 that the shorelines of the Great Lakes, the connecting channels, and the international St Lawrence River were all polluted in contravention of article IV of the Boundary Waters Treaty.[50] The IJC recommended that it be given 'ample jurisdiction' to regulate and prohibit sanitary pollution in the waters under study and that it be empowered 'to make regulations, rules, directions and orders as in its judgment may be deemed necessary' to ensure improvement in the quality of the waters.[51]

These recommendations for enhancing the functions and powers of the commission in relation to water pollution were never implemented by the governments and, following World War II, they again requested the commission to investigate boundary waters pollution problems, this time only in relation to the connecting channels of the Great Lakes, and to recommend measures to control pollution having transboundary consequences. This reference came to the IJC in 1946 and 1948 and, based upon the scientific conclusions of its joint technical boards, the commission reported in 1950 that all of the connecting channels (St Marys River, St Clair River, Detroit River, and Niagara River) were seriously polluted on both sides of the boundary by domestic and industrial effluents.

To remedy the problem, the IJC set out a series of scientific criteria (Objectives for Boundary Waters Quality Control) that it urged the governments to adopt as minimum standards for maintaining acceptable water quality. Instead of requesting any enforcement power for itself, the commission recommended that the governments authorize it 'to establish and maintain continuing supervision over boundary waters pollution' through joint control boards that the commission would create to monitor abatement progress and to report lack of satisfactory progress to the governments, with recommendations for necessary action by the 'appropriate authority having jurisdiction.'[52] Ottawa and Washington adopted the IJC recommendations in 1951 and the commission set up two joint advisory boards to carry out surveillance functions over the connecting channels waters. While considerable progress has thus been made in curbing transboundary pollution in these waters, the boards have recently reported to the IJC that the quality standards are still not being met in all parts of the waters.[53]

In 1964 the IJC was requested once more to study transboundary pollution problems in the Great Lakes. Specifically, the governments asked the commission to examine the state of water quality in Lakes Erie and Ontario and the international section of the St Lawrence River and to recommend the necessary remedial measures. Because a study of such magnitude would obviously entail several years of investigation and public inquiry, the IJC proceeded to issue a series of interim reports pointing out a number of specific problems (phosphate build-up, oil spills, and watercraft discharges) that required immediate action by the governments.[54]

In December 1970, following studies completed by its two water pollution boards and numerous hearings conducted by the IJC, the commission transmitted to the governments a comprehensive report on water conditions in the lower Great Lakes basin, wherein it documented the causes of the serious deterioration of the water quality and recommended a number of measures for immediate and long-range remedial action by all levels of government. Again the IJC detailed a series of scientific objectives to be achieved in order to restore the waters to an acceptable quality and urged that the two countries enter into agreement on programs, measures, and schedules designed to achieve these objectives. As for its own continuing role the commission proposed that it be assigned the task of ensuring co-ordination and co-operation among the various governments in measures taken to implement the programs of pollution control, with the power to 'review and make recommendations concerning legislation in each country relating to pollution of the Great Lakes System.'[55]

At a ministerial meeting in Washington on 10 June 1971 the two governments announced their intention to conclude an agreement to give effect to the main proposals of the IJC.[56] This intention became a reality on 15 April 1972 in Ottawa when President Richard Nixon and Prime Minister Pierre Trudeau signed the Agreement on Great Lakes Water Quality, which adopts water quality standards and obliges the two countries to develop and implement control programs 'as soon as practicable.'[57] The IJC was charged with establishing a Great Lakes Water Quality Board and was authorized to set up a regional office in the Great Lakes basin to assist it in carrying out its research, investigation, and reporting responsibilities. The commission was authorized to issue reports directly in its discretion rather than having to transmit them only to the governments. The effectiveness of this agreement will depend in large part on the extent to which the several governments involved are prepared to commit the necessary financial resources to the control programs.

Multipurpose projects
The IJC has received eleven references that may be classed as multiple-use cases: cases wherein the commission has been asked to consider all of the uses to which a particular body of water along the boundary may be beneficially put and to recommend to the governments the optimum regime of water resources planning and development that should be undertaken jointly by the two countries. In these cases the studies by the commission are obviously broad and complex and require the skills of many technical experts. They also require the commission to adopt a more policy-oriented stance than do many of the single-use cases. The multiple-use references have ranged across the continent from the Columbia River in the west to the St Croix River in the east. Three are described below to illustrate the functions of the IJC as an international water resources planning agency.

Columbia River basin reference   As early as 1944 Canada and the United States realized the need to rationalize the water resources development on the Columbia-Kootenay system to ensure the optimum beneficial uses. In that year the IJC was asked to 'determine whether in its judgment further development of the water resources of the [Columbia River system] would be practicable and in the public interest from the points of view of the two Governments, having in mind (A) domestic water supply and sanitation, (B) navigation, (C) efficient development of water, (D) the control of floods, (E) the needs of irrigation, (F) reclamation of wet lands, (G) conservation of fish and wildlife, and (H) other beneficial public purposes.' The commission was instructed to recommend desirable projects, to indicate interests in the basin to be benefited or adversely affected thereby, to estimate the costs of proposed projects including indemnification costs, and to propose the apportionment of costs between the two governments.

Because of the dearth of knowledge concerning the resources of the upper basin, it was many years before the International Columbia River Engineering Board created by the commission was able to complete its studies. In addition, the IJC itself became deadlocked for some time over the question of apportioning downstream benefits derived from any power or flood control storage developments upstream and over the question of the right of Canada to divert for its own uses the waters of the Columbia-Kootenay system before they flowed into the United States.[58]

Not until 1959 did the Engineering Board submit its report to the IJC on proposed development of the water resources of the Columbia basin. In it the board presented three alternate plans for joint development of the basin and recommended that one of them be undertaken co-operatively by the two governments to realize optimum benefits for water power, flood control, and irrigation uses. The board was also of the view that there existed no present need for co-operation between the countries in developing the water resources for other uses, but it believed that most other beneficial uses could be realized in each country under any one of the projected plans of development.

Before the commission could consider the board's report, the governments announced their intention to proceed to direct negotiation of a treaty for co-operative development of the Columbia basin, and in January 1959 they asked the IJC to prepare immediately a special report on principles for determining and apportioning between the two countries the downstream benefits that would result from the co-operative use of upstream water storage, particularly in regard to power generation and flood control. In the absence of any specific rules in the Boundary Waters Treaty on this matter, the IJC adopted two guiding rules. First, co-operative development of shared water resources should result in an overall advantage to each country as compared to separate development. Second, the benefits so derived should be shared equitably by the two countries. Having established these guidelines, the IJC proceeded to recommend a series of principles for the determination of power and flood control benefits to be derived by the downstream state as a result of storage works constructed and operated by the upstream state and for the apportionment of these benefits between the two countries in proportion to the resources contribution that each state made to the overall co-operative development. The commission reported these principles to the governments in December 1959.

With the Engineering Board and IJC reports in hand, the governments proceeded in 1960 and 1961 to conclude the Columbia River Treaty which provided for the co-operative development of the basin's water resources. Under it Canada was to develop a series of storage facilities in the upper basin, providing for increased power development and flood control downstream in the United States. In return, Canada was provided with compensation for one-half of the downstream power benefits and for the downstream flood control benefits according to the IJC principles. Under the treaty, the two countries also agreed to refer to the IJC for decision any dispute arising from interpretation of the treaty.[59]

Pembina River basin reference The Pembina River is a tributary of the Red River, rising in southern Manitoba and flowing into North Dakota where it joins the Red River south of the international boundary. In its undeveloped state, the river overflows its banks during spring runoff and carries insufficient water to supply needs during the rest of the year.

In 1962 the governments requested the IJC to determine 'what plan or plans of cooperative development of the water resources of the Pembina River Basin would be practicable, economically feasible and to the mutual advantage of the two countries, having in mind: (a) domestic water supply and (b) control of floods; (c) irrigation and (d) any other beneficial uses.' The commission was directed to estimate the costs and benefits of any such plans and to determine how costs and benefits might be apportioned between the countries.

In carrying out the studies through the International Pembina River Engineering Board, the commission defined three objectives to be realized: 1 / to devise a plan of co-operavive development that would assure a high degree of optimization of net benefits throughout the basin; 2 / to ensure that co-operative development would result in a net advantage to each country over separate development; 3 / to ensure an equitable apportionment of the benefits consistent with co-operative development.

In 1964 the board reported to the IJC three possible plans of development that would serve the multipurpose demands in the two countries and optimize the uses of the waters. Based on these studies and on public hearings, the commission in 1967 recommended to the governments a co-operative plan of basin development that involves joint construction by the two countries of storage reservoirs and supply facilities. In the commission's opinion, the proposed project would be to the mutual advantage of both countries, benefiting flood control, municipal and industrial water supply, irrigation, water quality, recreation, and game fishing in the basin.

The IJC proposed that the annual runoff or yield of the basin's waters above the uppermost reservoir site, less certain deductions, be shared 60 per cent by Canada and 40 per cent by the United States, reflecting each country's contribution to the river flow. As for cost sharing, the IJC proposed that initially each country pay for project works located in its territory and that subsequently there be a payment transfer from one country to another that would result in a balancing of operating costs of the project. Finally, the IJC recommended that Canada and the United States conclude an agreement based upon this proposed plan of co-operative development of the water resources and authorize the commission to exercise continuing supervision over the operation of the joint project works.[60] Thus far the governments have indicated no course of action on the report.

Great Lakes water levels reference   The IJC now has under consideration what is perhaps the most challenging and complex reference ever submitted to it by the governments, the study of fluctuations in the levels of the Great Lakes. Over the years the water levels have moved from very high to very low levels, adversely affecting the many interests dependent on the waters in the basin. In 1964, when the lake levels were at a low extreme, the governments requested the commission to ascertain the causes of level fluctuations in the Great Lakes basin and to determine whether measures might be taken within the basin in the public interest of both countries to bring about a more beneficial range of levels for domestic supply and sanitation, navigation, power, industry, flood control, agriculture, fish and wildlife, recreation, and other public purposes.

Because of the magnitude of the task, the commission divided the work into two phases. The first five years would be spent gathering data and developing methodology for testing regulation techniques. In the second phase, the commission would proceed to develop regulation plans, to design regulatory works, and to evaluate the economic and social data. The commission created the International Great Lakes Levels Board to undertake the first phase tasks and proceeded itself to gather information and opinions from the governments and the public.

To date the IJC has issued two progress reports which indicate the comprehensiveness of the studies being made of the multiple uses of the waters and which caution that the task of devising a plan to control the water flows in the basin which will be beneficial to the greatest number of interests will be a very difficult job.[61] Just how difficult the problem will be has been demonstrated by the seeming impossibility of taking any action to relieve the extreme high levels on the lower lakes experienced in 1973.

Air pollution and Point Roberts references

No consideration of the work of the IJC would be complete without mention of the air pollution cases and the Point Robers reference, the only cases that have not related to water matters.

The first air pollution case in 1928 involved the IJC in assessing the amount of compensation that should be paid to property interests in the state of Washington injured from sulphur fumes emanating from a smelter in Trail, BC. In 1931 the IJC recommended a lump sum payment of $350,000.[62]

In 1949 the commission was requested by the governments to determine the harm to health and property being caused on both sides of the boundary by smoke emissions from ships plying the Detroit River. The IJC advised that there were harmful effects from this source of air pollution and recommended in 1960 that the governments adopt and enforce against vessel operators a proposed code of emission standards, and empower the commission to exercise surveillance over vessels plying the river. The IJC also reported that the chief source of transboundary air pollution in the Detroit-Windsor area was not the ships but the land-based industries.[63] This last observation by the commission led to a broader reference in 1966, requesting the agency to study and report on all sources of transboundary air pollution in the Detroit-Windsor and Sarnia-Port Huron areas, with recommendations for measures to rectify the situation. The commission was futher empowered to take cognizance of any other air pollution problems along the boundary.

In 1971 the International St Clair-Detroit Air Pollution Board established by the commission reported that it found substantial transboundary air pollution, exceeding the level that is 'detrimental to the health, safety, and general welfare of citizens, and to property on the other side of the international boundary.' The board proposed that the IJC urge the governments to adopt uniform air quality standards in both countries and to take measures designed to enforce the standards.[64]

In July 1972 the IJC confirmed the seriousness of the air pollution problems along the industrialized portions of the boundary and urged the federal and local governments to adopt common air quality objectives and to enter into agreement for implementation of the standards and for co-ordination of preventative measures to control emission at the earliest practicable date.[65] The report is now under review by the governments.

The most recent case to be referred to the IJC is also its most unusual reference, for it deals neither with water resources nor with air resources along the boundary, but rather with problems involving a small group of human resources affected by the existence of the international boundary. In April 1971 the commission was asked by the two national governments 'to investigate and recommend measures to alleviate certain conditions of the life of residents of Point Roberts, in the State of Washington, existing by reason of the fact that the only connection by land between Point Roberts and other territory of the United States is through Canada.' As the terms of reference indicate, Point Roberts is a tiny (five square miles) piece of land on the west coast of the United States, the tip of a peninsula attached to Canada and physically separated from the United States, though a part of the United States because it is below the 49th parallel. Most of the property in Point Roberts is owned by Canadian summer residents, but approximately three hundred United States citizens live there and their daily life is complicated by the point's isolation from mainland United States.

The commission is now looking at the various problems – customs' laws and regulations, transportation, employment regulations, health and medical services, power and telephone services, law enforcement and 'any other problems found to exist on account of the unique situation of Point Roberts.'[66] In doing so, it is certainly venturing into new areas of concern and its proposed solutions to the problem will be awaited with considerable interest.

CONCLUSIONS

From the foregoing discussion, it is evident that, among the joint agencies created by the United States and Canada to facilitate effective relations between the two countries, the International Joint Commission has generally responded actively and positively in promoting co-operation in sharing the resources along the common frontier.

The commission, whether applying rules established by the Boundary Waters Treaty or formulating principles for co-operative action, brings to bear techniques and practices that would be difficult to duplicate in the traditional institutions of diplomatic intercourse. It not only ensures a degree of continuity and consistency in dealing with a series of similar problems but also, because of its detachment from political involvement, achieves an important element of objectivity in evaluating the issues involved in each case. As a result, matters that might otherwise exacerbate the relations between Canada and the United States are dealt with in an informed and dispassionate manner calculated to ensure a full consideration of the interests of both nations.

This is not to suggest that the IJC is without limitations and a number of these should be noted. Some of the shortcomings stem from provisions of the treaty; some arise from the composition of the commission and others result from the policies of the governments.

Looking at the treaty, the priorities of water uses set out in 1909 by article VIII in relation to boundary waters do not, perhaps, accurately reflect the priorities as we see them today. Indeed, in the present-day interests of environmental protection, we would probably assign sanitary needs a low priority and make conservation of the water resources the foremost priority. Again, article VIII makes no mention of the importance of industrial uses of the waters, and it is by no means certain that navigation would now take precedence over hydroelectric development in all parts of the boundary waters.

Article II of the treaty enables each country to divert all transboundary waters and waters flowing into boundary waters for its sole use rather than allowing them to flow in their natural course to the downstream state. This may be viewed as a somewhat anachronistic principle in view of the doctrine of 'equitable utilization' developed in the Helsinki Rules on water uses by the International Law Association. In any event, the further provisions of Article II dealing with the rights of injured parties downstream when such a diversion occurs are certainly in need of clarification if a meaningful protection of downstream interests is to be assured.

Third, the IJC is not permitted by the treaty to initiate studies of common resources problems on its own. While this is probably an essential restriction in the interests of national sovereignty, it has proven to cause delays that can be serious in the examination of environmental quality problems along the boundary. This limitation can be alleviated by a practice that has been adopted in the most recent water and air pollution references where the two governments have authorized the commission to draw to their attention similar pollution problems elsewhere along the international boundary, so that formal references may be transmitted if the governments consider such action appropriate. However, to carry out this responsibility effectively, the commission probably requires additional technical personnel.

As for the commission itself, the two main weaknesses have been the quality and concern of the commissioners and the limited number of support staff that the commission is authorized to employ. On the first point, for many years there was a tendency on the part of the governments to appoint as commissioners persons who were not particularly qualified for the important tasks of the commission or who tended to devote little of their time to the cases awaiting the commission's attention. This in turn led to a situation in which the legislative bodies of the two countries were reluctant to furnish the commission with adequate financial resources. The lack of support staff is a continuing problem for the IJC. The commission has traditionally been required by the governments to rely upon the technical services of regular government personnel to carry out both its investigative and its evaluative studies. While the quality of these services is unquestioned and, in its investigative role, they probably provide the commission with the best possible information and advice, other considerations arise when the IJC is charged with its task of evaluating the progress being made by the governments and industry in implementing the recommendations of the commission. Here, a serious question of potential conflict of interest arises where the commission's boards, staffed with regular public servants, are charged with responsibility under the direction of the IJC to carry out monitoring and surveillance of the pollution abatement programs administered by the government departments from whence the board members are drawn. Where the commission performs this independent monitoring and surveillance role, it would seem essential that it be free to employ its own technical personnel.

Finally, there are two practices by the national governments that may inhibit the effectiveness of the commission in the environmental protection field. First, the commission has no power to release its reference and evaluative reports to the public; it may only submit them to the governments. It might be preferable, in this area where public interest is so great, if the commission were authorized to publish its findings and conclusions directly.[67] Second, despite the provisions of article IX, the practice has developed of not making a unilateral reference on a matter of the commission; the two governments must agree on its terms beforehand. While this has the obvious advantage of defining the scope of the reference (and the resultant study and report) in terms acceptable to both governments, it does result in delays in getting problems under examination promptly and creates a situation where the scope of the reference subsequently proves to be inadequate in relation to the particular problem.

Most of these limitations are a question of the commission's independence from the governments. If the body is to perform its role in planning the co-operative or co-ordinated development and conservation of international frontier resources most effectively, it must enjoy a substantial degree of detachment from the national position of its masters.

NOTES

1 United States, Department of State, *Principles for Partnership: Canada and the United States* (1965). The study was undertaken by the late A.D.P. Heeney of Ottawa and Livingston T. Merchant of Washington.
2 'Canada-U.S. Interparliamentary Group' (1968), 20 *External Affairs* 212–15.
3 Exchange of notes signed at Washington, 12 November 1953, [1953] CAN. T. S. no 18.
4 'Canada-United States Ministerial Committee on Trade and Economic Affairs' (1970), 22 *External Affairs* 434–8.
5 Exchange of notes signed at Ottawa, 29 August and 2 September 1958, [1958] CAN. T. S. no 22.
6 United States Information Service, *Canadian-American Relations: A Selected List of Publications* (1966) 57.
7 Joint Declaration of the prime minister of Canada and the president of the United States, Ogdensburg, New York, 18 August 1940, [1940] CAN. T. S. no 14.
8 Canada, Department of External Affairs, *The Canada-United States Permanent Joint Board on Defence* (1965) Reference Paper 1965/116.
9 Agreement between the Government of Canada and the Government of the United States concerning the organization and operation of the North American Air Defence Command (NORAD), signed at Washington, 12 May 1958, [1958] CAN. T. S. no 9. This pact was extended in May 1973 for a further three year term.
10 'Renewal of the NORAD Agreement' (1968),

20 *External Affairs* 216–17 provides the text of the exchange of notes.
11 Convention between Canada and the United States of America for the Preservation of the Halibut Fishery of the Northern Pacific Ocean and Bering Sea. Ratified 28 October 1953, [1953], CAN. T. S. no 14.
12 Convention between Canada and the United States of America for the protection, preservation and extension of the sockeye-salmon fisheries in the Fraser River System. Ratified 28 July 1937, [1937] CAN. T. S. no 10; amended by Protocol of 3 July 1957, [1957] CAN. T. S. no 21.
13 Convention between Canada and the United States of America on Great Lake Fisheries. Ratified 11 October 1955, [1955] CAN. T. S. no 19.
14 Treaty between His Majesty and the United States of America concerning the International Boundary, 1 July 1908. 1 Malloy *Treaties, Conventions, International Acts, Protocols and Agreement between the United States of America and Other Powers* (1919) 815–27.
15 Treaty between Great Britain and the United States of America in respect of the Dominion of Canada, 17 July 1925. (1940), 1 *Papers Relating to the Foreign Relations of the United States* 544–50; CAN. T. S. no 720.
16 Treaty Between the United States and Great Britain Relating to Boundary Waters, and Questions Arising Between the United States and Canada, 1909. T.S. no 548; III Redmond, *Treaties* (1923) 2607–8; Can. c 28

(1911). (Hereinafter referred to as the Boundary Waters Treaty.)

17 Boundary Waters Treaty, articles III, IV.

18 Ibid, article VIII, para 3. Under paragraph 6, however, the commission may in its discretion permit unequal temporary diversions in cases where an equal division cannot be made advantageously.

19 Ibid, article VIII, paragraph 4.

20 Ibid, article VIII, paragraph 5.

21 Ibid, article VIII, paragraph 7.

22 Ibid, article VIII, paragraph 8.

23 Ibid, article VIII, paragraph 9.

24 Ibid, article IX. Under article X the IJC is empowered to arbitrate to a binding decision any dispute submitted to it by common agreement of the two governments. As this power has never been invoked, the commission's functions under article X are not considered in this study.

25 Ibid, article XII.

26 See IJC, *Rules of Procedure*, II, *Applications* (1964).

27 See IJC, *Rules of Procedure*, III, *References* (1964).

28 IJC Can. Sect., docket no 27. (The reference here and in subsequent notes is to the files of the Canadian Section of the IJC in Ottawa where each case has been assigned a docket number.) See also L.M. Bloomfield and G.F. Fitzgerald, *Boundary Water Problems of Canada and the United States*, (1958) at 125–128.

29 IJC Can. Sect., docket no 39, and Bloomfield & Fitzgerald, 130–1.

30 IJC Can. Sect., docket nos 43, 45, 47, 59, and 84. See Bloomfield & Fitzgerald, 132–3.

31 IJC Can. Sect., docket no 44. See Bloomfield & Fitzgerald, 158.

32 IJC Can. Sect., docket no 66. See Bloomfield & Fitzgerald, 196.

33 IJC Can. Sect., docket no 17. See Bloomfield & Fitzgerald, 107–10.

34 Exchange of Notes between Canada and the United States of America on Construction of Power Facilities on the St Lawrence River. Signed at Washington, 30 June 1952, [1952] CAN. T. S. no 30.

35 IJC Can. Sect., docket no 68. See Bloomfield & Fitzgerald, 199–202.

36 Under an earlier reference in 1948, the IJC had assessed the costs of carrying out feasibility studies for power development at Passamaquoddy Bay. In 1950 it reported that the cost of such studies would be about $4 million. See IJC Can. Sect., docket no 60 and Bloomfield & Fitzgerald, 182.

37 IJC Can. Sect., docket no 72. See also 3 Whiteman, *Digest of International Law* (1964) 867–8.

38 IJC Can. Sect., docket nos 2 and 12. See Bloomfield & Fitzgerald, 71, 96–7.

39 IJC Can. Sect., docket no 12. See Bloomfield & Fitzgerald, 97.

40 IJC Can. Sect., docket no 37. See Bloomfield & Fitzgerald, 150–1.

41 IJC Can. Sect., docket no 77. See IJC, *Report on the Improvement of the International Champlain Waterway for Commercial Navigation* (1967).

42 IJC Can. Sect., docket no 18. See Bloomfiield & Fitzgerald, 111–12.

43 IJC Can. Sect., docket no 54. See Bloomfield & Fitzgerald, 174–5 and IJC, *Report on the Sage Creek Reference* (1967).

44 IJC Can. Sect., docket no 7. See Bloomfield & Fitzgerald, 85–6.

45 IJC Can. Sect., docket no 89.

46 Treaty between Canada and the United States of America concerning the Diversion of the Niagara River. Signed at Washington, 27 February 1950, [1950] CAN. T. S. no 3.

47 IJC Can. Sect., docket no 64. See IJC, *Report on the Preservation and Enhancement of Niagara Falls*. (1953).

48 IJC Can. Sect., docket no 74. See IJC, *Interim Report on Remedial Works Necessary to Enhance and Preserve the Scenic Beauty of the Niagara Falls and River* (1961).

49 IJC Can. Sect., docket no 86.

50 Article IV, para 2 provides: 'It is further agreed that the waters herein defined as boundary waters and waters flowing across the boundary shall not be polluted on either side to the injury of health or property on the other.'

51 IJC Can. Sect., docket no 4. See IJC, *Final Report on the Pollution of Boundary Waters* (1968).

52 IJC Can. Sect., docket nos 53 and 55. See IJC, *Report on the Pollution of Boundary Waters* (1950).

53 See IJC Advisory Board, *Summary Report on Pollution of the Niagara River* (1967); IJC Advisory Board, *Summary Report on Pollution of the St. Marys River, St. Clair River and Detroit River* (1967); IJC Advisory Board, *The Niagara River, Pollution Abatement Progress* (1971).

54 The commission issued three interim reports between 1965 and 1970. IJC, *Interim Report on the Pollution of Lake Erie, Lake Ontario*

and the *International Section of the St. Lawrence River* (1965); *Second Interim Report on Pollution of Lake Erie, Lake Ontario and the International Section of the St. Lawrence River* (1968); and *Third Interim Report on Pollution of Lake Erie, Lake Ontario and the International Section of the St. Lawrence River: Special Report on Potential Oil Pollution, Eutrophication and Pollution from Watercraft* (1970).

55 IJC Can. Sect., docket no 83. See also IJC, *Report on Pollution of Lake Erie, Lake Ontario and the International Section of the St. Lawrence River* (1970).

56 See Department of Fisheries and Forestry, *Communiqué on Canada-United States Ministerial Meeting on Great Lakes Pollution,* Washington, 10 June 1971.

57 Agreement Between Canada and the United States of America on Great Lakes Water Quality. Ottawa, 15 April 1972; in force 15 April 1972.

58 See Bloomfield & Fitzgerald, 167–70 and 194–5 for a discussion of these issues.

59 IJC Can. Sect., docket no 51. For complete documentation on this reference, see *The Columbia River Treaty, Protocol and Re-lated Documents* (1964) and *The Columbia River Treaty and Protocol: A Presentation* (1964).

60 IJC Can. Sect., docket no 76, and IJC, *Report on the Cooperative Development of the Pembina River Basin* (1967).

61 IJC Can. Sect., docket no 82. See IJC, *Interim Report on the Regulation of Great Lakes Levels* (1968); IJC, *Briefing on Great Lakes Water Levels Study* (1970).

62 IJC Can. Sect., docket no 25. See Bloomfield & Fitzgerald, 137–8.

63 IJC Can. Sect., docket no 61. See IJC, *Report on the Pollution of the Atmosphere in the Detroit River Area* (1960).

64 IJC Can. Sect., docket no 85. See IJC, *Joint Air Pollution Study of St. Clair-Detroit River Area* (1971).

65 IJC, Can. Sect., docket no 85. See IJC, *Report on Transboundary Air Pollution: Detroit and St. Clair River Areas* (1972).

66 IJC, Can. Sect., docket no 92. See *Terms of Reference,* 21 April 1971.

67 This is now permitted under the 1972 Agreement on Great Lakes Water Quality but only in relation to pollution problems covered by the agreement.

S. JOSHUA LANGER

23/International Leases, Licenses, and Servitudes

The topic of leases, licenses, and servitudes in public international law is one which illustrates the danger as well as the futility that tends to accompany the introduction of municipal law concepts and analogies into international law, particularly when these concepts are introduced as terms of art with their train of special connotations. This topic has, furthermore, attracted a considerable, some think an excessive, degree of juristic attention, largely no doubt because of the vagueness and confusion that seem to be the subject's only consistent features.[1]

Anyone who essays to add, even to a modest extent, to the literature on the field has, therefore, to adduce a good reason. I can think of no better reason than that I come, like Mark Antony, not to praise, but to bury the use of these private law expressions in the international law context, certainly insofar as such usage imports rules or principles from municipal systems of property law; or if not to bury, then to contribute what I can to the hastening of the obsequies. What should replace that usage, in my submission, is open recognition and reliance on the underlying principles which govern the rights and duties of states in relation to territorial sovereignty; and the further recognition that a state's granting of privileges, or its agreement so to grant, over or upon some part of its territory is to be considered in accordance with the general rules on international agreements when the grantee is also an international person. At a time when communications, natural resources development, transport, and many other important international activities depend upon an ever widening variety of channels, frequencies, pipelines, and routes across state territories, the rationalization of the international legal arrangements involved and the discarding of needlessly complicating legal categories have practical utility.

This paper, which does not attempt to be exhaustive, is intended to outline a *prima facie* case for the thesis just proposed. Accordingly, the authorities and examples which I canvass are meant to be illustrative only. I have not attempted to enter into, much less to resolve, the details of the juristic controversies alluded to above, because they are largely beside the point and because of my respect for the advice of Koheleth: 'And further than these, my son, be admonished: of making many books there is no end; and much study is a weariness of the flesh' (Ecclesiastes XII, 12).

One author has remarked incisively that 'international law really amounts to laying down the principles of national sovereignty and deducing the consequences.'[2] In this world of territorial states and territorial imperatives, the most ancient and fundamental aspect of sovereignty is territorial sovereignty. While the doctrine of sovereignty, and the nationalism that accompanies it, has unfortunate implications from the point of view of achieving world order under the rule of law, nevertheless, sovereignty can have some beneficial uses. Among these is the legal underpinning that it provides for a country's position in maintaining ownership, control, and possession of its own inheritance.[3] Given that law and policy are inextricably interwoven, the sensitive nature of legal rules which purport to limit territorial sovereignty in favour of a foreign state is apparent to the international lawyer. It is with this in mind that any effort to update this particular corner of international law should be approached.

SCOPE OF THE PROBLEM

To make the most objectionable term first, an international servitude stems from the civil law of servitude, in particular a praedial servitude. This implied a right inhering in a dominant entity over or in relation to a servient entity, somewhat approximating the common law easement. The notion of a state servitude, arising only by treaty, which would run with the land as an *in rem* right independent of a change of sovereignty in the servient state, has been considered by international tribunals. References to it by writers date back to Wolff in 1764,[4] and in diplomatic correspondence its usage dates from the Anglo-American negotiations of 1818 regarding the Newfoundland fisheries. The *locus classicus* is, of course, the North Atlantic Coast Fisheries Arbitration, where the Permanent Court of Arbitration, while not rejecting the existence of servitudes in all cases, refused to agree with the United States contention that certain fishing rights granted by Great Britain constituted a state of servitude identical in construction with that of Roman law; the tribunal's finding on this point was based also in part on the absence of express evidence of international contract in this connection.[5] It is also difficult to ignore Judge Lauterpacht's pointed comment of 1927: 'Of all attempts to apply to relations between States conceptions taken from private law, none has caused more confusion or has brought the recourse to analogy into more disrepute than the efforts made to introduce the conception of servitudes into international public law.'[6]

A careful distinction should be made between this kind of exceptional conventional restriction on the territorial supremacy of a state and the undoubted general restrictions, which may be termed natural, by which all states are equally limited by certain rules of customary international law in the exercise of territorial sovereignty, for example, the right of innocent passage.[7] Even such general restrictions, it may be noted, are not without their limits in given circumstances. A state servitude was denied in the *Wimbledon* and in the *Right of Passage* cases.[8]

Accordingly, while the concept has its advocates,[9] its failure to gain general acceptance and approval and the discredit in which many hold it are such that the question really becomes, I submit, what should be put in its place? For, useless though the legal category may be, and unacceptable in its use of phrases such as dominant state and servient state, there undeniably exist some real problems in sorting out various treaty rights relating to territory. I have tried to give a general answer to this question at the outset and I will return to it with more particularity presently.

International leases present many of the same difficulties. The term lease has numerous associations, especially in common law systems, which are inappropriate to the international law context. Moreover, lease in the pre-World War I period was a euphemism for acquiring outright control of a part of another state without having recourse to the formalities of outright annexation, as in the case of the New Territories of China attached to the British crown colony of Hong Kong. The unreality of this approach was dramatized by the lease of the Canal Zone 'in perpetuity' to the United States in 1903. While there is technically a reversionary interest in the lessor state, for all intents and purposes there is a transfer of sovereignty for a term of years or indefinitely, and it is submitted that 'transfer of sovereignty' is a more accurate term than lease in this context if candour is to govern. This terminology can incorporate into the resulting rights the attribute of being unaffected by changes in the original parties to the agreement. Since even a lease in perpetuity can be terminated by agreement between the parties, I suggest that the most appropriate substitute expression would be defeasible transfer, *faute de mieux*.

The provisions for military bases and installations present special problems. Though known as leases, it may be argued that they are not international leases, as that term is wont to be used, but are municipal leases authorized, though not created, by the particular international agreement. Recent practice seems to support the view that no transfer of sovereignty takes place in these cases. In the agreement of 27 March 1941, by which Great Britain granted certain bases to the United States, the latter, while enjoying 'all the rights, power and authority ... necessary for the establishment, use, operation and defence' of the areas concerned, was conspicuously not granted powers to act as if 'sovereign of the territory,' the wording of the convention establishing the Panama Canal Zone. In fact, except as regards limited jurisdictional rights, there was no surrender of either sovereignty or the exercise thereof. This was confirmed by the Supreme Court of the United States in 1949 when it held that the United States did not possess sovereignty over the airbase in Newfoundland and that that base was part of the territory of a foreign country within the meaning of an American statute.[10] Further support for the view that such arrangements for military bases, space vehicle tracking stations, and the like are really *in personam* municipal leases and not *in rem* international transfers can be found in the practice followed when independence was granted to the late West Indies Federation, in the territory of which certain of the bases covered by the 1941 agreement were situated. At that time, the United States found it advisable to conclude an agreement with the federation on the future of these bases. For this type of case, I find appealing the term 'territorial facilities' suggested by Starke, who apparently had in mind a wider ambit for it than I have here delimited.[11]

Turning now to licenses. Using the term in an international context would be comparatively innocuous, since a license ordinarily connotes a privilege granted *in personam* on a contractual basis, rather than an *in rem* interest in land; of course, it would also be superfluous since, with this meaning, the term is not much different from the ordinary sort of provisions in a treaty. When one considers the difficulties that the development of this basically simple concept has produced in the common law, what with the distinctions between revocable and irrevocable licenses, bare licenses, and licenses coupled with a grant, and the like, it appears advisable to avoid using the term in the international context. The breach of such a term relating to territory would, as would the breach of any other term, give rise to a remedy for compensation against the state which undertook the obligation. On the other hand, license in the sense not of an agreement relating to land but as a privilege granted in return for payment of a fee, seems unexceptionable as a concept in an international setting.

An interesting adaptation of the license concept in a new context appears in the United States draft convention on the peaceful use of the seabed.[12] This draft has as its point of emphasis the idea that an international seabed area containing over 90 per cent of all seabeds should be recognized as the common heritage of all mankind, with an eye to obviating the possibility of peremptory appropriation by individual states of whatever resources and areas seem ripe for the taking.[13] The draft would make the littoral states trustees of the international community and would confer on them certain responsibilities over seabed areas close to their coasts. Out to a depth of 200 metres, the coastal state would exercise all sovereign rights given it under the Geneva Convention of 1958 to explore and exploit the natural resources of the seabed. Beyond that depth, to approximately the outer edge of the continental margin, the coastal state would act as a trustee. No precise seaward limit is yet defined for the area of trusteeship.[14] Beyond this seaward limit, the resources of the seabed would be administered exclusively by an international seabed resource authority.

All who seek to exploit the mineral resources of the seabed would have to be licensed by the trustees, acting on behalf of the authority, and by the authority itself. Furthermore, the trustees would turn over between a half and two-thirds of the revenue to the authority. The net income realized from this revenue, plus the revenue raised by the authority through its own licensing procedures and fees, would, after deduction of administrative expenses, be turned over to appropriate international organizations for the economic advancement of developing countries which sign the treaty. The latter refinement is presumably a carrot designed to attract developing signatories, as well as to make them feel, perhaps, that they will be partners sharing in the venture's profits rather than passive objects of the extractive process as often-delineated in Third World rhetoric. As well, this may be an oblique answer to the objections raised not only by underdeveloped nations but also by underprivileged groups within the United States that contemporary concern with ecology and the conservation of natural resources serves primarily to divert attention and financial support from their pressing human problems. In any case, the licensing provisions and revenue arrangements are such that exploiters of natural resources would pay amounts that would ordinarily go to individual governments, such as royalties, cash bonuses, and taxes; and such that the more thoroughly the seabed is exploited the larger the amount that will go towards economic development of emerging nations.[15] It cannot be denied that this is an innovative attempt to set up an independent source of revenue for international purposes, but its incidence has less appeal.

PRINCIPLES AND APPLICATION

It is clear that international law endorses the idea of one state's territory serving the interests of another state or states. There is no other way to explain the numerous situations, of unquestioned legal legitimacy, of treaty provisions for such privileges; for example, the Pipeline Agreement of 1945 between Canada and the United States.[16] In principle, the question then is, what general legal propositions can or should be advanced concerning the territorial interdependence of the members of the international community?

There are several possible ways to approach this question, of which the two most important are the functional and the doctrinal. Limiting the discussion to rights arising by treaty, and thus excluding such restrictions on sovereignty as the right of innocent passage in the territorial sea, the functional approach would postulate a conceptual framework of legal rules which would allow for the operation, with minimum friction, of international co-operation for goals agreed upon as generally beneficial. These include, apparently, the smooth flow of international commerce, the avoidance or quick settlement of disputes, and the optimum utilization of nature for human betterment consonant with ecological safeguards. Unfortunately, such inputs as power politics, economic disparities, and nationalism have also to be reckoned with, and the result is a pragmatic compromise, sometimes expressed in the form of a law-making treaty, and sometimes expressed as nothing more authoritative than an article in a learned journal. There is certainly room for arguing that treaty rights in foreign territory should, multilaterally, be the subject of an international treaty.

However, carrying forward the notion of a pragmatic compromise for the moment, and applying that spirit to the principles of international law which appear in the sources, it is possible to elaborate a position based on a doctrinal approach.

First of all, existing treaty rights in foreign territory can be explained by the ordinary principles of the international law of treaties and the doctrine of sovereignty. This is so regardless of the tag that is attached to these rights, even if they are described as servitudes in the treaty itself. When one of the parties is succeeded by, say, state x, as legal sovereign of the 'servient' parcel, any arrangement relating to the material rights of territory becomes a matter for agreement between state x and the state of the dominant parcel. This is evidenced by two instances often cited for the opposite conclusion. When the Alsatian town of Hüningen came under the Peace Treaty of Paris, 1815, which required that it never be fortified, it was yet to undergo two changes of sovereignty, becoming German in 1871 and French in 1918. While the town was never in fact fortified, that is in itself of no probative value whatever; it is quite consistent with the hypothesis that no one thought it worth fortifying or that fortifying towns in that area and elsewhere simply fell out of fashion. What is more important is that as a practical matter the question was considered to be a matter for tacit or express agreement between the parties, namely, France and Switzerland.[17] An even clearer case is the right which Switzerland was given to locate troops in parts of Savoy and Sardinia, under the act of the Congress of Vienna, 1815. After those territories became French, France and Switzerland agreed to abrogate these rights. As a practical matter, again, these states acted on a tacit assumption that the new situation called for a new difinitive agreement, as indeed a separate treaty so declared.[18] In brief, what I am submitting is that it is not the change in sovereignty which abrogates the *in rem* right – a submission which, incidentally, an advocate of state servitudes would also make but for different reasons and with a different conclusion – but that there is no *in rem* right to begin with, the treaty provision being *inter partes* and *in personam* from the beginning.

Second, there is no point in becoming involved with property analogies at all, because it is possible and preferable to avoid these complications by sticking to a straight contractual basis involving only the parties to the agreement and excluding third party acquisition of either benefit or burden.

An excellent example of this sensible and straightforward mode of handling a situation is the exchange of notes of March 1942 between Canada and the United States relating to the Alaska Highway.[19] The two governments agreed that the United States should build a military highway through Canada to Alaska. It was expressly and significantly agreed, however, that no rights over the highway were to be acquired by the United States. Since in treaty-making the form is usually at least as important as the substance, it is worth quoting the precise wording as a useful example of drafting. The two countries agreed that the Canadian government was to 'acquire rights of way for the road in Canada (including the settlement of all local claims in this connection), the title to remain in the Crown in the right of Canada or of the Province of British Columbia as appears more convenient.' Furthermore, it was agreed 'that the practical details of the arrangement be worked out by direct contact between the appropriate governmental agencies subject, when desirable, to confirmation by subsequent exchange of notes.' The emphasis on the contractual aspects and the clear avoidance of property complications make this agreement an efficient and business-like document. There is no reason why, in principle, peacetime arrangements should be any less business-like than this wartime example.

Third, it is evident that, on the basis of this reasoning, there are no valid distinctions about subject matter to be drawn in principle between rights in foreign territory – for example, rights of transit, fishery rights, water rights – or about whether such rights are for the benefit of a single state, a number of states, or the general international community. They are all the same, that is, insofar as their status as *in personam* treaty rights is concerned; certain other rules peculiar to the particular subject matter may certainly add their influence, and treaty rights embodied in multilateral conventions can acquire thereby a decided degree of *de facto* permanence and inviolability. However, all these rights and duties inhere, not in the land itself, but in the parties to the treaty.

It may be protested that this paradigm is too stark and simplistic and that provisions in this or that convention contemplate a more complex state of the law, to say nothing of the views of the writers. Nevertheless, the point I am urging is that complexity in this area is so much excess baggage. It would be helpful to discard it in future, while treating existing instances by the direct application of basic principles, subject of course to special treaty provisions which may lay down specific *ad hoc* regimes in certain cases.

CONCLUSIONS

From a functional as well as a doctrinal viewpoint, the concepts (and the concretized legal formulations which flow from them) in this area need to be revamped and streamlined. This should be done in such a way as to rationalize them at the same time. The modes for effecting this end lie in the hands of the international lawyer as writer, as treaty-drafter, and interpreter, and in other roles as well.

It is suggested that the concept of servitude in international law be discarded altogether. As circumstances may require, treaties could include appropriately delimited privileges which somehow impinge upon uses of territory but which are strictly *in personam* and contractual in nature and *inter partes* only. It would probably be advisable in certain cases to leave a fair number of the details to be worked out subsequently and confirmed by supplementary agreement. The keynote should be that of mutual benefit to the states concerned, in substance as well as in verbalization superseding the dominant-servient terminology, together with the confusing proprietary notions. It is to a significant degree a matter of replacing, as Maine thought in quite another context, status with contract.

It is further suggested that the concept of an international lease be similarly discarded and that there be put in its place the idea of a 'defeasible transfer' as spelled out above. Though this is a more accurate term, less encrusted with property notions that the word 'lease,' it would appear to be better practice to avoid its use in favour of authorizing by treaty the employment of municipal law leases whenever required. This, as already noted, is arguably the legal status at present of the 'territorial facilities' as defined in this paper, such as military bases and tracking stations. It should be possible, accordingly, eventually to exclude property analogies from this subheading insofar as the international law relations of the states concerned are involved. Regarding licenses, this category should also be done away with so far as territorial analogies with 'real estate' licenses are concerned. Such a category would be quite superfluous if the suggestions just given (with regard to replacing the concept of international servitudes) are accepted. This does not of course touch the other meaning of the word 'license' in the non-property sense, as already described.

While I have here set out an essentially theoretical treatment of the title topic, I do not wish to omit mention of the fact that the topic is of tremendous practical importance to Canada and to Canadians. This is so despite the absence to date of a clearcut enunciation of policy from the eyrie of the External Affairs Department in Ottawa. In taking the broad perspective of the problem, I have refrained from citing more than a handful of practical Canadian examples, but these abound. Included are the proposed Mackenzie Valley pipeline for transporting Alaskan oil and gas to the US, and the existing pipeline systems with both Canadian and American termini, eg, the Interprovincial Pipeline, the Trans Mountain Pipeline, and the Montreal Portland Pipeline (for oil), and the Trans-Canada Pipeline, the Westcoast Pipeline, and the Alberta Pipeline (for natural gas).[19]

The communications field includes the Canada-US convention relating to the operation by citizens of either country of certain radio equipment or stations in the other country, the Canada-US television and FM agreements, and the North American regional broadcasting agreement.[20] The space program is increasingly evident in this sector, as witness the new Canada-US agreement in force 23 February 1972 for the establishment and operation by the United States National Aeronautics and Space Administration of a tracking facility at Pouch Cove, Newfoundland, for the manned spaceflight Skylab program.[21] In civil aviation, Canada has air agreements on routes and landing rights, etc, with some twenty-five countries,[22] while in the field of electric power, huge voltages destined for American grids pass along Canadian transmission lines.[23] This list of examples could easily be lengthened to underline further the crucial economic and political importance which the international legal basis for all this possesses. The need for putting the legal basis in order is, certainly from a Canadian point of view, self-evident.

Taken all in all, these suggestions may seem to do violence to notions cherished in some quarters, and that is quite intentional. I have no difficulty in opting for clarity and efficiency over pedantry and, while I can do no more than hope that this particular precinct of international law will develop in a way consonant with the suggestions I have made, there are many encouraging signs of a fresh new approach to international law problems today, from a variety of directions.

NOTES

1 See, for example, D.W. Greig, *International Law* (1970) 145.
2 François Laurent, as quoted by Walter Schiffer in *The Legal Community of Mankind* (1954), at 157.
3 I developed this theme in a talk on Canada's natural resources delivered on *Viewpoint*, CBC-TV National Network, Montreal, 2 June 1970; see also Maurice Copithorne, 'The Development of Natural Resources' (1970), 22 *External Affairs* 398. Resource problems, and protection of rights in for example the Great Lakes and the Arctic, are key factors in the present development of Canada's approach to international law.
4 *Jus Gentium Naturale* (1764), at s 321.
5 U.N.R.I.A.A. 167 (1910).
6 Lauterpacht, *Private Law Sources and Analogies of International Law* (1927) 119.
7 See A. Donat Pharand, 'Innocent Passage in the Arctic' (1968), 6 *Can. Y.B. Int'l L.* 3; 'Historic Waters in International Law with Special Reference to the Arctic' (1971), 21 *U. Toronto L.J.* 1, esp. at 4–5; J.-Y. Morin, 'Le progrès technique, la pollution, et l'évolution récente du droit de la mer au Canada, particulièrement a l'égard de l'Arctique' (1970), 8 *C.Y.B. Int'l L.* 158, esp. at 215–20.
8 In the *Wimbledon* case the majority of the court considered the concept of an international servitude to be controversial, Judge Schücking dissenting. In the *Right of Passage* case, the limited right of access there found could scarcely qualify as a servitude in Portugal's favour.
9 In his *Principles of Public International Law* (1966), at 295, Brownlie lists in this category Reid, Váli, and Oppenheim. He finds that the majority of modern writers consider the concept of servitude to be useless and misleading, listing McNair, Schwarzenberger, Brierley, and others.
10 *United States* v *Spelar, Administratrix,* (1949) 338 U.S. Reports 217; see also Agreement Concerning Leased Bases in Newfoundland, 1941–52 (Canada-United States), [1952] CAN.T.S. no 14. Annex II at 26 gives the actual Forms of Leases.
11 J.G. Starke, *An Introduction to International Law* (6th ed, 1967) 205.
12 The full text is printed in (1970), 9 *International Legal Materials* 1046.
13 See Northcutt Ely, 'United States Seabed Minerals Policy' (1971), 4 *Natural Resources Lawyer* 597.
14 See John R. Stevenson, 'The U.S. Proposal for Legal Regulation of Seabed Mineral Exploitation beyond National Jurisdiction' (1971), 4 *Natural Resources Lawyer* 570.
15 However, interim protection for investment is provided for in article 73, para 6 of the Draft Convention.
16 Agreement Concerning the Canol Project, [1945] CAN.T.S. no 3; Exchange of notes, dated 26 February 1945.
17 However, Váli does make the point that the French Foreign Office in 1927 took the position that construction of the Maginot Line had, to protect Swiss neutrality, to take into account the demilitarized character of the town. *Servitudes of International Law* (2nd ed, 1958) 264.
18 An agreement among the Great Powers of the day (embodied in article 435 of the Treaty of Versailles) left it to France and Switzerland to agree on the matter. It also declared that the provisions of article 92 of the Final Act of the Vienna Congress and other provisions relating to the neutralized zone of Savoy were no longer consistent with conditions at the time of the Treaty of Versailles. Article 435 resulted in the separate controversy of the *Free Zones* case.
19 An Agreement Providing for the Construc-

tion of a Military Highway to Alaska, [1942] CAN.T.S. no 13. Exchanges of notes: U.S. to Canada, 17 March 1942; Canada to U.S., 18 March 1942; in force, 18 March 1942.

20 Convention Relating to the Operation by Citizens of Either Country (Canada-U.S.) of Certain Radio Equipment for Stations in the other Country, Ottawa, 8 Feb. 1951, [1952] CAN.T.S. no 7. Exchange of notes (Canada-U.S.) concerning the Allocation of Television Channels, Ottawa, 23 April, 23 June 1952, [1952] CAN.T.S. no 13. Exchange of notes (Canada-U.S.) concerning the Allocation of Channels for frequency modulation Radio Broadcasting, Washington, 8 Jan., 15 Oct. 1947, [1947], CAN.T.S. no 30. Exchange of notes constituting an Agreement Between Canada, the United States of America, Cuba, and Newfoundland, relative to the assignment of High Frequencies to Radio Stations on the North American Continent, Ottawa, 1 Feb. to 26 Sept. 1929, in force 1 March 1929, [1929] CAN.T.S. no 6.

21 Dept. of External Affairs, *Canadian Weekly Bulletin*, 15 March 1972, at 5. An important recent example which also deserves mention is the renewal of the lease at Goose Bay, Labrador. Department of External Affairs, (1973), 1 *Canada Weekly* 3. The Canadian and US governments agreed in principle, subject to the conclusion of mutually satisfactory arrangements, that the US Air Force may continue to use the airfield and facilities at Goose Bay until 30 June 1976, after expiry of the present lease. Significantly, discussions between representatives of the two governments were to proceed concerning the proposed arrangement whereby the Canadian Ministry of Transport would acquire the present US base facilities and operate the airfield for both civil and military purposes. This sort of arrangement seems to accord, in a satisfying manner, with the recommendations as to both form and substance contained in this article.

22 (1970–1), *Canada Year Book* 937–45; Statistics Canada, Information Canada, *Canada 1972,* at 295–7. See for example the Agreement for Air Services with Japan, Ottawa, 12 Jan. 1955, [1955] CAN.T.S. no 14.

23 (1970–1), *Canada Year Book,* 757 and 1094. See for example Treaty Between Canada and the United States of America relating to the co-operative Development of the Water Resources of the Columbia River Basin, signed at Washington, 17 Jan. 1961, with Annexes; also the Protocol and Attachment relating to terms of sale which were agreed to by Canada and the United States on 22 Jan. 1964. This and other relevant documentation is collected in Department of External Affairs *et al, The Columbia River Treaty, Protocol and Related Documents,* (1964). For an example of a lease of a railway route by Canada to the US, see exchange of notes, Ottawa, White Pass and Yukon Route Railway, 23 Feb. 1943, [1943] CAN.T.S. no 3.

CANADIAN

PARTICIPATION IN

INTERNATIONAL

ORGANIZATIONS

DOUGLAS M. JOHNSTON

24/International Environmental Law: Recent Developments and Canadian Contributions

ENVIRONMENTALISM AND INTERNATIONAL LAW

International environmental law has barely begun to be accepted as a legitimate new coinage in international law. Perhaps it is proper for an academic discipline to challenge concepts that are newly in vogue and hungry for recognition. But we live in an age of mounting concern for the human environment, and it seems fairly certain that this concern will have substantial impact on the development of international law.

The term 'international environment law' cannot be associated exclusively with any single limb of the body of literature on international law. It might be regarded rather as the responses of the body as a whole to the present accumulation of environmental disorders. Initially some of the most difficult questions are related to the allocation of authority among states and international organizations, but the legal problems inherent in international environmental policy go far beyond traditional issues of 'jurisdiction.' Most important of all is the task of creating new principles of responsibility and of making the necessary institutional innovations and adjustments for applying these principles in a world community which is increasingly incapacitated by enormous economic and social disparities. But the development of international law in response to environmental problems depends first on how 'environmentalism' is perceived.

Environmentalism as a concept

In general usage the concept of environmentalism is vaguely but emotively suggestive of a rearranged scheme of values that places life at the centre. If the grimmer warnings of credible scientists are to be taken seriously, it should be seen essentially as a crisis concept. Distinguished from the cognate principle of conservation, which is concerned chiefly with the management of renewable resources and the preservation of natural beauty, the concept of environmentalism has a global dimension and a more fundamental concern with the continuance of life itself on this planet. The real environmental challenge, in this new global sense, is not to enhance the quality of life, but to postpone the death of man.[1] Environmentalism may then be defined, for the purposes of this paper, as intellectual concern with the evidence that our planet and all its species are dying.

The environmental challenge is taken up at different levels of urgency. In a kind of prospective death watch, for example, some astrophysicists are now looking beyond the hope of planetary survival and searching for clues billions of light years distant about the fate of other technological civilizations that might have exhibited the tendency to self-destruct at a particular stage of their development as a species.[2] With a shorter time perspective, oceanographers try to estimate the finite capacity of the oceans to absorb hydrocarbons, just as biochemists for decades have tried to estimate the earth's finite capacity to produce food supplies for expanding populations.[3] Chemical engineers try to calculate the rate of evaporation of gasoline in air, while biologists study the effect of various pollutant compounds on phyto-plankton, the bottom of the food chain in the sea. In numerous ways, at different stages of remove from the concept of planetary death, the entire family of life sciences is engaged in the assessment of apparent threats to human survival.

The social scientist may be more difficult to persuade that in accepting the fact of environmental crisis he is witnessing the death of man as a species. Because of the number of variables affecting human behaviour, he is usually reluctant to make confident long-range projections and remains distrustful of intuition; the history of man is, after all, a history of survival. Not all social scientists are certain, however, that their traditional disciplinary techniques are adequate to meet the environmental challenge. Economists in particular are troubled by the flaws now apparent in their framework of analysis.[4] The need for a causal analysis of the problems of environmental decay is being recognized.[5] Some social scientists have found that the major danger to the survival of humanity lies in 'the growing gulf between capacity to control the environment, society, and individuals, on one hand, and, on the other, knowledge of how to design and operate policymaking systems so they can use these capacities.'[6] Other writers have emphasized that a vast, imaginative effort must be made to harness and co-ordinate human knowledge more efficiently if there is any hope of solving the various problems that threaten the continuance of life on this planet.[7]

The average lawyer, accustomed to operating within the limits of a particular jurisdiction, may find it especially difficult to relate professionally to the all-encompassing concept of planetary death. By virtue of his training in verbal analysis, he will feel he has less to contribute, as a lawyer, to the treatment of environmental problems than to the settlement of disputes they create. To him, environmental concepts are meaningful only if they are productive of principles that can acquire a cutting edge as tools of verbal analysis. The international lawyer is, however, something of a special case. As a student of international politics as well as law, he is familiar with the phenomenon of systemic failure and disintegration. He knows that organizations die: the League of Nations failed, and the United Nations is mortal. He has seen that central organs, like the World Court, may attract and repel at the same time: there is nothing inevitable in the centralization of authority. The perception of mutual advantage often changes, and with it the basis of common interest. The balance of power shifts, sometimes with disastrous consequences. Major treaties can foster illusions: arms control and disarmament have not obviously reduced the risk of nuclear disaster. Alliances are impermanent and may now be in decline, aggravating the instability of satellite political systems. Revolutions and violence occur, usually at an unpredicted time and place. The maintenance of world order is not assured. Ecocatastrophe would merely represent the culmination of a long line of calamities that man's talent for organization has failed to avert. Environmentalism may be readily accepted by the international lawyer as another crisis concept; and environmental protection as a new kind of crisis management.[8]

Environmentalism as a mood

Even to those most sceptical of planetary death, environmentalism represents a mood, a climate of opinion and expectations. The term conveys a critical attitude to growth and enrichment for their own sake, an attitude more widely shared in the western world than ever before. The environmentalist mood is said to reflect a newly urgent concern for the quality of life. But this popular mood concern for quality instead of growth differs in focus from the preservative concept of global environmentalism. Sometimes the environmental mood lacks any definite focus, like the cognate popular mood concern for 'relevance.' At this level of understanding, environmentalism is nothing more precise than an expanded sense of relevance, inflated by heightened awareness of ecological theory. Unfortunately, this expanded sense of relevance does not necessarily sharpen the awareness of crisis.

For many, the environmentalist mood projects a revival of the utopian hope for a new beginning. In expressing an optimistic belief in the possibility of profound change in human affairs, environmentalism provides an outlet for the reformist's impatience as well as the anger of the revolutionist.[9] If mood were all, we might look forward with confidence to the progressive development of international environmental law.

There is a danger, however, that the larger hopes for legal development cannot be realised, and that subsequent frustration and resentment will have the effect of accelerating the trend towards planetary death. There is already evidence that the complexity of environmental problems and the uncertainty of ecological 'facts' are a source of despair to lawyers trained in a tradition of precise, if not always clearcut, distinctions. The development of environmental law seems, however, to rest with lawyers who keep the faith in interdisciplinary approaches to law-making problems. It rests, therefore, with lawyers who can live with the certainty of occasional scientific error. The scientist's world of fact, dominated by the need for hypothesis and the danger of error, is essentially different from the lawyer's world of fact, which is dominated by the need for normative development and the danger of anarchy. Scientists, who have to experiment with facts, can accept more easily than lawyers the existing factual uncertainty about the rate and causes of deterioration in the biosphere. Environmental lawyers may tend to exaggerate the threat that factual error or uncertainty represents to normative development, unless the latter is seen as requiring the design of mechanisms for continuous review and evaluation of environmental data and of factual assumptions underlying environmental policy.

To become attracted to the hypothesis of planetary death, the lawyer may have to become more critical of the facile assumption that the deliberate pursuit of goals has much to do with the present state of the human condition[10] and that timely corrections can be applied by ingenious and rational forms of social engineering. He may also have to grasp the mathematics of exponential growth[11] and the history and mechanics of ecocatastrophe.[12]

Environmentalism as a perspective

Environmentalism is also a way of looking at things: a mode of perception that is global, relational, dynamic, co-operative, remedial, and political. The scope of environmental concern matches that of the biosphere, encircling the globe and encompassing all its resources. The ecological focus on the human environment is essentially a planetary perspective. Certain kinds of environmental problems, such as air pollution, are highly concentrated in certain areas, such as industrial cities, but the localization of effects merely provides a temporary practical excuse for a partial approach to a universal problem. Other kinds of environmental problems, such as marine pollution, have such a general impact on mankind that conventional notions of state territory and national sovereignty are irrelevant and dangerously destructive of rational solutions. Because of the emotional investment in these notions, the prospect of a global solution is especially dismal in the case of shore-generated sources of marine pollution, such as sewage, agricultural chemicals, and industrial wastes, which are so all-pervasive that they seem incapable of effective regulation except under a scheme of authority that transcends existing territorial limits.[13] Since some environmental problems seem to place unprecedented strain on the possibilities of international co-operation,[14] it may be more accurate to describe the environmental perspective as transnational, rather than international.

The environmentalist's relational perspective is derived from the nature of human ecology and the emphasis it places on factors of interdependence. This kind of focus inevitably raises factual questions of cause and effect and related judgemental questions as to blame or guilt. Because environmental abuses are so deeply rooted in our way of life, we may have to learn to broaden existing notions of responsibility. Where the same environmental problems are shared by neighbouring communities, rational authoritative response may be complicated by the co-existence of different traditions of political loyalty and obedience, each closed off from the other by ritualistic attachment to its own concept and system of political community. Environmental perceptions and judgments in each community may vary significantly with the range of political expectations. Even settlements in and around the Great Lakes basin, for example, have different views of their common environmental crisis, according to where they have learned to attach political responsibility: in Ottawa, Washington, or their respective subfederal political centre. Significantly, perhaps, in the Great Lakes society 'environmental community consciousness' is least discouraged at the high school level, where the constituency is judged too immature to exercise political influence.

Ecology is a study of dynamics. The factors of interdependence have no fixed ratio to one another, partly because human 'intervention,' in the form of technology, has constantly changing impacts on the natural environment. The measurement of environmental impact variables is certainly facilitated by the latest techniques in the use of computer technology, but history provides no assurance that these advantages will not be negated by familiar human failings of *hubris*.

Ecology, however, is also a study of co-operation, of synergic combinations in nature. Viewed holistically, an ecosystem which is stable is composed of mutually productive forces. Each component, functioning properly, contributes to the welfare and perpetuation of the entire population. Ecologically, success lies in systemic balance, inviting comparisons and contrasts with man-made systems of economy and government. It is important, if trite, to observe again that western technological societies have developed largely on the basis of inculcated respect for the virtues and efficiency of open competition among the individuals in the population. More co-operatively oriented cultures, such as the Chinese, may prove to be more naturally attuned to the imperatives of human ecology.[15]

The ecologist's view of the world tends, however, to support the belief that things can be fixed. At the very least, it suggests that by studying interactions within the environment, man can learn to cope. More optimistically, it inspires the belief that with proper scientific awareness man can learn to apply appropriate remedies, at least to postpone the inevitable death of his planet to the distant future. This view tends to underplay the possibility that man is biologically incapable of the degree of managerial genius that would now be required universally to ensure perpetual balance in the human environment.

Environmental management on a global level can only be an intergovernmental responsibility, and as such a function of politics. In most cultures, if not in all, politics tends to operate as an outlet for competitive rather than co-operative tendencies in human nature. Even the existence of a highly organized technocratic elite in the service of international organization will be no assurance of responsiveness to environmental distress signals.[16] Yet it seems fairly certain to the environmentalist that international politics will increasingly be dominated by ecological issues, as their impact on the planning goals of developing countries is more acutely felt.[17] These will certainly include such issues as the environmental consequences of high-consumption societies; resource depletion caused by high standards of living and poor rates of reclamation; population growth induced by the use of modern health measures without corresponding changes in other socioeconomic dynamics; and the economic and cultural domination of the world by wealthier nations.[18] In the developing world there will be a tendency to blame global pollution on more acquisitive cultures which have fostered an exploitive attitude towards nature. In the richer areas there will be a tendency to see pollution problems increasingly as the product of acquiescent cultures which reflect an indulgent attitude towards human reproduction.[19] The rich industrial nations responsible for past pollution will be expected to enforce higher standards of environmental quality than other countries in the name of pollution control, but resistance to this may be reinforced by the suspicion that part of the motivation is to impose higher costs, and competitive disadvantages in the short term, as a kind of penalty for past success in international trade.[20] Even with the acceptance of such a principle of compensation in the richer nations, they would still have domestic political problems in co-ordinating national environmental policy so as to distribute the costs of pollution control equitably in the corporate sector.[21]

RECENT DEVELOPMENTS IN INTERNATIONAL ENVIRONMENTAL POLICY-MAKING

Virtually all national problems of environmental policy have a transnational aspect. Extranational activities are a contributory cause of most environmental problems, and many forms of environmental damage spread beyond the limits of national territory. Even where the causes and effects of environmental harm are localized, the range of possible forms of treatment cannot be exhausted without raising questions of foreign policy and invoking the need for international co-operation. Problems of atmospheric and marine pollution, for example, can only be solved through international co-operation and the development of international law. The solution of other problems that might be characterized as national or regional in scope – soil erosion, urban decay, pollution of rivers and other inland waters – would be facilitated by wider international co-operation in such areas as technical and financial assistance, exchange of information, and the sharing of national experience.[22]

Environmental concepts are still so loosely conceived that it is virtually impossible to assert confidently when and how the making of international environmental principles began. Those who focus on interstate pollution incidents invoke the celebrated *Trail Smelter* arbitration[23] between Canada and the United States. Others, mindful of the history of attempts to prevent the misuse of shared resources, refer to early forms of planning by international drainage basin and fishery conservation commissions.[24] But it was only after World War II that there was a beginning of organized concern for the 'human environment' as a whole and of global efforts to treat special aspects of it. This concern and these efforts are closely related to the work of the United Nations and its various organs and specialized agencies.

United Nations and International Environmental Policy, 1945–67[25]

From their beginnings most of the UN specialized agencies have been involved in environmental studies and projects. UNESCO, for example, has long assisted governments in taking conservation measures, and in 1949 it sponsored the creation of the International Union for the Conservation of Nature (IUCN). Since then, UNESCO has initiated environmental studies in various ways; for example, through its International Oceanographic Commission (IOC), under its International Hydrological Decade Programme, and more recently under its Man and the Biosphere (MAB) Programme. WMO has long been engaged in the study of changes in atmospheric parameters of particular significance to weather and climate, and more recently it has stimulated other kinds of research under its World Weather Watch Programme. WHO has helped governments in identifying, measuring, and evaluating air and water pollutants and in solving waste disposal problems. In later years it has become concerned about diseases carried by mosquitoes, rats, snails, and other vectors which often accompany urbanization or are attracted by water resource and other development works. Along with other agencies, FAO has promoted and conducted studies of the accumulation of pesticides and radioactive fallout which may render foods unsuitable for consumption. The International Atomic Energy Agency (IAEA) has, of course, had a continuing program to combat radioactive pollution caused by nuclear power plants and the peaceful uses of atomic energy. Among its other functions is the promulgation of standards, regulations, codes, and manuals on nuclear safety and environmental protection. ILO has been concerned with problems of atmospheric pollution control in order to improve the environmental health of employees. ICAO has become deeply involved in studies of 'sonic boom' and aircraft noise.[26] The Intergovernmental Maritime Consultative Organization (IMCO) has taken a lead in sponsoring law-making efforts to regulate navigation on the high seas by providing remedial sanctions to reduce the threat of pollution by ships.[27]

Specialized agencies, by virtue of their specialized nature, are not, of course, equipped to take a holistic view of the global environment. The potential perils to the human race as a whole were first stressed under UN auspices at the Scientific Conference on the Conservation and Utilization of Resources held at Lake Success in 1949. The main emphasis was on finding the means to avoid waste and depletion of natural resources, to apply modern techniques to obtain the maximum use of resources, and to discover or create new resources. Although it was held in the 'atomic age,' the conference did not reflect the growing scientific concern about the impact of technology on the global environment. Questions of pollution, the residual effects of chemicals on plant and animal life, and the ecological balance between man and other living things were not yet matters of urgent international concern.

But within a few years the General Assembly was dealing more or less consciously with the danger of 'planetary death.' In 1955 it set up the UN Scientific Committee on the Effects of Atomic Radiation, which since then has given periodic reports on radioactivity levels in air, soil, and water, on the effects of radioactive emissions on plant and animal life, on the hazards of fallout, and on related threats to humanity in present and future generations. A planetary perspective has also been evident in UN conferences on the peaceful uses of atomic energy and on world population problems. At the UN Conference on New Sources of Energy, held at Rome in 1961, scientists considered the global significance of unconventional sources of energy – sun, wind, tides, underground steam, and hot water – which may eventually help to limit the air pollution attributable to current sources of energy.

In this same period (1945–67), the United Nations made important contributions to the making of the first international environmental agreements. A convention limiting the discharge of oil from ships, signed in 1954, came under UN auspices when it fell under IMCO's jurisdiction in 1958.[28] In 1958, at the first UN Conference on the Law of the Sea, several provisions on marine pollution were adopted.[29] In 1959, as a result of the UN's International Geophysical Year, states with claims to Antarctica signed the Antarctic Treaty, agreeing to ban all nuclear explosions and all disposal of radioactive waste material, and pledging to co-operate in preserving the living resources of the region.[30] In 1963 the UN disarmament talks produced what is probably the most important environmental measure to date, the Partial Nuclear Test Ban Treaty.[31]

The Stockholm Conference on the Human Environment

Background
By 1967 the 'cluster' of physical and social effects wrought by technology, industrialization, and population pressures began to be described in the United Nations as the 'problems of the human environment.' At the Twenty-second General Assembly, this overall concept emerged in the debate on a report by the UN Scientific Advisory Committee. Rapidly accumulating evidence that the global environment as a whole, the planet earth, was endangered soon produced a bold response from the organized world community. At the spring 1968 session of the Economic and Social Council (ECOSOC) Sweden proposed that a worldwide conference on the problems of the human environment be held at Stockholm in the spring of 1972. After ECOSOC endorsed the idea, the Twenty-third General Assembly gave

its approval in December 1968, in a resolution sponsored by fifty-five states.[32]

It was clear that a tremendous effort would be required to organize a conference of this magnitude in such a short time. The novelty of the undertaking would call for an unprecedented degree of organizational imagination. At the same time, the UN secretary general was asked to initiate preparations with a report on the problems of the human environment. This report was presented in May 1969.[33]

Participation

It was agreed, of course, that all members of the United Nations would be entitled to participate fully in the Stockholm Conference on the Human Environment, and it was hoped that as many as 130 delegations would attend. Difficulties arose immediately, however, on the issue of participation by non-member states and by non-governmental organizations.

By the end of December 1971 the question of participation by non-member states was still highly contentious, with the Soviet Union, Czechoslovakia, and other socialist states threatening to boycott the conference unless East Germany (GDR) received an invitation to attend as a full participant. The position of many western governments was that the secretary general should invite 'state members of the United Nations or members of specialized agencies and the International Atomic Energy Agency.' This would have included West Germany (FGR), which is a member of some specialized agencies, but excluded the GDR, which is not. The Soviet position was that invitations should be sent to 'all states' and that this formula need not become a precedent for other UN conferences. The western view was that the 'all states' formula would become a precedent anyway despite present assurances to the contrary; that the GDR was welcome to attend as an observer; and that if it genuinely wished to have full rights of participation it could have prepared an application for admission to a specialized agency of the UN, especially one interested in environmental problems. The Soviet threat of boycott was considered, at the time, a disturbing threat to the success of the conference, and many scientists were prepared to blame all the governments concerned for introducing what was regarded as an essentially trivial and extraneous political issue.

Before the fall of 1971, when the People's Republic of China (PRC) was admitted to the United Nations, it was widely hoped that a suitable formula could be found to invite the Chinese to participate at Stockholm. Mr Strong, secretary general of the conference, was known to be in favour of Chinese participation and apparently initiated inquiries about the interest of the Chinese government. It might have been possible, for example, for the Swedish government, as the host government, to invite the PRC to attend. This question became irrelevant, of course, when the General Assembly voted in favour of admitting the PRC, and in January 1972 the Chinese government announced its intention to attend.

The problem of accommodating many scientists who wished to attend Stockholm in a private capacity was solved by establishing plans for an Environmental Forum which would be an official part of the conference but organized to be held separately from, though concurrent with, the intergovernmental sessions. The forum would be available for the exchange of scientific data and ideas and the preparation of recommendations. It would be attended also by representatives of appropriate national non-governmental organizations as well as representatives of international non-governmental organizations not included on the list of accredited organizations entitled to send a representative in an observer capacity to the intergovernmental sessions.

Objectives

As defined in the original resolution,[34] the objective was 'to provide a framework for comprehensive consideration within the United Nations of the problem of the human environment in order to focus the attention of governments and public opinion on the importance and urgency of this question and also to identify those aspects of it that can only or best be solved through international co-operation and agreement.' Such a conference, it was agreed, would be essentially a promotional or educational undertaking organized to mobilize world public opinion and stimulate research and the exchange of ideas in all relevant branches of human knowledge. But the secretary general's report of May 1969, reflecting a growing sense of urgency, resulted in a significant shift of emphasis in the formulation of the conference's objectives. In December 1969, at its twenty-fourth session, the UN General Assembly decided that Stockholm 'should serve as a practical means to encourage, and to provide guidelines for, action by governments and international organisations designed to protect and improve the human environment, and to remedy and prevent its impairment, by means of international co-operation, bearing in mind the particular importance of enabling developing countries to forestall the occurrence of such problems.'[35]

The decision that the conference should provide guidelines for national environmental action meant in effect that Stockholm was also to be the forum for the formulation of international environmental policy. Even though it was not originally designed as a law-making conference, it was now to be construed as the first formative stage in the progressive development of general legal principles. More complicated than any recent law-making conference convened to approve draft articles prepared by the International Law Commission, the Stockholm conference would require foreign ministries to devise new strategies of law-making which would depend on the sophisticated interaction of lawyers, environmental scientists, and other kinds of technical experts.[36] The precise juridical role of the conference became more difficult to determine when the Third Law of the Sea Conference was tentatively scheduled for 1973 and when IMCO decided to convene its own conference on marine pollution. Interforum co-ordination and a sense of orderly sequence became essential to normative development, especially in the area of marine pollution where the three conferences overlapped.

Focus

The decision to hold these three major conferences within a short period reflected the view that international law should focus initially on the marine environment. The Stockholm conference was, of course, even broader in its range of concerns. By the end of November 1971, it seemed that the main agenda items would be seven in number: i / planning and management of human settlements for environmental quality; ii / environmental aspects of natural resource management; iii / identification and control of pollutants and nuisances of broad international significance; iv / educational, informational, social, and cultural aspects; v / development and environment; vi / implications for international organization; vii / Declaration on the Human Environment.

Early in the planning for Stockholm, it was suggested that the conferees should engage in problem identification and the development of a theoretical framework. Later, however, descriptions of the conferees' work became increasingly action-oriented, and it was emphasized that in some of the agenda areas there was already a sufficient amount of knowledge to permit the taking of particular actions immediately.

Secretariat

In December 1969 the UN secretary general was instructed by the General Assembly to set up a conference Secretariat. This remained a fairly small but expert group, largely drawn from the UN Secretariat, though some outsiders were brought in to perform key roles at a senior level. In 1970 Mr Maurice Strong, president of the Canadian International Development Agency, was appointed secretary general of the Stockholm conference, directly answerable to the UN secretary general. Under his vigorous leadership the Secretariat adopted an unusually broad interpretation of its own mandate, assuming overall responsibility for the organization of the conference. Intergovernmental groups established to prepare for Stockholm were regarded by the conference Secretariat as advisory to it and their reports and working drafts as subject to its final discretionary approval. In exercising this discretion, without express mandate, the Secretariat altered some of the preparatory papers, even on matters of substance, to the dismay of some governments. Its image was that of an activist secretariat, determined not only to master formidable problems of organization with maximum efficiency but also to have an influence on the course of the conference. In view of the rushed state of preparations, this attitude was perhaps understandable, and a reflection of the Secretariat's willingness and competence to serve after the conference as the nucleus of an agency charged with the task of implementing carefully considered recommendations.[37]

Preparatory Committee

In December 1969 the UN General Assembly also established a twenty-seven member Preparatory Committee. It was agreed that the committee would meet four times between March 1970 and March 1972.

At the first session, in March 1970,[38] the committee found itself divided on the question of priority between development and environmental protection. The developing countries naturally tended to favour the former, and some began to view the environmental movement as a threat to their development planning. Highest priority was given to the careful identification of environmental problems and the need to strike an appropriate balance between the problems of developed and developing countries. It was agreed, however, that the Stockholm conference should be action-oriented and that governments should be urged to approach the conference in the spirit of urgency. The committee called for the drafting of a Universal Declaration on the Human Environment, laying down basic international norms for preserving the global environment. Three preliminary areas were agreed upon: environmental aspects of human development; rational management and conservation of natural resources; and pollution and other nuisances. The committee stressed 'preventive' over 'curative' measures and called for a broad-gauged 'strategic assessment which takes full account not only of the effects on the environment but also of financial, fiscal, administrative, legislative, social, economic, scientific and technical factors.' Fearful that the conference might fail because of the apathy or resistance of developing countries, the committee concluded its first session by inviting the secretary general of the conference in his report to its second session to suggest steps to facilitate their active participation at Stockholm.

By the time of the second session of the Preparatory Committee, held in February 1971,[39] Mr Strong, of Canada, had galvanized the conference Secretariat into intense preparatory work. In his report to the second session Mr Strong expressed concern that the needs of the developing countries 'are fully taken into account' in preparations for the conference and in the agenda itself.[40] The meeting supported the approach that would provide a balance between a comprehensive overview of environmental problems and a basis for concrete action. It was agreed that the overview would take the form of a report on the *State of the Human Environment* to be drawn up before the conference by a 'representative group of the world's intellectual community.'[41] The group was asked to 'identify the major areas of intellectual consensus and the major gaps in present knowledge, point out priority issues for consideration by political leaders, and indicate directions in which action should proceed.' It was agreed that the conference should be expected to make recommendations to governments and other appropriate bodies for specific actions and institutional arrangements for implementation. The committee went further and identified several topics on which it felt substantive action might be completed, not merely begun, at the conference itself: i / Declaration on the Human Environment; ii / marine pollution; iii / monitoring of significant environmental variables; iv / soil reclamation and preservation; v / conservation (including the establishment of the World Heritage Foundation for areas of natural, cultural, or historical importance). Intergovernmental Working Groups (iwgs) were established for each of these five topics, and in some cases preparations for law-making were initiated.[42]

The third session of the Preparatory Committee, which took place in September 1971,[43] discussed the draft declaration and considered agenda items in five specific areas: i / pollutant release limits; ii / protection of endangered species; iii / training of specialists in environmental problems; iv / information exchange on environmental matters; v / pools of genetic resources.

At its fourth and final session, held in March 1972, the Preparatory Committee discussed further the draft declaration[44] and dealt at greater length with organizational and financial implications of the recommendations in the Action Plan. The latter, designed to further the principles enunciated in the declaration, was comprised of a framework for environmental action and recommendations for international action. The recommendations were organized within each of six subject areas: i / planning and management of human settlement for environmental quality;[45] ii / environmental aspects of natural resource management;[46] iii / identification and control of pollutants of broad international significance;[47] iv / educational, informational, social, and cultural aspects of environmental issues;[48] v / development and environment;[49] vi / international organizational implications of action proposals.[50]

Action recommendations were to be put in a 'framework for environmental action,' consisting of three categories: i / environmental assessment (evaluation and review, research, monitoring, information exchange) – this global programme would be entitled 'Earthwatch'; ii / environmental management (goal setting and planning, international consultations, and agreements); iii / supporting measures (education and training, public information, organization, financing, technical co-operation).[51]

Intergovernmental Working Groups (IWGS)

Declaration on the Human Environment   The first meeting of this working group ran into differences about the degree to which the conference should lay down specific guidelines for action. Members from developing countries felt that the first draft had unduly separated environmental issues from the general framework of development and development planning. Various reservations and objections were expressed and it became clear that protracted drafting sessions lay ahead for all members and for all other governments interested in submitting a national draft. It was hoped, however, that the IWG mechanism would help to reduce the proliferation of national drafts by presenting compromise language that would be generally acceptable at Stockholm itself.

Marine pollution   At its first session in June 1971,[52] the IWGMP agreed to consider general principles of state responsibility to prevent and control activities which caused damage to the marine environment. At the second session, held at Ottawa in November 1971,[53] this IWG discussed this problem largely on the basis of a working paper submitted by Canada and other papers prepared by the United Kingdom, Spain, and the conference Secretariat. As a result of these discussions the meeting adopted twenty-three guiding principles as the basis of a report to the conference on the preservation of the marine environment. The meeting also took note of four other principles which were not adopted by the working group as a whole, on the ground that twenty states, almost half of those represented, 'supported the general concept' contained in them.[54]

The second session of the IWGMP also considered a United States draft proposal for a convention on the regulation of transportation for ocean dumping, a memorandum on the components of a comprehensive plan to preserve the marine environment prepared by the conference Secretariat, and other papers. The IWG took note of the articles on dumping and expressed the hope that after further consultation among governments an agreement on concrete global action might be reached before Stockholm.[55] The meeting also suggested changes that should be made in the Secretariat's memorandum before it was reduced to the form of a final submission.

Monitoring   The first session of the Intergovernmental Working Group on Monitoring or Surveillance was held at WMO Headquarters in Geneva in August 1971.[56] Consensus appeared to emerge particularly on two points: first, the advantage of building upon and expanding existing national and international structures and activities; and second, the need to proceed with great selectivity in recommending that new variables be monitored. There was also general agreement that expansion of monitoring activities on a worldwide scale would, in most cases, require an intensive effort in training and involve a considerable degree of technical assistance. Two drafting groups prepared a series of thirty-nine recommendations, organized under seven headings: atmospheric monitoring; monitoring of the terrestrial environment; ocean monitoring; environmental health monitoring; needs and means for improving present monitoring arrangements; institutional needs for collecting, receiving, and evaluating global environmental data; and the question of pollutant release limits.

Soil The IWG on soil reclamation and preservation was established to consider the social, economic, legal, and institutional aspects of soil erosion or degradation, and to review a number of specific action proposals and suggested policy guidelines. Environmental problems of this kind, of special importance to developing countries with a large stake in a stable rural economy, were seen to require the strengthening of intergovernmental machinery in FAO and other agencies for the acquisition and transfer of knowledge and experience in soil capabilities, degradation, conservation, and restoration. It was hoped that the Soil Map of the World, being prepared under UN auspices, would indicate those areas where the transfer of this kind of knowledge would be most valuable.

Conservation The IWG on Conservation held its first session at New York in September 1971,[57] concurrently with the third session of the Preparatory Committee. The meeting reviewed three draft conventions prepared by IUCN – the draft Convention on Conservation of the World Heritage, the draft Convention on Conservation of Certain Islands for Science, and the draft Convention on Export, Import and Transit of Certain Species of Wild Animals and Plants; reviewed the Convention on Conservation of Wetlands of International Importance, especially as Waterfowl Habitat, which was adopted by eighteen states at the Ramsar Conference in Iran in February 1971; and heard a general presentation of the draft Convention on the International Protection of Monuments, Groups of Buildings and Sites of Universal Value, prepared by UNESCO. The draft Convention on Export, Import, and Transit of Certain Species of Wild Animals and Plants received criticism that had the effect of delaying action by the working group. Differences were also expressed concerning the scope of the proposed World Heritage and the method by which executive decisions should be taken, but it was agreed that the preparation of a convention on the conservation of the World Heritage should be pursued for completion at Stockholm in June 1972.[58] The IWG asked the conference Secretariat to keep UNESCO informed of progress, so that it could be taken into account at the UNESCO meeting of government experts in April 1972, when consideration would be given to the draft Convention on the Protection of Monuments, Groups of Buildings and Sites of Universal Value. The IWG also recommended that the secretary general of the conference take the necessary steps in order that the Convention on Conservation of Certain Islands for Science be opened for signature at the Stockholm Conference on the Human Environment; and it expressed the wish that the Wetlands Convention be opened for signature before Stockholm. The secretary general was asked to consider whether the Wetlands Convention should also be opened for additional signatures at Stockholm, or whether other steps should be taken to encourage states to become parties.

Committees of the conference

The formal working arrangements at the conference provided for concurrent sessions of three committees from 6 June to 14 1972. The committees were charged with considering the recommendations for inclusion in the Action Plan,[59] subject by subject, and preparing reports on their deliberations for consideration by the plenary session. Each of the committees was assigned two subject areas: Committee I was assigned Planning and Management of Human Settlements for Environmental Quality, and Educational, Informational, Social, and Cultural Aspects of Environmental Issues; Committee II was assigned Environmental Aspects of Natural Resources Management, and Development and Environment; and Committee III was assigned Identification and Control of Pollutants of Broad International Significance, and Institutional and Financing Questions.

Planning and Management of Human Settlements for Environmental Quality[60]
Of those recommendations under this heading adopted by Committee I without objection perhaps recommendation 138[61] has the widest potential juridical significance:

> Certain aspects of human settlements can carry international implications, e.g. 'export' of pollution from urban and industrial areas, effects of seaports on international hinterlands. Accordingly *it is recommended that* the attention of governments be drawn to the need to consult bilaterally or regionally whenever environmental conditions or development plans in one country could have repercussions in one or more neighbouring countries.

Recommendation 140[62] called for a central body to be given co-ordinating authority in this area of environmental research, but recommendation 141[63] asked governments to consider co-operative arrangements in such research whenever the human settlement problem areas have 'a specific regional impact.' It is interesting to note that 'noise pollution' was not overlooked, despite the obvious difficulty of subjecting such a problem to international regulation. In (new) recommendation 157,[64] which was adopted by Committee I without dissent, and with only four abstentions,

> *It is recommended that* the intergovernmental body for environmental affairs to be established within the United Nations ensures that required surveys be made concerning the need and the technical possibilities for developing internationally agreed standards for measuring and limiting noise emissions and that, if it is deemed advisable, such limitations be applied in the production of means of transportation and certain kinds of working equipment, without a large price increase or reduction in the aid given to developing countries.

Predictably, the issue of birth control was extremely divisive. In Committee I (new) recommendation 155,[65] for example, barely passed, by 23 votes to 17 with 62 abstentions:

> *It is recommended that* WHO and other United Nations agencies should provide increased assistance to governments who so request in the field of family planning programmes without delay. *It is further recommended that* WHO should promote and intensify research endeavour in the field of human reproduction so that serious consequences of population explosion on human environment can be prevented.

Educational, Informational, Social, and Cultural Aspects of Environmental Issues[66]
Under this heading various co-operative arrangements were agreed upon by Committee I without much difficulty. Most important, it was recommended that steps be taken to organize an International Referral Service for sources of environmental information, in order to assist in the successful implementation of the conference recommendations.[67] The Secretariat of the conference also brought to the attention of Committee I the progress that had been made in preparing the draft conservation conventions: the draft Convention on Conservation of the World Heritage, prepared by the International Union for Conservation of Nature and Natural Resources (IUCN); the draft international instruments for the protection of monuments, groups of buildings and sites, prepared by UNESCO; the draft Convention on Conservation of Wetlands of International Importance, prepared by IUCN; the draft Convention on Conservation of Certain Islands for Science, prepared by IUCN; and the draft Convention on Export, Import, and Transit of Certain Species of Wild Animals and Plants, prepared by IUCN.[68] The Secretariat's proposals for action on these draft instruments were referred to plenary by Committee I.

Environmental Aspects of Natural Resources Management[69]
Committee II approved by consensus (or unanimity) 38 recommendations dealing with a wide range of topics pertaining to the management of natural resources, such as agriculture and soils, forestry, wildlife, parks, and other protected areas, conservation of genetic resources, fisheries, water resources, minerals, and energy.[70] Of special interest in the context of international environmental law were a recommendation that governments 'give attention to the need to enact international conventions and treaties to protect species inhabiting international waters or those which migrate from one country to another,'[71] and a series of recommendations that governments, and the secretary general in co-operation with FAO and other UN organizations concerned, as well as development agencies, take steps to:

a support recent guidelines, recommendations and programmes of the various international fishing organizations;[72]
b ensure close participation of fishery agencies and interests in the preparation for the UN Conference on the Law of the Sea;[73]
c ensure international cooperation in the research control and regulation of the side effects of national activities in resource utilization where these affect the resources of other nations;[74]
d further develop and strengthen facilities for collecting, analyzing and disseminating data or living aquatic resources and the environment in which they live;[75] and to
e ensure full cooperation among governments by strengthening the existing international and regional machinery for development and management of fisheries and their related environmental aspects, and in those regions where these do not exist, encourage the establishing of fishery councils and commissions as appropriate.[76]

Innovative forms of international action were outlined in recommendations for the establishment of appropriate mechanisms for the exchange of information on national park legislation and planning and management techniques;[77] for the assistance of UN agencies to developing countries in planning the inflow of visitors into their protected areas 'in such a way as to reconcile revenue and environmental considerations';[78] and for the making of inventories of genetic resources 'most endangered by depletion or extinction.'[79]

Of the recommendations put to a vote in Committee II, by far the most highly publicized was recommendation 86, which was approved by 53 votes to none, with three abstentions.

> *It is recommended that* governments agree to strengthen the International Whaling Commission, to increase international research efforts and as a matter of urgency to call for an international agreement, under the auspices of the International Whaling Commission and involving all governments concerned for a 10-year moratorium on commercial whaling.[80]

In recomendation 159, finally adopted by 43 votes to 2 with 7 abstentions, five principles were endorsed and applied to water resources common to more than one jurisdiction:

a full consideration must be given to the sovereign rights of each country concerned to develop its own resources;
b when water resource activities are contemplated that may have an environmental effect on another country, the other country should be notified well in advance of the activity envisaged;
c the basic objective of all water resource use and development activities from the environmental point of view is to ensure the best use of water and to avoid its pollution in each country;
d the net benefits of hydrologic regions common to more than one national jurisdiction are to be shared equitably by the nations affected; and
e regional conferences should be organized to promote these considerations.[81]

Also divisive was recommendation 160, which was finally adopted by 44 votes to 9, with 2 abstentions. The most controversial part of this recommendation called upon the secretary general to take steps to:

d conduct an exploratory programme to assess the actual and potential environmental effects of water management upon the oceans, define terms and estimate the costs for a comprehensive programme of action and establish and maintain as far as possible.
(i) a world registry of major or otherwise important rivers arranged regionally and classified according to their discharge of water and pollutants; and
(ii) a world registry of clean rivers which would be defined in accordance with internationally agreed quality criteria and to which nations would contribute on a voluntary basis.[82]

Development and Environment[83]

This proved to be one of the more difficult subject areas, because of the fear of many developing countries that the conference would be largely an exchange of views on environmental policy by the richer countries, which would try to pass the burden of their environmental problems to the developing countries. This, it was felt, could occur in three ways: 'a / by the transfer of "dirty" industries to the developing world; b / by restrictions on exports from developing countries whose environmental standards were less stringent; and c / through the imposition of higher environmental standards, and thus higher costs, in the design and appraisal of development projects by donor countries.'

The issue of the probable impact of environmental controls on international trade proved to be particularly thorny. Finally, however, Committee II passed recommendation 32 in the following words, by 36 votes to 2, with 11 abstentions:

> *It is recommended that* governments take the necessary steps to ensure that:
> – all countries present at the Conference agree not to invoke environmental concerns as a pretext for discriminating trade policies or for reduced access to markets and recognize further that the burdens of the environmental policies of the industrialized countries should not be transferred, either directly or indirectly, to the developing countries. As a general rule, no country should solve or disregard its environmental problems at the expense of other countries.
> – where environmental concerns lead to restrictions on trade, or to stricter environmental standards with negative effects on exports, particularly from developing countries, appropriate measures for compensation should be worked out within the framework of existing contractual and institutional arrangements and any new such arrangements that can be worked out in the future.
> – all countries agree that uniform environmental standards should not be expected to be applied universally by all countries with respect to given industrial processes or products except in those cases where environmental disruption may constitute a concern to other countries. In addition, in order to avoid an impairment of the access of the developing countries to the markets of the industrialized countries due to differential product standards, governments should aim at world wide harmonization of such standards. Environmental standards should be established at whatever levels are necessary to safeguard the environment, and should not be aimed at giving trade advantages.[84]

Identification and Control of Pollutants of Broad International Significance[85]

In this important subject area Committee III endorsed over two dozen recommendations on pollution generally and on marine pollution in particular. Especially important in international environmental law were recommendations 233 and 239. The former was approved in this form:

> *It is recommended that* governments, with the assistance and guidance of appropriate United Nations bodies, in particular the Joint Group of Experts on the Scientific Aspects of Marine Pollution (GESAMP)
> – accept and implement available instruments on the control of the maritime sources of marine pollution;
> – ensure that the provisions of such instruments are complied with by ships flying their flags and by ships operating in areas under their jurisdiction and that adequate provisions are made for reviewing the effectiveness of and revising, existing and proposed international measures for control of marine pollution;
> – ensure that ocean dumping by their nationals anywhere or by any person in areas under their jurisdiction, is controlled and that governments continue to work towards the completion of and bringing into force as soon as possible of an overall instrument for the control of ocean dumping as well as needed regional agreements within the

framework of this instrument, in particular for enclosed and semi-enclosed seas, which are more at risk from pollution:
- participate fully in the 1973 Intergovernmental Maritime Consultative Organization (IMCO) Conference on Marine Pollution and the Law of the Sea Conference scheduled to begin in 1973, as well as in regional efforts, with a view to bringing all significant sources of pollution within the marine environment, including radioactive pollution from nuclear surface ships and submarines, and in particular in enclosed and semi-enclosed seas, under appropriate controls and particularly to complete elimination of deliberate pollution by oil from ships, with the goal of achieving this by the middle of the present decade;
- strengthen national controls over landbased sources of marine pollution, in particular in enclosed and semi-enclosed seas, and recognize that, in some circumstances, the discharge of residual heat from nuclear and other power stations may constitute a potential hazard to marine ecosystems.[86]

Recommendation 239 was approved in these words:

It is recommended that:
- Governments collectively *endorse* the principles set forth in paragraph 197 of Conference document A/CONF 48/8[87] as guiding concepts for the Law of the Sea Conference and the Intergovernmental Maritime Consultative Organization (IMCO) Marine Pollution Conference scheduled to be held in 1973 and also the statement of objectives agreed at the second session of the Intergovernmental Working Group on Marine Pollution as follows,

'the marine environment and all the living organisms which it supports are of vital importance to humanity and all people have an interest in assuring that this environment is so managed that its quality and resources are not impaired. This applies especially to coastal nations, which have a particular interest in the management of coastal area resources. The capacity of the sea to assimilate wastes and render them harmless and its ability to regenerate natural resources is not unlimited. Proper management is required and measures to prevent and control marine pollution must be regarded as an essential element in this management of the oceans and seas and their natural resources,'

and in respect of the particular interest of coastal states in the marine environment and recognizing that the resolution of this question is a matter for consideration at the Law of the Sea Conference, *take note* of the principles on the rights of coastal states discussed but neither endorsed nor rejected at the second seminar of the Intergovernmental Working Groups on Marine Pollution and *refer* these principles to the 1973 IMCO Conference for information and to the 1973 Law of the Sea Conference for such action as may be appropriate;

- governments take early action to adopt effective national measures for the control of all significant sources of marine pollution, including land-based sources, and concert and coordinate their actions regionally and where appropriate on a wider international basis;

– The Secretary-General, in cooperation with appropriate international organizations, endeavour to provide guidelines which governments might wish to take into account when developing such measures.[88]

A major political issue in Committee III was the question of nuclear weapons testing. A resolution co-sponsored by New Zealand and Peru, introduced in the hope of using the influence and publicity of the conference to halt the imminent French tests, was adopted in committee by 48 votes to 2 with 19 abstentions, before being referred to plenary. The text read as follows:

The United Nations Conference on the Human Environment
    Considering that there is radioactive contamination of the environment from nuclear weapons tests;
    Taking into account the reports of the United Nations Scientific Committee on the Effects of Atomic Radiation;
    Believing that all exposures of mankind to radiation should be kept to the minimum possible and should be justified by benefits that would otherwise not be obtained:
    Considering that the United Nations has endorsed world treaties such as the Partial Test Ban Treaty and the Seabed Denuclearization Treaty and regional treaties such as the Tlatelolco Treaty for the Denuclearization of Latin America, and has repeatedly called for the cessation of nuclear weapons tests,

Resolves:
1 To condemn nuclear weapons tests, especially those carried out in the atmosphere
2 To call upon those states intending to carry out nuclear weapons tests to abandon their plans to carry out such tests as they may lead to further contamination of the environment.[89]

Institutional and Financing Questions

The debate on these questions in Committee III was preceded by extensive informal consultations before and during the conference. These consultations, led by Brazil, US, Sweden, and Kenya, with drafting support from Canada, Indonesia, and Egypt, resulted in a draft recommendation which, after several votes in the committee, was sent to plenary for approval.

Several issues found the developed and the developing countries on different sides. For example, on the question where the new environmental body should be located within the United Nations structure, the developing countries plus Sweden wanted to have the General Assembly establish the relevant committee, while most of the developed countries preferred that the Economic and Social Council (ECOSOC) establish the committee and be the principal authority to which it would report. Agreement was finally reached upon a 'Governing Council for Environmental Programs' modelled on the Governing Council of the United Nations Development Program. This would be established by the General Assembly and report to it through the ECOSOC, which would transmit comments on the economic and social implications of environmental activities. In addition, there was a provision recommending that the General Assembly review these arrangements in 1976, keeping open the possibility that ECOSOC might assume prime responsibility for the Governing Council. The recommendation proposed that the executive director, to be elected by the General Assembly, would under the authority of the Governing Council seek co-ordination of United Nations environmental programs. To allay fears about the extent of these powers, it was pointed out that the Secretariat would not have authority to make recommendations directly to other United Nations bodies.

It was agreed that a voluntary fund – the Environment Fund – should be established in accordance with existing UN financial procedures in order to provide additional financing, outside the specialized agencies, for environmental programs. There were contrary proposals on how the expenses of the Secretariat should be met. The US, UK, Japan, and West Germany, citing the examples of the UNDP and UNICEF, urged that all such expenses should be met from the fund, whereas the majority of delegates wanted to have these expenses met from the regular budget of the UN. It was assumed on both sides that under the former arrangement the richer countries, as the chief contributors to the fund, would acquire more influence over the Secretariat's operation. As a compromise, it was agreed that part of the expenses – the 'hard core' administrative expenses – should be met from the UN regular budget, while program costs should be met from the fund.[90]

Plenary

Declaration on the Human Environment
In accordance with a resolution put forward by the Chinese delegation,[91] a Working Group was established to review the scope and content of the draft declaration prepared by the Intergovernmental Working Group. The purpose was to meet the objection that not all participants had had an opportunity to contribute to the drafting of the basic document to emerge from the conference, which would affect the interests of all people. The draft was, therefore, reopened to negotiation under the pressure of conference deadlines. Two problems dominated: the Argentinian-Brazilian dispute over principle 20 of the IWG draft on the duty of states to notify others of activities that may have an extraterritorial effect; and Chinese opposition to principle 21 on nuclear testing. The first question remained unsolved and was referred to the UN General Assembly. The Chinese were adamant but finally agreed not to demand a vote on a compromise formulation worked out in informal consultations, contenting themselves with reading into the summary record their own proposal. In effect, this cleared the way for adoption of the new amended text by consensus.

The text of the Stockholm Declaration on the Human Environment consists of a preamble and 26 principles.[92] Because of its historic importance in the development of international environmental law, the text is included as an appendix to this article. This is not a suitable place to make an extensive analysis. It may be sufficient here to underline some of the more important legal aspects.

Both the nature of the UN Declaration on the Human Environment and the circumstances of its birth, as the first universal attempt at policy formulation, seem to ensure that it will be invoked constantly in innumerable forums as the world community's most authoritative charter on environmental rights and duties. Like other charters of the world community, it is composed of principles that vary considerably in specificity and in degree of intensity of commitment. Some of the propositions are, essentially, scientific warnings to the world in general: for example, the first part of principle 6 states that 'the discharge of toxic substances or of other substances and the release of heat, in such quantities or concentrations as to exceed the capacity of the environment to render them harmless, must be halted in order to ensure that serious or irreversible damage is not inflicted upon ecosystems.' This statement is followed anticlimactically by a weak effort in environmental rhetoric which is empty of juridical potentiality. 'The just struggle of the peoples of all countries against pollution should be supported.'

The first part of principle 1 is somewhat more charter-like in its declaratory eloquence, though articulated at the highest level of generality: 'Man has the fundamental right to freedom, equality and adequate conditions of life, in an environment of a quality which permits a life of dignity and well-being, and bears a responsibility to protect and improve the environment for present and future generations.' In future law-making forums this kind of declaration may serve a useful rhetorical purpose to the extent it reflects a balanced consideration of related rights and duties, which might even be construed as interdependent. It is also important as a pledge by the organized world community to protect the environmental interests of succeeding generations, because the sense of obligation to the future is crucial to the concept of conservation and justifies the view that international environmental law is basically concerned with the postponement of the death of man.

Some of the principles in the declaration are really general recommendations applied to specific problem areas. Principle 13, for example, is an important and adroitly worded statement which advocates integrated planning as the best means of reconciling the separate but compatible objectives of development and environmental planning: 'In order to achieve a more rational management of resources and thus to improve the environment, states should adopt an integrated and coordinated approach to their development planning so as to ensure that development is compatible with the need to protect and improve the human environment for the benefit of their population.'

But only two principles are immediately and obviously conducive to the development of international environmental law. The first and stronger of the two, principle 21, purports not only to affirm but to extend the famous *Trail Smelter* principle of state responsibility for activities within the territory that cause environmental damage in the territory of a neighbouring state.

> States have in accordance with the Charter of the United Nations and the principles of international law, the sovereign right to exploit their own resources pursuant to their own environmental policies, and the responsibility to ensure that activities within their jurisdiction or control do not cause damage to the environment of other states or of areas beyond the limits of national jurisdiction.

The *Trail Smelter* principle is extended by virtue of the fact that responsibility arises not only when damage is caused in the territory of another state but also when it is caused in a non-territorial area such as the high seas. It is also extended by the apparent intention that responsibility should attach to activities under the state's control even if not under its jurisdiction. Presumably also the responsibility would be the same whether the state's jurisdiction was territorial, extraterritorial, or functional, as in the high seas, for example, under the regime of the continental shelf.

What is new and most important in this formulation is the extensive scope of state responsibility for environmental damage asserted. Equally noticeable, and perhaps as significant, is the lack of qualification in the assertion of state responsibility. Arguably, the prior invocation of the 'sovereign right' that states are declared to have 'to exploit their own resources pursuant to their own environmental policies' creates a potential 'conflict of laws' situation in which national and international environmental standards may compete for priority. No doubt we should accept the prospect of such difficulties as part of the inevitable problems that lie ahead in the development of international environmental law.

The 'compensatory' part of the *Trail Smelter* principle is also endorsed in the Stockholm Declaration. Principle 22 provides that 'States shall cooperate to develop further the international law regarding liability and compensation for the victims of pollution and other environmental damage caused by activities within the jurisdiction or control of such States to areas beyond their jurisdiction.' The language here is weakened by the operative clause which merely recognizes that states have an obligation to co-operate, but the phrase 'develop further' clearly implies that liability and the duty to compensate in these circumstances already exist in international law. It is worth noting also that environmental damage is not limited to the various forms of pollution.

Action Plan

Because of the pressure of time, the Secretariat was unable to present the plenary with a final version of the recommendations adopted in committee, but the plenary did adopt the committee reports on the adopted recommendations. In this way, the conference can be said to have adopted the context of the Action Plan.

Planning and Management of Human Settlements for Environmental Quality The plenary engaged in a long and vigorous debate of a recommendation that called on WHO and other UN agencies to provide increased assistance to governments in the field of family planning and overpopulation. Despite determined opposition from many countries, especially those with large Roman Catholic populations, the recommendation was finally approved. Another equally divisive issue arose from an amendment by India and the Libyan Arab Republic requesting that governments and the secretary general take immediate steps towards establishment of an international fund having the primary objective of assisting national programs for the environmental improvement of human settlements. Resulting in a polarization of developed and developing countries, this amendment was finally adopted by 58 votes (developing) to 15 (developed), with 13 abstentions.

Educational, Informational, Social, and Cultural Aspects of Environmental Issues None of the recommendations under this heading proved to be controversial in the plenary. Of special interest from a legal standpoint was the adoption of recommendations that governments examine the draft Convention on the Protection of the World Natural and Cultural Heritage with a view to its adoption at the next General Conference of UNESCO, and that governments should sign whenever appropriate, the Convention of Wetlands of International Significance.

Environmental Aspects of Natural Resources Management   Debate on these issues was sometimes quite emotional. Brazil, which frequently throughout the conference warned against the danger of sanctioning encroachments upon national sovereignty, opposed an amendment which its neighbour Argentina proposed to a recommendation on water resource management. This debate arose out of a border river dispute between the two countries. The amendment, which sought to make the recommendation more specific by proposing the creation of 'international river basin commissions' rather than simply 'appropriate mechanisms,' was finally approved.

One of the most emotional of all issues at the conference was that of whaling, and the specific recommendation that called for a ten-year moratorium was widely supported. In the absence of the Soviet Union, the other major whaling nation today, Japan had to stand alone against the tide of indignation, denying the existence of adequate scientific evidence that the types of whales being exploited were in danger of extinction to the point of justifying a total ban. A US amendment was adopted, with none in opposition and only Japan, Portugal, and South Africa abstaining. This puts the International Whaling Commission under considerable pressure to implement the recommended ban, or at least to take some other kind of drastic action.

Development and Environment   The chief difficulties under this rubric were debated more intensively in committee than in plenary. Perhaps the most important recommendation approved was that environmental concerns must not be invoked as a pretext for discriminatory trade policies. Surprisingly, the developing countries did not use the opportunity to press for promises of additional aid to finance environmentally related projects, possibly a reflection of their appreciation of the difficulty experienced by donor countries in increasing, or even maintaining, present levels of development assistance.

Identification and Control of Pollutants of Broad International Significance   All twenty-five recommendations under this heading were adopted in the plenary without a vote. Of major importance was the call, in recommendation 239,[93] for endorsement of the twenty-three principles of marine pollution which had been adopted at the Intergovernmental Working Group on Marine Pollution at Ottawa in November 1971[94] as guiding concepts for the Third UN Conference on the Law of the Sea and the IMCO Marine Pollution Conference. Along with recommendation 233,[95] this represented perhaps the most important legal outcome of the conference, providing in effect a new foundation for the reformulation of the law of the sea in favour of coastal states' rights and responsibilities with respect to pollution control and resource management.

Institutional and Financing Questions   The Plenary approved the report on these questions by Committee III, including the proposal for establishing a voluntary fund. The fund would be administered by an Environmental Secretariat under an executive director, who would be elected by the General Assembly, and the Secretariat would report to a Governing Council. While Committee III recommended a Council of 48 members, the plenary changed its size to 54. The plenary agreed that the question of location for the Secretariat headquarters should be referred to the General Assembly. It was agreed to recommend the convening of a second UN Conference on the Human Environment, the question of location again to be left to the General Assembly.

Implementation in the General Assembly

In the fall of 1972 the UN General Assembly adopted eleven resolutions on the human environment as recommended by Committee II. Some of these resolutions deserve particular notice.

In adopting resolution 2994 (XXVII) on the Stockholm conference, the Assembly drew the attention of governments and the proposed Governing Council for Environment Programmes to the Declaration on the Human Environment, and referred the Action Plan to the Governing Council for study and appropriate action.[96] The Stockholm resolution on the convening of a second UN Conference on the Human Environment was also referred to the Governing Council for similar purposes. Significantly, the vote on this resolution by the General Assembly was 112 in favour to none against, with 10 abstentions. Most of the abstention votes were cast by the eastern European states that boycotted the Stockholm conference.

Under resolution 2995 (XXVII) on co-operation between states on the human environment the Assembly emphasized that in the exploration, exploitation, and development of their natural resources, states must not produce significant harmful effects in zones situated outside their national jurisdiction. This resolution, which may be of fundamental importance in the development of international environmental law, was adopted by 115 votes to none with 10 abstentions.[97]

Resolution 2996 (XXVII) on the international responsibility of states declared that any resolution adopted at the Twenty-seventh Assembly could not affect principles 21 and 22 of the Stockholm Declaration on the Human Environment. As we saw above, these seminal principles seem to point to the general acceptance of the need to extend the *Trail Smelter* doctrine of state responsibility for environmental damage beyond territorial limits. The special treatment given by the General Assembly to these two principles suggests that they may evolve to the level of *jus cogens*. This legally important resolution of the General Assembly was adopted by a vote of 112 in favour to none against, with 10 abstentions (Bulgaria, Byelorussian SSR, Cuba, Czechoslovakia, Hungary, Mauritania, Mongolia, Poland, Ukrainian SSR, USSR).[98]

A four-part resolution 2997 (XXVII) on institutional and financial arrangements for environmental co-operation was adopted by 116 votes to none with 10 abstentions. Under part one, the Assembly decided to establish the fifty-eight member Governing Council for Environmental Programmes to be elected by the Assembly on the following basis: 16 seats for African states; 13 seats for Asian states; 10 seats for Latin American states; 6 seats for eastern European states; 13 seats for western European and other states. The function of the Council would be, *inter alia,* to promote international co-operation in the environment, to provide policy guidance for the direction and co-ordination of environmental programs, and to review the impact of national and international environmental policies and measures on developing countries. Under part II, the Assembly decided to establish a small Secretariat to serve as a focal point for environmental action and co-ordination within the United Nations system. The secretariat would be headed by the executive director, to be elected by the Assembly on the nomination of the secretary general for a four-year term. Costs of servicing the Governing Council and of providing the small secretariat would be borne by the regular budget of the United Nations, and operational program costs, support, and administrative costs of the Environmental Fund would be borne by the fund.

Under part III, the Assembly decided to establish a voluntary fund with effect from 1 January 1973 which would finance wholly or partly the costs of new environmental initiatives undertaken within the United Nations system. The fund would be used for financing such programs of general interest as regional and global monitoring and other programs as the Governing Council might decide upon. To ensure that development priorities of developing countries would not be adversely affected, measures should be taken to provide additional financial resources on terms compatible with the economic situation of the recipient developing country.

Under part IV, the Assembly decided to establish an Environmental Co-ordinating Board under the chairmanship of the executive director and under the auspices and within the framework of the Administrative Committee on Co-ordination. The board would meet periodically to ensure co-operation and co-ordination among all bodies concerned in the implementation of environmental programs and to report annually to the Governing Council.[99]

It is also worth noting that another resolution 3002 (XXVII) on development and environment emphasized that, in implementation and financing of the objectives of the environment fund, the environmental measures and programs might constitute a necessary part of the process of accelerating the economic development of developing countries and should receive special consideration in the formulation of programs and priorities by the Governing Council. It recommended respect for the principle that resources for environmental programs should be additional to the present level and the projected growth of resources contemplated in the International Development Strategy should be made available for programs directly related to development assistance.[100]

The General Assembly decided to locate the Environment Secretariat in a developing country, namely in Nairobi, Kenya. This resolution was adopted unanimously by 128 votes to none, despite unofficial misgivings about a new agency of this kind being so far from the specialized agencies of the United Nations in Geneva and elsewhere whose environmental research is to be co-ordinated by the Environment Secretariat.[101]

Post-Stockholm developments

By the end of 1972 it had become generally accepted by the participating governments that the conference, though ambitious, had realized their expectations as a useful and important first step towards the gradual evolution of international environmental policy. Even before this endorsement by the General Assembly, references to the Stockholm recommendations had already become common in other forums concerned with law-making issues, such as the July 1972 session of the UN Seabed Committee preparing for the Third Conference on the Law of the Sea and the Intergovernmental Conference on the Convention on the Dumping of

Wastes at Sea held at London in November 1972.[102] The influence of the Stockholm conference on the formulation of international environmental law remains, however, to be tested at the IMCO Conference on Marine Pollution and the Third UN Conference on the Law of the Sea, at the Intergovernmental Conference on Human Settlements, and at other policy-related conferences scheduled to take place in the mid-1970s.

Perhaps an even more reliable measure of the Stockholm legacy should be looked for at national and regional levels as national governments struggle to cope with the consequences of living with themselves and their neighbours in an age of increasing environmental sophistication. Whether pollution consciousness is a temporary cult should be discoverable within the next few years in the volume and mode of environmental legislation. Here too, as well as on international law-making efforts, the UN Environment Secretariat at Nairobi can be expected to focus much of its attention.

CANADIAN CONTRIBUTIONS TO INTERNATIONAL ENVIRONMENTAL POLICY-MAKING

If we were to define international environmental law so broadly as to encompass all international problems of resource use and management – law of the sea, air and space law, international river basins, weather modification, telecommunications, and so forth – Canadian contributions to these 'environmental' areas would represent the most conspicuous Canadian inputs to the practice and literature of international law in the last twenty years. But in this paper the concept of environmentalism is defined more narrowly as a scientific concern with the evidence that our planet and all its species are threatened with extinction; and the first evidence of international environmental law in this planetary sense is regarded as just emerging from intergovernmental preparations for the Stockholm Conference on the Human Environment. Canadian contributions to international environmental law will be treated in the same restrictive fashion.

The Stockholm preparations, however, involved a pooling of national experience in resource use and management in order to provide the broadest view of global environmental problems. Canadian resource scientists, administrators, lawyers, and economists were intensely engaged not only in the preparation of Canadian government positions for Stockholm and related conferences, such as the Third Law of the Sea Conference and the IMCO Conference on Marine Pollution, but also in international responsibilities. A Canadian, Maurice Strong, has been the most visible and most influential of all international civil servants in the environmental field as secretary general of the Stockholm conference. He was appointed to this position as a highly efficient resource administrator and as president of the Canadian International Development Agency in Ottawa. Canadians are also prominent in the work of those international agencies and organizations that have been most active in problems of the human environment, such as UNESCO, IUCN, IOC, WHO, WMO, FAO, and ICAO. Canadians have also been fairly prominent on the staffs of some agencies, such as ILO, FAO, and ICAO, that have particular interests in environmental problems. Canadian diplomats and government lawyers have taken important initiatives on environmental issues in political organs like ECOSOC, technical agencies like IMCO, and specialized bodies concerned with law-making problems, like the UN Disarmament Committee and the Seabed Committee.

In staking out government positions at international conferences and in diplomatic representations, Canada has become identified as a hardliner on the need for strict environmental controls and as one of the most insistent advocates of a systematic, comprehensive approach to the problems of the global environment. From the beginning, therefore, Canada was regarded, correctly, as strongly pro-Stockholm.

The strength of Canadian government interest in the Stockholm conference is more apparent from the scale of preparations in Ottawa than from the publicity devoted to it. The Department of the Environment, as lead agency, assumed the chief burden, especially in scientific preparatory studies. This was an appropriate assignment of departmental responsibilities, since this department employs over 60 per cent of scientific personnel in federal government service, including almost all those engaged in the environmental areas of oceanography, meteorology, forestry, and fisheries. Because of its longer experience and special expertise in diplomacy and international law, External Affairs assumed a major role in staking out the government position on conference strategy and in the execution of pre-Stockholm negotiations on environmental issues. Other departments involved in Stockholm preparations included Energy, Mines and Resources; Indian Affairs and Northern Development; Transport; National Health and Welfare; Agriculture; and Industry, Trade and Commerce. Interdepartmental co-ordination was facilitated by the Interdepartmental Committee on International Environmental Activities, chaired by Environment; the UN Environmental Affairs Sub-Committee, chaired by External; by various Interdepartmental Task Forces; and, in the field of marine pollution, by the Interdepartmental Committee on the Law of the Sea, chaired by External. In an advisory capacity, contributions were also made by a number of federal-provincial and national committees, and by an advisory committee on marine and environmental conferences composed of academic international lawyers.

Canadian approaches to marine pollution problems

Soon after the decision to convene the Stockholm conference it was generally agreed that marine pollution was one of the most serious environmental problems and one which might, because of the international areas involved, lend itself to some kind of effective treatment through global action at Stockholm. To Canada, possessing the longest national coastline in the world, the dangers of marine pollution were especially serious and an emphasis on the problems of the ocean environment in its Stockholm preparations seemed particularly appropriate. Accordingly, Canada took the initiative in offering to prepare a working paper on general guidelines and principles for the preservation of the marine environment for the second session of the Intergovernmental Working Group on Marine Pollution (IWGMP) held at Ottawa in November 1971.[103] This offer was accepted, and the Canadian working paper was presented as the basis of discussion, which culminated in the adoption of a text by the IWGMP and its submission to the conference Secretariat.

The process of preparing the Canadian working paper on marine pollution involved government officials of several departments, chiefly Environment and

External Affairs. More important perhaps is that it involved close co-operation between scientists and lawyers, since the subject matter raised difficult technical questions of both disciplines. The final result was, among other things, a testament to the fact that governments can conduct interdepartmental and interdisciplinary exercises more harmoniously and more effectively than universities, in situations where the national incentive is sufficiently high! Although this particular exercise is regarded today in Ottawa as something of a model, it should not be expected that it will be easy for the Canadian government to follow it in preparing its position in other areas of international law, for the Canadian cabinet's determination to make a major impact on development of marine pollution principles was exceptional and obviously attributable to its recent experience in having to bear the major part of the cost in the *Arrow* clean-up.

The IWGMP: Ottawa session

The nature and extent of Canadian influence at the Ottawa session of the IWGMP can, perhaps, be shown most clearly by reproducing the IWGMP and Canadian drafts of the 'general guidelines and principles for the preservation of the marine environment,' with the corresponding sections placed side by side.

1 *Definition of marine pollution*

IWGMP text	Canadian text
Marine pollution is defined as:	
The introduction by man, directly or indirectly, of substances or energy into the marine environment (including estuaries), resulting in such deleterious effects as harm to living resources, hazards to human health, hindrance to marine activities including fishing, impairment of quality for use of sea water, and reduction of amenities.	Identical

The definition proposed by Canada and the IWGMP is that accepted by the UN Group of Experts on the Scientific Aspects of Marine Pollution (GESAMP), which seems now to have become the generally accepted working definition during the preliminary (Stockholm) phase of law-making. It is, of course, open to question whether a definition of this term is necessary at all at this stage.[104]

2 *Basic premises*

IWGMP text	Canadian text
a The marine environment and all the living organisms which it supports are of vital importance to humanity, and all people have an interest in assuring that this environment is so managed that its quality and resources are not impaired.	Humanity as a whole has an interest in the preservation of the marine environment and its protection from all forms of pollution.

b This applies especially to coastal nations, which have a particular interest in the management of coastal area resources.

Coastal states have a priority of interest in and a special responsibility for the protection of the marine environment.

c The capacity of the sea to assimilate wastes and render them harmless, and its ability to regenerate natural resources, is not unlimited.

No counterpart

d Proper management is required and measures to prevent and control marine pollution must be regarded as an essential element in this management of the oceans and seas and their natural resources.

No counterpart

These four basic premises are, rather strangely, called 'objectives' in the IWGMP draft. In the Canadian draft the first premise, the principle of universal interest, is described as a 'basic premise,' standing alone along with the definition of marine pollution shown above. It might be inferred from both formulations of the principle of universal interest that all states and all marine-related international organizations have a responsibility to protect that interest in the preservation of the marine environment, since this derivation provides the link with the second basic premise, the principle of the particular interest of the coastal state. Neither draft is entirely satisfactory in the absence of a clear recognition that responsibility (and commensurate powers) should be derived directly from the nature and degree of interest in the preservation of marine environment. The third basic premise is confusing because the key concept of 'wastes' is not defined in the IWGMP draft. Until a clear definition is given it is impossible to test the scientific validity of the proposition. What is in question is the capacity of the sea to assimilate substances and energy that might cause 'marine pollution,' as defined above. The fourth premise, recognizing that the preservation of the marine environment must be subject to management, like resource development, looks like a bold step forward towards the view that the world's oceans must be managed, but 'management' is a very loosely used expression in the law of the sea and neither draft brings us any closer to a clear understanding of what it means.

3 *Principles of state responsibility (general)*
   IWGMP text   Canadian text

a Every state has a duty to protect and preserve the marine environment and, in particular, to prevent pollution that may affect areas where an internationally shared resource is located.

No state has a right to pollute the marine environment, in particular where such pollution may affect areas where an internationally shared resource is located or where other states have primary responsibility for marine environmental protection.

b Every state should adopt appropriate measures for the prevention of marine pollution, whether acting individually or in conjunction with other states under agreed international arrangements.

Every state should adopt appropriate measures for the prevention of marine pollution, whether acting individually or in conjunction with other states under existing or future international agreements.

c States should use the best practicable means available to them to minimize the discharge of potentially hazardous substances to the sea by all routes, including land-based sources such as rivers, outfalls and pipelines within national jurisdiction, as well as dumping by or from ships, aircraft and platforms.

To the extent that some states must, of necessity, use the marine environment for the disposal of wastes, these states should ensure that such disposal does not result in pollution.

d States should ensure that their national legislation provides adequate sanctions against those who infringe existing regulations on marine pollution.

Every state should, to the greatest possible extent, protect and preserve the marine environment and restore that environment where it has been seriously damaged by actions of that state or persons under its jurisdiction.

e States should assume joint responsibility for the preservation of the marine environment beyond the limits of national jurisdiction.

No counterpart

f States should discharge, in accordance with the principles of international law, their obligations toward other states where damage arises from pollution caused by their own activities or by organization or individuals under their jurisdiction and should cooperate in developing procedures for dealing with such damage and the settlement of disputes.

States should devise means to enable responsibility to be fixed with states or international organizations or agencies that have caused marine environmental damage or where such damage has been caused by the activities of persons under their jurisdiction. Compensation should be payable in such cases and should be provided for by international agreements which would also provide the necessary mechanism for the submission of disputed cases to existing and future international tribunals.

g Every state should cooperate with other states and competent international organizations with regard to the elaboration and implementation of internationally agreed rules, standards

Every state should cooperate with other states and competent international organizations with regard to the elaboration, implementation and enforcement of internationally agreed rules and standards for and procedures for the prevention of marine pollution on global, regional and national levels.

the prevention of marine pollution, on global, regional and national levels.

h States should join together regionally to concert their policies and adopt measures in common to prevent the pollution of the areas which, for geographical or ecological reasons, form a natural entity and an integrated whole.

No counterpart

i Every state should cooperate with other states and with competent international organizations with a view to the development of marine environmental research and survey programmes and systems and means for monitoring changes in the marine environment, including studies of the present state of the oceans, the trends of pollution effects and the exchange of data and scientific information on the marine environment.

Identical

j States should cooperate in the appropriate international forum to ensure that activities related to the exploration and exploitation of the seabed and the ocean floor beyond the limits of national jurisdiction shall not result in pollution of the marine environment.

All states should, in the areas of the seabed beyond the limits of national jurisdiction, refrain from engaging in or permitting persons under their jurisdiction to engage in activities related to the exploration and exploitation of seabed resources which may result in pollution of the marine environment, except in compliance with agreed international rules and standards for the prevention of marine pollution.

k States should assist one another to the best of their ability, in action against marine pollution of whatever origin.

No counterpart

The Canadian proposal denying a right (license) to pollute is replaced by the IWGMP affirmation that every state has a duty to protect and preserve the marine environment. More important than this change in wording is the retention of the clause stating that this principle has special application to the situation where two or more states share an economic interest in a particular area. It was hoped that this clause, if approved at Stockholm, would improve the prospects of a later attempt at the Third Law of the Sea Conference to enunciate the environmental responsibilities and powers of regional organizations and joint commissions that exercise managerial authority over shared marine resources.

Both versions of principle b are noteworthy insofar as they place equal emphasis on unilateral and joint measures for the prevention of marine pollution. Presumably 'agreed international arrangements' is intended to be broader than 'existing or future international agreements,' so as to include decisions taken under the auspices of international organizations and agencies.

The Canadian formulation of principle c conceded that the discharge of wastes in the sea could not be totally prohibited and accepted that the extent of permissible restrictions should depend on scientific arguments over the application of the GESAMP definition of marine pollution. The IWGMP substitute language is much vaguer and its weakness is underlined by the difficulty of interpreting 'national jurisdiction.'

The Canadian proposal for a duty to restore – a true environmental responsibility – was apparently unacceptable to many states which could not contemplate undertaking in advance to sustain the high costs that might be involved in environmental rehabilitation. The IWGMP's formulation, calling for 'adequate' sanctions, seems inadequate as a deterrent in the absence of agreement on reasonably stringent international standards with which the legislation of all states must comply. Again, in the absence of agreement on the extent of the limits of national jurisdiction, the IWGMP proposal for a principle of joint (common?) responsibility beyond these limits is of uncertain utility.

Neither formulation of principle f can be regarded as an advance towards the establishment of criteria or procedures for the attachment of liability. Admittedly a declaration of principles is not the most appropriate instrument for a detailed treatment of this problem, but it is unfortunate that the IWGMP could go no further than to assert in a tautologous manner that 'states should discharge their obligations.' The two versions of principle g are very similar, separated only by minor drafting changes influenced, for example, by the United Kingdom position that 'implementation' includes 'enforcement.' Principle h in the IWGMP draft calling for regional co-ordination of national policies was not, unfortunately, included in the Canadian draft, but its impact may prove to be considerably reduced by scientific difficulties of determining what constitutes a 'natural entity' or an 'integrated whole.'

The call for scientific co-operation does not provide much difficulty and, as worded here, does not require even the most cautious of states to reserve their position on the more controversial question of the freedom of scientific research. The duty of states to co-operate to prevent pollution arising from mineral exploitation of the seabed beyond the limits of national jurisdiction is, once again, an unexceptionable principle. The IWGMP version refers impliedly to the existing attempts to establish an international mechanism under a deep sea regime at the Third Law of the Sea Conference.

Principle k which was not included in the Canadian working paper looks, at first glance, like a catch-all principle of little interest, but it should be noted that it represents a warning that the effectiveness of an international system for the preservation of marine environment will vary widely with the ability of states to contribute to the pooling of preventive technology. This universal duty of assistance is derived, of course, from the principle of universal interest.

4 *Principles of state of responsibility (particular)*

IWGMP text | Canadian text

a In addition to its responsibility for environmental protection within the limits of its territorial sea, a coastal state also has responsibility to protect adjacent areas of the environment from damage that may result from activities within its territory.

In addition to its responsibility for environmental protection within the limits of its territorial waters, the coastal state also has primary responsibility for environmental protection in adjacent areas, particularly where it claims exclusive or special rights in such areas.

b Coastal states should ensure that adequate and appropriate resources are available to deal with pollution incidents resulting from the exploration and exploitation of seabed resources in areas within the limits of their national jurisdiction.

Coastal states should maintain and make available when required resources to deal with any pollution incident which may result from the exploration and exploitation of seabed resources in areas within the limits of their national jurisdiction.

c All states should ensure that vessels under their registration comply with internationally agreed rules and standards relating to ship design and construction, operating procedures and other relevant factors. States should cooperate in the development of such rules, standards and procedures, in the appropriate international bodies.

All states should ensure that vessels under their jurisdiction, ownership and registration, or sailing from their ports, comply with internationally agreed rules and standards relating to ship design and construction, operating procedures and other relevant factors. In the absence of internationally agreed rules and standards, states should ensure that vessels under their jurisdiction, ownership or registration comply with non-discriminatory rules and standards adopted by other states, in areas where such other states have primary responsibility for marine environmental protection.

d The states at higher levels of technological and scientific development should assist those nations which request it, for example by undertaking programmes either directly or through competent agencies intended to provide adequate training of the technical and scientific personnel of those countries as well as by providing the equipment and facilities needed in areas such as research, administration, monitoring or surveillance, informa-

States having attained an advanced level of competence in ocean sciences, offshore resource exploration and exploitation, and other areas of relevance to problems of marine pollution, should participate in programmes of assistance to interested states so as to improve their capability to fulfill their responsibilities for marine environmental protection.

tion, waste disposal, and others, which
would improve their ability to discharge
their duties consisting of protecting the
marine environment.

In addition to the general principles of state responsibility described above, particular principles of responsibility are also applied to three classes of states: coastal states, flag states, and states whose science and technology are highly developed.

Since Canada's general attitude to law of the sea problems is that of a coastal state, the Canadian wording of principles a and b is of special interest. In the first of these the coastal state would have 'primary,' but not necessarily exclusive, responsibility for environmental protection in (undesignated) areas adjacent to its territorial waters. This is, of course, part of the official rationale for the Canadian Arctic Waters Pollution Prevention Act of 1970.[105] The Canadian working paper adds that this principle is justified particularly where the coastal state claims exclusive or special rights in these adjacent areas. This final clause would have to be interpreted as referring to *acquisitive* (economic) claims by the coastal state to adjacent areas of the high seas. The rationale is presumably that primary environmental responsibility, including the costs that might arise from its discharge, is one kind of 'price' that the coastal state should pay for exclusive or special privilege. Though an acceptable kind of 'trade-off' for a highly developed coastal state like Canada, it is not so likely to be attractive to developing countries that aspire to fishery expansion on the high seas. Theoretically, however, there is a strong case for recognizing the primary environmental responsibility of a coastal state that has the demonstrated capability to exercise the exclusive or special fishery *conservation* authority that it claims in high seas areas adjacent to its territorial waters.

In contrast with the Canadian proposal, the IWGMP language is weak stuff, providing no coherent rationalization for the allocation of state authority over marine pollution prevention and control beyond territorial limits in situations where the pollution originates inside these limits. This weak wording must be judged a major flaw in the IWGMP draft, since most *accumulative* pollution originates within territorial limits and accumulative forms are much more serious than the total effect of the highly publicized *catastrophic* spillages.[106]

Principle b is much less controversial than the Canadian version of principle a. Developing coastal states which lack 'adequate and appropriate resources' to deal with pollution resulting from the exploitation of seabed resources are likely also to lack the technology for such exploitation. Being dependent on foreign corporations for purposes of development, they would, under this principle, be required in effect to negotiate with these corporations for the provision of anti-pollution 'resources.'

Principle c requires flag states to comply with 'internationally agreed rules and standards' of the kind that Canada has already signified its intention to apply unilaterally, pending their acceptance by other states or pending an international agreement on equally acceptable rules and standards. It should be noted that the IWGMP principle represents neither an acceptance nor a rejection of the Canadian policy for the interim period, which is justified by reference to the coastal state's 'primary responsibility.'

The IWGMP proposal spells out in greater detail the kind of assistance programs that the Canadian working draft advocates should be undertaken by 'have' states to improve the environmental capability of poorer countries. This principle has to be treated carefully by the highly developed states, but it is necessary to recognize that an effective international system for marine environmental protection will depend in large part on new and imaginative 'investments' in technical assistance.

5 *Rights of states*

IWGMP text

Canadian text

a No counterpart

A state may exercise special authority in areas of the sea adjacent to its territorial waters where functional controls of a continuing nature are necessary for the effective prevention of pollution which could cause damage or injury to the land or marine environment under its exclusive or sovereign authority.

b Following an accident on the high seas which may be expected to result in major deleterious consequences from pollution or threat of pollution of the sea, a coastal state facing grave and imminent danger to its coastline and related interests may take appropriate measures as may be necessary to prevent, mitigate, or eliminate such danger, in accordance with internationally agreed rules and standards.

Following an accident on the high seas which may be expected to result in major deleterious consequences from pollution or threat of pollution of the sea, a state facing grave and imminent danger to its coastline, offshore resources or maritime interests in areas where it has primary responsibility for marine environmental protection may take appropriate measures beyond such areas as may be necessary to prevent, mitigate, or eliminate such danger, in accordance with internationally agreed rules and standards.

c No counterpart

A coastal state may prohibit any vessel which does not comply with internationally agreed rules and standards, or, in their absence, with reasonable national rules and standards of the coastal state in question, from entering waters under its environmental protection authority.

d No counterpart

The basis on which a state should exercise rights or powers, in addition to its sovereign rights or powers, pursuant to its special authority in areas adjacent to its territorial waters, in that such rights or powers should be deemed to be delegated to that state by the world community on behalf of humanity as a whole. The rights and powers exercised must be consistent with the state's primary responsibility for marine environmental protection in the areas concerned: they should be subject to international rules and standards and to review before an appropriate international tribunal.

Only one of these four proposals in the Canadian government's working paper proved to be acceptable to the IWGMP in October 1971. Yet it should be noted that of the forty-two states represented at the meeting twenty 'supported the general concept contained in these [three] draft principles'[107] not adopted by the working group as a whole. These twenty states were Algeria, Argentina, Brazil, Barbados, Colombia, Chile, Cuba, Equador, Ghana, India, Spain, Iceland, Ivory Coast, Kenya, Mexico, Malta, Peru, Portugal, Guatamala, and Tanzania. Other states 'disagreed and still others considered that this forum was not the place for their discussion and accordingly reserved their position.'[108] The large minority vote of approval and the plea of *non forum conveniens* seem to guarantee that the principles advanced by Canada in Ottawa will continue to be debated, possibly in modified or expanded form, during preparations for the Third Law of the Sea Conference.

The one right that was granted to the coastal state in the IWGMP proposal is the relatively non-controversial one that allows an imperilled coastal state to take emergency action after the event of an accident on the high seas. What is permitted under this principle is the right to take preventive action on the high seas, but only in circumstances where it may already be too late to stave off the disastrous consequences of a major spillage. This is at least an advance in the right direction from the point of view of any coastal state and will help to improve the climate of expectations, which seems to be moving towards the point of tolerating the unilateral adoption of *a priori* preventive measures by coastal states such as those envisaged in recent Canadian and British legislation. It may be inferred from this that the attitudes even of shipping states are in the process of transformation, since principle b above was accepted at Ottawa by carrier and oil-producing countries such as Denmark, Iran, Japan, Libya, the Netherlands, Norway, South Africa, Sweden, the United Kingdom, the United States, and the Soviet Union. Belgium, France, and Italy, on the other hand, expressed formal reservations as to the entire undertaking to formulate general guidelines and principles for the preservation of the marine environment.

6 *Guidelines for law-making*

IWGMP text	Canadian text
a International guidelines and criteria should be developed, both by national Governments and through inter-governmental agencies, to provide the	No counterpart

policy framework for control measures. A comprehensive plan for the protection of the marine environment should provide for the identification of critical pollutants and their pathways and sources, determination of exposures to these pollutants and assessment of the risks they pose, timely detection of undesirable trends, and development of detection and monitoring systems.

b   Internationally agreed criteria and standards should provide for regional and local variations in the effects of pollution and in the evaluation of these effects. Such variables should also include the ecology of sea areas, economic and social conditions, and amenities, recreational facilities and other uses of the seas.

No counterpart

c   Primary protection standards and derived working levels – especially codes of practice and effluent standards – may usefully be established at national levels, and in some instances, on a regional or global basis.

No counterpart

d   Action to prevent and control marine pollution (particularly direct prohibitions and specific release limits) must guard against the effect of simply transferring damage or hazard from one part of the environment to another.

No counterpart

e   The development and implementation of control should be sufficiently flexible to reflect increasing knowledge of the marine ecosystem, pollution effects, and improvements in technological means for pollution control and to take into account the fact that a number of new and hitherto unsuspected pollutants are bound to be brought to light.

No counterpart

f   There should be ... cooperation in the exchange of technological information

No counterpart

on means of preventing marine pollution, including pollution that may arise
from offshore resource exploration and
exploitation.

g International guidelines should also be   No counterpart
developed to facilitate comparability in
methods of detection and measurement
of pollutants and their effects.

None of these criteria of law-making was explicitly included in the Canadian working paper, though some are implicit in Canadian attitudes towards the 'strategy' of international law-making in the law of the sea and environmental fields. Canadian officials have, for example, expressed interest in the possibility that some kind of international mechanism might be established for more or less continuous reappraisal of existing anti-pollution measures in light of the most recent scientific findings. This would facilitate the differential treatment of different kinds of pollutants, as proposed in guideline a, and help to ensure that international standards make sufficient allowance for local variations, as suggested in guideline b. The recognition of the need for establishing primary protection standards initially at national levels is also highly compatible with the general Canadian position on the making of international environmental law. Perhaps the most important of all these guidelines is the fourth, which emphasizes the crucial consideration that pollution measures must not be allowed to have the effect of simply transferring a problem from one area to another. For this reason there is no final solution to marine pollution problems other than a global solution that depends upon the integration or co-ordination of all environmental measures at national, regional, and local levels. A flexible approach to the establishment of marine pollution control measures, called for in guideline e, is essential because of the present state of scientific uncertainty. The comparability of data provides a problem that can only be treated effectively after the establishment of guidelines to determine the best scientific methods of investigation and appraisal.

The kinds of differences that emerged at the Ottawa session of the IWGMP seemed to indicate inadequate interdisciplinary preparations by most of the governments represented. Some of the criticisms of the Canadian draft by non-legal delegates of other governments were later abandoned after consultations with their legal advisers who did not attend the Ottawa meeting. This experience demonstrated the need for carefully co-ordinated government planning to develop a flexible and well-balanced strategy to prepare for a complicated, interdisciplinary, law-making conference such as Stockholm. It will be difficult, indeed impossible, for most governments to have an appropriate mix of disciplines represented at every stage in conference preparations.

The conference Secretariat: Post-Ottawa developments
The diplomatic difficulties experienced at Ottawa were complicated further by the decision of the conference Secretariat to play an activist role. Within weeks of the Ottawa meeting, in their own draft paper on the need for a comprehensive approach to the control of marine pollution, the Secretariat included principles which were

said to be patterned on those initially set down at the Ottawa meeting but which revealed an appreciable de-emphasis on the special interest of the coastal state in the management of the marine environment. Some of the new language introduced in the Secretariat redraft constituted a departure from what was agreed to by the governments at the Ottawa meeting. Particularly serious from a Canadian view-point was the new implication – not evident in the IWGMP draft – that the coastal state's protective rights over its marine environment were to be limited to the ter-ritorial sea, except in emergency situations after an accident on the high seas. This emphasis is closer to the British than to the Canadian position. Suspicions of British influence were strengthened by the introduction of new references to a 'regime of liability' and to the need for more precise and detailed measures at the regional level.

In the final resort, what the conference Secretariat did was to include the twenty-three principles agreed at the Ottawa session of the IWGMP in its own preparatory document, Doc A/CONF. 48/8 entitled 'Identification and control of pollutants of broad international significance.' It was these principles in their Ottawa form that were collectively endorsed at Stockholm itself and incorporated by reference in recommendation 239 of the conference. Moreover the Canadian contribution before the Ottawa meeting was further rewarded by the conference's endorsement of the Ottawa statement of objectives preceding the twenty-three principles. Even more significantly, as a measure of the Canadian diplomatic 'victory,' was the inclu-sion in recommendation 239 of a reference to the four principles of special concern to Canada in support of its unilateral action under the Arctic Waters Pollution Pre-vention Act:

> [It is recommended that Governments] in respect of the particular interest of coastal States in the marine environment and recognizing that the resolution of this question is a matter for consideration at the Law of the Sea Conferences, *take note* of the principles on the Rights of Coastal States discussed but neither endorsed nor rejected at the second session of the Intergovernmental Working Group on Marine Pollution and *refer* these principles to the 1973 IMCO Conference for information and to the 1973 Law of the Sea Conference for such action as may be appropriate.

At the time of writing, it seems highly unlikely that these formulations of coastal rights advanced by Canada will be supported at the 1973 IMCO Conference, since this form is largely dominated by shipping interests which feel threatened by pro-posals that would permit the imposition of restrictions on foreign shipping in offshore areas beyond the territorial sea. On the other hand, there is a high probabil-ity that in the universal forum of the Third UN Conference on the Law of the Sea, which will be influenced by the antishipping sentiments of developing coastal states, there will be some kind of recognition granted to the coastal states to impose such restrictions in the face of pollution dangers, within an exclusive economic zone or otherwise.

Canadian approaches to other developments in international environmental law

Limitations of space and time preclude a similar textual analysis of Canadian con-tributions to international environmental policy-making outside the context of the general principles of marine pollution prevention and control. Some Canadian views in three other areas should, however, be mentioned because of their interest to international lawyers.

Declaration on the Human Environment
Canadian government international lawyers shared the general view that the declaration should be regarded as an open pledge by the nations of the world, dressed in general terms but appropriately reflective of the common concern expressed at the Stockholm Conference on the Human Environment. It seems, however, that Ottawa may have been prepared to go further and insert in the operative part of the text a number of general environmental principles, which though not in conventional binding form would contribute the bedrock of international environmental policy. To accomplish this it would have been necessary to avoid giving the impression that these principles were intended to take precedence over developmental goals by an express acknowledgment to this effect or by a slightly firmer declaration that socioeconomic development and environmental protection are interdependent. It was apparently a Canadian preference to add that the irrational utilization of the limited resources of the biosphere is posing an accelerating threat to the human environment, though an overemphasis of this point was certain to encounter resistance.

Because Canada is known to be more fully committed to international environmentalism than many countries, Canadian government lawyers were aware of the danger of promoting their own draft declaration too vigorously. But Ottawa made known its preference to link the concept of environmental rights with the right to territorial integrity by introducing the concept of 'environmental integrity.' In a similar attempt to link territorial and environmental concepts, Ottawa suggested a declaration to the effect that every state has a sovereign and inalienable right to its environment and to dispose of its natural resources. It would have been consistent with Canadian Arctic policy to assert further that every state has the right to take all necessary and appropriate measures to protect its environmental integrity, but it was recognized that such a sweeping and indeterminate assertion was unlikely to win widespread acceptance.

Yet, as it turned out, the Stockholm conference was able to adopt a stronger declaration than most expected. The two most difficult controversies were those concerning principles 20 and 21 in the draft prepared by the Intergovernmental Working Group on the Declaration on the Human Environment. The first of these would have recognized the duty of states to inform one another of the probable environmental impact of their actions upon areas beyond their jurisdiction. The second was a fairly strong statement about the environmental effects of nuclear weapons testing. The first problem, aggravated by a dispute between Argentina and Brazil, proved to be insoluble. This was particularly regrettable from a Canadian viewpoint, for Canada adopted the position that this duty of notification already existed in customary international law.[109] The Canadian delegate also deplored the weakening of language on the nuclear issue, for it has long been the Canadian policy that nuclear tests should be stopped for environmental as well as security reasons. However the final version of the Declaration on the Human Environment, approved at Stockholm and endorsed by the UN General Assembly, was regarded by Canada as a satisfactory document and 'the first essential step in developing international environmental law.'[110] In the final analysis the declaration is regarded by Canada as important chiefly for its inclusion of principles 21 and 22, which are interpreted by the Canadian government as reflecting existing duties in customary international law, as evidenced by the *Trail Smelter* decision.

Environmental aspects of natural resources management

Canada was on the whole highly gratified with the outcome of the debate on the environmental aspects of natural resources management. For example, at Canada's suggestion fourteen recommendations on the conservation of genetic resources were passed *en bloc* without amendment or separate discussion. Canada's initiative in this technical area was greeted with enthusiasm by many of the delegates, adding to Canada's reputation as a pro-environmental protection state. More relevant to international law, four recommendations on international fishery management were also approved *en bloc* at Canada's suggestion. The Canadian delegation was successful in persuading the conference to take note of trends in favour of coastal state management not only over fisheries but also over marine pollution activities and ocean dumping. Even more important, the final recommendations of the Stockholm conference reflected Canada's strongly argued preference for the streamlining and co-ordination of environmental law-making exercises in post-Stockholm forums such as the 1973 IMCO Conference on Marine Pollution and the Third UN Conference on the Law of the Sea.

Canada was less happy, however, with the final conference outcome on the emotional issue of commercial whaling. The recommendations for a ten-year moratorium on all commercial whaling represented a departure from the North American policy and practice of conserving renewable resources on a sustained yield basis. A blanket moratorium on all whales including underexploited stocks was recognized to be unscientific: there is no scientific evidence to support a complete prohibition of commercial whaling for all species for an arbitrary ten-year period; the conservation logic was marred by the blanket exception in favour of native peoples; and the proposal in any event was not intended to be legally binding. But all these considerations finally had to yield to tremendous emotional and political pressures in support of a general moratorium, and Canada followed suit lest it end up paradoxically in virtual isolation with Japan. The Canadian vote in favour of a moratorium adds to the pressure on the International Whaling Commission to take strong action commensurate with the Stockholm recommendation. If such action results counterproductively in the withdrawal of Japan and the USSR from the commission, it will leave the commission emasculated of the two major whaling nations in the world and powerless to effect direct reforms upon them. This would be a double blow, to the cause of conservation by international management procedures, and to those who were conspicuous, including Canada, in recent successful efforts to produce the first of such reforms within the commission.

Treaty-making prospects

Contrary to earlier expectations expressed by the conference Secretariat, the Stockholm conference was unable to complete detailed considerations of the various environmental treaties in the making at that time. Little attention could be given, for example, to the draft of the forthcoming Convention on the Dumping of Wastes at Sea, but it might be said that the general mood of the delegations was conducive to proceeding with the intergovernmental conference held in October-December 1972 at London, which resulted in the opening of the convention for signature on 29 December 1972. The Canadian approach to this convention, and to marine pollution in general, was clearly reflected in its preparations for the Stockholm conference. It was also of interest to Canada that the Stockholm conference called for the immediate establishment of a working group to examine the need for a convention on the management of migratory game such as polar bears and migratory birds. Canada supported a proposal and is expected to participate in the working group. The various conservation conventions referred to above[111] were not open for signature at Stockholm, but the conference adopted resolutions with favourable references to them. The Convention on Conservation of Wetlands of International Importance, which was adopted by eighteen states at Ramsar in February 1971, addressed itself geographically to Eurasian areas important to waterfowl, and will therefore not be signed by Canada. It should be noted however that it was modelled on the Canadian-US[112] and Mexican-US[113] treaties on migratory birds, and to that extent Canada may be said to have contributed to the development of this area of international environmental law on a regional basis. Because no action was taken on the other conservation conventions at Stockholm, the Canadian approach to some of them is not yet known at the time of writing. The Convention on the Conservation of the World Heritage drafted by the IUCN has been criticized as vague, idealistic, elitist (in the sense that the designated areas would be seen by only a privileged few), and cynical (because it would lead to competition among countries for tourist benefits). On the Convention on the Conservation for Certain Islands for Science, also drafted by the IUCN, Canada has had difficulty in deciding whether to regard the conservation of threatened islands as a convention for purposes of biological science, or as only a special example of the need for affording international protection to over one hundred designated areas under the newer concept of a World Heritage Foundation.

CANADIAN APPROACHES TO INTERNATIONAL ENVIRONMENTAL LAW

Summary of trends

Generally identified as pro-Stockholm, Canada has cultivated the image of a country highly interested in the appropriate use of global processes for the development of international environmental law. From an early stage, the Stockholm conference was seen in Ottawa as an opportunity to take immediate action at the global level in areas of the most urgent concern. Transnational environmental problems were regarded, however, as requiring effective responses at regional, subregional, and national, as well as global, levels of authority. Stockholm was, therefore, also viewed as the necessary first step in the formulation of first-order principles that would govern subsequent measures adopted at subordinate levels. Like other countries, Canada was slow to commit itself on specific institutional questions, such as the case for a global environment protection agency, but it was hoped and expected that some kind of international mechanism would be placed on a continuing, preferably permanent, basis after Stockholm, so as to take maximum advantage of the momentum established at Stockholm and to facilitate co-ordination among the various existing agencies involved in the making and execution of international environmental policy.

In preparing for the Stockholm Conference, Canadian government departments were obliged not only to adopt multidisciplinary approaches to environmental problems, which is unavoidable, but also to experiment with interdisciplinary collaboration in the formulation of Canadian positions on questions of international environmental law. The decision to hold the Third Law of the Sea Conference and the IMCO Conference on Marine Pollution quite soon after Stockholm underlined the need for close and frequent consultation among the departments responsible for government planning, research, and preparations. The trends towards increased interdisciplinary collaboration and interdepartmental consultation have, predictably, met with some resistance where they seem to trench upon established lines of specialization and jurisdiction, but it seems to have been generally accepted at the senior level that there is no other way of formulating sophisticated policy on international environmental issues of great complexity. The certainty that these three conferences will be succeeded by other, equally important, environmental conferences ensures that increased interdisciplinary collaboration and interdepartmental consultation on policy questions of international environmental law are long-term trends.

Marine pollution
The Canadian government has been involved in virtually all Stockholm agenda areas, but that of marine pollution has had a particularly high priority for the international lawyers in Ottawa. In line with the general Canadian attitude to the making of international environmental law, the problem of protecting the marine environment is conceived as multidimensional, requiring action at global, regional, subregional, and national levels. It was therefore hoped in Ottawa that the adoption of general principles and guidelines for the prevention and control of marine pollution would be part of the 'action completed' at Stockholm, and that the formulation of a comprehensive plan for the preservation of the marine environment would be part of the 'action begun.' Both the general principles and the comprehensive plan were regarded as attempts to meet the need for a firm, but realistically flexible, normative framework within which more specific, and possibly more stringent, measures would later be adopted at various levels of action. The Third Law of the Sea Conference was envisaged, in part, as an opportunity to translate at least some of the Stockholm norms on the prevention and control of marine pollution into widely acceptable treaty form, and the IMCO Conference on Marine Pollution as a further opportunity to spell out more detailed regulatory and remedial measures with respect to international navigation.

In its systematic approach to the development of international law relating to marine pollution, Canada has emphasized the importance of developing the concept of state responsibility as the controlling normative element. The rights that a state may claim and exercise are to be viewed as those that can properly be derived from the responsibility that falls upon, and is accepted by, the claimant state. These rights should be limited by the consideration of what is reasonably necessary for the effective discharge of the state's responsibilities for preservation of the marine environment. When special protective rights are claimed by a coastal state, they should be governed by the consideration of what is reasonably necessary for the effective discharge of the special responsibility falling on the coastal state as the nearest adjacent state. This, in essence, is the rationale of the Canadian unilateral assertion of extraterritorial authority for the prevention of marine pollution in extensive areas of the Arctic marine environment. Since enactment of the Arctic Waters Pollution Prevention Act there has been growing support by other governments for this rationale, and the approach to international environmental law that it represents. But it is certain that this approach will continue to be challenged by the shipping states in diplomatic exchanges preceding the Third Law of the Sea Conference and the IMCO Conference on Marine Pollution.

Other environmental problems
The Canadian approach to the drafting of the Stockholm Declaration on the Human Environment has been to favour a strong statement of general principles that would be accepted thereafter as the authoritative premises of international environmental policy. One feature of the Canadian approach has been the coining of the concept of 'environmental integrity,' which it was hoped would develop as a correlative of 'territorial integrity.' To the extent that the former concept is larger than the latter, justifying state action beyond territorial limits, the allocation of environmental authority is, in the Canadian view, to be regarded primarily as a matter to be governed by an expanding sense of state responsibility. The state's responsibility for environmental protection is the proper measure of its environmental rights. The absence of an effective international body to discharge effectively its collective responsibility for environmental protection in a particular region underlines the responsibility of the individual states in the region and justifies their assertion of right unilaterally to take appropriate environmental action beyond territorial limits.

Canada has strongly supported the principle of international co-operation in environmental monitoring and has made important contributions to the study of the scientific and technological problems involved. There is no unanimity among Canadian scientists on priorities in international environmental research, but there seems to be a preference for specific shorter term, problem oriented projects rather than basic, long-range, systemic studies.

Canada has espoused a comprehensive approach to international environmental policy issues, which are seen as requiring treatment simultaneously on global, regional, subregional, and national levels. Yet this policy is not intended to rank organizational approaches in that order of preference. In fishery conservation, for example, multilateral regional approaches, such as that of the International Commission for the Northwest Atlantic Fisheries (ICNAF) are regarded as inadequate and Canada would prefer to exercise coastal management of stocks on both sides of Canadian territorial limits. There is little evidence of a strong Canadian interest in a regional, circumpolar approach to the problems of protecting the Arctic environment through an organization consisting of the six countries whose territories border the Arctic; and even less of a Canadian interest in a larger organization that would include extraregional user states. Instead Canada has been cultivating international co-operation on a bilateral basis, most noticeably with the Soviet Union.

Appraisal of trends

Canada's pro-Stockholm posture is a true reflection of its conception of environmental crisis as global in character, requiring sophisticated inter-disciplinary collaboration and intensive intergovernmental consultation. There is a danger, however, that in Ottawa, like elsewhere, the need to prepare for a continuous procession of environmental conferences in the 1970s and beyond will result in a de-emphasis on long-range policy research and planning. When a government makes a heavy investment of personnel and talent in conference oriented policy and strategy, it takes the risk of sacrificing long-term objectives to diplomatic gains. The Stockholm conference has already given birth to a new and intellectually exciting kind of diplomatic game. As future conferences become concerned with more specific issues, on the basis of a more restrictive mandate, there is an increasing danger that the trees will get more attention than the forest.

It is hoped that the best qualified academic environmentalists in Canada, and elsewhere, will be encouraged to participate in long-range government policy research and planning on a regular and continuing basis. In no other area of public concern is it more desirable to have organized interaction between government service and academic community without reducing the public responsibility of the former or violating the private integrity of the latter. Relatively few academics in Canada or elsewhere became involved in governmental or intergovernmental preparations for the Stockholm conferences, perhaps because of the crowded schedule that was forced on the governments. In the future, academic specialists should be encouraged to serve the public interest as long-range policy advisers, so that conference objectives can be placed in the larger context of 'planetary crisis research.'

Marine pollution
The Canadian emphasis on marine pollution is appropriate in a country whose environmental concern is greatly aggravated by the possession of an enormous coastline and an unusually vulnerable ecozone in the Arctic basin. The unilateralist image acquired by Canada through its Arctic policy of 1970 has been modified in 1971 by its prominence in helping to draft the IWCMP's draft principles on the prevention and control of marine pollution for the Stockholm conference, for these principles give proper weight to the need for international co-operation. In identifying itself publicly with coastal, rather than shipping, states, the Canadian government has improved the prospect of winning general support from the third world for its preventive approach to marine pollution and helped to supply the deficiencies inherent in the remedial (liability) approach associated with IMCO.

At regional and subregional levels, Canada has been less active in the development of international procedures for the preservation of the marine environment. In theory, there is an attractive argument that the Arctic (and possibly sub-Arctic) states should form some kind of pan-Arctic agency for the protection of the Arctic marine environment. The North Sea environmental regime to be discussed at a north European conference convened by the British government might provide a suggestive model that could be adapted to the different conditions of the Arctic. But, in practice, the desirability of this kind of regional approach to marine pollution depends on the outcome of global approaches at the Stockholm conference and on the potentiality of bilateral (subregional) approaches. The Canadian and US governments have begun to discuss the possibility of a bilateral agreement to regulate the passage of oil tankers to and from Alaska through the offcoastal waters of North America. Canada and the Soviet Union have also agreed in principle to an agreement for the exchange of Arctic environmentalists. But bilateralism seems a seriously inadequate substitute for a regional approach to the problems of preserving the Arctic environment.

Other environmental problems

Canadian officials were wise not to press too hard in promoting the Canadian draft proposal for the Stockholm Declaration on the Human Environment. Agreement on the formulation of general environmental principles is sufficiently difficult when confined to the problems of protecting the marine environment, where Canadian interests are most deeply involved and where it is most likely to establish some degree of international consensus, without arousing widespread fears of new encroachments on territorial sovereignty. 'Environmental integrity' is an unusually felicitous phrase, serving nicely to rationalize Canada's Arctic policy of self-protection beyond territorial limits, but the concept is difficult to develop logically without subverting the analogous principle of territorial integrity. This is, in a sense, precisely what needs to be subverted if the danger of 'planetary death' is to be met intelligently: the national boundary, in Falk's phrase, has to be deprived of its mystique. But the invocation of 'environmental integrity' by a leading proponent of the rights of coastal states is bound to be interpreted cynically by the shipping states; and the have-not coastal states of the third world have still to be convinced that their developmental interests are not best served by expanding the concepts of territory and territorial integrity. But if the trend to territorial expansionism at sea beyond twelve miles continues to be resisted and a new doctrine of environmental integrity is rejected, there seems to be no alternative to the establishment of a global environment protection agency with regulatory power.

This outcome seems desirable as well as necessary. Just as the environmental crisis cannot be resolved by expanding the ancient doctrine of territoriality, it seems unlikely it can be treated effectively by extending the mid-twentieth century state practice of making extraterritorial claims to limited jurisdiction for functional purposes. What is needed above all in the aftermath of the Stockholm conference is a global agency kept suitably equipped and empowered to meet the environmental needs of the last quarter century.

As these developments unfold it may be necessary to clarify the distinctions between resource use, resource conservation, and environmental protection. All three apply science to problems of welfare deficiency, but whereas the first emphasises the goal of development, the second stresses perpetuation, and the third survival. In resource use the critical problem, underdevelopment, is essentially economic; in resource conservation the chief challenge, instability of production, is managerial; in environmental protection the crucial difficulty, ignorance, is scientific. The three are in fact distinguishable by reference to the *primacy* of concern. To insist that in practice resource use, resource conservation, and environmental protection tend to overlap is to complicate the task of problem-solving in all three areas. The task of a global environment protection agency will be hopelessly complicated if it has to reconcile its obligations in the maintenance of the minimum life support capability of the global environment with other responsibilities for maximum resource development and optimal resource management practices. Other organizations, not necessarily global in scale, will have to be made responsible for protecting these central, but ultimately less vital, concerns.

With the enunciation of global environmental principles at Stockholm the most difficult phase of international environmental law is just beginning.

APPENDIX

A. DECLARATION OF THE UNITED NATIONS CONFERENCE ON THE HUMAN ENVIRONMENT,
   The United Nations Conference on the Human Environment
   Having met at Stockholm from 5 to 16 June 1972, and
   Having considered the need for a common outlook and for common principles to inspire and guide the peoples of the world in the preservation and enhancement of the human environment,

PROCLAIMS THAT:
1. Man is both creature and moulder of his environment which gives him physical sustenance and affords him the opportunity for intellectual, moral, social and spiritual growth. In the long and tortuous evolution of the human race on this planet a stage has been reached when through the rapid acceleration of science and technology, man has acquired the power to transform his environment in countless ways and on an unprecedented scale. Both aspects of man's environment, the natural and the man-made, are essential to his well-being and to the enjoyment of basic human rights – even the right to life itself.

2. The protection and improvement of the human environment is a major issue which affects the well-being of peoples and economic development throughout the world; it is the urgent desire of the peoples of the whole world and the duty of all governments.

3. Man has constantly to sum up experience and go on discovering, inventing, creating and advancing. In our time man's capability to transform his surroundings, if used wisely, can bring to all peoples the benefits of development and the opportunity to enhance the quality of life. Wrongly or heedlessly applied, the same power can do incalculable harm to human beings and the human environment. We see around us growing evidence of man-made harm in many regions of the earth: dangerous levels of pollution in water, air, earth and living beings; major and undesirable disturbances to the ecological balance of the biosphere; destruction and depletion of irreplaceable resources; and gross deficiencies harmful to the physical, mental and social health of man, in the man-made environment, particularly in the living and working environment.

4. In the developing countries most of the environmental problems are caused by under-development. Millions continue to live far below the minimum levels required for a decent human existence, deprived of adequate food and clothing, shelter and education, health and sanitation. Therefore, the developing countries must direct their efforts to development,

bearing in mind their priorities and the need to safeguard and improve the environment. For the same purpose, the industrialized countries should make efforts to reduce the gap between themselves and the developing countries. In the industrialized countries, environmental problems are generally related to industrialization and technological development.

5. The natural growth of population continuously presents problems on the preservation of the environment, and adequate policies and measures should be adopted as appropriate to face these problems. Of all things in the world, people are the most precious. It is the people that propel social progress, create social wealth, develop science and technology and through their hard work, continuously transform the human environment. Along with social progress and the advance of production, science, and technology, the capability of man to improve the environment increases with each passing day.

6. A point has been reached in history when we must shape our actions throughout the world with a more prudent care for their environmental consequences. Through ignorance or indifference we can do massive and irreversible harm to the earthly environment on which our life and well-being depend. Conversely, through fuller knowledge and wiser action, we can achieve for ourselves and our posterity a better life in an environment more in keeping with human needs and hopes. There are broad vistas for the enhancement of environmental quality and the creation of a good life. What is needed is an enthusiastic but calm state of mind and intense but orderly work. For the purpose of attaining freedom in the world of nature, man must use knowledge to build in collaboration with nature a better environment. To defend and improve the human environment for present and future generations has become an imperative goal for mankind – a goal to be pursued together with, and in harmony with, the established and fundamental goals of peace and of world-wide economic and social development.

7. To achieve this environmental goal will demand the acceptance of responsibility by citizens and communities and by enterprises and institutions at every level, all sharing equitably in common efforts. Individuals in all walks of life as well as organizations in many fields, by their values and the sum of their actions, will shape the world environment of the future. Local and national governments will bear the greatest burden for large-scale environmental policy and action within their jurisdictions. International co-operation is also needed in order to raise resources to support the developing countries in carrying out their responsibilities in this field. A growing class of environmental problems, because they are regional or global in extent or because they affect the common international realm, will require extensive co-operation among nations and action by international organizations in the common interest. The Conference calls upon the Governments and peoples to exert common efforts for the preservation and improvement of the human environment, for the benefit of all the people and for their posterity.

PRINCIPLES

STATES THE COMMON CONVICTION THAT

Principle 1

Man has the fundamental right to freedom, equality and adequate conditions of life, in an environment of a quality which permits a life of dignity and well-being, and bears a solemn responsibility to protect and improve the environment for present and future generations. In this respect, policies promoting or perpetuating *apartheid,* racial segregation, discrimination, colonial and other forms of oppression and foreign domination stand condemned and must be eliminated.

Principle 2
The natural resources of the earth including the air, water, land, flora and fauna and especially representative samples of natural ecosystems must be safeguarded for the benefit of present and future generations through careful planning or management as appropriate.

Principle 3
The capacity of the earth to produce vital renewable resources must be maintained and wherever practicable restored or improved.

Principle 4
Man has a special responsibility to safeguard and wisely manage the heritage of wildlife and its habitat which are now gravely imperilled by a combination of adverse factors. Nature conservation including wildlife must therefore receive importance in planning for economic development.

Principle 5
The non-renewable resources of the earth must be employed in such a way as to guard against the danger of their future exhaustion and to ensure that benefits from such employment are shared by all mankind.

Principle 6
The discharge of toxic substances or of other substances and the release of heat, in such quantities or concentrations as to exceed the capacity of the environment to render them harmless, must be halted in order to ensure that serious or irreversible damage is not inflicted upon ecosystems. The just struggle of the peoples of all countries against pollution should be supported.

Principle 7
States shall take all possible steps to prevent pollution of the seas by substances that are liable to create hazards to human health, to harm living resources and marine life, to damage amenities or to interfere with other legitimate uses of the sea.

Principle 8
Economic and social development is essential for ensuring a favourable living and working environment for man and for creating conditions on earth that are necessary for the improvement of the quality of life.

Principle 9
Environmental deficiencies generated by the conditions of underdevelopment and natural disasters pose grave problems and can best be remedied by accelerated development through the transfer of substantial quantities of financial and technological assistance as a supplement to the domestic effort of the developing countries and such timely assistance as may be required.

Principle 10

For the developing countries, stability of prices and adequate earnings for primary commodities and raw material are essential to environmental management since economic factors as well as ecological processes must be taken into account.

Principle 11

The environmental policies of all States should enhance and not adversely affect the present or future development potential of developing countries, nor should they hamper the attainment of better living conditions for all, and appropriate steps should be taken by States and international organizations with a view to reaching agreement on meeting the possible national and international economic consequences resulting from the application of environmental measures.

Principle 12

Resources should be made available to preserve and improve the environment, taking into account the circumstances and particular requirements of developing countries and any costs which may emanate from their incorporating environmental safeguards into their development planning and the need for making available to them, upon their request, additional international technical and financial assistance for this purpose.

Principle 13

In order to achieve a more rational management of resources and thus to improve the environment, States should adopt an integrated and co-ordinated approach to their development planning so as to ensure that development is compatible with the need to protect and improve the human environment for the benefit of their population.

Principle 14

Rational planning constitutes an essential tool for reconciling any conflict between the needs of development and the need to protect and improve the environment.

Principle 15

Planning must be applied to human settlements and urbanization with a view to avoiding adverse effects on the environment and obtaining maximum social, economic and environmental benefits for all. In this respect projects which are designed for colonialist and racist domination must be abandoned.

Principle 16

Demographic policies, which are without prejudice to basic human rights and which are deemed appropriate by Governments concerned, should be applied in those regions where the rate of population growth or excessive population concentrations are likely to have adverse effects on the environment or development, or where low population density may prevent improvement of the human environment and impede development.

Principle 17

Appropriate national institutions must be entrusted with the task of planning, managing or controlling the environmental resources of States with the view to enhancing environmental quality.

Principle 18

Science and technology, as part of their contribution to economic and social development, must be applied to the identification, avoidance and control of environmental risks and the solution of environmental problems and for the common good of mankind.

Principle 19

Education in environmental matters, for the younger generation as well as adults, giving due consideration to the underprivileged, is essential in order to broaden the basis for an enlightened opinion and responsible conduct by individuals, enterprises and communities in protecting and improving the environment in its full human dimension. It is also essential that mass media of communications avoid contributing to the deterioration of the environment, but, on the contrary, disseminate information of an educational nature on the need to protect and improve the environment in order to enable man to develop in every respect.

Principle 20

Scientific research and development in the context of environmental problems, both national and multinational, must be promoted in all countries, especially the developing countries. In this connexion, the free flow of up-to-date scientific information and transfer of experience must be supported and assisted, to facilitate the solution of environmental problems; environmental technologies should be made available to developing countries on terms which would encourage their wide dissemination without constituting an economic burden on the developing countries.

Principle 21

States have, in accordance with the Charter of the United Nations and the principles of international law, the sovereign right to exploit their own resources pursuant to their own environmental policies, and the responsibility to ensure that activities within their jurisdiction or control do not cause damage to the environment of other States or of areas beyond the limits of national jurisdiction.

Principle 22,

States shall co-operate to develop further the international law regarding liability and compensation for the victims of pollution and other environmental damage caused by activities within the jurisdiction or control of such States to areas beyond their jurisdiction.

Principle 23

Without prejudice to such criteria as may be agreed upon by the international community, or to standards which will have to be determined nationally, it will be essential in all cases to consider the systems of values prevailing in each country, and the extent of the applicability of standards which are valid for the most advanced countries but which may be inappropriate and of unwarranted social cost for the developing countries.

Principle 24

International matters concerning the protection and improvement of the environment should be handled in a co-operative spirit by all countries, big or small, on an equal footing. Co-operation through multilateral or bilateral arrangements or other appropriate means is essential to effectively control, prevent, reduce and eliminate adverse environmental effects resulting from activities conducted in all spheres, in such a way that due account is taken of the sovereignty and interests of all States.

Principle 25

States shall ensure that international organizations play a co-ordinated, efficient and dynamic role for the protection and improvement of the environment.

Principle 26

Man and his environment must be spared the effects of nuclear weapons and all other means of mass destruction. States must strive to reach prompt agreement, in the relevant international organs, on the elimination and complete destruction of such weapons.

NOTES

1 It should not be assumed, however, that environmental death is necessarily a gradual process of deterioration. The sudden collapse of some environmental systems, such as Lake Erie in North America, should be sufficient warning of the dangers of the 'gradualist fallacy.' Richard A. Falk, 'Toward a World Order Respectful of the Global Ecosystem' (1971), 1 *Envir. Affairs,* 251–65, at 252. See also Fadiman, Clifton, and White, eds, *Ecocide and Thoughts about Survival* (1971) 13–22.

2 'The dominant concept resulting from modern research into star formation and the origin of the solar system is that we must expect planetary systems to be extremely common in space. Many stars, perhaps 80 per cent of them, occur in binary pairs. Some investigators view this as merely another manifestation of the tendency for matter to orbit around stars in space; in this case, the stars orbit around each other. However, theories of the origin of the solar system now tend to place the origin of the planets in the general process by which the sun itself formed. Hence, there may be between 10^{10} and 10^{11} planetary systems in our galaxy.' A.G.W. Cameron, 'Recent Advances in Astronomy and Space Sciences,' in *Environment and Society in Transition,* Proceedings of International Joint Conference of the American Geographical Society and The American Division of The World Academy of Art and Science, held at the New York Academy of Sciences, 27 April – 2 May 1970 (1971), 184, *Annals of the New York Academy of Sciences* 20–5, at 24. When we consider also the number of planetary systems that may exist in other galaxies, there is an extremely high probability of intelligent life forms other than *homo sapiens.* The most

serious doubt is whether the vast distances separating co-existing technological civilizations would preclude the possibility of communication between them. See *Time,* 13 Dec. 1971, 40–6.

3 See L.R. Brown, 'The Environmental Consequences of Man's Quest for Food' in *Environment and Society in Transition, supra* note 2, at 62–72. The future of the recent agricultural revolution seems brighter in light of the phenomenon of 'yield take-off.' See L.R. Brown, *Seeds of Change: The Green Revolution and Development in the 1970's* (1970) 36–43. The question of the ocean's capacity to produce food is controversial. The annual world catch of fish will be over 100 million tons by the end of the 1970s – much earlier than suggested by projections made in the early 1960s. Some scientists believe that 200 million tons is the limit of world sustainable yield and that it may be reached before the end of the twentieth century. Others suggest that with proper management the oceans could sustain well over ten times this size of annual catch. There is now a tendency, however, for biologists to stress the problem of population control rather than food production. See, for example, the recent large-scale report on the state of the life sciences, P. Handler, ed, *Biology and the Future of Man* (Committee on Science and Public Policy of the US National Academy of Sciences, 1970) 889–911.

4 'While scientists keep offering new technologies to repair the damage done by the old, economists, in a sense, also rely on technological solutions when they offer their functional models of externalities and social versus private costs. Thus the technological solutions are more or less translated into economic terms, into cost-benefit calcula-

tions, and the entire discussion is conducted as if economics were still dominated by the marginal utility school. The concepts of rational allocation of resources and of rational calculation within a given economic system, fashionable in tne first decades of this century, come up again and lay claim to being adequate frameworks for the solution of contemporary socioeconomic problems. It is not surprising, therefore, that policy recommendations derived from these hollow categories are proving inadequate to restore the environment and prevent its further destruction.' G. Kade, 'The Economics of Pollution and the Interdisciplinary Approach to Environmental Planning' in *Controlling the Human Environment* (1970), 22 *Int'l Soc. Sci. J.* 563–75, at 570. Other economists have underlined the tradition of psychological and ethical hedonism in western societies based on competitive economies. Two writers recently argued that the conventional intellectual tradition in economic theory over the last two hundred years rests squarely upon hedonistic preconceptions, and have challenged the faith that self-interest has optimal utility. 'What needs to be accomplished is a persuasion of the populace away from the doctrine of self-interest and toward a doctrine of cooperation and conservation. A doctrine in which self-interest is realized but is not the dominant theme – where man is cognizant not only of his own gains but of nature's losses.' R.C. d'Arge and E.K. Hunt, 'Environmental Pollution, Externalities and Conventional Economic Wisdom: A Critique' (1971), 1 *Envir. Affairs* 266–86, at 284. For similar views expressed by an ecologist, see Bruce L. Bandurski, 'Ecology and Economics: Partners for Productivity' (1973), 405 *Annals of the American Academy* 76.

5 'Our damaged environment can only be saved from further destruction and possibly restored when we stop our imagination from being confined by technicalities. If we are not ready to enter into a causal analysis of the problems of environmental decay we shall not be able to develop long-term plans to prevent the self-destruction of mankind. Pollution cannot be attributed to mistaken technologies, population growth, consumption habits and economic growth, as such. These superficial phenomena are symptoms, not causes.' Kade, *supra* note 4, at 571.

6 Y. Dror, 'Policy Sciences: Developments and Implications' in *Environment and Society in Transition, supra* note 2, at 419.

7 See, for example, J. McHale, 'The Timetable Project,' ibid, 440–9.

8 For another lawyer's concept of environmental crisis, see Richard A. Falk, *This Endangered Planet: Prospects and Proposals for Human Survival* (1971), 1–19. Falk argues that we are confronted with a fundamental dilemma: '*Success* in industrializing the poor countries is likely to result in less poverty and turmoil, but in a rapidly and possibly decisive worsening of the ecological situation, whereas the *failure* to industrialize these countries is likely to generate political behaviour that would be likely to increase risks of general war.' Ibid. 33.

This book includes a bibliography that lists some recent works of 'conjecture, prediction and prophecy' that are highly pertinent to the theme of planetary death. See, for example, R. Buckminster Fuller, *Utopia or Oblivion: The Prospects for Humanity* (1967); Erich Jantsch, *Technological Forecasting in Perspective* (1967); Karl Jaspers, *The Future of Mankind* (1961); Jacques Ellul, *The Technological Society* (1964); Gerald Feinberg, *The Prometheus Project: Mankind's Search for Long-Range Goals* (1968); Herman Kahn and Anthony J. Wiener, *The Year 2000: A Framework for Speculation on the Next Thirty-three Years* (1967); John McHale, *The Future of the Future* (1969); Gordon R. Taylor, *The Biological Time-Bomb* (1968); and Alvin Toffler, *Future Shock* (1970).

9 But even the more optimistic scientists generally concede that man's best efforts to solve the environmental crisis are seriously constrained by his own biological and emotional needs. 'Scientific technology cannot and should not be uprooted; not only has it become indispensable for man's survival but it has enriched his perceptions, enlarged his vision, and deepened his concept of reality. To a very large extent the continued unfolding of civilization will depend on the imaginative creativity of scientific technologists. But it would be dangerous to assume that mankind can safely adjust to all forms of technological developments. In the final analysis, the frontiers of social and technological innovations will be determined not by the extent to which man can manipulate the external world but by the limitations of his own biological and emotional

nature.' Rene Dubos, *So Human an Animal* (1968), 28–9.

10 Bandurski, *supra* note 4, at 81.

11 See, for example, *A Blueprint for Survival*, an ecological manifesto by E.R.D. Goldsmith, R. Allen, M. Allaby, J. Daroll, and S.C. Lawrence, first printed in (1972), 2 *The Ecologist* 111–17.

12 See Fadiman and White, *supra* note 1, at 1–46.

13 To the international lawyer especially, the environmental challenge is 'to find ways to deprive the national boundary of its mystique, and thereby of its capacity to cut mankind off from lines of action that would assure human survival and even promote human welfare.' Falk, *supra* note 8, at 35–6. On the future of the nation state in environmental perspective, see Harold Sprout and Margaret Sprout, 'The Ecological Viewpoint and Others' in Cyril E. Black, and Richard A. Falk, *The Future of the International Legal Order*, IV, *The Structure of the International Environment* (1972) 568–605.

14 See Abel Wolman, 'Pollution as an International Issue' (1968), 47 *Foreign Affairs*, 164–75.

15. John Lear, 'Global Pollution: The Chinese Influence,' *Saturday Review*, 17 August 1971, 41–2.

16 R.St.J. Macdonald, Gerald L. Morris, and Douglas M. Johnston, 'International Law and Society in the Year 2000' (1973), 50 *Can. Bar. Rev.*

17 For a challenge to the conventional assumption that highly populated, urban-industrial societies with continuously growing economies are the proper goal of development, see Edward J. Woodhouse, 'Re-Visioning the Future of the Third World: An Ecological Perspective on Development' (1972), 25 *World Politics* 1. See also Harold Sprout and Margaret Sprout, *Towards a Politics of the Planet Earth* (1971), where the relationship between ecology and politics is most fully examined; and Donella H. Meadows, and others, *The Limits of Growth* (1972). Writers such as these question whether the commonly used indicators of political development, such as secularization, rationality, complexity, and modernization, are in fact the most appropriate concepts.

18 Woodhouse, *supra* note 17, at 3.

19 For a discussion of the probable impact of the future demand for large-scale resettlement

on international law, see Macdonald, Morris and Johnston, *supra* note 16.

20 For an extended discussion of the question whether environmental standard setters in the affluent countries will benefit in the long run, see A.V. Kneese, S.E. Rolfe, and J.W. Harned, eds, *Managing the Environment: International Economic Cooperation for Pollution Control* (1971). See also Frederic L. Kirgis, Jr, 'Effective Pollution Control in Industrialized Counties: International Economic Disincentives, Policy Responses, and the GATT' (1972), 70 *Mich. L. Rev.* 859.

21 Seymour Halpern, 'A Major Obstacle to World-Wide Environmental Accord' (1972), 10 *Atl. Commun. Q.* 239–46. To provide the mechanism for such co-ordination in the United States, Congressman Halpern proposes the creation of a Commission on International Trade and Environment.

22 Issues before the 26th General Assembly (1971), *International Conciliation* no 584, 71.

23 (1949) 3 U.N. Rep. International Arb. Awards 1905. On the need to develop international principles and procedures for the control of atmospheric pollution, see E.C. Lee, 'International Legal Aspects of Pollution of the Atmosphere' (1971), 21 *U. Toronto L. J.* 31–8.

24 On environmental planning by the International Joint Commission, see F.J.E. Jordan, 'Canada-United States Boundary Relations,' in this volume, *supra*, 522–43; and Richard B. Bilder, 'Controlling Great Lakes Pollution: A Study in United States-Canadian Environmental Cooperation' (1971), 70 *Mich. L. Rev.* 469. For regional experience in the regulation of drainage basins generally, see A.H. Garretson, R.D. Hayton, and C.J. Olmstead, eds, *The Law of International Drainage Basins* (1967). For a recent review of the evolving principles for the regulation of international water resources, see C.B. Bourne, 'International Law and Pollution of International Rivers and Lakes' (1971), 20 *U. Toronto L. J.* 21–30. For a current review of early international fishery commissions in which Canada has participated, see John A. Yogis, 'Canadian Fisheries and International Law,' in this volume, *supra*, 398–409; and more generally, Douglas M. Johnston, *The International Law of Fisheries: A Framework for Policy-Oriented Inquiries* (1965).

25 This section of the paper is based on the summaries provided in *New Challenge for the*

United Nations (UN Office of Public Information, 1971) and in 'Issues Before the 26th General Assembly,' *supra* note 22. For a documentary history of international environmental law, see James Barros and Douglas M. Johnston, *The International Law of Pollution: Selected Materials* (1973).

26 For a recent review of developments, see G.F. FitzGerald, 'Aircraft Noise in the Vicinity of Aerodromes and Sonic Boom' (1971), 21 *U. Toronto L. J.* 54–68.

27 For a critical review of IMCO contributions, see L.H.H. LeGault, 'The Freedom of the Seas: A Licence to Pollute?' ibid, at 39–49.

28 The 1954 Convention for the Prevention of Pollution of the Sea by Oil was signed in London at a major conference convened to deal with this problem at the invitation of the British government. IMCO was established in 1958, the same year that the 1954 convention came into force. A second conference on oil pollution was held at London in 1962 for the purpose of amending the 1954 convention. This revision provided the basis for further developments in public and private international law, prompted by the 1967 *Torrey Canyon* disaster, at the 1969 Brussels conference, convened by IMCO. Another IMCO conference on marine pollution is scheduled for 1973.

29 Only two provisions, articles 24 and 25 of the Convention on the High Seas, deal expressly with marine pollution, but others, such as article 5 of the Convention on the Continental Shelf, are equally applicable without explicit reference to pollution.

30 See, especially, articles V and IX of the Antarctic Treaty, [1959] 402 U.N.T.S. 71, at 76 and 79–80 respectively.

31 See article I of the Treaty Banning Nuclear Weapons Tests in the Atmosphere, in Outer Space, and Under Water, 480 U.N.T.S. 43, at 44.

32 G.A. Res 2398 (XXIII), 3 Dec. 1968.

33 U.N.Doc E.4667, 26 May 1969 21.

34 G.A. Res 2398 (XXIII), 3 Dec. 1968.

35 G.A. Res 2581 (XXIV), 18 Dec. 1969.

36 The importance of scientific contributions to foreign policy decisions in many capitals is reflected in widening participation of government departments in the field of foreign affairs. It is also reflected in the increasingly common practice of foreign ministries to send scientific attaches to their missions abroad. It was recently estimated that 27 countries have begun this practice, accounting among them for a total of 116 embassies in 23 world capitals. Surprisingly, no foreign ministry has so far accredited a scientific attache to its UN missions in New York or Geneva, but this is likely to change as UN organs become more permanently involved in environmental law-making. J.W. Greenwood, 'Scientists as Diplomats' (1971), 23 *External Affairs* 125–40.

37 The Secretariat's aspirations are revealed in its own cautious recommendations, in U.N. Doc A/CONF 48/5, at 37–39.

'Although most of the recommendations ... can be carried out by existing organizations, there is an important need at the international level to provide governments with the means to maintain continuous review and coordination of international activities, especially those of Earthwatch programmes, and to take initiatives when appropriate ... What is required is an institutional pattern that fills important gaps in the existing structure, minimizes overlapping and duplication, makes the most effective use of limited personnel and financial resources and focuses effort upon priority tasks. The appropriate machinery could consist of an intergovernmental body supported by a Secretariat that has access to the extensive work being done in governmental, intergovernmental, and non governmental organizations.' Ibid, at 38.

It was suggested that this body might be a subsidiary organ of the General Assembly or of ECOSOC under article 68 of the UN Charter or a subsidiary organ of the General Assembly with its report to the Assembly being submitted through ECOSOC. Ibid, at 39.

38 Reported in U.N. Doc A/CONF, 48/PC, 6 April 1970. For a summary of the session's work, see (1970), *International Conciliation* no. 579, 56–9.

39 Reported in U.N. Doc A/CONF 48/PC9, 26 Feb. 1971.

40 Ibid, annex IV.

41 The report was drafted by Barbara Ward, the British economist, and reviewed by a panel of one hundred scientists under the chairmanship of René Dubos, the American biologist.

42 It was recommended, for example, that preparations should be begun to draft a convention for the regulation of the export, import, and transit of certain species of wild animals

and plants. U.N. Doc A/CONF 48/PC9, paragraph 57. This was undertaken by the International Union for the Conservation of
Nature and Natural Resources (IUCN) and
formal drafts were prepared for comment by
governments and other organizations, such
as FAO, the Secretariat of GATT, the Customs
Cooperation Council, and the Scientific
Committee on Antarctic Research.

43 Reported in U.N. Doc A/CONF 48/PC, 13.
44 U.N. Doc A/CONF 48/4.
45 U.N. Doc A/CONF 48/6.
46 U.N. Doc A/CONF 48/7.
47 U.N. Doc A/CONF 48/8.
48 U.N. Doc A/CONF 48/9.
49 U.N. Doc A/CONF 48/10.
50 U.N. Doc A/CONF 48/11.
51 See U.N. Doc A/CONF 48/5, 26–41.
52 Reported in U.N. Doc A/CONF 48/IWGMP I/5.
53 Reported in U.N. Doc A/CONF 48/IWGMP II/5.
54 See *supra*, at 583 ff.
55 A global convention on ocean dumping was
opened for signature in December 1972, after
the conclusion of a conference held in London in the previous month. For a summary
see Douglas M. Johnston, 'Marine Pollution:
Law, Science and Politics' (1972-3), 28 *International Journal* 69–102.
56 Reported in U.N. Doc A/CONF 48/IWGM I/3.
57 Reported in U.N. Doc A/CONF 48/IWGC I/11.
58 In its formulation as of October 1971, the
World Heritage would consist of 'those areas
of outstanding interest and value which are
recognized as such in accordance with the
provisions of Article 1.' Such areas would be
principally natural areas, but might include
areas which have been changed by man. Any
area recognized as part of the World Heritage
would be inscribed in a register instituted for
that purpose. Each contracting state would
be responsible for protecting and managing
any such area that falls within its territory.
Recognition of such an area as part of the
World Heritage would not prejudice the
sovereignty of the state with such responsibility within its territory, but by adopting the
convention contracting states would 'be
deemed to have given their consent to the
principle that the conservation of the areas
forming part of the World Heritage shall be
a matter of common concern.' A fund – the
World Heritage Fund – made up of voluntary
cash contributions from intergovernmental,
governmental, and private sources, would be
established to support conservation of areas

of the World Heritage. U.N. Doc A/CONF
48/IWGC I/13, at 2–4.
59 U.N. Doc A/CONF 48/5.
60 See U.N. Doc A/CONF 48/6.
61 U.N. Doc A/CONF 48/CRP 13/Add 1, at 3.
62 Ibid.
63 Ibid, at 4.
64 Ibid, at 6.
65 Ibid.
66 See U.N. Doc A/CONF 48/9.
67 Recommendation 137, in U.N. Doc A/CONF
48/CRP 13, at 7.
68 See U.N. Doc A/CONF 48/C. 1/CRP 1.
69 See U.N. Doc A/CONF 48/.
70 See U.N. Doc A/CONF 48/CRP 12/Add 1.
71 Recommendation 84, ibid, at 6.
72 Recommendation 131, ibid, at 15.
73 Recommendation 132, ibid, at 15–16.
74 Recommendation 133, ibid, at 16.
75 Recommendation 134, ibid, at 16–17.
76 Recommendation 135, ibid, at 17.
77 Recommendation 96, ibid, at 7.
78 Recommendation 97, ibid.
79 Recommendation 108, ibid, at 8.
80 Recommendation 86, ibid, at 18.
81 Recommendation 159, ibid, at 19.
82 Ibid, at 21.
83 See U.N. Doc A/CONF 48/10.
84 U.N. Doc A/CONF 48/CRP 12, at 3.
85 See U.N. Doc A/CONF 48/8.
86 U.N. Doc A/CONF 48/CRP 14, at 6.
87 See *supra*, at 581 ff.
88 U.N. Doc A/CONF 48/CRP 14, at 8.
89 Ibid, at 9.
90 See U.N. Doc A/CONF 48/CRP 14/Add 1.
91 U.N. Doc A/CONF 48/CRP 8.
92 U.N. Doc A/CONF 48/CRP 26.
93 See *supra*, at 571–3.
94 See *supra*, at 581 ff.
95 See *supra*, at 571–3.
96 See (1973) 10 *U.N. Monthly Chronicle* 72–3.
97 Ibid, at 73.
98 Ibid.
99 Ibid, at 73–4.
100 Ibid, at 75.
101 Ibid.
102 See D.M. Johnston, 'Marine Pollution Control: Law Science and Politics' (1972–3), 28
International Journal 69.
103 U.N. Doc A/CONF 48/IWGMP. II/5.
104 For a proposed definition of 'pollution,'
without specific reference to the marine environment, see Carl A. Fleischer, 'An International Convention on Environment Cooperation Among Nations: Proposed Draft,

Policies and Goals' (1971), 7 *Texas Int'l L. J.* 73–88, at 78–80. For a proposed definition of 'polluting agent,' also without specific reference to the marine environment, see E.W. Seabrook Hull and Albert W. Koers, *Introduction to a Convention on the International Environment Protection Agency,* occasional paper no. 12 of the Law of the Sea Institute, University of Rhode Island (1971) iv. For an official definition of 'waste,' confined to a designated area of the Arctic marine environment, see s 2 (h) of the Arctic Waters Pollution Prevention Act of Canada.

105 R.S.C. c 2 (1st supp) (1970). For a recent Canadian analysis of this legislation see D. Pharand, 'Oil Pollution Control in the Canadian Arctic' (1971), 7 *Texas Int'l L. J.* 45. For a critical American comment, see R. Bilder, 'The Canadian Arctic Waters Pollution Prevention Act: New Stresses on the Law of the Sea (1970), 69 *Mich. L. Rev.* 1. A more general discussion is reproduced in the *Proceedings of the Fifth Annual Conference of the Law of the Sea Institute* (1971). See also *supra* note 61.

106 The flaw is perhaps less serious when seen outside the context of marine pollution, for the Action Plan presented to the Stockholm Conference is designed in numerous ways to attack pollution at its source. Most of these source directed methods of pollution control may not lend themselves to traditional treaty techniques. On international methods of standardsetting, see P. Contini and P.H. Sand, 'Methods to Expedite Environment Protection: International Ecostandards' (1972), 66 *Am. J. Int'l L.* 37. There is, of course, a role for treaty-making to curb pol-

lution originating in national territory. In each international river basin, for example, the riparian states should enter into agreements to deal with environmental problems relating to their shared river system. There might also be an international agreement 'requiring each nation to test specified products and processes, particularly those containing non-degradable, non-recyclable, or toxic components for their potential effects on the environment, and to publish the results of these tests before the products are introduced on the market.' International Parliamentary Conference on the Environment held in Bonn, June 1971, *Report,* 6–7.

107 U.N. Doc A/CONF 48/IWGMP II/5, 12.

108 Ibid, at 12–13.

109 Canada, Information Division, Dept of External Affairs, Doc 72/19. *Declaration on the Human Environment. A Statement on June 14, 1972, to the Plenary Session of the United Nations Conference on the Human Environment, Stockholm, concerning the Draft Declaration on the Human Environment, by Mr. J.A. Beesley, Legal Adviser to the Department of External Affairs.*

110 Ibid, at 1.

111 See *supra*, at 567.

112 Convention between His Majesty and the United States of America for the Protection of Migratory Birds in Canada and the United States (1916), [1917] G.B.T.S. no. 7; 110 BSP 767; U.S.T.S. no. 628.

113 Convention between the United States of America and the United Mexican States providing for Protection of Migratory Birds and Game Mammals (1936), U.S.T.S. no. 628; 50 *Statutes at Large* 1311.

JOHN HUMPHREY

25/The Role of Canada in the United Nations Program for the Promotion of Human Rights

In the booklet on the United Nations published by the Department of External Affairs after the recent review of Canadian foreign policy, less than two pages are devoted to human rights.[1] Conciseness is not necessarily a criterion of interest. The careful student of the foreign policy review will be more impressed by the place occupied by human rights in the overall picture. Human rights are not even mentioned in the list of policy themes which are said to reflect the ingredients of Canadian foreign policy. It is true that one of the themes is promoting social justice, which means, the paper says, 'focusing attention on two major international issues – race conflict and development assistance.' The paper also speaks of Canadian interests and 'values' which should be safeguarded in a world situation and says that 'external activities should be directly related to national policies pursued within Canada.' But it does not explicitly say that the promotion of human rights is one of these values or a policy pursued by the Canadian government.

I do not attach much importance to these omissions except perhaps insofar as they are an indication of the preoccupations of civil servants. There is no doubt that human rights are a value which the Canadian government wants to promote and that it is in the interest of Canada to promote their respect both at home and abroad. The proposition that human rights need to be defended at home hardly needs to be discussed. Why they need to be defended internationally and why Canada should join in the effort probably require more explanation.

The chief reason is a practical one. Violations of human rights, particularly where there is a consistent pattern of gross violations, can be and have been causes of international unrest and even war. One of the causes of World War II was the consistent violation of human rights in and by Nazi Germany. It is therefore in the interest of the international community of which Canada is a part to reduce these violations to a minimum. There is another reason, however, which at first blush is not so obvious. It is that, while the first responsibility for protecting human rights rests undoubtedly at the national level, in the final analysis human rights can only be protected internationally. This is because national laws protecting human rights can, even if imbedded in a constitution, always be changed. There is no national protection against a determined majority. There needs therefore to be some supranational standard by reference to which national law can be judged. Traditionally this supranational law was natural law. Today it can only be international law. Hence the importance, even from a national point of view, of international law for the protection of human rights, and hence the Canadian interest in contributing to building up such law.

It should have been unnecessary to demonstrate Canadian interest in the international promotion of human rights. I have done so only because of the equivocal treatment of human rights in the foreign policy review. It will be noted that I have kept the argument at the level of the major premise of the review, namely that the criterion of foreign policy should be national interest. I dislike this concept and some of its implications, although I agree that it can be expanded to include almost anything. A more generous and, I think, in the long run more realistic, criterion would be one based on the concept of community, because there will be no effective international order until there exists in fact a sense of community – and that perhaps can be translated by common interest – extending across national borders.

'Canada's general approach to human rights issues in the UN has tended to be cautious,' the foreign policy review goes on.[2] This is an understatement of the first order. The truth is that until quite recently Canada's approach to human rights issues in the United Nations was almost completely negative. As a country, we played no role whatsoever in the drafting of the Universal Declaration of Human Rights. In 1948, indeed, we distinguished ourselves by abstaining in the vote on the declaration in the Third Committee of the General Assembly – along with the communist countries, Saudi Arabia, and South Africa. When this position was reluctantly changed three days later in the plenary assembly, Secretary of State for External Affairs Lester Pearson rationalized our position. The declaration, he said, was often worded in vague and imprecise language, and he regretted that the International Law Commission had not been asked to review the text before it came to the General Assembly. He also mentioned the legislative limitations put on the federal authority by the Canadian constitution. Canada was a federation and many of the matters with which the declaration dealt fell under provincial jurisdiction: 'The federal government of Canada does not intend to invade other rights which are also important to the people of Canada, and by this I mean the rights of the provinces under our federal constitution.'[3] That, as interpreted by the Privy Council in the *Labour Conventions* case,[4] the Canadian constitution does put extensive limitations on the power of the Canadian parliament to implement treaty obligations cannot be doubted.[5] But Mr Pearson's explanation based on the distribution of powers under the Canadian constitution was hardly convincing in the context of the declaration, for whatever the situation may now be[6] there was no intention in 1948 that the Universal Declaration of Human Rights would be binding on states as part of international law.

The argument is even unconvincing as an explanation of Canada's reluctance to co-operate in the early stages of the drafting of the two international covenants on human rights which, according to stated policy, the government now intends to ratify. Many of the matters covered by these covenants fall within provincial jurisdiction, but once the instruments have been ratified Canada will be internationally obliged under them, notwithstanding the fact that under the Canadian constitution the federal authority does not have the power to implement all of their provisions.[7] It is for this reason that ratification is being held up pending negotiations with the provinces; for the federal government wants to be sure, before committing itself internationally, that provincial law meets the standards required by the covenants insofar as those matters which fall within provincial jurisdiction are concerned. Canada is one of the very few countries where the treaty-implementing power is not the same as the treaty-making power. It follows therefore that it is more difficult for us to ratify certain kinds of treaties than it is for most countries, and our difficulties have not been made any easier by the refusal of other countries in the United Nations to include so-called federal states clauses in such treaties. Under such clauses the obligations of federal states are limited to those matters to which the legislative authority of the federal government extends. Such clauses were once included in treaties almost as a matter of course; but more recently the majority in the United Nations has refused to include them on the ground that there is no equality in the burden of obligations assumed by the contracting parties under such treaties. Indeed, the two draft covenants not only contain no federal states clause; they specifically provide that their provisions 'shall extend to all parts of federal States without any limitations or exceptions.'[8]

It can be admitted therefore that the position in which Canada finds herself in relation to international human rights law is not an easy one. The point that I wish to make however is that we are now apparently on the point of ratifying the covenants in spite of these difficulties. But there has been no substantial change in the situation in the United Nations since 1954 when the Commission on Human Rights completed its work on the drafting of the covenants. What has changed is Canada's attitude, or rather the attitude of her officials. It has been suggested that the reason for the change in Canadian attitudes and policy is that it came to be seen

> as the work of the United Nations and its organs unfolded over the years, that the inability of Parliament to ratify international instruments dealing in part or whole with matters of internal provincial competence need not produce major hesitations in the United Nations insofar as participation in international negotiations is concerned. It would come to be better understood that many of the matters being dealt with fall largely or in part within federal legislative competence and, in situations where provincial competence is involved, full opportunities for consultation as to ratification exist after signature and in some cases even during negotiations. It would also be better understood that full and conscientious participation in preparing international standards could not be regarded as creating commitments as to formal adherence to treaties embodying these standards or as in any way infringing the unqualified right of provincial authorities to decide whether or not they wish to introduce legislation to correspond with these standards.[9]

This is undoubtedly partly true, but it is also partly a rationalization. The fact is that until the sixties neither the Canadian public nor Canadian politicians were much interested in the human rights program of the United Nations. If constitutional limitations were the only or the chief reason for the failure of Canada to play a more important role in the human rights program of the United Nations, conceivably the politicians and bureaucrats would have discovered earlier – as their homologues in other countries did – the truths outlined in the passage quoted above or, as in the case of the Americans in 1953, when they decided also partly for constitutional reasons no longer to support the covenants, they could have initiated or backed some alternative or supplementary program. The human rights program in the United Nations has never been limited to the quasi-legislative function of drafting and adopting treaties and declarations.

One wonders whether there may not have been motives other than the ones given by the secretary of state for external affairs for the Canadian reluctance to vote for the declaration in 1948. In the United States there was a well organized campaign against the declaration and the proposed Covenant on Human Rights (as it then was) which was led by the American Bar Association, and great pressure was put on the State Department not to support or vote for these instruments. The campaign in the United States against the declaration failed, although when the Eisenhower administration came to power Secretary of State John Foster Dulles undertook never to bring a human rights convention before the Senate for ratification.[10] There is evidence that after the American Bar Association had failed to influence the State Department against the declaration, its president came to Montreal where he saw the president of the Canadian Bar Association several times in 1948.[11] The latter was one of the chief Canadian opponents to the declaration. To what extent these influences helped to determine the Canadian position is an open question. It must be remembered that for many people, the declaration was a socialist instrument, since it enunciated and defined not only the traditional civil and political rights but also economic, social, and cultural rights.[12] It is of some interest in this connection to note that in 1950, when the question was being debated in the United Nations whether economic, social, and cultural rights should be included in the Covenant on Human Rights or whether there should be a separate covenant dealing with them, Canada voted against including these rights in any covenant.[13]

Not only was the Universal Declaration of Human Rights tainted, in the minds of some people, by socialism, but the very concept of an International Bill of Rights seemed to be foreign to common law traditions and the parliamentary system as they had developed in Canada. Bills of rights were republican institutions associated with the American war of independence and the French revolution. In the United States an imbedded bill of rights had upset the traditional balance between the legislature and the courts, which now had the final say in wide areas of human conduct. In the Canadian system it was parliament and the provincial legislatures which were the ultimate guardians of the liberties of the people. An entrenched bill of rights would also introduce undesirable rigidity into the law; it would be better to leave to the legislature and the courts the task of adapting the law pragmatically to the needs of society. These arguments are still heard in the great debate on whether a bill of rights should be entrenched in the Canadian constitution.

I would like to think that such reservations based on considerations of legal principle and constitutional practice were a principal factor in the Canadian reluctance to support the human rights program of the United Nations. But in the light of what I have already said regarding the rationalization based on the distribution of powers under the constitution and to the fact that Canadian participation even in the legislative activities of the United Nations would not have entailed any Canadian commitment under international law at the time, I doubt whether this was the case. If it was a major factor, then it must be said that considerations which might possibly have had some relevance in the debate for and against an entrenched national bill of rights were inapplicable to the proposed international bill. For there is no supranational parliament in the international community which could pragmatically adjust the law to the needs of society and the customary law of nations has very little to say about the promotion of human rights. Apart from a controversial and indeed doubtful rule which was said to permit humanitarian intervention on behalf of populations which were being persecuted by governments whose actions 'shocked the conscience of mankind' – but which in practice was resorted to only for political reasons – it was an established principle of customary international law that what a state did to its own citizens was its own business, within, that is to say, its domestic jurisdiction and beyond the scope of international law. Nor was there any prospect of developing pragmatically and by custom a body of international law which would fill the gap. So that whatever hesitations Canadian lawyers may have had regarding an entrenched national bill of rights, their arguments were quite foreign to the issues before the United Nations.

According to *Foreign Policy for Canadians* there was in the past 'an over-emphasis on role and influence obscuring policy objectives and actual interests.' Whether this is true or not, no one could ever suggest that Canada ever in the first fifteen years of the organization's history even attempted to play a role in the United Nations' program for the promotion of human rights. Although Canada could have easily been elected to the Commission on Human Rights, it was not until after the Diefenbaker government came to power that Canada became first, in 1958, a member of the Commission on the Status of Women and, in 1963, of the Human Rights Commission. Nor with the exception of the Subcommission on Freedom of Information and of the Press was a Canadian ever a member of either of the subordinate bodies of the Human Rights Commission until 1966. Members of these latter two bodies, moreover, act in their personal capacity and not as representatives of government, and when Mr George Ferguson, the editor of the *Montreal Star*, was elected to the Subcommission on Freedom of Information in 1947 it was on the suggestion of the United Nations secretariat and not because of any Canadian initiative. Canada is now again a member of the Commission on the Status of Women.

Not only has Canada only once been a member of the Commission on Human Rights – and this at a time when the commission had already completed its most important legislative activity – but during her membership she took no important initiatives or indeed any initiatives which produced any concrete result.[14] This is no reflection on Miss Margaret Aitken, who represented Canada on the commission, for she was there as a representative of the Canadian government and acted on instructions. During this period there was at least one small way that Canada could have shown an interest in the international promotion of human rights by supporting a useful United Nations program and that would have been by acting as host for one of the United Nations seminars on human rights. While this was often discussed, Canada never extended an invitation.

The Canadian contribution to the protracted debates on the many human rights issues in the Third Committee of the General Assembly has been equally uninspiring. And the same can be said of a number of conferences convened by the United Nations, beginning with the Geneva Conference on Freedom of Information in 1948, although Canada did play a certain role in the drafting of the Convention relating to the Status of Refugees. Not only was Canada one of the states represented at the 1951 Geneva conference which adopted the convention, but Mr Leslie Chance, a Canadian, was the chairman of the first session of the *ad hoc* committee which did the preliminary work on the convention.[15]

In 1965, however, Canada began to play an active role in the work of the Third Committee on the International Convention on the Elimination of All Forms of Racial Discrimination, in promoting the suggestion (already approved by the Commission on Human Rights and the Economic and Social Council in 1967) that the General Assembly appoint a United Nations High Commissioner for Human Rights, and also, for the first time, in the final drafting (the operation had begun in 1947) of the two Covenants on Human Rights.[16] Canada has now ratified the Racial Convention;[17] and, as indicated above, the secretary of state for external affairs has announced the intention of the government to ratify the covenants as soon as agreement can be reached with the provinces under whose jurisdiction fall many of the matters dealt with by the covenants.

There are probably three explanations for the change in Canadian attitudes and policy towards the human rights program of the United Nations. The first is that, whatever *Foreign Policy for Canadians* may say, Canada is preoccupied by her image abroad and her role in the United Nations. The second is a reflection of the preoccupation of a government which wants to entrench a bill of rights in the constitution. And the third is the changed Canadian attitude towards apartheid and racial discrimination in southern Africa. To quote *Foreign Policy for Canadians* again: 'At the United Nations, Canada's position on southern African issues has changed markedly during the past 20 years. During the immediate postwar period, its posture was one of relative detachment.'[18] By 1971, however, Canada had become a leading protagonist among the developed western countries in its opposition to these racist policies – to the point indeed that, at the recent Commonwealth Conference in Singapore, Canada played a leading role in opposing the sale of arms to South Africa by Britain.

This changed Canadian attitude towards human rights issues in the United Nations has become apparent only in the last half dozen years; how solidly it is embedded is a question that cannot yet be answered. According to *Foreign Policy for Canadians,* 'Canada's future approach to human rights at the United Nations should be both positive and vigorous.' That is the declared policy of the present government. It will take something more than words to make it credible.

In one important aspect of the United Nations program for the promotion of human rights, the opportunity for a 'positive and vigorous' approach has already been lost. The International Bill of Rights, which includes the Universal Declaration of Human Rights and the two covenants, has now been adopted by the General Assembly.[19] The United Nations and its specialized agencies have also adopted a large number of conventions, most of which are in force, which deal with specific rights and special aspects of human rights. It will be a long time before the international community engages on another legislative program of anything like the same scope.

But, while there now exists a considerable body of international human rights law, this law is still largely lacking in effective sanctions. The next stage which has already begun and which will be far more difficult than the process of reaching agreement on standards will be concerned with implementation. So that if the Canadian commitment to pursue a positive and vigorous approach has any meaning it will almost necessarily be directed towards the building of institutions and procedures for the implementation and enforcement of human rights which the international community has already catalogued and defined.

The covenants and some of the other human rights conventions contemplate certain procedures for their implementation; but, these are weak, even on paper,[20] particularly if they are compared with the relatively effective procedures created by the European Convention for the Protection of Human Rights and Fundamental Freedoms and contemplated by the recently adopted American Convention on Human Rights. Treaties, moreover, only reach and are only binding on states which ratify them and they are not likely to be ratified by all states, including those states with the worst records for violating human rights. It is for these reasons that efforts are now being made in the United Nations to establish implementation procedures the validity of which will be based directly on the charter itself and which will therefore be applicable to all member states, including states which will hardly ratify the covenants or the other human rights instruments. The Canadian approach, if it is to be positive and vigorous should be directed towards the establishment and strengthening of such procedures.

There are several possibilities, one of which relates to reporting. Under article 64 of the charter, the Economic and Social Council may make arrangements to obtain reports on steps taken to give effect to its own recommendations and to recommendations on matters falling within its competence made by the General Assembly, which includes the Universal Declaration of Human Rights. Early attempts of the council to establish procedures for receiving and examining such reports came to nothing, but in 1956 the council did request member states to report on developments and progress achieved in the matter of human rights. The council's resolution, as amended from time to time, is still in force; but, although many states do report, the United Nations has not been able to perfect any effective machinery for examining and acting on these reports such as exists, for example, in the International Labour Organization.[21] Another possibility relates to communications addressed to the United Nations by individuals and private organizations which allege violations of human rights. For many years the position taken by the United Nations was that it had no power to take any action on complaints relating to human rights; but recently the Economic and Social Council has authorized the Commission on Human Rights and its Subcommission on the Prevention of Discrimination and the Protection of Minorities to look at the communications with a view to identifying and indeed investigating situations which reveal a consistent pattern of gross violations.[22] In the summer of 1971, the subcommission put the final stages on the new system for dealing with communications by agreeing on rules of admissibility, but the system has yet to operate in practice and the danger is that like the reporting system it will be frustrated unless it receives the determined support of governments represented on the Human Rights Commission and the council. There are other possibilities such as the advisory services program and the proposed High Commissioner for Human Rights mentioned above.

If Canada's future approach to human rights at the United Nations is to be both positive and vigorous, the Canadian delegation at the United Nations will have to become more involved in institution building of this kind. It requires something more than simply taking positions, however good, in the General Assembly. What is required is a continuing presence and interest in the subordinate bodies where the new institutions are taking form.

NOTES

1 Department of External Affairs, *Foreign Policy for Canadians* (1970).
2 Department of External Affairs, *Foreign Policy for Canadians: United Nations* (1970) 27.
3 This remark could almost be interpreted as meaning that the Canadian government attached more importance to the rights of political collectivities than to the rights of individuals.
4 [1937] A.C. 326.
5 The matter is fully dealt with by Allan Gotlieb in his article 'The Changing Canadian Attitude to the U.N. Role' in Gotlieb, ed, *Human Rights, Federalism and Minorities* (1970) 16–53.
6 But many international lawyers now say that the declaration has become part of customary international law and is therefore binding on all states.
7 See article 27 of the Vienna Convention on the Law of Treaties.
8 Article 28 of the Covenant on Economic, Social and Cultural Rights and article 50 of the Covenant on Civil and Political Rights. Note that federal clauses are still incorporated into treaties negotiated outside the United Nations. There is, for example, a federal clause in the American Convention of Human Rights of 1969 (article 28).
9 Gotlieb, *supra* note 5, at 36.
10 Shortly after John Foster Dulles made this statement in the American Senate, the Americans sponsored the so-called 'action program,' which resulted in the creation of the advisory services program, including seminars, the institution of periodic reporting by governments, and the initiation of a series of studies of specific aspects of human rights.
11 See (1948), 34 *A.B.A.J.* 112. See also the president's report to the 72nd annual meeting of the association: 'In the last year there has been an important exchange of ideas [between the American and Canadian Bar Associations] with respect to the so-called 'International Bill of Rights' program of the United Nations, and the Canadian Bar Association has held five regional conferences in their country similar to those held in this country under the direction of our Committee on Peace and Law through the United Nations.' (1949), 74 *A.B.A. Rep.* 180. In its

report to the American Bar Association in 1948, its Committee on Peace and Law through United Nations drew attention to the fact that 'the Canadian Bar Association, at its annual meeting a few days ago, is reported to have taken action expressing generally similar views as to the Draft Declaration and Draft Covenant and urging that action be not taken by the General Assembly this year.' (1948), 73 *A.B.A. Rep.* 287. John T. Hackett, the president of the Canadian Bar Association, addressed the American association that year. The views of Frank E. Holman, the president of the American Bar Association, on the declaration are contained in an article 'An International Bill of Rights: Proposals have Dangerous Implication for U.S.' (1948), 64 *A.B.A.J.* 984.
12 See the editorial 'Human Rights on Pink Paper,' Montreal *Gazette,* 17 January 1949.
13 The reasons why Canada opposed inclusion of economic and social rights in the same covenant which included other human rights are given in *Canada and the United Nations, 1951–53,* 71–3. But these reasons were hardly applicable to the decision subsequently taken to have two convenants, since the systems contemplated for their implementation were different.
14 On the suggestion of the secretariat, Canada proposed the organization of a series of regional courses on human rights; but in the face of American opposition nothing came of it.
15 Canada ratified the convention in 1969.
16 See Gotlieb, *supra* note 5, and R. St J. Macdonald, 'The United Nations High Commissioner for Human Rights' (1967), *Can. Y.B. Int'l L.* 84.
17 14 October 1970.
18 *United Nations,* supra note 2, at 18.
19 The covenants will not come into force until they have been ratified by thirty-five states.
20 See my report to the International Law Association, *Proceedings of the 53rd Conference* (1968) 441, and my chapter, 'The World Revolution and Human Rights' in Gotlieb, *supra* note 5, at 147.
21 See my report to the International Law Association, *supra* note 20, at 441.
22 See my article, 'The Right of Petition in the United Nations' (1971), 4 *Human Rights Journal* 466.

J.P. WOLFE*

26/War and Military Operations

The desirability of re-examining the law of war has been recognized over the past years by publicists enjoying international respect and by learned societies and other international bodies such as the International Committee of the Red Cross (ICRC). However, up to now this interest has not apparently inspired any response from governments. Even the successes of disarmament talks, in whatever forum they have taken place, have in the final analysis been few; and what has been accomplished probably does not represent any real sacrifice on the part of the governments concerned. But now, twenty-two years after the coming into being of the Geneva Conventions of 12 August 1949 for the protection of war victims, governments are again bestirring themselves; and perhaps out of their initial cautious steps will come a full public scrutiny of what the law of war is, how it relates to modern practices of warfare (or more properly how these practices stand up to examination under what are still avowed to be valid principles of international law), and how much of this law should be reaffirmed or cast aside and new law developed.

The fact that active international attention is again being given to the problem of the conduct of war results, most immediately, from two 1969 resolutions: one was adopted by the United Nations General Assembly on 13 January 1969 at its twenty-third session;[1] and the other was adopted by the twenty-first International Conference of the Red Cross at Instanbul.[2] The General Assembly resolution invited the secretary general, in consultation with the ICRC and other appropriate international organizations, to study:

a Steps which could be taken to secure the better application of existing humanitarian international conventions and rules in all armed conflicts;
b The need for additional humanitarian international conventions or for other appropriate legal instruments to ensure the better protection of civilians, prisoners and combatants in all armed conflicts and the prohibition and limitation of the use of certain methods and means of warfare.

The Red Cross Conference resolution, *inter alia,* noted the importance of the General Assembly resolution, and requested the ICRC

to pursue actively its efforts in this regard with a view to
1 proposing as soon as possible concrete rules which would supplement the existing humanitarian law,
2 inviting governmental, Red Cross and other experts representing the principal legal and

*The views expressed herein are those of the writer and do not necessarily reflect either the policy or the opinion of the Canadian government.

social systems in the world to meet for consultations with the ICRC on these proposals,
3 submitting such proposals to Governments for their comments, and
4 if it is deemed desirable, recommending the appropriate authorities to convene one or more diplomatic conferences of States parties to the Geneva Conventions and other interested States, in order to elaborate international legal instruments incorporating those proposals.

The ICRC did not delay in responding to this request, and from 24 May to 12 June 1971 government experts from some forty countries, at the invitation of the ICRC, attended a conference in Geneva on the Reaffirmation and Development of International Humanitarian Law Applicable in Armed Conflicts.

The scope of the conference was unique and ambitious.[3] It was unique in the sense that the ICRC included in the agenda not only what is sometimes called 'the law of Geneva'[4] – the protection of war victims – but also that part of the law of war referred to as 'the law of the Hague'[5] – methodology of warfare. The introduction of the latter into conference deliberations may have an influence on the ultimate success of any diplomatic conference or, indeed, may have a decisive influence on whether a diplomatic conference is ever convened; it may prove easier to agree to explore how one might be more humanitarian to victims of war than to examine present-day weaponry and methods in the light of long-standing principles.

While possibly creating difficulties, the inclusion in conference deliberations of the law of the Hague created an opportunity to resolve, at least in part, problems that have arisen in the past from the practice of some states of distinguishing between being involved in a war in a factual sense and being 'at war' or in a 'state of war.' This problem was met in the 1949 Geneva Conventions by article 2 common to the four conventions, which provides in part: 'In addition to the provisions which shall be implemented in peacetime, the present Convention shall apply to all cases of declared war or of any other armed conflict which may arise between two or more of the High Contracting Parties, even if the state of war is not recognized by one of them.'[6] While this article resolves the problem as far as the law of Geneva is concerned, such is not the case with respect to the law of the Hague. It would be fortunate indeed if progress could be made towards a law of armed conflict in which the 'state of war' concept would be irrelevant with regard to the law applicable to the conduct of hostilities.

This conference, it is hoped, will turn out to have been the initial step in a process leading to further developments in the law of war. As far as Canada is concerned, the conference has undoubtedly already been beneficial, in that it has caused thought to be given as to what Canada's views are or might be with respect to the many perplexing problems considered. Some of these views will no doubt eventually find their way into an appropriate Canadian forces manual on the law of war.[7] At this point, perhaps Canadian perspectives on this branch of international law can best be considered by examining certain of the proposals put forward at the conference and some of the views expressed thereon by members of the Canadian delegation.[8]

INTERNATIONAL LAW AND NON-INTERNATIONAL CONFLICT

The amount of suffering to which the world has been witness as a consequence of internal strife occurring almost without interruption since the end of World War II appears to have awakened an international conscience and sparked a desire to diminish this suffering by bringing into force international rules and regulations to govern the conduct of such conflicts. The sanctity of paragraph 7 of article 2 of the United Nations Charter has perhaps been eroded by the 'international concern'[9] expressed as tragedy after tragedy has unfolded. The following statement by Canada's secretary of state for external affairs to the 26th General Assembly of the United Nations on 29 September 1971 is illustrative of this problem:

> Canada believes that domestic problems are best dealt with by domestic solutions, and others feel the same way. The question is, how can the international community best assist in a situation where an internal problem has got beyond the capacity of the government concerned? The mere fact that the nations are preoccupied with internal problems and questions of sovereignty in the foreseeable future does not excuse us from making the best possible use of the instrument we have, the United Nations.
>
> It can and should move promptly and effectively, as it has often done, to ameliorate human suffering and protect, to the extent possible, the innocent non-combatants that often bear most of the suffering. This is a noble end in itself, and can be a means toward the settlement of a conflict by creating a better and a saner atmosphere.

Because of past reluctance of states to intervene in situations of internal strife occurring in the territory of other states, little in the way of conventional law has been directed to civil wars and the like. Common article 3 of the Geneva Conventions represented a courageous break with the past. This article imposed obligations respecting the care and protection of victims on both parties to an internal conflict:

> 3 In the case of armed conflict not of an international character occurring in the territory of one of the High Contracting Parties, each Party to the conflict shall be bound to apply, as a minimum, the following provisions:
> (1) Persons taking no active part in the hostilities, including members of armed forces who have laid down their arms and those placed *hors de combat* by sickness, wounds, detention, or any other cause, shall in all circumstances be treated humanely, without any adverse distinction founded on race, colour, religion or faith, sex, birth or wealth, or any other similar criteria.
> To this end the following acts are and shall remain prohibited at any time and in any place whatsoever with respect to the above-mentioned persons:
> (a) violence to life and person, in particular murder of all kinds, mutilation, cruel treatment and torture;
> (b) taking of hostages;
> (c) outrages upon personal dignity, in particular, humiliating and degrading treatment;
> (d) the passing of sentences and the carrying out of executions without previous judgment pronounced by a regularly constituted court affording all the judicial guarantees which are recognized as indispensable by civilized peoples.
> (2) The wounded and sick shall be collected and cared for.

An impartial humanitarian body, such as the International Committee of the Red Cross, may offer its services to the Parties to the conflict.

The Parties to the conflict should further endeavour to bring into force, by means of special agreements, all or part of the other provisions of the present Convention.

The application of the preceding provisions shall not affect the legal status of the Parties to the conflict.

In its consideration of article 3, the ICRC stated: 'However useful Article 3 had proved, it had been shown to have numerous loopholes, and this made it no longer possible to ensure sufficient guarantees to the victims in question.'[10] In reporting on a comparative study of the protection afforded by the Geneva Conventions and various other UN instruments relative to the protection of human rights, the secretary general of the United Nations stated in part as follows:

25 One aspect of the question of scope and applicability concerns the types of armed conflict to which the instruments which are being compared apply. As stressed in the preliminary report, and as is reiterated in the study contained in Annex I, provisions of the human rights instruments of the United Nations, including, in particular, the provisions of the International Covenant on Civil and Political Rights from which derogation is not permitted in accordance with article 4, paragraph 1, of that Covenant, are intended to apply always and everywhere, in time of peace as well as in time of war, and to the full range of conceivable armed conflicts, irrespective of whether or not they are of an international character, while the application of many important provisions of the Geneva Conventions is confined to international conflicts, with conflicts which are not of an international character being governed by common article 3 of the Conventions, which in its generality affords substantially reduced protection. To the extent, therefore, that the Geneva Conventions make the protection of certain rights dependent upon the character of the armed conflict concerned, the protection derived from the United Nations instruments with respect to the rights in question is more encompassing.[11]

It should be noted with respect to the UN instruments that in paragraph 29 of the same report the secretary general also said:

One of the obvious conclusions to be derived from the observations made above is that the International Covenant on Civil and Political Rights being a main source of protection, respect for the rights of all persons in all armed conflicts would be strengthened by the acceleration of the process of ratification of the Covenant so that it might enter into force.

Whatever the strengths or weaknesses of article 3, the ICRC has proposed that a protocol to that article be drafted for two purposes: a / to broaden the scope of the article as to the minimum humanitarian rules to apply for the protection of war victims; and b / to broaden the applicability of article 3, as augmented by the substantive provisions of the protocol, either by providing for a means of determining when a situation exists which attracts the application of the protocol or by defining in the protocol the types of non-international conflicts to which it applies.

Applicability of non-international conflict provisions

Procedure for determining applicability
As noted in paragraph 158 of the secretary general's report, 'article 3 as presently worded leaves considerable latitude to the Governments concerned in determining whether a situation constitutes an armed conflict within the purview of this article.' In practice, several states in the past have refused to recognize the applicability of article 3 to conflicts[12] or internal disorders occurring in their territory. The ICRC proposed that this problem could be solved in one of two ways:[13] by formulating a procedure which would permit objective recognition of the existence of non-international armed conflicts; or by finding a better definition or specification of the concept of 'non-international conflict.' The secretary general has described the problem as 'complex and delicate ... since it concerns questions in which the States Parties may well wish to preserve their discretionary powers.'[14]

With regard to the first proposal, some of the suggestions put forward by the experts consulted by the secretary general were:

a That any given situation be regarded as coming under article 3 if the Government concerned makes an official proclamation of emergency along the lines of those provided in the International Covenant on Civil and Political Rights[15] or in the European Convention on Human Rights;

b That the International Committee of the Red Cross be allowed to collect evidence with a view to expressing a considerable opinion as to whether article 3 is applicable; and

c Alternatively – and considering that the International Committee of the Red Cross might not find it possible to do so – that some international body, already in existence or to be established for that purpose, and offering full guarantees of competence, independence and impartiality, be allowed to perform these functions.[16]

Article 15 of the European Convention on Human Rights is somewhat similar to article 4 of the International Covenant, paragraph 1 of which permits states to derogate in part from their obligations under the covenant during a 'time of public emergency which threatens the life of the nation and the existence of which is officially proclaimed.' Although article 15 does not require that the emergency be publicly proclaimed, paragraph 3 does provide that derogations and the reasons therefor must be reported by states to the secretary general of the Council of Europe.

It seems apparent that unless a declaration or report of a derogation were made by a state pursuant to the covenant or the convention, there would be a great deal of room for argument as to whether particular acts committed by states were along the lines provided for in those documents; it is also possible that a serious conflict could be taking place and measures could be adopted by a state relative thereto without its making any declaration or even imposing unusual restraints on civil and political rights. At the other end of the spectrum, a state might declare an emergency without actually resorting to other than normal police enforcement actions in dealing with the emergency. The 'official proclamation' approach, therefore, would not appear to be a satisfactory way to determine whether an internal conflict was of such a nature as to be governed by international laws of armed conflict.

Employment of the ICRC as a fact-finding body might well compromise the organization; moreover, if the ICRC undertook to render a judgment based on those facts, its non-political image would become tarnished and its present usefulness greatly diminished. Indeed, this role is one which the organization has stated it would not accept.[17] As for the employment of an existing international body, or the creation of a new body, to determine whether an article 3 situation exists, it is unlikely that any body along the lines of a 'mini' International Court of Justice could be created which would be capable of remaining, or at least appearing to remain, completely impartial and which would have the capacity to render decisions in a time frame appropriate to the urgency of all situations. Even should the possibility exist, it is doubtful if states would agree to be bound by the decisions such a tribunal would be called upon to make. The Security Council, though perhaps ostensibly the best equipped organ to take appropriate action, will continue to be hamstrung by the conflicting political interests of its members. In the final analysis, at this juncture the most useful organ available to pass judgment and bring opinion to bear would seem to be the General Assembly.

Definition of 'non-international armed conflict'
In its preparatory material for the conference, the ICRC did not appear to be too hopeful that procedures for an objective determination of the existence of an armed conflict within the meaning of article 3 could be either formulated or agreed upon. It was felt by the ICRC, therefore, that the answer lay in better defining those situations to which article 3 would apply. With respect to such a definition the ICRC has stated the following:

> The following situations, among others, will be considered non-international armed conflicts entailing the application of the provisions of the present Protocol [that is, the protocol it is hoped will be entered into] when they occur on the territory of one of the High Contracting Parties and involve military or civilian victims:
> 1 A hostile organized action
>   a) which is directed against the authorities in power by armed forces;
>   b) which constrains the authorities in power to have recourse to their regular armed forces to cope therewith.
> 2 Hostile organized actions which take place between the armed forces of two or more factions, whether or not these hostile actions entail the intervention of the authorities in power[18]

It should be noted that the circumstances described in paragraph 1 of the definition are not intended to be cumulative.

At first glance the proposed definition would appear to meet the requirements, but – perhaps like all definitions – it does contain weaknesses. One would have to determine what constituted a 'hostile *organized* action' (emphasis added) and what 'regular armed forces' were. Also, one would have to ask whether there had to be a causal connection between the use of regular armed forces and the nature of the hostile action, or whether such connection would be deemed to exist once regular armed forces were employed.

The ICRC did not intend its proposed definition of internal armed conflict to include *minor* incidents. Indeed, the experts consulted made it clear that there should be no suggestion that the principles of article 3, as they might be developed, would apply to internal 'disturbances' or 'tensions.'[19] Since exceptions to the rule therefore exist, and since such exceptions are themselves difficult to define or classify, perhaps the door to argument and uncertainty remains open, except that it will be the meaning of 'internal disturbance or tension' rather than that of 'internal conflict' which will be the subject of the debate.

In the view of the Canadian delegation at Geneva, if the problems inherent in attempting to define a non-international armed conflict were to be avoided, the only solution appeared to be to make the protocol applicable to *all* situations of armed conflict, whether described as civil war, internal tensions, disturbances, or in some other manner – although, of course, if the conflict were considered international, all the laws of war would apply. This approach was presented in the form of a draft protocol to article 3, which provided in part as follows:

Article 1   Purpose and Application of the Protocol
1) The present provisions which reaffirm and supplement existing provisions of the Geneva Conventions of August 12, 1949 (hereinafter referred to as 'the Conventions'), apply to all cases of armed conflict occurring in the territory of one of the High Contracting Parties, involving government military forces on one side and armed forces whether regular or irregular on the other side, and to which common Article 2 of the Conventions is not applicable.

It is quite likely this provision could be improved upon, for example, by changing the expression 'armed forces whether regular or irregular' to 'armed personnel whether regular or irregular.' The important point at this time is the philosophy behind the provision, namely, that whenever government military forces are employed in any situation against persons resorting to force of any kind to achieve their purpose, the protocol becomes applicable. It should be noted that the Canadian provision would not make the protocol applicable to conflicts between two or more factions within a state not involving the intervention of the authorities in power. In the view of the Canadian experts, it is unlikely that a state will fail to intervene where organized hostilities are taking place within its borders. Even if such is possible, however, and leaving aside the question of the applicability of the protocol to disputants of whom none would be party to the protocol, it is unlikely that governments would agree to provisions purporting to regulate what in effect would be private disputes and therefore on their face could be said to amount to intervention in the internal affairs of states.

Substantive non-international conflict provisions

It was realized by the Canadian delegation that if the proposed protocol to article 3 were to have the broad scope mentioned in their article 1, its substantive provisions would have to be kept to a minimum. With a few exceptions, the content of the Canadian draft protocol was limited to provisions which it was thought were of such a basic humanitarian nature that no government could, with good conscience, reject them. Moreover, many of the substantive provisions proposed by the ICRC were such as do not give rise to too much controversy, including those relative to the protection of the wounded and sick and medical personnel and facilities; similar provisions were included in the Canadian draft. However, certain proposals considered by the conference were controversial and will ultimately have to be resolved. These proposals and the views of the Canadian delegation thereon will be examined briefly.

Role of the ICRC

Article 3 provides in part that 'an impartial humanitarian body, such as the International Committee of the Red Cross, may offer its services to the Parties to the conflict.' This provision is not mandatory, and in the past the ICRC has experienced difficulty in accomplishing this task. With a view to strengthening the right to take the initiative in providing humanitarian aid, the ICRC submitted the following proposal to the governmental experts for study: 'The ICRC wishes particularly to emphasize the fundamental principle according to which the many victims of non-international armed conflict must, at all times, be able to receive the necessary relief, and to benefit from humanitarian aid under all circumstances.'[20] It should be noted that this proposal does not contemplate an agency fulfilling the role that a 'Protecting Power' would fill pursuant to the Geneva Conventions.

The ICRC has foreseen two possibilities for obtaining better protection for the victims of internal armed conflict through application of the 1949 Geneva Conventions: the first is that of calling upon existing bodies such as the ICRC or international or regional organizations to provide a presence where the conflict is occurring; the second envisages the parties to the conflict setting up a special *ad hoc* multinational supervisory commission, as was done in the recent conflict in Nigeria.[21] It is apparent that the ICRC contemplates the role of whatever body is employed as involving more than the mere provision of humanitarian assistance in whatever form that might take. The proposed role would appear to entail supervision of the conduct of the opposing parties with appropriate reports being made to some authority whenever breaches of humanitarian law occur.

The presence of representatives of the ICRC or some similar organization, whether created for the purpose or not, in the territory in which a conflict is taking place, is essential. Even with such observers present there will be breaches of the conventions, either through the ignorance or negligence of individuals or, unfortunately, through execution of the policy of those in authority. To say such presence is essential, however, is different from saying that governments will agree in advance to bind themselves to an obligation to permit such presence with the consequent observation of their activities.

Having regard to political realities, the Canadian delegates in drafting their protocol included a provision in Article 1 which, though somewhat stronger than the corresponding provision in article 3, was nevertheless not entirely satisfactory:

4 Each Party to the conflict should arrange for, or agree to, the presence in territory under its control of impartial observers who shall report to the Party who has so arranged for or agreed to their presence, on the observance by persons in the territory under the control of that Party of the provisions of this protocol. Where such action has not been taken by a Party to a conflict other states may request and encourage that Party to consider having recourse to such impartial observers.

In the hope of reinforcing the concept implicit in this paragraph, article 11 of the Canadian draft provided as follows:

1 All persons belonging to or under the control of a Party to the conflict shall have the right to make application to the ICRC, the National Red Cross (Red Crescent, Red Lion and Sun) Society or other organization in the country in which the conflict is occurring which might assist them.
2 The several organizations referred to in this article shall be granted all facilities for carrying out their purposes by the authorities within the bounds set by military or security considerations.

It is to be hoped that as negotiations on the draft protocol continue, any Canadian delegation involved in those negotiations will make its goal that of ensuring the strongest possible position for the ICRC or some similar organization in this regard.

Members of the armed forces: Penalties, prisoners of war
As the treatment afforded to captured combatants of either side can have an effect on the ferocity and perhaps even duration of a conflict, it is not surprising that the ICRC should have put forward proposals relative to this problem. Two of these proposals will be examined together as, while on their face they purport to deal with different things, they are in fact related. The first of these proposals concerns the imposition of penalties for having belonged to the armed forces of one of the parties to the conflict, and reads as follows:

The regulation [that is, international convention] envisaged should include the principle by which no one could incur the death penalty solely for having belonged to armed forces which have fought in accordance with the laws and customs of armed conflicts.
Generally speaking, the authorities in power should not punish the fighter solely for having belonged to armed forces, unless imperative security requirements make this necessary.[22]

The second proposal concerns the granting to captured combatants in internal armed conflicts treatment which prisoners of war would receive pursuant to the Prisoner of War Convention:

a Members of regular armed forces and combatants belonging to armed forces satisfying the conditions of the Interpretative Protocol[23] of Article 4 number 2 of the third Geneva Convention shall benefit of the treatment of prisoners of war provided by the terms of the said convention.
b Apart from the minimum guarantees of Article 3 common to the four Geneva Conventions of 1949, the combatants who belong to armed forces not satisfying conditions of the said Interpretative Protocol shall have the benefit of the protection afforded by the provision relative to the prohibition against capital punishment for the sole fact of having taken part in hostilities.

It would be unrealistic to expect a government to agree in advance to waive the death penalty or any other penalty for acts which in the eyes of that government amount to treason. Equally, it is unrealistic to expect governments to agree to any provision which would purport to equate rebel combatants to prisoners of war when these latter enjoy immunity from punishment for having borne arms. What one can perhaps realistically hope for at this time is agreement by governments that executions resulting from a death sentence for having taken part in hostilities could be postponed until they ended. When hostilities have ceased, one might reasonably expect that with the numbers involved and in the interests of facilitating an early return to normalcy, the majority of such penalties would not in fact be carried out. The Canadian draft therefore included the following provision:

Article 18 – Death Penalty
1 Death sentences imposed upon persons whose guilt arises only by reason of having participated as combatants in the conflict shall not be carried out until after hostilities have ceased.
2 Death sentences imposed on any person shall not, in any event, be carried out until the convicted person has exhausted all means of appeal and petition for pardon or reprieve.

With respect to the idea of affording captured persons the treatment afforded prisoners of war under the Prisoner of War Convention, it should be noted that a literal interpretation of this requirement could involve the imposition of obligations incompatible with other provisions of the draft protocol; for example, the draft protocol would not envisage the presence of a Protecting Power to protect the interests of prisoners of war. In addition, the full application of the Prisoner of War Convention would impose an administrative burden on the rebel forces which they would in all likelihood, at least in the initial stage of the conflict, be unable to carry out. This failure could result in accusations, reprisals, and counter-reprisals, thus escalating further breaches of whatever rules might eventually be applicable to such conflicts. The Canadian approach, therefore, was that rather than referring specifically to the treatment normally afforded prisoners of war as such, it would be preferable to spell out in the draft protocol certain basic requirements that would improve the lot of those captured and still would be possible for both parties to the conflict to satisfy. To this end the following provision was included:

Article 19 – Persons Whose Liberty Has Been Restricted
    All persons who for any reason are confined, detained, interned or whose liberty has otherwise been restricted shall be humanely treated, and in particular shall:
a receive necessary medical attention including periodical medical examinations and hospital treatment;
b be allowed to practise their religion and to receive spiritual assistance from ministers of their faith;
c be adequately fed, clothed and sheltered, having particular regard to their health, age, condition and employment;
d be enabled to receive individual or collective relief sent to them;
e be removed if the area in which they are confined, detained, interned or restricted, becomes particularly exposed to dangers arising out of the conflict;
f if female, be confined in quarters separate from males under the direct supervision of women; and

g shall be allowed to send and receive letters and cards, except that where it is considered necessary to limit the number of letters and cards sent by a person the said number shall not be less than two letters and four cards monthly.

A further ICRC proposal respecting the imposition of punishment was to the effect that *all* death penalties, not simply those in respect of having fought in the opposing armed forces, should be deferred until the end of hostilities, unless imperative security requirements dictated otherwise. It will be noted that this provision would cut across entire systems of national law and therefore would be unlikely to prove acceptable to governments.

Finally with respect to punishments, there was a proposal that encouragement should be given to the parties to a non-international armed conflict to proclaim a general amnesty at the end of hostilities, subject to exceptions for imperative security reasons. To the extent that the provision does not purport to impose a mandatory obligation it may prove acceptable to governments; on the other hand, it would appear that the provision is too broad in its scope. If it is to appear at all, perhaps it should be limited to amnesty in regard to the offence of participation as a combatant in the conflict.

MILITARY AND NON-MILITARY OBJECTIVES: THE CIVILIAN POPULATION

Distinction between military and civilian population

There is little likelihood any government will go so far as to suggest the abolition of the distinction between the civilian population and the military population with regard to these respective populations being made the object of direct attack. The practices of World War II may indicate that the distinction is not always respected; but generally when a violation is alleged, the perpetrator either tries to excuse it on the ground of error or denies the occurrence of the violation. The ICRC proposal that the distinction should be specifically set forth in any draft protocol relative to the protection of the civilian population in armed conflicts is therefore unlikely to meet with objection. The method of presentation, however, especially with regard to what constitutes the best approach to the problem, is an issue for which a unanimous resolution will be difficult to obtain.

Approach of the ICRC
Generally speaking, one could approach the problem by considering what persons, either because of their status or because of circumstances, should legitimately be made the object of direct attack. Another approach, and the one favoured by the ICRC, is to recite the principle of the distinction between those participating in hostilities and a non-participatory civilian population, with the latter being defined.[24] The principle as enunciated by the ICRC for inclusion in a draft protocol and two proposed alternative definitions read as follows:

> *Principle*
> In the conduct of military operations, a distinction must be made at all times between, on the one hand, persons who directly participate in military operations and, on the other

hand, persons who belong to the civilian population, to the effect that the latter be spared as much as possible.[25]

Alternative Definitions of 'Civilian Population'

a The civilian persons constitute the civilian population. Civilians are those persons who do not form part of the armed forces, nor of organizations attached to them or who do not directly participate in military operations (or: in operations of a military character). The above mentioned persons whose activities contribute directly to the military effort do not, for that reason, lose their status of civilians.[26]

b Persons who do not form part of the armed forces, nor of organizations attached to them or who do not directly participate in military operations (or: in operations of a military character), are civilians and, as such, they constitute the civilian population.[27]

In the ICRC proposed principle of distinction a new category of persons is contemplated: 'persons who directly participate in military operations,' whether in the armed forces or not, would no longer be civilians. What they would be or what rights and obligations they would possess is not stated, nor is help provided in the proposed definitions, which themselves raise further questions. Perhaps the problem arises in part because the expressed principle contains elements, albeit negative, of the definition of the civilian population. Rather than attempting to enunciate a distinction, it would be preferable for the principle simply to reaffirm that the civilian population is not, generally speaking, a lawful object of direct attack, and that it should be spared as much as possible.

There remains the problem whether there should be a definition of the civilian population. As a military man, I would prefer that no attempt be made to define that concept. At present the basic rule is that a civilian is inviolable. It is true that in certain circumstances, particularly those involving self-defence, a soldier can and will attack a civilian; but these circumstances are unusual and such attack is contrary to military tradition. In certain theatres of armed conflict soldiers will be faced with difficult decisions as to which civilians have forfeited their right to be considered inviolable; however, this difficulty is one that will have to be accepted. To introduce a new legal concept, that is, a sort of non-civilian civilian, is to introduce the possibility that the long-standing respect of the soldier for the civilian population will be eroded. Apart from the foregoing, which is essentially an argument involving principle, further problems might arise in the application of the definitions proposed by the ICRC.

Problems with the ICRC definitions

The two definitions quoted above appear to be approaching the problem from different points of view but essentially are really not that different. In both cases a civilian is a person who i / does not form part of the armed forces, ii / does not form part of an organization attached to the armed forces, or iii / does not directly participate in military operations (or in operations of a military character).

One question which arises is about the status of a member of the forces who through age, medical category, or trade is not likely ever to participate in military operations. It is unlikely that one would want to exclude as a lawful object of direct attack any member of the armed forces, except, of course, in circumstances where such member (for example, a medical officer) is already protected from attack pursuant to international law, particularly by the Geneva Conventions. Perhaps the ambiguity of the definitions in this respect could be removed in part by amending iii above to read 'does not *otherwise* directly participate in military operations (or in operations of a military character).'

The category comprised of persons belonging to organizations attached to the armed forces is much too broad. It is true that in the past armed forces have unfortunately found it necessary to employ civilians in roles which would constitute direct participation in military operations; for example, during the UN operations in Korea civilians were recruited in service battalions, and their duties included the carrying of ammunition in front line areas. However, the numerous civilians attached to the armed forces whose duties simply involve the provision of amenities, entertainment, administration, or the simple gathering of news should not be made the object of direct attack, even when these duties bring them in relative proximity to operations areas.

The concept of direct participation in military operations also raises problems. In the words of the ICRC

> 'directly' establishes the relationship of 'adequate causality' between the act of participation and its immediate result in military operations. According to this theory of 'adequate causality,' a person is only a 'combatant' – and thus a possible military objective – to the extent that his act, or activity, is a direct cause of damage inflicted on the adversary, on the military level; that is to say, when his act or activity is such as to cause damage of this nature in the ordinary course of events and according to experience of armed conflicts.[28]

Thus persons 'who are objectively useful in defence or adequate in the military sense, without being the direct cause of damage inflicted on the adversary, on the military level' while contributing to the 'military effort' would not lose their status as civilians. This distinction would not appear to be acceptable. Apart from the scope it leaves for argument between adversaries, if the theory of direct 'adequate causality' is interpreted literally it would lead to unrealistic conclusions; for example, civilian support personnel engaged in duties in a front line area who, although essential as far as the fighting troops are concerned, are not immediately required for purposes of harming or killing the enemy would be immune from direct attack even while engaged in these duties. It should be noted that such essential support personnel would not include the entertainment, welfare, and news personnel mentioned in the preceding paragraph.

Another question arises as to the rights and obligations of this new 'non-civilian civilian.' Since he is a legal object of direct attack, perhaps he should be entitled to take up arms, at least to defend himself; but if he does so, on capture he might be liable for trial as an illegal combatant. This problem has been recognized in a somewhat different sense by Professor Denise Bindschedler-Robert in a report submitted to the Carnegie Endowment:

> The principle that armed forces are the only legitimate human objectives and that civilians in groups (civilian population) or individually are not, is so well established that it is unnecessary to dwell on it. However, it has been pointed out that without workers,

military installations could not function; hence these workers have been called 'quasi-combatants.' It is quite generally admitted that the civilians who happen to be within military objectives incur a risk connected with those objectives and that their presence does not confer any immunity whatsoever on the objective. If the above notion implies that these workers – wherever they may be and at whatever moment – are lawful objectives, then the immunity of the civilian population as such is brought into question, for it is impossible to draw distinctions between civilians. This is an entirely new concept and one which must be fought energetically. It creates a class of non-privileged combatants whose activities, nevertheless, are not considered lawful, and it fails to account for the fact that workers are engaged in activities useful to the war only as long as war installations to that end exist. The lawful objectives to be destroyed are those installations rather than an elusive and easily replaceable labor force.[30]

Perhaps one can fairly conclude that while the distinction between civilians and military must be maintained, it may not be possible, in relatively concise definitions, to reflect the many and varied circumstances which significantly affect the status of either.

Protection of the civilian population

The ICRC considers it desirable that in any future international instrument relating to armed conflicts a provision be included respecting protection of the civilian population generally, even though such a provision may be redundant in certain respects especially if the distinction between civilian and military is otherwise provided for. The following was proposed:

> The civilian population shall enjoy general protection against dangers arising from military operations. The civilian population should not, in particular, be the object of attacks mounted directly against it. Neither should it be used, by its presence, to render certain points or areas immune from military operations.
>
> Nevertheless, civilians whose activities directly contribute to the military effort, assume, within the strict limits of these activities and when they are within a military objective, the risks resulting from an attack directed against that objective.
>
> The civilian population taken as a whole, like the individuals who constitute it, must never be made the object of reprisals.[31]

I do not intend here to examine the proposal in detail but rather to comment on the unique principles contained in it.

The first such principle is that which obliges the party attacked not to employ its civilian population so as to render certain points or areas immune from military operations. The seeds of this idea are already contained in existing provisions of international law, such as article 19 of the Wounded and Sick Convention which obliges parties not to situate medical establishments in such a manner that they might be imperiled by attacks against military objectives. The ICRC proposal will serve as a useful reminder that states have an obligation to their own populations. Perhaps, however, the third sentence of the proposal should be amended to read 'in an attempt to render certain points or areas immune from military operations.'

The second unusual principle contained in the ICRC proposal concerns the prohibition against making the civilian population the object of reprisals. On the face of it this is an attractive proposition and probably for that reason it elicited little comment during the conference – a result which, in many respects, was unfortunate. While it is true that no one wishes to appear to be against a proposal which is the very essence of humanitarianism, one has to be realistic and inquire whether states will, in practice, live up to the obligation when faced with the realities of war. It seems doubtful that a state will remain inactive if the party with which it is in conflict resorts to measures endangering the first state's civilian population, or to measures that are of such a heinous nature as to arouse the entire population of the country upon which they are inflicted. Apart from this aspect of the matter, when adopting a measure purporting to represent such a great step forward one must be careful to ensure that no loopholes exist whereby the obligation can, with ostensible legality, be avoided. This point will be pursued below in discussing the prohibition of attacks on non-military objectives.

Special protection
In addition to the general protection to be afforded to the civilian population as a whole, there invariably arises during discussions on this point the question whether certain identifiable categories of persons should enjoy particular or special protection, such as that afforded to persons entitled to wear the protective emblem of the Red Cross. The right of certain groups of persons to additional protection has been recognized to a certain extent in the Geneva Conventions; for example, article 16 of the Civilian Convention provides that the wounded, sick, infirm, and expectant mothers 'shall be the object of particular protection and respect.'

The concept of such special protection is not without merit; however, there are problems inherent in it. One has to consider the scope of the protection to be provided and upon whom the obligation to provide such protection is to be imposed. It is one thing to impose a certain obligation on an occupying power, but it might be unrealistic to impose the same obligation with respect to its own population on a state which may be fighting for its very existence. Further, one should resist the expansion of those categories that are to be afforded special protection (and there is little doubt that much lobbying for the inclusion of particular groups will take place) since the broader the list becomes, the more watered down becomes the respect shown to traditionally recognized categories of specially protected personnel.

One type of special protection is that to be afforded to children. The ICRC proposal in this regard is as follows: 'Children of less than 15 years of age (or: children, or: young children) shall be the object of special protection. The Parties to the conflict shall make every effort to keep them away and safe from military operations.'[32] The particularly interesting feature of this proposal is that implicit in it is the prohibition against using children of less than fifteen years in the armed forces of a party to the conflict. Whether it is reasonable or realistic to pick arbitrarily an age to which this prohibition is to apply is problematical. The age at which young persons mature and assume community responsibility varies from society to society; and it is perhaps unrealistic to attempt to cut a state off from a supply of manpower that in the normal course of events that state would feel it could properly employ in any capacity. While instinctively one feels some effort should be made to restrict the employment of children insofar as military operations are concerned, perhaps one should not expect or seek more than to apply the concept to 'young children.'

Structures and installations

Non-military objects and military objectives
Concerning the distinction between non-military objects and military objectives, the ICRC has said 'it implies in particular, the illicit objectives be identified when attacks are mounted and that all measures be taken to respect and safeguard protected things; secondly, it reinforces the protection of the civilian population.'[33] The ICRC further states that a rule for making such a distinction has not been expressly affirmed by written law.[34] It would appear that the distinction was first formally articulated in a resolution of the Institute of International Law in 1969,[35] the relevant paragraph of which reads as follows: 'The obligation to respect the distinction between military objectives and non-military objects as well as between persons participating in the hostilities and members of the civilian population remains a fundamental principle of the international law in force.' The ICRC enunciation of the distinction was put in a somewhat more positive manner and in a way that might suggest it was a rule *de lege ferenda*: 'In the conduct of military operations, the distinction must be made at all times between military objectives and non-military objects, so that the latter be spared as much as possible. Consequently, attacks must in all circumstances be restricted to military objectives alone.'[36]

There is little difficulty in accepting the foregoing principle, whatever language is employed, so long as the language clearly reflects the principle. Difficulties do arise, however, in attempting to provide guidance as to what falls within each particular category of objectives. For example, the first question to answer is whether one approaches the problem by identifying those objects which can be attacked directly, that is, military objectives, leaving all else immune from such attack, or whether the problem should be approached the other way around with an attempt made to identify what is immune. While it might be considered that the category of military objectives would be more limited in scope than that of non-military objects and thus easier to identify, either approach is satisfactory if it can achieve the purpose of providing the proper guidance to those responsible for carrying out military operations.

The ICRC adopted the second approach and attempted to define non-military objects:

> Objects reputed to be non-military are those necessarily or essentially designed for the civilian population, even should they subsequently assume a preponderantly military character following a transformation of their use.
>
> Non-military objects are those such as houses and constructions which shelter the civilian population or which are used by it, foodstuffs and food producing areas, and water sources and tables.[37]

Because of its apparent contradictory nature this is perhaps a somewhat confusing definition. The confusion may be somewhat lessened by reference to the distinction made by the ICRC between 'mixed objects' and 'mixed objectives.' Mixed objects are those that

> according to their usual purpose are non-military objects but which, by means of a simple transformation, may easily be used directly in the military effort or operations. These latter are so to speak, 'potential military objectives.' A mixed objective would be for example, a factory producing both civilian and military equipment and a mixed object would be a school turned into a barracks.[38]

The difference between 'mixed objectives' and 'mixed objects' is further explained as follows:

> a The mixed object would *only* become a military objective if it took on a direct military function following a change, despite its usual purpose.
> b The mixed objective, in the strict sense, would only become a military objective on two conditions: firstly, its function in support of military requirements must be preponderant; secondly, its military function, if it were preponderant, must represent an adequate cause in the military effort or operations for the party undergoing an attack.[39]

It is apparent that the substance of the two foregoing quotations would have to be incorporated into the ICRC definition of a non-military object, if that definition were to be reasonably understandable. In so doing, however, one would be going a long way towards defining a 'military objective.'

In the final analysis it would seem that the simplest approach would be to concentrate on trying to isolate the notion of the military objective. As noted by the ICRC, the essential criterion to apply in this regard is that of function,[40] although subsidiary criteria will also have to be identified. In this regard an important consideration will be the element of immediacy or directness. It is perhaps in this aspect of the matter that the concept of the 'strategic offensive' might come under critical review: one will have to consider at what point 'strategic bombing' becomes 'indiscriminate bombing.'

Along with the definition of the military objective, however, there could be a provision in the international instrument whereby it would be stipulated that certain objects would not be considered as military objectives *per se*. These could include such things as those presently mentioned in the ICRC proposed definition: 'houses and constructions which shelter the civilian population or which are used by it, foodstuffs and food producing areas, and water sources and tables.' It would probably not need stating that such objects would not be immune from *indirect* damage; nor perhaps would it be necessary to state that if the defending party utilized the objects or areas in question for defensive or other operational purposes, the immunity granted would be forfeited while such use continued. The ICRC has recognized this latter situation and has suggested the possibility of introducing the concept of giving a warning prior to withdrawal of immunity, as envisaged by article 21 of the Wounded and Sick Convention with respect to medical establishments.[41]

An interesting proposition put forward by the experts consulted by the ICRC was that non-military objects should as a general rule not be exempt from reprisals. While it is understandable that the same concern would not be shown for inanimate objects as would be shown for the civilian population, the practical differentiation would seem quite difficult; for example, it would be possible to inflict reprisals on a civilian population under the guise of attacking objects. The ICRC has attempted to meet this problem in part in a proposal respecting general protection of non-military objects: 'Among non-military objects, those indispensable to the survival of the civilian population must be neither destroyed, nor damaged, nor be made the object of reprisals in as much as the survival of the civilian population would be threatened.'[42] Nevertheless it is apparent that if reprisals are permitted with respect to non-military objects, the way is open to inflict reprisals on the civilian population.

Installations containing dangerous forces
Under this heading the ICRC, perhaps wisely, limited its proposal as follows:

> So as to spare the civilian population from the dangers which may result from the destruction of constructions and installations – such as hydro-electric dams, nuclear power stations and dykes – following the release of natural or artificial elements, the interested States or Parties are invited:
>
> a to agree on a special procedure, in time of peace whereby a general protection may be assured, in all circumstances, to such of these installations as are designed for essentially peaceful purposes;
>
> b to agree, during periods of conflict, on granting a special protection – possibly taking existing legal provisions as a basis – to such of these installations whose activity does not have any, or no longer has any, relationship with the conduct of military operations.[43]

This is a problem area that, in part, is again related to the question of the 'strategic offensive.' It is also a problem with respect to which one could look at article 22 of the Hague Rules and remind parties that 'belligerents have not got an unlimited right as to the choice of means of injuring the enemy.' The problem is difficult but must be examined because, as has been pointed out by some experts, 'apart from the terrible short-term effects that the destruction of such installations would have on the civilian population, the medium and long-term effects would be catastrophic for the economies of some countries, particularly the countries in course of development.'[44]

Unless the question of the 'strategic offensive' is resolved, perhaps all that can be done with respect to the protection of these installations is to prohibit attack on them except in cases of extreme military necessity. Coupled with this could be a requirement for warning (this concept is discussed further below), both as to the conditions that must be met to avoid attack, that is, what the defender must do to retain their immunity, and, if the destruction is considered militarily essential, the granting of adequate time to allow steps to be taken to alleviate the suffering it will cause the civilian population.

Specific precautions respecting the civilian population

Under this heading will be considered certain specific proposals designed to give effect to the general protection to be afforded to the civilian population.[45] The precautions to be taken are described by the ICRC as being 'active' or 'passive.' Active precautions are those which must be taken by the attacker and passive are those to be taken by the defender.

Passive measures
These would include such things as removing the civilian population away from danger areas and ensuring that military objectives are not constructed in places where the civilian population will be endangered.

Evacuation   Even in time of peace it would prove a difficult task for most governments quickly to effect an evacuation of any significant number of its population from a threatened area to a place of safety, at least other than temporarily. The required transport facilities alone would probably stretch existing resources to the limit. Even assuming this problem were surmountable, there would remain the problem of where the people would go. In certain climates shelter would perhaps be a minimal requirement; in others it would be of primary importance. Compound the task by imposing the logistical demands of a wartime situation and it can be seen that any provision to be included in an international convention in this regard can at most be in the form of a recommendation.[46]

Location of military objectives   This problem is intimately associated with the concept of military objectives generally, and similarly will ultimately be affected by any solution that may be reached with respect to problems arising out of the 'strategic offensive.' Even if the concept of military objectives is interpreted narrowly, certain concessions to reality will have to be made. A factory producing war material has to be located near people; it has to be serviced by adequate means of transportation, power, and other utilities. The placement of even those military objectives that *could* be located without much inconvenience outside major population centres, for example, defence establishments such as military headquarters, camps, or air fields, raises questions which influence the political decisions involved. The problem will have to be met of the effect on the economy not only of the locality from which a military objective might be moved, but also that of the locality upon which it will be imposed.

It is apparent that both of the foregoing passive measures involve practical problems that make it doubtful that they will be followed by states even if they are included in a protocol. Moreover, their insertion in an international instrument might also create a legal problem: the fact that measures are made obligatory or even recommended in an international instrument might give an attacking party a legal straw to grasp at with regard to any excesses it might commit if the so-called passive measures have not been carried out by the defending party.

Active measures
Included in measures the ICRC proposes should be imposed on the attacking party are those respecting identification, warning, proportionality, and choice of weapons and methods of inflicting injury on the enemy. The conference was unable to devote much time to these proposals; however, there is little doubt that they or similar proposals will have to be considered in more depth in the future. The proposals will be considered in turn.

Identification   'Those who order or launch an attack must ensure that the objective or objectives concerned are not civilian elements, but are identified as military objectives.'[47]

In its terms this proposal is too stringent, and the practical problems which it would impose on commanders was recognized by some of the experts. It should be limited to the requirement of 'taking all practical measures' to ensure that the object being attacked is in fact a military objective. Apart from the confusion which exists in a battle area, it must be recognized that states go to great lengths to camouflage the identity of those objects that they expect will be made the object of attack. It would be asking too much of the attacker to suggest that the ability of the defender effectively to camouflage a particular object would result in the entire area in which the object is known to be located becoming immune to attack.

Warning 'Those who order or launch an attack, must warn the civilian population threatened, whenever the circumstances permit, so that it may find shelter.'[48]

Many of the experts thought this provision should not be so general, but should be limited to those cases where objects that would otherwise enjoy a special protection were going to have that protection withdrawn and be attacked.[49] While this opinion undoubtedly reflects a realistic approach to the problem, it should be noted that the inclusion of the words 'whenever the circumstances permit' does take cognizance of the principle of military necessity. It is conceivable that in this technological age occasions will arise when, even with notice, one party to a conflict will be unable to prevent the destruction of an object or place that the other party has decided must be destroyed. This being so, it is not unreasonable that the civilian population should be given by way of warning, when circumstances permit, at least a limited opportunity to evacuate the area or take such other measures as they may be able to take for their survival.

Proportionality

Those who order or launch an attack must take into consideration the losses or damage which the attack, even carried out with the precautions laid down [in other articles] ... may inflict on the civilian population and non-military objects designed for its use (or: non-military objects indispensable to its survival).

When there is a choice between several objectives which will obtain the same military advantage, the choice shall fall upon that which entails the least danger to the civilian population and non-military objectives designed for its use (or: which are indispensable to its survival).

The attack shall be abandoned if it is found that the probable damage would be disproportionate to the military advantage anticipated.[50]

As a principle the foregoing is not objectionable and, indeed, is one that might well, even without its being specified in any convention, be followed to a large extent by a military commander, if for no other reason than that to do otherwise would present an uneconomic expenditure of his resources. If, however, the principle is expressed as a rule, it is apparent that military commanders might well be placed in positions involving judgment decisions beyond their capacity at all times to make. Rules have to be drafted with an eye to the circumstances in which persons who have the obligation to follow the rules might find themselves. Moreover, the rule must be practical. It is one thing to legislate that an attack must be abandoned in certain circumstances; it is another thing in the heat of battle to call off an attack once launched, particularly if the enemy force has been actively engaged and abandonment of the attack would adversely affect the attacker in terms of losses or tactical position.

Choice of weapons and methods of inflicting injury on the enemy

> Those who order or launch an attack, must take the necessary precautions in the choice of weapons and methods of attack, as well as in the execution of such an attack, so as not to cause losses or damage (or: at least to reduce them to a minimum) to the civilian population or individuals, or to non-military objectives designed for their use (or: non-military objects indispensable to their survival), in the vicinity of a military objective.
>
> The attack shall be abandoned, or suspended, if it appears that the conditions laid down in the present article cannot be respected.[51]

The same comments concerning the breaking off of an attack made under the proposal of proportionality are applicable to the second paragraph of this proposal. With respect to the question as to the choice of weapons to be employed, it is extremely difficult to describe in a few words an obligation in this regard that would be appropriate to all situations. To attempt to proscribe weapons by such generalities as that they are particularly dangerous to the civilian population can only lead to confusion, accusations, and reprisals. If the civilian population unfortunately must assume risks of suffering injury indirectly, it does not seem practical to attempt to specify by what weapons such indirect injury can or cannot lawfully be inflicted. In the final analysis the freedom of action of a commander can be limited only to the extent that international law has proscribed targets and weapons generally. Subject to this the commander must be free to attack targets with those weapons at his disposal that he considers will best do the job.[52]

The foregoing is not to say that a number of weapons presently included in the arsenals of some states should not be proscribed. Rather it is to say that any attempt to proscribe the use of particular weapons should adopt clear and precise language leaving no doubt as to the weapon or its illegality. Paragraph f of article 23 of the 1907 Hague Convention Concerning the Laws and Customs of War on Land already prohibits the use of 'arms, projectiles, or material calculated to cause unnecessary suffering.' Obviously an analysis cannot be made here of all current or recently current weapons to see whether in the light of that article they should be declared to be illegal; however, whenever weaponry is discussed there is one – napalm – which is almost automatically categorized as inhumane and illegal. Whether this is inspired by reasoned analysis or automatic response to man's general fear of fire is problematical; it is apparent, however, that this particular weapon should be made the subject of a study similar to that undertaken by the secretary general of the United Nations on chemicals and bacteriological weapons.[53] Such a study was called for in a resolution proposed by the Swedish delegate and passed by the Third Committee of the United Nations General Assembly during the twenty-sixth session. If the results of such an investigation indicated that napalm should be outlawed, then an appropriate international instrument should be drafted with this object in mind.

As to the choice of means of injuring the enemy, only two points will be considered here. The first concerns the overall question of the 'strategic offensive.' If the practice of both sides in World War ii, so far as their bomber offensives were concerned, can be considered as justifiable or at least not contrary to international law, there seems to be little point in drafting provisions calculated to ease the suffering of those who become prisoners of war or calculated to bring some order and humanitarianism into the conduct of non-international conflicts. In noting that in the bombing of the civilian population in that war the protection had become nominal, one commentator stated: 'That result was not due merely to the reciprocal adoption of the practice of reprisals. It was due to the general acceptance of a notion of military objective of an enlargement so vast as to lose in fact any legally relevant context.'[54] It has been alleged by one authority that, prior to the outbreak of hostilities, recommendations were put forward within the Royal Air Force which would have called for a bomber force capable of wreaking civilian casualties on a scale of 150,000 weekly.[55] The issues involved in this method of warfare must be faced; and if limitations are to be imposed, they must be imposed by international law, and then care should be taken not to reaffirm existing principles which in practice have become meaningless.

A further question which might be considered under this heading is that concerning the use of famine as a means of injuring the enemy. If modern news media have done nothing else constructive, they must surely have awakened an awareness throughout the world as to the cruelty of this form of warfare. Leningrad and Vietnam should have shown the ultimate futility of attempting to achieve military victory by starving the population. Perhaps the time has come to cease worrying about the fact that if food is made available to the civilian population some of it might find its way into the hands of the fighting troops.

This concern over the ultimate recipient of goods is reflected in article 23 of the Civilian Convention:

> Each High Contracting Party shall allow the free passage of all consignments of medical and hospital stores and objects necessary for religious worship intended only for civilians of another High Contracting Party, even if the latter is its adversary. It shall likewise permit the free passage of all consignments of essential foodstuffs, clothing and tonics intended for children under fifteen, expectant mothers and maternity cases.
>
> The obligation of a High Contracting Party to allow the free passage of the consignments indicated in the preceding paragraph is subject to the condition that this Party is satisfied that there are no serious reasons for fearing:
> a that the consignments may be diverted from their destination,
> b that the control may not be effective, or
> c that a definite advantage may accrue to the military efforts or economy of the enemy through the substitution of the above-mentioned consignments for goods which would otherwise be provided or produced by the enemy or through the release of such material, services or facilities as would otherwise be required for the production of such goods.
>
> The Power which allows the passage of the consignments indicated in the first paragraph of this Article may make such permission conditional on the distribution to the persons benefited thereby being made under the local supervision of the Protecting Powers.

> Such consignments shall be forwarded as rapidly as possible, and the Power which permits their free passage shall have the right to prescribe the technical arrangements under which such passage is allowed.

Surely our civilization has advanced enough and we have been made sufficiently aware of the horror of starvation that the free passage of food and medical supplies to the enemy could be made mandatory. Perhaps a system could be devised so that food ships might enjoy the same protection as hospital ships, although such a system would have to include suitable methods of inspection and certification to avoid the passage of contraband. Immunity from diversion or capture of such ships would also appear appropriate. If necessary, controls on distribution could be imposed. The important thing is that the entry of foodstuffs and medical supplies should not be left to the unfettered discretion of the blockading power or the power controlling access to the area in question. On the other side of the coin, the power being blockaded should be put under an obligation to receive the supplies. The suffering of the population under control of a party should not be permitted to become a means of gaining any ends whatsoever.

CONCLUSION

The foregoing does not by any means represent a complete survey of all the questions raised by the ICRC or other during the conference; nor does it represent an adequate presentation of the arguments presented by the ICRC in support of its proposals or by the various experts participating in the conference. The points of view raised herein are not intended to refute arguments that have already been made or that might be put forward by the ICRC or others. The only point I hoped to make here is that the task which the ICRC has taken upon itself is a vast one involving questions upon which agreement will be difficult to reach; indeed, on certain questions there will be states which will resist even having the question formulated. It is a task which cannot even be approached unless there is dialogue and understanding among politicians, officials, members of the military profession, and members of the academic community.

One can expect that Canada will participate actively in any future preparatory conferences that might be held. If these conferences culminate in the calling of an appropriate diplomatic conference, no doubt Canada will be active there also. One can hope that Canada's position will reflect the experience and wisdom of those who have so much to contribute. One would also hope that Canada will be in a position to present views that, although tempered with realism, are courageous and forward looking. Finally, I for one would hope that Canada will resist any attempt to adopt ambiguous compromising language that merely gives the illusion of progress and lends itself to glowing press releases at the conference end. If mankind's lot is to be indiscriminately bombed and napalmed, to have his foodstuffs poisoned, and his environment polluted by his enemies, let it be said in clear language.

NOTES

1 G.A. Res 2444 (XXIII), 13 Jan. 1969
2 Resolution XIII.

3 Prior to convening the conference, a questionnaire (ICRC Doc D1141b, 10 April 1970)

and a commentary on the questionnaire (ICRC Doc D1142b, 10 April 1970) were submitted to experts for reply. The replies received were used in the preparation of conference documents, the titles of which are indicative of the work covered: Book I (Doc CE/1b), *Introduction*; Book II (Doc CE/2b), *Measures Intended to Reinforce the Implementation of Existing Law*; Book III (Doc CE/3b), *Protection of the Civilian Population Against Dangers of Hostilities* [hereinafter cited as *Book III*]; Book IV (Doc CE/4b), *Rules Relative to Behaviour of Combatants*; Book V (Doc CE/5b), *Protection of Victims of Non-International Armed Conflicts* [hereinafter cited as *Book V*]; Book VI (Doc CE/6b), *Rules Applicable in Guerrilla Warfare*; Book VII (Doc CE/7b), *Protection of Wounded and Sick*; and Book VIII (Doc CE/8b), *Annexes*.

4   This part of the law of war is found in the four Geneva Conventions of 12 August 1949, Relative to the Protection of War Victims: Convention I, Geneva Convention for the Amelioration of the Wounded and Sick in Armed Forces in the Field (the 'Wounded and Sick Convention'); Convention II, Geneva Convention for the Amelioration of the Conditions of the Wounded, Sick and Shipwrecked Members of Armed Forces at Sea (the 'Maritime Convention'); Convention III, Geneva Convention Relative to the Treatment of Prisoners of War (the 'Prisoner of War Convention'); and Convention IV, Geneva Convention Relative to the Protection of Civilian Persons in Time of War (the 'Civilian Convention').

5   The Hague Conventions of 1907, with particular attention being given to the International Convention Concerning the Laws and Customs of War on Land.

6   There is perhaps an unfortunate drafting weakness in this provision as one could ask what is the situation if a state of war is not recognized by either party. However, the generally accepted interpretation is that even in this situation the conventions would apply.

7   To date the Canadian forces have sought guidance in this respect from a British forces manual: 'The Law of War on Land' *Manual of Military Law* part III.

8   In order that views might be freely exchanged, the proceedings of the conference were conducted on the basis that the views expressed by delegates would not be binding on their governments; moreover, no votes were taken with respect to any proposals submitted. In this paper views not attributed to the Canadian delegation are mine. It should be noted that the scope of the conference and the course its development took did not permit a co-ordinated approach on all points discussed.

9   McDougal and Reisman, 'Rhodesia and the UN: The Lawfulness of International Concern' (1968), 62 *Am. J. Int'l L.* 1.

10 *Book V*, at 7.

11 Report of the Secretary-General, *Respect for Human Rights in Armed Conflicts* (1970), A/8052, at 12.

12 France long insisted that the Algerian uprising which commenced in 1954 was not an armed conflict within the meaning of article 3.

13 *Book V*, at 37.

14 Report of the Secretary-General, *supra* note 11, at 49.

15 The relevant provision of the International Covenant on Civil and Political Rights referred to is undoubtedly article 4(1).

16 Report of the Secretary-General, *supra* note 11, at 50.

17 *Book V*, at 42

18 Ibid, at 46.

19 Ibid, at 52.

20 Ibid, at 75.

21 Ibid, at 78.

22 Ibid, at 57.

23 This proposed Interpretative Protocol would modify the conditions which members of existing groups must now meet in order to qualify for prisoner of war status: a / being commanded by a person responsible for his subordinates; b / having a fixed distinctive sign recognizable at a distance; c / carrying arms openly; and d / conducting their operations in accordance with the laws and customs of war.

24 The concept of 'civilian population' does not appear to have been defined in instruments of international law now in force. *Book III*, at 17.

25 Ibid, at 24–5.

26 Ibid, at 26.

27 Ibid.

28 Ibid, at 28.

29 Ibid, at 27.

30 *Report of the Conference on Contemporary Problems of the Law of Armed Conflicts*

(1969) 25–6.
31 *Book III*, at 38.
32 Ibid, at 47.
33 Ibid, at 51.
34 Ibid.
35 Session at Edinburgh, 4–13 Sept. 1969. *Ibid*, annex xxiv, at 76.
36 Ibid, at 52, 60.
37 Ibid, at 63.
38 Ibid, at 59 n 67.
39 Ibid, at 59 n 68.
40 Ibid, at 56.
41 Ibid, at 71.
42 Ibid, at 69.
43 Ibid, at 73.
44 Ibid, at 72.
45 Rules similar to these proposals are contained in the Report of the Secretary-General, *supra* note 11, at 17.
46 Related to this question is the further proposal of the ICRC for the creation of zones under special protection similar to those contemplated by articles 14 and 15 of the Fourth Geneva Convention (the Civilian Convention). This concept plus the concepts of the 'operation' and an 'undefended area' are discussed in *Book III,* at 89–102.
46 Ibid, at 82.
48 Ibid, at 83.
49 There is such a provision in article 21 of the Wounded and Sick Convention.
50 *Book III,* at 83.
51 Ibid.
52 The present situation whereby incendiary bullets can be used against *things* but not *persons* is an example of how unsatisfactory and unrealistic attempts to match weapon to target can become.
53 Report of the Secretary-General, *supra* note 11.
54 Lauterpacht, 'The Problem of the Revision of the Law of War' (1952), *Brit. Y.B. Int'l L.* 360.
55 A. Verrier, *The Bomber Offensive* (1968) 60.

27/International Peacekeeping: Canada's Role

BETWEEN THE WORLD WARS

The concept of collective security by means of an international peace force is certainly not an idea known only to the twentieth century.[1] However, the desire for peace was at one of its strongest peaks at the end of World War I, when the world was exhausted from the heavy expenditures in men and money which had gone before. Hence the leaders of the great powers sat down to talk of peace.

Up to this point Canada had been diplomatically under the protective wing of the United Kingdom. But because of the country's substantial participation in the war effort, Sir Robert Borden, Canada's prime minister, insisted that Canada should have an independent voice at the peace talks and ultimately in the proposed League of Nations;[2] this independence in the League was granted. Thereafter the House of Commons debated at length Canada's financial contributions to the organization, but any brief references to Canada's military obligations were dismissed by members of the government as being something to be discussed if and when a crisis arose. Canada would not be totally committed.[3] Members of parliament also appeared to have a basic mistrust of collective security.[4]

During the negotiations leading up to the founding of the League of Nations, most states proposed some sort of military sanction within the organization, but the French proposals went the farthest: they included an international army to enforce the peace imposed by the League, and a League staff to regulate national army sizes.[5] It is not surprising that the proposal was treated as an attempt to limit a state's sovereignty and was rejected outright. Ultimately the Covenant of the League of Nations made fewer demands on the member states than the original proposals and tended to be vague. Articles 10, 11, and 16 were the most important from the standpoint of keeping international peace. Article 10 stated that aggression upon the 'territorial integrity' of another state was unacceptable, and that in the case of such aggression, the Council of the League would determine the steps to be taken. Article 11 stated that the League was to take any action deemed wise to safeguard the peace of nations, while article 16 gave the League economic sanctions and military power: 'It shall be the duty of the Council ... to recommend to the several governments concerned that effective military, naval or air force of the Members of the League shall severally contribute to the armed forces to be used to protect the Covenants of the League.' Any decision made under article 16 had to be unanimous.[6]

Canadian representatives to the League disputed the wisdom of article 10, which was viewed as an attempt to usurp national sovereignty[7] – a thought most disturbing to a nation just recovering from the throes of a struggle for diplomatic independence. Indeed, the League itself was subject to criticism within Canada, being called 'a pious hope'[8] and later an 'utter failure.'[9] From time to time, however, government officials would reaffirm their faith in the organization,[10] and attempts would be made unofficially to gain public support for the League. As a result the Canadian Institute of International Affairs was founded in 1928, and it was from its ranks that government policy was most seriously criticized from 1931 to 1939.[11]

Efforts to gain support for the League were counteracted by the events of the 1920s and 1930s in Europe. Canada's foreign policy during this period has been aptly described as 'isolationist'[12] as Canadians feared another encounter with the European power struggle. The now famous statement by Canadian Senator Dandurand could easily be said to reflect Canadian opinion: Canada was a 'fire-proof house far from flammable materials.'[13] The isolationist policy was furthered by the 'no commitment' attitude of the governments during this period. Prime Minister Mackenzie King for most of the twenty years between the wars advocated that 'parliament must decide' all major policies; that is, the cabinet would not commit itself without such full support.[14]

As writers[15] and statesmen became disillusioned with the effectiveness of the peacekeeping machinery of the League, the concept of an international force became of interest once more. Small groups and individuals in the United States, France, United Kingdom, Germany, and Spain all voiced their approval of such a force,[16] with the most favoured idea including an international air force, a force with a new kind of mobility. As the 1940s approached the concept of fault which was prevalent in the 1920s lost its significance and peace enforcement became a positive concept.[17]

The Canadian reaction to an international force was consistent with its policy against obligatory sanctions. At a disarmament convention in 1932, the Canadian representatives voted against an armed force for the League of Nations.[18] In the House of Commons there were two positive referrals to an international force, but neither was made by a member of the government.[19]

The League of Nations itself attempted some form of keeping the peace with an internationally contributed force, but most of the operations involved simply the organization and supervision of plebiscites held in those territories left in a state of limbo after World War I. In 1920 plebiscites were held in Schleswig,[20] Allenstein, Marienwerder, Teuschen, and Klagenfurt; in 1921 plebiscites were attempted at Sopron and Upper Silesia.[21] The plebiscite in Vilna was a true League initiative, and a force of fifteen to eighteen hundred men was present.[22] The Saar plebiscite force of thirty-three hundred men has been described as the first truly international force.[23] Germany and France met the immediate expenses of this force and the remainder was paid for by the League. The Leticia dispute in 1933 was resolved by providing a face-saving League force to administer the territory until settlement.[24] Unfortunately, however, the successes of the League peacekeeping machinery were dwarfed by the trouble spots which remained undisturbed by any kind of League intervention: Bolivia and Paraguay in 1932–8,[25] Manchuria in 1931,[26] Ethiopia in 1935–6,[27] Spain in 1936–7, and Finland in 1939.

The Ethiopian dispute was not a quiet affair in Canadian politics. On 2 November 1935 Walter A. Riddell, Canadian representative to the Geneva Committee of Eighteen studying sanctions against Italy, proposed, without any authority from Ottawa, the extension of sanctions to oil, coal, iron, and steel. The proposals made news in Europe and caused the Liberal government great embarrassment, after which the proposals were denounced by the government. Canada's policy of 'no commit-ment' ruled the day.[28]

The deterioration of European relations had a slow but profound effect on the Canadian government. A policy speech made by Mackenzie King on 18 June 1936 stated: 'In the first place, we do not believe that isolation from interest in world affairs is possible for Canada. The world today is an interdependent world. No hap-pening of any magnitude abroad is without its repercussions on our fortunes and our future.'[29] From 1935 on there was an increase in the defence budget,[30] and the possibility of a second European war was subject of comment in the debates. The change in the policy of the government and Mackenzie King's talks with Hitler[31] would indicate that Canada was preparing for the eventuality of war as early as 1936. But in 1939 Canada did not declare war on Germany until 10 September, a week after the United Kingdom. The United States recognized Canada's indepen-dent status and did not invoke terms of her neutrality until after 10 September.[32]

THE UNITED NATIONS: FIRST FIVE YEARS

The hard and demanding years of the war brought Canadians forcibly, a second time, into the subtle coils of international affairs. Prime Minister King put into words the feelings of many Canadians: 'The fortunes of battle since the outbreak of war; the fate of nations that lie prostrate beneath the heel of the aggressor; the terrific tasks which face the nations since battling for their freedom – all these go to show that neutrality has become a snare and a delusion.'[33] Once the Canadian public realized this, the next step – a world organization dedicated to peaceful co-existence – was recognized as not only acceptable but necessary. Gallup polls indicated that Canadians generally supported such a move, but the kind of reaction varied considerably from one part of the country to another.[34]

Throughout the early 1940s, Mackenzie King appeared to be doing a tightrope act with regard to his foreign policy, which was accordingly inconsistent: on the one hand, as early as 1941 he advocated a new world order;[35] yet in the House of Commons in 1943 he was not prepared to make a definite policy statement and chose instead to dig up his old noncommittal, blasé statement of 1938.[36] Later that same year, however, it appeared that he at last realized that Canada must play a definite role in the new international organization in order to ensure that Canada would not lose its place in the power structure. In July 1943 he unveiled his 'func-tionalist' approach – that the authority of the organization should be spread among member nations not equally but according to the contribution each made to par-ticular aspects of the organization.[37] His formula would have ensured that middle powers like Canada would play an important role.

The rest of the world was also concerning itself with the ways and means of creat-ing lasting peace. The Moscow Conference in October 1943[38] and the Conference of Commonwealth Prime Ministers in May 1944[39] both readily accepted the idea of a strong international organization. At the same time, the American State Depart-ment was doing a study on the feasibility of an international force.[40]

The preliminary talks for a new international organization took place at Dumbarton Oaks from August to October 1944. Canada was not asked to be present, but there were Canadians in attendance as observers, one of whom was Lester Pearson.[41] And Mackenzie King indicated in the House on 11 August 1944 that Canada would support any security schemes agreed upon even if 'they involved the creation of an international police force.'[42] Such a force was an important item on the agenda, and both the Soviet Union and China proposed an international air force.[43] The studies of the American State Department were adopted at Dumbarton Oaks with very few changes in the original text.[44]

In Canada, there was a sincere effort to provide public education on the Dumbarton Oaks proposals in the hope that it would stimulate interest and support.[45] At the same time the government was working on improvements, notably Mackenzie King was pushing his functionalist approach[46] hoping to increase the status of the middle powers without jeopardizing the superpowers. The parliamentary debates were heated and lasted one week.[47] The proposals were ultimately accepted 200 in favour and 5 opposed, and all parties gave full support to the motion.[48] The debates indicated that the members of parliament took a pragmatic approach to the new organization and did not support it with an idealistic hopefulness; Canada's geographic position placed her as a possible 'battleground of the future.' Canada also took a lead in promoting the socioeconomic aspects of the United Nations. Putting the humanitarian element aside, it could be that Canadian politicians felt that in this area a middle power could best take the initiative.[49] The war had caused Canada to boom and its prestige had increased accordingly.

Prime Minister Mackenzie King, Minister of Justice Louis St Laurent, Gordon Graham (leader of the opposition), and M.J. Coldwell (leader of the federal CCF party) headed the seven-man parliamentary delegation to the talks in San Francisco. But since a general election called for 23 June brought the politicians back to Ottawa for most of the San Francisco negotiations, the alternate delegates were required to take over.[50] Pursuing a middle-of-the-road course, the Canadian delegates played a realistic role in negotiations;[51] their proposals were less radical than most and met with little opposition during debate. But despite their uncontroversial part in the proceedings, the prime minister insisted that the delegates present Canada as a middle power with a vital stake in the functions of the new United Nations.[52]

Canada made a valuable contribution to the articles of the charter. In the first place, Canada proposed a method of selection of non-permanent members for the Security Council: the stress, the Canadian delegation stated, should be on the contribution of members to the maintenance of international peace and security.[53] Canada's suggestion together with a consideration of regional representation became the criterion for the selection of non-permanent members of the Security Council.[54] Canada also sponsored a resolution requiring the Security Council to submit annual reports to the General Assembly; this proposal was adopted unanimously.[55]

One of Canada's most important contributions was the content of article 44 of the charter. The Canadian government feared compulsory military sanctions imposed by the Security Council.[56] As a result of Canada's proposals a committee report recommended that 'the council, before calling upon a member not on the council to provide armed forces ... [should] invite that member "if it so request," to participate in decisions concerning the employment of such forces.'[57]

Canada played only a minor role in the discussions of article 43 regarding the agreements for provisions of contingents of national armed forces.[58] There was considerable discussion of article 43 at San Francisco,[59] but few agreements were reached owing to the fact that a proposed Military Staff Committee was to deal with the practical matters of designating national contingents.[60] It was decided finally that rights of passage and numbers and types of forces pledged, together with degree of readiness and location, should be in special agreements between the Security Council and the nations involved. The forces were to remain part of their own national army until such time as the United Nations called them up for duty; proposals for the specific earmarking of forces were rejected, however, based on the opinions of national military authorities.[61] Proposals for the Military Staff Committee were largely a repeat of the Dumbarton Oaks proposals. The Big Four insisted, however, that since they would bear the burden of any enforcement action, their representatives should sit on the committee.[62]

Collective Security, 1945–50

Once the structural plans of the United Nations were complete, the problems of creating an efficient, workable organization began. The first few years after the war were full of hope and optimism for world peace: the war was over; the United Nations – a forum for peace – had been successfully agreed upon. During the first five years of the United Nations, however, problems developed which plague the organization to the present day. The unsatisfactory negotiations of the Military Staff Committee,[63] whose duty it was to provide the formula for an international force, created a vacuum in the peacekeeping capacity of the organization and forced the General Assembly into the role of peacekeeper.

Canada left no doubt that she wanted to see article 43 implemented as quickly as possible. On 28 November 1946 Dana Wilgress called for the creation of an international force, and a Canadian proposal in the General Assembly asked the Security Council to continue negotiations without delay.[64] By the following year, Canadian demands for an immediate decision were quite heated.[65] But under article 47 of the charter, the Military Staff Committee was to be responsible to the Security Council for the strategic direction of any armed forces placed at its disposal. The committee first met on 4 February 1946 and was given its first planning assignment on 16 February 1946. The talks proceeded very slowly, and ultimately, owing to lack of unanimity, broke down in August 1948.[66] The committee had, however, presented a report on 30 April 1947, showing their areas of agreement and disagreement.[67]

To counteract the negative effects of these talks, on 28 September 1948 Secretary General Trygve Lie proposed to the General Assembly the formation of a United Nations guard.[68] His original plans called for three hundred permanent men and five hundred on reserve, but after considerable opposition he suggested instead a three-hundred-man Field Service and a two-thousand-man Field Reserve Panel. In committee the idea received 'lukewarm approval,' and the resolution obtained a passing vote in the General Assembly on 22 November 1949.[69] Secretary General Lie continued his attempts to create an international police force, and under the Collective Measures Committee[70] he proposed a United Nations Legion of fifty to sixty thousand combat troops.[71] This proposal died from lack of interest rather than from strong disapproval; the idea was dropped as being 'administratively, financially and militarily impractical at the present time.'[72]

Canadian leaders in the late 1940s, disappointed with the attempts at creating means of collective security at the United Nations, began to look for some better method. In actual fact, many of their comments on such a need led to the formation of the North Atlantic Treaty Organization (NATO).[73] Despite their doubts, however, political leaders called for continued support of the United Nations from the Canadian people and blamed the organization's failures on its infancy.[74] It was a difficult period with a change in thinking and therefore policy.[75] Ultimately, Canada's new commitment to NATO resulted in this policy statement: 'NATO is intended neither to supercede nor to bypass the United Nations Organization, but rather to help create the conditions under which the United Nations may become an effective instrument of international peace.'[76] However, the international political instability of the period from 1948 to 1950 gave countries such as Canada reason to wonder how peace was going to be maintained. In fact there were many skirmishes which were brought to the attention of the United Nations.

Disputes commencing after World War II [77]

The Balkan crisis[78]
The Balkan dispute, lasting from January 1946 to May 1954, was managed most successfully by using observers.[79] In 1947 the General Assembly established the United Nations Special Committee on the Balkans with its own observation groups,[80] and in 1952 the Peace Observation Commission[81] established a Balkan Sub-Commission which was to observe the area on the request of any of the countries involved; the financing of this latter operation was done through the regular budget of the United Nations.[82] In May 1954 the observation ended with improved relations.

The Indonesian dispute[83]
The Indonesian crisis began in 1946 and was largely disposed of before 1950. A Consular Commission was established which used observers to supervize 'status quo' lines and to supervize the withdrawal of forces under the Renville Truce Agreement of 17 January 1948;[84] the expenses for this effort were met out of the regular budget.[85] The situation calmed down somewhat, and Indonesia gained her independence on 27 December 1949.

The Palestinian crisis (UNTSO)[86]
The conflict between Arabs and Jews over the status of Palestine has continued from early 1947 up to the present day. United Nations involvement in these lengthy hostilities has changed over the years as the crisis has increased or decreased in gravity. First a Palestine Commission and then a Truce Commission were established by the United Nations to help reach a settlement.[87]

Despite the fact that Canada felt sympathy towards the United Kingdom's problems in Palestine, 'Canadian policy ... [was] consistently pragmatic.' As the 1947 to 1948 debates continued, '[Canada's] representatives reached the conviction that of all the plans put forward, only partition stood any real chance of being made to work.'[88] Canada also supported ceasefire and conciliation attempts and the appointment of a UN mediator on 14 May 1948.

On this same date, the Jewish state was proclaimed, with an outright rejection by the Arab states. Count Bernadette, the UN mediator, established the United Nations Truce Supervisory Organization (UNTSO) of military observers.[89] UNTSO has been in existence since that time and its numbers have been modified to meet conditions.

Canada was not requested to provide observers until late in 1953. Four army officers were sent in February 1954, followed shortly by Major General E.L.M. Burns, who became chief of staff of UNTSO until 1956.[90] In 1956 five more officers were sent; in 1958 another five; and three more in 1959; by 1964 there were eighteen officers present. This was the largest single national contingent out of one hundred observers until the 1967 war, when the observer numbers increased[91] to help implement the ceasefire and survey the Suez Canal sector especially.

The financing of UNTSO has always been out of the regular budget of the United Nations and has been assessed among UN members in accordance with their scale of contributions.[92] For Canada, the estimated annual non-recoverable costs up to 15 June 1969 were $299,000 in addition to Canada's assessment for direct UN expenses.

The Kashmir dispute (UNMOGIP, UNIPOM)[93]

The conflict over the small but picturesque province of Kashmir has stormed since approximately January 1948. At this time a three-member commission[94] was established to investigate and mediate; and on 21 April it was given authority to use observers who supervized the subsequent ceasefire and truce agreements. The largest contingent was present in September 1949 and consisted of officers from Canada, United States, Belgium, Mexico, and Norway.[95] After the commission was disbanded in 1950, the United Nations Military Observation Group in India and Pakistan (UNMOGIP) continued to supervize the ceasefire line established in Kashmir.[96]

Canadian participation was kept very discreet.[97] The request for observers was not met with enthusiasm, partly because of Canada's new commitment to NATO and partly because of an inadequate army at home.[98] Supported avidly by Lester Pearson, however, the government sent four officers in February 1949, four in July 1949, and another one in 1963. Canada also lent a Caribou aircraft, three pilots, and a ground crew, bringing their contingent to seventeen in 1964.[99]

Brigadier Angle of Canada was the first chief of staff of UNMOGIP until he died in an airplane crash in 1950.[100] In 1965 UNMOGIP was increased by thirty and Canada sent ten more officers. At this same time, the United Nations India-Pakistan Observer Mission (UNIPOM) was created to supervize the cease fire and withdrawal of forces from areas outside the jurisdiction of UNMOGIP. Brigadier Bruce McDonald, a Canadian serving in Cyprus, was given command of the one hundred UNIPOM observers.[101] Canada supplied twelve officers and five aircraft plus crew and maintenance personnel; a total of one hundred and twelve Canadians were involved in UNIPOM. In 1966 UNIPOM was disbanded after allowing both sides to withdraw without losing face.

The financing of this operation was done through the regular UN budget. Each observer team received salaries from their own governments; and the United Nations provided a subsistence and equipment allowance plus clothing. Canada's estimated annual non-recoverable costs were $246,000 for UNMOGIP, with an overall total of $1,344,435 recoverable costs for air support for UNIPOM.[102]

Korea (UNTCOK, UNCOK)[103]

The Korean crisis had its beginnings just after World War II. Initially the General Assembly established the United Nations Temporary Commission on Korea (UNTCOK)[104] to find some peaceful method of holding elections; despite much controversy over the lack of co-operation from North Korea, elections were held in May 1948 in South Korea alone,[105] after which the United States restored government and military functions to the new government. In December 1948 UNTCOK was replaced by the United Nations Commission on Korea (UNCOK),[106] whose task it was to reunify Korea. It was not until 29 March 1950 that UNCOK requested military observers.[107]

After North Korea attacked South Korea on 25 June 1950,[108] the UNCOK observation team was responsible for making an immediate report to the Security Council. On the same day the United States called an emergency session of the Security Council and called for an immediate ceasefire and a withdrawal of North Korean forces. The resolution[109] was passed, nine affirmative, with Yugoslavia abstaining and Russia absent. The absence of the Soviet delegates from the Security Council[110] and the presence of the Pacific armed forces of the United States near Korea were factors allowing the Security Council to act so decisively. On 27 June President Truman ordered his air and sea forces to give Korean troops support; this initiative set the trend of the whole war.[111] Later that same day the Security Council passed another resolution recommending that 'the members of the United Nations furnish such assistance to the Republic of Korea as may be necessary to repel the armed attack and to restore international peace.'[112]

In Canada the North Korean invasion was mentioned in parliament on 26 June and the members were told that a Canadian representative had attended the 25 June Security Council meeting. On 28 June 1950 Lester Pearson reported to the House that he was sure parliament would support the action taken by the Security Council because it represented collective action for peace. On 29 June, when Trygve Lie asked each state for assistance, an overwhelming majority offered; in the House of Commons Lester Pearson said Canada was sending two observers. But the following day Prime Minister St Laurent stated that the government had decided to support the UN force if necessary, and three destroyers were being sent to the area;[113] the House of Commons gave full support to the statement of the government.[114] Parliament was prorogued on 30 June 1950 with promises that if the situation changed drastically it would be recalled.

On 7 July the Security Council named the United States head of the unified command, and General MacArthur was appointed commander of the forces the following day.[115] On 14 July the secretary general asked member states to supply more combat troops, particularly ground forces.[116] But since the Canadian government was faced with the already heavy burden of NATO and North American defence systems, it feared that any kind of commitment to UN peacekeeping would weaken

Canada's home defences.[117] On 19 July Prime Minister St Laurent stated that steps were being taken to strengthen the Canadian armed forces but, he continued, 'having in mind the other obligations for the employment of Canadian ground forces, the Cabinet has reached the conclusion that the dispatch, at this stage, of existing first line elements of the Canadian Army to the Korean theatre would not be warranted.'[118] An RCAF transport squadron was, however, sent to support the UN Command.[119]

During July there was public pressure at home and pressure by foreign governments for an all-out Canadian commitment to the United Nations.[120] Finally, on 7 August 1950 the prime minister announced the recruiting of a Canadian Army Special Force, which was to be specially trained and equipped to be available for use in carrying out Canada's obligations under the United Nations Charter or the North Atlantic Pact;[121] 'thus, in uncertainty, haste and improvisation was the Special Force born, the Cinderella of the Active Force family.'[122] The first troops arrived in Korea in December 1950, and the remainder were there by March 1951.

In name and in such things as flag and insignia, the force was a UN force;[123] but the lack of direct consultation[124] and the stringent requirements set by the American command for acceptable contingents[125] made the war practically an 'American-led war of alliance.'[126] This was the largest force ever to carry UN insignia, its largest number at any one time being 740,000 men. In all, 21,940 members of the Canadian Army served in Korea and Japan.[127]

The financing reflects the uniqueness of the operation itself: since all contributions were voluntary, no part of the military operations was charged to the UN budget; instead complex bilateral agreements were made between the United States and contributing states.[128] Canadian Army expenditures in Korea were heavy and by 31 March 1951 totalled nearly $200 million; by 1953 the Army was costing over $500 million annually. The RCAF budget for Korea in 1952–3 was $760 million and the Navy budget was $260 million.[129]

In July of 1951 truce negotiations began,[130] but a formal agreement was not signed until June 1953. By 1956 the Canadian military representation was reduced to one officer and one NCO.[131]

PEACEKEEPING FROM 1950

The 1950s

The Uniting for Peace Resolution
The absence of the Soviet Union from the Security Council, which had allowed the passage of the Korea resolutions in June and July 1950, ended in August when the chief Soviet delegate returned to assume his duty as chairman of the council for that month. The communist bloc was quick to point out that in their view all resolutions passed in their absence were illegal.[132] It was against this background that the Uniting for Peace Resolution was passed on 3 November 1950.[133] 'It was an effort to rectify the inability of the Council to act by providing for Assembly supervision of enforcement action under the limitations of recommendatory authority';[134] in effect, the resolution permitted the Assembly to do much of what the council was authorized to do under chapter VII of the charter. Canada, one of the seven co-

sponsors of the resolution, appeared to have been quite enthusiastic about its effects;[135] but it can be strongly argued that the resolution deepened the freeze in the cold war and was an immediate arm of American policy.[136]

The resolution established a Peace Observation Commission whose function it was to observe troubled areas endangering international peace.[137] It also recommended that member states should maintain earmarked units in their armies for prompt availability to the United Nations.[138] Finally, it established a Collective Measures Committee[139] to report on the best methods to be used to strengthen international peace and security; the committee eventually presented watered-down recommendations to the General Assembly, but they were merely noted and not accepted.[140]

In the course of its study the Collective Measures Committee asked each member state what assistance they could contribute. The total contribution came to only six thousand men: only Thailand, Greece, Denmark, and Norway made offers of national contingents, and Uruguay offered two destroyer escorts.[141] Canada's hedged reply was a disappointment after all the major policy speeches Lester Pearson had made in the fall of 1950 about Canada's 'special' earmarked force and after Canada had been set out as 'a valuable example and precedent.'[142] But although earmarking was to become a persistent Canadian theme, the Canadian government was certainly not consistent in its application of it.[143] The Soviet Union consistently denounced the resolution as a 'violation of the Charter' and an 'usurption of the Council's privileges'; as late as 1967 a Soviet memorandum was circulated to council members restating their opinion.[144]

The Uniting for Peace Resolution has been used, for example, in the Suez crisis of 1956[145] and immediately following in the Hungarian situation. Two years later in the Lebanon crisis application of the resolution, especially its legality, was debated openly before it was used.[146]

International Control Commission, 1954

French Indochina has been a scene of political upheaval since 1945, but it was brought to the forefront of the international scene in May 1954 when the French army surrendered to the communist North Vietnamese at Dien Bien Phu after eight years of war and one hundred years of colonial rule.[147] The outcome of events was a source of international concern and a conference was held in June 1954 in Geneva.

Thailand took the problem to the Security Council and requested the dispatch of observers from the Peace Observation Commission; the resolution was vetoed by the Soviet Union.[148] But the Uniting for Peace Resolution allowed Thailand to go to the General Assembly, and on 7 July she asked the General Assembly to reconvene. In the meantime, however, Geneva Conference agreements were reached for the withdrawal of Viet Minh forces from Laos and Cambodia. Accordingly Thailand withdrew her request from the General Assembly in August 1954.

At this point, the Canadian attitude towards Indochina was one of 'aloof interest – aloof because this country was not directly involved but interested because of the possibility that the conflict would spread.'[149] Canada had taken part in the Geneva Conference on Korea but had not taken part in the subsequent Indochina talks. On 21 July 1954 Canada, India, and Poland were asked to sit on an International Commission for Southeast Asia. The invitation was completely unexpected by the Canadian cabinet,[150] but an immediate reply was necessary. The government was faced with a rather serious policy decision: could Canada provide the necessary personnel required, and would Canada be compromising the American position on this situation?[151] Editorial opinion was divided on the issue and so did not play too strong a role in shaping the final decision.[152] Despite what could be termed reservations, on 28 July the Canadian government agreed to accept the invitation.[153]

The first meeting was held in New Delhi on 1 August with R.M. Macdonnell and two officers of the Department of National Defence to assist the High Commissioner to India, Escott Reid. The three members of the International Control Commission began operation on 11 August and the Canadian contribution was significant.[154] The urgent duties of the ICC were to supervise ceasefires, to restore order, and to shuffle belligerent military forces to designated areas of divided Vietnam.[155] It was agreed that Canada, Poland, and India would supply wages and allowances for their personnel; food, lodging, medical services, and transportation would be paid by China, France, United Kingdom, and Soviet Union; the local expenses would be paid by all parties to the Geneva agreements.[156]

In 1955 there were some suggestions that Canada should withdraw from the commission in protest against the communist obstruction they had experienced. However, Lester Pearson said that Canada would not withdraw because withdrawal would contribute to new tensions and would jeopardize peace.[157] This time newspaper comments voiced strong approval of Canada's remaining a member of the ICC.[158] By the year 1967, there were 37 officers and 29 ranks serving a one-year term of duty on the commission.[159] The expenditures by Canada up to 1964 were $10,219,305, with $8,052,715 not recoverable; the non-recoverable costs per year have been about $875,000.[160]

Vietnam and the involvement of the United States in a major war against the Viet Cong have been a constant problem for the commission and Canada in particular. In 1967 a CBC television reporter charged that 'Canadians on the ICC were passing information garnered in the North to the Americans.' The charge was flatly denied by Prime Minister Pearson and Secretary of State Paul Martin.[161] Despite, or perhaps because of, the growing discontent in Canada over the United States position, Canada continued to serve in Vietnam.[162]

United Nations Emergency Force (UNEF)
Canada's policy towards the crisis between the Arabs and Israelis has always been fairly consistent. Aside from participation in the early 1947 negotiations and representation on UNTSO from 1954, the Canadian government has taken the view that Canada's attitude should be equal to both sides of the dispute.[163] The Canadian government had not ignored the troubled area, however, and as early as 1953 had discussed with the United Kingdom the possibility of replacing UNTSO with a police force; in the fall of 1953 the idea was introduced at the United Nations but was dismissed by the secretary general as inappropriate at the time.[164] Again in 1955 Lester Pearson discussed the possibility with Major General Burns, chief of staff of UNTSO, but there was little favourable response from interested states.[165]

The nationalization of the Suez Canal by President Nasser on 26 July 1956 appeared to come as a complete surprise to users of the canal.[166] In the Canadian House of Commons the incident did not raise much debate, and when questioned

Lester Pearson merely stated that the action should be condemned.

At this point the United Kingdom began planning an operation to occupy the canal zone,[167] without consulting other Commonwealth countries although with a request for their support. The Canadian high commissioner in London represented to the United Kingdom that Canada could not support a policy of force in this matter, and the British government was aware of this position at all times.[168] France, United Kingdom, and the United States called a conference of those nations party to the Suez Convention as well as other nations who qualified by tonnage sent through the canal, but Canada was not included.[169] After this conference, the United Kingdom and France proceeded to lay further plans for the occupation of the canal zone[170] but did not communicate them to Canada. Lester Pearson, feeling the tension had eased somewhat, made no mention of the situation in a speech two days before the war began.[171]

Israel attacked Egypt on 29 October 1956, and a few hours later the United Kingdom and France delivered a twelve-hour ultimatum. Openly Canada did not criticize the United Kingdon and stated that it was hoped the United Nations could bring about a peaceful settlement.[172] The Security Council held a meeting that same day, and the United States called for an immediate withdrawal of Israeli forces from Egypt; the United Kingdom and France vetoed the motion, however. Meanwhile, the ultimatum expired and the Anglo-French landing began. The following day Yugoslavia presented a resolution under the authority of the Uniting for Peace Resolution asking for transfer of the issue to the General Assembly.[173]

At this point, before he left for the General Assembly meeting on 1 November 1956, Lester Pearson discussed with the cabinet the idea of a UN police force; he also had Canadian diplomats in Washington and London feel out the reception of the proposal in those countries. His original idea was to make the Anglo-French troops the nucleus of a UN force,[174] but he was forced to change his plans when he reached New York because several delegates had already labelled France and the United Kingdom aggressors.

Early on 2 November in the General Assembly the United States pressed a resolution calling for a ceasefire, which was easily passed.[175] Pearson decided to abstain so that he could use the opportunity of explaining his abstention to propose an international force.[176] Speaking to the Assembly, he outlined the reasons why he abstained and went on to lay the groundwork for his proposed UN force:

> I therefore would have liked to see a provision in this resolution ... authorizing the Secretary-General to begin to make arrangements with Member Governments for a United Nations force large enough to keep these borders at peace while a political settlement is being worked out. My own Government would be glad to recommend Canadian participation in such a United Nations Force, a truly international peace and police force.[177]

The American delegate supported Canada's proposal.[178] At a luncheon meeting the same day, Mr Pearson succeeded in convincing the sceptical Dag Hammarskjöld of the gravity of the situation and plans were set in motion.[179]

Pearson returned to Ottawa where, according to some reports, an international force was not discussed at the cabinet meeting; but Prime Minister St Laurent gave an informal approval to the plan before Mr Pearson returned to New York.[180] Before discussing specifics with the secretary general, he conferred with London and Washington and received encouraging help and suggestions.

Norway and Colombia agreed to co-sponsor the resolution, and, after a brief was constructed, it was presented to the secretary general.[181] On 4 November the General Assembly passed the resolution:[182]

> The General Assembly, bearing in mind the urgent necessity of facilitating compliance with the (United States) resolution of 2 November requests as a matter of priority, the Secretary-General to submit to it within forty-eight hours a plan for setting up, with the consent of the nations concerned, of an emergency international United Nations force to secure and supervise the cessation of hostilities in accordance with the terms of the above resolution.

The detailed planning of the United Nations Emergency Force (UNEF) commenced immediately after the resolution was passed,[183] with first the creation of a UN Command headed by General Burns, chief of staff of UNTSO, with temporary staff from UNTSO. The preliminary decisions concerning logistics were well under way when Dag Hammarskjöld presented his report to the Assembly, less than twelve hours after he was authorized to begin.[184] The final report was presented on 6 November,[185] and laid down the principles to be used in that and future peacekeeping operations:

1 Permanent members of the Security Council were not included on the force.
2 Political control remained with the Secretary-General assisted by an Advisory Committee.[186]
3 The force would be more than an observer corps but less than a military force.
4 The force would be neutral.
5 The host nation's rights would be respected.
6 Each contributing nation would supply wages and equipment. The United Nations would absorb other costs.[187]

By 7 November Dag Hammarskjöld had offers of troops from twelve countries.[188] On 8 November when General Burns went to Egypt, President Nasser had not yet agreed to let troops enter the territory,[189] but an official cable came from Egypt on 14 November allowing UNEF troops to enter Egypt. The force was created and implemented in less than fourteen days.

The Canadian government had stated on 7 November that it was preparing a battalion (Queen's Own Rifles) with complete auxiliary detachments; they also offered to fly the troops by RCAF and send equipment by H.M.C.S. *Magnificent*.[190] But at this point there were indications that Canadian troops might not be 'acceptable' to the Egyptian government. Both General Burns[191] and the secretary general opposed this position, but Egypt remained firm. This Egyptian reluctance to take Canadian forces was 'a severe blow to national pride' and a source of embarrassment to the government. Lester Pearson discussed the problem with the secretary general, who advised him to continue plans as decided upon; both agreed that no country should be able to determine the composition of the force.[192] On 15 November Egypt agreed to allow a Canadian air transport and field ambulance unit to participate.[193]

Meanwhile General Burns had come to New York to confer with the Advisory Committee. Studying his manpower he concluded that he was short of administrative and technical units and relayed this information to the Canadian government, which was able to comply with this UN request and save face by not having to back down from President Nasser's stipulations.[194] By 12 January 1957 Canadian strength exceeded one thousand men, or one-sixth the total of UNEF.[195]

In 1967 Canada's role in UNEF was brought to an untimely death; in fact the status of UNEF itself was becoming very shaky indeed. President Nasser asked on 18 May that UNEF leave Egypt because of the growing tension resulting from the buildup of arms on both sides of the border;[196] orders were therefore given for the withdrawal of UNEF.[197] At this point, access to the Gulf of Aquaba was a question of major importance; and Canada, since 1956, had supported Israel's right to the use of this area. To make matters worse, the president of Israel and President Johnson both spent time in Ottawa shortly after President Nasser's announcement; after President Johnson left, Pearson reiterated in the House that Israel must have right of passage through the Gulf of Aquaba. Canada was openly criticized by the Arabs for her stand, and the Canadian contingent in UNEF was told to leave Egypt in forty-eight hours. Accordingly the Canadian contingent of 774 men was withdrawm immediately, after spending $20,508,500 on recoverable costs and $44,276,500 on non-recoverable costs during its eleven-year stay.

The Diefenbaker era

In June 1957 the Canadian electorate ousted the Liberal party from office. There are varying opinions as to whether or not the decisive policy of the Liberals in the Middle East led substantially to their loss of power,[198] but without a doubt the Conservative party, led by John Diefenbaker, used the crisis as a means of embarrassing the government. They did not criticize the concept of an international force *per se*, but they condemned the attitude of the Liberal government towards the action taken in the Suez area by the United Kingdom and France.[199]

When the new government took office there was considerable speculation as to the possibility of changes in foreign policy. More specifically, what priority would the United Nations have in the Conservative caucus?[200] However, there was little significant change in foreign policy objectives except perhaps for a slight shuffling of priorities.[201] At the General Assembly on 23 September 1957 Prime Minister Diefenbaker made a commitment to the United Nations and said the organization was the 'cornerstone'[202] of Canada's foreign policy. In fact Canada kept her well-established position at the United Nations and played an especially important role when the discussion turned once more to the Middle East in the summer of 1958.

Lebanon (UNOGIL)[203]

The first international crisis to be faced by the Conservative government was in

Lebanon. It was a curious situation, a small country with a pro-western president who was seeking to retain control of his half-Moslem, half-Christian country in the face of the growing threat of President Nasser and the newly established United Arab Republic, composed of Egypt and Syria. Most reports indicated that internal revolt seemed imminent.[204] President Chamoun alleged that the United Arab Republic was smuggling arms into Lebanon and promoting insurgency,[205] and requested a meeting of the Security Council, which was held on 21 May 1958.[206] On 10 June Sweden proposed that an observer group be sent to Lebanon in order to ensure that no arms were being smuggled illegally across the border; the belligerents agreed to the resolution passed on 11 June.[207]

The secretary general named Major General Odd Bull the chief of staff and transferred ten men from UNTSO (including one Canadian officer) without prior negotiation with the governments involved; by 13 June the first patrols of the United Nations Observer Group in Lebanon (UNOGIL) were in action.[208] Canada was asked to sit on the Advisory Board and on 16 June was asked to provide ten more officers.

In the observer reports in July it was stated that there was no conclusive evidence of infiltration or smuggling. But the situation became more tense on 14 July when in nearby Iraq a pro-western government was overthrown. President Chamoun sought American aid, and on 15 July United States Marines landed at Beirut. Reaction in Ottawa to this intervention was not clear; one report said that John Diefenbaker approved,[209] and another report said that the Canadian reaction was not enthusiastic by any means.[210]

The situation in Lebanon was far from stable and the American presence made UNOGIL's work much more difficult. By 18 July the United States tried to have UNOGIL strengthened so that they could withdraw, and at the United Nations there were several abortive attempts to bring about a settlement.[211] Canada began to play a more forceful role, seeking to have a UN presence in Lebanon and Jordan in order to allow the United States and United Kingdom to withdraw.[212] At this point there was sharp criticism from the Liberal opposition that the Canadian government had turned to the United Nations only after realizing that supporting the interventions had not been wise.

The conflict in Lebanon started to subside almost as suddenly as it had begun. President Chamoun decided not to seek re-election, and in mid-August a new government requested the United States Marines to leave. On 19 August Canada, Colombia, Denmark, Liberia, Norway, Panama, and Paraguay submitted a draft resolution giving the secretary general authority to maintain peace, particularly by investigating the formation of a standby UN peace force;[213] the resolution was not accepted, however.

UNOGIL was increased in September[214] and Canada sent fifty more observers. On 27 September Lebanon and the United States reached a formal agreement to have United States troops withdrawn by the end of October, and withdrawal was completed on 2 November 1958. UNOGIL kept up strict surveillance, and in mid-November a report showed that infiltrations appeared to have ended. Therefore, by 9 December 1958 most of the UNOGIL observers had left.

The exact number of men contributed by Canada seems to be in question, but generally, 70 to 80 out of 591 people were Canadians during the eight-month existence of the force.[215] While UNOGIL was financed out of the regular budget of the United Nations, Canada itself spent $147,000 for the maintenance of men during this period.

Permanent peace force
The discussions favouring a permanent peace force seemed to revive during the 1957 to 1958 period, but the response to such suggestions was no better. Before the change in government in 1957, Lester Pearson said that he hoped that the experience of the 1950s could be drawn from and a more permanent force established.[216] In 1958 the secretary general presented a final report on UNEF in which he set down what he considered to be minimum conditions for peacekeeping operations. The communist bloc opposed any discussions on a permanent force, however, and other governments did not feel compelled to press the issue.

Nevertheless, in Canada the Queen's Own Rifles was put on standby for possible UN duty, and since that time a new battalion has been earmarked for this duty each year. The 1959 white paper on defence stated for the first time that it was the defence policy of Canada 'to provide forces for the United Nations to assist that organization in attaining its peaceful aims.'[217]

The Congo (ONUC)
Canada entered the sixties with a battalion in a state of readiness for UN service, the personnel of which were specially equipped and trained for overseas duty. The rest of the Canadian forces were not, however, prepared for a major contribution to a peacekeeping operation.[218] Therefore, although the Canadian government had officially committed itself to peacekeeping, in practice the government could not carry out its commitment. When the Congo crisis broke out in July 1960, the Diefenbaker cabinet hesitated to supply anything more for the proposed force than food supplies and the like.

The situation in the Congo was a direct result of the failure of a paternalistic colonial government to foresee its obligations to prepare a state for nationhood: independence was granted without any kind of transitional period,[219] and almost immediately the Congolese army rebelled against its white officers. To protect the lives and interests of fleeing Belgian nationals, the Belgian government sent in troops immediately. But Patrice Lumumba, leader of the new government, requested technical aid from the United Nations; and on 12 July after an unsuccessful attempt to obtain American assistance, he sought an emergency force from the United Nations.[220] On 13 July Dag Hammarskjöld, on his own initiative under the authority of article 99, called the Security Council into session to discuss the crisis. He recommended military assistance,[221] and on 14 July the Security Council passed a resolution embodying the secretary general's proposals and ordering the Belgian government to withdraw its troops.[222]

The United Nations was once again unprepared for a major peacekeeping operation, and the logistics problem was a headache for the secretary general and his small staff.[223] Major General Carl Von Horn of Sweden was transferred to the Congo from UNTSO, and within one month he had 15,000 troops[224] from twenty-four states under his command, the Organisation des Nations Unies au Congo (ONUC).

Meanwhile, on 12 July 1960, the possibility of Canadian participation in the Congo was raised. The prime minister said that the subject had not been considered because member states had not been requested for aid. He indicated that there was a standby battalion available on five days' notice, as well as one hundred officers from technical services; but these men would be deployed only if the government decided to do so. Shortly thereafter the prime minister stated that the secretary general had asked for two officers and possible RCAF help in transferring supplies and personnel. The government acquiesced, but it was obvious that it did not want to become too involved at this point.[225] Despite the government's misgivings, on 15 July requests for food and three additional officers were met; and a few days later RCAF planes were used to evacuate refugees.[226]

As the requests for personnel increased so did public participation.[227] The most important request was for bilingual signallers - one element vital in the Congo operation.[228] On 25 July the secretary of state for external affairs announced that certain personnel were being prepared for Congo duty, although no decision regarding the sending of Canadian troops had been made. Army officials now faced the problem of finding suitable men in the armed forces. On 30 July John Diefenbaker announced that, with parliament's approval, Canada was prepared to send five hundred men, two hundred of whom were signallers; the establishment and maintenance of UN communication was to be their main function. Also, two Caribou aircraft were to transport supplies, with another two to be made available in a few months.[229]

During this period the Soviet delegate lodged a complaint with the secretary general concerning Canada's participation in ONUC. Canada's unique bilingual signal corps provided the secretary general with the perfect explanation, and Soviet protests met with little support at the United Nations.

Just as the Canadian contingent arrived, the Congolese were beginning to abuse personnel of ONUC.[230] There were several occasions when the Armée Nationale Congolaise beat, humiliated, and forcibly detained members of a signal detachment; understandably, the Canadian government sent a strong note of protest.[231] Despite the specific problems Canadians had as participants in ONUC, the Conservative government on at least two occasions stated that the United Nations personnel were rightfully present in the Congo.[232]

In 1963 ONUC's financial base was very unstable, and by September plans were being made for the withdrawal of the force by June 1964. On 30 June 1964, the last 56 Canadians left the Congo by RCAF airlift. Approximately 1900 Canadians served in the Congo[233] at a total cost of about $13,000,000, with $7,240,000 recoverable and $5,760,000 non-recoverable.[234] Unfortunately, ONUC left the Congo in hardly any better shape than when it arrived. One problem was that the Congolese had failed to train officers for their army.[235] However, the United Nations did make provision for 200 technical personnel to give training in economic and social building.

The financing of ONUC was a major problem. On 24 October 1960 costs were estimated at $60 million, and the question arose of how to apportion these costs. The communist bloc said the 'aggressor' should pay the costs, while most of the western nations felt the financing was a collective responsibility.[236] A resolution was passed giving an *ad hoc* account for the expenses to be assessed on the regular scale, and the assessments were to be binding legal obligations.[237] The next cost estimate was $120 million, at which point the discussions on apportionment were more grave and the arguments were less frivolous. The end result was the passing of a resolution calling the expenses 'expenses of the United Nations.' They were not called a legal obligation and were in fact described as extraordinary expenses. The next budget called the expenses 'extraordinary and essentially different from the expenses of the organization under the regular budget.' ONUC also depended heavily on voluntary contributions of men, equipment, and money. The United States made voluntary contributions of $30.6 million between 1960 and 1962. In addition, the United States, the Soviet Union, Canada,[238] and the United Kingdom waived $12.7 million on airlift costs in 1960. The assessments made from 1960 to 1963, written in vague terms and lacking sanctions, became a mere adventure in semantics as the number of states in arrears – both out of protest and owing to an inability to pay – increased. The problem has not yet been resolved.

West Irian dispute (UNTEA, UNSF)

The Dutch-Indonesian dispute over West New Guinea originated out of the 1949 recognition of Indonesia as an independent state by the Netherlands.[239] The dispute continued throughout the fifties with no progress being made towards settlement. In 1961 and 1962 there were sporadic outbursts of violence between Dutch forces and Indonesian troops who had infiltrated West New Guinea. Ellesworth Bunker, a retired American diplomat, was appointed in March 1962 to negotiate a peaceful solution. On 16 August 1962 both parties agreed to sponsor a resolution which would give the secretary general the power to appoint a UN administrator to head a United Nations Temporary Executive Authority (UNTEA), which would administer New Guinea until 1 May 1963, at which point the area would be handed over to Indonesia.[240] U Thant was asked to send observers to the area at once to assist in the ceasefire and to prepare UNTEA.[241] The secretary general asked member states for administrators, and thirty countries responded positively. Despite this enthusiastic response, only a few volunteers had arrived in the area by 1 October.[242]

To assist UNTEA establish a peaceful transition, a United Nations Security Force (UNSF) was organized.[243] Initially a request was made to Malaya for troops, but that government said they could not spare men. Finally, a self-contained Pakistani unit – the 14th Punjab Regiment – consisting of six companies with a total of 1537 men was sent.[244] The Canadian contribution numbered twelve men and two Otter aircraft; the United Nations had made the request to Canada on 16 August 1962, and the planes and men reached Biak, New Guinea, at the end of the month.[245] The task of the Canadians was to transport supplies from Biak to Fak Fak. The United States also contributed three DC-3 aircraft and their crews to UNSF, completing the force.[246]

Total costs of UNTEA were $20 million over its seven-month presence. The actual costs of peacekeeping came to less than one-third of that amount, with the balance being used in administrative and developmental activities.[247] The entire costs of UNTEA and UNSF were borne equally by Indonesia and the Netherlands, so that the financial crisis of the United Nations was not affected by this operation.[248] On 1 May 1963 the UN administrator turned the territory formally over to Indonesian administration.

The Liberals and peacekeeping

Yemen (UNYOM)

On 26 September 1962 King Imam al-Badr of Yemen was overthrown by a military officer, Abdullah Salla. This tiny desert kingdom on the Sinai peninsula was not left alone with its internal problems, however, since the area was far too important strategically to be left in an unstable state.[249]

During early 1963 Undersecretary Ralph Bunche on behalf of the secretary general was sent on a fact-finding mission, and Ellesworth Bunker was sent by the United States to seek a negotiated settlement. As a result largely of Bunker's efforts the secretary general was able to report that the three immediate parties – the United Kingdom, Egypt, and Saudi Arabia – had agreed to disengage; there was to be a ceasefire and a withdrawal of hostile troops with a demilitarized zone of twenty kilometers on either side of the Saudi Arabia-Yemen border.

Major General Carl Von Horn was asked to ascertain the need for observers, and on 27 May 1963 the secretary general reported that UN observers were 'vitally necessary.'[250] On 7 June Saudi Arabia and the United Arab Republic agreed to meet a proportionate part of the costs of the observer mission. At this point there was no authorization from the Security Council, although the secretary general indicated he was planning to send men.[251] Then on 11 June a resolution proposed by Ghana and Morocco was passed[252] embodying all the proposals of the secretary general with regard to setting up the United Nations Yemen Observation Mission (UNYOM).

In the House of Commons T.C. Douglas, on 28 May 1963, asked if Canada would participate in a United Nations Yemen team; and at that point Paul Martin, secretary of state for external affairs, said he would be sympathetic to any such request.[253] Later, on 13 June, Mr Martin said that Canada was sending an RCAF air transport unit, two Canadian Caribou were being transferred from UNEF, and the United Nations agreed to provide three Otters. Canada was also asked to operate three UN helicopters. On 30 June fifty officers and men, as well as five Canadian Army officers from UNTSO and UNEF, reached Sana, Yemen.[254]

On 4 July 1963 UNYOM began its operations, its mandate being to check and certify the observance of the ceasefire agreement.[255] The conditions under which the observers worked were very arduous, and in August 1963 General Von Horn resigned.[256] UNYOM was extended on three occasions for two months in March, May, and July 1964,[257] during which period the fighting in Yemen had increased.

On 6 September 1964, the mission was ended after some of the fighting diminished, although for the most part the parties had failed to observe the agreement.[258] Thirteen states had provided personnel, with no casualties; and the total expense for the two-year period was $2 million.[259] Recoverable expenses for Canada were $120,000, with $135,000 non-recoverable expenses.

Cyprus (UNFICYP)

The London Agreement of 19 February 1959 and the Treaty of Guarantee of 16 August 1960 made Cyprus an independent state with a guarantee of independence, integrity, and security from Greece, Turkey, and the United Kingdom, but in 1963 trouble broke out between the two ethnic groups on the island and co-operation between the two governments ended.[260] Heavy fighting broke out between the two factions[261] on 21 December 1963, and a few days later the British government stepped in to mediate. A joint peacekeeping force was proposed under British command, but negotiations for this force did not go very well.[262]

In January, at the request of the parties involved and at the expense of the Cyprus government, the secretary general sent an observer to Cyprus for one month, the assignment subsequently being extended another month. In February, when it appeared that the British peacekeeping proposal was not meeting with any acceptance, the British government asked the Security Council to convene.[263] In the Security Council the British pressed for a peacekeeping force of only those parties concerned, rather than a diversified UN force;[264] eventually, however, they modified their position and favoured UN participation.

Canada had been asked to participate in the proposed United Kingdom peace force; and on 11 February 1964 Prime Minister Home of the United Kingdom announced, during a visit to Ottawa, that he looked forward to Canadian contribution to that force.[265] Canadians had more of an interest in Cyprus as a member of the Commonwealth, as opposed to the rather remote areas of New Guinea or Yemen,[266] but the reaction to the proposition of Canadian participation was not consistently either for or against.[267] On 19 February Prime Minister Pearson told the House that certain requirements would have to be met before Canada would participate in a UN force.[268] Never before had the Canadian government expressed such reservations before committing itself to a UN peacekeeping force.[269]

After lengthy negotiations the Security Council adopted a compromise resolution on 4 March 1964.[270] It called for an end to violence and recommended the creation of a UN peacekeeping force with a mandate for three months; finances were to be met by voluntary contributions as well as by the governments providing the manpower and by Cyprus.[271] At this point, the secretary general called on Brazil, Canada, Finland, Ireland, and Sweden to provide contingents.

In the meantime the situation had deteriorated, and on 11 March the Turks issued an ultimatum threatening to intervene if attacks on Turkish Cypriots did not end. Paul Martin, judging the urgency of the situation, took the initiative to begin the organization of the UN force. On 12 March, after he had consulted with U Thant about the preciseness of the mandate, the government of Canada announced it would participate in a UN force.[272] And upon his return to Ottawa, Mr Martin contacted Sweden, Finland, and Ireland and, although Sweden was the only other state to commit itself immediately, this was deemed sufficient for Mr Martin to tell U Thant that a force was ready.[273] The Canadian parliament was convened in an emergency setting on 13 March and, despite a few procedural setbacks,[274] approved the government decision to supply 1150 officers and men.[275] The prime minister stated that costs for the three months would be met by the government.

The first Canadians landed at Nicosia on 17 March 1964, and the rest followed in a few days; but despite their early arrival the troops were not operational as a UN force until 27 March. Besides the British, the Canadians were the only contingent present for nearly a month. Initially, their presence curbed any major outbreaks, but after a few weeks Canadian patrols were being fired on and were returning the fire. By June 1964 there were 6524 UN troops in Cyprus.[276] This United Nations Force in Cyprus (UNFICYP) was extended many times, although the numbers dwindled: by 1969 the force was down to 3650 men.[277] The Canadian contribution also diminished as the overall force fell in numbers: by 31 August 1967, it stood at 880 men[278] and at the end of 1969 it stood at 579.[279] UNFICYP is still present in Cyprus, and the dispute is no closer to settlement.[280]

The financing of UNFICYP has been a major problem.[281] The United Nations had paid $110 million and contributions had reached only $93 million up to the end of 1969. The expenses of UNFICYP for Canada up to 15 December 1969 are estimated at $2,953,800 in recoverable costs, $15,094,582 in non-recoverable costs, and normal pay and allowances of $24,413,164.[282]

Permanent peace force

The theoretical and practical aspects of a permanent peacekeeping force were under serious discussion once more in the early 1960s, in spite of or partly because of everpresent UN peacekeeping commitments. In Canada there were several references by both opposition parties in the House of Commons to a buildup of 'mobile Canadian forces' for future peacekeeping duties.[283] A reply from a cabinet minister stated that it would be impossible to train enough Canadian soldiers to meet all the possible kinds of UN service.[284]

At the superpower East-West Conference held 3 to 6 February 1961 the principle of an international police force to replace national armed forces was adopted. In 1962 at the United Nations Conference on Disarmament in Geneva both the Soviet Union and the United States drafted proposals for United Nations combat forces.[285] But on 13 June 1963, U Thant stated:

In my opinion, a permanent United Nations peace force is not a practical proposition at this time. I know that many serious people in many countries are enthusiastic about the idea, and I welcome their enthusiasm and the thought they are putting into the evaluation of the institution which will eventually and surely emerge.

Personally, I have no doubt that the world should eventually have an international police force which will be accepted as an integral and essential part of life in the same way as national police forces are accepted.[286]

On 19 September 1963 at the General Assembly Lester Pearson called once again for the earmarking of units for UN service. He said that peacekeeping should not be by hit and miss methods, but should be the result of advance planning, He stressed the sharing of technical knowledge among experienced countries in order that there could be 'the development in a co-ordinated way of trained and equipped collective forces for UN service.'[287] On 20 February 1964, during the height of the negotiations for peace in the Cyprus crisis, a conference was held in Oslo. It was a conference of experts who presented papers on various aspects of the feasibility of establishing a permanent peace force, with a view to determining the general consensus.[288]

In March 1964 the *White Paper on Defence* was presented by the minister of national defence. It was a vital paper from the standpoint of Canada vis à vis its peacekeeping commitments, since it was a recognition by the government that peacekeeping was a national responsibility: peacekeeping was not stressed as the greatest priority, but it was included in a statement of defence objectives.[289] The plan for an integration of the armed forces was also particularly suited for the mobile and flexible forces needed for peacekeeping operations.[290]

Lester Pearson on 7 May 1964 once more stressed the concept of some sort of preliminary planning for peacekeeping forces and stated that the Canadian government was preparing for a confidential conference of all those governments particularly concerned with military problems arising out of peacekeeping. On 11 May he stated:

> If the United Nations itself remains unable to agree on permanent arrangements for a stand-by peace force, members who believe that stand-by arrangements should be made could discharge their own responsibility, individually and collectively, by organizing such a force for use by the United Nations.
>
> The stand-by contingents which resulted from such an arrangement would not be used unless and until they had been requested by the United Nations to engage in one of its duly authorized peacekeeping operations.[291]

The conference of peacekeeping nations was originally planned for July 1964, but it was postponed because of criticisms directed at it.[292] The date of the conference was changed to late fall, and the only criterion for attendance was that a state must have contributed one hundred persons or more to a peace force; twenty-seven countries received invitations.[293] On 26 October Paul Martin stressed that the conference was solely to exchange views on technical and practical problems; all other issues of finance or politics were not to be discussed. The meetings were held in Ottawa from 2 to 6 November and were attended by twenty-two nations.[294] Three working groups were established which studied different aspects of peacekeeping and exchanged opinions but did not reach any formal conclusions.[295] Both Pearson and Martin addressed the delegates, reaffirming the informality of the meetings and stressing the concept of advance preparation for UN peacekeeping operations. Mr Martin later, in reiterating the earmarking aspect, said of the meetings that they 'had also shown that it is entirely possible to discuss the practical side of United Nations peacekeeping without diverging into the field of political controversy.'[296]

On 24 to 26 February 1967 the Canadian Institute of International Affairs sponsored a conference on peacekeeping with delegates from across Canada. A unique proposal arising from the conference was for a United Nations staff college to train and educate personnel for peacekeeping operations.[297] There were suggestions that Canada should take the initiative by establishing such a college and paying for the training expenses.

FINANCES AND PEACEKEEPING

The financial crisis

The United Nations financial crisis of the early sixties was deeply rooted in the financial arrangements for UNEF in 1956. During the Suez crisis the secretary general had recommended that a special account be created outside the regular budget, with costs to be shared by member states according to the scale of assessments for 1957. But although it was called a special account, the secretary general considered the expenses as 'United Nations expenditures within the general scope and intent of Article 17 of the Charter.'[298] After lengthy negotiations during which patterns of argument were set for future debates, resolution 1089 (XI) was passed on 21 December 1956 – The Assembly had voted for collective responsibility.[299] But each year up to 1962 arrears and defaults amounted to one-third the total assessment, despite the fact that from 1957 to 1962 over $26 million had been pledged by voluntary commitments.[300]

Essentially the same method of financing was used in ONUC as in UNEF, and the principle of collective responsibility was still being used, although its terms of reference were fading into obscurity. In April 1961 the Fifteenth General Assembly passed a resolution declaring that an examination of methods for covering peacekeeping operations was of the utmost importance. Then a Canadian draft resolution in the standing Finance Committee proposed the creation of a United Nations Peace and Security Fund to finance peacekeeping operations; this proposal sparked interest in the General Assembly.[301] A Working Group of Fifteen[302] made a study over the summer and on 15 November 1961 reported that the only conclusion they all were agreed upon was that the question of finances should be submitted to the International Court of Justice for an advisory opinion.

At the 1961 General Assembly the secretary general reported that the financial situation was extremely serious. The special UNEF account was 30 per cent in arrears for the 1960 and 1961 budgets, and the ONUC account was 40 per cent short in the 1960 budget. Only twenty-four members had paid their 1961 assessments, and in addition both France and the Soviet Union had openly stated they would not pay their assessments.

On 20 December 1961 a resolution was passed in the General Assembly asking the International Court of Justice for an advisory opinion on the question whether the expenditures authorized by the General Assembly for UNEF and ONUC were included under article 17 of the charter.[303] The resolution was not accepted without considerable debate, however, and although it was approved, the effect of the ultimate decision was in doubt even before the court sat to consider the question.

The legal implications of the financial crisis now being under consideration, U Thant turned to the practical maintenance of the two existing forces. Canada was one of nine to co-sponsor a resolution authorizing the secretary general to issue bonds of $200 million with interest at 2 per cent per annum.[304] Canada was the first state to respond to the issue and bought $6,240,000;[305] by 1 October 1963 sixty-five states had subscribed to the bond issue.[306]

The expenses case
In the meantime the ICJ had been in session. On 20 July 1962 there was a 9 to 5 advisory opinion that the costs of UNEF and ONUC *were* costs of the United Nations and were legally binding obligations on the entire membership.[307] Arguments had been presented to the ICJ in roughly three groups.[308] The affirmative pleadings said that these particular expenses were expenses of the organization under article 17; the method of apportionment was merely a matter of bookkeeping and had no special significance.[309] The negative side argued that these expenses did not fall under article 17 because that article refers only to the normal activities of the regular budget; they continued that the assessing resolutions were *ultra vires* since only the Secur-

ity Council could deal with matters such as breaches of peace;[310] lastly, both France and South Africa said that the question put to the court was ambiguous and the court could not express a legal opinion on it.

The court quickly dismissed the French and South African argument and drew the following conclusions:

I   And the plain meaning of the text of Article 17(2) referred to all expenses; although at various times in the history of the Organization a differentiation between 'administrative' and 'operational expenses' had been made, this differentiation did not result in the adoption of two separate budgets.

II i   The responsibility conferred upon the Security Council for the maintenance of international peace and security, under the terms of Article 24, is a primary responsiblity, but it is neither sole nor exclusive in character.

ii The effect of Articles 12 and 14 is to confer upon the General Assembly some dispositive authority in the 'peace and security' field, except when the Security Council is actually seised of a question.

iii [The Court] could find no support for the view that the distribution of functions and powers between the Assembly and the Security Council, provided for in the Charter, excluded from the Assembly the power to provide for the financing of measures designed to maintain peace and security.

III The Court had no difficulty in holding that the UNEF operation established a force that was non-coercive in character and function. This was not enforcement action under Chapter VII of the Charter: ... it was an operation to promote one of the prime purposes of the organization ... the year by year treatment of expenditures by the Assembly was indicative of a consistent intention to treat them as 'expenses of the Organization.'

IV These [ONUC] expenditures were only 'extraordinary' or essentially different from the items of the regular budget for the purposes of assessing procedures.[311]

On 19 December 1962 the General Assembly accepted and acknowledged the advisory opinion.[312] On the same day the Working Group of Fifteen was expanded to twenty-one members.[313] The group was to study special methods for financing peacekeeping operations, including a special scale of assessments for each operation; but after several meetings it was unable to come to an agreed solution.[314] This situation has plagued the ensuing peacekeeping committees up to the present time. For example, one result of the lack of agreement was that the financing of UNEF and ONUC was *ad hoc* for the remainder of their lives, with no definite decision reached on a set financial policy for peacekeeping operations.[315]

Article 19

By 1964 it became evident that if the assessments were not met, article 19 sanctions were probable; although that article would not be of any significance unless and until the General Assembly was in session, once it was in session the nations in arrears would lose their voting privileges. Faced with the possibility of a confrontation with the Soviet Union over the right to vote, the membership agreed not to open the new session of the General Assembly until mid-November. Meanwhile, the Working Group of Twenty-one tried informally to find a solution to the problem for both sides, but with no success;[316] under the circumstances the secretary general decided to postpone the opening of the General Assembly once more to

December 1. When the Assembly finally opened, there was a lack of agreement over the precise meaning of article 19; thus a 'no-objection' procedure was adopted to settle Assembly business, and issues requiring a vote were not dealt with. By February 1965 the Assembly decided a lengthy recess was in order since they had run out of business for which a vote was not required.[317]

Canada's position on the financing issue has always been very clear: all peacekeeping operations are a matter of collective responsibility, and the assessment level should be based upon the capacity of member states to pay.[318] But Canada's position on the application of article 19 has not remained constant over the years: in 1964 the Canadian government said article 19 must be applied to defaulting nations; but in 1965 and 1966 the government indicated that it would support the return to normal deliberations and voting regardless of the arrears of defaulting nations.[319]

The future of peacekeeping

Special Committee on Peacekeeping Operations
On 18 February 1965 a resolution was passed by the General Assembly authorizing the president to establish a Special Committee on Peacekeeping Operations, whose task was to make a comprehensive review of peacekeeping operations in all their aspects 'including ways of overcoming the present financial difficulties of the Organization.' Canada was chosen as one of the members of the committee.[320] This committee did not have any more success than had the Working Group of Twenty-one in finding a solution to these basic issues.[321] The first report [322] of the committee, presented on 15 June 1965, listed members of the committee and also urged that members of the United Nations make voluntary contributions 'without prejudice to their positions taken ... on the financial question.'[323] The second[324] and third[325] reports did not indicate any significant kind of progress.

At this point in the twenty-first session, Canada put forward a carefully considered and well-laid plan on peacekeeping.[326] This was deferred by means of a procedural resolution by some non-aligned delegations, and the whole matter was sent to the Committee of Thirty-three, from which no results have emerged owing to continued disagreements between the permanent members of the Security Council, notably the United States and the Soviet Union.

The fourth report of the committee,[327] issued on 17 May 1967, dealt with members' suggestions for finances[328] and provisions for facilities, services, and personnel,[329] and ended with recommendations. Canada's representative said that 'ideally, collective financing of peacekeeping operations should be the rule and other methods the exception'; he also stated that financing should be worked out prior to an operation taking place.[330] In the discussion of facilities, the Canadian delegate's opinions were highly regarded by most members. He went on to say that 'there was nothing sinister about preparations for peacekeeping.'[331] He felt that the idea of a permanent peace force was unrealistic and that, instead, members should earmark units;[332] he urged that a study should be done of the technical as opposed to the political aspects of a UN peace force, and also suggested that a new look could be taken at article 43 and its application. The United States and Netherlands delegates fully supported his opinions.[333]

Such a study was in fact carried out. Canada prepared and, on 19 June 1968, pre-

sented a report on Canadian participation in UN peacekeeping and observer missions.[334] A working group was set to study the material[335] and decided its first task
should be a study of the 'UN military observers established or authorized by the
Security Council for observation pursuant to Security Council resolutions.' On 3
November 1969 the chairman of the Special Committee on Peacekeeping Operations stated that the working group had made 'a certain amount of progress which,
although limited, was none the less significant.'[336] But on 1 October 1970 the working group reported in the seventh report of the Special Committee that it appeared
an impasse had been reached.[337] And so the story continues.[338] Perhaps this committee is destined to end as the Military Staff Committee did – in obscurity in a room
in the United Nations building.[339]

Canada and peacekeeping, 1964–71
From 1964 to 1967 most public statements of the Canadian government referring
to UN peacekeeping were directed towards Canada's consistent policy of collective
responsibility for the financing of peacekeeping operations.[340] But after UNEF was
disbanded and in the face of unexpected and growing criticism of Canadian support
in peacekeeping,[341] the tenor of speeches given by government officials began to
change. The benefits of maintaining the status quo in these troubled areas were
being questioned, since peacekeeping could be standing in the way of gradual and
peaceful settlement. The merit of future planning for peacekeeping was not ignored
altogether, but there was a shift in emphasis and peace-making became a more predominant theme.[342]

Despite the criticism, there seemed to be no doubt in the minds of government
officials that the public still supported Canada's peacekeeping role.

> Recently, there has been some confused criticism of the concept of peacekeeping and
> Canada's role in United Nations activities in this field. The position of the Canadian gov-
> ernment on this question is clear – we recognize that peacekeeping and efforts at 'peace-
> making' should be pursued simultaneously. Instead of belittling peacekeeping because
> of the problems which United Nations forces have encountered (for example in the Mid-
> dle East) critics should devote their energies to suggesting ways to strengthen the United
> Nations' ability to discharge its primary responsibility for peace and security and to
> ensure that future UN forces will have better terms of reference for carrying out their man-
> date ...
> I am convinced that Canadians want us to go on making a contribution to UN
> peacekeeping in spite of the undoubted difficulties.[343]

The Trudeau cabinet does not appear to have stressed Canada's contribution to
peacekeeping as much as Pearson's cabinet. Undoubtedly, from speeches given by
the secretary of state, peacekeeping is still a Canadian interest, but there has been
more emphasis placed on Canada's regional commitments.[344]

On 5 June 1970 the Eighth Report of the Standing Committee on External Affairs
and National Defence Respecting United Nations and Peacekeeping was presented
to the House of Commons. The Subcommittee on Peacekeeping stated in the report
that 'the Subcommittee cannot assert too strongly its conviction that strong and
tenacious advocacy of improved United Nations peacekeeping should remain a

foremost priority in Canada's foreign policy.'[345] The committee continued that peacekeeping missions were still going to be needed, and 'the development of new peacekeeping machinery therefore must necessarily conform to the principles of the present Charter and recognize that the Security Council has primary responsibility for the maintenance of peace and security.'[346] The subcommittee also made several recommendations as to the course Canadian policy should take in this area. Some of these are:

1   The Subcommittee urges that UN peacekeeping efforts in any particular situation be linked more directly with efforts at peaceful settlement of the issues underlying the dispute.[347]
2   The Subcommittee hopes that these discussions can be directed to the objective of establishing a stand-by force of 20,000 to 25,000 men from non-Permanent Members, supported by adequate earmarked reserves especially trained for UN service.[348]
3   The Subcommittee further recommends the formation on a permanent basis, of a UN international training center responsible for providing training courses for personnel of member countries designed to serve with any UN force.[349]
4   In order to ease the financial difficulties under which the UN has laboured, the Subcommittee recommends that a United Nations Peace Fund be established primarily with voluntary governmental contributions.[350]
5   In designing its defence posture the Subcommittee suggests that the Government of Canada place high priority on maintaining forces earmarked for UN duty. Since each peacekeeping operation is likely to differ from previous ones, flexibility should be the key-note to our military arrangements.[351]

One of the closing remarks is: 'For Canada now to lose heart and reduce its interests in peacekeeping would be an abdication of responsibility. No other country could fill the gap thus opened – and the development of effective peacekeeping would be set back with incalculable but certainly disastrous effects.'[352]

In August 1971 the federal government issued the white paper on defence which gave a positive although qualified renewal to Canada's role in international peacekeeping; international peacekeeping was labelled one of Canada's defence priorities, although it was the last of four:

> The Government continues to support the concept of peacekeeping and will seek to utilize Canada's experience to develop guidelines, within the United Nations and elsewhere, for effective peacekeeping operations. The Government will consider constructively any request for Canadian participation in peacekeeping ventures when, in its opinion, based on the lessons of the past and circumstances of the request, an operation holds the promise of success and Canada can play a useful role in it.[353]

The paper also indicated that for Canada to be involved in a peacekeeping operation there would have to be 'realistic terms of reference.'[354] In keeping with this policy, the government stated it would continue to maintain a standby unit of the Canadian armed forces for possible United Nations use. Canadian forces may also be used in what could be loosely termed peace-making missions in developing countries, since the defence department 'has capabilities to assist in such fields as engineering and construction, logistics policies, trades and technical training, advisory services, project analysis and air transport.'[355] One commentator on Canada's peacekeeping role has stated: 'All too often there has been a tendency for Canadians ... to look on their peacekeeping role as qualifying them for international sainthood. In fact, however, it can be argued that Canada's efforts are eminently practical ... Canada's only defence is peace. Anything that may lead to the attainment of this goal is in the best interests of the nation, and it is difficult to fault the argument that peacekeeping is Canada's most effective military contribution to peace.'[356]

Peacekeeping in the future

The white paper indicated the role of peacekeeping would probably be quite different in the next decade, predicting that most trouble spots would be a result of subversion and insurgency and would therefore be less amenable to the traditional approach to international peacekeeping.

In the future, the role of the middle powers as the mainstay of peacekeeping operations may be diminished and there may be more of a blending of middle- and super-power participation. If the decision-making power for peacekeeping returns to the Security Council under article 43, the superpowers will in all likelihood actively support peacekeeping operations. This support in return will likely lead to the resolution of the financial crisis. However, if peacekeeping decision-making returns to the Security Council, members may no longer have the luxury of going to the General Assembly for action if a veto prevents Security Council action.[357] It is a question of evaluation whether a possibly penniless United Nations is more lethal to world peace than a vetoed peacekeeping operation. In this context it should be borne in mind that it is possible there may be in the near future an independent source of income for the United Nations from revenues arising out of taxation and licensing of seabed resources. The possibility of such a move is being considered presently in UN committee hearings.

One new variable which has been injected into the United Nations political scheme is the presence of the People's Republic of China in the Security Council of the United Nations. The policy patterns of the other permanent members are known and thus can be subject to diplomatic manoeuvring. But this is not the case with the People's Republic of China, and time alone will determine the effect of this development on UN peacekeeping.

NOTES

1 For a historical discussion of attempts to establish international peace, see Passony, 'Peace Enforcement' (1945–6), 55 *Yale L.J.* 910. See also L.P. Bloomfield, *International Military Forces* (1964) 182–6; D.W. Bowett, *United Nations Forces* (1964) 4–7 [hereinafter cited as *Bowett*]; P. Van Slyck, *Peace: The Control of National Power* (1963) 44; W.R. Frye, *United Nations Peace Force* (1957) 46–7 [hereinafter cited as *Frye*]; J.

Johnsen, *International Peace Force,* 17(2) *The Reference Shelf* (1944).
2 Eagleton, 'The Share of Canada in the Making of the United Nations' (1948), 7 *U.Toronto L. J.* 329, 330.
3 'As far as Canada is concerned, she cannot be called upon to make a military contribution unless her Parliament authorizes it and her representative at the Council approves of it.' Canada, House of Commons *Debates,*

[hereinafter cited as *Debates*] 16 March 1920, at 502. See also *Debates,* 22 June 1920, at 3976.

4 See *Debates,* 22 June 1920, at 3975; 18 Feb. 1921, at 111; 1 March 1921, at 400.

5 Passony, *supra* note 1, at 927–8.

6 League of Nations Covenant, article 5.

7 'We are practically, when signing this Treaty, signing away our independence, not in relation to Britain but signing away our independence to the extent that we become subservient to the directions of the League of Nations.' *Debates,* 16 March 1920, at 492. Cf *Debates,* 18 June 1936, at 3870. The United States did not join the League largely because of its fear of the ramifications of article 10, which in fact was proposed by its own President Wilson.

8 *Debates,* 31 March 1920, at 938.

9 *Debates,* 18 April 1932, at 2139.

10 *Debates,* 8 April 1929, at 1334; 25 May 1932, at 3438.

11 *Canada and the United Nations, 1945–1965* (1966), at 6.

12 *Debates,* 21 Feb. 1921, at 186. See also *Debates* 18 June 1936, at 3862.

13 A.M. Taylor, A.M. Cox, and J.L. Granatstein, *Peacekeeping: International Challenge and Canadian Response* (1968) 95 [hereinafter cited as *Taylor*].

14 Mackenzie King has been quoted extensively for his policy of 'no commitment.' Eg, *Debates,* 10 Feb. 1927, at 161; 17 Feb. 1927, at 386; 14 May 1928, at 2965; 16 May 1928, at 3064. This policy was soundly criticized by Mr Woodsworth, who was very active in debates of external affairs. *Debates,* 11 Feb. 1929, at 51–2. For a discussion of Mackenzie King's approach to foreign policy, see G.P. de T. Glazebrook, 2 *A History of Canadian External Relations* (1966) 126–7. With the change of government, Conservative Prime Minister Bennett assumed a 'wait and see' attitude. *Debates,* 25 May 1932, at 3439; 21 Nov. 1932, at 1369–70. With regard to his policies, Mr Woodsworth said: 'He [the prime minister] seems to take for granted that the League of Nations is something apart from ourselves, something that has a more or less independent existence, and that we must stand aside and wait until the League takes action ... The League is only a sort of forum; it is an exchange. It cannot have a life apart from that of its members.' *Debates,* 25 May 1932, at 3435–7.

15 One of the most comprehensive books written in this period was Lord Davies, *The Problem of the Century* (1934). For an analysis of his proposals see *Bowett,* at 313.

16 For details see Johnsen, *supra* note 1, at 144–7; *Passony, supra* note 1, at 934–7.

17 'We therefore arrive necessarily at the conclusion that in case of war or threat of war, international society must possess an organ analogous to the internal police for the purpose of acting against acts of war, without raising the question as to which of the belligerents is at fault.' Kopelmanas, 'The Problem of Aggression and the Prevention of War' (1937), 31 *Am. J. Int'l L.* 244, 255. 'As long as we identify force and the use of force with war, and believe that peace is merely a period without the use of force, we shall never have peace and will always be the victims of force.' Johnsen, *supra* note 1, at 45.

18 See *Debates,* 16 May 1932, at 2979.

19 *Debates,* 15 March 1934, at 1535; 1 April 1935, at 2292.

20 See E. Luard, ed, *The International Regulation of Frontier Disputes* (1970) 43–53; D.W. Wainhouse, *International Peace Observation* (1966) 15–20 [hereinafter cited as *Wainhouse*].

21 See *Wainhouse,* at 33–5. For details of all seven plebiscites, see *Bowett,* at 9.

22 Ibid, at 9–10; *Frye,* at 50.

23 For details see *Frye,* at 51; *Bowett,* at 10–11; *Wainhouse,* at 20–9.

24 See *Frye,* at 51; *Bowett,* at 11; Luard, *supra* note 20, at 75–83; *Wainhouse,* at 64–8.

25 See *Frye,* at 50.

26 See *Wainhouse,* at 53–64.

27 Ibid, at 68–77.

28 Mackenzie King was quick to add, however, that particular sanctions against Italy would be considered individually. Glazebrook has pointed out that at this stage 'it was only from the fame of leadership that the government backed with such rapid steps.' Glazebrook, *supra* note 14, at 121.

29 *Debates,* 18 June 1936, at 3869. See also *Debates,* 25 Jan. 1937, at 250–1; 24 May 1938, at 3215.

30 Defence spending: 1935–6, $17,000,000; 1936–7, $22,923,000; 1937–8, $32,760,000; 1938–9, $34,432,000.

31 Mackenzie King told Hitler that in the event of war Canada would not remain neutral. Glazebrook, *supra* note 14, at 126.

32 *Canada and the United Nations, supra* note 11, at 5.

33 *The Inauguration of the Second Victory*

Loan (1942) 3.

34 A Gallup poll in 1943 showed 78 per cent of those interviewed favoured 'Canada playing an active part in maintaining world peace.' Polls on 20 November 1943 indicated that 62 per cent of Canadians believed that a new League of Nations which included the United States would succeed. Indications were that the maritimes, the prairies, and British Columbia gave avid support, whereas Quebec and Ontario registered a cooler response. (1943), 18 *Foreign Policy Assoc. Rep.*, at 310–23.

35 *Taylor,* at 96.

36 *Debates,* 19 March 1943, at 1396.

37 'Representation should be determined on a functional basis which will admit to full membership those countries, large or small, which have the greatest contribution to make to the particular object in question ... Some compromise must be found between the theoretical equality of states and the practical necessity of limiting representation on international bodies to a workable number.' *Debates,* 9 July 1943, at 4558.

38 The foreign ministers of the Big Four at this time recognized 'the necessity of establishing at the earliest practicable date a general international organization, based on the principle of the sovereign equality of all peace-loving states, and open to membership by all such states, large and small, for the maintenance of international peace and security.' F.H. Soward and E. McInnis, *Canada and the United Nations* (1956) 11 [hereinafter cited as *Soward*]. See also A. Boyd, *Fifteen Men on a Powder Keg* (1971) 56, 69–70 [hereinafter cited as *Boyd*].

39 The prime ministers agreed there should be an international force with military sanctions. 'There was general acceptance of the Canadian view that the stability and cohesion of the Commonwealth was linked with the creation of a strong international organization.' Commonwealth Prime Ministers' Meeting, *Declaration of 16 May 1944* (Dominions Office Pub.).

40 *Frye,* at 173–4. This is one of the earliest indications that the United States was dropping the isolationist policy it had been following for the last twenty years. For views on the change in American policy, see J.R. Beal, *The Pearson Phenomenon* (1964) 79.

41 *Soward,* at 14. Each day for two months during the talks the United Kingdom representatives briefed all the Commonwealth rep-

resentatives on the progress of the meetings and there was an exchange of views, but it is not known if Canadians in particular made any impression on the negotiations.

42 *Debates,* 11 Aug. 1944, at 6270–1.

43 Bloomfield, *supra* note 1, at 5. It was felt that such a force would be of strategic value and its mobility would be of great preventive value.

44 US Dep't of State, no 3580, *Postwar Foreign Policy Preparation, 1939–1945* (1949) at 602–3. See also *Frye,* at 174–5. For the entire text of the Dumbarton Oaks proposals, see R.E. Summers, *Dumbarton Oaks,* 18(1) *The Reference Shelf* (1945) 103–17.

45 *Soward,* at 14–15.

46 In April 1945 he presented his views at the Commonwealth meeting in London, and in March of 1945 he presented his changes to President Roosevelt. Ibid at 18; Eagleton, *supra* note 2, at 333.

47 *Debates,* 19 March 1945, at 10–14; 20 March 1945, at 18–60; 21 March 1945, at 63–106; 22 March 1945, at 110–47; 23 March 1945, at 151–89; 26 March 1945, at 199–240; 27 March 1945, at 243–84; 28 March 1945, at 294–312. See also C.C. Lingard and R.G. Trotter, 3 *Canada in World Affairs, 1941–1944* (1950) 250–55.

48 For details on the five dissenting votes, see *Soward,* at 19 n67. In the debates there was agreement by the House on the approach taken by Mackenzie King – that the position accorded to each state should correspond with the functions that it is able and ready to discharge, and that states not represented on the council should not have to take enforcement action without some say in the council.

49 It was Lester Pearson's enthusiasm which sparked Canada's actions in this regard. This element of the new organization was supported especially by the CCF party.

50 See D. Wilgress, *Dana Wilgress Memoirs* (1967) 138–40. Among the seven alternate delegates were Lester Pearson; Norman Robertson, high commissioner for Canada in the United Kingdom; Hume Wrong, Canadian ambassador to the United States between 1946 and 1953; and Mr Dana Wilgress. The conference lasted from 25 April 1945, to 26 June 1945.

51 The delegation remained discreetly reticent in controversial matters in which they were not directly concerned. *Soward* at 25–6.

52 See F.H. Soward, 4 *Canada in World Affairs, 1944–1946* (1950) 124–51. At the con-

ference, Mackenzie King stated:

> We shall not be guided by considera-
> tions of national pride or prestige and
> shall not seek to have changes made for
> such reasons as these. Peace ... is not
> exclusively concentrated in the hands of
> any four or five states, and the Confer-
> ence should not act on the assumption
> that it is. Experience has shown that the
> contribution of smaller powers is not a
> negligible one, either to the preserving of
> the peace or to its restoration when peace
> has been disturbed. U.N.C.I.O. Doc 20,
> p/6, at 30.

53 Eagleton, *supra* note 2, at 334.
54 'Although the sponsoring powers argued at
   the time that geographical distribution would
   be "a secondary consideration" such has
   certainly not proved to be the case in elections to the Security Council.' *Soward*, at 27.
   See also *Boyd*, at 189.
55 It was Canada's hope that this requirement
   would reduce the independence of the council and make it more functional. See
   U.N.C.I.O. Doc 555, III/1/227.
56 U.N.C.I.O. Doc 231, III/3/9 (1).

> Whereas each great power is assured of
> participation in the consideration of dis-
> putes from the beginning and can by itself
> prevent the imposition of sanctions, the
> other members of the organization are
> asked to obligate themselves to carry out
> the Council decisions without any assur-
> ance that they would be consulted rather
> than ordered to take action ... It might be
> advisable ... to write into the charter
> several alternative methods in order to
> permit the participation of members not
> on the Council in decisions which gravely
> affect them.

57 See Can. Dept. of External Affairs, *Report
   on the United Nations Conference of International Organization*, 2 *Conference Series
   1945*, at 37.
58 Eagleton, *supra* note 2, at 339–41.
59 Many states felt that the charter should
   specify the kind of contributions to be made
   to an international force. The French wanted
   to know, more specifically, when each contingent would be on call, where each would
   be situated and the means of communication
   to be used. U.N.C.I.O. Doc 2, G/7(0), at 4.
   Most of these proposed amendments to article 43 were rejected.

60 The Military Staff Committee, proposed at
   Dumbarton Oaks, was to plan an international force and carry out agreements with
   member states regarding the commitment
   each would make to it.
61 These men felt that the added psychological
   value of such earmarking would be outweighed by the loss of military efficiency;
   that is, the forces used to fill a country's
   quota should be those closest to the trouble
   spot and not necessarily those earmarked for
   the United Nations.
62 The committee consisted of the chiefs of staff
   or other representatives of the permanent
   members of the Security Council. For the
   composition of this group, see *Boyd*, at 79.
   Under article 47 the committee was to consult with participating states not permanently
   represented on it when such consultation
   was deemed necessary. There was also a
   provision for regional subcommittees.
63 One commentator said regarding the down-
   fall of this committee: 'Second only to the
   sacred veto itself, the MSC had been the apple
   of the great powers' collective eye, or
   perhaps the apple of their teeth. They were
   not only going to give the UN the "teeth" that
   the League had lacked; they were also going
   to make sure that the actual biting was done
   by themselves.' *Boyd*, at 78.
64 'The government and people of Canada are
   anxious to know what armed forces, in common with other members of the United
   Nations, Canada should maintain as our
   share of the burden of putting world force
   behind world law.' *Report on the Second
   Part of the First Session of the General
   Assembly of the UN*, 3 *Conference Series
   1946* (1947), at 165.
65 Secretary of State for External Affairs, Louis
   St Laurent, addressed the General Assembly
   on 18 September 1947:

> There is a growing feeling in my country,
> as in other countries, that the United
> Nations, because of the experience of the
> Security Council, is not showing itself
> equal to the discharge of its primary task
> of promoting international confidence
> and ensuring national security ... The
> Security Council ... has done little to
> strengthen the hopes of those who saw in
> it the keystone of the structure of peace.
> *Taylor*, at 99.

66 Since that time the 'Military Staff Committee

exist only in fortnightly fantasy on the 35th floor of the UN building in New York.' *Boyd*, at 362. Another commentator suggested that perhaps these talks failed because the Soviet Union feared that the UN would become something like a regional security organization such as NATO. He felt also that it may be that the Soviet Union did not want the UN to have any police force at all; their international policy may have been to keep the UN impotent. *Frye*, at 54–5.

67 See *Bowett*, at 13–18. The major conflicts were: 1 / the Soviet Union insisted that all five Security Council members should make matched contributions to the United Nations force, whereas the United Kingdom and the United States felt that each of the five should make a comparable contribution with the kinds of contributions (that is, navy, army, and air force) differing according to the strength of each country's capacity; 2 / the Americans wanted a force of over 300,000 men, whereas the estimates of the other countries were much lower. See also R.B. Russell, *United Nations Experience with Military Forces* (1964) 13–18 [hereinafter cited as *Russell*].

68 He wanted it to be a field guard offering minimum protection plus technical services with UN personnel carrying out observation or supervision. It was to be part of the secretariat staff.

69 See *Bowett*, at 18–21, 62–3; *Boyd*, at 124–5. Mr Lie has described the kind of opposition he had against the force, and has concluded that 'an internationally recruited police force was too radical an idea for many governments ... Ultimately, the Assembly agreed on something useful, but not at all what I had originally intended.' T. Lie, *In the Cause of Peace* (1954) 193.

70 This committee was authorized under the Uniting for Peace Resolution passed in November 1950.

71 The legion was to be composed of small units provided by smaller nations to work alongside the main UN force. The units would be based in each home state and would function as UN forces only when called upon and solely at the discretion of the contributing state. See *Frye*, at 62–4.

72 Ibid, at 64.

73 For some of the comments made, *see* Can. Dep't of External Affairs, *Statements and Speeches* 47/1, at 5; 48/35, at 5 [hereinafter cited as *Statements and Speeches*].

74 R.A. Spencer, 5 *Canada and World Affairs, 1946–1949* (1959) 98–9; *Debates*, 29 April 1949, at 2797; 28 March 1949, at 2077; 24 Nov. 1949, at 2173. The United Nations Charter was repeatedly called the 'cornerstone' of Canadian foreign policy. Eg, *Debates*, 17 Nov. 1949, at 1929.

For additional information on Canada and the UN see R.W. Reford, *Canada and Three Crises* (1968) 4–7 [hereinafter cited as *Reford*]; Spencer, *supra*, at 244–63; *Taylor*, at 100; Beal, *supra* note 40, at 90–5.

75 For a discussion of the change in Canada's policy, see Spencer, *supra* note 74, at 74–82.

76 Can. Dep't of Nat'l Defence, *Canada's Defence Program* (1949–1950) 67. But see *Taylor*, at 100: 'These statements notwithstanding, NATO marked a clear shift in Canadian policy. While not abandoned, the United Nations was no longer relied upon as the first, or even the second, line of Canadian defence. Canada's primary obligations were now NATO.'

77 In order to discuss various trouble spots as cohesively as possible, this section will deal with one problem as completely as possible without limiting the discussion to any particular time period.

78 See *Frye*, at 125; C.G. Teng, *Synopses of UN Cases in the Field of Peace, 1946–1967* (1968) 1–3; *Wainhouse*, at 221–3.

79 On 19 December 1946, the Security Council set up a Commission of Investigation which had authority for military observers. UN Doc s/339.

80 *Bowett*, at 61; *Frye*, at 126. There were four groups of observers consisting of personnel from Brazil, China, France, Mexico, the Netherlands, the United Kingdom, and the United States. *Bowett*, at 68. By 1 August 1949 there were thirty-four observers and additional technical backup staff.

81 The Peace Observation Commission, established in 1950 under the Uniting for Peace Resolution, was a corps of UN observers available on request.

82 For details on budgets and financing, see *Wainhouse*, at 229–30.

83 For a complete story, see *Frye*, at 130–5; 2 R. Higgins, *United Nations Peacekeeping, 1946–1967* (1967) 3–90 [hereinafter cited as *Higgins*]. For historical background see *Wainhouse* at 293–6.

84 *Bowett*, at 77, 78. The Consular Commission was formed on 25 August 1947 by the Security Council after a call for cessation of hos-

tilities failed on 1 August 1947. UN Doc s/525. The observers were military assistants of the Consular Commission but were used at the request of the Security Council; after a series of technical problems in fulfilling their assignments, the observer vehicles were marked and armbands were worn by the men. *Wainhouse*, at 301, 303. The observers established 'status quo' lines which were in turn adjoined by demilitarized zones; there were no front lines per se. Often the status quo lines would surround large pockets of Indonesian-held territory behind the Netherlands' positions. *Bowett*, at 74.

85 *Wainhouse*, at 304–5.

86 For details see *Boyd*, at 119–25; 2 *Higgins*, at 5–216; Teng, *supra* note 78, at 12–15. The Suez crisis, part of the continuing struggle between Arabs and Israelis, will be dealt with separately below.

87 The Palestine Commission was called to supervize the withdrawal of British forces by 1 August 1948. Colombia, New Zealand, and Guatemala proposed police forces for the area but nothing resulted. *Frye*, at 143. The Truce Commission consisted of Belgium, France, and the United States; these countries provided the first observers. *Bowett*, at 69.

88 *Soward*, at 109. There were many prominent Canadians working on this question. Mr Justice I.C. Rand sat on the original UN Special Committee on Palestine; Lester B. Pearson was prominent in committee hearings; and General Howard Kennedy acted as director of the United Nations Relief and Works Agency for Palestine Refugees in 1950.

89 For details on observer activities, see *Frye*, at 145–6.

90 'Press reports indicate that General Burns, while respected, was never popular with either side, and both sides demanded his dismissal on occasion.' His work was praised by the Security Council, however. *Taylor*, at 116–17.

91 For the controversy over why more Canadian officers were not requested at this time, see ibid, at 141–2.

92 For yearly expenses from 1953–66, see 1 *Higgins*, at 135–6.

93 For background informations, see *Wainhouse*, at 357–9.

94 The commission was originally composed of Czechoslovakia, Argentine, and the United States but was enlarged 21 April 1948 to

include Belgium and Colombia. For the role of General McNaughton, a Canadian, as a mediator in the dispute, see *Soward*, at 105.

95 American observers left UNMOGIP quite unceremoniously. *Wainhouse*, at 364. Later, observers came from Australia, Chile, Denmark, Finland, Italy, New Zealand, Sweden, and Uruguay.

96 The ceasefire line extended five hundred miles over mountainous terrain, and the observer group varied in strength from thirty to forty-two members.

97 'The government's policy, according to one unclassified army public relations guidance sheet, was "to give as little publicity as possible" to the dispute. As "both nations are Members of the Commonwealth, the dispute is embarrassing to Canada." ' *Taylor*, at 102.

98 Ibid, at 101–2

99 This was now the largest national contingent. The Caribou was destroyed on the ground in 1965 by Pakistani saboteurs.

100 Major General R.H. Nimmo of Australia was appointed to take his place and remained in it until his death in 1966.

101 Can. Dep't of External Affairs, [1966] *Canada and the United Nations* (1967) 57.

102 These estimates are as of 15 June 1969. Can. Dep't of External Affairs, *Eighth Report of the Standing Committee on External Affairs and National Defence Respecting United Nations and Peacekeeping.* (1970) 37. For the total UN expenditures, see *Wainhouse*, at 365–6; 2 *Higgins*, at 370–3.

103 See *Wainhouse* at 323–5; 2 *Higgins*, at 153–60; H.F. Wood, *Strange Battleground* (1966); Goldie, 'Korea and the United Nations' (1949-50) 1 *U.B.C. Legal Notes* 125–9.

104 The commission consisted of Australia, Canada, China, El Salvador, France, India, Philippines, Syria, and Ukraine.

105 Canada took a particularly strong stand that elections should not be held only in the South. The resolution to hold elections in the South was passed, however. *Wainhouse*, at 328.

106 Canada and Ukraine were dropped from the commission, but the rest of the members remained. Ibid, at 332.

107 For complete details on logistics, personnel, expenses, etc, see Ibid, at 333-49. All observation teams disbanded in June 1956, and today only the commission and secretariat remain.

108 See C.M. Eichelberger, *United Nations:*

The First Twenty Years (1965) 21–22. It has been indicated that American military observers warned of the North Korean buildup as early as 10 March 1950. Wood, *supra* note 103, at 7.

109 UN Doc s/1501.

110 The Soviet delegates had been boycotting the Security Council since early 1950 protesting the presence of representatives of Nationalist China.

111 Eichelberger, *supra* note 108, at 23; *Russell*, at 28.

112 UN Doc s/1511; see *Russell*, at 25. The resolution was passed by a vote of 7 to 1 (Yugoslavia) with 2 abstentions (India and Egypt) and the Soviet Union absent.

113 'On 5 July, H.M.C. Ships *Cayuga*, *Athabaskan* and *Sioux* sailed from Esquimalt bound for Pearl Harbor.' Wood, *supra* note 103, at n13. 'Canada's contributions came piecemeal, and then only after the U.N. itself made formal requests.' Ibid, at 12. St Laurent stressed strongly that any Canadian contribution would not be as a participant in a war against a state but as part of 'collective police action' under the United Nations.

114 Parliamentarians Drew and Graydon gave Conservative support, S. Knowles lent CCF support, and Mr Low gave Social Credit support. The sole disenchanted voice came from Jean-François Pouliot of Quebec, but his reaction was disparaged by Maurice Boisvert who said French-Canadians *did* support the government. *Debates*, 26 June 1950, at 4116–17 June 1950, at 4251–53; 29 June 1950, at 4383–92.

115 The United States unified command, under United Nations auspices, was asked to accept assistance from other states. *Russell*, at 26; *Frye*, at 56. But 'General MacArthur regarded himself as acting primarily in the role of Commander-in-Chief of United States forces in the Far East. His connection with the United Nations he viewed as largely nominal.' *Russell*, at 31.

116 See Can. Dep't of External Affairs, *Canada and the Korean Crisis* (1950) 12.

117 Wood, *supra* note 103, at 19:

On 30 June 1950, the day Parliament was prorogued, the strength of the Active Force was 20,369 all ranks; which did not even fill the restricted establishments ... [in July 1950 an appreciation of the force] stated that if the units were immediately brought up to strength, and allowed to concentrate on training, they should be reasonably efficient in six months' time. This meant that the Regular Army ... was not only unable to provide an expeditionary force at once, but could not hope to carry out with any degree of success its two peacetime roles.

118 Ibid, at 20.

119 Ibid.

120 Ibid, at 20–2.

121 *Soward*, at 127. For reaction of the Canadian public to this announcement, see ibid, at 129; Wood, *supra* note 103, at 24; *Debates*, 1 Sept. 1950, at 110–50; 2 Sept. 1950, at 156–94.

122 Wood, *supra* note 103, at 26. As for the future of the Special Force, 'those who regarded the Force as a temporary expedient required to discharge a transitory obligation, misjudged the nature and power of the influences at work on Canada. A continuing and increasing requirement for overseas forces, to which no end could be foreseen, forced important changes in the role of the Regular Army, and the status of the Special Force.' Ibid.

123 F. Seyersted, *United Nations Forces in the Law of Peace and War* (1966) 36.

124 For the channel of communications showing the extent to which the UN was in control of the operation, see ibid, at 35.

125 See *Russell*, at 28–9; *Bowett*, at 37.

126 'The mental image of Korea as a UN "police action," rather than an American-led war of alliance, survived reasonably well; this is to say, the UN's moral "umbrella" remained largely intact. At least, it did until many Americans, frustrated by the absence of total victory and mistakenly blaming the UN restraints for it, began to rip the umbrella to shreds themselves.' *Frye*, at 57. It has been estimated that the ground forces were 50.32 per cent American, 40.01 per cent Korean; the naval forces were 85.84 per cent American, 7.45 per cent Korean; and the air forces were 93.38 per cent American, and 5.65 per cent Korean. *Bowett*, at 40.

127 In January 1952 there were 8123 present, the greatest strength of the contingent. There were 1543 battle casualties: 11 officers and 298 other ranks were killed, and 59 officers and 1143 other ranks were wounded; 2 officers and 30 other ranks survived as prisoners of war. Wood, *supra* note 103, at 257–8. For a summary of military assistance, see 2 *Higgins* 199–201.

128 2 *Higgins,* at 246.

129 Wood, *supra* note 103, at 92.

130 In December 1950 Lester Pearson was asked to sit on a Three Man Commission to establish a ceasefire, and contributed to a large degree to the recommendations for a ceasefire presented to the General Assembly on 12 January 1951. Despite the refusal by the Chinese to negotiate on a ceasefire at this point, these preliminary negotiations helped to pave the way to the truce talks and ultimate ceasefire arrangements. For Mr Pearson's comments on his appointment to the commission, see *Soward,* at 136.

131 Ibid, at 257–8.

132 For a discussion of this view, see Goldie, *supra* note 103, at 131; 2 *Higgins,* at 174–8.

133 GAOR A/1775. The resolution passed by a vote of 39 to 5, with five members of the Soviet bloc voting against and India and Argentina abstaining.

134 *Russell,* at 19. One writer commented colourfully: 'This epochal action was a result of the organic imbecility of the Security Council whereby the Soviets obtained a strangle-hold on the proceedings through the veto and other tactics.' Woolsey, 'The 'Uniting for Peace'' Resolution of the United Nations' (1951), 45 *Am. J. Int'l L.* 129, at 143.

135 'Speaking to the Political Committee of the Assembly on October 11, the Canadian delegate expressed the hope that the resolution might ''provide the germ of an international force by making it possible to earmark national contingents for United Nations purposes.''' *Canada and the United Nations, supra* note 11, at 40.

136 See *Taylor,* at 43–4.

In terms of the *kind* of international security pursued, the Uniting for Peace Resolution A is more closely related to the North Atlantic Treaty Organization than to the collective security ... of the Charter; it represents a stage in the alignment of United Nations members in hostile military camps. It 'divides for war' even as it 'unites for peace.' Ibid, quoting from J. Stone, *Legal Controls of International Conflict* (rev ed, 1959) 275.

137 The members of the original commission were China, Colombia, Czechoslovakia, France, India, Iraq, Israel, New Zealand, Pakistan, Sweden, Soviet Union, United Kingdom, United States, and Uruguay. There were only two attempts at using this commission: it was successfully used in Greece in 1951; the second request was by Thailand in 1954, but the Soviet Union vetoed the resolution. See 'The Uses of the Uniting for Peace Resolution Since 1950' (1966), 3 *The Strategy of World Order* 257–9.

138 For the difference between this resolution and article 43 of the charter, see *Frye,* at 58.

139 The 14 members were Australia, Belgium, Brazil, Burma, Canada, Egypt, France, Mexico, Philippines, Turkey, United Kingdom, United States, Venezuela, and Yugoslavia.

140 *Russell,* at 22–3, 23 n 22.

141 Seventeen nations did not reply; 2 sent an acknowledgement of the request; and 21 replies ranged from negative to non-committal. 'That left only 20 replies which could be considered friendly, even in tone. Some of these, Canada's for example, appeared at first glance to be commitments, but on closer study were hedged. The United States reply was a model of skillfull obfuscation.' *Frye,* at 59–60.

142 'If other countries were in the same way to earmark a portion of their forces which might be made available to the United Nations for collective defence, there would be ready throughout the free world national contingents for a United Nations force which could be quickly brought together in the face of a future emergency.' *Debates,* 31 Aug. 1950, at 94–6.

At the United Nations Lester Pearson stated: '*So we decided,* therefore, that we would take this occasion to put ourselves in readiness not only to meet the appeal in Korea but to fulfil similar commitments under the Charter in the future.' Can. Dep't of External Affairs, [1950] *Canada and the United Nations* (1951) 163.

143 On 1 June 1951 the Canadian reply to the Collective Measures Committee was that any employment of a Canadian force would require the approval of parliament and 'the Canadian Government does not at present contemplate the recruitment and organization of further units of its armed forces specifically for service with the United Nations.' *Taylor,* at 106. The following year, the government withdrew even further from commitment to collective action and in a letter to the secretary general, dated 29 September 1950, Lester Pearson said that after the Korean War 'it will be for the Canadian Government to consider what measures

might be taken under the conditions then existing in further implementation of ... [the Uniting for Peace] Resolution.' Ibid, at 107.

144 *Boyd*, at 92–3. Note the inconsistencies of the Soviet claims and that they have on occasion supported the use of the resolution.

145 3 *The Strategy of World Order, supra* note 137, at 259–64.

146 Ibid, at 264–8. See generally Seyersted, *supra* note 123, at 45.

147 *Wainhouse*, at 489.

148 Thailand feared the Viet Minh would overtake Laos and Cambodia and then move into Thailand. *Boyd*, at 146. The Security Council met on 3 June 1954 to hear the complaint and on 16 June to hear the formal resolution; on 18 June the vote was 9 in favour, the Soviet Union veto, and a Lebanon abstention. Ibid, at 163–4. In the Security Council US Senator Henry Cabot Lodge spoke out indignantly against Russia's veto: 'I hope I will never live to see the day when a small country comes to the United Nations to ask for protection against war and is simply greeted with the question, "What's the hurry?"'

149 *Reford*, at 38–9. See also D.C. Masters, 8 *Canada in World Affairs, 1953–1955* (1959) 82–3. Lester Pearson stated: 'We have of course in Canada a very definite interest in this problem but no special or separate responsibility for Indochina or for Southeast Asia. We have no regional or special commitments in that part of the world and no question of accepting such has arisen at Geneva.' *Debates*, 28 May 1954, at 5189.

150 The Indian representative had suggested Canada's name to Chou En-lai, who found the nomination acceptable. Canada was chosen to represent the western viewpoint on the commission and was known for not following the 'American hard line on containment.' *Taylor*, at 108.

151 See Masters, *supra* note 149, at 84–5; *Taylor*, at 109.

152 Ibid.

153 The government issued a statement giving the reasons why it had accepted. First, the government had seriously studied the armistice and was well aware of the task ahead. Second, Canada regretted that the settlement was not under the authority of the United Nations. Finally, Lester Pearson stated that Canada accepted in order to contribute to world peace. *Statements and Speeches* 54/36.

154 By the end of 1956 the commission had 135

service personnel and 35 civilians from Canada. *Taylor*, at 110; *Wainhouse*, at 492–3.

155 For a closer look at the work of the commission, see *Taylor*, at 111; Masters, *supra* note 149, at 88–94; *Wainhouse*, at 493–4, 501.

156 *Taylor*, at 110. For members of the Geneva Conference, *Wainhouse*, at 500.

157 3 [1955] *Debates* 3389.

158 Masters, *supra* note 149, at 95.

159 *Taylor*, appendix B, at 196.

160 These statistics are only the expenses of the Department of National Defence, as received on 26 June 1964 from G.T. Murray, head of UN Division, Department of External Affairs, Ottawa.

161 'The Canadian delegation reports to the Canadian government and the Canadian government only; it is for the Canadian government to decide in the case of these reports ... what use is to be made of them in the course of normal diplomatic exchanges with other countries.' *Taylor*, at 113. But see N. Sheehan, C.W. Kenworthy, and F. Butterfield, *The Pentagon Papers* (as published by the *New York Times*) (1971) 236–49, 289–91 concerning the use of J. Blair Seaborn, Canada's representative on the ICC, to convey offer of United States economic aid to Premier Dong when Mr Seaborn visited Hanoi in June 1964.

162 At least one writer believed that Canada could avoid United States pressure to contribute more actively to the American war efforts in Vietnam by remaining a peacekeeper in that same war. *Taylor*, at 113–14. Early in 1973 Canada sent peacekeeping observers to Vietnam as part of the new International Commission for Control and Supervision (ICCS).

163 In early 1956 Lester Pearson was questioned as to sales of arms to both states. He replied: 'Our attitude is to do nothing that would disturb the military balance or add to their offensive strength.' He was also asked if he himself would take the lead in trying to achieve a settlement, to which question he replied in the negative. *Reford*, at 76. See also *Taylor*, at 83–4.

164 *Taylor*, at 118–19; *Reford*, at 80.

165 Israel and the Arab states did not favour the idea; the United States was hesitant; and the United Kingdom did not offer active support. *Taylor*, at 119; *Reford*, at 81.

166 Nasser had been mulling the idea over since October 1954, but no world leaders appeared to have obtained this information or to have

made any plans for such a contingency. *Reford,* at 82.

167 Ibid, at 85.

168 Ibid, at 85, 89, 92.

169 Ibid, at 86. The Pearson government was perhaps relieved by the absence of an invitation. But meanwhile the Conservative party insisted that Canada should play a decisive role in this dispute and offer the United Kingdom moral support and encouragement.

170 United Kingdom watched the growing mobilization of troops by the Israelis and Arabs. Plans were made that in the event of war between the two, United Kingdom and France would step in, issue an ultimatum to cease hostilities, and open the canal zone. Ibid, at 97.

171 Ibid, at 98, 100

172 Ibid, at 103. Louis St Laurent was openly angry at the move and sent a personal note to Anthony Eden strongly criticizing the action taken, whereas Lester Pearson continued his moderate statements in public.

173 For the complete story of this resolution, see 1 *Higgins,* at 227.

174 *Reford,* at 103. The idea was 'not to give United Nations respectability to the Anglo-French intervention but to change its character and make it serve different ends.' *Taylor,* at 121.

175 The vote was 64 to 5 (Britain, France, Israel, Australia, New Zealand) with 6 abstentions (Canada, Belgium, Netherlands, Laos, Portugal, South Africa).

176 Pearson was near the bottom of the speaker's list on the resolution so that he knew he would be unable to speak before the resolution was called; but by choosing to abstain he created the opportunity to be heard. He received cabinet approval of this move. *Taylor,* at 122.

177 For the full text of his speech, see Can. Dep't of External Affairs, *The Crisis in the Middle East Oct.-Dec. 1956* (1957), at 9–10. Pearson's initiative in this situation has been favourably commented upon: 'What the Suez situation called for was a ''floor manager'' who would guide it toward specific action, and this is what Pearson became.' *Taylor,* at 112. 'The incident illustrated more clearly than any other in which Pearson engaged how a middle power that is alert to its opportunities can move in and provide leadership when a clash among great powers leave international affairs disorganized.' Beal, *supra* note 40, at 111.

178 John Foster Dulles said: 'It is a phase of the situation which we see as of the utmost importance, and the United States Delegation would be very happy indeed if the Canadian Delegation would formulate and introduce as part of these proceedings a concrete suggestion along the lines that Mr. Pearson outlined.' *The Crisis in the Middle East, supra* note 177, at 10. See also *Boyd,* at 115.

179 *Reford,* at 106.

180 Ibid; *Taylor,* at 123.

181 *Frye,* at 6. The draft resolution was shown to as many influential delegates as 'Pearson and his aides could collar in UN corridors and lounges.'

182 GAOR A/3354 (passed 57 to 0 with 19 abstentions).

183 *Reford,* at 109. Canada, Colombia, Norway, and India were represented in Dag Hammarskjöld's office.

184 L. Gordenker, *The UN Secretary-General and the Maintenance of Peace* (1967), at 74–5, 144–7, 164–7, 238–55, 262–7. Canada, Colombia, and Norway recommended the adoption of the report, and the resolution was passed 57 to 0 with 19 abstentions.

185 GAOR A/3302 (passed 64 to 0 with 12 abstentions). Dag Hammarskjöld consulted Lester Pearson quite closely and used Canadian officials to secure the co-operation of Britain and France in a ceasefire.

186 Brazil, Canada, Colombia, India, Norway, and Pakistan were chosen.

187 *Taylor,* at 125. See also 1 *Higgins,* at 415–55; *Wainhouse,* at 282–3; Seyersted, *supra* note 123, at 54–5; *Bowett,* at 139–48; J.G. Stoessinger, *Financing the United Nations Systems* (1964) 106–13. The financing arrangements will be discussed in more detail below.

188 Canada, Ceylon, Colombia, Czechoslovakia, Denmark, Finland, India, New Zealand, Norway, Pakistan, Romania, and Sweden all volunteered troops.

189 The 5 November resolution had said there would have to be consent to the presence of troops by the host nation.

190 The aircraft carrier could also be used to evacuate troops if the Egyptians would not allow them entry. *Taylor,* at 126. Canadian public reaction to the sending of troops was not encouraging, at least in areas with a strong Empire background. Ibid; *Boyd,* at 116, 118.

191 General Burns said that it would be impossi-

ble for him to act as commander of UNEF if Canadians were not included.

192 *Taylor*, at 126; *Redford*, at 117.

193 Canada insisted that this was still not good enough. See *Frye*, at 29–31.

194 Whether the revised plan of General Burns was a diplomatic manoeuvre rather than a military necessity is difficult to say. See ibid, at 31; *Taylor*, at 131–2, 134. For the kinds and numbers of troops sent, see *Taylor*, at 132–4.

195 One writer feels that this period indicated the peak of Canadian influence after several years of quiet diplomacy. 'One starring role inevitably breeds expectations of a repeat performance ... [but] this was "a one-night stand, an exceptional turn staged amid circumstances unlikely to occur."' *Reford*, at 136–7.

196 This was after President Nasser had told UNEF to withdraw from the Israeli border, and Secretary General U Thant had informed him that UNEF would leave altogether if so requested. Paul Martin, Canadian secretary of state, took strong exception to U Thant's acquiescence. See *Debates*, 18 May 1967, at 342. Later, Pearson suggested that he thought U Thant took the right approach. *Debates*, 24 May 1967, at 534.

197 See Burns, 'Withdrawal of UNEF' (1967–8), 23 *International Journal* 1; Cohen, 'Demise of UNEF' (1967–8), 23 *International Journal* 18.

    For the story of UNEF in general, *see* Seyersted, *supra* note 123, at 47–60; *Russell*, at 50–71; E. Lauterpacht, ed, *The United Nations Emergency Force* (1960); *Bowett*, at 90–151 (very detailed and heavily footnoted for specifics on every area); *Wainhouse*, at 277–88 (for the relationship between MAC–UNTSO–UNEF); Luard, *supra* note 20, at 106–7 (consent); 1 *Higgins*, at 221–528; Bloomfield, *supra* note 1, at 268–89.

198 'No issue of foreign affairs affected Canada as deeply as Suez. Ten years later, one could still meet Canadians who would not vote Liberal because that party refused to support Britain's action and who regarded Pearson less as a man who won the Nobel Peace Prize than as the man who stabbed Britain in the back.' *Reford*, at 124. The Liberals seemed ready only to admit that the Suez was a marginal factor in their loss. The Conservatives felt it may have given them 6 to 8 seats in Ontario. Ibid, at 125; Beal, *supra* note 40, at 135; J. Meisel, *The Canadian General Election of 1957* (1962), at 57–8.

199 'In the tradition of this Party,' Diefenbaker said in his first major campaign address in Toronto, 'we did and do resent the British people being castigated and derisively condemned as those 'supermen'' whose days are about over.' *Taylor*, at 136.

200 T. Lloyd, 10 *Canada in World Affairs, 1957–1959* (1959) 131.

201 *Reford*, at 54.

202 *Statements and Speeches* 57/33, at 1. This was a well-used phrase of Liberal government officials in the late 1940s.

203 See generally 1 *Higgins*, at 533; Gordenker, *supra* note 184, at 210–25; A.L. Burns, *Peacekeeping by UN Forces* (1963) 9–15.

204 At this point President Chamoun sought assistance from the United States and the United Kingdom, who both guaranteed help even so far as armed intervention. This support seemed to alienate the Moslems further and the situation became critical.

205 *Taylor*, at 143.

206 The UAR insisted that the alleged 'plot' was only a method to get the internal problem of Lebanon before the Security Council. 'The Security Council meetings were stormy and conducted in a tense atmosphere. Canada, Colombia, Japan, Panama and Sweden avoided prejudicing the issue.' *Wainhouse*, at 375.

207 UN Doc s/4023 (10 to 0 vote, with the Soviet Union abstaining). Canada, sitting on the council, was in favour of the resolution.

208 Major General Odd Bull decided that he required 100 observers with jeeps, helicopters, and other aircraft. Observers came from Afghanistan, Burma, Canada, Ceylon, Chile, Denmark, Ecuador, Finland, India, Indonesia, Ireland, Italy, Nepal, Netherlands, New Zealand, Norway, Peru, Portugal, and Sweden. For details, see *Wainhouse*, at 376–86. See also 1 *Higgins*, at 566–8 (finances).

209 Loyd, *supra* note 200, at 140. One newspaper, obviously disillusioned, was quoted as saying: 'Canada may have lost international prestige when it too hastily condoned the landing of United States and United Kingdom forces in Lebanon and Jordan.' Ibid, at 141.

210 'The general opinion in Ottawa was that the American landings were legal but not wise.' *Taylor*, at 145. Other reports from Ottawa indicated that the government was preparing a brigade of troops to send to Lebanon under the UN if needed. Ibid, at 146.

211 Lebanon tried to have the Marines authorized as a UN police force (see *Russell*, at 76–7); Sweden tried to have the activities of UNOGIL suspended until further notice (UN Doc s/4054); and Japan tried to have UNOGIL strengthened to allow American troops to withdraw (UN Doc s/4055; *Bowett*, at 69; Burns, *supra* note 203, at 13.

212 Lloyd, *supra* note 200, at 143–4. With the United Kingdom Canada exerted considerable pressure on the United States for acceptance of a proposal by the Soviet Union for a summit conference on the Middle East; the Soviet Union a few weeks later withdrew the proposal, however. Ibid, at 142.

213 The resolution did not make reference to the withdrawal of troops, and in fact asserted the right of United States and United Kingdom governments to intervene. Ibid, at 143–4.

214 GAOR A/3893. UNOGIL was asked to supervize the withdrawal of American troops; in fact, the buildup of UNOGIL was largely to help the United States save face in the withdrawal.

215 *Taylor*, at 194; Lloyd, *supra* note 200, at 140.

216 *Canada and the United Nations, supra* note 11, at 45.

217 Ibid, at 46. Canada had been discussing earmarking since 1950 but, lacking support of other states, had not implemented the concept before this point. *Taylor*, at 148.

218 The Conservative government had instigated a new 'national survival' program of civil defence and this had drained the resources of the armed forces. Ibid, at 147.

219 The Belgian government withdrew leaving no trained administrators, governors, or army officials. The sitaution was chaotic. K.R. Simmonds, *United Nations Military Operations in the Congo* (1968), at 25–30; Teng, *supra* note 78, at 54–7.

220 Lumumba alleged that international peace was threatened by the 'aggression' of the Belgian troops. He also indicated he would seek Soviet aid if his request was not met.

221 '[The crisis] is a source of internal, and potentially also of international, tension ... and, in consequence, I strongly recommend to the Council to authorize the Secretary-General to take the necessary steps, in consultation with the Government of the Congo, to provide the Government with military assistance.' *Taylor*, at 151.

222 UN Doc s/4387. The resolution was passed 8 to 0 with 3 abstentions (China, United Kingdom, and France). The action taken by the secretary general was unprecedented. He had come to the Security Council under article 99; the Security Council gave assistance to a non-member; and the UN was providing assistance to restore internal order. For the story of the Soviet rejection of Dag Hammarskjöld's work, see *Boyd*, at 13–14, 41–5. See also Gordenker, *supra* note 184, at 49–50, 80–1.

223 Bloomfield, *supra* note 1, at 151, 165. See also *Russell*, at 91–5.

224 Seyersted, *supra* note 123, at 64 n193; but see *Canada and the United Nations, supra* note 11, at 49. See also Simmonds, *supra* note 219, at 140. In all, 100,000 men served on the force, and the total cost was more than $400 million.

For general material on ONUC with special attention to the UN aspects, see Seyersted, *supra* note 123, at 60–76; *Wainhouse*, at 405–13; Simmonds, *supra* note 219, at 25–241; *Russell*, at 86–126.

225 'The government is responding favourably to requests of this kind because it believes that this is the most useful contribution which Canada can make in the current situation. If there are additional requests of the same nature they will be considered seriously.' *Taylor*, at 153, 154.

226 On 20 July these aircraft were requested by the UN to transport food into the interior. The request was met and indeed, despite the government's anti-involvement policy, seemed to have been anticipated, since the squadron of 25 technicians sent on this request to the Congo had been immunized 15 July.

227 *Taylor*, at 155.

228 This request provided special problems in light of the civilian survival program already in full swing in Canada. See, *supra* note 218.

229 In fact the Caribou did not make it to the Congo but were used in UNEF to replace the older Dakotas there. *Taylor*, at 159. Preparations for sending the men were slow, and immunization and refresher courses took two weeks; but the airlift began on 9 August and was completed by 2 September. The RCAF North Star and USAF C-124 Globemaster aircraft transported all the personnel and supplies.

230 It appeared that this was reaction to their growing hostility towards outside intervention in their internal matters.

231 There were no serious Canadian injuries,

and at first Canadians did not resort to firing, following UN command headquarters orders. But although Canadians did not face the heavy casualties borne by other contingents, in March 1961 they were given orders to shoot to kill anyone trying to disarm them.

Lumumba's reaction to the harassment also changed: in the first instance he said the incident was trivial and did not deem so much attention; later, however, he said, 'I asked for the French-speaking technicians myself during my trip to Canada. It was not for this that I invited them.' *Taylor*, at 161.

232 On 26 September 1960, John Diefenbaker addressed the General Assembly and said that the Congo reinforced Canada's belief that nations should 'have military forces readily available for service with the United Nations when required.' In April 1961 the Canadian representative to the UN stated that 'the involvement of the United Nations was unquestionably right.' *Canada and the United Nations*, *supra* note 11, at 48.

233 *Taylor*, at 164.

234 *Eighth Report*, *supra* note 102, appendix 3, at 37.

235 *Boyd*, at 178–85. Towards the end of the ONUC operation the Canadian government was asked to lend 15 French-speaking officers to help train the Congolese army. The request came first from the Congolese government and then from the United Nations. On 29 January 1963 the Canadian government announced that it refused the request because not enough men were available to meet the demand. R.A. Preston, 11 *Canada in World Affairs, 1959–1961* (1965) 322.

236 See generally Stoessinger, *supra* note 187, at 113–21.

237 The resolution was sponsored by Pakistan, Tunisia, and Senegal, and was passed on 20 December 1960 by a vote of 46 to 17 with 24 abstentions.

238 Canada waived $650,000. See Stoessinger, *supra* note 187, at 120.

239 Indonesia said that West New Guinea was included in the agreement, but the agreement shows unquestionably that the status of that area would remain unchanged, with negotiations as to its fate to take place within a year. Negotiations failed, and the Netherlands said they would continue to keep control until the population of New Guinea decided its fate for itself. For background, see *Russell*, at

126–30; *Wainhouse*, at 414–15; 2 *Higgins*, at 93–100.

240 GAOR A/5170. This was a unique role for the UN in that UNTEA was to have complete responsibility for the administration of the territory, including keeping all the essential services running smoothly until the transfer of power. As for the future of the area, there was to be a plebiscite before 1970 in which the Papuans and indigenous peoples could decide if they wished to remain with Indonesia or not.

241 For the story on the observers, see *Wainhouse*, at 414. Brigadier-General Rikhye of UNTSO was appointed chief of staff, and there were 21 observers supplied by Brazil, Ceylon, India, Ireland, Nigeria, and Sweden; they were present from 17 August to 1 October 1962.

242 *Taylor*, at 166.

243 Gordenker, *supra* note 184, at 247.

244 Seyersted, *supra* note 123, at 77. See also Bloomfield, *supra* note 1, at 8; 2 *Higgins*, at 125. The force was commanded by a Pakistani brigadier general.

245 *Taylor*, at 166; Preston, *supra* note 235, at 325.

246 2 *Higgins*, at 125; *Bowett*, at 259.

247 Stoessinger, *supra* note 187, at 105.

248 *Bowett*, at 260–1.

249 President Nasser of Egypt, hoping to gain influence, supported the 'republican' resolution, while Saudi Arabia to the north gave full support to the king. The United Kingdom also supported the king to try to counterbalance the role of the UAR in the struggle, to protect their oil interests, and to protect the British colony of Aden to the south – 'the seat of the British Middle East Command.' *Wainhouse*, at 421. The United States offered support to the republican element, and the Soviet Union watched with growing interest. See *Taylor*, at 167.

250 *Wainhouse*, at 423. There were to be not more than 200 men required, some as observers plus a ground patrol unit of 100 men, and reconnaissance, transport, and other supportive units. The estimated time of the operation was four months and the chief of staff was Major General Carl Von Horn with personnel drawn from ONUC, UNEF, and UNMOGIP. The estimated cost was $1 million and the secretary general hoped that Saudi Arabia and the UAR would share the costs.

251 Gordenker, *supra* note 184, at 227.

252 UN Doc s/5331 (vote of 10 to 0 with the Soviet Union abstaining). For comments of the Soviet delegate, see *Wainhouse*, at 425–6.

253 *Taylor,* at 168.

254 Ibid.

255 There was a reconnaissance unit of 114 officers and men from a Yugoslav contingent serving with UNEF, as well as the air unit of 50 men provided by the RCAF. UNYOM's role was more restricted than its predecessor's as it did not deal with peacekeeping except strictly by observation.

256 He was supposed to have resigned as a protest against improper support for UNYOM. See *Wainhouse*, at 428.

257 This kind of periodic extension was due largely to the fact that UNYOM was dependent on Saudi Arabia and the UAR for financial backing.

258 The war continued for three more years after the withdrawal of UNYOM, and not until after the six-day war in 1967 did the situation begin to cool.

259 1 *Higgins*, at 638–40, 645–52.

260 Turkey threatened to intervene to protect its minority population, and the Greek Cypriots, in control of the government, said the old agreement was no longer workable. For general background information, see *Boyd*, at 270–98; *Bowett*, at 552–60; *Wainhouse*, at 436–7; Gordon, 'The UN in Cyprus' (1963), *International Journal* 326.

261 *Boyd*, at 227. The Turkish Cypriots suffered most, as thousands were injured and driven from their homes. Twenty-five Turkish warships sailed towards Cyprus and planes of the Turkish air force flew over Nicosia.

262 *Wainhouse*, at 439–40. The force was to consist of troops from the United Kingdom, Greece, Turkey, and Cyprus under a British commander. Ibid, at 437.

263 *Taylor*, at 170–1. The Cypriot representative to the UN reiterated that request.

264 *Boyd*, at 281. The Soviet Union representatives at this point charged that certain NATO powers were interfering with the UN charter. *Wainhouse*, at 442. *See also* Gordon, *supra* note 260, at 334 (was it to be a NATO operation 'under a UN umbrella' or a UN force?).

265 It is likely that the troops referred to were the Royal 22nd Regiment of 1000 men who were on standby. *Taylor*, at 171.

266 'The crises in Yemen and New Guinea had passed almost unnoticed by a Canadian public absorbed with domestic issues.' Ibid, at 169.

267 Ibid, at 171–2.

268 The mandate would have to be well-defined, the composition and terms of reference would have to be set, and there would have to be some possibility of a peaceful settlement coming out of it.

269 One commentator suggested that the Canadian government's brief hesitance to support a UN force was due to the fact that the government favoured a NATO force first. *Taylor*, at 172.

270 UN Doc s/5575. All members voted in favour except the Soviet Union, Czechoslovakia, and France, who abstained on certain parts of the resolution.

271 The Canadian government expressed disappointment that the terms of reference of the force were too vague and that the force was not given enough authority to carry out a difficult task in a delicate situation. The government also felt that costs of the force should be a collective responsibility of the membership and not only of the contributing governments. *Canada and the United Nations*, *supra* note 11, at 45.

272 *Taylor*, at 173.

273 *Boyd*, at 283–4.

274 See *Taylor*, at 176.

275 The forces committed were the standby battalion of Van Doos and the armoured reconnaissance squadron of the Royal Canadian Dragoon. The RCAF was to airlift to Cyprus and the H.M.C.S. *Bonaventure* was to bring supplies. Ibid, at 174.

276 There were 3500 UK troops (later reduced to 1792), 950 Canadians (some figures say 1126), 700 Finns, 600 Irish, 700 Swedes, and 74 Australians. *Wainhouse*, at 450. The commander was Lieutenant General P.S. Gyani.

277 None of the original contributors to the force, although impatient at the lack of any progress towards peace, indicated they would withdraw support. *Boyd*, at 289.

278 *Taylor*, at 196.

279 *Eighth Report*, *supra* note 102, appendix 4, at 39. Despite the gradual reduction in the Canadian contribution, UNFICYP has been a 'strain on the resources of the Army, increasingly short of trained soldiers.' *Taylor*, at 176.

280 *Boyd*, at 284–90.

281 'The council, as such, did nothing to relieve U Thant of the endless task of going around

like a Buddhist monk with a begging bowl, pleading for funds to sustain a UN operation which the Council had authorized and kept on extending.' Ibid, at 289.

282 *Eighth Report*, *supra* note 102, appendix 3, at 37.

283 Eg, *Debates*, 12 Sept. 1961, at 8231; 13 Sept. 1961, at 8235; 25 Jan. 1963, at 3124, 3141.

284 *Debates*, 13 Sept. 1961, at 8315–17.

285 Seyersted, *supra* note 123, at 87.

286 Address to the Harvard Alumni Association. For the whole text, see R.A. Falk and S.H. Mendlovitz, eds, 3 *The United Nations: The Strategy of World Order* (1966) 526.

287 (1963) 1 *J. of the UN Assoc. in Canada* 3–5.

288 For a report on the conference, see P. Frydenberg, *Peacekeeping: Experiences and Evaluation* (1964). A second and similar kind of conference was held in Oslo in December 1965.

289 Can. Dep't of Nat'l Defence, *White Paper on Defence* (1964) 24. For discussion of the white paper, see *Taylor*, at 87–91.

290 *White Paper on Defence*, *supra* note 289, at 18, 19. The principle of a single command is consistent with the actual practice of peacekeeping operations.

291 *Statements and Speeches* 64/12.

292 Invitations were initially sent only to Finland, Netherlands, Denmark, Sweden, and Norway; the Soviet Union complained that only NATO countries were asked, while U Thant pointed out that only Caucasian states had been invited.

293 *Canada and the United Nations*, *supra* note 11, at 52–3. Once again the Soviet Union levelled charges against Canada and her invited guests: the conference was labelled an attempt to organize a collective security machine that would carry out military operations under cover of the UN flag. *Taylor*, at 180.

294 Can. Dep't of External Affairs, (Dec. 1964) *Bulletin* 562–7.

295 The three groups studied 1 / composition, command, control, etc, 2 / environmental operating information and logistics; and 3 / personnel administration.

296 *Statements and Speeches* 64/36.

297 A training period of three to six months could bring together officers from nations with an interest and involvement in peacekeeping. For selected comments and opinions from the conference, see *Taylor*, at 63–92.

298 Stoessinger, *supra* note 187, at 108. On the special account generally, see also ibid, at 107; Gordenker, *supra* note 184, at 114–17; Simmonds, *supra* note 219, at 247–87.

299 The vote was 62 to 8, with 7 abstentions.

300 The United States pledged $23 million; the United Kingdom pledged $2.5 million; France pledged $400,000; Canada pledged $310,000; and there were contributions from 18 other states. In 1960 the assessment basis for UNEF was changed and those governments having the least capacity to pay were accredited with voluntary contributions pledged to UNEF up to 1960. This reduced their commitment by up to 50 per cent in some cases.

301 Stoessinger, *supra* note 187, at 133.

302 Brazil, Bulgaria, Canada, China, France, India, Italy, Japan, Mexico, Nigeria, Soviet Union, Sweden, UAR, United Kingdom, and United States were members of the group.

303 UN Doc A/5062. Brazil, Cameroons, Canada, Denmark, Japan, Liberia, Pakistan, Sweden, United Kingdom, and United States co-sponsored the resolution, which was passed 52 to 11, with 32 abstentions. Note that the court was not asked to pronounce upon the legality of the establishment or the conduct of the operations of UNEF and ONUC.

304 GAOR A/5076. The vote was 58 to 13, with 24 abstentions and 9 absent. The principal of the bonds was to be repaid in twenty-five annual instalments from the regular budget of each year beginning in 1963. This resolution was obviously of only a temporary nature, but at that point in time it was a critical and necessary decision. Stoessinger, *supra* note 187, at 125–6.

305 This amount is about the same as Canada's assessment to the UN.

306 Eighteen states agreed to purchase bonds despite the fact that they were in arrears in assessments. Out of $150 million pledged the United States had purchased $75 million. Stoessinger, *supra* note 187, at 131–2.

307 For a full description of the pleadings and documents, see Advisory Opinion, Certain Expenses of the United Nations, [1962] I.C.J. *Pleadings* (The Hague, 20 July 1962). For an analysis of the ruling, see Hogg, 'Peacekeeping Costs and Charter Obligations' (1962), 62 *Colum. L. Rev.* 1230; Gross, 'Expenses of the United Nations for Peacekeeping Operations' (1963), 18 *Int'l*

Organ. 1; Simmonds, 'UN Assessments Advisory Opinion' (1964), 13 *Int'l & Comp. L.Q.* 854.

308 Simmonds, *supra* note 307, at 862. The court received 20 written statements, and 9 states presented oral pleadings.

309 Ibid, at 863. The affirmative was pleaded by Australia, Canada, Denmark, Ireland, Italy, Japan, Netherlands, Norway, United Kingdom, and the United States. For the written statement of Canada on 16 February 1962, see I.C.J. *Pleadings, supra* note 307, at 210.

310 Simmonds, *supra* note 307, at 866–9. These arguments were adopted by Mexico, India, Portugal, Spain, Upper Volta, and the Soviet Bloc (USSR, Byelorussian SSR, Bulgaria, Ukranian Republic, and Romania).

311 Simmonds, *supra* note 307, at 871–5.

312 GAOR A/5380. The vote was 76 to 17 with 8 abstentions.

313 Argentina, Australia, Cameroons, Mongolia, Netherlands, and Pakistan were added to the original fifteen countries. See *supra* note 302.

314 The report simply outlined the positions taken by the various members of the group. The group was asked to continue its work, but the original position of the members had changed very little.

315 What is most important about this financial crisis is that it 'is financial only in form and reflects a deeper dissatisfaction with the manner in which peacekeeping is carried out in the Organization itself.' Simmonds. *supra* note 307, at 890.

316 Despite various proposals the Soviet Union and France refused to pay their assessments.

317 'It was not the least of the ironies of the nineteenth session that the only formal vote taken in two-and-a-half months was used to uphold the decision not to vote. The vast majority of the membership, divided on many points of substance about the financing of past, present and future peacekeeping operations, were nonetheless agreed that there was more to be lost than gained by pushing these issues to a decisive confrontation while the possibility of a negotiated settlement still existed.' Can. Dep't of External Affairs, [1964] *Canada and the United Nations* (1965) 21.

318 The Canadian delegation was quick to question the 'voluntary contributions' financing scheme for UNFICYP as a noticeable departure from the collective principle. Ibid, at 22.

See also Bishop, 'Canada's Policy on the Financing of UN Peacekeeping Operations,' (1965), 20 *International Journal* 463.

319 *Debates*, 25 June 1965, at 2848. Canada felt that rigorous application of the principle could lead to the withdrawal of major powers from the UN. Bishop notes that this about-face is a glaring inconsistency, and describes it as 'Divorce, Canadian style. Still wedded to the principle, but no longer living with it.' Bishop, *supra* note 318, at 480.

320 GAOR 2006 (XIX). For Canada's general approach to her role in the Peacekeeping Committee, see ibid at 23–4.

321 The committee came back to the General Assembly several times pointing out the problems it was having, and each time was sent back again to continue its work. UN Doc A/2053 (XX) (15 Dec. 1965); UN Doc A/2220 (XXI) (19 Dec. 1966); UN Doc A/2249 (23 May 1967); UN Doc A/2308 (XXII) (13 Dec. 1967); UN Doc A/2576 (XXIV) (15 Dec. 1969); UN Doc A/2670 (XXV) (8 Dec. 1970).

322 UN Doc A/5915.

323 Ibid, at 4.

324 UN Doc A/5916 (31 Aug. 1965).

325 UN Doc A/6414 (30 Sept. 1966).

326 For the statement made by the Canadian representative, Pierre Elliott Trudeau, in the Special Political Committee on 16 November 1966, see Press Release no 70 of the Canadian Mission to the United Nations, 1966. The following report was issued by the Canadian mission to be included in the 'Review of the Work of the Twenty-First Session of the United Nations General Assembly' concerning the Special Committee on Peacekeeping Operations:

Canada, after extensive consultations, had decided to submit a resolution which might serve to advance matters without disturbing the postions of principle of any delegation. While private consultations had suggested that our good intentions were accepted at face value, subsequent developments reflected an increasingly suspicious attitude on the part of the Soviet Union and France which, apart from disagreeing with certain specific elements in our text, e.g. the right of the Assembly to express an opinion on a special scale for the apportionment of costs among member states, interpreted the preamble of our resolution as an attempt to reassert the residual authority of the General Assembly to mount peacekeeping operations in a situation where the Security Council fails to act.

327 UN Doc A/6654.
328 Ibid, at 20–45.
329 Ibid, at 45–58.
330 Ibid, at 33–4.
331 Ibid, at 47–51.
332 'In his delegation's view, that was the minimum that should be asked of Member states in support of the United Nations in its fundamental peacekeeping role.' Ibid, at 48.
333 The American delegate stated: 'There again the Canadian representative had adopted a practical and sensible approach, pointing out that functions performed in peacekeeping more closely resembled those of police than military units. Since that type of role for an international organization was relatively new, it was of the utmost importance to prepare units to carry it out effectively.' Ibid, at 55.

The delegate from the Netherlands said: 'We fully concurred in the Canadian representatives' detailed proposals for a technical study along these lines. In any such study, the vast amount of information already collected by the Canadian Government on all organizational aspects of peacekeeping operations should be taken into consideration.' Ibid, at 58.

334 UN Doc A/AC 121/17.
335 UN Doc A/7131. The group consisted of Canada, Czechoslovakia, Mexico, UAR, France, Soviet Union, United Kingdom, and the United States.
336 Sixth Report, UN Doc A/7742. The group stressed that patience was needed to iron out the basic differences in principles which had been plaguing the UN for years.
337 UN Doc A/8081.
338 A press release dated 3 December 1971 announced that the Committee of thirty-three had concluded its year's work without yet fulfilling its mandate. The committee also noted that the working group had not concluded model I of its work nor had it been able to agree on model II. Nevertheless the report ended 'on a note of hope.'
339 There has been some optimistic comment on the committee, however:

Though progress in the Committee of 33 has been slow there are grounds for some optimism. There are indications that the

United States and the USSR are moving towards closer agreement on peacekeeping machinery. The USA now seems prepared to make more use of the Security Council ... because this best reflects the realities of great power influence. The Soviet Union has also moved from its previously rigid position. The USSR may have concluded that it is to its advantage to enter fully into the peacekeeping picture so that it can exercise control from within.' J.A. Stenga, 1970, 579 Int'l Conciliation, at 44–6.

For some additional work on the financial crisis, see Nathanson, 'The Price of Peacekeeping' (1965), 32 U. Chicago L. Rev. 621–58; A.M. Cox, Prospects for Peacekeeping (1967) 12–19; Rendall, 'Case Comment on ICJ Decision' (1963), 2 Osgoode Hall L.J. 539–58; Fines, 'Peacekeeping Costs' (1966), 15 Int'l & Comp. L.Q. 529–39; Bleicher, 'Financing Peacekeeping from IMF and IBRD Income' (1966–7), 42 Wash. L. Rev. 1017–64; Can. Dep't of External Affairs, [1964] Canada and the United Nations (1965) 11–24; 'Issues Before the 21st General Assembly' (1966), 559 Int'l Conciliation 12–20.

340 Eg, Paul Martin, Statements and Speeches 64/32, at 3; 64/35, at 5. 'It is becoming increasingly difficult for a united group of middle powers, of which Canada has been in the forefront, to carry the burden of serving in peace-keeping forces while others of greater resources and power not only refuse to pay their share of the cost but insist that the operation itself is illegal under the Charter.' Lester Pearson, Statements and Speeches 65/3, at 4.
341 See J.K. Gordon, ed, Canada's Role as a Middle Power (1966) 51; Taylor, at 183.
342 Eg, Statements and Speeches 65/22, at 7; 65/24 at 6. 'But peacekeeping by itself is not enough. Peace building is even more important.' Ibid, 65/27, at 5; 67/12, at 2. 'The UN is bound to be both a battlefield and a conference room. It must reflect as well as contain the impulse for change.' Ibid, 67/30, at 11. 'Unlike peace-keeping, the peaceful settlement of disputes has been neglected too long by us. It is easy to pay lip service, of course, to the concept of peaceful settlement, and more difficult to suggest how in practice it might be implemented.' Ibid, 68/14, at 5.
343 Paul Martin, Statements and Speeches 67/27, at 3–4.

344 Eg, Pierre Trudeau, *Statements and Speeches* 68/17. In a speech entitled 'Canada and the World' no mention of Canada and the UN is made. Pierre Trudeau, *Statements and Speeches* 69/17. Speaking on defence policy on 3 April 1969, Mr Trudeau mentioned peacekeeping in one sentence; the rest of the speech dealt with regional alliances.

> Our first priority is the protection of Canadian sovereignty, in all the dimensions that it means. And I don't accept the criticism of those who say this is a return to isolationism, or this is a return to the fortress Canada conception. This is not our purpose and not our aim.
>
> You can't talk of isolationism of Canadians, because, with the small manpower we have, with the economic means we have, we say we want to use the first part of it in terms of our own sovereignty, the second part of it in terms of the defence of our territory and continent and the third part of it in defence of other alliances such as NATO, peacekeeping operations which we will embark upon and we have embarked upon through the United Nations. *Statements and Speeches* 69/8.

345 *Eighth Report*, *supra* note 102, at 22.
346 This statement shows that Canada has moved along with the United States towards some kind of meeting with the Soviet position on how peacekeeping should be carried out.
347 *Eighth Report*, *supra* note 102, at 15.
348 Ibid, at 16.
349 Ibid, at 18. Compare *supra*,
350 *Eighth Report*, *supra* note 102, at 19.
351 Ibid, at 20.
352 Ibid, at 21.
353 Can. Dep't of Nat'l Defence, *Defence in the 70's, White Paper on Defence* (1971).
354 Ibid, at 40.
355 Ibid, at 14.
356 *Taylor*, at 181–2.
357 For the opposite point of view, see National Policy Panel of the United Nations Association of the United States, *Controlling Conflicts in the 1970's* (Brewster Report 1970) 41.

GEORGE IGNATIEFF

28/Canadian Aims and Perspectives in the Negotiation of International Agreements on Arms Control and Disarmament*

PERSPECTIVES

Perspectives have to be sought within a structure of time and space and their historical setting. In order to visualize the options of the future, we must perceive the determining trends of the past and realize why the negotiation of international agreements on arms control and disarmament – a process which undoubtedly creates international law – constitutes such an important but frustrating aspect of international co-operation.

World War I produced an explosion of new ideas sparked in large measure by the application in practice of the new ideas of Marx and Lenin in Russia, the world's largest country. Seen in historic perspective, the revolution in Russia has tended, over more than half a century, to divide the world into competing and mutually hostile systems, coinciding in our generation with the development of weapons capable of destroying civilization. A fear of Russia that was justifiable in the era of expansionism under Stalin in the 1940s projected into the 1960s and 1970s a sense of world struggle and bipolarity between exclusive alternatives of liberalism and totalitarianism.

This ideological bipolarity between the Soviet Union and the United States was reminiscent of the absolute divisions of earlier times on grounds of religion, creating personal attitudes which tend to persist even after circumstances in fact have rendered them obsolete and increasingly illusory. When Dr Johnson, in a discussion with Boswell about religion, was asked by what principles Turks were Moslems and Englishmen Christians, he replied: 'This now is such stuff as I used to talk to my mother when I first began to think myself a clever fellow, and she ought to have whipt me for it.' However, while both our thought patterns and the institutions of the cold war have tended to be conditioned by its bipolar tensions, persisting even after the historical circumstances have changed through the fragmentation of the communist world and the emergence of new powers like China and Japan, a new and co-operative mode of international relations through the United Nations, brought into being after World War II, has represented and still represents the main instrument for channelling human hopes for steady and peaceful progress towards global solutions.

It is a paradox of our times that the atomic age, which ushered in an era of

*The views expressed in this article are mine (when they are not explicitly set down as representing Canadian government policy) based on my experience as adviser to the Canadian representative to the Atomic Energy Commission from 1946 to 1948, and as Canadian representative to the Geneva Disarmament Committee from 1969 to 1972.

unprecedented scientific and technological revolution, at first reinforced the trend to bipolarity resulting from ideological differences by bringing two superpowers armed with nuclear weapons to the fore as the leading world powers, while at the same time rendering bipolarity in military terms compatible with the preservation of civilization from destruction only with a high degree of risk and at the cost of continuous diplomatic effort in order to reduce that risk. Realization of the implications of this paradox gave rise to the doctrine of deterrence, as well as the other restraints on the physical use of nuclear weapons by tacit or negotiated agreements.

The implications of the advent of atomic weapons have of course been global. But, from a Canadian perspective they have been especially important not only because of Canada's geographic location between the United States and the Soviet Union, but also because of Canada's pioneering role as a participant in the development of atomic energy during World War II. The transfer of an essential part of atomic research from the occupied or threatened countries of Europe to Montreal and later to Chalk River inevitably involved Canadians with the problem of trying to find ways to control this revolutionary and potentially devastating force. For it was realized from the start that atomic energy, like all physical forces, is both militarily and legally impartial and could just as easily serve destructive as constructive purposes – even though indeed its destructive use was at first paramount, leading to the development of the first atomic bomb. The problem has been and remains: how can we ensure that atomic energy and other agents of mass destruction should be used for peaceful purposes and that restraints and controls are established against their use for destruction? Our generation will be judged according to its ability to advance contemporary scientific and technological capabilities for growth and development, and at the same time to retard and restrict the application of these same capabilities for destruction. This looms as an inescapable personal responsbility for those who are concerned about the survival of civilized life.

The effort to find answers has been an essentially interdisciplinary challenge, involving as it does the physical scientist, the social scientist, the military, the lawyer, and the diplomat, as well as the politician. Each has tended to look for answers, drawn from his respective field of experience. Thus the lawyer and the diplomat, following their respective natural bents and realizing that any schemes for placing restraints on nuclear weapons (arms control) or eliminating them (disarmament) had to be based on voluntary agreements, set out on the path – the long and often frustrating path – to negotiate a series of international agreements.

Efforts to limit armaments by treaty over the years, have certainly not enjoyed brilliant success. But most of the time, there were quite understandable reasons why treaties were so difficult to conclude or failed to work out as expected. One reason which seems clear is that not much can be expected from attempts at limitation of armaments, which either are not tied closely in with the international political pattern of the times, such as bipolarity, or go counter to the basic policies of those powers which are most able to impose their will on the international community, especially the superpowers – the US and the Soviet Union. In other words, to understand the progress – or lack of it – in making law in the field of arms control and disarmament, it is necessary to bear in mind the reverse side of the coin, and realize that the forces which are at work tend to perpetuate the arms race. Let us see how these efforts have fared and what have been the aims that succeeding Canadian governments have followed in the negotiation of international agreements in arms control and disarmament.

BARUCH PLAN AND EARLIEST EFFORT AT INTERNATIONALIZATION
OF ATOMIC ENERGY

Canadian diplomacy has to its credit pioneered in the effort to develop international law in the field of arms control and disarmament. Canadian national interests, owing to Canada's geographic location and the availability of uranium – the principal natural resource used in atomic energy – were engaged, from the very dawn of the atomic age, in trying to develop international agreements to bring this new dread power under control, so as 'to ensure its use only for peaceful purposes.'[1]

This objective was first proclaimed in Washington by the president of the United States together with the prime ministers of Canada and the United Kingdom (Messrs Truman, King, and Attlee respectively) on 15 November 1945[2] just after the dropping of atomic bombs on Hiroshima and Nagasaki by the United States in August of that year. The three statesmen took this initiative, they stated, because of the progress their three countries had made during the war in the development and use of atomic energy. At Mr King's suggestion, the agreement stood between heads of governments rather than between the governments themselves. At Canadian initiative, also, the sharing of information about atomic energy was made contingent upon the development of international safeguards to prevent its use for destructive purposes. The problem of international control was thus posed as the main objective in the negotiations which were to follow.

The declaration of November 1945 was of historical significance. For one thing, it was the first major call for disarmament to be made after World War II. It set as the objective to seek to control the vast potential for evil of the atom, while also developing its potential for good. At the same time, the negotiations which the declaration envisaged sought to build a bridge across ideological differences between the US and the USSR, using the United Nations as the intermediary.

It is important to recall the role played by Canada at the time. Canada, together with the UK and US, alone represented 'the three countries which possessed the knowledge essential for the use of atomic energy' (Declaration, paragraph 4). Following up the declaration of the three heads of governments, the agreement of the Soviet government was obtained. Unanimous approval was then given on 24 January 1946 to the establishment of the Atomic Energy Commission as an organ of the United Nations, at the very first session of the General Assembly. It was Canada's role in these earliest efforts for atomic arms control which was responsible for her inclusion, despite the fact that Canadians laid no claims to being a 'great power,' in the UN Atomic Energy Commission and Disarmament Commission (composed of members of the UN Security Council) even when Canada was not a member of the Security Council.

At the first meeting of the Atomic Energy Commission which took place on 14 June 1946 in New York, the US representative, Mr Bernard Baruch, outlined a plan for the creation of an International Atomic Development Authority based on a State Department study (the Acheson-Lilienthal report) on atomic energy, prepared under the chairmanship of the then Undersecretary of State Dean Acheson. Mr

Baruch introduced the plan on a sombre note. Members of the UN Atomic Energy Commission (including myself in the capacity of adviser to General A.G.L. McNaughton, the representative of Canada) were called upon 'to make a choice between the quick and the dead ... If we succeed in finding a suitable way to control atomic weapons, it is reasonable to hope that we may preclude the use of other weapons adaptable to mass destruction.'[3]

The 'Baruch Plan,' as this first postwar plan on disarmanent came to be called, proposed that all dangerous atomic activities be placed in the hands of an international control authority. Internationalization amounted in effect to the elimination of all national atomic privileges. Under the plan the US would surrender its atomic monopoly. The authority envisaged in the plan would be entrusted with all stages of the development and use of atomic energy, including: 1 / managerial control or ownership of all atomic activities potentially dangerous to world security; 2 / power to control, inspect, and license all other atomic energy; 3 / the duty of fostering the beneficial uses of atomic energy; 4 / research and development responsibilities intended to put the authority in the forefront of atomic knowledge and thus enable it to comprehend, and therefore to detect, misuse of atomic energy.

In emphasizing the importance of immediate 'punishment' for infringement of the rights of the authority, Mr Baruch in a significant personal addition to the original Acheson-Lilienthal plan, stressed that 'there must be no veto to protect those who violate their solemn agreements not to develop or use atomic energy for destructive purposes.' In calling for international ownership and control of atomic energy and the effective surrender in this field of national sovereignty by the great powers, the plan had wide appeal among those who favoured an internationalist approach. The Canadian government gave its support to the principles and objectives of the Plan.

To a totalitarian regime, like that of the Soviet Union, the exercise of international control in a sector of the Soviet economy dependent on atomic energy for peace, as well as the threat of interference with its security by means of international inspection units, were totally unacceptable. Furthermore, the idea that a radical scheme of internationalization would provide a bridge across the bipolar chasm which was dividing the world and was essential to the preservation of world peace through the newly established United Nations must, in retrospect, have seemed hopelessly utopian to Stalinist Russia. As Robert Oppenheimer, who wrote part of the Acheson-Lilienthal report and was a member of the Baruch delegation, later said of the effect of the international control envisaged in the Baruch Plan: 'It would have meant that there could be no Iron Curtain.'[4]

At the second meeting of the AEC, 19 June 1946, Mr Gromyko, then the Soviet Union's permanent representative to the UN, made a counter-proposal in the form of a Soviet draft convention calling for a ban on the production and use of atomic weapons and for the destruction of all atomic weapons within three months of the entry into force of the draft convention.[5] The 'controlling organ' was to be subordinated to the Security Council with its veto, thus weakening the effective international control features of the Baruch plan. The proposal was not acceptable to the government of the US, as they would be called upon to destroy their atomic stockpile without the international safeguards which could assure them that these weapons, called 'absolute' at the time, would not be developed by their rival.

With the Soviet rejection of the Baruch Plan of internationalization of atomic energy, agreement had to be sought within the recognized bipolar pattern of US-Soviet rivalry. In a remarkably succinct and prescient speech to the Canadian Club in Hamilton on 31 March 1950, General McNaughton picked out surprise use of atomic weapons as the key danger to be guarded against in these circumstances.

> I think the members of the United Nations Atomic Energy Commission now clearly recognize the validity of the suggestion first given in the Acheson-Lilienthal Report, that in a war of long duration it would probably not be possible to prevent the use of atomic weapons; that the worst danger to be feared is the surprise use of these terrible contrivances and, in consequence, that the real objective to be sought is to free the world from secrecy in atomic matters and to allay suspicions by giving a certainty of warning to the world, if any nations should start to prepare for atomic war.

This reformulation of aims, consequent upon the Soviet rejection of the Baruch Plan, predicted with remarkable foresight the way in which nuclear disarmament would depend increasingly on negotiations between the principal nuclear powers, the Soviet Union and the US, including such measures as the Moscow-Washington 'hot-line,' the Non-Proliferation Treaty, and SALT.

ESTABLISHMENT OF THE GENEVA DISARMAMENT CONFERENCE SYSTEM

The breakdown of the efforts to find a truly international and global solution through the Baruch Plan to the threat posed by atomic weapons coincided with the freezing of the international system on bipolar lines, which characterized the cold war. The Berlin Blockade, confrontation in Greece, the war in Korea, and the Cuban missile crisis were all landmarks in the ice age which descended on the relations between Washington and Moscow. With international security dependent upon an equilibrium between the two opposing alliances – the North Atlantic Treaty Organization and the Warsaw Pact – the ever-changing military balance between the two systems was maintained primarily by means of the arms race and escalating military expenditures (a global figure of about $200 billion US annually), rather than by arms limitation and disarmament. But even under these unpropitious circumstances, governments on both sides recognized that disarmament offered a possibility for maintaining international peace and security. Hence the series of resolutions passed by succeeding sessions of the United Nations General Assembly.

Even during the height of the cold war under Stalin, the UN Disarmament Commission had as its aim the establishment of principles for the regulation and reduction of military arms and forces to achieve a global balance, as an adjunct to the international forces that were supposed to be established for peacekeeping under the Security Council and never were. But the machinery for the negotiation of arms control and disarmament agreements was to go through several changes before it was to emerge as the Conference of the Committee on Disarmament (CCD) in Geneva.

Canada, however, because of her pioneering role in atomic matters, was an active participant in each succeeding multilateral disarmament body as it changed its composition, its name, and its locale. The setting up of the UN Atomic Energy Commission was the first act of the first General Assembly to meet in New York; the Commission for Conventional Armaments was established in 1947; in 1952 these two commissions were merged into the Disarmament Commission. The Disarmament Commission established a five-power subcommittee consisting of Canada, France, the Soviet Union, the United Kingdom, and the United States. After the five-power subcommittee of the United Nations Disarmament Commission, which met in London from 1954–7, there came the eight-power conference of experts on the detection of nuclear tests and the ten-power conference of experts to prevent surprise attack, both of which met in Geneva in 1958; the Ten Nation Disarmament Commission (TNDC) which met in Geneva in 1960; the Eighteen Nation Disarmament Commission (ENDC) which met in Geneva from 1962–9; and finally the Conference of the Committee on Disarmament (CCD) which has been meeting in Geneva since 1969.

Moreover, because of the expertise Canadians had developed in the field of arms control and disarmament and Canada's reputation for being independent in its thinking and being willing to consider problems on their merits, Canadians were invited to serve on a succession of expert groups to advise the secretary general of the United Nations; these groups reported on the effects of nuclear weapons in 1967, on chemical and biological weapons in 1969, and on the economic and social consequences of the arms race and of military expenditures in 1971.

With the passing of Stalin and the beginning of serious efforts at negotiating arms control and disarmament agreements at the London subcommittee, there came in 1959, with the adoption of a unanimous resolution of the General Assembly on Khruschev's proposal, a shift towards general and complete disarmament as the aim, to be achieved by stages and to be accompanied with adequate international verification.

The McCloy-Zorin agreement on a Joint Statement of Principles for Disarmament Negotiations in 1961 set the stage for serious negotiations in Geneva. The forum for these negotiations was to be the Eighteen Nation Disarmament Committee. This body reflected in its composition the prevailing bipolar international system, but for the first time included a distinct group of so-called non-aligned states. In addition to the two co-chairmen, furnished by the US and USSR, the other members were drawn equally from NATO and the Warsaw Pact countries (at first four each, now six each in the CCD) and eight (now twelve) drawn from non-aligned countries to try to act in an intermediary role. While the tensions of the cold war were there to keep the lines of demarcation straight, this system more or less worked as it was intended to do.

The first hint of a possible breakup of this system came when President de Gaulle, on returning to power in 1958, refused to accept the idea of the US and USSR running the Geneva Disarmament Conference as co-chairmen. Such a concept was of course totally at odds with his ideas of France's place in Europe and the world. In fact, his idea of a *Europe des patries* was precisely aimed against bipolarity. France's chair, hitherto filled by a distinguished statesman, M Jules Moch, was never occupied at the Geneva conference.

An even more powerful challenge to the whole system of bipolarity from China may well spell the end of the present conference for arms control and disarmament negotiations in Geneva. Rejecting the domination of the so-called superpowers, China is seeking the extension of its diplomatic influence throughout the world on the basis of equality for all nations. The solution of the Chinese representation issue in the United Nations may bring in its train an end to the special privileges accorded to the co-chairmen in Geneva and new arrangements may emerge either before or after a world conference on disarmament, which China has called for at the level of heads of government.

Acting within the limitations of the Geneva system, in which the co-chairmen representing the two superpowers have not unnaturally sought to play a determining role in all negotiations, it is remarkable what has been achieved. Those of us who remember the convoys of the last world war will understand what it means to have to sail at the rate of the slowest ship or ships. We now have the anomaly that the slowest ships are also the escort vessels of the convoy – the Dreadnoughts being two superpowers represented by the two co-chairmen! But this anomaly only works so long as the Dreadnoughts enjoy virtual monopoly over military power and are not themselves the victims of obsolescence in strategy, as well as military power.

For the achievements at Geneva it is necessary to pay tribute not only to the untiring, patient efforts of outstanding representatives like General E.L.M. Burns of Canada, with his incomparable expertise, and Madame Alva Myrdal of Sweden, with her drive and inspiration, but to a succession of wise representatives of the superpowers too, like William C. Foster and Adrian Fisher (backed by a substantial effort from the Arms Control and Disarmament Agency – ACDA – in Washington) and such knowledgeable and competent negotiators from Moscow as Messrs Tsarapkin and Roshchin. Nor must one overlook the long-standing and continuing contribution made by Mr William Epstein, senior Canadian national in the UN Secretariat and director of its Disarmament Division, as well as the secretary general's representative at the ENDC and CCD.

The aims of Canada at Geneva have been pragmatic and have had to recognize the limitation imposed on Canadian initiative which results from being an ally of the US, both in Europe as well as for purposes of North American defence: a / active participation in the negotiations in the forum which had been created for this purpose; b / identifying specific issues which might be ripe at any time for initiatives in the negotiation of arms control or disarmament agreements; c / seeking to modify proposals put forward by others, especially by the two superpowers, in such a way as to be most helpful in finding practicable compromises; d / helping use the Geneva Conference machinery and the United Nations General Assembly (to which the conference reports) in order to gain public understanding of the issues involved in arresting and ending the arms race.

When I took over the job from General Burns in 1969, he particularly stressed the potential of Canada's role as a catalyst, when (using a mechanical rather than chemical metaphor) he said: 'In the CCD, it is the nuclear powers who apply the brakes, and countries like Canada have to provide the dynamo.'[6] It has always been Canadian policy to press ahead with initiatives on any subject which holds out the promise of progress. Thus in pursuit of our pragmatic but catalytic course, Canada has put first priority on ending the nuclear arms race, and first and foremost on ending nuclear testing, which is the outward and visible sign of the ongoing contest.

A recent and emphatic definition of Canada's aims in regard to the nuclear arms race was the statement made by Prime Minister Trudeau in the House of Commons in Ottawa on 24 October 1969 when, in opening a debate on national policy, he said: 'No single international activity rates higher priority in the opinion of this Government than the pursuit of effective arms control and arms limitation agreements. Canada refuses to submit without protest to the present nuclear hegemony.' This approach was maintained in the foreign policy white paper produced by the government in 1970.

GENERAL AND COMPLETE DISARMAMENT (GCD)

In the 1950s, with the cold war at its height, the approach to disarmament was basically one of 'all or nothing,' with the result that there was nothing. When the relaxation of tensions began after the death of Stalin, however, an effort was made at the United Nations to define the aims of disarmament more precisely and to set up more effective negotiating machinery.

During the days of the Disarmament Commission, the Soviets wanted to give priority to nuclear disarmament, the West to conventional disarmament. This commission, of which Canada was a full-time member, made the first approach towards a comprehensive disarmament program, synchronizing conventional disarmament, nuclear disarmament, and control. The Canadian delegation, at the time led by the Honourable Paul Martin, took the initiative in 1954 in getting all five members of the commission's London subcommittee to co-sponsor a General Assembly resolution (based on an Anglo-French plan of 11 June 1954 for comprehensive disarmament in three stages) calling for the conclusion of agreement on 'comprehensive and co-ordinated' proposals of disarmament – one of the few times during the cold war that the USSR concerted action with the western powers. But in attempting to implement this agreed resolution, there was divergence over its interpretation.

A joint western plan was submitted to the subcommittee in March 1955 in which the West continued to insist on 'foolproof' control. The detailed Soviet plan was presented on 10 May 1955 and stated that there was no way of ensuring complete international control over the elimination of nuclear weapons. The deadlock led to an emphasis on partial measures beginning with the ways of preventing a surprise attack, first discussed at the Geneva Summit of July 1955.

The Fourteenth General Assembly in 1959 declared GCD to be the most important question facing the world and called for governments to make every effort to solve the problem.[7] Just before the Assembly began, the foreign ministers of France, UK, US, and USSR, meeting to consider the Berlin problem, decided to establish a new Ten Nation Committee on Disarmament (TNCD), consisting of five western and five eastern powers. The committee convened in March 1960 in Geneva, instructed by the foreign ministers to explore possible ways of moving towards agreement on limitations and reductions, under international control, of all major types of arms and of armed forces. The western powers acknowledged GCD only as an ultimate goal and put forward proposals for a number of partial measures. The eastern powers called for immediate agreement on a plan for GCD. In June the five eastern powers walked out of the conference, charging that the western powers were not interested in GCD but only in measures of arms control. The walkout was also part of the aftermath of the U-2 incident.

On 20 September 1961 the US and USSR managed to produce a Statement of Agreed Principles (the McCloy-Zorin agreement) as a basis for multilateral negotiations. In the joint statement the list of principles began: 'The goal of negotiations is to achieve agreement on a programme which will ensure: (a) that disarmament is general and complete and war is no longer an instrument for settling international problems.'[8] It is worth noting that principles 5 (which seeks to ensure that no state shall gain military advantage over another as the result of implementation of the treaty) and 6 (that all disarmament measures should be implemented throughout under strict and effective international control) are concepts just as valid for measures of arms control as for GCD. On 13 December 1961 the General Assembly endorsed the agreement of the US and USSR and also agreed to the creation of the Eighteen Nation Disarmament Committee (ENDC) and recommended that the committee undertake negotiations 'as a matter of utmost urgency' with a view to reaching General and Complete Disarmament.

When the conference opened at the foreign minister level in Geneva on 15 March 1962 (without France), the main documents before it were: a 'Draft Treaty on General and Complete Disarmament Under Strict International Control,' submitted by the USSR on 15 March, and an 'Outline of Basic Provisions of a Treaty on General and Complete Disarmament in a Peaceful World,' submitted by the US on 18 April.

Both drafts envisaged a three-stage disarmament process, with progress from one to the next stage dependent upon the completion of disarmament measures and the advance preparation of inspection machinery for later measures. Both drafts also included reductions in conventional armaments and armed forces to set levels, as well as certain collateral arms control measures to build up international confidence, which were in fact negotiated separately from the GCD context. Each side accepted the need for inspection and control, although the Soviets, as usual allergic to outside intervention for whatever purpose, opposed the inspection of remaining stocks of armaments and insisted only on inspection of arms actually reduced or destroyed and on indirect inspection, eg, budgetary controls. The USSR also wanted the advantage of having its draft treaty adopted as the basis of discussion.

The Canadian delegation preferred the formulation of the US draft but was concerned, as usual, to look for and to try to bridge the major differences between the Soviet and US approaches. It soon became clear that the two sides differed over acceptable measures for the limitation and reduction of long-range nuclear weapon vehicles that had important implications for the strategic balance between the two superpowers. From the Canadian point of view, any solution would have to conform to 'the agreed principles of balance and effective international control.'[9] Throughout the debates, the idea underlining the Canadian approach was that 'the building of confidence between the two sides' was essential, and we sought clarification in particular of the Soviet position in order to try to eliminate differences between the two sides, a goal which proved elusive.

During the next two years, general and complete disarmament remained a lively but fruitless quest. Although this remains the ultimate objective of the United Nations, the co-chairmen's draft treaty proposals have remained static since 1964. A growing emphasis has in fact been put on the 'collateral' or 'confidence-building' measures such as Comprehensive Test Ban (CTB), Chemical and Biological Weapons Control (CBW), non-proliferation, and seabed arms control, etc, both at Geneva and in New York. This is evidence of an increasing realization, prompted by Canada, *inter alia*, that the 'all or nothing' approach does not work, especially in an environment of great power confrontation, and that attainable limited objectives might be missed while one chased the rainbow of GCD. The Canadian foreign policy white paper of 1970 pointed out that progress towards disarmament and for stopping the arms race was most likely to be realized through arms control and limitation agreements, even if GCD remained an ultimate objective of Canadian policy.

During its 1966 session the ENDC, 'in order to achieve the widest possible agreement at the earliest possible date,' had given priority to a comprehensive test ban and to non-proliferation.[10] Indeed until its signature in mid-1968, the Non-Proliferation Treaty (NPT) became the centre of attention. In the provisional agenda for its work adopted by the ENDC in its 1968 summer session (which was the first time that the western powers had formally given top priority to nuclear disarmament), GCD had slipped to fourth and final place after a test ban, chemical and biological (bacteriological) weapons (CBW), and the Seabed Arms Control Treaty.

That the goal of general and complete disarmament has not yet disappeared altogether out of sight is shown by the fact that, when at the Twenty-fourth General Assembly in 1969 consideration was being given to a call by Romania to proclaim the 1970s a 'UN Disarmament Decade' with GCD as the goal, some countries recommended the drawing-up of a long-term comprehensive program of disarmament. Canada, while being in favour of this concept, has since maintained opposition to any set timetable for the various measures to be achieved, again stressing that the committee should be free to tackle at any given time what seems most ready for solution. The US, UK, and Soviet Union share this view.

CONTAINMENT OF NUCLEAR WEAPONS

Three international treaties have been negotiated which seek by different methods to contain the spread of nuclear weapons to nations which do not yet possess them. While none of the three has fully accomplished its objectives, each represents at least a progression in the scope of arms limitation involved. The Partial Nuclear Test Ban Treaty, the Treaty Prohibiting Nuclear Weapons in Latin America, and the Non-Proliferation of Nuclear Weapons Treaty were all completed in the five years between 1963 and 1968. The first and the last were negotiated at Geneva, and the Latin American treaty was negotiated in Tlatelolco, a part of Mexico City. In addition, three other international treaties also prevent the spread of nuclear weapons to outer space or to uninhabited areas of the earth: the Antarctic Treaty, the Outer Space Treaty, and the Seabed Treaty, which are discussed below in the section on 'unmilitarized or demilitarized areas or environments.' Two more international agreements for the containment of nuclear weapons are still in course of negotiation. Negotiation to end all nuclear testing in all environments (a Comprehensive Nuclear Test Ban or CTB) has high priority on the agenda of the Geneva conference. At the same time, the governments of the US and USSR are engaged in bilateral talks on the limitation of strategic nuclear weapons and delivery systems (SALT).

Partial test ban

During the summer of 1962 while the ENDC was still discussing the provisions of a treaty of general and complete disarmament, it also dealt with collateral measures of more restricted scope which were already being referred to as arms control

measures. The most important of these was the prohibition of nuclear weapons testing. This had been urged at the United Nations General Assembly since 1954 and
the nuclear powers had been considering it since 1957.

Worldwide pressure had been mounting over the dangers of the atmospheric pollution and health hazards resulting from the fallout of radioactive wastes. Canada
was in the van of this pressure. The UN Scientific Committee on the Effects of
Atomic Radiation (UNSCEAR) was set up by the General Assembly in 1955 to carry
out an extensive fallout monitoring program. Monthly reports from air, precipitation, and milk samples, as well as the results of the examination of water, soil, and
human bone samples, are sent to the committee for their study of the problem of
preventing radioactive contamination, an undertaking of continuing importance in
the health and environmental contexts.

On 21 March 1962 the ENDC, a week after it had first come together, set up in
place of the defunct three-member Geneva Conference on the Discontinuation of
Nuclear Weapon Tests, 1958–9, a subcommittee of representatives of the same
three nuclear powers – US, USSR, and UK – to negotiate a test ban. The nuclear
powers were divided, as usual, on the problem of verification. On 16 April the eight
non-aligned countries submitted a Joint Memorandum, in an effort to find a basis
of compromise, which stated that a system could be established by agreement,
involving continuously operated observation posts.[11] This Joint Memorandum
originated the idea of 'verification by challenge' or inspection by agreement. An
international commission could be set up of qualified scientists to process all data
from the posts and report on any 'suspicious events.' A suspected party would be
under obligation to furnish information on request and 'could invite' the commission to visit its territory or the site of the suspected event. Canada considered that
the non-aligned proposals constituted 'a constructive effort to find a compromise'
solution.[12] The USSR accepted this Joint Memorandum as the basis for negotiations,
while the US and UK accepted it only as one of the bases for negotiation. Problems
arose over different interpretations, especially whether the memorandum set out
obligatory or permissive provisions for on-site inspection. The Soviets rejected
obligatory international inspection of national territory.

Three weeks later, on 27 August 1962, the US and UK submitted two alternative
draft treaties: one providing for a test ban in all environments, and a quota of on-site
inspections in cases of underground tests; the other proposing a partial test ban only
in the three non-controversial environments – atmosphere, outer space, and under
water – without international verification.[13] The latter was to be a first step while
the Soviet Union opposed compulsory on-site inspection in a comprehensive
treaty. The Soviet side again rejected any proposals that included obligatory on-site
inspection, insisting that national measures of detection would suffice. As for the
partial ban, they rejected it on the grounds that it excluded underground tests, but
they were prepared to consider it if a voluntary moratorium on tests could be agreed
upon, pending a comprehensive ban on testing. On 10 December in the ENDC, they
proposed the use of automatic unmanned stations, 'black boxes' (a concept
developed at the Tenth Pugwash Conference earlier in 1962), to supplement existing manned national detection means for verification of an underground test ban.
Two or three automatic stations could be established on the territories of each of
the nuclear powers and some in neighbouring countries.[14] The sealed instrument
boxes would be carried to the international commission for analysis. The US

accepted this as a positive idea under certain circumstances, but as one which could not rule out the need for on-site inspection. In face of an apparent deadlock, the subcommittee of the three nuclear powers ceased to function.

When it reconvened on 12 February 1963 the ENDC centred its discussions on a nuclear test ban in all environments. There was general acceptance of nationally manned seismic stations, of the installation of unmanned 'black boxes' in the territories of nuclear powers and adjacent countries to check the functioning of the manned seismic stations, and of an annual quota (unspecified) of on-site inspections to clarify suspicious events. The numbers of boxes and inspections were not, on the other hand, agreed upon; the Soviets proposed three automatic stations and two or three on-site inspections, the US seven and seven (at first eight to ten inspections) respectively. The Soviets insisted on prior agreement on the numbers concerned before they would discuss the composition of inspection teams. Meanwhile, the eight non-aligned appealed to the nuclear powers to resolve their differences, which they characterized as not unsurmountable, and on 10 June 1963 Ethiopia, Nigeria, and the UAR submitted a joint memorandum calling for talks between foreign ministers of the nuclear powers to help break the impasse.[15]

The same day it was announced by President Kennedy that the USSR, US, and UK would hold talks in Moscow in four weeks time on the cessation of nuclear tests. On 2 July, Khrushchev stated that since the US and UK insisted on on-site inspection, an underground test ban was impossible; the Soviet Union was prepared to sign a partial ban covering the three non-controversial environments. Talks began on 15 July with the Soviets no longer insisting on any voluntary moratorium on underground testing. Agreement on the text of a treaty banning nuclear weapons testing in the atmosphere, outer space, and under water, initialled on 25 July, was signed in Moscow on 5 August 1963 by the foreign ministers of the three nuclear powers, the US, USSR, and UK.

In a significant preambular phrase, parties to the treaty declared they were 'seeking to achieve the discontinuance of all test explosions of nuclear weapons for all time, determined to continue negotiations to this end.' Besides banning tests in the non-controversial environments, article I also prohibited those 'in any other environment if such explosion causes radioactive debris to be present outside the territorial limits of the state under whose jurisdiction or control such explosion is conducted.'

The Partial Test Ban entered into force on 10 October 1963. It must be described as 'partial' in application not only because the restraints it imposes did not include underground testing – which in fact has permitted the US and the USSR to step up their rate of testing of their nuclear weapons until they exceed the number of tests conducted in 1963 – but also because neither France nor the People's Republic of China acceded to its terms and continue their testing in the atmosphere. Nevertheless, more than one hundred countries have become parties to the treaty, including all the potential or near-nuclear powers.

Latin American nuclear free zone

In the wake of the Cuban missile crisis, the concept of regional denuclearization, first put forward by Poland in the form of the Rapacki Plan in late 1957,[16] with an eye on German rearmament, caught fire in Latin America ten years later. Negotiations initiated by Mexico bore fruit on 14 February 1967 when in the borough of Tlatelolco, Mexico City, the Treaty for the Prohibition of Nuclear Weapons in Latin America was signed.

The treaty, *inter alia*, defines the term 'nuclear weapon'; establishes an international agency to ensure compliance with the treaty, with a permanent system of control and verification including IAEA safeguards and special inspections; provides for the development of peaceful uses of nuclear energy (including its uses in explosions for peaceful purposes); and defines the zone of application of the treaty and measures in the event of a violation of the treaty.

An additional protocol I of the treaty provided for an undertaking by extraterritorial powers (France, Netherlands, UK, US) to apply the state of denuclearization in those territories in the Latin American zone for which they were responsible *de jure* or *de facto* (eg, French and Dutch Guiana, the Cayman Islands, and Guantanamo in Cuba). Additional protocol II provided that the nuclear weapons powers undertake fully to respect the denuclearization of Latin America and not to use or threaten to use nuclear weapons against parties to the treaty.

Canada, while welcoming the Tlatelolco Treaty, expressed reservations (as did certain other countries) about those provisions according to which explosions of nuclear devices for peaceful purposes were regarded as an exception to the prohibitions under the treaty. Mexico responded by stating that such explosions could be carried out directly by parties to the treaty only if they did not call for use of a nuclear device akin to a weapon as defined in article v of the treaty; that is, 'any device which is capable of releasing nuclear energy in an uncontrolled manner and which has a group of characteristics that are appropriate for use for warlike purposes.'

The treaty entered into force in June 1969 and the Agency for the Prohibition of Nuclear Weapons in Latin America (OPANAL) was established in Mexico City.

The Non-Proliferation of Nuclear Weapons Treaty (NPT) of 1968

The US had already incorporated the idea of a treaty to ban the spread of nuclear weapons on a global scale, in a package proposal on disarmament in 1957. This idea was also included in General Assembly resolutions in 1959,[17] in 1960,[18] and 1961,[19] by which time the UN had given unanimous support to it. Both the US and USSR draft treaties of GCD in 1962 contained provisions for non-proliferation of nuclear weapons. Negotiations, however, did not begin in earnest until 1964–5 after an important precondition for success had been arrived at; that is, recognition by the two superpowers that there was a real danger of nuclear proliferation and that it would serve their common interest to prevent it. The subject kept the ENDC busy from 1965 to 1968, when the NPT was opened for signature.

In the Canadian view, an agreement of this nature was a significant contribution to world peace and security if it would also contribute to halting the nuclear arms race between the superpowers. That Canada viewed the NPT not as an end in itself was evident from the statement made by General Burns on behalf of the Honourable Paul Martin in the ENDC on 18 January 1968: 'The conclusion of an NPT would put us in an excellent position to attack the more substantive problem of the control and reduction of existing nuclear arsenals.'[20]

Basically, antagonism to the treaty draft presented by the co-chairmen derived from what non-nuclear weapon states regarded as the inequality of sacrifice implicit in the treaty obligations. Thus lengthy debate arose even within NATO as to what restrictions an NPT should impose on non-nuclear members of NATO. When President Johnson decided to abandon the idea of a nuclear Multi-Lateral Force (MLF) (in which a fleet of twenty-odd ships of destroyer-frigate size armed with Polaris missiles would be manned by crews of mixed NATO nationality), which Canada did not support, the future looked brighter for the negotiation of an NPT.

To hasten progress in the ENDC, Canada prepared a draft NPT to help towards the tabling of a definite text in the ENDC in July 1965. The Canadian draft aimed particularly at attracting the non-nuclear states which were not keen to give up the right to acquire nuclear weapons without corresponding nuclear disarmament obligations being laid on nuclear weapons states. It was important that an NPT should not simply ensure a perpetuation of the monopoly of nuclear weapons for the existing nuclear powers.

The Canadian draft emphasized, *inter alia*, that all parties to the treaty should incorporate all their non-military nuclear activities under IAEA safeguards procedures. The final treaty did not oblige nuclear powers to do this, but the US and UK, unlike the USSR, declared they would do so voluntarily. The Canadian draft also provided an undertaking by nuclear powers to come to the assistance of a non-nuclear state party subjected to attack, in cases where that state was not allied with another nuclear state. This point was covered in a declaration by the nuclear powers party to the treaty and in Security Council Resolution 255 of June 1968 supported by them. The Canadian draft further stipulated that the entry into force of the treaty should require ratification by a number of 'near-nuclear' as well as nuclear states, the former being specified as: Canada, FGR, India, Israel, Japan, Pakistan, and Sweden. The final treaty did not include such a provision, though the desirability of this provision has been rendered obvious from the fact that the absence of ratification from five out of the seven specified, as well as from Argentina, Brazil, and South Africa, is holding up the full implementation of the treaty. Although France and China are not parties to the treaty, the former has officially announced that she will abide by the treaty and it is likely that China will also do nothing that might lead to nuclear proliferation, which is obviously against the interests of any nuclear power.

A major obstacle in the negotiations was the Soviet objection to any modification of NATO nuclear sharing arrangements which might lead in particular to a rearmed FGR. Throughout 1966 and 1967 the ENDC wrestled with the major problem of finding a formula which would quell Soviet fears over West Germany and yet would be acceptable to the European NATO allies as not compromising their defence arrangements or commercial civilian nuclear activities, or undermining their existing safeguard system in Euratom. Parallel negotiations of non-ENDC members of NATO were a vital part of the US effort, especially since the FGR was always concerned lest any agreement might curb US freedom to use tactical nuclear weapons in the defence of Europe.

The final wording of article I agreed between the US and the USSR must have convinced the Soviets that the US did not in fact intend to hand over, directly or indirectly to any of its non-nuclear allies, control of nuclear weapons.

Each nuclear-weapon State Party to this Treaty undertakes not to transfer to any recipient whatsoever nuclear weapons or other nuclear explosive devices or control over such weapons or explosive devices directly, or indirectly; and not in any way to assist, encourage, or induce any non-nuclear weapon State to manufacture or otherwise acquire nuclear weapons or other nuclear explosive devices, or control over such weapons or explosive devices.[21]

The phrase 'other nuclear explosive devices' was inserted to cover the desire of certain non-nuclear weapons states to develop such devices for peaceful purposes, partly as a result of expectations by the US AEC after its 'Plowshare' series of tests that nuclear explosions could facilitate recovery of underground minerals and the excavations of canals and harbours. Canada, while realizing the potential value of peaceful nuclear explosions, has persistently pointed out (as did other representatives) that such explosions are not distinguishable in effect from nuclear weapons tests, a point confirmed in the report on the effect of use of nuclear weapons of a panel of leading scientists convened by the United Nations secretary general. Article II of the NPT, prohibiting peaceful nuclear explosions, is still cited by India and Brazil as a major reason why they will not sign the NPT. Nevertheless, article v of the treaty ensures that when peaceful nuclear explosions can be carried out to economic advantage, states with nuclear weapons would make nuclear explosion devices available at low cost for projects in the territory of non-nuclear states party to the treaty. It is still a matter of discussion whether all peaceful explosions should be banned, except those specifically permitted by international treaty, and as to how they might be carried out.

Safeguards and verification were dealt with in the highly complex third article of the final treaty in which the US draft called for parties to apply IAEA or equivalent international safeguards to all peaceful nuclear activities. The Soviets came to support IAEA safeguards, too. However, Euratom members of NATO – non-possessors of nuclear weapons in western Europe (Italy, Germany, Belgium, Netherlands, and Luxembourg, excluding France) who co-operate in peaceful nuclear research and who had thus developed their own inspection methods – consider their own safeguards sufficient for an NPT. The Soviet Union and many non-aligned governments object to this approach on the grounds that this would amount to no more than self-inspection, since Euratom members are also in NATO. Since the USSR, unlike the US and UK, refuses to accept any IAEA safeguards on its territory, its objections have little persuasive force. Article III as finally worded sought, *inter alia,* to dampen fears of Euratom and others that IAEA inspectors might interfere with their peaceful atomic energy research, permit industrial espionage, or introduce unnecessary red tape into their inspections; it also enables Euratom to negotiate as a group collectively with the IAEA for safeguards.

Articles IV, V, and VI had to be added to the original Soviet and US drafts to meet the demands of non-nuclear states including Canada that 'the Treaty should embody an acceptable balance of mutual responsibilities and obligations of the nuclear powers' (General Assembly Resolution 2028 (xx) 19 November 1965), involving not least some concrete steps towards nuclear disarmament. Most important of all is article VI of the NPT which states that 'each of the Parties to this Treaty undertakes to pursue negotiations in good faith on effective measures relating to cessation of the arms race at an early date and to nuclear disarmament, and on a Treaty on General and Complete Disarmament under strict and effective international control.' The superpowers would not agree to accept any more substantive provision in the treaty which would commit them to actual nuclear disarmament, but this does at least constitute the first time they have accepted a legal commitment to seek a halt to the arms race and nuclear disarmament. The implementation of this commitment is regarded by the non-nuclear powers as a test of the sincerity of the superpowers and it opened the way to SALT.

Finally, it was necessary to provide assurance to non-nuclear weapon states about their security if they renounced the production or acquisition of nuclear weapons. Positive guarantees by the nuclear powers in the treaty would have amounted to the nuclear powers assuming alliance commitments to non-nuclear weapon states. This they were unwilling to do in a general way, although of course Canada is the beneficiary of specific guarantees under both NATO and NORAD. General Burns put the Canadian view, that it was 'important that steps be taken to meet the concern of the non-nuclear states with regard to security,'[22] to the ENDC on 12 September 1967. The nuclear powers should at least either have made declarations, when the treaty opened for signature, that they would assist any non-nuclear signatory state attacked with nuclear weapons or so threatened; or have such promises embodied in a UN resolution. The latter alternative was chosen, resulting in Security Council Resolution 255 of 19 June 1968, thereby constituting the only general security guarantees to non-nuclear states parties to the treaty, acceptable to the superpowers. Many non-nuclear states wished for more, and some called for a binding legal commitment in the NPT itself.

Comprehensive Test Ban (CTB)

In an effort to facilitate a resolution of the deadlock between the US and the USSR on the verification of an underground nuclear test ban, Canada has been taking the lead for the last few years in attempting to focus attention on the underground test issue and to inject some mobility into the negotiations, which have been stalled since 1963. In particular, Canada has initiated and carried out exploratory in-depth studies on the utility of an international exchange of seismic data and of ways to improve non-intrusive seismological means of identifying underground nuclear tests, that is, distinguishing them from natural earthquakes.

Negotiations have in fact been stalled since 1963 owing to the 'verification gap,' with the government of the US insisting that given the inadequacy of international seismological identification techniques on-site inspection was necessary, and the government of the USSR consistently refusing international on-site inspection on their territory and insisting that detection by national means only would provide sufficient guarantees that the terms of a comprehensive test ban treaty would be complied with.

Over the years, in the ENDC-CCD and the General Assembly, various suggestions have been put forward to resolve this verification controversy. Meanwhile, there has been a steady increase in the rate and magnitude of US and Soviet underground nuclear weapon testing, as well as continued testing in the atmosphere, at a much smaller rate but with its greater risk of radioactive contamination, by France and China. Thus, there is a risk that the PTB will increasingly become eroded; the need for a CTB becomes correspondingly greater.

Among the various suggestions advanced in the ENDC and General Assembly in the 1960s aimed at promoting an early conclusion of a CTB, the most important have been: a / the Swedish proposal of 1965 for the creation of a 'Detection Club' to promote international co-operation in the exchange of seismic data, and their submission of a draft CTB in 1969, revised in 1971;[23] b / the UAR suggestion for a threshold together with a moratorium on underground testing below this level;[24] c / the system for 'verification by challenge' put forward by the Swedish delegation in 1966;[25] d / the UK suggestion that a treaty should provide for an agreed annual quota of underground test explosions, the scale descending to nil in a period of four or five years;[26] e / the Canadian effort to establish improved detection methods for the verification of an underground test ban through an international seismic data exchange.

Indeed, ways of promoting international exchange of seismic data became the chief area of Canadian diplomacy, in addition to research to promote the end of nuclear testing in all environments. Thus, in 1962 the then Department of Mines and Resources set up seismographic stations designed to improve techniques for detection and identification of underground events, and Dr Kenneth Whitham, with comparatively modest resources, has put Canada in the forefront of international seismological co-operation. The Canadian delegation submitted a proposal at Geneva, and ultimately to the General Assembly of the United Nations, that a request be made to governments by the UN secretary general for the provision of information to facilitate the achievement of a CTB, which would involve, principally, providing a list of all seismic stations in a country from which its government 'would be prepared to supply records on the basis of guarantee of availability.' The proposal, contained in UN General Assembly Resolution 2604A (XXIV), was adopted on 16 October 1969. The Soviet Union, together with the Warsaw Pact countries, however, rejected the resolution on the grounds that any compulsory exchange of information on seismic stations must be accompanied by an acceptance that national means of detection, alone, sufficed to ensure compliance with an underground test ban, otherwise it was of no use.

Well over half the membership of the UN responded favourably in 1970 to this Canadian initiative, informing the secretary general about the quantity and quality of the seismic data they would be willing to supply from their seismic stations. On the basis of these new 'hard' data, Canadian experts have prepared further extensive original studies of the current state of the art of the seismological detection of underground tests. Unfortunately, the USSR declined to co-operate in this exercise and has consistently refused to present any scientific data to assist in establishing what in fact can be done by national seismic detection alone to ensure compliance with a comprehensive test ban.

The basic problem of an underground nuclear test ban is not merely the detection, but also the positive identification of underground tests, ie, distinguishing them from earthquakes. In the past few years there has been a marked improvement in scientific techniques, which can already identify at least a yield of twenty kilotons (in hard rock) in Eurasia and ten to twenty kilotons in North America, as the Canadian studies have shown, and the level of identification could probably be lowered to five kilotons in the northern hemisphere and perhaps less. It will probably not, however, be possible to detect and identify all seismic events of lower magnitudes by seismic means alone. As the difference between the positions of the US and the USSR is primarily political, rather than technical, we cannot simply wait for some technical breakthrough in the seismic field to solve the problem. Satellite surveillance adds another means of verification and, as already noted, various compromise ideas have been advanced. A combination of the 'Detection Club' idea (ie, the pooling of seismic data) together with 'verification by challenge' (ie, no provision for any obligatory on-site inspections, but an agreement that a party could challenge another to permit an inspection of an allegedly suspicious event and, if the challenge were denied, could withdraw from the agreement) or, alternatively, the acceptance of diminishing risks of non-compliance have been suggested as ways of resolving the political problem.

Meanwhile, Canada has taken the initiative of urging the superpowers to take certain interim or transitional measures to reinforce the Partial Test Ban Treaty of 1963 to prevent the situation from deteriorating further while efforts continue to put an end to all nuclear testing through a comprehensive test ban. In particular, the Canadian proposal of 6 April 1971 called on both the two major testing powers to undertake, whether unilaterally or on the basis of a bilateral understanding, some or all of the following steps: a / to announce in advance their annual test programs so that existing monitoring facilities could be more easily tested and improved; b / as an earnest of their good faith in working towards a comprehensive test ban, to begin as soon as possible to scale down their underground testing programs, beginning with high-yield testing that can be readily identified, and working downwards; c / to take special measures to guard against environmental risks connected with testing; and d / to undertake to co-operate in the use, development, and improvement of facilities for the monitoring of underground tests by seismological means.[27] The USSR undertook to study our proposals carefully but on 7 September 1971, in the CCD, they rejected step a on the curious ground that it would facilitate leakage of military information; the US was also reticent.

Latest public indications, however, are that the US is not prepared to give up its insistence on on-site inspection for the verification of a CTB, and that the Soviet Union will not change its position about reliance on national means of detection only. It is truly a *dialogue des sourds*. We therefore see a strengthening of the restraints on nuclear testing, based on the Partial Test Ban Treaty of 1963, as preferable to no progress at all towards a CTB. Consequently, Canada will continue to press for consideration and acceptance of the transitional measures we have suggested, together with any other restraints on testing that may prove generally acceptable, pending the resolution of the political issues between the nuclear testing powers that lie at the root of the present impasse.

SALT

The Geneva Conference on Disarmament risks suffering the fate of Lot's wife, while the superpowers deal elsewhere on a bilateral basis with regard to the threat posed not only to each other, but to the rest of the world, by their arms race in strategic nuclear weapons and delivery systems. Nothing better illustrates the advantages as well as the disadvantages of bipolarity than the Strategic Arms Limitation Talks taking place alternately in Vienna and Helsinki between the US and the

USSR. They owe their immediate existence to the pledge entered into by the two powers involved under article VI of the Non-Proliferation Treaty cited above.

At the signing ceremonies of the Non-Proliferation Treaty on 1 July 1968, Premier Kosygin and President Johnson first announced that the talks would be held forthwith, but the Soviet invasion of Czechoslovakia caused a postponement and the talks began in Helsinki, not in the best of circumstances, in November 1969. Given that such negotiations involve the vital security interests of both sides, the complexity of any discussion on limitation of strategic weapons is obvious. The talks in fact were apparently deadlocked for over a year until 20 May 1971 when the two sides made public their agreement 'to concentrate this year on working out an agreement for the limitation of the deployment of antiballistic missile system (ABM). They have also agreed that together with concluding an agreement to limit ABO, they will agree on certain measures with respect to the limitation of offensive strategic weapons.'

This somewhat limited undertaking in the agreement of 20 May was hailed throughout the world as a breakthrough when it was made public, not only because of the secrecy with which these talks are shrouded and the vital significance of SALT, but because it indicated that a stalemate had been broken and gave reason to hope for concrete results at a reasonably early date. The joint statement referred to the conviction of the two sides that the course they proposed to follow would 'create more favourable conditions for further negotiations to limit all strategic arms.' This is obviously so. For instance, the work being done in Geneva on CTB is to some extent linked with the outcome of SALT and the question arises whether the conference at Geneva has merely to sit back and wait until a breakthrough is reached in Vienna or Helsinki. The first teams of both superpowers have been fielded in the latter places rather than at Geneva.

A point to be borne in mind is that SALT is more a political than a technical exercise, and the conceivable motivations attributable to each of the superpowers are not to be explained merely through reference to the momentum of technology but involve the whole spectrum of issues affecting the equation which will determine the balance of power in the world and whether this balance is to be accomplished, at least at the nuclear level, through bilateral agreements of constraint or through an unrestrained arms race.

Canadians naturally have a tremendous stake in the outcome of SALT. We are kept informed through NATO consultations of what happens in SALT and have taken an active and constructive role in them. Our role in these consultations has been to emphasize both the urgent need to enhance security through effective nuclear arms control and the obligations of the superpowers under article VI of the Non-Proliferation Treaty. We have also repeatedly stressed that in addition to quantitative restrictions efforts should be made to achieve not only restrictions on qualitative improvements or new strategic weapons but, at least ultimately, reductions as well.

The success of these talks is clearly crucial to the whole future of arms control and disarmament. It would be wrong to suppose that the signing of a treaty is essential to indicate success. At best these negotiations might result in a reduction of the existing stockpiles of nuclear warheads and delivery vehicles – that is to say, in real terms, physical nuclear disarmament.

If, however, the talks fail, it is not too much to say that both existing and future arms control and disarmament agreements would be in danger. It is unlikely, for instance, that the near-nuclear powers would be prepared to accede to the Non-Proliferation Treaty, even if they had already signed it. It is clearly possible that even those which have signed and ratified the treaty would begin to have second thoughts about the wisdom of remaining bound by it. They might have to consider taking advantage of the withdrawal clause in the treaty either immediately or at the review conference that must be held by 5 March 1975 (five years after the treaty's entry into force). There would be little, if any, hope of a comprehensive nuclear test ban, and even the Partial Test Ban Treaty of 1963 would be in jeopardy; hence the significance of the interim or transitional restraints on nuclear testing that Canada has been advocating.

The factor of China and of Japan in these circumstances could have incalculable effects on nuclear proliferation. While China has developed its own nuclear weapons and has become the fifth nuclear power, Japan has signed the Non-Proliferation Treaty but has not yet ratified it. Given its advanced technology and industrial plant, Japan could become a nuclear power in a short time. There are, moreover, near-nuclear powers in other continents which may individually or collectively take up the nuclear option if the effort at containing the proliferation of nuclear weapons is seen to have broken down.

We would be left with only a few collateral measures to show for all the arms control and disarmament effort since World War II – useful but hardly crucial to the central problem of survival – for the potential threat to our survival is the weapon of mass destruction, and the nuclear weapon is still the core of that threat. The other problems of arms control and disarmament will remain subordinate and to some extent academic until the nuclear arms race between the superpowers is brought under control and the proliferation of nuclear weapons contained.

What is eroding bipolarity is the growing and worldwide concern, shared by Canadians, that the two superpowers should hold world hegemony and that they should be deciding *inter se* the fate of the world. But, meanwhile, there is no doubt at all that what happens in SALT holds the key to the main question in the field of the two areas central to this paper: arms control, and disarmament. Are these aims a myth, or are they to become a reality?

UNMILITARIZED OR DEMILITARIZED AREAS OR ENVIRONMENTS

Three international treaties have been aimed at preventing the extension of the arms race, and in particular nuclear weapons, into geographical areas or physical environments in which they do not at present exist and at trying to reserve these areas or environments 'exclusively for peaceful purposes.' The Antarctic Treaty was the first international instrument designed to 'reserve exclusively for peaceful purposes' an area which had not been militarized at all. Under the terms of the Outer Space Treaty, arms limitation provisions applicable to the moon and celestial bodies are very similar to those pertaining to Antarctica, but in space *per se*. However, only nuclear and other weapons of mass destruction are affected. These weapons may not be orbited around the earth and parties undertake not to 'station such weapons in outer space in any other manner.'[28] The Seabed Arms Control Treaty, like the Outer Space Treaty, only affects nuclear and other weapons of mass destruction, although it emerged from an international effort to 'unmilitarize' or reserve the seabed and ocean floor as a whole 'exclusively for peaceful purposes.'

Antarctic Treaty

The Antarctic Treaty, signed on 1 December 1959, was the first to set aside, at least temporarily, national claims in a new region of the earth. By the early 1950s seven nations claimed territorial sovereignty according to generally defined sectors over most of the Antarctic: Argentina, Australia, Chile, France, New Zealand, Norway, and the UK. However, other countries did not necessarily recognize these claims and the US, though the most active explorer in the region, made and recognized no claims. Further, Argentina, Chile, and the UK had overlapping claims and, while scientific co-operation flourished, potential political problems increased.

There was, however, a respite during the International Geophysical Year (IGY) between July 1957 and December 1958, when large-scale internationally co-ordinated research programs were undertaken in the area. On 2 May 1958 the US, after an extensive review of its Antarctic policy, sent identical notes to the eleven governments concerned to see if the region could be reserved for peaceful and scientific research, and to propose a conference at which a treaty could be concluded to ensure these results. The application of a number of principles – that Antarctica be used for peaceful purposes only and that freedom of scientific investigation in the area be maintained – was called for, and these principles were later reflected in the treaty.

All the states replied affirmatively, preparatory talks were held from June 1958 to mid-1959, and a conference was finally convened in Washington on 15 October 1959. In only six weeks, agreement was reached on a draft treaty based on previously prepared working papers, and it was signed on 1 December. The treaty entered into force on 23 June 1961 when the final ratifications of the twelve signatory states were deposited, and was to remain in effect for at least thirty years from that date.

In its first article the treaty provided that Antarctica would be used for peaceful purposes only. Article II provided for scientific investigation and for co-operation towards that end in the area. Article III provided for an exchange of information respecting plans for scientific programs to permit maximum efficiency, an exchange of scientific personnel between the various states, and free availability of any scientific observation or results obtained through research. All of this, of course, presupposed international co-operation without the pressing of any exclusive political claims in the region by any of the governments concerned.

A follow-up to the treaty is covered in article IX providing for periodic consultative meetings of representatives of contracting parties to consider and recommend to their governments 'measures in furtherance of the principles and objectives of the Treaty.' Measures so recommended once approved by all the participating governments come into effect throughout Antarctica, thus leading to the gradual development of a hitherto non-existent network of administrative arrangements and regulations. By the end of 1970 five consultative meetings had already been held, ensuring the continuing effect and efficacy of the treaty.

From an arms control and disarmament point of view, the most important article in the treaty is undoubtedly the fifth, which prohibits nuclear explosions in Antarctica and the disposal there of radioactive waste material while permitting the regulated use of nuclear energy for peaceful purposes. Article vii reinforces article v in providing for unlimited on-site inspection by observers of any contracting party to ensure the observance of the provisions of the treaty. For the purpose the observers are to have 'complete freedom of access at any time to any or all areas of Antarctica.' A number of inspections has in fact been carried out by the us and other countries under article vii.

For Canadians, it naturally comes to mind to what extent, if any, does the Antarctic Treaty have any relevance to our concerns in the Arctic. Admittedly, the problems of the Arctic and Antarctica are not entirely parallel. But Canada is indeed concerned to ensure peaceful uses of the Arctic and the furthering of scientific exploration there as well as the protection of the ecological environment within its area of jurisdiction. Moreover, the region is already used for military purposes under continental defence agreements with the us, and no doubt by the Soviet Union for their own reasons of defence. Demilitarization is more difficult than unmilitarization, just as prevention is easier than cure.

At an earlier stage, proposals were made for Arctic surveillance in the interests of reducing international tensions. The first was at the 1955 Summit Conference when President Eisenhower made an 'open skies' proposal, which suggested reciprocal aerial inspection of us and Soviet territory in order to guard against surprise attack.[29] In 1957 Prime Minister Diefenbaker suggested that a useful start at providing safeguards against surprise attack could be made in the Arctic area. He indicated that, provided the ussr would reciprocate, he would be agreeable to the inclusion of either the whole or a part of Canada in an equitable system of aerial inspection. He repeated this offer in May 1958 and February 1959. Secretary of State for External Affairs Howard Green again expressed willingness to 'throw open' the northern areas of Canada for establishment of a verified system of disarmament at the ENDC in March 1962.[30] The proposals of 1957 and 1958 for open skies and aerial inspection, particularly over the Arctic, were overtaken by the rapid development of spy satellites and long-range intercontinental ballistic missile delivery systems, which drastically reduced the usefulness of the surveillance of the Arctic as a safeguard against surprise attack.

The problem still has relevance to the possible verification of any international agreement dealing with delivery systems of shorter range and military activities located in the Arctic, including nuclear testing. It has been suggested by John Holmes, for instance, that control systems and radar networks might be erected in the Canadian Arctic to make possible a strategic arms limitation agreement with stronger 'teeth.'[31]

Any further examination of the Arctic problem in relation to arms control and disarmament would have to take into account factors such as a / Canadian sovereignty in the Arctic region, b / Canadian and allied defence interests, c / plans Canada might have for the economic development of the Arctic, as well as d / stimulating further momentum in international efforts to curtail the arms race.

Outer Space Treaty

Canada took the initiative in proposing a ban on placing weapons of mass destruction in outer space in the Ten Nation Committee on Disarmament at Geneva. The program for General and Complete Disarmament, put forward by the US on 27 June 1960,[32] had included such a ban, but Canada proposed this as a separate collateral measure in the absence of progress towards GCD. While in the end the successful conclusion of a complicated and technically proficient agreement was largely a matter of negotiation between the two superpowers. Canada played a catalytic role.

On 27 March 1962 the Honourable Howard Green stressed at Geneva that it was 'vital that agreement should be reached quickly at this conference on at least some measures which are not directly involved in the May negotiations – i.e. the negotiations on the treaty on general and complete disarmament.'[33] General Burns followed up this call with specific proposals concerning the reservation of outer space for peaceful purposes which would prohibit launching of mass destruction weapons into orbit and would provide for advance notification of the launchings of space vehicles and missiles. At the meeting of the General Assembly that year, the US declared itself willing to enter into such an agreement on outer space. In 1963 Mexico also followed up the question by submitting a draft treaty in the ENDC to ban nuclear and other mass destruction weapons from outer space. When the 1963 Assembly started work, the Soviet foreign minister suggested an agreement be reached between the Soviet Union and the US to ban weapons of mass destruction from outer space, and bilateral talks began. A joint draft emerged banning nuclear and other weapons of mass destruction from outer space, without calling for a halt to any space activities already underway. This draft was approved by the General Assembly on 17 October 1963, by acclamation, as Resolution 1884 (XVIII).

In it, the General Assembly solemnly called upon all states in effect to 'prevent the spread of the arms race to outer space.' The Committee on the Peaceful Uses of Outer Space and the General Assembly considered the question after that. In 1966 the US and USSR reached agreement on a treaty governing activities in outer space and the General Assembly commended the treaty in Resolution 2222 (XXI) which was unanimously adopted on 14 December 1966. On 24 January 1967 the treaty was opened for signature and entered into force on 10 October 1967.

Its principal disarmament provisions called for 1 / an undertaking by parties not to place in orbit around the earth any objects that carry nuclear weapons or any other kinds of weapons of mass destruction, install such weapons on celestial bodies, or station such weapons in outer space in any other manner (article IV); 2 / a prohibition of all military activities on the moon and other celestial bodies including establishment of military bases and weapon testing, but excepting the use of military personnel for scientific research or other peaceful purposes as well as the use of equipment needed for peaceful explorations (article IV); 3 / provisions that all stations, installations, equipment, and space vehicles on the moon and other celestial bodies would be open to representatives of parties 'on a basis of reciprocity' (article XII).

At the time of the conclusion of this treaty, landings on the moon, or the placing of space ships into orbit, may have seemed to be still in the realm of science fiction. The Canadian initiative under Mr Green led to an important preventive measure of unmilitarization, which has and will have increasingly far-reaching implications for peace as the moon and other celestial bodies are opened up to discovery and research.

Seabed Arms Control Treaty

The initiative for an arms control measure to apply to the seabed and deep ocean floor stemmed from a Maltese campaign at the United Nations between 1966 and 1968 calling for international action to preserve the seabed and ocean floor exclusively for peaceful purposes. This idea was reflected in the Soviet disarmament memorandum of 1 July 1968, which included a proposal for the demilitarization of the seabed and ocean floor upon which the USSR government considered action should be taken.[34] Actual negotiations began on 18 March 1969 with the tabling of a Soviet draft treaty for the complete demilitarization of the seabed and ocean floor.[35] The comprehensive scope of the treaty had a superficial attractiveness but, considering that all the seas and oceans are fully exploited for military purposes, both on the surface and by submarines, the sweeping scope of the Soviet draft posed serious defence and verification problems. The US draft on the other hand suggested that any agreement should be limited specifically to banning the emplacement of nuclear weapons and other weapons of mass destruction on the seabed and ocean floor.[36] It provided for a defensive zone for coastal states of three miles and limited verification rights.

Canada urged that any seabed arms control treaty should be specific as to what was to be prohibited, how compliance was to be verified, and how the rights of coastal states should be protected. On 13 May 1969 I outlined Canadian views on the three most important matters which would obviously be at issue: the scope of the treaty, its geographical limits, and the question of verification.[37] The Canadian statement suggested that the CCD explore the possibility of extending the ban to cover not only nuclear weapons and other weapons of mass destruction, but also all weapons, military activities, and undersea bases or fortifications designed for military action against the territory, territorial sea, or air space of another state, but stopping short of the complete demilitarization requested by the USSR in order to provide for defensive sensing devices required for protection against submarines. With regard to the geographical limits, Canada suggested a defensive zone of two hundred miles, in which only the coastal state would be allowed to undertake or authorize military activities which were not prohibited under the treaty. This suggestion obviated the potential concern of a coastal state at seeing other states undertake purportedly defensive activities in areas adjacent to its own coast. With respect to verification, Canada rejected the idea of reciprocity put forward as a basic principle in the US and Soviet drafts and contended instead that 'the verification procedure will need to have other characteristics (i.e. than reciprocity) in order to accommodate states which may feel threatened and allow them in some way to participate in the inspection procedures.'

Discussions during the summer and autumn of 1969 brought to light differences of view over the various issues covered in the two drafts. Although many delegations expressed interest in the Canadian ideas regarding a broader scope and defined prohibitions, the USSR in a sudden turnabout accepted the more restricted US position of limiting the prohibition to nuclear weapons and other weapons of mass destruction. In return for this Soviet concession, the defensive zone was agreed by the two co-chairmen to extend to twelve miles. These changes were reflected in a joint draft treaty submitted by the US and the USSR on 7 October 1969.[38]

Criticism of the joint draft then focused primarily on the restricted verification article, which in the joint co-chairmen's draft was based on the already existing rights of observation on the high seas and of consultation among parties, making no special concession to the rights of coastal states. Although the article also granted the right of parties to bilateral assistance in carrying out verification and recognized the ultimate right of parties to refer the matter to the Security Council, it did not lay down procedures by which all parties could obtain satisfaction in the event of a suspected violation.

In the expectation that this first joint draft would be further revised before submission to the xxivth UN General Assembly, the Canadian delegation argued, with support from virtually all aligned members and some of our NATO allies, in favour of a more thorough and equitable verification article. Despite obvious acceptance by the majority of the CCD members of the fact that any treaty without a fair and balanced verification article would have difficulty in obtaining broad support at the UN General Assembly, the co-chairmen at first appeared unwilling to compromise on this issue.

As a result, in close consultation with a number of other delegations from all political blocs represented in the CCD, the Canadian delegation developed and tabled on 9 October 1969 a working paper (CCD/270) outlining what a balanced verification article should contain. In introducing this working paper, I described it as a 'check list of the criteria required to give meaning for all parties to the phrase "right to verify." '[39] The verification system proposed involved specifying a step-by-step procedure to resolve doubts concerning compliance with the treaty, granting the right of all states to apply for assistance through the secretary general, and (perhaps most important in terms of Canadian national interests) providing detailed clauses to protect as fully as possible the rights of coastal states over their continental shelves. There was keen disappointment among CCD members when the co-chairmen, on 30 October, tabled a revised joint draft which, despite improvements on some articles, left the verification article unchanged. Support for the Canadian concept of verification including the rights of coastal states was widespread at the CCD, at the UN seabed Committee which was meeting concurrently, as well as in the General Assembly.

Discussion at the xxivth session of the General Assembly in 1969 also focused on two other problems which had been raised during CCD discussions but which had not been resoved in the co-chairmen's joint drafts. The first had been put up initially by Argentina and concerned the concept of delineating the geographical limits of the seabed arms control treaty, by using the language and systems set out in the 1958 Geneva Convention on the Territorial Waters and Contiguous Zone.[40] The other point, raised initially by Sweden, concerned the obligation to be assumed by the parties to undertake further negotiations leading to the complete demilitarization of the seabed.[41] Despite concentrated attention on these three specific problems, agreement proved impossible during the Fourteenth Session, and the treaty was referred back to Geneva for discussion during the 1970 session of the CCD.

As a basis for this new discussion at Geneva, the co-chairmen submitted a second revision of their joint draft which, while incorporating the Argentine amendment and most of the content of the Canadian working paper, omitted the Canadian proposal that parties had the right to seek international good offices, including those of the UN secretary-general, in the process of verification.[42]

As the summer session of the CCD drew to a close, the non-aligned delegations who had supported the Canadian verification proposal presented a working paper containing new compromise wording on the two remaining issues: the commitment to continue disarmament negotiations regarding the seabed, and the verification procedures. The co-chairmen accepted the compromise wording with minor revisions and a paragraph was added to the verification article which provided for international assistance in the verification procedure 'through appropriate international procedures within the framework of the United Nations and in accordance with its Charter.'

The third revised version of the draft treaty, containing the compromise verification proposal laboriously negotiated on the basis of the Canadian working paper, was presented to the Fifteenth Session of the UN General Assembly in November 1970. Canada co-sponsored the resolution commending this treaty for signature and was one of the original signatories when the treaty was opened for signature early in 1971. The problem of reserving the seabed and ocean floor 'exclusively for peaceful purposes,' or at least of seeking additional arms control measures for the seabed, remains on the agenda of the Geneva Conference as unfinished business.

Chemical and biological weapons

Canada, if only because of the casualties, albeit terrible, suffered from gas attacks by Canadian soldiers in World War I, has had an interest in seeking to prevent the use of CBW in warfare from the start of the efforts to control this type of weapon of mass destruction. Thus Canada was a signatory of the Geneva Protocol of 1925. After World War II, in its very first resolution on disarmament which Canada supported, the United Nations called for the elimination not only of atomic weapons, but also of 'all other major weapons adaptable now and in the future to mass destruction.'[43] The General Assembly no doubt had in mind the scientific possibilities for the improvement of chemical and bacteriological methods of warfare, building on the protocol 'prohibiting the use in war of asphyxiating, poisonous or other gases and of bacteriological methods of warfare,' which had been signed in Geneva in 1925.

At the Geneva Disarmament Conference, the question of CBW was really considered first in the GCD context. In 1961 the 'joint statement of agreed principles for disarmament negotiations,' agreed to by the US and adopted by the General Assembly, decided that a program for GCD should contain provisions for the 'elimination of all stockpiles of nuclear, chemical, bacteriological and other weapons of mass destruction, and the cessation of production of such weapons.'[44] The two draft GCD treaties submitted by the USSR and the US in March and April 1962 both contained provisions for the elimination of CBW. As a comprehensive agreement on GCD became increasingly unlikely, emphasis was placed on dealing with CBW as one of the collateral measures to be negotiated.

In fact, the delegation of the United Kingdom took the initiative in opening discussions on this issue by tabling a working paper (ENDC/231), asserting at the same time that the problem would be more manageable if chemical and biological weapons were dealt with separately.[45] The UK proposed, in order to 'supplement not supersede' the general protocol, the early conclusion of a new convention on microbiological weapons, the use of which had never been established but which had potential in warfare more terrible than chemical weapons.

In the introduction to his annual report on the organization's work for 1967–8, the UN secretary general pointed out that during the twenty-three years of the UN's existence, there had never been a thorough discussion in any UN organ of the problems posed by CBW, or any detailed study of them.[46] He welcomed a recommendation from the ENDC to the General Assembly that he appoint a group of experts to study the effects of the possible use of chemical and bacteriological methods of warfare. Canada, and initially nine other states, co-sponsored a draft resolution submitted to the Twenty-third General Assembly under the item 'Question of General and Complete Disarmament' that requested such a report to be prepared and submitted to the ENCD if possible by 1 July 1969. Consultant experts appointed by the secretary general were given the task of surveying the entire subject of CBW from a scientific and technical viewpoint in order to place modern chemical and bacteriological weapons in proper perspective. Canada took part in the study through the participation of a noted physiologist, Dr M. McPhail of the Department of National Defence.

The experts' report pointed out that the potential for developing an armoury of chemical and bacteriological weapons had grown considerably in recent years in terms not only of numbers but also of toxicity and diversity of effects. The experts concluded that 'were these weapons ever to be used on a large scale in war, no one could predict how enduring the effects would be and how they would affect the structure of society and the environment in which we live. This overriding danger would apply as much to the country which initiated the use of these weapons.'[47] Another important conclusion was that 'the prospects for general and complete disarmament under effective international control, and hence for peace throughout the world, would brighten significantly if the development, production and stockpiling of chemical and bacteriological (biological) agents intended for purposes of war were to end and if they were eliminated from all military arsenal.'

In a foreword to the experts' report, the secretary general urged the members of the UN:

1 To renew the appeal to all States to accede to the Geneva Protocol of 1925;
2 To make a clear affirmation that the prohibition contained in the Protocol applies to the use in war of all chemical, bacteriological and biological agents (including tear gas and other harassing agents) which now exist or which may be developed in the future;
3 To call upon all countries to reach agreement to halt the development, production and stockpiling of all chemical and bacteriological (biological) agents for purposes of war and to achieve their effective elimination from the arsenal of weapons.

These recommendations were accepted by a majority of the General Assembly and became the basis for the ensuing work in this field.

On 1 July 1969 the secretary general transmitted the experts' report to the General Assembly to the Security Council, as well as to the governments represented on the Geneva Disarmament Conference. This launched detailed negotiations on the issue in the ENDC. The United Kingdom tabled a draft Biological Warfare Convention which Canada supported in principle. At the same time, the Canadian delegation submitted a working paper proposing that detailed examination of the British draft should go hand in hand with consideration of the whole problem of chemical as well as biological weapons.

The Twenty-fourth General Assembly in 1969 had three basic documents before it: the secretary general's report; the CCD report including the UK draft treaty; and a draft treaty submitted by the nine communist member states, as co-sponsors, on the prohibition of development, production, and stockpiling of CBW.[48] The co-sponsors stressed the comprehensive nature of their draft and the fact that international control would amount to 'intrusion' of foreign personnel owing to its necessary complexity. The General Assembly adopted a resolution based on the Canadian working paper, which took note of the UK and Soviet draft conventions and called on the CCD to give urgent consideration to reaching agreement on the prohibition of chemical and bacteriological weapons.

The twelve non-aligned members of the CCD, however, submitted a draft resolution interpreting the Geneva Protocol, by which the Assembly declared as contrary to the generally recognized rules of international law as embodied in the Geneva Protocol the use in international armed conflicts of any chemical and bacteriological agents of warfare, whatsoever.[49] Certain governments, including the Canadian, expressed doubt about the propriety of the General Assembly undertaking to interpret the Geneva Protocol, whose ambiguity had been recognized since 1925, without a consensus of all the signatories of that Protocol. Nevertheless, the draft resolution was adopted by the Assembly by an overwhelming majority.

In an effort to work towards a consensus Canada, in a declaration in March 1970, unconditionally renounced the possession, development, production, or acquisition, of biological weapons, and the possession, production, acquisition, or use of chemical agents except in the event that these are used first against Canada or its allies (a reservation Canada and most other countries attached to their ratification of the Geneva Protocol).[50] Canada did not, however, include in its commitment tear gas and other crowd and riot control agents (for purposes of warfare), pending 'further studies.'

Soviet insistence on a comprehensive banning of chemical and bacteriological weapons, together with their rejection of inspection other than by national means, held up progress until recently when, in a sudden volte-face, the Soviet delegation tabled a draft convention covering the prohibition of biological agents of warfare only. Despite the fact that several non-aligned countries in Geneva were left disconcerted, this turnabout by the Soviet government broke the deadlock, and a treaty banning the development, production, and stockpiling, of Bacteriological (Biological) and Toxic weapons and on their destruction was concluded in 1971.

Indeed to the extent that existing stockpiles of bacteriological and biological weapons would be destroyed under a system of international verification, this treaty emerged as the first actual disarmament treaty – in the sense of the elimination of existing weapons – which has resulted from the Geneva Conference. Canada has supported the UK draft treaty on biological warfare from the start and we continue to consider that even a convention banning weapons that are not likely to be used will, once in force, add significantly to international law in the field of disarmament. At the same time we have urged continued efforts to resolve the problem of an international ban on chemical weapons, taking into account that many of the chemical components are in current use in industry and agriculture and that the verification of compliance with such a ban presents a particularly difficult problem.

CONCLUSIONS

If we are to find our way around in and, it is to be hoped, out of the maze comprising the whole complex of interlocking arms control and disarmament arrangements described in the preceding pages, it is essential to have our eyes turned to some guiding light, as well as to have our feet firmly planted on the ground. The latter means being grounded in an analysis both of the underlying world politics and their perspectives, as well as of strategy and current academic arms control theories; the former visualizing not only the ideal but what is realizable and vital for human survival in the atomic age.

My conclusions take the form mainly of questions, both because any answers can be no better than plausible guesses, and because this is a time for questioning – 'those obstinate questionings' Wordsworth wrote about:

> Of sense and outward things,
> Fallings from us, vanishings;
> Blank misgivings of a creature
> Moving about in worlds not realized.[51]

To the extent that the questionings about arms control and disarmament primarily involve international politics and can be illuminated by experience, I feel entitled to offer some conclusions, however tentative; legal aspects of arms control and disarmament mainly relate to the form of the agreements whether treaty, convention, or protocol, and in this field I claim strictly amateur status and prefer to refrain from comment.

Unrealized, and unrealizable, is a warless world in which no armaments or armed forces would be required, because it would be necessary to assume a world in which all national conflicts had been eliminated. But is it not possible to assume, as an objective, an international system of peace and security which could ensure equal protection of all states and their legitimate rights, and an impartial world authority directed by law and devoted to justice? It is necessary at least to conclude that any serious consideration of general and complete disarmament, which is the ultimate objective of all disarmament efforts, leads to a direct confrontation of the problem of world government and the, as yet unrealized, potential of the United Nations. Total nuclear disarmament probably carries the same implications.

On the other hand, the kind of limited partial and collateral measures considered above, and negotiated in the sixties, implies a continuation in some ways of the system of a bipolar world and superpower hegemony which we have been living with in the past quarter of a century. This has its advantages as well as its disadvantages. For, undoubtedly, the comparative stability of superpower relationships has given relative freedom to middle powers like Canada. But the unequal growth of technology and of population, as well as the awakening of Asia and Africa to sovereignty, have brought about an unprecedented change in the perspectives of world politics.

Nor should it be overlooked that some consider that the carefully fostered doctrine of nuclear deterrence, usually justified in terms of its necessity in a bipolar world and of the stability of the system, has its flaws. It is true that the world has endured for twenty-five years without the explosion of any nuclear weapons in war – but then the US has had a wide nuclear superiority over its nearest rival and has been content with the maintenance of the status quo. However, the nuclear balance between the superpowers, far from being a static concept, is one of precarious and ever-changing balance, a balance furthermore which might be irrevocably disturbed by any of a number of developments that are by no means unlikely to occur, such as some substantial advance in weapons technology, or gross political miscalculation, to say nothing of just accident or escalation of some local conflict. The danger is always present of an unstable status quo where rivals seek to gain nuclear superiority, particularly regarding their first-strike capability. Moreover, by far the most effective way to disturb what ever balance now exists, or that may emerge from SALT, would be to encourage or condone the emergence of new nuclear powers with primitive delivery systems highly vulnerable to pre-emptive attack and manipulated by governments often engaged in charged unneighbourly disputes.

Few would dispute that bipolarity is on its way out for various reasons. Bipolarity risks nuclear confrontation between the superpowers; it threatens hegemony for others. As President Nixon said in his inaugural address on 20 January 1969, 'the balance of nuclear power has placed a premium on negotiation rather than confrontation.' Since then, American reaction to the continuing ordeal of the war in Vietnam, has inclined the US towards retrenchment of its global power commitments and a resentment of foreign entanglements where rivals might perceive an incentive to launch a first strike. At the same time the USSR, faced with the growing fragmentation of the communist movement and a continuing upsurge of nationalism among its client states, has also shown signs of a continuing scaling down of its universal claims in favour of more limited and more enforceable spheres of influence under the Brezhnev doctrine.

While the ideological rivalry between the superpowers obviously persists, the US and USSR have been seeking stabilization not only through SALT but also by concurrently exploring the possibilities of mutually balanced force reductions in Europe between NATO and the Warsaw Pact. The two powers have been seeking accommodation in international politics too; the agreement on West Berlin being possibly a first instalment towards a settlement in Europe. The political alignments of the cold war, like the cold war itself, are loosening and breaking up. Indeed the cold war is finished; and with it the easy acknowledgment of world 'leadership' of the US and the USSR respectively as the champions on either side.

It is against this perspective of a changing relationship of the superpowers, based on a web of rival and collaborative interests, that China is seen emerging on the world scene. There are also western Europe, in the process of becoming further strengthened by the enlargement of the EEC and seeking a more active and independent role in world affairs through unification, and Japan, second only to the US in economic power. Japan has not yet ratified the Non-Proliferation Treaty; nor for that matter have several other near-nuclear states: the Federal Republic of Germany, India, Pakistan, Australia, Argentina, Brazil, Israel, or South Africa.

But have we survived the bipolarity of the cold war only to enter into an era of even greater uncertainty, while a growing number of great powers dispute for world control, and a growing number of middle or small powers challenge their hegemony with the ability to threaten the triggering of a nuclear holocaust over their national claims or disputes?

The first and obvious response is to strengthen the only world authority which now exists, the United Nations, and to do everything possible to seek the sort of international agreements that not only will prevent the further elaboration and spread of nuclear weapons but would help in constructing an international system in which the ineradicable knowledge of the atomic age can be put to use for peaceful purposes only, assuming that this means more than the 'peaceful' role played by nuclear weapons in deterrence of war.

There is an interrelationship between these two purposes. There are now five nuclear weapon powers: US, USSR, the People's Republic of China, France, and the United Kingdom. These are the same powers which are represented as Permanent Members of the United Nations Security Council. This coincidence provides a logical stage at which to call a halt to the spread of nuclear weapons and create a kind of watershed of non-proliferation. It also provides a certain logical opportunity to have the Permanent Members of the Council – acting collectively as they should – to start discharging their special responsibilities for the maintenance of international peace and security conferred upon the council under article 24 of the United Nations Charter. This should include finding a way of arresting the proliferation of nuclear weapons, a matter of profound importance to the maintenance of international peace and security, as well as of carrying out the day-to-day fire-brigade type of duties the council is called upon to perform in current international disputes.

The most important first step is to halt what is called the 'vertical proliferation' of nuclear weapons, that is, to stop the further sophistication, accumulation, and deployment of nuclear weapons by the nuclear powers. The cessation of the nuclear arms race may be a condition for preventing the 'horizontal proliferation' of nuclear weapons, that is, their spread to additional countries. Indeed something of the sort is implicit in the Brezhnev proposal for a conference of the five nuclear weapons powers which has been turned down by China. But it might be a different matter if it were presented, not as a privileged invitation from one of the superpowers to join a special meeting of the 'Nuclear Club,' but as the fulfilment of obligations among equals, as members of the Security Council. One of the first items for consideration would presumably have to be the question of China's accession to or association with such arms control and disarmament agreements that already exist.

It is surely in the interest of all the nuclear weapons powers to make the Non-Proliferation Treaty work. The success of the effort, however, also depends on the attitude of the non-nuclear weapons powers; for non-proliferation is really a synonym for the non-acquisition of nuclear weapons. Here Canada is certainly in a position to influence the outcome, both by the fact of Canada's example and as a supplier of nuclear power plants to a number of countries. Everybody knows that Canada, although possessing the scientific and technological basis for a nuclear weapons program from the earliest days, has deliberately foregone the nuclear option.

The advantages of non-proliferation from the standpoint of the near-nuclear powers may well outweigh the advantages of acquiring nuclear weapons. That is probably why the situation is by no means hopeless. While it used to be said of a bayonet, that you can do anything with it but sit on it, there is nothing you can do with atomic bombs, once you have acquired them, but sit on them. For to use them against another power similarly armed risks instant retaliation and suicide or, if used against a non-nuclear power, the intervention of a more powerful nuclear adversary. A near-nuclear power is in fact in its strongest bargaining position before taking up the nuclear option; afterwards it becomes merely the smallest and weakest member of the nuclear club.

There is, admittedly, a number of serious political concerns that have to be met among the near-nuclear powers, which seem to be hovering on the brink of 'going nuclear,' in which the world community can help: the critical state of the relations between India and Pakistan, the mutual concerns of Israel and her Arab neighbours which pose a threat to peace and security in the Middle East, and the problems of South Africa caused by her policy of apartheid and its repercussions on black Africa. But none of these problems is likely to be brought nearer to solution by the acquisition of nuclear weapons by one side or the other.

There are also concerns of an economic and technological nature among the non-nuclear powers which have to be met. In the atomic age it is natural that nations should seek to augment, from nuclear power, their sources of energy required for industrialization and thus accelerate their development. Here safeguard regulations, which are seen to be fair and equal in their application, can help and that is precisely what is being negotiated under the auspices of the International Atomic Energy Agency in Vienna.

I should like to suggest here that, peering down the long dark tunnel of negotiations which, it seems, we must follow in trying to halt the arms race, our way will be illuminated if, in our future efforts, we keep in mind the following lights or objectives. First, we take advantage of the fact that for the first time all five leading military powers in the world are permanent members of the Security Council. We should impress upon them their responsibilities to strengthen the Non-Proliferation Treaty through adopting restraints *inter se* on the future development and deployment of stockpiles of nuclear weapons, reporting the results to the General Assembly under article 24(3) of the UN Charter. Second, we strengthen the complex of interlocking arms control and disarmament arrangements by seeking the accession or association of China and France to such arms control and disarmament agreements as have already been concluded. Third, in having China and France participate in the Geneva Conference on Disarmament, or some other negotiating forum, as equal members with the other permanent members of the Security Council, we focus particularly on a halt in the nuclear arms race, a comprehensive test ban, and on nuclear-free zones, as well as on the completion of the ban on chemical warfare. Fourth, we recognize that the entry of China into the world community and the increasing Sino-American dialogue, together with the emergence of Japan as an economic power of prime importance, and with the movement in western Europe towards greater unity and coherence, have marked the replacement of a bipolar balance by a multiple power balance. Fifth, we seek to strengthen the NPT through early negotiation of safeguard agreements with more of the countries having or embarking on nuclear power programs, including nuclear weapon states, in order that NPT safeguards are implemented on a fair and equitable basis.

These lights, admittedly, are no stars. But at least they make a start in the process of adjustment away from bipolarity. They are all attainable objectives, moreover, which could take us through the period of transition into which we are now going, with great power relationships thrown into the melting pot, and with history accelerating faster than anyone seems able to control.

At a time when it is science and technology that set the pace, it seems appropriate to start thinking hard about trying to match that progress in human affairs and institutions. What seems to be involved is a revolution in political thought – still strongly influenced by nineteenth century and even earlier concepts – given the scientific revolution which seems to have taken all governments largely by surprise, confronted as they are by such symptoms as unemployment, pollution, urban degradation, as well as an arms race which absorbs scarce resources – some $200 billion (US) a year.

A quarter of a century ago, Albert Einstein had already pointed out that the settlement of disputes by war had become incompatible with survival in the atomic age: 'The release of atomic energy has created a new world in which old ways of thinking, that include old diplomatic conventions and balance-of-power politics, have become utterly meaningless. Mankind must give up war in the atomic era. What is at stake is the life or death of humanity.' Words which governments everywhere had better heed.

Some hard thinking is going on in Canada. But even more research is required if the thinking is to lead to action. It will be necessary to organize and utilize all available intellectual resources, including the newly founded private Political Research Institute, the CIIA and its Commission for Strategic Studies, the universities, lawyers, scientists and scholars, as well as the armed and public services. For, since the problems are interdisciplinary, touching as they do international politics, law, military strategy, science, technology, as well as public administration, the solutions have to be sought on an interdisciplinary basis, too. The costs of the continuing arms race in terms of both human and material resources, on the national and international scale, are staggering. Solutions to the problems of population, poverty, pollution, and all the other manifold questions of modern society are intimately interlinked with questions of the arms race, massive military expenditures, and the overall state of international peace and security.

One suggestion is that a panel of Canadians, each eminent in his or her speciality, might be set up to ask the right questions, for as Disraeli said: 'Ignorance never settles a question.' Under this panel, a director of research, assisted by a small staff, would set individuals or teams to work finding possible answers. These in due course, after consideration by the panel, would be submitted to the government and ultimately to the public, so as to contribute to the formulation of a broad consensus on these issues, which so profoundly affect our lives; particularly is this so, if something seriously goes wrong, as it has on a global scale twice in our lifetime.

For purposes of illustration, here in specific form is the basic approach and some of the kinds of questions that might be worth studying in the light of the discussion in this article. In considering the alternatives which Canada should adopt in future arms control and disarmament negotiations, the following components of Canadian interest would have to be considered as criteria: a / their impact on broader Canadian foreign policy objectives as already defined in *Foreign Policy for Canadians*;[52] b / their relationship to existing and possible future arms control and disarmament agreements, as well as defence arrangements; c / ethical and moral considerations; d / the military and economic consequences of alternative policies.

The central problem remains one of trying to bring atomic energy under control, to ensure its use for peaceful purposes only, and to prevent its use for military purposes. There are admittedly many vital questions to be examined and resolved if the threat of atomic catastrophe is to be lifted from mankind, as well as the threat of the possible use of other weapons of mass destruction, such as chemical warfare, and the possibility of the escalation of local conflicts in which conventional arms are the means of warfare.

1 Should the use of nuclear weapon be banned as the use of chemical and bacteriological weapons was banned by the Geneva Protocol of 1925?

2 How can non-nuclear weapons states, non-parties to the NPT, be persuaded to accept the same safeguards developed by the IAEA Safeguards Committee for non-nuclear weapons states that sign the treaty. (Under article 3(1) safeguards are designed to give assurance that a portion of the fissionable material required for domestic nuclear power reactors is not diverted to military purposes.)

3 What is to be done with existing stockpiles and to ensure the cut-off and disposal of the surplus of fissionable material now being employed for bomb-making?

4 Pending the reduction and elimination of nuclear weapons, what further restraints and disciplines can be devised so that the credibility of the nuclear strategic balance can be accompanied by a greater assurance that there will not be a nuclear war (granted that for the time being it is to SALT that we look for an answer)?

5 What new international institutions or world authority, including the strengthening of the United Nations, are required to give effect to the will of people everywhere that they should not continue to live under the threat of atomic annihilation?

6 How can non-proliferation of nuclear weapons among presently non-nuclear countries be made effective, while nuclear powers continue to retain and augment their weapons for deterrence and no adequate system of peacekeeping and enforcement exists for the rest of the world?

7 What safeguards can be devised of a national and international character to prevent the diversion of chemicals in current industrial or agricultural use to military purposes, for incorporation in weapons of mass destruction?

8 What should Canada's contribution be to the defence of the European region of our NATO alliance in the event of a new equilibrium emerging there as a result of agreement on mutual and balanced force reductions?

9 What measures of conventional disarmament, regional or global, should or could Canada propose?

10 What feasible and desirable measures of arms control and disarmament could be proposed for the Arctic region consistent with the maintenance of a military equilibrium between the US and the USSR?

Thus, peering into the near future, we can discern a vital period of transition ahead, in institutions as well as policies, for which Canadians need to prepare themselves. For one thing is sure – modern man, as population pressures increase at an alarming rate, in relation to resources, armed as he is with atomic and other weapons of mass destruction, has the capability of making himself obsolete in a flash, unless he reorganizes his needs and priorities, as well as his loyalties, so as to permit the settlement of international conflicts without resort to weapons of mass destruction.

Certainly more is necessary than is being done now to rethink and adapt human institutions and to develop and apply international law to international problems if we are to deal adequately with the enormous powers of destruction which modern science and technology have placed at our disposal. Especially is progress in arms control and disarmament important, in an age where nationalism and self-determination are increasingly dominant in the motivation of governments and peoples, and the harmonization of actions of states through the United Nations is still in such a rudimentary stage of development.

However, as President Kennedy said: 'We prefer world law, in the age of self-determination, to world war in the age of mass extermination.' Obviously Canadians will opt for this rational choice, but the development of world law and authority will take years. There is no excuse, in face of the perspectives before us, to waste any time.

NOTES

1 As in U.N. GA Res. 41 (I) 14 December 1946.
2 8 *Documents on American Foreign Relations, 1945–46* (1947) 547.
3 F.H. Soward, 4 *Canada in World Affairs: 1944–1946* (1950) 165.
4 AEC 'In the Matter of J. Robert Oppenheimer,' transcript of Hearing before Personnel Security Board (1954) 38–9.
5 *Official Records of the Atomic Energy Commission* (1946) 7.
6 Empire Club Speech, November 1969 in *Empire Club Addresses, 1969/1970* (1971).
7 U.N. GA Res 1378 (XIV), 20 November 1959.
8 UN, *The United Nations and Disarmament, 1945–1970* (1970).
9 ENDC/PV 30, 3 May 1962.
10 Official Records of the Disarmament Commission, Supplement for 1966, Doc DC/229.
11 Official Records of the Disarmament Commission, Supplement for January 1961 to December 1962, Doc DC/203, annex 1, section J (ENDC/28).
12 ENDC/PV 24.
13 Official Records of the Disarmament Commission, Supplement for January 1961 to December 1962, Doc DC/205, annex 1, section O (ENDC/58).
14 ENDC/PV 90.
15 Official Records of the Disarmament Commission, Supplement for January to

December 1963, Doc DC/208, annex 1, section A (ENDC/PV 94).
16 The Plan in elaborated form was circulated by the Poles on 14 February 1958 to Canada, the US, UK, France, Czecholsavakia, West and East Germany, Belgium, Denmark, and USSR.
17 U.N. GA Res 1380 (XIV), 20 November 1959, based largely on Irish efforts.
18 U.N. GA Res 1576 (XV), 20 December 1960.
19 U.N. GA Res 1665 (XVI), 4 December 1961, and Res 1664 (XVI), 4 December 1961 (Swedish draft).
20 ENDC/PV 357.
21 Official Records of the Disarmament Commission, Supplement for 1967 and 1968, Doc DC/230 and add 1, annex IV, ENDC/192 and ENDC/193.
22 ENDC/PV 329.
23 Official Records of the Disarmament Commission, Supplement for January to December 1965, Doc DC/227, annex 1, ENDC/154.
24 ENDC/PV 224.
25 ENDC/PV 247.
26 Official Records of the Disarmament Commission, Supplement for 1967 and 1968, Doc DC/231, annex 1, ENDC/PV 232.
27 CCD/PV 507.
28 Treaty on Principles governing the Activities

of States in the Exploration and Use of Outer Space, including the Moon and Other Celestial Bodies; signed 27 January 1967. *The United Nations and Disarmament, 1945-1970, supra* note 17, at 453–8.

29 A plan based on this proposal was presented by the US in August 1955, to the Five Power Sub-Committee of the Disarmament Commission. Official Records of the Disarmament Commission, Supplement for April to December 1955, Doc DC/71, annex 20 (DC/SC.1/31).

30 ENDC/PV4, 19 March 1962.

31 Before the External Affairs Committee, 4 November 1969.

32 Official Records of the Disarmament Commission, Supplement for January to December 1960, Doc DC/154.

33 ENDC/PV10.

34 Official Records of the Disarmament Commission, Supplement for 1967 and 1968, Doc DC/231, annex 1, ENDC/227 submitted to the ENDC on 16 June 1968.

35 Doc DC/232, annex C, ENDC/240.

36 Ibid, ENDC/249 22 May.

37 ENDC/PV 410.

38 Doc DC/232, annex C, CCD/269.

39 CCD/PV 441.

40 Doc A/c.1/997.

41 Doc A/c.1/994.

42 CCD/269/Rev.2 of 23 April 1970.

43 U.N. CA Res 41(I), 14 December 1946, adopted unanimously.

44 See *supra*, at 698.

45 Working Paper on Microbiological Warfare, ENDC/231 6 August 1968.

46 *The United Nations and Disarmament 1945 to 1970, supra* note 17, at 359–60.

47 Ibid, 363.

48 U.N. GA Doc A/7655.

49 Doc A/7890, paragraph 11.

50 CCD/PV 460, 24 March 1970.

51 'Intimations of Immortality.'

52 Department of External Affairs, *Foreign Policy for Canadians* (1970).

IVAN BERNIER

29/La Réglementation canadienne en matière de commerce et de douanes[*]

Depuis 1946 la politique commerciale du Canada semble caractérisée d'abord et avant tout par une volonté nette de multilatéralisation des échanges économiques.[1] Une telle attitude ressort nettement de la participation active du Canada au sein du GATT, des déclarations officielles de ses dirigeants ainsi que des nombreux traités de commerce signés depuis 1946.[2] Mais parallèlement à cette volonté de multilatéralisation des échanges économiques, et l'expliquant dans une grande mesure, existe aussi une volonté d'indépendance nationale. Le Canada, de par sa situation géographique, fait face à un délicat problème qui est celui de commercer avec un géant économique sans en même temps se trouver absorbé par ce dernier. Dans un discours prononcé à Ottawa le 20 février 1969, le secrétaire d'état aux affaires extérieures, M Mitchell Sharp, exprimait ainsi cette double préoccupation: 'Dans le domaine économique, il y a longtemps que le Canada aborde les problèmes du commerce mondial sous l'angle multilatéral ... Nous avons reconnu que, vu le poids accablant de nos liens économiques avec les Etats-Unis, il est de notre intérêt, et de celui de la communauté internationale dans son ensemble, de favoriser la création d'un régime multilatéral libéralisé de commerce mondial plutôt qu'un régime autarcique ou de blocs.'[3]

Toutefois, cette volonté d'indépendance nationale, qui incite le Canada à diversifier ses courants d'échanges commerciaux afin de trouver de nouveaux débouchés à ses produits primaires aussi bien que secondaires, lui impose aussi l'obligation de rationaliser sa production afin de mieux soutenir la concurrence étrangère. Car s'il désire obtenir de meilleures conditions de commerce sur les marchés extérieurs, le Canada doit lui-même ouvrir son marché intérieur. Or, ce processus de rationalisation de la production canadienne ne peut être réalisé qu'à long terme. Ainsi que le déclarait le ministre des finances du Canada, M Benson, lors d'un discours prononcé devant l'Association des Importateurs Canadiens réunis à Toronto le 24 mars 1971: 'Si la réadaptation doit se produire trop rapidement ou sur une trop grande échelle, il peut en résulter des difficultés considérables. La réadaptation signifie souvent fermer des usines pour en construire des nouvelles qui exerceront leurs activités en d'autres domaines et d'autres endroits. A court terme, il existe une

---

[*]La présente étude, préparée pour janvier 1972, ne tient malheureusement pas compte de certains développements qui se sont produits depuis. De plus, elle doit être complétée par deux monographies importantes entreprises sous les auspices du Canadian Economic Policy Committee of the Private Planning Association of Canada, soit: Klaus Stegeman, *Canadian Non-Tariff Barriers to Trade* (1973) et Rodney de C. Grey, *The Development of the Canadian Anti-dumping System* (1973).

limite à la capacité de l'économie de recycler de nombreux travailleurs et de les réintégrer.'[4] C'est donc dire que le Canada ne peut aborder le problème de la libéralisation des échanges commerciaux avec les pays étrangers sans une grande prudence. Comment il a procédé, depuis 1946, pour arriver à ses fins, c'est ce qui fait l'objet du présent chapitre.

LA STRUCTURE TARIFAIRE DU CANADA

Aperçu général du tarif des douanes

'Facilement l'un des plus complexes du monde,'[5] le tarif douanier canadien se présente à première vue sous la forme de trois listes distinctes, la première concernant les produits frappés de droits et produits admis en franchise, la deuxième les produits admis au bénéfice du drawback pour consommation intérieure, et la troisième les produits prohibés.

Les produits frappés de droits ou admis en franchise
Pour chacun des produits énumérés dans la liste A, soit ceux frappés de droits ou admis en franchise, trois taux sont prévus: le taux de préférence britannique, le taux de la nation la plus favorisée, et le taux général. La nomenclature des différents produits prévoit en outre, pour certains d'entre eux, l'existence d'un taux dit du GATT ou d'un taux spécial résultant d'accords préférentiels avec certains pays. C'est ainsi que sous le numéro tarifaire 810-1 (jambon en boîte), on trouve les cinq taux suivants: 1 / taux de préférence britannique, 15 pour cent; 2 / taux de la nation la plus favorisée, 22$^1/_2$ pour cent; 3 / taux général, 35 pour cent; 4 / taux du GATT, 20 pour cent; 5 / taux prévu par l'accord commercial avec la Nouvelle Zélande, en franchise.

Depuis 1946 le Canada a étendu le bénéfice du traitement de la nation la plus favorisée à la presque totalité des pays du monde.[6] De telle sorte qu'à l'heure actuelle, le tarif général a perdu sa signification originale pour ne devenir qu'une sanction éventuelle contre des pays faisant preuve de discrimination à l'endroit du Canada, ou ne respectant pas les engagements contractés avec ce pays. C'est ainsi qu'en 1968 Singapour s'est vu retirer le tarif de préférence britannique et le tarif de la nation la plus favorisée à l'égard de certains produits textiles exportés vers le Canada en des quantités supérieures à celles prévues aux termes d'un engagement contracté antérieurement avec le Canada.[7] Dans certains cas, le retrait du tarif de préférence britannique et du tarif de la nation la plus favorisée peut aussi constituer une sanction économique prise par le Canada conformément à ses responsabilités et devoirs en tant que membre de la communauté internationale. A la suite de la déclaration unilatérale d'indépendance de la Rhodésie, le 11 novembre 1965, et de la condamnation de celle-ci le lendemain par le conseil de sécurité des Nations Unies, le gouverneur général en conseil du Canada décrétait le 12 novembre que le tarif général s'appliquerait désormais à toutes les marchandises en provenance de la Rhodésie.[8] Cependant, au lieu de maintenir ainsi le tarif général comme sanction éventuelle à l'égard de certains pays, on peut se demander s'il ne serait pas plus simple pour le Canada de ne conserver que deux tarifs, quitte à recourir, au besoin aux articles 8(1) du Tarif des douanes ou à l'article 22(2a) de la Loi sur les douanes. Le premier prévoit la possibilité d'une surtaxe sur les marchandises en provenance d'un pays étranger qui traite les importations du Canada avec moins de faveur que celles d'autres pays. Le second permet d'interdire ou de réglementer l'entrée de marchandises dont l'exportation en provenance d'un pays quelconque fait l'objet d'un accord ou d'un engagement entre le gouvernement du Canada et le gouvernement de ce pays, lorsque cet accord ou engagement n'est pas respecté.

Ne peuvent bénéficier du tarif de préférence britannique ou du tarif de la nation la plus favorisée que les produits qui remplissent les conditions suivantes. Il doit d'abord s'agir de marchandises transportées sans transbordement d'un port de l'un quelconque des pays britanniques jouissant des avantages du tarif de préférence britannique dans un port du Canada, ou importées directement au Canada d'un pays auquel sont acquis les avantages du tarif de la nation la plus favorisée, selon le cas.[9] En outre, les marchandises en question doivent être authentiquement le produit de fabrication d'un pays britannique admis aux avantages du tarif de préférence britannique, ou d'un pays admis aux avantages du tarif de la nation la plus favorisée, et l'industrie de l'un ou de plusieurs de ces pays doit avoir produit une partie importante de la valeur de l'article fabriqué.[10] Cette dernière exigence, caractéristique des régimes préférentiels, n'est plus vraiment justifiée dans le cas des produits entrant sous le régime de la nation la plus favorisée, car la plupart des pays maintenant bénéficient de ce régime; mais elle conserve encore sa raison d'être pour les produits admis au tarif de préférence britannique. Le gouverneur général en conseil décide, par décret, de la proportion obligatoire dans la teneur en matières britanniques, laquelle peut varier selon les produits. A l'heure actuelle, cette proportion est fixée à 50 pour cent de la valeur totale, excepté pour un certain nombre de produits où elle fluctue entre $1/3$ et $1/6$ de la valeur totale.[11]

L'importateur de marchandises jouissant des avantages du tarif de préférence britannique a droit, en outre, à un escompte spécial de 10 pour cent sur le montant du droit calculé d'après ledit tarif, 'quand ces marchandises sont transportées sans transbordement du port d'un pays jouissant des avantages du tarif de préférence britannique à un port du Canada.[12] Une telle stipulation apparaît à première vue comme une anomalie, étant donné que toute marchandise jouissant du tarif de préférence britannique doit nécessairement être transportée sans transbordement du port d'un pays jouissant des avantages du tarif de préférence britannique à un port du Canda.[13] Son objet évident est d'accorder une certaine protection aux ports canadiens, mais aux yeux d'autres pays elle est déjà apparue comme une extension cachée de la marge de préférence britannique.[14] Il faut toutefois préciser que l'escompte en question ne s'applique pas aux vins, spiritueux, sucre, tabac, cigares, et cigarettes.[15] Elle ne s'applique pas non plus lorsque le droit n'excède pas 15 pour cent *ad valorem,* lorsque le taux du droit imposé en vertu du tarif de préférence britannique est le même que le taux de droit imposé en vertu du tarif de la nation la plus favorisée, ni aux marchandises bénéficiant des réductions concédées par l'Accord de 1926 entre le Canada et les Antilles.[16]

La nomenclature des différents produits que l'on retrouve sous la liste A du tarif des douanes prévoit pour certains d'entre eux, outre le taux général, le taux de la nation la plus favorisée, et le taux de préférence britannique, l'existence d'un taux dit du GATT ou d'un taux spécial résultant d'accords préférentiels avec certains pays. La mention d'un taux spécial dit du GATT, différent formellement du taux de

TABLEAU 1

Moyenne des droits ad valorem en pourcentage des importations

	En pour cent des importations imposables	En pour cent des importations totales
1946	21.2	12.4
1950	17.1	8.8
1954	18.1	10.5.
1958	17.5	10.2
1962	19.2	10.7
1964	16.8	9.0
1966	16.4	8.0
1968	16.3	6.6

Source: Bureau fédéral de la statistique, *Commerce du Canada: Tableaux sommaires et analytiques, années civiles 1966–1968,* vol I

la nation la plus favorisée, indique simplement qu'on se trouve en présence d'un taux négocié dans le cadre du GATT et incorporé, par arrêté en conseil, au tarif des douanes. Tant qu'il n'a pas reçu l'autorisation statutaire, ce taux conserve un caractère temporaire. Mais aussi longtemps qu'il demeure en vigueur, il s'applique de préférence au taux statutaire de la nation la plus favorisée. Ce dernier devient alors un taux de réserve qui ne prendra effet que si le Canada se retire de l'accord général sur les tarifs douaniers et le commerce ou rejette les taux du GATT par arrêté en conseil.[17]

Les pays du Commonwealth avec lesquels le Canada a conclu des accords commerciaux stipulant l'échange de droits préférentiels particuliers sont l'Australie,[18] les Bahamas, la Barbade, les Bermudes, la Guyane, le Honduras Britannique, les Iles du Vent et les Iles sous-Le-Vent, la Jamaïque ainsi que la Trinité et Tobago,[19] et la Nouvelle-Zélande.[20] En outre, le Canada a conclu avec l'Afrique du Sud un accord commercial aux termes duquel il accorde le régime de préférence britannique à certains produits en provenance de ce pays.[21] Ces différents régimes particuliers, non assimilables au régime général de préférence britannique, font exception avec ce dernier au traitement de la nation la plus favorisée.[22] Les préférences accordées visent surtout les importations de fruits, de légumes, et de viandes.

Si l'on se penche maintenant sur l'évolution du tarif des douanes depuis 1946, on constate que le niveau des droits perçus sur les importations a marqué une tendance sensible vers la baisse. Pour la période allant de 1946 à 1968, l'évolution a été comme au Tableau 1.

Pour la période couvrant les années 1968 à 1971, les données statistiques officielles ne sont pas encore disponibles. Mais à la suite des accords de Genève, en date du 30 juin 1967, on peut déjà affirmer qu'elles témoigneront d'une nouvelle

TABLEAU 2

	Importations en franchise	Importations imposables
	(milles dollars)	
1946	762,333	1,078,934
1950	1,503,697	1,621,534
1954	1,655,833	2,311,568
1958	2,097,778	2,952,714
1962	2,777,494	3,480,282
1964	3,452,804	4,034,903
1966	5,034,730	4,831,700
1967	5,978,279	5,096,920
1968	7,328,722	5,029,260

Source: Bureau fédéral de la statistique, I *Commerce du Canada: Tableaux sommaires et analytiques, années civiles 1966-1968,* vol I

baisse du niveau général des droits perçus à l'importation. On sait en effet que le Canada s'est engagé, dans ces accords, à réduire sur une période de quatre ans les droits douaniers visant plus d'un quart de ses importations, la réduction moyenne pour les seuls produits industriels étant de l'ordre de 24 pour cent.[23] Cependant, il ne faut pas nécessairement en conclure que la réduction de la protection offerte aux producteurs canadiens est proportionnelle à la réduction des tarifs nominaux. Au contraire, dans une étude publiée en 1968, les professeurs Melvin et Wilkinson suggèrent que, de façon générale, les transformations de la structure tarifaire attribuables au Kennedy Round ne sont pas susceptibles d'influencer sensiblement les taux de protection réelle offerts aux producteurs canadiens.[24] Leur argumentation est basée sur l'idée que c'est le tarif douanier réel, calculé en appliquant le tarif nominal à la valeur ajoutée au cours de la fabrication d'un produit quelconque, qui permet, plutôt que le tarif nominal applicable au produit fini, de déterminer le degré de protection réelle accordée à l'industrie fabriquant ce produit. Toutefois, certaines hypothèses de base formulées par les auteurs ont été critiquées (particulièrement en ce qui concerne la méthode de pondération des tarifs douaniers par industrie), de telle sorte que la question paraît encore loin d'être résolue.[25]

L'examen de l'évolution du tarif des douanes depuis 1946 révèle un autre phénomène important qui est l'accroissement rapide, depuis 1965, de la valeur des marchandises admises en franchise. Déjà dans le tableau 1, il était permis de constater que la moyenne des droits *ad valorem* sur les importations totales avait décru de façon marquée depuis 1965. Si l'on examine maintenant les chiffres concernant la valeur des marchandises admises en franchise, pour la période 1946 à 1968, on constate que cette valeur, inférieure jusqu'à 1966 à la valeur des marchandises frappées de droits de douanes, est maintenant supérieure à cette dernière, comme au Tableau 2.

Comment expliquer ce phénomène? La réponse est simple. L'accroissement subi de la valeur des marchandises admises en franchise à partir de 1965 correspond, dans le temps et dans les faits, à l'entrée en vigueur du pacte automobile canado-américain.

Ce dernier, signé le 16 janvier 1965 et entré provisoirement en vigueur le même jour, prévoit l'entrée en franchise, entre le Canada et les Etats-Unis, d'automobiles et de pièces détachées destinées au montage d'origine.[26] Dans le cas du Canada, cependant, la franchise ne s'applique que si l'importation est effectuée par un fabriquant remplissant les conditions suivantes: 1 / il doit avoir produit des automobiles au Canada dans chacune des quatre périodes consécutives de trois mois dans l'année de base (1er août 1963–31 juillet 1964); 2 / il doit s'engager à maintenir entre la valeur marchande nette des automobiles produites par lui au Canada (pour le marché intérieur ou pour l'exportation) et la valeur marchande nette des automobiles vendues par lui au Canada (produites dans le pays ou importées) une proportion qui ne soit pas inférieure à celle de la période de base, et de toute façon pas inférieure à 75 par rapport à cent; 3 / il doit veiller à ce que la valeur canadienne ajoutée dans sa production d'automobiles au cours de toute période de douze mois ne soit pas inférieure à la valeur canadienne ajoutée dans sa production d'automobiles durant la période de base.[27] Dans le cas des Etats-Unis, la franchise ne s'applique qu'aux produits automobiles contenant une certaine proportion d'éléments fabriqués au Canada ou aux Etats-Unis.[28] L'article v de l'accord prévoit en outre que l'accès aux marchés du Canada et des Etats-Unis 'pourra à des conditions semblables être accordé à d'autres pays.'

Le Canada ayant unilatéralement, dès le lendemain de la signature de l'accord, accordé la franchise aux automobiles et pièces originant de tout pays jouissant du tarif de préférence britannique ou du tarif de la nation la plus favorisée, l'article v n'avait de sens en pratique qu'en ce qui concerne l'accès au marché américain.[29] Or dans la mesure où les Etats-Unis, en vertu de l'accord, accordaient au Canada un traitement qui n'était pas immédiatement et inconditionnellement accordé aux autres pays membres du GATT, ils se trouvaient à violer le principe de base du GATT. L'accord entre le Canada et les Etats-Unis fut donc soumis aux parties contractantes du GATT pour examen. Un groupe de travail *ad hoc* écouta les explications des représentants des deux pays et soumit un rapport aux parties contractantes.[30] Tout au long de l'enquête, le Canada soutint qu'il appliquait l'accord de façon compatible aussi bien avec l'esprit qu'avec la lettre de l'article premier du GATT, étant donné qu'il accordait les mêmes avantages tarifaires, aux mêmes conditions, à toutes les parties contractantes.[31] Certaines questions furent soulevées en ce qui concerne l'exigence du maintien d'une proportion fixe de valeur canadienne ajoutée, laquelle pouvait paraître contraire aux exigences de l'article III(5) du GATT; mais l'objection ne fut pas retenue. Quant aux Etats-Unis, ils prétendirent que leur action pouvait être contraire à la lettre, mais non pas à l'esprit de l'article I du GATT.[32] Finalement, les parties contractantes acceptèrent, dans leur décision du 20 décembre 1965, d'accorder une dérogation aux Etats-Unis sur la base de l'article XXV(5).[33]

Aux yeux du Canada, le pacte automobile s'est avéré dès son entrée en vigueur un véritable succès. La figure 1 donne une assez bonne idée de l'évolution du commerce automobile entre les deux pays pour la période 1964 à 1968.

Côté américain cependant, cet accroissement important des exportations

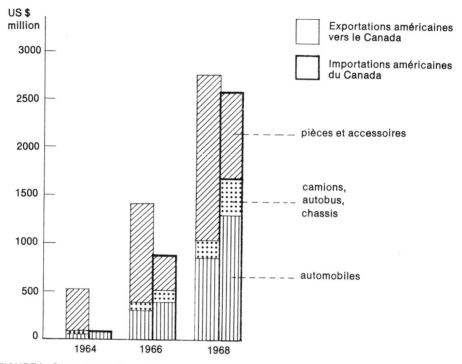

FIGURE I Commerce automobile

canadiennes vers les Etats-Unis n'a pas été envisagé d'un aussi bon œil. D'autant plus qu'une façon différente de calculer, de part et d'autre, les importations et les exportations d'automobiles et de pièces détachées venait singulièrement compliquer le problème.[34] Régulièrement depuis 1969, des pressions plus ou moins officielles ont été exercées sur le Canada pour qu'il accepte, sans conditions, l'entrée en franchise des produits automobiles fabriqués aux Etats-Unis. La récente surcharge américaine à l'importation pourrait fort bien, dans cette perspective, constituer le prétexte d'une renégociation de l'accord.[35]

Les produits admis au bénéfice du drawback

La liste B du Tarif des douanes, qui énumère un certain nombre de produits admis au bénéfice du drawback pour consommation intérieure, ne requiert pas de commentaires particuliers, si ce n'est pour observer qu'un résultat identique peut être atteint par la mention, dans la liste A du Tarif des douanes, que tel produit importé à des fins spécifiques entrera en franchise.[36] Ce qu'il importe de savoir, par contre, c'est qu'il ne s'agit pas là des seuls produits admis au bénéfice du drawback. En vertu des articles 275 et 276 de la Loi sur les douanes, le gouverneur en conseil peut autoriser, par règlements, le remboursement d'une partie ou de la totalité des droits payés sur les denrées importées et utilisées dans la fabrication de produits devant être exportés, ce qui a effectivement été fait.[37] Il s'agit là 'd'un moyen très ancien d'atténuer les répercussions des droits de douane sur le commerce, fondé sur le principe que les exportateurs ne devraient pas être empêchés de faire concurrence sur les marchés extérieurs par un accroissement de leurs frais de production imputable aux droits imposés à l'importation des pièces et des matières qu'ils doivent importer.'[38] En outre, des drawbacks visant des catégories particulières de produits ont été autorisés par le gouverneur en conseil agissant sous l'empire des articles 273-K, 274, et 275 de la Loi sur les douanes et de l'article 22 de la Loi sur l'administration financière.[39]

Les produits d'importation prohibée

La liste C du Tarif des douanes énumère les produits dont l'importation au Canada est prohibée. L'article 14 de la même loi précise que 'si ces marchandises sont importées, elles doivent être confisquées au bénéfice de la Couronne et être détruites, ou il doit en être autrement disposé suivant qu'en décide le ministre; et quiconque importe ces marchandises prohibées ou les fait importer ou permet qu'elles soient importées encourt pour chaque contravention une amende d'au plus deux cents dollars.' Les marchandises ainsi exclues le sont, de façon générale, pour des raisons d'ordre moral, sanitaires, ou de sécurité interne. Le fait d'en prohiber l'importation n'est pas contraire aux obligations internationales du Canada, car dans l'Accord général sur les tarifs douaniers et le commerce, une exception générale est prévue concernant l'adoption de telles mesures par les pays membres.[40] Dans certains cas, toutefois, l'interdiction d'importer peut équivaloir à une restriction cachée au commerce international. Certains doutes peuvent être émis, par exemple, à l'égard de l'interdiction d'importer les oléomargarines et autres succédanés du beurre, ainsi que les automobiles et avions usagés.[41]

Les surtaxes douanières

Le Canada ne perçoit pas, à l'heure actuelle, de taxes spéciales à l'importation. Les seules taxes perçues sur les produits importés au Canada sont les taxes d'accise et la taxe de vente, et elles s'appliquent tout aussi bien aux produits fabriqués au Canada.[42] Cependant, l'article 8 du Tarif des douanes prévoit la possibilité d'une surtaxe à l'importation dans certaines circonstances. Il y a d'abord la situation, déjà mentionnée, d'un pays étranger qui traite les importations du Canada avec moins de faveur que celles d'autres pays; les produits originant de ce pays pourront être frappés d'une surtaxe.[43] En outre, une surtaxe à l'importation peut être décrétée lorsque des marchandises provenant de l'extérieur 'sont importées au Canada dans des conditions où elles causent ou menacent de causer un préjudice grave à des producteurs canadiens de produits semblables ou directement concurrentiels.'[44] Dans ce cas particulier, le plus fréquent en pratique, le décret de surtaxe doit être approuvé par résolution adoptée par les deux chambres du parlement dans les 180 jours de son établissement, ou si le parlement ne siège pas dans les quinze jours de la reprise de ses travaux, sous peine de perdre tout effet.[45] Enfin, les produits d'un pays étranger importés au Canada sur des navires battant pavillon de ce pays peuvent être assujettis à une surtaxe si les marchandises importées dans le pays en question sur des navires immatriculés au Canada sont assujettis à des droits de douane plus élevés que des marchandises similaires lorsqu'elles sont importées sur des navires de ce pays.[46]

Il ne faudrait pas passer sous silence aussi le fait qu'entre juin 1962 et avril 1963, le Canada a imposé une surtaxe temporaire sur les importations de nombreux produits, y compris des numéros tarifaires consolidés aux parties I et II de l'annexe v de l'Accord général sur les tarifs douaniers et le commerce. Le recours à de telles mesures fut jugé alors nécessaire pour le maintien de la position financière extérieure et de la balance des paiements du Canada.[47] La façon de procéder fut la suivante. Agissant sous l'autorité de l'article 4 du Tarif des douanes, le gouverneur en conseil retira, pour les produits visés, le bénéfice du tarif de préférence britannique et de la nation la plus favorisée à tous les pays qui y avaient droit.[48] Le seul tarif applicable devint alors le tarif général. Puis, agissant cette fois sous l'autorité de l'article 22 de la Loi sur l'administration financière, il accorda une remise des droits de douanes payés en supplément des droits normalement applicables aux produits en question haussés de 5, 10 ou de 15 pour cent selon les produits.[49]

Les mesures ainsi prises par le Canada furent portées à la connaissance du GATT qui institua une enquête. Tout en admettant que la surtaxe temporaire à l'importation ne pouvait se justifier sous l'article XII de l'Accord général, qui autorise uniquement le recours à des restrictions quantitatives comme mesure de sauvegarde en cas de déficit de la balance des paiements, le Canada se défendit en alléguant qu'il avait agi de la façon qui lui paraissait la plus rationnelle dans les circonstances. Il souligna entre autres le fait que le recours à des restrictions quantitatives aurait exigé la mise en place d'un dispositif administratif important, ce qui n'était pas le cas pour une surtaxe. Il fit remarquer qu'une surtaxe, contrairement aux restrictions quantitatives, fournissait des revenus à l'état. Enfin, il soutint qu'une surtaxe avait un impact moindre sur le commerce international que des restrictions quantitatives. Ce qui équivalait, en somme, à remettre en question le bien fondé de l'article XII du GATT. Dans leur décision, les parties contractantes se contentèrent d'exprimer leur regret 'que le gouvernement du Canada ait dû juger nécessaire d'instituer des mesures temporaires incompatibles avec l'article II de l'Accord général.'[50] Elles tinrent compte de l'effort initial fait par le Canada en vue de la suppression des surtaxes temporaires et recommendèrent que les surtaxes qui restaient soient supprimées promptement. Dès la fin de février 1963, plus de la moitié des surtaxes étaient éliminées, les dernières disparaissant le 31 mars 1963.[51]

LES BARRIERES NON-TARIFAIRES AU CANADA

> A nontariff trade-distorting policy is any measure (public or private) that causes internationally traded goods and services, or resources devoted to the production of these goods and services, to be allocated in such a way as to reduce potential real world income.[52]

A partir d'une telle définition, il est possible d'élaborer une liste assez complète des obstacles non-tarifaires au commerce international.[53] Cependant, pour les fins de la présente étude nous nous limiterons à l'étude d'un nombre restreint de problèmes qui sont les suivants: les règles et formalités administratives relatives à l'importation, les droits antidumping, et les restrictions quantitatives à l'importation.

Les règles et formalités administratives relatives à l'importation

Les règles de classification
Les taux applicables à un produit en particulier dépendent de sa classification exacte dans la nomenclature du Tarif des douanes. Or, au Canada, les possibilités

d'erreurs de classification sont relativement nombreuses. Ainsi, un même produit peut très bien se trouver dans plus d'un poste tarifaire, dépendant de l'emploi définitif que l'on désire en faire.[54] En outre, un danger particulier de confusion résulte du fait que certains biens sont susceptibles d'entrer dans un poste tarifaire comme produits finis, et dans un autre poste tarifaire comme pièces détachées d'un produit fini.[55] Dans un certain nombre de cas, le taux applicable à un produit variera selon qu'il s'agit d'une catégorie de biens fabriqués ou non au Canada.[56] Dans d'autres cas, le taux variera selon la composition du produit en question.[57] Enfin, pour certains types de produits, essentiellement les fruits et les légumes, le taux pourra varier selon les saisons. C'est donc dire que la détermination exacte du taux de douane applicable à un produit en particulier n'est pas une tâche particulièrement aisée.

Un des problèmes de classification le plus complexe et le plus fréquent a trait à l'identification des marchandises 'd'une classe ou d'une espèce fabriquée au Canada.' Aux termes de l'article 6 du Tarif des douanes, 'les marchandises ne sont pas censées appartenir à une classe ou à une espèce fabriquée ou produite au Canada, à moins qu'elles ne soient ainsi fabriquées ou produites en quantitées importantes. Le gouverneur en conseil peut prescrire que ces quantités, pour être importantes, doivent suffire à fournir un certain pourcentage de la consommation canadienne normale, et a la faculté de fixer ces pourcentages.' Un ordre en conseil datant de 1936, toujours en vigueur, fixe à dix le pourcentage de la consommation canadienne normale devant être fourni par les producteurs du Canada.[58] Mais comme le soulignent bien F. Masson et H.E. English, le véritable problème n'en est pas un de pourcentage, mais bien plutôt de comparaison valable entre les produits importés et ceux fabriqués au Canada.[59] Avec le temps, des critères concrets de comparaison ont été élaborés, que la Cour Suprême du Canada, dans *Dominion Engineering Works Ltd.* v *D.M.N.R. et al.* a résumés ainsi:

> The Board heard evidence directed to the question whether these two machines were competitive, interchangeable or equivalent to such a degree as to outweigh the choice of classification by size. It did not adopt the trade classification automatically and without regard to the other evidence. It had before it evidence of comparative capacity, the weight of the machines, the comparative uses and performance of the two machines and the circumstances in which one machine would be used in preference to another, and with this evidence before it, concluded that the two and a half cubic yard shovel was of a class or kind not made in Canada.[60]

Pour simplifier la tâche, le Ministère du revenu national émet des memoranda annonçant le passage de certains types de produits de la catégorie 'classe ou espèce non faite au Canada' à la catégorie 'classe ou espèce faite au Canada.'[61] Mais outre le fait que le délai de transfert est relativement court, ces décisions sont susceptibles d'être renversées par la Commission du Tarif; ce qui n'est pas de nature à rassurer les importateurs.[62]

Que se passe-t-il en cas de doute ou d'erreur dans la classification? Disons d'abord que lorsqu'un article est désigné dans le tarif sous deux noms ou deux descriptions différentes, la règles générale d'interprétation statutaire s'applique, à savoir que les dispositions générales ne dérogent pas aux dispositions spéciales.[63] Autrement dit, le produit en question sera classifié d'après la description qui apparaitra la plus spécifique. Mais il se peut très bien que ces deux descriptions applicables à un même produit apparaissent également spécifiques ou également générales. Dans ce cas, la Commission du Tarif a décidé que:

> In our view, where an article is named or described under two tariff items in such ways that it is impossible to discover from the language of the items which of the items the legislator intended to apply to such article, section 50 governs the classification.[64]

Or, l'article 50 de l'ancienne Loi sur les douanes, maintenant renuméroté article 54, stipule que: 'Si un article est désigné dans le tarif sous deux noms ou deux descriptions ou plus, et s'il y a une différence de droits, le droit le plus élevé est imposé et perçu.'[65] A première vue donc, il semble qu'en cas de doute véritable, l'interprétation la plus favorable au gouvernement l'emporte. Cependant, dans une décision en date de juin 1949, la Commission du Tarif déclarait que: 'It is our view that in cases of serious uncertainty as to the correct classification, the benefit of the doubt ought to be given to the importer.'[66]

Quelle est la portée véritable de cette décision, face à l'article 54 de la Loi sur les douanes? Si l'on en juge par les faits soumis à la commission, il n'y a pas vraiment contradiction. En effet, le problème soulevé consistait à déterminer si certains produits pouvaient logiquement être classifiés dans un poste tarifaire donné. Aucune autre classification n'était proposée par les autorités gouvernementales. Dans l'incertitude quant à la signification exacte du poste tarifaire en question, la commission préfère accorder le bénéfice du doute à l'importateur.

Maintenant que se passe-t-il lorsque, de l'avis d'un importateur, un produit a été classifié par erreur sous un mauvais poste tarifaire? Dans un tel cas, l'article 46 de la Loi sur les douanes prévoit que la détermination de la classification faite au moment de la déclaration en douanes est définitive et péremptoire, à moins que l'importateur, dans les quatre-vingt-dix jours de la déclaration en douanes, ne fasse une demande écrite, selon la forme et de la manière prescrites, à un appréciateur fédéral des douanes en vue d'une nouvelle détermination.[67] S'il se croit lésé par cette nouvelle détermination de l'appréciateur fédéral des douanes, l'importateur pourra en appeler successivement au sous-ministre du revenu,[68] à la Commission du Tarif,[69] à la Cour fédérale,[70] et éventuellement à la Cour suprême.[71] Il est à noter que dans les deux derniers cas, l'appel ne peut porter que sur une question de droit. Dans l'ensemble, on constate que la procédure à suivre pour obtenir une nouvelle détermination du classement tarifaire d'un produit est assez complexe, et les délais pour ce faire relativement courts. Si l'on tient compte en outre de la complexité du Tarif des douanes, et des nombreuses possibilités d'erreurs qui en résultent, on peut voir dans les règles qui régissent la classification des produits d'importation au Canada une restriction involontaire, mais non moins réelle, au commerce international.[72]

Certains auteurs ont suggéré que le Canada pourrait éliminer en bonne partie les problèmes de classification simplement en adoptant la *Nomenclature Tarifaire de Bruxelles*.[73] Cette dernière, qui date de 1955, comprend trois parties principales: 1 / les règles générales d'interprétations; 2 / des notes explicatives sur les chapitres et les sections; 3 / la liste des différents postes tarifaires présentés selon un ordre logique. Les règles d'interprétation aussi bien que la présentation scientifique des différentes catégories de produits tendent à éviter qu'un produit quelconque se retrouve dans plus d'une catégorie tarifaire. Or, depuis 1969, le Canada a fait un premier pas vers l'adoption de la *Nomenclature de Bruxelles*. En effet, au cours des négociations Kennedy, le gouvernement canadien s'était engagé à donner suite aux concessions sur les produits chimiques et les matières plastiques. A la suggestion de l'industrie, la Commission du Tarif recommanda en 1968 l'adoption de la *Nomenclature de Bruxelles* pour l'ensemble de ce domaine complexe.[74] En décembre 1968, finalement, était sanctionnée une loi modifiant en ce sens le Tarif des douanes.[75] Faut-il voir dans cette initiative le présage d'une modification plus radicale du Tarif des douanes? Il est impossible de le dire.

Les dispositions relatives à la détermination de la valeur imposable

Lorsque vient le temps de calculer les droits à acquitter sur un produit en particulier, deux possibilités peuvent se présenter. Ou l'on se trouve en présence d'un taux spécifique, autrement dit d'un montant précis à payer pour une quantité déterminée d'un produit, et alors le calcul est relativement simple. Ou bien on se trouve en présence d'un taux *ad valorem,* auquel cas il faut déterminer la valeur en douanes du produit en question avant de procéder au calcul des droits à acquitter. Or, de l'avis de la Chambre de commerce internationale 'parmi les nombreux obstacles indirects, dits ''invisibles'' ' qui entravent le fonctionnement régulier du commerce international, il en est peu qui présentent autant de gravité que les dispositions législatives et administratives relatives à la détermination de la valeur des marchandises frappées de droits *ad valorem.*'[76] C'est pourquoi, il importe de s'arrêter un moment sur la pratique canadienne dans ce domaine.

Au point de départ, il faut savoir que le Canada, en tant que membre du GATT, est soumis à certaines obligations d'ordre général concernant la détermination de la valeur en douanes des produits d'importation. L'article VII de l'Accord général, en effet, énonce à ce sujet certains principes dont les parties contractantes reconnaissent la valeur et qu'elles s'engagent à respecter. L'objectif de base est de faire en sorte qu'aucune méthode d'évaluation ne soit conçue et appliquée par les autorités douanières nationales de manière à modifier l'incidence des droits de douanes et renforcer la protection que la loi assure aux industries du pays. A cet effet, l'article VII du GATT prescrit que la valeur en douane des marchandises importées 'devrait être fondée sur la valeur réelle de la marchandise importée à laquelle s'applique le droit ou d'une marchandise similaire et ne devrait pas être fondée sur la valeur de produits d'origine nationale ou sur des valeurs arbitraires ou fictives.'[77] Par la suite, la 'valeur réelle' est définie comme devant être 'le prix auquel, en des temps et lieu déterminés par la législation du pays d'importation, les marchandises importées ou des marchandises similaires sont vendues ou offertes à la vente à l'occasion d'opérations commerciales normales effectuées dans des conditions de pleine concurrence.'[78] Enfin, il est édicté que dans le cas où il serait impossible de déterminer la valeur réelle en se conformant aux conditions énoncées ci-haut, 'la valeur en douane devrait être fondée sur l'équivalence vérifiable la plus proche possible de cette valeur.'[79]

Comment le Canada s'est-il conformé à ces obligations? Le 30 juin 1948, soit à peine six mois après l'entrée en vigueur de l'Accord général, était sanctionnée une loi dont le but, selon les notes explicatives, était d'abroger certains articles de la

Loi sur les douanes nettement contraires à l'article VII du GATT pour les remplacer par des mesures plus conformes à l'esprit du dit article.[80] C'est ainsi que fut éliminé l'article 41 de la loi qui déterminait que lorsque des effets sont importés au Canada dans des circonstances ou conditions telles qu'il était difficile d'en déterminer la valeur imposable, le ministre pouvait déterminer de façon arbitraire la valeur imposable de ces effets. En fait, les amendements apportés par la loi de 1948 reprenaient pour l'essentiel le langage de l'article VII du GATT.

Entre 1950 et 1958, cependant, de nouveaux amendements furent apportés à la Loi sur les douanes qui modifièrent sensiblement la règlementation canadienne concernant la détermination de la valeur en douane des marchandises importées. Ainsi, en 1953, pouvoir fut accordé au ministre de déterminer, sans droit d'appel, la valeur des produits saisonniers.[81] En 1955, la clause de la loi de 1948 prévoyant dans certains cas l'utilisation de l'équivalent vérifiable le plus proche possible de la valeur réelle fut abrogée.[82] En 1958, l'ensemble de la réglementation concernant la détermination de la valeur en douanes fit l'objet d'une nouvelle rédaction et, mis à part quelques modifications, c'est cette réglementation qui demeure encore en vigueur à l'heure actuelle.

Par rapport à la législation de 1948 qui, ainsi que nous l'avons dit, reproduisait assez fidèlement l'article VII du GATT, la réglementation actuelle se présente de la façon suivante. Le principe de base demeure sensiblement le même, à savoir que la valeur en douane des marchandises importées

doit être la juste valeur marchande, au moment où les effets ont été directement expédiés vers le Canada et à l'endroit d'où ils l'ont été, d'effets pareils lorsqu'ils sont vendus

a à des acheteurs situés à cet endroit et auprès desquels le vendeur s'en tient rigoureusement à la lettre du droit, qui sont au même niveau commercial que l'importateur, ou sensiblement à ce niveau, et

b en mêmes quantités ou sensiblement en les mêmes quantités, pour la consommation intérieure, dans le cours ordinaire du commerce et à des conditions de concurrence.[83]

Lorsqu'une marchandise identique n'est pas vendue pour la consommation intérieure, mais que des marchandises semblables le sont, alors un deuxième principe s'applique, à savoir que la valeur imposable doit être le coût de production de la production importée majoré d'un pourcentage de profit brut égal à celui appliqué aux marchandises semblables vendues dans le pays d'exportation.[84] Cette dernière mesure diffère de ce que prévoyait la loi de 1948 et présente, par rapport aux objectifs de l'article VII du GATT, certains dangers. Ainsi, au dire de Francis Masson et H.E. English, 'To the extent that this method eliminates values established by selling prices in the country of export, it establishes arbitrary or fictitious values, since there is, of course, no fixed and typical relationships between cost of production and market price.'[85] Le même Francis Masson et J.B. Whitely écrivaient, quelques années plus tôt: 'Obviously, the application of a similar goods rule, without an allowance for the difference in production costs between the goods imported and the similar goods used for comparison, would be extremely limited.'[86] Enfin, la loi actuelle prévoit un certain nombre de cas spéciaux où, à défaut de pouvoir utiliser les principes exposés ci-haut, le ministre peut déterminer lui-même la valeur imposable.[87] Encore là, il faut noter une divergence avec la loi de 1948, qui ne prévoyait pas expressément de tels cas.

Dans l'ensemble, il faut reconnaître que l'estimation de la valeur en douane des marchandises importées est fondée, dans la grande majorité des cas, sur la juste valeur marchande de celles-ci.[88] Mais dans la mesure où certains produits sont évalués de manière arbitraire ou fictive, le danger de restrictions indues au commerce international persiste. Ce qui nous amène à étudier les recours possibles dans le cas où une évaluation est jugée erronée.

Au niveau interne, les recours formels prévus par la Loi sur les douanes sont identiques à ceux précédemment exposés concernant la classification des marchandises importées.[89] Il est à noter toutefois qu'il n'y a pas d'appel possible des décisions arbitraires rendues par le ministre lorsque celui-ci agit à l'intérieur de ses pouvoirs.[90] En pratique, l'estimation de la valeur en douane des marchandises importées a donné lieu à un nombre relativement restreint d'appel à la Commission du Tarif. Ceci s'explique en partie par le fait que la majeure partie des cas d'évaluation ne présentent pas de problème sérieux et que lorsque de véritables problèmes se posent effectivement, ceux-ci sont parfois solutionnés par le moyen de négociations directes entre l'importateur concerné et le ministre.

Au niveau international, l'article VII (1) du GATT prévoit que chaque fois qu'une partie contractante en fera la demande, une autre partie contractante examinera, à la lumière des principes énoncés dans l'article, l'application de toute loi, et de tout réglement relatifs à la valeur en douanes. L'article XXIII du GATT prévoit en outre un mécanisme de conciliation dans le cas où une partie contractante se jugerait lésée par l'action d'une autre partie contractante. Agissant sur la base de ces deux articles, les Etats-Unis soumirent en 1962 aux parties contractantes du GATT un différend avec le Canada concernant l'application des valeurs en douanes prévues pour les pommes de terre par la loi douanière canadienne.[91] Les faits étaient les suivants. Le 16 octobre 1962, le gouvernement canadien fixait une valeur en douane de $2.67 dollars canadiens par cent livres pour les pommes de terre nouvelles importées dans l'ouest du Canada. Aux termes de la législation canadienne, la différence entre la valeur à l'exportation moins élevée et la valeur en douane devait être perçue par les autorités douanières canadiennes à titre de droits de dumping lorsque les autres conditions exigées par la loi étaient remplies. Le gouvernement des Etats-Unis déposa alors une réclamation au sujet de l'application de cette imposition, perçue en sus d'un droit spécifique de 0.375 dollars canadiens par cent livres, qui avait été consenti aux Etats-Unis en 1957 à titre de concession tarifaire sur les pommes de terre.[92]

Devant le groupe spécial constitué par le GATT pour examiner la question, la délégation américaine soutint que la fixation de la valeur en douane des pommes de terre à la valeur moyenne, pondérée pour quantité, pendant la période de trois ans précédant immédiatement la date de l'expédition à destination du Canada, constituait une décision fondée sur une valeur arbitraire ou fictive, et était en conséquence incompatible avec les dispositions du paragraphe 2(a) de l'article VII du GATT.[93] La délégation canadienne prétendit au contraire que les dispositions en question de la loi douanière de son pays ne comportaient pas d'évaluation arbitraire ou fictive, mais se fondaient sur la valeur des importations réelles au cours des trois années précédentes et, de ce fait, étaient moins arbitraires que la législation précédemment en vigueur.[94]

Dans le rapport qu'il remit, le groupe spécial affirma que la notion de valeur en douane appliqué actuellement aux importations de pomme de terre en vertu de la loi canadienne différait de celle que les parties contractantes avaient présente à l'esprit en rédigeant le texte de l'article VII. A cause de cette différence d'interprétation, le groupe spécial préféra ne pas prendre en considération les dispositions de cet article dans le contexte de l'examen dont il était chargé. Se basant plutôt sur le fait que l'institution d'une imposition additionnelle par le Canada ne pouvait être considérée comme une mesure antidumping aux termes de l'article VI du GATT, et que d'autre part ladite imposition venait en sus d'un droit d'importation spécifique consolidé antérieurement, contrairement aux prescriptions de l'article II du GATT, le groupe spécial suggéra aux parties contractantes qu'elles recommandent au gouvernement canadien de supprimer cette imposition additionnelle.[95] Ce que ce dernier fit, le 2 janvier 1963.

La réglementation relative aux marques d'origine
Bien qu'il n'en ait pas toujours été ainsi, la réglementation canadienne en vigueur actuellement n'impose pas le marquage de tous les produits d'importation.[96] L'article 17(1) du Tarif des douanes spécifie en effet que le gouverneur en conseil peut, au besoin, lorsqu'il le juge à propos, décréter que des marchandises d'une classe ou d'une espèce quelconque spécifiée dans ce décret, importées au Canada, soient marquées. Donc, seules les marchandises mentionnées expressément dans le décret doivent être marquées. Le paragraphe 2 de l'article 17 ajoute que toutes 'les marchandises importées au Canada après la date de l'entrée en vigueur de ce décret du gouverneur en conseil et non conformes aux prescriptions de ce décret ne doivent pas sortir de la douane avant qu'elles aient été ainsi marquées.' Ainsi, il n'est plus question, comme ce fut le cas entre 1931 et 1950, d'une surtaxe de 10 pour cent *ad valorem* à prélever sur la valeur des marchandises importées ne respectant pas les prescriptions sur le marquage.[97] Enfin, le paragraphe 3 de l'article 17 prévoit certaines sanctions à l'égard de ceux qui violent une des dispositions relatives au marquage dans l'intention de supprimer l'information demandée.

Peut-on en conclure que la réglementation canadienne tend à 'réduire au minimum les difficultées et les inconvénients' résultant du marquage, ainsi que le prescrit l'article IX du GATT? A première vue, cette réglementation apparaît assez libérale. Le nombre de produits soumis aux dispositions relatives aux marques d'origine, en particulier, est restreint. Le décret présentement en vigueur sur le marquage des marchandises importées au Canada mentionne une cinquantaine de produits regroupés dans cinq catégories générales qui sont: marchandises pour usage personnel ou domestique, quincaillerie, nouveautés et articles de sport, ouvrages en papier, et vêtements.[98] Mais il n'en reste pas moins que le fait d'exiger que les marchandises en question soient 'marquées au fer chaud ou autrement, timbrées ou étiquetées lisiblement de façon à indiquer le pays d'origine en anglais ou en français' et que tel marquage, timbrage, ou étiquetage soient 'aussi indélébiles et permanents que le permet la nature des marchandises' et 'apposés sur les marchandises à un endroit bien évident' entraine pour les producteurs des frais additionnels suffisants dans certains cas pour décourager l'exportation occasionnelle.[99] De plus, les modifications relativement fréquentes apportées à la liste des produits soumis à la réglementation sur le marquage sont de nature à créer un climat d'incertitude même chez les exportateurs non touchés par cette réglementation.[100]

Aussi serait-il dangereux d'affirmer que la Canada, à l'heure actuelle, a déjà réduit au minimum les difficultés et les inconvénients résultant du marquage.

Les mesures antidumping

L'article VI du GATT stipule que le dumping, 'qui permet l'introduction des produits d'un pays sur le marché d'un autre pays à un prix inférieur à leur valeur normale, est condamnable s'il cause ou menace de causer un préjudice important à une production établie d'une partie contractante ou s'il retarde sensiblement la création d'une production nationale.'[101] Mais le but de cet article n'est pas uniquement de condamner le dumping. Il vise en outre à décourager le recours injustifié à des mesures antidumping en délimitant de façon relativement précise les cas de dumping.[102] En 1968, l'article VI du GATT a été complété par un Code international antidumping qui reprend ce deuxième objectif en proposant une procédure uniforme et détaillée de contrôle du dumping.[103] Or, ce code international antidumping visait de façon particulière le Canada. Pourquoi exactement, c'est ce que nous allons voir maintenant.

Le Canada a été le premier pays a légiférer contre le dumping, la législation originale datant de 1904.[104] Cette législation est demeurée substantiellement la même jusqu'en 1969, année où le Canada introduisit une nouvelle législation sur le sujet. Jusqu'en 1969, les mesures à prendre en cas de dumping se présentaient de la façon suivante:

> Dans le cas de marchandises exportées au Canada d'une classe ou d'une espèce fabriquée au Canada, si le prix d'exportation ou le prix réel de vente à un importateur au Canada est inférieur à la juste valeur marchande ou à la valeur imposable des marchandises établie sous le régime des dispositions de la *Loi sur les douanes,* il doit en sus des droits autrement établis, être prélevé, perçu et payé sur lesdites marchandises à leur importation au Canada, un droit spécial ou antidumping égal à la différence entre ledit prix de vente des marchandises pour l'exportation et leur dite valeur imposable; et ce droit spécial ou antidumping doit être prélevé, perçu et payé sur ces marchandises lors même que ces dernières ne seraient pas imposables par ailleurs.[105]

Cette législation soulevait un certain nombre de problèmes. Ainsi, pour qu'il y ait dumping, il fallait que les marchandises impliquées soient 'd'une classe ou d'une espèce faite au Canada,' détermination qui, dans certains cas, n'était pas toujours facile; car si les manufacturiers canadiens réclamaient une protection aussi étendue que possible, les consommateurs canadiens, eux, ne tenaient aucunement à acquitter des droits sur des produits non fabriqués au Canada.[106] En outre, il fallait que le prix d'exportation des marchandises en question soit inférieur à leur juste valeur marchande, ce qui, d'un point de vue étranger, posait le problème des valeurs en douane fixées de manière arbitraire ou fictive. L'exemple déjà mentionné des pommes de terre importées au Canada soulevait de façon très concrète ce type de difficultés.[107]

Mais le problème le plus sérieux que posait la législation antidumping d'avant 1969 avait trait à son caractère arbitraire face aux exigences de l'article VI du GATT.

En effet, nous avons vu que ce dernier article condamne le dumping 's'il cause ou menace de causer un préjudice important à une production établie d'une partie contractante ou s'il retarde sensiblement la création d'une production nationale.'[108] Or, la législation d'avant 1969 n'exigeait pas la preuve d'un dommage réel ou appréhendé comme condition de recours à des mesures antidumping. Commentant ce fait, K.C. Mackenzie écrivait en 1965:

> The absence of a statutory requirement of injury gives the Canadian anti-dumping legislation the appearance of being as ruthless in operation as any in the world. With strict enforcement there would be nothing to prevent a Canadian manufacturer from eliminating a foreign competitor selling goods in the same class in the domestic market, simply by cutting his prices below the section 6 value of the imports. The foreign exporter would be barred by dumping duties from following the domestic price down to maintain his share of the market, nor could he agree to indemnify his importer from losses upon resale because this would be considered a price discount not granted in the home market and would attract further dumping duties. The only barrier to abuse of the legislation in this portion at the present time, apart from the restraint in making class or kind determinations, is a judicious use of administrative inertia.[109]

Il n'est donc pas surprenant que lors des négociations Kennedy, lorsque fut discuté le problème des obstacles indirects au commerce international, de sévères critiques furent adressées à l'endroit de la réglementation antidumping du Canada. L'Angleterre étant dans la même situation, les Etats-Unis étant incriminés à un moindre degré, et le Marché Commun songeant déjà à une réglementation uniforme dans ce domaine, on en vint à la conclusion qu'un Code international antidumping s'imposait.[110] Celui-ci vit finalement le jour en juin 1967; la date d'entrée en vigueur fut fixée au 1er juillet 1968 pour let états ayant ratifié l'accord à cette date, et à la date de ratification pour les autres états.

Le Code international antidumping comporte cinq parties principales qui sont les suivantes: la détermination du dumping, la détermination du préjudice subi, les modalités d'enquête et les procédures administratives, les droits antidumping et les mesures provisoires, et finalement les mesures antidumping prises au nom d'un état tiers.[111] L'objectif général est d'éviter qu'il soit fait un usage abusif des droits antidumping. Le point de départ demeure évidemment l'article VI du GATT, mais de nombreuses précisions y sont apportées. C'est ainsi que l'article 3 spécifie 'qu'une détermination ne conclura à l'existence d'un préjudice que lorsque les autorités compétentes seront convaincues que les importations faisant l'objet d'un dumping sont manifestement la cause principale d'un préjudice important ou d'une menace de préjudice importante pour une production nationale ou d'un retard sensible dans la création d'une production nationale.' A l'article 5, il est demandé que l'instruction complète des affaires de dumping soit faite de façon ouverte. L'article 10 ajoute que des 'mesures provisoires ne peuvent être prises que lorsqu'une décision préliminaire concluant à l'existence d'un dumping a été prise et qu'il y a des éléments de preuve suffisants d'un préjudice.' Enfin, l'article 14 exige des parties contractantes qu'elles prennent toutes les mesures nécessaires pour rendre ces lois, règlements, et procédures administratives conformes aux dispositions du Code antidumping.

Pour le Canada, cela signifiait une révision complète de sa réglementation antidumping. Le 19 décembre 1968 était sanctionnée la Loi antidumping qui abrogeait toute réglementation antérieure sur le sujet pour la remplacer par de nouvelles normes conformes aux exigences du Code international antidumping.[112] Un décret en date du 31 décembre 1968 fixait l'entrée en vigueur de la loi au 1er janvier 1969.[113]

La première partie de la loi définit les conditions d'assujettissement aux droits antidumping. De tels droits sont payables sur toutes marchandises sous-évaluées entrées au Canada pour lesquelles le Tribunal antidumping a rendu une ordonnance portant que le dumping de semblables marchandises a causé ou est susceptible de causer un préjudice sensible à la production canadienne.[114] La loi définit par la suite les marchandises sous-évaluées comme étant celles dont la valeur normale excède le prix à l'exportation et élabore différents critères permettant de déterminer la valeur normale d'une marchandise ainsi que son prix à l'exportation.[115]

La deuxième partie de la loi porte sur la procédure d'enquête. Celle-ci est ouverte par le sous-ministre du revenu national pour les douanes et l'accise, de sa propre initiative ou sur réception d'une plainte portée par les producteurs canadiens concernés, lorsqu'il y a des éléments de preuve que des marchandises ont été ou sont sous-évalués et que le dumping qui en résulte cause ou est susceptible de causer un préjudice sensible à la production canadienne de pareils produits.[116] Si le sous-ministre est convaincu, à la suite de son enquête, que les marchandises ont été ou sont sous-évaluées et que la marge de dumping aussi bien que son volume ne sont pas négligeables, 'il fait une détermination préliminaire du dumping spécifiant les marchandises ou la sorte de marchandises auxquelles cette détermination s'applique.'[117] A la suite de cette détermination préliminaire, l'affaire est transmise au Tribunal antidumping qui est chargé de faire enquête dans les quatre-vingts-dix jours pour savoir si le dumping des marchandises qui font l'objet de l'enquête a causé, cause ou est susceptible de causer un préjudice sensible à la production présente ou éventuelle au Canada de marchandises semblables.[118] Les conclusions du tribunal sont subséquemment retransmises au sous-ministre qui fait une détermination définitive du dumping dans le cas de toutes marchandises décrites dans l'ordonnance ou les conclusions du tribunal.[119]Cette détermination est susceptible d'appel devant la Commission du Tarif et subséquemment, sur une question de droit uniquement, devant la Cour fédérale.[120]

En vertu de certains amendements apportés à la Loi antidumping, le 18 décembre 1970, le tribunal doit en outre 'faire enquête et faire rapport au gouverneur en conseil sur toute autre question ou chose relative à l'importation de marchandises au Canada, qui peut causer ou menacer de causer un tort à la production de toutes marchandises au Canada que ce dernier lui renvoie pour enquête et rapport.'[121] L'article 5 amendé de la Loi sur les licences d'exportation et d'importation permet subséquemment au ministre de l'industrie et du commerce d'utiliser les conclusions d'une telle enquête pour décider s'il y a lieu d'inclure les marchandises touchées par l'enquête dans la liste des produits d'importation contrôlée.[122] Une première enquête sous l'autorité de l'article 16 vient tout juste d'être ouverte au sujet des importations de chaussures.[123]

Du 1er janvier 1969, date de son institution,[124] au 1er janvier 1972, le Tribunal antidumping a rendu quinze décisions. De ces décisions, six ont été négatives, en

ce sens que le tribunal a conclu à l'absence de préjudice sensible causé, ou susceptible d'être causé, aux producteurs canadiens;[125] quatre décisions ont reconnu
qu'un préjudice important avait été subi par les producteurs canadiens; et quatre
autres ont conclu que le dumping allégué était susceptible de causer dans le futur
un préjudice important aux producteurs canadiens.[126] Enfin, dans une dernière
décision, le Tribunal antidumping s'est contenté de renvoyer l'affaire portée devant
lui au sous-ministre du revenu, après avoir soumis une nouvelle définition du champ
d'application de l'enquête.[127]

Dans l'ensemble, on constate que le Tribunal antidumping s'est acquitté de ses
tâches de façon relativement indépendante. La meilleure preuve en est peut être
la réaction des producteurs canadiens. Dans un éditorial du journal the *Financial
Post,* en date du 21 novembre 1970, les commentaires suivants, nettement pes-
simistes, suivent l'annonce d'une décision du tribunal:

> It is established that dumping took place. It is also known that domestic industry over
> a period of years experienced reduced profits and underused production capacity.
>
> But how much of the profit squeeze was attributable to imports and how much to other
> factors? Was all the unused capacity entirely due to the imports?
>
> In the end, the tribunal concluded: 'It is difficult to believe that the dumping of transfor-
> mers and reactors had no injurious effect on the Canadian manufacturers, but it is exceed-
> ingly difficult to isolate this effect from other factors bearing on the industry during the
> relevant period. There is reasonable ground for the view that many of the past difficulties
> of the industry are unrelated to the matter of dumping.'
>
> The tribunal found it easier to deal with the future than the past and decreed that future
> dumping is likely to cause material injury to Canadian producers of like goods.
>
> This is, to say the least, hardly a satisfactory finding from the viewpoint of domestic
> producers of transformer equipment. The confusion, moreover, is not a good omen, for
> other industrial producers entitled to protection under antidumping regulations.[128]

Cependant, moins d'un an plus tard, un autre éditorial dans le même journal com-
mentait dans les termes suivants une nouvelle décision du tribunal:

> Canada's antidumping tribunal, suddenly and with force, is shaping industrial policy.
>
> In a new ruling on women's shoe imports from Italy and Spain, the issue of dumping
> and material injury is barely visible. What stands out is the tribunal's firm instruction to
> Canada's shoe producers to revitalize their industry and get more competitive.
>
> 'It would appear that the principal problem which has troubled the Canadian manufac-
> turer of ladies' footwear in the immediate past does not arise in any material degree from
> the dumping of footwear from Italy and Spain, but rather arises from a fashion explosion
> which radically favored the kinds of footwear made in Italy and Spain and which, in large
> measure, domestic manufacturers were unwilling or unable to supply.'
>
> Canada's shoe producers will receive help in getting with it. For this reason, the tri-
> bunal decided that for 18 months sandals and other women's footwear from Italy and
> Spain could threaten injury and would henceforth be subject to dumping duties. So some
> price adjustments (up, that is) are now possible.[129]

Le seul fait d'avoir attiré, par ses décisions, aussi bien des éloges que des critiques constitue sans doute la meilleure preuve du rôle original joué par le Tribunal canadien antidumping. Toutefois, il faut souligner que dans la décision concernant les chaussures importées d'Italie et d'Espagne, ce dernier est venu bien près d'outrepasser la compétence que lui reconnaît la loi antidumping.

Les restrictions quantitatives à l'importation

Le Canada n'applique généralement pas de restrictions aux importations.[130] Mais il existe diverses lois qui rendent possible le contrôle des importations dans certains domaines précis. En outre, des accords dits 'volontaires' existent entre le Canada et des pays étrangers qui ont pour effet de restreindre les exportations de produits en provenance de ces pays vers le Canada.

Les mesures législatives rendant possible le contrôle des importations
Il faut distinguer ici deux types de lois. Il y a d'abord celles qui exigent l'obtention d'une licence pour l'exportation ou l'importation de certains produits spécifiques. Tel est le cas de la Loi sur les licences d'exportation et d'importation,[131] et de la Loi sur l'Office national de l'énergie.[132] Ensuite, il y a des loi qui créent des monopoles d'état; indirectement, elles permettent aussi de contrôler les importations. A titre d'exemples, mentionnons au niveau fédéral la Loi sur la Commission canadienne du blé[133] et au niveau des provinces, les diverses lois créant des régies provinciales des alcools.[134]
    En vertu de l'article 5 de la Loi sur les licences d'exportation et d'importation:

> Le gouverneur en conseil peut établir une liste de marchandises, appelée 'liste de marchandises d'importation contrôlée,' comprenant tout article dont, à son avis, il est nécessaire de contrôler l'importation pour l'une quelconque des fins suivantes, savoir:
> a assurer, selon les besoins du Canada, le meilleur approvisionnement et la meilleure distribution possible d'un article rare sur les marchés mondiaux ou soumis à des régies gouvernementales dans les pays d'origine ou à une répartition par arrangement intergouvernemental;
> b mettre à exécution toute mesure prise selon la Loi sur la stabilisation des prix agricoles, la Loi sur le soutien des prix des produits de la pêche, la Loi sur la vente coopérative des produits agricoles, la Loi sur l'Office des produits agricoles ou la Loi sur la Commission canadienne du lait, ayant pour objet ou pour effet de soutenir le prix de l'article; ou
> c mettre en œuvre un arrangement ou un engagement intergouvernemental.'

Un amendement récent apporté à l'article 5 par la Loi sur la Commission du textile et du vêtement prévoit en outre la possibilité d'inclure dans la liste en question des marchandises dont l'importation au Canada risque de porter un préjudice sérieux aux producteurs canadiens de marchandises semblables ou directement concurrentes.[135] La liste de marchandises d'importation contrôlée établie par le décret C.P. 1970–1376, en date du 31 juillet 1970, énumère treize catégories de produits dont dix sont des dérivés du lait, les autres étant le sucre, le café, et les marchandises de provenance rhodésienne.[136] Le contrôle des importations de produits dérivés du lait, dont le fondement juridique est le paragraphe (a) de l'article

5, remonte à 1951.[137] En pratique ce contrôle a été d'une importance très secondaire, étant donné que le Canada suffit à ses propres besoins dans ce domaine.[138] En ce qui concerne le sucre et le café, c'est la mise en œuvre d'accords internationaux, auxquels le Canada est partie, qui justifie leur inclusion dans la liste des marchandises d'importation contrôlée.[139] Dans le cas des produits d'origine rhodésienne, le contrôle exercé est fondé formellement sur l'existence d'un accord intergouvernemental intervenu entre le Royaume-Uni et le Canada à la suite de la déclaration unilatérale d'indépendance de la Rhodésie.[140] Mais un tel usage de la Loi sur les licences d'exportation et d'importation a fait l'objet, devant la Chambre des Communes, de sévères critiques comme étant contraire à l'esprit de la loi qui n'avait pas été prévue dans le but d'imposer des sanctions.[141]

Depuis le 31 juillet 1970, la liste des marchandises d'importation contrôlée a subi deux modifications importantes. Le 26 août 1971, le gouverneur général en conseil, agissant sous l'autorité de l'article 5(2) de la Loi sur les licences d'exportation et d'importation, ajoutait à la liste en question une 14ème catégorie de produits couvrant les filés et mêches de coton.[142] Plus récemment encore, un nouveau décret, dont l'entrée en vigueur était fixée au 30 novembre 1971, introduisait une 15ème catégorie de produits couvrant les chemises importées à bas prix.[143] Dans les deux cas, le Canada justifia son action en alléguant que l'article XIX du GATT lui permettait d'agir ainsi.[144] On sait que cet article permet le recours à des mesures d'urgence lorsqu'un produit est importé sur le territoire d'une partie contractante 'en quantités tellement accrues et à des conditions telles qu'il porte ou menace de porter un préjudice grave aux producteurs nationaux de produits similaires ou de produits directement concurrents.' Mais à la suite de l'annonce d'un contingentement global sur les importations de chemises, le Japon a laissé entendre récemment qu'il pourrait exiger du Canada certaines concessions équivalentes aux conditions prévues par le paragraphe 3 de l'article XIX du GATT.

La Loi sur l'Office national de l'énergie établit, à son article 81, que personne ne doit exporter du gaz ou de la force motrice, ou importer du gaz, que sous l'autorité et conformément à une licence délivrée selon la loi;[145] l'article 82(2) spécifie que la licence en question 'peut être restreinte ou limitée à l'égard de la région, de la quantité ou de l'époque ou relativement à la catégorie ou nature des produits.' Enfin, à l'article 87, il est prévu que le gouverneur en conseil peut, par proclamation, étendre au pétrole la partie de la loi ayant trait au contrôle des exportations et des importations. Or, depuis le 7 mai 1970, une telle proclamation est effectivement en vigueur, de telle sorte que l'importation de produits pétroliers se trouve à l'heure actuelle contrôlée.[146] Mais ce contrôle ne s'est pas fait sans aléas. Une première réglementation exigeant comme condition d'obtention d'une licence, que l'importateur intéressé ne transporte ni ne fasse transporter de l'essence à moteur de certaines régions du Canada à d'autres, sans le consentement de l'office, fut déclarée inconstitutionnelle.[147] Subséquemment, cette réglementation fut modifiée de manière à permettre à l'office de délivrer une licence d'importation de pétrole pour fins de consommation 'dans la région du Canada indiquée dans la licence en quantités, à l'époque et par les ports d'entrée qu'il juge appropriés.'[148] Le nouveau règlement fut déclaré constitutionnel, par la Cour de l'Echiquier d'abord,[149] puis par la Cour suprême.[150]

La Loi sur la Commission canadienne du blé est l'exemple parfait au Canada d'une loi créant un monopole d'état dans un domaine donné. Le contrôle des importations et des exportations est prévu aux articles 32 et 33 de la loi. Il a été étendu par décret à l'avoine et à l'orge, ainsi qu'aux produits contenant plus de 25 pour cent de blé, d'avoine ou d'orge.[151] En pratique, l'incidence de ce contrôle sur le commerce international peut être considérée assez secondaire, étant donné la surproduction canadienne de tels produits. Le plus grave problème, ainsi que le note le rapport Habeler préparé pour le compte du GATT, concerne les pays en voie de développement dont certains se voient ainsi fermer un débouché éventuel à leur producteurs agricoles.[154] Toutefois, si le système de préférence en faveur des pays en voie de développement proposé par le Canada à la Conférence des Nations Unies sur le commerce et le développement devient réalité, une réponse satisfaisante à ce problème pourrait être apportée. La proposition du Canada comporte en effet une offre de réduction – dans certains cas de suppression – du tarif douanier à l'égard d'une liste choisie du produits agricoles, ainsi qu'une offre d'élimination des restrictions quantitatives pour les produits jouissant du traitement préférentiel.[153]

Dans le cas des régies provinciales des alcools, il demeure assez difficile d'établir l'impact véritable du monopole qu'elles exercent sur les importations de boissons alcooliques étrangères. Mais si l'on en juge par un discours récent du ministre de l'industrie et du commerce, il semble bien que le problème soit réel. Parlant devant le Conseil économique des provinces de l'Atlantique à Fredericton, Nouveau Brunswick, M Jean-Luc Pépin déclarait, le 19 octobre 1971: 'Les commissions des alcools des provinces déterminent les genres d'alcools qui peuvent être vendus et fixent également les prix de ces produits. Leur action a donc une répercussion importante non seulement sur le commerce interprovincial mais international.'[154]

Les accords de restrictions 'volontaires'

Le 5 octobre 1971, le ministre canadien de l'industrie et du commerce déposait devant la Chambre des Communes un échange de lettres intervenu entre le gouvernement du Canada et l'ambassadeur du Japon au Canada, aux termes duquel le Japon consentait à limiter ses exportations au Canada dans les domaines des textiles et de la radio.[155] Le fait pour un pays de limiter ainsi volontairement ses exportations vers un autre pays est relativement fréquent et ne peut être considéré, à strictement parler, comme une restriction à l'importation originant du Canada. Cependant, comme le fait remarquer William B. Kelly, Jr, 'although neither Canada nor the United States applies discriminatory quantitative restrictions to imports from Japan, they, along with other industrial countries, have formally and informally pressured Japan to control exports of a number of products. These controls have the same purpose and effect as discriminatory import restrictions.'[156]

Dans le cas du Canada, il importe de savoir qu'en vertu de l'article 8(2) du Tarif des douanes, le gouvernement en conseil peut décréter une surtaxe à l'importation de produits étrangers qui 'causent ou menacent de causer un préjudice grave à des producteurs canadiens de produits semblables ou directement concurrentiels.'[157] La simple menace de recourir à une telle mesure, permise ainsi que nous l'avons vue par l'article XIX du GATT, constitue un moyen efficace de persuader les pays étrangers de restreindre certaines de leurs exportations vers le Canada. Et lorsque de pareilles restrictions s'avèrent inefficaces, ou ne sont pas respectées, il est loisible au Canada d'avoir recours aux prescriptions de l'article 8(2) du Tarif des douanes.[158] Il peut aussi, depuis le 25 mai 1971, interdire ou réglementer l'entrée de marchandises, 'dont l'exportation en provenance d'un pays quelconque fait l'objet d'un accord ou d'un engagement entre le gouvernement du Canada et le gouvernement de ce pays,' lorsque ces marchandises 'sont importées au Canada d'une manière qui circonvient cet accord ou cet engagement.'[159]

Toutefois, il faut préciser qu'en vertu de l'article 3 de l'Accord concernant le commerce international des textiles de coton, tout pays dont le marché est désorganisé peut demander au pays exportateur de limiter ses exportations à un certain niveau; et si un accord s'avère impossible, des restrictions peuvent être imposées pour empêcher que le niveau en question soit dépassé.[160] Or, un certain nombre de demandes de limitations introduites auprès de pays étrangers l'ont été en conformité avec cet accord. Comme le faisait remarquer le représentant du Canada au Comité des textiles de coton en 1966: 'Nombre de ces importations sont effectuées à des prix très bas et, dans certains cas, de graves problèmes ont surgi de ce fait. Aucun effort n'a cependant été négligé pour maintenir au minimum absolu les demandes de limitation au titre de l'article 3.'[161]

Cependant, dans un nouveau rapport présenté devant le même comité en 1970, le représentant du Canada faisait part de la déception de son pays. Celle-ci paraissait résulter 'd'une répugnance croissante de la part de certains pays exportateurs à reconnaître la nécessité de limiter leurs exportations de certains produits vers le Canada, même après avoir été informés de façon détaillée du préjudice causé aux producteurs canadiens.'[162] En outre, il soulignait le problème particulier occasionné par l'apparition sur le marché canadien, à partir de 1965, des tissus à base de fibres artificielles. Comme les dispositions de l'accord étaient insuffisantes pour régler le problème des produits de remplacement et que de nombreux pays exportateurs craignaient qu'une 'manifestation de bonne volonté de leur part ne soit interprétée comme sanctionnant une extension de l'Accord dans le domaine plus vaste des produits à base de fibres chimiques,' le Canada avait dû 'engager des négociations bilatérales séparées en dehors de l'Accord.' C'est précisément dans cette perspective que s'inscrit l'accord récent intervenu entre le Canada et le Japon en octobre 1971.[163] Mais il va de soi que la technique n'est pas nécessairement efficace dans tous les cas. Ainsi, le récent rapport de la Commission du textile et du vêtement sur les effets des importations de chemises à bas prix signale les tentatives déjà faites en vue de freiner les importations de telles chemises au moyen d'accords de restrictions volontaires, mais note la montée en flèche des importations malgré ces efforts.[164] On sait déjà comment, à la suite de ce rapport, fut décrété un contingentement global des importations de chemises.[165]

CONCLUSION

La présente étude ne prétend pas être exhaustive. En particulier, il faut souligner qu'aucune mention n'a été faite jusqu'ici de législations canadiennes ayant pour effet de fournir, directement ou indirectement, des subsides à l'exportation. Or, on sait que l'article XVI du GATT prohibe les subsides à l'exportation, excepté en ce qui concerne les produits de base.[166] Le même article fait en outre aux pays membres du GATT un devoir d'informer les parties contractantes de toutes subventions ayant pour effet direct ou indirect d'augmenter les exportations ou de diminuer les importations.[167] Si l'article III (8)b du GATT permet expressément le paiement de subventions aux producteurs nationaux, c'est seulement dans la mesure ou de telles subventions ne constituent pas une aide directe ou indirecte à l'exportation. Qu'en est-il au Canada?

Il est difficile de donner une réponse précise à cette question uniquement à partir du droit. Il n'existe pas vraiment au Canada de programme général de subsides à l'exportation. Il y a bien la Loi sur l'expansion des exportations qui prévoit un système de crédit à l'exportation; mais les conditions offertes ne paraissent pas favoriser indûment le Canada par rapport aux autres pays.[168] Dans le domaine spécifique des transports, la Loi sur les chemins de fer prévoit des tarifs réduits pour les expéditions de grains de l'intérieur du pays vers les ports de l'Atlantique, aux fins d'exportation.[169] Mais ce type de subsides qui vise en particulier les produits agricoles fait exception aux exigences de l'article XVI du GATT. Il en est de même d'ailleurs des diverses lois canadiennes qui accordent certains types de subsides aux producteurs agricoles du pays, dans la mesure où ces subsides constituent une aide indirecte à l'exportation.[170] Enfin, certaines législations comme la Loi sur les subventions au développement régional peuvent, dans des cas concrets, apporter une aide indirecte à l'exportation.[171] A titre d'exemple, mentionnons un contrat de $60 millions obtenu par la Davie Shipbuilding Co. de Québec pour la construction de navires grecs grâce à une subvention du Ministère de l'expansion économique régionale et à un prêt à long terme consenti aux importateurs par la Société pour l'expansion des exportations.[172] Peut-on vraiment parler de subsides à l'exportation dans un tel cas? Il s'agit manifestement d'un problème d'espèce qui relève autant de la science économique que du droit. Mais si l'on généralise à partir du problème des subsides à l'exportation, on ne peut que répéter ce qui était déjà affirmé plus haut, à savoir: une étude du genre de celle-ci ne peut prétendre être exhaustive. A un certain point, en effet, les problèmes deviennent multidisciplinaires, et c'est uniquement dans le cadre d'une étude multidisciplinaire qu'ils peuvent être abordés en profondeur.

Cependant, si l'on s'en tient uniquement au droit, que conclure de ce qui a été exposé précédemment? En ce qui concerne l'évolution du tarif des douanes, deux faits en particulier sont à retenir. Il y a d'abord l'abandon progressif du tarif à trois colonnes en faveur d'un tarif à deux colonnes. Ce qui a amené certains auteurs, comme nous l'avons déjà vu, à suggérer l'abandon formel du 'tarif général.'[173] La suggestion est valable, mais peut-être y aurait-il lieu d'attendre encore un certain temps. Car si le 'tarif de la nation la plus favorisée' apparaît assez clairement, à l'heure actuelle, comme le véritable 'tarif général,' il n'est pas certain du tout par contre que le 'tarif de préférence britannique' subsistera tel quel.[174] Les données de base dans ce domaine sont modifiées singulièrement, d'une part par l'entrée prochaine de la Grande-Bretagne dans le Marché commun, d'autre part par la perspective d'une préférence généralisée en faveur des pays en voie de développement. Donc si une modification générale du Tarif des douanes doit être opérée, mieux vaut attendre.

Une telle révision pourrait aussi tenir compte d'un autre fait qui est l'introduction, dans le tarif des douanes canadien, de la partie de la *Nomenclature tarifaire de Bruxelles* ayant trait aux produits chimiques. Ainsi que nous l'avons déjà noté précédemment, les problèmes de classification au Canada sont multiples et leur complexité est parfois telle qu'on peut voir là un obstacle indirect au commerce international.[175] Or l'adoption intégrale de la *Nomenclature tarifaire de Bruxelles* pourrait constituer, à cet égard, une solution partielle mais non moins valable à ce problème.

Pour ce qui est d'autre part de la réglementation canadienne en matière de commerce international, les conclusions suivantes peuvent être retenues. En premier lieu, le Canada semble, dans sa façon de procéder, accorder une importance au moins aussi grande à la réalité économique qu'au strict respect de ses obligations internationales. A titre d'exemple, on peut mentionner d'abord le fait que lors de la crise économique de 1962, il a imposé une surtaxe temporaire sur les importations, contraire aux exigences du GATT, plutôt que d'établir des restrictions quantitatives, explicitement prévues par le GATT, mais économiquement beaucoup plus difficiles d'application.[176] Un autre exemple serait l'absence, dans la réglementation antidumping antérieure à 1969, de toute exigence relative à la preuve d'un dommage réel ou appréhendé comme condition de recours à des mesures antidumping, ce contrairement aux prescriptions de l'article VI du GATT.[177] Dans d'autres domaines, on pourrait mentionner aussi l'adoption par le Canada d'un taux de change fluctuant contraire en principe aux exigences du Fonds monétaire international,[178] ou encore la législation canadienne sur la pollution dans l'Arctique qui semble aller au delà des normes présentes du droit international coutumier sur la question.[179] Il s'agit là d'une conclusion qui, pour certains, apparaîtra quelque peu surprenante.

Sur le plan interne, par ailleurs, le gouvernement du Canada semble avoir procédé avec tout autant de liberté. Nous avons déjà vu qu'à deux reprises par le passé, l'opposition parlementaire avait accusé le gouvernement au pouvoir d'utiliser des lois canadiennes à des fins autres que celles originairement prévues. La première fois, il s'agissait du recours au Tarif des douanes et à la Loi sur l'administration financière pour imposer une surtaxe temporaire à l'importation.[180] La seconde fois, c'est le recours à la Loi sur les licences d'exportation et d'importation aux fins d'imposer un embargo sur les produits d'origine rhodésienne qui fût critiqué.[181] Aussi bien au plan interne qu'au plan international donc, il apparait que le gouvernement canadien, dans la poursuite de ses objectifs commerciaux, a fort bien su adapté le droit à la réalité économique.

LES NOTES

1 Pour la période antérieure à 1946, voir W.T. Easterbrook et Hugh G.J. Aitken, *Canadian Economic History* (1956). Voir aussi John H. Young, *La politique commerciale du Canada,* étude préparée pour le compte de la Commission royale d'enquête sur les perspectives économiques du Canada (1958) 25–53.

2 Voir Young, *La politique commerciale du Canada, supra* note 1, 54–68; aussi Canadian-American Committee, National Planning Association (US), Private Planning Association of Canada, *A New Trade Strategy for Canada and the United States* (1966) 9–12.

3 Canada, Ministère des affaires extérieures, division de l'information, *Déclarations et discours,* no 69/3, 4.

4 Canada, Ministère des finances, *Communiqué* no 71–40, 24 mars 1971, à 5.

5 Young, *La politique commerciale du Canada, supra* note 1, à 111, citant les mots du président de la Commission du tarif Hector B. McKinnon, en 1948.

6 Voir (1970), *Annuaire du Canada* 1197–1205; les quelques rares pays ne jouissant pas

encore de ce bénéfice, tels l'Albanie ou la Mongolie extérieures, ne commercent pas véritablement avec le Canada.

7 Décret du 12 juin 1968 (DORS/68–194).

8 DORS/65–521.

9 Article 3(2) et 3(3) du Tarif des douanes, Statuts révisés du Canada, c C-41 (1970).

10 Article 3(6) et 3(7) du Tarif des douanes.

11 C.P. 1954-531; *Décrets, ordonnances et règlements statutaires* (1955), vol I, 878.

12 Article 5(1) du Tarif des douanes.

13 Semblable remarque est faite par L.D. Wilgress, *Canada's Approach to Trade Negotiations*, Canadian Trade Committee, Private Planning Association of Canada (1963) 58–9.

14 Voir G.A. Elliott, *Tariff Procedure and Trade Barriers: A Study of Indirect Protection in Canada and the United States* (1955) à 19, note 4.

15 Article 5(3) du Tarif des douanes.

16 Article 5(4) du Tarif des douanes.

17 Voir Young, *La politique commerciale du Canada, supra* note 1, à 113.

18 Accord commercial du 12 février 1960, entré en vigueur le 30 juin 1960 (Canada [1960] Recueil des traités, no 9); cet accord remplace un traité antérieur de 1931: [1931] Recueil des traités, no 5.

19 Accord commercial entre le Canada et les Antilles, signé le 6 juillet 1925 et entré en vigueur le 30 avril 1927; un préavis du Canada du 23 novembre 1938 dénonçant l'accord a été remplacé par un avis du 27 décembre 1939 le maintenant en vigueur. Le protocole signé le 8 juillet 1966 reconduit dans l'interim la partie I de cet accord en la modifiant et résilie la partie II.

20 Accord commercial signé le 23 avril 1932 et entré en vigueur le 24 mai 1932; les modifications les plus récentes sont incorporées à un Protocole signé le 13 mai 1970, voir 1970–1–2, Can., c 14.

21 Accord commercial signé le 20 août 1932, entré en vigueur le 13 octobre 1932 [1933] (Recueil des traités, no 4).

22 Voir l'article I(2) a ainsi que l'annexe A de l'Accord général sur les tarifs douaniers et le commerce.

23 19 *International Financial News Survey* (International Monetary Fund) 14 July 1967.

24 James R. Melvin et Bruce W. Wilkinson, *Protection effective dans l'économie canadienne* (1968).

25 Les auteurs eux-mêmes expriment certaines réserves quant à la précision de leur recherche, en particulier au chapitre 6 de leur monographie.

26 [1966] Recueil des traités du Canada no 14; la compatibilité de l'accord avec le GATT est examinée par L.J. Jahnke, 'The United States–Canadian Automotive Products Agreement' (1964–66), 2 *University of British Columbia Law Review* 378.

27 Annexe A du traité.

28 Annexe B du traité.

29 Décret en date du 16 janvier 1965 (DORS/65–42), article 1.

30 GATT, *Instruments de base et documents divers,* supp. 13, 1965, 118–32.

31 Ibid, à 131.

32 Ibid, à 130; voir aussi *Instruments de base et documents divers,* supp. 14, 1966, 192.

33 GATT, *Instruments de base et documents divers,* supp. 14, 1966, 39.

34 Voir *Financial Post,* 14 février 1970.

35 La surcharge de 10 pour cent imposée au mois d'août 1971 par le gouvernement américain a été abolie quatre mois plus tard en décembre 1971; mais des négociations sont toujours en cours concernant la revision du pacte automobile (janvier 1972).

36 Voir Wilgress, *Canada's Approach to International Trade, supra* note 13, à 58.

37 C.P. 125/4317: *Décrets, ordonnances et règlements statutaires,* codification 1955, vol I, 765.

38 Young, *La politique commerciale du Canada, supra* note 1, à 115.

39 L'objet précis de ces différents drawbacks est décrit dans McGoldbrick's *Canadian Customs and Excise Tariffs* (76° ed, 1968–9) 786–813.

40 Articles XX et XXI de l'Accord général sur les tarifs douaniers et le commerce.

41 Voir par exemple F. Masson et J.B. Whitely, *Barriers to Trade Between Canada and the United States,* Canadian-American Committee, National Planning Association (US) et Private Planning Association of Canada (1960) 22.

42 Voir Elliott, *Tariff Procedures and Trade Barriers, supra* note 14, à 21–2.

43 Article 8(1) du Tarif des douanes.

44 Article 8(2) du Tarif des douanes.

45 Article 8(4) du Tarif des douanes.

46 Article 8(5) du Tarif des douanes.

47 Sur ce sujet voir Kenneth C. Mackenzie, *Tariff-Making and Trade Policy in the U.S. and Canada. A Comparative Study* (1968) 202–4; F. Masson et H.W. English, *Invisible Trade Barriers between Canada and the*

United States, Canadian-American Committee, National Planning Association (US) et Private Planning Association of Canada (1963) 40–1; Kenneth W. Dam, *The GATT-Law and International Economic Organization* (1970) 29 and 32.

48 Mackenzie, *Tariff-Making and Trade Policy, supra* note 47, à 202.

49 Devant le parlement, l'opposition prétendit qu'une telle utilisation de la Loi sur l'administration financière et du Tarif des douanes n'était pas conforme à l'esprit de ces lois: voir Masson et English, *Invisible Trade Barriers, supra* note 47, à 41.

50 GATT *Documents de base et instruments divers,* supp. 11, 1963, 58.

51 Masson et English, *Invisible Trade Barriers, supra* note 47, à 41.

52 Robert E. Baldwin, *Nontariff Distortions of International Trade* (1970) 5.

53 L'auteur de la définition distingue lui-même douze types de barrières non-tarifaires: ibid, à 10–12.

54 Dans *Oppenheimer Bros. & Co.,* (1957), 2 *Tariff Board Reports* 21, porté en appel devant la Cour de l'échiquier, *Javex Co. Ltd* v *Oppenheimer Bros. & Co.* (1959) Ex. C.R. 439, et devant la Cour suprême, (1961) R.C.S. 170, ce problème a été abordé de façon très claire. Il s'agissait en l'occurence de déterminer si le produit 'Clorax,' un désinfectant utilisé couramment comme détergent dans le lavage, pouvait être classifié sous le poste tarifaire 219a, 'produits chimiques pour désinfecter.' Il fut décidé que le fait que le produit en question pouvait servir à d'autres fins que de désinfecter était sans portée sur la classification de ce dernier. Voir sur ce sujet K.E. Eaton et N.A. Chalmers, *Canadian Law of Customs and Excise* (1968) 68–70; Elliot, *Tariff Procedures and Trade Barriers, supra* note 14, à 114–16.

55 L'exemple typique est le moteur électrique. De nombreuses décisions ont porté sur ce problème; pour l'analyse de ces dernières voir Eaton et Chalmers, *Canadian Law of Customs and Excise, supra* note 54, à 72–84; voir aussi Elliott, *Tariff Procedure and Trade Barriers, supra* note 14, à 104–9.

56 Le problème est abordé de façon plus particulière au paragraphe suivant.

57 Voir sur le sujet Elliott, *Tariff Procedures and Trade Barriers, supra* note 14, à 130–6.

58 P.C. 1618, 2 juillet 1936.

59 Masson et English, *Invisible Trade Barriers, supra* note 47, à 19.

60 *Dominion Engineering Works Ltd* v *D.M.N.R. et al.* (1958), 1 *Tariff Board Reports* 152; pour une analyse détaillée de la jurisprudence, voir Eaton et Chalmers, *supra* note 54, à 85–119.

61 Memoranda D-51.

62 Voir Masson et English, *Invisible Trade Barriers, supra* note 47, à 19.

63 Les décisions sur ce sujet sont examinées par Eaton et Chalmers, *Canadian Law of Customs and Excise, supra* note 54, à 48–53.

64 *Federal Belting & Asbestos Co. Ltd.* (1955), 1 *Tariff Board Reports* 239, à 240.

65 La nouvelle numérotation se trouve dans les Statuts revisés du Canada c C-40 (1970).

66 *Canadian Housewares Ltd.* (1949), 1 *Tariff Board Reports* 8.

67 Article 46(1) de la Loi sur les douanes, Statuts revisés du Canada c C-40 (1970).

68 Article 46(3) de la Loi sur les douanes.

69 Article 47(1) de la Loi sur les douanes.

70 Article 48(1) de la Loi sur les douanes; la Loi sur la cour fédérale, 1970–1–2, Can., c 1 a remplacé le nom de 'cour de l'échiquier' par celui de 'cour fédérale': articles 3 et 64.

71 Article 48(20) de la Loi sur les douanes.

72 Voir Masson et English, *Invisible Trade Barriers, supra* note 47, à 17–18.

73 Voir par exemple Wilgress, *Canada's Approach to Trade Negotiations, supra* note 13, à 59; Masson et English, *Invisible Trade Barriers Between Canada and the United States, supra* note 47, à 60–2. Sur la Nomenclature Tarifaire de Bruxelles, voir 'The Brussels Tariff Nomenclature' (1970), 4 *Journal of World Trade Law* 803.

74 *Débats des Communes,* 14 novembre 1968, vol III, 2758–9.

75 Loi modifiant le tarif des douanes, 1968–9, Can., c 12, art 4.

76 Chambre internationale de commerce, *Entraves invisibles au commerce,* brochure 130 (1949).

77 Article VII(2) a du GATT.

78 Article VII(2)b du GATT; une note explicative ajoutée au paragraphe 2 de l'article VII précise qu' 'il serait conforme à l'Article VII de présumer que la "valeur réelle" peut être représentée par le prix de facture, auquel on ajoutera tous les éléments correspondant à des frais légitimes non compris dans le prix de facture et constituant effectivement des éléments de la "valeur réelle," ainsi que tout escompte anormal ou tout autre réduction anormale calculée sur le prix normal de concurrence': GATT, *Instruments de base et*

documents *divers*, IV, Texte de l'Accord général (1969), annexe I, 68–9.

79 Article VII(2)c du GATT.

80 Voir Masson et English, *Invisible Trade Barriers, supra* note 47, à 10.

81 Loi modifiant la Loi sur les douanes, 1953–4, Can., c 3.

82 Loi modifiant la Loi sur les douanes, 1955, Can., c 32, article 2.

83 Article 36(1) de la Loi sur les douanes. c C-40.

84 Ibid, article 37.

85 Masson et English, *Invisible Trade Barriers, supra* note 47, à 11.

86 Masson et Whitely, *Barriers to Trade, supra* note 41, à 53.

87 Article 39 de la Loi sur les douanes.

88 Masson et Whitely, *Barriers to Trade, supra* note 41, à 53.

89 Voir *supra*, 727 et seq.

90 C'est ce qui ressort de la décision de la Commission du Tarif dans *H. Bedos & Co. (Canada) Inc.* (1962), 2 *Tariff Board Reports* 264, à 267–8.

91 GATT, *Instruments de base et documents divers,* supp. 11, 1963, 90.

92 Des mesures semblables avaient été adoptées pour une première fois par le gouvernement canadien en août 1961; à la suite de plaintes américaines, elles furent subséquemment retirées, mais seulement à la fin de la période de commercialisation: ibid, à 91.

93 Ibid, à 92–3.

94 Ibid, à 94.

95 Ibid, à 96 et 55–6.

96 L'article 5 du Tarif des douanes, exigeait que toutes marchandises pouvant être marquées, timbrées, ou étiquetées, indiquent en français ou en anglais, de façon lisible et en évidence, le lieu de leur origine; voir Elliott, *Tariff Procedures and Trade Barriers, supra* note 14, à 227.

97 La surtaxe fut imposée en vertu de l'article 1 de la Loi modifiant le Tarif des douanes, 1931, Can., c 30, et abolie dix-neuf ans plus tard par l'article 3 de la Loi modifiant le Tarif des douanes, 1950, Can., c 14.

98 C.P. 1963–1775 (DORS/63–461), 5 décembre 1963.

99 Article 17 du Tarif des douanes.

100 Voir Masson et English, *Invisible Trade Barriers, supra* note 47, à 53–4.

101 Article VI(1) du GATT.

102 Voir à ce sujet Dam, *The GATT-Law and International Economic Organization, supra* note 47, à 167.

103 GATT, *Instruments de base et documents divers,* supp. 16, 1967.

104 Sur les mesures antidumping au Canada avant 1969, voir K.C. Mackenzie, 'Antidumping Duties in Canada' (1966), 4 *Annuaire canadien de droit international* 131.

105 Loi sur les douanes, Statuts revisés du Canada c 60, article 6(1) (1952).

106 Voir Mackenzie, 'Anti-Dumping Duties in Canada,' *supra* note 104, à 133.

107 Voir *supra*, à 739–40.

108 Voir *supra*, à 741.

109 Mackenzie, 'Anti-Dumping Duties in Canada,' *supra* note 104, à 159.

110 Voir Dam, *The GATT-Law and International Economic Organization, supra* note 47, à 174.

111 Sur le Code international antidumping en général, voir John B. Rehm, 'Development in the Law and Institutions of International Economic Relations: The Kennedy Round of Trade Negotiations' (1968), 62 *Am. J. Int'l L.* 403, à 427–34.

112 Loi antidumping, 1968–9, Can., c 10.

113 DORS/69–17.

114 Articles 3 à 7 de la Loi antidumping, Statuts revisés du Canada c A–15 (1970).

115 Articles 8 à 12 de la Loi antidumping.

116 Article 13 de la Loi antidumping.

117 Article 14(1) de la Loi antidumping.

118 Article 16 de la Loi antidumping tel qu'amendé par l'article 2 de la Loi modifiant la Loi antidumping, 1970–1–2, Can., c 3.

119 Article 17 de la Loi antidumping.

120 Articles 18, 19, et 20 de la Loi antidumping.

121 Loi modifiant la Loi antidumping, 1970–1–2, Can., c 3, article 3.

122 L'article de la Loi sur les licences d'exportation et d'importation, 1953–4, Can., c 27, tel qu'amendé par l'article 26 de la Loi sur la Commission du textile et du vêtement, statuts du Canada 1970–1–2, Can., c 39.

123 *Le Devoir,* 5 novembre 1971; *Financial Post,* 13 November 1971.

124 Sur le tribunal antidumping même, voir la partie III de la Loi antidumping, Statuts revisés du Canada c A–15 (1970).

125 Ces décisions portaient sur les produits suivants: 1 / Isooctanol en provenance des Etats-Unis; 2 / bottes, bottines, et souliers de cuir pour le travail et le sport provenant de Roumanie et de Pologne; 3 / Chlore liquide en provenance de Bellingham (Washington), E.-U.; 4 / Antigel en vrac, à base d'ethylène-glycol, en provenance du Royaume-Uni; 5 /

panneaux muraux en plâtre ordinaire et dotés d'un indice de résistance au feu en provenance des Etats-Unis d'Amérique; 6 / robe de mariées au Canada par les maisons Bridallure Inc. et Alfred Angelo Inc., Philadelphie, Pennsylvanie.

126 Le tribunal a conclu à l'existence d'un préjudice réel dans les affaires suivantes: 1 / cerises glacées en provenance de France; 2 / ouvre-boîtes électrique en provenance du Japon avec ou sans éléments additionnels pour aiguiser les couteaux et ouvrir les bouteilles; 3 / certaines aiguilles et seringues en provenance des Etats-Unis d'Amérique et du Japon; 4 / téléviseurs monochromes et couleurs en provenance du Japon et de Taiwan, à l'exclusion des téléviseurs dont la diagonale est de moins de huit pouces. Le tribunal a par ailleurs conclu qu'un préjudice était susceptible d'être causé dans les affaires suivantes: 1 / verre à vitre transparent, en provenance de Tchécoslovaquie, d'Allemagne de l'est, de Pologne, de l'Union des Républiques socialistes soviétiques, et de Roumanie; 2 / transformateurs d'une puissance nominale de plus de 500 KVA (0.5 MVA) et de réacteurs d'une puissance de plus de 500 KVAR (0.5 MVAR) en provenance du Royaume-Uni, de la France, du Japon, de la Suède, de la Suisse, et de la République fédérale d'Allemagne, et de réacteurs d'une puissance de plus de 500 KVAR (0.5 MVAR) en provenance de la Belgique; 3 / chaussures pour dames en provenance d'Italie et d'Espagne; 4 / bandages pleins industriels en caoutchouc à montage à la presse exportés au Canada par la société Bearcat Tire Company, Chicago, Etats-Unis.

127 La décision portait sur les transformateurs de puissance en provenance de la Grande-Bretagne et du Japon; le tribunal s'est prononcée ultérieurement sur le fond du problème. Ibid.

128 *Financial Post,* 21 November 1970.

129 *Financial Post,* 4 September 1971.

130 Voir Masson et Whitely, *Barriers to Trade Between Canada and the United States, supra* note 41, à 21.

131 Statuts revisés du Canada, c E-17 (1970).

132 Statuts revisés du Canada, c N-6 (1970).

133 Statuts revisés du Canada, c C-12 (1970).

134 Loi de la Société des Alcools du Québec, Statuts du Québec, c 20 (1970-1).

135 Article 26 de la Loi sur la Commission du textile et du vêtement, 1970-1-2, Can., c 39.

136 DORS/70-359.

137 Voir Mackenzie, *Tariff-Making and Trade Policy in the U.S. and Canada, supra* note 47, à 199.

138 Ibid.

139 Il s'agit d'abord de l'Accord international sur le café de 1968, signé le 29 mars et ratifié par le Canada le 17 juillet 1968 (C.P. 1968-1344); le traité est entré en vigueur définitivement le 30 décembre 1968. Pour ce qui est de l'Accord international sur le sucre de 1968, il a été signé par le Canada le 19 décembre 1968 et la ratification a été déposée auprès des Nations unies le 23 décembre 1968; l'accord est entré en vigueur définitivement le 17 juin 1969.

140 C.P. 1966-289 (DORS/66-236).

141 *Débats des Communes,* 26 avril 1966, vol IV, 4312.

142 C.P. 1971-1788 (DORS/71-441).

143 C.P. 1971-2190 (DORS/71-539).

144 Ministére de l'industrie et du commerce, *Communiqué,* 22 octobre 1971, no 73/71, 5.

145 Statuts revisés du Canada, c N-6 (1970).

146 DORS/70-206.

147 *Caloil Inc.* v *Le Procureur Général du Canada et al.,* (1970) R.C.E., 513.

148 *Gazette officielle du Canada,* 26 août 1970, no 16, vol 104, 961-2.

149 *Caloil Inc.* v *Le Procureur Général du Canada,* (1970) R.C.E. 535.

150 *Caloil Inc.* v *Le Procureur Général du Canada et al.,* (1971) R.C.S. 543.

151 Voir Mackenzie, *Tariff-Making and Trade Policy in the U.S. and Canada, supra* note 47, à 204-5.

152 Voir Dam, *The GATT-Law and International Economic Organization, supra* note 47, à 263-4.

153 Voir Canadian Institute of International Affairs, (1970), *International Canada* 221.

154 *Le Devoir,* 10 novembre 1971.

155 *Le Devoir,* 6 octobre 1971; voir aussi Ministère de l'industrie et du commerce, *Communiqué,* 5 octobre 1971, no 69/71.

156 William B. Kelly, Jr, 'Nontariff Barriers' dans Bela Belassa, ed, *Studies in Trade Liberalization* (1967) 265, à 274.

157 A titre d'exemples, mentionnons le Décret de surtaxe concernant les chemises fabriquées en République de Corée, en date du 3 avril 1969: C.P. 1969-672 (DORS/69-165); ou encore le Décret de surtaxe concernant les filés de coton de fabrication mexicaine, en date du 21 novembre 1969: C.P. 1969-2230 (DORS/69-591). De tels décrets peuvent aussi être général, ne visant aucun pays en par-

ticulier; voir par exemple le décret de surtaxe sur des chemises pour hommes et garçons, en date du 2 juin 1970: C.P. 1970–959 (DORS/70–230).

158 Ce rôle de deuxième ligne de défense est apparent dans le Décret de surtaxe concernant les chemises fabriquées en Corée mentionné à la note précédente.

159 En vertu d'un amendement apporté à l'article 22 de la Loi sur les douanes par l'article 27 de la Loi sur la Commission du Textile et du vêtement, 1970–1–2, Can., c 39.

160 Accord à long terme concernant le commerce international des textiles de coton, entré en vigueur le 1er octobre 1962, prorogé une première fois en 1967, et une seconde fois en 1970: Protocole prorogeant l'Accord concernant le commerce international des textiles de coton du 1er octobre 1970 au 30 septembre 1973, signé par le Canada le 8 octobre 1970 (C.P. 1970–1726).

161 GATT, *Instruments de base et documents divers,* supp. 14, 1966, 94.

162 GATT, *Instruments de base et documents divers,* supp. 17, 1970, 53–4.

163 Ibid, à 54.

164 Commission du textile et du vêtement, *Rapport sur une enquête relative aux chemises pour hommes et pour garçons* (juin 1971) 11–12.

165 Voir *supra,* à 746.

166 Sur l'application concrète de cet article, voir E. Bruce Butler, 'Countervailing Duties and Export Subsidization: A Re-emerging Issue in International Trade' (1969), 9 *Virginia Journal of International Law* 82.

167 Article XVI(1) de l'Accord général sur les tarifs douaniers et le commerce.

168 Statuts revisés du Canada, c E-18 (1970) tel

qu'amendé par la Loi modifiant la Loi sur l'expansion des exportations, 1970–1–2, Can., c 23; sur le problème général du crédit à l'exportation, voir l'étude préparée par le département des affaires économiques et sociales des Nations-Unies et intitulée *Export Credits and Development financing* (1967) (Documents E/4274 ST/ECA/95 et E/4274/ Add. 1 ST/ECA/96).

169 Statuts revisés du Canada, c R-2, article 272(4) (1970); voir de façon générale sur ce sujet A.W. Currie, *Canadian Transportation Economics* (1967), c 4: 'Rates on Export Grain.'

170 Par exemple, la Loi sur la stabilisation des prix agricoles, Statuts revisés du Canada, c A-9 (1970).

171 Statuts revisés du Canada, c R-3 (1970).

172 *Le Devoir,* 15 mars 1971.

173 Voir *supra,* à 736.

174 Voir *Le Monde,* 29 juin 1971: 'Un Commonwealth sans "préférences"?'

175 Voir *supra,* à 735–7.

176 Voir *supra,* à 734

177 Voir *supra,* à 742.

178 Voir à ce sujet Joseph Gold, 'Development in the Law and Institutions of International Economic Relations: Unauthorized Changes of Par Value and Fluctuating Exchange Rates in the Bretton Woods System,' (1971), 65 *Am. J. Int'l L. 113.*

179 Loi sur la prévention de la pollution des eaux arctiques, Statuts revisés du Canada, Supp. 1, c2 (1970); voir aussi sur ce sujet Louis Henkin, 'Arctic Anti-Pollution: Does Canada Make – or Break – International Law,' (1971), 65 *Am. J. Int'l L.* 131.

180 Voir *supra,* à 746.

181 Ibid.

D.H.W. HENRY

30/International Aspects of Competition Policy

'Competition policy' is the expression which evolved in the latter 1960s to describe those measures and policies adopted by a nation to give effect to its acceptance, in whatever degree, of competition as the central mechanism of its economic system. In Canada, competition policy is now widely discussed as a result of the Interim Report on Competition Policy published in 1969 by the Economic Council of Canada[1] and the subsequent introduction in parliament of a bill entitled 'The Competition Act,'[2] designed to modernize Canada's anticombines laws along the lines suggested by the council's report. Ideally, competition policy embraces the totality of policies having an impact on competition, including tariff and tax policy, subsidies, the laws relating to industrial and intellectual property, regional development programs, and direct regulation of industry through boards, commissions, corporations, and other government agencies. In practice, competition policy finds its primary expression in laws relating to restrictive business practices designed to give some degree of protection to the operation of the competitive market.

The discussion of competition policy in an international context is timely. Most countries of the western world rely on a competitive market system, in one form or another, to allocate resources within the economy: Canada and the United States have had anticombines and antitrust laws since the end of the last century, while the United Kingdom and most western European countries have adopted restrictive business practices laws since the end of World War II. Moreover, competition policy is rapidly becoming as important in the international or world economy as in the domestic market; indeed, it is likely that over the next quarter century the need for an international competition policy will far outweigh the need within a particular domestic economy. The Economic Council put the matter this way:

> The rise of the international corporation, controlling productive and distributive facilities in a number of countries, is an indication that there exists a recognizable entity called the world economy ... It is by no means naive to look on the world as such corporations do and to consider issues of the locus of productive and distributive facilities, the maximization of economic efficiency and other matters relating to competition policy from an international as well as a domestic standpoint. The fact is that if nations fail to pursue policies designed to promote more efficient resource use on a world-wide basis, and to act upon a recognition of the many different channels through which goods and service, including information, can with advantage be transferred, they will incur, both individually and collectively, a heavy cost in foregone output.[3]

As a country greatly dependent upon international trade, as a recipient of heavy foreign investment, and as the host country to many international corporations,

Canada has an unusually high stake in the successful application of competition policy, both domestically and internationally. As trade liberalization progresses, opening up new markets for Canadian products, tariffs may tend to be supplemented or replaced by non-tariff barriers to trade in the form of restrictive business practices of one kind or another. With an increase in world markets and new technology, scale becomes more important so that the world economy will become increasingly characterized by monopolies and oligopolies of large international firms. This situation was recognized in the late sixties by Thorkil Kristensen, then secretary general of OECD, who posed the critical question for the future: '[H]ow can we keep market power under control without doing harm to rationalization and economic growth? ... Behind the current trend towards big business, through mergers or otherwise, there is a mixture of two motives. Let us call them the *high price motive* and the *low cost motive*. If we would reduce the first and let the second play its full role we would have the best of both worlds. How is that possible?'[4]

Internally a nation can exercise some degree of control over anticompetitive structures and conduct, but there is at present no law or mechanism for dealing with the emerging international problem. In these circumstances, at least initially, individual nations will be forced to seek their own solutions to the international problem with resulting difficulties identified by the Economic Council as 1 / unwanted extraterritorial impacts of one country's competition policy upon the economy of another, and 2 / problems calling for competition policy action that are beyond the scope of any one country's policy to resolve.[5] The solution to these problems clearly lies in some form of bilateral or multilateral arrangements which may not be too far beyond the horizon.

It is hoped that the following comments will serve to assist in the development of solutions in this field, especially regarding the role in such development of Canada – which will inevitably be the victim rather than the aggressor with respect to international anticompetitive practices.

COMBINES INVESTIGATION ACT

Canadian competition policy is at present expressed in the Combines Investigation Act.[6] The legislation had its origin in 1889 in an act prohibiting combinations in restraint of trade[7] and which, in 1892, became part of the newly formed Criminal Code; this provision remained in the code until 1960. Meanwhile, in 1910, the Combines Investigation Act was enacted to provide the machinery for investigation of the activities prohibited; it contained provisions parallel to those in the Criminal Code. Both the code and the act continued to exist, with amendments from time to time, until 1960, when the two sets of provisions were consolidated into the present Combines Investigation Act. And now the Competition Act reflects the government's intention to undertake the first major revision of this legislation since 1923.

Economic aspects

It should be said at the outset that the anticombines laws are almost entirely directed towards anticompetitive situations or conduct in the domestic market;

conduct in Canada which has anticompetitive effects beyond her borders is not reached by the law. This principle has been reflected in the administration of the act to the present.

The economic rationale of the legislation has been identified in its essentials by the Supreme Court of Canada, which has held that the purpose of the legislation is to protect the public interest in free competition.[8] Such free and open competition is to be maintained as a prime stimulus to the achievement of maximum production, distribution, and employment in a system of private enterprise; the legislation therefore seeks to eliminate certain practices in restraint of trade which prevent the nation's economic resources from being most effectively used. The legislation is intended to create a situation in which those who wish to compete for economic gain are free to do so, and thus discourages the regulation in industry by its members while encouraging such regulation by the forces of competition.

The responsible minister expressed the economic rationale in these terms in 1966:

> The Combines Investigation Act is based on the principle that under normal circumstances competition provides the greatest spur to efficiency and to the best allocation of economic resources in the private sector of the economy. This is sometimes forgotten in the more immediate concern about possible exploitation of consumers or about the inequitable treatment of some economic units by others. Where competition is effective, efficiency is rewarded and inefficiency is penalized. In the long run, efficient corporations grow and inefficient ones decline. Scarce resources are therefore channelled into the hands of those who use them best.[9]

It should be added that the Economic Council has recommended that the objective of Canadian competition policy be shifted from the achievement of competition for its own sake to the objective of economic and industrial efficiency, with competition the most important means to the attaining of this objective.[10]

It is worth emphasizing that the competitive market in our economy is not the classical model characterized by fragmented industries but is based on the more practical concept of 'workable competition.' Moreover, although the competitive market affects the major part of the economy, large segments of the economy have been withdrawn from the competitive market and placed under direct regulation by administrative boards or commissions, which make choices, often relating to price and production, that would otherwise be made by market forces.

General legal aspects

The Combines Investigation Act is part of the criminal law of Canada. It prohibits certain conduct because of its impact on the competitive process and prescribes penalties for such conduct. The three major areas of activity which are dealt with in the act are:

1 Combinations that prevent or unduly lessen competition in the production, purchase, sale, storage, rental, transportation or supply of commodities, or in the price of insurance;
2 Mergers or monopolies that may operate to the detriment of the public; and

3   Unfair trade practices, including price discrimination, predatory pricing, certain promotional allowances, misrepresentation of the regular price and resale price maintenance.

There are two important areas of economic activity which are not covered by
the act. The first is what might be termed 'pure services': since the act is designed
mainly to prohibit restraints on competition in the manufacture and distribution of
goods, it does not apply to services except for those noted specifically in section
1 above. In the second place, it has been held by the Supreme Court of Canada[11]
and by the Supreme Court of Ontario[12] that to the extent that power is conferred
upon an agency to regulate an industry, the anticombines laws do not apply to that
industry; in effect, the agency replaces the market place *pro tanto* as the protector
of the public interest.

Constitutionality
The statute has been held in a series of constitutional decisions to be the valid exercise by parliament of the criminal law power.[13] Its criminal nature, however, has
the result that there is no discretion on the part of the administrators to proscribe
industry activities; particular activities are either lawful or unlawful. This has made
the law a somewhat blunt instrument for the development of a competition policy
through the courts. Moreover, Canadian judges, unlike their American counterparts, have been reluctant to embark upon sophisticated economic analysis for
determining the issues involved, with the result that the jurisprudence has tended
to develop somewhat mechanical tests to separate lawful from unlawful conduct.[14]

Enforcement
Enforcement of the act is left in the hands of three agencies: the Director of Investigation and Research, the Restrictive Trade Practices Commission, and the courts.
Under section 8, it is the duty of the director to commence a formal inquiry
whenever he has reason to believe that an offence has been or is about to be committed; he can also be compelled to commence an inquiry on application, in statutory
form, by six Canadian citizens, or upon the instruction of the minister of consumer
and corporate affairs.[15] The director is given very wide powers of gathering evidence, including the search of premises, the interrogation under oath of witnesses,
and by return of information. The director's inquiry is undertaken for the purpose
of ascertaining the facts; at this stage no person is accused or called upon to make
a defence. On completion of the inquiry, if the director is of opinion that the evidence discloses an offence, he may refer the matter to the Restrictive Trade Practices Commission or to the attorney general of Canada.
    If the director decides to go to the commission, he prepares a statement of the
evidence supporting his allegations, places it before the commission, and gives a
copy to all parties against whom an allegation is made. The statute requires the commission thereupon to hold a hearing at which the parties are given full opportunity
to be heard. At the conclusion of the hearing, the commission writes a report
appraising the effect on the public interest of the activities disclosed in the evidence
and making recommendations as to the application of remedies, either provided in
the act or otherwise. The commission's report is delivered to the minister and is
ordinarily required to be published.
    If the director refers the material to the attorney general of Canada, the latter

decides whether or not legal proceedings are called for; if he decides they are, he may prosecute or ask for an injunction or both, in accordance with the statute. Proceedings may be undertaken in either the federal or the provincial courts, which are empowered to impose a penalty of up to two years' imprisonment, or a fine which is in the discretion of the court and without statutory limit, or both. In addition, the court may prohibit the continuation or repetition of the offence by an order which may be made binding on all directors, officers, servants, or agents of a corporation; such an order is frequently imposed by the court and is regarded as one of the more effective remedies provided by the statute.

Offences under the act

Combinations
Section 32(1) of the act provides:

> Every one who conspires, combines, agrees or arranges with another person
> a   to limit unduly the facilities for transporting, producing, manufacturing, supplying, storing or dealing in any article,
> b   to prevent, limit or lessen, unduly, the manufacture or production of an article, or to enhance unreasonably the price thereof,
> c   to prevent, or lessen, unduly, competition in the production, manufacture, purchase, barter, sale, storage, rental, transportation or supply of an article, or in the price of insurance upon persons or property, or
> d   to restrain or injure trade or commerce in relation to any article,
> is guilty of an indictable offence and is liable to imprisonment for two years.

Essentially the combination offence is an aspect of the law of conspiracy: the jurisprudence holds that it is the *agreement* to limit competition that constitutes the offence, whether or not the agreement has been, or even is capable of being, carried out.[16]

Only agreements that prevent or lessen competition *unduly* are prohibited under this provision, and the jurisprudence has established that this concept is to be measured by the actual or intended effect of the agreement on competition. An important though somewhat mechanical test is the share of the market accounted for by the parties to the agreement; while the excessive share of the market has never been described in absolute terms, combinations held to have been unduly restrictive of competition embrace, at one end of the scale, a virtual monopoly resulting from the agreement and, at the other end, a share of the market in the neighbourhood of 60 per cent.[17]

A number of exceptions are provided in section 32. Subsections (2) and (3) provide as follows:

> (2) Subject to subsection (3), in a prosecution under subsection (1) the court shall not convict the accused if the conspiracy, combination, agreement or arrangement relates only to one or more of the following:
> a   the exchange of statistics,
> b   the defining of product standards,

    c   the exchange of credit information,
    d   definition of trade terms,
    e   co-operation in research and development,
    f   restriction of advertising, or
    g   some other matter not enumerated in subsection (3).

(3) Subsection (2) does not apply if the conspiracy, combination, agreement or arrangement has lessened or is likely to lessen competition unduly in respect of one of the following:
    a   prices,
    b   quantity or quality of production,
    c   markets or customers, or
    d   channels or methods of distribution,
or if the conspiracy, combination, agreement or arrangement has restricted or is likely to restrict any person from entering into or expanding a business in a trade or industry.

In making it clear that the activities excepted may not be the vehicle for an anticompetitive agreement, subsection (3) reflects the great importance that competition policy attaches to the preservation of competition in price, production, markets, or channels of distribution and, even more important, the freedom of entry of a newcomer to a trade or industry. This is, in a nutshell, what competition policy is all about, and the factors mentioned in section 32(3) in relation to the domestic market are equally important in any consideration of competition policy relating to international markets: these are the areas in which experience has shown that limitations on competition take place to the detriment of the economy.

One other important exception in section 32 should be mentioned:

(4) Subject to subsection (5), in a prosecution under subsection (1) the court shall not convict the accused if the conspiracy, combination, agreement or arrangement relates only to the export of articles from Canada.

(5) Subsection (4) does not apply if the conspiracy, combination, agreement or arrangement
    a   has resulted or is likely to result in a reduction or limitation of the volume of exports of an article;
    b   has restrained or injured or is likely to restrain or injure the export business of any domestic competitor who is not a party to the conspiracy, combination, agreement or arrangement;
    c   has restricted or is likely to restrict any person from entering into the business of exporting articles from Canada; or
    d   has lessened or is likely to lessen competition unduly in relation to an article in the domestic market.

This exception illustrates the concept mentioned above that under the act the significant protection is for competition in the domestic market rather than in foreign markets; it is considered 'fair ball' to subject foreign markets to restrictive agreements on the part of Canadian exporters. This game is played by most exporting countries who have restrictive business practices laws; in general it may be said that collusive arrangements to penetrate export markets are removed from the scope of such laws.[18]

Export agreements may achieve beneficial results for the parties by saving costs through common marketing programs and by attracting large orders from foreign buyers who can be confident that an export consortium can fill such orders on a regular basis. While some of the larger export consortia in Canada are well known, the full extent to which section 32(4) has been used is not known as there is no requirement that export agreements be registered. But it should be noted that under subsection (5) an export agreement cannot be used if it results in an undue restriction of competition in the domestic market.

Mergers
Section 33 provides: 'Every person who is a party or privy to or knowingly assists in, or in the formation of, a merger or monopoly is guilty of an indictable offence and is liable to imprisonment for two years.' Section 2 defines 'merger':

(e) merger means the acquisition by one or more persons, whether by purchase or lease of shares or assets or otherwise, of any control over or interest in the whole or part of the business of a competitor, supplier, customer or any other person, whereby competition
   (i) in a trade or industry,
   (ii) among the sources of supply of a trade or industry,
   (iii) among the outlets for sales of a trade or industry, or
   (iv) otherwise than in subparagraphs (i), (ii) and (iii),
   is or is likely to be lessened to the detriment or against the interest of the public, whether consumers, producers or others.

The jurisprudence under this provision has not developed well, partly because of the first two important decisions under it[19] and partly because of the reluctance of the administrators to devote resources to cases which have little chance of success.

Most mergers in Canada do not attract the application of the act: mergers are currently taking place at the rate of about 500 annually, of which not more than 20 would be regarded as sufficiently significant to warrant more than preliminary examination. The Economic Council, in its 1969 report, recommended that around 8 to 17 per cent of all mergers in Canada ought to be subject to close scrutiny under the act.[20] In practice, a number of mergers are examined annually by the director and his staff under the 'program of compliance' where the parties to the merger are in effect seeking an advance clearance. Moreover, it is probable that many mergers are rejected in the board rooms of corporations because of the existing merger provisions.

At present the following tests are generally applied by the director in deciding whether a merger should be brought before the commission or the courts:

(1) Is there a sensibly defined product for which there are no close substitutes?
(2) Is there evidence that a substantial market (even though this may be regional) is likely to be affected by the merger and is capable of fairly unambiguous definition?

(3) In the absence of competition among domestic suppliers, is there evidence in the form of a substantial tariff or statistics showing that only a small portion of the market is supplied by imports, that foreign suppliers cannot be looked to, to protect the public?
(4) Is there reasonable assurance that there is no significant government regulation?
(5) Is there evidence that existing concentration ratios are high or there is a large size-differential between the acquiring company and its rivals?
(6) Is there evidence that the barriers to entry in the industry are high or that they will be raised by the merger or that new firms have not in fact entered the industry for some significant period of time?
(7) Is there evidence that competition remaining in the market is likely to be ineffective?

(8) Does the acquiring firm have a history of growth by merger or a history of coercive or predatory action or any other anticompetitive behavior?
(9) Is there any evidence of intent to reduce competition or to dominate the industry?
(10) Is there any likelihood that there will be foreclosure of an important market or source of supply to firms unconnected with the acquiring company?
(11) To what extent is there evidence of a real possibility of increased efficiency via economies of scale or the transfer of assets from incapable into capable hands?
(12) Is there direct evidence of detriment such as excessive profits or price enhancement following the merger?

The combined effect of the *Beer* and the *Sugar* cases,[21] the first important cases in the merger field, was to discourage the application of the act to a merger which does not result in a very high degree of concentration; indeed, there is a widespread belief among defence counsel, which is not shared by the director and his staff, that the courts are likely to strike down a merger only if it produces a virtual monopoly. This question will ultimately have to be resolved in the Supreme Court of Canada, but in the meantime the director proceeds on the assumption that a reasonably high degree of concentration is necessary before a prosecution would be successful.

In fact, no merger has yet been struck down in Canada by the courts, although in addition to or in lieu of any fine that may be imposed, the court may make an order dissolving the merger. This would seem the appropriate remedy in the circumstances: if concentration is unduly high in relation to the state of competition in the market, the structure of the industry requires a change; hence machinery should exist to bring this about.[22]

The bill to enact the Competition Act set out in some detail criteria to be applied by the proposed Competitive Practices Tribunal, which would have the function of determining which mergers brought before it should be allowed to proceed and which should be enjoined. Special criteria to be applied in considering a foreign takeover were also set out; these relate to the international aspects of competition policy which such a merger may raise.[23]

Monopolies
Section 33 of the act also prohibits monopolies, which are defined in section 2:

(f) 'monopoly' means a situation where one or more persons either substantially or completely control throughout Canada or any area thereof the class or species of business in which they are engaged and have operated such business or are likely to operate it to the detriment or against the interest of the public, whether consumers. producers or others, but a situation shall not be deemed a monopoly within the meaning of this paragraph by reason only of the exercise of any right or enjoyment of any interest derived under the *Patent Act,* or any other Act of the Parliament of Canada.

While it is not entirely apparent from the words, the activity to be prohibited might best be described as 'monopolization' or abuse of monopoly. It is not an offence to be in a monopoly position *per se,* but it is unlawful to achieve a monopoly by predatory conduct, driving out competitors and destroying competition in the process, or to maintain a monopoly position by predatory activity which destroys competition.

The only example of a court case in which these elements or some of them were present is the *Eddy Match* case,[24] in which the accused was convicted of the offence of monopolizing. The facts before the court disclosed a long history of anticompetitive mergers accompanied by such flagrantly abusive practices as fighting brands, industrial spying, and secret discounts and rebates. In addition, the industry was characterized by international cartel arrangements.

In the *ERCO* case[25] a conviction was obtained on a plea of guilty in respect of a merger and monopolization activity relating to industrial phosphates. A report of the Restrictive Trade Practices Commission published in December 1966[26] revealed a history of restrictive business practices on an international scale in the industry dealing in sodium chlorate, red phosphorus, and industrial phosphates. While the legal proceedings ultimately taken did not involve the international ramifications of ERCO's association with its United Kingdom parent, Albright & Wilson, the court, besides imposing a fine on ERCO, prohibited specific activities which constituted monopolization, that is, arrangements with competitors or potential competitors relating to: the selling price of industrial phosphates to third parties, the allocation of customers and markets, the purchase by third parties of raw materials used in the production of industrial phosphates, and the determination of delivery charges. In addition, the order required ERCO to make available to any customer or potential customer its current pricing schedule for industrial phosphates, showing the full range of prices, and it limited the spread between the highest and lowest price which the corporation may charge. An important feature of the order was a prohibition against ERCO entering into contracts lasting for a period greater than one year for the supply of sodium tripolyphosphate; this was to stop the foreclosing by long-term contracts of substantial portions of the market to new entrants.[27]

A still more recent situation involved an oligopoly consisting of three manufacturers of electric lamps, all subsidiaries of foreign parents. The oligopoly was characterized by what might be generally termed 'conscious parallelism' of action, exemplified primarily by identical prices and tenders relating to these products. The Restrictive Trade Practices Commission found that the companies concerned were in breach of the monopoly provision of the act.[28]

Unfair trade practices
In the international context it is perhaps inappropriate to go into any detail concerning the provisions of the Combines Investigation Act relating to price discrimina-

tion, predatory pricing, disproportionate promotional allowances, resale price maintenance, and misleading advertising since, generally speaking, these provisions have importance mainly in the domestic field. However, they are mentioned here in order to complete the picture so far as the coverage of the act is concerned.

The prohibition against price discrimination[29] prevents a supplier of goods from discriminating in price between competing purchasers except on a basis of quantity or quality of goods. As the offence arises only when there is a *practice* of price discrimination, incidental or temporary discrimination does not give rise to a breach of the act. There are two major reasons for the inclusion of such a provision in the anticombines laws: on the seller's side, price discrimination can be a predatory device to eliminate or retard a competitor of the seller; and on the buyer's side, the provision is aimed at the power of the big buyer to extract from a seller more favourable terms than those available to the buyer's competitors – price concessions which reflect primarily the buying power of the purchaser rather than economies and cost savings achieved by the seller by reason of the large volume order. In both cases, the practice depends on some form of market dominance or financial power.

Predatory pricing[30] – selling at an unreasonably low price – is outlawed when the effect or the design of the predatory pricing policy is to lessen competition substantially or eliminate a competitor. It is an activity designed to monopolize the market. Similarly, promotional allowances,[31] which are given by a supplier to his outlets for advertising or display, must be conferred on all competing customers in proportion to the volume of business they do with the supplier; the entire promotional budget cannot go to a small number of the most powerful and hence the most persuasive buyers.

Resale price maintenance is prohibited outright.[32] It is an offence for a supplier by any means whatever to require or induce a resale outlet to resell the product at a stated price or at not less than a stated or agreed minimum; it is also an offence for the supplier to cut off or refuse supplies to an outlet because the outlet has refused to maintain the price. The purpose of this provision is to encourage competition particularly among retailers, notwithstanding the fact that their suppliers and other outlets wish to maintain the retail price structure and enforce what is called 'orderly marketing.' It should be noted that this offence has been charged in an international trade situation in the *Surgical Blades* case,[33] as will be discussed below.

Misleading advertising[34] has become one of the most prolific sources of complaints and actions in the courts, but it is mentioned here only for completeness.

International influences

Anticompetitive activities within the domestic economy are frequently made possible by the existence of a protective tariff or other barrier to trade. The more trade is liberalized and the more the domestic market is open to imports, the less opportunity there is for Canadian enterpreneurs to engage in anticompetitive activities; foreign competition will see to it that the market inhibits such activities. However, where there are international cartels, market-sharing arrangements, restrictive patent licensing arrangements, and international firms which dominate the world market, the impact of foreign competition on the domestic market may be nullified and domestic restraints may flourish even without the tariff barrier. Inevitably the working of the competitive market within the nation is affected by the working of the international competitive market; problems in the latter can therefore have detrimental effects in the domestic economy. Hence it is to the international aspects of competition policy that we now turn.

INTERNATIONAL RESTRICTIVE BUSINESS PRACTICES

Private international agreements or cartels placing artificial restraints on international trade began to emerge with modern industrial development prior to World War I. The further industrial expansion arising out of the war produced an emerging breed of industrial giants competing in world markets; governments tended to encourage or tolerate the development of large scale monopolies or oligopolies and to favour increased concentration through rationalization. The period of industrial development and expansion between the world wars was the heyday of international cartels, with international arrangements, often overt and formal, relating to raw material industrial products as well as finished consumer goods.

So far as Canada was concerned, private international agreements were known to exist in the following categories: 1 / those affecting commodities for which Canada is dependent wholly or in large part on imports, including fertilizers, tanning materials, flat glass, sulphur, dyestuffs, tools, cemented tungsten carbide, magnesia refractories and titanium pigments; 2 / those giving Canadian manufacturers exclusive enjoyment of the home market but barring them from exporting, involving products such as chemicals, soda ash, electric lamps, radio tubes and sets and matches; and 3 / those involving participation by Canadian exporters in the cartel arrangements, involving such items as base metals (copper, lead, zinc, and nickel), steel, aluminum, ascetic acid, radium, and newsprint.

The restrictive practices resulting from international arrangements are similar to those found in combines in the domestic market. They include fixing uniform prices, establishing standard discounts or classes of customers, allocating territorial markets, fixing maximum sales or production quotas, limiting exports or imports, limiting the establishment of additional productive capacity or the introduction of new products, exclusive exchange of patents, and setting up exclusive selling agencies or exclusive dealers.[35]

The period since World War II has seen the growth of the multinational corporation, with its own restraint of trade problems; international industrial stategy has become characterized more by the internal decision-making process of the multinational corporation than by adherence to the cartel principle. The Economic Council has described the situation thus:

It does appear that a combination of the increased importance of u.s.-based international companies in world business and the reluctance of such companies to enter into cartels, for fear of u.s. antitrust consequences if not for other reasons, may have reduced the scope for such [cartel] arrangements. But there is information, including some contained in written briefs to the Economic Council, that suggest the persistence of noteworthy international cartels.[36]

It is perhaps significant that since World War II many OECD member countries have adopted or strengthened laws against restrictive business practices: Japan (1947), United Kingdom (1948), France (1953), Ireland (1953), Norway (1953), Sweden (1953), Denmark (1955), the Netherlands (1956), the Federal Republic of Germany (1957), Austria (1959), Belgium (1960), Switzerland (1962), and Spain (1963). The existence of such laws has been or is likely to be an important factor in changing the course of international restrictive business practices, particularly with respect to the abandonment of overt and formal cartel arrangements and their replacement by oligopolistic behaviour, such as price leadership and conscious parallelism, in more concentrated markets.

Types of restrictive business practices

There are known to exist currently a number of restrictive business practices in international trade which it may be useful to describe. The examples cited are not exhaustive but are mentioned because they are public knowledge.

International export cartels
Collusive arrangements for the export of goods to foreign markets are usually promoted or tolerated by laws and governments in exporting countries, although they may not be so charitably viewed in importing countries where an anticompetitive effect may be felt. In three industries, formal cartels made up of European firms have been organized as Swiss corporations and publicly registered; the products concerned are nitrogen fertilizers (NITREX), cellulosic fibres (UNICEL), and aluminum semimanufactures (ASSOCALEX). Little is known about their way of operating except that they are understood to be price cartels.[37]

International export cartels can have unacceptable anticompetitive effects, however; two such clearly established cases have been disclosed in the results of investigations by national authorities: the international quinine cartel, and the international red phosphorus cartel. The international quinine cartel was investigated in the United States by the Senate Subcommittee on Antitrust and Monopoly in 1967.[38] The cartel was organized in 1959 by the Dutch Nedchem Group and the German producer Boehringer/Mannheim Consortium, and included British and French producers as well. Basic components of the cartel agreement were the following: 1 / co-operation in making purchases from the United States stockpile, with Nedchem to be the sole bidder on behalf of the group and the purchased material shared among them on an agreed basis; 2 / an export agreement fixing prices and imposing other restraints in world markets outside the EEC and the United Kingdom; 3 / a gentleman's agreement fixing prices and quotas within the EEC and the United Kingdom, reserving to the Dutch, French and German manufacturers their domestic markets and certain export markets, and reserving the production of quinidine exclusively to the Dutch and German firms; and 4 / an agreement for the purpose of holding down the price of the raw material, cinchona bark, and setting selling prices for cinchona bark.

The United States Senate committee considered that the cartel had the effect of raising prices of quinine and quinidine to an artificially high level (although the increase in 1964 and 1965 must be considered in the light of other factors as well) and resulted in the allocation of markets and the protection of home markets of the large producers. Proceedings were taken against the members of the cartel by the Department of Justice of the United States, one of the members of the cartel being a subsidiary of a United States parent.[39]

The cartel was also the subject of proceedings by the Commission of the European Communities[40] which resulted in an order prohibiting the cartel under article 85 of the Treaty of Rome.[41] The commission found that the agreement involved all the major quinine producers in the Common Market, and that the six enterprises concerned held a dominant position on the European quinine market and even on the world market. The commission also found that they agreed to charge common prices for quinine and quinidine in all countries, that they established export quotas for all countries, that the French companies were excluded from the manufacture of quinidine, and that the home markets of the members of the cartel would be protected against imports from the other members. The commission held that the agreements on prices, control of production and outlets, and market-sharing were clearly prohibited by article 85 of the treaty and, indeed, fell within the express examples of agreements that are 'inconsistent with the Common Market.' The fact that the agreements were not strictly applied after 1965 was attributed by the commission to market developments; a sudden increase in demand was accompanied by a simultaneous shortage of cinchona bark with a resulting sharp increase of prices both for quinine and for raw materials. The parties were subjected to substantial fines, concerning which the following comment was made: 'In imposing these fines, the Commission desired to make clear its determination to enforce vigorously the ban on cartels incompatible with the aims of the Treaties, especially large-scale secret agreements, so as to ensure observance of the Community's rules of competition.'[42]

The international red phosphorus cartel was disclosed in a report of the Canadian Restrictive Trade Practices Commission.[43] This product, used for the manufacture of matches, fireworks, and railway flares, is produced in the United Kingdom, United States, Canada, France, West Germany, Sweden, and Japan; substantial export markets exist outside these countries, the largest being India.

Following certain more limited international arrangements, a global agreement was negotiated in 1959 in the face of declining prices for amorphous phosphorus on the export market; this agreement, known as the 'Hunting Ground Agreement,' applied to the sales of amorphous phosphorus to the match industry. The parties to the agreement were the Albright & Wilson group of companies (the only manufacturer in the United Kingdom), the French firm Societé d'exploitation des produits chimiques Coignet, the German firm Knapsack-Griescheim, and Duff Chemical Company of the United States, which supplied the product as agent of the manufacturer, American Agricultural Chemical Company. (Duff also was the sole export outlet for Electric Reduction Company of Canada, Ltd. (ERCO), a Canadian subsidiary of Albright & Wilson; but it does not appear that Canada was affected in any significant way by this agreement and ERCO was apparently not a party to it.)

The Hunting Ground Agreement provided for the division of the export markets into five groups, four of which were allocated to the four parties respectively, with the fifth being left open to all owing to the strength of Japanese, Russian, and other competition in them. Each of the parties agreed not to export into a market reserved for the others, either by declining to bid or by placing a cover bid in an amount proposed by the owner of the 'hunting ground.' Since the agreement did not embrace all the competitors in the market, it seems to have run into substantial difficulty particularly because of inroads made by the Japanese, but the report of the commission indicated that the parties to the agreement at least were able to avoid competition among themselves and presumably were safe from each others' competition in their home markets.

National export cartels
As already mentioned, the restrictive business practices laws of most countries of the western world permit export agreements or consortia among nationals, and the existence of a number of such cartels is known. Examples in North America are the Canadian sulphur producers' export consortium 'Cansulex,' allowed under section 32(4) of the Combines Investigation Act, and the American counterpart 'Sulexco' set up under the Webb-Pomerene Act.[44] The existence of these cartels has in several cases caused buyers in other countries to form import cartels, such as the National Sulphuric Acid Association in the United Kingdom.

Export consortia, by limiting competition in exports by firms in the exporting country, may or may not significantly limit competition in the markets in which the exports are sold, depending upon the presence of other sellers producing in or exporting into those markets. But if the export agreement is a vehicle for lessening competition in the home market (as, for example, by including an agreement to hold supplies off the domestic market), it might be expected to be subject to the domestic laws. Similarly the creation of an import cartel to meet the threat of concerted or monopolistic exporting practices may well have the result of blunting the impact of that foreign competition in the importing market, even though such retaliatory tactics may have some national support.

Oligopolistic behaviour
In oligopoly situations in the domestic market we find the phenomenon of conscious parallelism or virtually uniform behaviour: where the market consists of a small number of fairly large sellers of a homogeneous product, each producer or supplier knows the minds of his competitors so well that he can predict with virtual certainty what their reactions will be to any market decisions that he makes; the result is that market behaviour has all the appearances of being collusive, even though there may in fact have been no actual agreement or collusion.[45]

The same phenomenon can be seen in the international field; indeed, the existence of important international oligopolies is one of the major characteristics of the world market now emerging, as mentioned above.[46] Although in the oligopoly situation it is usually difficult to establish definitely the existence of an agreement or of concerted action prohibited by anticollusion laws, competition may be affected in virtually the same way as if overt collusion in fact exists.

An interesting example showing the difficulties and the divergencies of view which surround the application of anticompetitive practices legislation to oligopoly situations is the *Dyestuffs* case.[47] In this case the activities challenged were simultaneous price increases of dyestuffs in the years 1964, 1965, and 1967 by major

European producers who accounted for 80 per cent of sales in the Common Market; the firms were BASF, Cassella, Bayer and Hoechst in Germany, Francolor in France, ACNA in Italy, Ciba, Geigy and Sandoz of Switzerland, and ICI of Great Britain. The situation came before the Commission of the European Communities, which in its decision in July 1969 found the activities concerned contrary to article 85(1) of the Rome treaty and subjected the parties within the EEC to substantial fines.

There was apparently no evidence of an overt or express agreement, so that the question for determination became whether the price increases at the times in question represented oligopolistic but non-collusive behaviour or were the result of collusion or concerted action. Of importance in the commission's review of the matter was the following evidence: the price increases were identical in all countries on each occasion; they were applied to the same product in each case; they were put into effect simultaneously; there was a similarity in the wording of the instructions given by the producers to their subsidiaries or representatives in the various markets; and the producers exchanged information on several occasions, particularly at meetings held in Basel and in London. On these facts, and given the dominant market position of the group, the commission concluded that the price increases were at least the result of 'concerted practices' within the meaning of article 85(1); thus a decision as to whether the increases were the result of an agreement was not required.

In 1967 the German Federal Cartel Office fined the four German manufacturers involved for an infringement of the national restrictive business practices laws;[48] the Cartel Office found that the price increases by the four firms were the result of an agreement prohibited by the legislation. In making this finding, the Cartel Office relied on the evidence that the firms met from time to time to discuss questions of common interest, and that, at a particular meeting in Switzerland in 1967, the habitual price leader, Geigy, indicated its intention to raise its price on a certain date; others indicated a similar intention, and shortly thereafter identical increases becoming effective on the same date were announced by all those represented at the meeting. Although the companies took the position that the price increases were the result of independent decisions by each manufacturer, the Cartel office deduced that the announcement by Geigy of its intended price increase was for the purpose of securing the assent of the others, and that a meeting of the minds to increase the prices by a given percentage was in fact achieved. Ultimately, however, this view of the facts and the finding of the Cartel Office were not accepted by the Berlin Court of Appeal, which concluded that no agreement had been reached.

The *Dyestuffs* case bears marked similarities to the *British Basic Slag* case,[49] in which the Restrictive Practices Court of the United Kingdom found that a mutual expectation that particular moves by one competitor would be met by predictable reaction on the part of others constituted an 'arrangement' so as to require registration under the Restrictive Trade Practices Act 1956.[50]

Restrictive use of patents
The field of industrial and intellectual property poses questions of particular difficulty in relation to competition policy, domestically and internationally. By their very nature, the exclusive rights conferred on the owner of a patent, trade mark,

or copyright by the legislation of the country concerned represent a type of monopoly; moreover, these property rights are protected internationally by agreements to which most nations of the western world are parties. The problem for competition policy does not lie in the protection of the owner's rights but rather in the anticompetitive abuses of those rights going beyond the protection intended by the legislation. The aim of restrictive business practices laws, then, is to prohibit the abuse of patent and trade mark rights, such as the extension of the patent monopoly in a given product to other products not covered by the patent.[51]

Combines or conspiracies among patent owners to restrain competition are another type of abuse of patent rights. Such arrangements have taken place in the field of radio and television technology, through patent pools and restrictive licensing agreements which have the effect of limiting competition internationally. Two important cases in the United States exemplify this problem.

In the *C.R.P.L.* case[52] a civil antitrust suit was filed against General Electric, Westinghouse, and Philips, alleging a conspiracy to restrain trade in radio and television receiving sets. When licenses for a number of patents must be obtained to produce a finished article, such as a radio or television set, the pooling of the patents enables manufacturers of the sets to obtain readily the necessary licenses; hence the Canadian subsidiaries of the defendants had organized a patent pool in Canada (Canadian Radio Patents Limited). But such a pool also can have restrictive results; and in this case it was alleged that the defendant firms, through their Canadian subsidiaries controlling the pool, prevented the importation into Canada of radio and television receiving sets manufactured in the United States, thus foreclosing the Canadian market for such products to United States manufacturers. A consent decree disposed of the case, the companies being prohibited from agreeing to prevent or restrict exports from the United States into Canada.

Zenith Radio Corporation v *Hazeltine Research Inc.*[53] involved the Canadian patent pool as well as patent pools in Australia and the United Kingdom. Originally commenced as an infringement action by Hazeltine against Zenith, it developed by counter-claim into a treble damage action against Hazeltine for breach of the Sherman Act.[54] Conspiratorial activities were alleged in the operation of the three patent pools, which had refused to license patents to Zenith and other exporters of radio and television sets manufactured in the United States. The patent pool, which embraced the leading international manufacturers, made it a practice to give outsiders package licenses subject to the condition that the licensees would not export the products manufactured under the license; thus the licensees were restricted to manufacturing and distributing in their home market and, with distribution reserved for licensees who manufacture in the particular market, the international market was divided up. So far as the Canadian pool was concerned, the Supreme Court of the United States agreed with the finding below that Hazeltine and CRPL *were* conspiring to exclude Zenith and others from the Canadian market, and that 'this clear violation of the antitrust laws' fully justified injunctive relief against Hazeltine with respect to the Canadian market. These judgments reflect a horizontal type of restrictive agreement going beyond the scope of the patent grant and constituting an abuse of the patent. Other vertical arrangements in international markets may restrict a licensee to the use of the patent in a particular territory, may require him to sell the products manufactured under the license at a particular price (a form of price maintenance), or by a tying arrangement may require him to use the products of the licensor or other designated products in conjunction with his exploitation of the license.

In Canada, the owner of a patent or trade mark may exlude the importation by others into Canada of the product subject to the patent or trade mark, notwithstanding that it may be an identical product manufactured by the same firm from whom the Canadian patent or trade mark owner imports it. This situation gave rise to amendments to the Patents and Trade Marks Act in 1969, with the intention of limiting the power to impose such restraints on international competition.[55]

Vertical export prohibitions

It is quite common in a domestic market for a manufacturer to restrict his outlets to distribution in particular territorial areas; in return the distributors may be guaranteed that they will have exclusive access to that territory, but in that case they may also be required to deal only in the supplier's products. Exclusive dealing arrangements of this type are known to exist in international markets as well.

A good example is the *Grundig/Consten* case,[56] in which the Commission of the European Communities found that Grundig, the leading German manufacturer of radio receivers, tape recorders, dictating machines, and television sets, appointed exclusive distributors in France and other EEC countries for these products. The agreements with the distributors provided, *inter alia,* for prohibition of sales to customers in other countries, and for the registration of the trade mark GINT (with which all Grundig products are marked) with the distributor's country in the distributor's name; in addition, Grundig imposed the obligation on its German dealers not to export. The purpose of these arrangements was to give each foreign distributor absolute protection against sales by others in his territory, and to make sure that products exported by Grundig itself would not be re-exported to Germany; in this way an international territorial allocation of the sales of Grundig products was to be achieved. The commission found that the distribution arrangements in question were undesirable from the viewpoint of the policy aims of EEC to remove trade barriers between member states and to establish a common market; they were therefore contrary to article 85 of the Rome treaty.

Monopoly selling

Generally speaking, the existence of a monopoly is not regarded in most jurisdictions as unlawful *per se*. But as in the case of oligopolies, the economic effects of monopoly situations may well be detrimental to the economy, whether national or worldwide, if the enterprise concerned seeks to maintain its monopoly power by destroying any actual or potential competition in its markets. Thus it is abuse of the monopoly position, or the action of monopolizing, that is generally regarded as the target of restrictive business practices laws as has been discussed above in relation to section 33 of the Combines Investigation Act.

An example of monopoly power in the world market is the International Diamond Syndicate, operated by the Central Selling Organization (CSO) in London within the framework of the de Beers group, and selling about 80 per cent of the world's production of natural diamonds. It is known that several restrictive business practices have been engaged in by the organization, such as restricting direct buying to certain customers, minimum purchase requirements, resale prohibitions, and allotment of specific qualities to different countries. These practices, the existence of which has not been disputed, may be characterized as those of a single powerful seller who determines practically at will the conditions under which he sells.

Summary

The foregoing are examples of agreements, arrangements, and situations which exist or have existed in the international market and which, although not necessarily unlawful, have or can have an inhibiting effect on international trade to the detriment of the world economy. In the various situations described, the main types of restrictions used were the following: market allocation (both territorial and product market), price fixing, limitation of output or sales, joint sales organizations and profit pooling, restrictions in the field of technology, and international joint ventures. All of these devices are designed to have an anticompetitive effect in international trade.

INTERNATIONAL PRACTICES AND CANADIAN LEGISLATION

The kinds of artificial restraints described in the preceding section and the techniques used to implement them on an international scale are basically the same as anticompetitive arrangements made within domestic markets, against which domestic restrictive business practices laws have been developed; hence it is obvious that individual nations, including Canada, should be concerned with such restrictive practices which originate outside the state but have an impact upon its domestic economy. This section will therefore give some attention to international situations that have arisen or might arise in relation to the Canadian market, and will examine the impact of the anticombines legislation on them.

Two points should be made at the outset. First, activities in Canada which limit competition are within the reach of the anticombines laws when the anticompetitive effects are felt or are intended to be felt in the Canadian domestic market; but generally speaking, the laws will not be enforced against such activities if those effects are felt only in markets outside Canada. Second, in order for the anticombines laws to be applied in respect of a particular anticompetitive activity, there must be some person or corporation within the jurisdiction of Canadian courts before enforcement proceedings can be effectively taken; a theory of extraterritoriality of the application of the anticombines laws has not yet been developed in Canada.

Combinations: Consortia, cartels, and conspiracies

Horizontal arrangements

Export agreements   Export agreements have been mentioned previously as being exempt from the Combines Investigation Act so long as they relate only to exports from Canada and do not have the result of lessening competition unduly in the Canadian market or limiting the volume of exports from Canada. There are known to be a number of such agreements and consortia, but their activities have not as yet given rise to any enforcement under the act. From this it may be assumed that such agreements are being administered in such a way as to avoid the effects on the domestic market which would attract an inquiry.

Price fixing An agreement among competitors to lessen competition unduly is, however, an offence under the Canadian law; therefore, a horizontal price fixing cartel, if it embraced a sufficiently large segment of the market, might expect to attract enforcement. Jurisdiction of the Canadian courts in this kind of collusive arrangement would depend on the presence in Canada of a person who has done an overt act in furtherance of the conspiracy.[57] Assuming that the person committing the overt act in Canada has knowledge that he was furthering the conspiracy, it might be expected that Canadian courts would enforce the law in a prosecution against that person.

A Canadian example of the horizontal price fixing type of arrangement was revealed in the report of the Restrictive Trade Practices Commission on Shipping Conferences.[58] The commission found that the agreements between the members of the eastbound and westbound Atlantic shipping conferences were contrary to section 32 of the Combines Investigation Act. These agreements fixed the rates to be charged by conference members for the carriage of goods in Canadian–United Kingdom trade, imposed a scheme of discriminatory rates applicable to conference members who used conference lines, and allocated berthing space in various ports to conference members. However, the commission found that

> Although the member lines lessened competition within the meaning of the Combines Investigation Act, the public interest would not be served by excessive rate competition and instability in the liner trade. The Commission considers, therefore, that the lines in the Canada-U.K. trade should be allowed to continue such arrangements as are necessary for the efficient handling of Canada's exports and imports subject to appropriate safeguards for the public interest.

Legislation was accordingly enacted in the form of the Shipping Conferences Exemption Act[59] to permit the conferences to operate lawfully in Canada, subject to full disclosure of the arrangements and other conditions. Hence the attorney general did not proceed with a prosecution.

In the *Quinine* case mentioned above,[60] if the conspiracy were knowingly furthered by acts of any person in Canada, it would be incumbent upon the director to undertake a formal inquiry into the circumstances in view of the *prima facie* breach of the Canadian act. In fact, no evidence has been forthcoming that Canadian interests are involved in this way.[61]

Market allocation Market-sharing arrangements may also be the subject of a conspiracy outside of Canada with Canadian participation. Recent press reports suggest that there have been international discussions in relation to the world supply of and trade in sulphur,[62] including discussions between sulphur producing countries for the purpose of allocating world markets to various producers, presumably with the intention of avoiding extreme price competition in a period of oversupply of this product. If such a scheme were participated in by Canadian producers voluntarily (that is, without a valid law to support it), such an agreement would certainly attract a formal inquiry under the Combines Act.

Patent pools In connection with the activities of patent pools, mention has already been made of the Canadian pool, Canadian Radio Patents Limited, which was involved in, among other matters, a United States action for treble damages in *Zenith* v *Hazeltine*.[63] While such an arrangement may be unduly restrictive of competition, as has been clearly held to be the case in the United States, it is not necessarily so. Over the years, the activities of CRPL have been conducted in a manner which has not attracted enforcement in Canada, through a liberal licensing policy. However, the patent pool is a situation which, if improperly handled, could give rise to proceedings in Canada under the Combines Act.

Vertical arrangements
Vertical arrangements, such as vertical price fixing and vertical allocation of markets, can also have anticompetitive effects. Generally speaking, vertical price fixing is carried out in the form of resale price maintenance, which may be collusive or may be imposed by the supplier on the distributor. This practice will be discussed separately below.

A Canadian example of vertical market allocation which bears some similarity to the *Grundig/Consten* case mentioned earlier[64] is described in the report of the Royal Commission on Farm Machinery which was tabled in the House of Commons in January 1969.[65] This report indicated that the prices of identical or virtually identical farm tractors for all horsepower sizes up to 75 hp 'are very much lower in Britain and a number of other countries in Western Europe than they are in Canada.' The report said that some of the price differences may be accounted for by the cost of shipping tractors to Canada and selling in the dispersed Canadian market, but the remaining differences allow for larger profits to the farm machinery companies on sales of tractors directed to the tariff-free Canadian market. The commission found that Deere and International Harvester, the two dominant sellers of tractors in the North American market, set a price in that market which was high enough to yield a satisfactory profit based on North American costs; and even though some of the other firms, such as Ford and Massey Ferguson, have lower cost supply sources in western Europe, they have elected to accept that price rather than bring price levels down closer to European levels. The commission found that because tractor prices in North America are kept at a much higher level than they are in western Europe, the companies had to take steps to prevent farmers from importing tractors directly from these countries. Thus manufacturers selling to dealers in the United Kingdom prohibited the export of the tractors to North America by the dealers concerned. The commission commented: 'While conspiracy may be too harsh a word, these data suggest at least a tacit agreement on the part of the manufacturers supplying tractors to Canada from Britain to maintain the price in Canada in spite of the advantage afforded by devaluation.'[66]

No prosecution has as yet taken place as a result of this report and it must be assumed that, in the view of the authorities, the evidence does not disclose an offence. However, speaking hypothetically, if the evidence were to establish that a collusive arrangement existed between United Kingdom manufacturers to restrain exports from the United Kingdom by their dealers, and this were participated in or implemented by any person in Canada, Canadian courts would have jurisdiction over such a conspiracy. There would, of course, be the practical problem of obtaining evidence outside of Canada for use in any Canadian proceedings.[67]

Mergers and joint ventures

General considerations

These examples of restrictive agreements and arrangements which affect international trade to not include mergers, but the importance of increasing concentration of industry both in international and domestic markets is clear. In the absence of international laws, the question becomes the application of Canadian law to mergers and joint ventures affecting international trade. It should be mentioned at the outset that any discussion of the anticompetitive aspects of mergers and joint ventures at this time is necessarily somewhat theoretical and speculative in view of the fact that no joint venture cases and only a few merger cases have been dealt with by Canadian courts. The principles to be outlined, however, are those which would guide the director under the Combines Investigation Act in determining whether or not a formal inquiry should be undertaken into any merger or joint venture.

Companies carrying on activities in Canada are subject to the Combines Investigation Act regardless of the nationality of the corporation or of its ownership or control. This fact is significant in view of the relatively large incidence of United States and other foreign ownership of companies operating in Canada. A second point that should be borne in mind is that under the anticombines legislation, the effect of the merger or joint venture on the state of competition in Canada is crucial. Canada is a relatively small economy with an industrial structure characterized by a relatively small number of firms; hence the impact of a large international firm can be very great. It is certainly likely to be more significant in any given industry than would be the case in the United States, for example, with its considerably larger markets and industrial structure. Therefore, a decision made by a large international firm to change its competitive policy in the Canadian market, or to refuse its Canadian subsidiary the right to penetrate export markets in which the parent is interested, or to withhold supplies from the Canadian market to protect a related company in Canada or pursuant to an international cartel agreement can have a very significant effect upon the state of competition in the Canadian economy.

Mergers and joint ventures produce in one form or another common control of enterprises or particular aspects thereof; and common control, it is submitted, inevitably produces, if not an elimination, at least a significant blunting of competition between the business units concerned: while it may appear to be outwardly vigorous, competition will tend, in fact, to be limited to salesmanship and promotion. Of course, if companies involved in a merger or joint venture are not competing with each other in the first place, and enter into the liaison for the purpose of combining complementary products and services or producing a merger conglomerate in nature, the adverse effect on competition prohibited under the Combines Act is not likely to be present; the particular facts would have to be examined, however.

Jurisdictional considerations

When the decision-making power is shifted abroad, as would be the case where a foreign company acquires a Canadian company and retains active control of policy, questions of jurisdiction may arise; the problem may become insoluble if the decisions or activities complained of in fact take place in the foreign country and are executed by a foreign company over which Canadian courts do not have jurisdiction. A very simple example of this jurisdictional problem – although involving resale price maintenance instead of a merger situation – is the *Surgical Blades* case.[68] An American manufacturer through its sole agent in Canada imposed resale prices for its product sold in Canada through jobbers. Since there was no plant or office of the manufacturer in Canada, it was not possible to charge the company with the offence; hence the charge was directed against the manufacturer's agent, who *was* within the territorial jurisdiction of Canada, and he was duly convicted and sentenced. Somewhat analogous problems may arise in connection with the shifting abroad of decision-making pursuant to a merger or joint venture.

It should be added that to the extent that a joint venture is viewed as a conspiracy or agreement in restraint of trade, any overt act taking place in Canada in furtherance of the conspiracy would give Canadian courts jurisdiction over the persons in Canada doing the act as parties to the conspiracy.

Hypothetical illustrations
A brief look at several hypothetical situations may serve to clarify the anticompetitive problems inherent in international mergers and joint ventures.

Mergers (1) Two competing American companies, each with a Canadian subsidiary, merge, with one acquiring control over the other. The two Canadian subsidiaries thereby come under common control and, by direction of the parent, harmonize their policies, with the net effect *prima facie* being the elimination or serious impairment of the former competition between them. Unless a monopoly is thus created in the Canadian market, however, this situation would not appear to fall within the Combines Act: the Canadian companies are not parties to a merger, nor do they necessarily act in collusion with each other; and in any event it is doubtful whether in law either of the subsidiaries could successfully be convicted of a conspiracy either with the parent or with each other.

(2) An American company located in the United States acquires a Canadian company located in Canada. Here the merger may well be said to be consummated in Canada, although control is shifted to the United States. The effect on competition in the Canadian market will depend upon the facts of the particular case. The result of the merger may be merely to substitute one competitor for another and competition may be unaffected; or competition may even be sharpened by reason of the control of the Canadian company by a more imaginative and aggressive competitor. However, competition may be lessened to the detriment of the public within the meaning of the merger provision: if the acquiring company was formerly exporting into the Canadian market in competition with the Canadian company, the merger may have the effect of eliminating a competitor, since it is unlikely that the American parent would continue to export to Canada as well as produce goods through its Canadian subsidiary; and if the acquired Canadian company is not a competitor but either a supplier or an outlet, a detrimental effect on competition in the Canadian market may result by the foreclosure of the source of supply or the outlet to competing firms. This type of merger, which has not as yet given rise to an inquiry in Canada, poses legal problems in effective enforcement, since proceedings could

not be taken directly against the parent located outside the territorial jurisdiction of Canada. In such a case, a *de facto* divestiture could be accomplished indirectly by obtaining an injunctive order against the Canadian subsidiary.

(3) A Canadian company located in Canada acquires an American company located in the United States. Here the merger presumably takes place in the United States and primarily affects competition in that market; it would not be of concern to the Combines Branch *unless* the effect of the merger were to lessen competition in the Canadian market, as, for example, by significant limitation of previously existing import competition from the American company. If the impairment of competition were sufficient to constitute a breach of the merger provision, it would seem that the Canadian authorities could proceed against the Canadian parent with the object of seeking a divestiture.

Joint ventures.   Turning now to joint ventures, we find some corresponding situations.

(1) Two American companies in the United States, competing with each other, form a joint venture in the Canadian market and jointly form a new company in Canada. Any competition that existed previously between the two companies in the Canadian market now has disappeared, and if the competition was significant, its loss may be detrimental to the public. However, the Combines Act may not be capable of effective enforcement: proceedings could not be initiated against the parties to the joint venture, since they are outside the territorial jurisdiction of Canada; and whether proceedings could succeed against the jointly formed Canadian company, for conspiring with its parent organizations, would have to be tested in Canadian courts. The joint venture might, of course, operate through Canadian subsidiaries of the two parties, in which case the subsidiaries may clearly be guilty of conspiracy; it is also possible that even without an express agreement there might exist between the two Canadian subsidiaries an unlawful understanding or tacit agreement sufficient to attract an inquiry and subsequent legal proceedings. Finally, if the effect of the joint venture is to produce in Canada a company falling within the definition of monopoly in the Combines Act, proceedings might then be taken against the monopoly if it is operated to the detriment of the public.

(2) A joint venture takes place between an American company and a Canadian company. If the effect of the joint venture is to limit competition unduly in the Canadian market, within the meaning of section 32 of the Combines Act, it would give rise to an inquiry and subsequent legal proceedings under the act. Since the Canadian company is within the territorial jurisdiction of Canadian courts, it can be brought before those courts notwithstanding that its American partner in the joint venture could not (unless, of course, it also is physically present within Canadian territory).

Vertical price fixing: Resale price maintenance
Vertical price fixing can be collusive, as in the case where a supplier and his outlet agree on a resale price to be maintained for the product, or it may be imposed by the supplier by threats or by actual disciplinary measures, such as refusing future supplies if the outlet does not maintain the price. This type of unfair trade practice ordinarily occurs within the domestic market, but it can become the subject of international concern, as has been seen in the *Surgical Blades* case.[69] To review that

case, a United States manufacturer, Bard-Parker Inc., shipped surgical blades into Canada for distribution to hospitals through wholesalers, who were required to adhere to a scheme of resale price maintenance; this requirement constituted the illegality alleged before the court. The manufacturer was wholly outside of Canada so could not be reached in the prosecution; and proceedings were therefore ultimately taken against the manufacturer's sole agent in Canada, who was in due course convicted and subjected to a fine. It should be noted that the unlawful conduct described in the charge was that of Bard-Parker in the United States; and the accused was charged as a party to the offence committed by Bard-Parker notwithstanding that the latter was not before the court.

Multinational firms

A few comments should be made about the multinational firm, although it is not intended to deal in depth with this subject in view of the full treatment given it by Professor Feltham elsewhere in this work.[70]

As has been said, the multinational firm poses special problems for competition policy. If we embrace within this expression a situation where a Canadian firm is either the parent or the subsidiary of a foreign firm, then it becomes apparent that a considerable area of Canadian industry consists of multinational firms. This situation is not unique to Canada but it has had an important impact in recent years on Canadian thinking, particularly in terms of the search for a Canadian identity and independence in economic development.[71]

In terms of competition policy, the significance of the multinational firm lies primarily in the mechanics and direction of control. If multinational firms had their headquarters in Canada and were controlled by decisions made in Canada, this situation would probably be hailed as entirely acceptable and as a means of controlling our economic destiny. In fact, the situation is the reverse: the Canadian arm of most multinational companies is owned abroad and is therefore subject to decisions made without regard to the whole development of the Canadian firm or its contribution to the Canadian economy.

As the Economic Council has said, the large international enterprise may well be replacing the international cartel in controlling world markets. These enterprises are, of course, an important vehicle for the transfer of technology, research, and the development of investment in world markets. At the same time they can be the cause of restrictive practices adversely affecting international trade, such as international product and territorial market allocation, restrictions on expenditures on research and development, and international price discrimination. Like any other enterprise, the multinational firm can, of course, be party to an international cartel or engage in a practice of monopolizing.

The Competition Act

Mention should be made here of provisions of Bill c-256, the Competition Act,[72] which gave to the proposed Competitive Practices Tribunal power to examine and adjudicate upon, *inter alia*, foreign takeovers; foreign judgments, decrees, or orders which may be implemented by some person in Canada; and foreign laws and directives of foreign governments which may be implemented by some person in Canada. The text of these provisions follows.

Foreign takeover:

33 (1) Every merger that is not required to be registered with the Tribunal under section 32 and in which control is acquired over the whole or part of the business in Canada

(*a*) of an individual resident in Canada,

or

(*b*) of a company incorporated by or pursuant to an enactment of the Parliament of Canada or of the legislature of a province, of which fifty per cent or more of the issued and outstanding shares having voting rights under all circumstances were, before the merger, owned or controlled by individuals resident in Canada or by companies incorporated by or pursuant to an enactment of the Parliament of Canada or of the legislature of a province, or by any combination of such individuals and companies or that was, before the merger, otherwise controlled by individuals resident in Canada,

by

(*c*) an individual not resident in Canada,

(*d*) a company that is not incorporated by or pursuant to an enactment of the Parliament of Canada or of the legislature of a province,

(*e*) a company of which fifty per cent or more of the issued and outstanding shares having voting rights under all circumstances are owned by an individual who is not resident in Canada, a company that is not incorporated by or pursuant to an enactment of the Parliament of Canada or of the legislature of a province or by any combination of such individuals and companies, or that is otherwise controlled by an individual or individuals not resident in Canada,

(*f*) any combination of individuals and companies mentioned in paragraphs (*c*) to (*e*)

shall, either before the date on which the merger becomes effective or within two weeks thereafter, be registered with the Tribunal by filing with the Registrar all information relating to the merger that is required by the rules ...

35 Without limiting the application of section 34, the Tribunal may, by order, prohibit or dissolve a merger that is required by section 33 to be registered with the Tribunal, or that would be required by that section to be so registered if it were not required by section 32 to be so registered, where the Tribunal is satisfied that the merger

(*a*) is likely to bring about the creation or entrenchment in, or the extension into, Canada of a firm that is able to influence significantly either prices or the volume of a commodity or service supplied in a market in Canada,

(*b*) is likely to extend into Canada the influence of an international cartel or oligopoly,

or

(*c*) is likely to restrict the production in or export from Canada, of a commodity or service,

unless the Tribunal also finds that the merger is likely to result in a significant improvement of efficiency, a substantial part of the benefits of which is likely to be passed on, through conditions imposed by the market or by order of the Tribunal, to the public within a reasonable time in the form of lower prices or better products.

Foreign judgment, decree or order:

49 Where

(*a*) a judgment, decree, order or other process given, made or issued by or out of a court or other body in a country other than Canada can be implemented in whole or in part by persons in Canada, by companies incorporated by or pursuant to an enactment of the Parliament of Canada or of the legislature of a province, or by measures taken in Canada; and

(b) the Tribunal finds that the implementation in whole or in part of the judgment, decree, order or other process in Canada would

    (i) adversely affect competition in Canada,

    (ii) adversely affect the efficiency of trade or industry in Canada without bringing about or increasing in Canada competition that would restore and improve such efficiency,

    (iii) adversely affect the foreign trade of Canada without compensating advantages, or

    (iv) otherwise restrain or injure trade or commerce in Canada without compensating advantages,

the Tribunal may, by order, direct that

(c) no measures be taken in Canada to implement the judgment, decree, order or process, or

(d) that no measures be taken in Canada to implement the judgment, decree, order or process except in such manner as the Tribunal prescribes for the purpose of avoiding an effect referred to in subparagraphs (b) (i) to (iv).

Foreign law and directive of a foreign government:

50 Where the Tribunal finds that a decision has been or is about to be made by a person in Canada or a company incorprated by or pursuant to an enactment of the Parliament of Canada or of the legislature of a province,

    (a) as a result of a law in force in a country other than Canada, or

    (b) as a result of a directive, instruction, intimation of policy or other communication to the person or company or any other person, from

        (i) the government of a country other than Canada or of a subdivision thereof that is in a position to direct or influence the policies of the person or company, or

        (ii) a person in a country other than Canada who is in a position to direct or influence the policies of the person or company, where the communication is for

    the purpose of giving effect to a law in force in a country other than Canada,

and the Tribunal also finds that the decision, if implemented, would have any of the effects mentioned in subparagraphs 49(b) (i) to (iv), the Tribunal may, by order, direct that

    (c) no measures be taken in Canada to implement the law, directive, instruction, intimation of policy or other communication, or

    (d) no measures be taken to implement the law, directive, instruction, intimation of policy or other communication except in such manner as the Tribunal prescribes for the purpose of avoiding an effect referred to in subparagraphs 49(b)(i) to (iv).

These provisions reflect the intention of the government of Canada to make a start at dealing with international restrictive practices. The step is a modest one but nevertheless indicates a growing preoccupation with the concern that Canadian economic affairs may be significantly affected by decisions made outside of Canada. It also recognizes, in express terms, the danger that the domestic economy, through a merger or takeover by a foreign firm, may become subjected to the anticompetitive effect of an external agreement, cartel, or oligopoly to the detriment of that economy. The minister of consumer and corporate affairs, in his public pronouncements, has emphasized that these provisions are an important aspect of the foreign ownership or foreign investment policy of the government but do not constitute that entire policy. These provisions reflect only the competition policy aspects of the foreign investment problem and say nothing about foreign investment by the creation of a new enterprise or new assets; it is only investment in Canada by merger or takeover which is subject to these provisions, and such a merger or takeover may be prohibited or dissolved only where the effect on competition in Canada is a significant limitation which is not outweighed by substantial increases in efficiency.

The provisions of sections 49 and 50 relate to the possible extraterritorial application of foreign judgments or decrees, such as at one time existed under the United States antitrust laws, and foreign directives or laws which may be implemented in Canada by subsidiaries of foreign parents. Again it will be noted that the jurisdiction of the tribunal depends upon a finding that the implementation of these matters would adversely affect competition, industrial efficiency or trade in Canada without compensating advantages.

CONTROL OF INTERNATIONAL RESTRICTIVE BUSINESS PRACTICES

It is now appropriate to consider what has been the response to the challenge of restrictive business practices having international effect and what means might be devised for their control in the future. These questions must be considered in terms of three possibilities: unilateral action by individual states; bilateral arrangements between states for resolving common antitrust problems; and multilateral arrangements for control of such practices, including the development of supranational laws.

National legislation

Extent
Prior to World War II the antitrust philosophy was basically a North American concept. The aftermath of that war, however, seemed to produce a growing awareness in the western world of the problems that antitrust laws were designed to meet, stimulated, no doubt, by appreciation of the adverse effects of the international cartels which had flourished between the two wars and the developing philosophy of competition as the means of reconstructing a war-torn society in Europe; hence there was a great development of restrictive business practices laws in the western world, particularly in the countries that are members of OECD (including Australia which has recently become a member). Professor Cairns writes with respect to the newcomers to the antitrust field:

> Typically, these countries previously had an attitude that was tolerant of, and in some cases sympathetic to, the restrictive activities of cartels and monopolies. The value of competition in providing an efficient solution to economic problems had not received the same support as it had in the United States of America and Canada. Nor had competition,

rather than, say, co-operation, or 'live and let live,' had the same appeal as a general principle of social organization. Co-operative (or restrictive) arrangements had considerable sympathy, judicial and political, as well as in the business community. Restrictions were seen not so much as a method of exploiting the public, but as a legitimate attempt to achieve some amount of security and protection against the upsetting threat of new competitors.[73]

Extraterritoriality
Such national laws designed to deal with activities within the jurisdiction affecting the domestic economy are of only limited assistance in controlling international practices, where the locus of decision-making and the parties to the trade-restraining conduct are outside the jurisdiction. But in the absence of international machinery to counter the effects of foreign anticompetitive conduct affecting the domestic and foreign trade of a nation, the state may have no recourse, in its efforts to protect its own economic interests, other than the extraterritorial application of its national laws. Unilateral extensions of antitrust laws in this way can result in the impact of one country's competition policy upon the economy of another; this situation obviously creates problems when the two countries' economic policies are not in accord, and it may also give rise to political questions in respect of an actual or supposed invasion of sovereignty.

The United States is the widely cited example of a country whose courts supposedly practise the extraterritoriality principle. The point was recently put this way by a distinguished member of the New York Bar:

> Our antitrust laws reach not only throughout the Atlantic community but wherever men engage in international trade, export or withhold their goods, or sail their ships, provided, of course, that the acts or failures to act affect United States foreign commerce, exports from or imports into this country, or otherwise have a 'definite nexus with significant interests of the United States.'
>
> How is it, the uninitiated might ask, that United States laws can apply to activities in England, Japan or Afghanistan? And how is it that nationals of those countries, acting lawfully in their own countries, can become subject to criminal sanctions in the United States, should they venture within our shores, or become liable for treble damages if our sheriff can find assets to levy upon? If our antitrust laws can cover the earth, what are the limits to their application to conduct outside the United States? These are very practical and controversial questions – the enduring problem of extraterritoriality.[74]

A distinction must be made between the legal reach of a United States antitrust law or decree beyond United States boundaries and the economic effects of such a law or decree in another territory. For example, in the *R.C.A.* case[75] the consent decree issued by the United States court purported to be binding not only on the parent company in the United States but its subsidiaries wherever situated, including a Canadian subsidiary which was placed under restraint in the management of its existing and future patents. On the other hand, in the *I.C.I.* case,[76] the United States court ordered, *inter alia,* that either Du Pont or ICI should divest itself of its interest in CIL as one of several companies they jointly owned; the decree was *not* directed to the Canadian jointly owned company, but it did have an economic effect in Canada: when Du Pont subsequently sold its shares in CIL to ICI, the result was that Du Pont and ICI became independent competitors in Canada.

The attitude of the United States courts to the extraterritoriality principle has evolved from the *American Banana* case,[77] in which the Supreme Court held that acts abroad could not form the basis of action under the antitrust laws, to its antithesis, the *Alcoa* case,[78] in which a Canadian company involved in European cartel arrangements adversely affecting United States imports was held to be amenable to proceedings under the Sherman Antitrust Act.[79] Briefly, the general effect of the jurisprudence on the antitrust laws is 1 / to make unlawful activities enjoined by the antitrust laws that adversely affect the foreign commerce of the United States, even though they take place outside the territory of the United States, and whether committed by United States or foreign owned companies; and 2 / to bring within the jurisdiction *in personam* of the United States courts corporations resident outside the territory of the United States but having some business dealings within the United States, through a subsidiary, a branch office, an agent or an even more tenuous connection.[80]

For example, in the *Swiss Watchmakers* case,[81] where service of process was made on the Swiss subsidiaries of American companies, the court took the position that jurisdiction over the Swiss companies was properly sought through the parent which assented to the illegal activities abroad. In effect, the court looks to the United States parent, being within the jurisdiction and having knowledge of the impugned conduct of its foreign affiliate, to act as a vehicle for enforcement of the court's judgment against the foreign participant. It should be mentioned that while United States courts regard the antitrust laws as applying even if the anticompetitive acts are lawful in the foreign country, they will not assert this principle where the impugned acts abroad are expressly *required* by a valid law of that country.[82]

One difficulty with the extraterritorial approach is that it will almost inevitably give rise to reactions by other countries, in the protection of their sovereignty or domestic economy, which tend to inhibit the global solution to the problem. For example, in the *Nylon Spinners* case[83] an American court had purported to order ICI, a United Kingdom company, to deal with its foreign patents in a manner inconsistent with a contract made and to be performed in England; but the Court of Appeal of the United Kingdom held that the matter was subject to the jurisdiction of the United Kingdom courts and did not recognize the jurisdiction asserted by the United States court.

Extraterritorial application of the antitrust laws also leads to procedural difficulties, especially with respect to the gathering of evidence for use in antitrust proceedings or in congressional inquiries relating to anticompetitive activities. For example, in the *C.I.P.* case in 1947,[84] it was sought to compel International Paper Company, a New York corporation, to produce documents in the control of two Canadian affiliates in the province of Quebec. The United States court found that CIP was doing business within the jurisdiction, itself or by an agent, and was therefore amenable to the process of the court for the production of documents within its control, even though they were located in Canada.

This kind of compulsion by United States courts in the production of documents gave rise to the enactment in Ontario of the Business Records Protection Act in

1948[85] and subsequently the enactment in the province of Quebec of the Business Concerns Records Act.[86] Both these statutes prohibited removal of corporate records from the province in compliance with any requirement, order, direction, or subpoena of a legislative, administrative, or judicial authority in a jurisdiction outside the province.[87]

Bilateral arrangements

Canada and the United States
Actual or incipient problems of sovereignty arising out of the extraterritorial effect of United States antitrust laws on Canada were sought to be eliminated by the adoption, in 1959, of the Anti-trust Notification and Consultation Procedure, originally set up as a bilateral arrangement between Canada and the United States. Its immediate origin lay in the *C.R.P.L.* case,[88] commenced in November 1958, in which a conspiracy was alleged between the defendant United States companies and a number of Canadian companies, who were operating a patent pool in a way not regarded by the Canadian authorities as contrary to the Combines Investigation Act. The Canadian government became concerned that the judgment sought in the United States courts might require the directors of the Canadian companies to take certain actions with respect to the operations in Canada of those companies in accordance with the requirements of United States rather than Canadian law and policy. The minister of justice met the United States attorney general in Washington early in 1959 and made it clear that, in his view, such a result could only be regarded as an infringement of Canadian sovereignty. Following assurances by the attorney general that the action taken by the United States government in this or any other antitrust suit was not intended as an infringement of the sovereignty of Canada but was merely a necessary discharge of the enforcement responsibility of the government, an understanding was reached:

> As a result of these talks it was readily agreed that in any similar situation in the future, discussions will be held between the two governments at the appropriate stage when it becomes apparent that interests in one of our countries are likely to be affected by the enforcement of the anti-trust laws of the other. Such discussions would be designed to explore ways and means of avoiding the sort of situation which would give rise to objections or misunderstandings in the other country. It was, however, made clear that each government would have to reserve its ultimate responsibility to decide for itself what action it should take, and that such consultations should not be regarded in any way as necessarily implying approval of the action ultimately taken.[89]

This Anti-trust Notification and Consultation Procedure is entirely informal, involving periodic meetings between officials of the respective governments and sometimes cabinet members. Yet since its adoption, there has been no case of enforcement of the laws of either country which has given rise to a sovereignty issue in the other. One interesting feature of the arrangement is that Canada has occasion to notify the United States authorities more frequently than the latter notify the Canadians since virtually every major case under the Combines Act involves at least one company that has an affiliate in the United States. But it is noteworthy that co-operation, even if informal and indeed voluntary, has thus far avoided confrontation on this issue.

In November 1969 the minister of consumer and corporate affairs, who had by now become the minister responsible for the Combines Investigation Act, and the attorney general of the United States met in Washington and confirmed and extended the informal understanding of 1959. A joint statement issued on 3 November 1969 read in part as follows:

> Canadian Consumer and Corporate Affairs Minister Ron Basford met today with United States Attorney-General John M. Mitchell for a discussion on co-operation between Canada and the United States in antitrust matters affecting the two countries ... Mr Mitchell and Mr Basford stated that in their views, the procedure adopted by the o.e.c.d. strengthens the United States-Canadian Understanding which has served to eliminate conflicts in antitrust enforcement and has provided a common approach to problems affecting both countries. Of course, each country has the responsibility to enforce its own laws and the discussions under these procedures do not in any way bind a country as to what action it decides to take. The two cabinet members expressed the view that, in this time of expanding international trade, with special problems being posed by the multi-national corporation, and when most industrial countries have enacted anti-monopoly laws, international co-operation in the antitrust area is essential for carrying out antitrust policy and to avoid conflicts in enforcement.
>
> In addition, therefore, to continuing the Notification and Consultation Procedure in accordance with the 1959 Understanding, the two cabinet members agreed that the o.e.c.d. Recommendation of 1967 should be actively implemented as between Canada and the United States in relation to restrictive business practices in international trade. Notification and consultation will continue under both arrangements. Each country will, insofar as its national laws and legitimate interests permit, provide the other with information in its possession of activities or situations, affecting international trade, that the other requires in order to consider whether there has been a breach of its restrictive business practices laws.
>
> A primary concern would be cartel and other restrictive agreements and restrictive business practices of multi-national corporations affecting international trade. The enforcement agencies of the two countries, each within its own jurisdiction, will where possible co-ordinate the enforcement of their respective laws against such restrictive business practices.[90]

Notification and consultation between Canada and the United States are now carried out under both the original arrangement and the recommendation of OECD described hereafter; moreover, in accordance with the OECD recommendation, the Basford-Mitchell Arrangement extends beyond mere notification and consultation to the exchange of information with respect to possible breaches of the restrictive practices laws of each country, as well as the co-ordination of enforcement of the respective laws against restrictive business practices. Notwithstanding that in both Canada and the United States there exist certain restraints with respect to the disclosure of information arising in investigations leading to prosecutions or other legal proceedings, it has been possible to work out a practical *modus operandi* for notification, consultation, and co-operation while at the same time complying with the requirements of confidentiality under the laws of the respective countries.

Canada and OECD

In October 1967 the Council of OECD recommended to its members a procedure similar to and derived at least in part from the original Canadian-American Understanding. That recommendation reads in part as follows:

> Considering therefore that a closer co-operation between Member countries in the form of consultations, exchanges of information and co-ordination of efforts on a fully voluntary basis should be encouraged it being understood that such co-operation should not in any way be construed to affect the legal positions of Member countries with regard to such questions of sovereignty, and in particular the extra-territorial application of laws concerning restrictive business practices, as may arise;
>
> I RECOMMENDS to the Governments of Member countries
>
> 1. (a) That in so far as their laws permit, when Member countries undertake under their restrictive business practices laws an investigation or a proceeding involving important interests of another Member country, they should notify such Member country in a manner and at a time deemed appropriate. Notification should, where appropriate, take place in advance in order to enable the proceeding Member country, while retaining full freedom of ultimate decision, to take account of such views as the other Member country may wish to express and of such remedial action as the other member country may find it feasible to take under its own laws to deal with the restrictive business practice.
>
> (b) That where two or more Member countries proceed against a restrictive business practice in international trade, they should endeavour to co-ordinate their action in so far as appropriate and practicable under national laws.
>
> 2. To supply each other with any information on restrictive business practices in international trade which their laws and legitimate interests permit them to disclose.
>
> 3. To co-operate in developing or applying mutually beneficial methods of dealing with restrictive business practices in international trade.
>
> II INSTRUCTS the Committee of Experts on Restrictive Business Practices to keep under review developments connected with the present Recommendation and to examine periodically the progress made in this field.[91]

Although the object of this recommendation is clearly multilateral participation, as a practical matter such a scheme is best implemented in the first instance by a series of bilateral understandings. Pursuant to the recommendation, Canada has from time to time notified several member countries of OECD of enforcement activities which might affect the interests of those countries.

Multilateral arrangements

The final question to be considered concerns the possibilities of developing some form of international machinery for the development and enforcement of antitrust laws to protect the world market. It is obvious that to overcome the limitations of national laws the only really satisfactory solution would be a supranational law binding all states, subject to enforcement and adjudication by a supranational court or other body.

Professor Corwin Edwards, whose views are not to be taken lightly, has suggested that there are grave difficulties involved in reaching a multilateral agreement by reason of the diverse philosophies of competition held by the various states, even within OECD.[92] He has suggested alternatives that might be considered, including a comprehensive treaty (probably not at present possible), a selective treaty covering areas that all or some can agree to, bilateral arrangements, exchanges of information, perhaps along the lines of the Basford-Mitchell Arrangement, and a multilevel treaty of the type found in the field of industrial and intellectual property.

A further discouraging note is the fact that historically multilateral arrangements have not proved successful. In 1947 to 1948 the International Trade Organization prepared a draft charter (the Havana Charter)[93] providing for complaints, investigation, and recommendation for remedial action, but this was not ratified by the necessary majority. In 1958 a consultative procedure was proposed by the members of GATT as a means of international co-operation to control cartels prejudicially affecting international trade, but this procedure does not appear to be in use. And, in 1959, an abortive *ad hoc* committee on restrictive business practices was set up in ECOSOC.

But on the positive side, there is a currently continuing body which gives regular consideration to anticompetitive practices: the Committee of Experts on Restrictive Business Practices of OECD, which meets twice yearly. This committee has published the *Guide to Legislation on Restrictive Business Practices*[94] as well as a number of other useful studies in the field;[95] it was also responsible for the development of the recommendation on notification and consultation in 1967. The committee is currently engaged in a considerable program of work relating to various aspects of restrictive business practices. Moreover, a study has been undertaken by UNCTAD into the adverse effect of restrictive practices on international trade from the somewhat more specialized point of view of the developing nations.

It is a matter for speculation whether, in the foreseeable future, any form of general agreement can be reached on the means of tackling anticompetitive problems. But it should not be overlooked that the European Economic Communities *have* managed to find a method of achieving a supranational law and the enforcement agency to apply it. Within the community, while national antitrust laws still exist and are applied within their own territorial jurisdiction, the Commission of the European Economic Communities has the authority to proceed with effect beyond the territorial jurisdiction of any of the states as, for example, was done in the *Dyestuffs* case.[96] Such an arrangement requires some surrender of sovereignty to the supranational agency, however, a step which many nations are as yet unwilling to take.

APPENDIX

CANADIAN ANTI-COMBINES LEGISLATION

Conspiracy in Restraint of Trade

1 An Act for the Prevention and Suppression of Combinations formed in Restraint of Trade, 1889, c 41.
2 *Criminal Code*, 1892, c 29, s 520.
3 An Act to amend the *Criminal Code*, 1892, with respect to Combinations in Restraint of Trade, 1899, c 46.
4 An Act further to amend the *Criminal Code*, 1892, 1900, c 46.
5 *Criminal Code*, R.S. 1906, c 146.
6 An Act to amend the *Combines Investigation Act* and the *Criminal Code*, 1952, c 39.
7 *Criminal Code*, 1953–54, c 51, s 750(1).
8 An Act to amend the *Combines Investigation Act* and the *Criminal Code*, 1960, c 45, ss 13 and 21.

Discriminatory and Predatory Pricing

1 An Act to amend the *Criminal Code*, 1935, c 56, s 9.
2 An Act to amend the *Combines Investigation Act* and the *Criminal Code*, 1952, c 39.
3 *Criminal Code*, 1953–54, c 51, s 750(1).
4 An Act to amend the *Combines Investigation Act* and the *Criminal Code*, 1960, c 45, ss 13 and 21.

Combines Investigation Act

1 *The Combines Investigation Act*, 1910, c 9.
2 (1) *The Combines and Fair Prices Act, 1919*, 1919, c 45.
 (2) *The Board of Commerce Act*, 1919, c 37.
3 *The Combines Investigation Act, 1923*, 1923, c 9.
4 *The Combines Investigation Act*, R.S. 1927, c 26.
5 (1) *The Dominion Trade and Industry Commission Act, 1935*, 1935, c 59.
 (2) *The Combines Investigation Act Amendment Act, 1935*, 1935, c 54.
6 *The Combines Investigation Act Amendment Act, 1937*, 1937, c 23.
7 An Act to amend the *Combines Investigation Act*, 1946, c 44.
8 An Act to amend the *Combines Investigation Act*, 1949 (2nd Sess.), c 12.
9 *The Regulations Act*, 1950, c 50, s 10 (Repeal of s 40(2) and (3) of the Act relating to Regulations).
10 An Act to amend the *Combines Investigation Act*, 1951 (2nd Sess.), c 30.
11 An Act to amend the *Combines Investigation Act* and the *Criminal Code*, 1952, c 39.
12 *Combines Investigation Act*, R.S. 1952, c 314.
13 *Criminal Code*, 1953–54, c 51, s 750.
14 An Act to amend the *Combines Investigation Act* and the *Criminal Code*, 1959, c 40.
15 An Act to amend the *Combines Investigation Act* and the *Criminal Code*, 1960. c 45.
16 An Act to amend An Act to amend the *Combines Investigation Act* and the *Criminal Code*, 1960–61, c 42.
17 An Act to amend an Act to amend the *Combines Investigation Act* and the *Criminal Code*, 1962–63, c 4.

18 An Act to amend an Act to amend the *Combines Investigation Act* and the *Criminal Code*, 1964–65, c 35.
19 An Act to amend An Act to amend the *Combines Investigation Act* and the *Criminal Code*, 1966–67, c 23.
20 An Act respecting the organization of the Government of Canada and matters related or incidental thereto, 1966–67, c 25.
21 An Act to establish a Department of Consumer and Corporate Affairs, 1967–68, c 16.
22 *Criminal Law Amendment Act*, 1968–69, c 38.
23 *Combines Investigation Act*, R.S. 1970, c C-23.

NOTES

1 Economic Council of Canada, *Interim Report on Competition Policy* (July 1969) [hereinafter cited as *Interim Report*].
2 Bill c-256, 3rd Sess., 28th Parl., 1970–1 Can. (introduced in House of Commons 29 June 1971).
3 *Interim Report*, at 174.
4 *International Conference on Monopolies, Mergers and Restrictive Practices*, Cambridge, England (1969) (Kristensen's emphasis).
5 *Interim Report*, at 176.
6 R.S.C. c C-23 (1970).
7 An Act for the Prevention and Suppression of Combinations Formed in Restraint of Trade, 1889, c 41. Citations of subsequent statutes are set out in the appendix hereto.
8 *Weidman v Shragge*, (1912) 46 S.C.R. 1, 36 (Duff J).
9 Can. House of Commons, *Debates*, 30 May 1966, at 5688.
10 *Interim Report*.
11 *Reference re the Farm Products Marketing Act*, [1957] S.C.R. 198.
12 *R. v Canadian Breweries Ltd.*, [1960] O.R. 601, 33 C.R. 1, 126 C.C.C. 133.
13 The following are the judicial decisions on constitutional aspects of the legislation: *In the Matter of The Board of Commerce Act and The Combines and Fair Prices Act of 1919*, (1920) 60 S.C.R. 456; *In Re the Board of Commerce Act, 1919, and The Combines and Fair Prices Act, 1919*, [1922] 1 A.C. 191, (1921) 60 D.L.R. 513, [1922] 1 W.W.R. 20; *Re Combines Investigation Act and S. 498 of the Criminal Code*, [1929] S.C.R. 409, 52 C.C.C. 223, 2 D.L.R. 802; *Proprietary Articles Trade Association v Attorney-General for Canada*, [1931] A.C. 310, 55 C.C.C. 241, 2 D.L.R. 1, 1 W.W.R. 552; *Reference re Section 498A of the Criminal Code*, [1936] S.C.R. 363, 3 D.L.R. 593; *Attorney-General for British Columbia

v Attorney-General for Canada et al.* (Reference re Section 498A of the Criminal Code), [1937] A.C. 368, 1 D.L.R. 688, 1 W.W.R. 317; *Reference re Dominion Trade and Industry Commission Act, 1935*, [1936] S.C.R. 379, 3 D.L.R. 607; *Attorney-General for Ontario v Attorney-General for Canada et al.* (Reference re The Dominion Trade and Industry Commission Act, 1935), [1937] A.C. 405, 1 D.L.R. 702, 1 W.W.R. 333; *Regina v Goodyear Tire & Rubber Co. of Canada Ltd. et al.*, [1953] O.R. 856, O.W.N. 828, 17 C.R. 252, 107 C.C.C. 88, 19 C.P.R. 75 (Trial); *Regina v Goodyear Tire & Rubber Co. of Canada Ltd. et al.*, [1954] O.R. 377, O.W.N. 436, 18 C.R. 245, 108 C.C.C. 321, 4 D.L.R. 61 (Appeal); *Goodyear Tire & Rubber Co. of Canada Ltd. et al. v The Queen*, [1956] S.C.R. 303, 114 C.C.C. 380, 26 C.P.R. 1, 2 D.L.R. (2d) 11; *Regina v Campbell*, [1964] 2 O.R. 487, 46 D.L.R. (2d) 83, 3 C.C.C. 112 (Appeal), 50 C.P.R. 142 (includes appeal to Supreme Court of Canada); *Regina v Campbell*, [1966] 4 C.C.C. 333, 58 D.L.R. (2d) 673 (Supreme Court of Canada).
14 See *Regina v Howard Smith Paper Mills Ltd.*, [1954] O.R. 543, 571 (Spence J). A cumulative list of the jurisprudence on the act is contained in the annual reports of the director of investigation and research, Combines Investigation Act.
15 This is the minister presently named in section 2 of the act. In the past the act has been under the jurisdiction of various ministers, including the minister of justice.
16 See eg, *Weidman v Shragge*, *supra* note 8; *Stinson-Reeb Builders Supply Company et al. v The King*, [1929] S.C.R. 276; *Rex v Container Materials Limited*, (1940) 74 C.C.C. 113; *Howard Smith Paper Mills Limited et al. v The Queen*, [1957] S.C.R. 403.
17 See eg, *Rex v McGavin Bakeries Limited*,

(1951) 101 C.C.C. 22; *Regina* v *Northern Electric Company Limited*, [1955] O.R. 431; *Howard Smith Paper Mills, supra* note 16; *Regina* v *Electrical Contractors Association of Ontario and Dent*, [1961] O.R. 265; *Regina* v *Abitibi Power & Paper Company, Limited et al.*, (1961) 131 C.C.C. 201, 36 C.P.R. 188.

18 See Organization for Economic Co-operation and Development, *Guide to Legislation on Restrictive Business Practices* (4 vols) (3d ed, 1971).

 This useful guide contains four sections as follows: 1 / legislation on restrictive business practices in force in participating countries, and international legislation applying to several states, with a brief introduction on the historical background and underlying basic principles, and an outline of the structure of such legislation; 2 / explanatory notes on the legislation; 3 / a selection of administrative and court decisions; and 4 / a selected bibliography. Information concerning the following countries and international organizations has so far been included: Austria, Belgium, Canada, Denmark, Finland, France, Germany, Ireland, Italy, Japan, Netherlands, Norway, Portugal, Spain, Sweden, Switzerland, United Kingdom, United States of America, European Coal and Steel Community and European Economic Community.

19 *Canadian Breweries Ltd., supra* note 12; *Regina* v *British Columbia Sugar Refining Company Limited et al.*, (1960) 32 W.W.R. (N.S.) 577.

20 *Interim Report*, at 86.

21 *Canadian Breweries Ltd., supra* note 12; *British Columbia Sugar Refining Company Limited, supra* note 19.

22 See *Concentration in the Manufacturing Industries of Canada* (published under the authority of the Honourable Ron Basford, Minister of Consumer and Corporate Affairs, 1971).

23 Bill C-256, *supra* note 2, ss 34, 35 (mergers and foreign takeovers).

24 *Rex* v *Eddy Match Limited et al.*, (1952) 13 C.R. 217, (1954) 18 C.R. 357 (appeal), leave to appeal to Supreme Court of Canada refused.

25 *Regina* v *Electric Reduction Company of Canada Ltd.*, (1970) 61 C.P.R. 235.

26 Restrictive Trade Practices Commission, *Report on Trade Practices in the Phosphorus Products and Sodium Chlorate Industries* (1966).

27 The terms of the order are set out in the *Report of the Director of Investigation and Research, Combines Investigation Act*, for the year ended 31 March 1970.

28 Restrictive Trade Practices Commission, *Report into Electric Large Lamps* (1971).

29 Section 34(1)(a) and (b).

30 Section 34(1)(c).

31 Section 35.

32 Section 38.

33 *R.* v *Campbell*, [1964] 2 O.R. 487 (appeal to Supreme Court of Canada dismissed). See *supra*, at 777.

34 Sections 36–7. Citations of reported cases on misleading advertising are included in the cumulative list in the Annual Reports of the Director of Investigation and Research.

35 For details of these arrangements, see Commissioner, Combines Investigation Act, *Report: Canada and International Cartels* (1945).

36 *Interim Report*, at 179.

37 For more detailed comment on these arrangements, see H. Kronstein, 'Das Recht der internationalen Kartelle' (1967), 5 *Recht der internationalen Verwaltung und Wirtschaft*.

38 'Prices of Quinine and Quinidine,' *Hearings Before the Subcommittee on Antitrust and Monopoly of the Senate Committee on the Judiciary* (parts I & II), pursuant to S. Res. 191, 89th Cong., 2nd Sess., and S. Res. 26, 90th Cong., 1st Sess. (1967); Subcommittee on Antitrust and Monopoly of the Senate Committee on the Judiciary, *Report: Prices of Quinine and Quinidine*, pursuant to S. Res. 26, 90th Cong., 1st Sess. (1967).

39 The Department of Justice subsequently brought a criminal action in the matter: *United States* v *N.V. Nederlandsche Combinatie Voor Chemische Industrie, et al.* Crim. 870 (S.D.N.Y. 1968). See also civil consent decree, [1970] Trade Cas. (CCH) no 73,181.

40 See *Official Gazette* no L 201 12 Aug. 1968.

41 The Treaty of Rome of 25 March 1957 established the European Economic Community (the Common Market). Articles 85 and 86 provide in part as follows:
Article 85
'(1) The following shall be deemed to be inconsistent with the Common Market and shall be prohibited, namely: all agreements between firms, all decisions by associations of firms and all concerted practices likely to affect trade between Member States and which have the object or effect of preventing,

restraining or distorting competition within the Common Market, and in particular those which:
   a) directly or indirectly fix buying or selling prices or other trading terms,
   b) limit or control production, marketing, technical development or investments,
   c) effect the sharing of markets or sources of supply,
   d) apply to trade partners unequal conditions in respect of equivalent transactions, thereby placing them at a competitive disadvantage,
   e) make the conclusion of a contract subject to the acceptance by trade partners of additional goods or services which are not by their nature or by the custom of the trade related to the subject matter of such contract.
(2) Any agreement or decision prohibited by this Article shall be automatically null and void.'

Article 86
'It shall be inconsistent with the Common Market and prohibited so far as the trade between Member States may be thereby affected for one or more firms to abuse a dominant position in the Common Market or any substantial part thereof.
   The following practices shall in particular be deemed to be an abuse:
   a) the direct or indirect imposition of buying or selling prices or other unfair trading terms;
   b) the limitation of production, marketing or technical development to the prejudice of consumers;
   c) the application to trade partners of unequal conditions in respect of equivalent transactions, thereby placing them at a competitive disadvantage;
   d) subjecting the conclusion of a contract to the acceptance by trade partners of additional goods or services which are not by their nature or by the custom of the trade related to the subject matter of such contract.'

42 4 *Guide to Legislation, supra* note 18, E.E.C. 3.1, at 68.
43 *Phosphorus Products and Sodium Chlorate Industries Report, supra* note 26.
44 40 Stat. 516 (1918), as amended; 15 U.S.C.A. ss 62–5.
45 For an interesting analysis of an oligopoly

situation, see *Electric Large Lamps Report, supra* note 28.
46 *Supra,* at 766–7.
47 *Official Gazette* no L 195 (1 Aug. 1969); 4 *Guide to Legislation, supra* note 18, E.E.C. 3.1, at 71.
48 It should be noted that this case points up an interesting question as to the relationship between proceedings brought by the Common Market authorities and those brought by the authorities of a member state.
49 (1963) L.R. 4 R.P. 116.
50 4 & 5 Eliz. II, c 68. See also *Electric Large Lamps Report, supra* note 28.
51 See eg, the *Union Carbide Case,* in the *Report of the Director of Investigation and Research, Combines Investigation Act,* for the year ended 31 March 1970. For a good treatment of the antitrust aspects of patents, see A.D. Neale, *The Antitrust Laws of the United States of America* (1960) 261 *et seq.*
52 *U.S.* v *General Electric Company, Westinghouse Electric Corporation, and N.V. Philips,* 82 F. Supp. 753 (D.N.J. 1949); [1948–1949] Trade Cas. (CCH) no 62,518 (D. Cal.).
53 395 U.S. 100 (1969).
54 26 Stat. 209 (1890), as amended; 15 U.S.C.A. ss 1–7.
55 *An Act to Amend the Patent Act, the Trade Marks Act and the Food and Drugs Act,* 1968–1969, Can., c 49.
56 [1964] *Official Gazette* 2545. The commission's decision was substantially upheld by the Court of Justice of the European Communities. 4 *Guide to Legislation, supra* note 18, E.E.C. 3.1, at 14; 3.0, at 1.
57 *See R.* v *Connolly & McGreevy,* (1894) 25 O.R. 151; *R.* v *Container Materials Ltd. et al.,* (1939) 4 D.L.R. 387.
58 Restrictive Trade Practices Commission, *Report into Shipping Conference Arrangements and Practices* (1965).
59 1969–1970, Can., c 72.
60 *Supra,* at 767–8.
61 According to the Office of the Director.
62 See the *Globe and Mail* (Toronto), 22 July 1970 (Alberta may discuss prorationing and marketing co-op for sulphur); *Globe and Mail* (Toronto), 12 Nov. 1971 (combines study will question sulphur firms); *Globe and Mail* (Toronto), 13 Nov. 1971 (Alberta cabinet plans meeting on federal probe plans); *Journal of Commerce,* 22 Nov. 1971 ('Chemical Markets').
63 *Supra* note 53.

64 *Supra,* at 772.
65 Royal Commission on Farm Machinery, *Special Report on Prices* (1969).
66 Ibid., at 42.
67 Section 17(7) of the Combines Investigation Act provides for the taking of evidence abroad on commission.
68 *R.* v *Campbell, supra* note 33.
69 Ibid.
70 'Economic Nationalism,' *infra*, at 885–917.
71 In this connection see the draft of the Gray Report published in (1971), *Canadian Forum*.
72 *Supra* note 2.
73 J.P. Cairns, *The Regulation of Restrictive Practices: Recent European Experience* (Economic Council of Canada, June 1971) 1.
74 Address by Carlyle E. Maw [American Bar Association], Section on Antitrust Law, 7 July 1971.
75 *U.S.* v *Radio Corporation of America*, [1958] Trade Cas. (CCH) no 69, 164.
76 *U.S.* v *Imperial Chemical Industries*, 100 F. Supp. 504 (S.D.N.Y. 1951), 105 F. Supp. 215 (S.D.N.Y. 1952).
77 *American Banana Co.* v *United Fruit Co.*, 213 U.S. 347 (1909).
78 *U.S.* v *Aluminum Co. of America*, 148 F. 2d 416 (2d Cir. 1945).
79 *Supra* note 54.
80 For further analysis of the jurisprudence, and references to scholarly writing, see Henry, 'The United States Antitrust Laws: A Canadian Viewpoint,' (1970), *Can. Y.B. Int'l L.*
81 *U.S.* v *Watchmakers of Switzerland Information Centre*, 133 F. Supp. 40, *modified*, 134 F. Supp. 710 (S.D.N.Y. 1955).
82 See, eg, *U.S.* v *Imperial Chemical Industries, supra* note 76 (Per Ryan J); *U.S.* v *General Electric Co.*, 82 F. Supp. 753 (D.N.J. 1949), 115 F. Supp. 835 (D.N.J. 1953); *Continental Ore Co.* v *Union Carbide and Carbon Corporation*, 370 U.S. 690 (1962); *U.S.* v *Watchmakers of Switzerland Information Centre*, [1963] Trade Cas. (CCH) no 70,600 (S.D.N.Y. 1962).
83 *British Nylon Spinners, Ltd.* v *Imperial Chemical Industries, Ltd.*, [1952] 2 All E.R. 780 (C.A.).
84 *In re Grand Jury Subpoena Duces Tecum Addressed to Canadian International Paper Company et al.*, 72 F. Supp. 1013 (S.D.N.Y. 1947).
85 R.S.O. c 44 (1960).
86 R.S.Q. c 278 (1964).
87 For a more recent reaction to the problem of extraterritoriality, see Bill C-256, *supra* note 2, ss 49, 50.
88 *U.S.* v *General Electric Company, supra* note 52.
89 Can. House of Commons, *Debates*, 3 Feb. 1959, at 619.
90 Can. House of Commons, *Debates*, 5 Nov. 1969, at 574.
91 O.E.C.D. Doc. no c(67)53 (Final) (10 Oct. 1967).
92 C.D. Edwards, *Control of Cartels and Monopolies: An International Comparison* (1967).
93 Charter of the International Trade Organization, US Dep't of State Pub. no 3206 (24 March 1948); Commercial Policy Series 114.
94 *Supra* note 18.
95 Under OECD rules, the work of the committee is not made public while it is in progress, but some completed studies and reports have been published by authority of the council and are available. These include *Annual Development Reports* of member countries on restrictive business practices, *Glossary of Terms, Market Power and the Law, Information Agreements* and *Inflation*.
96 *Supra* note 47.

LOUIS SABOURIN

31/Normes juridiques canadiennes en matière de développement international

> On n'échappe pas au droit. Dès qu'une pratique tend à se prolonger, à s'imiter elle-même, à se rationaliser, elle donne naissance à du droit. Les principes et les règles juridiques qui surgissent ainsi spontanément de l'action, la soutiennent. Le droit n'est pas, par nature, conservateur et rigide. Il est un instrument de l'action sociale.—Michel Virally

Il peut sembler paradoxal, qu'après avoir établi autant de liens de coopération avec les états du Tiers Monde et de programmes de développement international, aussi bien sur le plan multilatéral que bilatéral,[1] le Canada ne se soit pas encore donné de normes fondamentales précises, reconnues qui coifferaient l'ensemble de ces activités et représenteraient par le fait même le 'corpus' de son droit du développement international.

Aussi souhaitables qu'elles puissent paraître a priori, de telles normes générales ne pourront jamais être codifiées au même titre que bien d'autres secteurs du droit.[2] Ceci ne tient pas seulement au caractère particulier du processus juridique adopté par les principaux organes du gouvernement canadien mais à la nature même du droit du développement international – en particulier sa dépendance non seulement d'une entité, en l'occurrence le Canada, mais de plusieurs autres phénomènes, comme le droit international public, le droit des états avec qui le Canada veut coopérer sans oublier celui des institutions internationales vouées au développement.

Si d'une part il n'est pas possible, pour les raisons qu'on vient d'évoquer, de traiter du droit canadien du développement international au même titre que du droit administratif, par exemple, on peut, d'autre part, relever des institutions, des activités, et des programmes qui, par leur organisation, leur répétition, et leur rationalisation ont progressivement créé un cadre et des habitudes qui constituent déjà des sources importantes de la pratique canadienne en matière de développement international. En réalité on peut d'ores et déjà parler d'une pratique juridique canadienne en la matière.

Le but de ce chapitre est donc de 1 / préciser la nature du droit canadien en matière de développement international en faisant ressortir: (a) une définition; (b) l'évolution; 2 / brosser un tableau des principales dimensions juridiques des programmes canadiens d'assistance au développement sur le plan: (a) institutionnel et (b) des accords de coopération; 3 / déterminer les principales incidences de ce droit dans les domaines commercial et financier. La conclusion mettra en valeur les principales caractéristiques de ce droit.

NATURE

Définition

Certes le droit international public classique continue de régir les rapports entre le Canada et les pays du Tiers Monde.

> Il ne faut pas se hâter de proclamer périmé, au nom de la solidarité internationale, le principe de l'égalité souveraine des Etats. L'attachement à ce principe des pays nouvellement parvenus à la vie internationale devrait donner l'éveil sur ce point. Il ne s'agit pas d'une maladie infantile de l'indépendance, non plus que chez d'autres, une manifestation de sénilité. C'est bien plutôt la tradition juridique de ce qui demeure, quoiqu'on en ait, la structure fondamentale de la société internationale contemporaine. S'agissant de développement, ce principe reste particulièrement actuel, comme l'a affirmé la Conférence de Genève (de la CNUCED) de 1964, dans le premier principe général qu'elle ait adopté.[3]

Chaque peuple doit déterminer lui-même ses propres priorités pour assurer son progrès et son développement; il n'appartient pas au Canada, ou à tout autre pays industrialisé, d'imposer ses conceptions aux pays sous-développés, ici comme ailleurs. Il faut admettre par conséquent que l'on ne peut parler d'un droit international de la coopération qu'à partir du moment où un état a décidé de prendre en main son développement et qu'il se soit décidé à faire appel à d'autres états ou institutions internationales pour obtenir de l'assistance soit directement, soit par le biais du commerce ou des investissements ou d'une autre façon. C'est alors que le droit international public classique n'apporte pas tous les éléments nécessaires pour régir ces nouveaux rapports 'd'inégalités de fait' dans 'une égalité de droit.'

Le droit du développement international constitue ainsi une dérogation importante au droit international public classique à un tel point qu'on est en présence d'un nouveau secteur du droit international.[4] On parle déjà beaucoup du rôle du droit en tant que stimulant ou frein au développement sur le plan strictement interne. Ainsi, on s'interroge beaucoup actuellement sur l'influence que les normes juridiques, par exemple, le droit de la famille, le droit des successions, le droit fiscal peuvent avoir sur le développement, et la justice sociale dans les pays du Tiers Monde.[5] Cette approche, que l'on pourrait définir comme étant celle du 'Droit et du développement' connaît un certain essor présentement non seulement dans les pays sous-développés mais aussi dans les pays industrialisés.[6] Alors que la notion du 'Droit et du développement' s'exerce avant tout à l'intérieur d'un territoire, le droit international du développement, qui nous intéresse ici, implique essentiellement une interaction de normes juridiques de deux entités internationales ou un processus juridique de type inter-étatique ou transnational.

On a pu définir le 'Droit du développement' comme étant: 'l'ensemble des règles juridiques ayant directement pour objet de promouvoir le développement économique, social et culturel des pays sous-développés.'[7] Cette définition peut s'appliquer aussi bien au droit interne des pays en voie de développement qu'aux normes qui régissent les actions de toutes les entités extérieures – étrangères et internationales – qui souhaitent y promouvoir ce genre de développement.

En fait s'il est intellectuellement possible de séparer les normes juridiques reconnues dans les états du Tiers Monde, au Canada, et dans les organisations internationales, il faut admettre d'un autre côté que c'est de la rencontre, de la coexistence, de l'acceptation, ou du refus mutuel de ces normes que naît le droit international du développement, surtout en ce qui a trait aux normes contractuelles notamment aux accords de coopération et aux investissements dans le Tiers Monde.

Le champ d'application de ce nouveau droit est très vaste, puisqu'il doit, en principe, régir l'ensemble des rapports entre pays industrialisés et pays en voie de
développement.

> Toute une série d'institutions et de procédures ont été imaginées, soit pour aménager les
> règles suivies en matière d'investissements ou dans le domaine des paiements, soit en
> matière commerciale, soit pour permettre aux pays industrialisés de soutenir l'effort des
> pays du Tiers Monde. La règlementation de l'assistance technique et financière,
> bilatérale ou multilatérale, des prêts internationaux, des investissements privés, des con-
> trats commerciaux, des prix des produits de base, etc ... constitue un secteur de droit
> international nouveau et en pleine évolution.[8]

Cette branche nouvelle du droit international, le droit international du développement, a des implications importantes pour le Canada, dont les rapports avec les
pays en voie de développement n'ont cessé de croître depuis la dernière guerre
mondiale. On peut donc définir la pratique canadienne en la matière comme étant
l'ensemble des normes écrites et non-écrites, qui régissent ou affectent les relations
dites de coopération entre le Canada et les pays du Tiers Monde dans la mesure
où ces rapports visent à promouvoir le développement de ces états. En réalité, il
peut s'agir aussi bien des règlements qui régissent le statut et le rôle des coopérants
canadiens ou des boursiers du Tiers Monde au Canada que des ententes qui régissent les prêts accordés aux pays sous-développés ou encore certains traités commerciaux.

Evolution du développement international

En adhérant à la Charte des Nations Unies à San Francisco en 1945, le Canada s'est
engagé dans la voie de la coopération internationale en matière de développement
socioéconomique. Ainsi le Canada s'est engagé à favoriser 'le relèvement des
niveaux de vie, le plein emploi et des conditions de progrès et de développement
dans l'ordre économique.'[9]

Cet engagement pris à San Francisco, le Canada devait l'assumer d'abord par
le truchement des organismes multilatéraux aussi bien le cadre des programmes
spéciaux de l'ONU tel que le Fonds spécial, le Programme élargi, le PNUD, l'UNRWA,
l'UNICEF, que les institutions spécialisées, la Banque Mondiale et ses organismes
affiliés, les groupes consultatifs, et les consortia.[10]

Puis, avec l'établissement du Plan de Colombo et l'accession à l'indépendance
des nations du Tiers Monde, le Canada établit des programmes de coopération
bilatérale avec de nombreux états d'Asie (1950), des Antilles du Commonwealth
(1958), d'Afrique anglophone (1959), d'Afrique francophone (1961); en 1964 le
gouvernement canadien étendit ses programmes à l'Amérique latine par le truchement de la Banque Inter-américaine et en 1971 il le fit sur une base bilatérale.

Le Canada a considérablement étendu son action dans ce domaine en participant à plusieurs organismes régionaux qui s'intéressent au développement, tels que: l'OCDE, le Commonwealth, l'Agence de Coopération culturelle et technique (des pays francophones), les banques régionales d'Asie, des Antilles occidentales, d'Amérique latine. Le Canada ne peut devenir membre de la Banque Africaine de Développement mais participe au Fonds spécial de cette institution.

Pour l'année fiscale 1972-3, le gouvernement canadien a affecté près de 500 millions de dollars au chapitre de l'assistance au développement dont environ 25 pour cent sous la forme d'aide multilatérale.[11] Le Canada s'est engagé à atteindre l'objectif de 0.7 pour cent de son PNB tel que recommandé par la Commission Pearson, mais Ottawa n'a pas indiqué quand il le fera. Il ne fait aucun doute que le gouvernement canadien s'oriente vers cet objectif. C'est la raison pour laquelle, le Premier Ministre Trudeau souhaitait confirmer cet engagement dans le préambule de la future constitution canadienne:

> Dans un monde interdépendant, dans lequel les systèmes de communications permettent aux pauvres de prendre conscience de leur pauvreté, dans un monde où l'industrie, la finance, le commerce revêtent de plus en plus un caractère international, l'intérêt même du Canada justifierait que notre pays joue un rôle actif sur le plan international. Sans une paix mondiale solidement établie sur la compréhension, la coopération et la nécessité de venir au secours des régions sous-développées, les détails de notre constitution pourraient perdre toute signification dans la lutte pour la survie de l'humanité qui pourrait s'ensuivre. Mais ce n'est pas un intérêt égoïste qui doit inciter les Canadiens à formuler l'objectif suivant: contribuer à la réalisation de la paix et de la sécurité mondiale, au progrès social et à l'amélioration du niveau de vie de toute l'humanité.[12]

D'ailleurs à côté de ces programmes de coopération officielle, existant bien auparavant une coopération privée canadienne avec les pays et territoires du Tiers Monde. Cette coopération se manifesta aussi sur le plan commercial et financier et prit une envergure plus considérable une fois que ces pays devinrent indépendants.

En somme, la coopération canadienne avec les pays du Tiers Monde s'est accrue très rapidement, depuis 1960 en particulier. Au fur et à mesure que se développaient les relations entre le Canada et le Tiers Monde, se développait en même temps une pratique juridique en la matière. C'est ce que nous verrons maintenant.

Le droit institutionnel

Si, d'une part, il existe plus d'une centaine d'institutions privées qui s'occupent de coopération internationale, les programmes d'aide publique du Canada sont coordonnés par un organisme, l'Agence Canadienne de Développement international (ACDI).

L'ACDI

Sur le plan juridique, le statut de l'ACDI n'est pas très précis, quoique son rôle et ses fonctions soient assez bien définis 'en pratique.' En effet, si l'ACDI est considérée comme un ministère pour les fins de la *Loi sur l'administration financière*,[13] et bien que l'agence agisse en fait très souvent comme un ministère, aucun texte de loi ne lui a conféré officiellement ce statut. Un ordre en conseil du 17 août 1951[14] confia à un Comité du Ministère de l'Industrie et du Commerce la tâche de coordonner la participation canadienne au Plan de Colombo. Cette direction se développa rapidement mais garda son statut initial. Un autre ordre en conseil, du 28 octobre 1960,[15] transféra cette responsabilité au Ministère des Affaires extérieures et créa le 'Bureau de l'Aide Extérieure,' ayant à sa tête un directeur général. Par un troisième ordre en conseil, en 1968,[16] le Bureau de l'Aide Extérieure fut transformé en l'Agence canadienne de Développement international, avec un président à sa tête. L'ACDI demeure 'coiffé' d'un comité interministériel, le Conseil Canadien pour le Développement. Ce conseil est composé du président de l'ACDI, des sous-ministres des Ministères du Commerce et de l'Industrie, des Affaires extérieures, des Finances, et du gouverneur de la Banque du Canada. Ce conseil surveille les opérations de l'agence, assure la coordination avec les projets d'autres ministères, et discute de politiques nouvelles dans ce domaine. Le conseil n'est pas habilité, en pratique, à prendre des décisions importantes, puisque c'est le ministre des affaires extérieures ou le Conseil des Ministres qui décide en dernier ressort. Il joue néanmoins un rôle consultatif important.

L'ACDI s'occupe de l'organisation, du fonctionnement, et de l'administration des programmes canadiens d'aide au développement. L'agence peut déléguer une partie de ses responsabilités à un autre organisme. Ainsi l'ancien Président de l'ACDI, Maurice Strong, soulignait:

> The basic function of CIDA is to bring Canadian resources and services to bear on the needs of the less developed nations. To do this, CIDA must maintain direct and continuing relationships with all the resources available in Canadian society – universities, schools, businesses and co-operatives, farm organizations, the labour movement and professional groups. It must also become familiar with the requirements for development and the conditions of life within the less developed countries, and be able to work directly with governments and other organizations in these countries.[17]

Il ajouta à la même occasion: 'CIDA is an ever changing agency, gearing itself to meet new challenges in the highly complex field of international development. With a view to achieving maximum effectiveness in the administration of a growing aid programme, CIDA has been restructuring its organization.'[18]

L'ACDI en effet a connu de nombreux changements structurels au cours des dernières années. Plusieurs recommandations ont été formulées au sujet du statut qu'on devrait lui conférer. Le sous-comité de l'aide au développement international du Comité Permanent des Affaires extérieures et de la Défense nationale a étudié cette question et en est arrivé à la conclusion que le statut actuel de l'ACDI, malgré ses multiples lacunes, convenait mieux que celui d'un ministère ou d'une société de la couronne.

> Dans l'étude des diverses solutions qui se présentaient à lui, le sous-comité est parti de l'hypothèse que l'ACDI devait être à même d'exercer une influence marquée dans les hautes sphères gouvernementales de décision, si l'on voulait que l'ensemble des efforts officiels concernant l'aide soient concertés et efficaces ... Le sous-comité n'est pas con-

vaincu que l'ACDI exercerait plus d'influence qu'à l'heure actuelle si on l'élevait au rang de ministère secondaire. Il serait également possible, dans les conditions actuelles et pour accroître l'influence politique de l'ACDI, de nommer un ministre subalterne dépendant du Secrétaire d'Etat aux Affaires extérieures. Ce ministre, qui pourrait être un ministre d'Etat, ne siègerait pas habituellement au Cabinet et le Secrétaire d'Etat aux Affaires extérieures serait le porte-parole de l'ACDI dans cette assemblée. Ce ministre subalterne ajouterait à l'importance politique de l'ACDI dans les cercles gouvernementaux et permettrait une plus grande représentation politique aussi bien à l'intérieur qu'à l'extérieur du Canada.[19]

Quant au statut de société de la couronne, les membres du sous-comité soulignèrent qu' 'une société de la courrone pourrait, dans une certaine mesure, se sentir libre de critiquer les lignes de conduite suivies dans certains domaines qui relèvent de plusieurs ministères. Il ne lui serait pas possible, cependant, de recommander une action positive ou d'en prendre l'initiative, ou de participer de façon significative à la mise en application de changements formels.'[20]

Certes, l'ACDI a besoin d'une certaine liberté dans l'exécution de ses programmes particuliers. C'est pourquoi la Loi sur l'Administration Financière – qui établit d'une certaine manière la tutelle du Conseil du Trésor sur presque toutes les dépenses de plus de $25,000–devrait être revue. Cependant, une plus grande liberté *à priori* pourrait correspondre à des contrôles sévères *a posteriori*. Il faudrait aussi que l'ACDI puisse déléguer plus de responsabilités *de jure* à ses représentants en poste à l'étranger; à l'heure actuelle, tout doit être sanctionné par Ottawa. Ces normes juridiques constituent souvent des freins à une mise en œuvre rapide des programmes de développement international.

Autres organismes gouvernementaux
Si le Conseil du Trésor exerce une influence directe sur la coopération canadienne, par le truchement des lois portant sur l'administration financière, il faut signaler aussi le rôle très important que joue la Commission de la Fonction publique; en effet les règlements de cette commission affectent l'engagement et le statut des administrateurs de l'ACDI et, sur certains plans, celui des coopérants canadiens.

D'autres ministères jouent un rôle important dans le domaine de la coopération canadienne, en particulier le ministère des Affaires extérieures. Etant responsable de la formulation et de la mise en œuvre de la politique étrangère ce ministère participe ainsi à l'orientation générale de l'aide au développement international du Canada. Les ministères des Finances, de l'Agriculture, de l'Industrie et du Commerce, et de la Défense, ainsi que la Banque du Canada, sont directement intéressés par le programme de coopération, dans des secteurs précis. Il en est de même du Conseil des Arts et du Conseil national des Sciences. En réalité, presque tous les ministères du gouvernement collaborent à divers titres, en fournissant des experts et des conseillers dans le domaine de l'assistance technique.

Il faut signaler aussi le rôle grandissant des gouvernements provinciaux. Par exemple, le ministère de l'Education du Québec recrute les professeurs québécois que l'ACDI affecte dans les pays du Tiers Monde. A côté des provinces, un certain nombre d'entreprises publiques, comme l'Hydro-Ontario, ou parapublique, telles que les universités, collaborent avec l'ACDI, en vue de la mise en œuvre de programmes canadiens de coopération internationale. Il faut signaler enfin le rôle du nouveau Centre de Recherches pour le Développement international, qui tout en n'étant pas un organisme national, a tout de même été créé par une loi du parlement canadien.[21]

Ainsi on le voit, c'est à partir des règlements de tous ces organismes que progressivement s'élabore le droit institutionnel en matière de développement international. Néanmoins il faut ajouter que c'est surtout au sein de l'ACDI que s'élabore de plus en plus cette pratique.

Les accords de coopération bilatérale

A côté de tous les traités multilatéraux auxquels le Canada a adhéré dans le domaine du développement, le gouvernement canadien a conclu déjà de nombreux accords de coopération sur une base bilatérale avec des pays d'Afrique, d'Asie, et d'Amérique latine. Certains juristes soutiennent que ceux-ci ne tombent pas dans le domaine du droit international public. C'est un point de vue valable si on se place dans la perspective du droit international classique mais plutôt discutable dans l'optique du nouveau droit international.

On distingue plusieurs sortes d'accords de coopération: traité, entente intergouvernementale, protocole, lettres d'entente, simple contrat. Une telle classification est imparfaite en soi; en effet il arrive souvent qu'un accord de coopération contienne des dipositions que l'on retrouve aussi dans au autre genre d'entente.

Le cas des traités ne soulève pas tellement de difficultés car on reconnaît qu'ils font intégralement partie du droit international public: ils tiennent compte des normes définis par le 'Droit des Traités.' Les traités formels ne sont pas souvent utilisés dans le domaine de la coopération.

Habituellement, on a recours à une entente:

> This is an instrument less formal than a treaty or Convention proper, and generally not in Heads of State form. It is usually applied to agreements of a more limited scope (than treaties) and with fewer parties than the ordinary Convention. It is also employed for agreements of a technical or administrative character only, signed by representatives of a Government Department, but not subject to ratification.[22]

Le Canada a déjà signé un grand nombre de ces ententes avec presque tous les pays auxquels Ottawa accorde de l'aide bilatérale. Le ministère des Affaires extérieures a en fait préparé des projets – types d'accord où l'on souligne:

> The present agreement, of unspecified duration, shall come into force after ratification by the two Parties according to the customary procedure in each State and shall remain in force as long as one or the other has not denounced it by six months written notice.[23]

De tels accords constituent des sources importantes de la pratique canadienne en matière de développement international et, à ce titre, tombent dans le domaine du droit international public, aux yeux de l'auteur. On peut associer à cette catégorie les protocoles d'entente qui n'exigent pas aussi de ratification de la part des gouvernements. Plusieurs affirment qu'ils ne s'agit que d'arrangements administratifs qui ne tiennent pas en droit international public.

> The present Agreement, and all subsidiary Agreements and amendments hereto, shall be considered to be administrative arrangements only and not binding in international or domestic law. Differences and disputes arising from the present agreement shall be settled by negociation between the Government of Canada and the Government of ...[24]

Il existe en fait une très grande variété d'accords de coopération. Dans certains cas, des accords ont été conclus entre un ministère d'un pays et l'ambassade du Canada, et dans un cas assez exceptionnel entre le souverain d'un état et l'ambassadeur canadien accrédité dans ce pays.

Le gouvernement canadien tente cependant d'uniformiser la forme de ses accords de coopération. L'ACDI et le ministère des Affaires extérieures souhaiteraient conclure des 'accords cadres' avec le pays récipiendaire de l'aide canadienne; ceci permettrait ensuite à l'ACDI de conclure des ententes avec les ministères ou les agences de ces pays. Cependant, certains pays hésitent à accepter cette formule et préfèrent conclure un accord particulier pour chaque programme ou projet de développement estimant ainsi avoir plus de garanties juridiques.

Les accords de coopération sont des textes très généraux. Les premiers articles établissent la volonté du Canada de coopérer avec l'autre partenaire et prévoient habituellement que

> In pursuance of the objective of the present Agreement, the Government of Canada and the Government of ... acting directly or through their competent Agencies, may in due course conclude secondary Agreements, evidenced by letters, notes, or memoranda in writing, relating to the following questions: ... d) all questions as might permit the two governments to pursue jointly the objectives enunciated in this Agreement.[25]

On énonce ensuite les principes qui régissent l'assistance technique et financière canadienne. Le projet-type stipule que

> Unless the text thereof expressly states the contrary, subsidiary Agreements concluded in accordance with Article 4 of this Agreement shall be considered to be administrative arrangements only and not formal agreements binding in international or domestic law.[26]

Les protocoles d'ententes servent à des fins plus précises. Ils délimitent clairement les domaines des responsabilités de chaque gouvernement quant au partage des dépenses encourues lors de l'exécution du programme de coopération, alors que d'autres dispositions traitent par exemple de la nature, des conditions, du niveau de l'assistance.

Il faut s'interroger sur la nature des ententes administratives que l'on voudrait exclure du domaine du droit international public: on souhaiterait que les différends à ce sujet soient résolus par voie de négociation entre les deux gouvernements. Or, on peut se demander si les deux parties peuvent se soustraire à leurs obligations en soulignant qu'un tel accord ne tombe pas dans le domaine du droit international public. Un état, à qui le Canada aurait retiré son aide pour des raisons politiques, pourrait-il, à la suite d'une plainte portée devant un tribunal international, obliger le gouvernement canadien à continuer ses programmes d'assistance au développement? Une telle question peut paraître hypothétique aux yeux de plusieurs mais elle peut devenir une réalité à l'avenir.

Si, d'une part on peut douter de la valeur de certains de ces accords au regard du droit international classique, d'autre part il est certain que ces ententes font partie de la pratique canadienne en matière de développement international. En second lieu, l'évolution présente favorise une reconnaissance de ces ententes dans le domaine du droit international public. A cet effet, la Commission de Droit international

> took the view that the Convention should apply to 'treaty' whatever its particular designation. In its 1962 draft, the Commission emphasized the generality of its definition by including the parenthetic catalog '(treaty, convention, protocol, covenant, charter, statute ... exchange of notes, agreed minute, memorandum of agreement, modus vivendis or any other appellation)' immediately following the word designation ... At the second reading of the articles in 1965, the Commission decided to use the generic term 'treaty' to cover all forms of international agreements concluded between states. The definition proposed by the Commission was: 'Treaty' means an international agreement concluded between states in written form and governed by international law, whether embodied in a single instrument or in two or more related instruments and whatever its particlar designation.[27]

Ainsi, selon la Commission du Droit international, de tels accords administratifs, même s'ils ont trait à des sujets très techniques, peuvent tomber dans le domaine du Droit des Traités; par conséquent, ils ne peuvent être exclus complètement du domaine du droit international public.

Il serait bon d'analyser quelques-unes des positions qui régissent certains programmes de coopération du Canada.

L'assistance financière du Canada est octroyée sous deux formes: les prêts et les dons. Jusqu'en 1965 l'aide bilatérale du Canada se faisait surtout au moyen des dons. Les procédures suivies étaient et sont encore simples. A la suite d'une requête d'un pays du Tiers Monde, l'ACDI étudie une telle demande et émet un avis. Si l'avis est favorable, un accord est alors conclu; le contrôle de l'emploi des fonds est limité au contenu des biens et services achetés au Canada par le pays bénéficiaire.

Le Canada a toujours préféré accorder des dons plutôt que des prêts, car le service de la dette de la plupart des pays du Tiers Monde accapare une grande partie des devises qu'ils obtiennent ainsi. Cependant, étant donné que plusieurs états du Tiers Monde préfèrent emprunter, pour des considérations de dignité nationale, le Canada a mis sur pied un système de prêts au développement.

Les prêts canadiens au développement sont des 'prêts à long terme, à faible taux d'intérêt (soft loans). Les fondements juridiques de ce système de prêts se trouvent dans plusieurs décisions du Conseil du Trésor.'[28] En 1965 on établit des prêts à très long terme, remboursable en cinquante ans, avec une période de grâce de dix ans. Le taux d'intérêt n'était que de $^3/_4$ de un pour cent par année. Ces prêts étaient semblables à ceux de l'Association internationale de Développement. Avec l'échéance lointaine, et le dépréciation monétaire, la proportion de don dans ces prêts atteint 90 pour cent. Le Secrétaire d'Etat aux Affaires extérieures fut chargé de l'administration de ces prêts.

> The Board further recommends that Your Excellency in Council grant general authority to the Secretary of State for External Affairs (and to such persons as may be specifically designated to him in writing) to conclude loan agreements for approved projects with eligible borrowers, without reference to your Excellency in Council, where the loan agreements incorporate the terms and conditions described above.[29]

Cependant, il apparut clairement aux dirigeants du programme canadien de coopération qu'il serait sage de modifier quelque peu le système des prêts au développement afin de placer l'ensemble des pays sur le même pied. Un autre ordre en conseil instaura un régime des prêts qui se situent à mi-chemin entre les prêts de l'AID et ceux accordés par la Banque Mondiale.[30] Ces prêts sont remboursables en trente ans, avec une période de grâce de sept ans. Le taux d'intérêt s'élève à 3 pour cent; ce même ordre en conseil supprima l'intérêt de ³/₄ de un pour cent sur les prêts remboursables en cinquante ans.

Un autre aspect qui a des incidences juridiques importantes est le contenu de l'aide canadienne. Jusqu'à tout récemment, ceux qui bénéficiaient de l'assistance financière canadienne devaient obligatoirement dépenser la plus grande partie de cette aide au Canada, sous forme d'achats de biens et de services. Un récent rapport annuel de l'ACDI traitait de ce problème dans les termes suivants:

> Canadian bilateral aid continues to be used mainly to provide Canadian goods and services for the less developed countries. But two important changes have been made which mitigate the unfavourable implications of aid-tying for the recipient countries, and increase the number of Canadian suppliers who can share in the business available under the Canadian program. Now, under certain circumstances, up to 25% of Canada's contribution to a development project may be used to cover local costs – such as local labour and materials – normally by the receiving country. Also, the minimum Canadian content of goods supplied has been reduced from 80 to 66%, permitting our aid funds to be used for a much wider range of Canadian goods under competitive conditions.[31]

Ce texte illustre bien les problèmes soulevés par l'aide liée. En effet, jusqu'en 1968, 80 pour cent des fonds fournis par le Canada devaient servir à l'achat de biens et services purement canadiens. Ce montant est maintenant diminué à 60 pour cent. De plus, 20 pour cent de l'ensemble de l'aide bilatérale peut être complètement 'déliée.'

'L'aide liée' est étroitement régie par des règlements qui régissent l'achat de biens et services au Canada. Les procédures ont varié considérablement depuis l'instauration de l'aide financière canadienne. D'une façon générale, le pays commande ses biens et services au Canada d'après une liste qui lui est remise par l'ACDI. Une procédure encore plus courante consiste à émettre des appels d'offres, selon les règlements qui régissent les achats du gouvernement canadien. Les paiements s'effectuent au moyen de crédits disposés dans des banques à charte canadiennes qui effectuent les paiements aux compagnies, sur ordre de l'ACDI. L'ACDI demande l'exécution des paiements sur réception des rapports de dépenses préparés par les sociétés ou les pays concernés. Certains pays, l'Inde notamment, ont demandé de pouvoir faire directement affaires avec certains fournisseurs sans avoir à émettre des appels d'offres, et à disposer des fonds de coopération, comme ils l'entendent, pour acheter des biens et services canadiens.

Une autre décision du Conseil du Trésor[32] a modifié les normes et procédures dans le domaine des procédures d'aide. A l'heure actuelle, les pays bénéficiaires de l'aide canadienne peuvent effectuer leurs achats au Canada chez un seul fournisseur, sans appel d'offres, selon la procédure dite 'sole source procurement':

> It is therefore recommended that the Treasury Board authorize the External Aid Office to waive tendering procedures and permit recipient countries to enter into sole source procurement provided:
> a funds have been approved for the project, goods or services in question;
> b the External Aid Office is satisfied that opportunities for competition have been made known to all Canadian suppliers;
> c that the suppliers certificate regarding fair pricing has been checked and accepted by the External Aid Office;
> d that Canadian content regulations are respected;
> e that the External Aid Office approve specific financing before contractual obligations are entered into.[33]

Il est bien entendu cependant qu'en règle générale que les achats de services et de biens par les pays bénéficiaires doivent donner lieu à des appels d'offres; 'to the degree practicable, tender calls would be made in accordance with Canadian Government regulations.'[34]

Un autre problème existe au niveau des dispositions juridiques qui ont trait aux dépenses dites 'locales.' Jusqu'en 1968 le pays bénéficiaire devait fournir la totalité des devises locales nécessaires à la mise en œuvre de certains programmes de coopération. Etant donné que ces montants étaient souvent trop élevés pour le pays bénéficiaire, bien des pays hésitaient à s'engager dans des projets de grande envergure, faute de fonds locaux suffisants. Le Canada accepta donc de modifier ces règlements et d'assumer jusqu'à 25 pour cent des dépenses locales. De plus, dans certains cas, l'ACDI défraie toutes les dépenses.

NORMES JURIDIQUES DANS LE DOMAINE DU COMMERCE ET DES INVESTISSEMENTS

L'ampleur des problèmes auxquels ont à faire face les pays en voie de développement est telle que l'assistance seule, bilatérale ou multilatérale, ne représente qu'un élément dans leur développement. En effet, les pays sous-développés tirent principalement leurs ressources en devises par la voie du commerce et des investissements étrangers. Les dirigeants canadiens sont conscients de ce phénomène:

> L'aide est très importante mais les investissements et le commerce le sont encore plus. Les pays en voie de développement obtiennent 80% de leurs devises par l'intermédiaire du commerce international. M. Pearson disait un jour: 'Où est la logique si nous stimulons

la croissance des pays en voie de développement en leur accordant une aide financière alors que d'un autre côté nous ne laissions pas entrer librement les produits que ces pays sont en mesure de fabriquer sur une base concurrentielle.' Cette notion est généralement acceptée. Le Canada et les autres pays du monde commencent à mieux comprendre dans quelle mesure le Tiers Monde est dépendant de ses exportations pour pouvoir financer l'importation de ses biens d'équipement. Les pays industrialisés doivent diriger leurs efforts de développement de telle façon à permettre aux pays moins riches de se développer économiquement sans devoir faire appel à l'aide extérieure. Le commerce est le chaînon manquant dans leur évolution de la pauvreté à l'affluence.[35]

Depuis la première Conférence des Nations Unies sur le Commerce et le Développement à Genève qui s'est déroulée en 1964, le Canada s'est interessé de près à ce problème et a formulé des recommandations en vue d'éliminer les barrières douanières et d'autres entraves qui réduisent le commerce des pays sous-développés.

Il en est de même au sujet des investissements dans le Tiers Monde. Certes l'expropriation de la Demerara Bauxite, filiale de l'Alcan, en Guyane, dont il sera fait question plus loin, a mis en lumière les problèmes qui surgiront de façon de plus en plus aigue au cours des prochaines années. Il s'agit en effet, pour les pays en voie de développement, d'attirer les capitaux et la technologie étrangère, tout en n'aliénant pas leurs richesses naturelles et les ressources humaines de leur pays, au profit des grandes sociétés multilatérales. Le conflit inhérant à cette situation trouve sa source dans le désir légitime des pays du Tiers Monde qui veulent contrôler leur développement socio-économique; ceci entre souvent en conflit avec les impératifs des grandes sociétés multilatérales pour qui les frontières existent peu ou pas. En tant que pays exportateur de capitaux privés et de technologie dans les pays du Tiers Monde, le Canada se trouve directement impliqué dans cette situation.

Le Canada a reconnu que:

> Depuis toujours, le secteur privé a joué un rôle très important dans le développement. Les institutions de bienfaisance ont consacré des sommes considérables à l'instruction, à la santé et au bien-être social des pays en voie de développement. L'industrie privée a contribué à en accroître le potentiel commercial et industriel. L'aide dispensée par le secteur privé possède un avantage déterminant: elle permet aux organismes et aux compagnies des pays en voie de développement d'établir des relations de travail directes avec leurs homologues du Canada. Ce contact direct facilite la transmission du savoir et des connaissances spécialisées et en assure l'utilité pour l'entreprise. Le Gouvernement se propose donc d'appuyer davantage l'activité du secteur privé qui contribue au développement international.[36]

Le droit canadien du développement international se trouve donc une de ses composantes essentielles dans les dispositions et règlements qui ont trait au commerce avec les pays sous-développés et aux investissements canadiens dans le Tiers Monde. Il s'agit à la fois des mesures existantes ou recommandées en vue de favoriser ou restreindre l'entrée des produits du Tiers Monde au Canada, et l'exportation de produits du Canada vers ces pays, sans oublier naturellement les normes juridiques qui affectent les investissements canadiens dans ces pays, de même que les mesures prises par le gouvernement canadien pour inciter les hommes d'affaires à agir en ce sens.

Commerce

Le commerce avec les pays du Tiers Monde ne représente pas un chiffre très important par rapport à l'ensemble du commerce extérieur canadien. En 1969 le Canada a importé pour un milliard de dollars de marchandises des pays en voie de développement, ce qui représentait environ 8 pour cent des importations totales du Canada.[37] Les exportations canadiennes vers le Tiers Monde s'élevaient à $900 millions, soit 7 pour cent du total. Le Canada reçoit environ 2 pour cent des exportations du Tiers-Monde, ce qui représente un chiffre équivalent, à peu de choses près, au pourcentage des importations du Tiers Monde provenant du Canada. Le commerce import-export du Canada représente 5 pour cent des échanges mondiaux avec le Tiers Monde. En réalité le Canada n'occupe pas une place très importante dans l'ensemble du commerce entre pays développés et en voie de développement. Le commerce entre le Canada et les pays du Tiers Monde est à l'avantage de ces derniers, puisque le Canada subit un déficit de $100 millions.

Le cadre juridique général qui régit le commerce extérieur canadien est celui qui découle de la participation du Canada à l'Accord Général sur les Tarifs douaniers et le Commerce (GATT).[38] Le GATT est caractérisé surtout par *la clause de la nation la plus favorisée* :

> GATT provides that each Member country should give the other Members fair and equal treatment in trade and not discriminate against any of them. This provision removes one of the major sources of discord among nations.[39]

En pratique, ceci signifie que si l'un des pays membres concède des avantages tarifaires à un pays membre, il doit les concéder à tous les autres états membres. Ces dispositions ont mené à plusieurs séries de négociations générales sur l'abaissement des tarifs douaniers, dont la plus célèbre fut le *Kennedy Round,*[40] lequel amena une diminution générale des barrières douanières de tous les pays membres (50 pour cent dans le cas de plusieurs produits finis).

D'une façon générale, le Canada applique la clause de la nation la plus favorisée à tous les pays en voie de développement, soit parce qu'ils sont membres du GATT, soit sur une base de réciprocité. Les pays membres du Commonwealth constituent un cas spécial, dont il sera question plus loin. Il reste un petit nombre de pays du Tiers Monde, l'Arabie Séoudite par exemple, qui ne sont pas membres du GATT et qui n'accordent pas de préférence sur la base de la clause de la nation la plus favorisée aux produits canadiens. Le 'tarif général' canadien s'applique aux importations en provenance de ces pays-là; les barrières érigées, par ce tarif, sont parfois prohibitives, de telle sorte que le commerce entre le Canada et les pays astreints au tarif général est très faible. Il ne fait pas de doute que la survivance de ce tarif est anachronique et qu'il y aurait peut-être lieu de l'abolir entièrement dans le cas des pays en voie de développement; il ne représente en fait qu'une éventuelle mesure de représailles envers des pays qui pourraient établir des politiques discriminatoires à l'endroit des produits canadiens.

LA CNUCED

L'attitude du Canada à l'endroit de la CNUCED constitue un dossier important dans les relations avec les pays du Tiers Monde. Les Nations Unies établirent, après de multiples demandes des pays du Tiers Monde, une conférence spéciale afin d'étudier en profondeur les problèmes posés par le commerce et le développement. La plupart des pays industrialisés accueillirent cette décision de l'Assemblée Générale de l'ONU avec certaines réserves; le Canada fut l'un de ceux-là.

Le Canada accorda son appui aux recommandations de la première conférence de la CNUCED qui eut lieu à Genève en 1964.[41] Celles-ci portèrent surtout sur la généralisation des 'préférences commerciales.'

> Le Canada n'est pas particulièrement attiré par l'élaboration d'arrangements commerciaux à caractère régional. Nous sommes préoccupés par la prolifération d'arrangements préférentiels négociés par la CEE avec un grand nombre de pays africains et méditerranéens. Il y a un risque sérieux que l'adhésion éventuelle du Royaume-Uni à la CEE donnera naissance à des arrangements discriminatoires similaires avec de nombreux pays en voie de développement du Commonwealth. La discrimination commerciale sur une base hémisphérique aboutirait à une concentration de l'activité économique dont seuls profiterait quelques blocs d'influence économique. Le genre d'arrangement, qui ressemblerait étrangement au bon vieux protectionnisme d'antan mais appliqué à une plus grande échelle, donnerait certainement lieu à des rancunes et à des confrontations politiques entre blocs économiques.[42]

Le Canada s'est donc prononcé en faveur d'un système de préférences généralisées à l'égard de tous les pays du Tiers Monde. Ces derniers, réunis à Alger en 1967, réclamèrent qu'à la deuxième conférence de la CNUCED, qui devait avoir lieu à la Nouvelle Delhi en 1968, des mesures concrètes soient adoptées.

Le Canada indiqua qu'il était prêt à réduire ses barrières douanières jusqu'au niveau des préférences déjà accordées aux pays en voie de développement, membres du Commonwealth; dans d'autres cas, Ottawa se dit prêt à accorder une préférence douanière qui ferait en sorte que plusieurs produits pourraient être importés au Canada au 2/3 du taux accordé en vertu de la clause de la nation la plus favorisées.

Si à prime abord, les propositions canadiennes semblaient assez généreuses, ce ne fut pas là l'avis de Perez Guerero, secrétaire général de la CNUCED.

> In preferences, we cannot say, however that the Canadian offer has been among the best. It falls short of the offers received from a number of other countries, particularly the Scandinavian countries that are always, I would suggest, in the forefront of international cooperation. And other countries, members of the OCED, have been able to give offers that would, indeed, permit the developing countries to export their manufactures to the developed countries without having to pay any duty at all. In the case of Canada, we know that this has not been possible, that you did not consider – your government and you –

and your country did not approve of it, that you could start with that situation, so that, in most of the items, the developing countries would enjoy a preferential system which would carry to 33 percent.[43]

Malgré la timidité relative des propositions canadiennes en matière de préférences douanières, le parlement canadien n'avait pas encore été appelé à adopter la législation nécessaire à la mise en œuvre des recommandations proposées en 1968 à la veille de la troisième conférence de la CNUCED, qui débuta à Santiago en avril 1972. Le Canada se prête ainsi à des critiques de la part des pays du Tiers Monde, critiques d'autant plus fondées que la plupart des pays industrialisés ont d'ores et déjà mis en application un système de préférences douanières pour les produits manufacturés des pays du Tiers Monde. Le Canada fait figure de retardataire dans ce domaine, au même titre que les Etats-Unis.

Les accords sur les produits de base

Une question étroitement reliée au problème posé par le commerce et le développement est celle des accords sur les produits de base. En effet, les pays du Tiers Monde sont principalement exportateurs de produits de base. Il est donc de la plus haute importance pour eux que des prix équitables leur soient accordés pour ces produits et que les marchés des matières premières soient stabilisés afin de leur permettre de mieux planifier leur développement.

Le Canada est partisan de la conclusion d'accords internationaux sur les produits de base. En effet, le Canada a adhéré aux accords suivants: Arrangement international sur les céréales, Accord international sur le sucre, Accord International sur le café, Accord international sur l'étain.[44] D'autres accords sont en voie de négociation tels que l'accord sur le cacao, et des études auxquelles participe le Canada, se poursuivent quant à la possibilité de signer des accords sur le caoutchouc, le plomb et le zinc, les huiles végétales. Ces accords stabilisent les prix au moyen de quotas et de l'établissement de stocks. Des fonds sont établis afin de diversifier et augmenter la production; dans le cas de l'accord international sur le café, on prélève des contributions sur les exportations qui dépassent les montants prévus dans le cadre de l'accord.

Ces ententes constituent des sources importantes du droit canadien du développement international.

Investissements et exportations vers le Tiers Monde

A côté des accords commerciaux avec les pays du Tiers Monde, le droit canadien en matière de coopération internationale s'inspire aussi des normes qui régissent les investissements privés canadiens dans les pays sous-développés. Le gouvernement canadien a reconnu que

Un meilleur accès aux marchés industrialisés présenterait intrinsèquement peu de valeur pratique pour les pays en voie de développement surtout dans les secteurs spécialisés. Les investissements privés à l'étranger ont donc un rôle important à jouer dans la mise en place d'installations de productions génératrices de biens d'exportations à haute valeur technologique. Le secteur industriel canadien doit participer activement aux programmes de développement.[45]

A l'heure actuelle, un certain nombre de pays bénéficiaires désirent accroître et diversifier leurs sources de capitaux. Nombreux sont ceux qui en sont rendus à une étape où leur développement exige l'établissement d'entreprises industrielles de faible ou de moyenne envergure. L'expérience que le Canada a acquise dans ce genre d'opérations et dans des domaines comme le traitement des produits alimentaires, les produits forestiers et la transformation des matières brutes peut se révéler particulièrement précieuse. Le Gouvernement adoptera donc d'autres mesures pour encourager le secteur commercial et industriel du Canada à étendre ses opérations aux pays en voie de développement ou à les y accroître, en aidant à surmonter les obstacles particuliers d'une telle entreprise, sans perdre de vue les difficultés que pourrait créer un apport sans discernement de telles ressources.[46]

A cette fin, un certain nombre de mesures propres à stimuler les investissements canadiens dans les pays du Tiers Monde ont été prises: financement d'études de pré-investissements, assurances, etc.

L'Agence canadienne de Développement international a établi un programme de subventions pour les études de démarrage et les études de rentabilité effectuées par les entreprises canadiennes dans des pays en voie de développement. Seules les entreprises 'dûment établies au Canada avec siège social légalement constitué, et reconnues dans le monde industriel et le monde des affaires'[47] peuvent présenter des demandes de subventions à l'ACDI. L'ACDI s'engage à rembourser les dépenses encourues par la société jusqu'à concurrence de $2,500. L'entreprise, d'autre part, s'engage à respecter les normes et les exigences de l'ACDI, se rapportant à l'étude et aux critères de rentabilité qui doivent être analysés. Si la société décide de ne pas donner suite à son étude, celle-ci est remise à l'ACDI, qui peut la communiquer à d'autres sociétés intéressées.

L'ACDI met aussi à la disposition des entreprises un grand nombre de renseignements ayant trait aux possibilités d'investissements dans les pays du Tiers Monde. L'ACDI fournit aussi des renseignements au sujet des contrats accordés par les organisations internationales comme la Banque Mondiale, le PNUD ou les pays en voie de développement qui bénéficient de l'aide de ces organismes.

Dans ce domaine, il faut signaler le rôle de la Société pour l'Expansion des Exportations. Cette société fut établie en 1969 dans le but de faciliter et d'accroître le commerce entre le Canada et un pays étranger. La SEE peut:

a   conclure en contrat d'assurance avec une personne faisant des affaires ou ayant d'autres activités au Canada afin d'assurer cette personne contre tout risque résultant, dans le cadre d'une opération d'exportation, d'une cause qui ne peut être éliminée ni par elle ni, le cas échéant, par son affilié étranger.
b   fournir à une personne, au moyen de l'endossement approprié d'effets ou autrement, des garanties relatives à une opération d'exportation pour laquelle un contrat d'assurance a été ou pouvait être conclu en vertu de l'alinéa (a).[48]

Cette société est appelée à jouer un rôle de plus en plus important dans les relations avec les pays du Tiers Monde. Ses règlements deviendront une source importante de la pratique juridique canadienne en matière de coopération.

Certains efforts ont été faits depuis la fin de la guerre en vue de trouver un régime de garantie et de compensation des investissements expropriés par des gouvernements étrangers. La rédaction de conventions sur ce sujet s'est avérée extrêmement pénible, étant donné que les pays en voie de développement ne veulent pas hypothéquer leur avenir et le développement de leurs ressources en concluant des ententes qui les obligeraient à indemniser les entreprises étrangères qu'ils nationalisent selon des normes et des taux fixés par les pays industrialisés. La tentative la plus sérieuse dans ce sens a été la Convention de la Banque Mondiale sur le règlement des différends concernant des investissements. Cette convention fut signée par une vingtaine d'états en 1965. Cinquante-sept pays y avaient adhéré en 1968 dont trente pays du Tiers Monde. La convention prévoit la mise sur pied d'un centre de conciliation et d'arbitrage pour les disputes impliquant des investissements de nationaux d'un état dans un autre état; ce centre fonctionne sous l'égide de la BIRD et seuls les états signataires peuvent en devenir membres. Le droit en vigueur est celui du pays où sont faits les investissements. Le droit international s'applique aussi 'dans la mesure du possible.' Le Canada n'a pas adhéré à cette convention. Comme plusieurs dispositions de cette convention relèvent de la compétence des provinces, il n'est pas certain que celles-ci accepteraient de se conformer aux dispositions de la convention.[49]

Le gouvernement canadien ne s'est jamais vraiment prononcé officiellement sur le sujet. On peut toutefois considérer que le Canada est d'accord avec les principes énumérés dans la convention rédigée par un Comité spécial de l'OCDE qui prévoit que:

> Each Party shall at all times ensure fair and equitable treatment to the property and nationals of the other parties. It shall accord within its territory the most constant protection and security to such property and shall not in any way impair the management, maintenance, use, enjoyment or disposal thereof by unreasonable or discriminatory measures. The fact that certain nationals of any State are accorded treatment more favourable than that provided by the Convention shall not be regarded as discriminatory against nationals of a Party by reason only of the fact that such treatment is not accorded to the latter. The provisions of this Convention shall not affect the right of any Party to allow or prohibit the acquisition of property or the investment of Capital within its territory by nationals of another Party.[50]

D'ailleurs, jusqu'à tout récemment, le gouvernement canadien n'avait pas eu à faire face à la nationalisation d'avoirs canadiens par un pays du Tiers Monde. Mais il eut à prendre position quand le gouvernement de la Guyane nationalisa les installations de la Demerara Bauxite Ltd, filiale de l'Alcan. La prise en charge de ces installations fut cependant différée, en attendant la conclusion d'un accord avec la compagnie. L'Alcan refusa d'abord les conditions proposées par la Guyane, mais accepta en 1971 l'indemnisation offerte le gouvernement Burnham. La compagnie l'accepta enfin parce que le gouvernement canadien n'avait pas manifesté une très grande sympathie à l'égard de la position de l'Alcan.

En effet, après avoir averti le gouvernement guyannais qu'il s'attendait à ce que

Alcan reçoive une indemnité 'raisonnable,' le gouvernement canadien n'intervint pas dans le conflit; les porte-parole du gouvernement se déclarèrent satisfaits de l'accord intervenu en 1971 entre le gouvernement de Georgetown et l'Alcan. Lors d'une visite qu'il fit aux Antilles en 1970, l'Honorable Paul Martin déclara: 'En ce qui concerne l'avenir, on peut prévoir des conditions plus strictes moyennant lesquelles les investisseurs canadiens seront favorablement accueillis dans ce pays, de même qu'une insistance plus grande pour que les investissements canadiens qui existent déjà se conforment aux politiques du pays.'[51]

Le gouvernement canadien a donc adopté une attitude réaliste, en se rendant compte qu'il valait mieux ne pas s'immiscer trop directement dans de tels conflits, si l'expropriation était suivie d'une indemnisation raisonnable.

CONCLUSION

Cette étude permet de mettre en valeur cinq caractéristiques principales de la pratique juridique canadienne en matière de coopération internationale. Il faut d'abord mettre en relief l'*état embryonnaire* de ce droit; en effet, contrairement aux autres grandes puissances, le Canada a eu très peu d'échanges officiels avec les territoires du Tiers Monde, à l'exception des Antilles occidentales et certains territoires de l'empire britannique avant la seconde guerre mondiale. De plus, ce n'est que vers la fin des années 60 qu'on a commencé à rationaliser les politiques en matière de développement international et à favoriser une concertation entre les nombreuses entités canadiennes intéressées à cette action. Par conséquent, il existe encore peu de 'pièces juridiques maîtresses' en matière de coopération internationale au Canada. Dans bien des cas, on se réfère aux normes du droit international public classique, normes que de nombreux pays en voie de développement refusent de reconnaître aujourd'hui.

En second lieu, il faut signaler le caractère hautement *règlementaire* de cette pratique juridique du Canada en matière de coopération internationale. Malgré ses mérites évidents, la déclaration du gouvernement Trudeau sur 'Le Développement international' ne touche pas à l'ensemble du problème, en particulier à toutes les questions ayant trait au commerce avec le Tiers Monde.[52] Comme on l'a vu, la pratique canadienne dans le domaine de la coopération internationale repose sur toute une série d'accords multilatéraux et bilatéraux, d'ordres en conseil, de règlements et de décisions de plusieurs ministères, et en particulier des décisions de l'Agence canadienne de développement international et du Conseil du Trésor. En effet, c'est par le biais d'ordres en conseil[53] et de décisions administratives et non par le truchement de législations dûment adoptées par le parlement que la plupart des programmes canadiens de coopération du Canada ont été établis et sont régis.

La jeunesse et le caractère règlementaire du droit canadien ont eu un double effet: si d'une part on a assisté à très peu de conflits dans ce domaine, d'autre part la jurisprudence est encore très limitée et les études des juristes canadiens sur le sujet le sont encore davantage. Face à l'absence de lois-cadre et d'une institution centrale, au début, ces pratiques ont été développées sur une base *ad hoc* par les nombreuses entités mentionnées plus haut et bien d'autres encore.

De là découle le *pragmatisme* et l'*éclectisme* du droit canadien du développement international.[54] Ces caractères ont été très évidents au cours des deux dernières décennies mais ces deux phénomènes seront moins apparents à l'avenir, à la suite d'une meilleure concertation entre les unités intéressées au développement international y compris les provinces, et à leur souci d'améliorer la qualité des programmes de coopération.

Ces quatre premières caractéristiques pourraient peut-être conférer une place secondaire à la pratique canadienne en matière de droit international public. Or il faut reconnaître que l'*importance* d'une telle pratique ne cesse de croître.

Tout comme dans le cas du droit de l'environnement, la pratique canadienne en matière de développement international a progressé très rapidement au cours des dernières années et continuera de progresser à un rythme très rapide à l'avenir. Les liens de toutes sortes – diplomatiques, culturels, commerciaux, financiers – avec le Tiers Monde et en particulier l'engagement du gouvernement canadien à multiplier ses programmes de coopération sont autant de signes qui indiquent que le droit du développement occupera une place très grande dans la pratique canadienne en matière de coopération internationale.

LES NOTES

1 Sur l'ampleur du programme d'aide canadien avec les pays du Tiers Monde, consulter: Agence canadienne de développement international, *Le Canada et le monde en voie de développement*, Rapport Annuel de l'ACDI, 1970–1971 (1971).

2 Pour avoir une idée des travaux dans ce domaine, consulter: *La Coopération Internationale*, Bulletin d'information et de documentation de l'Institut de Droit de la Paix et du Développement de l'Université de Nice, semestriel.

3 Gérard Virally, 'Vers un Droit international du développement' (1965), *Annuaire Français de Droit International* 10.

4 Consulter à ce sujet: Gérard Virally, 'La notion de programme – un instrument de la coopération technique multilatérale' (1968), *Annuaire Français de Droit International* 530–53.

5 Voir à ce sujet: Peider Könz, 'Legal Development in Developing Countries' (1970), 8 *Development Digest* 61–70.

6 On pense aux problèmes posés par la 'socialisation du Droit' au Québec par exemple. Voir aussi: 'Potpourri of Speculations on Law and Development' (1970), 8 *Development Digest* 75–81.

7 R.G., 'Développement économique et social: Droit' in 5 *Encyclopédia Universalis* (1969) 510.

8 Virally, *supra* note 3, à 6.

9 Charte des Nations Unies, article 55.

10 Pour avoir un aperçu de la participation canadienne aux activités de ces organisations internationales, consulter, *Le Canada et le monde en voie de développement, supra*, note 1, à 57–69.

11 Pour saisir l'évolution du budget canadien dans ce domaine, consulter ibid, à 79–87.

12 Pierre Elliott Trudeau, *La Constitution canadienne et le citoyen* (1969) 13–15.

13 D'après l'ordre en conseil P.C. 1968–923, du 8 mai 1968.

14 P.C. 212/4211 du 17 août 1951.

15 Entra en vigueur le 1 novembre 1960.

16 P.C. 1968/1760.

17 ACDI, *Rapport annuel 1969* (1962) 2.

18 Ibid. Consulter aussi Paul Gérin-Lajoie, 'CIDA in a changing government organization' (1972), 15 *Administration Publique du Canada* 46–59.

19 Chambre des Communes, Comité permanent des Affaires extérieures et de la Défense nationale, sous-comité de l'aide au développement fascicule no 29: *Troisième rapport à la Chambre*. Troisième Session de la 28e Législature, juin 1971, 29–51.

20 Ibid, à 29–53.

21 1970, Can., c 36: 'Loi portant création du Centre de Recherches pour le Développement International,' sanctionnée le 13 mai 1970.

22 J.-G. Castel, *International Law, Chiefly as Interpreted and Applied in Canada* (1965) 816.

23 Ces clauses font partie d'un accord-type que l'ACDI a rédigé en collaboration avec le

Ministère des Affaires extérieures.

24 Clauses tirées de l'accord-type de l'ACDI.

25 Ibid.

26 Ibid.

27 R.D. Kearny and R.E. Dalton, 'The Treaty of Treaties' (1970), 64 503–4.

28 Surtout P.C. 1965 – 8/220 et P.C. 1966 – 13/1573.

29 Recommandation du Conseil du Trésor, TB 635672.

30 P.C. 1966 – 13/1573.

31 ACDI, *Rapport annuel 1969, supra* note 17, à 9. Voir aussi *Le Canada et le monde en voie de développement, supra* note 1, à 15.

32 TB 683100, modifiant, TB 650422.

33 EAO – 262, demande d'autorisation du Bureau de l'Aide extérieure adressée au Conseil du Trésor le 11 août 1967. (annexe A, à 5).

34 TB 683100, du 28 août 1968, à 3.

35 Jean-Luc Pépin, Discours prononcé à Windsor le 6 novembre 1970, distribué sous forme de polycopié par le Bureau du Ministre, à 2–3.

36 Mitchell Sharp, 'Développement international' brochure de la série *Politique étrangère au service des Canadiens* (1970) 22.

37 Ces chiffres sont tirés du discours de M Pépin dont nous avons fait état, et de *Le Canada et le monde en voie de développement, supra* note 1, à 86.

38 Le Canada a signé le Protocole d'application provisoire de l'Accord général sur les Tarifs douaniers et le Commerce le 30 octobre 1947, et l'Accord général est entré en vigueur le 1er janvier 1948.

39 Castel *International Law, supra* note 22 à 134.

40 Ces négociations débutèrent en 1963, pour arriver à un certain nombre d'accords en 1967–8 entre le Marché Commun et les Etats-Unis. Voir Mitchell Sharp, 'Les perspectives d'une politique commerciale,' *Déclarations et Discours*, no 67/23 (1967).

41 Pour avoir un aperçu de la politique canadienne dans ce domaine à la suite deux premières CNUCED, consulter Grant L.

Reuber, *Canada's Economic Policies towards the Less-Developed Countries* (Research Report 7038), evidence submitted to the Parliamentary Sub-Committee on International Development Assistance, 17 December 1970.

42 Pépin, Discours du 6 novembre 1970, *supra* note 35 à 17.

43 Chambre des Communes, Comité Permanent des Affaires extérieures et de la Défense nationale, sous-comité sur l'aide au développement international. *Fascicule No 6*, du 10 décembre 1970, 6:8–6:9. 'Le Canada n'a rien à offrir aux pays sous-développés,' *Le Devoir,* le 10 avril 1972, à 14.

44 Pour la liste complète des accords dont le Canada est signataire dans ce domaine, consulter *Le Rapport Annuel du Ministère de l'Industrie et du Commerce, 1969–1970* (1971), 109–31.

45 Pépin, Discours du 6 novembre 1970, *supra* note 35, à 25.

46 Sharp, 'Aide au développement,' *supra* note 36, à 23.

47 Consulter la brochure de l'ACDI: *Etude de démarrage, Etudes de rentabilité* (1971).

48 *Statuts du Canada* (17–18 Elizabeth II), Chapitre 39: Loi créant la Société pour l'expansion des exportations, 1969, Can., c. 39, article 24, à 973–4.

49 Consulter pour plus de détails à cet égard, George Schwarzenberg, *Foreign Investment and International Law* (1969).

50 Ibid, à 156.

51 Cité par Boris Miskew, *Le Droit* du 17 août 1971.

52 André Vinette, *Evolution de l'idée d'un système préférentiel généralisé en faveur des pays en voie de développement et analyse de la position du Canada*, Thèse de maîtrise présentée à l'Université Laval (1973).

53 1973, Can., c 172: 'Loi modifiant le Tarif des douanes,' sanctionnée le 13 avril 1973.

54 CIDA, 'Juridical Aspects of Canadian International Co-operation' (miméo) Ottawa (1972).

BRUCE C. MCDONALD # 32/Intellectual Property*

Article 27(2) of the Universal Declaration of Human Rights declares that 'everyone has the right to the protection of the moral and material interests resulting from any scientific, literary or artistic production of which he is the author.' In view of the fundamental nature of this principle, upon which protection of intellectual property is partly grounded, it is less surprising than it might otherwise be to find both western and communist countries, developed and developing, co-operating through international institutions to achieve a degree of harmonization and interrelationship of domestic laws as a basis for effective worldwide protection. The reason it might be surprising at all is that the economic nature of intellectual property rights means they are usually instruments of private economic power, with consequent political implications. Also, they can affect balances of payments and foreign exchange reserves to an extent capable of impeding the flow of technology and information to the areas of the world in greatest need.[1]

Article 2(viii) of the 1967 Convention Establishing the World Intellectual Property Oganization (WIPO) defines the subject matter as follows:

'intellectual property' shall include the rights relating to:
– literary, artistic and scientific works,
– performances of performing artists, phonograms and broadcasts,
– inventions in all fields of human endeavour,
– scientific discoveries,
– industrial designs,
– trademarks, service marks and commercial names and designations,
– protection against unfair competition,
and all other rights resulting from intellectual activity in the industrial, scientific, literary or artistic fields.

The WIPO administers the Convention for the Protection of Industrial Property (Paris 1883) to which approximately eighty countries including Canada are party, and the Convention for the Protection of Literary and Artistic Works (Berne 1886) to which over sixty countries including Canada are party. It also administers a series of more limited treaties relating to international classification and standardization in intellectual property systems, appellations of origin, the international deposit of industrial designs, and similar matters. The WIPO, led by a permanent

*I wish to acknowledge the co-operation of the Patent and Copyright Office and the Department of External Affairs in permitting me to review their files in the course of preparing this essay. Needless to say the views expressed here are my own and have in no way been suggested or approved by government officials.

secretariat that is both diplomatically and technically expert and active, is currently working towards concluding and bringing into force additional treaties to facilitate co-operation in the efficient acquisition of foreign patent protection,[2] to establish a system for the international registration of marks, to protect type faces, and to protect computer programs.

As a result of their interest in international education and development the United Nations and several of its agencies are becoming increasingly involved with intellectual property. This activity, accompanied by increasing co-operation with the WIPO, is largely a development of the last decade. The significant exception is the Universal Copyright Convention, negotiated in 1952 and in force as of 1955, to which approximately sixty countries including Canada are party. Problems of jurisdiction and dovetailing between the UCC and the Berne Convention have led to a certain amount of co-ordinated work between the two organizations. This has been particularly true in connection with the 1971 Paris revisions of both conventions to establish special copyright status for developing countries. The WIPO and UNESCO are also co-operating closely on new multilateral treaties to protect phonograms against unauthorized reproduction and to prevent the unauthorized use of television signals transmitted by satellite.[3] With the ILO, they are jointly responsible for administering the Rome Convention on Neighbouring Rights.[4]

In addition to the WIPO, which is the dominant international organization in the field and which might conceivably become a specialized agency of the UN within the next decade, a number of much smaller, regional intergovernmental organizations exist for the purposes of limited co-operation.[5]

The existing network of multilateral treaties, designed to secure standardized reciprocal rights in foreign countries, is a development of the last century. The international relations and legal harmonization they establish are now important aspects of the global distribution and use of educational, cultural, and scientific information. Exclusive domestic rights conferred pursuant to the treaties, and which almost invariably protect against imports, provide the legal basis for international exploitation of the subject matter through branch plants, licensing arrangements, assignments, or other appropriate means. China is the only major country not party to the Paris Convention. Neither China, the Soviet Union, nor the United States is party to the Berne Convention, although the United States and, as of 27 May 1973, the Soviet Union belong to the Universal Copyright Convention.

Apart from treaty, foreigners would not be entitled under international law to intellectual property rights in Canada and, even with the treaties, they can only assert rights in Canadian courts to the extent that parliament implements Canadian treaty obligations or rights are otherwise conferred by Canadian law. Beyond that, they must rely on diplomatic channels.

The type of impact the treaties have on legislation can perhaps be illustrated by reference to Canadian patent law. One of the basic principles of the Paris Convention, requiring that nationals of member countries be treated as favourably as one's own nationals, is reflected in the Patent Act. Primarily, however, the international significance of the convention lies in its requirement that inventors gain a twelve-month priority right in all member countries dating from their first application for that invention in another member coutry.[6] This means, for example, that if an inventor files an application in Canada on 1 September 1972 for protection of a better mousetrap he should have the benefit of that date, for the purpose of priority of applications, for an application disclosing substantially the same invention filed in Japan up to 1 September 1973. Applications filed within the twelve-month period in other convention countries should not be invalidated by any act occurring during that period, such as publication or another filing. This requirement is implemented in the Canadian Patent Act.[7] A variety of less significant provisions are also implemented, such as exempting from possible infringement actions the use of patented inventions in ships and aircraft that temporarily enter Canadian jurisdiction.[8]

ADMINISTRATIVE ORGANIZATION

The Paris and Berne conventions are among the more senior of the world's growing collection of multilateral treaties. Both treaties are open and, subject to possible implications for recognition,[9] any country may accede at any time. Each of the treaties has been revised several times since its original negotiation,[10] however, and while existing parties to the conventions may remain with older texts rather than accepting new revised versions, new members can accede only to the most recent text in force. This gives rise to some difficult questions of defining treaty obligations, which could be important to Canada. To appreciate the problem it is useful to understand the institutional structure created by the treaties.

From the beginning, the membership of each of the Paris and Berne conventions has been constituted into a 'union,' which by the late nineteenth century had become the most popular institutional form for intergovernmental co-operation.[11] Indeed, unions were an important step forward in international legislation. Their membership was large, and the sanction for disobedience was exclusion from the organization. Beginning with the Telegraphic Union, which was the first important international administrative union and which was followed shortly by the Postal and Metric unions, a pragmatic pattern was emerging by the 1880s when the intellectual property unions were created. The 'union' form has also been continued for each of the several more specialized agreements negotiated as subsidiary to the Paris Convention.[12]

The Paris and Berne unions each established a permanent administrative body, or bureau, under the general supervision of the isolationist, multilingual Swiss government. In 1893 the Swiss government combined the administrative offices and secretariats of the two unions into one unit, called the Bureaux internationaux réunis pour la protection de la propriété intellectuelle (BIRPI). One of the purposes of the 1967 treaty establishing the WIPO was to relieve the Swiss government of its supervisory obligations by creating a new structure of legislative and executive organs responsible directly to the membership.

The main features of the union concept as a form of international organization appear to be as follows:

1   Each member state has a treaty relationship with all other members, even though they have not signed the same document. The theory is that only one treaty is involved and each revision constitutes merely a successive act passed by the union. Therefore a treaty relationship exists between all union members even

though any given two member countries may not be bound by a common act. (For example, Canada, bound by the Rome Revision of the Berne Convention, has a copyright treaty link with countries which have signed only the Berlin Act on the one hand or the Brussels Act on the other hand.)

2   The union forms a single administrative and financial unit, there being only one budget and set of accounts. All member countries contribute on the basis of the same budget, regardless of the fact that many countries are members of the union at different revision levels.

3   Accession may take place only with relation to the latest text of the convention in force, and denunciation only with respect to the latest text binding the particular country, but they are valid in respect of the entire union. (Consequently, just days before the Stockholm Conference in 1967, Mexico and Argentina joined the Berne union by acceding to the Brussels text.) Members of the union remain as such even though they choose not to ratify the latest revision.

4   Revisions are adopted by the organs of each particular union according to the rules of quorum and majority as set out in the treaty. Out of deference to the principle of sovereignty most unions require unanimity. (For example, article 24(3) of the Brussels text of the Berne Convention specifies that no alteration of the convention shall be binding on the union 'except by the unanimous consent of the countries composing it.' This has been taken to mean unanimity amongst those 'present and voting,' with Rules of Procedure for conferences specifying that this phrase excludes abstentions. The Paris Convention specifies no majority requirements but as a matter of practice unanimity in the same sense has been taken to be necessary and is commonly required by the Rules of Procedure accepted at revision conferences.)

It is interesting that after all these years some of the more basic legal questions arising from the union principle remain unsettled. For example, what are the precise terms of the treaty link between Canada, participating at the Rome level in Berne and the London level in Paris, with other members of the unions which are bound only by different texts? Are Canadian nationals entitled abroad to different protection (usually a higher level) than Canada is obliged to extend to foreign nationals? In the case of France, for example, it can be argued that since France was once bound by the Rome text of Berne, Canadians are still only entitled to Rome level protection in France even though France is, at least for other purposes, now committed at the higher level of the Brussels text.[13]

But the situation where a country first joins the union by acceding to the most recent text is even less clear. In practice, that subsequent text has tended to be a higher level, in the sense that the minimum standards of protection are more favourable to creative people, but this may not be true in all respects[14] and in any event may not be true of future revisions. Indeed, as between any two given texts the protection may be higher in one text on some questions and lower on others. Should the lowest common denominator apply as to each particular issue that arises?[15]

Another interesting feature of the unions concerns the interpretative role of the permanent secretariat. While the officials disclaim competence to interpret the treaties authoritatively, they are both influential and knowledgeable and do not hesitate to recall the 'intention' behind certain provisions and 'past practice' in applying them, as part of their responsibility to provide information. For example, the secretariat appears to hold the view that the latest common text defines the treaty obligations between two countries participating at different levels in a union.

Nor is the general matter of state succession any more settled within the context of the intellectual property conventions than it is in international law generally. Many developing countries have recently gained independence from European countries which have been members of the conventions since the nineteenth century. Indeed, the conventions have probably applied to Canadian territory since the time of Great Britain's original membership, though Canada purported to adhere independently in the 1920s.[16] As a general matter, however, does a newly independent state remain in the relevant union until it denounces the convention, or must it adhere specially? Since the latter does not appear to have been the practice, despite Canada's own course of action, how far does Canada have patent and copyright treaty links with newly independent states? If it does have treaty links, what are they? The question is complicated somewhat in the case of the copyright treaties because the Berne Convention, which sets higher minimum standards than does the Universal Copyright Convention, is protected by a safeguard clause in the UCC against countries denouncing Berne and staying with the UCC.[17] If a newly independent state does not want to be bound by the rigorous standards of Berne must it denounce Berne specifically and thereby lose the benefit of the UCC?[18] Kenya, for example, considers itself fully covered by the UCC yet not bound in any way by the Berne Convention.

POLITICAL AND ECONOMIC ISSUES

General diminution of tariff barriers may be one factor that has resulted recently in increased attention being paid to such non-tariff barriers to trade as intellectual property. In many ways, however, the issues associated with intellectual property are more complex than those relating to other types of international trade. One reason is that with intellectual property physical things do not necessarily move across borders and therefore control is more difficult. The item of value is not a physical thing but rather the exclusive right to imitate the thing, whether it is a machine, a chemical process, a design, or an opera. Another reason why the question is more complex is that the barrier to trade lies not in an artificial border tax but rather in the intrinsic worth of the right of imitation, claimed by the creator himself. Further, that worth stems ultimately not from physical control over an object in demand but from exceptional rights created entirely by legislation in each state pursuant to the values and priorities of that state.

Given the wide variations among countries in their population, standard of living, wealth, educational and technological needs, and so on, it is not surprising that the degree of interest in and enthusiasm for the intellectual property treaties varies widely. The first clear manifestation of these differences occurred at the Stockholm Revision Conference in 1967 when the developing countries, impelled by their desperate need for educational and scientific material and at the same time to conserve foreign exchange, put up a strong united front demanding special treatment within, particularly, the Berne Convention. Bitter division between the have's and the have-not's became evident at that time, and the first of what will no doubt be many compromise solutions[19] was finally worked out at the Paris Conference in 1971.

Not surprisingly, much of the debate has been cast in emotional terms about how the 'other' group of countries really misconceives its own long-term interest. The United States is one of the few countries in which educational and cultural productivity have risen dramatically since achieving independence. Particularly in copyright terms it was a pirate country internationally until the late nineteenth century and now is heavily protectionist. Different aspects of its experience are used by each side in the debate. The Canadian government does not appear to have an overall policy concerning the intellectual property treatment of developing countries.[20]

To separate the economic camps into only two does not reflect the realities in a very refined way, and some countries, including Canada, have expressed an interest in exploring the possibility of multilevel conventions to accommodate so-called 'intermediate' countries which, while 'developed' by UN standards, are nevertheless net importers of protected material. There are many such countries, among them Australia, Sweden, Israel, and Austria, but their views are not uniform, and they also lack the political force of the developing countries in this field. Accordingly, further refinement of obligations according to general economic circumstances seems unlikely.

Some flexibility does result from the union concept whereby countries may remain in the union at 'lower' levels of protection, as does Canada in the case of both Paris and Berne. Increasingly, too, there appears to be a tendency to negotiate treaties of more limited scope[21] so that, although the general rule is against reservations, countries gain flexibility by being able to decide separately on each general area. This is, in effect, a partial alternative to an integrated multilevel treaty.

One of the intriguing and important questions about the international scope of the Berne and Paris conventions has been the membership of the Soviet Union. Soviet intellectual property law is remarkably like that of western countries,[22] differing primarily with respect to compulsory licenses and other forms of state interference. Indeed, communist countries have long been members of Paris and Berne. The Soviet Union, however, is not a member of Berne and only joined Paris in 1965 when that union accepted the principle of the inventor's certificate.[23] The primary obstacle to Berne union membership is that the Brussels text of Berne sets a minimum term of protection of life plus fifty years, whereas Soviet policy is only life plus fifteen years. There are also important differences relating to translations.

The USSR has always assumed a rigid attitude towards foreign authors. Unlike the United States it has not negotiated a superstructure of bilateral copyright treaties,[24] and only very recently acceded to the Universal Copyright Convention. The implications of this accession are not yet clear, for over the years the Soviet Union has gained a reputation for piracy and distortion of foreign works; the countries hardest hit by these practices have been the United States, the United Kingdom, France, and Germany. Canadian works have also been affected, though to a much lesser extent.[25] Particularly since 1940 consistent attempts have been made by western countries through diplomatic channels, performing rights societies, and in the Soviet courts to secure royalty payments – without success. Over the same period, however, there has been a steady, if erratic, increase in 'gratuitous' payments by Soviet publishing houses to foreign authors. There have also been bilateral agreements bordering on copyright which constitute a limited recognition of foreign rights in this area. One such agreement was entered into on 26 April 1967 between the CBC and the USSR·Council of Ministers Committee for Radio and TV Broadcasting concerning the exchange of programs.[26]

PERFORMING OBLIGATIONS AND SETTLING DISPUTES

No operative text of the Paris Convention provides for the settlement of disputes, though at the Brussels Revision Conference in 1948 a provision was added to the Berne Convention requiring that any dispute between two or more member countries as to the interpretation or application of the convention, not settled by negotiation, 'shall' be taken to the International Court of Justice unless the countries concerned agree on some other method of settlement. Despite the fact that no dispute has yet been submitted to the court under the Berne Convention, the compulsory jurisdiction provision is probably one reason why the communist membership of the union (Bulgaria, Czechoslovakia, Hungary, Poland, and Romania) remains at the Rome level and has not acceded to the Brussels text.[27] The disputes clause was amended at Stockholm to provide for optional jurisdiction, though the revised text is not yet in force.

In determining the extent to which Canada performs its treaty obligations it is important to bear in mind the principle of statutory interpretation, that where a statute is ambiguous the court will consider our treaty obligations as an extrinsic aid to interpretation, on the presumption that parliament would not intentionally legislate in derogation of those obligations but rather would seek to implement them. This principle could, for example, be important to the construction of the words 'and if' in section 4(1) of the Copyright Act.[28] Its application is quite distinct from that of statutory provisions requiring that a specific power not be exercised so as to contravene a treaty, such as is found in section 68(d) of the Patent Act and section 29 of the Combines Investigation Act relating to orders affecting patent or trade mark rights.[29]

Despite Canada's appearing to be clearly in breach of some of its treaty obligations under the intellectual property conventions,[30] no serious dispute appears to have arisen over these delinquencies. The Department of External Affairs does receive about a dozen requests per year relating to intellectual property matters, but most of these relate to the use of trade marks in Canada or abroad that might be either belittling or taken to imply some government approval of the wares or services.[31] These are handled on the basis of comity, so one of the more serious sanctions is to record 'displeasure.' Occasionally private Canadian businesses request assistance to learn about foreign laws, such as those of China, and on very rare occasions the Canadian government may be requested by a foreign government to support a particular position in court proceedings.[32]

CANADIAN PARTICIPATION

The Berne and Paris unions were created largely as a result of initiatives from the private sector and throughout their histories the main initiatives, as well as much of the technical expertise at the negotiations, have continued to come from the private sectors of the member countries. The private sectors communicate both through their national governments and through international non-governmental organizations.

For a country to maximize its return from international relationships in the field of intellectual property the private sector must work closely with government. Government possesses the resources for continuity and treaty information, and it supplies the diplomatic contact. Also, of course, it is responsible for policy and for accepting and performing international obligations. A fundamental requirement of sound policy formation, however, is that good processes of communication exist between government and whatever interests in the private sector are or may be organized to present information and a point of view.

Canadian initiatives and contribution to international developments in the field of intellectual property have been minimal, and the probable reason for this has been inadequate liaison between the government and the private sector. The primary responsibility for ensuring this liaison rests with the government, but until the late 1960s there appeared to be little interest or knowledge at the governmental level. Canadian contributions internationally came from one or two outstanding individuals from the patent profession. Despite recent improvement in the level of official knowledge and participation, and in the processes of communication, both the treaties and the subject matter are technically complex, and improvement will be gradual at best. At the same time, the commercial significance of the subject matter is continuing to grow and, with an increased tempo of international activity, Canadian competence is becoming more and more important.

Good liaison between government and the private sector also requires, of course, an interested private sector, and in some areas the government appears not to have had the benefit of the informed, responsible contribution required for effective Canadian representation abroad. Still other parts of the private sector have seemed insensitive to the range of interests government must weight in formulating policy, with the result that some needless antagonism has developed and communication has been impeded.

It appears that the processes of communication between the government and the private sector are slowly becoming more firmly established and more productive. Also, in some areas such as patent system administration, broadcasting, computers, and satellites there is a considerable degree of expertise within the Canadian government itself, or its agencies, which is brought to bear on those limited aspects of intellectual property questions.

The United Kingdom, Germany, Italy, and France have always been the most influential countries in the intellectual property unions, and they have recently been joined by the United States. This influence is attributable largely to the personal competence of their representatives, which doubtless results in part from the commercial significance of the subject matter to those countries. Their negotiators are effective diplomats with a thorough grasp of the law, practice and policy objectives at home, the complexities of the treaties, and the basic requirements of other major countries. Canada, by contrast, has in the past lacked the advantage of one or two able representatives who have made careers out of the requisite knowledge and experience.

Another complication in recent Canadian participation internationally has been the abnormally prolonged government review of its intellectual property policy, which began with the 1954 (Ilsley) Royal Commission on Patents, Copyright, Trade Marks and Industrial Designs. Following the reports of that royal commission and a period of legislative inactivity, the Economic Council of Canada was requested in 1966 to review the policy of the entire area, 'in the light of the Government's long-term economic objectives.' The council's *Report on Intellectual and Industrial Property,* which was issued in 1971, was sufficiently different, and general, that it could not be quickly endorsed as a basis for policy.[33] Accordingly, work is currently being done at the departmental level to formulate specific policies and legislative proposals. During this entire period the lack of a clear government policy has had an obvious impact upon Canada's international posture, reducing its role practically to that of an observer.[34]

The formulation of government policy, particularly with respect to copyright, will of course be closely related to treaty requirements and options. The Berne Convention is complex and, owing to both its rule against reservations and the safeguard clause on the UCC, is an all-or-nothing proposition as to multilateral copyright relations. Within Berne, however, the choice is available, for a short time, to adopt the Brussels text before the 1971 Paris revisions take effect. The obvious appeal of the Rome text, on the other hand, is that it leaves more options open to legislate as we please, which may be the best position available for a so-called 'intermediate country.'

In most respects the character of Canadian participation in international intellectual property matters looks more promising for the future than it has at any time since independence.

NOTES

1 Cuba is both communist and developing, and perhaps it was the combination of the two forces that inspired the Cuban government in 1967 to repudiate any and all treaty obligations requiring it to compensate foreign creators when their material was imitated in Cuba. It was at least consistent for Premier Castro to declare, as he did, that all Cuban creations were free to the rest of the world.

2 The Patent Cooperation Treaty (Washington 1970) is not yet in force.Canada is one of several countries that has signed but, as of the date of this writing, has not yet ratified it.

3 The UN Outer Space Committee and the ITU are also working on legal aspects of satellite transmissions.

4 International Convention for the Protection of Performers, Producers of Phonograms and Broadcasting Organizations (Rome 1961).

5 Eg, Pan-American Copyright Union (to which the United States and countries from Central and South America belong), and the African and Malagasy Industrial Property Office (OAMPI) (which administers a common system of industrial property for several African countries which have recently gained independence from France). For a discussion of regional intellectual property organizations see Gould, 'The International Intellectual Property Organization' (1972), 3 *Canadian Patent Reporter* (2d) 249, at 267–73.

6 Article 4. The priority period is of much less significance inside Canada and the United States than it is elsewhere because those two countries grant patents to the first inventor only. In all other countries entitlement to protection is influenced more by the date on which an application is filed.

7 RSC c P–4 (1970): sections 29(1), 28(2)(b), 38(3), 43, 63. The Patent Act deals with priority in terms of 'invention' and so at least may be consistent with the treaty requirement that the priority date goes to the disclosure rather than the claims. Also, by section 12(1)(b) of the Patent Act, the rules and regulations power extends specifically to carrying into effect the terms of any treaty, though

this would not confer authority in cases where legislation may make express provision in contravention of the Paris Convention (see note 30, below.)

8 Paris Convention, article 5 *ter*; Patent Act, section 23.

9 Since 1956 the German Democratic Republic has sought full status in relation to the Paris and Berne conventions, but the secretariat keeps its contributions in a separate trust fund. The German Democratic Republic is not invited to revision conferences and most parties, including Canada, do not regard themselves as having treaty relations with it. Canadian inventors, however, receive the priority benefit under East German patent law.

10 For example, the Paris Convention of 1883 was revised at Brussels in 1900, Washington in 1911, The Hague in 1925, London in 1934, Lisbon in 1958, and Stockholm in 1967. The Berne Convention of 1886 was revised at Berlin in 1908, Rome in 1928, Brussels in 1948, Stockholm in 1967, and Paris in 1971. For substantive purposes Canada participates in the Paris union at the London level, and in the Berne union at the Rome level. For the purposes of union administration it participates in both at the Stockholm level.

11 See generally, Reinsch, *Public International Unions* (1911).

12 Membership in Paris is a precondition to membership in the subsidiary agreements. Canada is not party to any of the subsidiary agreements.

13 This indeed is France's position on the general question. France emphasizes the normal treaty principles of bargain and reciprocity. On the other hand, the United Kingdom also participates at the highest level in both the Paris and Berne conventions and takes the position that each member of the union is obliged to extend to all other members the protection specified in the texts it has adopted.

One of the reasons why the question has not been settled may be that in practice countries do not seem to distinguish, in their implementing legislation, between countries that participate in the union at different levels. Another reason may be that the question is better settled diplomatically and bilaterally if and when it arises rather than risking division by trying to formulate an answer in treaty form. Also, of course, any written solution would only bind parties to that text.

14 The question surfaced in an acute form at the 1967 Stockholm Conference in connection with the proposed Protocol Regarding Developing Countries, which would have entitled developing countries to offer severely reduced copyright protection by filing reservations respecting the term of protection and the rights of translation, reproduction, broadcasting, and education.

15 See generally Ringer, 'Relationship Between Two Texts of the Universal Copyright Convention' (1971), *EBU Review*, no 125B. Accession practice may bear directly on entitlement under Canadian law inasmuch as section 4(1) of the Copyright Act refers only to nationals of countries which have adhered to the Berlin text of the Berne Convention. Accession practice varies: see Bodenhausen, 'Paris Convention: General Questions' in *BIRPI Lecture Course on Industrial Property* (1965), at 9, 11. See also (1970), *Copyright*, at 2–3 (BIRPI). *Quaere*, the application or effect of articles 30 and 40(5) of the Vienna Convention on the Law of Treaties, especially in view of article 4 of that convention.

16 For a legal and political account of Canada's international copyright posture in the period 1886–1931, see Ladas, *The International Protection of Literary and Artistic Property* (1938) 900–9. Also see Fox, *The Canadian Law of Copyright and Industrial Design* (2nd ed, 1967), XXIII.

17 Article XVII and appendix declaration.

18 The Paris revisions of 1971, not yet in force, deal specifically with this problem for developing countries only. When the safeguard clause was negotiated in 1952 at the behest of Berne Union countries, Canada and Japan were the main opponents to it, but they refused to insist on their opposition.

19 Accommodation of the special needs of developing countries for intellectual property is receiving growing attention and study. See particularly, *Symposium on International Copyright: Needs of Developing Countries* (Government of India 1967); *The Role of Patents in the Transfer of Technology to Developing Countries* (Report of the Secretary General, United Nations, 1964, UN Doc E/3861/Rev 1); *The Application of Computer Technology for Development* (UN Doc E/4800, 1970). Special status is also being urged by developing countries in the negotiations for a treaty to protect satellite signals carrying television programs.

20 The 1970 white paper, *Foreign Policy for Canadians,* is much too general to provide guidance in specific situations.

21 For example, separate instruments for each of phonograms, type faces, satellite transmissions, and computer programs. This tendency, rather than negotiating solutions within the framework of the Berne Convention, may be due in part to continuing doubt about whether domestic copyright law in the United States will be changed to permit that important country to subscribe to the 'no formalities' rule of Berne. Also, of course, the subject matter is slightly different from the traditional scope of 'copyright' and, in this respect, certain Canadian constitutional problems are suggested for the implementing legislation. Federal legislative competence under the BNA Act relates to 'Copyrights.'

22 With specific respect to copyright, see Woltmann, 'The Author and the State: An Analysis of Soviet Copyright Law' (1966), 14 *Copyright Law Symposium (ASCAP)* 1–50.

23 Essentially, the inventor's certificate separates the exclusive right to an invention from the right to remuneration for its use. The state owns the exclusive right of exploitation and it pays royalties to the inventor. Patents are granted in the Soviet Union but the financial incentives are such that 99 per cent of inventions are covered by inventor's certificates rather than patents.

24 Its first bilateral copyright treaty was entered into in November 1967 with the Hungarian People's Republic. The treaty is discussed in Timar, 'The Hungarian-Soviet Copyright Convention' (1968), *The Canadian Composer.*

25 During the period 1919–60, 6,386,000 copies of the works of seven Canadian authors were reproduced in the Soviet Union. Levitsky, *Introduction to Soviet Copyright Law* (1964), 240.

26 For a summary of the terms, see Canada, HC *Debates,* 29 May 1967, 715.

27 With respect to Canada, the Royal Commission on Patents, Copyright, Trade Marks and Industrial Design, in its *Report on Copyright* (1957), at 15, objected to the compulsory jurisdiction clause in the Brussels text. This attitude is inconsistent with Canada's general position concerning compulsory jurisdiction of the court.

28 Section 4(1) provides as follows:

Subject to this Act, copyright shall subsist in Canada for the term hereinafter mentioned, in every original literary, dramatic, musical and artistic work, if the author was at the date of the making of the work a British subject, a citizen or subject of a foreign country that has adhered to the Convention and the Additional Protocol thereto set out in Schedule II, or resident within Her Majesty's Realms and Territories; *and if,* in the case of a published work, the work was first published within Her Majesty's Realms and Territories or in such foreign country; but in no other works, except so far as the protection conferred by this Act is extended as hereinafter provided to foreign countries to which this Act does not extend.

In *Ludlow Music Inc.* v *Canint Music Corp. Ltd. et al.,* [1967] 2 Ex. C.R. 109, at 114–15, Jackett P considered the effect of the Berne Convention on the ambiguity in section 4(1) of the statute.

As to the general principle see *Salomon* v *Commissioners of Customs and Excise,* [1967] 2 Q.B. 116, 130 (C.A.); *CAPAC* v *CTV,* [1968] S.C.R. 676.

29 Another possibly relevant principle of statutory interpretation is that where the terms of an international agreement have been incorporated into a statute, that statutory provision will, so far as possible, be construed with a view to attaining uniformity with the law in other jurisdictions in which the agreement is operative. This principle could, for example, be important to the construction of section 7(e) of the Trade Marks Act ['No person shall do any other act or adopt any other business practice contrary to honest industrial or commercial usage in Canada'], which clearly was intended to implement our obligation under article 10 *bis* of the Paris Convention on Industrial Property and which is mirrored in the domestic legislation of several other countries.

30 For example:

i The marking requirement under section 14 of the Industrial Design Act probably contravenes article 5(D) of the Paris Convention (London).

ii Whether section 41 of the Patent Act, providing for compulsory licensing of food and medicine patents, contravenes article 5(A)(4) of the Paris Convention, or whether it should be interpreted in the light of that provision, depends upon whether Canadian courts will follow the House of Lords decision in *Parke Davis & Co.* v *Comptroller General et al*, [1954] A.C. 321 (holding that the convention requirement that compulsory licenses only be available after three years of a patent's life was limited to licenses granted for abuse of rights).

iii The procedural and remedial advantages of registration conferred by sections 22, 36, and 40(3) of the Copyright Act probably contravene article 4(2) of the Berne Convention (Rome).

iv The fourteen-day definition of 'simultaneous publication' in section 3(4) of the Copyright Act appears to be in contravention of the thirty days requirement of article IV(6) of the Universal Copyright Convention.

v Also with respect to the UCC it has been suggested that section 4(1) of Canada's Copyright Act breaches the obligation to confer copyright on works first published in a non-contracting state where the author is a national of a contracting state: Bogsch, *The Law of Copyright Under the Universal Convention* (3rd ed, 1968), at 252.

31 See article 6 *ter* of the Paris Convention.

32 See, for example, the recent litigation to require Chateau-Gai Wines Ltd, to stop using the appellation 'champagne,' which was registered in the name of the Government of the French Republic in accordance with the Canada-France Trade Agreement of 1933: *Chateau-Gai Wines Ltd.* v *Le Gouvernement de la Republique Francaise* (1967), 52 C.P.R. 39 (Exch.); *Re Chateau-Gai Wines Ltd. and Attorney-General of Canada* (1970), 63 C.P.R. 195 (Exch.). See also *Institut National des Appellations d'Origine des Vins et Eaux-de-Vie* v *Chateau-Gai Wines Ltd.* (1968), 57 C.P.R. 93 (Que. S.C.).

33 The Economic Council did not, by and large, take treaty obligations as 'givens,' and some of its recommendations contradict those obligations. The council's basic view was that intellectual property should be treated as an integral part of total innovation and information policy, and that in the past there has tended to be too much emphasis placed on the social benefits of intellectual property without enough attention to the social costs. As a result, it tended to discourage further increases in protection and recommended more extensive use of compulsory licenses.

34 It should perhaps be noted that in 1970 Canada was elected to the Executive Committee of the Berne Union, thus automatically gaining membership in the Co-ordination Committee of the WIPO, as well.

JOHN E.C. BRIERLEY

33/International Trade Arbitration: The Canadian Viewpoint

Canadian business interests and Canadian governments appear to have little interest in the subject of international trade arbitration. Indeed, commercial arbitration generally is in no sense an important feature even of Canadian internal business practices. The two phenomena – resort to arbitration in the domestic forum, and participation in arbitration at the international level – are not necessarily linked, but a review of the developments in arbitration law and practices since the 1920s in a number of other countries suggests that there is an important connection between them. In France and the United States, for example, the modernization of the law on the subject, the creation of institutionalized arbitration centres providing arbitration machinery, and participation in the elaboration of international conventions on various aspects of arbitration are developments that have coincided to some degree.[1] These efforts have facilitated, and perhaps even encouraged, arbitration as a dispute-solving process for American and French business interests.

To examine the subject of international trade arbitration from the Canadian point of view is to seek out the Canadian experience in these same matters and to attempt to ascertain their relationship. What is the configuration of the Canadian law on arbitration; what organized initiatives to promote the practice of arbitration have been made; and, finally, what is the position of Canadian law with regard to the emerging internationally recognized norms of international commercial arbitration? The answers to these questions may provide some understanding of the Canadian perspective on this increasingly important method for the regulation of disputes arising within the context of international commerce.

CANADIAN ARBITRATION LAW

There is in fact no 'Canadian' arbitration law, in the proper sense of the term, common to all ten Canadian provinces. And this diversity of provincial legislation has not been attenuated by either of those techniques available to federated unions, that is to say, by either a uniform arbitration statute adopted by each province or a federal arbitration law applicable throughout the whole country. Each of these aspects of the present state of Canadian law requires some comment.

Provincial legislation

The main features of the legislation on arbitration in the ten Canadian provinces have not substantially changed over the years since their original enactment.[2] And in most respects both the common law and the civil law of Quebec have remained closely approximate to the legal traditions of England and France from which they issue. The main features of both systems can be succinctly outlined.

Common law provinces
The arbitration statutes of the nine common law provinces, because they are inspired by the English enactment of 1889,[3] are substantially similar on those points now generally accepted as necessary to the proper functioning of arbitration.

The arbitration contract, termed the 'submission agreement,' whether or not it designates an arbitrator and whether or not it concerns a present or a future dispute, is valid; and, saving a contrary stipulation or the leave of the court, is binding and enforceable. Although it need not be in any particular written form, it is considered clothed with the same authority as if made an order of the court. The parties to the contract are therefore bound to proceed to an arbitration, and a court seized of a matter or dispute anticipated by the agreement may order the stay of the proceedings if there is no valid reason shown why the arbitration should not proceed. The court has the power further to remedy the possible paralysis of the arbitration by reason of disagreement over the nomination of an arbitrator, refusal to proceed thereto, or the supervening incapacity of an arbitrator. The arbitral award, finally, is obligatory (saving a contrary stipulation) and may, upon leave, be entered as a judgment of the court and enforced in the same manner as an order or judgment to the same effect. In four provinces an appeal of the award is however envisaged.[4]

These legislations, moreover, conform to the English legal tradition according to which the court is vested with the power to direct the arbitrators on the law applicable to the difference or dispute. The arbitrator may, at any stage of the proceedings, and shall if so directed by the court at the request of a party, state in the form of a 'special case' any question of law arising in the course of the arbitration or, in some provinces, the award itself,[5] for the opinion of the court. The award may therefore, in theory at least, be set aside for 'error' of law if the reasons for the award are stated.

For all practical purposes, therefore, there is true uniformity of legislation within common law Canada on the three points essential to a system of arbitration: the validity of the contract, the power of the court to assist in the implementation of the arbitration, and the enforcement of the award. The real diversity in Canadian law on the matter is thus found when this commonly shared tradition is contrasted to that of the civil law of Quebec.

Quebec civil law
The law of Quebec on contractual arbitration, as originally contained in the Code of Civil Procedure of 1867 and even as reformulated in 1966, has proved almost wholly deficient. Upon the same points as those outlined above, it still provides no adequate basis for the proper functioning of arbitration.

In the first place, Quebec law, like that of France, truncates the arbitration agreement. For a hundred years the code only provided for the contract to arbitrate present disputes (the *compromis* or submission) and the courts therefore rejected, as unenforceable, the agreement to arbitrate future disputes (the *clause compromissoire*): it was considered a *nudum pactum* and, in the last phases of this development, against public order. And, despite the 1966 reform of the Code of Civil Procedure which *appears* to admit its validity (or which could be so interpreted), the point is still unsettled.[6] It follows, therefore, that the court seized of a matter with respect to which there is such an agreement will not stay the proceedings or dismiss the action in order to allow the arbitration to take place. Before 1966 the courts refused further to appoint an arbitrator in those circumstances where this assistance was necessary; the reformed code, however, now anticipates such nomination at least in the context of a submission and, so it would seem (curiously enough), in that of the promise to arbitrate. The former code provided that a 'suit brought in the ordinary manner' was necessary for the enforcement of the award; this unfortunate rule, carried over into the reformed code of 1966, was only amended by legislation of 1970 which replaced the procedure by way of action with that of a 'motion for homologation.' It has however never been open to the court under Quebec law to 'enquire into the merits' of the contestation and so an appeal is, effectively, excluded.

Quebec law is to be distinguished further from the common law tradition in that it authorizes the parties in an arbitration agreement to exempt the arbitrators from deciding according to the rules of law, either by way of an express clause or insofar as they empower the arbitrators to act as 'mediators' (*amiables compositeurs*); that is to say, to decide *ex aequo et bono*. There is moreover no procedure such as the 'special case' whereby the arbitrators might be directed as to the applicable law. And under the former law there was no obligation that arbitrators give reasons for their decision; since the 1966 reform, the decision or award must, however, in all cases, whether the arbitrators are dispensed or not from observation of the rules of law, contain the reasons for their decision.

The Quebec position on this last point therefore is exactly the converse of that in the common law provinces; and, more important, on the mechanisms capital to the development of commercial arbitration, Quebec law has been, and still is, seriously out of step with the law of the other provinces.

Uniformity of Canadian legislation

This summary exposition of the principal characteristics of the provincial arbitration laws illustrates in a Canadian context that connexity, observed elsewhere,[7] between two aspects of the legal regulation of arbitration: on the one hand, the binding nature of the arbitration agreement and award and, on the other, the freedom of the parties to dispense the arbitrators from observance of the rules of law. Where an arbitration agreement is not fully binding and the award not enforceable as a judgment of a court (the case in Quebec ever since 1966), the arbitrators may be relieved of the obligation to decide according to the rules of law; where, on the contrary, the agreement is in principle binding and the award, upon leave, is enforceable like a judgment (the case in the common law provinces), the arbitrators do not possess such freedom. They are in principle obliged to decide according to the rules of law and the award may be set aside if they do not.

The elaboration of a truly Canadian arbitration law, bringing about a synthesis of these two conceptions of arbitration by admitting at one and the same time that the arbitrators are not obliged to decide in law and that, moreover, the agreement and award will have all the authority of a court order or judgment, appears at this time a very remote possibility. It is of course a characteristic development of the so-called 'modern' arbitration law of a number of American jurisdictions,[8] but there is no indication that the appropriate Canadian authorities would be interested in or, if they were, even able to bring about such a *rapprochement* in Canada. The question can however be examined from two points of view.

The Conference of Commissioners on Uniformity of Legislation in Canada[9]
This body considered the matter of uniform arbitration legislation in 1930-1 upon the occasion of a brief submitted to it by the Canadian Chamber of Commerce. The latter, aware of the importance of arbitration to the commercial community, submitted for study to the conference a draft uniform law based upon the American Draft State Arbitration Act.[10] The study by the conference, embracing only an examination of the law of the common law provinces and omitting any reference to Quebec law,[11] reached the conclusion that the Canadian arbitration law was of an 'advanced' type, that it replied sufficiently to the needs of the time, and that 'probably in no other subject of legislation [was] there a more marked degree of uniformity existing in Canada, Great Britain and throughout the Empire' than that obtaining already in arbitration.[12] No action was taken therefore on any of the draft propositions submitted.

While this study did have the merit of emphasizing the quasi-uniformity of the provincial common law legislation, it is curious that it made no particular study of the technique of the 'special case,' for it was on this point that the draft of the Canadian Chamber of Commerce did possess some originality. This feature of the traditional English scheme of arbitration did not figure in the draft because the latter was inspired by the then modern American conception that arbitrators should not be held to apply the rules of law, and that the procedure of the special case, which could oblige them to do so, be dropped as a feature of the legal regulation of arbitration. It is of course significant from the Canadian point of view that while the development of arbitration in England could not be said to have been hindered because of this aspect of English law, it is generally believed that arbitration has only developed significantly in those American states where it has been dropped and has not progressed in those where the technique of the special case, and therefore the duty to decide in law, has been retained.[13]

But the implications of this last observation in respect of Canada are not necessarily self-evident. The fact that arbitration has not, seemingly, gained in importance to the commercial community at large may very well be explained by quite different factors, legal or commercial. Among other possible legal factors, is the absence of a federal law on the subject, common to the whole country, and similar in function to that in the United States, to be counted? To this question some attention must now be given.

Absence of federal law
The subject matters of legislation upon which uniformity is assured for the whole of Canada are those confided to the federal legislative authority, the Canadian parliament. A first reading of the provisions of the British North America Act, 1867[14] could suggest, or so it might seem to one unfamiliar with their interpretation, the

possibility of a federal law on the subject of arbitration insofar as it relates to inter-provincial and international commercial and trading activities.

The federal parliament's exclusive authority extends to all matters coming within the rubric 'The Regulation of Trade and Commerce' (s 91:2) and 'Navigation and Shipping' (s 91:10). These are the only two likely heads of competence upon which legislative activity could be envisaged. But, as one author has put it, they either have been affected with the 'atrophy of disuse'[15] or have been severely limited in their possible scope by other provisions of this basic constitutional document and its judicial interpretation. The subject of commercial arbitration in any one pro-vince, whether characterized as a matter of 'procedure,' or as a matter of 'contract,' would undoubtedly be seen as an invasion of provincial legislative competence which extends to 'Property and Civil Rights in the Province' and to 'The Adminis-tration of Justice in the Province' and 'Procedure' (under s 92:13 and 14), and therefore unconstitutional as *ultra vires* of the federal power. It is, indeed, by virtue of these heads that the provinces have enacted their present arbitration legislation.

The case for constitutional validity of a federal arbitration law under the trade and commerce rubric could therefore only rest on the proposition that the subject matter of arbitration transcends the bounds of provincial competence; that, in other words, the arbitration contract and award, and their enforcement, as adjuncts to trade and commerce both interprovincial and international, constitute regulation of trade and commerce rather than an invasion of an exclusive provincial field. To rest the argument on this ground is to affirm that the subject of commercial arbitra-tion goes beyond the subjects of contract and/or procedure and touches upon com-merce, such that federal authority can be seen to begin. This is a mode of reasoning that is unlikely to be followed in the present Canadian climate of opinion.[16] These same considerations also seriously impinge, of course, on the possibility of federal implementation of an international treaty obligation assumed by the federal au-thority.

It has been suggested that these same objections might fall away in regard to federal legislative activity respecting arbitration contracts in relation to 'Navigation and Shipping' or maritime matters, with respect to which the federal power has exclusive competence to legislate in all respects. The general field has in fact been occupied by federal legislation since 1891 but its authority has not yet been exer-cised in regard to arbitration as a feature of maritime contracts or the resolution of maritime disputes.[17]

There is, therefore, no Canadian arbitration law if by that is meant a 'mixed' arbitration legal system participating in both the civil and the common law tradi-tions and either the work of the federal authority or a collaboration of the provincial authorities. But the absence of any evolution in this sense is not to be explained only by the constitutional difficulties and the distinctive features of the two private law traditions on the subject. It is conceivable that such difficulties could be resolved, and such peculiarities reconciled, were commercial arbitration practices so developed that Canadian uniformity in this field was a matter of some urgency. That such is not the case is demonstrable.

CANADIAN ARBITRATION PRACTICE

Arbitration, it has been remarked, is not in its essence a juridical phenomenon; it is rather a phenomenon distinct from law.[18] The observation is certainly true when any attempt is made to survey the amount, types, and characteristics of arbitration practice in any given area or at any particular time. It is, after all, a dispute-settling process which, because it is ideally voluntary in its mechanisms and private in its nature is also, if the term be permitted, clandestine – that is to say, if an arbitration is successful, it leaves little or no trace which can be recorded, measured, and then compared to other procedures for the settlement of disputes. This clandestinity may very well be one of its principal attractions;[19] it is nonetheless an obstacle in the way of an attempt to seize upon its real practice with any pretension to scientific accuracy.

Bearing these limitations in mind, it is instructive to endeavour to assess the Canadian experience in the practice of arbitration, both internally and in regard to international commercial arbitration, by examining the arbitration machinery available in Canada, and what appear to be Canadian attitudes to the arbitration process itself.

Arbitration machinery in Canada

The development of organized arbitration machinery through the efforts of a number of well-established non-governmental organizations such as the International Chamber of Commerce (ICC), the American Arbitration Association (AAA), and the London Court of Arbitration of the London Chamber of Commerce requires no demonstration here.[20] It is the fact that their institutionalized procedures are available to the general business community (rather than merely to members of specialized groups or particular trade associations) that is of interest because the continued existence of such bodies indicates to some extent a general need for arbitration facilities. What, in this respect, has been the Canadian experience?

There is no such organization of national dimension in Canada. And, it seems to follow, Canadian business interests are not apparently in need of such organized arbitration machinery for the resolution of commercial disputes *at any level,* whether wholly internal, interprovincial, or international. The creation some years ago of arbitration machinery within the framework of a Canadian institution of the type functioning elsewhere, specially designed to complement Canadian trade relations, has proved a failure; and no effort to renew the attempt within existing suitable structures is seemingly contemplated.

Failure of the 'Canadian-American Commercial Arbitration Commission'
This body was created by virtue of an agreement concluded in 1943 between the Canadian Chamber of Commerce and the American Arbitration Association.[21] These two organizations, inspired by the desire to promote further the good trading relations which have always existed between Canada and the United States, collaborated in the setting up of procedures whereby arbitration facilities could be put into operation as a means of solving disputes between Canadian and American business interests. The CACAC had two sections: on the Canadian side in Montreal at the head office of the Canadian Chamber of Commerce, and on the American at the AAA in New York. Each section was to draw up and maintain lists of suitable persons in the major centres from among whom those apt to act as arbitrators could be selected by those who seized the commision of their dispute. The CACAC itself

therefore, like other similar organizations, was not called upon to act as an arbitrator but merely to organize the means whereby the arbitration could take place; and the rules of the commission, again as in the case of the AAA or the ICC, ensured the operation of the arbitration by way of the incorporation into the contract of the parties' intention that they be ruled thereby.[22]

The arrangement, while still cited by some as an 'important' example of institutional arbitration, has in fact been disaffected for many years and may be written off as a failure.[23] While its facilities were apparently employed on a very limited number of occasions during a short period after 1943, the CACAC has been definitely inoperative since at least the mid-1950s – the lists of arbitrators are not maintained and the Montreal secretariat no longer functions. No steps are envisaged at the present time to revive it. An agreement dating from 1961 between the Vancouver Board of Trade and the Japanese Commercial Arbitration Association, of interest because it might have signified a revival of interest in the earlier arrangement (since it was inspired by the CACAC structure and rules), appears to have enjoyed only modest success.[24]

Structures suitable for arbitration
These do exist now and have been in place for some time. The Canadian chambers of commerce or boards of trade consitute precisely that type of non-governmental organization which could fulfil in Canada, as they have elsewhere,[25] the role of a suitable arbitration forum or agency within which to organize arbitration facilities and promote its practice: economically, they are bodies generally representative of the commercial interests of the milieux in which they are located; juridically, they are capable of creating arbitration courts or facilities open to all.[26] It would be normal, therefore, that arbitration, the classic dispute-solving process for members of a commercial community, originate within these bodies. And in addition to providing arbitration forums in any given locality, they can naturally constitute a national network of arbitration facilities through affiliation with the Canadian Chamber of Commerce.[27] The long-standing association of the Canadian Chamber of Commerce with the International Chamber of Commerce could extend their connection, again quite naturally, to the international scene. A survey of the chambers and boards reveals, however, that arbitration procedures almost never originate through their offices; and this absence of arbitration in particular localities is duplicated at both the interprovincial and international levels.

The quantity and types of commercial arbitration practised in Canada generally cannot, in all probability, ever be determined unless, as in certain American studies,[28] one were to proceed to a census of a wide number of individual commercial or trading enterprises or commodity trade associations. It is nonetheless very significant that the structures and facilities described above have either failed or remained almost wholly unused over the years. These facts indicate that the commercial community at large has not in the past, and apparently does not now, experience any pressing general need for commercial arbitration. But is it not, to say the least, at first sight curious that this should be so at the local, interprovincial, and international levels and even in the more important commercial centres of Vancouver, Toronto and Montreal?

Canadian attitudes to commercial arbitration

To describe Canadian attitudes on this subject is undoubtedly an even more elusive task than that of ascertaining Canadian practices. And yet some element of the explanation of the Canadian experience assuredly lies in the realm of the attitudes of Canadian business circles.

Since there is no demand by Canadians or non-Canadians[29] for arbitration facilities within Canada itself, one may perhaps assume that Canadian business interests are either forced to acquiesce in, or are content to assent to, arbitration outside Canada, and that the existence of highly respected arbitration organizations in London, Paris, New York, and Japan are sufficient for all Canadian needs. 'Arbitration in London [or New York or Paris]' rather than 'arbitration in Canada' is likely to be the preference of course of those foreign business or governmental concerns with which Canadians do business. And for the Canadian party as well it may be more desirable to agree to arbitration under the aegis of some recognized body in those international centres than to agree to resolve a possible dispute according to the national law of the other contracting party or by means of arbitrators of his nationality. The question is, undoubtedly, settled in large part as a function of the strength of the bargaining position of the parties involved.[30]

Thus, with respect for example to the so-called 'penetration contracts' in a number of developing nations, in which some large Canadian enterprises have been involved, the compromise position on this matter would be the stipulation of some such internationally recognized arbitration facility. It is of interest to note however that the records of these bodies do not in fact reveal anything but an insignificant Canadian participation in arbitration procedures even though it is commonly accepted wisdom that the ICC arbitration clause (for example) is frequently inserted in international business contracts of one kind or another.[31] Again, with respect to Canadian importation contracts, the majority of which are concluded with American exporters, it may very well be, as a result of an inferior Canadian bargaining position, that an eventual arbitration is stipulated in New York or some other American centre, rather than at the point of Canadian entry and according to Canadian law. But once again American sources do not reveal any noticeable involvement of Canadian interests in American institutionalized arbitration facilities.[32]

Arbitrations involving Canadians may of course, as suggested earlier, occur outside these institutionalzed facilities and on a purely *ad hoc* basic or within a particular trade or commodity association; or the arbitration clauses may, as it is often desired, exercise a preventive effect such that a business difference never degenerates to the level of a dispute which the arbitration is designed to resolve. Then again some business disputes of international character involving Canadians may not be arbitrable at all. One thinks, for example, of the case of a dispute between an American parent company and a Canadian affiliated company, where quite different dispute-solving mechanisms would be employed; or, again, of the activities of a number of Canadian state-controlled bodies or crown corporations, some of which are increasingly involved in aspects of foreign trade where provision for arbitration may be included, but with respect to which the cloak of confidentiality is all enveloping.[33]

It nevertheless remains true, from my experience, that Canadian businessmen have the reputation of being largely ignorant on the subject of arbitration and that their advisers, Canadian lawyers, have the misfortune of enjoying the general reputation of being hostile to arbitration as a process, even if provision for it is included in many contracts more or less as a matter of routine.[34] The hostility may of course be explained by a number of factors: the difficulty of naming suitable arbitrators, the high cost of arbitration, and the risk that some aspect of the arbitration, or the award itself, may ultimately or even inevitably, lead the parties into a court of law – a likely possibility, at least in the present state of Canadian law. But this attitude, whether justified or not, is in all probability a contributory factor in the explanation of the position occupied by Canada and Canadian law when assessed at the level of developments in international commercial arbitration.

CANADIAN LAW AND THE EMERGING NORMS OF INTERNATIONAL ARBITRATION

Given the configuration of the Canadian law, practices, and attitudes on the subject of commercial arbitration as analysed in the preceding pages, it is now appropriate to consider the degree to which there has been, or is likely to be, Canadian participation in the emerging body of international treaty law and, therefore, Canadian recognition of what have come to be accepted as those minimal requirements for the satisfactory functioning of international arbitration itself.

Participation in treaty law

The growing scope and importance of the international treaty law on arbitration is apparent. Within fifty years, since 1923, the conclusion of four multilateral conventions[35] on the subject is ample evidence of its important place in the complex of relations to which international trade gives rise. These developments are largely yet another manifestation of that typically European receptiveness towards the elaboration of close ties between a growing number of trading countries more than ever before linked by common interests. International agreements having arbitration as their object could be equally expected on the North American continent between Canada and the United States which are associated by all kinds of factors and, in particular, commercial and trading interests. In addition to this obvious Canadian-American connection, it would moreover be natural for Canada, as it reaches out to expand its sphere of commercial relations beyond those with its immediate neighbour, to endeavour to involve itself in this new international arbitration law.

Canada however is a party to none of the multilateral conventions mentioned above.[36] Indeed only in regard to the latest in date of these agreements did Canadian representatives participate in any of the preliminary discussions.[37] Nor has Canada, with one exception, become a party to any bilateral agreements of the type developed in the United States[38] with some of its more important trading partners. This exception is the bilateral commercial treaty of 1956 with the USSR, where arbitration is mentioned as an available means of solving disputes for the nationals of either country.[39] The significance of the clause is however doubtful, given the fact that it does not establish any new arbitration procedures for settling disputes that might arise in the course of Canadian-USSR trade, or oblige any party under any circumstances to resort to arbitration.[40] There is no available record indicating that it has ever been invoked.

The explanation for this inactivity, as suggested earlier and as demonstrated more fully by others in this volume, lies in the realm of Canadian constitutional law. Thus, while the federal government is the sovereign authority constitutionally empowered to participate in the creation of a treaty with another state, and the only Canadian authority able to assume international obligations thereunder, it does not thereupon acquire the constitutional competence to execute that obligation if its subject matter is a provincial matter. The subjects of commercial arbitration agreements, procedures, and enforceability of awards are, primarily, matters within a class of subject matter with respect to which the Canadian parliament lacks exclusive jurisdiction. And it is not because a particular subject may have attained a national or even international commercial importance that these distinctions as to legislative competence will dissolve away.

Thus, for example, the New York Convention of 1958 on the Recognition and Enforcement of Foreign Arbitral Awards would *prima facie* apply to arbitral awards rendered in one Canadian province of which enforcement is sought in another (article I). And this subject, a matter to be characterized as wholly internal or even interprovincial, would be one upon which the federal parliament could not proceed to implement legislation. Again, in the Convention on the Settlement of Investment Disputes of 1965, it is provided that a contracting state with a federal constitution may enforce an award in or through its federal courts and may provide that such courts shall treat the award as if it were a final judgment of the courts of its constituent state or province (article 58). But the fact that the convention so specifies does not have the effect of attributing to the federal parliament a power to see to the enforcement of such awards through Canadian federal courts when the latter are not invested with such jurisdiction as to the subject matter in the first place. If the government of Canada would have to implement legislation to fulfil its obligations under such treaties, it can easily be seen that the subject matter involves both the administration of justice and procedure in the province and property and civil rights.

The Canadian position is thus very different from that in the United States where a federal arbitration law exists by virtue of federal legislative competence, and federal implementation of treaty obligations on the subject of international arbitration is, to whatever extent may be necessary, possible.[41] The only obligation that the Canadian federal authorities can assume and effectively discharge under a multilateral or bilateral convention on arbitration is, therefore, that of bringing to the attention of the appropriate provincial authorities that which is within their own competence with a view to the several provinces implementing the real substance thereof. Given the constitutional problem, Canadian legislation on international arbitration must be the work of all the provinces, and it will only be brought about to the extent that each province is prepared to co-ordinate its own internal law in whatever respect may be necessary to the international norms commonly accepted by all other provinces.

It falls however to the federal government to take the initiative in involving the provinces in those consultative processes leading up to the point where internal implementation of such international norms embodied in a convention is possible to envisage. This, it is important to note, it has already begun to do by sending delegations to the Hague Conference on the Unification of Private International Law and the Rome Institute for the Unification of Private Law (UNIDROIT). Continued participation by Canadian delegations in the deliberations of such assemblies devoted to private law matters, and the co-ordination of this work with Canada's own efforts to achieve uniformity of Canadian law, may ultimately enable Canadian arbitration law to adjust itself to the imperatives of international commercial arbitration law.

Canadian recognition of minimal imperatives

The international conventions on arbitration constitute a body of 'international private law' composed of what have come to be recognized as minimal imperatives to the arbitration process in the international sphere. In the absence of Canadian adherence to these agreements, Canadian recognition of such imperatives is measured as a function of the extent to which Canadian provincial law can be found to do so. The judgment must be made in regard to two cardinal questions in the chronology of the arbitration process: Will the arbitration agreement providing for a non-Canadian arbitration be respected by Canadian courts? Will the foreign arbitration award be enforceable in a Canadian court if required?

Validity of the arbitration agreement

This feature is of course as necessary to an international arbitration process as it is to a domestic arbitration process. And it has long been a recognized feature of the treaty law on arbitration that the agreement, whether relating to future or existing disputes between parties subject to the jurisdiction of different states, whereby they agree to submit to arbitration those differences arising in connection with their dealings will be respected by their respective courts. On being seized of a dispute in respect of which there is such an agreement, such a court is obliged, at the request of a party, to stay the action and refer the parties to arbitration unless it finds the agreement null or the arbitration incapable of being performed.[42]

The deficiency of Quebec law on this point has already been evoked: in that jurisdiction, the dominant view is that the arbitration agreement respecting future disputes is void, and therefore unenforceable, insofar as it provides that the award to be rendered in virtue thereof is final and binding. This view has been endorsed by the Supreme Court of Canada in a decision which, while adding no new element to the debate in Quebec law, has however deduced a new application of the clause's invalidity. The case concerned an agreement to arbitrate a future dispute in New York according to the law of that state and whether an application for a stay of action or dismissal of suit could be obtained in respect of an action brought in Quebec on the same subject in violation of the agreement. The application was dismissed on the ground that the clause was contrary to public policy, and thus void according to the applicable Quebec law which, as the *lex fori*, governed the matter characterized by the court as one of 'practice and procedure' rather than substantive law.[43] The characterization in the latter sense would have enabled the court to apply a law favourable to the clause – the proper law of the contract, American law.[44]

Thus, according to the majority view of Canada's highest court, to give effect in Quebec to the arbitration agreement stipulated under a favourable foreign law was to violate Quebec public order. That, it will be recalled, is a position to which the French courts, during the long history of their hostility to such agreements in French internal law, never arrived insofar as an *international* arbitration agreement was concerned.[45] The Supreme Court of Canada thus chose to harden, rather than attempt to relax, the position of the Quebec courts on a point of incontestable importance to international arbitration. The law of Quebec is therefore today even more out of step with that of the other Canadian provinces where, in all certainty, the opposite conclusion would have been reached in view of the rule that the court has a discretion to exercise in such cases. Quebec courts, until there is further legislative clarification on the point, do not posses such discretion.

Enforcing the award

The efforts of international treaty law have been directed over the years to bringing about an assimilation of the foreign award to that of the domestic award. In this way it is possible to arrive at the position where a foreign arbitration award will not be subject to more onerous conditions in respect of its recognition and enforcement than would be imposed on a domestic award.[46] The desired end, in other words, is to treat the foreign award as though it were an award of the jurisdiction where its enforcement is sought and to enforce it in the same way.

There would appear to be no obstacle to this assimilation under the laws of the several Canadian provinces. None of them lays down any special procedures or requirements in regard to foreign awards. Neither Canadian common nor Canadian civil law demands, for example, that the foreign award in addition to being final and conclusive according to the foreign law by which it is ruled also be enforceable under that law before its enforcement can be sought in a Canadian court. There is no authority for a system of 'double *exequatur*.' The domestic procedures for enforcement of final foreign awards are thus, on the legislative face of things, fully available: in the common law, by the summary proceeding of applying for leave of the judge to enforce the award in the same manner as a judgment or order to the same effect; and in the civil law, upon a motion for homologation of the award in order to have the party condemned to execute it.

But while this would appear to be the position in Canada, and one conformable to both English[47] and French[48] law quite apart from international convention, there is no Canadian judicial authority to this effect. The two Canadian decisions on the subject of foreign arbitration awards, one from a common law province and the other from Quebec, deal only with those foreign awards which were ratified or confirmed by the court of the place where they were rendered and which were, consequently, sued upon in Canadian courts as foreign judgments[49] which thereupon made applicable to such awards those rules applicable to foreign judgments. In neither instance was the issue whether such foreign ratification was necessary to its 'final' character in that foreign jurisdiction even raised; nor was there, consequentially, any ruling on the question of the characterization of the award either in the *absence* of such confirmation or *despite* that confirmation. The characterization one way or another is particularly important in respect of enforcement in Quebec because there the regime of execution of an award is considerably more favourable than that applicable to a foreign judgment.[50] In sum, the law applicable to the enforcement of foreign awards is still largely unexplored by Canadian courts.

CONCLUSION

What, then, is the Canadian perspective on the subject of international commercial arbitration? A first conclusion to draw may be that at whatever level, and in whatever locality, Canadian business interests are involved in this process of solving disputes, theirs is not such a *practice* of arbitration that has, as yet, had any influence on the *law* of arbitration in Canada. If the practice of arbitration, whether wholly intraprovincial, interprovincial, or international, were to have gained an important dimension, it is surely no exaggeration to suggest that some 'movement' in the law on the subject would be perceptible – a developing case law or *jurisprudence,* a modernization of the provincial laws, a renewed effort towards uniformity, or even (it may be no rash thought) some attempt to resolve the constitutional difficulties in the path of participation in the evolving international law on arbitration.

Does it follow that Canadian business interests are not equipped at this time to participate in arbitration as an instrument for solving international commercial disputes? Here an answer cannot be readily deduced from the present state of Canadian arbitration law and practice. Canadian businessmen may, as suggested earlier, be either inclined or forced to provide for an arbitration in some third or unconnected country and may, like those elsewhere, generally tend to observe and respect both the jurisdiction of the tribunal of their own creation and its award, and do so to such an extent that the problems regarding the validity of the agreement and the enforcement of the award have presented themselves even more infrequently before Canadian courts than those of other countries.

NOTES

1 The American Arbitration Association (AAA) was founded in 1926 shortly after the enactment in New York of a modern arbitration law (N.Y. Sess. Laws 1920, art 84 c 275) which has served as a model law for other American states. The founding in 1923 of the International Chamber of Commerce, and its arbitration facilities, coincided with France's adhesion to the 1923 Geneva Convention on the validity of arbitration agreements and assisted in the movement of French opinion towards the acceptance of the validity of the agreement to arbitrate future disputes (*clause compromissoire*) in domestic commercial matters, finally achieved by the law of 31 décembre 1925 which amended article 631 of the French Code de commerce.

2 The present sources (with the date of original enactment in parentheses) are: Alberta (1909), R.S.A. c 21 (1970); British Columbia (1893), R.S.B.C. c 14 (1960); Manitoba (1911), R.S.M. c A-120 (1970); New Brunswick (1909), R.S.N.B. c 9 (1952); Newfoundland, R.S.N. c 114 (part 6) (1952); Nova Scotia (1895), R.S.N.S. c 12 (1967); Ontario (1897), R.S.O. c 25 (1970); Prince Edward Island, R.S. P.E.I. c 12 (1951); Quebec Code of Civil Procedure, 1867, articles 1431–44 now C.C.P. articles 940–951 (1966); Saskatchewan (1898), R.S.S. c 106 (1965). A review of these legislations as they stood in the 1940s is given by B. Claxton, 'Commercial Arbitration under Canadian Law' (1943), 21 *Can. Bar Rev.* 171.

3 52 & 53 Vict. c 49; as modified in 1934, 24 & 25 Geo. v, c 14; now the Arbitration Act, 1950, 14 Geo. vi, c 27.

4 Manitoba, s 32(1); Ontario s. 16; Prince Edward Island, s 21; Saskatchewan, s 14, where it may be so provided in the terms of the submission.

5 According to the laws of Saskatchewan, s 7(b); Ontario, s 9(b); Nova Scotia, s 8(b) and Alberta, s 7(b); Prince Edward Island, s 9(b), unless the submission expresses a contrary intention.

6 The text (c.c.p. 951: 'An undertaking to arbitrate must be set out in writing') is, admittedly, ambiguous in the light of its legislative history; for an examination of the matter, see J.E.C. Brierley, 'Aspects of the Promise to Arbitrate in the Law of Quebec' (1970), 30 *Rev. du Barreau* (Québec) 473.

7 E.J. Cohn, 'Commercial Arbitration and the Rules of Law: A Comparative Study' (1941), 4 *U. Toronto L.J.* 1.

8 For a review of these, see M. Domke, *Commercial Arbitration* (1968); L. Mayers, *The American Legal System* (1955), 549; A.B. Carb, 'The Need for Uniform Laws on Arbitration' (1960), 15 *Arb. J.* 65.

9 An unofficial (i.e, non-governmental) agency, grouping representatives from all the provincial governments and a selection of law professors and practitioners, which has met annually since 1918 to draft model uniform statutes on matters within provincial legislative competence.

10 'Proceedings of the Conference of Commissioners on Uniformity of Legislation in Canada' in 15 *Proceedings of the Canadian Bar Association* (1930) 287, 358 Appendix i; and 16 *Proceedings of the Canadian Bar Association* (1931) 274.

11 Quebec, it should be noted, manifested a certain hostility or indifference to the work of the conference prior to the mid-1940s.

12 16 *Proceedings, supra* note 10 at 276.

13 Mayers, *The American Legal System, supra* note 8, and (rev ed, 1964), 549; F. Kellor, *Arbitration and the Legal Profeseion* (nd) 27; M. Domke, 'Arbitral Awards without Written Opinions' in *XXth Century Comparative and Conflict Law* (1961), 256.

14 30–31 Vict. c 3, ss 91, 92.

15 A. Smith, *The Commerce Power in Canada and the United States* (1963), 177.

16 See in general, ibid.

17 Admiralty Act, originally s.c. 1891, c 29 and now R.S.C. c A-1 (1970); the federal parliament has exercised its power under s 101 of the BNA act, 1867 to create admiralty courts.

18 R. David, 'Arbitrage et Droit comparé' (1959), *Rev. int. droit comparé* 5, at 14.

19 Thus it is said that the best arbitrations are those of which one hears the least ('Les arbitrages les mieux réussis sont ceux dont on parle le moins'). The arbitrations of which we possess some judicial recognition, through reported cases, may thus be considered, in some respects, as having failed: the initial purpose, at least, of an arbitration is frustrated if resort to the courts is necessary.

20 Of the more recent and comprehensive surveys, see Ph. Fouchard, *Arbitrage Commercial International* (1965).

21 'Note' (1944), *Arbitration Magazine* (AAA) 16; the address of B. Claxton, in (1943), 1 *Arb. J.* 14, and (1943), 21 *Can. Bar Rev.* 171, at 186; W.H. Coverdale, 'A Unique Experiment in Fact' (1945), 1 *Inter. Arb. J.* 49: M. Domke and F. Kellor, 'Western Hemispere Systems of Commercial Arbitration' (1946), 6 *U. Toronto L.J.* 307, at 325.

22 The text of the rules in the brochure entitled 'Canadian-American Arbitration Facilities (Rules of Procedure)' is reproduced, in part, in Domke and Kellor, *supra* note 21; Coverdale, *supra* note 21, at 49; F. Kellor, *American Arbitration* (1948) 134; F.E. Klein, *Considérations sur l'arbitrage en droit international privé* (1955) 24; Fouchard, *supra* note 20, at no 360 *et seq.*

23 R. Marx, 'Normalisation internationale des règlements arbitraux,' Rapport à la Session des 15 & 16 mai 1950 de la Comm. de l'arbitrage commercial international in CCI brochure *Arbitrage commercial et liberté contractuelle*; Kellor, *American Arbitration, supra* note 22, at 134; Fouchard, *supra* note 20, at no 342. Only G.L. Morris, 'The Problems of Uniform Arbitration Legislation in Canada (1958), 13 *Arb. J.* 103 has drawn attention to the real fate of this co-operative effort.

24 These statements are based on communications to the writer.

25 See the role of the chambers of commerce under the 1961 Geneva European Convention on International Commercial Arbitration, article iv; the roles of the ICC/CCI and the London Court of Arbitration in the development of arbitration practices are well known.

26 Either by virtue of their statutes of incorporation and by-laws (as illustrated by the long-

standing provisions anticipating arbitration facilities in the case of the Montreal Board of Trade and the Board of Trade of Metropolitan Toronto); or, if need be, either under special provincial legislation (cf, the Ontario Boards of Trade General Arbitration Act, 1894, s.o. c 24 (1894), now repealed) or federal enactment (Boards of Trade Act, R.S.C. 1970, c B-8, ss 32–35 (1970)).

27 Boards of Trade Act, R.S.C. c B-8, ss 38–41 (1970). Some 1000 such organizations are registered with the Canadian Department of Consumer and Corporate Affairs.

28 For example, that of S. Mentschikoff, 'Commercial Arbitration' (1961), 61 *Col. L.R.* 846.

29 Communications from the Canadian Department of Industry, Trade and Commerce (Trade Commissioner Service) indicate that, to its knowledge, there is no particular interest manifested by foreign businesses as to arbitration laws or facilities in Canada.

30 Cf I.R. Feltham, 'Export Sales Contracts' in I.F.G. Baxter and I.R. Feltham, eds, *Export Practice* (1964), at 29.

31 Communications from the London Court of Arbitration and the International Chamber of Commerce (Paris). No arbitration involving a Canadian element is recorded by the former; in the latter, for 1970, only 3 cases out of 150 implicated any Canadian interests, and none is recorded for 1971.

32 Communications from the American Arbitration Association.

33 This is the case for example of the Canadian Wheat Board, established under the Canadian Wheat Board Act, R.S.C. c c-12 (1970), which buys and disposes of huge amounts of Canadian wheat; and, to a lesser extent, the Export Development Corporation (successor to the Export Credits Insurance Corporation), R.S.C. c c-18 (1970), in respect of the financing agreements it supports which may contain an arbitration clause.

34 American practitioners have indicated to me that Montreal and Toronto lawyers are known for their suspicious attitudes and unco-operativeness respecting arbitration.

35 Geneva Convention of 24 September 1923 on the Validity of Arbitration Clauses; Geneva Convention of 26 September on the Execution of Foreign Arbitral Awards; the United Nations Convention of 10 June 1958 on the Recognition and Enforcement of Foreign Arbitral Awards; the Washington Convention of 18 March 1965 on the Settlement of Investment Disputes between States and Nationals of other States. The texts are conveniently located in L. Kos-Rabcewicz-Zubkowski, *East European Rules on the Validity of International Commercial Arbitration Agreements* (1970) 239 *et seq.*

36 Newfoundland however was able to give effect to the two early Geneva conventions by the Arbitration (Foreign Awards) Act, 1931, 22 Geo. v c 2, ie, prior to its entry into the Canadian confederation in 1949.

37 Canada was represented at the Consultation Meetings of Legal Experts in Santiago, Chile, 3–4 February 1964, preparatory to the 1965 Treaty of Washington. 'Summary Record of Proceedings' in *Convention on the Settlement of Investment Disputes between States and the Nationals of other States, Documents concerning the Origin and the Formulation of the Convention,* (1968), vol II, part I, Document 27, 298 *et seq.* No observers from Canada attended the meetings for the 1958 New York convention on the enforcement of arbitral awards; according to the Canadian Department of External Affairs, the Canadian business associations consulted on the matter expressed little or no interest in Canadian presence or adoption.

38 The American practice in regard to treaties of 'friendship, commerce and navigation' is documented by C.H. Sullivan, 'United States Treaty Policy of Commercial Arbitration, 1920–1946' and by H. Walker, for the period 1946–1957 in M. Domke, ed, *International Trade Arbitration* (1958), at 35, 49.

39 Canada/USSR Trade Agreement of 29 February 1956, [1956] *Can. T.S.* no 1, article VI.

40 See the remarks of the then minister of trade and commerce, *Canada,* H.C. *Debates* 18 April 1956, 3041 moving approval of the ratification of the agreement.

41 Regarding American judicial enforcement of awards handed down under the 1965 Washington Convention on the Settlement of Investment disputes, see Public Law 89–532 (11 August 1966), s 3498. As to the US implementation of the UN 1958 Convention, see Public Law 91–368 (31 July 1970), and M. Domke in (1971), 19 *Amer. J. of Comp. L.* 575.

42 1923 Geneva Convention, articles. 1, 4; 1958 New York Convention, article II; 1961 European Convention, article VI.

43 *National Gypsum Co.* v *Northern Sales Ltd.,* [1964] S.C.R. 144; (1964), 43 D.L.R. (2d) 235; (1963), 2 Lloyd's Rep. 499. Commented upon in (1964), *J. Bus. Law* 298; (1965), 3 *Colum.*

J. Transnational Law 246.

44 See the dissenting judgment of Cartwright J, relying upon *Hamlyn & Co.* v *Talisker Distillery*, [1894] A.C. 202.

45 See in particular Cass. civ. 19 février 1930, Dalloz Heb. 1930.228; Sirey 1933.1.41; Cass. civ. 27 janvier 1931, Sirey 1933.1.43; a general discussion is found in Fouchard, *supra* note 20, at no 95; Klein, *supra* note 22, at no 102; cf also J-G. Castel, 'Quelques questions de procédure en droit international privé québecois' (1971), 31 *Rev. du Barreau* (Québec) 134, at 143.

46 1927 Geneva Convention on the Execution of Foreign Arbitration Awards; 1958 United Nations Convention on the Recognition and Enforcement of Foreign Arbitral Awards.

47 Russell on *The Law of Arbitration* (18th ed, A. Walton, 1970) 337, and C. Schmitthoff, *Export Trade* (1969) 358; Dicey and Morris, *The Conflict of Laws* (8th ed, 1967) 1051 and rule 177, 1054–5. All are in agreement that the procedure for enforcement of domestic awards (Arbitration Act, 1950, s 26) is available to the foreign award as well.

48 Cass. req. 9 juill. 1928, Sirey 1930.1.17; Fouchard, *supra* note 20, at no 727.

49 *Stolp* v *Browne*, [1930] 4 D.L.R. 703 (Ont. Supreme Court); (1930–31), 66 O.L.R. 73; 38 O.W.N. 400. *Orsi* v *Irving Samuel Inc.*, [1957] C.S. 209 (Que. Superior Court). Cf J-G. Castel, 'Recognition and Enforcement of Foreign Judgments *in Personam* and *in Rem* in the Common Law Provinces in Canada' (1971), 17 *McGill L.J.* 11, at 183 *et seq*, and 'Quelques questions de procédure dans le droit international privé québécois (1971), 31 *Rev. du Barreau* (Québec) 134, at 144–5.

50 The Quebec Code of Civil Procedure, articles 178–80 (formerly articles 210–12) allows a Quebec court to hear defences set up to the original action to be pleaded to an action brought upon a foreign judgment, whereas article 950 does not permit the court to enter into the merits of the contestation.

34/International Civil Procedure

This chapter deals with special domestic or conventional rules designed to assist Canadian litigants in obtaining legal remedies abroad and foreign litigants in obtaining legal remedies in Canada in civil and commercial matters. It is mainly concerned with the taking of evidence abroad and the service of judicial and extrajudicial documents on defendants residing outside the country where the action is brought. Security for costs and judicial assistance for poor persons are matters which sometimes are mentioned in international conventions to which Canada is a party.

SOURCES

There are presently in force in Canada many bilateral conventions[1] regarding legal proceedings in civil and commercial matters. Practically all of them were concluded by the United Kingdom government before World War II and were made applicable to Canada at the time of conclusion or subsequently. Now that Canada has joined the Hague Conference on Private International Law,[2] reference should also be made to some of the conventions prepared by this international organization that are concerned with civil procedure.[3] None of these conventions has yet been signed by Canada.

In Canada, the rules of practice apply[4] as well as statutes such as the Evidence Act[5] of the various provinces and territories. In Quebec the Code of Civil Procedure[6] and certain rules dealing with 'international civil procedure' are in force.

TAKING EVIDENCE ABROAD

When it becomes necessary to take evidence abroad there are several procedures available: 1 / a person may be appointed and authorized by the courts of the country of origin (usually by commission or by appointment as examiner) to take evidence abroad; 2 / the evidence may be taken by the courts of the country of execution pursuant to Letters of Request. These two procedures are available in countries with which Canada has not signed civil procedure conventions. 3 / The evidence may be taken by an examiner appointed and authorized by the courts of the country of execution pursuant to Letters of Request. This procedure is generally restricted to some countries with which Canada has signed a convention.

The first procedure is usually employed for willing witnesses. It is expeditious and effective as the witnesses may be examined and cross-examined by the legal representatives of the parties. The second and third procedures are used when unwilling witnesses must be examined, since the authorities of the country of execution can exercise their compulsory powers. The second procedure may be used in nearly every country of the world. However, it often involves considerable delay.

Commission evidence

Originating in English practice, the commission is generally to be used where necessary for the purposes of justice.[7] Now the English practice is to appoint a special examiner in place of the more cumbersome commission. This change has been reflected in Canada but to a lesser degree.[8]

Application
The first step in obtaining an order for a commission is to make out an application. The onus of establishing the necessity for this mode of examination is on the party applicant.[9] Along with the application should be an affidavit, made by the party applicant himself,[10] generally setting forth who is to be examined and stating that these witnesses can prove facts and circumstances supporting the applicant's case. It may be necessary to show the nature of the evidence or facts intended to be proven on the application.[11] In countries where the taking of evidence by a consul or by any other person appointed by the court of the country of origin is not permitted by the domestic law, the procedure by Letters of Request is the only one available. Thus, if it is intended to take evidence in a particular country by a commissioner or by appointment of a special examiner, the Department of External Affairs should be consulted in order to ascertain whether or not this procedure is authorized in that country. It should be noted that the department does not normally authorize its diplomatic or consular officers abroad to act as commissioners for taking evidence.[12]

Granting the order
Once the court is appraised of the application, the granting of the order for a commission is a matter of discretion.[13] The application must be made during a pending proceeding[14] and usually after the issue is joined.[15] The court must be satisfied a / that the application is made *bona fide*,[16] b / that the issue in respect of which the evidence is required is one which the court is to try,[17] c / that the witnesses to be examined can give evidence material to the issue,[18] d / that there is some good reason why they cannot be examined within the jurisdiction,[19] e / that the examination abroad will be effective.[20]

A commission is more readily granted in the case of a witness than a party,[21] and of a defendant than a plaintiff.[22] Where some of the plaintiffs reside within the jurisdiction and some without, the latter may be examined by commission.[23] If the court considers attendance at trial a necessity the commission will not be granted, for instance if the issue between the parties hinges largely on credibility,[24] or if from the nature of the case cross-examination in open court is a necessity.[25] The discretion of a court or judge in granting or refusing an order will not be readily interfered with but is capable of review on appeal.[26]

The power to appoint foreign commissioners may also reside with the government.[27] Where an authorized person takes evidence abroad there is usually a statutory provision to validate the oaths given and make the evidence admissible as if taken in Canada.[28] It seems that a master has no jurisdiction over admitting commission evidence, rather it is a matter that involves the trial judge directly.[29]

Form of the order

When a commission order is granted for a foreigner to examine witnesses abroad, there must be the formal issuing of the commission from the appropriate authority or the commission is rejected.[30] The form of the commission shows wide variation, for example the court may order that the subject matter of the action be sent abroad so that it may be identified by the foreign witnesses,[31] or it may call for certain documents to be sent abroad with the commission, so long as these are not *sub judice* in the action.[32] Furthermore, the court often imposes conditions on the issuing of the commission. Where information concerning the whereabouts of a foreign witness was slender and it seemed doubtful whether he would attend the examination, the plaintiff-applicant was required to give security for the costs of the commission.[33] In another case where the court felt that the application was not made in good faith, but was reluctant to interfere with the master's order for a commission, the court required the names of the foreign witnesses to be given to the opposite party and that the commission be returned within four months with no further delay in the trial proceedings.[34]

The order may also direct the commissioner as to how to conduct the examination. It has been held that *prima facie* the examination is to be upon interrogatories, and when an order for a commission makes no provision for the mode of examination, the depositions which had been taken *viva voce* are not to be admitted.[35] The directions in the commission are not considered obligatory, and therefore substantial compliance may be sufficient.[36] For non-compliance with a formal requirement a separate motion should be submitted to quash the depositions.[37] In a case where a foreign notary public failed to affix his official seal, the affidavits sworn before him were rendered inadmissible.[38] Other examples of improper commissions occur when no notice is given to the opposite party of the execution of the commission,[39] when no opportunity is given for cross-examination,[40] or when the examination is carried out by an unauthorized person.[41]

The examination abroad

The mode of examination is generally uniform throughout Canada. The authorized commissioner first takes an oath, then examines the witnesses, places his seal on the documents, swears out an affidavit of due taking, and returns the commission to the proper officer of the court.[42] During the examination a witness who refuses to answer certain questions is protected by the Canada Evidence Act.[43] If a party applicant refuses to attend the commission, judgment may pass against him.[44]

The commission returned

When the commission is returned, it is opened without need for an order in the presence of all the parties, it is filed for the inspection of all the parties for a reasonable length of time, and all the parties may obtain copies of the commission.[45] In a situation where a plaintiff was precluded from joining the examination or a witness on commission because of financial limitations, he was allowed to open the commission before trial.[46] At the trial each party may read into the record the evidence of witnesses examined on commission. It is in the trial judge's discretion as to how much of the evidence may be allowed in;[47] and if neither party chooses to read in any such evidence, it forms no part of the trial record.[48]

Costs of the commission

The matter of the costs of the commission often depends on the nature of the particular facts. Generally each party who wishes to join in the commission will pay the costs consequent upon the examination of his witness.[49] If the party applicant is insolvent, he may have to furnish security for the costs of the commission.[50] On occasion, the courts have ruled that commissions were unnecessary and so the costs have been disallowed. However, the party applicant will not necessarily lose the costs just because the commission evidence is not used at trial.[51]

Letters of Request (Commissions Rogatoires)

This form of taking evidence abroad can be used nearly everywhere,[52] except the United States where commissions or special examinations must be used. A strong drawback to consider is that it is difficult to ensure that the evidence is taken in accordance with the procedural rules of the original jurisdiction. Furthermore, this method may involve added expense and delay.

How to proceed

The recommended practice is to address Letters of Request

> to competent authorities of the country of execution rather than to a named court; it then becomes the business of the Department of External Affairs to see that the documents are transmitted through the local authorities to the proper judicial tribunal in the country of execution that is competent to take evidence. The documents should be transmitted with at least one copy, together with an undertaking as to costs, to the Under-Secretary of State for External Affairs ... If the parties are represented by agents in the country of execution, their names and addresses should be disclosed. Where they are not so represented, the documents should in all cases, be accompanied by complete interrogatories and cross-interrogatories.[53]

In addition, the applicant is obliged to satisfy the court of the facts of which the evidence is required.[54]

When is the order made?

Once again the court order is based on the exercise of discretion. But here it has been said that Letters of Request are only ordered where absolutely necessary for the purposes of justice.[55] The court is apt to look more favourably at the application of a defendant resident abroad than a plaintiff who has had the opportunity to choose the tribunal himself.[56] In an Ontario case where the plaintiff applied for a commission to examine witnesses abroad, it was held that the requirements for its issuance were *prima facie* met, but that the issuing of letters rogatory was denied because nothing was shown in the motion to the effect that the proposed witnesses were adverse or had an unwillingness to attend and testify at the commission.[57] In another Ontario case on an application to take evidence in Yugoslavia the court held that orders for a commission or letters rogatory were inappropriate because such procedures were not used in Yugoslavia; but that the court had power to order by analogy to rule 276 Letters of Request directed to a competent judicial authority in Yugoslavia for assistance in obtaining the testimony of the witnesses. The letter would be issued by the registrar containing the formal authorization of the chief justice of Ontario.[58]

The effect of international conventions on civil procedure
In each of Canada's bilateral conventions on civil procedure there are provisions on how and to whom Letters of Request issued in Canada should be transmitted to the competent foreign authority. For example, in the convention with Italy,[59] article 9 states that a Canadian consular officer must transmit the letters in Italy to the *Procuratore Generale presso la Corte d'Appello* of the district of execution. In case the authority to whom the letters are addressed is without jurisdiction, they will be forwarded without any further request to the competent authority of the same country in accordance with the rules laid down by its law. The Letters of Request must be drawn up in the language of the authority to whom the request is addressed or be accompanied by a translation in such language certified as correct by a diplomatic or consular officer of the country making the request or by an official or sworn translator of one of the two countries concerned.

The usual mode of procedure to be used by the requested state is exemplified in article 9 (i) of the convention between Canada and Italy which gives the requested authority the power to apply its own procedure. However, the authority may give effect to special demands in the Letters of Request if not incompatible with its own law. In addition, some conventions describe in detail the form the Letters of Request are to take. For instance, article 8(a) of the Canada-Denmark convention[60] declares that ' "Letters of Request" shall state the nature of the proceedings for which the evidence is required, the full names and descriptions of the witnesses. They shall also either be accompanied by a list of interrogatories ... and a translation thereof ... or shall request the competent authority to allow such questions to be asked *viva voce* as the parties or their representative shall desire to ask.'

A universal provision in these conventions to ensure the effectiveness of the request is represented by article 9(d) of the Italy-Canada convention[61] which states that the judicial authority to which Letters of Request are addressed must give effect thereto by the use of the same compulsory measures as are employed in the execution of a commission or order emanating from the authorities of its own country. Certain situations may arise where the requested country cannot or will not execute the request. Article 9(f) of the convention with Italy[62] lists three of the common grounds for refusal: a / if the authenticity of the Letters of Request is not established;[63] b / if in the requested country, the execution of the letters in question does not fall within the functions of the judiciary;[64] c / if the High Contracting Party applied to considers that his sovereignty or safety would be compromised thereby.

The consular officer by whom the Letters of Request are transmitted shall, if he so desires, be informed of the date and place where the proceedings will take place in order that he may inform the interested parties who shall be permitted to be present in person or be represented if they so desire.

Most conventions provide that evidence may also be taken, without any request to or the intervention of the authorities of the country of execution, by a person in that country directly appointed for the purpose by the court of the country of origin. A consular officer acting for the country of origin or any other suitable individual may be so appointed;[65] of course such a person lacks any compulsory powers.[66] The evidence may be taken in accordance with the procedure recognized by the law of the country of origin.[67]

A person appointed by the requested authority may exercise compulsory powers where needed.[68] In such a situation the local laws of procedure apply. In particular the convention with Spain specifically declares that those examined shall be subject to the local perjury laws.[69] An interesting point to note here is that the conventions give a right to those examined which many countries have seen fit to deny their own citizens in domestic cases, that is the right to counsel upon being examined.[70]

With regard to costs, the requesting country does not pay a fee for the execution of the Letters of Request, but pays the expenses of witnesses, translators, and the costs of obtaining documents and so on, according to the tariff in the requested state.[71]

The Department of External Affairs is of the opinion that from past experience the most satisfactory method of the alternatives provided for in the conventions on civil procedure is to secure a Letter of Request from the appropriate Canadian court addressed to the appropriate foreign court asking that the desired evidence be secured by summoning the witnesses for questioning and returning the answers to the court trying the case: 'Although there is a provision for a diplomatic or consular officer to be appointed to take such evidence, the Department is not in a position to offer this service because of a shortage of staff. Moreover, this method is not desirable because the diplomatic or consular officer does not possess any powers of compulsion to summon witnesses, or secure answers to questions and consequently in many instances, the securing of evidence is difficult if not impossible in such circumstances.'[72]

In every instance where the Letters of Request are not executed by the authority to whom they are addressed, the latter will at once inform the consular officer by whom they were transmitted, stating the grounds on which the execution has been refused, or the judicial authority to whom they have been forwarded.

The Hague International Convention, 1970

A multilateral Convention on the Taking of Evidence Abroad in Civil or Commercial Matters was signed at the Hague in 1970. Chapter one of the convention deals with Letters of Request. Only a 'judicial' authority is entitled to issue a letter for the purpose of obtaining evidence or performing some 'other judicial act.' Excluded from the latter term are service of documents, enforcement of judgments, and provisional and protective measures. Under article 2, each country is to establish a central authority which, upon receipt of a letter, will transmit it to the local authority competent to execute it. Article 3 sets out what shall be the contents of the letter, including the nature of the proceedings and the parties thereto, the evidence required, and also where appropriate the names and addresses of persons to be examined, the questions to be asked, any requirement that the evidence is to be given on oath or affirmation, and any special form to be used. If the requesting authority desires, it may be informed under article 7 of the place and date of the proceedings so that the parties or their representatives may attend. Article 8 permits judicial personnel of the requesting country to be present at the proceedings if the country of execution files a declaration of consent. Fees paid to experts and interpreters and costs occasioned by 'a special procedure' under article 9(2) are alone reimbursable by the requesting authority. In addition, because of constitutional limitations, a requested country may, by article 26, ask for reimbursement of witness fees, the costs of compelling the attendance of witnesses, and the costs of the transcripts of the evidence.

Chapter two deals with the taking of evidence by diplomatic officers, consular agents, and commissioners. They are allowed to take evidence of their own nationals under article 15, but as regards others, article 16 says express permission of the executed country is required. Article 18 shows a significant departure from Canada's previous bilateral conventions in the fact that it allows such agents to apply to the competent local authorities for aid in compelling unwilling witnesses. Article 23 allows common law countries to refuse executing Letters of Request issued for the purpose of obtaining pre-trial discovery.

Each of the rules concerning consuls and commissioners may be varied by particular countries by side agreements, less restrictive internal law, and practice or treaty. Thus the convention has served the function of codifying much of the previous case law in the area, and has added certain provisions to clarify and expedite international judicial assistance.

HELPING FOREIGN TRIBUNALS

International legal assistance rests on the comity of nations. In the case of *National Telefilm Associates Inc.* v *United Artists' Corp.*,[73] the Ontario Court of Appeal ruled that in the interests of comity a foreign request should be given full force and effect wherever possible. Szaszy[74] is of the opinion that if the requested court recognizes an international customary obligation to give judicial assistance, and this obligation has been incorporated in an international convention or municipal statute, or both, that court may deny legal assistance on the ground of public policy only if a / the legal act requested is not within the powers of the requested court, or b / the legal act conflicts with the local regime or local notions of justice and security, or c / the state requesting refuses to guarantee reciprocal treatment.

The Canadian practice here to a great extent has been modelled on the English example. Saskatchewan has gone so far as to implement literally the relevant British statute, the foreign Tribunals Evidence Act.[75] In the Canada Evidence Act,[76] section 48 gives a court the rule-making power to put into effect a foreign court's request. Thus, where it is made to appear to a Canadian judge that a competent foreign court has duly authorized the obtaining of testimony in relation to a proceeding pending before such foreign court of a witness out of the jurisdiction thereof and within the jurisdiction of the court applied to, such court may order the examination of such witness and command his attendance and the production of such documentary evidence as he may have in his possession or under his control. The general procedure is exemplified by section 60(1) of the Ontario Evidence Act[77] in which the foreign applicant must first establish that under its own rules the requesting court has the power to direct the taking of evidence in a foreign jurisdiction, and also its inability to obtain such evidence without the intervention of the Ontario court. The *National Telefilm* case[78] states that in the absence of evidence to the contrary, the foreign order (here it was from New York asking for an examination and production of documents) is to be assumed regular and in accordance with the rules of practice in the requesting jurisdiction.

The Ontario act contemplates nomination by the foreign court of the person by whom the evidence is to be taken whereas under the federal act, the requested court may also name such person. In order to obviate the difficulty that would arise when the foreign court did not appoint a person before whom the witness is to be examined, the application should be made under both the federal act and the provincial act.

One of the key rules that local courts follow is that aid is normally only given to a *proper* foreign court. Thus it has been held that the only foreign tribunal within the contemplation of the Canada and Ontario Evidence Acts is a court of law or equity. Furthermore, an administrative tribunal without the power itself to make requests for depositions to be taken abroad, and having limited sanctions in respect of its orders, cannot be considered a proper tribunal to which an Ontario court should give assistance.[79]

In responding to letters rogatory from a foreign court pursuant to section 43 of the Canada Evidence Act or section 60(1) of the Ontario Evidence Act, the court will order the examination of a witness only if it is clear that what is intended is the taking of that evidence for the purpose of trial.[80] No such order will be made if the principal purpose is to use such proceedings to search out evidence and information in the same way as on examination for discovery.[81]

A further rule to note is that the foreign request must be in such a form as to be acceptable to the requested court. For example, in *National Telefilm*[82] the court ruled that the request for the taking of testimonial evidence should stand, but it rejected the one asking for documents on the ground that the request was too broad and vague. Hence it is also apparent that the foreign request is severable.

Foreign applicants must be careful that they comply with local statutes or court orders relating to the taking of evidence within the jurisdiction. For instance, when a Swiss magistrate asked for an Ontario commission to take evidence for the Swiss court, it was held that he failed to place the proper seal of the court on the request and hence did not comply with section 23 of the Canada Evidence Act. The application was therefore refused.[83] Similarly, after an Ontario court had ruled that no action could be taken against a particular bankrupt company unless the receiver was made a party and the court gave its leave, a Spanish court in its application failed to comply with the order, and so its request was stayed until the requirements were met.[84] Finally, where a Civil Procedure Convention is in effect between the requesting country and Canada, the foreign court must comply therewith or the request will not be answered.[85]

On the other hand, the requested court is obligated to conform to the provisions in conventions which apply, so as to give full effect to proper requests. Also when a local court has knowledge of the rules for taking evidence in the requesting jurisdiction, it should accommodate itself to the mode requested, although it is not limited to the specific foreign statutes which comprise that method of examination.[86] For instance, it has been held that local witnesses cannot be subjected to a broader form of inquiry for a foreign action that would be the case in a domestic action.[87] Often provincial statutes will specifically afford protection to local witnesses examined for foreign tribunals.[88]

In giving effect to the foreign request, the local court may comply with a directive from the requesting court to appoint a named examiner; or if none is specified the local court may appoint its own examiner.[89] The final rule to note is that the local court is not to decide on the relevance of the evidence to be adduced, because that function belongs solely to the trial court.[90]

To conclude, the facilities to enforce the giving of testimony for the use of foreign courts under the Canada Evidence Act and the provincial Evidence Acts will usually be invoked when the witness may or does prove unwilling to give the testimony requested. When the witness is willing, Canadian law will not prevent the foreign courts from appointing whomsoever they may wish as examiner and from taking depositions in whatever manner they desire.[91]

SERVICE OF JUDICIAL AND EXTRAJUDICIAL DOCUMENTS

In order to serve documents abroad validly one must follow the requirements of the law of the place where such service is to be effected. Even when a convention permits several forms of service in a foreign country, the mode of service must conform to the requirements imposed by the Canadian court which has ordered it.

Provincial law

In Ontario, service of a writ may be made on a foreigner anywhere in British dominions,[92] but service of a writ instead of a notice on a foreigner not in British dominions is a nullity.[93] According to Rule of Practice 30, where service is to be effected upon a person other than a British subject in a foreign country to which this rule is by direction of the chief justice of Ontario made to apply, the following procedure shall be adopted:

1   The notice of the writ and statement of claim shall be transmitted by the Registrar of the Supreme Court to the Under-Secretary of State for External Affairs for Canada with a copy thereof, translated into the language of the country in which service is to be effected, with a request for further transmission of the same to the government of the country in which it is to be served, with the request that service, either personal or in such manner as is consistent with the practice and usage of that country when personal service cannot be made, be effected and that return be made showing how such service has been effected.
2   Any such official return shall be regarded as proof of the facts therein stated.
3   The plaintiff's solicitor shall, before the papers are transmitted, pay or secure to the satisfaction of the Registrar a sum to answer the fees and charges in connection with such service.

This rule applies to countries to which it is expressly made applicable by order of the chief justice of Ontario.

Service of process of foreign court

Rule of Practice 31 provides as follows:

> Where in a civil or commercial matter pending before a court or tribunal of a foreign country a letter of request from such court or tribunal for service on a person in Ontario of any process or citation in such matter is transmitted to the Supreme Court of Ontario, the following procedure shall be adopted:
> 1 The letter of request for service shall be accompanied by a translation thereof in the English language and by two copies of the process or citation to be served, and two copies thereof in the English language.
> 2 Service of the process or citation shall, by a direction of a judge, be effected by any sheriff or his authorized agent.
> 3 Such service shall be effected by delivering to and leaving with the person to be served one copy of the process to be served and one copy of the translation thereof or may be effected in such other manner as is directed by the letter of request.
> 4 After service has been effected, the process shall be returned to the Registrar of the Supreme Court, together with the evidence of service by affidavit of the person effecting the service, sworn before a notary public and verified by his seal, and particulars of charges for the cost of effecting such service.
> 5 The Registrar of the Supreme Court shall return the letter of request for service, together with the evidence of service, with a certificate appended thereto (Form 17) duly sealed with the seal of the said court.
> 6 Nothing in this rule prevents service from being effected in any other manner in which it may now be made.

This rule prescribes the procedure to be followed for serving the process of a foreign court in Ontario.[94]

International conventions

Canada

As yet Canada is not a party to a multilateral convention on civil procedure but, as noted previously, is bound by several bilateral ones whose provisions are generally quite similar. First, the documents to be served abroad must be sent through the diplomatic channels of the requesting state for proper authentication.[95] These documents must be written not only in the language of the state of execution. Herein are included descriptions of the original parties to the action, of the recipient, of the nature of the documents themselves, and copies thereof.

Each state specifies to whom the request should be forwarded, for instance, in Austria it is the federal Ministry of Justice, and in Spain, the president of the competent Territorial Court. Service is effected according to the local laws of the state of execution, but the latter may comply with special requests where these are not incompatible with its own law.[96] In addition many conventions allow other methods of service without any direct intervention such as 1 / service by diplomatic or consular officers of the requesting state, 2 / service by an agent appointed for that purpose either by a judicial authority of the requesting state, or by a party on whose application the document was issued, 3 / by the post,[97] 4 / any other mode of service recognized as valid in the requesting state,[98] or the state of execution.[99]

But of course, with these methods no compulsion may be used, and the validity of the service is a matter to be determined by the respective courts of the High Contracting Parties. If the request is sent to an authority who is incompetent to execute it, he is under an obligation to send it himself to the proper competent authority where it can be executed.[100] Most treaties provide that a requested state may refuse assistance if the authenticity of the request is not established and the sovereignty or safety of the requested state may be compromised by executing the request, or the latter provision alone may be stipulated. The requested authority is obliged to furnish a document proving that service was executed, or giving the reason why the request was not carried out.[101] Finally, all the conventions stipulate that although there is to be no fee for complying with a foreign request, nevertheless the requesting state is obliged to pay for the service according to the local tariff in the state of execution.

Hague International Convention, 1965

The Hague Convention on the Service Abroad of Judicial and Extrajudicial Documents in Civil or Commercial Matters, concluded on 15 November 1965, creates appropriate means to ensure that judicial and extrajudicial documents to be served abroad shall be brought to the notice of the addressee in sufficient time. It also improves the organization of mutual judicial assistance for that purpose by simplifying and expediting the procedure.

In each contracting state a central authority shall be designated which will undertake to receive requests for service coming from other contracting states. The authority competent under the law of the state in which the documents originate shall forward to the central authority of the state addressed a request conforming to the model annexed to the convention without any requirement of legislation or other equivalent formality. The document to be served or a copy thereof shall be annexed to the request. The request and the document shall both be furnished in duplicate. The central authority of the state addressed shall itself serve the document or shall arrange to have it served by an appropriate agency. The central authority of the state addressed or any authority which it may have designated for that purpose shall also complete a certificate in the form of the model annexed to the connection stating that the document has or has not been served. This certificate shall be forwarded directly to the applicant.

According to articles 15 and 16:

Article 15:
    Where a writ of summons or an equivalent document had to be transmitted abroad for the purpose of service, under the provisions of the present Convention, and the defendant has not appeared, judgment shall not be given until it is established that:
a   the document was served by a method prescribed by the internal law of the State addressed for the service of documents in domestic actions upon persons who are within its territory, or

b the document was actually delivered to the defendant or to his residence by another method provided for by this Convention, and that in either of these cases the service or the delivery was effected in sufficient time to enable the defendant to defend.

Each contracting State shall be free to declare that the judge, notwithstanding the provisions of the first paragraph of this article, may give judgment even if no certificate of service or delivery has been received, if all the following conditions are fulfilled:

c the document was transmitted by one of the methods provided for in this Convention,

d a period of time of not less than six months, considered adequate by the judge in the particular case, has elapsed since the date of the transmission of the document,

e no certificate of any kind has been received, even though every reasonable effort has been made to obtain it through the competent authorities of the State addressed.

Notwithstanding the provisions of the preceding paragraphs the judge may order, in case of urgency, any provisional or protective measures.

Article 16:

When a writ of summons or an equivalent document had to be transmitted abroad for the purpose of service, under the provisions of the present Convention, and a judgment has been entered against a defendant who has not appeared, the judge shall have the power to relieve the defendant from the effects of the expiration of the time for appeal from the judgment if the following conditions are fulfilled:

a the defendant, without any fault on his part, did not have knowledge of the document in sufficient time to defend, or knowledge of the judgment in sufficient time to appeal, and

b the defendant has disclosed a *prima facie* defence to the action on the merits.

An application for relief may be filed only within a reasonable time after the defendant has knowledge of the judgment.

Each contracting State may declare that the application will not be entertained if it is filed after the expiration of a time to be stated in the declaration, but which shall in no case be less than one year following the date of the judgment.

This article shall not apply to judgments concerning status or capacity of persons.

Countries with which Canada has no conventions

Service of court documents abroad is possible provided the law of the place where the service is to be effected is followed.

Role of the Canadian Department of External Affairs

In all cases to serve a document abroad the solicitor should request the assistance of the undersecretary for external affairs. The latter will then send his instructions to the Canadian mission in the country where service is to be effected.

The solicitor should simply include in the letter an undertaking to defray all costs and expenditures, the title of the cause, the name of the court, etc., a request that service of the document be effected in a particular country and an indication of his preference as to the mode of service. When service has been ordered by a court of justice, the document should be accompanied by a copy of the order. Of course, complete information as to the name and address of the person upon whom service is to be effected should also be included in the letter. The requirements as to the number of copies and translations vary in different countries; thus, the solicitor should send three sets of the documents and should authorize the Department to make provisions for translations if necessary (with the general undertaking as to costs extending to such matters) ... The authority should be broad enough in terms to enable the Department to follow its ordinary practice and so leave to the mission in the country of execution the decision of the necessity for translation ...In taking out an order for service it is desirable, if possible, to make provision for the proof of service, or failure to effect service, by certificate rather than be affidavit ... Where, however, affidavits are insisted upon by the courts, the solicitor should give adequate instructions to this effect.[102]

LEGALIZATION OF FOREIGN DOCUMENTS: HAGUE INTERNATIONAL CONVENTION, 1961

In 1961 a Convention Abolishing the Requirement of Legalisation for Foreign Documents was signed at the Hague. It has not yet been signed by Canada. The convention applies to public documents which have been executed in the territory of one contracting state and which have to be produced in the territory of another contracting state.

The public documents referred to in the convention are documents emanating from an authority or an official connected with courts of the state; administrative documents; notarial acts; and official certificates which are placed on documents signed by persons in their private capacity, such as official certificates recording the registration of a document or the fact that it was in existence on a certain date and official and notarial authentications of signatures. Not included are documents executed by diplomatic or consular agents and administrative documents dealing directly with commercial or customs operations.

The basic principle of the convention is to be found in article 2, which provides that each contracting state shall exempt these documents from legalization if they are to be produced in its territory. Legalization means only the formality by which the diplomatic or consular agents of the country in which the document has to be produced certify the authenticity of the signature, the capacity in which the person signing the document has acted and, where appropriate, the identity of the seal or stamp which it bears.

The only formality that may be required is the addition of a certificate described in the convention, issued by the competent authority of the state from which the document emanates. However, this formality cannot be required when either the laws, regulations, or practice in force in the state where the document is produced, or an agreement between two or more contracting states has abolished or simplified it or exempted the document itself from legalization.

The certificate which shall be placed on the document itself or on an 'allonge' must be in the form of the model annexed to the convention. It may, however, be drawn up in the official language of the authority which issues it. The standard terms appearing therein may be in a second language also.

The certificate shall be issued at the request of the person who has signed the document or of any bearer. When properly filled in, it will certify the authenticity of the signature, the capacity in which the person signing the document has acted, and where appropriate the identity of the seal or stamp which the document bears.

The signature, seal, and stamp on the certificate are exempt from all certification.

Each contracting state must designate by reference to their official function the authorities who are competent to issue the certificate. These authorities shall keep a register or card index for the purpose of recording the certificates issued, specifying the number and date of the certificate, and the name of the person signing the public document and the capacity in which he has acted, or in the case of unsigned documents, the name of the authority which has affixed the seal or stamp.

At the request of any interested person, the authority which has issued the certificate shall verify whether the particulars in the certificate correspond with those in the register or card index.

JUDICIAL ASSISTANCE FOR POOR PERSONS: IMPRISONMENT FOR DEBT, AND SECURITY FOR COSTS

According to article 12 of the Canada-Denmark Convention regarding Legal Proceedings in Civil and Commercial Matters, 'the subjects of one High Contracting Party shall enjoy, in the territory of the other High Contracting Party a perfect equality of treatment with subjects of that High Contracting Party as regards free judicial assistance for poor persons and imprisonment for debt; and provided that they are resident in any such territory, shall not be compelled to give security for costs in any case where a subject of such other High Contracting Party would not be so compelled.'[103]

This article does not modify the common law with respect to security for costs since, in Canada, security will only be ordered where the plaintiff is ordinarily resident abroad and has no assets within the jurisdiction to answer for the costs. The plaintiff's nationality is not a relevant consideration. An alien plaintiff resident in Ontario cannot be compelled to give security for costs on the ground that he is not a Canadian citizen.

The wording of article 11 of the Canada-Greece convention[104] is slightly different but has the same practical effect: 'The subjects of one High Contracting Party resident in the territory of the other High Contracting Party shall not be compelled to give security for costs in any case where a subject of such other High Contracting Party would not be so compelled.' In other words, these conventions do not dispense with security for costs in all cases. They only assimilate a foreigner to a national resident within the jurisdiction where the action is pending. A Canadian citizen residing in Greece will have the same rights in Greece as a Greek citizen residing in that country. Conversely, a Greek citizen residing in Ontario will have the same rights in Ontario as a Canadian citizen residing in Ontario.

NOTES

1 Eg, between Canada and Austria, Belgium, Czechoslavakia, Denmark, Finland, France, Germany, Greece, Hungary, Iraq, Italy, the Netherlands, Norway, Poland, Portugal, Spain, Sweden, Turkey, and Yugoslavia. Note that in 1948 the government of Canada notified Italy, Hungary, and Finland that the civil procedure conventions with these countries which had been suspended by the war were to apply to all the provinces other than Quebec.

2 See Castel, Canada and the Hague Conference on Private International Law: 1893–1967 (1967), 45 *Can. Bar Rev.* 1.

3 Analysed *supra*, at 852–3.

4 Eg, Ontario, rules 30–1; also Williston and Rolls, 2 *The Law of Civil Procedure* (1970) 976 *et seq*.

5 Eg, Saskatchewan Evidence Act, R.S.S. c 80, s 49 (1965).

6 See articles 426–37. Also Special Procedure Act, R.S.Q. c 22, ss 16–27 (1964).

7 Supreme Court Rules order 37, rules 5–6; Evidence on Commission Act, 1859, 22 Vict. c 20.

8 In Prince Edward Island, for example, by order 37, rule 7 of the Supreme Court Rules appointing a special examiner has replaced taking commission evidence. *Clow* v *Clow,* [1947] 2 D.L.R. 75 (P.E.I.). In Ontario the court may order a special examination under rule 270 instead of issuing a commission under rule 276 of the Supreme Court Rules of Practice.

9 *Staples* v *Miloff,* [1927] 2 D.L.R. 847.

10 *Kennett* v *Gill* (1969), 71 W.W.R. 1 (Alta C.A.) held that the solicitors' affidavit was unacceptable here.

11 *Smith* v *Murray* (1912), 1 W.W.R. 764 (Man.). See also *Kleiman* v *Cannon,* [1938] O.W.N. 106 for the opposite view. Where the affidavit simply cited information and belief as to why a particular witness should be examined abroad, it was held insufficient in *Lawson* v *Vacuum Brake Co.* (1884), 27 Ch. D. 137. It is no longer obligatory to name all the witnesses to be examined before a commission will be granted, as long as the examination is not 'a fishing expedition'. *Mamarbachi* v *Cockshutt Plow Co.,* [1953] O.W.N. 44 and *J.R. Watkins Co.* v *Cafferky,* [1925] 2 W.W.R. 588 (Alta). It is also to be noted that an application may be made under certain statutes like the Dependent's Relief Act of Ontario, R.S.O. c 126 (1970) in which case the particular statutory requirements must be met. *Re Martin,* [1951] O.W.N. 691. If the need arises to examine expert witnesses abroad, the party must show in his affidavit the lack of a comparable expert within the jurisdiction. *Lea* v *Stuart,* [1950] O.W.N. 733. Generally courts disapprove of such examinations abroad. *Mamarbachi* v *Cockshutt Plow Co., supra,* and *Washburn and Moen. Mfgn. Co.* v *Brooks* (1885), 2 Man. L.R. 44. In addition, if the party desires to examine a large number of witnesses abroad, he must obtain prior leave of the court. *French's Complex Ore Reduction Co.* v *Electrolytic Zinc Process Co.,* [1929] S.C.R. 463.

12 'International Civil Procedure: Role of External Affairs' (1962), 14 *External Affairs* 93; (1966), 4 *Can. Y.B. Int'l L.* 301.

13 *Warner* v *Mosses* (1880), 16 Ch. D. 100 (C.A.).

14 Ontario rule 270. The court may in any cause or matter where it appears necessary for the purposes of justice make an order for the examination upon oath before an officer of the court or any other person and at any place, of any person, and may permit such deposition to be given in evidence. (Form 77). Ontario rule 276:

(1) Where the testimony of a person or persons resident out of Ontario is required and for any reason an order under rule 270 is not sufficient, the court may order the issue of a commission to take such testimony (Order: Form 74; Commission: Form 61).

(2) Unless otherwise ordered or the parties otherwise agreed, if the name of any person to be examined is not set out in the order, notice of such name shall be given by the party who intends to conduct such examination to the opposite party or to the agent named by him under subrule 1 of rule 279 five days before the time fixed therefor.

Similar provisions are found in rule 169 of the former Exchequer Court of Canada now rule 477 of Federal Court and s 90 of the Supreme Court of Canada Act, R.S.C. c S-19 (1970). Where the Manitoba legislation allowed an order in any cause, it was held that an *action* was defined as a proceeding commenced by a writ of summons, and a *cause* was a wider term which included 'any suit, action, matter or other proceeding competently brought before and litigated in a particular court'. *Grant* v *Hunter* (1890), 6 Man. L.R. 610. In New Brunswick the decision whether to make a rule *nisi* final or not was held to be a proper 'action' in which a foreign commission could be ordered. *Pictou Bank* v *Trueman* (1894), 14 C.L.T. 267. In Ontario a judge of the Court of Appeal has no power to order a commission to take evidence abroad for use upon a compulsory arbitration pending before an arbitrator named by a judge of that court, *Re Macpherson and City of Toronto* (1894), 16 P.R. 230; whereas in Alberta it has been held that a district court judge acting as arbitrator under the Workmen's Compensation Act has authority to direct a foreign commission to take evidence which he can use in granting the award. *Bodner* v *West Canada Collieries* (1912), 3 w.w.r. 529 (Alta.).

15 *Clutterbuck* v *Jones* (1848), 6 Dow. & L. 251. But the order may still be granted before the issue is joined where justice requires, *Braun* v *Mollett* (1855), 16 c.b. 514, and where the applicant discloses the nature of the evidence to be adduced by the foreign witness, so that the court may gauge whether it is likely to be material and necessary. *Morrow* v *McDougald* (1894), 16 p.r. 129.

16 *Robins* v *The Empire Printing and Publishing Co.* (1892), 12 c.l.t. 199. Where the application is not *bona fide*, for example in order to keep a witness out of the witness box *(Lawson* v *Vacuum Brake, supra)* or to cause an unreasonable delay in the trial *(Antiseptic Bedding Co.* v *Gurofsky* (1913), 4 o.w.n. 1552), then the commission will be refused.

17 *Williams* v *Williams*, [1949] 1 w.w.r. 916 (Sask.). But where the court considers it necessary to examine the matter directly and orally, for instance when the issue involves, *inter alia*, complicated accounts executed within the jurisdiction, then the commission will not be granted. *Porter* v *Boulton* (1893), 15 p.r. 318 (Ont. c.a.).

18 *Ehrmann* v *Ehrmann*, [1896] 2 Ch. 611. Ontario courts no longer consider the controversiality of the facts in dispute to be a criterion in the exercise of their discretion. *Miewiadomski* v *Langdon*, [1956] o.w.n. 762, *Copps* v *Time International of Canada Ltd.*, [1964] 1 o.r. 229. But in Manitoba, this criterion is used in exceptional circumstances to justify refusing an order for a commission. *Tilton Tanning Corp.* v *Victoria Leather Jacket Co. Ltd.* (1969), 71 w.w.r. 477 (Man. c.a.). Where there were some witnesses in Ontario and a commission was applied for to examine others outside the province, the court refused to determine then whether the Ontario witnesses could give all the evidence that the proposed foreign witnesses could give, because doing that would amount to an evaluation of the evidence. *A.J. Freeman Ltd.* v *Springfield Fire Insurance Co.*, [1943] o.w.n. 574.

19 *Williams* v *Williams, supra* note 17. Where the only reasons given for inability to attend trial were 'engagements in England,' these were held to be inadequate in *Porter* v *Boulton, supra* note 17. The practice has been to consider the expense of coming to trial as a reason for non-attendance, for example, in

Haynes & Haynes v *Haynes* (1962), 35 d.l.r. (2d) 602 (b.c.) (where the witness was also old and infirm). But expense of travel is not of itself sufficient legal ground for granting a commission. *Macaulay* v *Glass* (1902), 47 Sol. J. 71.

20 *Williams* v *Williams, supra* note 17.

21 *Laing* v *Northern Life Assurance Co.* (1918), 14 Alta. l.r. 140.

22 *New* v *Burns* (1895), 64 l.j.q.b. 104; *Lunney* v *Welland Securities Ltd.*, [1939] o.w.n. 80; and see *Dow & A.C. Canada* v *Brady*, [1944] o.w.n. 633. An exception to the rule is found where the defendant is resident within the jurisdiction at the start of the action and afterwards goes abroad. *Ferguson* v *Millican* (1905), 11 o.l.r., at 41. One should also note that on a counter-claim the plaintiff 'becomes' a defendant and thus fits into the rule. *Levi* v *Edwards* (1905), 5 o.w.r. 83.

23 *Banque Franco-Egyptienne* v *Lutsher* (1879), 41 l.t. 468. There the foreign plaintiffs' interest was comparatively small and they were unwilling to prosecute their claim. Whereas in *Mills* v *Small* (1907), 9 o.w.r. 307 when a nominal plaintiff in Ontario sued on behalf of the real plaintiffs in the us, the latter were allowed to be examined on commission provided the defendant was paid security for costs of the commission.

24 *Stewart* v *Battery Light Co.* (1913), 25 o.w.r. 189. In *Kenneth* v *Gill* (1969), 71 w.w.r. 1 (Alta. c.a.), the court held that an application by a defendant resident outside the jurisdiction to have his evidence taken on commission should not, if there are good reasons for the application, be refused on the ground only that the plaintiff would be deprived of his right to cross-examine the defendant in open court. This consideration, though important, ought not to outweigh others.

25 *Re Boyse* (1882), 20 Ch. D. 760.

26 *Ehrmann* v *Ehrmann, supra* note 18; *Giberson & Brown* v *Atkins (E.C.) & Co.* (1917), 24 b.c.r. 19.

27 Supreme Court Act, r.s.c. c s-19 (1970). S 86 gives the governor general in council such power. Similar provisions are found in the Ontario Judicature Act, r.s.o. c 228, s 55 (1970) which gives this power to the lieutenant governor in council.

28 See Canada Evidence Act, r.s.c. c e10, ss 49–51 (1970); The Exchequer Court Act, r.s.c. c e11, s 61 (1970), of Federal Court Act, 1970, Can., c 1, s 54. Ontario Evidence Act, r.s.o. c 151, s 46 (1970); Commissioners

for Taking Affidavits Act, R.S.O. c 72 (1970); Notaries Act, R.S.O. c 300 (1970); Saskatchewan Evidence Act, R.S.S. c 80, s 49 (1965); Manitoba Evidence Act, R.S.M. c E150, s 63 (1970); New Brunswick Commissioners for Taking Affidavits Act, R.S.N.B. c 32, etc (1952).

29 *E.R.C.O.* v *Crane,* [1959] O.W.N. 241.

30 *Newman* v *Martin,* [1952] O.W.N. 786.

31 *Chaplin* v *Puttick,* [1898] 2 Q.B. 160.

32 *Clark* v *Union Fire Insurance Co.: Chabot's Case* (1884), 10 P.R. 413.

33 *Coleman* v *Bank of Montreal* (1894), 16 P.R. 159.

34 *Lemoine* v *MacKay* (1903), 2 O.W.R. 408 (S.C.).

35 *Mulligan* v *White* (1887), 7 C.L.T. 416. See also Ontario rules:

279 1 Unless otherwise directed, the examination shall be upon oral questions to be reduced into writing and returned with the commission; and notice of the execution of the commission shall be given to the opposite party, if, within the time prescribed by the order, he gives the name and the address of a person resident within two miles of the place where the commission is to be executed, on whom such notice may be served.

2 If no agent is named or the name or address given proves to be illusory or fictitious, or if the party so notified fails to attend pursuant to the notice, the commission may be executed ex parte.

280 Where the examination is to take place upon written interrogatories, the interrogatories in chief shall be delivered to the opposite party eight days before the issue of the commission, and the cross-interrogatories shall be delivered to the opposite party within four days after the receipt of the interrogatories in chief, and in default of cross-interrogatories being so delivered, the commission may be executed without cross-interrogatories.

281 The witnesses shall be examined on oath, affirmation or otherwise in accordance with the law of the country in which the commission is executed.

Also, s 64 Exchequer Court Act, *supra* note 28, allowed examination on interrogatories if unable to attend trial, but this provision does not extend to examination of a party giving evidence on his own behalf. Now see rule 477 of the Federal Court.

36 *Darling* v *Darling* (1880), 8 P.R. 391.

37 *Decrean* v *Vancanneyt* (1913), 4 W.W.R. 1235 (Alta.). But s 89, Supreme Court Act, *supra* note 28, and s 47, Ontario Evidence Act, *supra* note 28, declare that informality is not to be an objection to the admissibility of commission evidence. Furthermore, it seems that objections to the admissibility of evidence (*Robinson* v *Davies* (1879), 5 Q.B.D. 26 (D.C.)) and to answering certain questions at the examination (*Hickey* v *Le Gresley* (1906), 4 W.L.R. 40 (Man.)) should be raised at the time. But even if the commissioner accepts inadmissible evidence, the court can exclude it at trial. *Tinney* v *Tinney,* [1945] 1 W.W.R. 390 (Man.). And rule 339 of P.E.I. Supreme Court rules obliges the examiner merely to note any questions objected to but he is powerless to decide upon their materiality or relevancy.

38 *A.C. Spark Plug Co. Ltd.* v *Logan,* [1934] O.W.N. 358.

39 *Loveden* v *Milford* (1794), 4 Bro. C.C. 540.

40 *Colville* v *Johnston* (1871), 5 P.R. 462.

41 *Mulholland* v *Spratt,* [1952] Ex. C.R. 233.

42 *Reford* v *MacDonald* (1864), 14 C.P. 150; *Gendron* v *Manitoba Milling Co.* (1891), 7 Man. L.R. 484. See Ontario rules 270, 279, 286, and s 4, Ontario Evidence Act, *supra* note 28. Also s 97, Supreme Court Act, *supra* note 28, declares that commission evidence taken abroad must be proved by an affidavit of due taking. Rule 339 of P.E.I. Supreme Court Rules details the following: 'If the witness shall refuse to sign the depositions the examiner shall sign the same. The examiner may put down any particular question or answer if there shall appear any special reason for so doing, and put any question to the witness as to the meaning of any answer or as to any matter arising in the course of the examination.'

Similar provisions are found in rule 401 Nova Scotia Supreme Court Rules, rule 494 British Columbia Supreme Court Rules, order 37 rule 12 New Brunswick Supreme Court Rules. Furthermore, rule 346 Prince Edward Island Supreme Court Rules allows the examiner to submit his own special report touching the examination. Similar provisions to this section are to be found in rule 299 Saskatchewan Queen's Bench Rules, rule 499 British Columbia Supreme Court Rules, order 37 New Brunswick Supreme Court Rules, rule 271 Alberta Supreme Court Rules. Finally, it is to be noted that rule 291 of the Queen's Bench Rules of Saskatchewan obliges the party applicant to provide the commissioner with a copy of the pleadings or other documents necessary to inform him of the issue in the cause. Also rule 288 of the Alberta Supreme Court Rules provides for sending a copy of the relevant rules to the examiner abroad.

43 *Supra* note 28, ss 45–6. In addition where a petitioner in a divorce action was examined on commission in Ontario, she was afforded the full protection of the Manitoba Evidence Act with respect to questions of adultery. *Purdy* v *Purdy*, [1944] 2 w.w.r. 486 (Man.).

44 Rule 277 Ontario Rules of Practice.

45 *Smith* v *Greey* (1886), 6 c.l.t. 88, in which case the court allowed the commission to be opened before trial and ruled that the parties were thereupon free to make use of the knowledge so obtained. See also *Richardson* v *McMillan* (1908), 9 w.l.r. 632 (Man.).

46 *Wessels* v *Wessels* (1941), 56 b.c.r. 239.

47 *Marks* v *Marks* (1907), 13 b.c.r. 161. In this connection it should be pointed out that documentary evidence may be included here. It seems the forum will more readily allow in this type of evidence where it is valid by the *lex loci actus*. For example, in a claim for an estate located in Saskatchewan a document referred to as 'an act of testimonial disposition' which was a statement made by independent witnesses as to the family history of the applicant was admissible under s 49 (1) (g) Saskatchewan Evidence Act because it was properly deposed before a Soviet notary public. *Stasun* v *Nesteroff et al.* (1966), 57 w.w.r. 586 (Surr. Ct.) (Sask.). See also s 50, Ontario Evidence Act, which declares that a person probating in Ontario under a will made abroad can, after one month's notice to the opposite party, annex the will or a copy under seal of the foreign court which will act as *prima facie* evidence of the will and the validity of its contents in the Ontario probate court.

48 *Alberta Wheat Pool Elevators Ltd.* v *Ship Ensenada*, [1952] Ex. C.R. 61.

49 Rule 287 of the Ontario Rules of Practice. But in *Fergus* v *McIntosh* it was held that the costs of the commission were costs in the cause ((1835), 2 n.b.r. (Ber.) 173). In another case, when the defendant left the jurisdiction at the start of the action and obtained a commission to be examined in the Northwest

Territories, he was obliged to pay part of the plaintiff's costs. *Ferguson* v *Millican, supra* note 22, at 35. Also in *Kleiman* v *Cannon*, [1938] o.w.n. 106 it was stated that usually a plaintiff applying for a commission will have to pay the defendants costs but the same is not true in the reverse circumstances.

50 *Hawes, Gibson & Co.* v *Hawes* (1911), 3 o.w.n. 1229.

51 *Rondot* v *Monetary Times Printing Co.* (1898), 18 p.r. 141 (c.a.). See *Bartlett* v *Higgins*, [1901] 2 k.b. 230, where the commission was ruled necessary for justice even though unnecessary with regard to the particular event; and see *Kelly's America Ltd.* v *Smith* (1956), 19 w.w.r. 580 (Sask.).

52 Evidence was secured in the ussr on the basis of a Letter of Request from the Supreme Court of British Columbia to which was attached documents and a series of questions to be answered by the witnesses to be examined, all of which documentation was translated into the Russian language and transmitted to the Foreign Ministry in the ussr requesting that the documents be transmitted to the appropriate Soviet judicial authorities for completion and return (1966), 4 *Can. Y.B. Int'l L.* 297.

53 'International Civil Procedure: Role of External Affairs,' *supra* note 12, at 93.

54 *Ehrmann* v *Ehrmann, supra* note 18.

55 *Keogh* v *Brady* (1905), 6 o.w.r. 552 (d.c.).

56 *Ross* v *Woodford*, [1894] 1 Ch. 42.

57 *Quality Steels (London) Ltd.* v *Atlas Steels Ltd.*, [1950] o.w.n. 24.

58 *Nacevich* v *Nacevich*, [1962] o.w.n. 105.

59 Eg, between Canada and Austria, [1935] can. t.s. no 16 and [1952] can. t.s. no 3; Belgium, [1928] can. t.s. no 16 and [1937] can. t.s. no 4; Czechoslovakia, [1928] can. t.s. no 7 and [1937] can. t.s. no 5; Denmark, [1936] can. t.s. no 4; Finland, [1936] can. t.s. no 5; France, [1928] can. t.s. no 15; Germany, [1935] can. t.s. no 11 and [1953] can. t.s. no 17; Greece, [1938] can. t.s. no 11; Hungary, [1939] can. t.s. no 6; Iraq, [1937] can. t.s. no 12; Italy, [1935] can. t.s. no 14; the Netherlands, [1936] can. t.s. no 2; Norway, [1935] can. t.s. no 15; Poland, [1935] can. t.s. no 18; Portugal, [1935] can. t.s. no 17; Spain, [1935] can. t.s. no 12; Sweden, [1935] can. t.s. no 13; Turkey, [1935] can. t.s. no 19; Yugoslavia, [1939] can. t.s. no 4.

60 Ibid. For similar provisions see Canada-Austria convention, article 7(b); Canada-Netherlands convention, article 7(b).

61 See also Canada-Sweden convention, article 8(d); Canada-Portugal convention, article 7(d); Canada-Norway convention, article 7(d).

62 See also article 7(f) Canada-Greece convention.

63 Article 7(f) of the Canada-Netherlands convention excludes this ground of refusal but includes the others.

64 Article 6 of the Canada-France convention excludes this ground of refusal but includes the others.

65 Article 8(a), Canada-Greece convention.

66 Canada-Italy convention, article 11(b).

67 Canada-Greece convention, article 8(d).

68 Article 12 of the Canada-Germany convention states in addition that 'the court applied to shall, in the case of subjects or citizens of the Contracting Party making the request, take the necessary steps to secure the attendance of and the giving of evidence by witnesses and other persons to be examined, and the production of documents, making use, if necessary, of its compulsory powers.' See also Canada-Italy convention, article 12.

69 Canada-Spain convention, article 9(d).

70 See Canada-Denmark convention, article 9(d).

71 Article 10, Canada-Italy convention, and Canada-Germany convention, article 10.

72 (1965), 3 Can. Y. B. Int'l L. 345.

73 (1958), 14 D.L.R. (2d) 343. Also B. Sischy, 'Evidence in Aid of Foreign Tribunals' (1959), 1 Osgoode Hall L. J. 49.

74 Szaszy, International Civil Procedure (1967), at 652.

75 (1856), 19 & 20 Vict., c 113. In Saskatchewan see rule 310 of the Queen's Bench Rules. See also s 65(1) Nova Scotia Evidence Act, R.S.N.S. c 94 (1967). In Quebec see Special Procedure Act, R.S.Q. c 22, ss 16–27 (1964). See also L. Kos-Rabcewicz-Zubrowski (1964), 13 Int. & Comp. L. Q. 270.

76 Supra note 28.

77 Supra note 28, s 43 et seq.; Canada Evidence Act, supra note 28, s 49; Saskatchewan Evidence Act, supra note 5, c 80 which allows the local court to make appropriate orders to comply with the foreign request once it is satisfied of the authenticity of that request. Also see s 64, Nova Scotia Evidence Act, supra note 75, s 84, Manitoba Evidence Act, R.S.M. c E150 (1970), and rule 71 of the British Columbia Supreme Court Rules.

78 Supra note 73.

79 Re McCarthy and Menin v U.S. Securities and Exchange Commission, [1963] 2 O.R. 154 (C.A.).

80 Re Geneva v Comtesse, [1959] O.R. 668, 23 D.L.R. (2d) 506.

81 R.C.A. v Rauland Corp. et al., [1956] 1 Q.B. 618; Re R.C.A. v Rauland Corp. et al., [1956] O.R. 650, 5 D.L.R. (2d) 424, 26 C.P.R. 29, 16 Fox Pat. c. 46; Re Raychem Corp. v Canusa Coating Systems Inc., [1971] 1 O.R. 192, reversing [1970] 1 O.R. 448, 8 D.L.R. (3d) 614. Re General Fire Services Ltd. v Foundation of Canada Ltd. (1971), 17 D.L.R. (3d) 501 (Sask.).

82 Supra note 73.

83 Geneva v Comtesse, supra note 80.

84 Re Barcelona T.L. & P. Co., [1960] O.W.N. 415.

85 Ibid.

86 Re Isler (1915), 34 O.L.R. 375.

87 National Telefilm Associates Inc. v United Artists Corp. et al., supra note 73.

88 For example, see s 84(3) Manitoba Evidence Act.

89 Paramount Film Distributing Corp. v Ram, [1954] O.W.N. 753 (H.C.J.).

90 R.C.A. v Rauland Corp., [1956] O.R. 630.

91 Sischy, supra note 73, at 57.

92 Spink v Sill (1916), 10 O.W.N. 404.

93 Henderson v Hall (1880), 8 P.R. 353; Bedell v Gefaell (No. 2), [1938] O.R. 726, at 729.

94 In Quebec see Code of Civil Procedure, article 136.

95 Article 3 (a), Canada-Austria convention.

96 Ibid, article 3(e).

97 See Canada-Turkey convention, article 6.

98 Canada-Austria convention, article 4(d).

99 Canada-Poland convention, article 4(a).

100 Canada-Greece convention, article 3(d).

101 Canada-Austria convention, article 3(g).

102 See 'International Civil Procedure: Role of External Affairs,' supra note 12, at 94–5.

103 [1936] CAN. T. S. no 4.

104 For other countries see article 14, Canada-Germany convention; article 11, Canada-Austria convention; article 12, Canada-Turkey convention; article 11, Canada-Sweden convention; article 13, Canada-Spain convention; article 11, Canada-Portugal convention; article 12, Canada-Poland convention; article 11, Canada-Norway convention; but not so far with France or Italy. See also the 1954 Hague Convention on Civil Procedure, articles 17–19 and 1965 Hague Convention on the Service Abroad of Judicial and Extra-Judicial Documents in Civil and Commercial Matters, article 12, not signed by Canada.

35/Sovereignty and Canada-US Co-operation in North American Defence

The Foreign Policy Review went well beyond considerations of security. Of necessity much of it was devoted to the central problem facing Canada – how to live distinct from but in harmony with the United States, the greatest power on earth. – Secretary of State for External Affairs, Ottawa, 14 December 1970.

After a period of reappraisal probably unprecedented in its range and depth in Canada's history, the government announced in 1971 the shape of defence policy for the years ahead. The review began in April 1968 with the assumption of office of Prime Minister Trudeau, who was committed to a thorough review of Canada's defence policies and of possible options or alternatives. The review culminated three years and four months later with the publication of the government's white paper on defence in August 1971. During the intervening years the review had engaged a wide range of Canadians in a lively debate between the government (and occasionally between members of the government), parliament, the bureaucracy, armed services, press, academics, and the public at large. A flood of statements, reports, hearings, seminars, articles, editorials, and books on foreign and defence policies lifted public debate of the issues to a new level of understanding and sophistication.

Concurrently, the process of policy formulation within the government was gradual and cumulative. The prime minister's statement of 3 April 1969 outlined in broad strokes future defence priorities, including a reaffirmation of Canada's participation in NATO and in the joint Canada-US agreements for the defence of North America, a partial redeployment of Canadian forces stationed in Europe, and a new emphasis on protection of sovereignty at home. Over the months a succession of decisions were announced by the Department of National Defence, elaborating on these policies in operational and budgetary terms: for example, force levels, organizational changes, and capital programs. On the premise that defence policy flows from foreign policy, the government's approach to defence issues was placed in a conceptual framework and received further refinement in the white paper entitled *Foreign Policy for Canadians*, published in June 1970. The appointment in September 1970, of Mr Donald S. Macdonald as minister of national defence in succession to Mr Léo Cadieux gave fresh impetus to the development of the 1971 defence white paper, as a logical follow-on and companion piece to the foreign policy paper.

One of the basic postulates adopted by the government in these papers was that 'the United States is Canada's closest friend and ally and will remain so.'[1] The foreign policy paper described the rationale for the decision to remain an ally and to continue to co-operate in continental and NATO defence in terms of 'the Government's determination to help prevent war between the super-powers by sharing in the responsibility for maintaining stable nuclear deterrence and by participation in NATO policy-making in both political and military fields.'[2] And the defence white paper elaborated further:

> ... co-operation with the United States in North American defence will remain essential so long as our joint security depends on stability in the strategic military balance. Canada's objective is to make, within the limits of our resources, an effective contribution to continued stability by assisting in the surveillance and warning systems, and in the protection of the U.S. retaliatory capability as necessary. Co-operation between Canada and the U.S. in the joint defence of North America is vital for sovereignty and security.[3]

SOVEREIGNTY AND SECURITY

While reasserting the importance of defence co-operation with the United States and other allies, the government's white papers also focused on a closely related aspect which had been highlighted in public debate. This was the question of Canadian sovereignty which became a major theme in the new Canadian defence posture. At an early stage in the review, the prime minister set defence policy in this new context: 'Our first priority in our defence policy is the protection of Canadian sovereignty in all the dimensions that it means.'[4] The first of four basic roles for the Canadian forces was described as 'the surveillance of our own territory and coastlines, i.e. the protection of our sovereignty.' The second priority was the defence of North America in co-operation with US forces, followed by NATO and peacekeeping roles.

The white papers identified various dimensions of sovereignty which had implications for future defence planning. First of all the defence white paper recognized that security against the threat of armed attack, the traditional concern of military forces, was at the core of the meaning of sovereignty for Canada as for any other nation: 'Canada's sovereignty and independence depend ultimately on security from armed attack. In this sense, the contribution of the Canadian Forces to the prevention of war is a vital and direct contribution to safeguarding our sovereignty and independence.' This objective was to be pursued through collective security arrangements. But there were other challenges to Canada's sovereignty, 'mainly non-military in character,' which 'may be more likely to arise during the 1970s' and which 'must be met exclusively by Canada.' Greater emphasis was to be placed on the role of the forces in responding, together with the civil agencies, to non-military challenges such as possible infringements of Canadian fisheries regulations, dangers of oil or other pollution, especially in the north, threats to civil order, and generally 'on projects which relate to their capabilities to respond efficiently and promptly to their basic defence roles.' Emphasis was also to be placed on carrying out defence activities in Canada by Canadian personnel: 'The Government has decided that in normal peacetime circumstances the guiding principle should continue to be that, to the greatest extent feasible, defence activities on Canadian territory will be carried out by members of the Canadian Armed Forces.'[5]

The defence white paper also made reference to the surveillance role of the forces in the context of the government's objective 'to continue effective occupation of

Canadian territory.' Here was another dimension of sovereignty, more familiar to international lawyers than to military officers; that is, upholding sovereign title of a state against any competing claims of other states under international law.[6]

The government had thus decided to initiate a 'process of adjusting the balance between Canadian defence interests to ensure that priorities for defence were responsive to national interests and international developments.[7] The balance was to embrace purely national interests as well as collective security interests and traditional military roles as well as quasimilitary, police, or civilian roles in a variety of fields of domestic interest.

At first sight, sovereignty and collective security might seem to be a contradiction of terms. The concept of sovereignty, whatever else it may mean (and jurists have debated this at length and inconclusively), implies freedom of action, freedom to deploy forces for independent purposes. Collective security requires, on the other hand, political solidarity and military co-operation between allies and therefore voluntary limitations on the freedom of action of each. If either principle were to be pressed to its logical extreme, they would come into collision. If the Canadian armed forces spent all their time and resources on purely domestic or civilian missions, they would have little capability to respond to any military threat. They would be unable 'to respond efficiently and promptly to their basic defence roles.' If they spent all their time in training and readiness for a military threat under mutual defence arrangements, they would have little contribution to make to other Canadian concerns. One can, however, identify activities where there is little or no incompatibility. For example, greater use of the Dew Line and Pine Tree Radar Line in support of the civilian air traffic control network (as envisaged in the white paper) need not impair and may in fact contribute to a high level of effectiveness of the system in its primary military function. Similarly, employment of a destroyer escort on part-time fishery protection patrol need not downgrade the effectiveness of the ship as a submarine killer. On the other hand, it is clear that it would be inefficient to utilize highly sophisticated, specialized, and expensive military equipment and personnel on a continuing basis on jobs which could be performed as effectively and more cheaply by a civilian agency or private contractor. The defence white paper indicated that the government intended to see the problem as that of striking an appropriate balance between a totality of national needs which must be met by deployment of relatively limited national resources – military and civilian – in accordance with overall priorities.

Involvement in domestic or civilian tasks was not, of course, new to the Canadian forces. They had always been involved to some degree in such tasks, including the administration of unemployment centres during the great depression, map surveys and communications in the early postwar years, and national disaster and search and rescue activities whenever the need arose. What the defence white paper outlined was therefore less a new departure than a shift of emphasis, a heightened responsiveness on the part of Canadian forces to domestic demands on government.[8]

The new responsiveness may be traced to yet another aspect of sovereignty which ran like a thread through the review and which had important implications for Canadian defence policy and Canada-US defence relations in particular. This was a growing concern amongst Canadians about American influence. In public statements at home and on visits to Washington and Moscow, the prime minister expressed this concern about Canadian dependence on the US, including military dependence. The foreign policy paper spoke of the economic, military, and political dominance of the United States. Here, too, there was a need for balance, and a 'continuing search for countervailing factors to offset the pressure of its complex involvement with the United States.'

> The problems the European nations face in their relationships with the predominant power are magnified in Canada by geographic location, economic interdependence, the shared defence of the continent and the growing homogeneity of North American Society ... Canada contributes to its own defence but, like the countries of Western Europe, relies ultimately on American military power for its security.

The white papers offered no final answers but they did pose the questions with a fresh emphasis. Interdependence and independence; can we have both? How much of each? If hard choices have to be made, how do we maintain a proper balance? What are the countervailing factors? These questions were implicit in the way the situation was defined as 'the complex problem of living distinct from but in harmony with the world's most powerful and dynamic nation, the United States.' In this situation, the white papers in effect asked: How does the government 'manage its complex relations with the United States, especially as regards trade and finance, energies and resources, continental defence?'[9]

There have, of course, been those who have questioned whether it is possible to 'manage' our defence relations at all. It has been asserted that Canada, having become locked into a system of military dependence, must accept that any decision-making of consequence will take place in Washington rather than in Ottawa. This pessimistic refrain is not new to Canadians. Frank Underhill expressed his concern in a historical perspective: 'In 1940 we passed from the British century to the American century. We became dependent upon the United States for our security. We have, therefore, no choice but to follow American leadership.' And in *Lament for a Nation* George Grant spoke in harsher terms: 'Of all the aspects of our society, the military is the most directly an errand boy for the Americans.'[10] Further, an American scholar recently described Canada as being 'caught in a dilemma of Kafkaesque proportions':

> ... the closer Canada's defence association with the United States, the greater the danger of United States influence and loss of Canadian identity ... The one force (United States) that guarantees Canada's security, and thereby eliminates a second possible security threat (USSR), itself then constitutes a national security threat of a different nature and magnitude, but of no less relevance to Canada's existence and identity.[11]

To put these fears into perspective, it is useful to recall that there has existed in Canada since the Ogdensburg agreement of 1940 a broad acceptance of the desirability of a Canadian involvement in continental defence arrangements. As John Holmes has pointed out, the defence partnership was never forced on an unwilling Canada; it was a compact based upon mutual interest in the face of a commonly perceived threat.[12] This is not to say that over the years there has been no controversy over the nature and extent of Canada's contribution to the North American Air Defence Command (NORAD) and continental defences generally. One of the most turbulent political controversies in Canada's history was precipitated in 1963 by a dispute over the acquisition of nuclear weapons for Canadian forces in NORAD and NATO. For the second time in Canadian history a government was obliged to resign following a vote of non-confidence in Parliament. Throughout this period, however, general public support for the principle of NORAD as a joint command system for close defence co-operation with the US remained fairly constant.[13] In spite of differing views on nuclear weapons there was no significant disagreement between political parties on the underlying issue of defence co-operation. All-party agreement was reached for example on the first report of the Special Committee on National Defence following the fall of the Diefenbaker government in February 1963 and the return of the Liberals in the elections of April 1963. This report recommended unanimously that 'Canada remain a member of NORAD, since the defence of North America is a joint responsibility,' and as long as the bomber threat continued 'Canada must share in the defence against that threat.'[14]

In more recent years this underlying consensus has been subject to serious strain. A primary cause has been technological: the shift from bombers to missiles in the strategic nuclear balance. Canadian territory and airspace interposed between the US and USSR was of vital importance when the strategic balance rested entirely on long-range bombers. In the years following Sputnik in 1957 intercontinental missiles gradually became the main element of the balance, followed by an increasing number of missile-launching submarines and a declining number of bombers.[15] When a new parliamentary committee examined North American air defence in 1969, all-party agreement was no longer obtainable. The majority report of the committee recommended that Canada should remain in NORAD without fundamental changes in existing arrangements.[16] However, three New Democratic party members and one Liberal member of the committee issued dissenting opinions calling for Canadian withdrawal from continental bomber defence.[17]

Other factors were also at work, chipping away at the edges of the consensus. An increasing Canadian concern about economic and cultural dependence on the US led to a more critical view of joint defence arrangements. The Vietnam war eroded one of the basic assumptions Canadians had held through the postwar period that there was a fundamental identity of interest and a 'sense of shared purpose' with the US on major world issues. It was assumed that if the US was at war, Canada was bound to be at war as well. Now the US was in fact at war and Canadians wished to have no part of it. And yet could they say they had no part in it as long as components of the Canadian input to the defence production sharing pool found their way, however unobtrusively, to Vietnam? With a moderation of East-West antagonisms and growing signs of north-south divisions, Canadians saw new avenues opening up in the pursuit of peace: arms control negotiations, political reconciliation, and development programs in the third world. A contribution to defence and deterrence was only one way to help strengthen international security. According to some, it was perhaps not the most effective, especially for a middle power with greater freedom to manoeuvre and experiment than the superpowers. Finally, internal problems of national unity and regional disparities forced Canadians to re-examine their priorities in the allocation of limited national resources.

Nevertheless the compact held. The Trudeau government's decision to continue to play a part in joint continental defence created few ripples on Canadian political waters, and was generally well received by defence critics.[19] The theoretical alternative of non-alignment had been rejected by Canadian parliamentary and public opinion, even while recognizing that alignments were loosening up in an increasingly polycentric world. The announced changes in policy within the continental framework demonstrated, once again, that compact did not mean passivity and that Canadians were not relieved of the need to make their own judgments and consult their own interests in national terms. The white papers could thus be viewed as representing yet another stage in the progressive redefinition of the terms and conditions of the compact.

DEFENCE FOR WHAT PURPOSES?

Given a broad commitment to joint defence, what are the real choices open to Canada? James Eayrs has suggested that, historically, states have maintained military forces for one or more of six basic purposes: in a *strategic* role, to attack or to deter or defend against attack; for *insurance* purposes, just in case they might be needed; to help maintain internal *law and order*; for *modernization and development*; in a *ceremonial* function; and finally in a *diplomatic* role.[20] This is a useful way of looking at the first layer of broad choices open to governments and voters. Although one could argue, as Eayrs does, that the Canadian military establishment serves as a form of insurance as well as in a diplomatic role, successive Canadian governments have viewed it primarily as fulfilling a strategic purpose, namely, to deter or defend against attack by the Soviet Union. As we have seen above, the present defence white paper places the Canadian contribution to North American defence in the context of the strategic military balance, while at the same time stressing the side benefits which can flow from the forces in domestic fields akin to Eayrs's 'law and order' and 'development' categories. Given this fundamental and long-standing decision to maintain forces in a co-operative framework primarily for strategic purposes, a further layer of options presents itself. In which of a multiplicity of possible joint defence programs (or, in today's defence parlance, weapons systems) should Canada participate? To what extent? And under what ground rules?

STRATEGIC DUEL: CANADA'S CHOICE OF WEAPONS

The present intercontinental strategic balance between the two superpowers is made up of six elements; three offensive systems and three defensive. The response to the intercontinental missile (ICBM) is the antiballistic missile (ABM). The submarine-launched ballistic missile (SLBM) is tracked by antisubmarine warfare (ASW) ships and aircraft, and the bomber has its counterpart antibomber defences. Because of the cost of military technology, it is well beyond the reach of middle powers such as Canada to maintain forces in all six systems. Only the two superpowers, at great cost, can maintain a panoply of both offensive and defensive weapons, and they are groping their way towards agreements which will perhaps enable them to put limitations on their arms competition.

Canada has chosen to take active part (that is, with a force contribution) in two systems: antibomber and ASW defences. Canada also co-operates passively in two other systems by granting US Strategic Air Command bombers overflight facilities, and by allowing the Ballistic Missile Early Warning System (BMEWS) communications link to pass through Canada to NORAD headquarters in Colorado Springs, Colorado. Canada has decided not to participate in ICBM, ABM, and SLBM forces. These choices reflect a range of political decisions or preferences not only in the domain of military strategy but including historical considerations (Canada's specialization in the ASW field during World War II) as well as geographical (long coastlines, territory interposed on the main bomber approach routes between the USA and USSR) and economic (the prohibitive cost of missile weaponry) factors. In 1946 Canada opted to refrain from producing an independent nuclear weapon capability, even though Canada emerged from the war with an advanced nuclear technology and large uranium resources. In 1968 Canadian reluctance to take part in the embryonic US plans for an ABM system found formal expression in the text of the renewal of the NORAD Agreement. In the 1971 white paper it was announced that the BOMARC antiaircraft missiles located in Canada would be retired, taking into account changes in the strategic situation. Furthermore, the government gave notice that it was 'not prepared to devote substantial sums to new equipment or facilities for use only for active antibomber defences in the future.'

At a more fundamental level the white paper recognized that increased military strength did not necessarily mean increased security; strength could undermine security, by provoking suspicions, tensions, and a futher spiral in the arms race: 'The fearsome logic of mutual deterrence is clearly not a satisfactory long-term solution to the problem of preventing world conflict.' Again a balance was to be struck between a contribution to the system of stable mutual deterrence and efforts to promote political reconciliation and arms control agreements between East and West.

Thus an assessment of what Canada's strategic role should be flowed from a number of interrelated and overlapping questions: What is the strategic threat? In what areas can Canada best contribute to deter or defend against that threat? What can we do best, as distinct from our allies, given our location, resources, manpower, and skills? What effect will our choices have on the stability of the strategic balance and on our capacity to contribute to arms control negotiations and the pursuit of détente? These questions involved difficult and complex strategic issues. The expertise and resources of the US government in the intelligence gathering and technological fields were formidable; in the words of one observer, there was a tendency 'to turn bilateral discussions into briefing sessions in which Canadians are awed into sceptical silence.'[21] But information, however essential and however skilfully sifted and marshalled, does not provide political answers. The tragedy of Vietnam highlighted the limitations of military technology and systems analysis. During the review there was a greater recognition that policy depends ultimately upon judgment and perspective, where the smaller ally is at no special disadvantage, and may in fact be able to cut through the inertia and distortions which can beset the more unwieldy policy-making machinery of the larger ally.

HOW MUCH DEFENCE IS ENOUGH?

Having accepted certain roles and rejected others, Canadians must further determine the *extent* to which they wish to contribute. The only firm rule is that there is no firm rule. The 1958 NORAD Agreement states that the command 'will include such combat units and individuals as are specifically allocated to it by the two governments.' Canada has for some years contributed, *inter alia*, three fighter interceptor squadrons totalling 48 aircraft. This now represents 11 per cent of NORAD's interceptor strength, since the US interceptor force declined from 40 squadrons in 1964 to 27 in 1972.[22] Cost-sharing arrangements for the three major electronic warning networks set up in the postwar period varied in each case. The Pinetree Radar Agreement (1951) provided for 'approximately' one-third Canadian and two-thirds US financing.[23] The Mid-Canada Line or 'McGill Fence' (closed down in 1964) was constructed and operated by Canada. The DEW Line (operational in 1957) was constructed and has been operated at US cost with a Canadian contribution limited to provision of the sites and Canadian military personnel. In 1969–70 Canada contributed approximately 8 to 10 per cent of the overall costs of maintaining and operating the NORAD system at an overall level of approximately $135 million in annual operating costs, while the US contributed in the order of $1.76 billion.[24] Although impossible to quantify, the equation would be incomplete if there was no mention of the use of Canadian airspace, territory and facilities by US forces for aerospace defence.

Canada's stake in maritime defence of North America is considerably larger, but in relative terms the contribution of the two countries in the maritime field is more difficult to measure since ships and maritime aircraft can be used not only in defence of North America against submarine-launched ballistic missiles but also in other roles including purely national or non-military roles, as well as in distant waters on military missions unrelated to North American defence. Moreover the Canadian contribution is changing. The defence white paper announced that 'the present degree of emphasis on anti-submarine warfare directed against submarine-launched ballistic missiles (SLBMs) will be reduced in favour of the maritime roles.' In 1969/70 the total operating cost of Canada's maritime forces, virtually all of which were assigned to roles in defence of Canada and North America, amounted to $242 million.[25]

In testimony before the House Committee in 1969, Minister of National Defence Léo Cadieux was asked: 'How do you decide what is the right basis?' He replied: 'That is the problem. We contribute deployment forces which we think are adequate. The bill happens to be what it is ... We have been negotiating many times, as a matter of fact, for the manning of the radar stations. At times we have different trading arrangements with the Americans.' He concluded that it would not be in the Canadian interest to apply any fixed criterion or ratio, based on relative population or GNP.[26] The calculation of such a ratio would be enormously difficult and ultimately arbitrary, taking into account the variety of purposes – national, continental, and international – to which military forces may be put. Even if a realistically proportionate figure could be arrived at, it is doubtful that the Canadian public would accept the assumption that defence policy should be defined in terms of how much should be spent rather than what should be achieved, particularly if it were to involve a substantially bigger defence budget (the Canadian defence budget is currently about one-twenty-eighth that of the US, excluding the direct costs of the war in Vietnam).[27]

Part of the difficulty in measuring what may be a 'fair' or 'adequate' share is that a particular joint program may have costs or benefits for Canada which do not appear in the defence estimates. There may be related economic, political, and social issues which will affect the final bargain which is struck. For example, after studying Canada's maritime forces, the House Committee 'rejected the view that the development of maritime forces solely in terms of effective support for defence and foreign policy is either possible, given the economic, technological and social linkages existing, or desirable, given the order of national resources involved and the potential side benefits attainable through such linkages.'[28]

Again the principle was underlined that there was no necessary contradiction between making a contribution to the prevention of war through collective security arrangements on the one hand, and promoting purely national interests on the other. What was required was a calculation of possible trade-offs which might achieve benefits of different kinds at the same time. It might be considerably cheaper to have a new destroyer escort built outside the country, but in so doing the government would forego an opportunity to strengthen Canadian industrial and scientific capabilities (and inject capital into a hard-pressed maritime community). Similarly it might be cheaper to have interceptor aircraft engines overhauled in Dayton, Ohio, but the contract could be an important boost to the Winnipeg economy. The McGill Fence was undertaken at Canadian cost, but the program was seen to have important advantages in technological spin-off for the Canadian scientific community who designed it. Conversely, decisions which seek to maximize the ancillary benefits or non-military 'feedback' may, of course, impose some penalty in higher costs or reduced military effectiveness. Thus even though there may be a broad identity of views between Canada and the US on the military or strategic basis for a given joint program, there are often a variety of national interests – sometimes competing interests – at play in addition to the shared interest which brought the two parties to the negotiating table in the first place.

There are other 'linkages' which help determine, at least indirectly, what may be an appropriate Canadian or US contribution to joint defence. Both governments recognize that defence spending (and its side benefits) cannot be looked at in isolation from other non-military programs in an overall allocation of national resources. The US defense secretary in recent statements to Congress has laid new stress on the need to relate defence spending to the overall government effort in domestic programs as well as in furtherance of foreign policy objectives.

> Planning in the revised and revitalized National Security Council context now takes into account all assets available for achieving foreign policy objectives. The goals we seek for the enhancement of American and world interests – peace, freedom, social, economic and political development, broadening opportunities ... obviously cannot be achieved by means of direct military power alone.[29]

Similarly, the Canadian defence white paper stated: 'A decision on the appropriate size of the defence budget can be made only in the context of the Government's national priorities ... a judgement must be made on proposed defence activities in relation to other Government programmes.'

The new emphasis on sovereignty in Canadian defence policy necessarily implies some diversion of effort and capability from roles concerned with threats of armed conflict to roles concerned with peacetime or civilian tasks. The scale of the diversion remains to be seen as new equipment and roles are developed over a period of years. It need not be dramatic. As we have seen, multipurpose forces have in the past performed useful peacetime tasks in a number of areas without any significant diminution of their professional skills. It is not an either/or proposition but a question of optimizing the contribution which resources allocated to defence can make at the same time to the civilian sector, without unduly impairing their military effectiveness. There is a built-in 'regulator' in the form of basic budgetary principles: undue diversion of a military unit to a peacetime task will not in the long run be cost-effective; beyond a certain point it will be apparent that this may be an expensive way to get things done and that it might be better to hand the task over to a civilian agency of government or to a civilian contractor who does not require an elaborate and costly military training, discipline, and infrastructure. Another regulator is the assessment of needs for military forces in a high state of combat readiness. Units which spend most of their time on non-military employment will obviously begin to lose their specialized skills. An assessment of national needs in terms of the level and readiness of forces required for defence and deterrence is again ultimately a political judgment. Such a judgment was made by the minister of national defence in his preface to the 1971 defence white paper:

> There has been increasing scepticism about the traditional roles of the Armed Forces as we move further and further from the last time the Forces were engaged in combat operations. Moreover, at a time when national social and economic needs are considerable, there is substantial pressure to cut defence expenditures.

A judgment of this kind is also implicit in the government's decision to freeze the budget on the Department of National Defence over the past three years, while increasing, for example, allocations to the Canadian International Development Agency in the same period by 28 per cent.[30]

THE ADMINISTRATION OF JOINT CANADA-US DEFENCE PROGRAMS

Finally, having decided in which joint defence programs Canada should participate, and to what extent, our theoretical Canadian policy-maker must consider how these programs are to be implemented, co-ordinated, and directed in terms of a continuing process of intergovernmental relations.

The unique complexity of the Canada-US defence relationship is reflected in the intergovernmental machinery which has been set up over the years for the conduct of these relations. During the foreign and defence policy review, the Department of External Affairs prepared a memorandum for the House Committee describing the various instruments for conducting relations with the US.[31] Apart from the traditional diplomatic channels, the memorandum listed seventeen joint Canada-US institutions. Of these, eight were concerned in whole or in part and at various levels with aspects of continental defence co-operation. In addition, as the memorandum pointed out, ministers and officials have developed the practice of direct, informal discussions with their counterparts in Washington or Ottawa. A statistical summary of visits during 1968 and 1969 suggested that more official business has been conducted in this manner by the two defence departments than by any other pair of governmental departments or agencies.

The NORAD system, with its headquarters at Colorado Springs, Colorado, and its radars and operational units spanning the continent, is commonly regarded as the core of the defence partnership. But as its name indicates it is restricted to air defences and it is the only joint program which is fully integrated for operational purposes, under the command of a single commander (US) and deputy commander (Canada). In the language of the Norad Agreement:

> Arrangements for the coordination of national plans requiring consultation between national commanders before implementation had become inadequate in the face of a possible sudden attack, with little or no warning. It was essential, therefore, to have in existence in peacetime an organization, including the weapons, facilities and command structure which could operate at the outset of hostilities in accordance with a single air defence plan approved in advance by national authorities.[32]

Canada's maritime forces co-operate closely with units of the United States Navy and they engage in frequent joint exercises. However, their respective plans are co-ordinated rather then integrated. Only those Canadian units assigned to NATO would come under joint command arrangements, namely under the Supreme Allied Commander, Atlantic (SACLANT) with headquarters in Norfolk, Virginia, and then only in the event of a NATO-wide emergency.

As for the third strategic weapons system, the retaliatory bomber forces of the US Strategic Air Command, Canada's contribution is limited to overflight and refuelling facilities. Canada has permitted SAC bombers (unarmed) to use Canadian airspace for peace-time training. In the event of an international crisis, 'as determined by the Government,' SAC bombers (nuclear-armed) can be given permission to overfly Canada and to refuel from tanker aircraft stationed at Goose Bay. The 1971 defence white paper announced that the government was preparing to negotiate further base facilities for dispersal of SAC refuelling tankers in an emergency. It was made clear that the right of overflight is not automatic; it is subject to a determination by the Canadian government that such overflights are justified by the nature of the crisis. An important criterion in this regard is the general reservation expressed at the outset of the defence white paper: 'With a view to ensuring the protection of Canada and contributing to the maintenance of stable mutual deterrence, Canada's resources, its territory, and its Armed Forces will be used solely for purposes which are defensive in the judgement of the Government of Canada.'

These three systems are the operational or 'business' end of the defence compact. Behind them, helping in various ways to support, co-ordinate, or direct them, we find the organizational web of joint Canada-US agencies as described to the House Committee: the Canada-US Ministerial Committee on Joint Defence, the Canada-US Inter-Parliamentary Group, the Permanent Joint Board on Defence, the Military Co-operation Committee, the Canada-US Regional Planning Group, the Canada-US Civil Emergency Planning Committee, the Senior Committee on US-Canadian Defence Production-Development Sharing Programme.

The seeming proliferation of these cross-border agencies has been a special subject of critical attention by commentators during the review period. Concern has been expressed as to whether their respective activities are adequately co-ordinated. In its report on Canada-US relations, the House Committee confessed it had

> an uneasy feeling that this is a problem which needs further attention. With such a multitude of contacts which are carried on daily by telex, telephone, direct air flights, and mail between the Canadian departments and agencies and the US governmental and private concerns, there seems to be a serious danger that decisions could be taken and policies formed which would work at cross-purposes with each other to the detriment of bilateral relations.[33]

Concern has also been expressed as to whether these joint bodies are subject to adequate direction by Canada or, to put it the other way around, subject to undue direction by the predominant partner, the United States. These arrangements have been criticized as resulting in a fragmentation or diffusion of Canadian political authority and thus lending themselves indirectly as instruments which serve to strengthen US domination. In its report on NORAD, the House Committee warned that 'Canada, as the very much smaller partner, must be particularly careful not to prejudice its independence unnecessarily within arrangements which, closely examined, might turn out to be not so much of a cooperative as a "take-over" relationship.'

The committee acknowledged that Canadian and US ministers had frequent and easy contact, including semi-annual NATO ministerial meetings where bilateral questions could be taken up informally. The committee stated, however, that during the 1962 Cuban missile crisis 'in spite of the close relations between the responsible ministers of the two countries, the Canadian Government was only informed of U.S. decisions by a diplomatic emissary at the same time as the other NATO countries.' The committee accordingly concluded 'that the present practice for political consultation within NORAD has proved to be inadequate in the one serious test to which it was put.'

The committee's recommendation was not, however, to reduce or disband existing co-operative arrangements. In the view of the committee, it was important to ensure that Canada would be fully consulted on and not just informed of US decisions, and to this end it would be desirable to reactivate one of the joint bodies which had fallen into disuse – the Ministerial Committee on Joint Defence, which was set up in 1958 and which had not met since 1964. The Committee noted that 'NORAD as presently constituted compares unfavorably with NATO in that it has no political forum for the joint consideration of international, political and security problems.'

Others have raised related questions: Has there been too much informality and intimacy in the relationship which have inhibited Canada from defining and asserting its own interests? Has the search for consensus in defence (as in economic) matters obscured differences between the two countries essential to the maintenance of Canadian sovereignty?

In any government, co-ordination of large, interrelated and multifaceted programs is a matter of continuing concern. Adam Yarmolinsky has described the problems of internal co-ordination within the US Defense Department in earlier years as being that of 'a loose confederation of independent fiefdoms, uneasily presided over by the Secretary of Defense.' The McNamara reforms moderated some of the internal bureaucratic conflict but, as Yarmolinsky pointed out, 'what has emerged is by no means monolithic'; many field-grade officers consider the secretary of defense and his staff as 'a separate and alien entity with which their organization is forced occasionally to deal, rather like a foreign power.'[34] By comparison, the senior defence policy-makers in Ottawa form a highly compact and close-knit community. It is too small for feudal fiefdoms to develop. The key policy agency is the Cabinet Committee on External Affairs and Defence, with the secretary of state for external affairs as chairman and the minister of national defence as vice-chairman. Senior officials in the various agencies (Department of National Defence, Department of External Affairs, and, on wider policy questions, the Privy Council Office and Treasury Board) have informal personal working (and often social) relationships with each other. When they must assemble together for more formal deliberations or briefings they can easily be accommodated in a medium-sized committee room.

Institutional arrangements have been developed over the years within the Ottawa community to reinforce habits of co-ordination and consultation. Unification of the Canadian armed forces has undoubtedly helped to break down artificial departmental or service divisions. In April 1972 the Department of National Defence was reorganized to introduce greater civilian control of policy, under the direction of an integrated military and civilian staff. The Defence Council of the Department of National Defence has been throughout an important policy clearing-house for the minister of national defence and his senior military and civilian officers (meeting usually every week, on Monday mornings). The undersecretary of state for external affairs or his delegate (usually the director-general of the Bureau of Defence and Arms Control in the Department of External Affairs) is a member and recipient of the minutes of the meetings of the Defence Council. As a result of recommendations of the Glassco Commission, an exchange program was instituted in 1966 for reciprocal secondment of middle rank (lieutenant colonel or equivalent) officers between the planning staff of the Canadian Forces Headquarters and the Defence Relations Division of the Department of External Affairs. There is also overlapping membership in joint Canada-US bodies. Some of the military members of the Canada-US Permanent Joint Board on Defence (PJBD) are also members of the Military Co-operation Committee. The above-mentioned director general of the Bureau of Defence and Arms Control Affairs in the Department of External Affairs is also a member of the Canadian Section of the PJBD. Many of the Canada-US committees are mixed in composition not only in the sense of two national components but also in having civilian and military members, drawn from various departments and branches, in each national component. While the problems of internal co-ordination and consultation require constant attention on the Canadian side, they are of an entirely different order of magnitude than those on the US side. The joint Canada-US bodies, instead of adding to problems of co-ordination, serve to tie together various elements in the service and bureaucratic machinery.

A more serious and recurring charge is that the patterns of cross-border contacts and agencies are somehow unresponsive to Canadian political direction; that given the disparity in size and power between the two countries, they serve unduly to diminish Canadian freedom of action and facilitate US penetration and domination. We are reminded that 'good fences make good neighbours' and that our international fence is highly porous and riddled with mutual access points.[35] Much better it would be for Canada, some say, if we dismantled some of this intergovernmental structure and reverted to a more formal manner of dealing with each other at arm's length, perhaps by restricting contacts as much as possible to 'traditional' diplomatic channels.[36]

In judging what forms the relationship should take, one must first ask what purposes or objectives are being sought by Canada in the relationship. It is difficult to come to grips with abstractions about an overall pattern of 'intimacy' or 'aloofness'; another way to look at the problem would be in terms of the efficacy of existing arrangements in promoting the objectives which Canada wishes to achieve. Only then does it become apparent that the intergovernmental structure is made up of different moving parts performing a number of different functions, some in close and interlocking embrace, others in competition and bargaining, and some in vigorous debate. The network of intergovernmental and interagency contacts can be examined in terms of four basic functions: co-ordination, conciliation/arbitration, consultation, and negotiation.

CROSS-BORDER CO-ORDINATION

The major part of the business transacted across the border consists of co-ordination of defence activities at the technical or operational level. Having decided, for example, to maintain an integrated air defence command, the two governments and their various agencies must deal with each other daily on a host of housekeeping questions relating to equipment maintenance, personnel appointments, training exercises, etc. Similarly, cross-border planning for civil defence or emergency relief of civilian populations in the event of a disaster – peacetime or wartime – is a complex and detailed matter. If emergency planning is to be effective, it must go well beyond an exchange of notes through the embassy. Officials at various levels – federal, provincial, state, and municipal – must co-ordinate their respective plans and exchange information on food stocks, medical supplies, communications, transportation etc.

Policy questions seldom arise, since joint programs such as these are administered within precise directives or terms of reference agreed to in advance by governments. Much of this co-ordination takes place on a day-to-day basis between planning staffs at the working level either in direct communication with each other between Ottawa and Washington and between the command or regional headquarters concerned, or through their respective embassies in Ottawa and Washington.

The joint committees meet periodically to pull the threads together in their respective fields. The joint Canada-US Military Cooperation Committee (MCC), for example, normally meets three times a year to review joint military activities. Each national component has representation from the three services (or environments) at the colonel level, headed by a brigadier general. The committee serves as a kind of 'early-warning' sensor where any problems at the working or operational level can be brought up by either side in an informal and frank manner. If it is a staff matter it can be dealt with by the service member concerned as part of his normal staff duties. If it involves policy questions the problem is flagged for attention of more senior staff or ministers and can be brought forward for higher level consideration at the next meeting of the Permanent Joint Board on Defence (PJBD.)

The PJBD provides an overview of defence relations in a forum with mixed military and civilian membership. On the Canadian side, it consists of a chairman without departmental affiliations appointed by the prime minister (currently Senator John Aird, who succeeded the late Arnold Heeney), three representatives from the Canadian Armed Forces, two officials of the Department of External Affairs, and, as observers, officials of the Ministry of Transport (air traffic control, arctic supply), and the Department of Industry, Trade and Commerce (defence production programs branch).

The board has described its own role as that of

> helping to mesh military requirements with political, economic and other considerations in order to facilitate the implementation of continental defence programmes in ways satisfactory to the two governments ... The task of reconciling the requirements of continental defence with the various other objectives of North American society is a complex and delicate one, involving the careful consideration of many sensitive factors which often cannot be separated by the normal dividing-line between military and political matters.[37]

The emphasis of the defence white paper on the interrelationship between military and civilian responsibilities and programs suggests that the PJBD could, if governments desired, become increasingly involved as a focus for interagency and intergovernmental co-ordination. Its terms of reference, as set out in the Ogdensburg declaration, are broad and flexible.[38] As an instrument of the two governments, it can readily be adapted to meet their changing needs and interests.

CONCILIATION/ARBITRATION

Conciliation or arbitration may be regarded as another function of the joint bodies. Views may differ in capitals on the direction which a continuing program might take and on whether it should be expanded, modified, or terminated. Such differences can be aired quite informally in the appropriate body and can often be composed without formal action. In addition, the PJBD has been formally designated in a number of Canada-US agreements as a kind of court of first instance to consider differences which might arise under these agreements. For example, the Nanoose Torpedo Test Range Agreement of 12 May 1965 provides: 'Following the ten year period, if either government concludes that the facility, or any installations, which are a part thereof, are no longer required, and the other government does not agree, the question of continuing need shall be referred to the Permanent Joint Board on Defence.'[39] In effect, as long as the Board is seized with the matter, neither party has a right to take unilateral action. Similar provisions calling for reference of 'the question of continuing need' to the PJBD are found in the Haines-Fairbanks Defence Pipeline Agreement of 30 June 1953, and in a number of other formal agreements concerning defence co-operation.[40]

A decision of the PJBD is not binding on governments, since the board can only make recommendations. However, its members are also members of the decision-making community in their respective capitals. They are thus in a position to anticipate what outcome would be acceptable to governments and, on their return from meetings, to seek approval and implementation. In practice the chairman of each national section of the board acts according to instructions prepared in capitals and if a matter arises which lies outside of the scope of his brief, he will seek instructions before taking a considered position for the record in the Board.

Joint machinery for settlement of bilateral problems is, of course, a well-established and familiar feature of Canada-US relations, dating back to the arbitral commission set up under Jay's Treaty of 1794.[41] From a Canadian viewpoint it is particularly important that the two governments agree to refer differences to a body with equal representation. Canada can thereby help safeguard against hasty decisions by the preponderant partner which might not fully take into account Canadian interests. For example, at times of budgetary retrenchment it can be tempting to US defence planners to trim programs outside the country in preference to domestic programs supported by an active and vocal political lobby. They are well aware that a Newfoundland community, which may be dependent on the local US-financed radar or naval station for jobs, has no congressman in Washington. A recommendation to cut back would, however, be subject to close scrutiny by the Canadian authorities, including members of the Canadian section of the PJBD who are well-informed both as to the military considerations and as to the need to cushion an adverse impact on the local community.

CONSULTATION

The NORAD agreement stressed 'the importance of the fullest possible consultation between the two governments on all matters affecting the joint defence of North America.' Unlike the NATO agreement, it did not, however, create any specific channel or forum for such consultations. One reason was that, as the Merchant-Heeney report pointed out, effective consultation in a bilateral relationship depends less on machinery and procedures than on the will to consult.

Much greater care must be devoted to machinery within a multilateral framework such as NATO, where each of the fifteen members must be assured of an equal opportunity to participate, inform, and be informed. This requires a centralized hierarchy of organs tied in with each other and serviced by an international secretariat, all under the direction of a standing political forum – the North Atlantic Council. When Canadians and Americans want to consult it can be a direct and much simpler process. Moreover, the council serves as a consultative forum for the whole of the North Atlantic Treaty area, which of course also includes North America. An institutional reflection of this is the Canada-US Regional Planning Group (CUSRPG), which is a subordinate body of the NATO structure and which is also linked directly to the Military Cooperation Committee (MCC), a purely bilateral committee which predates NATO. Ministers meet with each other twice yearly at NATO meetings. These meetings can be useful occasions for Canadian and US ministers to exchange views on bilateral defence issues, but with the pressure of other multilateral business and other interests in a European setting, ministers usually prefer to arrange for an *ad hoc* meeting in one or the other capital to deal with a particular bilateral subject in a timely fashion as the need arises.

The recommendation of the House Committee concerning reactivation of the Canada-US Ministerial Committee on Joint Defence should be examined in this light. This committee would consist of three ministers on each side: defence, external affairs, and finance. Any gathering of six cabinet ministers requires considerable advance preparation. It inevitably involves some publicity; at least a press briefing if not a formal release or communiqué. For emergency or 'crisis management' consultations, governments are more likely to make use of readily available channels which are less publicity prone: direct minister-to-minister telephone calls, diplomatic channels between the two capitals, or through the NATO Council. It is difficult to envisage a crisis in North American defence which is not at the same time a major international crisis involving the NATO alliance as a whole. Even the Cuban crisis, which was played out almost exclusively through direct Washington-Moscow communications, was accompanied by intensive consultation in the NATO Council, as well as, of course, in the UN Security Council. On the other hand, for 'non-crisis' consultations on future defence planning, the need is normally at a level below ministers, where policies are still in a process of formulation and where the Canada-US consultative machinery is already well developed. These drawbacks help to explain why ministers have not, in fact, resorted to the committee since 1964. They also help explain why this committee could hardly have contributed to advance consultations (ie, prior to announcement of the 'quarantine') in the 1962 Cuban crisis, when the US authorities took extreme measures to minimize the risk of disclosure of the situation before confronting their adversary.

Another reason why the NORAD agreement did not set up new consultative machinery was the fact that such machinery already existed. The principal continuing forum for intergovernmental consultations on North American defence plans and policies continued to be the PJBD. As a consultative forum, the PJBD has played an indispensable part in the 'management' of the Canada-US defence relationship. From the Canadian viewpoint it has served two important functions by facilitating a process of consultation whereby the Canadian authorities may receive timely information about new trends in US defence planning and may in turn transmit Canadian plans, viewpoints, or concerns into the US decision-making complex.

To exercise independent judgment in defence matters, the Canadian authorities need to be fully and accurately informed on strategic and technological trends. Only on the basis of the most reliable information available can they expect to make sound assessments as to where the Canadian interest lies on issues such as the ABM question or future air and maritime defence needs. Even with the best of intentions and good will, the US authorities cannot be expected to initiate *ad hoc* consultations with Canada through diplomatic channels in advance on all matters of direct interest or concern to Canada. The Canadian interest may not at the outset be apparent to the US agency concerned. The State Department, which is the traditional channel for consultations through the Canadian embassy in Washington, will not necessarily be aware of thinking developing elsewhere in the US defence community.

Conversely, to influence US decisions, Canada must have adequate access to various levels of decision-making in the US government. A former Canadian ambassador to Washington has pointed out that the US government is both 'the most approachable and the most immovable government in the world.'[42] Because of the size and complexity of that government, Canada must make its viewpoint or interests known at the earliest possible stage in the decision-making process. A British observer has described the process:

> American public servants are perhaps the most open-minded in the world, are less hampered by traditional conception than their European counterparts, and are closely linked to a system of academic discussion and research on public policy of great vitality. This means that in the preliminary stages of the evolution of a new policy or strategy, or reaction to an external challenge, the discussion is a relatively free one ... in which the views of allies are welcome. But so difficult is the process of reconciling the views of different departments, agencies and branches of the government that the further it moves up the chain of authority the more inflexible positions become. By the time the President has made 'a determination' on a particular policy, there is little that an allied government, however powerful, can do to change it.[42]

The PJBD normally meets three times a year for a period of three to four days each time, at defence bases throughout North America. In addition, it can meet for a shorter period in capitals, or elsewhere to study a particular subject in depth directly with government officials or military officers concerned. It is clearly not a forum for emergency consultation, nor does it deal with a great volume of day-to-day consultation or co-ordination of defence matters which, as we have seen, takes place through a multiplicity of channels and at a range of levels. However, because of their authority and expertise in their respective defence communities, and their mixed military and civilian backgrounds, members of the PJBD have unique opportunities during their informal contacts to exchange views and information and sound each other out on matters of policy. The two chairmen of the board, as appointees of the prime minister of Canada and the president of the US respectively, have access to all levels in their own government, including the highest level if the need arises. From the Canadian viewpoint, the board thus affords an opportunity to make maximum use of the 'approachability' of the US government, and to minimize the 'immovability,' if important Canadian interests should be brought to the attention of higher levels of the US government.

It should be noted that the integrated NORAD headquarters at Colorado Springs was created for operational purposes and not as a forum for intergovernmental consultations. The Canadian and US military personnel assigned to NORAD headquarters are not in direct line of communication with their respective governments; they are under the command of the commander-in-chief NORAD (CINCNORAD) who in turn is responsible to the Canadian chief of the defence staff and the US joint chiefs of staff. As part of his function, CINCNORAD frequently discusses his operational needs with defence staffs in the two capitals, but he has no mandate or indeed need to represent the views of one government to the other on policy matters.

NEGOTIATION

Excellency: I have the honour to refer to discussions which have taken place in the Permanent Joint Board on Defence, and subsequently between representatives of our governments, concerning a proposal for ...

An introduction of this kind is a familiar feature in Canada-US agreements on defence co-operation, indicating an important negotiating role of the PJBD, as well as other joint bodies.[44] As the quotation suggests, the joint bodies have no monopoly in this respect. What begins informally at one meeting in a particular forum at a particular level may pass for consideration, study, negotiation, and formal agreement through various bodies and channels. Traditional diplomatic channels are inevitably involved, and any intergovernmental issue or problem of any importance is bound to be reflected in the telegram traffic to and from embassies, as well as in the less formal discussions of the joint body concerned. The more important or sensitive the problem, the greater the tendency to channel communications through diplomatic channels. This is because embassies are there every day, while committees may or may not be meeting (meetings are often scheduled weeks or months ahead to ensure participation of all members) at the time when a decision is needed, and because there is no better way to ensure that the communication (or the 'message') goes through speedily and accurately, with dissemination to the various agencies of the recipient government which may be affected or interested. Representations made to the committee member may be difficult to follow up if he goes on leave or on an inspection tour of overseas bases. He may or may not recognize a responsibility to co-ordinate with other agencies involved. The State Department (or the Department of External Affairs) is always there, ready, if need be, to be reminded of an interest or a reply, and well aware of its co-ordinating responsibility on behalf of the government as a whole vis à vis the foreign embassy.

BILATERAL OR MULTILATERAL NEGOTIATIONS

It is sometimes assumed that, given a choice of channels, Canada will instinctively favour a multilateral setting in which to negotiate with the US.[45] It has frequently been said: there is less chance of rape when there are 15 in the bed.[46] Certainly on a number of international issues Canada, as a middle power, has been able to bring its views to bear more effectively on the US (or on the USSR) by acting in concert with like-minded middle powers within a multilateral organization such as NATO or the United Nations. Canada regards, for example, the UN Conference of the Committee on Disarmament (CCD) in Geneva as the primary focus for Canadian efforts to promote arms control agreements, including issues which have direct and important implications for continental defence, such as negotiations towards a comprehensive ban on all nuclear weapons tests. However, this is not so much out of any undue concern for our virtue in a bilateral encounter, but because the CCD happens to be the most effective forum available for arms control negotiations, which, if they are to make even faltering progress, must involve not only the US but also the USSR and the international community as a whole.

Canada has also been able to make its views known through NATO on the US-USSR negotiations concerning limitations on antiballistic missiles (ABM s) and strategic offensive weapons (the SALT talks). In addition to urging restraint within the CCD and NATO, Canada has not hesitated to make its views known directly in Washington (and in Moscow). In spite of what the US government considered were 'over-riding reasons of national security for proceeding with the test' Canada vigorously protested against plans for a nuclear detonation on Amchitka.[47] The bilateral way is usually the preferred way or the only effective way to resolve a problem of concern chiefly to the two parties. There is room for greater candour, less concern about 'face' and, as General Foulkes has pointed out, a wider exchange of intelligence and technical information on a bilateral basis than in an alliance of fifteen members, where security may be doubtful.[48]

The essential point is that Canada-US defence relations are carried on through a multiplicity of instruments which, like musical instruments, have different qualities. The Canadian government, like a skilful conductor, must make the best possible use of each of them within an overall orchestration of effects.

CONCLUSIONS

The white paper on foreign policy defined foreign policy as 'the product of the Government's progressive definition and pursuit of national aims and interests in the international environment.' In pursuing these aims and interests in the defence field, there are a range of choices open to Canada – in the formulation of the purposes of a Canadian defence policy, in the level and nature of the forces to be maintained, and in the instruments to be drawn upon in the conduct of relations with the US and other allies. The scope for independent judgment is not as narrow as some would have it. As John Holmes has said, our freedom of movement is circumscribed not by orders from Washington but by our own calculation of where our interests lie.[49]

This calculation involves a continuing process of hard work and vigorous exploration of alternatives. A defence review is over, in the sense that a set of policies and attitudes which seemed valid at a given point in time were articulated and published as government white papers. But the process of reviewing defence policies is unending; the strategic situation changes, equipment needs replacement, and agreements come up for renewal. In his 1971 report to Congress on US foreign policy, Mr Rogers reminded us that the NORAD agreement would be subject to renewal in 1973 and that 'discussion of the agreement will be one of the major items on the bilateral agenda for next year.'[50] By an exchange of notes of 10 May 1973 the NORAD agreement was extended for a further period of two years, from 12 May 1973. The exchange of notes contemplates further studies and consultations on modernized air defences and on the strategic situation in North America.[51]

A capacity for independent judgment on this issue and others involved informed discussion by Canadians outside of the small community of decision-makers in Ottawa. One of the lessons of the political crisis of 1963 was that a defence posture without the backing of public opinion, whatever may be its intrinsic flaws or strengths, is sooner or later untenable. Since then the policy process has opened up beyond recognition. A reactivated parliamentary committee has made an essential contribution to this process. More can be done, perhaps along the lines of the highly developed exchanges of ideas and personnel which take place in the US between government, the universities, and specialized 'think tanks.' A hopeful sign was the recent establishment and government sponsorship of the Canadian 'Institute for Research on Public Policy.' Strategic issues which are important to Canadian security and which make large demands on Canadian resources should receive their due share of attention.

In the field of defence, the search for sensible policies also involves consultation with allies. Such consultation does not involve any surrender of the right to dissent. It is sometimes forgotten that the Merchant-Heeney report, which described timely consultations as 'the cornerstone of a healthy relationship between our two countries' also sounded a cautionary note: 'To consult in this fashion, however, cannot be taken to imply that agreement must always result. The purpose rather is that each be enabled to hear and weigh the other's views. The outcome will depend upon the circumstances of the case and, ultimately, upon the judgement by each of its national interest.'[52]

One of the most effective safeguards of the Canadian interest may be, paradoxically, the enlightened long-term US interest. If the preponderant partner is heavy handed and insensitive to the junior partner, the defence relationship will not have the support of the majority of the Canadian people. It will not be harmonious and it may not be viable. Canadians will increasingly pursue their national interest outside the co-operative framework, to the detriment of both parties. There is thus a fundamental need for US policy-makers to continue to recognize, as they have in the past, that the American interest lies in ensuring that the defence relationship, like other aspects of the continental relationship, is based on a true consensus flowing from a perceived mutual interest and a mutual respect for inevitable divergencies.

NOTES

1 Department of External Affairs, 2 *Foreign Policy for Canadians: Europe* (1970) 14.
2 Department of External Affairs, 1 *Foreign Policy for Canadians* 38.
3 Department of National Defence, *White Paper on Defence* (August 1971) 25.
4 Prime Minister Trudeau, Calgary, 12 April 1969, *Statements and Speeches* no 69/8.
5 1971 *White Paper on Defence*, at 30. The number of US servicemen stationed in Canada has decreased over a period of years. At the height, in 1957, there were 14,000 stationed in Canada; at the present time they number less than 2,000, the majority of whom are located at Goose Bay, Labrador, and Argentia, Newfoundland. A formerly touchy issue of 'sovereignty' had thus become a non-issue.
6 The defence white paper was read by some critics as implying that there was some direct threat to Canadian sovereignty in the north; eg, J.L. Granatstein, 'Defence in the 70s: Comments on the White Paper' (1971), 30, *Behind the Headlines* 12. The paper speaks, however, in general terms of 'challenges which could occur' and 'potential challenges to our interests ... By creating a capability for surveillance and control which is effective and visible, the intention is to discourage such challenges.' On the strength of Canada's claims to sovereignty as legal title under international law in respect of northern territory and the Arctic Archipelago, see article by Ivan Head, 9 *McGill Law Journal* (1963) 200.
7 1971 *White Paper on Defence*, at 16.
8 In examining a growing tendency of the US military to become 'civilianized,' Yarmolinsky has commented: 'There are important limits on how far the military can become civilianized or non-militarized. According to Janowitz [*The Professional Soldier* 33] "The military establishment has not lost its distinctive characteristics ... The need for heroic fighters persists. The pervasive requirements of combat set the limits to civilizing tendencies." Whatever new and challenging tasks the military have to assume, their ultimate responsiblity is to the demands of combat.' *The Military Establishment* (1971)

83. A recognition of similar limits in respect of the Canadian military seems implied in the white paper reference to 'basic defence roles.'

9 *Foreign Policy for Canadians* 38.

10 *Lament for a Nation* (1965) 9. A similar concern was expressed, in more measured terms, by the Standing Committee of the House of Commons on External Affairs and National Defence in its Report on Canada-US Relations of June 1970 (the 'Wahn Report'): '... the Committee is concerned that the extent of military, economic and cultural dependency upon the US may, in time, become so great that Canada may be unable to make the kind of independent decision characteristic of autonomous nations.'

11 Roger F. Swanson, 'The United States as a National Security Threat to Canada' (1970), 29 *Behind the Headlines* 10.

12 John W. Holmes, 'Canada and the United States: Political and Security Issues' (1970), 29 *Behind the Headlines* 3. 'The basis of the compact was the simple belief that defence would be more effective and also less costly if resources were pooled and that an aggressor would be more effectively deterred if he had to take into consideration an alliance with a disposition on the part of its members to go to the defence of each other.'

13 Between September 1961 and February 1964, 66.8 per cent of Canadians polled felt Canada should follow a joint defence plan with the US, while 17.0 per cent wanted Canada to look after her own defence. Canadian Institute of Public Opinion, no 306, February 1964. As for the controversy over nuclear weapons, Professor Peyton Lyon expressed the view that it 'had less to do with the content of the government's defence policy than with its inability to articulate and implement a clear line of action. Given firm leadership, the country could have been persuaded to accept either a nuclear or nonnuclear role. Similarly, the Americans would have accommodated themselves to a clear decision by Ottawa to withdraw from its commitments which acquired nuclear ammunition.' *Canada in World Affairs*, vol. 12, *1961–1963* (1968) 77. An American scholar, Professor Jon McLin, concurred: 'It seems that an early decisive choice for either course would have aroused less turmoil than the prolonged indecision.' 'Review Article,' (1969), *International Journal* 381.

14 On public and parliamentary attitudes towards NORAD and NATO see R.B. Byers, *Canadian Foreign Policy and Selected Attentive Publics*, monograph prepared for Department of External Affairs (1967).

15 According to evidence submitted by US Defense Secretary Melvin R. Laird to the US House Armed Services Committee on 9 March 1971, the Soviet Union had, at the end of 1970, some 1,440 operational intercontinental missile launchers, more than 272 operational nuclear submarine-borne missile launchers (mounted on 17 submarines), and an intercontinental heavy bomber force of 'around 200' which 'continues its slow downward trend of the past few years.'

16 Standing Committee on External Affairs and National Defence, Ninth Report to the House, 26 June 1969.

17 CIIA, (1969), 7 *Monthly Report* 180.

18 Michael E. Sherman, 'Continental Defence in the Seventies: A Canadian View,' paper presented at the Wingspread Conference on Canada-US Relations, Racine, Wisconsin, October 1969.

19 Among critics on the left there was some questioning of the relevance of air defence but it was usually muted by expressions of satisfaction about the decision to retire BOMARC antibomber missiles. See, for example, Andrew Brewin, MP, 'Defence in the 70's: Comments on the White Paper' (1971), 30 *Behind the Headlines* 3: 'Neither traditional nor radical critics are likely to be enthusiastic about the substance of the paper. On the whole it represents a middle-of-the-road choice.'

20 James Eayrs, 'Future Roles for the Armed Forces of Canada' (1969), 28 *Behind the Headlines*.

21 John W. Holmes, *The Better Part of Valour: Essays on Canadian Diplomacy* (1970) 154.

22 Statement of Secretary of Defense Melvin R. Laird before House Armed Services Committee, on the FY-1973 Defense Budget, 17 Feb. 1972, 74.

23 Pinetree Radar Agreement, [1951] CAN. T.S., no 31, article 2.

24 Testimony of Lieutenant General F.R. Sharp, deputy commander of NORAD, 6 May 1969. House Committee Proceedings no 41, 1393. See also appendix XX, paper prepared by the Department of National Defence, which states that Canada contributed about 8 per cent of the total NORAD interceptor

forces (at 1416) and about 10 per cent of the total NORAD personnel (14,000 of 144,000) (at 1412).

25 Defence Estimates for 1969–70 tabled in the House of Commons, February 1969; cost of personnel, operations, and maintenance of Maritime Command was estimated at $242,927,000.

26 Léo Cadieux, Minutes of Proceedings and Evidence no 42, 8 May 1969, 1454. Based on this and other testimony 'The Committee found it difficult to determine whether consistent principles have been followed in allocating total NORAD costs between Canada and the U.S. up to the present time. Cost allocation for each facility and programme appears to have been determined on an *ad hoc* basis.' House Committee, Report on NORAD, 26 June 1969.

27 J.C. Arnell, 'The Development of Joint North American Defence' (1970), *Queen's Quarterly* 15.

28 Tenth Report of the Standing Committee on External Affairs and National Defence, on Canadian Maritime Forces, 26 June 1970, 1139.

29 Melvin R. Laird, Statement before House Armed Services Committee, 9 March 1971, 21.

30 The budget of the Canadian International Development Agency increased from $383.7 million in 1970/71 to $426.4 million in 1971/2 and $491 million in 1972/73. According to figures of the Development Assistance Committee of the OECD, Canada contributed 0.77 per cent of GNP to international development assistance in 1971, as compared with 0.61 per cent of GNP by the US.

31 'Canadian Governmental Instruments for Conducting Relations with the United States,' Department of External Affairs, Ottawa, 9 October 1969, Minutes of the Proceedings and Evidence of Standing Committee on External Affairs and National Defence, 20 November 1969.

32 NORAD Agreement, 12 May 1958, [1958] CAN. T.S. no 9; renewed 30 March 1968 and again 10 May 1973.

33 Eleventh Report of the Standing Committee on External Affairs and National Defence, on Canada-US Relations, 27 July 1970, 65.

34 Yarmolinsky, *supra* note 8, at 19.

35 'What is really required is a certain reserve, a sense of live and let live, even of aloofness on occasion, in the treatment of the smaller country by the larger.' James Eayrs, 'Sharing a Continent: The Hard Issues' in John Sloan Dickey, ed, *The U.S. and Canada* (1964) 94.

36 'Her relationship should be vigorous, obviously allied, but inevitably at arms length because Canadians think differently, have different relationships and a different history.' Leonard Beaton, 'Declaration of Independence' (1968), *Canadian Forum* 3.

37 *The Permanent Joint Board on Defence 1940–1965*, commemorative booklet prepared on the 25th anniversary of the establishment of the Board at Ogdensburg, New York, on 18 August 1940 (1965).

38 'It will consider in the broad sense the defence of the north half of the Western Hemisphere.' Ogdensburg Declaration, 18 August 1940. Colonel C.P. Stacey, writing in 1954, distinguished between four different ways in which the PJBD was used during the war years: consultation, negotiating, co-ordinating, and supervisory. (1954), 9 *International Journal* 120.

39 Exchange of Notes (with annex) Constituting an Agreement between the USA and Canada Relating to the Establishment, Operation and Maintenance of a Torpedo Test Range in the Strait of Georgia (Ottawa, 12 May 1965), paragraph 3. [1965] CAN. T.S. no 6.

40 Haines-Fairbanks Pipeline Agreement, [1953] CAN. T.S. no 5, article 3; Distant Early Warning (DEW) Line Agreement, [1955] CAN. T.S. no 8, article 9; Continental Air Defence System Improvements (CADIN) Agreement, [1961] CAN. T.S. no 9, article 10 annex.

41 In assessing the record of harmonious settlement of Canada-US issues by diplomatic, judicial, or quasijudicial methods, Professor Corbett had reassurance for Canadians 'who are still prone to assume that we have invariably lost in our litigations with the United States, and accordingly that no confidence in ultimate justice can be entertained when our interests come into conflict with theirs ... There is keen trading and clever advocacy on both sides: the record is no story of wolf and lamb.' Percy E. Corbett, *The Settlement of Canadian-American Disputes* (1937) 4.

42 A.E. Ritchie, undersecretary of state for external affairs. House Committee Proceedings no 26, 5 May 1970, 7.

43 Alistair Buchan, *Crisis Management: The New Diplomacy* (1966) 47.

44 The example quoted is from the Haines-

Fairbanks Pipeline Agreement, cited above. Similar language appears in the DEW Line and the Nanoose Torpedo Test Range agreements, amongst others.

45 See, for example, Ramsay Cook: 'It is surely an axiom of Canadian diplomacy that it is safer to deal with the U.S. as part of a multilateral organization than it is to deal with her unilaterally.' *The Maple Leaf Forever* (1971) 185.

46 This maxim was attributed by General Foulkes (chairman, Chiefs of Staff, 1951–60) to 'a former Minister.' See Testimony before the Standing Committee on External Affairs and National Defence, 12 February 1969, Committee Proceedings, 942.

47 In his 1971 report to Congress on US foreign policy, Secretary Rogers noted that in the case of the US nuclear test on Amchitka Island 'widespread public opposition in Canada, voiced in terms of possible environmental and public safety hazards and the relationship of the test to progress in disarmament, was reflected in repeated expressions of concern by the Canadian Government. When the United States decided that there were overriding reasons of national security for proceeding with the test, many Canadians felt that Canadian views were not being given due weight.' Report of the Secretary of State on U.S. Foreign Policy, 8 March 1972, 141.

48 General Charles Foulkes, *supra* note 46.

49 The case for more Canadian strategic studies has been well stated by Colin S. Gray, 'The Need for Independent Canadian Strategic Thought' (1971), *Canadian Defence Quarterly* 6. A favourable trend in recent years has been the establishment in a number of universities of chairs of strategic studies.

50 Report of the Secretary of State on U.S. Foreign Policy, 8 March 1972, 140.

51 Department of External Affairs Press Release no 48, 10 May 1973; '… additional time is required to examine the component elements of the concept for a modernized air defence system now under development. Further joint consultations will undoubtedly be needed in order that our two Governments will be able to consider and decide upon the extent of modernization that will satisfy future requirements for the joint defence of North America, taking into account the evolving strategic situation, including developments in the Strategic Arms Limitation Talks.' Letter from Canadian Ambassador to the United States Marcel Cadieux to Deputy Assistant Secretary of State for Canadian Affairs Rufus Z. Smith.

52 A.D.P. Heeney and Livingston T. Merchant, 'Canada and the United States: Principles for Partnership,' 28 June 1965.

IVAN R. FELTHAM AND
WILLIAM R. RAUENBUSCH

36/Economic
Nationalism

Over the past several years in Canada there has been a spirited ongoing debate over the question of foreign ownership of Canadian resources and industry. These discussions have included the phenomenon of the multinational enterprise (MNE) as it affects Canada, as well as the widespread activities in this country of United States-based enterprises which do not strictly qualify as multinational. Much of this debate reflects a general dissatisfaction with the performance of the Canadian economy as a whole. One side of the debate attributes the poor economic results directly and indirectly to the fact of foreign ownership, while the other side blames poor economic policies generally. Assuming, as is usual in such debates, that neither side is entirely correct, it appears that a more balanced approach to foreign ownership and its relationship to the economy is in order if Canada is to develop coherent and effective economic policies.

Canada shares with many other countries concern about the power of MNEs to establish priorities and follow practices inconsistent with national interests. Countries in which these giants have their principal centre of management share some of these anxieties. The peculiar features in Canada are that Canadian industry is marked by a relatively large activity of MNEs, most of which are US-based. The significance of this is heightened, of course, by the fact that the presence of the United States is apparent in every aspect of Canadian life.

The notion of foreign investment and trade involves the conception of each nation as a distinct unit. Trade is the exchange of goods among nations. But even in the case of trade, transportation and distribution arrangements necessary for the exchange of goods involve some penetration of each state from other states. Foreign direct investment may be contrasted as penetration which involves investment for more than merely transportation, warehousing, and distribution. Other foreign investment (portfolio investment) may be defined as capital investment, which does not involve significant participation in the management of the enterprise invested in.

The national policy aspect of trade in goods involves the tariff, quotas, and other impediments to free trade. Canadian duties are generally established within the framework of the General Agreement on Tariffs and Trade. There are, in addition, bilateral arrangements with certain countries, the USSR for example, as well as the British preferences which are recognized and sanctioned by the GATT. Canada has had and still maintains a relatively high tariff which has had an effect on foreign direct investment. This tariff has protected both foreign and Canadian owned producers. Many manufacturing plants were originally established to overcome the tariff wall and to take advantage of access to British preferential markets. The alternative of free trade, which would expose all domestic producers to foreign exports, has not been thought attractive.

The national policy regarding foreign investment is another aspect of economic foreign policy. Every nation has some reaction to investment from abroad, and most have some positive policy regarding investment abroad by its corporate and individual citizens. Foreign direct investment might be limited by a variety of controls, such as limits on non-resident control of assets and exchange controls. A survey of practice in the world discloses that such controls have been adopted to a greater or lesser degree by most countries. Canada, by contrast, is characterized by relative freedom from controls on foreign direct investment.

The world comprises a number of nation states which have in reality only semi-autonomous decision-making power and which are not, therefore, fully independent, whether that would be desirable or not. We in Canada wish to preserve to a substantial extent our power to act independently as a nation. There is no acceptable or workable alternative in the form of a multinational or world government. Given this state of desired political goals, we wish to curtail influence on our decision-making power which is not consistent with our own interest.

Among the many factors linking our political and economic behaviour to that of other nations, the existence and behaviour of two forms of international economic relations are particularly evident; namely, the MNE, and the overlapping phenomenon of ownership and control of enterprise in Canada by non-residents, particularly by residents of the United States.

There is in the world increasing trade, economic integration, economic interdependence, and to a lesser extent, increasing political co-ordination and interdependence. This is generally desirable because it reflects a tendency towards the most efficient use of resources and to harmonious relations, and therefore provides the best opportunity for improving conditions in all nations.[1] The peculiar characteristic of the MNE in this world of economic integration is that many have achieved transnational integration and are more co-ordinated than any of the political organizations. This is certainly the case with international organizations, including even the European Economic Community at its present stage of development. Moreover, the highly integrated federal states such as the United States and Canada, in terms of efficient co-ordination of policies of the several political units, do not exhibit the unity of the most highly efficient multinational enterprises.

It is now fashionable to describe the MNE as a 'challenge' to national policy and to international relations. Is it in reality a challenge? To us, the excitement of the situation lies in the existence of the phenomenon of the MNE in the total perspective of world affairs and international relations. In a world of creaking relations and tensions politically, and of somewhat less creaking and tense economic relations, the MNE appears to be the most highly effective and successful vehicle for transcending national boundaries.

All business activity requires constant observation to identify conflict and potential conflicts between the behaviour of the firm and the public interest. The latter should prevail, and regulatory devices need to be employed to see that the public interest does prevail. But to describe every potential difference of interest as a challenge assumes a certainty of public interest which is not evident and which probably cannot be demonstrated. To create an imagined challenge may be necessary to attract attention, but hardly assists in the analysis of the situation and the determination of measures necessary or desirable to achieve public-interest goals.

A fundamental problem is to define the national interest. Were such a definition achieved with a substantial measure of precision, the criteria would then be established against which to evaluate the characteristics and behaviour of the MNES. Still, without a precise definition of national interest, we must examine the MNE to attempt to determine what aspects may pose a threat to reasonably clear national interests.

The capacity of multinational enterprises to improve the lot of the people of all nations through expansion of technology and efficient management of resources – that is, to provide the wherewithal for social progress – is immense and can hardly be denied. No practicable alternative exists. Given this, what needs to be done is to refine further the identification of the hazards of MNE operation and devise effective and efficient safeguards against those hazards.

There is a strong case for international regulation of the world economy and for developing a multinational response to multinational enterprises. In order to develop a truly world economy there must be multinational public pressure as well as multinational enterprise. Such a presence is necessary not only to countervail the power of multinational enterprise, but also to facilitate the orderly development of the world economy, for there are pressures now afoot throughout the world for parochial response to multinational enterprise which may parallel what happened in the trade field during the 1930s, although perhaps not on the same scale. Therefore, Canada should encourage swift international discussion of, and action on, these problems.

There are indications that international organizations, such as OECD, are beginning to take up these issues. However, the prospects for effective discussion and agreement in the foreseeable future are not encouraging. Meanwhile, the economic exigencies and the political realities in Canada are such that we cannot wait for international discussion and action before we develop a policy in respect of foreign ownership in general and MNES in particular.

A major response to the debate in Canada was the publication of the Gray Report, which we believe is by far the best treatment of the subject to date.[2] The report expressed concern over the extent of foreign ownership and control of Canadian industry and suggested, among other things, the establishment of a screening agency to ensure that Canada's national goals would be protected. Bill C-132, the Foreign Investment Review Act, based largely on the analysis and recommendations of the Gray Report,[3] received second reading in the House of Commons on 4 April 1973 and was at the time of writing in committee stage; enactment is expected.

PERSPECTIVES ON NATIONAL GOALS: THE SEARCH FOR CANADIAN POLICY

It is readily apparent that this subject involves every aspect of Canadian economic, social, cultural, and political development. There is much established legal content, in the sense of statutes, regulations, and legal processes, but the questions remain fundamental and pervasive.

Although Canada has had a considerable degree of foreign ownership for a long time, the emergence of the MNE adds new and pressing dimensions to the foreign ownership debate. Through its worldwide system involving planning, research, production, and marketing, the MNE has the power, within certain constraints, to avoid any one government's control. This is the point where the Canadian dilemma begins. On the one hand, we want to be part of the world economy and we want to ensure that Canada achieves its place in it; yet, on the other hand, we are awed by the dimensions of the challenges that the world economy presents. We are afraid that if we commit ourselves fully to the world economy we shall not be able to hold our own. The fear is deepened by the spectre of Canada being swallowed up politically, economically, and culturally by the American giant. To be sure, a commitment to the world economy will involve serious adjustments for Canada. However, to remain a viable political and economic entity, Canada must accept the challenge which the new world economy presents. With appropriate policies, such a commitment need not erode – indeed it will strengthen – Canadian political, economic, and cultural independence.

It is not sufficient merely to catalogue and describe the activities of the multinational enterprise in Canada. Nor is it sufficient to catalogue and describe the hazards that these enterprises may pose for national policies. We need first of all a definition of national policy, of national goals, and of norms of behaviour against which to measure the behaviour and predict the effect of foreign ownership and of the MNE. The lack of definitive statements of national policy makes very difficult any evaluation of MNEs and foreign ownership of industry in Canada.

In the search for general guidelines, many commentators have concentrated too much on ownership and its traditional corollary, control, and too little on regulation of behaviour of enterprises to achieve defined goals. There is already a high level of regulation for economic, safety, and other social purposes. All business is subject to some regulation and some industry to a large amount of it. Regulation should be based on well-reasoned and well-articulated principles indicating the goals to be served by regulation and should be re-examined from time to time to determine whether it is achieving its intended purpose.

It cannot be assumed that indigenous ownership without regulation of business behaviour will produce desired results, although in some special cases this may well be so. For example, in connection with the export from the US of its peculiar laws and regulations dealing with "trading with the enemy,' it may be assumed that a Canadian manager free of the restraint of US law would behave differently from his American-controlled counterpart. But, in the debate on foreign ownership, we are concerned with much more than merely the extraterritorial application of foreign law.[4] Effective devices can be developed to counteract such foreign influences when they are thought to be undesirable. The debate about foreign ownership is concerned with something more fundamental and more pervasive.

It is not evident that Canadian owners and managers behave generally differently from non-Canadian owners and managers so that we must be wary of declarations by those now in control of major aspects of Canadian industry on the virtues of Canadian ownership. However, there is no doubt that the desire for increased Canadian resident ownership, or at least holding the line, is widespread. Although Canadian ownership is not a sufficient end by itself, overall national satisfaction does, we believe, require a substantial amount of indigenous ownership and management. The problem is to analyse the circumstances in any given industry to determine the long-run public interest.

Looking at the Canadian scene as a whole, we conclude that priority should be given to defining and articulating, much better than we have, a set of principles to improve our industrial organization. Study after study demonstrate the need to rationalize Canadian industry and to develop specialization in order to serve the domestic market better and to penetrate foreign markets more effectively. These economic goals are entirely consistent with other social goals and, indeed, the achievement of the economic goals is in practical terms an essential ingredient of success in achieving social goals.[5]

We need immense improvement in the efficiency of our industry and in export performance. Trading arrangements conducive to these goals should be actively pursued as national policy. Selective development of free trade with the United States and other countries appears desirable. We should also seek to increase processing in Canada of Canadian mineral and other resources which may be exported as raw materials. For this purpose each industry needs to be analysed in detail and rules appropriate to that industry developed.

Whatever the problems brought with foreign ownership, preoccupation with them tends to divert public attention from the more fundamental economic problem of productivity of the Canadian economic machine compared with levels achieved in other national economies. We agree with those who emphasize that growth figures are not necessarily indicative of good or bad social results, but relatively high productivity is important to give us the wherewithal to achieve desired social goals.

Much of the discussion in Canada about foreign ownership implies a state of underdevelopment not only of our economy, but also of our distinctive Canadian culture (whatever that may turn out to be).[6] However underdeveloped it is, building a protective wall is hardly conducive to the development of a vital, distinctive culture. Creation of any barrier implies a weakened condition that cannot stand competition and potential influence from outside. What we need is more positive strength and not more generalized protection. Protection may be justified in selected cases, the traditional 'infant industry' policy being an example. But how long must protection be maintained to achieve desired goals? Protection implies some inefficiency, at least in the short run, as far as industry is concerned, and protection implies something less than the best so far as cultural development is concerned. There is, of course, widespread concern that the 'best' will not survive without protection.

Our goal for Canada and one which we believe is widely held – indeed, we believe it to be the prevailing view – is that we should have a vital mix of indigenous enterprise together with the stimulating presence of enterprise based in other countries and of its personnel. Indigenous activity has to be sufficiently large to be obvious and to provide that psychological and basic political satisfaction which is the substance of a nation. But indigeneous activity does not need to be spread uniformly among all firms in any industry, or among all industries.

We are faced with a situation in which there is in Canada a high level of foreign participation. Although the degree of participation and the nature of it varies from one industry and activity to another, it is apparent that some control of participation in Canadian industry by non-Canadian interests is required. The foreign ownership debate has now progressed to a point where it is irrelevant to ask if foreign investment should be controlled. The question now is how it should be controlled. The political climate in Canada now is such that those who direct their attention to the former question to the exclusion of the latter are in danger of having little influence in shaping the legislative response to the foreign ownership debate. The Watkins Report, the Wahn Report, and the Gray Report all recommended retrenchment from the existing 'open-door' policy, and all political parties now accept a more restrictive policy with respect to foreign ownership as evidenced by the virtually assured passage of Bill c-132 in substantially the form in which it was introduced.[7]

But in any restrictions on the acquisition of existing Canadian-controlled operations by foreign enterprises, there is inherent the disadvantage that the Canadian economy might be deprived of the benefit of better management in the hands of the foreign enterprise than under existing Canadian management. Prohibition or substantial restriction of acquisitions might thus be self-defeating if there is no alternative Canadian acquirer in the market. The significance of these factors in any given case should be the subject of analysis appropriate to that case. Such individualistic treatment indicates the establishment of a control mechanism with discretionary power rather than the promulgation of inflexible regulations of general application. Bill c-132 seeks to establish such a flexible control mechanism.

In the broadest perspective, Canadian concern may be identified under the heading of 'economic and cultural nationalism.' This is indeed reflected in the establishment recently of a Select Committee of the Ontario Legislative Assembly of that name. Implicit, if not explicit, in the whole range of discussion is the concept of nationalism, the search for national distinctiveness. Manifestations of this concern, particularly among Canadian 'intellectuals,' are abundant in recent writing in Canada.

At the root of the concern lies the notion of sovereignty. This is not an absolute concept, but is essentially a notion of the relative power of self-determination of a nation in relation to other nations with which the nation must interact. Governments in Canada, both federal and provincial, are sensitive about the scope of their spheres of authority, both between themselves and between Canada and other nations. Issues of sovereignty range from the relatively straightforward questions of authority over Arctic waters and the continental shelf to complex and difficult-to-define questions of authority and effective control over economic affairs. And concern about the content of sovereignty is further complicated by considerations of the nature of Canadian culture and society.

Attempts to define Canadian culture and society tend to result in vague generalizations. Many Canadians are concerned that Canada does not manifest a cultural distinctiveness of its own. This is often attributed in large part to the predominance of the American media. Concern about economic dominance is linked with the fear that any distinctive features of Canadian national identity will be lost unless great care is taken to preserve them. Fear of cultural domination, indeed of being overwhelmed in that sphere of life, feeds the emotional element of economic nationalism. The presence of things American in the cultural sphere would, of course, exist regardless of economic relations. The obvious facts of proximity and the prevalence of the English language determine this. But there is widespread concern that distinctive Canadian elements in the cultural mix should be fostered by policy that involves not only measures designed to promote Canadian cultural factors but also to reduce the opportunities for influence from the United States. Containment of US investment is thought by some to be a necessary part of any package of policies designed to develop Canadian distinctiveness. However, it is obvious that the United States is, and will continue to be, the most important factor in determining Canada's cultural, political, and economic policies.

There are many references to the problem of maintaining or developing a distinctive Canadian culture, but few analyses of what is encompassed within that notion.[8] Certainly, 'culture' cannot be merely considered coincident with the arts,[9] for it essentially encompasses the quality of life for all people, their customs, and their distinctive characteristics. These customs and characteristics are influenced by and, indeed, are a part of the economic environment just as social, political, cultural, and economic aspects of life cannot be neatly compartmentalized.

The recent literature arising out of the foreign ownership debate has performed the useful function of searching out every aspect of Canadian life which might be directly affected by foreign investment. From this survey, one must conclude that there is no predominant connection in any one aspect. This is apparent when one attempts to isolate the questions from the all-too-obvious presence of the United States as Canada's proximate neighbour. Were there not one dollar of US investment in Canada, what would Canada look like socially, culturally, and politically? Not largely different, one might well assume, given the free flow of information and ideas via the English language media in both countries.[10]

Apart from questions of cultural distinctiveness, vague at best, there are the more tangible aspects of economic relations with other countries and the effect on the development of Canadian industry, technology, and managerial capability. It is beyond the scope of this chapter to discuss the attempts to measure these factors.

PATTERN AND PROBLEMS OF FOREIGN INVESTMENT IN CANADA

Take a large measure of activity by MNES. Note that most MNES are based in the United States. Add a substantial measure of activity by other US-based companies (that is, those that do not qualify as MNES, but have some international operations including Canada). Add a measure of activity by European and Japanese companies which do not fall within the MNE category. (This activity is, of course, in addition to those European and Japanese companies which are MNES.) The result is a mix of control of industry in Canada which is distinctively not indigenous, although there are notable Canadian companies of substantial size, including a few that qualify for, or are close to having, multinational status.

The mix varies by industry. Finance, transportation, and communication are largely owned and controlled in Canada. Petroleum production and refining are almost wholly foreign controlled as is the automobile industry. Other aspects of manufacturing exhibit a pattern of about 50 per cent Canadian and 50 per cent foreign, although foreign ownership predominates in highly technological industries such as chemicals (the Polymer Corporation is a notable exception) and electrical products.

The details are set out in numerous publications and will not be repeated here. What is notable for the purpose of generalization is that the level of foreign investment is very high in relation to investment owned and controlled by residents of

Canada and that by international comparisons Canada has by far the highest level of foreign investment of any industrially developed country. These facts justify treating the question of foreign ownership as a major factor in Canadian international relations.

It is highly desirable to have control of 'the domestic economic environment' (as the Gray Report calls it). It is also desirable to preserve relative freedom of movement for capital, labour, and goods so that residents of Canada may enjoy the benefit of international competition and the products of the best technology. Participation in the international marketplace inevitably involves some 'costs' as well as 'benefits.' Canada should use its bargaining power to achieve the best results for itself, having due regard to all relevant factors including physical environment and world social problems. All of the analyses published to date confirm the position that the costs or constraints of foreign investment are best dealt with by flexible selective policy. No one can reasonably deny the advantage of MNE participation in the world to the extent necessary to gain the benefit of management and technical skills which the MNES have to offer to any national economy in which they participate. But with the 'good' there is 'bad' in varying degrees. The national goal should be to optimize the good. As the Gray Report concludes, this is most likely to be best achieved by a process of discretionary control. The report calls it a screening process.

The most striking characteristic of the whole picture is that everything is a matter of degree. Only for the doctrinaire socialists is the picture simple. Their solution, as advanced by the Waffle Group, formerly a wing of the New Democratic party, is not predominant even in that party.[11]

CANADIAN POLICY AND REGULATION: A CURRENT REVIEW

Entry into business activity in Canada has been generally open and free of restrictions for citizen, resident, and foreigner alike. In practical terms, anyone could establish a branch of a foreign enterprise, incorporate a subsidiary, or acquire an existing corporation without concern for exchange controls or controls on direct investment. But within this general framework of freedom of establishment, there developed a key sector approach to restriction or prohibition of foreign control in certain industries.

Some controls have existed for a relatively long time; for example, the Railway Act amendment of 1904 added a provision that 'the majority of the directors of any company which has heretofore received, or hereafter receives, from the Government of Canada, under any Act of the Parliament of Canada, aid towards the construction of its railway or undertaking, or any part thereof, shall be British subjects.' Controls exist for financial institutions subject to federal jurisdiction where the 25–10 formula has been applied. Under this rule, non-residents collectively cannot hold directly or indirectly more than 25 per cent of the outstanding shares, and no individual or his associates may own more than 10 per cent. The 25–10 rule was first adopted by the federal government in 1964. Since then, some of the provinces have adopted it for financial institutions and in the case of Ontario for periodicals and paperback distributors. This 25–10 rule appears to be regarded as an almost magical formula, and it may be extended to other areas of the economy.[12]

Control or ownership of shares is usually coupled with citizenship and/or residence requirements for directors. Typically, legislation which imposes director qualifications requires that a majority or a greater proportion of directors be Canadian citizens ordinarily resident in Canada. Such director qualifications are to be found in both federal and provincial legislation. Another mechanism used to control the ownership of firms is the requirement that firms that wish to operate in a certain industry must be incorporated by special act or under the new provisions of the Canada Corporations Act. The special act or charter may restrict the ownership of shares of the corporation to residents or the issue of shares may be subject to approval by a regulatory body.

All industry is subject to a panoply of regulation and other government influence which applies without regard to the ownership or control of the enterprise. Some industry is more highly regulated than others. The Canadian regulatory scene resembles in general terms that of other industrialized countries of the western world.

The guidelines approach has also been attempted to induce desired behaviour on the part of foreign controlled firms. The 'Guidelines of Good Corporate Citizenship,' issued by the Department of Trade and Commerce in 1966, represent a blend of ownership and control regulation with regulation of behaviour. They were sent only to subsidiaries of foreign parents. Along with the questionnaire periodically sent to medium- and large-sized Canadian subsidiaries, the guidelines, to the extent that they are effective, represent behavioural control over foreign-owned firms.[13]

The federal government and Ontario have taken specific and selective steps to prevent the sale of controlling interest of a number of corporations to non-residents. The proposed takeovers of Home Oil and Denison Mines were thwarted by federal government action, and the Ontario government provided financial aid to McClelland and Stewart, which was said to have been considering selling out to foreign interests. In these situations in which the government acted there has been an element of political urgency involved. It is interesting to note, however, that that element was not apparent in the takeover of Supertest by British Petroleum.

In addition to controls on ownership and management, there has also been a variety of incentives to encourage research and development in Canada and Canadian participation in industry. The provinces have generally maintained an open-door policy, and at least several have actively promoted investment from abroad.

The Foreign Investment Review Act

Bill c-132, the Foreign Investment Review Act, is based to a large extent on the analysis and recommendations of the Gray Report.[14] The act received second reading on 4 April 1973 and was, at the date of writing, in the committee stage. Indications were that the act would be passed by parliament with some amendments but in substantially the same form in which it received second reading.

The bill requires that all proposed acquisitions of control of Canadian business enterprises by non-eligible persons and the establishment of new businesses in Canada, including the expansion of existing foreign businesses already in Canada into unrelated areas, must be registered with the Foreign Investment Review Agency established under the act.[15] The requirement to register acquisitions is, initially, to be subject to threshold limits; that is, if the gross assets of the Canadian enterprise are below $250,000 and if the gross revenue is below $3 million the takeover need not be registered.[16] The threshold provisions will become inoperative when the 'new business' provisions are brought into effect. All acquisitions will then have to be registered. The minister designated under the act (minister of industry, trade and commerce) must review the investment[17] to determine whether or not it is or is likely to be of significant benefit to Canada, having regard to five criteria:

a   the effect of the acquisition or establishment on the level and nature of economic activity in Canada, including employment;
b   the degree and significance of participation by Canadians in the business enterprise or new business and in any industry or industries in Canada of which the business enterprise or new business forms or would form a part;
c   the effect of the acquisition or establishment on productivity, industrial efficiency, technological development, product innovation and product variety in Canada;
d   the effect of the acquisition or establishment on competition within any industry or industries in Canada; and
e   the compatibility of the acquisition or establishment with national industrial and economic policies, taking into consideration industrial and economic policy objectives enunciated by the government or legislature of any province likely to be significantly affected by the acquisition or establishment.[18]

The power of final approval is given to the cabinet.[19] The minister may recommend approval or he may give notice to the parties that he is not prepared to recommend approval. The parties are given the right to a hearing and, in this connection, bargaining relevant to the criteria set out above is expected. The bill provides for written undertakings by the parties, and it is clearly intended that the minister should negotiate for the best deal for Canada before recommending approval. If there has been no cabinet order and the notice from the agency to the parties, which in effect commences formal negotiation, is not given within ninety days of registration, the investment is deemed to be allowed.[20]

The bill provides for the implementation of the screening process in stages. The screening of acquisitions is to begin when the act is proclaimed. However, the screening of the establishment of new businesses and the expansion of existing businesses into unrelated fields can be proclaimed separately.[21] The minister has indicated that he intends to consult with the provinces and to gain experience with the screening of takeovers before the screening of new businesses and expansions into unrelated activities is undertaken.

Non-eligible persons are defined to be all individuals other than Canadian citizens ordinarily resident in Canada and landed immigrants of less than six years' standing, and corporations controlled directly or indirectly by such individuals or by a group of persons any member of which is a non-eligible person.[22] A corporation is presumed to be non-eligible if, in the case of a corporation, the shares of which are publicly traded, 25 per cent or more of the ordinary voting rights are held by non-eligible persons or 5 per cent or more are held by any one individual or group of associates who are non-eligible persons, and in the case of other corporations, 40 per cent of the voting rights are so held. The fact of control by eligible persons can be established to rebut the presumption.[23]

Control of a Canadian business enterprise is acquired by the acquisition of substantially all of the property of the enterprise used in carrying on the business (a division capable of being operated separately constitutes a business enterprise for this purpose)[24] or by the acquisition of control through voting shares of a corporation.[25] As in the case of corporations presumed to be non-eligible unless the contrary is shown, the same 25 per cent (publicly traded shares) and 40 per cent poration.[25] Unless the contrary is shown, control is presumed acquired by acquisition of 5 per cent of the voting rights of corporations with publicly traded shares and 20 per cent for other corporations.[26] In addition, control is conclusively deemed to be acquired by the acquisition of more than 50 per cent of the ordinary voting rights.[27] On amalgamations, except in the case of a corporate reorganization without change of control and not related to purposes of the act, the amalgamated corporation is deemed to acquire control of the business of the constituent corporations.[28]

The bill contains a procedure to obtain advance rulings from the minister. If there is any question whether a party is a non-eligible person or whether a particular business would be related to another business carried on by a party, upon application of an interested party, the minister is required to issue an opinion forthwith for the guidance of that party.[29] There are two major problems with this advance ruling procedure. First, the need for speed and secrecy in negotiations involving takeovers and new investments is frequently crucial. Experience with advance ruling procedures such as those under the Income Tax Act have not been entirely satisfactory. Officials administering advance ruling procedures involving unconsummated transactions tend to be more negative in their positions and rulings than they would be if faced with a consummated transaction. Second, an opinion from the minister which is not binding on him is next to useless. The minimum that would be required to render the advance ruling procedure effective is for the minister to issue rulings which are binding on him. The minister has proposed an amendment which would make rulings binding on him for one year.

The act, when passed, is to be administered by the Foreign Investment Review Agency to be set up in the Department of Industry, Trade and Commerce and headed by a commissioner appointed by the cabinet.[30] The bill appears to contain adequate and reasonable provisions for its enforcement, including powers of investigation and provision for court orders to nullify investments in appropriate circumstances.[31]

As the bill is based on the recommendations and analysis of the Gray Report, the effect that the bill will have on the Canadian economy must be analysed in terms of the Gray Report. Much of what is said in the report makes a great deal of sense; indeed, it, together with Bill c-132 which it fostered, represents a more balanced view and constitutes a major step forward in the foreign ownership debate. Yet upon closer analysis of the crucial proposals of the report, it becomes clear that Bill c-132 can constitute only a first step in the development of policies that are appropriate and workable on the practical level.

One of the major and crucial shortcomings of the report which is reflected in the bill involves a failure to relate in a sufficiently systematic way the purposes of the screening agency to economic goals such as full employment, efficiency, and growth, and to conduct an analysis of the relationship. The consequences of such a failure are threefold. First, there is the danger that the mechanism will be regarded, both by Canadians and foreigners, simply as a device to keep out foreigners without a full appreciation of the economic consequences. Second, the agency itself may sooner or later see its own role as precisely that. Under the bill, the decision whether to accept or reject foreign investments rests squarely on the cabinet, a political body. Without well developed and well understood industry policies, it may be difficult to resist political demands to keep foreigners out regardless of the economic consequences even if the cabinet were inclined to. Finally, the agency may develop into an instrument of incrementalism, in that it attempts to bargain with non-residents for a little more of everything – a little more Canadian participation; a little more R & D; a little more exports. Incrementalism may not be appropriate if, as is likely, it is in Canada's long-term interest to concentrate its resources.[32]

These considerations lead to the conclusion that a policy of regulating foreign direct investment must be accompanied by well articulated industry policies. Indeed, it may be more appropriate to consider foreign ownership policy as being ancillary to industrial policies rather than the other way around. At any rate, throughout the Gray Report it becomes increasingly clear that the effectiveness of the proposals depends on the development of well defined industrial goals and strategies.[33] Recent ministers of industry, trade and commerce (both Mr Gillespie and his predecessor M Pépin) have stated repeatedly that specific industry policies are being developed. At the time of writing, we expected that there would be a public announcement in this connection during the fall of 1973.

Broadcasting

Only Canadians, or corporations all of whose directors are Canadians and 80 per cent of whose shares are owned by Canadians, can be granted broadcasting licenses.[34] Section 2(b) of the Broadcasting Act articulates the rationale for foreign ownership controls and illustrates the key sector approach: 'The Canadian broadcasting system should be effectively owned and controlled by Canadians so as to safeguard, enrich and strengthen the cultural, political, social and economic fabric of Canada.' Although some Canadians would argue that our broadcasting policy as currently executed is misguided in many respects, few would argue that the system should not be effectively owned and controlled by Canadians. Such a consensus demonstrates that the Canadian public has accepted the key sector approach.

The formulation and administration of broadcasting policy are highly complex undertakings and are beyond the scope of this paper. It is interesting to note, however, that the Canadian Radio Television Commission found it necessary to issue Canadian content regulations despite the existence of the comprehensive foreign ownership controls.[35] Does this not illustrate the point that Canadians are not necessarily more responsive to Canadian needs, culture, and policy than are foreigners? What is the point of having foreign ownership controls when a comprehensive regulatory scheme for the industry exists? If we do not have a regulatory scheme for an industry, what is the point of limiting foreign ownership? These con-

suggests that if we want certain kinds of conduct and results, we will not get them simply by limiting foreign ownership.
siderations highlight the distinction between limiting foreign ownership as such and regulating the activity of firms in an industry. Our experience with broadcasting

Pride of ownership is an important consideration, particularly in broadcasting. We suggest that that element figures large in the wide acceptance of foreign owner-ship limitations in broadcasting. But we must clearly understand that those limita-tions are protection, nothing more, of Canadian ownership. It is not evident that Canadian ownership somehow makes broadcasting more sensitive to Canadian values and policy.

In any review of the broadcasting industry, it must be noted that there is substan-tial competition along the Canada-US border from radio and television stations located in the United States. Moreover, relatively distant signals from US television stations are picked up and distributed to local receiving areas in Canada by the cable TV operators.[36] Another special feature of the Canadian broadcasting industry is the prevalence of the publicly owned corporation which maintains the largest net-work of radio and television broadcasting services. Notwithstanding the facts of indigenous ownership and the public broadcasting system, a major concern in reg-ulation of the industry centres upon program content.

Publishing

A large proportion of the publishing and distribution industry in Canada is owned and controlled by non-residents, and it appears that the trend is towards increased foreign control in the absence of government action. Except for the income tax and customs tariff provisions concerning special editions of foreign periodicals that con-tain advertising directed specifically at the Canadian market, the federal govern-ment has not responded to the problem. Canadians purchasing advertising space directed at the Canadian market in foreign periodicals are not permitted to claim the expense as a deduction for income tax purposes.[37] The Customs Tariff prohibits entry into Canada of special editions of foreign magazines,[38] *Time* and *Readers' Digest* being two well-known exceptions to those provisions.

But there have been indications that governments are concerned about the pub-lishing industry and that they may be prepared to take further action as Canadians come increasingly to regard publishing and distribution of printed material as a key sector for many of the same reasons as broadcasting.[39] The sale of Ryerson Press to McGraw-Hill in 1970, following shortly after the sale of W.J. Gage to another American firm, prompted a great deal of concern about Canadian-owned publishing, or what was left of it. In Ontario, the expression of concern led to the appointment of the Royal Commission on Book Publishing to inquire into the industry and to make recommendations.[40]

In a display of haste uncharacteristic of royal commissions, this commission issued two interim reports and urged immediate action on two fronts. In its First Interim Report, dated 23 March 1971, the commission recommended that the pro-vince make a loan of $1 million through the Ontario Development Corporation to McClelland and Stewart, the large Canadian-owned book publisher which was in financial difficulty and threatened with takeover by American interests.[41] In its Second Interim Report of 8 June 1971, the commission urged immediate action to prevent US interests from taking over Ontario magazine and paperback distributors. With equally uncharacteristic haste, the Ontario government produced legislation on 14 June, effective immediately, establishing a system of licensing.[42] Under the scheme, licensees are allocated territories and no license is to be issued to a corporation if more than 25 per cent of its voting shares are held by non-residents and if any one non-resident and his associates own more than 10 per cent.[43] The commission recommended breaking up the paperback and magazine distribution system controlled by Metro Toronto News Company. It also recommended continuation of the restrictions on new entrants into the distribution business and extension of restrictions to cover all retail bookstores in Ontario.[44]

The legislation accomplishes its purpose of preventing further takeovers. However, it does not address itself to the question of why we want Canadian-owned distributors. The purpose surely must be to facilitate and encourage distributors to place Canadian materials before the public. But Canadian ownership does not necessarily accomplish that. It is possible that Canadian-owned bookstores and newsstands want the 'tried and true' US publications.[45] This predilection for American material may reflect a lack of demand in Canada for Canadian works.

In its final report the commission made a number of recommendations including the establishment of an Ontario Book Publishing Board which would, among other things, administer a system of subsidies and grants to publishers and writers.[46] It suggested that all books receiving subsidies and grants should be required to be printed and manufactured in Canada. Training courses in all facets of the book publishing industries were recommended. The commission also thought that the 25–10 formula should be applied to ownership of book publishers and export sales should be encouraged, and it made a number of valuable recommendations concerning the marketing of Canadian books.

The problems of publishing and distribution of Canadian works are very complex. The recommendations of the commission illustrate that we must not delude ourselves into believing that a simple solution such as prohibiting foreign ownership will solve them. Just as in broadcasting, if we want specific results it may be necessary to provide a positive, regulatory framework to achieve them, and/or appropriate incentives to promote them.

Banks and other financial institutions

The board of directors of a chartered bank must be 75 per cent Canadian, and non-residents collectively are not permitted to own more than 25 per cent of the outstanding shares of a bank, with an additional stipulation that no one person and his associates (resident or non-resident) can own more than 10 per cent.[47] Similar restrictions with minor modifications have been applied to life insurance, loan, trust, and sales finance companies under federal jurisdiction.[48] Some of the provinces have followed the federal lead. Ontario[49] and Alberta[50] have citizenship and residence requirements for directors and they apply the 25–10 formula to non-resident shareholders of loan and trust companies.

The justification for key sector treatment of financial institutions is that Canadian ownership and control of these institutions are essential for the proper implementation and execution of economic policy. One result of the restrictions inherent in key sector treatment has been that competition by foreign-controlled firms is severely limited if not altogether precluded. In the case of banking, while the Canadian public is the most highly over-serviced one in terms of the number of branches, it is under-serviced in merchant banking functions. Moreover, the Canadian banking system appears to operate on the basis of conscious parallelism, despite frequent protestations by bankers to the contrary. Canadian banks are insulated as a system from direct foreign competition on the domestic market and they have managed to minimize competition between themselves.[51] To be sure, Canadians have an interest in preventing foreign takeovers of existing banks. However, the case for protecting them from new foreign competition is not strong, especially with the emplacement of a mechanism to screen foreign takeovers and new foreign direct investment.

It is not evident that banks whose shares are owned by Canadians are more responsive to public policy or are better citizens of the financial community than if the shares were held by non-residents; there is no automatic mechanism which ensures that result. First, the nexus between ownership and management has been severed in fact. Indeed, the law explicitly recognizes this fact by prohibiting any one person and his associates from holding more than 10 per cent of the shares. Moreover, as we have seen in the case of the broadcasting and publishing industries, ownership limitations do not induce desired conduct. Substantive regulatory devices are required. In broadcasting it is the regulatory powers of the CRTC; in banking it is a combination of factors – specific provisions contained in the Bank Act, the surveillance and regulatory powers of the Bank of Canada, parliamentary surveillance, and the decennial revisions of the Bank Act, among others.

It is frequently argued that foreign-controlled banks have access to foreign sources of funds and hence would be in a position to thwart Canadian monetary policy in periods of constraint. However, Canadian banks also have foreign credits at their disposal.[52] It is also said that domestically owned banks are more susceptible to moral suasion. That proposition is subject to serious question. At any rate, with the existence of a screening mechanism to monitor the operations of a foreign-controlled bank, it is likely that such a bank would find it in its interest to be highly responsive to Canadian policies. The existence of the screening agency combined with the regular tools available to control the operations of banks should be more than adequate to ensure the responsiveness of a foreign controlled bank.

The fear that Canadian banks would succumb to foreign competition does not appear to be justified. The 'Big Five' Canadian banks are among the largest in the world,[53] and they have substantial operations abroad where they appear to be successful. It may be true that they are inefficient on the domestic market, but, if that is so, it surely cannot be because of their small size. The absence of effective pressures to promote efficiency would appear to be a major factor. A limited foreign presence in the banking system may well provide the pressures needed.

The Royal Commission on Banking and Finance, which reported in 1964, was concerned about encouraging competition in the banking system when it made the following observations:

It should be remembered that competition is an uneasy state and that, however much they thrive under it, businessmen have an inclination to protect themselves against it.

> We must therefore be alert to development which would lessen competition or threaten its vigour ...
>
> The community as a whole stands to benefit from more open competition and it is this advantage rather than the comfort of any one group of institutions which should be sought.[54]

To inject competition into the banking system, the commission recommended that 'near banks' – institutions such as trust companies which take deposits – be permitted to incorporate their banking activities as *bona fide* banks. This has not happened.

The history of comfortable, gentlemanly co-operation between the banks and the size of the Big Five render it highly questionable whether it is possible to set up new banks to compete effectively with them.[55] To be sure, the Bank Act prohibits certain kinds of anti-competitive arrangements such as common directorships, interbank shareholdings, and outright collusion, and the application of the proposed Competition Act would prohibit anti-competitive behaviour of banks which is not subject to regulation by the Bank of Canada. Nevertheless, by and large, combines policy tends to be negative in nature and ill-suited to the purpose of injecting fresh competition into an industry which has long experienced comfortable co-existence.

The establishment of the screening agency envisioned in Bill C-132 will provide a more flexible control mechanism. The key sector approach, reflected in legislation such as that relating to banking, results in an all or nothing policy. Once a sector is designated as key, we exclude all foreign controlled firms regardless of the anti-competitive effects. However, the screening mechanism is an approach which is capable of being calibrated to a finer degree. Even if we conclude that an industry is a key sector, there may still be a role for a properly supervised foreign-controlled presence. The screening agency is a device whereby we could inject a limited foreign presence into the banking system to encourage efficiency while maintaining an adequate degree of control over foreign-controlled banks.

The screening agency could select foreign banks on the basis of the capabilities that would fill particular gaps in the Canadian capital markets. In order to provide for controls over its operation, it could be stipulated in the bank's charter that at some future point in time it may be necessary to limit the bank's growth, and that it may be subject to special regulation whenever public interest demands. If a foreign-controlled bank grew to such an extent, for example, that the effectiveness of monetary policy was impaired, a limit on its size could be imposed. The mere existence of these powers would be a strong inducement for foreign-controlled banks to be highly responsive to Canadian policy.

These special regulatory and limiting powers are also necessary because the voting shares of the foreign-controlled banks would be concentrated in a few hands, whereas the shares of Canadian-owned banks must by law be widely dispersed. The screening agency will also wish to restrict the transfer ability of the shares held by non-residents to ensure that the foreign owners who control the bank remain acceptable to Canada.

The introduction of a screening mechanism constitutes a selective process which would permit a more finely calibrated policy response than does the key sector approach. Whereas the screening mechanism constitutes a more restrictive approach to foreign direct investment generally, it can result in a more liberal response in the sectors we now protect as key. Once we decide that a sector is key, we must identify the interests we are trying to protect and decide precisely how far we need to go to protect them. We must be careful not to extend the protection beyond a point where protection is no longer justifiable in terms of those interests. If we protect a sector beyond that point necessary for public policy purposes we are really protecting industry because it is Canadian and not because of any other public policy imperatives.

Securities industry

Recently there has been concern about non-resident ownership of securities firms. In 1969 soon after Merrill Lynch of New York took over Royal Securities, one of Canada's largest and oldest investment houses, the Moore Committee was appointed by the Investment Dealers' Association and the major stock exchanges to study the securities industry, particularly in relation to public participation in ownership and to foreign ownership. The committee submitted its report in May 1970.[56]

The committee concluded that further foreign control over Canadian firms should be prohibited.[57] To accomplish this the committee recommended that ownership outside the firm should be limited to 25 per cent, any one individual and his associates being limited to a maximum of 10 per cent.[58] Foreign securities firms would be prohibited from investing in Canadian firms to any extent.[59] Liberal grandfather provisions were recommended to prevent the retroactive application of those recommendations.[60]

One is inclined to agree with the Moore Report's conclusion that the securities industry is a key sector for the same reasons that obtain in banking.[61] However, as is the case with banking, key sector analysis does not lead automatically to the conclusion that there is no room for direct foreign investment.[62] A limited foreign presence in the industry is desirable to ensure that the self-regulating securities industry maintains efficient operations by world standards. Moreover, outright limitation of foreign direct participation in the securities industry has serious regional economic implications. It must be recognized that the Quebec securities industry has been suffering severely in recent years. There may be a vital role for non-resident direct investment in developing the securities industry in that province and elsewhere, notably British Columbia, if Canadian firms, largely centred in Toronto, are not prepared to do so. The battle lines are being drawn.

In 1969 a Quebec committee to study financial institutions, under the chairmanship of Jacques Parizeau, recommended that Quebec decline to follow Ottawa's lead in limiting foreign ownership of provincially controlled financial institutions for two reasons. First, it asked, why distinguish between American intrusion into such provincial companies and intrusion from interests in other Canadian provinces? Second, the committee saw competition from without as healthy for economic development.[63] The Quebec authorities rejected the Moore proposals, published in 1970, and actively invited direct non-resident investment.[64] In addition, the Quebec government appointed the Bouchard Committee to study the Moore proposals. This committee rejected the Moore proposals and recommended that Quebec securities firms should have easy access to outside capital and that, within limits to be set by the Quebec Securities Commission, foreign-controlled firms should be welcome in Quebec.[65] By the time the Bouchard Committee reported the Quebec government had already introduced legislation to consolidate and strengthen the control of the QSC over the two Montreal stock exchanges to prevent them from adopting the Moore proposals.[66]

The Ontario government adopted the Moore proposals that no company may be registered after 14 July 1971 as an adviser, dealer, or underwriter if more than 25 per cent of the shares are held by non-residents and any one non-resident and his associates hold more that 10 per cent.[67] Exemptions may be allowed. At the same time, the Ontario government requested the Ontario Securities Commission to study the Moore Report with particular reference to 'the question of public partici-pation in investment companies and the continuing status of existing registrants which are foreign controlled.'[68]

At the end of July 1971 the Investment Dealers' Association and all the major stock exchanges, including the two Montreal exchanges, released a report which essentially recommended adopting the 25–10 formula of the Moore Report. However, far less liberal grandfather provisions were recommended.[69] Basically, a foreign-owned firm would be given an option. If it chose not to conform to the required ownership ratios, the firm's capital base would be frozen at the minimum required by the IDA and stock exchanges, during a recent fiscal year ending not later than 31 March 1971, and its growth would be limited to 10 per cent of net earnings thereafter. If the firm were willing to conform to the required ratios, it could grow at a rate of 1.2 per cent of earning for each 1 per cent of equity sold to Canadians. There was a schedule for disinvestment with a minimum Canadian participation of 15 per cent in 1974 and 75 per cent in 1985. In the latter year, the dominant non-resident would be permitted another three years to reduce his holdings in the required maximum of 10 per cent. Canadian subsidiaries of foreign parents which have gone public would have no option. They would have to Canadianize under the proposed formula.

After a series of public hearings in the fall of 1971, the committee of the OSC, established in response to the government's request, published its report in April 1972.[70] The OSC committee concluded that permitting foreign firms to operate branch offices 'in effect, merely diverts business originating in Canada from Cana-dian firms, which in turn reduces their ability to compete.'[71] At the same time, the committee stated that it was not 'in the public interest to provide Ontario firms with protection from the innovative and efficient practices suggested for the existing foreign controlled firms.' Thus, the committee justified a compromise prohibiting new foreign firms – enough foreign-controlled competitors are enough. The commit-tee also recommended the continued application of the 25–10 formula to all classes of registrants, the 25–10 limitation to apply not only to voting shares, but also to non-voting shares and debt.[72] However, where the non-resident owner is a firm which holds registration in a similar capacity in a foreign jurisdiction, and the OSC is of the view that the relationship facilitates reciprocal trading and research arrangements, subject to the approval of the OSC, the non-resident dealer and his associates may own up to 25 per cent of the voting shares, or of the non-voting shares or of the debt of the Ontario registrant, notwithstanding the 10 per cent restriction.

While we believe that a certain degree of control of foreign ownership in the securities industry is required, the controls must be based on reason and analysis. In the securities industry as well as elsewhere, the public interest in controlling foreign ownership lies not in protecting the comfort of any one group, but in the preservation of a viable industry responsive to public policy and efficient by world standards. Once we go beyond the point necessary to ensure a responsive industry, we are in effect protecting the comfort of one group at the expense of the public interest in maintaining an efficient industry. To prohibit the establishment of new foreign-controlled firms and to apply the 25–10 rule retroactively is not justified on the evidence presented. The public interest does not demand that each and every firm be controlled by Canadians. The public interest in a responsive, competitive, and efficient industry will best be served if there is a balance between Canadian-owned and foreign-owned firms. In order to achieve such a balance, foreign takeovers of existing Canadian owned firms should be prohibited and the 25–10 rule applied to them. New foreign-owned firms, should be permitted the right to establish, subject to regulation with regard to raiding Canadian firms of staff and perhaps other matters. Firms whose foreign parents are publicly owned should be limited to a growth rate permitted by Canadian earnings. In the long run, when Canadian-owned firms are permitted to go fully public, that restriction could be removed. The screening agency to be established under Bill c-132, as well as the osc, would appear to have a role in achieving a balance of ownership in the securities industry.

Transportation

Domestic air, rail, and water transport are, for all practical purposes, 100 per cent Canadian controlled. Whatever the foreign holdings of shares in the public corporations (eg, Canadian Pacific, Canada Steamships), management and control is clearly centred in Canada and satisfies the test of being truly Canadian.[73] The situation with regard to highway transport is different. There is significant non-Canadian control of intercity bus operations (Greyhound) and intercity trucking operations (eg Direct Winters, Gill Alltrans Express), although the trucking field is characterized by strong Canadian-owned carriers as well. The degree and significance of foreign ownership in highway transportation urgently requires further study.

Existing law and administrative practice provide for discretionary control over both acquisitions and new service by foreign operators, or at least contain the potential for such control. In most aspects of intercity transportation, new services, whether foreign owned or not, must obtain a franchise from a regulatory tribunal. In addition, there exists significant control or potential for control over acquisitions of Canadian enterprises which hold operating licenses.

Under the National Transportation Act,[74] a railway company, a company engaged in water transportation, or a person operating a motor vehicle undertaking or an air carrier to which the legislative jurisdiction of the parliament of Canada extends that proposes to acquire directly or indirectly an interest by purchase, lease, merger, consolidation, or otherwise, in the business or undertaking of any person whose principal business is transportation, whether or not such business or undertaking is subject to the jurisdiction of parliament, must give notice of the proposed acquisition to the Canadian Transport Commission (section 27.) Public notice is then given of the proposed acquisition, and any person affected by the acquisition may file an objection to it. When objection is received, the commission is required to investigate the proposed acquisition and is empowered to disallow it if in its opinion 'such acquisition will unduly restrict competition or otherwise be prejudicial to the public interest.' Thus, a foreign enterprise already engaged in transportation in Canada may be subject to section 27 if its operations are interprovincial. A foreign enterprise which is not engaged in transportation in Canada may well not be subject to this jurisdiction even if it is engaged in transportation outside Canada, nor does the section come into operation unless objection to a proposed acquisition if received.[75]

The public-interest test of section 27 would appear to be broad enough to enable the commission to take into account the fact that the proposed acquirer is a foreign enterprise. Nowhere is the notion of public interest limited. The national transportation policy set out broadly in section 3 of the act should be given full consideration in each case by the commission and this might well lead the commission to conclude that foreign penetration of the industry through the proposed acquisition would not be in the public interest.[76] Objection may be filed by 'any person affected by the proposed acquisition' and by 'any association or other body representing carriers or transportation undertaking affected by such acquisitions.' This is presumably broad enough to enable objection to be filed by any person reasonably interested in the proposed acquisition, and it might be said to follow reasonably from lack of objection in the case of a proposed acquisition by a foreign operation that none of the affected parties thought that the fact of foreignness of the acquirer was relevant to their interests. Foreignness would very likely be made an issue by one of the persons entitled to object in a case where that fact is relevant to any interests that might be adversely affected. And in those cases it seems entirely appropriate for the commission to take the element of foreignness into account. Foreign ownership is obviously a matter of public interest and where the commission can be satisfied that a proposed acquisition would be prejudicial to the public interest by reason of the fact of the foreignness of the acquirer, it should act accordingly.[77]

Under the Aeronautics Act, the commission is given power to make regulations, *inter alia*, prohibiting the change of control, transfer, consolidation, merger, or lease of commercial air services except subject to such conditions as may by such regulations be prescribed.[78] The Air Carrier Regulations[79] provide that no person shall enter into a transaction that is intended to or would result in a change of control, consolidation, merger, lease, or transfer of any commercial air service unless notice of the proposed transaction is given to the Air Transport Committee.[80] The regulations supplement section 27 of the National Transportation Act[81] with the result that the committee may review any such transaction to determine whether its consummation 'will unduly restrict competition or otherwise be prejudicial to the public interest.'[82] The Commercial Air Services Regulations,[83] superseded by the Air Carrier Regulations, contained a similar provision. It is not known whether the question of foreign ownership has ever been considered in this connection. Certainly the regulatory jurisdiction as conferred by the statute and regulations is broad enough to enable the Canadian Transport Commission to consider any factor in a proposed acquisition which it thinks relevant. Under the Air Regulations, two-thirds of the directors of a corporation must be Canadian citizens for the corporation to qualify as owner of a Canadian aircraft.[84]

At the moment, the federal power to regulate interprovincial highway services is delegated to provincial boards by the Motor Vehicle Transport Act,[85] and the provincial boards are directed to regulate interprovincial transport as they regulate intraprovincial transport. Most provinces, as noted, have a comprehensive system of franchising new service. Provincial laws and regulations governing acquisitions vary. Some, as in the case of Quebec, have very specific power to control acquisitions. Under the Quebec Transport Board Act,[86] any merger, sale, or transfer of any transportation service or any transaction, agreement, or contract of such a nature as to bring about a change in the control of such service, must have prior approval by the board. The Ontario provision[87] is not so clear but does appear to give unqualified general power to the Ontario Highway Transport Board to approve transfers or control of highway transport operations. The question of its practical operation is somewhat complex and difficult.[88]

Although entry into the business of providing rail services in Canada is restricted both legally and practically, there are in addition restrictions on the management of a railway enterprise subject to federal jurisdiction which would effectively limit acquisition of a substantial interest by foreign persons. One assumes that the question will never arise in connection with the publicly owned systems (Canadian National, British Columbia, Ontario Northland), and the provisions of the Railway Act[89] would effectively prevent foreign domination of Canadian Pacific, were that ever to become a practical possibility.

Although some major inland water service is subject to the usual requirements of the certificate of public convenience and necessity, there is no specific power to control acquisitions or to regulate penetration by foreign interests. There are, however, restrictions on the right of cabotage and ownership of vessels registered in Canada.[90]

Communications

Telephone services regulation has been undertaken at the federal, provincial, and municipal levels. At the federal level, only telegraph and telephone services for which charges were made to the public were under the jurisdiction of the Canadian Transport Commission until very recently.[91] However, the regulatory jurisdiction was expanded to include 'private wire' services, such as telex, TWX, and computer-data transmission, which are connected to telegraph and telephone systems under federal jurisdiction.[92]

Control over federal telegraph and telephone operations is accomplished in two ways. First, the Railway Act provides that tolls are subject to the approval of the CTC and that the operations of companies are otherwise subject to regulations by the CTC in much the same way as are railways. Second, the special acts of incorporation for federal telephone and telegraph companies contain authorizations, limitations, and restrictions. For example, the charter of Bell Canada makes the issue of shares subject to the approval of the CTC. Regulation and control of provincial telephone systems proceeds along similiar lines.[93]

The Canadian government is concerned about the extent of non-resident participation in Canadian computer industry, particularly software and data transmission facilities. The Department of Communications has undertaken a study of the tele-communications industry.

Energy

Recently there has been a worldwide concern over energy supplies, particularly fossil fuels. The so-called energy crisis in the US, whether real or manifactured, has brought the question of Canadian energy policy dramatically into public view. This a highly complex question which is only now beginning to receive the kind of atten-tion required to develop appropriate long-term policies. The problem in Canada is complicated by the fact that a number of energy industries are foreign controlled, particularly from the US.[94]

Energy policy is subject to the jurisdiction of the federal government and the pro-vinces. The provinces have jurisdiction by virtue of their control of resources within the province. However, once those resources move across provincial boundaries, federal jurisdiction comes into play.[95]

The National Energy Board regulates in the public interest the construction and operation of oil and gas pipelines, transmission charges, export and import of gas and oil, export of electric power and construction, and operation of power lines.[96] In considering applications for the construction and operation of pipelines, the National Energy Board is directed to take account of all relevant matters. Specific-ally, it is directed to have regard, among other things, to the extent to which Cana-dians will have an opportunity of participating in the financing of the lines.[97] There is nothing to indicate that the board has interpreted this direction to mean that only Canadian-owned firms should be permitted certificates for pipeline construction and operation.[98] At any rate, only companies which have been incorporated by special act of parliament or under the new provisions of the Canada Corporations Act may apply for certificates.[99] This is the point where the ownership of pipeline companies may be controlled.

The ownership and development of resources located within the provinces are under provincial jurisdiction. There do not appear to be any provincial restrictions on the nationality of ownership and control. One of the major concerns is the lack of processing within the provinces. The Alberta government has indicated that it has used informal means to encourage more processing within the province. However, the success of these informal means is doubtful, and there are pressures developing to adopt ownership restrictions. It is unlikely, however, that ownership restrictions will result in increased processing. What may be needed are not owner-ship restrictions but processing regulations and incentives similar to the ones Ontario has adopted in relation to mining. Such measures get at the heart of the problem by substantively regulating and encouraging appropriate activity, a result not guaranteed by simply limiting foreign ownership.

Oil and gas leases under federal jurisdiction may not be granted to a corporation unless at least 50 per cent of its shares are held by Canadians or the shares are listed on a Canadian stock exchange and Canadians have an opportunity of participating in the financing and ownership of the corporation.[100] Water resources and the gen-eration and distribution of electrical power are largely under public ownership.

Mining

Mining falls largely within provincial jurisdiction. There appear to be no provincial ownership restrictions in respect of mining operations. However, there is considerable concern that ore is not sufficiently processed in Canada.[101]

Ontario has enacted legislation and regulations to encourage the processing of ores to the metal stage. The Mining Act was amended in 1969 in order to permit the lieutenant governor in council to cancel mining leases if mining operations did not meet the processing-in-Canada requirements. There are provisions which enable the lieutenant governor in council to exempt any lands from the processing requirements.[102] The Mining Tax Act was amended at the same time to permit an annual deduction for mining tax purposes of 10 per cent of the costs of development provided that processing-in-Canada requirements are met. Again, there are provisions which permit selective exemptions from the processing requirements[103] and which have been liberally used.[104] There are indications that the regulation provisions already have had an effect, although the nature and size of the effect may be subject to dispute. At any rate, the Ontario provisions, being a blend of tax incentives, selective exemptions, persuasion and negotiation, and the legislation backing them up constitute a reasonable first step towards a long-term solution to the problem.

This approach does not unduly focus on the ownership factor, which may in reality be irrelevant to the degree of processing of minerals in Canada. It permits us to achieve a fine balance between our interest in promoting mining development and our interest in achieving a higher degree of processing in Canada. Perhaps the most important aspect of the Ontario approach was summarized by Mr Allan Lawrence, then Ontario minister of mines and northern affairs: 'It is going to take a long time ... I really do not think that the thing will start bearing measurable fruit, as far as the economy of the North is concerned, for 20 years. But at least the cards are on the table; the rules are out where all can see them and read them. People who are making investments in this country now know what the rules of the game are.'[105] British Columbia subsequently enacted similar legislation which requires that the processing be done within the province.[106]

Under federal mining provisions, mining leases in the Northwest Territories[107] and mineral exploration grants in northern Canada[108] may be granted only to Canadians or corporations, a majority of whose shares are held by Canadians or whose shares are listed on a Canadian stock exchange. As in the case of the oil and gas regulations, the purpose of these provisions is to ensure that Canadians have an opportunity of participating in the development of the natural resources of the north.

Laws of general application[109]

Companies legislation
The Canada Corporations Act [110] and the Ontario Business Corporations Act[111] permit public corporations to restrict the transferrability of their shares where such restriction is necessary pursuant to the provisions of other legislation to ensure that

a certain proportion of their shares are held by Canadian residents. The Ontario Business Corporations Act also requires that a majority of directors of every corporation shall be resident Canadians.[112] A number of other provincial governments have enacted or are in the process of enacting similar legislation. On 18 July 1973 the federal government introduced legislation requiring companies to have a majority of resident Canadians on their boards.[113] Moreover, both provincial and federal companies legislation have requirements with respect to the holding of directors' and shareholders' meetings within Canada.

It is notable that the Gray Report considered that residency requirements with respect to directors would not be 'a step of great significance.'[114] It appears that such requirements are more cosmetic than substantive. However, the Gray Report did concede that 'mandatory provisions relating to Canadian directors could possibly contribute in some measure to an improvement in the performance of foreign controlled firms – particularly if this step were adopted in conjunction with other approaches.'

Income Tax Act
The basic policy question is the determination of how much of the revenue of multinational or other foreign-based enterprises should be exacted by Canada, or by any other country with which the enterprise has contact. The Income Tax Act has many detailed rules dealing with this question. In addition, bilateral conventions have been worked out with some twenty countries to deal with allocation of income and expenses between Canada and the other countries and with the taxation of dividends, interest, royalties, management, and technical fees.

Degree of Canadian ownership
The Income Tax Act presently imposes generally a 15 per cent withholding tax on dividends paid to non-resident shareholders. The rate will increase to 25 per cent in 1976 subject to renegotiation of treaties. If the payor corporation has a 'degree of Canadian ownership,' the tax is reduced to 10 per cent (20 in 1976).[115] The legislative history of the present provisions provides an interesting lesson in the difficulties surrounding the drafting of effective legislation to prevent circumvention.[116] Most of the problems result from the highly flexible corporate vehicle.

The degree-of-Canadian-ownership provision has been ineffective in achieving its stated purpose. Even in the immediate post-1963 period when the inducements were substantially greater than they currently are, very few corporations complied, for there are several strong pressures for foreign owners to retain 100 per cent control. First, corporations with low earnings and new operations subject to the risks inherent in a new venture would find it difficult and uneconomic to float an equity issue. Second, foreign parents tend to fear the managerial problems which might arise because of the presence of a minority; these problems may result not in a conflict between national and corporate goals, but from conflicts over earnings retention, expansion, dividends, and purchasing policies. Third, a corporation may simply not be in need of capital provided by an issue of equity shares. It may have sufficient funds available to it from other sources such as retained earnings and debt.

To overcome all of these factors, the tax incentive would have to be substantial. A reduced withholding tax would not be enough because many foreign-owned corporations are under no pressure to pay dividends, or the additional 5 per cent withholding tax has no effect on their worldwide tax position. Other tax incentives would be required, would have to be available to all Canadian corporations, and tax cost of those incentives could be very high. And what of the proceeds of such issues? They could simply be paid to the parent. This may have adverse balance-of-payments effects as well as capital market implications. The proceeds could be used to initiate new direct investment thereby in effect increasing effective foreign control (albeit not 100 per cent), a situation which may not be desirable in terms of Canadianization policy.

An even more important cost in terms of Canadian economic development is that a minority interest may make the availability of capital, new products, research and development, and access to markets and R & D less free and more costly to the Canadian subsidiaries than was the case before dilution of the parent's ownership. This effect is extremely difficult to quantify and to illustrate precisely, for matters such as these depend to a very large extent on informal relationships, tacit understandings, and modes of operation. When Union Carbide Canada Limited offered shares to Canadians, its president said that the company could no longer expect to receive patent preferences, low-cost loans, or free access to the parents' export sales arrangements.[117]

It is generally agreed that this effort to 'Canadianize' industry through the tax system has been fruitless. Even the process of tax reform from which Canada has just emerged has not removed this ill-conceived effort from the tax system.

Small business deduction
The new Income Tax Act permits a 'Canadian-controlled private corporation' to enjoy a 25 per cent rate on the first $50,000 of business income, compared with the general rate of 50 per cent.[118] The low rate is available as long as the accumulated taxable income remains below $400,000. Thus, under normal circumstances, if the corporation pays sufficient dividends to keep accumulated taxable income below $400,000, the low rate will be available indefinitely.

The small business incentive is available only to Canadian-controlled private corporations. The stated purpose of this restriction is to 'encourage Canadian ownership of our expanding business.'[119] If control of the business is acquired by non-residents, the corporation will be required to repay, over five years, all the tax saving it has received.[120] By removing the small business incentive when accumulated taxable income exceeds $400,000, these provisions encourage the distribution of earnings. Consequently, the claim that this provision encourages *expanding* business is subject to doubt. In fact, the bias seems to be such that Canadian controlled private business may remain relatively small.[121] The repayment of the small business incentive when control is acquired by non-residents can be circumvented since section 190 applies only to share purchases. Non-residents need only purchase the assets of the corporation.

The proposed section seems to have accomplished little beyond requiring that future foreign takeovers of small business be conducted in the form of an asset rather than share purchase. Asset purchases might involve other complications.

Interest

The tax legislation new permits Canadian corporations to deduct interest on money borrowed to acquire shares in other corporations.[122] This provision is said to put Canadian corporations in the same position when competing in takeover bids as foreign corporations which can deduct such interest in the home country.[123] Under the old legislation, a number of techniques had been developed which in effect made the interest deductible.[124] The proposed provision makes such interest deductions less cumbersome, and makes it possible to deduct interest in situations where the earlier techniques were not available or impracticable. The result of the change, while significant in terms of law, may not be as great on the practical level as one would suppose.

Thin capitalization

The thin capitalization rule imposes a limitation on the deductibility, for tax purposes, of interest paid by a resident corporation to the extent that its foreign held debt exceeds three times the equity of the corporation.[125] This rule appears to encourage direct investment as opposed to investment by way of debt. In this way, the rule is inconsistent with the government's policy of reducing foreign direct investment. In any event, the rule can be circumvented to the extent that the Canadian corporation can borrow from a Canadian source on the parent's guarantee.

GUIDELINES FOR GOOD CORPORATE BEHAVIOUR

In 1966 the Department of Trade and Commerce set out twelve principles of good corporate behaviour for subsidiaries of foreign parents in response to President Johnson's 'voluntary' guidelines.[126] In addition, procedures were established to obtain information on a voluntary basis from large- and medium-sized subsidiaries of foreign parents to determine the extent of foreign influence in Canada and the performance of foreign-owned corporations.

If we feel that guidelines are necessary, we should give them the force of law and apply them to all corporations regardless of ownership. Some steps along these lines are being taken such as the amendments to the corporation and securities laws requiring a greater degree of disclosure, but more remains to be done. It is too easy to issue voluntary guidelines which have the ring of rectitude and to apply them to foreign-owned operations. But when we judge the performance of our own firms against the guidelines or when we try to translate them into law, the questionable value of the guidelines becomes evident. The Gray Report concluded that these 'Winters guidelines' have had no significant effect.

CANADA DEVELOPMENT CORPORATION

The Canada Development Corporation had a long and difficult gestation period. It was first proposed as government policy in 1963. Since then, there has been every variety of reaction to it. At last the CDC appears to be with us for better or worse, established by an act given royal assent on 30 June 1971. The CDC has now been in operation for about two years.

A good summary of the purposes which most people have in mind for the CDC was given by the Commons Committee on External Affairs and National Defence:

> The main purpose of the Canada Development Corporation should be that of a large hold-ing company with entrepreneurial and management functions; it should assume a leader-ship role in Canada's business and financial community in close co-operation with exist-ing institutions; it should help to organize consortia of investors domestic and foreign to carry out large projects beyond the capacity of a single institution, while throughout maintaining a clear Canadian presence.
>
> Its main purpose should not be to buy back Canadian businesses now owned by Americans.[127]

In addition, when the CDC issues shares to the public, Canadians will have an addi-tional opportunity to invest in Canadian industry. The act as passed by parliament reflects these purposes.[128]

The act requires that all directors must be Canadian citizens and that the majority reside in Canada.[129] Only Canadian residents and non-resident Canadian citizens are permitted to hold voting shares; non-resident foreigners are permitted to hold non-voting preferred shares.[130]

The success with which the CDC fulfils its purpose will ultimately depend upon the quality of the management personnel. To fulfil a dynamic and entrepreneurial function, an unusual kind of person is required. Moreover, the temptation for gov-ernments to view the CDC as a political tool will be ever present. It will take strong management to resist government pressures to meddle in the affairs of the CDC.[131] Judging from the two years during which the CDC has been in operation, there is every reason to be hopeful that the CDC will ultimately fulfil its purposes.

EXTRATERRITORIAL EFFECT OF LAWS

Extraterritorial extension of law is inherent in the complex of world legal and economic relations. To a greater or lesser degree the operations of a MNE are affected by the laws of each nation state with which it has contact, and the national laws which come into play at each point of contact have some effect, however minor, throughout the operation in other states. Each state needs a mechanism of countervailing power to contain unwanted intrusions of foreign law. The existence of such a mechanism would likely inhibit the propensity of the United States to extend its laws through the instrumentality of US-based enterprises.

No Canadian legislation can change the fact that foreign laws affect Canadian operations. What we can do is to spell out clearly how we want Canadian firms, regardless of ownership, to act and to back up those prescriptions with appropriate sanctions. The screening agency to be established under the Foreign Investment Review Act (Bill C-132) may have a role in this regard not only with respect to the initial screen, but also with respect to monitoring the activities of firms after they are permitted entry. The screening agency should be empowered to set up countervailing techiniques whenever a manifestation of extraterritoriality arises or threatens to arise.[132]

CANADIAN CONSTITUTIONAL QUESTIONS

In much of the discussion surrounding foreign ownership, constitutional questions have received scant attention. The constitutional picture in Canada is far from clear. Judicial interpretation of the British North America Act to date hardly permits simple answers to questions about the federal capacity to regulate foreign ownership. The uncertainty centres around the federal power to legislate in relation to trade and commerce and the general power to make laws for the peace, order, and good government of Canada, on the one hand, and the exclusive jurisdiction of the provinces to legislate in relation to civil rights and property, on the other hand.[133] Nor do the recent negotiations on constitutional reform indicate that the federal government is likely to acquire increased power in this area.

The constitutional situation is such that a particular policy instrument may not be available to be effectively legislated and administered by the federal government alone but may require the co-operation of the provincial governments. On an issue like extraterritoriality, such co-operation may be realized relatively easily. On the issue of limiting or otherwise controlling foreign ownership, such co-operation is not likely to be forthcoming in view of the fact that a number of provincial governments have served notice that they will strongly oppose a general limitation on foreign ownership of industry. Federal-provincial co-operation is a highly desirable goal, but it is not likely to be realized in the near future to the extent necessary to make policy instruments work that are dependent upon a high degree of federal-provincial co-operation.[134]

CONCLUSION

While the establishment of a screening agency as proposed under the Foreign Investment Review Act is an appropriate response to foreign direct investment, the success of that agency as a policy instrument in the context of the Canadian economy as a whole depends upon the development of well-reasoned and well-articulated industry policies. Too much attention to ownership, and Canadian ownership as an end in itself, tends to ignore fundamental questions about the behaviour of firms and how that behaviour may be influenced in the public interest.

NOTES

1 It is no doubt true, as is often said of the Contracting Parties to the General Agreement on Tariffs and Trade, that the rich get richer and the poor get relatively poorer. But this does not of itself demonstrate that the GATT arrangement is bad. The problem side of that picture merely indicates that additional positive measures are required to improve the lot of the not-so-rich.

2 Government of Canada, *Foreign Direct Investment in Canada* (1972) (Gray Report). The Gray Report was tabled in the House of Commons on 4 May 1972. However, the report had been 'leaked' to the editors of the *Canadian Forum* who published a condensed version in that periodical in December 1971. The Gray Report was the third of three official or officially sponsored federal reports in a period of five years. Each of these reports has identified similar con-

cerns and has recommended the establishment of some machinery to regulate the growth of foreign control. The other two reports are the *Eleventh Report of the Standing Committee on External Affairs and National Defence Respecting Canada-U.S. Relations*, Second Session, 28th Parliament (September 1970) (Wahn Report); and Canada, Privy Council Office, *Foreign Ownership and the Structure of Canadian Industry*, Report of the Task Force on the Structure of Canadian Industry (February 1968) (Watkins Report).

3 The Gray Report was officially released on 2 May 1972. Bill c-201, the Foreign Takeovers Review Act, was released on the same date and given first reading in the House two days later. It died on the order paper when the election was called in October of 1972. The bill became a major election issue, the opposition parties claiming that it did not go far enough since it sought to control only takeovers without regulating in any way new foreign direct investment. On 24 January 1973 the minority government under pressure from opposition parties introduced Bill c-132, which is a somewhat expanded version of Bill c-201.

4 The Watkins Task Force considered the 'intrusion of American law and policy into Canada' as the 'most serious cost of Canada resulting from foreign ownership.' Watkins Report, *supra* note 2, at 345, 360. This misplaced emphasis tended to distort the perspective of the report.

5 Economic Council of Canada, Seventh Annual Review, *Patterns of Growth* (1970), introduction.

6 John Porter offers some interesting reflections on this point in *The Vertical Mosaic: An Analysis of Social Class and Power in Canada* (1965).

7 See also Canada, Senate, *A Science Policy for Canada*, Report of the Special Committee on Science Policy, vol 2, 'Targets and Strategies for the Seventies' (1972) 506.

8 One recent analysis of the relationship between foreign ownership of book publishers and Canadian culture has been published: Ontario, Royal Commission on Book Publishing, *Canadian Publishers & Canadian Publishing* (1972).

9 As one might have assumed from the papers presented at the Ontario Conference on Economic and Cultural Nationalism 23–25 June 1971, published by the Ontario Department of Treasury and Economics.

10 The French language media are too small to have much effect on the characteristics of an English-language group numbering in all over 200 million. In any event, it must always be noted that the English-language group is itself made up of many and different subgroups, some linguistic and ethnic, others religious, etc.

11 Indeed, the Waffle Group was expelled by the NDP.

12 The Prime Minister of Ontario, The Honourable William Davis, in announcing the application of the 25–10 rule to new entrants in the investment industry made the following statement: 'This policy of using a 25-10 formula for non-Canadian ownership is consistent with that now in effect in the Loan and Trust Field and which we used in connection with distributors of paperback books. It is a sound yardstick for use in most areas involving foreign ownership, enabling the encouragement of foreign investment and funds while protecting our own Canadian interests.'

13 The guidelines questionnaire is to be distinguished from Corporations and Labour Unions Returns Act (CALURA) returns. Information under the guidelines questionnaire is obtained on a voluntary basis, whereas CALURA has the force of law. The Wahn Committee suggested that there might be some duplication of effort and insufficient coordination between the Guidelines Branch of the Department of Industry, Trade and Commerce and Statistics Canada. Wahn Report, *supra* note 2, at 3.24.

14 *Supra* note 3.

15 Canada, House of Commons, 1st Session, 29th Parliament, Bill c-132, Second Reading, 4 April 1973, section 8.

16 S 5. The figures are for the last completed fiscal year and are to be calculated according to regulations.

17 'Investment' is defined to include acquisitions, new investments, and expansions into unrelated areas. See ss 3(1), 8(2), 8(3).

18 Ss 9 and 2(2).

19 S 12.

20 S 13.

21 S 31.

22 S 3(1).

23 S 3(2).

24 S 3(6) (g).

25 S 3(3).

26 S 3(3) (b) and (c).

27 S 3(3) (d).

28 S 3(3) (e). The text reflects the expected amendment.

29 S 4.

30 S 7.

31 Ss 14 to 27.

32 See the Gray Report, *supra* note 2, at 456.

33 We have considered above the essentials of such industry policies.

34 Broadcasting Act, [1970] R.S.C. c B-11, ss 22(1) (a) (iii), 27 and *Direction to the Canadian Radio-Television Commission*, SOR/69–590 as amended by SOR/71–33. Specific restrictions on foreign ownership and control of private broadcasting stations were first introduced in the Broadcasting Act, 1958, Can., c 22, s 14; these restrictions were essentially the same as those under the present act. For a summary of federal legislation and regulations affecting foreign ownership, see, Department of Industry, Trade and Commerce. *Selected Readings in Laws and Regulations Affecting Foreign Investment in Canada* (April 1971).

35 See for example, the requirement that at least 40 per cent of television programming between the hours of 6 a.m. to 12 midnight and 6 p.m. and 12 midnight be Canadian. SOR/71–558 as amended by SOR/72–242. Somewhat similar Canadian content requirements have been made with respect to AM and FM radio broadcasting. The chairman of the CRTC has also indicated that Canadian content requirements will be made with respect to commercials aired on TV and radio.

36 In this area too, the CRTC has promulgated regulations concerning the carrying of signals from US stations on cable.

37 Income Tax Act, [1970] R.S.C., c 1–5, as amended, s 19.

38 Customs Tariff, [1970] R.S.C., c-41, schedule c.

39 *Globe and Mail*, 12 July 1971.

40 The Special Senate Committee on Mass Media under the chairmanship of Senator Keith Davey undertook a study of the mass media generally. Canada, Senate, *The Uncertain Mirror: Report of the Special Senate Committee on Mass Media* (1970).

41 Ontario, Royal Commission on Book Publishing, *First Interim Report*, 23 March 1971. Reproduced in the appendix of the commission's final report; *infra* note 46.

42 The Paperback and Periodical Distributors Act, 1971, Ont., vol 1, c 82.

43 Individual licensees or all partners of partnership licensees must be Canadian residents: ss 8 and 9. The act does not apply to distributors in respect of the distribution of periodicals and paperbacks that are published, printed, or distributed primarily in Canada: s 1(2). The act is deemed to have come into force on 14 June, 1971, s 17.

44 Ontario, Royal Commission on Book Publishing, *Final Interim Report*, 27 March 1972. Reproduced in the appendix of the commission's final report.

45 'Ontario probes US takeover of our paperback distributors,' *Toronto Star*, 12 July 1971.

46 Ontario, Royal Commission on Book Publishing, *Canadian Publishers & Canadian Publishing* (1972).

47 Bank Act, [1970] R.S.C., c B-1, ss 10(4), 18(3), and (4), 20(2) (b), 52(1), 53–6. Since 1871, until the 1967 revision of the act, the only requirement was that a majority of a bank's directors be British subjects ordinarily resident in Canada: Bank Act, 1953–4, Can., 48, ss 21, 23, 25. The present restrictions became effective on January 1968; however, before that date, the First National City Bank of New York took over the Mercantile Bank by buying out Dutch interests. The new act in an important sense applied the new provisions retroactively to the Mercantile by severely limiting its growth, s 75(2) (g). The Mercantile has indicated that it is prepared to comply ultimately with the 25-10 formula.

48 Canadian and British Insurance Companies Act, [1970] R.S.C., c 1–15, as amended by [1970], R.S.C., c 19 (1st supp.), ss 37–41. Loan Companies Act, [1970] R.S.C., c L-12 as amended by [1970] R.S.C., c 24 (1st supp.), ss 19, 44–8. Trust Companies Act, [1970] R.S.C., c T-16, as amended by [1970] R.S.C., c 47, (1st supp.), ss 37–41. Sales finance companies: Investment Companies Act, 1970–1, Can., c 33, ss 10–15, was proclaimed in force as of 1 January 1972. The act provides, among other things, that shares transferred to non-residents after 17 October 1969 in excess of the limits cannot be voted while in non-residents' hands.

49 Loan and Trust Corporations Act, [1970] R.S.O., c 254, as amended by 1970, Ont., c 84, s 2 which adds ss 52a–52f applying the 25–10 formula and by 1970, Ont., c 129, s 10 which changes ss 34(3,4) by requiring that a majority of directors must be resident Canadians.

50 Trust Companies Act, [1970] R.S.A., c 372, s

30(6) provides that 3/4 of the directors of a trust company must be resident Canadians. The 25–10 rule first enacted by s 8 of 1969, Alberta, c 112 is now contained in s 67 of the act.

51 The proposed Competition Act (Bill c-256) provides that competition policy should be applied, to some extent, to banks which have enjoyed and currently enjoy an exemption. Whether or not the proposed legislation will be reintroduced remains to be seen.

52 Canadian banks have in fact drawn on foreign sources of funds to finance Canadian assets in periods of official monetary constraint in Canada.

53 The Royal Bank, Canada's largest, ranked seventh and the Toronto-Dominion, the smallest of the Big Five, ranked thirty-ninth of the top fifty banks outside the us. If American banks are included, Royal ranked fourteenth and the Toronto-Dominion fifty-sixth. (May 1971), *Fortune* 192 and (August 1971), *Fortune* 157.

54 Royal Commission on Banking and Finance, *Report* (1964), (Porter Commission report) 369.

55 The only bank established since then which can be said to have had any degree of success is the Bank of British Columbia. The degree of success that it has had can be attributed to strong support from the provincial government. Whether the recently established Unity Bank can survive remains to be seen.

56 *Report of the Committee to Study the Requirements and Sources of Capital and the Implications of Non-Resident Capital for the Canadian Securities Industry* (May 1970) (Moore Report).

57 Ibid, 6.32.

58 Ibid, 6.45, 1 and 2. These proposals would be applied to all outside participation, whether foreign or domestic, in the ownership of a firm.

59 Ibid, para. 6.45, 4 and 5. This prohibition results from the concern by the majority of the committee that any investment by a foreign firm would constitute undue and disproportionate influence over the Canadian firm (6.33).

60 Ibid, 6.45, 6–11.

61 Ibid, 6.29– 6.31.

62 Indeed, leading bankers now appear to favour a relaxation of the restrictions on foreign-controlled banks imposed under the Bank Act.

63 Government of Quebec, *Report of the Study*

Committee on Financial Institutions (June 1969), at 203, 204.

64 *Globe and Mail*, 19 June, 1970. The government of Quebec and members of the industry were concerned that the Moore proposals would strengthen the already predominant position of Toronto-based firms.

65 Quebec, Department of Financial Institutions, Companies and Cooperatives, *Study on the Securities Industry in Quebec, Final Report* (June 1972), vol 1 (Bouchard Committee).

66 On 6 July, 1971, Quebec Financial Institutions Minister Tetley introduced a bill in the Quebec legislature which provides for appeal to the qsc against decisions of the exchanges. The minister said he opposed the Moore proposals and described them as 'a disaster for Montreal – we want to attract financiers from all over the world.' *Globe and Mail*, 30 July 1971.

67 o.r. 296/71. See also statement by the Honourable William Davis on 13 July 1971, o.s.c.b. (July 1971).

68 Statement by the Honourable William Davis in the Legislative Assembly 13 July 1971. See Ontario, Ministry of Consumer and Commercial Relations, *Report of the Securities Industry Ownership Committee of the Ontario Securities Commission* (1972) (osc Report), at (v).

69 *Report of the Joint Industry Committee on the Moore Report*, released 29 July 1971 (Joint Committee Report).

70 osc Report, *supra* note 68.

71 Ibid, at 111–12.

72 Ibid, at 113.

73 A 1970 study determined that 63.17 per cent of cpr shares were held in Canada. Research Branch, Library of Parliament, *Laws and Regulations Preventing Undue United States Influence on Canadian Financial Institutions, Transportation, Communications and Energy Industries* (1970) 11.

74 National Transportation Act, [1970] r.s.c., c n-17.

75 For a fuller discussion of the act, see I.R. Feltham, 'Common Ownership in Canada with Particular Reference to Regulation of Acquisition of Motor Carriers' (1970), 2, *Transportation Law Journal* 113.

76 However, see *Kenosha Auto Transport Corporation*, Canadian Transport Commission, Decision mv-20-15, 23 March 1971. Commissioner Magee's reasoning in that decision is, with respect, not convincing. He argued

that since the power of the commission to intervene is limited to cases where objection is received, parliament could not be taken to have intended that foreign ownership be a relevant consideration. He stated that between 29 January 1968 and 1 March 1971 the commission received 159 notices of proposed acquisitions of motor vehicle transport undertakings to which objection was registered in only fifteen cases. These fifteen proposed acquisitions were the only acquisitions that under the statute the commission was empowered to investigate, and he therefore reasoned that on such limited scope for review it would be unreasonable to apply a foreign-ownership test when the cases in which there were no objections might well have included a number of acquisitions by foreign based companies.

77 In the *Kenosha* case, the facts revealed in Commissioner Magee's 'Report' do not indicate prejudice; indeed, quite the contrary.

78 Aeronautics Act, [1970] R.S.C., c A-3, s 14.

79 SOR/72–145.

80 Ibid, ss 19 and 20.

81 Discussed above.

82 National Transportation Act, [1970] R.S.C., c N-17, s 27; Air Carrier Regulations, SOR/72–145, s 20.

83 SOR/65–369, as amended.

84 Aeronautics Act and Air Regulations, Department of Transport, 1967, and amendments thereto (Amendment 11 24/3/69, at 11).

85 [1970] R.S.C., c M-14.

86 [1964] R.S.Q., c 228 as amended, s 35.

87 Public Commercial Vehicles Act, [1970] R.S.O., c 375, ss 6, 5(6) and 11.

88 See Feltham, *supra* note 75.

89 [1970] R.S.C., c R-2.

90 Canada Shipping Act, [1970] R.S.C., c S-9, ss 6 *et seq*, s 663.

91 Railway Act, [1970] R.S.C., c R-2, s 320.

92 [1970] R.S.C., c 35 (1st supp.).

93 For a history of both federal and provincial regulation and control of telephone services, and for a list of provincial legislation see *History of Regulation and Current Regulatory Setting,* a submission by Trans-Canada Telephone System, published by the Department of Communications, Study 1(b).

94 For example, the latest statistics indicate that petroleum and refining are almost wholly controlled from abroad.

95 Ontario has challenged on constitutional grounds the recently announced two-price policy of Alberta with respect to natural gas. Ontario claims that the two-price system attempts to regulate interprovincial trade and commerce which is within the exclusive jurisdiction of the federal government.

96 National Energy Board Act, [1970] R.S.C., c N-6 as amended by [1970] R.S.C., c 27 (1st Supp.). See also National Energy Board, *Annual Report 1968.*

97 Ibid, s 44 (d).

98 The potential, however, is there that the direction could be interpreted in this manner.

99 National Energy Board Act, [1970] R.S.C., c N-6, s 25, and [1970] R.S.C., c 10 (1st Supp.), s 30 which amends the definition of 'Special Act' in s 2 of the NEB Act to include letters patent of companies incorporated under s 5.1 or 5.4 of the Corporations Act.

100 Canada Oil and Gas Regulations, SOR/61–253, s 55. Restrictions on exploratory licenses and permits are less demanding. Companies need only be incorporated or licensed in Canada or a province. These regulations relate to lands in the Yukon and the Northwest Territories (Territorial Lands Act, [1970] R.S.C., c T-6) and other lands under federal control (Public Land Grants Act, [1970] R.S.C., c P-29).

101 The Gordon Commission made suggestions to promote Canadian processing of minerals. Canada, Royal Commission on Canada's Economic Prospects, *Final Report,* (1957), at 227.

102 1968–69, Ont., c 68, s 6 amending s 106 of the Mining Act.

103 1968–69, Ont., c s 2 (3, 4) amending s 3 of the Mining Tax Act, ss 5, 6 amending ss 13, 14.

104 Ontario Mining Association, *Director's Report* (1969–70), at 8. See also *Hansard,* 19 May, 1970, 2877–81. The opposition in the Ontario Legislature has made much of the way the exempting powers have been used. See for example, Mr Lewis statement in the House, *Hansard,* 20 April 1970, 1763–4.

105 *Hansard,* 20 April 1970, 1758.

106 The initial draft of the Ontario legislation required processing in Ontario. However, it was argued that such parochialism is not appropriate and the requirement was subsequently altered to read 'in Canada.'

107 Canada Mining Regulations, SOR/61–86, SOR/62–294, SOR/66–80. Recent government action has resulted in the application of similar provisions to mining in the Yukon.

108 Northern Mineral Exploration Assistance Regulations, SOR/66–404, SOR/67–584.

109 Bill C-132, The Foreign Investment Review Act, has been discussed above.

110 [1970] R.S.C., c C-32, Schedule. Such corporations are called constrained share companies.

111 [1970], R.S.O., c 53, s 47.

112 Ibid, s 122 (3). This provision was to take effect 1 October, 1973.

113 *Globe and Mail*, 19 July, 1973.

114 Gray Report, *supra* note 2, at 516. The report commissioned by the federal government in respect of revising the corporate laws concluded that residency requirements were a 'futile gesture', Robert W.V. Dickerson, *et al, Proposals for a New Business Corporations Law for Canada* (1971), para 201.

115 Income Tax Act, [1970], R.S.C., c I-5, as amended, s 212; Income Tax Application Rules, s 10.

116 For a discussion of the legislative history of s 212(5) and the ease with which the provisions could be circumvented, see A.R.A. Scace, 'The Degree of Canadian Ownership: An Exercise in Futility? (1965), 3 *Osgoode Hall L.J.* 295.

117 *Financial Post*, 3 October, 1964.

118 Income Tax Act, [1970], R.S.C., s 125.

119 Budget Speech of the Honourable Edgar Benson when he introduced the new tax legislation, 18 June 1971.

120 Income Tax Act, [1970], R.S.C., s 190.

121 The dividends were to be taxed at personal rates. The 33–1/3 per cent dividend tax credit would offset the effective 25 per cent tax rate of small private corporations. Conceivably, the net dividend could be returned to the company in the form of a loan.

122 Before 1972 interest was not deductible since dividends received by one Canadian corporation from another were tax free; the Income Tax Act prohibited a deduction of expenses incurred to generate exempt income. Now, the definition of exempt income expressly excludes dividends. Income Tax Act, [1970], R.S.C., s 248.

123 *Supra* note 119, at 15.

124 'Tracking' was one such technique. An asset purchase, where possible, avoided the problem in some instances.

125 Income Tax Act, [1970], R.S.C., s 18(4).

126 For a complete text of the guidelines and the accompanying letter by Mr Winters, see Wahn Report, *supra* note 2, at 80.

127 Ibid, at 134.

128 Canada Development Corporation Act, 1970–71–82, Can., c 49, s 2.

129 Ibid, s 12.

130 Ibid, s 20 and schedule I, s 1.

131 The performance of the CDC will be judged according to business standards. Consequently, it must be permitted to operate as a business notwithstanding the obvious interest the government has.

132 Countervailing power in the form of positive policies can be effective in curtailing unwarranted manifestations of extraterritoriality. This was demonstrated, for example, in the *Watchmakers of Switzerland* case in respect of US anti-trust law, 1965, C.C.H. Trade Cases, para 71, 352 (S.D.N.Y. 1965).

133 The British North America Act, 1867, 30 and 31 Vict. c 3, ss 91, 92.

134 Bill C-132 may be amended to provide that the screening agency notify any province affected by a proposal it receives under the act. The minister of industry, trade and commerce has, at the time of writing, proposed amendments that would require that he and the cabinet take into account representations received from a province that is likely to be affected by a proposed investment.

J.A. BEESLEY

37/The Sixties to the Seventies: The Perspective of the Legal Adviser

The perspective of the foreign ministry legal adviser presumably varies from country to country and from one historical period to the other. The vital interests of one or more countries may be directly engaged during certain periods by major international issues such as the Korean police action, the Hungarian uprising, the Suez invasion, the Bay of Pigs incident, the Cuban missile crisis, the Dominican Republic intervention, the Czech invasion, the Biafran civil war, the Rhodesian declaration of independence, and the Vietnam war. Such issues and the responses to them reveal the extent to which international law influences the basic foreign policy of the countries concerned. There were no such war and peace issues directly engaging Canada's vital national interests during the sixties and early seventies. There has, however, been a series of international legal problems of a different order which have touched directly or indirectly on Canada's national interests, particularly Canada's personality as a single state on the international plane and Canada's jurisdiction, sovereignty, and territoriality.

What follows is a purely personal appraisal of the responses by Canada over the past decade to a representative range of issues, with a view to determining whether they indicate a distinctive Canadian approach and, if so, its relevance to the problems of the seventies. While the views are personal the optic is nevertheless that of the legal adviser to the Department of External Affairs, and it is useful, therefore, to consider the perspective before discussing the perceptions.

THE FUNCTION

The point of departure of any foreign ministry legal adviser and the distinguishing feature of his role is the solicitor-client relationship arising out of his official position. The basic function of the Canadian legal adviser is to attempt to safeguard Canadian interests as they may be affected by international law. To perform this function he must not only provide advice to the foreign minister and the government on issues of international law touching on Canada's interests but must also attempt to ensure that through Canadian participation in the progressive development of international law the law reflects Canada's interests to the maximum degree attainable.[1]

THE RESOURCES

In the case of Canada, the legal adviser to the Department of External Affairs is also the director general of the Bureau of Legal Affairs, and the bureau provides the supporting staff for both the advisory and operational aspects of his area of responsibilities. The bureau has been greatly strengthened over the past decade since the days when it comprised a single legal division with a relatively small staff. It is now composed of the Legal Advisory Division, consisting of 12 officers serving in 4 sections (treaty and constitutional, advisory, economic, and claims), and the Legal Operations Division, consisting of 12 officers serving in 4 sections (law of the sea, environmental law, UN and legal planning, and private international law). In addition there is a resident academic doing long-term research, and provision for two such positions to be filled at the same time (as was the case in 1972). The bureau is staffed in part by rotational legally qualified foreign service officers, most of whom spend approximately two-thirds of their career doing legal work in Ottawa and approximately one-third doing related work abroad, and in part by non-rotational legal advisers whose whole career is spent in the Legal Bureau.

THE PARAMETERS

There is a high degree of political content embodied in international law, both in its development and its interpretation.[2] No problem in international law can be viewed realistically in isolation from related economic, social, scientific, technical, and political factors. No solution to an international law problem can be achieved which does not take into account these considerations. This presupposes a close relationship between the legal adviser and the other foreign policy decision-makers. If this were true in the past it is increasingly true today, particularly with respect to such highly topical problem areas as environmental law, law of the sea, outer space law, hijacking, international terrorism, and humanitarian rules of war.

There is an interpenetration of national and international law. Acts on either plane can have constitutive legal effects on the other. Every legal adviser must therefore view questions of international law with a kind of double vision, focusing at one and the same time on both the domestic scene and the international world. If this is true as a generality, it is particularly true for Canada where this interpenetration exists not only on such classic issues as the legality in international law of unilateral assertions of marine jurisdiction but on peculiarly Canadian problems such as the constitutional validity of provincial action on the international plane. Examples of two-dimensional problems raising both kinds of complexity and illustrating the link between them can be seen, for example, in the differences existing between the federal and provincial levels of government concerning offshore mineral rights jurisdiction.

There is no automaticity in international law-making. Policy is not law on the international plane. Even major world powers must seek and obtain the acquiescence of the international community in the legality of their actions, failing which such action may be considered to be outside the law. Every policy option must be considered, therefore, not only in terms of national objectives but in the light of its acceptability internationally. As a consequence, there is at a relatively early stage of policy-making on international law issues a need to perceive the possibilities of attaining a reconciliation of national objectives with those of other states and even, in some cases, with the general interest of the international community.

There is a large element of responsiveness embodied in many foreign policy decisions, arising out of the organic link in this field between positive acts and reaction to acts of others. Not infrequently policies are developed primarily in response to policies of other countries or to more general trends and developments in international law. More often, policies reflect a blend of action and reaction. Responsiveness can be of many kinds, and even deliberate passivity can be a form of reaction (as, for example, with claims of other states neither accepted nor challenged). Even where the policy is essentially responsive, however, there must be a clear perception of the policy objectives at stake.[3]

International law is dynamic. It is nearly always in a state of flux on at least some major issues. At times a state must be in motion merely to keep abreast of the law. Nothing is immutable, nothing completed, nothing certain. By the same token, there is a great scope for progressive development of the law through creativity, determination, skill, and common sense in translating ideas into reality.

There is an interrelationship between seemingly discrete fields of law on the international plane even more perhaps than on the municipal plane, where law is more highly developed. Unrelated subject areas draw upon one another for both doctrine and procedure. Air law, for example, may influence the future law of the sea. The development of law in particular fields can often be seen to double back and draw upon its early origins, as appears to be also occurring in the law of the sea. This process of 'cannibalization' and cross-fertilization is thus both horizontal and vertical. It imposes on the part of those concerned an open-mindedness, a willingness to question first principles, and a need for a continuing 'overview.'

There is no continuing stream of authoritative and binding judicial decisions in international law. In most cases the law must be determined from sources other than judicial decision. There is no doctrine of *stare decisis* in international law. Apart from article 94(2) of the UN Charter, there is no authority to impose decisions of the International Court. States may even accept or reject voluntarily the jurisdiction of the International Court with the consequence that it is often impossible to determine an issue by reference to the court. There is no legislature, in the usual sense of the term, laying down the laws to be enforced. International law is enforceable only by consent.

The foregoing characteristics suggest rather more freedom for states than may actually pertain. Given the vast interlocking network of bilateral and multilateral treaties on a variety of subjects, these apparent weaknesses in the legal system are not fatal. There is much evidence that states take their treaty obligations seriously and only rarely violate them. Every system of law relies for its enforcement ultimately on the will of the community it purports to regulate, and this is particularly true of international law. Thus the weaknesses in the legal system tend to reflect the relatively primitive stage of development of the international society but not of the law itself, and, as Percy Corbett points out, 'legal advisers draw uhon a body of law which they treat as binding upon states' whether it originates from the customary or conventional law-making processes.

The international law-making process, whether customary or conventional, is complex, laborious, uncertain, and often painfully slow. Exceptions exist, such as the rapid emergence of the continental shelf doctrine during the period between the 1945 Truman Proclamation and the 1958 Geneva Law of the Sea Conference, perhaps because of the merging and coalescing of the customary and conventional processes through the agencies of the International Law Commission and the 1958

UN Law of the Sea Conference.[4] This situation imposes at once on the legal adviser the need for sensitivity to changes in international law and also to the possibilities for future changes in the law. Changes in the law may necessitate long-term planning and consistent and determined pursuit of goals through a variety of means, perhaps over a lengthy period.

The national interest on any particular issue of international law may not be clear-cut, and many factors may have to be considered in order to determine even the relevance or significance of an issue, yet alone the appropriate policy option. This is particularly true for Canada. At the simplest level an option which may appear to coincide with Canada's domestic interests may not coincide with Canada's national interests after the international consequences for Canada of the option in question are taken into account.

Canada is a complex country with a wide range of interests at stake on the international plane. Although a relatively small country in terms of population Canada encompasses a vast territory which must be 'protected.' At one level protection of Canada's 'sovereignty' takes the traditional forms of protection through the armed forces, alliances, and diplomacy; at another level the protection may consist of the kinds of action required to protect a specific range of interests, such as the quality of the environment and Canada's long-term economic interests. The range of factors to be included, for example, in seeking to determine the Canadian position on multilateral consideration of multinational enterprises might be that Canada is a major trading nation, a technologically advanced country with vast untapped natural resources, a considerable manufacturing capacity with no real lack of capital but recurring problems of inflation and unemployment, both a 'head office' country for Canadian-based multinational corporations and a 'branch plant' country with many foreign-based multinational enterprises operating in Canada. These considerations, when taken together, might justify a policy of inaction but instead resulted in a Canadian initiative at the XVI and XVII UN General Assemblies calling for the study of the implications for international trade law of the activities of multinational enterprises. It can readily be perceived from this single example that what is required in determining the policy options to achieve national objectives is a balancing of many factors coupled, ideally, with a sense of direction and timing concerning the subject matter, based as much on subjective considerations concerning the mood of the international community as on an appraisal of concrete factors.

CANADIAN INTERESTS

It would be idle to attempt to summarize the range of Canadian interests at stake on the international plane since they are as variable as the issues which may engage one or more such interests. Indeed, there are probably few states whose interests are more diverse and even at times conflicting or contradictory. In determining the Canadian interest which might be affected by a particular issue of international law, it may be necessary, for example, to take into account that Canada is a federal state with three levels of government (in some provinces four); two founding peoples with two languages (but encompassing many other ethnic groups); problems of regionalism rarely encountered short of whole continents; and belongs both to the Commonwealth and La Francophonie while maintaining continuing ties with both 'mother countries.' On another issue other factors may be relevant, such as the links between the Canadian economy and that of the United States at a time when a new form of Canadian economic nationalism appears to be welling up, or that Canada is both a substantial foreign investor and one of the world's greatest recipients of foreign investment.

Other problems may raise even broader considerations. Canada is physically located between the two major superpowers, facing both northwards and south-wards, not merely geographically but in the sense of the north-south development gap, as Canada remains a country both developed and developing, with consider-able scientific, technological, and industrial capacity but with natural resources in need of development; facing both eastwards and westwards in many senses other than the merely geographical, with long-established social, cultural, political, and economic links with western Europe and Commonwealth countries, and newly developing political, economic, and even cultural links with Africa, Asia, and Latin America, while strongly influenced politically, culturally, and socially as well as economically by the United States.

With respect to other problem areas, much more specific and particular factors may be relevant. Canada is a coastal state with an extremely long and vulnerable coastline and is not a major maritime power. It is a coastal fishing nation with few distant water fishing interests, and with an extensive and deeply glaciated continen-tal shelf. While a major trading nation concerned to protect freedom of passage, Canada is sensitive about the status of the waters of the Arctic archipelago, par-ticularly the Northwest Passage. On other matters, military-political considera-tions become relevant. Canada is a member of NATO allied to the great powers of the West but with a long-standing interest in bringing about a complete ban of nu-clear testing, and thus opposed to such tests, even by her allies; at the same time Canada is developing closer relations with the USSR and China while sharing many common interests with smaller 'non-aligned' countries which, like Canada, are essentially non-space, non-nuclear, non-maritime powers. On some issues, such as the Vietnam war, Canada has had little or no direct interest and yet a continuing commitment to peacekeeping and a highly developed capacity for it which could result in Canada's involvement in a further peacekeeping mission.[5] It is not surpris-ing, in the light of the range of complex and seemingly unrelated considerations which must be taken into account in determining the Canadian position on a par-ticular issue, that some Canadians may still wonder whether they have a clearcut national identity or why non-Canadians find it difficult to put Canada in an ideologi-cally neat package or in a particular 'geographic' or economic pigeon-hole.

In such circumstances, and in the light of the parameters discussed above, it might be understandable if Canada were to play little or no role on the international plane, if only because of the difficulties in determining Canadian priorities in clear and unambiguous terms. It is suggested, however, that the range of seemingly con-flicting considerations, contradictions, and inconsistencies concerning the Cana-dian national interest have required Canadian policy-makers to take a very hard look at one time or another at most of the contemporary international legal problem areas, ranging from the traditional war and peace issues to very particular and even highly technical legal problems in order to determine what are its particular implica-tions for Canada, and at what point the Canadian interest and the interests of the international community as a whole might appear to coincide. It is suggested further that as a consequence of this inability to make automatic assumptions about the Canadian position on any issue of international law, the Canadian approach to international law must necessarily be somewhat distinctive. It follows from this particularity of the Canadian outlook that Canada must be active in the development of the law if Canadian interests are to be protected.

THE ADVISORY FUNCTION

The nature of the issues requiring the advice of the legal adviser to the secretary of state for external affairs can vary from the strictly legal (the validity of a reservation to a treaty) through the highly technical (the precise point of criticality in legal terms of a nuclear energy plant at which time safeguards must begin to be applied) to the almost wholly political (the nature, form, and timing of recognition of a state or government). The problems can range also from the almost solely domestic (the permissibility under Canadian constitutional law of acts by a provincial government on the international plane) through the range of bilateral issues with other states (the liability for acts affecting the environment incurred pursuant to a treaty obligation or under customary international law) to the very general and most international of legal issues (the interpretation to be given to an advisory opinion of the International Court).

New questions can arise suddenly concerning areas of law regarded as settled, such as the precise nature and extent of the duty of a protecting state towards a kidnapped diplomat of another state. A legal opinion may be required as a matter of urgency on issues as delicate as the status of one of the belligerents in a civil war or whether the conflict itself is international or non-international. The precise language chosen to confer recognition emerging perhaps through a lengthy process of negotiation based on continuous legal as well as political advice on a variety of formulations can have a wholly disproportionate effect on issues as important as the admission of a state to the UN if enough other countries follow the precedent. Advice may be required in an area of law which is undeveloped or even virtually non-existent with consequences as serious as the submission of a new reservation to the jurisdiction of the International Court and as important as the development of a whole new concept in international law. Thus, the legal, political, and even economic consequences of a legal opinion on a practical issue may be extremely significant. It follows that the legal adviser must participate at a formative stage of the decision-making process on matters involving issues of international law.

Obviously, the political element in international law is so preponderant as to at times be predominant, necessitating a close relationship between the legal adviser and policy-makers on international legal-political issues. Nevertheless, the legal adviser must fulfil an essentially legal role in advising his foreign minister or government on matters of international law. Although there is often a dearth of clearly defined jurisprudence upon which advice may be based, there may be an overabundance of materials reflecting this jurisprudence, be they evidence of divergent state practice, disputed treaty provisions, conflicting views of authors, or contentious decisions of tribunals. These materials rarely provide certainty, in part because of the dynamic nature of international law itself. It does not follow from this, however, that the legal opinions offered can be correspondingly vague or ambiguous, since policy decisions may have to be made on the basis of such opinions (together, of course, with other relevant factors). An opinion, for example, as to the legality of the twelve-mile territorial sea given in 1964 might lead to the assertion of a lesser claim, such as a twelve-mile fishing zone, while six years later an opinion on the same issue might lead to a twelve-mile territorial sea claim without even the protection of a reservation to the jurisdiction of the International Court. State practice may account for the substantive change in international law in such a short period. However, state practice itself, which must take into account public statements, protests to claims, and even resolutions and debates of the UN, on occasion, rarely provides a solid basis for a clearcut opinion. As a consequence, international law is often elusive and difficult to define or to determine, and it requires, ideally, a feel for international law to ensure the weighting of all the legal, moral, political, economic, and even military factors which are in continuous interplay in the birth, development, and crystallization of law on any single issue.

The advisory function would appear to be simpler for the Canadian legal adviser today than for his predecessors in at least one respect: the materials and the sources of advice of Canadian origin are now much more numerous than heretofore, as the Canadian interest in international law increases and more and more able academics contribute to the sources of international law. The present volume provides evidence both of the richness of these sources and of the variety of Canadian perspectives. In at least one respect, however, the converse is true and the role of the Canadian legal adviser becomes more demanding as the range of international legal issues of importance to Canada continues to multiply, in part because of the increase in the number of law-makers as more and more countries emerge from colonial status, and in part because of the increase in law-making activities in the UN, which in turn reflect the growing diversity and complexity of international law as the foreign policy of states expands into fields never contemplated when foreign policy was seen essentially in terms of war, peace, and trade.

The range of problem areas considered and the nature of the opinions given by successive legal advisers during the sixties and the early seventies is indicated in the sections on Canadian Practice in International Law appearing in the *Canadian Yearbook of International Law* for these years. Even the selection of materials contained in that source, necessarily restricted for a variety of reasons, includes opinions and statements of the Canadian position on an extremely wide variety of issues of international law. It is interesting to note the range of action in two major areas of law which have required much of the attention of the successive legal advisers during the sixties and which will undoubtedly continue into the seventies; namely, questions touching on the nature and extent of the right of Canadian provinces to participate in action on the international plane and problems relating to the jurisdiction, sovereignty, and territory of Canada.[6]

It is central to the advisory function that the legal adviser must attempt to ensure that Canada's role in international affairs is conducted in accordance with recognized principles of international law.[7] Ideally, there is no conflict between this aspect of his responsibilities and his basic 'solicitor-client' function of protecting his country's national interests. Even from a purely national point of view, international law, as the basis for the developing world order, or even the lesser goal of stable relations between states, benefits all states. Far from being incompatible with the protection of national interests, adherence to the rule of law may be seen as a specific and valuable form of protection of national interests. Occasions may arise, however, when international law does not reflect the national interests and even, perhaps, the general 'international' interests, when, for example, the law is undeveloped or out of touch with contemporary needs. In such instances, it may be necessary to seek to bring about changes in the law.[8] It is the role of the legal adviser to guard against the law being regarded as a mere instrument of policy, an approach inimical to the very concept of the rule of law. The interests of the international community must, in any event, be taken into account in order to achieve the accommodation of interests which is the prerequisite to the emergence of a new rule of law, however it is developed, whether by state practice or by multilateral law-making. Thus, the legal adviser must often pursue 'international goals' as part of his function of protecting his country's national interests, while conversely he must pursue 'national goals' in a manner which takes into account the interests of the international community as a whole.[9] Much turns, therefore, on how the national goals are pursued and the extent to which a particular policy does, in fact, embody a blend of national and 'international' interests, a point which will be examined later.

THE OPERATIONAL FUNCTION

A major distinction between the advisory and operational functions of a foreign ministry legal adviser is that the former is his particular and sole responsibility, in consultation, of course, with appropriate experts within and outside the government service; in the case of the operational function, however, the legal adviser carries out instructions of his government in the same way as do other public servants. Bureaucrats make recommendations but governments decide policy. If the legal adviser represents his country in bilateral or multilateral negotiations, he does so in a purely representative capacity. The implementation of a particular policy máy fall to him and his colleagues in his own and in other government departments, but the policy is that of his country as determined by its government. The operational function may nevertheless be complex and involve, in the case of Canada, the hammering out of positions through consultations with a number of other government departments at the federal level, and on occasion (such as the Stockholm Conference) representatives from provinces and from industry. His operational function therefore usually consists of co-ordination, preparation, persuasion, and legal diplomacy, as compared to the essentially advisory nature of his other major function. The distinction is not unlike that between barristers and solicitors pertaining in the UK and some other parts of the world.

The legal adviser must look to a variety of sources for background information and advice. An area involving deep ideological differences may require the advice and expertise of political scientists in academic circles and the foreign service familiar with the historical background and the semantics involved on a particular issue. An attempt to develop an appropriate response on hijacking necessitates close consultation with civil aviation and security experts. An attempt to develop international environmental law requires a multidisciplinary approach presupposing close collaboration between scientists, technicians, economists, political scientists, and lawyers (both domestic and international) and consultation with other departments, the provinces, private industry, and concerned members of the public. An initiative in the UN calling for the development of space law on a particular issue is the outcome of a series of discussions with experts on communications, within and outside the government service. The position to be adopted on the legal measures to be taken to combat terrorism must take into account the views of a whole range of experts concerned with security, the airlines, and the airline pilots association, as well as those familiar with the methodology of legal diplomacy in the UN, including in particular knowledge of the positions of various countries and groups of countries on such highly political issues. The development of proposals on the law of the sea requires consultation with experts on fisheries, naval strategy, mineral resource exploitation, hydrographers, cartographers, and related sciences, as well as representatives of industry, and members of the public and parliamentary committees.

The advisory function is presumably as effective for one country as another, assuming that the necessary resources are available. In the case of the operational role, whatever the availability of resources and the degree of success in coordinating action, the influence of any one country on the progressive development of international law, whether by custom or by convention, is necessarily limited. It is, accordingly, an important fact of life for the Canadian legal adviser that Canada is neither a major power able to impose its view on the law of other states nor a ministate helpless to influence events which may shape international law.[10]

The success of the advisory function is often, although not always, measurable by events, whereas the success of the operational role is more difficult to appraise since its effectiveness depends on subjective considerations, particularly in the case of conference diplomacy, including on occasion such intangibles as timing of a statement, mood of the conference, and even personal relationships with other delegates. On other occasions where it is necessary to join forces with representatives of other states sharing a similar position, the influence which has been or can be exerted on a particular area of developing law is more readily identifiable.

The advisory function is nearly always a confidential one, although public answers must often be given with respect to letters from the public, questions in House of Commons committees, debates in the UN, and in certain other situations. The operational 'role' is more often a public one and becoming increasingly so as foreign ministry legal advisers are participating more and more in open or semipublic debates on matters of international law. This is particularly true in the case of Canada in the light of the attention focused in recent years upon Canadian approaches to international environmental law and the law of the sea as reflected in Canadian legislation.

CANADIAN ACTIVISM

In the light of these considerations, any resumé of Canada's role during the past decade in both the codification and progressive development of international law, and also the customary law-making process, through state practice in particular, indicates what may be to some a surprising range and intensity of activity. Although it is fashionable to talk of international law having fallen into disrepute since the days of the League of Nations, there is in fact a tremendous resurgence of codification and progressive development of international law. At the same time the development of customary international law by state practice has not fallen into desuetude nor can it, as new problems thrown up by technological developments continue to force governments to make decisions having constitutive legal implications on the international plane. The pace of both processes has, if anything, accelerated during the 1960s and shows every sign of continuing to do so during the 1970s.[11]

Over the past decade Canada has participated in virtually every important multilateral law-making activity. During this period, for example, a distinguished Canadian, Marcel Cadieux, was very active in the law-making activities of the International Law Commission in its studies on the law of treaties and special missions. Canada has also participated actively in the UN Human Rights Commission and the Third Committee of the UN on human rights problems; the major diplomatic conferences on diplomatic relations, consular relations, and the law of treaties; the 1969 Brussels IMCO Conference; the diplomatic conference on special missions; the UN Sub-Committee on the seven charter principles of 'friendly relations'; the legal committee of IMCO and a succession of IMCO conferences on maritime law; the UN Special Committee on the Definition of Aggression; the sessions of the UN Outer Space Legal Sub-Committee which have elaborated the outer space treaty, the return of astronauts convention, and the outer space liability convention, and is now working on a registration convention; the UN working group on direct broadcast satellites; the series of intergovernmental conferences leading to the establishment of Intelsat; the Ad Hoc and subsequent Standing Committee of the UN on the Seabed (which is also the preparatory committee for the Third Law of the Sea Conference); the several preparatory groups, including in particular those on marine pollution and on the Declaration on the Human Environment, established to prepare for the Stockholm Conference itself; the several preparatory conferences on the Ocean Dumping Convention, including the London conference at which the convention was concluded; a series of ICNAF conferences leading to new regional rules of law to conserve fisheries; the series of francophone conferences on education and cultural matters; the ICAO legal committee and subcommittees and the subsequent Montreal and Hague conferences on sabotage and hijacking of aircraft; the ICRC conference in Istanbul which started the process of up-dating humanitarian law in armed conflicts, and the subsequent ICRC conferences of government experts, in which Canada chaired the commission set up to further develop international humanitarian law in non-international conflicts; and the Sixth Committee studies on protection of diplomats and on international terrorism. Canada has also participated actively in the revision of the GATT, in the preparation of the GATT anti-dumping code, in the development of legal norms for the protection of foreign investment, and the range of conventions intended to facilitate international trade, from customs through the international combined transport of goods (TCM). Canada has also been active in recent years in the development of intellectual and industrial property conventions and in the preparation of the UNESCO conventions directed to the protection of the cultural heritage. Canada is also a member of UNIDROIT and the Hague Conference, which are both working actively on questions of private international law. Canada has made substantial contributions to the Sixth Committee studies on technical assistance in international law and on the role of the International Court of Justice (with considerable input from Canadian academics). Canada now expects to be appointed to the recently established UN Committee on Terrorism.

Merely to mention Canadian participation in the relevant commissions and committees and international conferences is no indication, of course, that Canada has been particularly active in these organizations or has made a substantive contribution in any of these diverse fields. Such evidence may, perhaps, be found in the other articles in this publication. The comments below will accordingly be directed to a few representative examples.

MULTILATERAL 'LAW-MAKING' ACTIVITIES

Canada has actively pursued a distinctive approach on a number of subject areas over the last decade, on some of which the Canadian national interest appeared to be directly engaged, on others merely indirectly, while on still others the Canadian interest was not markedly different from that of any other responsible member of the international community concerned to contribute to the development of the rule of law amongst nations.

In the first category of issues engaging the Canadian interest directly, an obvious example was the stance taken by Canada at the Law of Treaties Conference concerning the need to safeguard the constitutions of federal states against external interpretation and intervention. The Canadian member of the International Law Commission, Marcel Cadieux, had pointed out, together with some other members, the potentially serious, albeit unintended, dangers raised by the language of article 5 of the Law of Treaties Convention. The convention nonetheless went forward to the Law of Treaties Conference with the controversial language intact. The Canadian delegation, ably led by Max Wershof, deliberately refrained from active efforts to influence other states at the first session of the Law of Treaties Conference on the assumption that the view of federal states, that is to say those states directly affected by the article, would prevail. This did not prove to be the case, however, and Canada therefore worked actively both prior to and during the second session, together with other federal states (including in particular India, Mexico, and Australia) to persuade the delegates at the conference of the inadequacies of the article as drafted. In the event, the controversial language of the article was deleted by an overwhelming majority vote.

Another issue clearly involving the Canadian national interest was the nature and extent of participation by Canadian provinces in international francophone organizations. In spite of difficulties leading in one case to the suspension of relations with another state, it proved possible to work out accommodations which were sufficiently responsive to the real needs of the provinces to satisfy them and sufficiently flexible in legal terms to avoid doing violence either to the Canadian constitution or to international law. The contributions of Marcel Cadieux, Allan Gotlieb, and André Bissonnette during their time as legal advisers to the resolution of these problems were extremely significant.

A further such instance is the recent Canadian proposal in the Sixth Committee that the UN Commission on International Trade Law begin to consider the implica-

tions for the harmonization of trade law of the activities of multinational enterprises. The proposal was preceded by careful interdepartmental consultation on a
range of matters. UNCITRAL was chosen as the appropriate organ for action in this
field in spite of possible doubts concerning its mandate, because of its high professional competence in law-making on technical trade issues, and because it might
be expected to adopt a workman-like approach divorced from polemics. A gradualist approach was adopted whereby the matter was first raised at the Sixteenth UN
GA and put forth as a concrete proposal only a year later at the Seventeenth UN GA.
The proposal was a deliberately modest one not likely to alarm the economic sector
in Canada or abroad but intended nonetheless to provide an adequate basis for a
serious study of some of the relevant legal issues. In the intervening period, subsequent to the initial suggestion by Canada and prior to the specific proposal, Chile
and other countries put forth proposals that ECOSOC and UNCTAD consider certain
aspects of the phenomenon of the multinational enterprise, but Canada was the first
country in the UN to raise the legal issues.

Another such example was the Canadian proposal that the UN Outer Space Committee begin considering the range of problems raised by remote sensing of the earth
by satellites. Apart from other considerations, including the general desirability of
multilateral law on a highly technical matter on which existing technology is confined to relatively few states, the interest of Canada lies in safeguarding its own
'sovereign rights' to the information gained through such satellites concerning the
national resources of Canada. Similarly, in pressing so long and so hard for a
'victim-oriented' liability convention for damage by space objects, Canada
reflected its immediate national interest in protecting itself from damage by such
objects, which was not seen as incompatible with Canada's long-term interests as
a country with a developing space capability and thus a potential space power.

The Canadian position in the UN discussions on permanent sovereignty over
national resources provides a further interesting example. Early in the UN discussions on permanent sovereignty it was concluded that Canada did not fit neatly into
the categories either of developed or developing countries, and the Canadian position was therefore intended to reflect the fact that Canada was at once both a
developed and a developing country. The most recent illustration of this position
was the affirmative vote of the Canadian delegation to the XXVII UN GA on a resolution on permanent sovereignty over national resources which was supported
by very few other 'developed' states.

Numerous similar examples can be found in the field of disarmament.[12] Canada
took a lead and indeed was almost alone for a period in pressing for the Non-
Proliferation Treaty and the Partial Test Ban treaties (which were regarded even
in those early years as both environmental and disarmament measures), at a time
when some of Canada's allies resisted or were lukewarm towards such action by
Canada. More recently Canada adopted a distinctive and controversial position
with respect to the seabed arms control treaty; Canada was the first country to call
for the application of the treaty to the widest possible area of the seabed including
even areas within national jurisdiction. Canada also proposed in the face of opposition from other western countries the banning of the implanting of all offensive
weapons from the seabed and not merely weapons of mass destruction; Canada also
took a lead in pressing strongly for effective rights of inspection by coastal states

to ensure compliance with the treaty. In all of these activities the Canadian position reflected the interests of Canada as a coastal state, not a major maritime power, not a great power, not a nuclear power, and not a space power; but a NATO country experienced in peacekeeping and with a strong interest in developing effective arms control measures. Similarly, in the adoption of a strong stance on outer space issues long before Canada had any space capability of its own, the Canadian position reflected an awareness of the future implications for Canada of conventions which at the time appeared to be essentially bilateral agreements between the two space powers sanctioned by the rest of the international community.

There may be a second category of issues which engage both a direct and an indirect Canadian interest. An example of a Canadian position on such matters was the early and consistent Canadian insistence at the diplomatic and consular conferences on the functional approach to diplomatic and consular immunities whereby only those immunities essential to the performance of the function would be admitted. Another such example was the active collaboration by Canada with Sweden in the preparation of a joint paper on the legal aspects of direct broadcast satellites. Another is the current Canadian initiative proposing an outer space registration convention. These policies have been vigorously pursued with the conscious recognition of the Canadian interest, both direct and indirect, but, it is suggested, in ways not inconsistent with the general interests of the international community.

A particularly apt example of a problem area engaging Canada's interests both directly and indirectly is provided by the attempts made over the past decade in the OECD and the IBRD and in the International Law Commission, which will undoubtedly continue on into the next decade, to produce legal norms concerning the protection of private foreign investment. Canada is both an exporter and an importer of capital but is a net importer. In recent years, however, Canada's interests have become more directly engaged as Canadian investments abroad have been subjected to expropriation. The Canadian position has, however, not been on all fours with that of the major capital exporting states and has tended to go further towards meeting the preoccupations of developing countries on such issues as 'promptness' of compensation while adhering in general to traditional concepts of state responsibility.

There may also be a third category of problem areas engaging Canadian interests only indirectly. Such was the case with respect to the 'Friendly Relations' committee's deliberations in the UN, in which there was an active and distinctive Canadian involvement in the negotiations leading to the establishment[13] and the subsequent deliberations of that committee over a seven-year period, resulting ultimately in the 25th anniversary declaration of the UN on friendly relations. The Canadian approach was motivated originally by the indirect interest of a western state desirous to channel the pressures for the codification of the principles of peaceful coexistence into a less ideologically motivated direction, and at the same time to involve developing countries directly in the elaboration of charter principles as a means of responding to the widespread feeling that they had not had a hand in the development of the law of the charter. Subsequently, the Canadian interest in the formulation of specific principles, such as non-intervention and self-determination, became more direct, while the Canadian interest in other principles such as the non-use of force became less direct.

An analogous example was the lead taken by Canada in the UN Special Committee on the Definition of Aggression in pressing for a western definition (in the face of thirty years of western resistance to such action), in order to ensure that any definition produced adequately safeguards the discretionary powers of the Security Council and also that the most common forms of twentieth century aggression, such as the incursion of armed bands across frontiers, would be covered. Canada's position on hijacking similarly reflected at the outset only an indirect interest although more latterly a direct interest, after the hijacking of Canadian aircraft and of non-Canadian aircraft in Canadian territory. The Canadian approach on this question has been from the outset based on the need for concrete action to combat hijacking which does not do violence either to existing bilateral air agreements or the general principles of treaty law concerning the right to apply treaties against non-parties. The Canadian approach on this issue falls between those who consider that pre-existing multilateral agreements such as the Chicago Convention provide an adequate foundation for sanctions and those who argue that sanctions can be taken only by the Security Council. While on some of these questions the Canadian interest may be merely indirect, the common element in the Canadian approach is clearly the general desirability of developing international law on the non-use of force as an end in itself as part of the process of developing a world order.

It is possible to discern a fourth category of issues of no direct Canadian interest and little or no perceivable indirect interest, on which there are, nevertheless, examples of a distinctive Canadian position, such as the Canadian proposal at the Istanbul Red Cross Conference for the establishment of an international legal aid fund for human rights litigants. A similar example is provided by the very early Canadian co-sponsorship in the Human Rights Commission of the proposal for the establishment of a human rights commissioner. The proposals by Canada at the Istanbul conference for concrete follow-up action to develop humanitarian laws of warfare by drafting protocols to the 1949 Geneva Red Cross Conventions on the rules applicable to non-international conflicts is another such example. The Canadian position on the rules of succession of states in respect of treaties was also, at the point in Canadian history when the Canadian government's comments were submitted to the International Law Commission, based in large part, if not entirely, on the general interest of Canada in ensuring certainty and stability of treaty relations. The general Canadian posture at the Law of Treaties Conference on such issues as coercion, *rebus sic stantibus* and *jus cogens* and perhaps, more important, Canada's early accession to the convention on the law of treaties, provide concrete evidence of Canada's continuing commitment to the development of international law, in this case the constitutional basis for much of existing international law.

It is mentioned above that there are two major problem areas which have occupied the attention of successive legal advisers during the last decade[14] and which it may be assumed will continue to do so over the next decade; namely, questions touching on the participation of the Canadian provinces in action by Canada on the international plane and questions of jurisdiction, sovereignty, and territoriality. Although both are discussed in depth elsewhere in this volume, it is necessary to refer, albeit briefly, to these two fields of law of particular interest to Canada in any attempt at an overview, however cursory, of Canadian approaches to international law.

Canadians appear to have realized at an early stage in the evolution of the Canadian nation state that it would be necessary to modify both internal 'empire' law of the British Empire and international law in order to lay the basis for Canada's gradual and peaceful evolution from colony to nation. The temerity of Canadian politicians and statesmen is surprising in retrospect when one considers the extent of the changes they wrought. Certainly there was no precedent for their action in consistently moving towards independence by peaceful means, policies bold and inventive in concept, however gradualist in implementation. The development of the Canadian nation state has continued to reflect these early characteristics of willingness to bend both constitutional and international law in order to achieve acceptable accommodations.

The Canadian provinces have been accorded something tantamount to, while falling short of, a right of legation through their separate offices in London, Paris, and in Washington, while provincial representatives are now included in the offices of a number of Canadian embassies in other countries. One would search in vain for a precise rule of constitutional or international law for such a development. Similarly, while Canadian provinces have always been able to work out 'administrative arrangements' with member-states of the union south of the border, in recent years Canadian provinces have been able to conclude 'agreements' with France and other states resting for their validity upon umbrella treaties concluded by Canada and these other states. Once again, outside precedents from domestic, constitutional, or international law will be sought in vain. Even with respect to participation in international conferences, arrangements have been worked out for the inclusion of provincial delegates within the Canadian delegations to a series of francophone and other international conferences. No precise parallel exists in the state practice of other countries. In all these activities Canada may not have sought deliberately to alter international law but it has not hesitated to bend it where necessary. Similarly, Canada has not sought to postpone such developments until a formal constitutional solution is achieved but has developed practices within the existing constitution. Whether such practices have had constitutive legal effects either on the municipal or international legal plane is a moot point. What is of interest is the approach adopted (which will be referred to later).

The Canadian approach to questions of jurisdiction, sovereignty, and territory over the last decade provides a rich source of issues engaging the national interest directly in some cases, indirectly in others, and only peripherally in still others. There are numerous examples of a distinctive Canadian position on environmental law and on the law of the sea based on a readily discernible Canadian interest. Canada as a coastal state with an extremely lengthy coastline has an understandable concern in protecting its marine environment and has reflected this objective not only in its national legislation (and the accompanying reservations to the jurisdiction of the International Court) but in such multilateral action as the declaration of marine pollution principles presented by Canada to the Stockholm Marine Pollution Preparatory Committee and subsequently pursued at Stockholm, and the tabling of a working paper in the Seabed Committee on a comprehensive approach to marine pollution. Canada's more general interests in protecting its environment as a whole were reflected in the draft declaration of legal principles on the human environment submitted by Canada to the Stockholm Conference Preparatory Committee on the Declaration on the Human Environment. On both these issues, however, the Canadian position reflects also the environmental interest of every member of the international community in the development of law to prevent the degradation of the environment.

Similarly, on the law of the sea, Canada, as a state with an extensive and deeply glaciated continental shelf, has consistently supported the 'exploitability' test, embodied in the Geneva Continental Shelf Convention, to which Canada is a party, during the debates of the Seabed Committee. At the same time, Canada has put forth radical revenue-sharing proposals intended to benefit the international community as a whole. With respect to some issues cutting across both fields of law, such as the doctrine of innocent passage, Canada has proposed that the concept be revised and expanded so as to include the protection of the coastal state's environmental interests as well as its more traditional security interests. On fisheries questions Canada has protected its national interests by establishing new fishing zones by national legislation and negotiating bilaterally for the phasing out of the fishing activities of other countries in such zones. Canada has also proposed in the Seabed Committee the recognition of coastal state managerial rights and responsibility well beyond the territorial sea, together with coastal state preferences with respect to the living resources of the sea in areas adjacent to coastal states. Canada has also, however, opposed the extension of sovereignty as a means of protecting the living resources of the sea because of the effect such claims have on the interests of the international community as a whole. The Canadian working paper on scientific research principles tabled in the Seabed Committee was put forth as a deliberate attempt to strike a balance between coastal state interests and the general interest of the international community in freedom of research. There are equally numerous examples within these same two closely related fields of law where the Canadian interest is less direct, such as the regime for the resources of the seabed beyond national jurisdiction, with respect to which Canada has submitted a working paper postulating a functional approach directed towards economic exploitation subject to effective controls and leading to equitable distribution of proceeds.

The Canadian position on the Ocean Dumping Convention provides a recent and illustrative example of the way in which Canada's national interests are perceived and pursued. Throughout the year of preparatory discussions and the succeeding conference in London, the Canadian delegation pressed for an effective convention that would not leave the determination of the right to dump noxious substances to the discretion of the dumping state, as had been proposed by some delegations in early drafts. Thus the Canadian delegation strongly supported the 'black list-grey list' approach which banned the dumping of some substances and set up very strict controls over the dumping of other substances. On the jurisdictional issue, the Canadian delegation argued that the convention should be enforceable by all parties, whether coastal or flag state. No attempt was made by Canada to include the concept of pollution zones in the convention but the way was paved for consideration of such a solution by a provision referred for consideration to the Law of the Sea Conference on the nature and extent of coastal state rights. The demonstrable Canadian interest in recognition of the right and responsibility of coastal states to protect their marine environment was thus maintained while at the same time the interests of the flag states, in many cases the major dumpers, were also accommodated.

The Canadian position on all of these environmental and law of the sea issues can be seen as clearly reflecting Canada's national interests, both direct and indirect, but also the need to safeguard the 'international' interests at stake. Indeed, Canada is one of the few members of the UN Seabed Committee which has argued consistently that the interests of the international community as a whole, as well as the specific interest of coastal states, maritime states, and landlocked states, should be safeguarded in the future law of the sea. In an attempt to provide a conceptual bridge between the rights and responsibilities of states and between conflicting interests of states, Canada has put forth the notions of 'delegation of powers' by the international community to coastal states and the concept of 'custodianship' by the coastal states. Thus, while not hesitating to act 'unilaterally' when necessary, Canada has also engaged in bilateral negotiations with those countries directly affected by such action and has also acted multilaterally, participating actively in the negotiations in IMCO, the Stockholm Conference, the Seabed Committee, and the London Dumping Conference, in an attempt to work out accommodations on unresolved issues of environmental law and the law of the sea. The Canadian 'pluralistic' approach to these two fields of law may be indicative of basic Canadian attitudes towards international law.

STATE PRACTICE

Canadian contributions to international law by state practice similarly relate to a wide spectrum of fields of law and have been made through a variety of means. Evidence of the continuing and specifically Canadian contributions in the development of international law through state practice can be found in the successive issues of the *Canadian Yearbook of International Law* in the Canadian Practice sections, and the quotations from the yearbook and from direct Canadian sources in UN publications (such as, for example, the International Law Commission report on the succession of states in respect of treaties).

More public examples can be found in the series of national legislative measures and related public statements concerning the marine environment, such as the 1964 legislation establishing the nine-mile exclusive contiguous fishing zone; the series of orders in council based on that legislation establishing the straight baseline system along Canada's east and west coasts; the 1970 legislation laying down the basis for Arctic waters pollution prevention zones; the establishment of a twelve-mile territorial sea, the establishment of 'adjacent fishing zones,' and the extension of pollution control under the Canada Shipping Act to Canadian fishing zones. In addition to this series of unilateral acts, Canadian state practice includes a series of bilateral fisheries treaties with the United States, the USSR, France, the United Kingdom, Norway, Denmark, Portugal, and Spain, and the possible basis for the delineation of continental shelf limits with Denmark (Greenland) and France (St Pierre and Miquelon).

A relatively little known but highly significant example of Canadian state practice ranking in importance almost with Canada's decision to agree to arbitrate the *Trail Smelter* case was the decision to set up a special tribunal to arbitrate the damages suffered by US citizens from Canada's construction of Gut Dam. As a concrete example of a willingness to accept for the second time responsibility for damages to citizens of another state without the necessity of prior exhaustion of local remedies by the individuals concerned, the case is extremely important. Not surprisingly, Canada requested the US immediately after the conclusion of the Stockholm Environmental Conference to respond in similar fashion, on the basis of the Stockholm principles, and accept responsibility for the damage suffered by Canada from the Cherry Point oil spill.

A much better known and highly controversial example of Canadian state practice was the reservation submitted by Canada to the International Court of Justice concerning Canadian environmental protection and living resources conservation legislation. Government spokesmen made clear at the time that the reservations had been made because of the lack of existing environmental and conservation law on the international plane, and that the reservations were intended to be temporary and analogous to interim injunctions pending the development of the law. The statements made clear also that Canada would take complementary action multilaterally to develop the law in these two fields, and Canada has since been extremely active in developing the law in these fields.

As mentioned above, Canadian state practice on federal-provincial and international issues may also have had a constitutive legal effect not only domestically but on the international plane, particularly with respect to the working out of the *accord cadre* mechanism enabling Canadian provinces to conclude arrangements with foreign states under the aegis of the umbrella treaties concluded by the Canadian government. As is the case with organized multilateral law-making activities, Canadian state practice provides considerable evidence of the implications for Canada of international law issues and the need to respond accordingly.

CONCLUSION: A CANADIAN APPROACH?

The following passage occurs in the late Lester B. Pearson's memoirs:[15]

> Everything I learned during the war confirmed and strengthened my view as a Canadian that our foreign policy must not be timid or fearful of commitments but activist in accepting international responsibilities. To me, nationalism and internationalism were two sides of the same coin. International co-operation for peace is the most important aspect of national policy. I have never wavered in this belief even though I have learned from experience how agonizingly difficult it is to convert conviction into reality.

Over the past decade Canada has been extremely active, indeed activist, on a wide range of issues of international law. The policies pursued have been goal-oriented and directed towards the attainment of Canadian objectives. Where particular issues have engaged the Canadian national interest, the objectives have reflected this interest; in other cases the objectives appear to be almost wholly internationalist. In many cases the perception of the national interest clearly takes into account the interdependence of states. Positions adopted are not always those of other 'western' or 'developed' states and have often been distinctive to the point that on some questions Canada has parted company with friends. There is an emphasis on concrete problem-solving and a lesser concern with doctrinal attitudes, particularly those stemming from traditional concepts. On a number of continuing problem areas, there is evidence of consistency and perseverance over a lengthy period. There are many illustrations of a close co-ordination of Canada's positions on the same or similar issues arising in different fora. An innovative approach can be seen on many questions. On certain problems, such as environmental law and the law of the sea, a bold and dynamic approach is evident. There is a deliberate attempt on virtually every issue to develop the basis for accommodations between conflicting interests, in particular between the interests of Canada and those of the other members of the international community. A common characteristic throughout is a conscious tendency towards pragmatism, functionalism, and flexibility, most notably in responding to the need for change.

It is suggested that these characteristics, which, in my view, together comprise a distinctive Canadian approach to international law in the sixties, will continue to be required by Canada in the seventies, particularly with respect to the two main problem areas touched on briefly here: federal-provincial relations, and questions of jurisdiction, sovereignty, and territoriality.

NOTES

1 'In essence, foreign policy is the product of the Government's progressive definition and pursuit of national aims and interests in the international environment. It is the extension abroad of national policies.' Department of External Affairs, *Foreign Policy for Canadians* (1970) 9.

2 *Legal Advisers and Foreign Affairs* (1964), proceedings of the Princeton Conference. Marcel Cadieux' article on the role of the legal adviser, entitled 'An Inside View,' comments, at 35, as follows: 'As pointed out by the Royal Commission on Government Organization, which recently examined the Canadian Civil Service, "international law is intimately bound up with high policy questions and relationships with other nations." The Commission went on and concluded that "there is need ... to preserve a balance between policy considerations and legal implications." '

3 'Flexibility is essential but so too is a sense of direction and purpose, so that Canada's foreign policy is not over-reactive but is oriented positively in the direction of national aims. This is one of the main conclusions of the policy review.' *Foreign Policy for Canadians, supra* note 1, at 32.

4 A view on the interrelationship and interpenetration of customary and conventional law is contained in the following passage from a statement by the Canadian representative in the First Committee of the XXIV UN GA on 4 December 1970:

The contemporary international law of the sea comprises both conventional and customary law. Conventional or multilateral treaty law must, of course, be developed primarily by multilateral action drawing as necessary upon principles of customary international law. Thus multilateral conventions often consist of both a codification of existing principles of international law and progressive development of new principles. Customary international law is, of course, derived primarily from state practice, that is to say, unilateral action by various states, although it frequently draws in turn upon the principles embodied in bilateral and limited multilateral treaties. Law-making treaties often become accepted as such not by virtue of their status as treaties but through a gradual acceptance by states of the principles they lay down. The complex process of the development of customary international law is still relevant and indeed, in our view, essential to the building of a world order. For these reasons we find it very difficult to be doctrinaire on such questions. The regime of the territorial sea, for example, derives in part from conventional law, including in particular the Geneva Convention on the Territorial Sea (which itself was based in large part upon customary principles) and in part from the very process of the development of customary international law. During the period when it was possible to say, if ever there was such a time, that there existed a rule of law that the breadth of the territorial sea extended to three nautical miles and no further, that principle was created by state practice, and can be altered by state practice, that is to say, by unilateral action on the part of various states, accepted by other states and thus developed into customary international law.

5 'There could be further international demands for Canadian participation in peacekeeping operations – especially in regional conflicts. The Government is determined that this special brand of Canadian expertise will not be dispersed or wasted on ill-conceived operations but employed judiciously where the peacekeeping operation and the Canadian contribution to it seem likely to improve the chances for lasting settlement.' *Foreign Policy for Canadians, supra* note 1, at 23.

6 The following is a partial list of opinions or position statements in these two fields taken from the *Canadian Yearbook of International Law* for the years 1964-72:

Subjects of International Law:

Participation by provincial ministers of labour in the Canadian delegation to the annual conference of the International Labour Organization; participation by Canadian provinces in treaty-making and implementation (with particular respect to the Skagit River project); consultation with the provinces concerning Canadian accession to the 1949 United Nations Road Traffic Convention; procedure respecting ratification of International Labour conventions, touching in particular on the constitutional division of authority between the federal and provincial governments; the capacity of individual states of the United States to enter into agreements with the Canadian federal government concerning unemployment insurance; capacity of the state of Alaska to enter into an arrangement with a Canadian government department concerning the maintenance of an international highway; the legal status of the Portuguese overseas territories; the status of the Order of Malta; the role of the Canadian federal government in providing for the reciprocal enforcement of judgments between a Canadian province and an Australian state; the competent authorities under the Canadian constitution for the reciprocal enforcement of judgments and maintenance orders of foreign jurisdictions; the procedures for the reciprocal enforcement within the Commonwealth of maintenance orders; the legal basis for the

Franco-Quebec educational entente and the form of the assent of the federal government; the Canadian constitutional authority concerning the treaty-making power and the appropriate procedures; the lack of harmony between treaty-making and treaty-implementing powers; the constitutional historical development of the process whereby the *accord cadre* procedure evolved; the legal basis for the making of ententes on cultural matters by provinces; the requirement for and form of consent by the federal government to the Franco-Quebec cultural entente; competence of the provinces concerning reciprocal enforcement of foreign adoptions; validity of 'informal arrangements' between provincial governments and foreign states; Franco-Quebec entente on cultural co-operation; role of provinces in treaty-making; federal government, the sole treaty-making authority; arrangements for representation of provinces in Canadian delegations to conferences of specialized agencies.

Jurisdiction, sovereignty, territory:

Requirement for consent of the government of Canada to overflights by US nuclear-armed aircraft; right of Canadian government to regulate broadcasting beamed at Canada from US stations; the basis of Canadian sovereignty over Arctic islands; nature of agreement between Canada and British Columbia respecting the Columbia River; legal basis for implementation of straight baseline system for delimiting Canadian territorial sea and contiguous fishing zones; legal implications for foreign fishermen of establishment of Canadian exclusive fishing zones; legal basis for 'abstention principle' embodied in north Pacific treaty; sovereign immunity of foreign state aircraft carrying foreign head of state through Canadian air space; non-requirement for registration of foreign lobbyists; status of Geneva Law of the Sea Conventions; status of Gulf of St Lawrence and Hudson Bay under Canadian Territorial and Fishing Zones Act; date of acquisition of Canadian independence and sovereignty; extraditability of foreign national for crime committed in Canadian embassy abroad; territorial boundaries of another state as a fact of state; Arctic sovereignty; Canadian sovereignty over Arctic islands and seabed; status of waters of Arctic archipelago; implications for Canadian sovereignty of voyage of s.s. *Manhattan* through Northwest Passage; applicability of doctrine of innocent passage to waters of Arctic archipelago; legal effect of establishment of straight baseline system for delimitation of Canadian territorial sea; limits of Canadian jurisdiction over seabed; delimitation between continental margin and oceanic basin; Canadian position in Seabed Committee on limits of national jurisdiction over seabed; validity of unilateral extensions of jurisdiction over marine environment; role of unilateral action in customary law-making process; legal basis of Canadian assertion of marine pollution control jurisdiction over Arctic waters; Canadian exclusive fishing zones; legal validity of issues raised in us protest note to Canadian Arctic Pollution Prevention Act; legal content of concept of common heritage of mankind.

Similar examples can be found in the annual yearbook with respect to other broad special areas such as diplomatic and consular relations, recognition of states and governments, rights and duties of states, state responsibility, extradition law and procedures, treaty law, nationality, asylum, secession of states and governments, human rights, law of international organizations, civil procedure, outer space, judicial settlement, war and international conflict, general principles of international law, treatment of aliens, consular matters which are too numerous to list in terms of specific issues, etc.

7 Cadieux, *supra* note 2, comments at 36 as follows: 'The function of the Legal Adviser to the Department of External Affairs might be defined in general terms as attempting to ensure that Canada's role in international affairs is conducted in accordance with generally accepted legal principles, practices and processes.'

8 'In sum, while basing its foreign policy on recognized principles of international law, Canada will continue to introduce constructive innovations (as Canada has done on the law of the sea and on the Arctic environment) where international law is not sufficiently responsive to present or future needs.' *Foreign Policy for Canadians, supra* note 1, *United Nations*, at 30.

9 'Canada has less reason than most countries to anticipate conflicts between its national aims and those of the international community as a whole. Many Canadian policies can be directed toward the broad goals of that community without unfavourable reaction from the Canadian public. Peace in all its manifestations, economic and social progress, environmental control, the development of international law and institutions – these are international goals which fall squarely into that category ... Canada's action to advance self-interest often coincides with the kind of worthwhile contribution to international affairs that most Canadians clearly favour.' *Foreign Policy for Canadians, supra* note 1, at 11.

10 Ibid, at 19: 'Foreign policy can be shaped, and is shaped, mainly by the value judgments of the Government at any given time. But it is also shaped by the possibilities that are open to Canada at any given time – basically by the constraints or opportunities presented by the prevailing international situation. It is shaped too by domestic considerations, by the internal pressures exerted on the Government, by the amount of resources which the Government can afford to deploy.'

11 'The impetus for change has ... been reflected in the progressive development and codification of international law within the United Nations. The various organizations within the u.n. system have increasingly turned to the drafting of multilateral conventions as the best method of achieving this end.' *Foreign Policy for Canadians, supra* note 1, *United Nations*, at 7.

12 An excellent analysis of the role of the law and lawyers in disarmament negotiations is contained in Allan Gotlieb's well-known publication *Disarmament and International Law* (1965).

13 These developments, including in particular an exposition of the Canadian approach to the problem and the methodology of Canadian diplomacy on the issue, are outlined in an article by the Honourable Paul Martin entitled 'Co-Existence or Friendly Relations? The Canadian Approach,' and my accompanying article entitled 'Canadian Initiatives in East-West Legal Relations in the United Nations,' which appeared in the collection of essays, *Law, Policy and the East-West Détente*, edited by Edward McWhinney (1964). These articles, together with others appearing in the same volume, provide a useful basis for measuring the

nature and extent of the Canadian interest in the item at its outset as against the Canadian interest as it may be seen in retrospect.

14 The Canadian legal advisers over the period in question were: Marcel Cadieux, Max Wershof, Allan Gotlieb, André Bissonnette, and J. Alan Beesley.

15 *Mike: Memoirs of the Right Honourable Lester B. Pearson* I (1972).

R. ST J. MACDONALD,

GERALD L. MORRIS AND

DOUGLAS M. JOHNSTON

38/Canadian
Approaches to
International Law

As its title may indicate, this chapter constitutes something other than a review and assessment of the preceding essays. It is, instead, an attempt by the editors to survey the 'state of international law' in Canada. We intend to approach this question in the context of historical development, focusing on levels of apparent interest, main lines of recent activity, uses made of international law, characteristics of national style and philosophy, values and priorities, perceivable trends, possible pitfalls, and potential opportunities.

During a score of 'brainstorming' sessions the editors repeatedly examined aspects of basic questions about the subject: How have we Canadians arrived where we seem to be today? Why? Where do we appear to be headed? Why? Should we be following a different course? What can we do to improve our contributions to the strengthening of the international legal order? To these questions we elicited responses from colleagues in various parts of the country. The views of non-lawyers and of law students were sought. Letters from numerous individuals, including several 'elder statesmen' among the international lawyers in Canada, provided historical perspective and a measure of factual accuracy which might not otherwise have been obtainable. A variety of written sources was consulted.

Despite the effort devoted to this exercise, certain limitations were inevitable. So far as we are aware, no previous study of quite the same dimensions has been attempted in Canada and the ground was relatively uncharted. Central facts are not available in some cases, or remain ambiguous. Underlying factors, motives, and attitudes (and their significance) can frequently only be guessed. Those whom we consulted were by no means unanimous. On occasion, respected colleagues disagreed with us vigorously. Judgments on this topic must be tentative and speculative. It will be obvious that our comments involve assessments which other observers might well challenge, Debatable though they may be, we set forth our views in the hope of stimulating discussion and inquiry. We are convinced that the points at issue have considerable significance for Canada.

THE DEVELOPMENT OF INTERNATIONAL LAW STUDIES AND PRACTICE IN CANADA

Although Canada is a relatively recent arrival as a significant participant in the international arena, the number of international lawyers in Canada has already reached respectable proportions. This is true both of academic and government lawyers and it is now possible to convene a meeting of more than seventy Canadian officials and academics whose professional interest centres on international law. If political scientists and other non-lawyers with some background and working experience in international law are included, the number approaches one hundred.

As yet it is hardly possible to speak of a section of the Canadian international law community in private practice. Nonetheless, the several practitioners who might claim a specialization in international law are joined by an increasing number of other practitioners who, from time to time, find themselves required to dabble in the black arts of international law. As letters received by the Department of External Affairs and other federal agencies frequently reveal, however, many practitioners remain largely uninitiated in the concepts, principles, and terminology of international law.

The Canadian universities

The teaching of public international law in Canada can be traced back as far as the mid-nineteenth century. Among the common law faculties, it appears that Dalhousie University in Halifax may claim to have led the way. Dean Weldon taught an international law course at Dalhousie from 1885 until 1914 and, since that time, at least one elective course in international law has been offered there, except for two short periods when no one suitably qualified was on the teaching staff.

The earliest international law teaching program in Canada was probably located at Laval University, although available information leaves some uncertainty as to whether Laval in Quebec City or the Montreal branch of Laval (now the University of Montreal) can claim the honour. The first lecturer in international law at Laval in Quebec City was appointed for the academic year 1883–4. The Montreal branch of Laval had as its first professor of international law Sir Adolphe Chapleau, who died in 1899. The year of his first appointment could not be ascertained, but it is conceivable that it may have preceded the first appointment at Laval in Quebec City.

It seems that by the turn of the century McGill University had also become active in the field of international law and it is certain that in the years following World War I it had become the major centre in Canada of teaching and research in this field. Whereas other universities tended to limit themselves to the provision of a basic course, McGill developed a broader program. Percy Corbett was the major figure in international law at McGill.

Although not recognized as a professional law school until some years after World War II, the University of Toronto was another pioneer in the teaching of international law in Canada. The teaching program begun in 1889 was strengthened early in this century by the appointment of N.A.M. MacKenzie and John Falconbridge and was progressively broadened in the postwar years.

It is noteworthy that Osgoode Hall, the other law school in Toronto, did not introduce international law into its curriculum until 1955–6. Several of the law faculties established in Ontario since 1957 have developed significant strength in the field, with Queen's University perhaps being most notable. The University of British Columbia has an important international law program of relatively long duration.

The federal government of Canada

The Canadian government has, to an extent not commonly matched by other governments, developed an 'elite cadre' of international lawyers whose intellectual calibre equals the best academic minds in the field. This represents a considerable change from the situation twenty years ago when, as one or two veteran international lawyers recall, it was not easy to find experienced colleagues in government with whom views could be usefully exchanged. A generation ago, for one thing, there was a greater tendency than today to utilize the services of government constitutional lawyers or general solicitors with little training or prior interest in international law. At that time, of course, it was not always easy to find lawyers in Canada with specialized qualifications.

The first legal adviser in the Department of External Affairs was appointed in 1913. His task was to advise the government on policy matters involving questions of international law and on related legal issues in consultation with the Department of Justice and other appropriate departments. In the early decades of the office, the legal advisers played an important technical and policy role in resolving significant problems, which incorporated both constitutional and international law aspects, of the developing Canadian participation in the Commonwealth and the general international community. Until after World War II, the legal side of External Affairs remained very small. Prior to 1945 Loring Christie and John Read were the dominant figures. Subsequently, Max H. Wershof became a prominent legal officer and one of the most notable postwar legal advisers.

As the need for legal services in External Affairs grew, an expanded Legal Division became increasingly essential. It was not always easy, in a rotational service, to ensure that legal officers with specialized training and a desire to emphasize legal work during their careers were available to fill every position in the division. A consistent, determined recruiting policy was necessary if the right individuals were to be attracted and retained.

In the early 1950s, when a career in the Canadian diplomatic service was gaining high prestige, a number of able people with a particular interest and background in international law began to be recruited as foreign service officers. The professional capacity of these new officers in Legal Division more consistently matched the demands of their function, and the division itself became more influential than before. Admittedly, a number of urgent legal problems (law of the sea being the outstanding example) began to demand attention at about this same time, thus ensuring a central role for Legal Division and for law-trained officers in other branches such as United Nations Division. Several individuals, notably Wershof and his equally vigorous colleague, Marcel Cadieux, should be given considerable credit for capitalizing on the new opportunities to develop the international law component of the service as a focal point of influence on policy development. A culmination of this growing role was reached in the mid-1960s when trained international lawyers occupied senior levels in the department: Paul Martin as secretary of state; Marcel Cadieux as undersecretary; Max Wershof as assistant undersecretary and legal adviser, and Allan Gotlieb, as head of Legal Division (and shortly to become legal adviser). The compatibility of these men virtually ensured that considerations of international law would be included as central elements of policy.

The temporary existence of a law-oriented 'power axis' at External Affairs during a substantial part of the 1960s was probably an abnormal development attributable as much to coincidence as to the impressive competence of the key individuals involved. It could hardly be expected that the department would normally be led by both a minister and an undersecretary who were international lawyers. Once that situation had altered, the policy-making role of the international law hierarchy was bound to be modified, with much depending on the character and capacity of two or three legal officers just below the top level in the department. At present the team appears to function capably and effectively.

Perhaps the team of international lawyers developed in Ottawa during the fifteen years prior to 1968 could have come into being only under a succession of External Affairs ministers who were similarly oriented and had the strong support of their prime ministers. For two decades such a situation existed. Lester Pearson, as minister, had the advantage of being the handpicked choice of his predecessor, Louis St Laurent, when the latter became prime minister. While Pearson was not a lawyer, he had been a career diplomat who thoroughly understood international organizations and most of the legal underpinning of international relations. His successors after the change of government, Sidney Smith and Howard Green, were both lawyers interested in and generally receptive to creative uses of international law. Both ministers had notable influence with Prime Minister John Diefenbaker, a lawyer whose long concern with human rights appeared to be parallelled by a sympathy for the general viewpoint espoused by the government's international law advisers.

A new plateau in the role played by the legal service at External Affairs was reached with the installation of Paul Martin as minister in 1963. He was oriented in much the same way as his three predecessors but had a more professional view of international law. Martin was a fully trained international lawyer with experience extending back to the League of Nations and was interested in the development, as well as the day-to-day practice, of international law. In this respect he closely resembled his Undersecretary, Marcel Cadieux, with whom he seems to have developed an easy, harmonious working relationship. They probably responded instinctively as international lawyers to virtually all problems that came across their desks. Martin also had the benefit of having Lester Pearson as his prime minister, with all the understanding and support which that implied.

It is our impression that Pearson, Smith, Green, and Martin provided an environment hospitable for international lawyers and that the latter moved with relative speed to make the most of a favourable situation. In the years prior to 1968 there grew up a sort of natural creative tension between senior law-trained officials and their political masters which was highly productive. It seems equally clear that there has been a change, at least in degree, since 1968. Mitchell Sharp is not a lawyer, for one thing, but came to his portfolio with a background in business and trade problems. Like his Undersecretary, A.E. Ritchie, who is an economist, Sharp cannot be expected to react as a lawyer might. In consequence, the development of policy and the formulation of priorities will take place within a different set of conceptual parameters and the role played by legal advisers may be somewhat different. In this connection we might recall the 1970 white paper, *Foreign Policy for Canadians,* which (to the extent that an emphasis can be perceived in the Delphic obscurity of many of its passages) appears to stress economic interests and priorities. This preoccupation with economic concerns may explain Canada's emphasis on the law of the sea and related environmental questions as the principal current issues in international law.

Mr Sharp has faced an obvious difficulty in his relationship with Prime Minister

Trudeau, who is both strong-willed and of a notably different temperament. Trudeau has shown a readiness to rely on the advice and negotiating skill available in the self-contained advisory staff in his own office, instead of turning to External Affairs. In fact, it is only recently that the prime minister has curbed the obvious scepticism about the department and its personnel that he displayed on assuming leadership of the government. It seems fair to suggest that Mitchell Sharp has found himself burdened, to an unusual extent, with foreign policies conceived elsewhere in the government apparatus and imposed whether or not the career experts in External Affairs concurred.

The role of the present prime minister may give some cause for concern. Although we cannot be certain what he thinks of public international law, we are doubtful of his essential commitment to legal solutions as a primary frame of reference. Frequently he appears more interested in 'cost-benefit' analyses than in law. In respect of both domestic and international issues, the prime minister seems often to have emphasized economic arguments, while introducing legal rationales only to the extent that they provide a convenient supplementary argument. In international affairs the prime minister has not been markedly law-oriented in his approach, despite his training and background.

We are unable to discern a strong pattern of concern for the development of international law, under the present administration, except where it would serve Canada's immediate national interests. There does not appear to be much interest in the development of a legal regime as such. While international lawyers of the highest calibre are available in the public service, we conclude that they are called on to employ their talents in a somewhat narrower range of issues than in past years and are more frequently used as adjunct-technicians after policy has been discussed and settled on non-legal bases. Except in relation to certain issues of great and direct concern to Canada, international lawyers may have difficulty in finding interest or support for suggested policy initiatives. To the extent to which this impression may be accurate, we find it a discouraging diminution of the potential contribution that can be made by skilled international lawyers.

National style and philosophy in Canadian approaches to international law

In a period of rising national consciousness in Canada it is interesting to consider whether a distinctively Canadian approach to internationl law is evolving in this country. Government international lawyers might be regarded as pursuing a 'national' approach to international law when they are more or less consciously acting out a distinguishable national philosophy, which is established in government policy. The academic international lawyers in a particular country might be regarded as exhibiting a national approach by showing more or less unconsciously a significant number of assumptions and characteristics of style in the practice of their craft.

National style
National style can exist without the emergence of a national philosophy. Style in international law is more personal and may be more ephemeral. In government service international legal style can be altered quite abruptly by changes of personnel

at the senior levels of legal policy-making. In the academic community, individual style evolves, affected by changes in the scholar's perception of his role in the world of scholarship and in society at large. At the most appropriate time, one man's style could be adopted by an entire generation. At other times, a stylist may have to plough a lonely furrow. In Canada it is not yet possible to hail the emergence of a major Canadian legal theorist who is likely to attract a national following of Canadian students on the strength of his distinctive style in international law. There is no Canadian 'school' with an identifiable leader.

No doubt the non-existence of a Canadian academic style in international law is due in part to the arrival in Canada within the last fifteen years or so of several European scholars and graduate students. Though most of these European-Canadian international lawyers have in varying degrees been influenced by their involvement in the Canadian academic community, some of them still retain a work style associated with the European school or tradition to which they were first exposed. A few, on the other hand, seem to have become thoroughly North American in approach after graduate studies in American or Canadian law schools.

A more important factor, however, is the nature of Canadian legal education in general, and the method of teaching international law in particular. To discuss this, it is necessary to draw a sharp distinction between the past and present. Up to the end of World War II there were five distinctive patterns in the Canadian law school treatment of international law. First, at Dalhousie University, where international law was first taught in English-speaking Canada, the approach was 'common law Anglo-American,' with an emphasis on tribunals and treaties and the Harvard case-analysis method of teaching. This method was favourably received in a period of increasing familiarity with prestigious American law schools in New England.

Second, in the francophone faculties of law in Quebec the approach was 'traditional civil law,' with an emphasis on the body of doctrine and the textbook method of teaching. The influence was mostly continental European and the style of presentation was 'schematic.'

Third, at the anglophone civil law faculty of law at McGill, a stronghold of international law since the 1920s, the approach was different again, an approach that might be described as 'neo-classical.' The influence was chiefly European, reflected in the emphasis on historical development. Lectures drew upon the contributions of the great jurists of the past and contemporary writers such as Kelsen, Lauterpacht, de Visscher, and Anzilloti. At the same time the McGill approach was influenced also by neo-classicists in the United States, such as Hyde and Moore, who were especially interested in the work of Anglo-American and international courts and tribunals. The development as well as the application of classical doctrine was regarded as the proper function of courts and arbitration tribunals. At McGill, therefore, more than elsewhere in Canada, there existed an awareness of the opportunity to provide a synthesis between civil law and common law contributions to international law, and perhaps in this way to develop a distinctively Canadian style.

In Ontario, where legal education was controlled by the bar, international law was barely tolerated as an 'extra' course that provided no visible benefits to the practising profession. As an educational experience it ranked beside, or possibly somewhere below, 'jurisprudence' in an environment where Austinian strictures on international law were accepted more or less uncritically. Innate conservatism in the profession, reinforced perhaps by an English tradition, was too strong for the Ontario Bar to encourage exploration of the practical benefits of the problem-oriented approach to international law that was already developing in bar-dominated systems of legal education in the United States. Those individuals who were allowed to teach international law in Ontario up to the mid 1940s, at the then non-accredited faculty of law at the University of Toronto, were unable to impress their personal style on a significant number of graduate students.

In western Canada the opportunities for teaching international law and developing a regional style were even more resticted than in Ontario. In those provinces most law school courses were provided by practitioners on a part-time basis. In that setting international law had a low priority. Those few who taught international law were essentially lonely torchbearers, with little influence on the development of the subject in the region. Yet several international lawyers did emerge from the west in this period and, as in Ontario, some of them went on to make distinguished academic careers in other regions.

Although there was very little sense of community among the Canadian teachers of international law before the mid-1940s, some of them, such as P.E. Corbett, H.A. Smith, George Curtis, and N.A.M. MacKenzie, did move around from one region to another. Since each of the five systems remained largely unaffected by the others, the relative mobility of these international lawyers did not have the effect of contributing to a Canadian national style. Moreover, all of Smith's and most of Corbett's writings on international law were carried out in other countries, in England and the United States respectively.

Before the end of the 1940s some variations were beginning to appear. After the arrival of Maxwell Cohen, who had been trained in the common law in Manitoba and in public law at Harvard, the McGill approach to international law changed to a more contemporary concern with international policy issues, especially those confronting the United Nations and other international organizations established in the postwar years. This trend to an institutional, problem-solving orientation marked a decline in McGill's traditional interest in the European doctrinal approach to international law. As in many other law schools of North America, increasing relevance was found in the sociological school of jurisprudence, which emphasized the social science aspect of law and presented international law as an approach to decision-making in semi-organized international society. Treaty-making on a vast scale was envisaged as the direct method of remedying organizational deficiencies in the world society. The attention of international lawyers was now concentrated increasingly on the constitutional-administrative problems arising out of the new network of postwar international agencies. Since this approach to international law has become prevalent throughout North America, it is less easy to discover a distinctively Canadian style, other than in the emphasis on issues of immediate Canadian interest.

The late 1940s and the 1950s saw the emergence of a dominant university role in legal education. This had a generative effect on law school curricula, especially in Ontario and the western provinces. In the majority of Canadian provinces international law became widely accepted as a legitimate area of scholarship. By the 1960s over six hundred Canadian law students each year were taking at least one course in international law. Yet even in the period of expansion of international law, in a university law school setting, it was difficult to detect the emergence of a distinctively Canadian style of scholarship. In its absence, Canadian students of international law became susceptible to intellectual influences discovered, often by accident, in graduate law schools outside Canada, especially in the United States, Britain, and France.

Most of those teaching international law in Canada today have had graduate training in one of the major American law schools. Over the last twenty-five years Harvard Law School has attracted more Canadian graduate students than any other, but like Columbia and Michigan, Harvard has not attempted to develop a distinctive 'school' or style in international law. On the contrary, these US law schools have preserved a mixture of approaches to the subject: European doctrinal, charter reformist, rule of law, American transactional, crisis managerial, and others. Under these hybrid influences, it should not be surprising if Canadian international lawyers trained in these graduate schools show little sign of developing a common style which is distinguishable from that of colleagues in the United States. On the other hand, in recent years there has been some evidence of an increasing Yale influence on international lawyers in Canada, especially among those with earlier training outside North America. Reflected in academic style or methodological technique, this influence has its roots in the systematic policy science school of jurisprudence developed at Yale by Myres McDougal and Harold Lasswell.

With the exception of Yale, American graduate law programs, until recently, have done relatively little to overcome the Canadian law-teacher's disregard for interdisciplinary collaboration and for systemic perspective. Canadian academic distaste for systemic perspective extends beyond the field of international law. In the field of international relations, for example, systemic perspective has been imported from the United States, partly by Americans in Canada, but systemic methodologies have not yet been adopted by many of the political scientists trained exclusively in Canada. Somewhat similarly, among Canadian economists macroanalysis tends to have a lower status than microanalysis, development studies, and historical monographs. Only a few Canadian international lawyers have shown increasing interest in the possibilities of collaborative studies with fellow social scientists. Most, apparently, do not even think of their discipline as a branch of the social sciences. There may be developments that will change this attitude, but this possibility is more easily discussed at the level of national philosophy.

National philosophy
Few countries in the world have presented views on international law that are sufficiently consistent and distinctive to be regarded as the product of a national philosophy. Canada could certainly not be included among those that have. It might even be said that the *absence* of a tradition that could sustain such a philosophy is characteristically Canadian. The reasons for this are familiar to all Canadians who have joined the national exercise in self-analysis. Cultural diversity is both a fact and, at present, a creed in Canadian society. The Anglo-Saxon and Celtic subcultures in Canada, unlike the French, have never been strongly attracted to 'philosophy.' The ideas of a settled tradition and a national philosophy are perhaps considered alien by many Canadians, who may even view them as in some way antithetical to social mobility and economic development.

Nationalism itself can be thought of as a kind of national philosophy, with potential effects on the nature of national contributions to international law. But until recently relatively few Canadians were strongly moved by nationalist sentiment, though in many other countries nationalism is concomitant with an emphasis, such as the Canadian, on economic development and social mobility. Until the early 1960s the idea of nationalism was largely of interest to small groups of intellectuals in various regions of the country. For most Canadians, who continued to place a high value on the virtue of moderation, nationalism denoted a form of political extremism. Since then, however, many Canadians at different levels of society have come to believe that a separate 'national identity' must be secured in order to be freed of the economic and cultural influences of the United States.

Sharing a critical view of nationalism as a political force, at least until recent years most Canadian international lawyers have shown little interest in the possibility or desirability of a Canadian national (or cultural) influence on the development of international law. Both in government service and the academic community, they seem on the contrary to have taken some degree of professional pride in the growth of Canada's non-nationalist reputation in the world of diplomacy. Like their counterparts elsewhere, Canadian government international lawyers have, of course, always been required to keep an eye on the compatibility of international law and national interest, but the internationalist element in government policy enabled them to escape the appearance of pursuing a restrictive view of Canadian national interest. Canadian diplomatic activity in the United Nations, especially in response to peace-keeping problems, earned Canada much goodwill and credibility as an internationally minded state. No doubt this reputation helped to encourage Canadian government international lawyers to engage conspicuously in the quest for international solutions. Viewed from the United Nations, at least, Canada seemed respectably distant from the danger of overcommitment to a philosophy of 'national purposes.'

Canadian academic international lawyers were on the whole content to accept praise for Canadian diplomatic contributions to internationalism. Until the mid-1960s their ranks were still thin and they lacked the professional opportunities to 'monitor' Canada's legal operations abroad. Even today, of course, the possibilities of 'counter-research' are largely unexplored by international lawyers in Canada.

Whether a peculiarly Canadian national philosophy evolves in international law during the last three decades of the twentieth century may depend chiefly on whether there emerges a distinctively Canadian mix of social attitudes towards technology and a distinctively Canadian set of political responses. Succeeding Canadian governments will find themselves required to focus on shifting points of balance between developmental and environmental demands on the political community. Canadian positions on international law will, to this extent, be regarded as responses to the political need to reconcile growth and quality philosophies in Canadian society. For an international lawyer, the growth-quality dilemma is part of the larger confrontation between the rich and the poor countries of the world. It is difficult to see how Canada can avoid becoming increasingly embroiled in rich-versus-poor antagonisms. Accordingly, we can expect Canadian international legal idealism to be put to increasingly painful tests in this context.

A Canadian national philosophy in international law might then be characterized by reference to the critical point of emphasis on a 'technological-ideological' continuum. At one extreme, the 'technological' pole, international law is identified as a preferred problem-solving technique available to national governments, international organizations, and other major participants in the global process of decision-making. At the other extreme, the 'ideological' pole, international law is identified as a system of values applicable to the most threatening issues between the rich and poor areas of the world. The first of these different, though not necessarily conflicting, approaches to international law would be essentially pragmatic and specific in concept, favouring empirical methods of research, often in conjunction with the social sciences and other disciplines. The second approach, the ideological, would be essentially systemic in concept and lean more heavily on value commitment in the abstract, favouring the personal involvement of international lawyers in interna-ional causes related to social welfare problems which are aggravated by the widening economic and technological disparities in the world community.

We expect that a Canadian national philosophy will evolve on the technological side of the continuum. For a wide variety of reasons – historical, cultural, political, social, and geographical – Canadian international lawyers are not likely to acquire sophistication on the ideological side of international law. They are perhaps unlikely even to try to match their counterparts in, say, socialist countries in the rhetorical, emotive, system-justifying uses of international law. It remains doubtful how strongly Canadians will even want to learn how to use international law for purposes of reinforcing long-range expectations, for example in the area of human rights and fundamental freedoms or in relation to peaceful coexistence. The ideological use of international law just does not seem likely to become the Canadian way. Canadian government officials will continue to live for tomorrow's crisis, concentrating on the practical rather than the theoretical side of the exercise. Canadian academic international lawyers will continue to write mostly in response to events of direct Canadian significance rather than on the basis of long-range expectations or on theoretical questions of general interest.

The chief dangers are, then, that Canadian academic international lawyers will remain unnecessarily remote from international welfare issues aggravated by widening disparities between rich and poor areas of the world, and continue to neglect important questions of legal theory; and that Canadian government international lawyers will find themselves required to practise legal technique increasingly as a branch of political economy, serving mostly acquisitive purposes and gradually impairing Canada's reputation as a genuine internationally minded state.

Canadian officials have taken bold and imaginative initiatives on the technological side of international law – especially in the law of the sea, communications, and environmental protection – and have thus accentuated the problem-solving functions of the lawyer's craft. This is an appropriate emphasis, since the chief needs and opportunities of Canadian society are still generally understood in technological terms, despite the ideological protests of many young citizens and of some intellectuals. Neither of these protest groups have the right kind of knowledge or sophistication to spell out the implications of their antitechnological position in terms of a Canadian approach to international law. Moreover, not a single Canadian academic international lawyer has so far attempted a critical, systemic view of international law along the lines, for example, of Richard Falk in the United States. This may be attributed to a Canadian tendency to avoid or moderate ideological positions, or to a Canadian distaste for interdisciplinary collaboration and systemic perspective, as suggested above. The technological emphasis in Canadian approaches to international law may have the effect of reducing the difficulty of interdisciplinary collaboration in joint studies of international problems. Unfortunately, this advantage may be more apparent then real, for the lack of systemic perspective may prevent such studies from struggling above the level of superficiality. Interdisciplinary collaboration is likely, however, to be encouraged by the present federal government policy favouring government-academic interaction in policy-related studies. This policy, it might be added, is regarded as ethically acceptable by many Canadian political scientists, lawyers, and economists.

SUGGESTIONS AND RECOMMENDATIONS

Drawing on the foregoing summary of the state of international law in the academic community and at the governmental level, we now offer a number of suggestions and recommendations.

At the outset, we wish to record our conviction that Canada can best prosper and flourish within an orderly international community. Contrary to current government views, reflected for example in the 1970 white paper, we believe that the building of a sound international order, based on a flexible system of law and organization, must remain Canada's first priority in the field of foreign policy. We would go even farther and suggest that Canada has a special interest in promoting the development of a rational international structure: a special interest because we are the neighbour of a superpower whose views we cannot assume will be identical with our own; a special interest because we do not fit neatly into any geographical community, such as exists in Europe and Latin America; a special interest because, as an economically advanced country whose wealth is likely to become suspect, it is probable that we will come under increasing criticism if we pursue a narrow self-interest; and a special interest because, as a technologically advanced country, we are obliged to contribute to the solution of international problems of resource allocation and management. For all of these reasons Canada as a vulnerable state would lose out more significantly than most if the world were allowed to organize itself on an *ad hoc* political basis. That way lies the danger of subordination to the philosophies, interests, and values of less vulnerable states. The higher realism, in our view, requires us to dedicate ourselves to the continuing quest for the development of world order.

In our opinion Canadian international lawyers have not only the incentive but also the resources and opportunities to make more substantial contributions to the development of the international legal order. At the governmental level there is a need for more sustained, systematic, long-range planning in the area of international law and organization. We believe that it is necessary for government policy-planners to get beyond immediate issues and conference deadlines to a more generalized conception of basic disorders in the international community. A vulnerable middle-sized state such as Canada seems to have a special interest in the restructuring of world society on the basis of international law but can play a special role in this effort only through the deliberate invention and assessment of new policy alternatives. Institutional and procedural innovations resulting from systematic studies would provide Canada with a clearer idea of how to orchestrate its foreign policy and how to employ international law as a shield as well as a sword.

We admit to a concern about the fragmentation of foreign policy and the consequential extension of international law into an increasing number of governmental departments. The proliferation of international lawyers throughout government departments is a worldwide phenomenon, following quite naturally from the increasing complexity of international relations and the tendency to decentralize the making of foreign policy to a variety of lead agencies, usually in the technological and scientific fields. We welcome the rise of 'houses' of international law within the technological departments because of the technical and legal expertise that is likely to emerge. We suspect, however, that this evolutionary trend means that in the future decisions will be made increasingly on a functional basis, and that this trend may impair the prospects of developing an overall philosophy of world order. Each functional 'house' of international law will be too limited to produce a comprehensive ideological framework of reference for policy-makers. The consequent need for effective co-ordination by individual departments and by interdepartmental committees will reinforce the case for such a framework built on the foundations of long-range systematic studies.

A number of recommendations flow from these premises. We suggest that there be established within the Bureau of Legal Affairs of the Department of External Affairs, or perhaps within the Policy Analysis Group of the same department, a special research unit with wide-ranging responsibilities for identification, clarification, and analysis of problems of long-range interest to Canada. Indicative of the specific intellectual tasks that might be discharged by the personnel of this unit, we emphasize the following outstanding needs: 1 / the promotion and articulation of a higher degree of conceptualization about the future of the international legal order; 2 / the examination of selected areas of international law and organization from a comparative point of view; 3 / the projection of trends and the planning of strategies beyond the imperatives of immediately pending conferences and negotiations; and 4 / the provision of conceptual and research assistance to Canadian officials concerned with the progressive development of international law in specific areas.

The unit we are envisaging would be staffed by a small number of career officials who have had experience either in foreign service or in technological functions. It should also include an academic visitor in residence for the year and a few other members of the academic community imaginatively selected for shorter visits. All personnel should be chosen with a view to preserving a strong interdisciplinary capability. Presumably the practical experience of the official component would mitigate the danger of the unit becoming an ivory tower. At the same time, we believe that the officials in the unit must be free to address themselves to policy questions of the broadest kind. Consequently they must be insulated as much as possible from the day-to-day pressures of the departments. For this reason it may be necessary to locate the unit outside the area occupied by the Bureau of Legal Affairs.

The report of the research unit might be annexed to the annual statement that the minister for external affairs makes to the House of Commons. It might serve also as one of the background documents for presentation by the legal adviser and the director general of UN affairs to the Cabinet Committee on External Affairs and Defence, to which we will refer presently. It would also be useful to convene an annual meeting of government and academic lawyers to review and assess the work that is being carried out by the research unit, perhaps under the auspices of the Canadian Council on International Law. This recommendation is in line, happily, with the present policy of the Department of External Affairs to encourage the exchange of international lawyers between Ottawa and the universities.

Especially for a vulnerable state such as Canada, it is important to cultivate a sophisticated appreciation of the relevance of international law to the making of foreign policy. In addition to the reasons already indicated, we believe that the object of bringing considerations of world order to bear on policy-making in a regular and systematic manner is to broaden the national perspective, promote the international legal order, and contribute to Canada's image as a responsible participant in the international arena. The question arises whether we have adequate procedures available for bringing the international law perspectives to the attention of our decision-makers.

A number of procedures already exist for this purpose. The most direct is the procedure by which the legal adviser to the Department of External Affairs has personal access to the undersecretary and, through him, to the minister. An example of the impact of the work of the legal adviser on the operation of the decision-making system is found in the Canadian memorandum protesting the suspension of innocent passage by the United States and its creation of a 50 mile closing zone at the time of the Cannikin nuclear test on Amchitka Island in 1971. This memorandum was prepared on the initiative of the legal adviser, examined by the undersecretary, reviewed by the minister, and then communicated by cabinet to the United States State Department as the comment of the Canadian legal adviser on this particular point.

There are a number of less direct procedures involving the use of cabinet committees, such as the Cabinet Committee on External Affairs and Defence. It is evident that the committee system of the House of Commons is also available. In recent years this system has been strengthened and diversified and members of the House now have better opportunities to specialize in foreign affairs. Officials, including international lawyers, from the Department of External Affairs frequently appear before these committees. In this way, committee members are in a position to inject international law considerations into foreign policy discussions both inside and outside the House. There are other committees which have a significant international law input. We understand that the Legal Planning Committee has been revived. This interdepartmental committee, established at the time that Mr Marcel Cadieux was appointed to the ILC in order to advise him on government policy, comprises representatives from External Affairs and other departments. It is to be hoped that this additional procedure will become a significant contribution to overall legal planning and strategy, and that there will be fruitful interaction between the committee and the proposed research unit.

An extradepartmental procedure exists by virtue of the appointment of Mr Ivan L. Head, formerly of the University of Alberta, who is currently serving as special adviser to the prime minister on foreign policy. In this unique position, Mr Head enjoys unprecedented opportunities for advising the prime minister on matters of international law and organization. Another kind of extradepartmental procedure is provided by the Parliamentary Centre for Foreign Affairs and Foreign Trade, financed partly by the Canadian Institute of International Affairs. The centre arranges meetings between parliamentarians and officials, often in order to brief non-partisan groups, and advises on sources of information and on the organization of studies. At these meetings there are frequent presentations by legal officers from External Affairs.

Despite the number of such procedures, we are doubtful that the full range of mechanisms has been devised for the regular presentation of the international law perspective on the making of Canadian foreign policy. We appreciate that law has restricted uses and that it is all too possible to be overly legalistic. But the lead role that we would prefer for Canada, as a law-dependent state, requires a kind of pioneering in opening up additional routes for the transmission of relevant legal criteria to those who make or influence policy decisions. Our first recommendation is, therefore, that the legal adviser and the director general of the Bureau of United Nations Affairs be requested to appear at least once a year before the Cabinet Committee on External Affairs and Defence in order to review the major issues in international law and organization pertinent to the formulation and execution of Canadian foreign policy. These presentations might focus not only on the history and implications of Canadian attitudes to these problems but also on alternative approaches to the longer range development of the international legal order. The work of the Canadian delegations to the United Nations and other international organizations might be examined, and current priorities in the progressive development of international law reappraised, perhaps on the basis of the report prepared by the research unit referred to above.

If such a procedure were established, it might be appropriate for the cabinet committee, or a subcommittee thereof, to assume responsibility for surveillance of the government's performance in international law. This responsibility would include occasional re-evaluation of government machinery to ensure that international law considerations are brought to bear on relevant issues. It should also be concerned with the possibility that certain areas and problems of international law may not be receiving appropriate attention in day-to-day policy-making. In some cases it might be found useful to set up a task force or special study group to examine the prospects of preventive as well as remedial 'legal diplomacy.'

Second, we believe that more should be done to ensure that the internal legal order is kept consistent with current developments in the international legal order. For example, we suggest that a monitoring procedure might be established on the model of that in the Canadian Bill of Rights whereby the minister of justice is obligated to examine every proposed regulation submitted in draft form by the clerk of the Privy Council, as well as every bill presented to the House of Commons, in order to ascertain any inconsistency and to report thereon to the House.

Third, in this age of complexity in international affairs there is surely a need for a national advisory committee to the Department of External Affairs which would be composed of international lawyers as well as other kinds of specialists on foreign policy problems. This might be constructed on the model already established by the Canada Pension Plan Advisory Committee and similar committees serving other departments of the federal government.

We recognize that the adoption of these recommendations, resulting in heightened awareness of international law considerations, cannot be expected if they are interpreted as another row of hurdles to be overcome by those responsible for the execution of Canadian foreign policy. Nor should these recommendations be presented as if international lawyers possess a special kind of wisdom. But we see these suggestions as contributing to the Canadian search for an appropriate and realistic role in world affairs.

Returning to the state of international law in the universities, we should like to reiterate our concern about the capability of the law faculties in Canada to encourage and support a flourishing program of international law teaching and research. More specifically, we are disturbed about the levelling off in the number of full-time professors in international law and even more so about the decline in the number of able students in the field. International law research seems threatened by the absence of adequate research materials, especially in foreign languages, and the lack of funds for extended graduate training, for the promotion and exchange of articles in the learned journals, and for an adequate number of conferences, seminars, and visiting lecturers. Although Canadian international lawyers are bound to retain a North American orientation we believe that they should be absorbing wider influences and responding to innovative contributions from developing countries. In short, there seems to be a need to provide a more balanced input into Canadian international law thinking.

In order to provide a broader perspective in Canadian international law thinking we urge federal agencies to make available each year to outstanding law graduates at least two prestige scholarships of sufficient value to enable their holders to study for periods of two or three years at the leading centres in Europe, Asia, Africa, and Latin America. A program of this nature could not fail to enrich the Canadian academic community of international lawyers and broaden the perspectives of future Canadian government specialists. We also believe that the time has come to establish a number of chairs in international law at universities across Canada. At least two of these chairs should be in the province of Quebec, so that a vigorous effort can be made to strengthen the influence of the civil law tradition in the mainstream of Canadian international law.

We realize that these recommendations are more likely to be implemented if they are endorsed by an impartial and independent inquiry into the deficiencies of international law in Canadian universities. Such an investigation, which might be commissioned by the Canada Council, must inevitably touch on the financing and rationalization of research in the universities. Ideally it should be undertaken by a senior academic with experience in government operations as well as administrative service in the academic community. We believe that his report could be prepared within two months of a cross-country tour in which the requisite interviewing and fact-finding could be done. Altogether we are suggesting a commitment of time of approximately four months, one-third of the annual salary of a senior academic, which would not represent an obstacle to such a study.

INDEXES

Subject Index

Index of Cases